The Dartnell Handbook

for

SALES,
ADVERTISING and
SALES PROMOTION
EXECUTIVES

DARTNELL is a publisher serving the world of business with business books, business manuals, business newsletters and bulletins, training materials for business executives, managers, supervisors, salesmen, financial officials, personnel executives and office employees. In addition, Dartnell produces management and sales training films and cassettes, publishes many useful business forms, conducts scores of management seminars for business men and women and has many of its materials and films available in languages other than English. Dartnell, established in 1917, serves the world's whole business community. For details, catalogs, and product information, address: DARTNELL, 4660 N. Ravenswood Avenue, Chicago, Illinois 60640, USA—or phone (312) 561-4000.

OTHER DARTNELL HANDBOOKS

Advertising Manager's Handbook
Direct Mail and Mail Order Handbook
Marketing Manager's Handbook
Office Administration Handbook
Personnel Administration Handbook
Public Relations Handbook
Sales Manager's Handbook

The Dartnell

SALES PROMOTION Handbook

Editor...

Ovid Riso

Seventh Edition

 THE DARTNELL CORPORATION
Chicago • Boston • London

FIRST EDITION—APRIL 1950
Second Printing—January 1951
SECOND EDITION—JANUARY 1953
Second Printing—January 1954
Third Printing—April 1955
Fourth Printing (Revised)—April 1957
THIRD EDITION—SEPTEMBER 1960
Second Printing—January 1962
FOURTH EDITION—MAY 1964
Second Printing—June 1965
FIFTH EDITION—OCTOBER 1966
Second Printing—March 1969
SIXTH EDITION—JANUARY 1973
SEVENTH EDITION—FEBRUARY 1979
Second Printing—July 1982
Third Printing—September 1987

ISBN 0-85013-103-0

Printed in the United States of America by Dartnell Press, Chicago, IL 60640-4595

63,827

FOREWORD

Seventh Edition

IN THE first Dartnell Sales Manager's Handbook, edited almost 40 years ago by John Cameron Aspley, founder-president of Dartnell and former chairman of the board, the subject of sales promotion was treated as a function of sales management. However, within a decade, sales promotion had become so advanced and ramified that it had outgrown the confines of a single chapter and warranted a book in its own right.

The rate of growth of sales promotion activities has continued to accelerate, to the point where new media—especially television—and new methods of presentation through older media, combined with an ever-growing audience of more sophisticated consumers, have demanded a new type of practitioner: the sales promotion expert.

Ever increasingly, sales managers and other sales executives are dependent for guidance in their advertising and other promotional techniques on a different set of abilities than those required for sales planning and administration. In those companies where the sales manager wears the hat of sales-promotion executive as well, he must add to his sales-managerial ability the skills, knowledge and talents required in the sales-promotion field.

The increasing complexity of modern marketing calls for ever new and different approaches to sales promotion, as a supplement to such managerial activities as recruiting and selecting salesmen, market analysis, developing and managing territories, devising compensation plans, and the myriad other activities that concern the sales manager.

Thus, this Sales Promotion Handbook, whether it is to be used by one sales executive who "doubles in brass" or by a specialist in sales promotion, is both a companion and a supplement to the Sales Manager's Handbook. For, just as the sales manager must today understand, if not execute, the operations of sales promotion, the sales-promotion executive can work most effectively only if he has a ready understanding of sales-management problems as well.

When, in 1917, Mr. Aspley organized the company which has since become The Dartnell Corporation, he prepared a memorandum in which he set forth the policy which has guided Dartnell ever since. An understanding of this policy should be helpful in deriving the greatest usefulness from this HANDBOOK:

"We are a clearinghouse for information, not a manufacturer of plans, notions, and opinions. This is an important distinction to bear in mind. Other publishers will bring out textbooks by authors who theorize on how a job should be done, and there is an important place for such books. We, however, will operate as an experience exchange, securing information from various sources on what they do, how they do it, and the results they obtain, and passing this information on to our readers. Every Dartnell editor must keep before him always the basic operating principle that we are reporters, not originators."

In preparing the current edition of this HANDBOOK, Dartnell editors wish to reaffirm this principle. A book such as this does not presume to tell the reader *what to do;* it tells him *what has been done*—the unsuccessful as well as the successful—so that he may set his course with due regard to the hidden reefs as well as to the helpful currents.

It is also important to bear in mind, in consulting this HANDBOOK, that styles, trends, and fads in sales promotion come and go, and a plan which succeeded greatly a generation ago may fail utterly tomorrow. The reverse, of course, is equally to be kept in mind.

Premium plans and promotions have, likewise, waxed and waned, and the plans that flopped miserably for the ABC Company last year may be just the thing that the XYZ Company needs this year—the necessary changes, of course, being made.

Finally, like all Dartnell HANDBOOKS, this volume is intended as a desk-reference book—a book to be consulted as the need arises. It has, therefore, reproduced details that are not intended for "light summer reading," but to give the sales-promotion practitioner all the information he may need to evaluate the probable success of a promotion in his own operations, and to develop the plan if and when it seems to be adaptable or adoptable.

Comments and criticisms from readers are always welcome, and will be gratefully received, promptly acknowledged, and carefully considered.

THE PUBLISHERS

THE EDITORS

THIS HANDBOOK, like its companion the SALES MANAGER'S HANDBOOK, was first compiled by J. C. Aspley. Mr. Aspley, former chairman of the Dartnell board of directors, was president of The Dartnell Corporation from its founding, in 1917, until his retirement in 1959. Previously, he had been a member of the editorial staff of *Printers' Ink* and subsequently an editor of that publication. He was also associated with Swift & Company and the Addressograph Company in sales and public relations capacities. He had been a member of the public relations committee of the board of managers of the Young Men's Christian Association of Metropolitan Chicago.

Mr. Aspley was also founder-publisher of *Sales Management, American Business, Industrial Relations,* and other national periodicals.

The present revision was edited by Ovid Riso, advertising consultant and former vice president, advertising and sales promotion, Philco Corporation, International Division. Previously, Mr. Riso was advertising manager of RCA International, manager of the international division of Young & Rubicam, and a staff editor of McGraw-Hill Publishing Company. He is editor of *Poor Richard's Almanack,* monthly publication of the Poor Richard Club of Philadelphia; was formerly president of the Philadelphia chapter of the International Advertising Association, former vice-president of the Philadelphia chapter of the Public Relations Society of America, and member of the U.S. Regional Expansion Council.

Special acknowledgment is due to the several hundred sales management and sales promotion executives who have generously contributed the details of their promotional activities. It is, in the final analysis, the cooperation of such contributors that enables such a book to become a reality.

CONTENTS (Condensed)

Continued on next page

CONTENTS

INDEX

SALES PROMOTION . . .

Those sales activities that supplement both personal selling and advertising, coordinate them, and help to make them effective, such as displays, shows and expositions, demonstrations, and other nonrecurrent selling efforts not in the ordinary routine.

American Marketing Association

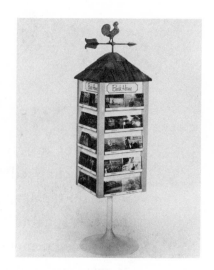

Sales promotion brings people to the retail store. That's the climactic point in any consumer-goods promotional campaign. It's where the sales promotion manager gets his final chance to help the dealer make the sale through effective store displays. Here are some excellent examples of good store merchandisers selected for awards by the Point-of-Purchase Advertising Institute.

PART 1

THE
RESPONSIBILITIES
OF
SALES
PROMOTION

Chapter 1

SALES PROMOTION TODAY

CHANGE is a basic factor in business as in any other form of human endeavor. The computer has already wrought tremendous improvements in market research and direct-mail techniques and the door to further progress in these fields has barely been opened.

In other areas are such broad developments for the future as greatly increased government concern in business practices which include, among others, advertising and sales promotion, i.e. contests.

Franchising and diversification are running full-speed ahead into new fields with greater promotional opportunities and methods to be explored.

Direct-mail executives are challenged to find new ways to overcome the startling increases in postal rates.

Over-riding all these trends is the fast-spreading force of "consumer protection." At a meeting of the Association of National Advertisers, in Pebble Beach, California, the association was "exhorted to update its thinking" according to the headline in *Broadcasting,* the industry magazine.

Members and guests were told that business communicators must be more aware of what's happening in society; how government is becoming very much a part of advertising and promotion.

D. C. Bowman, advertising manager, Hughes Aircraft Company, Los Angeles, indicated that understanding the state of society as it relates to business leads to recognition that consumer needs, worries and ideas must not be disregarded. "We cannot fall back into our technological sanctuaries and ignore them," he said. "They are reading, viewing, thinking, listening people who are greatly concerned with the problems confronting them in today's turbulent society."

ANA General Counsel Gilbert H. Weil, taking part in a panel discussion of current public and governmental pressures stated that the Federal Trade Commission and Congress are politically responsive to the pressures coming from their constituencies; and from idealistic economists.

Business, too, must respond.

The Changing Nature of the Market

A new economic development, with strong implications for the future, is the subtle shift in the nature of the market from goods to services. It is estimated that in 1979, services accounted for over 64½% of the Gross National Product, with forecasts of sizable annual increases. To keep pace with the expansion in the economy, companies now selling products alone will have to diversify into services.

New social forces have come into play, creating new public services markets. "The Federal government will be a much bigger factor in both the personal and business services areas," states Thayer C. Taylor, *Sales & Marketing Management's* senior editor. In the industrial area, he cites the services that the government will tackle as including pollution control, urban reconstruction, mass transit, crime, new towns, environmental protection, to name just a few.

The change of emphasis will produce new meanings and new objectives for sales management. Products will be sold from the standpoint of systems selling, or as some are calling it, "orchestrated selling," with greater stress on customer service.

The impact on sales promotion managers is that "Communication plays a much stronger role than distribution in the marketing of services," according to Dr. Peter Bennett, head of the marketing department at Pennsylvania State University.

A Decade of Opportunity

In an address before the Philadelphia Marketing Conference of the Association of Industrial Advertisers, Arno H. Johnson, vice-president and senior economist of J. Walter Thompson Company, said:

"The framework of American markets in general is being shaped right now by the rapid and dynamic changes so evident in the whole social and economic structure in the United States, as well as in other areas of the free world. Indications are that these changes will accelerate in the next decade and that there will be an opportunity for a major surge upward, world-wide, in consumer standards of living and in the levels of education, as productivity per capita mounts.

"Businessmen and marketing men in particular should be aware of these trends since it is the consumer and the potential upgrading of his standard of living that is fast becoming the real key to economic growth.

"There has been a deteriorating relationship between investment in creating consumer demand (i.e., advertising and public relations efforts) and the growth of investment in new plant and equipment. Hence, consumer demand has not been growing as rapidly as it should to keep up with the expansion of productive capacity or production efficiency implied by new plant and equipment expenditures.

"This rapidly increasing capacity to produce and the rapidly growing pressure for employment should revolutionize our ideas of needed growth in consumer demand, and the amount of investment in public relations, advertising and selling effort needed to educate, encourage, and stimulate that consumer demand."

All this is by way of saying that (barring war), marketing and its essential ingredient, sales promotion, will play an ever-increasingly important role on the economic stage of the country in the next 10 years.

According to the Quarterly Review of Economic Prospects, the average 1990 household will have disposable personal income of $24,000 compared with $13,200 in 1980. The Review authors said that in 1990, 36% of households will have pre-tax incomes of more than $20,000 in 1980 dollars, twice the 21% with that income in 1980.

Average personal income will increase 20% to $14,321. The baby-boom generation will be coming on strong during the eighties. They will be in their thirties. As a result they will have more experience in making a living. Not only will this cause better productivity and higher income but of necessity many thousands will be two-income families.

"The larger share of households in upper brackets broadens markets for income-sensitive commodities. This group will be able to pay for quality in big ticket durable goods, afford better housing, and expand their consumption of services—travel, medical care, and education."

Marketing Management and Planning

As an integral part of marketing, advertising and sales promotion executives should never lose sight of the fact that their functions have very definite relationships with corporate marketing goals and with long-term marketing policies, as well as immediate sales objectives.

As an indication of these close relationships, and how they intermingle, following is a list of the topics covered in an American Management Association seminar on the subject:

I. INTRODUCTION
   A. Marketing Plan Defined
   B. Establishing Policies, Objectives and Goals
   C. Assigning Responsibility and Authority
   D. The Product Manager Function
   E. Sources of Information
   F. Relations to Other Departments

II. SITUATION ANALYSIS
   A. The Size, Scope and Share of of the Market
   B. Sales, Costs and Profits on the Product
   C. The Distribution Channels
   D. The Consumer or End Uses
   E. The Product

III. IDENTIFICATION OF PROBLEMS AND OPPORTUNITIES
   A. What Are the Major Problems Restricting Profit and Sales Growth?
   B. What Are the Opportunities for:
      1. Overcoming the problems?
      2. Improving the product line?
      3. Increasing penetration or entering new markets?
      4. Improving operating efficiency?

IV. ESTABLISHING OBJECTIVES
   A. Assumptions Regarding Future Conditions
   B. Primary Objectives Regarding:
      1. Sales and share of market
      2. Profits
      3. Turnover
      4. Return on investment
   C. Development of Over-all Marketing Strategies
   D. Detailing of Supplementary Objectives

V. ACTION PROGRAMS
   A. Establishing Priorities and Schedules
   B. Test Marketing
   C. Advertising and Sales Promotion
   D. Acquisition
   E. Distribution Changes, etc.

VI. CONTROL AND REVIEW PROCEDURES
   A. What Information Is Required
   B. Frequency of Reports
   C. Format of Information
   D. Review and Modification of Marketing Plan

VII. OPERATING STATEMENT
   A. Basic Assumptions
   B. Development of Cost Information
   C. Profit Projection
   D. Estimate of Cash Flow

From the standpoint of personal advancement, the sales promotion executive who displays genuine interest in, and demonstrates an appreciation of, his company's broad marketing problems will advance more rapidly up the corporate ladder.

The Role of Promotion

Any discussion of sales promotion, its practices, applications, principles and techniques, must necessarily start with its role in the over-all marketing structure, whether in the institutional, service, industrial, or consumer fields.

The fate of any company obviously depends on its marketing policies and how efficiently they are carried out.

Management is a question of efficient executive personnel; production is controllable and predetermined; both rest and depend heavily on successful marketing. Without sales, naturally, nothing else matters.

How can a company be sure, or at least have some indication, that its marketing policies are well-directed?

In manufacturing, the engineers have their slide rules, the factory people know exactly how many units to produce, the purchasing agents know precisely how many components to buy, but who will tell marketing groups how many they will sell?

Increasingly, most companies and their advertising agencies are conducting intensive market research studies to determine consumer needs and preferences.

The A. C. Nielsen Company of Northbrook, IL states:

"Companies selling through retail outlets today face distribution problems that are increasingly complex . . . and competition that grows constantly keener. So the advertising and promotional appropriations must work with greater efficiency than ever before. Both the product and its production schedules must be even more closely geared to changes in consumer preference and consumer demand.

"Ineffective marketing methods can cause substantial losses—or even extinction in today's marketplace. For these reasons, men who make marketing decisions want to make them with facts—accurate facts—at their disposal."

Nielsen provides a variety of services now widely used to market goods more efficiently. The Nielsen Retail Index provides continuous factual marketing data on foods, drugs, pharmaceuticals, toiletries, cosmetics, confectionery, tobacco, photographic and other products. This type of Nielsen service, rendered in 15 countries on three continents, is used on a continuous basis by over 700 manufacturers.

Another company which provides several market research services is Burgoyne Index, Inc., Cincinnati. Its services include:

Measurements of consumer sales by product category through retail outlets including grocery, drug, discount, department, hardware, variety, etc., in over 100 U.S. markets. In addition, Burgoyne provides distribution and observation checks in any U.S. market. Consumer studies with nationwide interviewing facilities through personal, telephone or mail techniques; specialize in custom-tailored in-store interviewing techniques. Specialized marketing research is available for specific client problems; also statistical analyses and data processing.

One well-known company which provides "custom" research services to "help management achieve sales and communications goals" is Gallup & Robinson, Inc. Other firms specialize in specific fields such as publication readership, political problems, industry-wide surveys.

The role of sales promotion was the subject of a survey conducted by Professor Albert W. Frey, the results of which were analyzed in a booklet published by the Amos Tuck School of Business Administration of Dartmouth College. Although published some years ago, the report contains comments and observations which effectively apply with equal force today; in fact, more so because time has proved their soundness.

The survey was based on a questionnaire which was sent to 652 persons: 197 sales promotion managers in companies with separate advertising managers, 130 sales-promotion managers in companies with no advertising managers and 325 combined-advertising-and-sales-promotion managers. Fifty-three in the first group, 40 in the second and 139 in the third responded.

Respondents' companies included producers of consumer goods (about 39%), industrial goods (about 27%) and both (about 34%). The answers showed no significant differences in practice or viewpoint between consumer- and industrial-goods manufacturers.

The first point to become clear was that a great majority of the companies covered do distinguish between advertising and sales promotion. Of the 232 respondents, 180 (77%) said their firms distinguish formally; thirty-two (14%) indicated their companies do not distinguish formally but they themselves do informally; one said his company "doesn't distinguish, but—"

Of the companies that distinguish formally, one hundred (57% of those for which respondents gave this information) have separate sales-promotion budgets. Sixty-six (37%) provide for sales promotion in their advertising budgets, seven (4%) in salesmen's-activities budgets and three (2%) in other budgets.

In defining sales promotion, some of the comments received were:

"Neither advertising agencies nor sales departments have a full understanding of what is involved."

"A sales-promotion manager's responsibilities are to do the thinking to negotiate the marketing program which the sales manager is too busy to do and the advertising manager doesn't know how to do."

"It must by its nature be close to both advertising and selling, but neither ad agencies nor sales departments have a full understanding of what is involved."

"Sales promotion is the other half of the job begun by national advertising, which, by itself, cannot complete the sale—at least in our business."

"Sales promotion should always be treated as a separate function —no matter how interrelated and connected to advertising it becomes —because it's so important to support sales on a broad front and the whole idea of sales promotion is conducive to the broader thinking and action that modern merchandising requires."

"Sales promotion is the catalyst of business, big or small. It is the agent that gives direction to an advertising campaign, gives drive to a dealer organization, gives enthusiasm to a sales force . . . It can speed up sales in a specific area or throughout the country. The efforts of sales promotion thrive on one ingredient —enthusiasm. Any sales organization feels the impact of promotional efforts."

Albert W. Frey, Professor
Amos Tuck School of Business Administration
Dartmouth College

"In the soft-goods industries, sales-promotion activities are more important than national advertising, which serves nevertheless to give stature and focus to the sales promotion at the retail level. The best national advertising campaign fails without intensive sales promotion at store level in our industry. A sound budget in soft goods provides more money for local sales promotion than for national advertising. It is costing industry millions of dollars because its sales-promotion effort is weak as a result of lack of interest on the part of agencies and failure of management to do the job if the agency neglects doing it."

How do They Differ?

IN BRIEF, an overwhelming majority seemed to feel that advertising and sales promotion differ in many ways.

Advertising consists in (1) choosing the media through which a company will transmit its message to consumers and the trade, (2) buying space or time in those media and (3) composing and presenting the message. The media typically are owned and controlled by others, who sell their space and time at established rates.

Sales promotion, on the other hand, "educates" and arouses the enthusiasm of salesmen, middlemen, consumers and perhaps others through a variety of materials, tools and devices *that the company itself controls.*

Every marketing program, of course, has two other major components: merchandising and personal selling. The first deals with the company's products, prices and service, the second with salesmen and individual customers.

The four are not equally essential. While few firms could exist without personal selling or merchandising, and many could not without advertising, most could survive without sales promotion, and not a few do. But sales promotion buttresses and strengthens a marketing operation, thereby magnifying a company's profits and success.

The reason is that, while merchandising can produce and present an attractive product and personal selling and advertising can effectively inform and persuade dealers and the public about it, only sales promotion can add an *extra* element of persuasion and *engender enthusiasm.* As one respondent put it:

"Sales promotion is the catalyst of business—big or small. It is the agent that gives direction to an advertising campaign—gives drive to a dealer organization—gives enthusiasm to a sales force. Its addition to a company can speed up sales in a specific area or throughout the country . . . The efforts of sales promotion thrive on one ingredient—enthusiasm . . . Any sales organization feels the impact of promotional efforts. The spread of enthusiasm is a powerful weapon that can carry the sales force forward each year in its sales at an ever-increasing pace."

Unlike personal selling, which typically is directed at individuals, sales promotion is beamed at groups; but unlike advertising, which aims at masses of people, sales promotion aims at comparatively small, well-defined groups. While advertising, then, is "constant for the long pull," sales promotion seeks specific immediate objectives; it represents a rifle, rather than a shotgun, approach. Therefore it operates largely in periodic pushes, for any of which every individual among its targets—salesmen, distributor, dealer—may be specifically identified.

Organization for Sales Promotion

How DO we fit sales promotion into the marketing structure?

The survey revealed great diversity in current practice. Of 162 respondents, forty-nine report to general-management executives, seventy-four to sales executives, fifteen to marketing executives, ten to advertising executives, nine to merchandising executives and five to sales-and-advertising or sales-and-merchandising executives.

The chart probably explains why so many report to sales executives: The bulk of the sales-promotion effort is beamed at "own salesmen" and middlemen, both of whom are primarily in the sales department's province.

But this arrangement may not be the most rewarding. Let us outline a different one, the advantages of which will become apparent when we talk about "Sales Promotion in Detail."

In this arrangement, the sales-promotion manager—like the merchandising, sales and advertising managers—reports to the top marketing executive. This executive—a vice-president for marketing, a director of marketing, a marketing manager or whatever—is responsible for over-all marketing objectives. Each department head, for his own department, (1) sets up objectives attuned to the company's objectives, (2) sees that adequate programs are drawn up and carried out. For best results, of course, all four will co-operate; each will do his best, under the direction of the chief marketing executive, to co-ordinate and synchronize his efforts with the others'.

Jointly, they have four targets: company salesmen, middlemen (distributors, dealers and distributors' and dealers' salesmen), consumers and "others" (including, for example, engineers, architects and public officials).

The percentage of effort directed at each of these groups is likely to vary according to a company's product, as this chart, derived from respondents' answers, shows:

Percentages of Sales-Promotion Effort
Directed at Various Targets

Kind of product manufactured	Number of companies	Own salesmen	Middlemen	Consumers	Others
Consumer goods	70	22.4%	44.8%	32.4%	0.4%
Industrial goods	32	21.7%	26.0%	44.3%	8.0%
Both	59	18.0%	40.4%	32.8%	8.8%
Unspecified	5	23.0%	26.0%	31.0%	20.0%
	166	20.7%	39.1%	34.8%	5.4%

The narrowness of the range for "own salesmen" is rather striking. In contrast, industrial-goods producers seem to devote comparatively more of their effort to consumers and "others," comparatively less to distributors and dealers—partly, at least, because many of them operate without middlemen, selling directly to consumers.

But we shall best understand the sales-promotion manager's job if, before we describe it in detail, we go over some of the special skills and qualifications he brings to it.

Sales-Promotion Skills and Qualifications

LET US MAKE one point clear first: While out of respondents' replies came a picture of sales promotion as a sort of "department of enthusiasm," the sales-promotion man does not need to *be* more enthusiastic than his advertising or sales counterparts. Enthusiasm is desirable in any department, at any level. What sets the sales-promotion man apart is his ability to *engender enthusiasm in others.*

That he may do this, respondents generally agreed, he must above all be *creative:* "One of the keynotes of sales promotion is creativity," one typical comment ran, "and this point is being recognized more and more by management."

Of course creativity, too—especially if we define it broadly—is desirable in any manager. But if we define it rather narrowly—as merely the capacity to produce and introduce new ideas—its special applicability to sales promotion becomes clear: Within any given period the sales-promotion man will probably have to "think up" more new ideas than anyone else in the business will. Respondents undoubtedly were thinking in terms of this narrower definition.

A sales promotion manager must also be intimately familiar with the situations in which his creative efforts will work. Said one respondent:

"A good sales-promotion man needs field selling experience and a full knowledge of dealers' problems as well as the salesmen's in order to prepare practical promotional aids that will help the sale. Advertising can bring them in, but promotion does the 'on-the-spot' selling. An advertising man only needs to know copy, media, distribution, layout, art work and agency functions; he does not have to be a fieldman."

Many felt that the sales-promotion manager must be able to work, and enjoy working, under constant pressure, especially the pressure of almost continuously imminent deadlines. (Only comparatively few—no more than one might have expected—suggested they did *more* work than anyone else.) "It's an interesting business that keeps one on his toes and reaching for the bicarbonate of soda," wrote one man. Also implying this difference—and perhaps others—another wrote, "The ad manager wouldn't fill out this questionnaire on the train as I'm doing."

Unlike the advertising manager, the sales-promotion manager must be able to carry most of his burden himself; advertising agencies take relatively little part in their clients' sales-promotion programs. This is probably partly because (1) agencies consider sales promotion outside their proper scope and are reluctant to deal with the mass of detail it involves and (2) best sales-promotion performance requires close proximity to internal operations.

Sales Promotion in Detail

WHILE THE FOUR department heads must all co-operate for best results, the sales-promotion manager—creative, intimately acquainted with his company's over-all operation, self-reliant, efficient under pressure—*especially* works with the other three. His function, in fact, is essentially nothing but *to enhance the others' effectiveness.*

The merchandising manager ensures that the company's product and service are sound; the sales-promotion manager, starting where the merchandising manager left off, finds ways to make them more attractive and exciting. The advertising manager prepares an interesting, imaginative advertising campaign; sales promotion may give it an *extra* fillip of interest and imagination.

But the bulk of the sales-promotion effort, we have seen, is beamed at company salesmen and middlemen. Therefore the sales-promotion manager works *especially* with the sales manager.

Salesmen's basic education about product, price, company policies and how to sell is a sales-department function—but sales-promotion personnel, equipped and trained to do more than sell, create and provide visual aids that sharpen the teaching. The sales department can devise sales contests, manuals, portfolios and other equipment—but sales promotion can create better ones. The sales department can run conventions and meetings, but sales-promotion people, trained in ways to hold and move audiences—and adept at "thinking up" new ways—can make them more stimulating and educative.

The increased sales-force enthusiasm that sales promotion thus engenders is inevitably reflected not only in increased sales to distributors but also in greater distributor enthusiasm. But sales promotion is not content only to influence distributors so indirectly. It also wins their attention, interest and co-operation through skillfully prepared direct mail, catalogues, house organs, product-information sheets and service bulletins, through trade shows and exhibits, through merchandised advertisements, through contests and premiums for distributors' salesmen, through films and other visual aids company salesmen will use at distributor salesmen's meetings.

The increased enthusiasm of distributors and their salesmen, in turn, is reflected in greater sales to dealers and greater dealer enthusiasm—but dealers are also targets of *direct* sales-promotion activity. In so far as this seeks merely increased enthusiasm, its techniques are much like those it uses on the distributor level. But it seeks also to help the dealer sell, and to do this it gives him window and interior display material, advertising mats, radio copy, TV films, direct mail, demonstrations and educational material for his salesmen.

And increased dealer enthusiasm inevitably influences consumers—but sales promotion goes directly to the consumer, too. Typical tools include premiums, samples, coupons, contests and, for the industrial market, catalogues and technical bulletins. Some companies channel some of their consumer-beamed sales-promotion material through distributors and dealers, and unquestionably the consumer enthusiasm that results warms the distributors and dealers as well.

The Definition

Assuming the trend will continue—and reason and results to date indicate it will—we now find sales promotion not nearly as hard to define as it once was. This definition probably reflects today's majority opinion; it almost certainly reflects tomorrow's:

Sales promotion is that component of the marketing mix that continually creates and applies materials and techniques that, reinforcing and supplementing the materials and techniques provided by the other components, *increase* the capacity and desire of salesmen, distributors and dealers to sell a company's product and make consumers *eager* to buy it."

Sales Promotion Defined

In its broadest sense, sales promotion includes all those functions which have to do with the marketing of a product or the promotion of a service—personal selling, advertising, displays, exhibitions, and all other activities designed to increase sales and expand the market.

In point of fact, sales promotion differs from advertising only in terminology; advertising is a form of sales promotion and sales promotion is a form of advertising. Yet there is a convenience in making a distinction even where no great difference exists, in that sales promotion is a somewhat broader term.

The advertising manager of a large manufacturing company defined these terms as follows:

"Sales promotion moves the product toward the buyer, while advertising moves the buyer toward the product."

An executive of a retail chain-store organization has called sales promotion "merchandising the advertising."

It is significant of the difficulties of definition to note that some companies use the title "Manager of Advertising and Sales Promotion," while others reverse the words to read "Manager of Sales Promotion and Advertising."

The Committee on Definitions of the American Marketing Association offers the following definition:

SALES PROMOTION:

1. In a specific sense, those sales activities that supplement both personal selling and advertising and coordinate them and help to make them effective, such as displays, shows and expositions, demonstrations, and other nonrecurrent selling efforts not in the ordinary routine.

2. In a general sense, sales promotion includes personal selling, advertising, and supplementary selling activities.

This definition, while good, puts emphasis on sales promotion as a nonrecurrent selling effort. Most sales managers agree that the great weakness of sales promotion in business today is the "campaign" psychology which surrounds it. Sales promotion is no different from any other form of selling; it requires a continuing effort, for it has been amply demonstrated that "shot in the arm" techniques leave much to be desired. Then, too, the illustrations used in the definition belittle the function. There is a too-evident desire to subordinate sales promotion to advertising, when the trend is the other way, and advertising is being subordinated to sales promotion. While it is true advertising usually involves a larger expenditure of money, modern usage of the term tends to regard trade, consumer, and industrial advertising as a part of the over-all sales promotional program. We have so considered it in planning this HANDBOOK. For regardless of whether sales promotion is to be the tail that wags advertising, or advertising the tail that wags sales promotion, prevailing practice combines the two functions, at least so far as production is concerned.

Increased Importance of Sales Promotion

"Promotion investment is big business, any way you look at it," stated an editor of a prominent advertising magazine. Recent surveys show an increased percentage of the marketing budget being spent on sales promotion. A recent ANA (Association of National Advertisers) report showed that almost $36 billion were being spent in sales promotion, with the growth rate in promotion spending increasing faster than the advertising growth rate. Obviously sales promotion has become a more important marketing tool than ever and is still gaining momentum. The $36 billion figure compares favorably with the almost $43 billion spent on media advertising in the U.S. in 1978. The media estimate for 1979 is nearly $47 billion.

Making up the total of sales promotion expenditures were:
Business meetings and travel, $8.2 billion;
Premiums and incentives, $7.8 billion;
Trade shows and exhibits, $6.1 billion;
Direct mail, $5,340 million;
Point of purchase, $3.6 billion;
Specialties, $1.7 billion;
Printing, paper and production not included above, $1.9 billion;
Business films and audiovisuals, $1 billion;
Agency fees and services, $350 million.

Ed Meyer, Sr. Vice-President, Director of Merchandising for Dancer-Fitzgerald and Sample, in the May 1, 1978 issue of *Advertising Age* pointed out the tremendous increase in sales promotion investment and incidentally gave some excellent advice to all marketing managers. He pointed out how important it was to get an expert sales promotion person, or use an agency that specializes in sales promotion. Also, he emphasized how imperative it is to plan your promotions correctly. In your planning, he suggests running a promotion testing program and being sure you follow through in communicating your promotions effectively.

It is possible to go down a list of major U.S. companies' investments to prove that promotion is a vital factor in each firm's marketing scheme. For example, one of the large razor companies spends around $30 million in sales promotion. And the number of firms which spend a million dollars or more in point-of-purchase alone has grown to more than 300. The latest figures show that General Motors leads the way in p-o-p expenditures.

Interestingly, in a recent survey over half of the respondents said that their sales promotion budgets had grown faster than their media budgets and the overall expenditures quoted above verify this. An average of 48% of the total marketing budget was spent on promotion, up from 34%. The accelerated growth of the sales promotion function may be partially attributed to two chief causes:

Our population statistics of almost 218 million with 75 million, 250 thousand households make a remarkable market and the number of Americans who will be engaged in selling in the year 1983 should top 7.5 million according to a study of the nation's job outlook made by the U.S. Labor Department's Bureau of Labor Statistics.

The need for retail sales workers, the largest sales group, is expected to go up to 4.5 million in 1983, contrasted with 2.8 million employed in 1968 (longer hours in metropolitan and suburban areas will be chiefly responsible for the additional manpower).

This increase in manpower reflects, of course, the projected growth in output of goods and services which must be sold and the successful accomplishment of which dictates the need for more and better sales promotion material in all categories.

The second factor in the expansion of sales promotion programs is the ever-rising increase in advertising costs. The cost of a thirty-second commercial on NBC-TV winter prime time, (1978-79) ranges from $33,500 to a high of $66,500. Of course, one has to remember that such a broadcast is aimed at 62 million, 100 thousand households with an audience of almost 72 million. This is a 17.4% increase of such households over six years ago.

Sales Promotion as a Customer Service

Sales promotion is actually a service to the customer. It is designed to help him buy. Thus we find an astute merchandiser like the Scott Paper Company planning its principal sales promotional efforts: (1) To help industrial users of its products to plan washrooms; and (2) to help the retailer who sells Scott paper products to do a more effective merchandising job, not alone on Scott products, but on everything sold in the store.

The purpose of sales promotion is to increase sales; the corollary of this is that it also tends to reduce the costs of distribution by expanding markets. This is evidenced by the experience of colonial America. In those days most products were imported from England and other countries. As these products found wider markets, local production of the same products started and prices were reduced.

If the promotion of sales is regarded as a means of helping customers sell more of our products, or making better use of our products, the function becomes more constructive and, on the theory that those who serve best profit most, eventually becomes more profitable. That is why some companies approach sales promotion from the customer angle, rather than as just another way to sell. They designate the department or the operation as the "Customers'

Service Department," "Merchant's Service Department," "Washroom Advisory Service," etc. One important manufacturer has gone so far as to group advertising, sales promotion, publicity, and personal sales under a vice president in charge of "Customer Relations." When a customer receives a communication or a proposal from a department of the business which, its name implies, was set up to help him become more successful, his reaction is decidedly favorable; and his feeling toward the company is more kindly.

This distinction is important because sales promotion is not so much a department of the business as it is a concept of doing business. In any successful business which depends upon selling, everyone should be a sales promoter. The aim of sound sales promotion, therefore, extends beyond the mere stimulation of sales to making everyone in the organization sales-conscious.

Beginnings of Sales Promotion

Perhaps the earliest form of sales promotion was handling the inquiries which came in as a result of the company's advertising. It became the job of someone in the organization to answer such inquiries, send out the proper printed matter, and then forward the inquiries with the essential information to the salesman in the territory to follow up and sell. This is still the principal function of a great many sales promotion departments.

Then it was found that a good opportunity for increased sales existed in the inactive accounts on the ledgers. Many of these were not serviced by salesmen for one reason or another. So the man who handled the inquiries also took on the job of following up the inactive accounts. This required the preparation of special promotional literature, such as explaining the application of an office device to various types of business, or specific uses of a product to meet certain situations. With the realization that the sales organization could do its job better if the way were paved with educational literature and buying helps, sales promotion was broadened to include a wide variety of special projects mainly designed to expand existing markets or uncover new ones.

One of the earliest "indirect" sales promotions was the "Merchant's Service Department" of the National Cash Register Company. It was in 1895 when John H. Patterson, founder of that enterprise and "daddy" of modern sales management, concluded his sales agents, while doing very well selling cash registers to new prospects, were overlooking the potential business from merchants who had already bought cash registers. It occurred to Mr. Patterson that if he could in some way help these merchants to become more successful they would soon need more and better cash registers to handle their increased business. This was the job originally given to the N.C.R. Merchant's Service Department, which became a vitally important factor in the future operations of that company, through offering counsel to store managers on all phases of store management.

Sales Penetration

As the tempo of competitive selling increases, the need of covering all factors in the sale grows apace. Consumer advertising can and usually does do an important market-conditioning job, thus making it easier for the salesman and the dealer (if distribution is through that channel) to sell the product. But the influence of advertising is limited. Not all the people whom you hope to influence read advertisements, listen to radio broadcasts, or have television receivers. They may not even observe outdoor bulletins. Yet in many instances it is most important to the eventual success of a distribution program, to make sure that every buying factor is covered, and the more important factors *thoroughly covered.*

This is a "sharpshooting" undertaking which can usually be best done by sales promotional techniques, including selective (direct mail) advertising, trade shows, demonstrations, and service promotions. It is especially important in negotiated selling, but it becomes essential in all types of selling when there is keen competition for the customer's dollar. For example, in selling a product not presently carried by department stores it is necessary to get the story across to: (1) The store owner or manager; (2) the section merchandising man; (3) the department buyer and (perhaps) the manager of store promotions. Since it is improbable these executives will act until they observe some evidence of consumer demand, local advertising, either direct or through the store, may be required. It could be, as some advertising agents like to think, that high-powered general advertising will give a manufacturer all the penetration needed, but with advertising costs where they are, it is too expensive for most marketing operations.

One company's program serves to illustrate the importance which some sales executives attach to promotional penetration: "We have more than doubled our advertising in trade publications, to at least partially sell the dealer before the salesman calls. We are currently using two weeklies, one bimonthly, and two monthly trade papers, which are the five with the largest circulations, and, we think, with the most constant readership.

"We have stepped up the tempo of our direct-mail campaign to dealers. We now have a weekly mailing to 22,000 dealers, consisting of solicitations for business on unadvertised items, institutional copy, and reprints of all our trade-paper ads.

"We have more than doubled the number of point-of-sale pieces developed, and more than doubled the quantity prepared of each. They are all distributed to our dealers free of charge. We have quadrupled the amount of printed material that we supply to our dealers without charge, to be used as envelope stuffers, or for distribution in the stores."

The promotion program of a leading television manufacturer likewise concentrates on dealer penetration: "At the dealer level," an official of that company said, "we are putting into effect a merchandising type of advertising, which is the type of selling copy producing greater volume sales during the current buying season, as well as in preparation of proportionately greater sales in the new year to follow. This, also, is further supplemented by additional effort which is now being made in the development of a dealer 'awareness' in the effective use of window displays, local representation in community publications, participation in all advertising of a pamphlet nature edited by social clubs and other organizations, etc.

"In addition to these items, a great deal of emphasis is being placed upon the development of a stronger and more loyal dealer organization which is prompted by a greater interest in the coordination of all affairs pertaining to the distributor-dealer chain of relationship. Further, we are conducting a greater number of the type of dealer meetings which provides each attending member with the most current and advanced sales analysis, sales promotion, and sales administrative programs, which are interpreted as accurately as possible as they pertain to the tangible problems of our retail outlets."

Sales Promotion Grows Up

A very important development in sales promotion has been in the selling of "big-ticket" merchandise, such as household appliances, and in working with distributors' dealers to make them a more effective part of the over-all sales program. In fact, one of the significant developments in sales promotion is the outstanding succes of manufacturers, such as the Armstrong Cork Company, in getting wholesale distributors to take over an increasingly larger part of the sales promotional job.

In the case of companies selling through established dealers, where the unit of sale is large enough to justify the expense, most current promotional projects are aimed at helping dealers to rebuild and expand their outside sales organizations, on the theory that as competition deepens, an increasingly larger share of a dealer's volume must be obtained by ringing doorbells.

With that thought in mind, one company selling home appliances through public utilities retained the services of The McMurry Company, even before appliances were in good supply, to develop a "packaged" sales recruitment and selection program for gas appliance dealers. It was offered to the industry in cooperation with the American Gas Association. The purpose of the program was twofold: (1) To help dealers to recruit salesmen qualified to successfully sell gas appliances; and (2) to eliminate, so far as possible, the turnover of salesmen in dealers' organizations through more careful selection. Unlike most selection programs, Dr. McMurry placed emphasis on the interview rather than upon so-called psychological tests. He endeavored to bring out information about the applicant which would permit measuring his qualifications. From these interviews the dealer can determine to what extent the applicant has exhibited possession of those nine traits which investigation established as being necessary to ensure success in selling gas appliances, namely: (1) Stability, (2) industry, (3) ambition, (4) ability to get along with others, (5) loyalty, (6) perseverance, (7) maturity, (8) leadership, (9) motivation.

The program was well received by the industry and proved invaluable in assisting retail dealers to maintain sales under the competitive conditions which came after the pent-up demands for appliances were filled. The project was noteworthy in that it came to grips with the problem faced by every dealer handling products which depend upon creative salesmanship for a market—*manpower*. Few dealers know where to get good salesmen, how to select them, or how to train them. As a result they do not have the manpower to make the most of the franchise they hold. This underselling not only limits the dealer's earnings but, just as certainly, restricts the manufacturer's profits from the territory.

Another example of a "grass roots" promotion now in vogue was the driver selection and training program offered to operators of truck fleets by The White Motor Company. As is true of so many manufacturers White's largest potential market was among users of White trucks. The key to that market is customer satisfaction, and, in the case of motor trucks, customer satisfaction depends upon the performance of the truck under varying conditions. Satisfactory performance, however, involves more than the truck itself, for no matter how well engineered and built a truck may be, it will not show a low operating cost unless it is driven by men who have natural aptitude for the work and who know how to get the best out of it. So White developed, and offered to fleet operators, regardless of the make of trucks they were presently using, a streamlined program for: (1) Selecting drivers having natural aptitude for the work, and (2) training them to care for the trucks so as to avoid break-downs and needless maintenance expense. As a result of this farsighted promotional activity, fleet operators were able to control costs at a time when operating expenses were out of hand, and thousands of drivers of White trucks enjoyed greater job satisfaction by virtue of the experience they shared through White's *Driver's Manual,* and the training program built around it.

It will be noted in both of the foregoing cases, typical of the many promotional programs now current, they are not designed so much to promote the sale of one product over competitive products, but to help dealers or users, as the case may be, to better profit from the customer relationship. It is this characteristic which makes modern sales promotion effective. Dealers who are only mildly interested in devices which promote the sale of one product on their shelves, at the expense of another, respond favorably to a promotion aimed at helping them to correct basic weaknesses in their business operations. By helping to make them more successful, the manufacturer automatically ensures his own success, which is another way of saying that the type of sales promotion that we have today is in fact profit insurance. It is creative selling at its best. It is rapidly taking the place of high-pressure selling which seeks only to appropriate business which someone else has created. It thus serves society and the industry, as well as the individual manufacturer and distributor.

Kroger's Philosophy of Sales Promotion

One of the outstanding sales promotional activities is that of The Kroger Company, operating a national chain of food stores. One reason for the effectiveness of Kroger sales promotion is the philosophy behind it. This philosophy is summed up in a vest-pocket expediter card supplied to every Kroger employee who has anything whatever to do with distribution:

1. Create the *value.*
2. Plan distribution so the product is a *value* at the point of sale and at the point of use.
3. Present the value to the organization and to the customer.
4. Follow through to maintain the value at point of sale and point of use to continue successful sales.

It will be observed that the Kroger philosophy is a two-way proposition. It includes "selling" the value to: (1) The organization, and (2) to the customer. This is a too-little-appreciated responsibility of good promotion. It too often begins and ends with "selling" the customer.

On this point, Steven A. Douglas, director of sales promotion for the Kroger stores, says: "We think of sales promotion as a concept rather than a department of the business. We sell everyone on our company, its policies, and its products just as hard as we can, and usually before we sell the consumer. We never expect any employee to promote or sell anything by instruction or by direction. We *sell him* on the product or the idea first, and arouse his enthusiastic desire to in turn sell 'Mrs. Smith,' as we refer to the customer in all our promotions. This 'sell the man who sells the customer' idea is carried through all our promotions. Ours is a highly competitive industry and we believe that our success during the coming years will require the same accent on real *value,* well distributed and with careful follow-through, that successful selling has always required, *only more of it."*

To implement this philosophy Kroger utilizes every known promotional tool, depending to a larger extent than is true of most merchandising organizations upon dramatizing values. For example, one successful promotion was centered around a carefully worked out skit which was put on by every branch, called "The Greatest Value Show on Earth." It had a showboat theme and staging.

A philosophy of sales promotion which has stood up many years, and is as sound today as it was 30 years ago, was developed by William H. Ingersoll of dollar watch fame. According to the late Philip S. Salisbury, editor of *Sales Management* Magazine and one time sales promotion manager for Ingersoll watches, it was about like this:

1. A good product.
2. Priced right to the public.
3. Made easily available.
4. Well and consistently advertised.
5. Good store identification.
6. Dealers who know *how* to sell.
7. Dealers who *want* to sell it.

The Danger of Half-Baked Surveys

It is to the credit of sales promotion and advertising men that they are placing more dependence on hard facts, and less on hunches, in planning promotions. But, as in most selling methods, there is a danger that too much reliance may be placed on inconclusive or inadequate surveys. Just as a little knowledge can be a dangerous thing, so too small a sample when it comes to making a survey can be equally dangerous. In that connection a sales promotion executive with General Motors Corporation offers the following suggestions regarding direct-mail surveys:

> Never try to appraise the results of a survey without first studying the questionnaire—with special reference to such points as the following:
>
> 1. Was the questionnaire skillfully developed?
> 2. Were the questions easy to understand—with a minimum chance of being misunderstood?
> 3. Are the questions properly arranged?—consider not only the construction and arrangement of each individual question, but
> 4. Is the sequence or continuity such as to avoid confusion and facilitate the respondent's "flow of thought"?
> 5. Are questions or similar items asked the same way?—especially important as regards any series of items where the answers are to be compared on a *relative* basis.
> 6. Do the questions cover the subject adequately?
> 7. Do they afford the opportunity for the respondent to give any kind of answer that may reflect his individual reaction?
> 8. Does the questionnaire provide for all the data that will be needed for an adequate statistical break-down?
> 9. Does it invite the respondent to qualify his answers with remarks and comments?—extremely helpful in enabling the researcher to properly interpret the statistical findings. (See item 25.)
> 10. Is the questionnaire short enough to ensure high returns?
> 11. Is it attractive and inviting or does it look as though it were developed by a bureaucratic statistician?
> 12. Do you think that you yourself would have bothered to fill it out?
>
> And here's another practical method of appraisal:
>
> 13. How does the quality and attractiveness of the questionnaire stack up against the *finished report or formal presentation of the results?*
>   All too frequently there's a tendency to skimp on the questionnaire itself—then "shoot the works" and spend any amount of time and money on dolling up the report. (Don't get me wrong: Attractive presentations are important, but it's even more important to have an attractive questionnaire!)
>
> SAMPLES:
>
> 14. How was the questionnaire distributed and to whom?
> 15. Was it directed to the particular group or groups of people who are best qualified to give the answers?
> 16. Was the sample adequate as to size?
>   This depends primarily on the degree to which the data are to be broken down—or cross-indexed. The finer the break-down, the greater the number of samples required.

17. Was the sampling scientifically controlled so as to properly reckon with
    —territorial locations?
    —makes of cars?
    —ages of cars?
    —new car buyers vs. used car buyers?

    This does not necessarily mean that the mailings (or the returns) shall
    be in exact proportion to the characteristics of the market. Frequently it is
    more logical to take care of this by "weighting" the data incident to the
    statistical complications. But it is important that the incoming question-
    naires be properly identified as to the classifications that need to be
    reckoned with.

REPORTS:

18. Does the report include all the essential information that is needed for
    proper understanding and interpretation of the results?
19. Were the statistical procedures sound?
20. Were the returns properly "weighted" so as to compensate for distortions
    in the distribution of the sample?
21. Are the questions as quoted in the report exactly the same as they appeared
    in the questionnaire?
22. Are the statistical column headings consistent with the real meaning of
    the figures?
23. Are the data intelligently and effectively presented—in a manner that is
    conducive to proper interpretation and practical action?
24. Are any of the findings out of line with what you *positively know to be
    the facts?*
25. How does the report stack up as regards what we might call "internal
    consistency"?

    In other words, do its various parts hang together and tend to support
    one another, or is it contradictory in any respect?

SPONSORS:

    And last, but not least, here's a general question that it's always well to
    bear in mind:
    Did the agency responsible for the survey have an "axe to grind?"
    But that's not quite the right way to express it. Nobody makes a survey
    without having some reason for making it and the fact that these people
    had an "axe to grind" should not within itself be taken as a negative
    factor.
    But in appraising the results it's always well to consider—

26. Just *what* KIND *of axe* did they have to grind?—then scrutinize the
    results in the light thereof.

Coordinating Sales Promotion

Another important recent development in sales promotion is the
way it is being geared into other marketing activities to produce a
balanced sales program. This is particularly true of sales research.
The approved formula for successful business management is to find
out what the customer wants to buy and sell it to him rather than try

to sell him what you want to make. This philosophy is demonstrated in the customer research activities of the General Motors Corporation. The surveys which this department of GM is continually making to determine customer preferences not only provide all divisions of the corporation with data useful in designing new models, but provide a solid foundation upon which the company bases its sales promotional activities.

Similarly, consumer testing of new products is depended upon by some sales managers to give them the best "angle" to use in planning the promotional effort. It is a well-established fact in sales management that the first step to the order should be to find out *why* old customers bought the product and how it is used. Very often we find, to our amazement, that the real reasons people buy are quite different from those we think caused them to buy, or even reasons the salesmen give for their buying. For example, for years cash registers were sold as "thief catchers." An analysis of buying reasons showed that an overlooked factor in selling a merchant a cash register was that it removed the temptation any employee might have to pilfer the cash drawer.

Research as a Tool

Tremendous strides have been made in this area within the last few years. The business demand for more accurate market-penetration information, buying motives, and customer purchasing power stimulated the growth of national research organizations whose findings become the basis of the clients' marketing programs. This, in turn, determines the scope and objectives of advertising and sales promotion programs. Advertising agencies, particularly, base their campaigns on the results of market surveys, and sales promotion activities are naturally, closely affected.

A well-coordinated sales promotion program even includes the credit department. One sales promotion manager has the credit manager write a letter to a salesman every week, mentioning a specific retail account in that salesman's territory. The letter tells why that merchant's credit is ace high with the company. Salesmen show the letter to the merchants with excellent good-will results. In some instances the letter so flattered the salesman's customer, that it paved the way for a more substantial order than otherwise might have been secured.

One of the first, and very important steps, in coordinating sales promotion with the other departments of the business, is to get the entire organization from the president down to the shipping clerk sold on its importance as a sales stabilizer, and, more specifically, its importance to them. Even the man on the production line, who probably thinks it would be more to the point if the money which the company is now "squandering" on sales promotion went into workers' pay envelopes, needs to understand that were it not for sales promotion there might be weeks at a time, when orders lagged, that he would have to be laid off. And the same goes for the sales organization. Salesmen need to be "sold" and resold, because it is not unusual for salesmen to feel the company would get more business if the advertising and sales appropriation were used to raise salesmen's pay, and thus get more and better salesmen on the firing line.

Coordinating sales promotion with advertising is not an easy problem for the sales executive. In many companies the two functions are successfully combined and are the joint responsibility of one executive who thus serves as the director of advertising and sales promotion for the business. This often works out quite well, especially in cases where the sales promotional effort consists mainly of printed literature and dealer helps. Joint administration is almost universal in the case of companies whose advertising is confined to specialized rather than general media, as for instance companies making engineering specialties. In the case of a company doing extensive consumer advertising, as well as doing an aggressive job of promoting its products, it is extremely difficult to separate sales promotion from advertising because the overlapping functions and responsibility involved eventually cause difficulty.

One solution is to have a sales promotional section in each sales division of the business which is responsible for recognizing the need for a certain kind of promotional activity, and able to "put it over" when crystallized. The unit promotion man, upon approval of the division sales manager, gets all the facts and background material needed to develop the project. The advertising department then creates all the required promotional material, working in close cooperation with the divisional sales promotion unit. When the materials are ready they are turned over to the sales promotion manager of the unit and that executive, along with the division sales organization, is then responsible for the successful conduct of the campaign in the field. This division of responsibility, for example, is practiced with satisfactory results by Armstrong Cork Company and others operating on a product divisional plan. Some companies follow the same procedure in the case of geographical sales divisions. Westinghouse Electric, for example, has a sales promotional unit in each major territory of its wholesale division. In this case, however, the principal job of the divisional promotion unit is to carry through a national program developed in Mansfield.

Gearing Sales Promotion to Personal Selling

Integrating the sales promotional program with personal selling begins with "selling" the sales organization (including the dealers' salespeople in the case of companies selling through established trade channels) on the company, its policies, and its products. This may or may not include formal sales training. Usually it does, although in some large organizations this function is performed by a sales personnel officer. However, there is a growing tendency to bracket sales training with sales promotion, since modern selling is becoming more and more promotional in its concept. This is especially true in training dealers and their sales personnel. Most sales promotional programs depend upon the wholehearted cooperation of the field organization to "put them over." The sales promotional department therefore has a direct interest in training all those responsible for selling the product to the customer or at the point of sale. For example, in the marketing of Hoover cleaners, where a large force of salesmen selling direct to the home is required, the recruiting, selection, and training of these salesmen is a very important responsibility of the sales promotion manager. It is, in fact, the crux of the whole Hoover promotional program.

Modern practice therefore contemplates the sales promotional job as having three steps: (1) planning, (2) production, and (3) execution. It is extremely important that any sales promotional undertaking, if it is to attain a full measure of success with a minimum of cost, be painstakingly coordinated with the company's sales research operation to assure wise planning; the company's advertising department and advertising counsel, to assure economical and skilled production of sales promotional materials; and finally with sales field operations to make sure that after the plan is conceived and the required materials produced, it will be followed through intelligently and enthusiastically by the salesmen.

Some Industry-Wide Promotions

Another important trend in promoting a business is seen in the many instances of competitors pooling their efforts to develop business for the whole industry, on the theory that competition comes from rival industries as well as rival companies. For example, securing wider markets for coal would be a difficult and costly undertaking for the average coal producer. Yet his profits are continually under pressure from oil, piped natural gas, and other fuels. Some time ago all those who had a stake in maintaining the market for coal joined to form Anthracite Industries, Inc. Contributing to the work of the institute were equipment manufacturers, coal distributors, as well as mine operators. An engineering laboratory was established at Primos, Pennsylvania, to develop more efficient methods of using coal, and a field organization was formed to "sell" these improved methods to architects, heating engineers, and other interested persons. Similar promotional activities have been undertaken by the California wineries, the meat packers, the gas industry, and others too numerous to mention.

While some of these promotions have been confined to "putting over" a national "week" or "day" with hit-or-miss newspaper publicity, some have been outstanding. For example, the list of projects undertaken by the electrical industry's promotional institute includes :

Sales financing	Producers councils
Rural electrification	Commercial electric cooking
Federal construction projects	Electrical water heating
Residential wiring	Industrial electrification
Rural sales outlets	Commercial wiring
Federal housing	Better light—better sight
Electrical kitchen promotion	Electric range promotion
Electric application handbook	Highway lighting, etc.

These industry promotions have the highly desirable effect of doing a job which is fundamental to the success of all those in an industry, with minimum expense to the benefiting companies. They permit concentrating more of the sales promotional budget on promotional programs to improve the company's leadership position within the industry. It is not a question of "contributing" to a common cause, but of making the sales promotional dollars go further. This becomes evident if you study the promotional activities of companies in an industry which does not have a centralized promotional agency or institute. At least one-half of the money they appropriate for sales promotion is directly or indirectly spent for doing something which could be done for a fraction of the cost if those in the industry joined forces, employed capable promotional talent, and appropriated an adequate amount of money to carry through a minimum program.

The Age of Electronics

The impact of the computer and the advent of two-way cable television communication, mentioned in Chapter 44, will propel sales promotion to new heights of revolutionary achievement. Electronic technology daily widens the boundaries for innovative programs and techniques and offers the sales promotion executive new, exciting, challenges and opportunities.

Chapter 2

NEW BUSINESS DEVELOPMENT

AT A White House Conference on "The Industrial World Ahead," the Department of Commerce estimated that, by 1990, the population of the United States will rise to over 270 million. It follows that year by year, this will create increased markets and greater opportunities for reaching them through the introduction of new products and services.

Basically, new business development falls largely into three categories: the introduction of new products; expansion into new markets; and the pumping of new ideas into established pipelines of distribution.

The stimulation of new business by introducing new lines and new products is exemplified by the automobile industry which traditionally launches new models every year. The food and cosmetic industries constantly offer new products to increase sales or to maintain competitive positions.

The relentless search for new markets for established products has the advantage that it is not necessary to incur the costs of new designs and production. Often, new markets may be created by promoting new uses for existing products or utilizing new channels of distribution.

A prime example of this is the utilization of the credit-card systems of major oil companies by manufacturers of totally unrelated products.

Credit Card Promotions

The widespread use of credit cards, a concomitant of the computer, has opened up vast new fields of promotional opportunities in practically every industry. In fact, the credit card system is a store of golden opportunities yet to be mined, with still undreamed of practical applications. Looking ahead (and not too far!), consider the sales possibilities of credit cards in connection with television demonstrations by department stores, with Picturephone of the Bell Telephone System and, of course, the electronic transfer of funds.

Oil companies are making extensive use of their credit card lists. Gulf Oil Company makes periodic mailings to its customers, offering unrelated merchandise at special prices, with payments charged on monthly statements. One offer consisted of a 4-piece set of luggage at $4.99 a month for eight months plus a nominal shipping and handling cost, plus taxes, with a 15-day free examination period. Another Gulf offer featured a Hercules indoor-outdoor power-vac cleaner at $4.99 a month for eight months plus handling and taxes, with a ten-day free trial. Shell featured a deluxe AM/FM/-FM stereo radio system with 8-track record player and built-in digital clock at $9.99 a month for 12 months and a 30-day free trial. Esso (now Exxon) card holders were made eligible for membership in the Humble Travel Club which included accident insurance, a quarterly travel magazine, a travel atlas, routing service, vacation guides, arrest bond service, and merchandise discounts, for "as little as $2.25" billed monthly.

Department stores are making good use of charge account customer lists with many innovative applications as well as conventional uses such as pre-sale privileges and announcements to credit card customers.

Some major banks, of course, have long been in the field with credit cards acceptable in many areas of business.

Franchising Opportunities and Pitfalls

In a hearing before the Federal Trade Commission, the general counsel of the Small Business Administration declared that "the franchising area is a highly important one to small business. It has been estimated that annual sales of more than 400,000 franchise establishments exceed $131 billion, covering a wide range of products and services. The franchise industry however, has been plagued by numerous cases of abuse and misrepresentation."

This of course is not true of well-known, reputable companies such as the great hotel, motel chains, or companies in many other fields. Franchise operations such as Burger King, Gino's, Dairy Queen and Kentucky Fried Chicken seem to be thriving; Howard Johnson is a well-known name and Holiday Inns have expanded world-wide.

Advertising and sales promotion assistance is a feature of the major franchising operations which provide signs, newspaper advertisements, promotional literature and other sales aids. Manufacturers often receive the benefit of franchisers' advertising and promotional programs which feature the type of equipment they provide.

The Importance of Market Analysis

The introduction of new products as a means of developing new business is a time-honored practice. Many of the new products fail to establish a market position, however, because of inadequate market analysis, especially for products in the mass consumer field where competition is intense. This is particularly true in the drug and grocery industries.

"There is no longer any doubt in the minds of manufacturers regarding the importance of new products with respect to the maintenance of a growth position in the grocery industry today," states the A. C. Nielsen Company in describing its New Product Services.

"There are, however, many questions as to what product areas offer the greatest potential—and the point in time when this potential can be best realized.

"A study of a panel of United States supermarkets revealed that of the total number of items handled, in one year, 6,392 were discontinued—and replaced by 7,303 new items. And even more important, those new items accounted for nearly eight billion dollars —the equivalent of twice the actual dollar gain achieved by the retail grocery industry between the two years. Obviously, of the 6,000 plus items discontinued (many recently introduced), some were plainly inadequate in terms of quality and consumer satisfaction. Many, on the other hand, had been introduced into somewhat static product groups in which there was little or no growth potential for new items at that particular time. Others were introduced into categories already overcrowded by established products. Still more failed because they were of the wrong type or improperly priced. Nielsen New Product Services enable manufacturers to avoid many of these pitfalls and direct their attention and efforts only to those fields offering the greatest possible opportunity and potential."

To accomplish this, Nielsen provides a Directory Service and a Consulting Research Service—each available separately or combined to any company interested in appraising new product opportunities. The data are based on the product preferences of over 750,000 consumers from all sections of the country.

The Directory Service provides a complete listing of all package products purchased by a weighted sample of large supermarkets dispersed across the United States representing over 70 different warehouses and close to 100,000 items. The service is designed to offer growth-oriented companies the means of exploring and appraising profit opportunities in today's supermarkets.

The Consulting Research Service utilizes the same data developed for Directory Service, but is directed toward those companies with more specific interests in terms of product fields.

Nielsen Market Lifts is an intermediate service designed to help a manufacturer who, although not currently involved in a given product category, is interested in securing accurate measurements of yearly volume totals and trends to determine the basic potential for possible brand introduction.

There are, of course, other research organizations engaged in market investigation, some of which specialize in product analysis, consumer studies, pretesting and other areas which may be of specific interest.

Sales Forecasting Problems

If there be any area of the greatest importance to business and the one in which the least dependable progress has been made it is in sales forecasting. "What? In this day and age of the computer?" The answer is "Yes, in this day and age of the computer."

The most outstanding example of the failure of management properly to evaluate sales is the RCA* withdrawal from the computer field, the very instrument which could be useful in developing sales projections.

The computer division had projected its sales for the next three years when corporate management took a hard look at the situation and closed out the division and all its operations.

The fact is that, in the United States and abroad, sales forecasting has not yet even approached the status of a science. It never will, because sales depend on people, on customers, who do not act unless properly motivated. People must have good reasons to buy! With no attempt to indulge in psychological or philosophical dissertations, the fact is that people will not buy without an appropriate inducement of some kind, whether it be price, quality, a specific need, or an advantage to buy now.

It is not enough for a company arbitrarily to establish a goal of 10 or 15% over last year's sales. There are important factors to consider. Is the product any better? Is it a new product? Do we have more distributors and dealers to sell it? Can the advertising and sales promotion budget be increased to stimulate additional sales? Most important of all, what do we have to offer the customer in terms of quality, price and service features?

Next, how do we stimulate the field organization, the distributors and dealers to achieve extra sales? It is easy enough to put figures on paper but what about some realistic appraisals of the ways and

*Has also had marketing problems with its videodisc.

means of reaching them? The controller looks at the figures submitted to him but their substantiation is something else. For one thing, general economic conditions may completely invalidate them. For another, product deficiencies may distort them. A third factor is competition, with its capacity for sudden, unsettling moves. So, add 10%, or more if you like, but dont' count on it.

New products played a major role in doubling Procter & Gamble sales in a ten-year period. In an address before the Los Angeles Society of Financial Analysts, Dean P. Fite, P & G vice-president, corporate affairs, pointed out that more than 30% of the company's domestic household business came from products which had been on the market for less than 10 years. He attributed P & G's growth to "success in finding new ways to broaden our service to the public."

He cited Procter & Gamble's record of successfully introducing new products in the past 10 years as being good evidence that "any consumer product field can be changed overnight by the introduction of a product that represents a real and recognizable advance in service to the consumer."

"But," he continued, "first and foremost, marketing success requires a product that is worth marketing. It's impossible to have a steadily growing and successful business with products that are simply 'me-too' brands; items inferior to, or only equal to the competition."

Procter & Gamble, Fite emphasized, "will continue to place heavy emphasis on research and development programs, not only to develop new products and manufacturing methods, but to improve managements and organizational methods as well."

New-Concept Values

Hanes Corporation, leading manufacturer of women's hosiery, marketed its brand for many years through department stores and specialty shops until it noted a strong growth in hosiery sales through mass outlets, as in the food and drug industries.

Intensive market analysis disclosed that over 600 hosiery brands were found nationally in food and drug outlets; no brand enjoyed more than 6% share; the only form of promotion used was based on price; out-of-stock conditions (size and color) were prevalent; that there was no consumer loyalty to any particular brands; and that displays were common and undistinguished.

As a result, the company determined to enter new markets by developing an integrated program, including a distinctive brand name, innovative package, new display designs and advertising and promotion techniques to complement each and every element.

The chief consideration was to find a name that would clearly define not only the product, but its use. The display was to be the focal point of consumer attention at retail and had to be designed so that from any distance in the store its identity would be instantly known.

The name adopted was L'EGGS. It is feminine, descriptive, contemporary and of distinctive character. With the name came the package—colorful, modern, modular and outstanding. It comes in the shape of a plastic egg which is held in color-coded cylinders. The basic stocking cylinder color is red, with different shades of red used for the various stocking colors offered. The same is true for panty hose which are packaged in blue cylinders.

Finally came the new concept in display. Designed and manufactured by Howard Displays, New York, it is eye-catching and immediately identifiable with only one product—L'EGGS. It has a two-foot diameter and carries 24 dozen products. Importantly, it lends itself to island locations in high-traffic areas of the store where consumer exposure is great. It makes an attractive addition to store decor and is functional for drug outlets as well as food stores.

Paint Finds a New Market

Usually these opportunities for expanding the sale of a product are of the sort which lie in our own front yard. All that is needed to uncover them is someone who is promotion-minded. For years on end it had been the practice in manufacturing plants to paint inside walls white. White reflected light, it was clean, and there were any number of inexpensive "whitewashes" on the market which could be sprayed or slapped on the walls with a big, wide brush by a man with a strong back. Then along came one of the paint companies to challenge the idea of white walls for factories. If the walls and equipment were painted a soft green, or some other appropriate shade, it would be far more restful to the employee. It would also make a better-appearing plant. No one would think of painting the rooms of their home flat white, it would be too tiresome and crude. Yet people working in these plants spent more of their waking hours on the job than they did in their homes. Why not make the places where they worked just as attractive and pleasing as the places where they lived?

Putting the idea to work, the Pittsburgh Plate Glass Company began a nation-wide crusade for color in the factory. It undertook an extensive educational campaign, directed at top management and those responsible for employee welfare, to make them dissatisfied with whitewashed walls, messy looking machinery, and dirty ceilings.

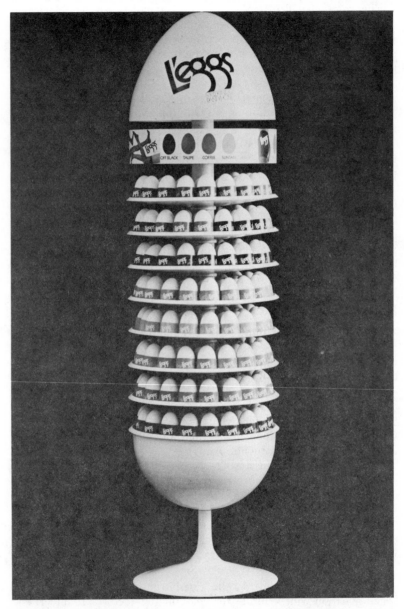

The extraordinary package for L'EGGS hosiery and the distinctive, eye-catching, display-and-stock unit, played an all-important role in the successful entry of mass markets through food and drug outlets by Hanes Corporation.

(Courtesy: Howard Displays, New York)

It contended employees who had pride in their surroundings took more pride in their work, they did more work, and were better employees.

A few plants thought well enough of the idea to try it out. In cooperation with the paint company's business development department, color plans were worked out. The ceilings were painted with light shades of the same color used on the walls. The machines and the trim were painted in another shade. The result was a plant interior that put to shame the traditional whitewashed plant interiors, forcing the owners of such plants to clean-up and paint-up in the interest of employee relations. Thousands of gallons of paint were thus sold which otherwise might never have been sold. Thousands of employees enjoyed the eye-comfort and pleasing appearance of their workplaces. And hundreds of companies profited because their employees took more pride in their work and the places where they worked. Everybody won. Even competitors of the paint company which pioneered the idea got business which otherwise they would not have had.

Lever Brothers Market Exploration Department

In marketing a long line of products sold through established channels of trade, the time lag between introducing the product and attaining a profitable sales volume presents a difficult problem. Lever Brothers, and others, have found it profitable to maintain a special department for that purpose, with a director responsible for the development, testing, and introduction of new products.

An important phase of this work is pretesting both the product and a variety of sales plans before the product is turned over to the sales department to be put in the line. In this way salesmen are relieved of tedious introductory work, which all too often is done at the expense of selling established products.

The Copy Machine Boom

An example of a revolutionary business development was found in the electrostatic-copier industry. With sales increasing 20% throughout the industry, the pioneering company, Xerox, enjoyed a phenomenal increase in business from $40 million to $400 million in the first six years. The potentials of this business tool are boundless. It has radically altered business procedures.

Copying machines are now reproducing over 47 billion copies and the industry volume reached over 13 billion dollars in 1980. Desk-top copiers are the regular equipment of many secretaries.

Publishing companies, too, are affected, and some are beginning to express concern over such matters as copyrights and circulation. These are some of the results of the introduction of a new product which performs a service not previously, or readily, available.

Order Analysis Uncovers New Uses

Perhaps the most fertile source of information which points the way to new business is the orders which come in every working day. Some companies pass these over the desk of the sales manager so that he can keep posted on what is happening in the field. But in many cases incoming orders go directly to the order desk, where they are priced, extended, billed, and then shipped. Too often no one in authority sees them. Yet these orders are a veritable gold mine if screened by a sales-development-minded member of the sales department. The following example will show the profit potential in such an approach to the otherwise routine flow of orders:

An office duplicating machine manufacturer, who published a weekly bulletin for salesmen, uncovered a market for several thousand machines as a result of the editor of the sales bulletin bumping into an order from a company which bought a duplicator to process orders. The purchaser had need of a large number of copies of each order for various executives and department managers, more copies than could be made with carbon paper. So he hit upon the idea of making an electrotype of the order form, having a supply of stencils cut from the electrotype, and then typing the order data directly onto the prepared stencil. The stencil was then slapped on a duplicator, the required number of copies struck off, and the stencil filed for further use, if necessary. The idea saved the purchaser hundreds of dollars and greatly expedited the handling of orders. That happened some years ago. Today the use of duplicators in processing orders is quite common. The point is that the use was uncovered by an alert bulletin editor who just happened to have a nose for that sort of sales opportunity. This is a talent to be encouraged and developed in any sales organization.

There is a growing practice, now that sellers are searching for new markets, to make an extra copy of all orders for some sales executive to check for sales opportunities. When such opportunities are found a bulletin is released to the sales organization, after checking with the consumer to obtain as much factual information as possible. These bulletins not only help to keep salesmen on their toes, but provide them with valuable ammunition they can use in their work. Of course, salesmen themselves uncover considerable information of this kind, but you cannot depend upon them. Not all salesmen are promotion-minded. Others realize the importance of what they have learned, but for one reason or another wish to keep it to themselves. This is especially true when salesmen are scored in competition with others in the organization.

Special Salesmen to Open New Accounts

Another noteworthy trend in new business development is the use of training in sales negotiation, and asking special home office representatives to work with the territorial salesmen in opening new accounts.

Basis for the use of new account salesmen is that it permits the employment of territorial salesmen of less skill to service accounts. Furthermore, it is an accepted fact that territorial salesmen are notoriously indifferent to opening new accounts. They are inclined to spend most of their time in calling on regular customers where they are known, and where they are reasonably certain of getting an order. Calling on new accounts is a chore they dodge as long as possible.

Qualifications for New Account Specialist

While the territorial salesman who does a customer service job needs to be of the "plugger, one-track-mind type," the new account specialist should be more intelligent, a good sales strategist, resourceful, and of the trader type.

The best place to recruit these men is from the army of small businessmen who at one time or another were in business for themselves. Perhaps you have among your former customers several men of the sort required. That kind of background is ideal, because the salesman is able to talk the customer's language from having been in business for himself. He knows the buyer's problems, and from his experience quickly determines the best and most effective approach.

Helping Salesmen to Open New Accounts

Smaller organizations, it was found, are thinking along different lines. As a rule they cannot afford, or think they cannot afford, to employ a salesman full time just to open new accounts. So they contemplate helping their present territorial salesmen to put desirable new accounts on the books through direct-mail cooperation.

While each company has its own idea of how to do this job, only a few have any definite plan. In the building field we found one company which has already checked every prospective account now in business to determine whether or not that account is desirable to cultivate and close.

The accounts which the credit department and management feel will develop and grow, and can be depended upon to buy in large volume, are set up on a special Addressograph list, carefully classified by lines of business and sales desirability. By use of a system of plate tabs or signals, any group of these accounts can be selected and worked when and as the occasion warrants.

"Sharpshooting" with Personalized Letters

A hardware specialty manufacturer who sells direct, added hundreds of desirable accounts by "sharpshooting" tactics of this sort. In connection with the list, which is maintained on McBee card records, this manufacturer employs a young man whose job is to maintain mail contact with every hardware merchant on the list. His department, outside of the file of McBee cards, consists of a stenographer and a battery of 4 automatic typewriters and 2 typists. There are about 5,000 names on the new business list. Whenever the company makes a new product, the business development department has the advertising department prepare a special folder slanted at opening new accounts, and then opens a barrage of personal letters (using the battery of Auto-typists) to selected prospects. The selection, of course, is a simple matter when McBee cards are used. It is only necessary to run a pin through the proper hole in the drawer of cards and all cards in any desired classification are automatically selected. The effectiveness of the plan depends upon the skill with which the letter is tied in with the needs of the prospect.

For best results such a list should be carefully checked for: (1) Credit rating to be sure the new customer will pay for what you sell him. (2) Names of all buyers or executives in a position to instigate as well as place the order—you would want to write a different letter to a foreman who merely requisitions the product than to the vice president in charge of operations who has to okay the expense. The arguments might be the same but the angle would be different. (3) Nature of competition. (4) Previous purchases, if any. (5) If a supposedly "dead" account, how long has it been inactive and why. (6) Type of products (if you make a line) in which the prospect is most interested. (7) Salesmen who will service the account after you put it on the books. You will also need information, if the account is a dealer, on the size and type of store, trading area data, etc.

IDEAS FOR GETTING LIVE NAMES

Agents of the Connecticut Mutual Life Insurance Company use the birth announcements in the newspapers as a source of live leads by writing a miniature letter of greeting to the new arrival with a return card enclosed which the parent signs and mails if interested.

Household appliance manufacturers secure the name of each purchaser of equipment, either through salesmen's orders or, if through dealers, by attaching a tag to the appliance which must be returned in order to get a guarantee certificate or some useful piece of literature. Card these names. Plan a series of at least three letters to each name to go out during the first 6 months of ownership. The first letter can be a personal note of interest from an officer of the company. It should be produced on an automatic typewriter, the number of the machine or appliance being filled in to give it a personal touch.

A magazine publisher determines how much he can afford to pay for three names of possible subscribers. He prepares a little folder offering some useful premium for the names of three friends who might be interested in subscribing to the magazine. These enclosures are sent out with a preliminary letter to all subscribers in advance of their expirations, signed by the editor, asking specific questions concerning the editorial contents and the advertising section.

A manufacturer selling through jobbers packs a dealer co-operation certificate in each package or with each shipment. When filled out by the dealer these certificates entitle the dealer to a window display, or a counter card, or something equally helpful to him in moving the merchandise off his shelf. If the dealer helps are well chosen, you will be surprised how many of these certificates come home.

A department store gets lists of people who are contemplating spending money for luxuries through various aggressive women's organizations, especially church societies whose main activities deal with raising money. The store provides each member with a book of blanks. On the side of each blank are listed items which carry a large mark-up and on which the store could afford to pay a small percentage.

The members keep these books handy and every time any of their friends mention they are thinking of buying an electric refrigerator, radio, or whatever it might be, they fill out a blank card, check the proper item, and mail it to the store. It is then circularized. If a sale is made the organization will be credited with the amount shown on the blank. If a sale is not made the organization is charged back to cover the postage on the circular matter. At the end of the organization's fiscal year a check is sent to the treasurer for an amount equal to the money earned less the cost of the postage. Every month a list of sales with the names of the women who had turned in leads is mailed to the organization to post or read. This is necessary to sustain interest in the plan.

A roofer in a sizable New England town wanted more business. At some time, of course, every roof in town would need repair or replacement—unless the house itself were torn down and a new one with a new roof erected in its place. But when? Tin roofs have been known to last a hundred years—and the durability of slate, shingle, or even tar paper is great enough to irritate a roofer.

Obviously, the best prospects for roofing were people living in old houses, whose roofs presumably had more or less disintegrated. There was only one way to locate these houses and that was by actual observation; so the roofer was advised to drive over every street in town, noting the number of every house, the roof of which might come under suspicion. After that, the name of the owner was obtained from the real-estate records. A tedious process, but it is the only possible method of getting a fairly practical working list.

A Checklist for Mailing Lists

It is natural to suppose that a mailing list is good enough if it is producing even a fair volume of returns. Yet it is entirely possible that the returns could be materially increased, even though they may be satisfactory, by carefully checking it to determine its efficiency rating. While no hard and fast rules can be laid down for checking the list for any particular business, the following suggestions may prove helpful:

Is your list classified according to the potential profit which each account will yield, or are you spending the same amount of money to circularize all names regardless of their buying possibilities? Do you spend as much to circularize "fringe" names as "preferred" names?

Has your mailing list been checked with current credit rating books to make sure that you would be warranted in accepting business from every name on the list, even if you did get an order? The last 6 months have changed the picture for many companies.

Are you confining your mailings to one man in larger companies, disregarding the fact that today several people are usually involved in the placing of an important order?

If you use individual names on your mailing list, do you know for sure if they are the names of men holding the deciding vote, or were the names placed on the list at the suggestion of salesmen who "think" they are the men to be sold?

When you send out mailings under third-class postage—do you mark your envelope so that all undelivered mail will be returned? Do you follow up the clerk to be sure that these dead names are being pulled from the list promptly?

In the case of individual names for large companies, when mail is returned for nondelivery, do you have some plan for automatically finding out the name of whoever succeeded to his work, or do you allow the name of the company to be killed with the name of the individual?

Have you some key or system to tell how long a name has been on a list, so that a periodical audit can be made and the mailing list cleansed of all names which have been worked for 2 years or more without response? Do you use it often?

How do you provide for getting new blood into a list? Do you depend entirely on hit-or-miss reports from salesmen or is it the duty of somebody in the organization to watch and clip the trade papers to be sure that reorganizations, new companies, and management changes are caught?

Have you ever sent a personal letter to each name on the list over the signature of an officer of the company to find out if you are wasting your money circularizing names of people who are not even prospects?

An indication of the wide range of lists and the quantities of names offered by list brokers is afforded by this very brief sampling of advertisements in an issue of *Direct Marketing:*

- 27,000 Farm Equip. Dealers, Wholesalers, Mfgrs.

- 46,000 Lat. Am. Farms, Ranches, Dists.

- 27,500 East. Hemisphere Farms, Ranches, Dists.

- 10,000 Golf Course Supers.

- 18,000 Grounds Care Mgrs.

- 14,500 Landscape Contractors

- 42,000 Lawn & Garden Retail Outlets, Buyers, Dists.

- 33,500 TV, AM, FM, CCTV Station Mgrs. & Engrs.

- 10,500 Lat. Am. TV, AM, FM Station Mgrs. & Engrs.

- 15,000 Video Mgrs. in Industry, Medicine, Ed., Studios

Another sampling provides a summary of typical costs, as follows:

List	Cost per M
Puzzle Contestants	$45
Record Buyers	45
Agricultural Report Subscribers	50
Grade School Teachers	45
Outdoorsmen	50
High-Priced-Gift Buyers	45
Senior Citizens	45
Business Magazine Subscribers	50

It should be noted that special requirements often entail extra charges, such as "state/zip select, $4 per M extra." List brokers also specify minimum orders, usually from three to five thousand names.

Building Sales Through Direct Mail

While good lists are extremely important in contributing to the success of direct mail campaigns, equally necessary is the quality level of the mailing in terms of "the offer," the inducement to buy and the ease of response. Other than price, some companies offer free trial or credit card purchase; the inducement may consist of a gift or sweepstakes ticket or price discount; to facilitate response, a postpaid card or envelope is enclosed in the mailing.

One interesting, yet simple, mailing was that of Lanier Business Products. In contrast to the usual white or color envelope, the company used a distinctive black-and-gray scheme with the imprint "Free Gift Certificate Enclosed for": over the opening for the address. Enclosed were the sales letter, a leaflet describing a free Business Dictionary and the return card, postpaid.

Other examples of direct mail promotions are described in following chapters on individual marketing subjects.

Chapter 3

SALES PROMOTION ORGANIZATION

WHAT are the responsibilities and functions of a sales promotion department? Perhaps the question may best be answered by drawing up a list of purposes and objectives and of the tools and materials with which to meet those objectives. Following is a comprehensive list:

Major Functions of a Sales Promotion Department

Audio-Visual Programs	Exhibits
Budgeting	Export Promotion
Catalogs	Fairs
Coordination with:	House Magazines
Advertising Department	Mail Order Selling
Sales Department	Manuals
Production Department	Meetings
Contests	Merchandising
Copywriting	Motion Pictures
Coupon Promotions	Premiums
Conventions	Retail Advertising
Dealers and Retailers	Sales Aids For Dealers
Demonstrations	Sales Training Materials
Direct Mail	Sampling
Displays, Posters, Signs	Special Service Agencies
Distributors	Trade Relations
Educational	Trade Shows

. In organizing for sales promotion the changing needs of the business are all-important. During the development stage a single executive, working with and through the sales department, might carry through the sales promotion program. Then as full distribution is attained, and more intensive market cultivation is required, it might be advisable to expand the facilities, perhaps going so far as to establish sales promotion units in the major sales districts to work more closely with territorial salesmen and distributors.

Sales Promotional Authority

All-important in any scheme of organization is the position and authority of the responsible executive. In a highly technical operation, such as selling ships, the promotional effort may be restricted to a few top officials who maintain close contact with transportation companies that use ships. In the case of engineering specialties sold to converters, a company may depend upon its headquarters and field engineering staffs to get its products specified. But in the marketing of products sold for resale, and most equipment used in the office, shop or store, sales promotion is an important sales function, and is so regarded by the management. The same is true of products and services sold direct to the user or consumer.

While there are still a number of important companies which proceed on the theory that everyone in the business is, or should be, a part of the sales promotional organization, there is a growing tendency to center sales promotional functions in a qualified executive. Usually, but not always, such an executive reports to the officer responsible for distribution, or he may report directly to the chief executive and, in a few instances, to the board of directors.

Again, some companies prefer to make sales promotion a branch of the advertising department, since it is the common practice to entrust the production of sales promotional materials

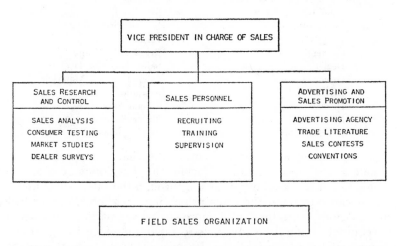

A widely used type of sales organization. The sales research director, manager of sales personnel, and the advertising and sales-promotion manager report directly to the coordinating sales executive.

SALES PROMOTION ORGANIZATION

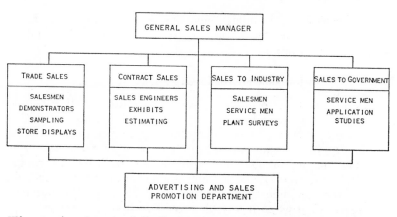

When varying channels of distribution are used in marketing the product, it is not unusual for each division to operate independently of the other, with sales promotion production for all divisions centered in the advertising department.

to the advertising executive. In such instances the advertising executive usually carries the title of Director of Advertising and Sales Promotion. There is no hard and fast rule for organizing sales promotion. It differs with the nature of the business; the size of the sales operation; and to a very great extent, upon the qualifications, experience, and capability of the individual.

Some sales managers have a flair for promoting sales that eminently qualifies them to supervise the activity. Others are anything but sales promotional minded. In the same way some advertising men have sufficient experience in sales work to understand and appreciate the needs of the salesmen and the distributing organization. Others lack this understanding. In that case a complete absorption of the sales promotional function by advertising, whether it be the headquarters department or the company's advertising counsel, is unwise. The advertising department is usually just far enough away from the actual selling operation to miss the extremely intimate coordination that good sales promotion demands.

So while some measure of organization is necessary to effective sales promotion, it by no means requires a large department with a high-powered idea man at the head, pushing buttons with a score or more of clerks dancing to his tune, and a sales department hanging on his every thought. There are, to be sure, such departments. Yet some of the most resultful sales promotional jobs are being done by companies with no formal organization whatever. But as the business grows, and competition becomes acute, the tendency in modern management is to recognize sales promotion as a specialized function of sales management and to organize accordingly.

Type of Operation as a Factor in Organization

The blueprint for organizing sales promotional activities obviously is determined by the ways in which the company distributes its products. Thus a manufacturer selling through mass distributors requires an entirely different sales promotional setup than one making a similar product, sold exclusively through independent dealers. If the product is sold through a field organization direct to industry, the promotional needs of the business are greater than when it is sold through mill supply houses.

Then there is the problem of the manufacturer who sells multiple lines through unilateral sales organizations. These might function by product divisions or by the distribution problem involved. The big packers, for example, operate separate sales organizations, requiring special sales promotional assistance, for such widely different products as fertilizer, dairy products, soap and cleansers. They also sell food staples to the trade through branch plants and branch houses. The product divisions may, and usually do, employ "specialty" salesmen who sell only the products of their division. The sales promotional activities of such operations are quite complex.

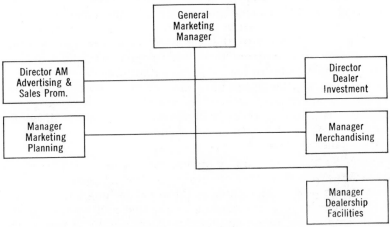

This organization chart indicates the important role of advertising and sales promotion in the American Motors marketing structure. The chart establishes the close liaison between sales promotion and four other divisions under direct supervision of the general marketing manager.

So far as products sold for resale are concerned, there are many ways of distributing them and as many ways of promoting their sale. Among the outlets to be considered in planning promotions for this type of operation are:

1. Independent specialty stores.
2. Independent general or department stores.
3. Mail-order stores.
4. Auto supply store chains.
5. Variety stores.
6. Voluntary chain stores.
7. Manufacturer's chain stores.
8. Chain department stores.
9. Chain specialty stores.
10. Co-operatives (particularly in certain areas).

A manufacturer or factory may sell to these stores by the following methods:

1. Direct to independents and chains.
2. Through old-line wholesalers.
3. Through specialty wholesalers.
4. Through distributors selling limited lines.
5. Through wholesalers serving voluntary chains.
6. Through manufacturer's exclusive wholesalers.
7. Through truck wholesalers.
8. Through manufacturers' agents.

What to Call the Department

While the function remains essentially the same, the sales promotion department may come under a different name in different companies. Thus the A. P. Green Fire Brick Company has a domestic sales department, in charge of a domestic sales manager; an export sales department in charge of an export manager; the merchandise department in charge of the merchandise manager; and a traffic department in charge of a traffic manager. The several departments are coordinated by a vice-president in charge of distribution. Under the merchandise manager are the following sections, each in charge of a manager:

1. Advertising and Sales Promotion.
2. Market Research.
3. Sales Service.
4. Sales and Construction Engineering.

Subsequent sections of this HANDBOOK will discuss sales promotion methods which have proved to be most effective in reducing distribution costs in the most important of these channels. But the way a product is to be distributed should be definitely established before the sales promotional machinery, whether it be a department or a method of operation, is set in motion.

Centralized and Decentralized Setups

A study of the sales promotional organization of several hundred companies in various industries shows two different approaches. One group centralizes all sales promotional activities in a home office organization, responsible for planning, production, and the execution of all undertakings of a promotional nature. Others decentralize sales promotion so far as planning and execution are concerned, but centralize production. They may operate through sales promotion units in each product division; that is to say, where a company operates several sales

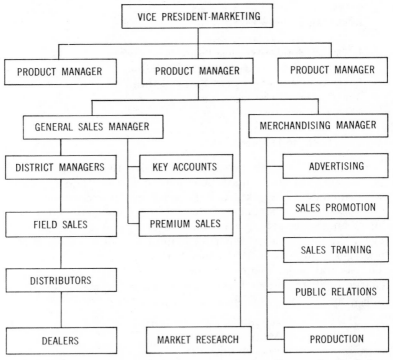

Where a company has a number of brands or product lines, as in the package goods, pharmaceutical or appliance industries, the product manager is responsible for all activities in his division, including advertising and sales promotion.

departments as a part of its over-all marketing operation, each department has its own sales promotion unit. Or, as is quite customary in the marketing of home appliances, each territorial division may have its own sales promotion unit which works closely with distributors and dealers in the field, helping them to devise ways and means of promoting sales. In such cases, of course, the supervision of these units is the responsibility of the sales executive of the business, or one of his assistants.

This decentralized type of organization is particularly favored when the principal promotional effort centers around the distributor, and where the aim is to assist the individual distributor or dealer to carry out sales promotional activities at the local or district level. At least one national organization finds it profitable to assign sales promotion specialists to distributors, for a limited time, to assist them in establishing a sales promotion operation of their own, in conformity with a national plan. In such cases the sales promotion man, while employed, trained, and directed by the manufacturer, is usually carried on the

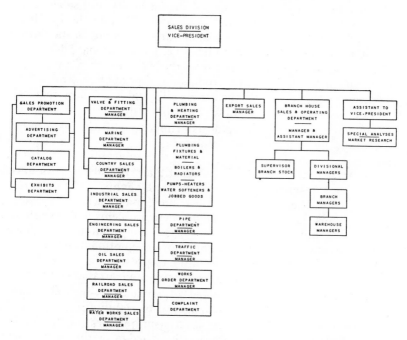

The organizational setup of a large company in the building supply field. The sales promotion department, advertising department, catalog department, and the exhibits department report through the sales promotion manager to the sales head.

distributor's payroll until the new department is able to function under a man whom the manufacturer's representative has trained.

Since sales promotion is, in fact, a form of service to the customer, it is sometimes advisable to have more than one sales promotion executive, each skilled in a particular operation and each responsible to the sales executive for promoting sales in that unit. Thus the Standard Oil Company of Indiana had one "sales promoter" for its wholesale operations; and another, with equal authority, to promote the sale of Standard Oil products and specialties through filling stations and other retail outlets. This dual responsibility has certain advantages, although it does create a division of authority.

Who Should Head Up Promotion?

Regardless of whether the promotional organization is centralized or decentralized, results depend, as they do in any activity, upon the man who directs the operation. He should be a man of high caliber and should command the authority and salary commensurate with a job of such importance. While the qualifications of a sales promotion manager vary according to the nature of the business and the job to be done, most national advertisers attach considerable importance to the skill which a promotion man has, or acquires, in the production of promotional literature. To some extent these are the same skills and know-how required in an advertising manager, but with this difference:

The advertising executive deals primarily with the mass mind. The copy he prepares for consumer groups is not so much designed to get action, as it is to create buying impressions. On the other hand the sales promotional man, who deals with such groups as salesmen, dealers, distributors, agents, and to a lesser extent with the consumer, must understand what influences these groups. He must understand their problems and be able to talk their "language." He must prepare copy that will convince and motivate a type of customer not so emotional as the consumer. Yet he must have the ability to present his ideas clearly and dramatically, through good layouts and arrangement.

It is noteworthy that classified advertisements in local newspapers for sales promotion managers invariably stress the need for creative imagination. This is a basic qualification too often overlooked. While experience and knowledge of the techniques of sales promotion are important, the capacity of a sales promotion manager to grow with the business and to measure up to his full responsibilities depends upon his ability to formulate and carry through broad promotional projects. In other words, the job calls for a man with a lot of initiative.

Specifications for Sales Promotion Manager's Job

While the job of sales promotion manager varies with the business, the man, and the time, the following job description, issued by the U.S. Employment Service in its *National Roster of Scientific and Specialized Personnel,* is interesting:

SALES PROMOTION SPECIALISTS (56.4.20)

> Sales promotion specialists plan and direct sales, that is they predetermine the sales effort needed and control the sales effort during the course of operations. They also control advertising campaigns and expenditures. The best kind of formal training for specialists in this field appears still to be the subject of some doubt. It is clear, however, that special knowledge of advertising, marketing, programming, and scheduling, together with detailed familiarity with the particular product is required.

Speaking before the marketing division of the American Management Association, a prominent editor of *Sales & Marketing Management* Magazine, told his audience that the man who heads up the sales promotion in a modern marketing operation should be not only a leader so far as keeping his organization alive, but he must keep his company alive *and kicking,* moving ahead all the time, constantly enlarging its viewpoint, developing its contacts, expanding its horizons. "He is the coordinator as well as the promoter of everything between all phases of top management on one hand, and field selling and the ultimate consumer on the other.

"He should be the type of man who combines these qualities: (1) Personal sales ability and sales experience, (2) a broad background in the use of advertising and promotion techniques, (3) a vigorous, aggressive mind that thinks constantly in terms of how the company can make more sales, (4) the common-sense approach that the increased sales must be made at a profit.

"The man who should be heading up your promotion activities is a man well able to put your company's best foot forward. In the moderate-sized company he may also be in charge of advertising, possibly also of public relations and employee relations. In the large company he will coordinate many and varied activities so that the ultimate in sales value is secured from each. In short, he will be the guy in the packing plant who finds a way to extract value from the one thing that now has to be thrown away—the pig's squeal.

"He will find every last bit of byproduct value in your consumer advertising, for example, and if you are a large advertiser, that one

TELEPHONE CHECK ON EXECUTIVE APPLICANT_____

Name of Applicant

_____

Person Contacted   Position

Company   City and State   Telephone Number

1. I wish to *verify* some of the information given to us by Mr. (name) whom we are considering for an executive position. Do you remember him? What were the dates of his employment with your Company?   From_____ 19___ To___ 19___
   Do dates check?

2. What was he doing when he started? _____
   Did he exaggerate?

   When he left? _____
   Did he progress?

3. He says he was earning $___ per___ when he left. Is that right?   □ Yes,   □ No; $_____
   Did he falsify?

4. What was basis of his compensation? _____
   Any profit sharing? Bonus? Evidence of ownership?

5. What did you think of him? _____
   Did he get along with his superiors?

6. Did he have any supervision of others?   □ No,   □ Yes;   How many?___
   Does this check?

   (If yes) How well did he handle it? _____
   Is he a leader or a driver?

7. How closely was it necessary to supervise him? _____
   Was he hard to manage? Did he need help constantly?

8. How willing was he to accept responsibility? _____
   Did he seek responsibility? Was he afraid of it?

9. Did he have any responsibility for policy formulation?   □ No,   □ Yes;   How much?___

   (If yes) How well did he handle it? _____
   Good judgment? Realistic? Able to plan ahead?

10. Did he develop or initiate any new plans or programs? _____
    Initiative? Creative? Realistic?

11. How well did he "sell" his ideas? _____
    Self-reliance? Ability to adjust to others' needs?

12. How hard did he work? Did he finish what he started? _____
    Is he habitually industrious? Persevering?

13. How well did he plan his work? _____
    Efficient? Able to plan?

14. How well did he get along with other people? _____
    Is he a troublemaker?

15. How much time did he lose from work? _____
    Conscientious? Health problems?

16. Why did he leave? _____
    Good reasons? Do they check?

17. Would you re-employ him?   □ Yes,   □ No;   Why not?___
    Does this affect his suitability with us?

18. Did he have any domestic or financial difficulties which interfered with work?   □ No,   □ Yes;   What?___
    Immaturity?

19. How about drinking or gambling?   □ No,   □ Yes;   What?___
    Immaturity?

20. What are his outstanding strong points? _____

21. What are his weak points? _____

22. For what type of position do you feel he is best qualified? _____

Checked by_____   Date_____

Form No. ET-302   Copyright 1949, The Dartnell Corporation, Chicago, Printed in U. S. A.

Selecting the sales promotion executive requires painstaking screening, searching, interviewing, and a thoroughgoing telephone check. The above form, developed for Dartnell by The McMurry Company, Chicago, will prove useful. It suggests the type of question to ask a former employer, and provides a permanent record of the information secured. It is filed with the application and interview blank in a personal history folder.

service alone can pay his salary several times over. At a time when many suppliers are competing for somewhat lessened demand, the merchandising of advertising becomes big-time. Any man who can make your branch and district managers, your salesmen, your wholesalers, your dealers really enthusiastic about your consumer advertising can increase the real value of that advertising by anywhere from 20% to more than 100%, because it will result in more orders, more displays, more 'push' by retailers and their salespersons."

While a knowledge of layout and copy writing is important, those are functions which can be delegated. But he should know how to get ideas across in the printed form and upon the public platform. With the growing importance of trade conventions and trade shows, and their place in sales, a sales promotion man who can talk well on his feet, and has "platform presence" is in a position to do his company a lot of good. In fact, organizing and staging dealer meetings is fast becoming one of his important duties in many companies.

For that reason, too, the title given to the sales promotion manager is important. Unfortunately, the title "Sales Promotion Manager" does not suggest anything constructive to a trade convention audience, nor does it greatly impress dealers called in to hear about a new sales plan. It may describe the functions of the man from an organization point of view. But to the customer it suggests a promoter, and promoters are evaluated differently by different people. One well-known food company gives its sales promotion man the title of "Sales Counsel," another labels him "Merchandising Manager," and in at least one instance he is the "Vice President in Charge of Dealer Relations." In the engineering field, a not unusual platform title is "Director of Research." This serves well if the nature of the promotional work has to do with new uses for the product.

THE SALES PROMOTION STAFF

In the case of a well-organized company where the sales promotional function covers planning and production as well as carrying out the plan in the field, the department usually includes, in addition to the director, several assistants, each of whom specializes in certain phases of the work. In the smaller organizations these activities may be combined. Briefly they are as follows:

Manager of Research

This executive has the job of contacting customers to determine their needs so far as sales helps are concerned; to keep informed as to what competitors and companies in related fields are doing in the way of sales promotion; to conduct consumer studies and tests to obtain factual data for preparing sales promotional material, talks to be delivered before customer groups, and for over-all planning. One duty of this executive is to attend meetings of sales executives' organizations, to keep in touch with general trends of value to the company in expanding its markets. Another duty is to measure the results of sales promotional activities at point of sale.

Exhibit Manager

Some companies find it profitable to use county and state fairs, trade shows, and conventions to promote sales. In recent years, the activities of sales promotion executives have been further broadened through participation in the overseas trade fairs sponsored by the United States Government, in various parts of the world, and by trade fairs in major U.S. cities.

The exhibit manager arranges for the display space required, plans the exhibit, has it built with the help of a firm specializing in this type of sales promotion, and is responsible for setting up the display as well as manning it. If the salesmen are on duty at the exhibit, they report to him. The usual practice is to give this job to a veteran salesman who has spent a good deal of time at conventions or trade shows, who knows the important customers and, if need be, can get up in front of an audience and give a good account of himself. When not engaged in work of this kind, this executive often organizes and conducts distributor and dealer meetings.

Contest Director

Under normal conditions most national sales organizations find it profitable to conduct various kinds of sales stimulating contests or campaigns. These may be contests between salesmen, between district offices, or they may be contests intended to get leads for dealers. One of the large utility companies enlists the help of non-selling members of its organization by awarding prizes for sales leads which are turned over to its salesmen to follow up. Sales contests are usually dramatized and promoted intensively, so that interest is maintained at white heat while they are under way. Registering contestants, scoring them, stimulating them to put forth the required extra effort, as well as purchasing and awarding the prizes, can well be a full-time job for someone with a flair for that sort of thing. When the operation is made the responsibility of a trained promotion man, it is customary to have some kind of contest going all the time, but each sufficiently different to avoid monotony.

Sales Training

This activity may or may not be assigned to the sales promotional department. Very often it is set up as a department by itself under the manager of salesmen. However, when the work consists principally of training dealers and their salespeople, either on the job or bringing them into the factory for specialized training, it belongs in sales promotion. It is important that the executive who has this responsibility should have the ability to impart his ideas to others, in other words, teaching ability. That sort of sales promotion consists of taking the principles of successful merchandising, as they are formulated by the company's sales command, and teaching them to those who distribute the product. The aim is to raise the standard of salesmanship at the point of sale. Too many sales trainers, engaged in resale work, make an excellent impression upon the dealers, and do a pretty good job of "trading up" those who take the course, but they forget that the real reason they are on the company payroll is to promote sales and not merely entertain customers. A good source for promotion men who are required to train dealers, is clerks and others who have done a good job selling the product behind the counter and who have experience in conducting a successful retail business.

Merchandising Manager

Some products require intensive merchandising at the point of sale. Store demonstrations, store arrangements, window displays, community promotions are just a few of the techniques. If much of this type of sales promotion is used it might well be a full-time job for somebody. Demonstrators must be hired and trained, routed, and supervised. Displays must be planned and purchased, to say nothing of being properly distributed. Store display men as well as salesmen must be shown how to get dealers to put in displays, modernize their stores, and increase store traffic. It means working with salesmen and display men in the field, all for the purpose of making sure that the money a company spends for this promotion is producing results commensurate with the cost. Sampling campaigns are usually entrusted to the merchandise manager, since an important consideration in such a promotion is the effect on the dealer. The job calls for a man who knows how to move merchandise off the dealer's shelf or floor and into the channels of distribution. He should have had sufficient experience in retailing to know the value of store display and store arrangement. And with it all he must be a good manager, for this is one of those operations where it is easily possible to spend a lot of money without getting very much in return.

There are other specialized jobs in sales promotion, such as preparing and producing educational film strips and moving pictures; managing the lecture bureau which supplies speakers to luncheon clubs, women's clubs; arranging and conducting trade trips. Some companies even place the responsibility for improving the tone of business correspondence, to the end that every letter will sell something, either goods or good will, upon the sales promotion manager. It all depends upon the kind of business, and what a company can afford to spend for this sort of thing. But sales promotion, like anything else, if worth doing at all is worth doing well. It is for that reason that more and more companies are breaking down the functions of sales promotion into simple tasks, and employing men skilled in that particular task to get the job done *right*.

Training for Sales Positions

An important consideration in selecting sales promotional personnel is the potential ability of the men for sales supervisory positions. The sales promotion department is an excellent training school for future sales managers since it grounds the staff in the home office point of view. If a man's qualifications are such that he is fitted only for sales promotional work, and qualities of a general sales executive overlooked, a company may deprive itself of an excellent source of branch managers, sales agents, and other operating sales executives. It is noteworthy that in some of the hard-fought fields, such as home utility appliances, it is customary to fill nearly all vacancies in the sales supervisory staff from the sales promotion department.

Outside Counsel

Rather than take on the expense of a specialized staff, some companies prefer to get along with fewer people in the sales promotion department and use outside specialists as needed. For example, in checking the results of a sales promotional or advertising campaign at the point of sale, the services of organizations like A. C. Nielsen Company are available on a fee basis. The Nielsen organization has arrangements with merchants in certain lines of business, at carefully determined points, whereby its research men go into the store every week and analyze the sales slips. The results of these studies are tabulated and furnished clients in the form of trade reports. By serving a number of companies in this way, the cost to each client is much less than if the client undertook to obtain the information himself. Similarly, in ascertaining new methods being used by competitors or others to promote sales, services like the Dartnell Sales and Marketing Service are available. Other research organizations specialize in consumer testing and in making studies of buying habits useful in sales planning. Unless there is a continuing need for this type of information, it is usually more economical to call in outside organizations than to maintain a full-time research staff at headquarters.

The same thing applies to producing sales manuals, planning books and other literature required in sales promotion. Unless a company uses enough of this material to warrant employing a capable executive, and good ones come high, it is better to arrange with some advertising agency to do this. While the fee may seem high, compared with the cost of doing the work under your own roof, you pay only for what you need when you need it. The need of "making work" to keep a staff man busy is avoided. There are also free-lance sales promotion men who work on a job-to-job basis. While they may lack the intimate contact with your sales problems which an insider would have, they do bring an outside point of view to your problems, and when the particular job for which you engage them has been completed, the expense stops. This is particularly true when conducting occasional sales contests or sales promotional campaigns. In the large centers there are sales promotional agencies skilled in planning, promoting, and operating sales contests. Such agencies assist sales executives in planning all manner of sales promotional and business development activities. They furnish stock materials for promoting sales contests. By using these standardized mailing pieces as a vehicle for a sales message, substantial savings are effected. Results, too, are usually better.

There are also organizations which specialize in store display. That is their business. They can be engaged on a consulting basis to develop point-of-sale promotion plans. The specialized experience they offer is most helpful. In the same way, large lithograph companies are able to help in the creation of window and store displays, either on a fee basis or in consideration of the purchase of materials from them. Others specialize in the distribution of display material, even renting wall and window space from merchants which they make available on a yearly contract basis for hundreds of stores in key cities.

THE FIELD ORGANIZATION

Field men are used in sales promotion where the product is sold through distributors and dealers. They are also used, but in a lesser degree, by manufacturers of technical products which require shop tests and demonstrations. Companies selling equipment used in offices and shops, where the continuing purchase of supplies is a factor in territorial profits, also use field men to call on users and stimulate wider use of the equipment. For example, a manufacturer of addressing equipment, where the sale of address plates is important, might profitably use men to call upon users and suggest more ways to use the equipment which the company has purchased. This type of promotional work theoretically should be done by the salesman, but salesmen are notably lax in calling back on old customers. They are more interested in finding new buyers, especially if the commisison received on supply sales is relatively small. By getting present users to put their equipment to better use, it is not long before those users will need more equipment as well as more supplies.

The companies which maintain large-scale field promotional organizations are mainly in the food, automobile, electrical appliance and related fields *where the neck of the sales bottle is the dealer.* In the case of big-ticket merchandise the crux of the sales problem is to get dealers to organize outside sales forces and to go out after business rather than sit around waiting for business to come to them. Then, too, there is the never-ending problem of increasing the sales effectiveness of dealers and their salespeople. It is an axiom of good sales management, that the surest way to build the kind of business that will stay with a company year in and year out is to build *better* dealers. That means more than getting dealers enthusiastic over some sales promotional campaign, which produces some immediate results but after all may be just a shot in the arm. It means helping them to be successful on all fronts, to buy more intelligently, to merchandise more skillfully, to control expenses and credits, and in other ways to improve their leadership and financial position. It takes time and money to carry through that type of "grass roots" program, but it pays off in the long run. It is noteworthy that in so-called bad times, those companies which have done a job of building financially strong dealers have weathered the storm more comfortably than others.

The sale of bowling equipment, for example, depends upon local enthusiasm. If there are a number of bowling teams in a locality, it is inevitable that some enterprising person will build a bigger and better bowling alley. So manufacturers making bowling equipment employ "organizers" in industrial centers to organize bowling teams in plants, churches, and other likely institutions. These organizers do little or no actual selling, but *indirectly* their efforts produce sales for their employer just as surely as any salesman's.

Another use for field men, as a supplement to personal selling is found in the distribution of office furniture. Enterprising dealers offer an office arrangement service at no cost to customers, which results in a saving on office space. Space in a mill-constructed building in a low-rent area costs much less in annual overhead than in a high-rent area. The "service" man, who has nothing to sell, interests a prospective buyer of furniture in the possibility of saving rent. He offers to come in and make a survey of his office arrangement without obligation but with the understanding, of course, that if the survey shows that substantial savings can be made by purchasing certain special-purpose furniture, his company will get first chance at the business. When the survey is completed, the salesman in the territory gets a copy and he carries on from there.

While an experienced salesman could make such a survey himself, the use of specialists on office arrangement seems to work out well. Actually the cost is about the same, since a good salesman's time is just about as expensive to the house as an efficiency man's. He may not be paid as much, but if you figure his cost on the basis of business lost while engaged in survey work, the odds favor the specialist. Most important of all, however, is the good-will value which accrues to a dealer when his representative is an expert, and not an amateur, on office management and arrangement.

One reason some report disappointing results from the use of field men in sales promotion is they fail to "spark" the men with new ideas for building sales which they can pass along to customers. A sales promotion man is no different from a salesman. He must have something to sell about which he can get excited. He needs something *important* to talk about. In far too many cases companies have set up field units in connection with some sort of a sales program, and then after that program was completed, or lost its edge, the management kept the men on the payroll on the theory that they could do the company a lot of good calling around on dealers and suggesting ways to increase sales. In theory they can. Actually, however, when men are left to their own devices, they tend to ride off in all directions. If there is no way of measuring the results of their efforts, they soon relax and get into a rut. So it might be said, with much truth, that unless there is a well-integrated plan for keeping a field organization stepping month in and month out, year in and year out, the cost of the operation might well be out of all proportion to the results obtained.

General Objectives of Management

OBJECTIVES	REQUISITE CONDITIONS
1. ORGANIZATION — To develop and maintain a sound and clear-cut plan of organization through which management can most easily and effectively direct and control the enterprise.	a. Organization structure (organizational components) designed best to facilitate management, prevent overlapping of functions, and duplication of effort. b. Function, responsibilities and authority, and relationships clearly defined for each management position. (See Management Guide.) c. Proper delegation of authority by management to permit decisions to be made at the lowest practicable level of management. d. Thorough understanding of the requirements and responsibilities of their positions on the part of personnel. e. Proper coordination of the entire organization plan.
2. PERSONNEL—To develop and administer a constructive personnel development and training program which will gradually ensure that all positions in the organization are filled by individuals fully qualified to meet the requirements of their respective positions.	a. Adequate control to ensure selection of best-qualified personnel available for the different types of work, first from within the organization, and then, if necessary, through outside hiring. b. Effective training by superiors, with the assistance of appropriate staff agencies, of all employees to meet the requirements of their jobs. c. Comprehensive annual rating of all employees in terms of job requirements. d. Positive action to correct deficiencies in qualifications and assignments as disclosed by the rating program. e. Carefully planned personnel utilization program to take the best advantage of demonstrated abilities, develop each individual's full potentialities, ensure adequate potential material for responsible positions, and to ensure placement of the best-qualified individual in each job. f. Adequate control to ensure that all promotions and appointments are made from among the best-qualified candidates available. g. Full cooperation in effecting the most advantageous placement of personnel. h. Proper coordination of the entire personnel development and training program.
3. PLANNING—To formulate well-considered plans and objectives, covering all operations, activities, and expenditures for each year or longer ahead, as a basis for authorization, a guide to achievement, and a measure of performance.	a. Clear conception of essential needs and worth-while objectives. b. Clear-cut plans for accomplishing these objectives. c. Sound analysis of requirements in terms of manpower, costs, facilities, and money. d. Good business judgment as to justification and extent of proposed undertakings. e. Effective participation of subordinates in formulation of their respective parts of the program. f. Proper coordination of each program. g. Appraisal of results compared with planning for these results.
4. ADMINISTRATION—To accomplish all functions and responsibilities fully, effectively, and harmoniously.	a. Guiding policies clearly stated, and well understood by all. b. Effective coordination and control of results. c. Prompt, well-considered management decisions. d. Close supervision affording first-hand familiarity and appraisal of operations, activities, and management problems on the ground without relieving subordinates of their proper responsibilities. e. Maximum use of best thought and capabilities of the entire organization in accomplishing the program.

General Objectives of Management

OBJECTIVES	REQUISITE CONDITIONS
ADMINISTRATION—*Cont.*	f. Assumption of proprietary responsibility for successful conduct of all activities under his control, relieving superiors of details, and presentation of matters of justifiable importance. g. Active cooperation in furthering the proper interest of other organizational components and of the enterprise as a whole. h. Maintenance of good public relations. i. Proper coordination of operations and activities.
5. COSTS—To keep all costs and manpower at an economic minimum, consistent with essential purposes.	a. Periodic analysis and appraisal of all functions and activities as to justification and required effort. b. Elimination of all unessential or ineffectual work, expense, and manpower as disclosed by such analysis. c. Establishment of most efficient methods for performing operations and activities. d. Establishment of suitable standards and measures as to what constitutes optimum performance and cost in regard to all operations, activities, and expenditures. e. An adequate control system, through which actual results are currently evaluated against the optimum or planned expectations, and all deficiencies are brought to the attention of the proper person for corrective action. f. Proper coordination of cost and manpower control programs.
6. BETTERMENT—To plan, stimulate, and develop improvement in methods, products, facilities, and other fields as applicable, keeping abreast of the best thought and practice throughout the industry, and to ensure that outmoded procedures and uneconomical facilities are abandoned.	a. Clear-cut recognition of needs and limitations. b. Well-planned betterment program with clearly defined objectives. c. Solicitation of best thought and suggestions from the entire organization. d. Keeping abreast of best thought and practice throughout the industry. e. Effective action in putting desirable improvements into effect. f. Proper coordination of betterment program. g. Periodic appraisal of results.
7. EMPLOYEE RELATIONS—To make sure that all employees are accorded fair and equitable treatment, and that they are inspired to their best efforts.	a. Personnel policies and practices (including benefit plans, wage and salary schedules, and working hours and conditions) kept up to date and in favorable relation to competition, through well-considered changes as necessary. b. Enlightened supervision, ensuring that each employee is treated fairly and justly as an individual, with helpful consideration for his personal feelings, ambitions, and problems, within the scope of reasonably interpreted rules and policies. c. Adequate control to ensure that each employee is fairly and appropriately compensated in general conformity with the established rate structure and policies. d. Maintenance of close touch with personnel and their problems. e. Effective leadership and stimulation of morale. f. Confidence and respect on the part of superiors, subordinates, and associates. g. Proper coordination of entire employee relations program.

Courtesy: Standard Oil Company of California

Chapter 4

THE BUDGET FOR SALES PROMOTION

A BUSINESS aphorism is that "nothing can happen without an order." Its counterpart in advertising and sales promotion is that nothing can happen without a budget. It is, or should be, the first and most basic step in any promotional program.

The budgeting process embraces three major phases: preparation, management approval, and control.

Marketing executives often observe that, in preparing budgets, sales promotion managers usually limit themselves to a review of the previous year's experience, to which they add a percentage of anticipated sales increases. They know that this procedure will win management approval, but it is no longer adequate. Broader concepts form the real starting point. They include:

Product market share.

Distribution pattern and depth.

Customer and prospect categories.

Competitive programs.

Susceptibility of product to treatment.

General market data.

Economic conditions.

Present or potential "profit contribution" is increasingly cited as a criterion. The vice president-marketing of a company in diversified metals manufacturing states:

"In general, we recommend that budgets be justified on the basis of each product's contribution to the division's overall sales and profits."

Other companies give strong advertising and promotion support to products that are faring poorly in terms of volume or profit. The vice president-sales in one manufacturing company describes its practices as follows:

"Although we split our budget roughly in proportion to the volume of the individual lines, wide deviations are possible when it becomes obvious that one product appears weak in the marketplace due to lack of exposure, etc. Occasionally a special allocation may be made for particular promotional projects on an individual product line which might require a disproportionate degree of support."

Another marketing executive expresses an interesting viewpoint in assessing allocations.

"Sometimes a product line that has little actual sales potential, but a lot of 'glamour,' may be advertised out of proportion to its sales prospects in order to generate inquiries and leads for our salesmen. What this boils down to is a 'common sense' approach to budgeting."

In the last two years, many companies have been headlined in the financial pages of the press as reporting "sales up but earnings down." Maximum sales may not always be profitable and management has come to realize that such terms as market share, increases in sales volume and maintenance of a leading position in the industry must be definitely related to profit.

"When sales are driven up to the point of profitability, or held there," states Mack Hanan, managing director of Hanan & Son, management consultants, "the sales function is operating at its greatest degree of cost effectiveness. The point of optimal profit for most products and services is usually well below a maximum share of market."

There are some exceptions. Violations of standards of profitability may be justified in such instances as new product introductions or market strategy, to meet keen competition.

A business cannot be long successful, however, or its management effective, if sales increases are sought without regard for considerations for the achievement of optimal profit. Sales promotion managers must plan and budget accordingly.

When it comes to obtaining management approval, it is extremely important that one be prepared to explain and justify all proposed expenditures on the basis of need and objectives. The Aluminum Corporation of America, for instance, requires budgets to be supported by individual product summaries which show sales objectives, advertising objectives and advertising strategies.

Budget controls take many forms. Most sales promotion departments naturally maintain records of expenditures against budget balances but only a few make provisions for future commitments, emergencies or reserves. These are just as much a part of the budget-control procedure as actual expenses. In larger companies, at least, the computer is a valuable means of avoiding over-expenditures.

It is essential that there be precise definitions of the expenditures chargeable to a sales promotion budget. As in the case of advertising and public relations budgets, there will be attempts by other departments to avoid cost responsibilities by diverting them to the sales promotion budget. The way to prevent this is to establish firm responsibilities for the approval of all charges against the budget.

If the appropriation for sales promotion includes operational expenses, these costs should be separated into a departmental budget. The promotion budget should consist only of those costs involved in the purchase of materials and services.

The departmental budget will detail the operating costs and expenses of the department, such as salaries, payroll taxes, travel, entertainment, office supplies and maintenance.

Usually the sales promotional budget and the budget for advertising are considered together. The advertising may be the sales promotion budget, or sales promotion might be included with advertising. But both are considered "indirect" selling expense and are seldom included with those items which relate specifically to direct sales cost—that is to say, the cost of operating the sales force. This is for the purpose of control. From an accounting standpoint all are, of course, a part of the cost of sales.

At certain times, there creep into sales budgeting many unhealthy practices. When money is easy and taxes high, companies allow branch managers and others to buy space in church and civic club programs as a gesture of interest in local affairs. Such expenditures, since they are purportedly advertising, are charged to the advertising appropriation. As advertising is not expected to carry a heavy load at such times, no harm is done. The same is true of many similar expenses, such as gifts and merchandise donations. But in times of competitive selling, and the need of making every advertising dollar stand on its own feet, sales managers insist that all such expenditures be charged to a special item in the general budget, such as "contributions and donations." It is held that charging such items to advertising or sales promotion penalizes the sales promotional activities, and makes it more difficult for the department to show results. The same applies to novelties given away at trade shows and state fairs. In a sense they are advertising, but more specifically they come under the head of "conventions and exhibits," which may or may not be charged against the appropriation for advertising. Some companies consider that expense as public relations.

Another item that may be charged differently by different companies is research work. Some research has to do with product development. Some has to do with market analysis. Some has to do with allocation of the advertising appropriation among various media. Some has to do with the preparation of sales manuals and sales tools. And perhaps more than we suspect may be for the benefit of the advertising agency. In the case of one company the research department worked for 6 months in gathering material for an operators' manual. Yet, in spite of the various departments which benefit from such research, the entire operation as a rule is charged to sales when it would seem only fair that the expense should be carefully computed and charged against the benefiting department.

Indeed, a well-thought-through scheme for measuring not only the need but the cost of all sales promotional activities is the first step in budgeting them. It is impossible to lay down any hard and fast rules, such as determining by percentage of sales how much a company should spend for sales promotion, or even which items should be charged to sales promotion. For example, if a new product is to be launched in a highly competitive field, two or three times as much as might normally be considered adequate should be spent for advertising, in order to shorten the time of introduction. However, companies which are enjoying a satisfactory ratio of profits to sales usually appropriate 3% of last year's sales for advertising and sales promotion. This figure might be higher in some instances as, for example, in pharmaceutical specialties; and lower in the case of engineering specialties. A general average might be 2% for consumer and trade advertising; 1% for sales promotion.

A newer trend in planning the sales promotional budget is to take the last year's sales figures, add to it the projected sales for the coming year, and divide by two. The percentage is then applied to this average. Advantage of this method is that if the company expects to sell a good deal more in the new year, the funds based on last year's sales will be inadequate; at the same time, giving equal weight to last year's figures will prevent overoptimism.

Preparing the Budget

No matter which budget-planning system is followed, and there are several, the over-riding consideration is that the total expenditure be in proper relation to sales and profits. While this might seem obvious, a corporate executive, in discussing the subject, said: "The difference, in this connection, between a company president and the advertising and sales promotion manager is that the president is, and must be, profit-conscious while promotion people, understandably, are largely interested in bigger and better budgets." Then he added, "And, perhaps, they should be."

As Charles G. Mortimer once stated: "There is no dollar-and-cents answer as to how much should be spent on advertising . . . It all depends on the selling task to be accomplished and the tools available, *including dollars.*"

This same profit-conscious factor applied by top management in appraising sales promotion budgets is reflected in the following summaries of reports and comments by corporate executives, including the results of a survey by the National Industrial Conference Board:

Without questioning advertising's role in determining the company's earnings, a number of NICB panel members stated unequivocally that the need for satisfactory profits in the current year will sometimes limit the advertising appropriation. One vice president, for example, said:

"We often find ourselves unable to provide an advertising budget that would do all the things we would like to do, and still produce the improving profits that are expected by our stockholders. Consequently we carefully delineate our advertising needs and then establish our budget according to our financial ability as best we can."

David L. Hurwood, NICB Division of Business Practices, in reporting the survey in the NICB "Record" made the comment that:

"Profit considerations are strongly implied in the use of such terms as probable funds available, overall operating budget of the company, the need for compromise, the amount we can afford." An executive in the packaging field comments, "Final programs and budgets, of course, are then subject to considerable negotiations between the advertising and sales promotion group and divisional management."

Before beginning his planning, the budgeter must know whether his overall budget will be limited to a maximum dollar amount or ceiling. There are few, if any, companies with resources so unlimited that no competition for funds exists between sales, marketing, production and the other areas of company operation. As a practical matter, therefore, a budget ceiling always exists and the advertising executive should be aware of the approximate dollar limit for his operation.

Other management executives stated:

The planning function is perhaps the most important first step in allocating funds. Planning for the efficient allocation of the resources of the firm is the primary task of the business leader. It requires an imaginative evaluation of the internal and external environment of the enterprise. It also requires flexibility and effectively overcoming many psychological impediments to innovation and change.

A long-range plan, possibly five years, should be built product by product. This would show the range of growth thought possible with various levels of marketing and advertising costs, for both established and new products. Pricing levels must be established, and inflationary factors in all costs should be included.

* * *

The allocation of advertising expenditures must be related to the allocation of all other corporate resources. Each function in the corporate system interacts with the others. These comments will attempt to describe: (1) The importance of planning and the over-all interaction between the functions of the company. (2) How the advertising appropriation then relates to the other marketing variables.

* * *

Advertising and sales promotion is perhaps the largest single item in the marketing appropriation. The question of how much to spend, and how to allocate that expenditure, is subject to continuing debate. Most executives agree that it is high time that procedures are established to assure top management that a recommendation to spend a given number of dollars on advertising is based on more than judgment and intuition.

Many new methods have been and are being tried, both quantitative and qualitative. Yet most have not yet proven fully capable, and old methods of budgeting and allocation are slow to disappear.

* * *

Promotional spending should be planned according to two distinct purposes: (1) to sustain the sales performance of a product in each of its market areas; and (2) to help develop or expand the brand's strength, especially in areas where its performance has been unsatisfactory.

While all promotional activity has the purpose of increasing sales (and ultimately, of course, profits), this focuses specific attention upon the dual goals of maintaining and expanding a brand's franchise in each geographic area where it is sold.

* * *

All areas do not possess the same potential. The possibility of future development (along with reasons for poor performance) should be analyzed before pouring development dollars into weak areas.

* * *

There is a wide gap between theory and practice in the development and allocation of advertising expenditures. The so-called "best" solution is elusive, and is difficult if not impossible to achieve. The information needed is not always available. When it is available, its worth is discounted by time, control and the presence of many variables.

In the large, modern corporation, the result is inevitably some sort of compromise. Top management must, however, make sure that the final result contains as much objective thinking as possible, that there is enough experimentation and innovation in all of the facets of advertising to insure that the corporation is moving closer to the goal of maximizing profits on a continuing basis.

At our company, we believe that the advertising allocation must be extended beyond the traditional one-year budget. We tend to think in terms of two years. The allocation of funds is closely tied to our long-range schedule of new product introductions and product improvements. It is also closely related to profits and profit potential.

* * *

Only through continuous experimentation with advertising variations will the advertiser ever know the effect on sales. However, this is expensive. You need people, research funds and patience.

When the total advertising budget has been established, we must turn to the problems of allocation of funds within the total, with the ever-present need to maximize profits.

The questions that must be considered here include product allocation, geographic allocation, media mix, scheduling and copy.

Product allocation poses some interesting challenges. What does each product or product group contribute to profits? What is the sales history and trend? What is each product's potential? What improved products do we have? What new products? What promotions do we have in mind? This will yield a range of possibilities to which some factors must be assigned.

Geographic allocation resolution will include historical industry sales, company sales trends and profits by area, and local media costs. All too often it does not include enough thought to future sales potential, and to the many differences between local markets.

* * *

Three different methods for deciding how much a company should spend on advertising were revealed in the survey of The Conference Board's Panel of Senior Marketing Executives:

The task approach—Marketing objectives are established, for the company or division as a whole, or for individual products, services, or markets. The role advertising is to play in helping to achieve these objectives is spelled out, and the cost of producing this advertising, and disseminating it via media, becomes the tentative advertising budget.

Budgeting by fixed guidelines—A formula is adopted which, when applied to some controlling figure, automatically establishes the advertising budget. The base figure is, most often, the volume of sales expected, and the formula is either a percentage or a specific amount per unit of sales. In relatively few instances, the base is the amount spent on advertising the preceding year, and the formula then becomes, simply, "what we spent last year," adjusted upwards or downwards as conditions appear to warrant.

Occasional doubts are expressed about the logic of fixing advertising budgets as a percentage of sales—particularly when based on last year's volume. "This procedure may be applicable in the case of a rising trend of sales, but presents problems in the case of declining sales," comments the spokesman for a consumer company. And a marketing executive in the industrial field declared:

"Our divisional ad managers are fighting the traditional use of a fixed percent of sales, or worse yet, the 'we're having a good year so we can afford to spend more money advertising, and vice versa' method."

One marketing executive in a chemical manufacturing company made the point that the preceding year's budget should exert a strong influence on the next year's appropriation, even if a percentage relationship is usually observed and sales have gone up sharply. The burden of proof rests on the advocate of a higher spending level. "For example, if we had an exceptionally good year and our sales increased by 25%, we would not be inclined to increase our advertising 25% the following year. At least, the people in charge would have to make a very strong case to sell such an increase."

On the other hand, it is pointed out that rising media and production costs must be kept in mind. Otherwise, spending the same amount as last year will represent a decline in the effective rate of expenditure. A sales vice president in the construction products industry states, "We make provision for these increased costs to sustain our current program before we consider that we are increasing our true dollar budget."

Subjective budgeting—Management decides, largely by judgment and experience, how to divide an available sum between advertising and other activities, vying for shares of the corporate purse.

The three approaches are not mutually exclusive. For example, emphasis may be placed on working out advertising tasks and needs, while another criterion, such as a customary percentage formula, may be used to establish a ceiling above which the budget is not to go.

PREMIUM STRENGTH & PRECISION FORGINGS

Sales Objective: Alcoa seeks to increase the specification of precision forgings and encourage the design of larger precision forgings by the aerospace industry.

Advertising Objective: Continue to announce among 65,815 engineers, 479 designers, and 4,934 purchasing agents the reasons for considering Alcoa as a source of aluminum precision forgings and premium strength/precision forgings. Have them contact Alcoa for further technical information and quotations.

Advertising Strategies:

1. Reach more than 55% of these aerospace material specifiers through 8 messages citing the advantages of precision and premium strength forgings to the purchaser and designer, and of doing business with Alcoa.

2. Provide salesmen with customer presentation material to communicate these advantages to above audience.

Advertising Budget:

1. Space		
Aviation Wk & Sps Tech 8-1p4cb		$27,040
Prep 2-1p4cb		10,000
2. Collateral		
Customer presentation material		4,000
Research		1,200
Total PS & P Forgings		$42,040

Aluminum Company of America requires the advertising and sales promotion department to include the reasons for expenditures in the budgets for all product sections. In addition to the budget, each sheet shows Sales Objective, Advertising Objective, and Advertising Strategies.

Courtesy: Alcoa

And although many companies use research techniques to help in arriving at the spending level for advertising and promotion, judgment inevitably plays a part in the ultimate decision.

In most instances, flexibility is the most notable feature of advertising budget policy. Two widespread practices are the provision of supplemental budgets for new products, and the establishment of contingency funds for unexpected needs and tactical opportunities.

In summary, it may be said that the preparation of the formal advertising plan and budget for presentation to the company's budget approval authorities is the culmination of the fact-gathering and advertising planning process. The formal budget is the translation of the advertising plan into monetary terms and is one of the chief means by which management appraises the advertising recommendations. The preparation and presentation of the formal budget is thus a most important part of the advertising executive's job. Management approval of a well-conceived advertising plan can be jeopardized by a budget which is insufficiently substantiated or poorly presented.

Breaking Down the Budget

For purposes of comparison and control it is good practice to break the total budget down by operations according to the nature of the business and the type of advertising and sales promotion employed. Advertising expenses (aside from administrative salaries) are usually broken down as follows:

1. General Advertising
   a. Newspapers
   b. Magazines
   c. Radio—Time
   d. Radio—Talent
   e. Television—Time
   f. Television-Talent
   g. Outdoor (incl. Car Cards)
2. Business and Trade Papers
3. Class Publications
4. Farm Journals
5. Direct Mail
   a. Consumer
   b. Trade
   c. Professional

6. Dealer Helps
7. Displays
8. Free Goods and Allowances
9. Samples
10. Premiums
11. Novelties
12. House Organs
13. Sales Literature
14. Conventions and Exhibits
15. Motion Pictures
16. Price Lists
17. Publicity
18. All Other

In the same way the budget for sales promotion, where a company sells through dealers, usually includes the following items of expense excluding departmental payroll:

1. Research	7. Fairs and Exhibits
2. Travel	8. Educational Material for Schools
3. Sales Education	9. Sales Contests and Campaigns
a. Training Literature	10. Dealer and Other Meetings
b. Films and Visuals	11. Community Relations
c. Housing and Administration	
4. Promotional Literature	12. Speakers' Bureau
5. Dealer Services	13. Publicity
6. Sales Tools and Equipment	14. Trade Associations

When business is running along on an even keel, and there are no special circumstances to be taken into consideration, budgets are usually prepared on an annual basis, well ahead of the end of the fiscal year. This is important, since a full-scale promotional activity requires considerable time to get under way. Until the department knows what it is going to have to spend, it cannot make hard and fast plans. In a period of rising prices, for example, it is desirable to contract for advertising space and TV and radio time before the first of the year when new rates usually become effective. In the same way it takes several months to prepare the printed matter required to carry through a plan after the exependiture has been authorized.

In changing times, however, and in times of uncertainty it is good sales-strategy to operate on a quarterly budget, rather than an annual appropriation. This permits fitting the budget to the needs of the business.

A sharp drop in sales during the winter might require a stepped-up appropriation for spring and summer promotions. On the other hand, an unexpected shortage of raw materials might make it wise to curtail promotional activities for the next quarter. The need for advance planning makes the quarterly budget impractical in most businesses.

GEARING THE BUDGET TO THE PROGRAM

Before an appropriation for sales promotion can be determined, it is necessary to have an objective and a plan to attain it. This may seem trite, yet there are an amazing number of companies which approach the problem in exactly the opposite way. On the theory that every business needs advertising and sales promotion, just as it needs insurance against fire, the directors allocate a sum of money, usually a percentage of last year's sales, for a sales promotional program to stimulate sales at the point of purchase, or to create new markets, or some similar purpose. The money having been appropriated, it then becomes the job of the sales promotion department or the advertising department, as the case might be, to "hit upon some scheme" for spending the money to good advantage. Usually it is spent to poor advantage. Management is justified in withholding any appropriation for promotion until a well-coordinated plan of action, with estimates as to results expected and the cost, has been prepared and has the approval of the sales executive.

The Idea Is the Thing

There is a saying in salesmanship that a good salesman doesn't sell life insurance, he sells protection for the widow. Neither does a good shoe clerk sell shoes, he sells foot comfort. In the same way a good sales promotional program or campaign "sells" an idea about the product and its use, rather than the product itself. The most successful effort to increase the sale of electric light bulbs pivoted on the idea that they were bought upon "impulse." Heretofore, lamp manufacturers laid a great deal of sales emphasis on the economy and life of their bulbs. The promotional effort was founded on the idea of making people want better light.

Then one of the companies devised a merchandising plan for light bulbs which was tested out by a large chain-store system. The plan was very simple. Counter and store displays of a reminder type were developed, and store supervisors were "sold" on the idea of putting these displays up where store traffic was heaviest, *disregarding* the fact that light bulbs were usually sold in the electrical goods section. It was found that where this was done, sales increased 70% the first year, and 35% the second year.

The theory was that people seldom go to a store to buy a light bulb. But when passing a lamp display in a store they are reminded of a burned-out bulb at home, will purchase a replacement, and can be easily induced to buy a few extra bulbs for a reserve supply. The merchandising plan of this manufacturer is to get dealers to set up displays of "impulse" merchandise, including light bulbs, at heavy traffic points in the store. The promotional program is built around that central idea.

Generally speaking, there would seem to be little in common between light bulbs and dictating machines. One is sold through dealers, the other is sold direct to the user. One sells for a few cents, the other for two hundred dollars. But just as the sales of light bulbs were increased by promoting a sales idea, so the sales of dictating machines have been increased by promoting a sales idea. Here is how it was done:

Experience of Dictaphone

The principal sales resistance to dictating machines is the opposition of the secretary of the man to whom the machine must be sold. Dictating machine salesmen only waste time talking to either the business executive or his secretary about the mechanical qualities of the product. Yet that is what some dictating machine salesmen were trying to do, because of the competitive situation in that field.

To meet this situation the Dictaphone Corporation developed a promotional program in which the machine was quite incidental. A sound film entitled "Two Salesmen in Search of an Order" was produced. This picture dramatized the right and wrong ways to sell a dictating machine.

Ostensibly, it was a sales training film; but actually it was a dramatic and convincing demonstration of how the Dictaphone saved time and money for the user, made the secretary more valuable to her employer, and enabled the executive to handle his correspondence with greater ease and dispatch. It was an excellent picture.

Prints of this film were furnished to the principal Dictaphone offices, which were also provided with portable sound projectors for showing the picture. A carefully planned program was prepared, involving the use of direct-mail, magazine advertising, and personal solicitation, to get businessmen to permit the Dictaphone salesman to show this film to the executives of local business organizations. It was explained that the selling principles dramatized in this picture could be applied to selling any product. And they can be.

Hundreds of these exhibitions were given in the offices of prospects, as well as at business shows, meetings of sales managers' clubs, Rotary clubs, etc. Naturally, a great many sales resulted. It was an indirect approach built around an *idea,* rather than around the product.

The Johns-Manville Guild System

Another interesting example of a promotion built around an idea rather than the product is a merchandising plan developed by the Johns-Manville Corporation of New York.

The system was defined by the Johns-Manville company as a "union of the merchandising power of manufacturer, dealer, contractor, architect, realtor, and financing agency into a cooperative selling operation which protects the identity and the prerogatives of each." Its objective was to organize all the sales promotional forces in the building industry behind the retail dealer, and by making him pros-

Examples of Sales Promotion Budgets

Line of Business (Number of Companies Investigated)	Folders and Broadsides	Catalogs and Booklets	Window and Store Display	Letters and Postage	All Other Forms
Store fixtures (28)	22.2	17.3	3.6	9.8	47.1
Food products (35)	13.9	10.7	16.3	4.1	55.0
Building materials (52)	22.0	14.0	1.0	11.0	52.0
Leather goods (21)	12.8	15.2	11.2	21.2	39.6
Household equipment (83)	28.4	11.1	2.3	18.0	40.2
Machinery manufacturers (45)	18.0	15.0	0.0	13.0	54.0
Jewelry (20)	27.9	40.9	0.7	16.8	13.7
Clothing (75)	13.2	6.8	6.1	39.8	34.1
Office equipment (27)	13.4	18.1	0.6	18.5	49.4
Chemicals (19)	13.5	28.0	1.5	21.0	36.0
Steel supplies (18)	12.5	14.3	0.0	12.5	60.7
Investment houses (27)	16.4	5.3	0.2	24.0	54.1
Scientific instruments (10)	9.0	11.7	0.9	7.8	70.6
Confectioners (10)	16.7	12.8	22.5	1.6	46.4
Automobile accessories (12)	26.8	10.9	1.5	7.9	52.9
Hardware (41)	15.7	30.6	1.1	15.6	37.0
Drug supplies (7)	15.1	5.7	4.7	15.3	59.2
Sporting goods (7)	13.3	14.7	0.8	7.3	63.9
Novelties (14)	15.3	20.9	4.0	19.1	44.3
Associations (11)	27.8	17.8	0.7	21.2	32.5
Textiles (13)	14.3	17.4	0.4	44.6	23.3
Musical instruments (13)	17.6	23.4	0.4	8.2	50.4
Fuel products (13)	7.5	6.8	0.9	25.2	59.6
Miscellaneous (57)	19.5	21.3	2.0	12.4	44.8
Average	17.2	16.2	3.4	16.5	46.7

perous, promote the prosperity of the entire building industry, including the Johns-Manville Corporation.

The plan provided for undertaking, in several regions, an aggressive training program for dealers' salesmen. Complete sales kits were furnished these salesmen, including estimating books, management handbook for sales managers, sales manuals for salesmen, etc. The guild salesmen, under the direction of the dealer, sold the services and products of all guild members to the consumer. This plan was discontinued during the war, and was later taken over as an industry activity.

Marshall Field's Store Promotions

This same principle of building promotions around an idea is also found in the prevailing practice of leading retail establishments. Marshall Field & Company of Chicago, for example, in an effort to "trade up" its customers staged a "quality" exhibition. A special section of the store was used for the purpose. Manufacturers of quality products were invited to cooperate. Merchandise of high quality, suitably tagged and explained, was featured beside similar products made to sell at a price. The greater values offered by the higher-priced products were thus clearly shown and demonstrated to the thousands of customers who saw the exhibition. Promotions of this sort have a decided effect in stepping up the unit of sale, and tend to focus purchases on merchandise most likely to enhance the reputation of the store. The National Retail Merchants Association's Sales Promotion Budget Planning Calendar (suggesting promotions for each month) is useful for this purpose.

FITTING PROMOTION TO MARKETING POLICY

It will be noted from some of the foregoing experiences that in most cases the program was focused on the *one* main objection encountered in selling the product. So we conclude that the first thing that should be done before spending any large sum of money for promotion, is to determine what this *one* main objection is to the sale of your product.

Most sales executives think they know the principal reason more people do not buy their product. In only a few cases, however, has any systematic effort been made to determine the exact reasons. In a number of cases, the men were told one thing by one executive, and another by some other executive of the same company. Salesmen had one idea; sales managers, another; and the head of the business, still another. These reasons should be more accurately determined.

Another fundamental that must be considered in setting up a marketing budget, of which sales promotion is to be a part, is the markets which you can profit *most* by serving. Then concentrate sales promotional effort on those markets.

Order Analysis as a Basis of Planning

This can be done by an analysis of orders. What group of customers is giving you a type of order that yields a good profit? Are you dissipating too large a portion of your sales promotional effort on a segment of your total market which produces less than 20% of your business? Are you spending too much for promoting sales to customers whose purchases are so small that all the profits are absorbed in service?

Then analyze your orders to see what happens to your product from the time it leaves the source to its final use. Some amazing discoveries have been made when such research has been undertaken. Obstacles which no one suspected as existing have thus been brought to light. Facts so obtained can be used to increase the results from a sales promotional effort.

Still another point to be considered is the extent of the sales promotional effort, with relation to the markets which can most profitably be served. Very often there are markets in which competition is firmly entrenched, where selling costs are excessive, or freight rates unfavorable. These can profitably be passed over in the planning, and the money spent more advantageously in other markets.

Similar studies should be made prior to spending any sizable sum of money for sales promotional effort. The facts required can often be gathered by somebody in the sales department; more often it is advisable to employ the services of a research organization equipped to do this sort of job. Again, the services of your advertising agency may be employed. In any event, make sure that whoever is making the analysis has no axe to grind. Otherwise he might set out to prove a preconceived opinion.

Using Salesmen to Survey Customer Needs

Valuable information may also be obtained for planning sales promotional activities by requiring periodical reports from salesmen. It was observed that some companies feel salesmen should not be asked to do any "paper work" whatever, such as making out reports, for fear it will take time away from selling. Going to the other extreme, some sales managers load salesmen with so much "paper work" they have to devote most of their evenings to that.

Is there a happy medium? In the case of salesmen calling on established trade, a periodical check-up, such as the Westinghouse dealer merchandise survey, is as helpful to the salesman himself as it is to the management. It forces a salesman to sit down and concentrate on each customer for at least 20 minutes once a year. In order to intelligently make out this survey sheet, a salesman must get certain information that will be useful in handling that account. The survey enables him to get that information.

The Coca-Cola Store Survey Plan

This same survey plan, your investigators found, has been successfully used by the Coca-Cola Company in promoting the sale of coolers. Wagon salesmen are furnished with survey forms, asking certain vital information from the dealer. The salesman devotes one call to getting this survey sheet filled out. Then he takes it home and studies it. From it he gets data upon which to base his sales talk. A few days later he goes back and, with the data from the survey sheet, makes the sale. Later these survey sheets provide the home office sales promotional department with useful information for planning promotional and advertising activities.

Use of Mail Questionnaires for Gathering Data

In former years many companies depended largely upon information which could be obtained by mail as a basis of planning a sales promotional program. But this practice is waning. There are two reasons: (1) The unreliability of information obtained through questionnaires, (2) the increasing percentage of customers who go berserk when it comes to taking the time to fill out questionnaires. The multiplicity of questionnaires from governmental agencies seems to have created a hearty dislike for that method. This is particularly true of dealers.

However, many lines of business and many types of buyers will cheerfully fill out questionnaires, if confined to a few intelligent "yes" and "no" questions. We found a number of companies using questionnaires of this type for getting essential information in connection with advertising media; suggestions for improving utility value of dealer-helps, etc. The trend, however, is away from this type of research work.

How U.S. Tire Schedules Promotion by Seasons

One company which arranged its efforts into an organized series of promotions, rather than making them a continuing proposition, was the U.S. Tire Mutual Corporation, dealer-help subsidiary of the United States Tire Company of New York.

This company used *four* distinct promotions during the year. These four promotions were scheduled at one time, and full information about them was released to dealers 2 months prior to the time the first promotion was scheduled to start. These campaigns were sold to the dealer by the promotional subsidiary company; thus any sales promotional contract made by the independent company had nothing to do with the sale of tires or the contracts of the tire company.

It is not too much to say that the success of any program for enlisting dealer support for promotions is dependent on timing. The whole series of promotions should be organized and submitted to distributors and dealers at least 60 days prior to the beginning of the first promotion.

Most of the companies which meet with poor success in getting sales promotions work too close to schedule. Local cooperators *must* be given ample time to make all local arrangements, build mailing lists, and develop acceptance within their own organizations for the necessary expenditure of time and effort.

How to Get Dealers to Set Budgets

The first thing in timing a promotion, as for example in the program of the United States Tire Company, is to get dealers to resolve to get a definite volume of increased business in a certain period. This is called a "loading" or a "bogie" or an "objective." It is best not to use the term "quota" as that smacks of high-pressure methods.

In the build-up for the promotion, supply dealers with data on the probable increase in business for the industry and endeavor to get them to "get their share of the increased business which is going to be available this summer." Send them something so that they can pledge *themselves* to get more business.

Point out to dealers that in order to get this increased volume of business, they must make an increased sales and sales promotional effort. In other words, if the average expenditures for sales promotion among the leaders in your industry is 3% of purchases, then they should increase their sales promotional budget to line up with their sales expectancy for the period.

Get dealers to break that budget down into a series of promotions, allocating a fixed amount for each promotion. The amount should be in relation to the seasonal sales opportunity. For example, the U.S.

Tire campaign was based on the following flow of retail tire sales through the year:

First Quarter—January, February, March................................19.4%
Second Quarter—April, May, June................................31.3%
Third Quarter—July, August, September................................29.1%
Fourth Quarter—October, November, December................................20.2%

Such figures for national averages will vary greatly, of course, in different sections of the country. But in every line of business there are average figures which can be used in helping the distributor plan his programs. In many cases he is able to supply his own percentages from his own records and experience.

COST RATIOS ACCORDING TO SIZE OF DEALER

	All Dealers	Sales Over $500,000	Sales $250,000 to $500,000	Sales $150,000 to $250,000	Sales $75,000 to $150,000	Sales Under $75,000
Net Sales...................	100.0 100.0	100.0 100.0	100.0 100.0	100.0 100.0	100 0 100.0	100.0 100.0
Gross Margin...............	32.9 32.0	34.9 32.6	33.0 31.4	33.9 31.4	29.9 31.6	34.6 31.3
Total Operating Costs.......	30.6 28.8	31.3 29.7	31.3 29.6	31.3 27.0	25.2 28.9	28.7 33.1
Administrative.............	21.2 20.6	21.3 21.5	22.4 20.8	21.8 18.5	16.5 20.1	19.6 20.4
Managerial Pay..........	3.4 3.6	3.2 3.7	3.6 2.9	2 4 2.7	3.3 6.5	4.4 5.3
Office Salaries...........	2.2 2.1	2.2 2.2	2.5 2.1	2.5 2.0	1.3 1.6	1.6 1.1
Salesmen's Pay..........	5.6 5.7	6.3 6.2	5.9 6.0	4.8 5.2	3.8 3.6	2.5 2.6
Servicing...............	6 0 5.1	5.7 5.4	6.2 5.5	7.5 4.4	5.1 4.3	4 7 7.5
Vehicle Expense..........	2.4 2.4	2.4 2.3	2.4 2.4	3.2 3.0	1.7 2.5	4.8 2.3
Other Administrative Costs	1 6 1 7	1.5 1.7	1.8 1.9	1.4 1.2	1.3 1.6	1.6 1.6
Occupancy Expense........	2.5 2 5	2.3 1.8	2.6 3.0	2.7 2.6	2.9 3.3	3.3 4.6
Advertising Costs..........	2.5 2 6	2.6 3.0	2.3 2.6	2 9 2.7	2.4 2.3	2.8 4.1
Bad Debt Losses...........	0.4 0.2	0.5 0.3	0.3 0.2	0.3 0.2	0.2 0.2	0.2 0.1
All Other Expense..........	4.0 2.9	4 6 3.1	3.7 3.0	3.6 3.0	3.2 3.0	2.8 3.9
Net Operating Profit........	2.3 3.2	3.7 2.9	1.7 1.8	2.6 4.4	4.7 2.6	5.9 −1.7

Dealer Advertising Ratios in One Line

As an example of how cost ratios relate to sales, the preceding table had been compiled from figures supplied by the National Appliance & Radio-TV Dealers Association. While these figures apply for only two particular years in a certain line, they show a pattern of allocation which is generally typical.

Rating Dealers and Distributors

A lot of good "heat" goes up the chimney as a result of failure to classify those upon whom the sales promotional money will be spent. It is well known, for example, that most companies get 70% of their business from less than 30% of their customers. It is also a fact, not so well known, that most sales promotional programs do not distinguish between these "bread and butter" customers and those who buy in relatively small amounts and whose value to the business, so far as future growth goes, is negligible. While it is true that the big accounts of today were once small accounts, there is a danger in helping any customer who asks for help of dissipating too large a portion of what is budgeted for sales promotion on fringe accounts.

To gear the promotional effort closely to those customers who give us most of our business, more and more companies are using dealer ratings. By means of questionnaires, filled out by the salesman or the dealer himself, an estimate is reached as to a customer's potential value to the business, his ability to make good use of promotional materials furnished to him, and his standing in the community. An incidential benefit from such a plan is that it establishes, without prejudice, a dealer's rating so no one can say one dealer is being rendered a service which the company is not offering to his competitors. It also helps to resolve the question of status: Does the account measure up to the company's definition of a wholesaler, retailer, or what have you? Most sales executives leave it to the territorial salesman to decide a buyer status. Naturally they are prejudiced in favor of getting an order. When the customer is required to fill out a rating blank for the salesman to mail with the initial order, salesmen are more critical of the nature of the buyer's business.

A good many retailers, who sell a few products locally in a distributor capacity and insist upon having the wholesaler's discount, are forced to admit they are not really wholesalers according to the company's rating plan. It protects the salesman, other legitimate wholesalers, and the company.

Rating forms usually bear down heavily on the ability of the prospective dealer or distributor to cooperate in sales promotions undertaken by the company. For example, one manufacturer rates prospective dealers for its line of farm machinery on such points as those shown.

1. Approximate wholesale value of machines and parts.
   (last year)   (this year)   (next year-est)

2. How much did dealer invest in all kinds of advertising?
   (last year)   (this year)

3. How much will the dealer spend on local advertising next year?
   $................................   How will he spend it? ....

4. What is dealer's attitude toward modern merchandising?
   ☐ enthusiastic   ☐ moderate   ☐ negative

With a rating plan in operation, distributors and dealers can be grouped and tabled in such a way that the more expensive dealer helps can be restricted to those groups most likely to use them to best advantage. The bulk of the appropriation is thus concentrated on customers from whom the company gets the bulk of its business and who hold out the most promise of growth, Dealers or customers rated as negative so far as modern merchandising methods go, can be helped less expensively.

Information Needed to Rate Distributors

In order to set up a rating scheme for a distributor organization, factual information is needed, depending upon the nature of the business. One company requires its salesmen to secure this information, either when the account is opened or as soon after as is practicable. Each salesman is furnished a list of questions as a basis for obtaining the information. The questions follow:

DISTRIBUTORS SALES ORGANIZATION

1. Wholesale men. Number employed.   ....

2. Wholesale men having received initial sales training and demonstration instruction.   ....

3. Wholesale salesmen actually proficient in demonstration. ....

4. Wholesale men with a fundamental knowledge of service and repairs.   ....

5. Wholesale men able to instruct and train retail dealers. ....

6. Wholesale men using training films, how-to-sell book, and other material with dealers.   ....

DISTRIBUTORS SERVICE ORGANIZATION

1. Service manager and servicemen instructed in service and repair. ....
2. Service and repair setup completed. ....
3. Repair parts stock purchased. ....
4. Supplies stock purchased. ....
5. Parts and supplies merchandising program undertaken. ....
6. Guarantee procedure understood. ....

DISTRIBUTORS ADMINISTRATION OF 50-50 AD FUND

1. Assignment of responsibility made. ....
2. Explanation of fund use understood. ....
4. Dealer program scheduled. ....

DISTRIBUTORS DEALER ORGANIZATION

1. Dealers franchised. ....
2. Dealers receiving one or more machines monthly. ....
3. Dealers sold and using:
   a. Background display. ....
   b. Neon sign. ....
   c. Parts display case. ....
   d. Parts and supplies deal. ....
   e. Wall banner. ....
   f. Window decal. ....
   g. Window trim. ....
   h. Full line folders. ....
   i. Yarn crafters. ....
4. Dealers given demonstration and sales training. ....
5. Dealers given service instruction. ....
6. Dealers supplied with presentation catalog. ....
7. Dealers supplied with how-to-sell book. ....
8. Dealers who have seen film "Sewing Machine, Domestic & You." ....
9. Dealers who have seen film "It's Big Business." ....
10. Dealers receiving "Domestic Affairs." ....

DISTRIBUTORS MONTHLY REPORTS

1. Assignment of responsibility made. ....
2. Reports completed. ....

What are this Distributor's recommendations and suggestions?

If it is not deemed practical to use salesmen to secure this type of information, the use of special men may be considered. Some companies have used undergraduates from colleges specializing in marketing to obtain rating information during summer vacations. But care must be used to make sure it is accurate. This requires supervision and some spot checking.

CONFIDENTIAL

DEALER POINT SURVEY REPORT

BASIC DATA:

Date...19.........

Town.. County.. State.................................

Population (town) ....Population (trading area).............................

Nearest large city...Distance ....Mi ....Transportation ....

Municipal water supply..Water pressure ....

No. Electric Meters.................................Gas Meters.............................. Water Meters.......................

Does surrounding country have utility power?......................................

What chains have stores in town?..

How many washer dealers?.........................Makes ....

Estimate total potential market for laundry equip. —next 12 months ....

Automatics ....Agitators.. Ironers............................

SPECIFIC DATA:

Dealer's Firm Name.. Address.................................

Type of Business ....

Years in business ....Years selling laundry equip............................

Did dealer previously sell the Speed Queen line?........................... When.....................

Brands Now Selling:

Automatic washers .... Non-Automatic..........................

Refrigerators .... Freezers .... Ironers ....

Electric Ranges..............................Gas Ranges.................................

Water Heaters, Electric.. Gas.........................

Radios .... Cleaners.........................

Other major appliances...

Character of location ....Parking facilities ....

Character of property, size........................... age................. appearance...................

Store layout (good or poor) ....Space for S. Q. line (approx.) ....sq. ft.

Does dealer have complete service dept?......................... Val. washer parts inv. $..................

If no service Dept. now, will he set up S.Q. service? ....

Any outside business interests?.................................

Is dealer of aggressive type?.............................

How does he stand in community?.............................

FINANCIAL DATA:

D-B Rating.........................Credit Limit.................................... Terms............................

Bank Reference ....

Credit Reference ....

Credit Reference ....

App. Value Inventory, as of..........................19............. $...........................

Facilities for financing sales...

Does dealer own or rent store?.................................

Does he plan any store expansion?.............................

FORM 279

To effectively cooperate with dealers and distributors, it is important that the sales promotion department, as well as the credit department, have a complete picture of each account. The above form is typical of many used for this purpose. It is filled out either by the salesman or by a sales promotion fieldman and used for rating the dealer. On the basis of these ratings both salesman's time and sales promotion are allocated.

SALES DATA:

Previous volume—   **Washers**   **Ironers**

           19............... ....

           19............... ....

           19............... ....

Sales Methods Employed:

Home Demonstration?.. Store Demonstration?...............................

Canvassing .... Other...

Hot and cold water for demonstration of S. Q. Automatic? ....

No. sales people, inside .... outside...

Method of remuneration ....

Territory covered regularly ....

Type of Advertising: Direct mail...........................Local paper ....

      Point-of-sale Displays ....Bill boards ....

      Local Theatre Trailers.......................Tel. Solicitation ....

Facilities for servicing major appliances...

Facilities for handling trade-ins..

Will this dealer sell the Speed Queen line exclusively ....

What quantities will he order? Washers: Wringer................... Automatic.................. Ironers..............

How to ship........................From which S. Q. warehouse ....

Does dealer have adequate warehouse space?..

Additional information ....

....

....

CONFIDENTIAL DEALER RATING

		Fair			Good			Excellent			Rating
Standing in Community	4	5	6	10	11	12	13	14	15	16	
Management Ability	1	2	3	4	5	6	7	8	9	10	
Financial and Credit Standing	4	5	6	10	11	12	13	14	15	16	
Character of Location	0	0	1	2	3	4	5	6	7	8	
Size and Attractiveness of Store	0	0	1	2	2	3	4	5	6		
Display and Demonstrating Facilities	1	2	3	4	5	6	7	8	9	10	
Knowledge of Specialty Selling	1	2	3	4	5	6	7	8	9	10	
Sales Aggressiveness	0	0	1	2	3	4	5	6	7	8	
Promotional Effort	0	0	1	2	3	4	5	6	7	8	
Service Facilities	0	0	1	2	3	4	5	6	7	8	
										Total	

NOTE: Obviously, all dealers can not be alike and some will rate higher than others on certain qualifications. The accompanying chart provides a quick, fair means of evaluating a dealer in laundry equipment, and you will notice that some qualifications are considered of greater importance than others. In using this chart, above all BE FAIR and be thorough. You will find this method of rating very helpful in screening your dealer franchises.

40-60 Inferior   60-80 Average   80-100 Superior

Survey made by:

....

Reviewed and Approved by:

Date..19.......   ....
                                                              Division Manager

Original: Office copy

Reverse side of the form shown on page 104, used by a manufacturer company to rate dealers for sales promotional purposes. The summary provides the sales executive with a quick method of evaluating the account, and determining its potential worth to the business. It is of particular value when selective sales methods are used to market the product. It permits accurate screening of dealer franchises.

Information Needed to Rate Dealers

The procedure in getting the information necessary to rate dealers for sales promotional purposes, when the product is sold directly to dealers, is similar to the procedure used in rating wholesalers. In the case of the new dealer, the information required is used by both the sales promotional department to establish a rating, and by the credit department to establish the line of credit.

How One Manufacturer Sets Distributor Quotas

Another popular method of setting the "loadings" for distributors and distributors' salesmen is to chart each sales territory, and furnish distributors with "exposure" charts to point up their sales effort. These charts, which are 17 by 22 inches in size according to an explanatory letter of transmittal, give the following sales information about a territory:

1. State.
2. County.
3. City. (All cities of 1,000 population or over are listed.) Let me point out here that we show in the "city" column, the *number* of radio dealers for whom we received radio franchises last season. This is a guide for your performance this year.
4. Population.
5. Radio Quotas. (Dealer Quotas, and Sales Quotas by units for each county.)
6. Salesman. (Each salesman's territory is to be numbered.)
7. Number of Refrigerator Dealers Franchised. (Your Radio Dealer Prospects.) On your chart we have typed the names of those dealers for whom we have received refrigerator franchises.
8. Other Radio Dealer Prospects.
9. Radio Dealers Franchised.

It is evident, therefore, that the foregoing analysis affords:

1. An instant analysis of your complete territory as to the cities and towns where you should secure radio dealers.
2. Your Radio Sales Quotas by units for each county.
3. By cities, the number of radio dealers franchised last year.
4. The names listed by cities of all the refrigerator dealers franchised this season—an extremely important factor, *as every one of your present refrigerator dealers is a potential Stewart-Warner Radio Dealer Prospect this coming year.*

The charts are sufficiently large to provide a distributor with a complete master record upon which he can make notations as salesmen report on each call. The charts are bound in a large hard-cover binder, so that they will not be folded up and misplaced. They are always ready for use. Distributors are also furnished with blank 8½-by 11-inch forms which they are instructed to fill out and hand to each salesman. From these salesman's sheets the master "Exposure" chart is posted. These individual salesman's sheets list the towns which the salesman covers; give the population of each town and the radio sales quota for each town; list the names of the present refrigeration dealers and the names of the prospective radio dealers: and carry a space where the salesman notes the disposition to be made of each name—that is, whether the prospect was sold, not sold, deferred, etc. The sheet also shows the name and number of salesman's territory, as posted on the "Exposure" chart at the office, and his quota or task for the current year.

It has been found by the manufacturer using this particular device that the chart, together with the salesman's quota forms, affords a distributor definite sales control of each territory; and for the same reason, provides the manufacturer with the control he needs to establish a reasonable factory quota.

How Much Should the Customer Pay?

We find there are three schools of thought on this question. One group, the most numerous, believes that the dealer should pay half the cost of a sales promotional campaign. Another group, not so numerous, believes the manufacturer should pay all and add it to the selling price. The third group, the minority, believes the dealer should pay all. There are even some in this group who expect to make enough on advertising helps sold to dealers and customers to cover the entire production cost of the units.

The trend varies a great deal from decade to decade. At one time, manufacturers are willing to pay a substantial share of the promotional costs and to exercise a large degree of control over the use of it. At other times, dealers are expected to stand for at least half of the costs of promotion efforts. However, some of the most successful operations have been those in which it has been consistently held that store promotion is a primary responsibility of the manufacturer, the cost of which comes out of increased sales volume, and consequently greater profits. Dealer turnover is also reduced, these manufacturers claim, through such services.

When the Dealer Pays All

It seems to be only the exceptional companies which make the dealer pay all, although a large number of companies have tried to do so. The local dealer and even the local distributor are seldom good promotion people. Except in rare cases, they do not know what's good for their own interests. For that reason, it would seem that many of the companies now trying to push this work onto distributors are making a mistake if they want to get maximum results from the big expenditures that they are making in national advertising.

An increasing number of companies have set up subsidiaries for the express purpose of helping distributors or dealers to promote the sale of their products, in the nature of a cooperative venture. The cost of operating the division or the company is prorated among the participating customers. There is much to be said in favor of this plan, especially if a company is operating in a price market, where increased service would have to be reflected in higher prices to the customer.

CONTROLLING EXPENSE AGAINST BUDGET

A budget is only as good as the way it is used. This is especially true of sales promotional budgets because of the pressure from with-

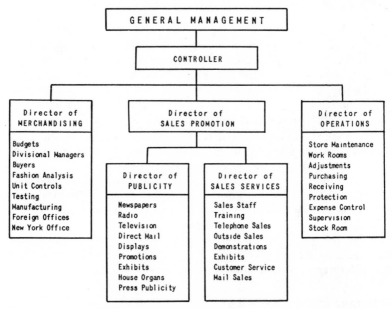

When the control of sales promotional expenses is essential to a marketing operation, some check of expenditures against the budget is necessary. A growing number of companies clear all sales expense through a controller who functions as an assistant to the sales officer. This is a chart of a retail store operation.

in the organization and outside of it to undertake some "special" promotional project which is "bound to produce a sales increase." There is only one way to operate a budget and that is to stick to it. But, by the same token, before the budget is drawn and approved, great care should be taken to make sure the activities it covers are important to the long-range marketing program of the company, and that the first things have been put first. Too often it has been discovered too late that some activities were put in the budget out of habit, or because some highly placed executive thought they ought to be done. Another bad habit in budgeting is to draw it up on the basis of what was spent last year. If budgeting has a weakness, it is the pressure exerted on those whose spending it controls, to come out at the end of the year with the appropriation 100% spent. They, perhaps with good reason, seem to fear unless they spend all the money that was allotted to them, they will be penalized next year.

Budget controls are therefore not only necessary, but they should be set up so that there will not be too much of a gap between the time the money is spent and when it is charged to a running total on the budget. This is especially important in multiple sales division operations. In that connection, a management engineer called in to evaluate one company's method of controlling budget expenditures made the following report:

> Studies of your advertising expense disclosed such a variation in costs for the same groups of products under similar conditions, that these recommendations are made:
>
> 1. A flexible standard unit cost is proposed for each product group by sales divisions. A spread in the allowable cost permits the less developed areas to spend more in proportion, realizing that a somewhat different advertising job is required.
>
> 2. The advertising budget should be balanced by product groups within sales areas as well as by total.
>
> 3. The expense for advertising, set up in the price of each product, should be no greater than the expense needed properly to advertise that product.
>
> 4. Advertising expense by product groups should be distributed to the sales areas in proportion to probable advertising income on the tonnage expected.
>
> Each product group seemed to have its own distinct pattern. Naturally the pattern for some products was much larger than for others. Limited demands or markets naturally limit the amount which one can afford to spend in advertising. Plans should be made to test advertising at the point of sale. In the meantime the flexible cost standards by product groups provide a valuable profit control.

Monthly Checkups

One corporation makes it a practice to have its financial analysts interview department heads about the middle of each month to determine whether budgets will be exceeded for the current period. While "budget vs. expense" remains the controlling factor, forecasting results before the end of the month serves three purposes: It emphasizes the overexpenditure to the sales promotion manager; it alerts the financial department so that it may defer optional expenses for that month; and provides, in advance, explanations for top management when monthly budgets are exceeded.

Expense Control Records

To operate the budget it is customary to have a hard-hitting control system. Depending upon how the budget is set up, records are maintained which will give the *essential* control information and no more. There is a tremendous loss of profits by businesses which go on year after year compiling sales information which is never used, or else not used frequently enough to warrant the expense of preparing it. When the expenses are "spread" against distributors or dealers, one of the simplest systems is to keep a "control" folder for each account. The folder, in addition to providing information of value in servicing the account, shows what the company can afford to spend in a calendar year to promote that dealer's sales. This service (in code) is shown on the front of the folder, and as expenses, direct or indirect, are incurred, the charges are posted and the remainder available is shown. This type of record is especially valuable where the sales agent type of distributor is used, or in the case of branch offices where the branch manager shares in the net profit of his branch operation. Red clip-on signals are used when an agent or distributor has spent his advertising allotment.

Job Control Envelopes

Another leaky faucet in sales promotional operations is the excessive cost of corrections on printed jobs, spending too much for unimportant display pieces, etc. It is advisable to run a control on every job of this kind. Most companies use cards. But there is much to be said in favor of using $8\frac{1}{2}$- by 11-inch Manila envelopes for this purpose, filed in a regular desk side cabinet by number, with card index cross-reference. On the face of the envelope full information appears concerning the quantities printed, the way the materials were used, the cost, source of supply, and a summary of the returns.

The advantage of the large envelope is that it enables a sales promotion man to place in it samples of the letters, enclosures, etc., as well as carbon copies of letters of instruction and other information concerning that particular piece of promotion.

Record sheets, showing the day-by-day returns on the mailing, if such records are required, may be kept in the sales promotion manager's desk until the returns from the mailings are completed. After that they may be transferred to the large envelope.

Customer Records on McBee Cards

Where promotional campaigns must be broken down so that a different effort is used for a different group of prospects or customers, there are advantages in keeping these records on McBee cards. This is a regular card index record on which any desired information may be written, but notches are punched around the edge of the card according to the way it is to be selected. To select one or more classifications for addressing or following up, the selecting device is set for those classifications and the cards automatically picked out. These advantages can also be obtained by the use of the Findex system, which is somewhat similar in principle, except that the cards are larger and not quite so convenient.

Customer Records on Addressing Stencils

Where the need for recording information on cards is limited, control may be obtained by the use of signaling and tabbing devices on either Addressograph plates or Elliott stencils. The same plates or stencils, of course, are used for the addressing.

The majority of companies checked used the Addressograph system, with the new type of address plate which has a pivot tab that can be quickly put in position for selecting any required names. These tabs pivot, and as a sales promotion manager goes through the list, he can push over the tabs with his pencil on all plates to be addressed. This device is very valuable in promotional work.

The compactness of the Elliott system makes it popular with many sales promotional departments. This system uses a fiber stencil which can be cut on any typewriter. Selections can be made in a number of groups at one setting of the selector. For example, you can select names for ratings, line of business, and position of individual at one time. Large record cards may be used with this system which also carry the addressing stencil.

Visible Control Through Card Records

While there are a few concerns which still depend upon the old map-and-tack systems and washable maps for controlling sales promotional effort, the most common practice is the use of visible

Typical Operating Budgets for Retail Businesses

SOURCES OF INFORMATION: Harvard University Bureau of Business Research; Florists' Telegraph Delivery Association; Retail Druggists Association of Greater St. Louis; National Retail Hardware Association; United States Department of Commerce; Druggists' Research Bureau; *Food Merchandising;* and *The Progressive Grocer.*

Items of Expense	Auto Tires and Accessories	Drug Stores						Electrical	Florist	Grocery Stores (Independent)			
		Eastern	Central	North Central	Western	Southern	Middlewest Group			Service	Cash	Complete Food Market	General Store
Total Salaries	15.2	19.5	17.8	15.8	17.6	16.4	18.9	12.71	18.0	7.2	6.8	9.8	8.3
Direct and General Selling ¶	....	10.0	10.1	7.1	11.1	....	11.2	8.48	....	....	....	7.9	....
Buying, Management, etc. ¶	....	9.5	7.7	8.7	6.5	....	7.7	4.23	....	....	....	1.9	....
Rent	2.5	4.0	3.8	3.4	3.8	3.1	5.1	1.51	4.0	1.33	1.0	1.0	1.2
Advertising	1.1	0.6	0.8	1.0	1.1	0.3	1.1	1.01	5.0	0.50	0.8	0.7	0.4
Wrappings and Supplies	0.4	....	....	....	....	....	....	0.41	....	0.34	0.6	0.6	0.3
Delivery	0.9	0.1	....	....	....	....	....	0.88	3.0	1.64	....	1.8	0.5
Heat, Light, Power, Water	0.9	1.1	1.0	1.2	1.0	0.8	1.5	0.34	....	0.41	0.3	0.6	0.6
Insurance	0.5	0.2	0.5	0.5	0.4	1.4	0.6	0.62	1.0	0.41	0.3	0.5	1.0
Taxes	0.3	0.2	0.4	0.7	0.9	†	0.4	0.43	....	†	†	†	†
Telephone and Telegraph	0.3	....	....	....	....	....	....	0.43	....	0.08	....	0.2	0.1
Repairs	0.4	0.2	0.2	....	0.3	....	0.1	0.68	....	0.48	0.5	0.8	0.6
Depreciation (Total)	1.0	1.4	1.2	0.6	0.7	0.4	1.4	0.65	....	‡	‡	‡	‡
Interest	1.3	....	....	....	0.4	....	....	0.56	....	0.16	....	0.1	0.3
Donations	....	....	....	....	....	....	....	....	....	0.12	....	0.1	0.1
Losses from Bad Debts	0.8	....	....	....	0.3	0.4	....	0.72	1.0	0.62	....	0.5	0.6
Unclassified	1.2	0.5	1.4	2.3	2.6	5.4	2.0	2.10	6.0	0.51	0.4	0.5	0.6
TOTAL EXPENSE	26.8	27.8	27.1	25.5	29.1	28.2	31.1	23.05	38.0	13.8	10.7	17.2	14.6
MARGIN	28.8	36.0	32.0	32.9	35.2	35.1	32.3	....	45.6	17.8	14.7	20.6	17.8
NET PROFIT	2.0	8.2	4.9	7.4	6.1	6.9	1.2	....	7.6	4.0	4.0	3.4	3.2
Stock-turn (times a year)	5.7	2.6	3.6	2.2	2.8	3.3	3.1	....	....	11.5	13.0	18.5	4.5

¶—The sum of these equals total salaries.　　†—Taxes included with insurance.
‡—Depreciation included with repairs.

card records, with signal tabs along the lower edge of the card.

One company which depends upon the cooperation of its salesmen in getting distribution for promotional literature and store material, uses envelopes instead of cards for this record. The envelopes are arranged in steps just as the cards would be, but they are open at the right end so that the reports from the salesmen, sales slips, and other documents can be slipped into the envelope to provide a complete working control.

Budget vs. Expense Analysis

Each month, the Sales Promotion Manager of each division of RCA received a report from the accounting department showing the budget figure for individual promotional classifications and the expenditures charged against them. The report was in five columns against each subject: (month) budget and actual; (year-to-date) budget and actual; over or under budget. Thus the executive could see at a glance the necessity for any adjustments that had to be made to stay within budget limits.

This also gave the department heads the opportunity to detect unauthorized charges against their budgets, such as sales department costs, "good will" expenses and other items not properly allocatable to the budget.

Chapter 5

SALES PROMOTIONAL CAMPAIGNS

THE many aspects of sales promotion are treated individually in the various chapters of this HANDBOOK; here we take a look at promotional campaigns as a whole, together with some underlying marketing philosophies. The word campaign denotes completeness. One definition is: "a series of planned, related, activities for a special purpose." For our consideration here, these purposes include: maintenance of market position, overcoming sales problems, expanding sales volume, meeting inroads of competition, introduction of new products. Campaigns begin or should begin, with market studies, consumer field tests, retail surveys; and end with the figures on the sales reports to management. Although all campaigns have the purpose of increasing sales; many are aimed at specific objectives.

To introduce its new fiber glass roofing shingle to the trade, Johns-Manville developed a complete campaign package to mail to its dealers. The outside of the carton was imprinted: "Inside: 1. The first ad in a campaign designed to generate a lot of interest in a brand new kind of fiber glass roofing shingle. 2. The second ad. 3. The third ad. 4. A brochure showing how roofs have changed over the years and how a certain new shingle design is perfect for the contemporary home. 5. A counter card that ties in with the advertising to help you make the sale. 6. A supply of consumer brochures. 7. A card you can send in to get more information, more counter cards and more brochures."

In the package, each ad had a tag affixed which read, respectively:

1. This ad (in the April, May and June issues of Southern Living and Sunset) will generate a lot of interest in Rampart, Johns-Manville's new Class A fiber glass shingle.

2. We're running this ad in the trade magazines so that you will know about the Rampart ad all your customers are reading.

3. You'll learn even more about Rampart fiber glass shingles from this ad in trade publications.

The tag on the brochure read: This brochure shows you how

Rampart's design is perfect for the contemporary home. The sample counter card, which included a holder for the consumer brochures, had a tag reading: Put this counter card right to work. It ties in with the consumer advertising for Rampart fiber glass shingles to help you make the sale.

Toastmaster's Campaign

The Toastmaster Division of McGraw-Edison Company organized a successful promotional campaign which prompted advertising manager D. W. Moran to report that "We were pleased enough with the results that we are continuing the same program, with some refinements, for the first half of this year and probably the second half." He described the origin of the plan and its implementation as follows:

"Toastmaster settled on 'Good Things That Last' as a company philosophy phrase or signature statement to be used everywhere possible.

"At the same time, we wanted to come up with something dramatic to set Toastmaster toasters apart from others, because of their excellence in making toast and also heating perfectly the dozens of toaster convenience-foods on the market—hence, the repositioning of the name from 'toaster' to 'food toaster' and the 'split-toaster' and '4 different foods in the slots' visual approach to sell the '2 elements per slot' and inside quality story.

"In another of our large-volume product categories, broiler-ovens, we wanted to set ours apart from competition and also to achieve consumer recognition of a wider range of uses for this product. 'Tabletop' was the result.

"During this same period we capitalized on the fast-building toaster convenience-foods business, by publishing a 20-page booklet specifically on these foods. These booklets were offered 'no charge' to consumers in our national ads. We also made quantities available to retailers along with little toaster-topped displays selling the 'Toastmaster Toaster-Toaster foods' quality story.

"These ideas were carried out from national advertising to point of sale."

The various campaign elements included:

Full-page advertisements in seven women's magazines, featuring the term "Food Toaster";

Sixty-second live TV spot announcements broadcast during the holiday season;

Four-page ads in leading trade publications;

GOOD THINGS THAT LAST.

In this repair-it, replace-it, throw-it-away world, people are questioning why. Why can't things work better? Last longer? There's a word for this challenging stance. Consumerism.

At Toastmaster, we have a word, too. Quality. If the public remembers when things lasted, so do we. Because we still build Toastmaster products that way.

But we aren't resting on our quality. Quality does no one any good when it sits on your shelves. So we mean to speed up your turnover.

With three new tapered toaster models.

A new way of positioning Toastmaster toasters: as <u>food</u> toasters, working day and night.

A new way of dramatizing all the uses of broiler-ovens.

Aggressive new ad, point-of-sale, and packaging efforts. Plus a new promise that characterizes Toastmaster products...

"Good things that last."

Maybe all this doesn't sound like the Toastmaster you know. But it's a new ballgame now.

So read on. You'll find we've included plenty of lasting good things for you.

TOASTMASTER®
Division of McGraw-Edison Co., Elgin, Ill. 60120

As part of an over-all campaign with the theme "Good Things that Last," the Toastmaster Division of McGraw-Edison Company ran a four-page ad in leading trade papers and sent reprints, in folder form, to its distributors and retailers. The second page described product features; the third page presented the various elements of the campaign, which included store displays, transparent stickers, a Food Guide booklet, ads in women's magazines and TV spot announcements. The back cover featured another trade ad.

Reprints of the trade ads were mailed to the company's distributors and retailers;

Transparent stickers for use with Food Toasters at the point-of-sale;

Larger-size four-color stickers were developed for application to the sides of shipping cartons and for display in retail appliance departments on walls, counters and shelves.

Tent-shaped toaster-topped displays selling the quality story and featuring an illustration of the free Foods Guide booklet.

A Comprehensive Campaign

Helbros Watches announced its complete Earth Time and Moontime promotional drive in a twelve-page 2-color brochure, 11 by 14

Date_____

We're interested, Helbros!

☐ Please send me all promotional material on your **ELECTRIC DAY-DATE** watch.

☐ Let's hear from your salesman.

☐ Keep me on your mailing list.

☐ Send complete assortment of in-store Dealer-aids.

☐ Send me your Catalog with latest Confidential Price List.

☐ We can use your complete assortment of newspaper ad-mats.

☐ I am interested in Helbros watches as Business incentives.

My Name_____Title_____

Company Name_____

Address_____

City_____State_____Zip_____

Signature_____

On the inside back cover of the brochure announcing its Earth and Moon campaign, Helbros Watches printed 4 of these all-purpose reply cards for dealers' use.

inches in size. The cover carried the message "Helbros literally gives you the Moon. And brings you the biggest, brightest, stars. The ideas you'll find here are absolutely down-to-earth when it comes to influencing the Earthmen (and Women) to buy. Use them all . . . use them well . . . and get ready for astronomical sales."

Inside, the company presented the various phases of the campaign with announcements of a radio broadcasting schedule over 400 radio stations covering 553 cities; four-color, two-page ads in leading magazines; a special radio program featuring its "Up to the Minute" show; local tie-in dealer ads; 1-minute commercials for dealer use; and counter and window display cards. A sound recording of the retail spot announcements was bound into the book. The inside back cover carried 4 business reply cards for dealers' to use in ordering promotional material.

Avid Corporation, which manufactures electronic and visual-aid equipment conducted a successful promotion directed at schools which it called "Search for Creativity." The campaign started with a two-page ad in educational publications, with the heading: "Join in Avid's nationwide search for creativity. Share in Avid's $60,000 worth of awards." In the body of the ad, the company announced that "Avid will award hundreds of educational products to schools showing the most practical or innovative use of Avid products (or similar products from other manufacturers). The products included were filmstrip projectors, cassette tape recorders, cassette tape players, listening centers and headsets.

Next, the company sent an announcement of the program, together with a reprint of the advertisement, to 80,000 schools. The announcement included a coupon with which educators could readily request entry forms and details of the Awards.

The entry form, which was also the official reporting form and a copy of the rules and regulations, were then sent out with a letter signed by Albert C. Allen, Chairman.

Joint Responsibility Campaigns

There is a growing tendency to look upon distribution as a joint responsibility of the manufacturer and the wholesale distributor. Moreover, there is a corresponding tendency on the part of the wholesaler to go along with that thinking. As a result most promotions are now set up so that the wholesaler feels he is definitely in the picture, and consequently receptive to standing a share of the cost. There is, however, a considerable difference of opinion among wholesalers as to what the manufacturer can do to help them in a

AVID CORPORATION
IS GIVING AWAY
$60,000 OF AWARDS TO SCHOOLS

Programming Tape Recorders	Headsets	Programmed Learning Lessons
Cassette Tape Players	Avidesks	Space/Science Travelab
Filmstrip Projectors	Filmstrip Viewers	Audio-Visual Mini Travelab
Cassette Recorders	Filmstrip and Slide Storage Cabinets	Av Centers
Wireless Listening Labs		Listening Centers

Dear Educator:

If your school system is creatively applying AVID Audio-Visual products (or other manufacturers' products similar to AVID'S) you can qualify for the above awards.

If your school system is planning to use creative ways to make better use of AVID products (or other manufacturers' products similar to AVID'S) you can qualify for the above awards.

AVID Corporation is instituting a national search for practical and innovative methods of using AVID'S audio-visual equipment. If your school system is creatively using A/V tools to educate, AVID wants to hear about it!

Awards will be given from selections made by independent organizations and educators. To receive additional information and entry forms, return the coupon below to:

AVID CORPORATION, P.O. Box 4263, East Providence, R.I. 02914

Yes, I would like to enter my school in Avid's $60,000 search for practical and innovative methods of using audio-visual equipment manufactured by your organization. Please send me your entry kit.

Name..

Title...

School...

City...State..................Zip............................

Our A/V Dealer...

Avid Corporation's announcement of its "Search for Creativity" campaign prominently featured a listing of its products and included a coupon for educators interested in submitting entries in the contest.

119

sales promotional way. One group of distributors, the National Supply and Machinery Distributors Association, sent a questionnaire to its members on this point. The summary of returns, as presented to a convention of the association, follows:

a. CATALOGS AND BULLETINS

Summary of principal comments with frequency:

Eliminate multicolored high-pressure advertising and issue good literature that tells the story simply, plainly, and shows prices—15.

Manufacturers cooperating with more catalogs, bulletins, imprinted material—11.

Of good help, be sure they are clear—8.

Condensed information—7.

Envelope stuffers, etc., light but effective—3.

Keep up to date—2.

Other composite excerpts from comments in order of frequency:

Distributor's name imprinted on front cover.

Clear catalog pictures of the items, distinct specifications, list of typical installations.

Sales features of article should be incorporated in any printed matter, price books, bulletins to be mailed or larger bulletins to be left with the interested customers.

More, especially by the valve manufacturers.

Greater difficulty getting complete catalogs from suppliers.

Ample application illustrations.

$8\frac{1}{2}$- by $10\frac{5}{8}$-inch catalog sheets covering line in brief.

b. PRODUCT DISPLAY MATERIAL

Summary of principal comments with frequency:

Occasional floor or counter—8.

Good store and window—4.

Not important—5.

Manufacturers cooperating—3.

Appealing and limited in size—2.

Other composite excerpts from comments in order of frequency:

New items only.

Cutaway samples, salesmen's samples.

Something new every 3 months.

c. DIRECT MAIL

Summary of principal comments with frequency:

Of good help—12.

Should tie-up with distributor—10.

Should be colorful and carry name of distributor on front—6.

Distributor would rather handle—4.

Do not use direct mail—3.

Mention distributor in manufacturers' direct mail—3.

Important if sent to proper persons—2.

Other composite excerpts from comments in order of frequency:

Manufacturer cooperating and furnishing upon request.

Small doses only, if at all.

Not too often, and only to a selected list.

We issue bulletins with lists attached each week.

O.K. if name is used as the consumer source of supply.

Distributors' own mailing lists, own letterheads, return cards addressed to them.

The manufacturer should be furnished with accurate mailing lists.

Only when you have a message of special importance.

More of it.

d. PUBLICATION ADVERTISING

Summary of principal comments with frequency:

Of good help—11.

Direct to industrial distributor—7.

Stressing the distributor—7.

Proper trade publications—6.

Nationally—4.

Other composite excerpts from comments in order of frequency:

Eliminate some magazine advertising, a lot of inferior literature, and put some money into good men who can go to a customer with good sound story of product.

Don't flood distributors with too many advertising reprints.

Show list of distributors when advertising in trade journals.

Not advertising experts.

In right channels.

Adequate.

Take advantage of trade-mark and trade name listings available in classified sections of telephone directories.

With a slogan "Buy it through your distributor."

e. SHIPPING PRACTICES

Summary of principal comments with frequency:

Shipping promises; advise of any delays—11.

Satisfactory—7.

Use packing lists showing contents and number—5.

Prompt mailing of invoices and shipping documents—3.

Size of article packed so they can be reshipped in original containers—3.

Material properly packed and follow distributor's routing—2.

Other composite excerpts from comments in order of frequency:

Ship products properly and so packed that our clerks can handle the goods, identify the merchandise, and put it away without calling a board of director's meeting.

Not too much weight in one package.

Group shipments to eliminate duplicating freight charges.

Simplify packages and papers as much as possible.

Allowance of freight charge—100 lbs. and over.

f. PRICE LISTS

Summary of principal comments with frequency:

As simple as possible, yet with adequate information so you will not refer to 10 pages and 2 indexes to arrive at prices—9.

Make understandable—7.

Standardize and cut out 50% of sizes—5.

Should be separate from descriptive sheets used in distributors', salesmen's catalogs—4.

Price lists with discounts preferred to net setup—2.

Other composite excerpts from comments in order of frequency:

Net resale price schedules.

Prices to user, distributor discounts left off.

Only as requested.

Better arrangements by valve manufacturers.

Difficult to get price lists from some suppliers.

Always 8½- by 11-inch size (or 8½ by 10⅝ inches).

Prefer showing only consumer prices. Dealers' and jobbers' discount from lists to be on separate list.

Customers' price list should be furnished with distributors' price list.

When sending price changes, kindly specify changes to assist rechecking for changes.

Manufacturer to index lists numerically by catalog numbers.

In addition to price of complete unit, show prices on replacement parts.

Programmed Merchandising

When a Sealy Mattress Company salesman calls on a retailer, he doesn't just sell him mattresses. He sells him "programmed merchandising."

Freely translated, this means that, along with a mattress order, the salesman is likely to sell:

A newspaper advertising campaign
A direct-mail program
A window display

This programmed merchandising changed Sealy from a "manufacturing-oriented" to a "marketing-oriented" company. The change in sales promotion emphasis, together with a new advertising approach, produced results. In four years, Sealy sales volume soared nearly 34% vs. an industry gain of less than 10%.

Sealy's programmed merchandising operates on a continuous basis, providing the factory branch salesman with a complete new advertising and sales promotion package once every three months. These sales kits are so complete, yet so flexible in application, that a salesman calling on a retailer can provide him with an integrated, custom-made promotion campaign to boost his mattress sales.

How the Jewelry Industry Expanded Its Market

After the war the jewelry industry, along with other luxury lines, took a beating. To meet the situation, the industry subscribed to a sales promotional fund. The purpose was to make better merchants out of thousands of retail jewelers throughout the country, who during the sellers' market had gone soft and flabby. They clung to the idea that all they had to do was to stock a product and the people would queue up to buy it. A cross-sectional study was made of consumers' jewelry buying habits and a campagin developed to achieve six specific purposes:

1. Increase store traffic.
2. Get retail jewelers to push gifts.
3. Induce jewelers to put in better window displays.
4. Sell more inside the store by creative sales techniques.
5. Improve selection and display of merchandise.
6. Train store personnel to be pleasant.

RETAIL DISPLAYS ARE AN IMPORTANT ELEMENT IN EVERY CAMPAIGN

Prize winners in the Point-of-Purchase Advertising Institute's Twelfth Annual Merchandising Awards Contest.

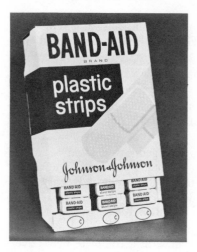

A. Counter display by Johnson & Johnson; B. Counter unit by Shulton, Inc.; C. Promotional floor stand by Hoffman-La Roche; D. Display unit by Shulton, Inc.

The study showed that only 20% of the American public buy their gifts from retail jewelers. The public does not think of the retail jewelry store as a place in which to "look around" for gifts—of those who like to look around only 5% do so in jewelry stores. People prefer to do their looking around in a gift shop, or a department store, where the store personnel are usually more patient and pleasant with folks who come to look before they buy. While it cannot be said that the campaign solved all the many problems of this industry, it did help to make retail jewelers appreciate that most of their difficulties were self-made and that the lack of business was in large measure due to their own lack of sales initiative.

An interesting angle of study upon which the Jewelry Industry Council based its program was the analysis of dealer-helps most popular with retail jewelers. Three-quarters of the 2,000 jewelers checked stated that they were dissatisfied with the assistance furnished to them by manufacturers for seasonal promotions, other than Christmas. On the kinds of dealer-helps most widely used the survey showed:

94% use manufacturers' window display materials.

80% use manufacturers' mats.

77% use manufacturers' counter displays.

72% use manufacturers' stuffers for envelopes.

49% get help from their local newspaper advertising departments.

38% use reprints of manufacturers' advertising.

24% use outside help in preparing window displays.

27% use outside help in preparing direct mail.

Dealer Helps Objectives

If it is not practical to conduct a trade study to establish objectives for a promotional program designed to "trade up" customers—and especially dealers—the following suggestions, prepared as a service to merchants by National Cash Register Company, may prove helpful. It enumerates 10 ways a merchant can increase his sales, and which should be considered in any sales promotional program designed to help retailers:

Train Salespeople: Encourage training to stimulate enthusiasm and increased earnings.

Sell "Associate Items": Many additional sales can be made by suggesting associated goods, articles that naturally go together.

Pay a Bonus: Nothing induces an assistant to work harder, sell more and make more money for himself and the store than a bonus.

Give Customers Service: Show them how to care for purchases.

Talk Quality: Encourage salespeople to sell high-grade merchandise to customers. It should always be pointed out that high-grade goods last longer.

Place Goods Near the Wrapping Counter: Place self-selling lines near the wrapping counter and a surprising number of sales will result.

Sell Bigger Packages: When a customer asks for an article which comes in different sizes, the larger size can usually be sold.

Teach Salespeople the Merits of Goods: This builds enthusiasm.

Push Seasonable Items: Certain items sell only at certain seasons. Displays, advertising, and sales talk can push them along.

Use Modern Showcases: People will buy many goods displayed which they had not thought of buying when they entered the store.

Retail Campaigns

Another use for intensive sales promotional campaigns is to level off seasonal fluctuations. This is especially important in a retail store operation. At a meeting of the National Retail Merchants

The Campbell Soup Company provides merchandising assistance and helps dealers to increase sales in every possible way. These brochures announce in-store promotions and acquaint dealers with the availability of merchandising aids.

Association (Sales Promotional Division), store promotions to even off sales peaks and valleys were rated high on the lists of "musts" for a well-managed retail store. "Too much emphasis is now placed," said one speaker, "on store-wide sales events at the expense of getting business every day of the year where it is most needed to secure a balanced operation." He singled out anniversary sales, spring sales, harvest sales, and "founder's whisker sales" as promotions which depend upon price cutting to get results. Such promotions, while they may move out merchandise, do not have the long-range benefits of a well-planned promotional program. The most successful campaigns are those which boost the average sale, eliminate waste in the fall and winter selling season, and build lasting good will for the store. Promotions with the greatest appeal to merchants play up store service and the merchant's prestige in a big way. Storekeepers turn thumbs down on campaigns that overplay the product. They like to see themselves in the picture.

Soup 'N Crackers

Among the most modern organizations in the food field, at every level from the plant to the retail store, is the Campbell Soup Company, Camden, New Jersey. It engages in year-round promotions as well as periodic campaigns. The company provides the retail stores with a wide variety of sales aids, banners, posters and other display material, promotional pieces of every description and merchandising information designed to increase store sales.

One of the biggest campaigns in Campbell Soup history was the company's annual Soup 'N Cracker Sale in January and February, when soup sales are at their peak.

It supplied the food stores with a complete collection of point-of-sale display material promoting cracker sales as well as soup.

To publicize the sale to consumers, Campbell ran 40 four-color ads in magazines and broadcast over 100 radio commercials a week during an eight-week period. One hundred TV spots were also broadcast.

PLANNING THE CAMPAIGN

The first step, naturally, in planning any sales activity is to determine exactly what the campaign is supposed to do. Usually the idea of conducting a sales drive, as contrasted to a week-in-and-week-out sales promotional program, arises out of a situation about which "something has to be done." Sales slump badly in certain territories while they hold up well in others. Perhaps an intensive campaign backed by advertising in those areas might be the answer. Or a department of a big store seems unable to get out of the rough and show a satisfactory profit. Perhaps an intensive campaign to build up the sales of the department should be undertaken. But whatever the need, it should be kept in mind that whatever merit a campaign for sales may have, it is after all only a campaign. It may achieve an immediate objective, but unless it is integrated with an over-all promotional program, its benefits are not likely to be lasting.

The purposes for which intensive sales campaigns best lend themselves are many; among them are:

1. Broadening the base of distribution.
2. Meeting a particular competitive situation.
3. Activating a dealer organization.
4. Overcoming seasonal slumps.
5. Introducing a new product or model.
6. Opening up new acocunts.
7. Increasing size of orders.
8. Getting salesmen to sell the full line.
9. Enlisting support for national advertising.
10. Getting dealers to make better use of advertising helps.
11. Pushing sales of "neglected" products.
12. Educating dealers and store personnel.
13. Reclaiming "lost" accounts.

Whom Is It Supposed to Influence?

The second step, after determining what the campaign is supposed to do, is to consider the type of people to whom it will be directed,

This is the complete window display kit which formed part of Admiral's color TV campaign featuring a "lucky number" to attract prospects to the dealers' stores. The company reported that "the response was fantastic."

and how best to influence them. What appeal will be most effective? The campaign might involve the participation of only a manufacturer's own sales force, or it might require "selling" a broad group of people in varying classifications, such as: (1) Housewives; (2) farmers; (3) business executives; (4) distributors; (5) wholesalers; (6) wholesalers' salesmen; (7) dealers; (8) dealers' salespeople; (9) route men; (10) county agents; (11) car owners, etc. Each type requires specialized treatment.

Color TV Promotion

One excellent campaign, which was aimed at consumers but required distributor and dealer support, was conducted by Admiral Corporation to promote sales of color TV and refrigerators.

As reported by Mr. John E. Meegan, the company's sales promotion manager, "It is one of the finest sales promotion efforts ever in the appliance industry."

The company developed a deluxe, 24-page, four-color consumer mailer, and announced to its distributors that they could be sold or given away to the dealers. The cost to the distributor was $85 per thousand, 50% of which would be charged back to a special cooperative fund, making the net cost to the dealer a little more than 4 cents per copy.

Later, at the company's distributor convention, two great new stimulants were added to the campaign. These were a cream-and-sugar set, which achieved the highest premium sales to distributors for one item in one year, and a "Lucky Number" insert in the mailer in which 3,000 Admiral products were offered as prizes. When people visited a dealer for their premium, they checked their numbers against a list which had been included in a complete window-display kit.

"The response was fantastic," said Mr. Meegan. "We have already given away eight color TV sets, seven Duplex refrigerators, 21 stereo consoles and 57 FM/AM clock radios.

"The timing of the mailer and the followup of the window premium and Lucky Number programs gave us a terrific competitive advantage."

Presentation Material for Salesmen

No matter how extensively consumer and trade advertising is used to "put across" the campaign, full value from the approppration cannot be obtained unless the salesmen are brought into the picture in such a way that they will feel it is their "baby" too. Some companies call in a few top-flight salesmen and have them sit in on the planning. Not only are their ideas worth while, but it helps to overcome the prejudice salesmen in the field feel for any promotional activity "dreamed up in the office." The agenda for such a meeting should include the presentation pieces to be provided for the salesmen to take out and show to customers.

There is, for example, the matter of a working guide, or brief, outlining the campaign so that each salesman will understand what it is all about and what he is supposed to do. Then there is the piece the salesman uses to explain the purpose of the promotion, and its benefits to the customer. Should it be an easel-type portfolio, a pull-out timetable folder, a loose-leaf book, or what? Will the salesmen use it? How will they use it? What do they want in it?

Then there will be a need for some pass-out literature which the salesman can leave with a customer after he has explained the promotion to him. What should it cover? Should it be a step-by-step account of what the customer should do, with a blank for ordering the materials needed to put the plan into effect, or will the salesmen be supplied with order books which they can flash on the customer? What about cost? Shall a token charge be made for cooperative materials furnished, or shall they be given to customers who agree to use them without charge?

The Kick-Off Meeting

When the material necessary to put over the campaign is ready, all those who are to have a part in "selling" the promotion are usually brought together at the factory, or at convenient regional hotels, to learn about the campaign and get up the enthusiasm needed to put it over. Where shall these meetings be held? What kind of a program should be developed? Shall there be talks or discussions? What about visuals? Entertainment?

How should the meeting to kick-off the campaign be buttoned up and packaged? A common fault with most of these meetings is that they are long on pep but short on the solid stuff a man needs to properly "sell" it to his customers. Perhaps it might be well to furnish ringbinders and then as the meeting proceeds hand each man material to put into the binder so that he can carry it back home.

The Follow-Through After the Promotion Begins

No matter how carefully a promotional campaign is planned, how thoroughly the salesmen and the distributors are coached, or how well the printed material is prepared, the job is only half done unless there is a hard-hitting follow-through. Without a follow-through the salesmen are likely to go back to their territories or stores, as the case may be, and get lost in the doing of their daily chores. It is easy to forget, and there is so much to remember. How can those upon whom the success of the campaign depends be made to remember and motivated to action?

There should, depending upon the appropriation, be periodical mailings to each group of participants. If it is an interstore competitive campaign, for example, there should be a series of mailings to dealers with a bulletin which they can tack up on the store bulletin board for the salespeople to read. If the salesmen are in the picture, they should get a firm but gentle prodding at regular intervals to make sure they do their part. Perhaps a sales contest of some sort might be used to introduce a competitive angle. Perhaps those salesmen who do certain things required of them will get credits good for merchandise prizes of their own selection. But whatever procedure is followed, it is most important that interest in the campaign be maintained. There should not be any slow-down, any dead-center. A well-rounded plan provides not only for participant education but assures participant action—two very different things.

BLUEPRINTING THE CAMPAIGN

In order to properly schedule production, and to make sure every operation in the execution of the campaign is completed on time, some sort of a working chart or timetable is desirable.

First of all the advertising must be scheduled far enough in advance of the opening campaign to permit the advertising agency to contract for the space, prepare the copy, and get out plates to the publications. Since some magazines close several weeks before they are in circulation, about 4 months should be allowed. As a rule, the usual way of visualizing the coverage of consumer advertising is to have the advertising agency proof up the various ads that are to appear, and then imprint at the bottom of each proof the publications in which that particular piece of copy is to run, with circulation figures.

"Try Before You Buy"

Emphasis at the point of sale was the focus of a well-organized campaign by the Ronson Corporation, as described by Robert H. Jorgensen, sales promotion supervisor for Ronson.

"First, we devised a try-it-yourself demonstrator display which would allow consumers to 'try before you buy.' This display was finely crafted in wood, metal and glass. An actual shaver is held in a nest under a sanitizing bulb and a 'magic mirror' flashed a sales message. We called it the Ronson S-4 demonstrator.

"Next came the deal: Buy four Ronson '400's and get the display free.

"Our trade ads merchandised the deal and the display to the wholesaler and retailer, via the leading trade magazines and in dealer mailings. National magazine ads featured the try-before-you-buy theme, urging consumers to come in and try the Ronson '400' for themselves at their local dealers. Retailers who bought the deal and a requisite minimum quantity of backup merchandise were listed alongside a newspaper version of the same consumer ad. These dealer-listing newspaper ads were run in major-market cities across the country. Ad reprints and store banners were provided to bring customers into the store for a demonstration.

"So the sequence goes: The dealer is shown the display and proposed support via mailers and trade ads. Consumers are informed by magazine ads that their dealer has the ultimate shaver and a means of trying it. Then the prospect sees a newspaper ad which not only reinforces the magazine impression, but shows him which dealers have it. Consumers are invited into the store by window streamers and at the point of sale the demonstrator display closes the deal. (For those not ready to buy, informative, colorful folders are available to take home.)

"I think this campaign illustrates how aimed sales promotion . . . the close coordination of point-of-purchase display, merchandising deal, trade promotion, direct mail, P.R., and consumer advertising, pays off.

"Results: A sellout of all deals and displays for Ronson along with the increased distribution the promotion was designed to create."

TIMING THE CAMPAIGN

The advantages of proper timing are obvious. There are some products which can be sold more easily at certain seasons of the year. In selling to department stores, for example, it has been found that campaigns timed to hit just *before* the department buyer goes into the market are twice as effective as those which are not so timed. Products designed for gift use go better in early fall than they do after Thanksgiving.

The headquarters of the Eastman Kodak Company's Exhibits Division. During the course of an average year, the Exhibits Division will make up displays for 125 conventions and trade shows, as well as about 75 miscellaneous exhibits.

A promotion man with a line of shoes for retailers would get best results in July, when orders for fall and winter styles are usually placed for deliveries in August and September. In the same way a promotion man for a national magazine times his campaign to sell space in August and September, when lists of media are usually prepared by the advertising agency for approval by the advertiser. A campaign timed to reach prospective advertisers after his list for the next year was made up would not be as effective as one which hit in July and August.

Most campaigns to stimulate the sale of automobiles are timed to break in the early spring, when people begin to think about buying a new car for the summer months. Factors which influence timing are: (1) Seasonal buying habits; (2) employment needs of the business itself; (3) climatic conditions; (4) special weeks, days, and events.

Leveling Off the "Slack" Season

A primary consideration in timing a promotion is the sales needs of the business. If, for some reason, it is desirable from an operating standpoint to step up sales on a certain product or group of products, say to use materials carried too long in inventory, that might be a good reason for putting on a sales drive. In the same way, with organized labor insisting upon guaranteed annual wage contracts, some companies depend upon intensive promotions to level off seasonal unemployment. It has been found, for example, that electrical refrigerators can be sold just as well, with the right promotional effort, in winter as in summer. By shifting promotional emphasis automobile manufacturers have been able to step up sales in the slack fall months, just before a model change-over. Procter & Gamble, soap manufacturer, by rearranging its sales promotional effort, has been able to sell its products in almost even volume the year around, thus getting rid of costly slack seasons in production. It may take more promotional steam to bring about these results, but production economies thus made possible might well offset the cost of getting the out-of-season business.

Tying-In with Special Days and Weeks

Some industries have made the promotions of their member companies more effective by "breaking" them simultaneously. A period is designated for the purpose and given an appropriate promotional name, as for example: "Insurance Week," "Apple Week," "Honey Week," etc.

At that time as much promotional effort as is practicable is undertaken by concerns in the industry, and an aggressive effort is made to get newspaper and other types of tie-in publicity. Newspapers will often give an industry publicity which they would hesitate to give to an isolated advertiser.

An All-Industry Example

More than 3,000 dealers throughout the country participated in the first annual National Office Products Week. Twenty-one manufacturers of nationally-advertised branded merchandise cooperated in the industry-wide program designed to promote specific office products.

A giant sweepstakes, with a grand prize of a free, all-expense vacation in Europe for two, was one feature of the promotion. Hundreds of other prizes were offered, including color TV sets, furs, portable TV's, and cameras. Thousands of dollars' worth of merchandise was given away to customers who visited dealers' stores.

Each dealer received a complete merchandising kit that included window streamers, pennants, counter cards, envelope stuffers, ad mats, sweepstakes entry forms and a complete guide in setting up the promotion.

A four-page color insert appeared in "Business Week" announcing the program. Other business publications reaching office managers, secretaries and purchasing agents carried special advertising to bring the promotion to the business community. All these ads carried entry blanks for the sweepstakes.

"This is the most practical promotion package ever offered to the office products dealer. It provides a promotional program that dealers could not afford to provide for themselves," stated A. W. Gurner, general manager of Olympic Office Supplies, New York City.

How One Company Times Mail Promotions

Another important factor in sales promotion is timing the frequency of mailings. A check of several companies indicates that the most popular interval is 1 month. While there are a number which use bimonthly frequency in their follow-up efforts, the majority seem to favor the monthly interval..

A check of the number of mailings in a sales promotional effort that can be made profitably brought out varying opinions and very little dependable experience. Much, of course, depends upon the unit being promoted, and the margin of profit available for promotion. The following schedule, used by a manufacturer of autographic registers in the reclaiming of old accounts, is based on careful tests and may be of interest:

INVOICE FOLLOW-UP: Six months after order is shipped, if no reorder has been received, a series of five follow-up letters (four-page illustrated pieces) is started. Letter No. 2 goes 3 months later, and the remaining three letters are sent at 2-month intervals. Copies of these letters are sent to the sales agent as mailed, with a request for a report.

DANGER LETTERS: If the invoice "Follow-Up" is completed without results, a second series of four-page letters, called "Danger Letters," begins. There are six letters in this series. They are mailed at 3-month intervals. The copies of these letters sent to the sales agents are especially printed so as to remind them forcibly that the customer has not ordered for 18 months, 21 months, etc.

RECLAMATION LETTERS: After the "Danger Letters" have been mailed the names go into a central file with all previous inactive accounts tabbed by years. This list is worked continuously. For example, customers who have not reordered for a year receive five letters; older customers receive fewer letters; but the entire list is worked systematically.

"PULLED" LIST: When a report comes in from an agent stating that a customer has gone over to a competitor, or is buying from another source, the McBee card is pulled and placed in a separate "reservoir." Address plates are tabbed to permit careful working in groups according to the situation involved. These groups of names are worked twice a year.

PERSONAL FOLLOW-UP: In addition to this automatic follow-up, all reports from agents are classified and turned over to a junior executive for special handling. This executive analyzes each case and decides which follow-up letters shall be used.

The purpose of this follow-up is to obtain reorders for forms used in the register. The high potential value of an account warrants a heavy follow-up. In other cases, where the unit is small, as, for example, subscriptions to magazines, it has been found that 5 follow-ups, timed at monthly intervals, are the most profitable. Some publishers, however, find it pays to follow up an old subscriber as many as 15 times.

It is recommended that tests be made before establishing a follow-up timetable to determine the point when it is no longer profitable to send follow-up literature. To carry a series of promotional mailings beyond the point of diminishing returns may prove costly over a period of years. That also applies to too frequent mailings.

Computerized Letters

One of the country's largest medical mailing-list houses, Clark-O'Neill Inc. of Fairview, N.J., embarked on a campaign designed to increase the use of its services among present clients and to expand to new clients. Three computers plus the acquisition of a Cheshire R-9000 had considerably increased the company's capabilities in creating, producing, and mailing promotional material for pharmaceutical manufacturers.

As told in "Direct Marketing," the direct mail magazine, mailings were sent every two weeks to a select list of 2,000 individuals, primarily members of the marketing departments of every pharmaceutical house in the country. Emphasis was placed on advertising and production personnel, and where the name of the individual was not known, a letter was addressed to the title and asked for the name by return mail. Response to this request was 90%.

Heart of the mailing effort was the company's Compu-Letter, a letter written by a computer printer with personalized information programmed into the middle of the letter: e.g., "If it becomes necessary, Mr. Jones, could you absolutely identify each physician, etc.?"

Although many pieces of literature were sent out in this program, the personalized Compu-Letter was a key element in each mailing. These letters are low in cost and quickly produced.The P.S. at the bottom of the second page of the two-page letter which kicked off the campaign read: "Did you notice that this was a Compu-Letter . . . produced on our computer in less than 3 seconds?" Compu-Letters are produced by Clark-O'Neill on company computers by the data processing department in less than 3 seconds. The letters are written by a computer printer with personalized phrases programmed into the body of the letter.

TYPICAL "WEEKS" FOR PROMOTION "TIE-INS"

Amateur Radio Week	Fire Prevention Week
American Camping Week	Girl Scout Week
American Education Week	Hardware-Housewares Week
Archery Week	Harmony Week
Be Kind to Animals Week	Holy Week
Book Week	Honey Week
Boy Scout Week	Humor Week
British Week	Jaycee Week
Brotherhood Week	Lath & Plaster Week
Campfire Girls Birthday Week	Let's Go Fishing Week
Cat Week	Library Week
Catholic Book Week	Lighthouse Week
Chemical Progress Week	Macaroni Week
Children's Book Week	Merchant Marine Book Week
Civil Rights Week	National Advertising Week
Cleaner Air Week	National Arts and Crafts Week
Clergy Week	National Baby Week
Comedy Week	National Beauty Salon Week
Constitution Week	National Bible Week
Diabetes Week	National Boys' Club Week
Dog Week	National Cherry Week
Electrical Week	National Civil Service Week
Employ the Handicapped Week	National Coin Week

National Crime Prevention Week
National Easter Seal Week
National Engineers Week
National Farm Safety Week
National Flag Week
National 4-H Club Week
National Frozen Food Week
National Hearing Week
National Highway Week
National Home Week
National Hospital Week
National Kraut and Frankfurter Week
National Latin American Week
National Laugh Week
National Letter Writing Week
National Model Railroad Week .
National Music Week
National Negro History Week
National Noise Abatement Week
National Panic Week
National "Pay Your Bills" Week
National Peanut Week
National Pharmacy Week
National Poison Prevention Week
National Pretzel Week
National Root Beer Week
National Salesmen's Week

National Salvation Army Week
National Save Your Vision Week
National Secretaries' Week
National Smile Week
National Sweater Week
National Transportation Week
National Wildlife Week
National Wine Week
Pan American Week
Paul Bunyan Week
Pickle Week
Police Week
Printing Week
Public Relations Week
Publicity Stunt Week
Small Business Week
Spring Clean-up Week
Tableware Week
United Nations Week
Universal Week of Prayer
Volunteers of America Week
Weights & Measures Week
World Trade Week
Youth Appreciation Week
Y-Teen Week
YMCA Week

Other Industrial and Consumer Campaigns

In addition to the campaigns already mentioned, other promotions designed for specific channels of distribution are described in following sections. Among them are industrial, distributor, retail and consumer sales promotion programs for a variety of products in different fields.

When Promotions Are Generally Prepared
(Month-to-Month Percentages)

Line of Business	Jan.	Feb.	Mar.	Apr.	May	June	July	Aug.	Sept.	Oct.	Nov.	Dec.	No time set
Store fixtures	6.8	6.8	6.8	6.8	5.6	4.5	3.4	5.6	10.2	9.1	8.0	5.6	20.8
Food products	5.5	5.5	6.6	5.5	6.6	6.6	6.6	6.6	8.7	5.5	5.5	5.5	25.3
Building materials	1.6	4.1	5.8	5.8	6.6	3.3	3.3	6.6	11.6	11.6	7.4	3.3	29.0
Household equipment	4.2	5.8	9.6	8.3	7.1	5.4	4.2	5.0	9.6	7.9	7.1	4.6	21.2
Jewelry	6.9	7.7	7.7	6.9	6.9	6.9	6.9	6.9	9.3	10.0	9.3	8.5	6.1
Machinery	5.4	5.4	7.8	7.8	7.8	5.4	5.4	5.4	5.4	6.7	7.5	4.7	25.8
Leather goods	5.9	8.2	8.2	7.1	5.9	5.9	4.7	7.1	15.3	11.7	7.1	4.7	8.2
Clothing	6.1	15.7	12.5	3.7	2.5	4.1	4.1	10.9	13.7	8.1	4.1	3.7	10.8
Novelties	4.3	4.3	4.3	4.3	4.3	8.7	4.3	0.0	0.0	4.3	13.0	8.7	39.5
Associations	3.4	3.4	7.0	10.3	10.3	7.0	3.4	3.4	10.3	10.3	3.4	3.4	24.4
Miscellaneous	1.1	4.4	4.4	5.5	4.4	0.0	0.0	6.5	8.8	7.7	7.7	1.2	48.3
Drug supplies	15.4	7.7	7.7	0.0	0.0	0.0	0.0	0.0	7.7	7.7	7.7	7.7	38.4
Sporting goods	4.6	13.9	16.3	11.6	9.3	4.6	4.6	7.0	9.3	7.0	4.6	4.6	2.6
Scientific instruments	5.3	10.5	5.3	0.0	5.3	5.3	0.0	0.0	5.3	5.3	5.3	5.3	47.1
Confectioners	7.9	7.9	7.9	5.3	5.3	5.3	5.3	7.9	7.8	7.9	7.8	7.9	15.8
Auto accessories	2.6	5.3	13.2	10.5	8.0	5.3	2.6	2.6	7.9	7.9	2.6	2.6	28.9
Hardware	4.7	5.6	9.3	12.1	11.2	1.8	1.9	3.7	5.6	7.5	6.5	3.7	26.4
Office equipment	2.0	2.0	2.0	4.0	4.0	6.0	4.0	4.0	6.0	6.0	8.0	10.0	42.0
Chemicals	6.8	9.1	9.1	9.1	4.5	2.3	4.5	6.8	6.8	4.5	4.5	4.5	27.5
Textiles	0.0	9.1	9.1	0.0	0.0	0.0	0.0	4.5	13.6	13.6	9.1	4.5	36.5
Musical instruments	5.4	7.1	5.4	7.1	10.7	5.4	5.4	10.7	10.7	8.9	8.9	7.1	7.2
Fuel products	3.1	6.5	3.1	6.5	9.4	9.4	9.4	9.4	6.5	3.1	6.5	6.5	20.6
Steel supplies	0.0	4.0	12.0	12.0	8.0	4.0	4.0	0.0	0.0	0.0	0.0	0.0	56.0
Investments	4.5	6.8	6.8	11.3	9.1	4.5	2.3	0.0	2.3	2.3	4.5	4.5	41.1
Average	4.7	6.9	7.8	6.7	6.4	4.6	3.8	5.0	8.1	7.3	6.5	5.1	27.1

PART 2

TECHNIQUES
AND
TOOLS
OF
SALES PROMOTION

Chapter 6

SALES LEADS AND INQUIRIES

IN AN ADDRESS before the Eastern Industrial Advertisers, in Philadelphia, W. A. Phair, Director of Information Services, Chilton Company, quoted a statement by the Marketing Communications Research Center which read:

> "Inquiries can be thought of as a means by which the market is talking to suppliers. If the supplier will only listen carefully, he can learn much about the market's changing needs and problems with great profit to himself."

Every advertiser receives inquiries; the question is how may one obtain the best results? Before you can hope to get a payoff, you have to invest some time and money in setting up procedures for handling the inquiries. That raises the next question: is it worthwhile? The preponderance of the evidence is that it certainly is.

What makes a good inquiry-processing system? In his talk, Mr. Phair presented the following guidelines:

1. Do not send raw inquiries to a salesman or distributor for follow-up. When you send out your literature, use a return post card to locate prospects with current needs. Then send these on for mandatory follow-up.

2. Be sure that everybody in your sales organization understands what you are doing—and that an inquiry represents only a prospect with a greatly varying degree of interest in a purchase. The goal of your inquiry fulfillment program is to segregate those with a current need from those with a long-term interest. Then the salesmen should be brought into the picture to work on the hot leads. Inquiries do a bird-dogging job; they supplement, but do not substitute for the job of face-to-face selling.

3. Set up a good accounting system so you will know the exact cost of your inquiries and the cost of the sales that result from them. Do the same with all your other sources of prospects, including trade shows and direct mail lists. "Acquisition cost" is the name of the game, and until you can talk about this with some precision,

you cannot really make an intelligent judgment as to which is the most efficient way to get good prospects for your company.

4. Don't sneer about "catalog collectors." If a man is serious enough to ask for your catalog, send him one. Perhaps you should have a shortened version for this purpose. But at least get your product catalog in his file.

5. Set up your system to get as much marketing intelligence as possible out of it. This is a phase of inquiry handling that is generally overlooked. The Marketing Communications Research Center tells you to listen to what inquiries tell you. When you do this, you'll be amazed at how much you can hear.

The newest stage in industrial inquiry processing is the Ad-Recap Program of the trade publication *Product Design & Development*. In referring inquiries to its advertisers, the magazine gives the prospect's SIC number and employment size. After two months, the advertiser receives a summary of all inquiries according to SIC. This gives the advertiser the opportunity to spot potential new markets, select specific inquiries for special follow-up and to discover changes in personnel in customer organizations.

Kodak's Inquiry-Handling System

The Business Systems Markets Division of Eastman Kodak Company employs a thorough, efficient, inquiry-handling procedure. Based on the use of a four-part inquiry form, it provides a continuous source of prospective buyers for a nation-wide group of sales representatives.

The company requires that inquiries receive a prompt reply, and that the salesmen receive notification for prompt follow-up. The BSMD inquiry system is also designed to *measure* advertising effectiveness through a simplified and efficient reporting system.

The inquirer is replied to by personal letter or by form letter depending on the nature of the request. He is sent, by first class mail, the literature he requested along with a listing of the company's Marketing Centers. Requests for sales representative calls receive priority handling and are processed the same day as received. Where information is required immediately, the District Sales Manager is notified by telephone. At the same time that the inquiry is answered, a four-part BSMD Inquiry Form is completed. This form is used to notify the salesman who the inquirer is, to provide a record of the source for computer input, and for the salesman to report the result of the initial contact. Each inquiry is accounted for by a preprinted 5 digit inquiry number.

For easy reference, space conservation and security, part 1 of all inquiries processed daily are microfilmed in numerical sequence by inquiry number. The inquiry is then forwarded to data processing, where a tab card is punched and the data read into the computer by inquiry number.

Parts 2-4 of the inquiry form are forwarded to the District Sales Manager. The DSM retains Part 2 in his tickler file and forwards Parts 3 and 4 to the sales representative. After the salesman contacts the inquirer and completes the inquiry form, he forwards Part 4 to his District Sales Manager. The DSM removes Part 2 of the form from his tickler file. He can then make notations on the form concerning the outcome of the call, or he may wish to destroy it, thus indicating that Part 4 has been received from the salesman. The DSM then forwards Part 4 of the inquiry form to BSMD Advertising in Rochester.

The information supplied by the salesman is keypunched into an EAM card and read into the computer along with the inquiry number. This information is used at the end of each month in compiling management reports. If the salesman classifies the inquirer as a "PROSPECT," a name and address card is punched and this information is entered into the system.

Salesmen are requested to make initial contact with the inquirer, complete, and return Part 4 of the inquiry form within 30 days from the date sent. The computer recognizes all outstanding inquiry numbers at the end of the 30 days and prints out a listing in inquiry number sequence. This printout is forwarded to the District Sales Manager for immediate follow-up and reporting by the salesman.

Every two months the salesman receives an 11" x 8½" printout listing names and addresses of those inquirers he has classified "PROSPECT." The salesman can then note any changes which have taken place since his previous contact by simply checking boxes and making short entries. This Prospect Report is returned to BSMD Advertising via the District Sales Manager. It is reviewed and forwarded to data processing for updating the computer file.

Most important are the monthly reports which management receives. These reports contain information which affects advertising and marketing decisions. For example: which conventions should be dropped from the convention schedule? Which ads are showing the best results? Which trade publications are giving the most value for the advertising dollar? Which target areas for direct mail campaigns are drawing the best response? Finally, how many dollars resulted from advertising inquiries and sales follow-up?

BSMD LEADS SUMMARY

BSMD ADVERTISING	PANORAMA ADDS YTD	TOTAL LEADS THIS MONTH	TOTAL LEADS THIS YTD	TOTAL LEADS LAST YTD	PERCENT CHANGE
INFORMATION TECHNOLOGY					
PUBLICITY ITEMS	8	321	496	781	36.5-
DIRECT MAIL	2		18	7	157.1
PUBLICATION ADVERTISING	10	314	391	656	40.4-
UNIDENTIFIED	8	39	113	26	334.6
	28	674	1,018	1,470	30.8-
MICROGRAPHICS					
PUBLICITY ITEMS	16	403	661	1,753	62.3-
DIRECT MAIL	12	5	95	52	82.6
PUBLICATION ADVERTISING	24	210	435	733	40.7-
UNIDENTIFIED	23	261	446	319	39.8
	75	879	1,637	2,857	42.8-
PHOTO REPRODUCTION					
PUBLICITY ITEMS		496	687	306	124.5
DIRECT MAIL		121	470	1,480	68.3-
PUBLICATION ADVERTISING		1,164	2,025	942	114.9
UNIDENTIFIED		5	30	11	172.7
		1,786	3,212	2,739	17.2

Each month, the number of leads obtained from all sources is analyzed in a report to Kodak's BSMD management. The summary figures are listed in separate pages for conventions, media, publicity, direct mail and by type of product.

EASTMAN KODAK COMPANY
BUSINESS SYSTEMS MARKETS DIVISION
ROCHESTER, NEW YORK 14650

HERE IS AN INQUIRY FROM A POTENTIAL PROSPECT IN YOUR SALES TERRITORY. TO HELP MAKE OUR ADVERTISING MORE PRODUCTIVE FOR YOU, COMPLETE AND RETURN PART 4 OF THIS FORM TO YOUR DISTRICT SALES MANAGER *within 30 days.*

BSMD ADVERTISING

LITERATURE SENT_____

INQUIRY NO. 45625 _____

DEPT. NO._____DATE SENT_____

MKTG. CNTR._____

SALESMAN REQUESTED ☐ _____

☐ PROSPECT   ☐ NO PROSPECT

☐ SOLD   ▶ $_____

☐ RENTED   ▶ $_____

☐ BOUGHT FROM
  OTHER VENDOR

TERR. NO.	SALESMAN

1   FOLLOW-UP PLEASE REPLY IMMEDIATELY

The inquiry handling process of the Business Systems Markets Division of the Eastman Kodak Company is based on the use of a four-part inquiry form. Each page plays a role in follow-up, field reports, district supervision, data processing, management reports and in the measurement of advertising effectiveness. (See chart)

BSMD INQUIRY SYSTEM

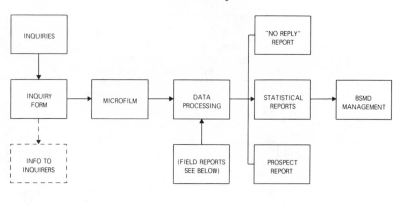

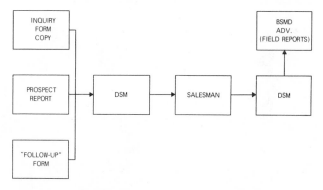

This chart shows the channels followed and the flow of information produced in processing the four parts of the inquiry form developed by Eastman Kodak Company's Business Systems Markets Division.

Methods of Getting Inquiries

The cheapest way to get inquiries for a product or service is the postpaid reply card. An offer to send some helpful booklet, or to send some articles of use, to a list of prospects has been known to produce as high as 37% replies at a cost of less than 54 cents each. Returns of 5 to 10% on reply cards of this kind are common.

Such inquiries, however, are usually of questionable sales value because they result from a desire to get something for nothing—even the cost of the return postage being paid by the seller. Sending inquiries of this sort to salesmen soon disgusts them, and unless great pressure is used they will only follow up those which for one reason or another impress them as as being hot. Since it is the practice in most sales departments to put the names of those making inquiry on a permanent mailing list, it is easy to see how over a period of time inquiries obtained by the use of government reply cards are likely to prove expensive from the standpoint of net sales cost.

Getting Worth-While Leads

In setting up an inquiry-getting program, make it necessary for an inquirer to qualify himself as a prospect in some way. High-pressure methods in securing inquiries are just as objectionable, and just as likely to back up on you, as high-pressure sales methods. The best inquiries are those which come with the least prodding, usually those which come from magazine or trade paper advertising where no direct play is made for inquiries. This may seem contrary to the ideal of most advertising departments which glory in being able to cut the cost of inquiries, but experience shows that cluttering up a mailing list with a large number of lukewarm names of supposed prospects can reach a point where a very substantial proportion of the entire advertising appropriation goes for "nesting on china eggs."

The best plan is to hand-pick a list of prospects, checking them first for application and second for ability to buy. The list may be as large or as small as the appropriation warrants. Lay out a series of mailing pieces backed by advertising in publications which your prospects have indicated they read. The object of both the direct-mail and publication copy should be educational. The use of publication advertising will serve to increase the returns from the mailings, and at the same time contact casual prospects who may not be on a mailing list.

Take the case of a manufacturer making lumber mill machinery. The backbone of his campaign for inquiries would naturally be a list of mill operators who he has reason to believe are now or will shortly be in the market for new equipment. It is not difficult to get such a mailing list, nor is it difficult to check it against Dun & Bradstreet to make sure that too much effort is not spent in trying to sell a prospect who could not pay for the equipment even if he could be sold. But every month somewhere in this country there are men who have accumulated some capital and are thinking about setting up a sawmill. They are valuable prospects for this manufacturer. But how is he to find them? When this chap with the money to buy sawmill equipment gets the idea of starting up in business for himself, the very first thing he will probably do is to write for a sample copy of the trade papers in the lumber field. He will be interested, of course, in the articles which they carry about operating a sawmill successfully, but the primary reason he wants those magazines is to get the names of manufacturers of sawmill equipment so that he can write for catalogs and literature. He will get this information from the advertising pages. Those manufacturers of sawmill equipment who advertise regularly in these papers are likely to receive an inquiry from this person. Those who do not may never know about him until after he has bought his equipment.

Some companies, such as USM Corporation, in responding to inquiries, include a qualification card with their literature and a common experience is that between 10% and 15% of these cards are returned.

These are then considered hot leads and salesmen are required to follow-up. "These qualification cards can form the basis of an excellent direct mail list," states Mr. Phair, "especially when coded for product interest."

Many industrial magazines offer direct mail services which permit companies to select names and build lists on the basis of function and industry. Many publications now ask for the reader's telephone number and print this on the inquiry sent to the advertiser. A surprising number of companies hire special services to call each inquirer, acknowledge the inquiry, determine the degree of interest and, if possible, the proposed use or application of the product.

Acknowledging Inquiries

In responding to inquiries, an interesting application of its product is made by Jeffco Industries, Middlesex, New Jersey. The company manufactures "Tab-Binders" featuring a glassine pocket on the front cover for a business card, so it naturally includes specification sheets and illustrations in one of its binders, with a printed letter in two colors, offering a free label-maker with each order received. The letter reads:

Gaining your prospect's attention is the first step to the sale! This new binder-folder does it! Placing your business card in the pocket on the front cover leaves no doubt who's looking for the order. And placing your sales presentation in an easily read—easily referred to manner can only build a favorable impression.

This is Jeffco's new "TAB-BINDER" with emphasis on your business card.

Your customer will like this unique presentation technique. He'll like the easy way he can file the folder for easy reference and he'll like the fact that your business card is up front where he can reach it without searching through his desk.

Torture your sample, if you can. Feel the plastic material. It's as tough as iron, strong as steel and flexible as leather. It's Jeffco's new "Ruf-Tuf" plastic and it's guaranteed for 5 years not to tear, dog ear, crack or crumple. Who would dare make such a guarantee?

The Tab-Binder comes in 5 attractive colors and has a binder grip strip that holds 25 pages, up to 8½ X 11, nice and snug.

Give your salesman a break. Order today. And watch his morale rise when his presentations start warming up his pockets with new commission checks.

And, you enjoy direct factory prices, too. Note the low cost. Add that slight investment to your important proposals and you've gained a new image. Try it. Our money back guarantee applies. You must be satisfied.

We've enclosed a postpaid order card for easy ordering. Do send it in today. We'll give your order prompt attention.

> Sincerely
>
> William J. Clark

P.S. The handy-sized Dymo Labelmaker is just perfect for home, office, or carry-out use. It's yours free with your order.

Notable for its consciseness and matter-of-fact content, yet stressing the advantages to the prospect dealer in handling the company's products, is the reply letter used by the American Footwear Corporation reading:

"Thank you for your inquiry regarding our new LIGHT-WEIGHT SAFETY FOOTWEAR. The response to our ad has been overwhelming. An American Footwear representative will be contacting you soon.

Enclosed for your appraisal is our current Safety Shoe Brochure and Distributor Price List. We're sure the following benefits extended to you through our Distributor Program will be of interest and value to you:

- Broad Distributor profit margin.
- Increase in sales.
- New and profitable accounts.
- Distributor program to fit your needs.
- Personalized assistance from us.
- Inventory requirement—you tell us.
- Every pair is UNCONDITIONALLY GUARANTEED.
- All exceed ANSI Class 75 standards as adopted by OSHA.

If you have any questions, or need more information, please call us collect at the above number."

Ask Prospects to Help

Most people are responsive to a request for assistance if it appears to be reasonable and genuine. In many instances, concerns have pulled replies by asking prospects to criticize the advertising they have received or to suggest the sort of information that might appeal to them. Others have attached to the letter a copy of the "prospect card" bearing the prospect's name and showing a record of several past mailings with a request to indicate what ought to be done with it. Good results have also been obtained by listing "Reasons for not replying" at the top of the letter and asking the prospect to check and return. Straight requests for aid in "keeping our list up to date" have helped secure definite information from prospects.

Premiums for Special Information

When the selling proposition depends upon knowledge of the prospect's circumstances, and the list is blind, inexpensive and attractive premiums can often be used to get the desired information from the prospect. Insurance companies have used diaries for obtaining qualifying data from prospects whose names are taken from various sources. With information concerning the prospect's age, business connection, etc., the company can make a definite proposition which otherwise would be impossible. A manufacturer of oil burners for household heating has made an adaptation of this plan by supplying his local dealers with information cards to be filled out with data of prospect's present equipment and pays the dealers 10 cents apiece for all cards returned. High school seniors are also used to obtain "qualifying" information about names on the prospect list.

When acknowledging inquiries, or orders, many concerns enclose one or two extra return cards with the request that they be passed along to somebody else who may be interested. This is particularly effective in connection with a high-grade product.

Exhibits Produce Leads

The main objective of a manufacturer's display in an exhibit is to produce leads. This is especially true of trade shows. While immediate direct orders may also be written in some cases, most manufacturers selling through distributors or dealers will refer the

THANK YOU FOR YOUR RECENT REQUEST FOR INFORMATION.

We are sending your inquiry to your authorized A. B. Dick products distributor whose name and address are shown at the lower left. As duplicating specialists, handling a complete line of duplicating and copying products, they can answer any questions you may have—and quote prices. If you have requested a demonstration you will be contacted to arrange

A·B·DICK.

I'd like to take a closer look at the 650.

Please arrange my showing for _____, or call me to set a date.
(Date)

NAME_____

POSITION_____

COMPANY_____

ADDRESS_____

CITY_____   STATE   ZIP #

TELEPHONE_____

☐ We now have a _____

Model # _____

of copies is about_____

☐ We *do not* have a copi

RESERVED!
Complete and mail this card now to reserve your 650 showing . . . and to get your free Executive Taskmaster

A request for product information addressed to the A. B. Dick Company produces a catalog booklet, together with a printed "thank you" note which also provides the name and address of the local office. Enclosed with the material is a reply card to indicate whether the prospect is interested in seeing a 12-minute color film demonstrating the product. To prompt response, the company offers a vinyl-bound executive memo book.

There are 3 steps involved in making a buying decision

We're enclosing the second step.

You recently learned about a Beseler product in a magazine (1st step)... and asked us to send you information.

The 3rd and most important step is for you to see the product for yourself. We'll arrange this, of course, without cost or obligation.

Just fill out and send in the postage-free reply card.

To: **Charles Beseler Company, 219 S. 18th Street, E. Orange, N.J.**

YES...I would like to see the following Beseler products demonstrated. Please arrange an appointment. Products:_____

name/title_____
school/company_____
address_____
city_____ state_____ zip_____
telephone_____
Our Beseler A-V dealer is:_____

An impressive two-color card-folder is employed by the Charles Beseler Company, manufacturer of projector equipment, in sending literature to inquirers. The postage-paid reply card at the bottom of the message is made part of a three-step process.

152

THANK YOU for your interest in our "POP" rivet line of blind fasteners.

Please fill out the attached postpaid reply card so that we may be of further assistance.

Product(s) Manufactured _____

Material Being Fastened _____

Hole Size/Fastener Diameter _____

Grip Range (total material thickness) _____

Fastener Now Used _____

Additional Information _____

☐ PLEASE HAVE YOUR REPRESENTATIVE CALL.

NAME_____ TITLE_____

COMPANY_____ PHONE_____

ADDRESS_____

CITY_____ STATE_____ ZIP CODE_____

The value of an inquiry is determined by USM Corporation through the use of this combination acknowledgement and qualification card.

more sales leads from . . . 42

CHILTON'S

PD&D

ONE DECKER SQUARE, BALA CYNWYD, PA. 19004 215-748-2000

PRODUCT DESIGN AND DEVELOPMENT

TO:
MR ARTHUR JONES
MARKETING DIVISION
PRECISION MFG. CO.
100 MAIN STREET
NEW YORK, N.Y.

ISSUE DATE JAN 70   ITEM NO. 180 A

ITEM DESCRIPTION VARIABLE SPEED PULLEYS

PRODUCT CODE **5508**

IMPORTANT MARKETING INFORMATION FOR YOU

To make these sales leads more useful as marketing intelligence, significant details about the inquirer's company are given in the box to the right of each name.

The first line gives the Standard Industrial Classification (SIC) of the plant. The second line gives the most recent employment data from our Census File; it may vary slightly from the current figure. The third line indicates whether the inquirer is a subscriber or pass-along reader. The fourth line gives the telephone number, when supplied by the reader.

4 DIGIT SIC

PLANT EMPLOYMENT

TYPE OF READER

PHONE NUMBER WHEN GIVEN

R JENKE   DES ENGR
PIONEER ENGINEERING & MFG
P O BOX 87
SAN DIEGO   CALIF   92112

SIC 3544
EMPLOYS 900
PRIMARY SUBSCRIBER
TELEPHONE ▶

SIC
EMPLOYS
TELEPHONE ▶

E L WOLF   MECH DES
TELEDYNE ENGINEERING
SOUTHSIDE DRIVE
POINT PLEASANT   CAL   93014

SIC 3602
EMPLOYS 250
PRIMARY SUBSCRIBER
TELEPHONE ▶
703-834-5831 EX375

SIC
EMPLOYS
TELEPHONE ▶

W G FOSTER   ELECTRONICS ENGR
VEGA PRECISION LABS
239 MAPLE AVE
LOUISVILLE KY   40214

SIC 3662
EMPLOYS 200
PASS ALONG READER
TELEPHONE ▶
703-938-6240 EX54

SIC
EMPLOYS
TELEPHONE ▶

J BURNS   CHF DES ENG
FORD MOTOR CO
DEARBORN RD
DETROIT   MICH   48202

SIC 3711
EMPLOYS 10000
PRIMARY SUBSCRIBER
TELEPHONE ▶
214-867-9000 EX 524

SIC
EMPLOYS
TELEPHONE ▶

N L NORMAN   PRES
N L NORMAN ASSOCIATES
537 W OAK ST
NEWARK N J   07114

SIC UNIDENTIFIED
EMPLOYS
TELEPHONE ▶
201-243-3765

SIC
EMPLOYS
TELEPHONE ▶

J SMUGGS   DES SPEC
RCA RESEARCH LAB
* 17 SHADYSIDE DRIVE
CHERRY HILL N J   08034

SIC 3651
EMPLOYS 6000
PRIMARY SUBSCRIBER
TELEPHONE ▶
804-648-2298

SIC
EMPLOYS
TELEPHONE ▶

---

* IN STREET ADDRESS DENOTES HOME ADDRESSED INQUIRY

SAMPLE

NOTE — Names and addresses have been mixed up and are for illustrative purposes only.

TOTAL INQUIRIES THIS PERIOD 6   TOTAL INQUIRIES TO DATE 154

When sending inquiries to advertisers, the trade publication "Product Design and Development," fills in the prospect's SIC number and plant employment size. The inquiries thus become a form of market intelligence.

names and addresses of interested people to local companies for followup.

This means, naturally, that provision should be made for inquiry cards to be distributed at the point of display, yet it is astonishing to find that this is not always done. Notebooks, scraps of paper, business cards are often resorted to by exhibit personnel in recording the necessary information.

Exhibits may also be made to produce leads and inquiries in another way. Large cities and resorts are the sites of important conventions and trade shows with large numbers of major exhibitors. The exhibit of the American Association of School Administrators, for instance, held in conjunction with its convention in Atlantic City, N. J., required a 96-page booklet merely to list the names, addresses and products of more than 600 exhibitors. Such a list would be useful to prospective suppliers to the exhibitors, but they are not always readily available as their distribution is usually controlled.

Additionally, major cities maintain Convention Bureaus which announce coming conventions and exhibits to the press. These publicity notices signal the advent of important gatherings which could also serve to help build up lists of prospects.

Special Offer for Limited Period

This is a tried and true device for speeding up the laggards, if the special offer or concession appears to be genuine and the time limit is definite and emphatic. The phrase, "for a limited period only," doesn't mean much, but a return card printed in big, red type, "Good Until Saturday the 25th Only," may mean a good deal. A publisher who offered a premium book with subscriptions to a forthcoming set of reference works found the ratio of inquiries increased when he changed "order before the supply is exhausted" to "we have only 550 books left to sell." Statements of this sort must be truthful and be able to stand Federal Trade Commission investigation.

Dramatize the Argument

One of the outstanding successes of the past few years is the enormous sales of such outwardly commonplace books as the *Book of Etiquette*, for example. Books of etiquette had been on the market for 50 years, and the only new element in the campaign was the advertising copy that made the prospect see herself in embarrassing situations from which she could be rescued by knowledge of social conventions. In other words, the appeal was dramatized from the personal standpoint of the reader.

Timely Mailings

Oftentimes the success of a campaign is increased by close attention to the time of mailing. A number of concerns report that they are giving more attention to this than in the past, especially when those addressed are businessmen. Care should be taken, they say, to avoid reaching the businessman's desk on Monday, or any day following a holiday, when there is likely to be a large accumulation of letters needing attention. Also, it is wise to avoid reaching him Friday or Saturday when he is tired after a week's steady work, or perhaps absent over the week end. The best day is Tuesday, and Wednesday is next best.

It pays to watch folds and enclosures carefully, to see that the proper continuity of argument is secured and especially to guard against the prospect's seeing the return card first. A good many prospects instinctively look for the return card or coupon first, in order to size up the proposition quickly, and some ingenuity is necessary to get their attention first for the argument it is desired to convey. It is, therefore, worth some extra effort to see that the mailing clerks have definite instructions as to the proper method of placing enclosures in the envelope and to make sure they are carried out.

It is also wise to avoid sending important features "under separate cover." Interest is likely to cool between the receipt of a letter and the later arrival of a catalog to which it refers, and there is also a chance that the recipient of the letter may not get the catalog at all. Where separate mailings cannot be avoided, it is advisable to adopt some highly distinctive color of wrapper or some striking device that will identify the catalog when it comes in as belonging with the letter already received. One plan is to attach a "Notice to Mail Clerk" card to the letter.

Memory Joggers for Salesmen

One of the most fruitful sources of leads for a salesman who sells intangibles to a large cross section of people in his own community, insurance for instance, is a memory jogger. These memory joggers are usually lists of possible prospects whom, for one reason or another, the salesman may not have thought of as sales prospects. Such a list, used by Investors Diversified Services, Inc., of Minneapolis, is shown on page 157. It lists over 80 possible people whom the salesman should know well enough to approach for an order. An executive of the company reports this type of memory jogger has worked remarkably well for them. It is a simple idea which can be adapted by a wide number of businesses.

WHOM DO YOU KNOW?

Can you list at least 100 gainfully employed persons in your community whom you know, and who would be willing to give you a hearing about a sound financial program in which you believe thoroughly yourself?

It may be difficult to remember 100 acquaintances at once. If so, we suggest you take a day or two to develop the list. Members of your family may be able to help. As you think of names, jot them down on a piece of paper or pocket note-book you carry with you — then enter them on the forms on the following pages.

Before starting your list read these

Memory Joggers

Whom do you know?
- from your old job?
- from school or college?
- because of your favorite sports or hobbies?
- from your church?
- from civic activities?
- because you rent or own your own home?
- because you lived in other neighborhoods?
- who sold you your automobile?
- who sells you gas, tires, or lubrication?
- through your children?
- through your wife?
- from lodge or club?

Whom do you know?
- who sells you meat?
- who sells you groceries?
- who sold you your wedding ring?
- who fixes your watch?
- who sells you hats?
- who sells you suits?
- who sells you shoes?
- who sold you your dog?
- who sells you office supplies?
- who is on your Election Board?
- who is your painter and decorator?
- who sold your wife her fur coat?

Whom do you know?
- who runs your delicatessen?
- who manages your local theater?
- who tends your dog when he is sick?
- who appraises real estate?
- who sells you used cars?
- who made your awnings, storm windows, screens?
- who is your physician?
- who is your dentist?
- who is your druggist?
- who heads your Draft Board?
- who is your son's or daughter's Scoutmaster?
- who sold you your piano?

Whom do you know?
- who gives your children music lessons?
- who sold you your refrigerator?
- who is a nurse?
- who is your lawyer?
- who owns the hotel nearest you?
- who made your latest family photograph?
- who edits your local newspaper?
- who is your best luncheon club friend?
- who are your buddies in the American Legion?
- who heads the local Parent-Teachers' Association?
- who owns the dairy where you buy milk, eggs, butter?
- who sold you your furniture?
- who stores your rugs?
- who does your dry cleaning?
- who sold you spectacles?
- who is your florist?
- who is the most popular undertaker?
- who is chief of your fire department?
- who is your local Building and Loan man?

Whom do you know?
- who is on your police force?
- who heads the Lions Club, Kiwanis, etc.?
- who manages or owns the Five & Dime store?
- who sold you your lightning rods?
- who insulated your house?
- who is your public stenographer?
- who is your telegraph man?
- who is your express man?
- who sold you your fence?
- who owns your lumber yard?
- who scrapes your floors?
- who is your postmaster or letter-carrier?
- who serves you lunch?
- who cuts your hair?
- who bought that new house in your neighborhood?
- who plays the organ in your church?
- who prints your stationery?
- who is principal of your high school?
- who sharpens your lawn mower?
- who hung your venetian blinds?

Whom do you know?
- who is your Justice of the Peace?
- who services or sells oil burners?
- who does your plumbing?
- who screened your porch?
- who reupholstered your chair?
- who soles your shoes?
- who heads your bank?
- who owns your bowling alley?
- who repairs your radio?
- who owns your hardware store?
- who is your local job printer?
- who plays bridge with your wife?
- who dresses your wife's hair?
- who sells you tobacco?
- who sells you railroad tickets?
- who lives next door to you?
- who was best man at your wedding?
- who sells you coal or oil?
- who was the groom at the last wedding you saw?
- who sells you fishing tackle?

LEADS FOR DISTRIBUTORS TO FOLLOW UP

Most dealers are notoriously lax when it comes to following up leads sent them by manufacturers. Sometimes it is because they do not have the manpower to do it; sometimes it is because they have followed up a few leads and concluded the results were not worth the effort; but usually it is just plain laziness on the part of the dealer or his outside salesmen.

There are three rather important principles involved in getting dealers to cooperate in following up leads: (1) Only good leads should be forwarded to the dealer for follow-up. Mere requests for a catalog or a free booklet should be handled direct by the manufacturer, using a request-for-further-information card with the mailing. When these cards come back they are immediately passed along to the dealer. (2) The lead or inquiry should be carefully and promptly acknowledged, mentioning the dealer by name, and stating the inquiry has been forwarded for his attention and that he or one of his representatives will call. A carbon copy of this letter should be sent to the dealer along with the *original* inquiry. (3) If a dealer does not follow up an inquiry or a lead within 10 days he should get some sort of a memory jogger. If he does follow up the lead, a letter over the signature of the territorial salesman should go to him offering further help if he needs it. The purpose of this is to let the dealer know you attach importance to the lead and the way he handles it. Naturally, if the manufacturer places little value on the inquiries he receives, the dealer won't think much of them either.

Distributors are inclined to cooperate more fully in follow-up advertising leads than dealers, who do not always have the outside organization to do it. Patterson Brothers, a New York machinery distributor, goes so far as to make a report, on a form of its design, to all manufacturers who send in inquiries to follow up. Along the right-hand margin of the form a thermometer chart is printed. This is used by the Patterson sales manager to indicate the potential sales value of the inquiry, after he receives the report on a call from his salesman. This plan of evaluating the worth of the inquiry, and informing the manufacturer's advertising department of it, is greatly appreciated by the manufacturer. It also works to the advantage of Patterson Brothers, since manufacturers send more leads when they know the leads sent will be intelligently followed up. Advertising managers are glad to get these estimates since it helps them to convince the company that the money spent for advertising is producing actual sales.

A simple plan used by Robert H. Clark Company, Beverly Hills,

California, to advise distributors of inquiries received from advertising, and at the same time make it easy for their salesmen to report *directly* to the manufacturer, is to use double government post cards. The message side of the card gives the name of the person making the inquiry, stating the product in which he is interested. There is also a brief "sales" talk about the growing demand for this particular product and its principal sales points. The reply side of the double card is used for the report. The salesman who makes the call indicates: (1) The size of the order obtained; (2) if no order was placed, when the prospect might be in the market again; (3) what further technical information was required to close the sale; or (4) if the salesman lost the order, the reasons why he lost it.

OTHER WAYS TO GET INQUIRIES

An analysis of methods commonly used in securing inquiries and leads shows 13 variations of plans, all of which are well known to advertising men. The following methods are in general use:

1. Customary advertising campaigns with appeal for inquiries, which are turned over to salesmen.

2. Mailing reprints of advertisements to buyers with enclosure of return card calling for more information.

3. Mailing letters to selected mailing lists, particular success being secured when separate letters are mailed to each class of buyer and the letters made more applicable to buyer's business.

4. Offering a small sample, either in the general advertising or the letter work, to find out who is interested in the product.

5. Featuring service and selling help in trade-paper advertising.

6. Preparing book with unusual appeal to buyer or his clerks, making it deal with some problem with which the buyer is confronted; this book to be offered free or at a very low cost to develop leads.

7. Watching the local newspapers for leads or employing a clipping bureau to furnish the right kind of items on a bigger scale.

8. "Club offers" or special assortments offered in broadcast manner.

9. "Booster" and "Associate Salesman" plans based on prizes to cooperating customers.

10. Taking advantage of fairs, exhibits, food shows, business shows, etc.

11. Placing on return post card a choice of several plans, any one of which will be furnished upon return of card.

12. Offering to send advertising novelty, such as address book, quota card case, billfold, old-fashioned quill pen, etc., to any executive who sends information needed to determine class of prospective buyer.

13. Sending card to present users requesting them to give you names of two other executives who should be interested in same proposition.

Love-A-Fair

PARTICIPA...
INDICATIC...

NO COST. NO OBLIGATION. PLEASE RETURN THIS CARD

YES, I PLAN TO USE YOUR LOVE·A·FAIR MATERIALS SOMETIME [
COMING YEAR. PROBABLY DURING THE MONTH OF _____

PLEASE ANTICIPATE MY REQUIREMENTS FOR APPROXIMATELY _____
FULL-COLOR INSERT/MAILERS WHEN MAKING YOUR PRODUCTION R...

LOVE,

SIGNED _____

DEALERSHIP _____

ADDRESS _____

CITY _____

Bell & Howell No-Risk Reservation Certificate

☐ **YES** Please accept my order to rush the complete Bell & Howell Super 8 Zoom Movie Outfit for my two week's free trial—mine to examine and use and enjoy without cost or obligation! If I'm not completely satisfied, I will return the entire outfit at your expense, and owe nothing.

If I decide to keep the movie outfit, I can have it for the cash price (amount financed) of $249.00, or charge it over 25 months at $9.96 per month. This adds up to a total of payments (deferred payment price) of $249.00 which includes shipping. Sales tax extra, where applicable. Imagine owning this fabulous Home Movie Outfit for less than $240 a week. There are NO FINANCE CHARGES . . . NO DOWN PAYMENT . . . NO DEPOSIT.

I understand that this order must be accepted by you and I have no obligation to buy anything, no salesman will call, and I can return the complete outfit at the end of two weeks, at your expense, no questions asked. In either case, any movies I take are mine to keep.

_____nature _____(Please write plainly)_____
_____ress

_____ Zip Code
_____ode) Home Phone No.

We'd like to know more.

Please send us more complete information on the equipment checked.
☐ Table Top Collator Model _____
☐ Semi-Automatic Collator Model _____
☐ Automatic Collator Model _____
☐ Auto Sorter Model _____
☐ Automatic Stitcher
☐ Automatic Stapler
☐ Booklet Stapler-Folder
☐ Booklet Stitcher-Folder
☐ Electric Paper Jogger
☐ Folding/Inserting Machine
☐ Postage Meters
☐ Addresser-Printer
☐ Tickometer
☐ Copier
☐ Mailing Scale

☐ Without obligation, I would like to see a demonstration in my office.
☐ Please have your local office supply price information.

_____ title
name _____
firm name _____
street address _____ state _____ zip _____
city _____

THIS KEY CAN OPEN THE DOOR

To A Storehouse Of Ideas
Summon your man from Omega and get involved with the idea people. Remove the token card below and paste it on the spot of your choice. FILL IN THE CARD AND MAIL TODAY.

Name _____
Company _____
Title _____
Address _____
City _____
Telephon... _____

Burns has an answe...

Send for free information that may save your comp...
thousands of dollars.

☐ Guards, Special Services —crowd control, usherettes
☐ Electronic security —burglary, fire
☐ Investigation and undercover services
☐ Insurance investigatio...
☐ Computer security
☐ Burns security analysis
☐ Please have representative call

Name _____
Company _____
Address _____

RESERVATION FORM

THE DARTNELL CORPORATION
4660 Ravenswood Avenue, Chicago, Illinois 60640

Please send us your full-color "Think Win" film on the plan checked below, along with Sales Campaign Package of exciting meeting aids.

☐ **PLAN 1—EXECUTIVE PREVIEW** Send on 10-day preview basis for screening by our executives, and bill us only $20.00 for the preview. We understand this may be applied against the purchase or rental price if we decide to use the film within 60 days of our preview.

☐ **PLAN 2—RENTAL FOR** _____ (date) Send the film in plenty of time for this meeting date. Bill us at $1.00 per person per showing with a minimum charge of $75.00 per showing, plus postage and handling.

☐ **PLAN 3—PURCHASE ON APPROVAL** Send on 10-day approval basis, and bill us $365.00 plus postage and handling. We understand film may be returned for full credit if it does not more than fill the bill, in which case we will pay only the $20 preview charge.

Name _____ Title _____
Company _____
Address _____
City _____ State _____ Zip _____

Reply cards take many forms and range from matter-of-fact styles to more complete, imaginative content. They should not be casually treated because they often supply the final push to lead-producing action.

FOLLOW-UP THIS SACONY CUSTOMER

Here's a potential sale. The card below is addressed
to a really interested customer who took the time to
write us asking where to buy Sacony fashions. We've
already given her your store name, but she's much
more likely to come in if you send her this personal
invitation.

Sacony

SIGN, TEAR OFF AND MAIL THE CARD BELOW, TODAY!

we invite you to see
the new Sacony fashions
you asked about at:

Lord & Taylor

Fifth Avenue

New York, N.Y.

*Mrs. John Bates,
1 East 70th St
New York, N.Y*

*Form used by one national advertiser in referring consumer inquiries to dealers. It
not only provides dealer with data on the inquiry, but serves to impress upon him
the extent of the advertising support he is getting from the manufacturer. Previously, this advertiser had used a questionnaire type of form, which had a place
to check the source of the inquiry, the publication in which the advertising was
seen, and other information. Experience with the form indicated that a shorter,
simpler method of passing along inquiries was just as effective, and saved considerable work in the advertising department.*

Regularity of Appeal

A series of mailing features of timely interest, such as blotters carrying monthly calendars, for example, or snappy testimonials, often serve to stimulate interest and make inquiries easier to get.

Teaser Features

Mail an attention-getter to stimulate curiosity a day or so in advance of main appeal. In one case two post cards reproducing news items were mailed in advance of the announcement of new styles. Successful use has also been made of "stunt" letters, unusual in size or striking in color.

Fictitious Personality

When used with tact and discretion, this often brings results where straight selling tactics fail. Jim Henry, Mennen salesman, can put over arguments and make direct appeals which would sound offensive if signed by an officer of the company. A fictitious character of this sort can freely indulge in humor, sarcasm, and good-natured "kidding"—powerful weapons, at times, but generally dangerous over a sales manager's signature.

Using Old Customers to Get Leads

One never-failing method for getting new business is to capitalize the good will of old customers. In the insurance field salesmen are trained to do this themselves, and it has been estimated that more than half the new business written every year is the result of leads passed along to a salesman by a friendly policyholder. This idea has been carried even further in some of the high-priced equipment fields, such as automobiles and household appliances, where "Booster Clubs" are organized among present users, and a definite program set up to make it worth while for them to put salesmen in touch with friends and others considering purchasing a new car, refrigerator, radio, or whatever it might be.

The Automobile "Sales Associates" Plan

Several automobile companies have used owners as "bird dogs." Each salesman is urged to build up a sales organization of his own, composed of 10 owners. A book detailing the plan, selling the salesman first of all on the general idea, and then giving him concrete suggestions for training associates, serves as the backbone of the campaign. The book, in this case, carried the load for the salesman. The plan follows:

1. You are privileged to choose and appoint not more than ten "Sales Associates"—men or women who, because of the nature of their occupations or

CHAPTER III

SECURING LEADS AND PROSPECTS

SUGGESTED ACTION	METHOD UNDERSTOOD	PERFORMANCE (Effective)
Plan the Survey of Physical Prospects in your territory	☐	20%....40%....60%....80%....100%
Master the various Classifications of Human Prospects	☐	20%....40%....60%....80%....100%
LEARN HOW TO USE THE FOUR GUILD PROSPECT CARDS	☐	20%....40%....60%....80%....100%
Assist your manager in securing a maximum number of Interested Prospects	☐	20%....40%....60%....80%....100%
DEVELOP THE CUSTOMER LEDGER PLAN IN YOUR TERRITORY	☐	20%....40%....60%....80%....100%
DEVELOP THE PLANNED CANVASSING PROGRAM IN YOUR TERRITORY	☐	20%....40%....60%....80%....100%
Conduct neighborhood canvass around every job you sell	☐	20%....40%....60%....80%....100%
Make observational surveys turn into sales	☐	20%....40%....60%....80%....100%
Secure leads from your satisfied customers	☐	20%....40%....60%....80%....100%
ENLIST THE COOPERATION OF CONTRACTORS, ARCHITECTS, AND REALTORS	☐	20%....40%....60%....80%....100%
Ask each prospect for a prospect	☐	20%....40%....60%....80%....100%
Plan your procedure for following fire, flood and storm losses	☐	20%....40%....60%....80%....100%
Capitalize on the Property Transfers in your territory	☐	20%....40%....60%....80%....100%
Develop the art of reciprocal sales relations	☐	20%....40%....60%....80%....100%
Make your friends and acquaintances your boosters	☐	20%....40%....60%....80%....100%
PLOT THE FOLLOW-THROUGH ON YOUR PROSPECT WORK	☐	20%....40%....60%....80%....100%

A step-by-step program for helping agents to get more and better leads used by an insurance company. Note provision on the plan sheet for agent to rate himself on performance as well as understanding of each particular step in the proposed plan.

their locations, will be able to put you in touch with as many prospective car buyers as possible.

2. These "Sales Associates" are to be paid, within twenty-four hours, whenever a sale results from their aid or information. The following rate of payment is recommended:

(The schedule of compensation cannot be shown here. It began at $7.50 for any used car valued at $200 or more,

and $10.00 for the lowest priced car in the company's line.
The compensation for the highest priced car was $25.00.)

Compensation is to be paid only upon actual deliveries of cars to persons whose names have not been previously filed and canvassed within thirty days. You must make every effort to convince your sales associates of your good faith in this respect—arrange to let them see your actual records of prospect cards showing the exact dates of your contacts with each prospect.

(Amounts are recommended for this reason: If they are made higher, it is often difficult to make the sale because the margin of profit becomes too narrow, while if the amounts are reduced to any considerable extent, the whole proposition becomes less interesting to your sales associates, and you will not get any real cooperation from them.)

3. The compensation to your sales associates will be guaranteed in writing by the house, and actually paid out by the house, but will be prorated or split between yourself and the house, the house paying one-half and you paying one-half.

This system has a big advantage. Since the commissions are pledged by the house instead of by the individual salesman, your sales associate is bound to feel more secure and is far more likely to work harder.

4. The best kinds of sales associates are to be found among the following:

Storage Garages
Repair Garages
Tire Companies
Oil and Gasoline Stations
Apartment House Janitors
Salesmen of Lower-Priced Cars
Employees of Beauty Parlors and Barber Shops
Telephone Operators in Apartment Hotels
Laundry Wagon Drivers
Chain Store Managers

These are just suggestions—use your own judgment bearing in mind that what you are after is the type of person who gets a chance to meet car owners and to overhear car discussions.

5. In order that the sales associates shall have, in writing, a definite pledge over a responsible signature, assuring them that the agreed commissions will be promptly paid you should see that the following letter is sent by the dealer or distributor, to each of your new sales associates:

Dear Sir:

Mr. Blank, sales representative of this company, told me this morning that you are willing to act as a Sales Associate on the basis of the plan that he explained to you.

The Etaion Shrdlu Sales Company of Blankville hereby agrees to pay you for furnishing the name and information regarding any prospect for a new car or a used automobile valued at $200 or more, provided (1) we are able to sell the prospect such car at retail within thirty days after you register it, (2) and that we have not actually solicited the prospect within thirty days previous to your turning in the name.

Our actual dated records of all such solicitations are open to your inspection at any time, and we pledge you our utmost fairness in this respect under all circumstances.

In every case, the sum due you for furnishing the name and whatever other useful information you can provide will be paid to you either on the day the car is delivered or on the following day.

This agreement may be terminated without previous notice by the Etaion Shrdlu Sales Company of Blankville in case you are unable to maintain reasonable activity. However, if this agreement is terminated you will be paid any amounts that may be then due you for names previously furnished and for such deliveries as may within the next thirty days be made to prospects you have turned in.

I am delighted to welcome you into our happy car family, and I hope and expect that our mutual relations will be both pleasant and profitable.

Sincerely yours,
(Signed)

Accepted:

....

(Signature of Sales Associate)

Merchandise Prizes for Leads

Another manufacturer has organized a "Booster League," the purpose of which is "to intensify and profitably direct the force of owner good will." A part of the program is to get customers to report names of prospects. For each prospect sold the owner is awarded a certificate indicating credits earned and having a wholesale merchandise value of about $5 to $15 depending on the make or model of car sold.

A large building materials dealer in Chicago pays manicurists, barbers, beauty parlor workers, and other people who have opportunities to visit or do business with women for the names of people who may be planning on building new homes or making general repairs.

Employees have friends, many of whom may be in the market for the products you make or sell. These leads when followed up by a salesman often result in sales. To avoid conflicting with the Wages and Hours Act, employees should be allowed to make such contacts on company time, or at least not encouraged to do it on their own time *after* working hours.

A local distributor of refrigerators, ranges, dishwashers, etc., in Buffalo, New York, offers a 2% cash commission to the employees of a large, nationally known organization for information leading to the sale of one of its products within 60 days. Printed slips were prepared for names of prospects and distributed to employees.

Five Dollars in Cash or Merchandise

A refrigerator manufacturer encourages users to send in the names of friends and acquaintances who may be prospects for the company's product. Rewards take the form of either cash or merchandise to the value of $5 for each sale completed with a prospect within 30 days after the name has been submitted by the user. Customers are given a booklet of 10 coupons to be used in sending in names of prospects. Should a check-up show that the prospect has already been approached, the user is so informed and is told that his name is ineligible for a reward if a sale is consummated. Another feature of this reward plan is an accessory merchandise catalog which lists material suitable for merchandise rewards.

Employee Contests

During a period of slow business, household appliance manufacturers rolled up a lot of highly desirable business by offering prizes of their own products to employees who turned in hot leads. All employees were furnished with special blanks, which they made out in duplicate. On these they reported the names of any friends or acquaintances interested in purchasing an electric fan, percolator, waffle iron, mixer, refrigerator, electric range, or any other electrical product. One of these blanks was turned over to the local dealer to follow up and sell; the other was turned over to the salesman calling

Public service companies, both gas and electric, find it profitable to use employees as "bird dogs" for the sales department. Employees turn in leads on slips like this which salesmen follow up. Employee is credited with a certain number of points for each lead closed, the accumulated points are good for merchandise prizes.

upon that dealer to make sure that it was followed up. The same idea has been used by a number of public utility companies to promote sales during an off season. As a rule such drives center upon one particular product which the dealer distributes exclusively in his community. The promotional matter and sometimes the prizes for such a campaign are furnished by the interested manufacturer.

Press Clipping Bureaus

In this way it is possible to receive clippings from papers all over the country which may suggest opportunities for sales. An office building in Omaha burns down; here is a chance for some salesmen and dealers to sell a lot of new office equipment, loose-leaf books, stationery, etc. Some businessman is promoted in a big industrial concern, dozens of others get a step up and corresponding salary increases. These are prospects for bond salesmen, life insurance salesmen, real-estate agents, photographers, and automobile salesmen.

New Incorporations and Business Expansion

Many trade papers and financial publications contain departments giving this information. It is an excellent plan to send salesmen weekly bulletins giving a digest of all such news (concerning their industry) so that they can in turn pass the tip on to local dealers and distributors.

Systematic Sifting of New Orders

In this way new leads for sales can be opened up. When one salesman finds a new outlet for your product, a letter should at once be dispatched to all salesmen urging them to get after that line of business. This tends to encourage salesmen to go after new avenues of distribution because of the credit they will get. An auto blanket manufacturer has sold enormous quantities of blankets through men's furnishings stores by following this plan.

Cooperation with Salesmen in Related Lines

In almost every line of business there are other products, the sale of which paves the way for selling your line. When a duplicating machine, for instance, is sold, it is a simple matter to sell the same buyer an addressing machine. When a druggist agrees to stock electric razors, it is easy to sell him beard preparations. Some concerns find it profitable to put the salesmen in these related lines on their mailing lists to receive all advertising matter. They find it stimulates better relations, and quite often results in these salesmen putting in a good word for them.

Capitalizing Advertising Good Will

Where a mailing list of either customers or prospects is worked by a concern systematically, it is quite often possible to get many live leads by an appeal for cooperation. A man may not be in the market himself, but will be glad to tell you of someone who is if you ask him in the right way. A good plan to get leads in this way is to publish some sort of helpful booklet, with only an incidental advertising flavor, and mail this out to the list with a tactful letter. Such a plan will invariably bring in a lot of testimonials when worked on a list of old customers. Much of the success of this plan, however, depends on the utility value of the book.

FOLLOWING UP LEADS AND INQUIRIES

Since inquiries, as well as leads, cost the company real money, salesmen should be required to follow them up promptly and report on them regularly until the prospect has been sold. Some opposition to this plan exists, principally among concerns that are not careful as to what kind of inquiries they forward to their salesmen. It is obviously impossible to expect a commission salesman to spend his entire day chasing leads sent to him by the home office, the great majority of which are nothing but curiosity seekers, when he has live prospects of his own to follow up. Yet the fact remains that salesmen operating under a plan where leads, after being sifted, are forwarded to them and definite reports are required, make more money and close a higher percentage of leads than when they are just passed along to the salesmen and forgotten. Sending a salesman a stream of leads keeps him from becoming discouraged. He can usually plan his day's work so that in addition to making the calls he had planned, he can take care of an inquiry or two besides. In that way a definite reduction of sales cost results. But it is important the leads be screened to get out curiosity seekers, who only waste the salesman's valuable time.

National Cash Register Plan

Getting leads effectively followed up is a more acute problem for sales executives under present business conditions than it has ever been, and in many organizations specific plans for checking up the work of salesmen have been developed to ensure prospects being carefully followed up and every effort possible made to turn such interest into new business. An interesting plan that makes a daily check-up on salesmen's efforts is used by some branches of the National Cash Register Company.

This plan is developed around two 3½- by 5-inch cards. One of these is a "master card" and is printed on white stock. The other is known as the "salesman's card" and is printed on blue stock. The master card is a permanent record and remains in the file all of the time. Besides keeping all the information concerning the prospect where it will always be available, it acts as a check in following up the salesman's work with the prospects which the sales manager can use.

As soon as the prospect is located, both cards are completely filled in. In the event he has been discovered by the salesman, which is the usual method, the salesman sees that all of the information he has been able to uncover about the prospect is entered on the blue card. This information is then transferred to the master card by a clerk whose whole duty is to keep the file in order and to see that salesmen follow up prospects promptly. Space has also been allowed on the cards for noting other ways in which the prospect may have been located and this information is shown on the face of both cards.

Each morning the clerk in charge of the prospect file runs through his file and pulls out all of the salesmen's cards for prospects which should be called on that day. These are then placed in a smaller file where salesmen are required to pick up the cards belonging to them each morning after they leave the daily sales conference.

When a salesman makes a call on the prospect, he is required to note the date of his call and the date of the next call in the event he was unable to close with the prospect on the first call. He is also required to report what he did when he called and to explain why he did not get the order. Space for all of the foregoing information is provided on the reverse side of the card.

All salesmen are required to turn in the "salesman's card" as soon after making the prospect call as possible and when the file clerk finds such a card missing from his file, he checks up with the salesman to find out why it has not been returned and to see if the proper information has been entered on it. In this way a daily check-up is made on each salesman in the organization as to his activity with prospects, and this arrangement ensures that prospects will be followed up carefully at the proper time.

Determining the Cost Per Inquiry

When it is desirable to know how much leads cost—particularly leads developed through circularizing large lists—some sort of office record should be kept. The most practical method to do this is to print up some 9- by 12-inch envelopes (see Chapter 38—"Controlling Sales Promotional Expenditures"). This permits keeping a record of returns and costs on the face of the envelope, and copies of the mailing piece, enclosures, etc., may be filed within the envelope.

The importance of a systematic method of developing leads from a carefully selected mailing list is evidenced by the experience of those companies selling equipment direct to the user. In the case of one large office equipment company, more than half of its prewar sales were the result of inquiries or leads developed by the sales promotion department. In addition to turning over this large volume of leads to the sales force, this company was able to close enough leads by mail in open territories not assigned to salesmen to pay the entire cost of operating the department; that is to say, the margin in the selling price for salesmen's commissions was sufficient not only to cover the cost of the mail sales effort, but to carry the cost of operating the sales promotion department as well.

INQUIRIES FROM NATIONAL ADVERTISING

Large national advertisers, as a rule, do not seek or desire inquiries from consumers. While they are interesting as an indication of the "pulling power" of an advertising medium, these advertisers usually sell through dealers who look down their noses at leads. The big packers, for example, are restricted by the Federal Government as to the classes of buyers they can sell. It is a policy of such companies to lean over backwards to avoid giving the impression they sell to consumers. They usually have no established procedure for handling inquiries received from consumers, except to pass them along to a wholesaler. But even that is not as simple as it may seem, because a company whose products are widely distributed and sold might alienate a number of wholesalers in a locality, if he sent a lead to only one of them. A manufacturer selling through exclusive dealers would not, of course, have this problem.

Yet these people who write in to get information about what an advertised product costs and where to buy it locally, offer both a sales promotional and a public relations opportunity. A food company uses a form letter, with a colorful little booklet describing the products it makes, for this purpose. The letter states that the product is sold by "nearly all the better grocers but if you find your grocer does not stock the product, return the card giving the grocer's name and address." The card is then referred to all wholesalers serving grocers in that locality, and usually results in a wholesaler's salesman opening a new account.

Another national advertiser, after finding wholesalers did not thank him for sending inquiries to them, refers the inquiry to the company's public relations department. A suitable booklet about the product and its many household uses is promptly mailed to the inquirer with the suggestion the product can be purchased at the leading food stores, such as Jewel Tea, Kroger, or Atlantic & Pacific. This company contends it pays to make friends of anyone sufficiently interested to spend the time and postage to answer its ads.

A recent check made by a Dartnell staff editor of 35 national advertisers, however, shows that only 10 of them take the time or trouble to even acknowledge inquiries received from magazine advertising. They consider that the cost of handling such inquiries is out of proportion to the sales resulting. What they overlook is the loss of sales occasioned by consumers who feel slighted by not receiving an answer to their letter. They go out of their way to tell their friends about it.

"Operator 25" Dealer Inquiry Service

In cooperation with the Distribution Council of National Advertisers, Inc., a nonprofit organization sponsored by the Association of National Advertisers, the Western Union has developed an inquiry service, whereby advertisers may mention in their national advertisements that the names of local dealers selling the product will be furnished over the telephone by calling Operator 25. The service covers cities where there are independent W.U. facilities. The advertiser using the service furnishes Western Union 3- by 5-inch cards listing its dealers in the cities that it wishes to cover, stating (1) the name of the city, (2) the name of the dealer, (3) the name of the national advertiser, and (4) the name of the advertised product. These cards are sent to the New York headquarters office of Western Union. The basic charge for the service is on an annual contract basis.

This service solves the problem of tying dealers directly into a national promotional campaign. Advertisers who have used the service seem to feel that it is of real help, not only from the standpoint of making it easy for consumers to buy a product, but in making national advertising more important and profitable to the dealer. An executive of the A. H. Pond Company reports the following experience with the use of the service in promoting the sale of "Keepsake Diamond Rings":

Our fall campaign consisted of 55 ads in 16 leading magazines, spearheaded by 6 full-page ads in *Life* magazine—some in full color—the defunct *Post* and *Look* magazines, and 13 others. Now the results that I know you are interested in are as follows:

The total number of calls received in August, the first month, was 352; in September, 312. We know that in those first 2 months there were many test calls, dealers checking to see if they were identified, prospects who had read our trade ads and wanted to see who was being identified in their trading areas. When we reached October, and we feel that October was the average month, we had 373; November, 267; December, 452. I'd like you to keep in mind that a diamond ring is a lifetime purchase. There is possibly one in each household. It is not an item that is purchased frequently, where there are two or three owned by every member of the family. So, on the basis of inquiry possibly these numbers could be multiplied by a hundred times to your local product or the one that you are interested in selling and advertising. But, roughly, these 1,500 to 2,000 inquiries were very important to us. That number of diamond rings would run into a good share of money.

The next important result was the new dealers. We know that we opened many new dealers on the basis of this plan. We had a strong increase in mail orders this fall season. It was indicated to us as a result of this program, because our dealers ordered by advertised set names and not by code numbers that they usually order by. This was an indication to us that the public had been demanding our product by the trade name.

The fourth result was that dealers have frequently written to us that they made sales as a direct result of calls to "Operator 25." Therefore, we have realized an increase of business as a result of the Operator 25 program and this demand by the public for our brand name has increased the value of our franchise in the minds of dealers.

Follow-Up to the Customer Only

For small companies or organizations with no direct control over their eventual point-of-sale outlets, it is difficult if not impossible to stimulate aggressive follow-up by the dealer organization, and it becomes necessary to depend upon the initiative of the customer.

The S. and Z. Manufacturing Company, maker of women's undergarments, invites inquiries by offering a color selector which shows the colors in which its slips are made and also contains small swatches of the materials used. These inquiries are not referred to the dealers, but when the company sends the booklet to the consumer it encloses a letter giving the name of the nearest dealer.

An ingenious way of cutting down the home office's work in assigning such inquiries to dealers is employed by The American Fluresit Company. The acknowledgement letter invites a second, more detailed letter after receipt of the initial inquiry. The prospect is asked to fill in and return a form attached to the letter. His doing so is pretty good proof of genuine interest.

In addition, the form asks the customer to give the name and address of his dealer. If the prospect is already on buying terms with one retailer, he will probably go there first no matter what the company suggests. Secondly, paper work in the home office can be substantially reduced if the inquirers who know their dealers can be pulled from the general group before further checking. In the third place, the charge of possible favoritism by the manufacturer in assigning prospects can be avoided. Finally, the percentage of inquirers who already know their dealers offers an interesting check on the effectiveness of the company's distribution pattern and on the effectiveness of local tie-in advertising.

Mail Follow-Up to Customer and Dealer

Most smaller companies not only send an acknowledgment to the prospect, but use some method of getting the prospect's name to the nearest retailer as well. Among the organizations which do this primarily by mail is the Charis Corporation. An officer of the company commented:

> In our national magazine advertising we offer a free copy of a style booklet. The customer receives a copy of the booklet and a form letter acknowledging her request and giving the name of the nearest distributor. A copy of the inquiry itself is sent to the Charis distributor in that particular territory, together with another form letter.
>
> The company as a general rule does not follow up to see what the dealer has done about inquiries. Until now, the only record we have kept has been of the total number of inquiries received from each magazine.
>
> Our zone department is now starting to use an interesting follow-up system. It is a book called "Record of Inquiries." This offers, we believe, a thorough follow-up.

The "Record of Inquiries" is a book containing numbered reply post cards. In the front of each book is a sheet with columns headed "Source, Prospect's Name and Address, Phone, Date Issued, Deadline for Return, Corsetiere, and Results." This end sheet, which is on the same heavy stock as the post cards, thus becomes a complete history of each inquiry listed in the book.

A maker of women's dresses uses a similar technique. In response to an inquiry the prospect receives a booklet with a hand-written personal note across the cover addressing her by name and listing the dealers in her area—a much more human approach than the usual form letter, and probably no more expensive to handle. In addition, all the nonexclusive dealers in the area receive a follow-up form giving essential information about the prospect.

This organization has made double use of its advertising inquiries by an adaptable device. The promotional booklet sent to the prospect bears this note on the front page:

> Here is your "Folio of Fall Fashions" . . . actual photographs of the latest Sacony fashions as featured in *Vogue, Harper's Bazaar, Good Housekeeping, Mademoiselle, Charm,* and *Glamour.* If you would like forthcoming issues of *Sacony Fashion Folios,* please write us—Sacony, 328 E. 42nd St., New York 17, New York.

Although most of the products discussed in this study are of a type which can expect repeat sales, only a few of the manufacturers indicated that any attempt was made to build a permanent list from inquiries for mail advertising.

Follow-Up by Company Salesmen

Instead of attempting to check on use of leads by the dealers by mail, some companies place the chief responsibility for checking upon their own salesmen. This is done in the hard goods field by the St. Charles Manufacturing Company. Inquiries are sent to those dealers who request them, and who agree to follow them up. In order to make the distribution efficiently and also as a means of ensuring the dealer's active cooperation, each dealer is required to submit an alphabetical list of the communities he serves and for which he wishes the names of inquirers. When dealers have a definite program for following these leads they get excellent results. Other dealers, either because they already have more prospects than they can handle or for lack of the necessary staffs, do not consistently follow up these leads.

Companies with branch offices or a chain of wholesale distributors ordinarily have the assignment of inquiries to individual dealers done at the branch or distributor level. This is the method followed by Libbey-Owens-Ford Glass Company and The Glidden Company, for instance. An interesting point was brought out by T. H. Turney, advertising manager at Glidden:

> In general, we do about what other companies do: Advertising invites the request for a booklet, and the names of inquirers are passed down through the organization to the nearest dealer. The booklet suggests that the consumer consult the dealer to get help in filling out a Color Recommendation Questionnaire. When this form is sent to us, an individual color scheme is worked out by our decorators for the prospect.
>
> Because we do go one step farther than most and offer this service, we are in personal communication with many of our customers. It is a matter of pride with us that all these letters receive individual response. Most of the replies I write myself.
>
> This has given us a great deal of good will. I am thinking of one woman in particular with whom I have been corresponding for years. Her husband's work has required them to move several times, and she has carried our story to her friends in each new community. Multiply this by several hundred cases and the result is the best kind of advertising.

Another company which makes a point of getting individual customer reactions is Evinrude Motors. Inquiries are sent to the nearest dealer; the purchaser gets a registration card with his motor. When this is filled in and sent to the factory, a warranty certificate is issued. A second letter is sent 6 weeks later—a friendly note, asking how the motor is behaving.

Rating the Value of Inquiries

One way to reduce the number of curiosity seekers, or worthless inquiries, is to charge for advertising pieces.

> "Our national advertising invites inquiries," said one sales manager, "but we also ask that the inquirer send us 10 cents to cover part of the cost of the book which we send and the mailing expenses.
>
> "We have followed this procedure for the past 2 years. Previously we had offered our literature without charge, and still earlier we had used coupons in our advertisements, but we were obliged to discontinue both those practices in order to eliminate the more casual inquiries and produce response from those definitely interested in our product."

On the other hand, the experience of Libbey-Owens-Ford may be cited. Current advertising contains a buried offer of two booklets, one of which is sent without charge and the other is sent for a dime. The company reports: "Offering a free booklet or charging for it has made no difference in our volume of response."

Most sales promotion men agree, however, that a buried offer —that is, a booklet offered in the body of the copy and without any coupon—seems to produce a higher quality of inquiries. At least the prospect who replies to such an offer has been sufficiently interested to read the whole ad.

Another rating technique is to reply to the initial inquiry in such a way that the interested prospect can get further information by doing a little work himself. This is the technique described by The American Fluresit Company and The Glidden Company. It is also used by Minneapolis-Honeywell Regulator Company, according to William B. Walrath, Jr., advertising manager: "We did attempt during the war to rate inquiries by including a post card with the booklet sent out. These cards included space for the person making the inquiry to give us information as to the type of home and heating system he had, or information about his intentions in building. We thought it safe to assume that anybody making a second inquiry in this way was a particularly good prospect, and as soon as we were in a position to supply the equipment we forwarded these cards to our branches for allocation to the dealers."

Present thinking in regard to advertising inquiries is in agreement on the following points:

1. The inquirer should receive a prompt response, offering a specific reason for visiting the dealership to get further help.

2. A copy of the inquiry should go to the nearest dealer, and to the salesman or wholesaler's salesman who will follow up.

3. In most cases the quality of leads can be improved by burying the offer in the copy and by charging a nominal mailing fee.

4. Annual study of results from a cross section of inquiries can lead to valuable suggestions for improving sales promotion.

Telephone Selling Through Automatic Systems

Obtaining leads by telephone is a long-established sales technique, successfully used by salesmen in all industries. In recent years, semi-automated systems have allowed a recorded message to be played once the potential customer gets on the line, allowing the telephone solicitor free to dial again.

Equipment has now become even more sophisticated, with machines capable of dialing thousands of telephone numbers without human assistance. Automatic dialing machines may be programmed to dial through every number in a selected telephone exchange.

Consumer resistance to the new system, already labelled "junk telephone calls," has been such as to arouse Congressional and FCC interest in controlling or restricting its usage. In fact, as reported by the National Retail Merchants Association, the FCC is looking into the problem created by unsolicited commercial telephone calls, whether by automatic dialers or those initiated by human dialers.

Chapter 7

SALES PROMOTIONAL LETTERS

LETTERS, the mainstay of business, deserve far more attention and recognition of their importance than they normally receive. Every letter may be judged according to its content and appearance, but as so many secretaries can testify, appearance is sometimes rated more highly than what the letter says and how.

Every letter that goes out on the company's letterhead should be a sales letter. Either it should sell goods or it should sell good will.

That is why the standards of correspondence in any business are so important. The letter is the most useful tool in the modern sales promotion manager's tool kit, for it enables him to multiply his contacts with customers and prospective customers a thousandfold. Even businesses which regard their sales force as all-important could hardly operate without letters. The right kind of letters paves the way for the salesman, and enables the management to communicate overnight with the selling organization, including dealers and distributors. They provide a means of contacting and selling customers in out-of-the-way places where salesmen cannot profitably call. Yet, in spite of their importance to business, the majority of the business letters are colorless, drab, and ineffective. They are cluttered up with foggy ideas, useless words, and platitudes. They are stuffy, high-hat, and talk *at* people rather than talking *with* them. Where friendliness and good humor are so important, they are curt and tactless, giving one the impression whoever wrote them was carried away by his own importance.

Considering the thousands of letters which are written and mailed every month by even moderate-sized business establishments, it is unfortunate that so few companies make any systematic effort to take advantage of the opportunity their letters offer, to make friends for the business. What could be more profitable from a sales promotional and public relations angle than to have each letter, even if only a "thank you" from the credit department for a prompt remittance, carry a friendly handclasp and show appreciation for a mutually beneficial business relationship. It costs no more to write, type, and mail a friendly letter than it costs for one which leaves the recipient cold. And it is of selfish concern to the sales promotion department to do what it can to make the letters sent out by all departments, no matter how trivial the purpose, be sales letters. At least they can sell good will.

Letters to Salesmen

Most important of all letters sent out by the sales promotion department are those to salesmen. The nature of the salesman's work and the need of maintaining his morale in the face of great discouragements require that any letter addressed to him should be

---

Dear Jim:

Did it ever occur to you that June is the biggest month in the year for promises? If you don't agree with me, think of the thousands of June brides who promise at least to love and honor--if not obey--this month!

Somehow or other, this business of promising seems to get into the air during June. You promise yourself that you are going to get into some real fishing or that you are going to cut at least ten strokes from your game this summer. The people you call on are promising themselves that it's going to be the seashore, the country, or Pike's Peak or bust before the summer is over. They get into the habit of promising so deeply that they commence to "promise" orders.

Just the other day, I overheard a buyer telling a salesman, "Yes, sir, I am not going to do anything until later, after I come back from the cottage at the lake. But, I can PROMISE that you will get the business." The buyer was full of good intentions, but the salesman did not get an order.

You know the old saying that "Hell is paved with good intentions." Maybe that's why our summers seem to be getting hotter!

The point is this: The extent to which we fulfill our promises depends upon the sincerity with which we make them and the effort we put forth to carry them out. While you are in the mood for promising, let me suggest that you promise yourself the best summer's business you have ever written, and then strive to keep that promise.

The June bride makes a promise for life. I am only asking you for a 3 months' promise. Think it over and then sit down and write on the back of this letter what you are going to promise yourself in sales during the next 3 months.

I am going to expect you to keep your promise, too.

Sincerely,

A letter to a salesman who is long on intentions, but short on execution.

Scott Paper Company has developed special promotional letterheads for each of its major product lines. The letterheads are lively and attractive, with large four-color illustrations of the individual product being featured.

morale-building. Too often some thoughtless person in the office becomes exasperated with a salesman, and writes an ill-tempered letter which throws him off his "feed" for days. What such letters cost a company in lost business cannot be estimated. But they do untold damage. While there are situations which make it necessary to reprimand salesmen in writing, usually that can better be done when the salesman comes into the office. If it must be done by letter, the letter should be written by his sales manager *and no one else.*

Another bad practice is writing general letters which imply the recipient of the letter is loafing on the job. The salesman is urged to "pull up his socks" and get twice as much business next week just to prove that he can do it. Such letters may go over all right during a sales contest where it is to the salesman's interest to put forth an extra effort in order to win, but they are sour as a steady diet. Merely telling a salesman that the company expects him to do his duty only suggests to him that whoever wrote the letter thinks he is not doing it. The letter should be constructive, appreciative, and hopeful—without slopping over.

The principal objection to the use of personalized general letters is that anything said in the letter is likely to be construed by the salesman to whom it is addressed as a "crack" at him. Some sales executives, for example, use letters of this type to tell about the nice business certain salesmen sent in during the week. In a general broadcast such items would not do any harm and may do considerable good. But if used in a personal letter, those salesmen who have tried their best without succeeding immediately jump to the conclusion that the sales manager is telling them about the other fellow in order to put them to shame. As a rule it is poor policy to do or say anything in a letter to a salesman which will break down a man's self-respect and self-confidence.

A recent survey made by the Sales Managers' Club of Boston to find out what salesmen wanted from their sales manager put appreciation high on the list. The feeling was general that too many sales managers are too prone to criticize a man for what he failed to do; too slow to recognize what he did well. Some sales managers refrain from too much back-patting on the grounds that it gives salesmen swelled heads. That is sometimes the case. However, there is a way of patting a man on the back, so that he will feel his good work is appreciated without causing him to feel that he has arrived.

Backing Up the Salesman

Most salesmen, rightly or wrongly, feel that their work is not appreciated and that they are not getting the support they should be getting from the house. They secretly resent the fact that most of the letters they receive from the office imply, even if they do not come out and say so, that they are not doing their part. But, they ask, what about the company? Is it doing its part to back me up? A salesman traveling out of Monroe City, Missouri, wrote as follows, to the editor of this HANDBOOK: "I have read many of your books and articles on selling and must say they are very good. But no matter how good a salesman is or how well he does his work, if his company does not back him up it is hopeless for him to try to build up his territory. It will surely slip away from him. For example:

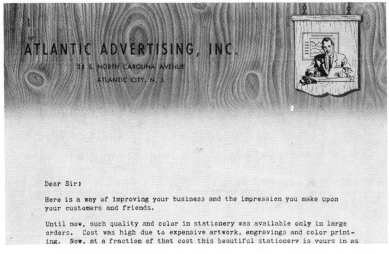

> Dear Sir:
>
> Here is a way of improving your business and the impression you make upon your customers and friends.
>
> Until now, such quality and color in stationery was available only in large orders. Cost was high due to expensive artwork, engravings and color printing. Now, at a fraction of that cost this beautiful stationery is yours in as

Illustrated two-color stock-letterheads are provided by a number of suppliers. Here, Atlantic Advertising uses its own product as the first page of a four-page folder showing the variety of designs available.

"In a territory where the salesman contacts his customers every 6 to 8 weeks, he calls on a merchant and the first thing the merchant throws at him is something that has transpired with the home office but which the salesman knows nothing about. Why is it that so many companies treat their salesmen like outsiders? Why don't they send them copies of letters written to customers? Why don't they do something to keep customers warm between calls? Why don't they do their part, as well as needle us to do ours? Why don't you write a book needling the sales manager for a change?"

It is easy for anyone who has sold goods on the road to understand this salesman's point of view. Some salesmen are truly the forgotten men of business. But it is not so much that they are forgotten, as it is that nobody at the home office takes the time or the trouble to write them an occasional letter telling them what is being done to back them up and make their job easier. Most of the things which a company does to back up its salesmen—such as good products, right prices, strong advertising, sound policies, etc.—are taken for granted by the salesmen. The smart sales manager or sales promotion man finds a way to make these taken-for-granted activities take on real importance in the eyes of the salesmen. The letters sent out to the field from the sales department deftly discuss projects and activities which directly or indirectly back up the salesman and make it easier for him to sell. Take such a small matter as sending out letters or cards to pave the way for a salesman's call. After a year or so, the salesman accepts this kind of help as routine. He, perhaps, never considers what it costs, or how much it would mean to him sales-wise if the practice was discontinued. But just stop it and see what happens!

In the same way, sales promotions which a company undertakes to stimulate sales at certain seasons of the year, or to tie in with special weeks or occasions, all too soon are taken for granted. They are just something the sales promotion department does to make money for the company. Salesmen are apt to over-look that in making money for the company the promotion makes money for them, because it makes their job easier. This fact needs to be stressed in writing salesmen regarding the company's sales promotional program.

Because of the sensitiveness of salesmen to criticism, and the danger of sooner or later saying or implying something that will throw them off their feed, most experienced promotion men prefer to intersperse the dictated letters sent to salesmen with obviously general bulletins which are frankly broadcasts. It gives them an opportunity to say things that will be of a somewhat critical nature without hurting anyone's feelings.

There are many other ways that friendly, constructive letters can be used to build sales by building salesmen. Among these are the following:

1. Educate prospective customers as to the value of goods, and pave the way for the call of the salesman.

2. Secure new inquiries, which may be turned over to the salesmen for individual, personal effort.

3. Notify customer of approaching call of salesman in such a way as to break down sales resistance.

TO ALL DISTRIBUTORS:

A lot of talking has been done for years about "Seasonal slump" in the refrigeration equipment business. So much talk and thought has been given to it that it has become in many organizations an accepted fact. Salesmen have been sold on it. They believe it. What is more regrettable--they practice it.

I have "doctored" the subject of this bulletin to indicate what I think it is. It is salesmen's slump. Of course, the food merchant may be harder to sell but that is where real salesmanship comes into worth-while play. During the winter months the merchant is making money and during the holiday season he is doing more business which should put him in a receptive frame of mind for new or replacement equipment.

He is at the turning point where he can look back over his last summer's business and correct weaknesses in the way he conducted his enterprise and get set for doing a better job next year.

Have you told him how he can invest in capital goods and not only have a better looking, more efficiently run business but can actually save money next year by so operating--also that he'll make a tax saving? Try it! Most of them will listen-- and act!

Then, too, how about selling the entire Sherer line? Send your salesmen out to call on all the bakeries in your territory. Not only will they sell Retardos but you'll be agreeably surprised at the prospects they'll turn up on regular coolers, combination and freezer coolers and reach-ins.

Here's another one to try. Send the boys out to call on florists. Here again you will be floored by the number and variety of good sales and sales leads.

Cold canvassed all the drug stores in your territory lately? No seasonal slump here. It's the time for striking pay dirt on reach-ins and coolers.

Now what brought all this up in the first place? One of our salesmen inquired if it would be okay for him to take Thanksgiving week off. The usual talk occurred--"There isn't anything doing during Thanksgiving week anyway." Before I thought it all out I had AGREED! But it's the bunk! I can tell from the number of interested prospects dropping in at the factory. Also our incoming coupons answering national advertising DO NOT DROP OFF. So if your organization is experiencing seasonal salesmen's slump, go to work on them. Now there's equipment for you. Money in your pocket. More money for the sales force. Get yours while the going is good.

Sincerely yours,

Distributors welcome constructive letters giving them sales ideas which they can pass along to their salesmen. Above is a good letter of this type.

4. Remind salesmen to send in items for the sales bulletin, which effort will not only help the manufacturer and please the customer but incidentally aid other salesmen.

5. Coach salesmen on the proper extending of credit, so that there may be no doubt as to how far they may go in this direction.

6. Help salesmen make collections.

7. Follow up the call of the salesman, expressing appreciation of order, and so on.

8. Keep customers satisfied and happy in between the calls of salesmen.

9. Follow up old customers who failed to buy at the time the salesman called.

10. Follow up prospective customers who failed to buy when called on by the salesman.

11. Keep in touch with people or firms who were once customers but who have not bought for a long time, trying to find out why they have not bought, so as to overcome whatever obstacle may be in the way of a continuance of business relations.

12. Getting from successful customers experiences and expressions which may be used in letters to prospective users or as suggestions to less successful customers.

13. Work on customers who are buying less than they once did, and make suggestions as to the disposition of goods, and so on.

14. Explain special offers, unusual opportunities, etc., to the trade, making it easier for the salesman to get action when he calls.

15. Inject new life into discouraged salesmen.

16. Explain to salesmen about contests, prizes, etc.

17. Keep salesmen informed as to what is being done in their territories to help them, letting them know that the house is supporting them and ready to help wherever opportunity affords.

Letters to Distributors

Keep in mind when writing promotional letters to wholesalers and others who distribute your product that they are in business to make a profit, and there *may* be a way to make a bigger profit than by pushing your line to the exclusion of competitive lines. Of course, that is not true in the case of exclusive distributors—those who handle only your line—but it is amazing how many sales promotion men seem to think every distributor is "dead from the neck up" just because he is not continually pushing the sale of their product. Nothing will so neutralize interest in a manufacturer's line as letters which even mildly suggest a man doesn't know his business, or that you know it better than he does. He may not value his connection with your company nearly as much as you think he does. This is especially true since the sellers' market came to an end.

As in personal selling, salesmen and sales letters are most welcome when they come to grips with a problem which at the moment is uppermost in the mind of the recipient. These are called "live nerve" contacts. For example, conditions might have taken a turn and sent the distributor's sales force into a tailspin—perhaps a sudden fear on the part of customers that prices are going to drop. Such a situation calls for a factual letter from the wholesaler's suppliers, and you need have no fear the letters won't be read with interest. Or it might be a seasonal slump. That is a headache for many distributors.

Letters to Distributors' Salesmen

Even though the distributor's salesman is not on the company payroll, he is very much a part of the company's sales organization. In fact, he might easily be the bottleneck in the company's sales operation. This is especially true in the case of a company which distributes almost entirely through wholesalers, and depends upon the wholesaler to push its products. The problem is complicated by the fact that the average wholesale salesman sells a thousand or more items, usually from a catalog or price list, and so far as he is concerned your products are just one more item in his line. But if there are good reasons why the wholesaler and his salesmen should push your products, perhaps in preference to competitive products, it is good sales strategy to find some way to keep those reasons before them. Writing them friendly, helpful, and factual letters may not be the best way to do this, but it is an easy and usually an effective method when the company cannot afford more elaborate promotions.

The type of letters which best motivate distributors' salesmen are those which aim to help the salesman improve his sales opportunities and make more money for himself and his company. Some of the most effective letters which manufacturers have sent out to wholesale salesmen have not mentioned the product in the letter. The theory is that anything a manufacturer does to help the wholesaler's salesman to greater success helps the wholesaler to operate more successfully, and thus he helps himself. It is not possible to write a salesman friendly letters about problems which bother him, without the salesman appreciating the lift. The name on the letterhead, the signature at the bottom of the letter, the occasional enclosures which accompany the letter all remind him of the company and the product it makes. He is bound to develop a friendly feeling for the company, and its products, and by the same token he is bound to reflect that kindly feeling in his conversations with customers.

A paper manufacturer selling an advertised line of book papers through jobbers, exclusive and otherwise, found that something more than trade-paper advertising was needed to get the volume required to operate the mill at a profit. This was before the war when paper had to be sold in a tough competitive market. So the sales manager for the mill hit upon the idea of employing a man who had been a top-flight paper salesman, but who had recently retired, to do a fortnightly letter built around his experience as a book paper salesman. The idea was to bombard salesmen selling book paper to printers and publishers with selling suggestions, advice, and counsel. The only mention to be made of the mill brands which the company sought to promote was on the letterhead.

At first glance this indirect approach might seem like taking the long way home. But wholesalers are not inclined, as a rule, to get excited about giving out lists of their salesmen to manufacturers. In the first place, they prefer that communications clear through them. In the second place, they have their own ideas as to what brands of book paper they wish their salesmen to push. They probably have private brands which they like to think return a greater profit. Then, too, being human they harbor the suspicion that if they give out a list of their salesmen there is always a possibility it will fall into the hands of competitors who will promptly try to hire their men away by offering a better "deal." But the wholesaler, no matter what he distributes, has the problem of keeping his salesmen on their toes. He knows only too well that most of his salesmen are order takers. Few of them are doing a really creative selling job. But those who are using creative methods are getting more business. So, naturally, he is receptive to any plan or proposal which will help him to correct bad work habits in his sales organization, raise sights, and build the men into hard-hitting business getters. He has to decide between his natural reluctance to give out the names and addresses of his salesmen, and his desire to increase the stability and earnings of the business.

In the case cited, when the paper manufacturer explained that the letters he proposed to send out would be purely educational, and not "plug" either the company, or its brands excepting as they might be listed on the letterhead, the wholesaler could hardly turn down an opportunity to give his salesmen such practical help. Of course, the fact that the mill was well and favorably known to the wholesaler, who valued the franchise and hesitated to appear noncooperative, was also a factor. But at any rate, this mill was able to get 100% of its wholesalers to cooperate, and the "Letters from an Old Paper Salesman to His Friends" went over with a bang. It was one of the most effective promotions the mill ever undertook. And the idea is just as good today as it was then.

This case is cited to impress upon sales promotion men, who are bubbling over with enthusiasm for the products they are promoting, that in preparing letters for mailing to distributors' salesmen, too much shouting about the product's virtues and the house's reputation is unwise. This is especially true when left-handed jabs are taken at competitors whose lines may be distributed by the same wholesalers. The letters that ring the bell with distributors' salesmen are those which strive first to help them to be better salesmen, and second to sell more of a product or service.

Letters to Dealers

An examination of nearly 100 letters from manufacturers received by a hardware merchant in a suburban community, saved for the editors of this HANDBOOK, shows 70% of them misfired. Only 30 letters out of the entire bunch were set aside by the merchant as being of sufficient interest or appeal to do anything about. The rest would have found their way into the furnace.

The most common fault in these letters was that they were too general. They did not get to first base, for to reach busy dealers, who like to "size up" incoming mail by the corner card on the envelope, the opening paragraph is all-important. If the letter doesn't come to the point quickly, and touch upon a problem close to the merchant's pocketbook, its chances of escaping the wastepaper basket are slim indeed. But, on the other hand, if it hits the merchant "where he lives" and talks *his* language, it has a mighty good chance of being answered. At least it will get favorable consideration. Even though a dealer gets a lot of mail, and a lot of long-winded letters from those who seek to sell him something, he is still eager for suggestions which help him make money or expand his influence in the community.

There are dealers and dealers. But by and large they are not moved by general statements about the merit or selling qualities of a product. They discount such statements as "self-pleading." Merchants are more interested in what other merchants have done with a product, and how they did it, than they are in what a manufacturer thinks about his own product. Merchants, perhaps more than most people with whom the sales promotion department deals, are profit-minded. It is not unusual to see a merchant go through his mail and read only the return card or order blank enclosed with a letter. He figures that he can get the profit information he wants more quickly that way and not have to read through what he calls a lot of "sales talk." Another fault in many letters is they talk too big, use too many $10 words and superlatives. It is better to understate your case than to overstate it.

Dealers want their facts straight and they want them simple. An advertising manager connected with a large manufacturer once said: "I was, until a few years ago, a retail merchant in a small town. I believe that a great deal of the appeal to the small-town dealer misses the mark because the letter is cluttered up with advertising jargon that the small merchant just doesn't understand, or if he does understand it, it fails to impress him. 'Distribution,' 'localized circulation,' 'broadsides,' 'consumer acceptance,' may impress the promotion man who wrote the letter, but they leave the merchant on Main Street cold." In the same way letters that preach, patronize, and assume that the merchant is not a smart operator are certain to find their way into the yawning wastepaper basket.

A study of letters used in promoting sales for a large manufacturer shows the wide application of letters in modern sales management and suggests ways in which you could use personalized letters more effectively in your own sales promotional activities:

1. To Reduce Resistance to Salesmen
   (a) Letter developing new prospective customers.
   (b) Letter to precede call of salesman.
   (c) Letter acknowledging initial order to salesman—to customer.
   (d) Letter to prospective customer who did not buy.
   (e) Letter to prospective customer who promised to buy later.
   (f) Follow up to both "d" and "e" prospects.
   (g) Letter to customer by salesman back in house.

2. To Increase Sales to Present Customers
   (a) Letter to trial customer to head off complaint.
   (b) Letter to old customer who is buying spasmodically.
   (c) Letter to old customer who had stopped buying.
   (d) Letter to customer regarding special offers.
   (e) Letter to old customers soliciting full line orders.
   (f) Letter inviting old customers "to come to market."

3. To Stimulate Mail Orders
   (a) Letter to "open territory" prospects about to start in business.
   (b) Letter in answer to requests for catalog.
   (c) Letter following up catalog emphasizing specials.
   (d) Letter to nonresponsive inquiries requesting return of catalog.
   (e) Letter to eliminate deadwood in mailing list.

4. To Ensure Use of Dealer Helps

    (a) Letter asking for "dealer help" suggestions.
    (b) Letter soliciting dealer's active cooperation.
    (c) Letter acknowledging dealer help requests.
    (d) Letter suggesting new ideas for dealer helps.

In the handling of correspondence of this type it is generally wise to use automatic typewriters. The letters are cut on paper rolls in the same manner as player piano rolls. After cutting, the rolls are filed, and when several letters of one kind have accumulated, the roll for that particular letter is placed in the machine. The machine automatically stops, whenever desired, at any place in the letter so that the operator can insert amounts, names of companies, or other subject matter.

Letters to Customers

An interesting success story is presented by the summer mailings to customers of Kozak Auto Drywash, Incorporated, Batavia, New York, manufacturers of Kozak Drywash Cloths, Kozak's Helper Washdry Cloths and Lady Kozak "furniture facial." The letter is in the form of a four-page folder in two colors, with an unusual sequence. Page 1 features the offer of the Drywash Cloth at $6.00. Page 2 is devoted to a discussion of the origins and processing of sheepskins to produce chamois; page 3 continues the letter with a presentation of the advantages of Kozak's Helper. Page 4 makes the final bid for the order and at the bottom are four testimonials from satisfied users.

States Marion W. Harding, Kozak executive: "Kozak customers were never 'mailed' during the summer months. The original summer letter (G 12) was written and mailed in 1968. It worked. It also won an award in the National Association of Direct Mail Writers Contest, presented at a luncheon meeting at the Advertising Club in New York. It was later revised by our letter G 64.

"Last year, we asked a consultant to write a customer letter (G 63) which we tested against our revised summer letter and G 63 out-pulled beautifully."

Mrs. Harding summarized the results as follows:

Letter Number	Mailings (Over 6 Months)	Orders Received	Result (per Thousand)
G 64	15,736	345	$157
	21,212	408	135
G 63	16,549	531	$233
	21,798	575	190

The company was so pleased with results that revised versions of the letter were later sent to volume buyers, funeral directors and Christmas customers.

Letters to Prospects

Merrill Lynch, Pierce, Fenner & Smith Inc., uses at least four different sales promotion letters in its quest for prospective customers. Three get right to the point with a question and end with an offer of free service. The different questions in each letter are, respectively: "Do you really know how to read a financial report?" "Would you like to know which stocks Merrill Lynch analysts recommend for current purchase?" "Would you like to know what the world's leading brokerage firm thinks are good investments for you?" The fourth letter starts immediately with the free offer: "I'd like to offer you a free Merrill Lynch service: a research opinion about any stock you're especially interested in or concerned about." An inquiry form and postage-paid envelope are enclosed with each letter.

FOLLOW-UP LETTERS

Present-day selling, except in the case of products sold on a one-call basis, resembles a siege. The salesman first has to investigate and build his plan. Then he has to decide just what plan of attack to follow, and how much effort he will have to spend on that account. No thinking salesman today follows the "once in a while" method of calling for business. He goes after it systematically, deliberately, and keeps after it with the utmost intelligent perseverance. The same should be true of mail follow-up work. The sales problem should be carefully considered: (1) As regards the product and the margin of profit available for mail work, and (2) as regards the market and the opportunity to dispose of a sufficient volume to make the campaign pay. There are, of course, different factors in every business that must be considered, but the following will apply to most lines of industry:

1. MARGIN OF PROFIT: Cost to manufacturer, plus fixed overhead (omitting sales cost) deducted from selling price. Use average unit of sale for computing this item.

2. REPEAT QUALITIES: How often will the product repeat (or supply business) during the average life of an account? Use average figures. Multiply margin of profit on initial sale by repeat profit to arrive at a gross profit per account placed on books.

3. GOOD-WILL VALUE OF NEW ACCOUNTS: Determine roughly the extra business that will result through the establishment of additional good-will units. These figures may be secured by making an analysis of increased volume in any typical territory where number of new accounts has been materially increased over preceding year. Add to gross profit per account.

When you have decided just how much you can afford to spend to make a sale, the next step is to decide on the range of the campaign, always keeping in mind that in direct-mail work the larger the mailing the smaller the cost per sale. In other words, after the cost of preparing and creating the mailing pieces has been absorbed, you only have presswork and paper to add on to every additional thousand pieces you send out. A campaign that will pay on one thousand names can be made to pay equally well on ten thousand names, if the names are of equal quality. Proceed as follows in analyzing your proposition to determine the size of your mailings for a given campaign:

1. NUMBER OF KNOWN BUYERS: Compiled from counts furnished by market surveys, list houses, directories, your mail lists, rating books, census figures, etc.

2. NUMBER OF BUYERS ALREADY SOLD: Deduct from known buyers an amount equal to the number which have already bought or are using your product. Figures from your own sales records.

3. NUMBER OF UNDESIRABLE BUYERS: Concerns or individuals who would be unable to purchase and pay for product; accounts located in inaccessible territory, etc.

4. NUMBER OF BUYERS SOLD BY COMPETITION: Use production of competitors as a basis, multiplying by the time they have been in business, and such other factors as life of product, etc.

5. NUMBER OF POSSIBLE BUYERS: Found by deducting items 2, 3, and 4 from the number of known buyers. These names should be classified according to sales appeal. If sales appeal is geographical, classify geographically—if vocations differ, classify by vocations.

The following are good types of mailing pieces which can be produced at a very nominal cost and have been found to be especially effective:

LARGE BROADSIDE: Gives utmost display at lowest cost of printing, as all the type matter is printed at once. Especially valuable when it is desired to literally sweep away doubt by hurling a great array of facts at the buyer at one time. When folded will go through the mails without envelope. Best to use color in a mailing piece of this kind.

FOUR-PAGE ILLUSTRATED LETTER: Gets the letter and the descriptive matter to the prospective customer together. Most effective when the letter on first page is multigraphed on, and the letter carefully filled in and personally signed. In using this type of mailing piece much depends on the illustrated qualities of the inside spread, which should be in color.

SELF-ADDRESSED REPLY CARD MAILERS: There are several forms of these

CENTRAL INFORMATION BUREAU
WALL STREET STATION, BOX 333
NEW YORK, NEW YORK 10005

MERRILL LYNCH, PIERCE, FENNER & SMITH INC

Dear Mr._____

Do you really know how to read a financial report?

Not everyone does. But to the experienced investor,
a company's financial report is a revealing window on
that company's inner workings. And worth.

Especially in today's market, you as an investor
need all the facts you can get about companies you
might invest in. So we've written a useful 24-page
booklet called HOW TO READ A FINANCIAL REPORT. I'd
like to send you a free copy of it.

The booklet explains in clear and simple language
how to interpret the facts and figures in a financial
report with a view to determining not only the company's basic soundness, but its future growth possibilities and the attractiveness of its securities.

Among other things, you'll learn about the net book
value of securities, leverage, capitalization ratios,
price/earnings ratio, and cash flow. Sound complicated? Not after you read the booklet.

To get your free copy of HOW TO READ A FINANCIAL
REPORT, just return the enclosed reply card. Why
not do it today?

                              Sincerely,

                              J. F. Bardsley, Jr.
                              Director
                              Central Information Bureau
          JFB/PD

*To build its list of qualified prospects, Merrill Lynch, Pierce, Fenner & Smith
offers a free booklet of special interest to investors.*

mailers; some are cut with a slot so that the address which is typewritten on the return card also serves as an address on the mailer itself. Some of these cards are patented, but there are many which cannot be protected. A good piece to use where reply cards are essential, as all the prospect has to do is to O.K. the card and toss it into an outgoing mail basket.

SINGLE PAGE ILLUSTRATED LETTER: Used in place of the ordinary company letterhead in order to provide a change of dress. It is generally unwise to use the same letterhead more than once in any given campaign. Prospects too often pass on the contents of a letter as soon as their eyes rest on the letterhead, the design of which can be remembered more easily than the text.

STAMPED GOVERNMENT POSTCARDS: A very valuable part of a direct-mail campaign too often overlooked. Can be used effectively in many ways. The most economical advertising piece to produce, as the stock is furnished free by the government and the stamp is affixed. Also has the advantage of going first class.

One sales manager suggests the following letter ideas:

LETTER NO. 1: This presumably is the letter in which you will outline your proposition so that it may be accepted or rejected. There is no need of using a "strategic" letterhead for it. The ordinary house letterhead will do, only be sure that it is dignified and of the kind which will establish confidence—the prime requisite in every sale.

LETTER NO. 2: For this letterhead I would use something which would show the product in use. It would be of the single page illustrated variety. A touch of color will add materially to its pulling power, and the name should be subordinated to the product.

LETTER NO. 3: In the next of the series get away entirely from the usual. A very effective third follow-up can be made by reproducing a clipping on the letterhead. Make an ordinary zinc etching of the clipping, and then print the zinc over a faint greenish gray tint that resembles newsprint paper. Draw a pin on the copy when the engraving is made so that when it is printed it will look as though the clipping has been pinned to the letterhead. Don't use any name whatever on this letterhead. Put the company name and address under the signature at the foot of the letter.

LETTER NO. 4: If you have sent a man three letters without getting a rise out of him it is plain you have to resort to strategy. So I would make the next letter something radical. Quite often I use a strip of cartoons across the top, which sympathizes with the recipient. The letterhead: "Movie of a Sales Manager Opening His Morning Mail" is a good example. This stunt at least gets you a favorable consideration, and if your opening paragraph is good, you have a fairly good opportunity to sell your man.

LETTER NO. 5: As this will be the final letter in the series, I would make it a personal message from the head of the house to the recipient asking him to tell you personally why he has not shown any interest in the proposition. Make it clear that you feel your advertising manager has been at fault for not properly explaining the proposition, and asking the man if he won't write you confidentially his opinion of the letters. This letter should be individually typed, and a high-grade engraved letterhead carrying the president's name used. This plan has been found highly effective.

A well-planned follow-up should eradicate common objections to

OLD AMERICAN INSURANCE COMPANY
4900 OAK STREET • KANSAS CITY, MISSOURI 64141

YOU MIGHT CALL THIS
A "NIGHT LETTER"...

... because we are really in the dark.

But you can shed some light on the subject by letting
us know whether you actually wanted your OLD
AMERICAN policy to lapse.

Whenever anyone lets a policy lapse, as yours just did,
it's a cause for great concern to us because it may mean
we have disappointed you in some way.

But it's entirely possible that you have just been too
busy to attend to the matter of renewing your Old
American policy.

So if that is the case, you can remedy it in a hurry by
mailing the enclosed reinstatement form right away.

Then -- just as soon as your reinstatement application
is received and approved -- your lapsed policy will be
put back into effect.

Won't you mail the form TODAY?

Sincerely,

Joseph J. McGee

Joseph J. McGee
President

JM:bl
Enc: L613

A truly striking and attention-getting letter from Old American Insurance Company. The black background carries out the opening theme: "You might call this a night letter" ... because we are really in the dark.

the proposition, covering only one point at a time. Suppose that you were planning a follow-up for some kind of duplicating machine. The first thing to do would be to arrange your follow-up by vocational applications, as we know that the prospect is interested in what a product will do for him, rather than in the machine itself. If our follow-up is to go to banks we will want to use a different appeal and a different series of letters, than if they go to laundries. The next thing to do is to find out what the main objections are in each line of business. Before planning the follow-up for banks find out the main objections the banks have to buying duplicating machines. One of the great, if not the greatest, troubles with sales letter writing today is downright laziness. It is also true of most salesmen today. They just won't do any preliminary work.

Making the Letter Seem Important

Letters intended to get action from businessmen need some unusual touch to make them stand out in the day's mail, to get them read and acted upon. Yet this must be done without resorting to stunts which are likely to make a businessman say "how clever" rather than "maybe I ought to do it." Because names are usually meaningful to businessmen it is possible, for example, to have several different people sign the letter. Another device is to send the letter, which may be two pages or more long, with a short covering letter from someone well and favorably known to the recipient. It should be personally typed, calling attention to the importance of the letter. This technique is successfully used by Junior Achievement, Inc., in soliciting funds. It can be used in many ways.

Common Faults in Letters

"Most of the letters that I see, and my observation covers about 40 years of office experience," said one business executive, "fall into one of four classes:

"The puzzle letter which is a challenge to the reader; the letter that is not clear but is reasonably understandable; the letter that is clear; and the letter that is good because it transmits the thought of the writer to the reader. Roughly, the first class accounts for 10% of the letters; the second and third classes for 40% each; and the fourth class not over 5 %.

"If any one studies the incoming and outgoing mail in an office of reasonable size, I think he will agree that there are four reasons why good letters do not constitute a larger percentage of the total mail.

"The first and most common offense is haste in reading and signing one's mail. If you go through almost any office just before closing time, you will see people hurriedly glancing through their mail and signing it, and you will see, at the same time, some mail being signed by clerks who did not dictate it and know little about the subject matter. I contend that there is no way that a person can improve his mail more quickly than by reading each letter carefully before he signs it, and discovering his own weaknesses. In the majority of cases there is no necessity of rewriting the letter. It can be allowed to go out as it is, but a caution can be set up in the writer's mind to avoid a repetition of some particular fault in future mail.

"Another cause of weakness in letters is the lack of clearly defined thought at the time of writing. The evidence of this in many letters is a wandering or a shifting of position instead of a direct path from the opening to the closing, and this weakness tends to make letters longer and less concise—and, by the way, a writer should distinguish between brevity and conciseness.

"A third cause for poor letters is interruptions. A man who is interrupted, especially if he is writing a long letter, loses the continuity of his thoughts. Related to this are diverting thoughts; many things pass through a man's mind when he is dictating, entirely foreign to the subject matter of the letter. Similar also in its effect is preoccupation because a man has found it necessary to interrupt some absorbing piece of work long enough to answer his morning mail. A somewhat different fault, but annoying to the reader, is the grammatical error. Errors of this type are surprisingly common, and they invariably take the reader's mind off the subject matter of the letter, and induce speculation as to the type of man who wrote the letter.

"The fourth cause of poor letters, like the first, is one that I have never seen mentioned and yet it is a serious fault. There is no name for it but laziness. Frequently when a man is writing, the word that he knows he ought to use, and the word that will express his meaning exactly, flits through his mind without registering; he misses it and knows that he has missed it, but is too lazy or too indifferent to hunt for it, so he uses some other word, with a slightly different meaning and perhaps an entirely different connotation, and lets it go because it is good enough."

Letterhead Content and Form

Except for color and size, why are letterheads so much alike? Also, with rare exceptions, why do they reveal so little, if anything, of the company's products or services? These questions bring to mind the old precept that if another company's signature may be readily subsituted at the bottom of an advertisement without affecting the message and its relationships, it is not doing an effective job and is not a good advertisement.

The Taylor Instrument Division of Sybron Corporation uses a letterhead with an imprint at the top reading:

Temperature Last 24 Hours
Max.   Min.
68   34

Since they change every day, the degrees of temperature were typed in. This innovative touch ties in with the company's products which include thermometers and barometers of all kinds.

Another letter, short and to the point, from the Sta-Rite Products Company, is of interest because printed at the bottom are a brief user-instruction section and a separate order coupon, all on a 6" by 9" letterhead, making full and effective use of the available space.

The 3M Company adds a pleasant tone to its letterhead by using a circle at the bottom enclosing the phrase "Have a good day." It not only makes the letterhead more distinctive than the usual run-of-the-mill letterhead, but gives it a more personal touch.

Production of Form Letters

Sales-promotion letters produced in quantity, popularly—though incorrectly—called "form letters," are generally prepared by one or another of the several processes which give the appearance of a typed communication. The various kinds of equipment used for this purpose are described in detail in Chapter 41 of this HANDBOOK, "Sales Promotion Equipment."

The most recent development in this field is the computer-programmed letter, in which the individual name is not only typed at the beginning of the letter but may also be inserted in the body of the letter.

In many of the systems of reproduction, the letter is typed through a ribbon, as on a conventional typewriter. Best results in processing

---

A. B. DICK COMPANY

The best designed business form
is no good to anyone unless it's
where it is wanted, when it is wanted

Ross-Martin Company of Tulsa, discussed in the enclosed Case History, built its business on that premise. It maintains finished inventories of business forms for its customers in eight warehouses around the country.

But it does not bill for those forms until they are delivered, and it maintains an "ever normal" inventory of the forms its customers need.

This unusual business, serving customers all over the country, is based on forms research for prospects – forms surveys that may take as long as six months before any recommendations are made. The drive is always to simplify, which in one case resulted in the elimination of over 18,000 different forms.

Much of Ross-Martin's forms printing is done on five A. B. Dick offset duplicators – four Model 360's and one Model 385. More than 500 jobs a week are scheduled on these machines with the aid of an efficient production control system that reduces lost time to a minimum.

Obviously this progressive firm has mastered the problem of keeping its equipment and employees busy at all times – and the savings benefit not only Ross-Martin but all of its customers as well. Part of the plan is dependable offset machines, A. B. Dick equipment, producing perfect work 24 hours a day, five to six days a week.

May we send you more information about these reliable A. B. Dick offset presses? Check the enclosed card and it will be sent at once. Or, if you would like to see them in operation that can easily be arranged.

Naturally there is no obligation. Explaining the advantages of A. B. Dick equipment is always a pleasure.

Sincerely,

V. R. Anderson

V. R. Anderson
for
A. B. Dick Company

AB·DICK.

COPYING/DUPLICATING PRODUCTS   A.B. DICK COMPANY • 5700 TOUHY AVENUE • CHICAGO, ILLINOIS 60648   71-152 (7)

In a national direct mail campaign, A. B. Dick Company sent out a total of 500,000 letters in one week to eleven different markets. Each mailing included a reply card and a case history appropriate to each specific field. Shown is the letter mailed to companies in the business-forms printing industry.

with such systems as Multigraph can be obtained when an inking attachment is used constantly to re-ink the ribbon (which is held stationary over the type form) rather than using a moving ribbon, which becomes lighter and lighter as it is used. Variation of color makes it difficult to match first and second sheets and to match fill-ins if they are required. The secret of getting nicely matched fill-ins is to use a typewriter ribbon of the right color and change ribbons as frequently as necessary to maintain the match. For best color control of fill-ins use electric typewriters, adjusting the touch to suit the color of the letter.

It is a great help, when processing form letters which are to be filled in by a typist, to place a *low* period at the point on the left-hand margin where the first line of the address should be filled in. This saves the typist having to realign the letter after locating the first line of the letter. The period used for this purpose must be taken down so that it just "kisses" the paper, leaving a very faint spot. This is covered up by the inside address. To save addressing envelopes, filled-in letters can be used with window envelopes and thus be made to do double duty.

The use of filled-in letters is diminishing. Many sales promotion men find that they can get equally good results with a caption to flag attention. Few people are fooled by fill-ins unless they are expertly done. In the larger cities there are letter shops which use special presses for producing letters to be filled in. The typewriter ribbons are cut from the same press ribbon. While letters produced in this way are relatively expensive, the work compares favorably with letters produced on automatic typewriters, except that changes in the body of the letter are not feasible. The most effective form letters, of course, are those which are individually written on automatic typewriters. These are operated in batteries of four, manned by one operator. It is not profitable to use a single automatic typewriter for promotional letters. It is less expensive to send them out to be processed.

TESTS FOR A SALES LETTER

By Cameron McPherson

How do the letters sent out over the signature of your company rate as media for promoting sales and good will? Just as every member of a business organization is ex officio a member of the sales promotion department, so every letter, regardless of its purpose, should aim to create acceptance for the policies and products of the company.

STA-RITE PRODUCTS CO.
P. O. BOX 1949. G. P. O.
NEW YORK. N. Y. 10001

Dear Customer:

It has been over a year since you last ordered our STA-RITE Temple Holders. For best results they should be replaced every three or four months.

If you want to continue to get the correct results from your glasses, don't delay, use the order form below for quick delivery.

Glasses that slip and slide cannot fulfill the purpose for which they were intended. Order your STA-RITE Temple Holders NOW.

- -

$1.00 $1.00

STA-RITE
TEMPLE HOLDERS

Renews tension

Restores that snug fit

Slide snugger over temple
piece until it fits
over hinge and pin

STA-RITE
TEMPLE HOLDERS

Mail this order blank with $1.00 check or money order enclosed and we pay postage.

For Two or more, 69c packs
(3 pair per pack)

No. of Packs at 2 packs for $1.00 net

No. (..........packs) $........./ ....Enclosed.

Your Name ....

Address ....

City .... Zone .... State..............

STA-RITE PRODUCTS CO.
P.O. Box 1949, N. Y., N. Y. 10001
U.S.A.

Here is a letter which, although printed on a small-size letterhead, serves a three-fold purpose: follow-up of an old customer, instructions for the user and a coupon for reordering the product.

1. Are Your Letters Neatly Typed and Easy to Read?

Is the letter set up with wide margins? or is it crowded up on the letterhead with too much white space at bottom? Is the type clean, sharp, and in good alignment? Are the paragraphs short? Remember that first impressions are lasting.

2. Do Your Replies Cover All the Points Raised?

It is a good idea to mark or number all the references in a letter which require answering, so that in your hurry to get through your dictation none will be overlooked. Nothing is more disastrous to good will than the careless handling of requests for specific information.

3. Are Your Letters Free from Vague Terms?

Study Emerson and Theodore Roosevelt and note their simplicity of thought and directness of statement. Note that they use short, concise sentences. They use a new sentence to express each new thought, and don't try to crowd three or four ideas into one sentence. What you are saying may be very clear *in your own mind,* but will the recipient see the same picture?

4. Do Your Letters Come to the Point Quickly?

The opening and reading of mail is making more and more demands on your customer's time. He is in an impatient mood when he reaches your letter. So come to the point quickly. Keep on the main track. Don't take your customer on needless side excursions. Say what you have to say, in a friendly, good-humored way, and sit down.

5. Are Your Letters Free from Hackneyed Phrases?

Are you still "begging to advise," "wishing to state," and "hoping to hear" in your letters? You don't *talk* that way, so why write that way? Endeavor to be yourself in your letters and studiously avoid these threadbare and moss-covered mean-nothings which mar so many business letters. They waste your time, the time of the person who has to transcribe your letters, and the time of the customer.

6. Are Your Letters Cheery or Coldly Commercial?

In your desire to be concise be careful not to give a "curt" tone

AMERICAN *Fly Away* SERVICE
Inc.

DAYTON MUNICIPAL AIRPORT
P. O. BOX 1, VANDALIA, OHIO
PHONE DAYTON: MO 4621

Roll 'em. .You can't lose.

We call these gallopin' dominoes "American" dice, because .no matter how
long you use 'em...you can't lose.

They're "naturals" ... and 100% dependable.

American Fly Away Service is as dependable as these dice, too   And, because
it takes the entire problem of plane delivery off your shoulders,

You can't lose

Frankly, you can lose your shirt - or at least your profits - with some
methods of delivery. No matter what price you quote your customer, personal delivery might cost you much more, especially in winter weather
And no matter what an amateur or "jitney" pilot quotes, "casual" delivery
might cost you plenty   Either way, your profits are subject to chance

It's only when your price is guaranteed by a reliable, responsible, careful
company which has your investment covered 100% that..

You can't lose

It's not immodest to say, "That's American" For our price is guaranteed
exactly as quoted...it's complete .it's good for all 12 months..
and you're covered 100%.

There's no "gamble" when you use American   Like these dependable little
dice, no matter how long you use 'em,

                                        You can't lose,

                                        Leon W. Wilder
                                        Leon W. Wilder
lww/gs   President

*Small dice were enclosed in a cellophane envelope and stapled to this letter. They
served as a "peg" on which the letter was "hung" and dramatized the "You can't
lose" theme of the letter. Salesmen were enthusiastic about this letter, reporting
that most dealers carried the dice in their pockets. Useful "gadgets" have long
played an important role in getting letters read and stimulating interest in product
uses. They are likely to backfire, however, if they are too clever.*

to your letter. No matter what your position may be, whether you are the general manager of the business or only one of many stenographers, you are here to serve.

7. Have Superlatives Been Toned Down?

Are you working "best" and "very" overtime? Are you using such expressions as "made from the very best materials obtainable" instead of stating specifically the materials used? Are you using adjectives that have lost their effectiveness?

8. Do Your Letters Anticipate Further Questions?

A really good correspondent puts himself in the place of the man with whom he is corresponding. He not only gives the information for which the man asks, but any other information which he thinks the man needs to reach a decision.

9. Do You Appeal to the Recipient's Self-Interest?

There is always a temptation to talk about what we are doing, what we hope to do, and what we have done. We think everyone is interested in our problems, our troubles, our distractions. Forget yourself. Think about the man to whom you are writing. He is not interested in you.

10. Do Your Letters Create Confidence and Ring True?

It is a real knack to be able to make the recipient feel that here is a man who is telling him unvarnished facts, and not painting a beautiful picture of something that does not exist. To do this, be careful not to overemphasize; impress without seeking to impress.

11. Do Your Letters Ask for Specific Action?

We write business letters to get business. Sometimes we write them to get orders; sometimes we write them to get information; sometimes we write them to give information; but always to build our business. We can get more business if we close every letter with a specific request for action. If you want an order ask for it. If you want a reply ask for it.

Letterheads and Envelopes

It is always a puzzle as to why more companies do not use their letterheads and envelopes to advertise or promote their products and services. With the millions of business letters in the mails every day, they could be a valuable promotional medium, at very little extra cost. Probably, some company managements feel that it would be a less-than-dignified practice for their organizations, but the fact is that their products or services are the "raison d'etre" for their business, regardless of all other considerations.

Why should the reverse side of an envelope be absolutely blank? TWA, for instance, uses it to display a chart showing its world-wide flights, with emphasis on domestic connections. In fact, even on the front of the envelope, it advertises its "New Ambassador Service."

A few companies make a timid approach to the opportunity through the use of their postage imprint machines, but this is not a very satisfactory utilization.

Promotion managers who wish to capitalize every means of "selling" their company products, could well begin by exploring and developing all the internal applications so readily available to them.

Uses for Letters in Building Business

SUPPLIER RELATIONS

A good supplier usually is your best potential customer—give him an opportunity to reciprocate.

Your suppliers have friends. Many of them need your products and would buy them from you if urged by your supplier.

Do you periodically "sell" your suppliers on your square deal buying policy, so that they will value your business all the more and serve you all the better?

Treat your suppliers, in your letters, as you would like to have them treat you if your positions were reversed.

Some day there will be a merchandise shortage when it will pay to be on your suppliers' blue list—the time to get on it is NOW.

CUSTOMER RELATIONS

A satisfied customer is your best advertisement—a 100% letter will keep him a booster for you.

When you get a new customer make a fuss over him—a 100% letter will make him feel he has found a friend.

Your front yard is full of uncovered opportunities for getting more business—100% letters will find them for you.

DAVID K. HOROWITZ STUDIO
920-22 CHESTNUT STREET, PHILADELPHIA 19107

WA 5-3600

Gentlemen:

"The world is moving so fast these days that the man who says it can't be done is generally interupted by someone doing it."

We're doers!

At Horowitz Studios we're completing photographic assignments ... that "couldn't be done".

We shoot, process, and deliver the "toughies" - everyday.

Perhaps it's because we don't scare easily?

When you have the photo talent Horowitz has - all under one roof - it's easier to do-the-job (on time) than be impressed by the complexity and challenge.

We specialize in ... photography at your place or ours, tough or easy, products or people.

Horowitz & team, can also supply design, copy, composition, mechanicals and printing - on a project management basis. We'll take catalogs, bro- chures, and reports from concept through completion. One source for all- of-your photographic and sales promotion needs.

Challenge us! We'll show you how we can help sell product or service.

Call WA5 - 3600 today - or complete and mail the enclosed card.

Very truly yours,

Wayne S. Spilove

Wayne S. Spilove
DAVID K. HOROWITZ STUDIOS

This sales letter has a forceful theme and stresses that the company can do "jobs that can't be done." The easy-to-read copy moves smoothly to the request for a phone call.

205

Everyone has a different idea about your company and your policies—good letters will correct any misconceptions.

Some customers and prospective customers cannot be sold economically by salesmen—give letters that job.

Keep feeding your customers new ideas for using your product or service so that they will be able and glad to buy.

It costs money for a salesman to sell a buyer who never heard of you before—letters will break down that resistance.

80% of your customers buy only 30% of their requirements from you—go after the other 70% with 100% letters.

Your present customers have friends—the right kind of letters will get their names so you can sell them too.

The best salesmen and the best territories get sinking spells—100% letters will pick them up.

Your customers are continually exposed to your competitor's sales lures—use more letters between your salesmen's calls.

A sale is not completed until the product moves out of your dealer's store—letters to his customers may help.

When a customer pays his account promptly, write him a letter—give him a reputation for being prompt pay and he'll try to live up to it.

GENERAL LETTERS

Before you start to dictate, do you underscore points in the letter you are answering to make sure you will not overlook any?

Do you strike at the heart of the proposition; or do you hem and haw, and beg to state, before you really get going?

Do you write differently than you talk? Are your letters natural and easy, or are they stilted and dull?

Is your tone simple and frank, or do you talk AT people? It's much better to talk WITH them.

When there is an objection to be overcome, do you use the "yes-but" technique, or do you contradict?

Does your letter reflect self-esteem or does it sound apologetic and weak?

Are you considerate of the other fellow's point of view?

Is your letter honest or do you say you are "surprised" and "dumbfounded" and "amazed" when you really are not?

Do you try to be pompous by using big words that few people understand, including perhaps yourself?

Are your sentences short and your paragraphs brief? Avoid getting the "and" habit.

How about the dead phrases—the "beg to advise," the "wish to state," the "instants," and the "ultimos"? Beware of cluttering your letters up with deadwood.

Are there enough "for instances" in your 100% letter to make it interesting and convincing?

Do you anticipate the reader's "so what" attitude with which he reads every letter—yours included?

How about the sequence of your points? Are they orderly and logical or do they hop-skip around?

After you have secured interest and conviction, do you follow through with a request for action?

Does your letter make it easy for the man to do what you want him to do?

How does the letter look? Is it neatly typed on good stationery, or is it just another "one of those things"?

Above all, is it the kind of letter you would like to have somebody write you, were you on the receiving end of the line?

DIRECT SELLING LETTERS

Does the opening paragraph touch a "live" nerve?

Will it shock the casual reader out of his indifference?

Is there a quick appeal to the reader's self-interest?

After awakening interest, does the letter proceed quickly to create desire?

Is the selling strategy simple—does it concentrate on *one* dominant buying motive?

Or, is its effectiveness dulled by attempting to cover too many buying reasons?

Is there sufficient proof to build up confidence in the proposition?

Does the letter show a keen understanding of the buyer's problem?

Has an overuse of superlatives given the letter a boastful or bragging tone?

Does it sound honest, or has a touch of "hokum" crept in to hurt it?

Have you painted the lily? Understatement is usually more effective than overstatement.

How about the price? If it might seem high, have you handled it as a matter of values?

Is the offer clear-cut and straightforward? Assume the buyer is honest until he is proved otherwise.

Finally, does it tell the reader exactly what you wish him to do?

And does it make it easy for him to order?

FAIRCHILD 221 FAIRCHILD AVENUE, PLAINVIEW, L.I., N.Y. 11803 · 516 WE 8-9601 · TWX: 516 433-9151 · CABLE: FAIRGRAF-PLAINVIEW, N.Y.

INDUSTRIAL PRODUCTS
A DIVISION OF FAIRCHILD CAMERA
AND INSTRUMENT CORPORATION

                                        RE: Fairchild AV 400 Continuous
                                             8mm Film Projector

Dear Sir:

Thank you for your recent inquiry for information concerning the Fairchild
AV 400 continuous 8mm film projector. Technical specifications, literature
and price information are enclosed for your inspection.

Fairchild's AV 400 stands foremost and alone in the fields of sales aids,
message communication and continuous film display systems. It operates
dependably for thousands of cycles without appreciable film wear. It weighs
only seventeen pounds, takes up less than two square feet (wide open) and
shows up to 20 minutes worth of color sound film. Fully transistorized, it
requires no warm up, utilizes a continuous loop cartridge and never has to
be rewound. With the 400, the need for darkened rooms, bulky projection
equipment and trained operators is eliminated.

Since its introduction in 1961, the AV 400 projector has set the standard for
the field. Industrial firms by the hundreds have entered the film market and
supplied their salesmen, distributors, dealers and showrooms with this unit.
Schools, churches, and agencies have accepted this perfect way to get across
their message conveniently, quickly, orally and visually.

I have also included information describing the MoviePak system with the
Mark IV rear screen projector and the Mark V front screen projector. These
units provide completely automatic projection and are indispensable when the
projection of several films may be required. Changing film with the MoviePak
is simpler than changing a phonograph record.

Fairchild maintains a nationwide staff-service capability and franchised
service dealers are established in most major metropolitan centers. We
would welcome the opportunity to discuss your plans with you and look forward
to hearing from you again.

                    Sincerely,

                    FAIRCHILD CAMERA & INSTRUMENT CORP.

                    Nat C. Myers, Jr., Director
                    Communications Products & Services

*When a prospect writes for information about a product, he is not familiar with
related products in the manufacturer's line. This letter brings them to the
reader's attention. Note the reference to staff representatives and service dealers
waiting to help the customer.*

LETTERS TO THE TRADE

Does your letter put the dealer right up front in the picture, and do it quickly?

Does the cash register begin to jingle before he has finished two paragraphs?

Is the letter written in the dealer's language? Does it show sympathy for his problems?

Dealers are hard to keep hitched—is the tempo of the letter fast enough to hold interest?

Dealers are skeptical of what sellers tell them—do you use concrete cases to prove your points?

Does your letter talk profits, and profits, and then more profits? And do you prove it to him?

Do you show him exactly how he can make a certain profit by doing a certain thing?

Do you talk about profits in amounts rather than in percentages which are hard to visualize?

Does your letter sell the sizzle, rather than the steak?

Can a busy dealer read your letter and get its message in 3 minutes? Four minutes is probably more time than he will give it.

Is your proposition supported with dramatic enclosures based on the "What One Dealer Did" principle?

Do you ask for action without pussyfooting?

And do you make it just as easy as possible for the lazy dealer to say "Yes"?

NEWSLETTERS ARE PRODUCTIVE

Many companies send newsletters to their distributors and dealers. These range from typewritten facsimiles to two-color multipage folders, with elaborate layouts and illustrations.

They are useful for two principal reasons. First, they summarize product announcements, often compensating for sales department failures for prompt communications; and secondly, they serve as a ready-reference source for the dealers. One company found that dealers were referring to newsletters rather than to sales department letters, probably because of filing problems.

Chapter 8

LETTER IMPROVEMENT PROGRAMS

EVERYONE has experienced, at some time or other, the frustration of receiving an unsatisfactory letter. Poorly-written letters penalize a company by losing customers or creating ill-will so management must do two things: (a) exercise greater supervision over correspondence and (b) take steps to establish higher standards of quality through training programs.

Poorly-written letters usually have one or more faults or weaknesses in common. They fail to be effective because they are:

Cold, unsympathetic or even unfriendly;

Curt and excessively brief; unhelpful; stereotyped;

Incomplete; promised enclosures are omitted; no details given when required;

Ungrammatical in construction;

Unconvincing; insincere;

Cliché-ridden;

Unclear; puzzling.

Such letters may be especially damaging to the sales department.

It is not unusual to hear a salesman complain that after working his head off to get some account onto the books, he lost it as a result of some letter written by an unthinking correspondent in the factory. The same is true so far as a company's sales promotional effort is concerned. Thousands of dollars can be spent building up accounts through various promotional methods, only to have the work undone by clumsy letters received by the customers from persons at the home office. They should know better, but they don't.

On the other hand, it would be hard to calculate the hundreds of old friends of the business who placed their first order as a result of a friendly handclasp extended in a business letter. Likewise, the same kind of good-will-building letters, even though they deal with routine matters, can play an important part in holding customers on the books by making them feel more kindly to the company whose name appears on the letterhead.

Opportunities for making friends for the business by well-tuned letters was never greater than they are right now. Which is the reason so many companies are undertaking programs designed to make all those who write letters to customers—and not just sales correspondents—letter-conscious. It is a fact well known to those responsible for public relations that a company develops character just as an individual develops character as he acquires wisdom and experience. A most important factor in giving character to a business is friendly letters—letters a company can be proud to send out, letters a customer will be happy to receive. Such letters can best be developed by a company-wide program for improving correspondence. Such a program will cut down the cost of handling inquiries, reduce the overhead burden of excessive correspondence which inevitably results from badly trained letter writers who do not understand the fundamental principles of good letter writing.

A regular and sustained program for improving letters will hold good will and build up a sound foundation of friendship toward your company to back up the personal and direct-mail sales work. It will constantly show all correspondents how tactless, ill-advised, thoughtless letters may lose customers who have been gained only through years of sales effort.

Finally, a program of this kind will more than pay for itself by teaching your correspondents to organize their work, to turn out a maximum of good letters daily. It will show them how to reduce the length of letters, to save the time of stenographers and typists. It will create more pride in the work of everyone who writes letters. People who are intensely proud of their work and who understand its importance make fewer mistakes, create more ideas, and turn out better work. These are but a few of the most obvious reasons for a systematic better letters program.

Points for Letter-Writers

The best approach to better sales letters, according to specialists in the field, is based on the following points:

1. Preparation: Don't write a single word of copy before you make notes.

2. Organize the notes according to (a) selling points, (b) appeals, (c) possible offers or propositions.

3. The lead should promise the most important benefit offered to the reader. Get to the point as quickly as possible. When he reads

your letter, he wants to know what the "Deal" is. It is highly significant that many people read the reply cards rather than the letters, for quick information.

4. In writing copy, it is often possible to improve it by eliminating the first line and, sometimes, the entire first paragraph! Follow the formula of promising a benefit, tell the reader what he will get, prove your statements, summarize the benefits and induce action.

Sales letters produced in quantity usually receive the attention and professional scrutiny not ordinarily accorded to individually-written everyday letters. Yet all letters, as previously mentioned, sell either product or "good will." Aside from content and sales values, it is interesting to note that the average cost of a business letter, according to the Dartnell Institute of Business Research, was $4.77 in 1978.

Considering the hundreds of letters written every day in a large corporation, this cost factor alone would be good reason for improving their effectiveness and quality.

In the preparation of this HANDBOOK, several hundred letters were received from businesses of all kinds, resulting in two observations. The first is that, unless specifically requested, the marketing, sales or promotion managers of very few companies enclosed so much as a product leaflet. Secondly, promotion or administrative executives of three large package-goods companies wrote negative letters with the excuse that it was "against company policy to reveal information." They did not have the imagination to enclose product literature or photos of counter cards or window displays on public view throughout the United States at its retail outlets. This certainly could have been done without violating the most restrictive company policy.

The First Step in a Better Letters Program

One widely used plan does not call for any formal course of study. Nor does it require a lot of textbooks. It costs next to nothing and *does not* require the use of a trained or skilled letter expert.

It *does* require the attention of the best letter writer in your business. That man may be the president of the company, he may be the sales manager, or the advertising manager. Or, in the case of larger companies, he may be the chief correspondent or the head of the correspondence department. The first step is to put your finger on this man—whoever he may be. This person must, of course, be able to write a good letter. He must be patient, tactful, and courteous by nature. He should be the kind of person who can show another where a mistake has been made without robbing that other person of his or her self-respect and confidence. He should have a natural flair for teaching, if possible.

When you have decided on the man best qualified to criticize the letters now being written by the various members of your departments, call him in and explain that beginning at once he is to receive a carbon copy of every letter written. He is to check these carbons for the most glaring errors, for the most obvious opportunities for improvement. Explain to him that he isn't to worry about an occasional split infinitive or a slight error in grammar. What he is to look for are the curt, snappy, tactless errors in letters that antagonize customers. He is to cull out the letters that are obviously too long, clumsy, or vague.

When you have instructed him how to begin, issue a statement to all members of the staff who write letters. Tell them that they are to furnish this man—the appointed correspondence critic—with a carbon copy of every letter (except those obviously personal or confidential).

The bulletin should state that the critic will be requested to confer with various correspondents from time to time concerning ways and means for improving letters. Make it plain that his word is to be final and that no one, not even a higher executive, should resent the friendly criticism which may be aimed at him after the carbons of his letters are read.

It is vital to a program of this kind that the man in charge of it have the support of the heads of the business. Otherwise, his hands will be tied and the program will soon become an office joke. It is essential that all employees be given to understand that the head of the business himself is taking a keen interest in the program and expects the utmost cooperation from everyone, department heads included.

TO ALL THE MEMBERS OF THE OFFICE STAFF:

On next Monday morning we are going to begin a Program of Correspondence Improvement.

Mr. .... has been appointed Correspondence Supervisor and will have complete charge of the work. I will take a keen personal interest in this work and shall expect the utmost from every member of the staff.

In reading carbon copies of many of the letters we send out, I find many opportunities for improvement. Some of our letters are too long. Others are too curt and brief. Occasionally I find a letter that isn't clear.

Because our letters are the only means many of our customers have of judging us, I am very anxious that every correspondent and member of the office staff join hands with Mr. .... in improving our correspondence to the point where our customers will be favorably impressed by every letter they receive from us--no matter from what department.

To begin this work it will be necessary for every stenographer and typist to make an extra carbon copy of every letter (except personal or confidential letters). These copies are to be given to my secretary, Miss .... for study and criticism.

Mr. ......'s criticisms and suggestions are offered to you with only one purpose--that of helping you make your work more valuable to us. I am sure you will accept his criticism in the spirit in which it is intended.

Don't forget to have an extra carbon copy of every letter you dictate sent to Miss ....

Yours truly,

Second Step—Lay Out a Definite Program

The surest way to kill a program of this kind and to discourage everyone connected with it is trying to do everything at once. Good letter writers are not trained in a day. In laying out a program, take up one step at a time. Just what step to take first will depend largely on the present efficiency of your correspondents and stenographers. If your letters at present are not written after a uniform style or setup, perhaps it will be best to begin with the appearance of your letters.

It is a mistake to assume that just because your staff members are writing letters every day that they know how to write a good letter. Begin the program with the assumption that most of them know comparatively little about letter writing. With this idea in mind start in to teach them how to begin making improvements in their daily task of writing letters.

It is not only necessary to help correspondents improve their letters, but their methods of work also should be studied. Below is a suggested outline of general subjects to be taken up. It is usually best to begin with the form and appearance of letters. However, if your letters are already written according to a standard form and their appearance is satisfactory, this step may be omitted.

We suggest that you lay out your program as follows:

1. Cost-Cutting Correspondence Methods.
2. The Arrangement and Appearance of the Letter.
3. The Construction of the Letter.

4. The Tone and Spirit of the Letter.
5. Opening and Closing Paragraphs.
6. Putting a Sales Slant in Every Letter.
7. Letters to Salesmen.
8. Letter-Writing Opportunities.

To this suggested outline you will want to add several other ideas of your own. You may want to devote some time and thought to House Policies in Correspondence. There may be a dozen or more house policies which have to do with handling various matters which ought to be understood thoroughly by everyone who writes letters. If this is true, by all means make this one of your subjects.

You may find it necessary to divide up your different classes of customers and prepare instructions about writing to them. If this true it would be a good idea to have bulletins on "Writing to Wholesalers," "Letters to Retailers," "When We Write the Consumer," etc.

Other suggestions will occur to you as you develop the program. It may be well to devote some time and instruction to the matter of form letters, methods for using them, and policies with reference to them.

Preparing the Bulletins and Talks

After the announcement of the better letters program has been handed to members of the staff or posted on office bulletin boards, we suggest that you issue a second bulletin or hold your first meeting of correspondents. In this letter or bulletin explain briefly what you expect to accomplish. If you start with Correspondence Methods, tell some of the things that correspondents can do to improve their letters and to speed up their work.

By all means get over the idea that the entire program is one of mutual self-help—not a plan for checking up errors or finding fault with members of the staff. This first meeting or bulletin will often determine the degree of success you will have. Make it plain that no staff member need feel hurt or unduly criticized if his letters are selected for the first criticisms—remind them that all will be criticized in due time.

Let the facts from this talk or bulletin sink in for a few days, then start reading the carbon copies which have accumulated. Select a few of the worst letters containing the most obvious faults and mark the carbons, calling attention to the faults, in personal conference with the offenders.

Confine your first criticisms to the point brought out in the first talk or bulletin. If your first bulletin dealt with appearance and form, confine your criticisms to mistakes in form and appearance. Disregard other faults.

Whoever talks with the correspondents whose letters are first criticized should be careful not to fall into the error of petty faultfinding or bickering. Never, under any circumstances, do or say anything that will rob a man of his confidence or self-respect. If the critic or supervisor is more interested in impressing a correspondent with his superior technical knowledge or his mastery of English than in helping his fellow workers, he will be useless in this program.

Those carbons which show only minor faults should be checked with a blue pencil directing attention to the faults, initialed, and returned to the correspondents. Those which are not corrected or commented on should be thrown away.

The Third Step—Hold Group Meetings

If your organization is small, hold meetings of all correspondents and executives who write letters. If the organization is larger, get together smaller groups whose work and correspondence requirements are similar.

These meetings should be brief and informal. Appoint a leader for each group. The leader should be responsible for attendance and necessary arrangements.

Meetings may be held during the noon hour, for a few minutes after regular working hours, or during office hours. If the meetings are held outside office hours, be sure that everyone comes willingly. Do not "order" employees to attend. Rather "sell" them the idea that the meetings are for their benefit as much as for the company's.

One of the most effective methods of stimulating interest at meetings is to employ one or another of the several sound-slide-films that have been developed on the subject of improving business correspondence.

A number of these are available, but as they go out of date rather rapidly, it would be well to inquire of Dartnell, when and if you wish to consider the use of such films, as to what ones are currently available.

Most companies nowadays are equipped with sound-slidefilm projectors; but in concerns which are too small to warrant the purchase of such machines, projectors are available on a rental basis from photoequipment dealers or other similar distributors.

There are several methods for adding life and interest to the meetings. Ask members of the group to bring letters they are anxious to have analyzed or discussed. Ask them to bring letters which they have revised after suggestions from previous meetings. Suggest that members write letters, then rewrite them and read both copies before the group.

Another good plan to keep up interest is to select a difficult letter that requires considerable judgment, tact, and skill in answering. Select an actual letter from current correspondence if possible. Ask each member of the group to answer this letter and bring it to the following meeting. Then read the various answers, discussing the strength and weakness of each letter.

As the meetings progress you will find an increasing interest in the problems. You will be able to be more critical and delve more deeply into the finer points of letter writing. But for the first few meetings confine the discussions to simple, obvious faults and problems.

Fourth Step—Compile a Manual of Standard Practices

From the meetings you will collect a number of oft-repeated errors—errors in the use of words, mistakes in handling or describing company policies—mistakes in tact, in openings and closings of letters. As you encounter these common faults make a note of them. Before the meetings have been conducted very long you will begin to see the need for compiling a manual which covers some of these common faults and shows how to correct them.

This manual should be more than a stenographer's instruction book. There is, of course, a place in the correspondent's manual for instructions to stenographers, but it should be far more than just a manual of style, spelling, and punctuation.

The nucleus for the manual will be found in the records of the meetings and in the bulletins and talks. To this data may be added collections of words frequently misspelled, words and phrases frequently used erroneously, definitions of technical terms, industrial abbreviations, and other material of use to new employees.

The work of improving letters is never done. Do not think that a brief campaign to improve your letters will result in perfection or anything approaching it. Any improvement resulting from a well-planned program will, in some respects, be lasting, but the good work you have done will not bring perpetual results. The problem of obtaining better results from letters may be compared with the problem of cutting down tardiness, inefficiency, or waste. It requires constant treatment.

After your first program has ended, some of the correspondents will immediately lapse into old, bad habits. The moment you cease prodding your staff members about improving their letters, some of them will begin to lose interest. You would not think of conducting a brief campaign among your salesmen, then forget all about them for a year.

We suggest that you have a bulletin board for correspondents. On this bulletin board post unusually good specimens of letters. When a letter brings unusual results or wins back a disgruntled customer, post the complaint along with the answer and the customer's answer and publicly praise the correspondent.

Occasionally select good letters and send copies with your comment and analysis to all members of the staff (executives included). This will go a long way toward keeping up interest in better letters.

Do not be afraid to comment favorably on an occasional letter.

LETTER IMPROVEMENT METHODS

A. Surveys by letter counselors. Especially useful in large organizations to show clearly just where the weakness in the correspondence is located, and to quicken the interest of the executive personnel in correspondence activities.

B. Lecture courses or discussion groups. By outside specialists who come into the organization for the purpose. (Such efforts need to be followed immediately by other measures to secure solid and permanent results.)

C. Courses by correspondence or in local schools. Very effective if the courses are standard and if the correspondents can be induced to take such work and to carry it through to a finish. The difficulty is that many courses are either too academic to hold the correspondent's interest or too general to have much practical value.

D. Part-time service of letter counselor in reviewing letter carbons and coaching correspondents individually. A very good arrangement when the letter counselor is a competent person and when the number of correspondents is not very large. In a firm where the number of employees is too great for the letter counselor to cover adequately, it may be worth while for him to concentrate on a small group, as, for instance, the sales correspondents, the adjustment correspondents, etc.

E. Weekly letter bulletin services. May be effective in building up an interest in better letters and may give correspondents many helpful ideas. Bulletins cannot, however, take the place of a training program or of personal coaching of correspondents.

F. Books and magazines on correspondence and English. These have the same advantages as bulletin services, though not usually to so great a degree, as the correspondent must invest more time and effort to get a similar amount of benefit.

G. Syndicated sound-slidefilms. This method of training was widely used by the Armed Forces, especially the air corps. The cost of preparing a series of sound-slidefilms especially for one company would be prohibitive, but when the production cost is spread over a number of companies the prorata cost is nominal.

H. Compiling of manual by letter counselor. May do much to establish consistent practice in typing and to bring recognition of general policies and letter-writing methods. A manual, though, should not be thrown together hastily. Above all, it can only serve its purpose adequately if it is compiled by a person with enough experience to have a thorough understanding of the needs of business letter writers.

Any intelligent beginning should show definite results in the quality of a firm's letters within a comparatively short period. On the other hand, it would be unreasonable to expect that any plan can bring about an overnight transformation. The elements which contribute to the effectiveness or ineffectiveness of business letters are too many and too complex for this.

It takes time, thought, and consistent tactful effort to develop in correspondents a real grasp of the sales point of view and a mastery of working methods. And, too, there are many important factors to be dealt with in building up correspondence quality besides the correspondents themselves. The suggestions here are only ways and means of making a practical start.

The Qualifications of a Correspondence Supervisor

The keystone of any successful better letter program lies in the selection of one individual who will perform the duties of correspondence supervisor. Here is a list of qualifications which such executive should have:

PERSONAL QUALIFICATIONS:

Imagination to understand his problems.

Aggressiveness to "tackle" them.

Tact to avoid antagonizing the organization.

Dignity to win the respect of the organization.

Sincerity to win the friendliness of the organization.

Cheerfulness to win the friendliness of the organization.

Talking ability to "sell" ideas to the organization.

Writing ability to set an effective example.

Adaptability to meet varying situations.

Patience to await opportunities to develop program.

TRAINING QUALIFICATIONS:

Practical and theoretical knowledge of grammar.

Broad and thorough knowledge of letter technique.

Extended experience in some kind of writing.

At least one year of college or university training.

At least one year's experience in teaching.

Intensive practical experience in salesmanship.

General familiarity with business methods.

Definite knowledge of particular company.

SUGGESTED BULLETINS TO CORRESPONDENTS

Every Letter Ought to Make a Friend

When "Bill" Galloway was president of a farm implement company in Waterloo, Iowa, he made a fortune for himself and others because he knew how to write a good letter. I think Bill's chief qualifications for letter writing were that he *knew* people and *liked* people. He would always find time to stop and talk with a visiting farmer.

Galloway never wrote a "form" letter. Every letter, even though the same copy would go to a hundred thousand farmers, was a personal letter from him. Bill was a great believer in friendliness in every letter. Even in form letters he would manage to put in some personal touch. One time he had some letterheads printed with a picture of his office building in the upper right-hand corner of the sheet. One of his favorite stunts was to draw a crude cross in pen and ink right over one window. Under this cross he would write "Here is where I sit."

There was a sample of the Galloway touch in a letter. This and similar ideas brought a golden stream of money in the mail to "Bill" Galloway. Instead of having his letterheads printed, "Office of the President," as so many do, he simply wrote, "Here is where I sit."

That simple cross-mark and phrase added a friendly note to a letter that made a deep impression on farmers. They are accustomed to doing business in a personal way. This idea made "Bill" into a human being that almost reached out from the envelope and shook hands with every reader.

He put himself into every letter. Sometimes he would begin a letter with, "Gee it's hot in this old office today, but I must get this letter off to you before I go home." Ideas such as this probably do not fit in our business because we haven't developed the personal equation as far as Mr. Galloway did. I mention these examples to show that a business letter, even though it is but a routine answer to a simple inquiry, need not be stilted, dull, or formal. There is no law against being friendly through the mail.

Let me show you how this business of putting a handclasp into a letter works in actual practice. A friend of mine went to a New York hotel last year and spent a very pleasant week there. He decided to return and wrote to ask if he could reserve the same room. Here is part of the answer he received:

> In reply to your valued favor we beg to state that we will reserve Room 1106 as per your instructions.

Just how a hotel, good enough to please a man well enough to make him want to return, could employ such dumb correspondents, I quite fail to understand. The letter doesn't read is if it were dictated by a human being. Suppose it had been written like this:

Dear Mr. Wilson:

> It was a real pleasure to know that you liked Room 1106 when you were here last year.

> Of course, we will be glad to reserve it for you. Since you were here we've had the room completely renovated and redecorated and I am sure you will like it better than you did last year.

The second letter is a trifle longer, but it sounds as if a man with flesh on his bones and blood in his veins wrote it. To the man who dictates from 40 to 100 letters a day any given letter may be just another task in the day's work. Yet to the man who reads that letter it may be of vast importance. He has gone to the trouble to write a letter. He may not have a dictating machine at his elbow or a stenographer at his beck and call. It may be the only letter he has written for weeks.

What will he think when he opens the envelope and reads the letter? Will he think you are curt, snappy, and a trifle discourteous? Will he think you are a little too busy or important to bother with him? Or will he think that you are a friendly, accommodating person, anxious to serve and willing to go out of your way to see that his money is well spent with this company?

A Misplaced Comma That Cost a Fortune

A famous lawsuit for many thousands of dollars once hinged on the interpretation of a sentence. With a comma the sentence meant one thing. Without the comma it meant something entirely different. The stenographer, in writing the contract, forgot the comma. No one noticed it until the case went to court.

In our business we may write ten thousand letters and never have the misfortune to have one of them used as "Exhibit A" in a lawsuit. But there is always that possibility. Many large companies employ legal staffs whose duty it is to check all letters that are, in any way, out of the ordinary. They have found that it is necessary for letters to mean exactly what they say. There must be no possibility of a double meaning or the chance of a customer interpreting the letter in any but the way it was meant.

While we cannot stop to have our letters checked by a legal expert, it is important that every letter be accurate and clear. If we pay the freight, we must say so. If the customer is to pay the freight we must not let him think that we intend to pay it. Where any terms are mentioned they must be clearly outlined. Writing "Usual Terms," may mean one thing to you, another to the customer or prospect.

It isn't necessary to burden a letter with many legal terms and phrases to make it clear and impossible of misinterpretation. Sometimes I think it is better to say, "You are to pay the freight," instead of "f.o.b. factory." The customer doubtless knows the meaning of "f.o.b." but writing it the other way seems a bit less stilted and formal, although the term "f.o.b." and similar abbreviations are correct through wide and repeated usage.

Some correspondents have a positive genius for writing letters that leave the customer in doubt. Imagine you had just placed a first order with a company and received this letter from it:

Dear Sir:

Your recent valued order has been shipped today.

We trust that you will find the goods entirely satisfactory and that you will favor us with more of your business.

As the recipient reads this letter here are some questions that must occur to him. Did the shipment go by parcel post, air mail, express, freight, or motor truck? Just what did I order from these people? When will the goods arrive? Of course, you can check back in your memory and recall just what it was you bought. You can probably guess that the shipment went by freight, but you can't be sure. And you can estimate when the goods will arrive. In this case the letter is of no value whatever.

Suppose we see if we can't improve that letter:

Dear Sir:

The order which you gave our Mr. Hanson for two dozen black bill folds was shipped prepaid by parcel post this morning.

You ought to receive them March 15 at the latest.

These black bill folds are double stitched, lined with silk. They are cut from a new pattern. Only selected hides are used. I am sure your customers will prefer them above any others we have in our lines. You made a good selection. While we do not want to tell you how to run your business, it occurred to me that you would be glad to know that the best stores everywhere are selling this number for $3.50 to $3.95 each.

The man who reads this second letter knows, without your telling him so, that you are interested in his business. Furthermore, you have given him all the information he needs. He doesn't have to look up the copy of his order to remember that he bought bill folds. The extra bit of information in addition to the routine facts makes everything clear to him.

The second letter has none of the vague and stilted phrases which dominated the first letter—"your valued order"—"we trust"—"favor us with more of your business." Brush out these cobwebs from your dictating vocabulary.

Turning Kickers Into Boosters

The customer who takes the trouble to write a complaint is frequently the most valuable customer we have. He may help us unearth a situation that is driving customers away from us every day. We must remember that for every customer who writes a complaint there are from 10 to 25 who were dissatisfied for the same reason but who did not complain. They simply stopped buying.

Every complaint brings a correspondent a problem filled with vast potential possibilities for good or for evil. Tactful, thorough, pleasant handling of a customer's complaint may turn a disgruntled customer into a friend for life. Careless, slipshod, or snappy letters in answer to a complaint may do more harm than good, even though you concede the customer everything he asks.

Here are some things to remember when answering a complaint of any kind:

Reply to a complaint promptly.

If we are wrong, admit it at once. Do not try to pass the buck, alibi, or attempt to argue with the customer.

If there is an adjustment to make, tell the customer about it immediately. Do not ask him to read through several paragraphs before you give him the good news.

Never use expressions such as "your claim," "you allege," "according to your contention," etc. Such phrases only irritate the customer because it seems as if we are casting doubts on his honesty.

Do not grovel or apologize too profusely. Almost any customer will be reasonable in excusing us for a mistake. He makes mistakes himself. He doesn't want anything more than fair treatment.

Some correspondents fall into the habit of adjusting a complaint as if they were doing the customer a big favor. That is the wrong attitude to assume. There's an old saying that the Lord loves a cheerful giver, and to this we might add that a customer respects a cheerful adjustment. He is not going to appreciate any adjustment if you try to make him feel that you think he is putting something over on you.

If you know the customer is actually dishonest, that brings up a different situation calling for firm, strict treatment, probably to be handled by an officer of the company.

A customer wrote to a wholesaler, complaining that an error had been made in shipping two dozen shovels, when he ordered only one dozen. In his letter he asked that his account be credited for the amount of the extra dozen shovels.

The correspondent answered him as follows:

> In your letter of April 4 you claim that we shipped 2 dozen shovels instead of 1 dozen as ordered. Investigations of our records show that you are correct in your claim. However, we cannot give you credit on our books for the item until we receive the shovels. Kindly return them to us at once and we will have a credit memorandum issued for the amount in question.

This correspondent infuriated the customer. After all it was a mistake of the house. The customer is told that the house thought him a liar until they made an investigation. Then he is ordered to return the shovels "at once." To add insult to injury the correspondent practically tells the customer that the house wouldn't trust him with a credit memorandum until the shovels are received. This complaint could have been handled much more tactfully by a letter similar to the one that follows:

> We are glad to cancel the charge for the extra dozen shovels we shipped you by mistake. Credit memorandum for the amount is enclosed.
>
> Will you please keep these shovels until our salesman, Mr. Willet, calls? It is possible that he can dispose of them to some near-by customer and save the extra cost of returning them to us. We are writing him about the error today.
>
> Please accept our thanks for calling this mistake to our attention. We are mighty sorry, Mr. Conway, that it put you to this trouble.

The correspondent wrote the salesman, sending him a copy of the letter. He suggested that perhaps Mr. Conway could use the extra dozen shovels, and urged the salesman to try to sell them to him. If that couldn't be done, the salesman could put them in his car and sell them to a near-by customer. When the salesman called, he found that Conway had sold more of the shovels than he had anticipated and was glad to keep the extra dozen.

The Difference Between a Brief Letter and a Curt Letter

We must remember that a long letter can be curt, and that a brief letter can be friendly, polite, and courteous. Brevity is one of the most important qualifications of a good correspondent, yet too many men think that to be brief is to be curt. That is not true. A brief, concise, one-paragraph letter can be as courteous as a preacher soliciting contributions. A long, rambling, unplanned letter can be curt and irritating to the point where every paragraph read makes the reader madder and madder.

I saw a letter from a finance company the other day which read:

> Dear Sir:
>
> Your payment due February 4 is 10 days overdue. Kindly remit by return mail.

The man who received that letter was ready to make his payment which was the final installment on an automobile. He knew that the company would hesitate before going to court over the last payment which was for $33.47. So he decided to see what would happen. Three days later another letter was received. He didn't answer. Two days later came a third letter. In 2 more days a man telephoned and my friend gave him a piece of his mind.

When he finally sent a check for the last installment it was a month late. There were three letters and two telephone calls and one threatening letter written on "Legal Department" stationery. Only one letter would have been necessary had the first one been a good one. Suppose the bright young man in the collection department of this finance company had written:

> Dear Mr. Brown:
>
> I know that you'll breathe a sigh of relief when you pay the final installment on your automobile. The payment must have been overlooked by you because it is now 10 days past due.
>
> So that we can send you your final papers and cancel your note promptly I am sure you will accept this letter as a reminder to mail that check tonight.

The second letter is less irritating than the first. We must remember that the customer has the whip hand. We can write a curt and snappy letter any time we want to. And the customer can get his revenge for our discourtesy by giving his trade to a competitor.

One of the chief reasons some customers find fault with brief letters is that they seem too mechanical. Hackneyed phrases are inexcusable at any time, but in a brief letter they stand out like a boil on the end of your nose.

Here is an example:

> In reply to your letter of May 12, we beg to state that our discount is 50 off list, 2 per cent, 10 days.
>
> Hoping to be favored with your valued orders, we are,

"In reply to," "we beg to state," "hoping to be favored," "your valued orders," are four phrases which have been gathering moss for several generations. In a longer letter they might go unnoticed. But in this brief letter they sound as if they were ground out of some machine. They ruin the entire letter.

There are many better ways to answer this inquiry about discounts. Isn't the following letter a big improvement?

> We are glad to tell you that our liberal discount is 50 per cent off of our list prices. For payment in 10 days we allow a cash discount of 2 per cent.
>
> Your orders will be shipped the same day we receive them and we are sure you will be pleased with our merchandise and our service.

If this suggestion seems too long, perhaps you'd prefer the one that follows:

> Thank you for your inquiry of May 12.
>
> Our list prices are subject to a discount of 50 per cent, less a cash discount of 2 per cent for payment in 10 days.

Is It Possible to Write as You Talk?

Many letter authorities claim that every correspondent should write as he talks. This isn't always possible. Nor is it always good business. While there is no excuse for putting big words, hackneyed phrases, or stiffly formal sentences into a business letter, there should be a certain amount of restraint in every letter.

In their effort to be friendly and natural in letters some correspondents go too far. Their letters are too familiar and in some cases are actually flippant and lacking in good taste. Al Smith once referred to President Roosevelt as "You old Potato," but I doubt if it would be good policy for any of us to use this manner or phraseology in addressing our customers.

I have found it a good rule never to write anything in a letter you wouldn't say if you were face to face with the man to whom you are writing. If you are the kind of person who would say, personally, "We will hold the matter in abeyance until receipt of further instructions," it may be permissible to write such language in a letter. But the chances are that you would, if you were talking, say, "We will do nothing about this matter until we hear from you"; or you may even say, "We will keep this proposition on ice until you give us the 'go ahead' signal." Either of the two latter sentences is much better than the phony formality of the first.

Harry Tammen, famed owner of the Denver *Post,* made $10,000,000 out of his various enterprises, partly because he was shrewd, and partly because he had the audacity to address anyone and everybody just as he saw fit. He called famous women "sister," just as some of us would call a ten-year-old girl "sister," but he had the personality to go with such audacity. While not all of us can be as audacious as Mr. Tammen was, we can dispense with much of the stiffness in the letters we write without being audacious or clownish.

When a chorus girl says to another, "Be yourself, dearie," she is giving mighty good advice. We must "be ourselves" in writing letters. We mustn't try to put on a false face and write as if we were imitating Daniel Webster.

A sales correspondent wrote to a list of customers about a special offer that was to be withdrawn in a few days. He ended his letter, "Call us on the telephone today and place your order for your fall requirements." Another correspondent wrote, "Pick up your phone, call Hemlock 4000, and tell us how much you can use."

Another sales correspondent wrote in answer to a customer who complained about slow shipments: "We have completed a thorough reorganization of our shipping facilities so that in the future your orders will be greatly expedited." "Greatly expedited," my eye! Why doesn't he write something like this? "We have added two more shipping clerks to the gang in the shipping room and from now on your orders will be shipped the same day we receive them."

A policyholder of an insurance company couldn't pay his premium on the due date. He didn't know that he had 30 days of grace. Hoping to obtain some sort of extension, he asked if he could delay payment for 2 weeks. A correspondent wrote:

> Inasmuch as your payment on our Policy No. MA31234 is due on March 20 your period of grace does not expire until April 20. Therefore, permission is hereby granted to delay remittance until that date.

An executive whose head was filled with more common sense saw the letter and changed it to read:

> We are glad to tell you that you are allowed 30 days of grace after the due date of March 20 for your payment on your policy No. MA31234. It will be perfectly all right for you to wait 2 weeks after March 20 to send us your payment.

I am sure that the policyholder felt much better when he read that second letter than he would have had he read, "Therefore, permission is hereby granted to delay remittance until that date." The second letter is more human. It leaves no question in the recipient's mind as to what date was really meant.

The Art of Getting Your Letters Read

Nothing gets me more out of patience than to hear a man say, "People won't read long letters." The truth is that people will read letters, three or even ten pages long, if they are interesting. One of the best paying letters ever written by Cameron McPherson, the nationally known letter expert, was a three-page, single-spaced letter. It sold thousands of dollars' worth of educational material, admittedly difficult to sell by mail.

So don't worry about the length of your letters if you really have something to say and can put a dramatic wallop in every paragraph. The trouble with most long letters is that the men who write them use words to cover up instead of uncover ideas.

Of course, in the ordinary run of correspondence, long letters are seldom needed. The point I am trying to get over is that the length of a letter has nothing to do with its readability or its power.

The knack of writing a good letter consists of setting up a train of imagination in the mind of the reader. How many times have you heard a person, in recommending a book or a magazine say, "It was a very interesting book—I read it from cover to cover"? There's a phrase you've heard time and again until it no longer means very much. Recently a friend wrote me, "It was half past three in the morning when I clicked out the light and put down *Men Against the Sea*." That one phrase made me want to read the book.

If you are trying to sell a merchant something, make him hear the ring of the cash register. If you want to sell a farmer, paint a picture of bountiful harvests. If your words start an imaginative train of thought in the prospect's mind, his own imagination will do far more to make him buy than anything you can say. A letter to sell gas heating started off: "Gas heating is now available to every home owner." Home owners didn't go wild with excitement at this news. A more expert letter writer changed the lead of this letter to read: "How would you like to start your furnace going full blast on a cold morning without getting out of bed?" That was an improvement. Then another correspondent cut up the opening into several short sentences:

> February weather--Below Zero.

> 7 A.M.--the house is Klondike cold.

> But you stretch your arm and turn on the furnace with a twist of your wrist.

> WITHOUT EVEN GETTING OUT OF BED.

Any home owner who has ever suffered through winter after winter, getting up half an hour early just to attend to the furnace is going to read that letter.

Letters must set down the common experiences of the people who are expected to read them. A sales book and register salesman once went into a store where the owner had refused to talk with him. Before introducing himself or even mentioning the delightful weather, the salesman said: "Are you sure you charged Mrs. Jones with that pound of coffee she asked you to bring out to her car?"

That question started the grocer's mind working. Yes, he had taken a pound of coffee in a big hurry to a customer's car one day last week. Was it Mrs. Jones? Or was it Mrs. Wilson, or Mrs. Mather? He was pretty busy that day. Did he forget to charge it? Does this sort of thing happen very often? Is that where his profits were going—forgotten charges? He listened to the salesman explain how his system prevented forgotten charges. He ended by buying the system.

The salesman told his sales manager about the sale. They sent out several thousand letters beginning, "Did you charge that pound of coffee you handed to Mrs. Jones in her car one day last week?" The letter pulled splendid returns.

Letter Appraisal Form

This appraisal form is intended to assist you in revising your own letters or in indicating to others the specific weaknesses of the letters that are submitted.

Before appraising a letter, be sure to determine its exact purpose. What message is it expected to convey? What response is desired from the addressee?

Place a check mark in the colmun "Yes" or "No" opposite each question which applies to the letter you are appraising.

IS THE LETTER:	Yes	No
1. COMPLETE		
a. Does it give, in the most effective order, all information necessary to accomplish its purpose?	......	......
b. Does it answer fully all the questions, asked or implied, in the incoming letter?	......	......
2. CONCISE		
a. Does the letter include *only* the essential facts?	......	......
b. Are the ideas expressed in the fewest words consistent with clearness, completeness, and courtesy; have irrelevant details and unnecessary repetition been eliminated?	......	......
3. CLEAR		
a. Is the language adapted to the vocabulary of the addressee?	......	......
b. Do the words exactly express the thought?	......	......
c. Is the sentence structure clear?	......	......
d. Are the paragraphs logical thought units, arranged to promote easy reading?	......	......
4. CORRECT		
a. Is the accuracy of all factual information beyond question?	......	......
b. Are all statements in strict conformity with policies?	......	......
c. Is the letter free from: (1) Grammatical errors, (2) spelling errors, (3) misleading punctuation?	......	......
5. APPROPRIATE IN TONE		
a. Is the tone calculated to bring about the desired response?	......	......
b. Is the tone calculated to build or protect good will?	......	......
c. Does the entire letter evidence a desire to cooperate fully?	......	......
d. Is it free from antagonistic words or phrases?	......	......
6. NEAT AND WELL SET UP Will a favorable first impression be created by: (1) Freedom from strike-overs and obvious erasures; (2) even typing; (3) position of letter on the page?		

To what extent is the letter likely to accomplish its purpose, obtain the desired response, and build good will? In other words, how do you rate its *general effectiveness?* Underline the word which best expresses your rating:

A. OUTSTANDING   B. GOOD   C. PASSABLE   D. UNSATISFACTORY

IN RATING ANOTHER'S LETTER:

If the letter is "unsatisfactory," be sure to indicate the specific weaknesses which necessitate revision. Similarly, if the letter is only "passable," indicate clearly the weaknesses to which attention should be given in future letters.

WHAT IT COSTS TO WRITE A BUSINESS LETTER

COST FACTOR	AVERAGE COST	YOUR COST	DETERMINING COST
Dictator's Time . . . For this cost, it is assumed that the executive receives a weekly salary of $558, and takes approximately 8 minutes to dictate a single business letter.	$1.86		Based on a 40-hour week, this cost is determined by dividing an executive's salary by 8 minutes. For example at a salary of $558 a week, the executive earns $13.95 an hour or 23.3¢ a minute. Thus, 8 minutes of time costs $1.86. ($558÷40 hrs.=$13.95 per hour) ($13.95÷60 min.=23.3¢ per min.) (23.3¢ × 8 min.=$1.86 per letter)
Secretarial Time . . . Based on a salary of $257 a week this figure includes all time. It is estimated that the total figure is 19 minutes, including filing and copying.	$2.03		The cost is determined by dividing the secretary's salary (40-hour week) by 19 minutes to learn the total cost of taking dictation, doing "extra" work and transcribing the letter as well as addressing envelope, filing, etc.
Nonproductive Labor . . . This is the time consumed by both dictator and secretary in waiting, illness, vacations, etc. This has been set at 15% of labor costs for both.	$0.58		This cost is a basic percentage arrived at from previous studies. It includes absenteeism factors but does not include all fringes. It does include interruptions due to phone calls.
Fixed Charges . . . A catchall charge that wraps up overhead, depreciation, cost-per-square-foot, taxes, interest and such things as maintenance and light and heat. Fringe benefits are included. This is now 52% of total labor costs.	$2.02		This particular cost is the most difficult to determine, but studies have indicated that the 52% of labor factor is about as close as you can come. It is a combination of time charges and fixed charges.
Materials Cost . . . Stationery, envelopes, carbon paper, copy machine sheets, typewriter ribbons, and other types of necessary supplies.	$0.24		This cost is fairly easy to arrive at if you maintain records covering your supplies. It reflects the fact that many firms make machine copies as well as carbons.
Mailing Cost . . . First class postage (20 cents). Includes the work of gathering, sealing, stamping, sorting done by personnel other than the secretary.	$0.38		The number of letters sent Special Delivery can change this given figure. It includes wages of mailroom help and mail pickup, also delivery to post office in majority of cases.
TOTAL COST	**$7.11**		**YOUR COST**

It should be pointed out that the costs figures here are strictly for the traditional boss-secretary type of business letter. The use of Word Processing is gaining momentum, but it is still generally accepted that most businesses use the secretary with steno pad and typewriter as their mode of business correspondence.

Rules for Business Punctuation

THE COMMA

1. Use a comma after each word or phrase of a series of three or more words or phrases. (The final comma, however, is often omitted.)

He will visit Buffalo, Syracuse, and Albany.

2. A comma accompanying a quotation mark is placed inside it. (This is true also of a final period.)

"Your order," John insisted, "was mailed yesterday."

"Now that we are here," Jim asked, "where do we go?"

3. Where the needed emphasis so demands, use a comma (a) after a noun clause when long, and (b) after a short noun clause ending with a verb.

(a) That the work of carrying on an extensive business and attending to all the details is difficult, no one will dispute.

(b) That he has failed, does not concern you.

4. Use a comma before a clause beginning with *who* or *which* only when the meaning is "and he" (*she, it, etc.*).

Your employer, who is a man of strict integrity, would agree to these terms. "Who is a man," etc., is equivalent to saying, "and he is a man," etc.

The goods, which were in perfect condition when purchased, were entirely ruined in transit.

5. Omit the comma before *that, who,* or *which,* when "and he" (*she, it, etc.*) cannot be substituted.

This is the man *that* called yesterday.

This is the man *who* called yesterday.

These are the goods *which* were ruined in transit.

NOTE—*That* is generally regarded as preferable to *who* or *which* when "and he" (*she, it, etc.*) cannot be substituted.

6. A transposed participial phrase is set off by a comma.

Replying to your letter of July 5, we quote you the following prices.

NOTE—It is incorrect to use any punctuation mark other than a comma in constructions like the foregoing.

7. Use a comma after the following adverbs introducing a sentence: *Again, besides, first, secondly, thirdly, lastly, finally, moreover, indeed.*

NOTE—The adverb introducing the sentence modifies the entire construction.

8. Adverbs used parenthetically are set off by commas.

Nothing, *however,* can mend this defect.

9. Adverbs that modify some other part of speech are not set off by commas.

However necessary it may be, it can be postponed.

NOTE—In the foregoing sentence, *however* modifies *necessary,* and so is not set off by a comma. In the following sentence, *however* modifies the entire construction, and so is set off by a comma:

However, it is not necessary to decide this question.

The rules that apply to adverbs apply also to adverbial phrases and clauses; for example:

At the end of April, we mailed you a final statement. (Transposed adverbial phrase.)

In looking over our accounts, we find that we mailed you, at the end of April, a final statement. [(a) Transposed adverbial phrase; (b) intervening adverbial phrase.]

Before we can send you a statement, we shall be obliged to go over the accounts. (Transposed adverbial clause.)

We are sorry to say that, before we can send you a statement, it will be necessary, etc. (Intervening adverbial clause.)

10. A comma may be used to separate the parts of a compound sentence.

The books were mailed on the day that the order was received, and the bill was sent at the same time.

THE SEMICOLON

A semicolon usually separates clauses or phrases that are equally important. The semicolon is ordinarily preferable to a comma in such situations if there is no conjunction between the equally important items, or if they themselves contain commas.

The books were mailed the same day; the bill was sent immediately.

Singapore, being near the equator, has a hot climate; but Nome, lying near the Arctic Circle, can be very cold.

We will stop at Sheridan, in northern Wyoming; at Butte, in southwestern Montana; and at Spokane, in eastern Washington.

THE PERIOD

Use a period after each sentence not ending with a question mark or exclamation point, and after each abbreviation.

Write me in care of John Smith, M.D., Rome, Ga., until further notice.

THE INTERROGATION POINT

Rule: Use an interrogation point after every direct question.

When shall our representative call, in the morning or in the evening?

NOTE—When two or more questions have a comma dependence, usage varies as to the repetition of the interrogation point. The following styles are both used:

What is the meaning of all this delay, of all this neglect of our interests?

What is the meaning of all this delay? of all this neglect of our interests?

Chapter 9

CATALOGS AND MICROFILMS

NEXT to a dividend check, the catalog is probably the most important piece of literature a company sends out. Whether it be an eight-page booklet or a Sears Roebuck catalog, its one and only job is to sell. Catalogs take many formats, dictated by needs or costs.

Some catalogs, such as those produced by automobile and land-development companies are things of beauty, justified by high-ticket prices. Others, popular with mail order houses, are in the easy-to-mail, 6" by 9" size, with color and black-and-white sections.

Large, expensive, full-color catalogs are often used not only to help sell products but to impress financial organizations and prospective shareholders as well.

The trend is toward less extravagant catalogs in most lines of business. It used to be that manufacturers felt it necessary to outdo their competitors and put out catalogs which were really works of skill and art. But as the cost of producing the "de luxe" type of catalog rose, one company after another found it advisable to spend the appropriation for catalogs and price lists more carefully. They would rather have more catalogs to distribute even if wider distribution might mean a less distinctive piece of literature. In fact, some companies found they were able to get just about as good sales results with simple black and white catalogs, produced by the offset process on tough paper, as from the elaborate publications they had been using.

In the last analysis the job of a catalog is to present the products in the line, and give prospective buyers essential information about them. To be sure, an expensively produced catalog helps to sell a product which is colorfully illustrated in an atmosphere of quality. Certainly it contributes to the impression of quality in a prospective buyer's mind. It is also a source of pride to the company whose name graces the cover, as well as to the printer and the manufacturer who supplied the paper. And, it goes without saying, the salesmen like a certain amount of "swank" in sales literature of any sort. But the question which the company that foots the bill must ask is: "If we spend the extra money it will cost to prepare a superlatively fine catalog, will it produce enough plus business to justify the expense?" It is not an easy question to answer.

The big mail-order houses, like Sears, Roebuck & Company, which have built businesses by catalog selling, know almost to a dollar what they can afford to spend, in space and production cost, to sell a piece of merchandise profitably. By the process of careful testing and checking they know the extra business which results from the use of color. They have found that there is a point of diminishing returns in preparing their big catalogs; when it becomes unprofitable to "punch" a product. Yet when they have something to sell like a new freezer upon which they wish to build a quick volume, the catalog department does not hesitate to go all out in featuring it on the cover, with special four-color inserts, or in other ways to attract maximum interest.

This same principle applies to any catalog. If it is important to surround the product with an atmosphere of elegance and quality, as in the case of quality-priced table silver, it would be short-sighted indeed to economize. In the same way, if the manufacturer is a newcomer to the field, or has not established leadership, then obviously it needs a catalog which will create an impression of reliability and progressiveness. In such cases the extra cost of an outstandingly fine catalog would be justified. But to issue an expensive catalog, just because a competitor elects to spend his sales promotion appropriation that way, is neither wise nor necessary.

The catalog does, however, represent the house in the eyes of the customer. It is your silent salesman. You want your salesmen to dress neatly and to conduct themselves in a way to create a favorable first impression of the company they represent. But you do not want them to overdress. You do not want them to scream at their customers. You do not want them to oversell or brag. So it is with your catalog. It should be neat, but not gaudy. Dignified, but not stuffy. Impressive, but not extravagant. By taking advantage of the many new techniques and processes which have been developed in the graphic arts, you can have a catalog that will meet these specifications without lavish spending. In fact, by careful planning, watching processes, and cutting out unnecessary frills it is possible to hold unit catalog costs to prewar levels, in spite of the fact that materials and wages have drastically increased.

Whether the catalog is distributed by salesmen, mailed direct to customers and prospects, or used by dealers' or distributors' salesmen as an active sales tool, the supporting promotional program is geared up to the job of keeping it alive and in steady use. For maximum usefulness a catalog must be: (1) Easy to handle and to refer to, which means that products listed are conveniently grouped and thoroughly indexed; (2) complete with respect to descriptions, uses, styles, sizes, colors, packaging, prices, and other clear answers to purchasers' logical questions; (3) well illustrated and well written, with pictures that show the products to best advantage and copy that goes beyond mere description to tell what they will actually do for purchasers; and (4) pleasing in appearance and durable in construction, so that it will have frequent attention and long life.

Purposes for Which Catalogs Are Used

Practically every business requires a catalog of some sort. In the mail-order field the catalog is the backbone of the business. Millions of dollars are expended upon its preparation, production, and distribution. Before costs increased to present high levels, it was customary for the big mail-order houses to send catalogs upon request, and once a person had requested a catalog, he automatically received successive issues. But mail-order catalogs have become so large, and represent such a substantial outlay of money, that it has become common practice to restrict the distribution of them to actual customers, or make a nominal charge which is credited on initial purchase. These big catalogs are standard equipment in millions of homes, especially in rural and small-town areas. They are perhaps the most important printed sales literature. They are usually issued annually, with seasonable supplements featuring special merchandise at special prices. In thousands of communities throughout the world, the mail-order catalog sets the prices at which "shopping" merchandise is sold.

Another type of mail-order catalog, also widely distributed, is isued by companies selling a limited line of specialties, such as the Frank E. Davis Fish Company, the New Process Company, direct-selling cigar manufacturers, and others. These are smaller pieces, featuring a limited selection of products, but they are mailed out by the millions. Then there are the inexpensive consumer catalogs issued for dealer or agent distribution. There is a great variety of these. In this classification would be catalogs issued by automobile manufacturers, some of which are highly effective pieces of sales promotion and all of which play an important part in a marketing operation.

Then there are the "general line" catalogs used to promote sales through dealers. This type of catalog usually presents, in as attractive a way as possible, a manufacturer's line of products. It is used to sell the dealer, but may also be used by the dealer in selling the consumer. The general line catalog is not, however, intended for widespread distribution and is usually painstakingly produced. It may, or may not, include data on the use of the product. A difficulty in the use of dealer catalogs is their cost. Obviously if the price to the dealer were quoted it would be impractical for the dealer to show it to a prospective retail buyer. So "list" prices are used, either in the catalog itself or in an accompanying price list. The dealer is allowed a discount from these prices, which discount represents his mark-up. Instead of printing new catalogs every time there is a price change, the discount is adjusted or a new price list is issued. The same catalog may be used to promote sales through wholesale distributors, but the discounts, of course, will be different.

On the other hand, catalogs designed for industrial selling, that is to say for promoting the sale of products for conversion or use by contractors and industrial establishments, frequently carry prices, except during a period of fluctuating prices, when a separate price list is enclosed with the catalog. This type of catalog is usually far more detailed, and gives purchasing agents, engineers, and other technicians the specifications and working information they need about the product and its uses. Because of the problem involved in maintaining a file of catalogs in the purchasing department, there has been a tendency lately to standardize the size of industrial catalogs at 8½ by 11 inches.

Keeping a file of catalogs is so complex and such a headache for the average purchasing agent, architect, engineer, or buyer that it has led to the development of multiple-company catalogs. Typical of these is the "Sweet's Architectural Catalog," which assembles in bound form, catalog sections of a number of companies manufacturing building supplies and materials. These sections follow a standard pattern, and are supplied to the publisher in quantity, bound by him into numbered volumes, and selectively distributed. In that way an architect or purchasing agent has a central, organized file of relevant catalogs covering the principal sources of supply, which is *always* up to date. The catalog publisher charges so much a page for this service. It relieves the manufacturer of many problems connected with giving catalog service to buyers or specifiers, and assures him full coverage.

New Catalog Uses

An interesting development is the growing tendency to find new uses and additional applications for such a valuable sales tool. It has inspired a number of companies to get extra mileage from their catalogs by giving them double duty and additional scope.

Ford Motor Company, for instance, produced a separate, special catalog to mail to its stockholders. The inside front cover was devoted to a letter addressed to "Dear Stockholder" signed by Henry Ford II, chairman; and Lee A. Iacocca, former president. The back cover included a coupon offering a free copy of the Ford book entitled "Car Buying Made Easier."

The marketing philosophy which inspired the special catalog was described by Mr. Frank A. Grady, Stockholder Relations Representative, as follows:

"The reason for publishing a separate product brochure for stockholders is very simple: Ford has about 340,000 stockholders of record and these people are a natural market for Ford products since they have already demonstrated an interest in and favorable attitude toward the Company by investing in its stock.

"Sending stockholders a special brochure rather than the regular showroom car catalogs already available has been thought necessary for several reasons. First, no single showroom catalog covers all of our car lines since these are produced by two separate divisions, Ford and Lincoln-Mercury, and sold by separate dealership chains using separate promotional literature. Second, normal showroom catalogs are rather "hard-sell" promotional pieces and we feel that a lower key approach is more appropriate in promoting our products to stockholders. Third, the mailing cost for this separate and condensed brochure for stockholders is considerably less than the cost of mailing a number of divisional showroom catalogs covering the same product lines to each stockholder."

Another application was found by Sunset House, the California mail order firm which, as described in Chapter 40, covered its catalog with an over-wrap announcing a contest for customers ordering products from the catalog.

Catalog Showrooms

Catalogs are put to special use by retailers who mail colorful books to business organizations, institutions, homes and industrial plants for consumers to browse through and then make their purchases at a showroom. These retailers often create the impression that they are wholesalers who sell only to preferred customers; a few even issue special-discount cards.

Usually, each item in the catalog has a stock number and a coded price. The last four numbers in the code are the price of the product; the higher, "regular" price may also be shown.

One showroom owner stated that "we don't make money on small appliances and general merchandise; we make our profit on fine jewelry and we depend on high-volume business."

These showrooms easily compete with department stores because they have fewer labor costs, less taxes and occupy less expensive quarters.

PLANNING THE CATALOG

The first step in planning a catalog is, as they say in military circles, to "make an estimate of the situation." It is not unusual when the catalog spearheads a new selling strategy, as is often the case, to begin by making a survey of the customers' needs as well as the way the catalog will be used by the sales organization as a promotional tool. This, for example, was the procedure followed by General Electric Supply Corporation when it was necessary to get out a new catalog covering the company's line of fluorescent lighting equipment. It was found, as a result of such a survey, that buyers wanted more functional information than the usual catalog included. Salesmen wanted a catalog which they could use in selling the "idea"

With sixteen pages in four colors and a white, black and gold cover, The Helbros Watch Catalog is a masterpiece of design and illustration. The cover artistically lists selling features between the repeated name lines. The inside front cover makes a dramatic start with a presentation of the first lunar-time watch in the industry; the inside back cover features the company's life-time guarantee.

of better lighting to prospective buyers, and they wanted the product benefits clearly set out, with the necessary technical information and price data so organized that they could use it quickly over the telephone or in personal calls. This information was not only helpful in preparing the catalog, but equally helpful in getting top management approval for the expenditure required.

Catalog Colors and Sizes

Since most of its Centura Dinnerware products are in white or light-color hues, Corning Glass featured them against black-background pages with dramatic effects. The illustrations were in four-colors and the descriptive details were in white on black. Although this was an expensive process, the natural effect produced well-justified the cost.

The most popular page size, naturally, is 8½" by 11" but common exceptions are to be found in the wallpaper and floor-covering industries which prefer jumbo sizes, with swatches and color cards. There are also many types of covers and bindings. Large mail-order retailers use the adhesive-bound soft covers; books with many inserts are side-wired and the thick counter catalogs used in the industrial supply trades necessarily use metal post styles. Three-ring binders are necessary for constantly-changing products or seasonal requirements which demand the loose-leaf format for quick and easy replacements.

General Electric's Master Catalog

As a result of the survey, General Electric issued what is called a "Master Catalog." It showed the company's line of fluorescent lighting equipment, including important product data useful to salesmen. In fact it presented all the basic information, plus the application data, needed by a salesman or a contractor to intelligently plan and sell lighting installations. In short, it was built to the specifications of those who used the catalog, and not those of some advertising man who looked upon the preparation of a catalog as an opportunity to demonstrate his advertising skills.

While a catalog of the type mentioned, indexed so that it functions as a sales manual as well as presenting the line, served General Electric in this particular case, there is a danger of putting too much "application data" in a catalog. The trend is toward breaking the catalog down into functional sections, rather than attempting to do too many things under one cover. This reduces waste in distributing it. The sectional catalog, with a different unit for each application, permits sending a prospective buyer only those pages which directly interest him. If he is a banker, he gets information on how banks use the product and the products adapted to use by banks. Catalog sections are punched for ring binders, so that wholesalers or contractors who sell the full line can bind the various sections together under a tabbed index, and keep the information in one place.

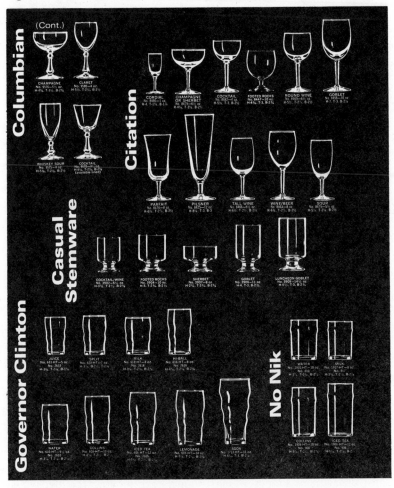

Depending on the product, black-and-white is sometimes preferable to color in catalog production. In this Owens-Illinois catalog, the black background effectively contrasts the white silhouettes of Libbey glassware. All of the company's sales offices are shown alphabetically at the bottom of each two-page spread.

In the case of a wholesaler whose salesmen sell several thousand different products from a catalog, the problem is to condense the catalog so that it will be as compact and easy to "tote" as possible. Catalogs for use by wholesalers' salesmen are usually bound in tough leather covers with handles attached, so they can be carried into the store by the salesman just as he would carry a sample case. They are printed on tough, lightweight (long fiber) paper to give minimum weight with maximum life.

A manufacturer selling the buyer direct by mail might find his customers depend upon his catalog for a wide range of information beyond descriptions of the products. Thus the A. I. Root Company, manufacturer of beekeeping supplies, scatters "how to" information through its catalog on such beekeeping problems as: "When to take off honey," "How to fold sections," "When to requeen a colony," etc. This sort of information makes the catalog useful. Anything which adds to the usefulness of a catalog and increases its span of life is a desirable customer service, provided it does not detract from its purpose of presenting the line. How far to go in that direction should be determined by a careful analysis of customers' needs.

Other questions which arise in planning a catalog, and which likewise can best be determined by customers' needs, are: How much color should be used in presenting the product; how the catalog is to be kept up to date and alive after it gets into the customer's hands; how prices are to be handled; and the procedure to be followed to make it easy for the customer to order. For example, some companies find it pays to enclose an order blank in the catalog, which can be folded and mailed without an envelope. This type of order blank might be of little value when the catalog is used by dealers who usually keep carbon copies of orders, but it might be very helpful to the type of customer who has no facilities for writing letters and does not have to make copies of orders.

Then there is the important question, which always comes up in the lay-out of a catalog, of space allocation. The usual practice is to leave this up to the advertising department or printer. It does simplify production, but it is not the best approach. Allocate space on the basis of customers' needs rather than a copywriter's whim. The sales department knows which products are moving rapidly, which are showing the highest percentage of repeat sales, and which have the most desirable competitive advantages. These products should be featured aggressively. They should be fully dramatized, given extra space in the lay-out, and preferred position. This places the emphasis where it belongs, on products which give the greatest customer satisfaction and turnover most rapidly. It is better business to "punch" such products rather than those which return the largest "book" profit. Manufacturers rail at dealers who balk at stocking a nationally advertised product, because they can buy a long-profit orphan brand for less money. But they do the same thing in planning their catalogs. The most profitable merchandise is not always the items with the longest profit, but those which build satisfied customers and repeat orders. With volume playing the important role it does in business today, catalogs and salesmen alike should emphasize turnover.

When the customers' needs have been determined, and a catalog to meet those needs laid out, it is then possible to estimate how much of an appropriation will be required. Too many appropriations for catalogs are based upon "what we usually spend" or "what we spent last year" rather than upon the job to be done. The cost of a catalog, as is true in all sales promotional literature, is not its first cost, but the business good it does a company. The most expensive catalog of all is the one that looks pretty but because of poor planning produces too little business.

A 16-page, four-color catalog describes the features and specifications of Kodak's Miracode II system for coding, storing, and retrieving microfilmed information. The booklet describes how the system scans coded images at rates up to 350 documents per second to locate specific images on 16 mm roll microfilm.

The Single Product Catalog

When the "line" consists of a single product, as for example a gas range, the catalog really becomes a sales presentation book. An excellent book of this type was developed for Roper gas ranges, the manufacturer of which claims to be the oldest maker of fine gas ranges in the country. To support its claim to fame, Roper issued to its dealers a carefully planned 8½- by 11-inch loose-leaf brochure. It was produced by offset process, spiral bound, and in full color. Following a brief foreword, the book set down 15 points a purchaser should consider in selecting a gas range. Then, one after another, each of these 15 points was covered, 1 point to a page. While there are several models in the line, the usual practice of picturing each model (all more or less alike) was not followed. Instead a page in the book explained that there was a Roper range to suit your particular desires, in which ovens, broilers, drawers could be arranged to please. Charts were used to show the oven arrangements available.

Engineering Catalogs

Industrial buyers, especially in highly technical fields, like to have catalogs which can be kept up to date by adding inserts furnished by the manufacturer describing newly developed products or appliances. It is not unusual for such manufacturers to issue catalogs in serial form, each appliance or product being described on a separate sheet, or folder, as the case may be. It is helpful when that procedure is followed to use the Dewey decimal system in indexing such releases. Customers are supplied with a post binder containing the current material, with tabbed and numbered indexes. The first digit on the release indicates the main classification or tab under which the insert belongs. The second digit, following the first decimal point, indicates the subclassification, and the digit following the second decimal point indicates the position of the sheet in the subclassification. Thus an electrical switch for high-voltage use might be indexed 4.7.18. This would be filed in the binder under tab 4, which covers switches of all types, subclassification 7 which relates to switches for use on high-voltage lines, and 18 denotes it should be filed after the insert numbered 17 under subclassification 7. One advantage of using this method of indexing loose-leaf catalog material is that it not only tells where the insert should be placed, but at the same time informs the customer if the material in that particular classification is complete or not.

Catalogs for Foreign Markets

Aldens, Inc., is one of many companies which have begun adapting their catalogs to international selling. The company is developing mail-order markets in Central America and the West Indies, as a beginning, for these reasons: (1) The improved living standards in Latin American countries; (2) faster transportation of mail, travelers, and merchandise, resulting in increased trade; (3) the pent-up demand for American goods; and (4) the nonexistence of large department stores as they are known in the United States. Potential customers for catalog sales are planters, ranchers, professional people, high-salaried workers and merchants, and the members of foreign colonies. Despite difficulties of market studies to determine the customs, styles, and preferences of different countries, of copy translation for different countries, and of local-color illustrations, both consumer and industrial catalogs are literally going abroad at a greater rate than ever before.

PREPARING THE CATALOG

As a sales promotional production job, the preparation of a catalog usually represents by far the biggest, most complex, and most time-consuming single piece of work the department handles. In general it is a different kind of job as well, calling for closer cooperation with the sales, manufacturing, and purchasing departments than do the average run of sales promotional pieces. For that reason, the planning, creating, and producing of catalogs do not necessarily follow quite the same course as the other forms of sales promotional literature outlined in the following three sections.

For one thing, there is the matter of size. While a 32- or 48-page booklet is a pretty fair-sized project as booklets go, it is not uncommon for catalogs to run from 2 to 10 times that number of pages, with a proportionately greater number of illustrations to be obtained, pieces of copy to be written, and layouts to be made. Certain short-cuts and organizational procedures must be devised in catalog production, consequently, which are not considered essential in other sales promotional jobs.

Steps in Laying Out a Catalog Dummy

Most catalogs are departmentalized, and frequently different departments are placed under the supervision of different individuals. After the amount of space to be devoted to each department has been determined, and after supervisory control over the entire operation has been established in order to keep track of progress all along the line, the actual building of the different sections begins to take shape. The following procedure is common:

1. Dummies of the exact page size, either in the form of single sheets or of bound signatures of 8, 16, 32, or whatever number of pages are to be printed in one form, are obtained from the printer, binder, or paper merchant.

2. In the case of very large catalogs, these sheets or bound signatures may be printed with rules to indicate type-page sizes and margins. Otherwise, the lay-out man will open out the signatures to the center spread and rule the right- and left-hand pages to the exact page size and then, at the four corners of each page, will push the point of a divider through the remaining pages. Thus size; position; and inside, outside, top, and bottom margins are kept uniform throughout the entire section. Even if he is working with single sheets it is important to distinguish between the inside and outside margins of facing pages, especially if bleed illustrations are used or if rules, decorations, and other elements of facing pages are aligned and arranged in balanced lay-outs.

3. The contents are allocated according to the general plan of the catalog. Illustrations, text, captions, descriptions, prices, headings, and whatever else must be contained in that particular section are assigned specific pages, with due regard to continuity, and to avoid overcrowding some pages and going too light on others.

4. Next comes the actual work of laying out individual pages, which is done before the type is set or the engravings made if costs are to be kept at a minimum. By determining spacing and positioning in advance, the cuts can be ordered to size, the copy can be lengthened or shortened, and the right type sizes specified.

5. When the engravers' proofs (or photostats, or Vandykes, if it is to be an offset job) and the galley proofs of the type are ready, they are cemented in position on each page, the captions and display type are added, and the section is ready for the finishing touches. This is the time to cut and fill rather than waiting until the pages are actually made up, although if the original typewritten copy was accurately cast up beforehand, cutting and filling after the type is set will be slight. This also is the time for any final copy corrections, alterations, or price changes. Few corrections should be necessary on the final page proof, to avoid needlessly running up the cost of the job.

6. The finished pages are finally assembled into the proper units for printing, so laid out as to combine the same colors in the same forms, and to permit the greatest economy in binding.

Many of the illustrations in modern catalogs are not limited simply to product photographs. Here is an example of how Roper Corporation employs human-interest values to produce an interesting catalog.

How One Company Solved the Organization Problem

As an illustration of the organizational problems involved in producing an exceedingly large catalog, the experience of the Physicians' and Hospitals' Supply Company, Inc., with its modern multipage book, offers some helpful suggestions. The catalog contains illustrations and descriptive copy of literally thousands of pieces of hospital equipment, supplies, instruments, and drugs. Most of the copy was rewritten from manufacturers' literature in as concise a style as possible so that it could be set in readable 8- and 10-point type rather than the less legible 6-point.

One practical device that proved helpful in keeping the pages in order and facilitated the assembly of the various signatures was the use of an oversize loose-leaf binder. As each page or each bound section was completed, it was folioed, inserted into its proper place in the binder, and kept there until ready for the printer. When enough consecutive pages were ready to complete a signature, they were delivered to the printer in marked file folders clearly identified as to page numbers, signature number, and section. This procedure prevented confusion all along the production line, as hundreds of pages were in work at the same time; and without proper organization it is easy to lose track of pages between the typesetting machines, the composing room, the proofroom, and the customer's office.

Photographs Favored as Catalog Illustrations

Photographic illustrations lend themselves so effectively to catalog use that comparatively few companies now use line or wash drawings. In some cases, photographs are so retouched as to look like wash drawings, but in general the more natural the photograph the more productive it is. In the majority of cases, also, it is not considered sufficient just to show the product. It is better, from an interest standpoint, to show the product in use; but, lacking the opportunity to do that, most products show up better in an appropriate setting than they would without benefit of background or atmosphere.

Since a catalog comes closer to a retail newspaper advertisement than any other piece of sales promotional literature, the same principles of merchandise illustration that have proved successful in newspaper advertising prove equally successful in catalog selling. And a recent survey by the American Newspaper Publishers Association and the American Association of Advertising Agencies showed photographs to be far ahead of drawings in boosting advertising readership. In food advertising, for example, food photographs them-

GENERAL AIRCRAFT
SUPPLY CORPORATION

Dear Mr. Russell:

You have asked us to send you one of our new aircraft supply catalogs. This catalog is being sent to you by prepaid parcel post and should reach you in a few days.

We feel sure that you will find the book helpful. It was designed just for people like youself. Products are arranged in the order of prominence on an airplane. For example, the first pages deal with hardware, and then they build up to tires, tubes, tailwheel accessories, propellers, batteries and other electrical units; then to instruments, and so on down the line.

Your General Aircraft catalog is somewhat unique as it contains a Handbook Section which begins on Page 228. The General Handbook is a swell reference guide. It contains useful tables on many of the day-in and day-out questions that you may have. For example, if you plan to mount some instruments on a panel, Page 234 of the Handbook Section will indicate the type of template to make up. It will give dimensions between screw holes--the exact diameter for the panel cut-out--the angles between the holes and a few other important items. Many other tables are included and the very comprehensive section on aircraft finishes has been mighty popular with shop operators.

With just a few moments checking, we believe you will agree with other top-notch aviation people, that this catalog is one of their mighty useful tools. Many of them refer to it as their "green bible."

GENERAL AIRCRAFT SUPPLY CORPORATION

Lawrence F. Zygmunt

HT

Here's a letter that increased the value of a catalog mailing. Instead of just sending a parts catalog when requested, Mr. Zygmunt carefully explains some of its workings and resells the prospect on the catalog. Results were excellent.

selves attracted the greatest attention—followed, in order, by babies, celebrities, animals, children, families or couples, pin-up girls, product packages, and men. In picturing products in use, the nature of the product will determine what pictorial treatment is most resultful, but it is worth discovering which subjects are of greatest interest to buyers in particular cases. Further illustrative principles developed in the survey were that reverse plates, while sometimes favored by designers, are below average in attention value, and that a single illustration is more effective than multiple illustrations. Second choice is a single large illustration dominating one or more smaller illustrations. The wisdom of using color in illustrations depends on the importance of color as a selling factor for the product. Catalogs showing flowers, fabrics, furniture, or other products with color as a sales appeal will profit from the use of color pictures; catalogs devoted to machinery, hardware, electrical equipment, will not so profit.

A Catalog Promotion

An effective promotion, based on its catalog, was the Spiegel 32-page, four-color "Get Acquainted Book," a form of condensed catalog, with a number of sales-stimulating features. First, the cover proclaimed: "Try anything in this catalog 30 days free! Order any item in this catalog. Use it 30 days. If you decide not to buy, return it—no questions asked. Otherwise we will add it to your new account after 30 days."

Bound into the center fold were:

1. An offer to send the complete catalog upon receipt of an order, or, with no buying requirements, an application for the full catalog.
2. A letter from the Chairman of the Board inviting orders for a trial period.
3. Order forms and applications to open new accounts.
4. Application forms for the full catalog.
5. Postage-paid envelope.

Thus, everything was done, and more, to carry out the old precept to make it as easy as possible for the buyer to place an order for merchandise.

A Deluxe Catalog for Special Customers

One of the finest catalogs ever designed has been produced by Steuben Glass for its high-quality artistically-superb crystal pieces for customers with good taste and good incomes. In keeping with the fine nature of the products, ranging in price up to $6,000 for an 8¼" high cut crystal block enclosing the sculptured figure of a woman, the book has a handsome, tasteful, gold-stamped red cover with a beautiful four-color illustration of its famed "Partridge in a Pear Tree" crystal, hot-stamped in the center. Inside, each work is given a full-page color illustration, with facing descriptive pages in two colors. Classic type and ample white space fully reflect its typographic craftsmanship. Appropriately, there is no attempt to sell; the illustrations, brief descriptions and prices easily convey the story of quality. The catalog is sent in the Spring and Fall of each year to established customers.

Advertising the Catalog

Because of the small-order nature of the seed business, W. Atlee Burpee Company features the catalog in its mail-order advertising in the garden sections of newspapers and Sunday supplements and in garden magazines. Currently, over 2.5 million catalogs are distributed free.

TL577JWA

That's a model number? Eight letters and figures? With only a slight variation to avoid indentification, that's actually a typical designation used in the numbering systems of large television manufacturers as well as in some other industries. Advertising, sales and promotion department people like to consider themselves as being customer-conscious and creative, but when it comes to model numbering, they leave it to the factory and fail to consider the customer's point of view.

Those letters and numbers mean something to the production people, or to the sales department, but they are cumbersome and confusing to the customer, especially on a long price list with numbers which vary by only one figure or letter.

This is not unimportant; consider the cost, in time and money, when retailers order merchandise in volume from distributors, or distributors from the factory, and a clerk or typist makes an error in listing those long, confusing and unnecessary numbers. The system places factory requirements ahead of customer considerations; the reverse should be true.

PRICES AND THE CATALOG

The reason catalog users refer to their books most frequently is to check on prices, which is also the chief reason, in all probability, why it was published in the first place. Without minimizing the importance of the proper handling of all the other things that go into its making, prices constitute a catalog's biggest use factor; it is changing prices even more than changing styles or the addition or deletion of lines that necessitate new editions and create the demand for the various types of catalog binders which permit pages to be replaced when they become outdated.

An illustration of the emphasis placed on price when there is a price story was provided a few years ago by the fall and winter catalogs of the mail-order houses. After 8 or 10 years of steadily rising prices, Sears, Roebuck & Co., Montgomery Ward & Co., Aldens, and Spiegel's found it possible in the following summer to reduce the prices of much of their merchandise for the coming season. Sears discarded its customary illustrated front cover in favor of a price message to customers which stated that Sears' prices really were lower, that "we guarantee to save you money," and "we guarantee to give you the immediate benefit of any lower prices after the catalog is printed." The 1,380-page book was the largest general catalog issued by Sears for several years, and price cuts averaging 8% below the previous year were made on 62% of the 100,000 or so items listed. Ward's emphasized the fact that the price reductions in its new 1,136-page catalog were more extensive than at any time in years, and that more than half the items listed were priced "very substantially below" the previous year. Prices in the 836-page catalog of Aldens ranged from 15 to 40% lower than the previous book and the number of pages was up nearly 10%. In every case, price was played up as the big news of the fall and winter season.

All catalog users aren't as price-conscious as mail-order buyers, of course, and all concerns issuing catalogs, even if they had such substantial price reductions to offer, wouldn't want to stress them so heavily. But under normal conditions—and disregarding such abnormal conditions as have caused the omission of prices from recent automobile catalogs, for instance—price is as indispensable a feature of catalogs as it is of retail merchandise advertisements in newspapers. The relatively small percentage of catalogs which do not include prices actually become style books, reference books, product listings, or indexes rather than catalogs.

Making Provisions for Price Changes

Where a catalog is necessarily so expensive that it can't be revised and reprinted periodically and where price structures are subject to frequent change, these considerations affect the planning of the entire sales promotional strategy. They are solved through any of the following devices, depending on a company's particular problem:

1. The publication of a separate price supplement keyed to and accompanying the catalog without actually being bound into it. This method has the obvious danger of the supplement's becoming separated from the catalog proper and not being at hand when needed.

2. The use of loose-leaf catalog covers of various ring-binder or mechanical-binding styles in which individual sheets or whole sections may be inserted in case of changes. When the burden of inserting the new material falls on buyers, the system is usually less satisfactory than when salesmen are responsible for making the changes, although even salesmen have been known to grow lax in the matter.

3. The issuance of several small catalogs in place of one big catalog, especially if the line is so diversified that different groups of products are sold to separate groups of buyers. The costs of revising and reprinting individual sections is proportionately less than redoing an entire catalog and those sections which do not require changing can be kept in longer use.

4. The issuance of special catalog supplements covering all necessary changes in both products and prices which are intended to be filed with the main catalog but not to be inserted in it. The disadvantage here is that the user is required to look up an item in one or more supplements in addition to the catalog itself in order to make sure that he is getting the latest information about it.

Price lists are usually inserted loose in the catalog, and are prominently dated and numbered. The serial number of the price list (usually a letter rather than a numeral) precedes each catalog number in the price list, so that the customer when ordering automatically indicates the price list used. To avoid confusion it is customary to change the color of each new price list, and request customers to destroy the old "yellow" list which is superseded by the "blue" list enclosed with the letter. Some promotion men arrange for a pocket in the catalog, usually a slot in the back cover or one of the last pages, to hold the price list so that it will stay with the catalog. The same pocket may be used for keeping order blanks and return envelopes.

Before proceeding with the production of a catalog it is well to get the advice of a catalog specialist who has no axe to grind. You may get good advice from your engraver or your printer, but then again you might not. After all, the engraver could hardly be expected to recommend that it be produced by a process which would deprive him of the engraving business, and a printer equipped only with flat-bed presses for relief printing would prefer to keep them busy rather than see the job go to an offset house or be produced by some other competitive process.

EVINRUDE MOTORS ■ DIVISION OF OUTBOARD MARINE CORPORATION ● MILWAUKEE, WIS. 53216 ● AREA PHONE 414 ● HILLTOP 5-0843

FIRST IN OUTBOARDS

HOORAY FOR SNOW!
(Skeeter owners welcome it)

We hope you'll join the fun...and we're glad to send you the Skeeter literature you asked for.

Evinrude's 32 page catalog features the Skeeter on the back cover, and pages 30 and 31. You'll find complete specifications on page 31.

Introduced last year, Evinrude's Skeeter caught the imagination of Sportsmen and outdoor-loving families throughout the snow country. This year, you have a choice of three Skeeter models---standard, wide track, and electric starting models. There's also an extension kit if you want more cargo space and more flotation.

We've enclosed the name of your nearest Evinrude Skeeter dealer with this letter.

We don't mean to be sneaky by sending you literature on our new motors and boats. It just happen that all of our products are in one catalog. Of course, we don't mind if you get the urge to own a new boat or motor.

We're in favor of fun all year 'round.

We invite you and your family to stop in at your Evinrude dealer--- and see and fun-test the Skeeter.

Cordially,

EVINRUDE MOTORS

Robert M. West Jr.

Director of Sales

R.N. West, Jr.

When an inquiry is received for a seasonal model, Evinrude sends out a complete catalog with an accompanying letter. The message stresses the model, invites attention to the entire line, and urges the prospect to visit the nearest dealer, whose name and address are enclosed—all in a cheery, informal tone.

Distributing the Catalog

A catalog is only as valuable, in the eyes of a possible buyer, as you make it. If you send it to him "cold," it is not likely he will attach much value to it. It is therefore good sales promotional practice to make the customer want the catalog before you send it to him. There are exceptions to this rule, of course. Some inexpensive catalogs, which are really not much more than illustrated price lists, can be mailed broadcast without involving much loss so far as the cost of the catalogs is concerned. But there is also the question, entirely aside from waste, of how much more business would result from the distribution of the catalog if the promotion department had "set the stage" for it.

It is not suggested that the distribution of an expensive catalog be limited only to those who ask for it. Obviously every probable buyer should have a copy, *provided he will use it*. But that is an important proviso. The best practice seems to be to depend upon publication and direct-mail advertising to get as many requests as possible for a newly issued catalog, on the theory that such names are valuable in other ways, and then after that distribution has been made to use special letters to get the catalog into the hands of important customers under the most favorable conditions.

Formulating catalog procedure, then, involves many factors of timing, press runs, length of service, costs, and pricing policy. It accounts for the trend away from regular yearly catalogs to a more flexible "as needed" schedule on the part of industrial companies which are not affected by seasonal considerations. The intervals between catalogs may be only 9 or 10 months in some periods and then 2 or 3 years in others, depending on circumstances at the time. General line mail-order companies necessarily base their operations on regular fall-and-winter and spring-and-summer catalogs, with special supplements in between; in industries where yearly models are the practice, so are yearly catalogs; retail stores and mail-order specialty houses invariably need annual Christmas and other timely catalogs for spring weddings and graduations, summer sports and vacations, fall back-to-school outfits, etc.; seasonal styles in any line of business require seasonal catalogs. But where real reasons for definitely spaced catalogs do not exist, most companies find that their catalogs produce more business in relation to their cost if they are scheduled according to specific needs rather than according to arbitrary dates.

Catalogs on Microfilms

Industrial buyers, wholesalers, parts suppliers and other volume purchasers are now able to enjoy the benefits of microfilm in catalog applications. Marvin Spike, Marketing Director of National Business Services, points out that during the past decade, an entire information retrieval science has grown up around the catalog business. Complete with new terms like microfiche, random access and the rest of the 20th-century phraseology, the micropublishing industry is busily converting the catalog published today into the business encyclopedias of tomorrow.

Because so many influential professional and business people rely on information contained in commercial and industrial catalogs to make daily decisions, they have discovered the increasing importance of systematic ways to maintain catalogs for easy reference. For example:

Specialty advertising and premium distributors serve their advertising clients' requirements through daily reference to more than 1,000 different catalogs, illustrating and describing the products manufactured by the suppliers they represent. Ordinarily, if the distributor could obtain and maintain these catalogs each year, they would fill over 10 feet of filing space and would be extremely unruly and difficult to handle.

A new micro-image system, published by Micro-Graphix, a division of National Business Services, reproduces every one of the nearly 10,000 catalog pages, in precise detail, at a 5X reduction, so that the entire file fits into a portable, office size 3-ring binder. And every product illustrated or described in each of the 1,000 catalogs is systematically indexed by manufacturer and page number for the added convenience of the user.

Information Handling Services, a micropublisher in Denver, Colorado, is successfully marketing a similar type service, reproducing thousands of pages of original equipment products catalogued for use by defense suppliers.

National Cash Register recently contracted to produce a micro-image catalog, reproducing Ford Motor Company parts manuals and catalogs for use by dealer service departments.

McGraw-Hill, one of the nation's leading industrial publishers, recently announced plans to market a Micro-Graphix type library consisting of micro-image reproductions of 25,000 pages, representing 2,600 construction products catalogs. Nearly 70,000 architects, engineers, draftsmen and builders rely on such a file for vital information, on which to base daily management and purchasing and design specification decisions.

Similar micropublishing programs are cropping up in every industry and profession where catalogs exist. In fact, it is generally assumed that micropublishing techniques will soon even be supplied at the consumer level.

In the not too distant future, it won't be unusual for a housewife, considering the purchase of a pair of shoes, to open a book or binder that will contain the reduced image reproductions of every department store catalog in which she conceivably might be interested. She'll look up the style, color, size and price range that meet her needs and have instant access to hundreds if not thousands of selections. Already, there are more than a dozen prime manufacturers of reading and viewing devices, for use with just such systems, feverishly involved in the development and manufacture of the ideal viewer to meet shopping needs.

Microfilm Readers

Great strides have been made in the design and production of microfilm reading equipment. At a press conference called in connection with the introduction of two new readers by Eastman Kodak Company, Van B. Phillips, vice president and general manager of the company's marketing division, made the following comments on developments in the fast-growing field:

"A ten-year back-issue file of a 325-page monthly journal," he said, "could be contained in a 4 x 6-inch card file. If an issue ever became lost or misplaced, a copy could be ordered at very little cost. While it might cost considerably more than a dollar to mail one copy of such a journal at first-class postal rates, over 1,000 pages on microfiche can be mailed first-class for eight cents. When compounded by thousands of mailings, the cost savings are impressive. When mailing overseas or by special delivery, the benefits are even greater."

Mr. Phillips pointed out comparable benefits for companies which publish massive amounts of literature for distribution to their sales and service personnel. To a company that must provide field support for the equipment it produces, micropublished materials provide an easily updated system for cheaply producing and mailing service manuals. To an appliance manufacturer who must keep his dealers informed on product changes, replacement parts, and new applications, micropublishing can be a happy solution to the problem of publishing thousands of pages of material yearly.

The two new readers announced by the company are the 20X Ektalite 120 and the 40X Ektalite 140. Both units employ front-projection optics; the light source is a 12-volt lamp and the Ektalite screen permits image contrast levels comparable to those of printed paper read in a well-lighted room. The model 120 accepts standard 4 x 6 microfiche or Recordak jackets containing up to 98 images; the model 140 accommodates microfiche containing up to 325 images.

The Kodak Ektalite 120 reader is designed for reading microfiche containing up to 98 images. A 40X Kodak Ektalite reader, model 140, can contain up to 325 images.

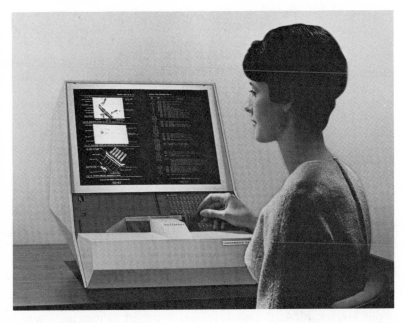

The Recordak Easamatic Reader, by Kodak, provides fast retrieval of microfiche images. To project a microfiche image, a pointer is guided by fingertip control to a letter-number on an index card.

Microfilm Readers at Colleges

Most colleges and universities, especially in the larger cities, offer, through their libraries, microfilm reading equipment facilities. While primarily for the benefit of the students, they are also available to the business community. Many colleges offer courses in business administration and maintain indexed files of available films, tapes and slides on marketing subjects, including advertising and sales promotion. These are also drawn upon by instructors for use as visual aids in classroom instruction.

Some manufacturers offer their complete catalogs on microfilm. Purchasing personnel and sales promotion executives in companies which do not have the necessary reading equipment may avail themselves of the college library services at no cost.

Chapter 10

SALES PROMOTION LITERATURE

I—Planning

REGARDLESS of product, type of service, or channel of distribution, a business organization may have to do without special campaigns, broadcasting or other forms of promotion but at the very least, it must have literature to present, describe or promote its products.

Determining size, colors and other elements, such as artwork or photography for a promotional piece of literature depends on three major factors. First: the market. Does it consist of men or women? Are they professional people, retailers, or part of a mass consumer audience? If the product is intended for use in industrial production, does the folder, booklet or catalog go to buyers, engineers or management?

A booklet intended to reach high-income prospects, promoting the sale of high-price products, such as a car, a house or a yacht, naturally requires a better, higher-grade and more expensive piece of literature than one for a mass-consumption product. The kind of market to be reached is thus the first consideration.

The second factor is cost. The size of the budget, based on sales and profits, places limitations on any effort, whether for a single unit or a whole campaign. Should the budget be small, expensive artwork cannot be used and printing, for instance may be limited to one or two colors instead of four.

Many companies attempt to make their literature, or its components, serve more than one purpose, as when an advertisement prepared by an advertising agency is also used as a reprint for mailing or as the back page of a booklet. Artwork is often used several times to spread its cost among different pieces.

The third consideration is that of distribution. The physical aspects of a promotional unit are often determined by its projected use. Is it to be made available in a dealer's store, distributed by salesmen in calling on customers, sent out by mail with or without a letter, or enclosed in shipping cartons? Those are some preliminary questions to be answered. A booklet or folder to be mailed may be designed as a self-mailer in which case it must meet postal regulations. If it be intended for distribution by retailers, space must be allowed for imprinting their names and addresses.

KINDS OF PROMOTIONAL LITERATURE

Sales promotional literature may be represented as encompassing four different fields of business literature, any one of which accounts for a tremendous volume of printing:

1. *Direct-Mail Advertising Literature*, which is familiar to everyone as the letters, folders, post cards, booklets, broadsides, and other pieces sent through the mails to advertise all manner of products and services. Direct mail is a distinctive medium of advertising in the same sense that magazine, newspaper, business paper, radio, television, outdoor, car card, and business film are distinctive media of advertising, direct mail having the particular advantage of controllable selectivity and personal attention value.

2. *Unmailed Advertising Literature,* which consists of substantially the same types of printed pieces as direct-mail advertising but is distributed by means other than the mails. In this case the pieces may be handed out to shoppers in retail stores; inserted in packages, bundles, or statement envelopes; passed out from house to house or office to office; placed in parked automobiles; given to pedestrians on the street; or delivered personally by salesmen or messengers. Included as unmailed advertising literature are many forms of window, counter, floor, wall, and package displays.

3. *Mail-Order Literature,* which differs from direct mail in that its purpose is not simply to advertise a product or service by mail but actually to sell it by mail, without benefit of salesman or retail store. Mail-order literature ranges all the way from post cards and simple sales letter-order form combinations to the gigantic catalogs of the big mail-order houses.

4. *Educational and Instruction Literature,* which is designed neither for direct advertising nor for mail-order selling yet occupies an exceedingly important place in sales promotion strategy. Sales manuals, sales training courses, instruction manuals, bulletins, and other material for the training and education of salesmen, dealers, wholesale and retail salespeople, sales correspondents, etc., are examples of this type of literature.

Combining, coordinating, and consolidating these four fields of business literature into one over-all sales promotional operation, consequently, is one of the most responsible functions of the executive in charge of sales promotion. The scope of the job is great, greater perhaps than even most managements realize. From the standpoint of the planning, creation, and production of the huge volume of printing demanded by an all-out promotional program, more time, more money, and more manpower are required than in the preparation of all the other components of a complete advertising campaign.

Retail promotion literature must be attractive and impelling. These representative samples of mailings by Zale Jewelry Co., massive Southwest retail operation, are designed to sell by direct mail as well as to attract new customers. Many of the items offered cost well over $300.

The objectives usually suggest several physical forms the literature may take; the budget usually decides which form is preferable in size, quantity, manner of treatment, and frequency of use. Final decisions are made difficult not because there are so many forms from which to choose but because there is such an infinite variety of ways for handling each form. Actually, almost any piece of sales promotional literature that can be devised falls within one of these ten major classifications:

1. Post cards and self-mailers.
2. Letters and enclosures.
3. Folders and broadsides.
4. Booklets and brochures.
5. House organs and bulletins.
6. Catalogs and price lists.
7. Portfolios and presentations.
8. Samples and specialties.
9. Reprints and publicity releases.
10. Window and store displays.

In each classification, however, are limitless possibilities for original and distinctive variations, depending again on the job to be done and the appropriation available for doing it. Those are the factors which govern whether the piece shall be economical or expensive, large or small, in color or black and white, 8-page self-cover or 96-page plus cover, a thousand run on a multigraph or a million run on 2- or 5-color rotary presses.

How Pharmaceutical Advertisers Plan Their Literature

An interesting case study of the types of sales promotional literature selected by one industry for mailing to its customers and prospects is afforded by the 5-year analysis compiled by a company of medical mailing list specialists. During each of the 5 years surveyed, as shown in the accompanying chart, this company collected, classified, and tabulated all of the promotional pieces received through the mails by the typical general practitioner. For the periods ending April 30 of these 5 years the totals were:

1st year, 2,199 pieces or 42 per week
2nd year, 1,919 pieces or 37 per week
3rd year, 1,774 pieces or 34 per week
4th year, 1,826 pieces or 35 per week
5th year, 1,263 pieces or 24 per week

Analysis of Direct-Mail Advertising Received by General Practitioners During Five 1-Year Periods

Percentage of Total

	First Year	Second Year	Third Year	Fourth Year	Fifth Year
Type of Advertiser					
Pharmaceuticals...................	82.3	83.2	85.0	85.9	86.5
Medical books and journal subscription solicitations.................	3.6	4.3	3.3	2.1	2.4
Medical equipment and instruments...	2.9	1.7	1.1	2.0	1.4
Miscellaneous—including all mail of a nonmedical nature...............	11.2	10.8	10.6	10.0	9.7
	100.0	100.0	100.0	100.0	100.0
Type of Postage Used					
Printed permit.....................	48.5	50.3	48.3	50.9	48.1
Postage meter......................	23.2	27.5	29.9	27.2	29.7
Third and fourth class.............	11.7	9.6	11.8	14.9	14.9
First class........................	4.3	3.9	2.9	3.0	2.1
Government post cards..............	12.3	8.7	7.1	5.3	5.2
	100.0	100.0	100.0	100.0	100.0
Corner Cards					
Usual style—name and address in upper left-hand corner............	62.2	64.8	68.3	70.2	73.4
Name and address on flap or reverse side................................	4.7	6.7	5.5	5.5	14.0
P. O. box or street address used—no company indicated...............	3.7	5.4	4.1	4.3	3.6
No corner card or return address......	29.4	23.1	22.1	20.0	9.0
	100.0	100.0	100.0	100.0	100.0
Self-Mailers and Mailing Cards					
Sealed............................	3.6	3.0	3.3	2.9	3.2
Unsealed..........................	8.4	7.8	5.5	7.1	7.4
Mailing cards......................	7.8	8.8	9.9	9.9	8.1
Government post cards..............	12.3	8.7	7.1	5.3	....
Sample Request Cards Enclosed					
Not prepaid.......................	0.6	2.1	2.8	2.3	3.7
Business reply cards................	17.4	17.3	12.2	12.3	10.9
Samples............................	14.4	14.2	9.3	9.3	8.6
Leaflets (1 or more) enclosed...........	11.1	14.6	15.5	15.4	15.8
House magazines.....................	5.6	6.0	6.3	7.0	7.8
Letters enclosed.....................	24.2	26.3	26.8	22.4	20.7

Since the 5-year study was made, the volume of mail to physicians has tended to increase annually, yet the significant fact remains that the percentages of the various types of material are found to have remained fairly constant, except for an increase in the mailing of samples.

The conclusions which can be drawn from the studies made in this particular field are of interest to all producers of sales-promotion literature, as indicative of both the possibilities and limitations of such literature. It should be noted, by the way, that much additional literature for physicians is not mailed but is delivered personally by detail men who call on physicians, to describe new products.

The post card and self-mailer classification, for example, represented 32.1% of all mailings; samples made up another 14.4%; and house magazines, 5.6%. These three classifications accounted for 52.1% of the total, the remaining 47.9% being in letters and enclosures, folders and broadsides, booklets and brochures, catalogs (but few price lists), and reprints (but no publicity releases) which are widely used by the pharmaceutical houses in the form of papers from the medical journals. Since it is not common practice in this field to enclose letters with such publications as booklets, brochures, house organs, and catalogs, it is fairly certain that most of the 24.2% of the mailings in which letters were enclosed belong in the

A New Size—100 ml.—ERYTHROCIN® Granules for Oral Suspension
erythromycin ethyl succinate,
A Logical Size For 5-Day Pediatric Therapy
PEDIATRIC DOSAGE

BODY WEIGHT	ERYTHROCIN CHEWABLE*	ERYTHROCIN GRANULES	ERYTHROCIN DROPS
Children under 10 lbs.			20 mg./lb./day in 4 divided doses
10 to 20 lbs.			½ to 1 dropper** q.i.d.
20 to 40 lbs.	½ tablet 4 to 5 times daily	½ tsp. 4 to 5 times daily	1 dropper 4 or 5 times daily
40 to 60 lbs.***	1 tablet q.i.d.	1 tsp. q.i.d.	
DOSAGE SHOULD BE INCREASED IN SEVERE INFECTIONS			
HOW SUPPLIED	200 mg. chewable tablets, scored for half doses. Bottles of 50.	60 ml. & 100 ml. bottles. 200 mg. per 5 ml. tsp.	30 ml. bottles. 100 mg. per 2.5 ml. dropper

*For full therapeutic effect, Chewable tablets should not be swallowed whole.
**Dropper calibrated at 1.25 ml. (half) and 2.5 ml. (full).
***60 lbs. or more, 1 chewable or 1 tsp. 5 times daily.

An example of promotional enclosure in the ethical-pharmaceuticals field— a 3 by 5 card which can be filed for quick reference. Note that it contains information but no "touting" of the product.

"letters and enclosures" classification, leaflets (describing new pharmaceuticals) being by far the most popular type of enclosure. Consequently, somewhere between 20 and 30% of the mailing pieces remain to be divided between the three classifications of folders and broadsides, booklets and brochures, and catalogs, with the third being the least prevalent of the three.

The fact that so much of the mail directed to physicians takes the form of inexpensive pieces is one of the most remarkable points developed in this study. As a group, the pharmaceutical companies, which are responsible for 82.3% of these mailings, are noted for the high quality of their sales promotional literature. They usually dominate the annual Direct-Mail Leaders awards of the Direct Mail Advertising Association, and frequently account for a disproportionately high percentage of awards in other contests.

They are probably the foremost examples of class advertisers among direct-mail users, one reason being that they are limited by ethical considerations in their use of newspaper and other popular forms of advertising and put most of their appropriations into direct-mail and medical journals; another reason is that the physicians who make up their particular market represent the best-educated and most affluent group of its size in the country and have the cultural and artistic interests to appreciate fine literature. It is therefore significant to other sales-promotion executives, those in mass markets as well as class markets, that in mailings to such a group the following practices prevail:

> Sealed and unsealed self-mailers make up 12% of the mailings; government post cards,12.3% ; and mailing cards,7.8%.

> Except for government post cards, only 4.3% of the direct mail is first class; third and fourth class account for the other 82.4%.

> Letters are included in practically one-fourth of all mailings.

> Samples are included in practically one-sixth of all mailings.

> Leaflets are included as enclosures in over one-tenth of all mailings.

1. POST CARDS AND SELF-MAILERS

The simplest and most economical of all mailing forms, of course, is the government post card. It is also the quickest to get into the mails in case of a timely news message, because it doesn't require stamping, metering or printing with a postage indicia; and is the quickest to get to its destination because it travels as first class mail. It can be printed, multigraphed, mimeographed, or processed by any other method, one at a time or any number of units up to full sheets of 40.

Post cards of all varieties are ideal for brief copy of a reminder nature; for quick series of repetitive sales points; for notices, announcements, instructions, invitations, and other short messages; for teaser build-ups or even for mail-order offers of inexpensive items. They are not suitable for confidential messages; for informative data to be filed for reference; for mailings intended to create prestige; or for propositions requiring a sustained sales story or a complete selling job.

Self-mailers have most of the same advantages and disadvantages as post cards so far as subject matter is concerned, although they do provide greater space for text and illustration. Double post cards and sealed mailing cards, however, are simply small-sized self-mailers and even the more elaborate pieces of this classification are generally regarded as being in the same category and are treated accordingly by their recipients. Many self-mailers are printed on sheets as large as 17 by 22 inches, then folded to 8¼ by 11 or 5½ by 8 inches for mailing. It is important that good tough paper stock be selected to withstand rough handling in the mails and that they be substantially sealed. Frequently, bristol or cover stock is selected of such weight that one corner may be perforated for tearing out and mailing in as a reply card. Regardless of the precautions taken, though, a self-mailer seldom reaches its destination in as fresh or clean a condition as if it had been mailed in a sturdy envelope supported, if necessary, by a stiffener.

A noteworthy post card promotion campaign was that of Capital Airlines, which obtained lists of the members of and delegates to conventions held anywhere along the routes it served. Those individuals who lived in Capital territory were then sent post cards, inviting them to make the trip by Capital Airlines. Each post card was tailored pictorially to fit the convention subject. Copy was brief and illustrations as large as the post card allowed. A typical card carried a cartoon of a telephone lineman at the top of a pole with accompanying text reading: "We're merely suggesting you go to the meeting of the AMERICAN INSTITUTE OF ELECTRICAL ENGINEERS (in display) at Pittsburgh, January 26-30, by Capital Airlines." Each individual mailing ran from 100 to 10,000, depending on the number of known delegates' names that were obtained. Costs were extremely low, but results were extremely high.

The 50 or so individual mailings in one year produced something over $150,000 in traceable one-way and round-trip reservations, and measurable returns came to over 25%.

2. LETTERS AND ENCLOSURES

Of the many types and varied forms of sales promotional literature, letters, of course, are by far the most widely used. In fact, there is practically no form of mailing piece aside from a post card itself which isn't, more often than not, accompanied by a letter. Even self-mailers are frequently made up to incorporate a letter either as the entire inside section, or in the case of the larger pieces which open out into veritable broadsides, as an integral part of the design. The familiar appearance of a standard letter form made up to resemble typewriting and reproduced on a conventional letterhead design contributes something to a mailing which nothing else can duplicate.

Since a letter may accompany any form of sales promotional literature, then, and since all these other forms thereby become enclosures, the classification of "Letters and Enclosures," may need clarifying. Here "enclosures" are distinguished from these other forms as being pieces which, because of their size or their design or their very nature, normally would not be mailed alone. Such enclosures would include blotters, index cards, business cards, coupons, tickets, order forms, reply cards and envelopes, picture cards and simulated photographs, poster stamps and stickers, single-page leaflets, and all the various printed novelties used to dramatize the so-called "gadget letters." The term refers primarily to those letter-and-enclosure combinations in which each is more or less dependent on the other for its effectiveness. It refers to the wide variety of plain and ingenious "envelope stuffers" which are enclosed with bills from public service companies and retail stores, with insurance notices and with bank statements, but which are hardly complete or impressive enough to stand on their own feet as mailing pieces. It refers to package enclosures as well as to envelope enclosures. In the aggregate, therefore, the volume of pieces designed to be used as enclosures and nothing else is tremendous, and they serve a wide number of important purposes.

The many different types of letters regularly employed in sales promotional programs and the objectives they are written to accomplish are covered elsewhere in this volume. (See also Chapter 7.) The letter is literally the foundation of direct-mail advertising and mail-order selling, and is more widely used in practically every other sales promotional function than any other piece. Many comparative tests in these fields have shown the letter to exert a more powerful influence on returns than any other element of the mailing—enclosure, envelope, reply form, color combination, form of postage, or even all of them together—with the single exception of the list. Nothing can cut returns like a poor list, and nothing can build them up like a good one.

Today, with the advent of computers and other electronic list-sorting machines, working with lightning speeds, there is little excuse for a poor or obsolete mailing list.

With the great variety and tremendous volume of folders and broadsides to compete with, this well-designed accordion-type folder claims ready attention. It was issued by the Colorado Division of Commerce to promote the serving of Colorado beef by restaurants and hotels.

3. FOLDERS AND BROADSIDES

When post cards, self-mailers, small folders, or other simple letter enclosures are no longer adequate to give proper length, proper display, or proper impressiveness to a sales promotional message, the next step is the preparation of a folder or a broadside, which is simply a large-size folder usually designed to unfold by progressively dramatic stages until the final fold releases a big smash climax or "broadside." Folders and broadsides are the standard pieces of printed advertising, and compare more closely to newspaper or magazine advertisements in style of copy and lay-out than do any other of the sales promotional forms. Since they are printed on single sheets which are folded and trimmed rather than gathered and bound, they are relatively inexpensive to produce and are highly flexible so far as size, shape, and style are concerned.

Many, probably a majority of, direct-mail campaigns are based on folders as the means of doing the specific job of illustrating and describing the product or service in detail, a job which can't be performed by a letter unless it is of the illustrated or four-page letterhead variety. Folders used to precede and follow up the more elaborate booklets, brochures, catalogs, and presentations permit the advertiser to make more frequent mailings, to deliver his sales points in more rapid succession, and to gain quicker advantage from the cumulative effect of a series or campaign. Folders are the "mass" medium of sales promotion, intended to establish contact with the widest possible number of prospects by distribution through the mail, through dealers' stores, and through salesmen's calls.

Broadsides go a step further than folders in the graphic presentation of a complete story. Their use makes it possible to inject a note of extraordinary emphasis at certain stages of a campaign such as the beginning or, as an abrupt change of pace, the closing stages or the final climax. They provide a larger printing surface for bold pictorial and copy expression and give the impression of bigness when there is a psychological advantage in doing so. Successful

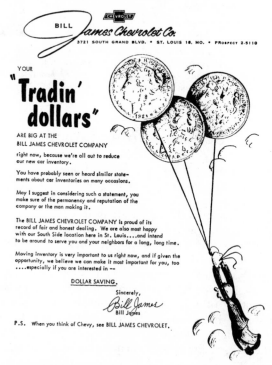

A promotion letter combining cartoon with copy, produced by M. W. Finkenbinder, of Lisle M. Ramsey & Associates, Inc., for the Bill James Chevrolet Company of St. Louis, Missouri.

broadsides are designed to capture interest immediately with a forceful opening, and then follow through in orderly, accelerating sequence to a rousing finish. At the same time, care must be taken to avoid confusion in following the story and to prevent difficulty in handling the piece.

4. BOOKLETS AND BROCHURES

Sales promotional literature of this classification is selected in preference to other forms for any or all of the following reasons:

a. Because the copy—the term "copy" including illustrations, captions, headlines, tables, charts, graphs, and other display matter as well as text—is too long to fit comfortably into the limited space of a folder or broadside.

b. Because the purpose of the piece is to establish the need and create the want for the thing being promoted rather than simply to give its specifications and prices, as is done with catalogs and price lists. Where a catalog *informs* and *describes,* a booklet *instructs* and *inspires.*

c. Because no other style of piece will convey the same feeling of dignity, prestige, and intrinsic value when those qualities are important.

d. Because it is desirable to impart information in a form which can be kept for thorough reading and study and which will be filed for future reference. Booklets, like catalogs, are usually planned for permanence; while cards, enclosures, folders, and broadsides are intended to deliver a flash message and are expected to live a shorter life.

e. Because the subject matter naturally lends itself to orderly page-by-page sequence and to more or less departmental organization. Where several related subjects or products are handled in a single piece under separate chapter headings, the booklet is the piece of choice.

Brochures Merely De Luxe Booklets

A brochure, according to commonly accepted sales promotional definition, is merely a de luxe booklet, just as a broadside is a de luxe folder. The distinction between them is one of degree rather than basic function. Elaborate, oversize, or extraordinary booklets are called brochures, which gain in impressiveness through sheer richness of design, illustration, typography, paper stock, color, bindings, or other physical attributes.

When to Use and When Not to Use

The same qualities which give booklets and brochures their advantages over other kinds of literature also set their limitations. Their greater length and their added cost make it impractical to issue them as frequently as simpler, less expensive pieces, especially for mailing purposes. A series of booklet mailings is of necessity spaced more widely than, say, a series of folder mailings, and its cumulative effect is slower in developing. More time is required both to prepare and produce them, so they do not lend themselves as effectively to situations where timeliness is a factor. Also, more time is required to read and digest them, so they seldom get the same fast response as a piece which can impart its message quickly and then be either discarded or acted upon at once.

As its name signifies, "booklet" is the diminutive of "book" and follows the traditional book format more closely than it does the advertising format. Booklets and brochures point up the distinction between editorial and advertising treatment, a distinction which is developed more fully in the following section on creating sales promotional literature.

Many types of special booklets to fit many special needs are required in sales promotional programs. Among the most prevalent are the following:

Product Booklets, which may be planned either singly or as a series; which may be devoted to all the uses for each different product in the line or to the different uses for the same product among various classes of customers; which may cover any angle of invention, discovery, raw materials, research, or production of the product having sales significance. There are almost as many kinds of product booklets and brochures as there are products, and they represent probably the widest use of this classification.

Yearbooks, Annual Reports, and Anniversary Books, which are regarded as "institutional" pieces as distinguished from "product" pieces. As the concept of sales promotion has broadened to encompass public relations and even personnel relations, the importance of institutional literature has become more and more widely recognized. Company yearbooks and annual reports receive greater attention and more generous treatment than they ever did before; they go beyond bare profit-and-loss statements to interpret financial operations graphically and to cover such other phases of the business as sales and marketing, production procedures, industrial relations, expansion and development programs, products and product development, reseach and community support. Many old established concerns are now looking for opportunities to issue anniversary booklets or brochures where for years they studiously avoided them. In addition to conventional twenty-fifth, fiftieth, or one hundredth anniversaries of a company's founding, institutional books are prepared to commemorate such other important dates in the development of a business or of its industry as these:

The introduction of new materials or processes.

The opening of new foreign or domestic markets.

The establishment of new plants and branches.

The birthdays or anniversaries of chief executives.

The occasions of "open houses" or other events calling for "Trip Through the Plant" booklets.

Any significant "firsts" in the company's past record.

Such literature appropriately combines historic milestones with contemporary accomplishment. It supplements product booklets and other strictly sales pieces by providing a background of prestige and good will which makes selling easier over the entire line. It enhances a company's position among customers, stockholders, and employees alike.

Instruction Books. Wherever there is a need for conveying information to owners or users about how to operate a product, how to service it, or how to use it in a variety of ways, a sales promotional booklet is usually selected as the most suitable vehicle. Many splendid examples of operation booklets which keep customers sold while instructing them in the proper way to operate their purchases are supplied by the automobile manufacturers, the washing machine companies, and concerns in the office equipment field. Many industrial firms prepare excellent booklets on the servicing of their products. And the best illustrations of booklets which stimulate the wider sales of products by showing different ways of using them are the recipe books of the food companies, the drink-mixing manuals of the distillers, the travel literature of the railroads and steamship lines, and the color charts and decorating combinations of the paint companies.

In all instruction literature the chief considerations are: (1) To keep it simple, readable, and understandable by avoiding technical jargon and overdetailed explanation; (2) to illustrate as well as describe; and (3) to hold customers' friendship and loyalty in the expectation that they will keep buying over and over again. In other words, whether it deals with operating, servicing, or using the product, the booklet prepared for that purpose is treated as a sales instrument rather than simply as routine technical data.

Reference Books. Closely allied with instruction books, yet serving a broader if somewhat less utilitarian purpose, are the reference books issued by many companies to supply present and prospective customers with the sort of informative material on general subjects which they might want to keep for permanent reference. The subject matter of such booklets need not directly concern a specific product or service in the sense that instruction booklets do, but it is sufficiently related to the sponsor's interests to be appropriate and to produce sales results. Outstanding examples which have been prepared in recent years include:

> The United Air Lines' elaborate booklets of "Air Maps," which are preserved and treasured by travelers because they contain excellently prepared and beautifully printed relief maps in full color of vast segments of the country. They bring geography to life in a manner which both instructs and entertains and will remain useful for many years to come.

> A monumental work by James Gray, Inc., direct-mail advertising specialists, called "Carrying the Mail: The Historic Drama of the Growth of the Postal System," which also contained much useful postal rate data and general postal information. Issued at a time of important rate changes, the book presented timely reference data, and the sections on historic steps in the development of mail service—starting with the earliest recorded methods of delivering messages, tracing the origin of postage stamps and postal delivery, and winding up with "the miracle of air mail"—were of practically timeless interest.

> "A Look at Peptic Ulcer," a so-called "Trans-Vision" booklet of Wyeth Laboratories, ethical pharmaceuticals, which described this condition to doctors by means of a series of anatomical drawings printed in color gravure on sheets of acetate which built up the picture step by step in cross-sections until the full image emerged. Surveys in the medical profession have shown that as many as 75% of the recipients of such reference books keep them in their permanent files.

In all these cases and, in fact, in the cases of most reference booklets which do really effective jobs for their sponsors, company and product names are greatly subordinated to the subjects presented, and the term "sponsor" is entirely accurate in this connection because worth-while reference literature actually is "sponsored" to the same degree that educational or entertainment features are sponsored on radio and television; brief mentions at the front of the book and short "commercials" at the back are usually as far as the sponsor feels he should go. Companies whose sales promotional programs have not yet taken advantage of the good-will possibilities of reference books would probably find it profitable to do so if there exist among their customers certain special applications for such specific reference data as the following:

> Mathematical tables like metric and apothecaries' measures; decimal equivalents as applied to particular problems; rate, cost, and pricing figures peculiar to a business, trade, industry, or profession, etc.

> Standard forms similar to the type styles and sizes, halftone and Ben Day screens, engraving and electroplating scales, etc., of the graphic arts industries, or the grades and cuts of the packing industry.

> Period styles such as exist in the furniture and home furnishings industries, or color combinations as used in these industries as well as in the clothing, paint, printing, automobile, and other industries.

> Performance records comparable to the batting, fielding, and pitching

averages of baseball players; team standings by years; track and field marks, etc., as they have been related to the sale of sporting goods.

Charts and graphs depicting periodic trends in markets, building, sales, production, income, expenditures, taxes, or any other data pertinent to the audience being reached.

Photographic records of persons or places of importance to individual groups, as a textbook publisher uses a portrait book of distinguished educators or a seed and nursery company uses a picture book of celebrated gardens.

Historic events and personages in any field that can be reconstructed by words or pictures and have sufficient bearing on present-day conditions to be of continuing interest.

Facsimiles of famous documents; reproductions of famous paintings, statues, and architectural studies; reprints of the outstanding literature of a business or profession—in short, appropriate printed keepsakes and souvenirs of any sort that possess qualities of permanence, usefulness, and lasting value.

Emphasis on reference literature becomes especially important when, as at the present time, competition for attention and reading time is so keen. Booklets which give the appearance of containing a substantial enough body of facts, figures, and specimens to make them seem worth keeping for future use have better than an even chance of holding their own against other matter in the daily mail; they provide salesmen and dealers with an appreciated form of literature for personal distribution; they get the biggest play at business shows and exhibitions; and they make the most productive offers for publication and radio advertising from an inquiry-getting standpoint.

Sales Manuals and Training Booklets. Corresponding to the instruction books for owners and users previously discussed, sales manuals and other forms of training booklets constitute the instruction literature for salesmen, district managers, dealers and distributors and their salesmen, sales correspondents, branch office personnel, or whatever parts of the entire distributing organization benefit from training in the more or less standardized procedures of handling their jobs. While the actual details of preparing and using sales instruction literature are covered thoroughly in another section, the funds to pay for them come out of the sales promotion budget and they must be correlated with all the other elements of the complete sales promotion program.

Whether it is prepared in the form of bound booklets or, as is more commonly the case, of loose-leaf binders, sales instruction literature nearly always follows the booklet style both in the way it is written and illustrated and in the way it is produced. And the same rules of simplicity, brevity, and graphic illustration which apply to consumer instruction books apply just as forcefully here. Even sales correspondence manuals, if they are to be of maximum effectiveness, must be easy to use and so indexed that the answers to any problems may be referred to quickly.

5. HOUSE ORGANS AND BULLETINS

An integral part of practically every sales promotional program is some sort of company periodical. Variously referred to as "house organs," "house magazines," "salesmen's, dealers', or employees' bulletins"—they all have certain definite characteristics in common:

- a. They are issued at regular weekly, monthly, bimonthly, or quarterly intervals.
- b. They appear in substantially the same format issue after issue, thereby building up cumulative recognition value and continuing reader interest.
- c. They make use of the editorial techniques that have been developed by newspaper and magazine publishers.
- d. They are literally business papers serving individual companies, comparable in purpose, preparation, and production to the general business papers serving individual industries, trades, or specialized groups.
- e. They are journals of news, information, inspiration, or instruction first and advertising media second if they are fulfilling their objectives; in other words, their first responsibility is to their readers because the advertising value of a periodical is in direct proportion to its reader-interest.

External and Internal Company Periodicals

For convenience, company periodicals are customarily divided into two major groups, both of which represent sales promotional functions: *Internal house organs* circulating inside an organization to its own salesmen, its own branch, district or divisional office people, its own employees and their families, and its own stockholders; and *external house organs* circulating outside an organization to owners and users, dealers and distributors, suppliers, community leaders, libraries, schools and colleges, selected prospects, and anyone else whose good will toward the company is considered an asset.

In actual practice there is often considerable overlapping between these two major groups, as many of the best-edited house organs are of broad enough general interest to be worth distributing both internally and externally. And even house organs whose primary purpose is to reach outside audiences should be pretty freely circulated inside the organization; if it is a sales publication, for instance, certainly the entire sales force should know what is going into it; and if it is a good-will and institutional publication, all personnel— sales, office, and production alike—will benefit by reading it regularly.

Four Principal House Organ Formats

While successful house organs have been prepared in almost every conceivable size, shape, and style that can be printed or processed, the great majority in current use fall into one of four general formats, the one selected being determined by the publication's subject matter, its audience, and its budget:

1. *The Popular Magazine Format* is preferred for periodicals in which most of the editorial material is handled in feature article style. This format permits impressive typographic and illustrative display, high-quality printing, and variety and flexibility of make-up. It is especially suited for circulation among customers and prospects in class markets, although a number of excellent salesman and dealer papers are done in this style as well. The average size is 8½ by 11 inches, a few publications going as large as 9 by 12 inches, or even 11 by 14 inches, and some as small as 6 by 9 inches with the same sort of design treatment. Nearly all of them are printed in color, at least for the covers, and they range anywhere from 16 to 32 pages in thickness.

2. *The Digest Magazine Format* has grown in popularity the last few years and has definite advantages when illustrations and type display can be subordinated to straight reading matter. Since such house organs are obviously capitalizing on the prestige of *The Reader's Digest, Coronet,* and the many other magazines in the small 5½- by 7½-inch size range, it is important for them to maintain the standard digest editorial formula as well as the standard digest format. Original articles or articles selected for reprinting must be terse, condensed, and of sufficient interest to the publication's readership to stand on their own feet without benefit of illustrative material. The *Coronet* style, however, does allow more pictorial latitude than the *Reader's Digest* style, but since illustrations are regarded as such a vital part of house organ publications, those of the digest format should be confined to above-average audiences.

3. *The Daily Newspaper Format,* usually of the 5-column tabloid style of approximately 11 by 17 inches, is by far the most popular kind of house organ for dealers and distributors and their salesmen, and ranks high among the publications for company salesmen and employees. The reason for this preference, of course, is that news makes up the bulk of their editorial content, and no better medium has yet been devised for the dissemination and emphatic display of news than the newspaper. For house organ purposes, the standard 8-column newspaper page is too big for convenient handling and, besides, the tabloid format is ideally adapted to photographic lay-outs and big headlines, and those are the lifeblood of aggressive sales publications. Except in rare cases where recurrent news is the prime factor, newspapers are not as satisfactory as magazines for the good-will and institutional periodicals that go to owners, users, and general lists.

4. *The News Letter Format* is an outgrowth of the conventional 8½- by 11-inch multigraphed or mimeographed bulletins, modified by the comparatively recent popularity of the so-called "Washington letters." Originally consisting of individual sheets clipped or stapled together—a form, incidentally, which is still widely used when economy is imperative—the contemporary news letter format is a 4-page affair folded down from a 17- by 22-inch sheet. While some house organs of this style are printed

with an extra color and make use of simple line drawings, cartoons, or charts and graphs, they have the same disadvantages from an illustrative standpoint as do the digest magazine styles. Because of their connotation, however, they do suggest last-minute news of a somewhat confidential nature and consequently are successfully used in both internal and external periodicals to all kinds of audiences. But in spite of the fact that it is the least expensive of all house organ formats, it is also the least widely used.

Importance of Selecting the Right Editor

It is a truism that a house organ is no better than its editor and a corollary that an editor is primarily a journalist rather than an advertising man, a salesman, a personnel man, or a sales executive— or, of course, their feminine equivalents. That doesn't mean that persons with these other qualifications can't also be capable and experienced journalists, but it does mean that if one of them is selected to edit his company's house organ, the selection must be based on his ability as an editor and not on his record in advertising, sales, or personnel work. Editing a house organ is a many-sided job consisting of either writing or selecting manuscripts of greatest interest to a particular group of readers; cutting, adding, revising, and getting them in shape for publication; obtaining the best illustrative materials to present them most interestingly; writing headlines and captions for them; and bringing out successive issues which have both variety and balance. The results of an editor's work speak for themselves and the extent of his ability is apparent in the success of his publication. A professional editor usually knows through instinct, training, and experience what his readers' interests are, but if he doesn't, he knows how to find out.

What Readers Want

Reader preferences in house organ contents naturally vary according to lines of business, types of publications, and classes of audiences, but surveys of various groups have revealed certain averages of response which are helpful in the selection of editorial material. The following subject listings for both internal and external house organs indicate the general order of preference:

I. INTERNAL HOUSE ORGANS:

    a. For Salesmen:

        1. Experiences of Salesmen, reported by 51% of total concerns.
        2. Personal News Items, reported by 19%.
        3. Inspirational, reported by 11%.
        4. Salesmen's Standings, reported by 4%.
        5. Service, reported by 3%.
        6. Home Office Cooperation, reported by 2%.
        7. Users' Experiences, reported by 2%.

b. For Employees:

1. Personal News Items, reported by 38%.
2. Organization News, reported by 18%.
3. Human-Interest Stories, reported by 9%.
4. Welfare, reported by 9%.
5. Semihumorous, reported by 8%.
6. Technical Articles, reported by 8%.
7. Educational, reported by 5%.
8. Inspirational, reported by 5%.

II. EXTERNAL HOUSE ORGANS:

a. For Owners or Users:

1. How to Use the Product, reported by 36%.
2. Testimonials and Stories About Well-Known Users, reported by 31%.
3. Human Interest Stories, reported by 15%.
4. Market and Trade News, reported by 5%.

b. For Distributors and Dealers:

1. Merchandising Plans and Methods, reported by 22%.
2. Reports of Dealers' Experiences, reported by 20%.
3. General News, reported by 16%.
4. Technical, reported by 12%.
5. Educational, reported by 9%.
6. Human Interest, reported by 9%.
7. Personal News Items, reported by 5%.
8. Inspirational, reported by 3%.
9. Service, reported by 2%.
10. Humorous, reported by 2%.

c. For Jobbers' and Dealers' Salesmen:

1. Sales and Merchandising Methods, reported by 41%.
2. Stories of Individual Success, reported by 29%.
3. Inspirational, reported by 10%.
4. Testimonials from Other Salesmen, reported by 10%.
5. Personal Experiences, reported by 3%.
6. Sales Contests, reported by 3%.
7. Service, reported by 2%.

How Users Appraise House Organ Results

While there are notable exceptions, relatively few house organs make any attempt to get direct returns in the form of inquiries or orders. Any voluntary response from readers is expressed in terms of occasional "Letters to the Editor" which are welcomed more as interesting contributions for that department of the paper than as an accurate index of reader interest. Unlike other sales promotional pieces sent out in general mailings for specific order- or inquiry-getting purposes, house organ results are difficult to appraise. Consequently, readership studies have been undertaken by a number of companies and several formulas developed for determining how many readers an external house organ may have.

An unusual mail survey plan was conducted some time ago among the readers of the Socony company magazine, *The Compass*. The following letter went out from the research offices, accompanied by the two self-addressed post cards reproduced on page 279.

ALFRED POLITZ RESEARCH, INC.

400 Madison Avenue, New York 17, N. Y.

Dear Sir:

We act as the research agent for Socony-Vacuum Oil Company, Inc. The Marine Sales Department of this company publishes a magazine entitled "The Compass" which has been coming to you or your organization with the compliments of the marketers of Gargoyle Marine Oils.

"The Compass" is not intended to compete with specialized trade papers and magazines which are devoted to the marine field. Its objective is to bring stories of the world's ships and the shipping industry to those whose livelihood and interests are related to the sea. The Gargoyle Marine Oil marketers realized that their magazine must have definite interest, as well as informational value, if it is to accomplish its objective.

Since "The Compass" is intended and distributed wholly as a courtesy and is not sold, there is no measure of the magazine's popularity or lack of popularity. Therefore, we have been asked to find out what the people who get the magazine think of it. The company feels that if they attempted to get this information themselves, the answers might be influenced by politeness. In our undertaking we are in a position to assure those who give us an opinion that their names will never appear. The answers will remain in our office and only a statistical report will be given to our client. Putting the facts squarely before you is, we believe, the most intelligent approach, as it will enable you to appreciate the problem.

We would like to have you give us your opinion frankly, without any reservations. To avoid any undue burden on you, we are enclosing two return post cards on which there are five statements about "The Compass". You can use card A or card B, depending upon whether you receive "The Compass" as an individual or for an organization. Please return only one of them. Would you kindly put an "X" behind the statement or statements that best describes your reactions or the reactions of your organization. If your time permits you to comment on the problem yourself, we will be very thankful for any additional statement you may want to make. But even if you only mark an X or X's, it will be of great help.

Sincerely yours,

ALFRED POLITZ RESEARCH, INC.

Socony engaged an outside research organization to make a survey of reader interest in its house publication, The Compass.

A (For your individual opinions)

1. I don't know anything about the magazine "The Compass". ☐

2. The intention of "The Compass" may be good, but I don't read it. ☐

3. I read "The Compass" once in a while. ☐

4. I read "The Compass" rather regularly. ☐

5. "The Compass" is interesting enough to make me want to receive it in the future. ☐

6. Your position or job ....

7. Comment, if you wish ....

....

....

....

B (For opinions of your organization)

1. We don't know anything about the magazine "The Compass". ☐

2. The intention of "The Compass" may be good but no one here reads it. ☐

3. To the best of your knowledge, about how many persons in your organization read "The Compass" once in a while? ....

4. About how many persons read "The Compass" rather regularly? ....

5. "The Compass" is interesting enough to make us want to receive it in the future. ☐

6. Type of organization ....

7. Comment, if you wish ....

....

....

....

The two return cards enclosed with the Politz letter reproduced on page 278. The high return was largely because only 10 questions were asked—5 on each card. Too many questionnaires misfire because they ask too many questions.

Other Readership Studies

A similar type of study done by Starch/Inra/Hooper for the Shell Oil Company magazine indicated a readership of 87%. Three thousand retailers, wholesalers, and manufacturers, out of a total of 17,300 on the list of the Pepperell Manufacturing Company to receive its *News Sheet,* once checked an enclosed post card and returned it in order to stay on the list. A double post card similar to that employed on behalf of Socony was used by the Squibb organization to check the readership of *Today In Pharmacy* among retail druggists, and was likewise very effective.

The B. Manischewitz Company, Cincinnati, Ohio, reported in a trade publication that it had found the free gift offer the best and most economical way of checking readership. By offering a free gift in the pages of its house organ and enclosing a business reply card for readers to use in asking for it, the company arrived at a method of determining the percentage of names on its list that represented actual readers. "The gift has to be some object of wide appeal to your particular audience," explained Howard Manischewitz, sales promotion director, "and the reason for offering the gift must be explained—the celebration of an anniversary, expressing thanks to faithful readers, etc. Do not, however, tie in the gift with an effort to obtain information of some sort." The formula for translating the reply cards into terms of actual readers was given in the following chart:

Value of Gift	*To Determine Number of Readers*
Under .05	multiply requests by 12
.05 to .10	multiply requests by 5
.10 to .25	multiply requests by 3
.25 to .50	multiply requests by 2
.50 to $1	multiply requests by 1½

It was Mr. Manischewitz' contention that a company which offers, say, a 10-cent key chain in its house organ and receives 500 business reply cards could claim it has a total active readership of 5 times 500, or 2,500.

Tests of the Mead Corporation

During a Presidential election, the Mead Corporation arranged to insert a sample ballot in every copy of its external company magazine, *Good Impressions,* used to promote the sale of high-grade printing papers. Readers were asked to cast their ballots—and, at the same time, to answer a number of other questions aimed at learning whether the magazine was read. Something over 70% of those replying stated that they had adapted ideas, art work, editorials, and copy from *Good Impressions*. The publication is a quarterly, and 60% of the replies favored having it issued 6, 12, or as many times a year "as you can keep up the present standard." Three out of four said that they specified Mead paper of the brands promoted in the house organ as a direct result.

In another Mead test of readership the company made a free offer of general interest and close application to the paper business; it offered a free tree! The offer wasn't displayed and it appeared inconspicuously on an inside page along with a business reply card, but the results were astonishing. Out of a circulation of 11,500, requests for free trees amounted to 4,017. Handling the shipments turned out to be a whole lot more than the company had bargained for, due to the limited time during the spring and fall when trees can be shipped; the necessary damp moss, moisture-proof paper, and 3-inch diameter cylinders for shipping them; and unexpected Japanese beetle regulations; but it found out about house organ readership. Commenting on the experience, Allen Converse of the Gray and Rogers Advertising Agency, editor of *Good Impressions*, interpreted the results in the light of the readership chart of the Manischewitz Company. "There is an article on how to estimate the readership of your house organ," Mr. Converse reported, "and it says, 'Offer them an article of this sort.' It has a table worked out, and for an item under 5 cents—and our tree costs 3½ cents—you multiply the returns by 12 and that gives you the readership. On that basis we have 48,000 readers for a magazine of 11,500 circulation!"

User and Consumer Magazines

Some house organs have proved so effective as a means of promoting sales that they have grown into full-scale publishing projects. It is estimated that automobile manufacturers alone, in a typical year, published nearly 20 million copies of magazines designed to increase user satisfaction with cars which they have purchased, and thus prepare the ground for users to buy the same make of car when they are ready to trade in their old one.

Some companies have their internal advertising staffs edit and publish the external magazine; others depend on advertising agencies or special publishing services. As might be expected, such publications appear and disappear, publishing policy being determined in each company by annual sales, budgets, and customer response.

International House Organs

The effectiveness of external company magazines in helping to establish new markets overseas has been illustrated many times, notably by such concerns as Coca-Cola, United Fruit, and others doing considerable business through foreign branches or associates.

Some of these publications are published in English only, others in the language of the country to which they are sent, and still others are bilingual—English and one foreign language—or even multilingual (as English-French-Spanish).

Especially noteworthy are the foreign-language company periodicals published by some of the American petroleum-products companies operating abroad. An executive for one of these companies said recently, "Our overseas magazines have been doing an educational job for us which we could not have accomplished through any other form of sales promotion."

6. CATALOGS AND PRICE LISTS

While the catalog in most selling operations is too important to be classified as a sales promotional device, it very often is a key piece in promoting the sale of a product by mail or through salesmen. Because of its over-all importance, and the investment involved, it has been treated separately in this HANDBOOK.

7. PORTFOLIOS AND SALES PRESENTATIONS

The use of this type of sales promotional literature is limited largely to salesmen's operations. They are sometimes made a part of a promotional campaign, as in the case of portfolios for use of dealers and dealers' salesmen, but to be really effective they require a salesman.

8. SAMPLES AND SPECIALTIES

Many sales executives contend, with sound reason, that it is desirable in promoting a product or service to put something into the hands of a prospective buyer which he can see and feel. The swatches and samples sent out by mills and merchants in the textile and paper fields are but one example of the use of samples in sales promotion. There are many others. Where the product does not lend itself to sampling, specialties demonstrating what a product does are employed. Both samples and specialties are being used more and more extensively as competition becomes keener, and their use has been treated at some length in other sections of this HANDBOOK.

9. REPRINTS AND PUBLICITY RELEASES

As publicity, like public relations, becomes more and more widely recognized as a sales promotional function, the importance of correlating publicity releases and editorial and advertising reprints with the over-all sales promotional program increases proportionately. A high percentage of the literature distributed as direct mail takes the form of news stories to the editors of newspapers, magazines, farm papers, and business and professional journals; of news photos; of feature articles or material to furnish the basis for individually written feature articles; of reprints of news and feature stories that have already appeared; of material for salesmen, dealers, and distributors to furnish their local newspapers and radio stations; of reprints and preprints of advertisements and advertising campaigns, with stories about them for the publications to carry as business news if they wish to do so. Once begun, an intelligently planned publicity campaign, tied in with other sales promotional literature, keeps refueling itself. Items of real interest in the newspapers are picked up by the radio news commentators and grow into requests for follow-up stories or for magazine and business paper feature articles, which in turn provide the material for reprint mailings. At almost every stage of the sales promotional program opportunities crop up for intensifying its effectiveness with well-handled publicity.

Several precautions, however, need to be observed in planning a publicity operation:

a. As is the case with house organs and, to a certain extent, book and booklet preparation, publicity is an editorial rather than an advertising function and should be under the direction of trained newspaper reporters or magazine writers with an understanding of what the public wants and a knowledge of how to present it professionally.

b. The releases should be limited to items of real news or feature material of recognized human interest value. Enough events are actually happening in most organizations to provide timely news, and there are enough remarkable people, unusual processes, dramatic pictures, and other extraordinary side lights in a business to be uncovered by alert publicity people who are really digging for stories, so that there will be no need for resorting to trumped-up news or padded, overcolored features.

c. Too much material should not be sent to the same editors and commentators too frequently. Even if it is all good, there is a limit to the amount of space or time that can be devoted to one company, and a sound publicity program is organized to cultivate different fields at different periods. No company can afford to acquire a reputation as an inveterate publicity seeker.

d. All material submitted for publication should be prepared according to the accepted editorial technique of the publication to which it is submitted.

In the case of news stories, opinions, interpretations, and editorializing are avoided; sources of information are cited; copy conforms to standard news style; photographs are glossy prints with complete captions attached.

Most published magazine and business paper articles and many newspaper stories about a company deserve reprinting and distributing at least among its own employees and salesmen, and probably among its dealers and customers. Most people are human enough to take what a company says about itself with a grain of salt but to accept without reservation what an outside agency says about it, especially if that agency has prestige.

10. WINDOW AND STORE DISPLAYS

Companies manufacturing products which are sold through most of the retail outlets in their fields—drug, grocery, hardware, and electrical stores; barber and beauty shops; garages and service stations—handle their display campaigns on as large a scale as their outdoor advertising, car card, or even publication or radio advertising campaigns. However, the efficient operation of window and store display programs is so closely connected with the merchandising activities of salesmen, and is so dependent on their support for its success, that it becomes an important responsibility of the sales promotion department.

As pieces of sales promotional literature, displays involve the same problems of planning, creation, production, distribution, and use that are common to all the other classifications covered. They usually come out of the same sales promotional budget, and are correlated with all the other ramifications of the program, their particular niche being, of course, the establishment of point-of-sale contacts which frequently is the final factor in completing the sale begun by some other activity. There are so many varieties of window, counter, floor, and wall displays, with such variations in cost, materials, and methods of construction that they cannot be as conveniently classified as other types of literature, but they are an indispensable part of the sales promotional picture in most dealer campaigns.

Another practical reason for having the sales promotion department responsible for window and store displays is that modern marketing campaigns make much use of identifying themes, slogans, symbols, cartoon characters, logotypes, etc. It is often important, also, that color schemes be the same in all aspects of a sales promotion effort. The sales promotion department, therefore, should have the decision-making authority over all window and in-store displays in order that the desired consistency of approach can be maintained.

I. Literature for Holding Present Customers

OBJECTIVES	1 Post Cards and Self-Mailers	2 Letters and Enclosures	3 Folders and Broadsides	4 Booklets and Brochures	5 House Organs and Bulletins	6 Catalogs and Price Lists	7 Portfolios and Presentations	8 Samples and Specialties	9 Reprints, Publicity Releases	10 Window and Store Displays
To acquaint customers with the services behind the product		X		X	X					
To maintain customers' interest in the product after the purchase		X		X	X				X	
To increase consumption or use of the product	X	X	X	X	X	X		X	X	X
To suggest new uses	X	X		X	X		X	X	X	X
To inform customers where stocks and services are available	X	X	X							X
To instruct customers in the proper use of the product		X	X	X	X					
To offer suggestions on servicing of the product		X		X						
To revive inactive accounts	X	X	X		X	X		X		X
To step up the size of customers' orders	X	X	X	X		X				X
To step up the frequency of customers' orders	X	X	X		X	X		X		X
To sell the full line, or other items in the line	X	X	X	X	X	X		X		X
To introduce new products or new policies		X	X	X	X		X		X	X
To acknowledge orders and payments	X	X								
To collect accounts		X								
To maintain contact between salesmen's calls	X	X	X	X	X	X		X	X	
To announce new addresses or telephone numbers	X	X	X							
To give customers news of special occasions or coming events	X	X	X		X				X	X
To notify customers of imminent price changes and new styles or models	X	X	X		X					
To welcome new customers		X	X							

II. Literature for Winning New Customers

OBJECTIVES	1 Post Cards and Self-Mailers	2 Letters and Enclosures	3 Folders and Broadsides	4 Booklets and Brochures	5 House Organs and Bulletins	6 Catalogs and Price Lists	7 Portfolios and Presentations	8 Samples and Specialties	9 Reprints, Publicity Releases	10 Window and Store Displays
To reach prospects whom salesmen have been unable to see	X	X	X	X	X	X		X	X	X
To offer charge accounts or other credit accommodations		X	X							
To get merchandise into the hands of prospects								X		
To bring buyers to the plant or showroom	X	X	X							X
To time sales messages to reach prospects at definite buying periods	X	X	X	X	X	X		X		X
To break down sales resistance through repetition of important points	X	X	X	X	X		X		X	X
To re-emphasize and summarize the sales arguments presented by salesmen		X	X	X						
To provide information which prospects file for permanent reference value		X	X	X	X	X		X	X	
To remind prospects of a steady source of supply	X	X	X		X	X				X
To overcome objections before they are raised		X	X	X	X		X	X		
To associate the name of the company with the leaders in its field									X	
To get the jump on competition	X	X	X							
To enable prospects to study claims without influence by salesmen or competitors		X	X	X		X		X		
To gain recognition for leadership and superiority		X	X	X	X	X	X	X	X	
To establish identity of products		X	X	X	X	X	X	X	X	X
To create confidence in minds of prospects		X	X	X	X	X	X	X	X	

III. Literature for Supporting Salesmen

OBJECTIVES	1 Post Cards and Self-Mailers	2 Letters and Enclosures	3 Folders and Broadsides	4 Booklets and Brochures	5 House Organs and Bulletins	6 Catalogs and Price Lists	7 Portfolios and Presentations	8 Samples and Specialties	9 Reprints, Publicity Releases	10 Window and Store Displays
To pave the way for salesmen's calls with material that educates the prospect in advance		X	X	X	X	X	X			
To obtain direct inquiries for salesmen to follow up	X	X	X							
To confirm salesmen's verbal statements with printed statements from the company		X	X	X			X		X	
To thank customers and prospects for courtesies extended salesmen	X	X								
To multiply a salesman's contacts	X	X	X	X		X	X			
To introduce and "build up" the salesman in advance of his calls	X	X								
To train salesmen in the most effective selling procedures		X	X	X	X		X		X	
To stimulate extra effort through special drives and contests		X	X	X	X					
To establish a reputation that makes it easier for salesmen to get interviews		X	X	X	X	X		X	X	X
To supply salesmen with a steady source of selling helps to make their interviews more productive		X	X	X	X		X	X		
To encourage the exchange of sales experiences among salesmen		X			X					
To provide media of inspiration and instruction		X			X					
To support salesmen with literature for them to leave with customers and prospects			X	X	X	X	X	X	X	X
To promote sales meetings and conventions		X	X		X					
To keep salesmen's prospect lists up to date	X	X								
To attract the highest type of salesman		X		X	X		X			
To enable salesmen to concentrate on their best prospects and territories				X	X	X	X			X

IV. Literature for Strengthening Dealer Relations

OBJECTIVES	1 Post Cards and Self-Mailers	2 Letters and Enclosures	3 Folders and Broadsides	4 Booklets and Brochures	5 House Organs and Bulletins	6 Catalogs and Price Lists	7 Portfolios and Presentations	8 Samples and Specialties	9 Reprints, Publicity Releases	10 Window and Store Displays
To obtain new dealers		X	X	X			X			
To acquaint dealers with the selling points of the product	X	X	X	X	X	X	X	X	X	
To provide dealers with merchandising plans and ideas		X	X	X	X		X			X
To enlist dealer support of the advertising program	X	X	X	X	X		X			X
To educate retail clerks in better selling methods		X	X	X	X		X			
To refer inquiries from national advertising to local dealers	X	X								
To explain house policies which safeguard dealers' interests		X		X	X		X		X	
To sell the dealers to their communities	X	X	X	X	X				X	X
To give distributors' salesmen helpful facts and suggestions which they can pass along to dealers		X			X		X			
To furnish ideas and materials for window and store displays		X	X	X	X		X	X	X	X
To offer dealers advisory assistance in matters of advertising, collection, financing, etc.		X		X	X					
To direct customers to dealers' stores	X	X	X					X	X	X
To supply dealers with literature for store and mail distribution		X	X	X		X		X	X	X
To promote contests among dealers and clerks		X	X	X	X		X			
To identify dealers with the product	X	X	X	X					X	X
To stage local exhibits, merchandise shows, and other affairs in dealers' communities	X	X	X					X	X	X

V. Literature for Intensifying the Advertising

OBJECTIVES	1 Post Cards and Self-Mailers	2 Letters and Enclosures	3 Folders and Broadsides	4 Booklets and Brochures	5 House Organs and Bulletins	6 Catalogs and Price Lists	7 Portfolios and Presentations	8 Samples and Specialties	9 Reprints, Publicity Releases	10 Window and Store Displays
To distribute copies of newspaper, magazine, and business paper advertising to salesmen and the trade		X	X	X	X		X		X	
To tie up local advertising with national advertising	X	X	X	X					X	X
To give radio and television advertising visual printed support		X	X	X	X			X	X	X
To convert advertising inquiries into sales	X	X	X	X		X		X		
To teach salesmen and distributors how to merchandise the advertising to dealers		X	X	X	X		X			
To teach dealers how to capitalize on the advertising through local direct-mail campaigns	X	X	X	X	X					
To stimulate inquiries by offering informative booklets, folders, and premiums	X	X	X	X	X	X		X		
To engage the merchandising cooperation of newspapers, magazines, radio stations, poster plants, etc.	X	X	X						X	
To reproduce advertisements and posters for point-of-purchase display purposes			X				X			X
To follow up dealers about inquiries	X	X								
To gather facts, testimonials, etc., to use in advertising	X	X	X							
To supply mats, proofs, copy, electrotypes, etc., for dealers' tie-up advertising		X	X	X	X		X	X		

VI. Literature for Broadening the Market

OBJECTIVES	1 Post Cards and Self-Mailers	2 Letters and Enclosures	3 Folders and Broadsides	4 Booklets and Brochures	5 House Organs and Bulletins	6 Catalogs and Price Lists	7 Portfolios and Presentations	8 Samples and Specialties	9 Reprints, Publicity Releases	10 Window and Store Displays
To obtain direct orders from territories not covered by salesmen	X	X	X	X		X		X		
To make possible the intensive cultivation of weak territories	X	X	X	X		X		X	X	X
To develop new types of buyers		X	X	X	X			X		
To reach new buyers and executives in the organizations of present customers and prospects	X	X	X	X	X	X				
To reach various members of buying committees who control purchases	X	X	X	X	X	X	X	X		
To go over the heads of buyers and reach "the man higher up"		X	X	X	X	X		X		
To develop a steady source of names from salesmen, dealers, etc., to be added to the permanent mailing lists	X	X	X		X					
To keep lists constantly up to date	X	X	X							
To provide for the efficient distribution of catalogs and other mailing pieces	X	X	X				X			
To make market surveys to determine the course of future sales and advertising expansion	X	X	X	X						
To facilitate the conducting of test campaigns on an inexpensive scale	X	X	X	X		X		X		X
To get the product specified or recommended as "standard"		X	X	X		X	X	X		

Typical Time Table

Mailing Date	First 100 Names	Second 100 Names	Third 100 Names	Fourth 100 Names	Fifth 100 Names	Sixth 100 Names
March 7	Mail Piece No. 1					
March 21	Mail Piece No. 2					
April 4	Mail Piece No. 3	Mail Piece No. 1				
April 18	Mail Piece No. 4	Mail Piece No. 2				
May 2	Mail Piece No. 5	Mail Piece No. 3	Mail Piece No. 1			
May 16	Mail Piece No. 6	Mail Piece No. 4	Mail Piece No. 2			
May 31	Mail Piece No. 5	Mail Piece No. 3	Mail Piece No. 1			
June 13		Mail Piece No. 6	Mail Piece No. 4	Mail Piece No. 2		
June 27			Mail Piece No. 5	Mail Piece No. 3	Mail Piece No. 1	
July 11			Mail Piece No. 6	Mail Piece No. 4	Mail Piece No. 2	
July 25				Mail Piece No. 5	Mail Piece No. 3	Mail Piece No. 1
August 8				Mail Piece No. 6	Mail Piece No. 4	Mail Piece No. 2
August 22					Mail Piece No. 5	Mail Piece No. 3
September 6					Mail Piece No. 6	Mail Piece No. 4
September 19						Mail Piece No. 5
October 3						Mail Piece No. 6

Salesmen call on first   100 names May and June
second 100 names June and July
third 100 names July and August
fourth 100 names August and September
fifth 100 names September and October
sixth 100 names October and November

This page from a Culligan dealer instruction book on direct mail gets right down to cases by giving dealers a practical mailing schedule to follow.

WHO PLANS THE LITERATURE?

The 10 major classifications of sales promotional literature just discussed constitute the tools of the job. How to use them most constructively, what part each one is to play, where they fit together to form a complete program—those are decisions to be worked out by the person or persons responsible for producing sales promotional results. This responsibility may be centered in any one of the following groups or may be shared by them all:

1. The sales department.
2. The sales promotional department.
3. The advertising department.
4. The advertising agency.
5. The service printer.
6. The sales promotion or direct-mail consultant.

The Advertising Agency Viewpoint

Many general agencies subscribe to the opinion that their facilities are keyed to the mass media like newspapers, magazines, radio, television, and so on, and that the planning and preparation of sales promotional literature is better handled by the client, either through its own organization or in cooperation with other outside agencies specializing in that specific activity. There are several reasons for this attitude on the part of advertising agencies, one of which was cited before a national convention of the Direct Mail Advertising Association by W. S. McLain of Fuller & Smith & Ross, Inc. Speaking primarily of the direct-mail aspects of sales promotional literature Mr. McLain said:

> To me, direct mail's first original weakness is the fact that it is usually eliminated from the annual budget of a manufacturing or business concern. I don't know why this is true. I sometimes think that we in the general agency business don't do as much selling on direct mail as we should. Our own particular organization, I believe, has done a very effective job in direct mail. We started out primarily as an industrial advertising agency, and developed into quite an extensive consumer goods advertising business. Even we don't take adequate advantage of direct mail, particularly at the point where the budget is being made up.

Why Some Agencies Concentrate on Sales Promotion

Among advertising agencies which have been active in the direct-mail and other sales promotional problems of their clients' businesses, the fact that this specialization has enabled them to integrate all the different media to their own and their clients' advantage seems to be the point of greatest importance. Julian P. Brodie of the former New York agency of Green-Brodie has stated:

> Almost every advertiser uses printed promotion to advantage. It seems to us that no conscientious advertising agency can or does evade its responsibility to serve clients in this field simply because the field is more challenging and hence treacherous. We have found the rewards commensurate with the risks. By taking the trouble to study the medium and explore its many

opportunities, we find we can produce certain results that are otherwise unattainable. Most of all, perhaps, we have thereby been enabled to offer clients a well-rounded program to integrate the direct advertising with the other phases of the client's campaigning and not set him adrift to fumble and experiment on his own. We think it is a more complicated medium than any other. But that's all the more reason for thinking that it *is* part of the agency's job!

Cases of agency participation in sales promotional campaigns which produced outstanding results for clients were reported by the president of the advertising agency. In 8 years the Woman's Institute of Scranton, Pennsylvania, as an illustration, sold $12 million worth of home study courses to develop it into the largest women's education institute in the world. Another campaign helped Harry and David of Bear Creek, Oregon, build the first business of selling fruit by mail, thus pioneering an idea which has since become a national industry. "Through direct mail and coupon advertising," the agency head told a conference, "we helped Richard Hudnut make the DuBarry Success Course the most popular of all methods for personal improvement. In 8 years, 10% of all the women in the United States between the ages 15 and 60 had requested information on this course. By direct mail exclusively, more than 10% of those inquiring had been sold. That means that, at one time, 1% of all the women in the United States had taken or were taking the DuBarry Success Course and each was sold by direct mail. That proves its power."

Why Many Companies Prepare Their Own Literature

While these and a number of other advertising agencies are both willing and able to shoulder many of the sales promotional responsibilities of clients, and while there are a few creative printers and qualified sales promotion consultants who do a good job of handling parts of campaigns, most companies depend on their own resources for nearly all the planning and a large share of the creation of their sales promotion. Where the volume of work is not great enough to require the services of a sales promotional staff, members of the advertising or sales departments who possess the necessary sales promotional talents are delegated to handle it. The ideal arrangement is the maintenance of a separate sales promotion department, whose duties are clearly differentiated from those of the sales department on one hand and the advertising department on the other. In many cases, even though the advertising department works with a capable and experienced agency, the sales promotion department draws on other sources when in need of outside assistance. Whether his organization is large or small, one individual should assume the responsibilities of "sales promotion manager," if not the title.

The objectives of all three departments—sales, sales promotion, and advertising—are the same, but they are arrived at in different ways. The abilities required to plan and produce a general advertising campaign are not the same as are required to plan and produce sales promotional literature or to operate a sales force. Each department is allotted its share of the total appropriation set aside for business development, but must work out its own solutions to the best methods of spending it, keeping in mind the best interests of the other departments and working in close cooperation with them.

PLANNING PROCEDURES

When it comes to the question of determining specifically which pieces of literature to schedule for a sales promotion program, the answer depends on the program's basic objectives. Each individual piece of literature is planned to accomplish some one of the following six objectives; each sales promotional program is planned to accomplish any or all of them. The six objectives for which sales promotional literature is used are:

1. For supporting the salesmen.
2. For strengthening dealer relations.
3. For intensifying the advertising.
4. For holding old customers.
5. For winning new customers.
6. For broadening the market.

The selection of literature for any of these six objectives is further affected by such additional considerations as whether it is promoting the company itself or the company's products or services; whether it is promoting one product or a line of products; whether the price is high or low; whether purchases are regular or spasmodic, frequent or infrequent; whether the product is a necessity, a luxury, or a convenience; whether it is used by many people or by a few. These and related factors help narrow down the choice of pieces by dictating how many and what kind will be required to do the whole job, how often they will need to be issued, how much copy and illustration will need to be provided for, what quantities will be involved, how much cost the budget will stand.

As has been noted, each of the 10 major classifications of sales promotional literature previously described possesses certain definite advantages and limitations which govern its suitability under these different conditions. Based on their comparative qualifications for performing certain kinds of jobs, charts have been prepared to show which literature classifications have been found effective in all the different functions making up each of the six basic sales promotional objectives listed.

LITERATURE THAT SUPPORTS THE SALESMEN

Companies operating their own sales forces use promotional literature to support their salesmen in several different ways. Some of it is directed to the salesmen themselves as a means of training them, giving them information about their products and the best ways of selling them, and inspiring them to put forth their best efforts; sales manuals, sales training course booklets, contest materials, house organs, and bulletins are examples.

Another kind is the literature that is furnished for them to use as selling aids in their everyday work; it consists of printed evidence for showing to buyers, visual sales presentations and portfolios, handout pieces for them to leave with prospects, and various forms of sample literature and specialties to create good will among all the people on whom they call.

Still another class of literature is that mailed out by the home office to make the salesman's work of selling easier; pieces that pave the way for his calls, that keep buyers reminded of him between calls, and that follow up the calls he has already made can be of tremendous help in getting interviews.

All these uses of sales promotional literature in supporting the sales force are covered more thoroughly in an accompanying chart. Together they represent one of the most powerful uses for printed pieces in the whole promotional program.

Promotion Material That Opens Doors for Equitable Life Agents

Consistently an award winner for its sales promotion material, the Equitable Life Assurance Society of the United States uses a variety of tested promotion ideas and methods to help its agents make sales.

The Equitable agent's enthusiasm for the sales aids in his kit is kept up by the periodic receipt of new sales pieces for all of his markets.

Equitable promotion ranges all the way from premium stuffers sent to policyholders, and direct mail cards and letters for new prospects, through to complete proposals; and from simple "package" presentations to elaborate kits containing many pieces for a particular market or unique policy.

Among the many such promotions used, two of the most effective were a complete sales kit service and the "package" presentations of specific policies.

Sales kits directed at many markets are used by new and experienced agents alike, but by their very nature are an ideal sales training medium. The makeup of a kit includes instruction sheets, prospecting and selling hints, preapproach material, visual sales presentations, a suggested sales talk, and materials to be used in closing the sale. New kits are prepared every year.

The "package" presentations are a series of booklets showing cost projections at various ages for the most popular policies. With the booklet, an agent is able to present his entire sales story by referring to a single page.

Backing the agent's individual sales efforts is a national advertising program concentrated in the big-circulation magazines. To obtain maximum results from the advertising, a comprehensive merchandising campaign is conducted. Agents receive reprints of ads for distribution to prospects; sales aids are tied in with the ad schedule; and devices such as posters and displays reproducing the current ads are widely used.

Interest in the advertising program is further developed and maintained by frequent reminders in Equitable's field magazine and by mailing direct to the agent media promotion pieces.

Essential to the success of the Equitable's sales promotion and advertising program are continuing market research and field testing of sales aids, as well as a close tie-in of promotion efforts with other agent activities, such as training and campaigns.

Experience of Reliance Life and Lumbermens Mutual

Like Equitable Life, most insurance companies have found sales promotional literature a very effective means of getting leads for salesmen, of following them up, and of making interviews more productive. According to the director of sales training of one of the major life insurance companies, even the largest insurance companies, which use newspaper, magazine, and radio advertising for prestige and institutional purposes, devote at least 25% of their budgets to supporting literature. In the average company the appropriation for literature goes as high as 50 to 90%, he states, and in his own company it is 30%, which is spent largely as a preapproach to a salesman's call; it helps to sell the interviewer rather than to sell the insurance itself.

One interesting plan, used by Reliance Life, totaled more than a million individual mailings for salesmen within 4 years after its introduction. It operated in this way: The salesman made up a list of from 25 to 100 prospect names and addresses from city directories, club directories, telephone books, new home owners, and other sources, and sent it in to the home office. The company then sent a multigraphed letter by first-class mail to those names and enclosed a booklet describing the seven basic needs for life insurance. With the booklet went a reply card listing the seven basic needs and asking the prospect to check the one he was most interested in and also to give his exact date of birth and his occupation. A business reply envelope was enclosed for him to use in mailing the card.

To stimulate replies the letter offered the inducement of a genuine leather memorandum book with the prospect's name imprinted in gold. If he sent in the card, the company made up the memorandum book and sent it, with the reply card, to the salesman who submitted his name. The salesman then delivered the books as the opening wedge for his interview.

How successfully the plan operated is shown in a comparison of the results between newspaper advertising and literature mailings. One year the company conducted a newspaper campaign which included coupons for getting inquiries and, at a cost of $60,000, produced 10,500 inquiries from prospects who bought $1½ million of life insurance. One year's operation of the prospecting plan, on the other hand, cost only $30,000 but produced 16,700 inquiries—6,200 more inquiries at half the cost. From the 16,700 inquiries, sales of life insurance reached between $12 million and $13 million, which the company attributed entirely to the mailings.

The greatly increased ratio of sales to inquiries from the literature mailings is accounted for by the much higher quality of leads. "We have found from experience that if we get over 10% returns, we are getting quantity and not quality leads," an officer explained. "The returns we get run about 5 to 6%. If we get over 10%, we begin to worry, but if we get less than 4% we begin to worry too. As long as returns stay between 4 and 10%, we think that everything is all right."

The Reliance Life program was also unusual in that the salesmen not only instigated the mailings but also paid for them. The company charged each salesman $5 for each 150 letter-booklet-and-reply-form mailings sent out to his prospect lists, including the postage. There was also a bonus arrangement in effect whereby the man who sold a certain amount of insurance from his 150 letters was given free another 150 as his bonus.

The Lumbermens Mutual Casualty Company is another of the many insurance companies which has found literature to be the backbone of a successful agent's sales promotional program. The company makes available to all agents information on how to set up a promotional program and supplies them with the brochures, folders, broadsides, mailing cards, and visual selling presentations to use in their own campaigns. It advocates that they make a practice of using an enclosure with every piece of mail they send out for any purpose.

Why Salesmen Need to Select Their Own Names

One of the important reasons the promotional literature of insurance companies produces such high returns is that the names of prospects are selected by the salesmen. Some of the dangers of supplying salesmen with names of prospects obtained from less selective general mailings or from newspaper and magazine advertisements were cited in a talk by J. S. McCullough, sales promotion and advertising manager of The Yale & Towne Manufacturing Company, at a Direct Mail Advertising Association convention. Mr. McCullough made the point that literature mailings which produce inquiry cards to the tune of 20, 10, or even 5% may look exceedingly good, from a results standpoint, to the inside promotional staff who prepared and mailed them, but exceedingly bad to the outside salesman who receives those cards and is expected to follow them up. Relating the case of the salesman who put in a long-distance call to ask the home office what to do about a big pile of inquiry cards that just landed on his desk and would take 2 solid months to follow up, Mr. McCullough asked his audience: "Do you know what results you should expect? What is your sales or results potential? What is your sales quota in a specific market or territory? What percentage of the actual business does your product enjoy in a specific market? If you get a sizable inquiry return, is your sales coverage sufficient to cash in properly on your inquiry return or is your campaign geared to follow up inquiries by mail until a proper sales call can be made?"

A salesman who travels long distances to follow up inquiries only to find that the inquirers could never buy the product or even influence its purchase soon loses interest in salesmen's support literature. A few calls on referred prospects who couldn't possibly use his product because of the nature of their business will sour a salesman on the whole campaign.

Referring primarily to the industrial field Mr. McCullough concluded, "Probably the best method of selection is to make the local representative responsible for his own list. The local man knows more about his own territory, its potential market, the types of business in it, the application of his product and the big purchasing factors in most plants. He must be given every possible assistance in keeping in action on his lists, because that is where a terrific loss occurs."

How United States Steel Gets Salesmen's Cooperation

Another industrial concern which is especially careful to avoid referring unlikely inquiries to salesmen is the United States Steel Corporation. Its well-integrated plan for maintaining contact with thousands of prospects by mail is designed to accomplish three things: (1) Provide thorough market coverage of individuals who influence sales; (2) conserve sales representatives' time for actual selling; and (3) reinforce the advertising and other promotional efforts in specific channels as need arises.

While all promotional mailings go out from the home office, the letters which are to accompany them are localized to the extent of being signed by the appropriate district sales manager. Prospects receiving them, therefore, see that they come from their own or nearby cities rather than from far-away Pittsburgh and from men whom they probably know either personally or by reputation. It isn't practical to go further and sign individual salesmen's names to the letters, but the company sees to it that copies of all mailing pieces go to the individual salesman, with a red imprint giving the date of the mailing and the list to which it was sent, and that the salesman receives his copy before the mailing reaches his customers and prospects. Realizing that salesmen find nothing more annoying than to have customers refer to something from the home office about which they know nothing, United States Steel bends every effort toward having its salesmen pull for, rather than against, its literature-mailing program.

Film Salesmen Save Time Through Using Literature

One of the most consistent users of sales promotional literature in the motion-picture industry has devised many unique pieces to assist its salesmen in presenting new movies to exhibitors. One of them was a big broadside used both for mailing and for salesmen's distribution which was so constructed that, in addition to selling the picture to exhibitors, it could be retained to provide part of their lobby displays. It could be converted into a poster, a set of photographs, a die-cut hanger or a streamer. With variations, this same idea was kept in use a long time after it was first proposed by an Ohio theater manager in a display idea contest which drew over a thousand entries.

The sales promotion manager of this company believes that unusual literature like this paves the way for fieldmen and delivers the kind of sales talk to local exhibitors that only a topnotch salesman could approach. The salesmen support the promotion program solidly because they say it eliminates cold calls and lessens their work by cutting down the time they spend with each exhibitor, enabling them to cover their lists faster and increasing the number of exhibitors they can see.

Literature Makes Calls for Johnson's Wax When Salesmen Can't

Since 1886 S. C. Johnson & Son, Inc., has manufactured a long line of industrial waxes, many of which are applied in such thin coatings that the firms using them buy too little to justify the expense of salesmen's calls. Those accounts which the salesmen in the territory can't afford to call on because of the small size of the orders are reached through a combination of sales promotional literature, business paper advertising, and radio and television features.

The literature itself is extremely simple, usually employing some special "gadget letter" device as a means of getting attention. In order to identify these comparatively unknown industrial waxes with the widely known Johnson's Wax which is advertised to the general public, the standard company letterhead is used to convey the mailings. The promotional theme is the increased sales appeal of an industrial product with a wax finish. For that reason each piece goes to the sales manager of a firm as well as to those directly responsible for purchasing; in fact, mailings usually reach at least four individuals in a firm at regular intervals—and still amount to only a fraction of what it would cost the salesman to make a single call.

Literature That Substitutes for Samples

Like so many other manufacturers of equipment that is far too big and bulky for salesmen to show as samples, the R. K. LeBlond Machine Tool Company solved the problem of introducing its Regal metal working lathe by means of printed literature instead. The literature also was required to take the place of floor models for distributors, who couldn't carry complete lines because of the capital tied up on low turnover items.

Since the Regal is a lathe specifically adapted to finishing the rubber rolls used in the printing trades by printers, paper mills, printing press manufacturers, and the manufacturers of the rubber rolls themselves, a series of three mailing pieces was prepared to reach the 5,000 likeliest prospects in those fields. The first two pieces, which took the form of simple self-mail folders with one fold comprising a reply card, went to the entire list; the third mailing went to only a hand-picked thousand names from the original list.

Actual inquiries from the three mailings amounted to less than 10%, but the ratio of sales to production costs of appromixately 100 to 1 was considered so successful that the company formulated a continuous promotional campaign consisting of additional literature, a small amount of business paper advertising, and publicity on other machines in its line. It also revamped and revitalized its monthly news letter called *Sales News* which goes to its domestic and international distributor organizations as well as the industrial bulletins which are mailed out periodically to prospect and customer lists. The LeBlond company's experience provides a typical example of the way initial promotional ventures, conceived on a small scale as the solution to a particular sales problem, sometimes lead to the formulation of diversified campaigns requiring a variety of literature pieces.

STRENGTHENING DEALER RELATIONS

Products sold through dealers and distributors are promoted by special kinds of literature which supply merchandising assistance both by giving these retail and wholesale outlets helpful ideas and suggestions on successful selling methods and by furnishing the selling materials for them, in turn, to mail out to their own customers and prospects, or to use in their stores and showrooms. Producing literature for dealers' use is only half the promotional program; the other half is showing them how to use it properly and get maximum results from it. Putting these two halves together forms the basis for most dealer campaigns.

Direct-Mail Instruction for Culligan Dealers

An unusually complete and informative dealer instruction book was prepared by Culligan, Inc., to tell the whole story of "Direct Mail: Your Direct Route to Prospects for Culligan Service." It was an 8½- by 11-inch booklet of 24 pages and cover, and its thoroughness was indicated by its chapter headings and subheadings:

SALES PROMOTION HANDBOOK

PART 1—The role that direct mail plays in your promotion program:
Direct mail offers you 6 important advantages.
Direct mail as an occasional medium. (4 uses.)
Direct mail as a basic medium. (5 uses.)
Direct mail as an occasional medium (4 uses.)

PART 2—How to develop productive direct-mail lists:
General lists.
Selected lists.
Using the lists.
Checking your lists.

PART 3—Selecting the proper material for your mailings:
Local identification sticker and/or imprinting.
Rate card.
Postage-paid reply card.
Service folder or farm booklet.
Reprints and/or letter.
Selection and classification of material:
Your own literature.
Testimonial type literature.

PART 4—Helpful hints for handling direct mail:
First class vs. third class.
Third class mail requirements.
Third class rates and regulations.
How to get a permit.
Postal rates effective January 1.
Mechanical equipment can help you handle your Culligan program. (With pictures, descriptions, and prices of Master Addresser, Class 700 Addressograph, Multipost Stamp Affixer, Elliott Addresserette, Weber Addressing Machine, and Pitney-Bowes Postage Metering Machine.)

PART 5—How to make a direct-mail program fit your particular needs:
Have a planned program.
Make many repeated mailings.
Timing your mailings.
Your choice of material.
Costs of the program.
Typical timetable.

PART 6—Direct mail gets results—the case history of a Culligan dealer:
Sixty-six new customers for Carl Leonard.
The cost: $4.84 per customer.

Each subject is handled clearly, simply, and as briefly as completeness will permit, and a full understanding of the contents enables any dealer to operate every phase of a professional direct-mail campaign. Several features are especially noteworthy because they illustrate novel ways of handling problems which are common to all dealer instructions on direct-mail procedure. One is the listing of 16 separate reprints of magazine articles under the "Testimonial Type Literature" section and the recommendation that dealers use them to supplement their own and the company's literature; another is the mailing timetable; still another is the manner of presenting the sources of lists.

Mailing List Information for Sylvania Dealers

"A direct-mail campaign with a carefully accumulated list of television owners in their territory is the best answer to the TV serviceman's problem of keeping in contact with the people in his trading area," stated *The Sylvania News,* house organ for its dealers, in an article on the importance of keeping mailing lists in first-class condition. Here again the suggestions for compiling and maintaining lists are of such wide general application that they deserve the careful study of all sales promotion people who handle dealer literature. The sources of lists recommended to Sylvania dealers were as follows:

Customer Lists: Satisfied customers are chief assets and should be included often. They can also give the names of other interested parties.

Directories: Both city and telephone directories are address-indexed. City directories are usually available in libraries and some drug stores. Telephone directories can be rented from the company for a small fee.

Public Records: Official, hence usually very accurate. Access to most costs nothing. They include: Voter's registrations, city tax lists, license and permit records, county clerk's records, county tax lists, and income tax lists.

Local Postmaster: Can yield names for mailing list and many sound suggestions for correct mailing procedures, as well as the service of checking your list for the charge of 1 cent per name.

Membership Lists: Local churches, clubs, lodges, and other social groups.

Purchased Lists: In addition to the regular sources lists can sometimes be rented from noncompeting retailers.

Other Tradespeople: Mailmen, milkmen, and newspaper carriers are usually the first to know when families move in or out. Their friendship can be very helpful.

Personal Contact: Telephone solicitation and house-to-house canvassing can be done by high-school students at the rate of so much per name.

Advertising: The offer of catalogs, premiums, etc., on the return of a coupon through other mediums will add names to the list.

Clippings: Clipping bureaus can supply news of moves, marriages, or deaths in your market area. Personal reading can supply much of this information also.

List Maintenance: Most of the preceding methods will keep a list accurate, but direct mail can be automatically self-correcting. Using Form 3547 on every third-class mailing will secure the new addresses of those who have moved at the rate of 3 cents per name received. When names are recorded incorrectly, misspelled, bear wrong initials or wrong titles your mailing to that group does more harm than good. If the list is incomplete, skipping several residents on each sheet, good prospects, and subsequent sales are missed.

What Is Wrong with Dealer Literature?

Vitally important as good mailing lists are in determining the success or failure of dealer mail campaigns, equally important is the literature manufacturers furnish for those campaigns. The retailer's side of the story as presented by Miss Nan Findlow, advertising manager of the L. Bamberger & Co. department store in Newark, New Jersey, is that much of the promotional material sent to retail stores by manufacturers is so unsuited for the job, so elaborate without cause, or so poor in quality that it winds up in the paper baler without being read or used by the retailer.

As Bamberger's is a large store which not only prepares a great deal of literature of its own but receives an even greater volume from manufacturers, Miss Findlow's conclusions are based on observations of dealer literature from all angles. Pointing out that the present trend of manufacturers is to make promotion kits as large, expensive, and bulky as possible, she advises them to pay less attention to the kits and more to the caliber of the promotional material they contain. She believes that mailing pieces for retailers should be divided into two groups—large and small outlets—because the larger stores with their own art, copy, and production facilities for preparing literature cannot or will not use the mats, imprinted pieces, and other ready-made promotions that are sent to the smaller stores without those facilities. Another fault of manufacturers in sending out their promotional kits, especially to department stores, is that they frequently are not addressed to the right people. Miss Findlow contends lists should be corrected to contain the full name and title of all the key people concerned with promotion in each retail outlet, including the general merchandise manager, divisional merchandise managers, advertising managers, copywriter, and fashion coordinator. Dealer literature can be promoted by mail to large as well as small stores, but it must be done in a different way.

Other Evidences of Waste by Dealers

That much direct advertising material provided by manufacturers as dealer aids shows a very poor batting average was the opinion expressed by Edwin F. Thayer, former publisher of an advertising magazine, in commenting on the evidence produced in that magazine's "Continuing Report on Direct-Mail."

"This is not necessarily a reflection of the quality of the material produced," he stated. "Rather it indicates that smaller retailers in particular do not take advantage of the promotional material at their disposal, either through ignorance, lack of interest or the sheer pressures of running a small business. Many of these so-called dealer helps are not used or, even worse, are misused.

"In a recent study among hardware dealers, for example, it was found that the vast bulk of promotional literature supplied to them merely gets stacked on the counters. The reason for this, apparently, is that it would cost money to do it any other way. When the dealers were asked, 'Which method of distribution of literature do you favor?' virtually all selected the least expensive one, which explains why most of their promotional effort is aimed at the present customers while not much effort is being made to find and interest new customers.

"Thus, unwillingness to invest money in advertising, or just not knowing how to use a manufacturer's promotional aids, has lost for these retailers a large share of the potential value of the material. It would indicate that money spent for the education of dealers on how to use these aids to real advantage would be money well spent, even if it had to come out of the product promotion budget."

A Successful Use of Manufacturer's Literature

Really aggressive retail merchandisers, on the other hand, have built up successful businesses through the use of dealer literature furnished by manufacturers. An outstanding example is the store of Garver Brothers, which sold over $1 million worth of goods a year in the small town of Strasburg, Ohio, which had a population of only 1,305. Beginning years ago with the aid of handbills to build up mailing lists for the farm areas in a radius of 15 to 25 miles, Garver Brothers attracted shoppers from cities like Canton, 18 miles away, with a much larger population and several big department stores of its own. The store had no art department and used no agency. It got whatever art work it needed from advertising services and its mats and literature from manufacturers. Its lists were all gathered from school district correspondents hired to send in data on newcomers to each district, names of persons who did not trade at Garver's, names of those planning to build new homes, etc. Letters were sent to people about to be married, to parents of newborn babies, and to everyone who was known to have experienced an important event. The efforts of this form of mail promotion are apparent in the results.

An interesting and intriguing headline is used in this four-page folder produced by American Can Company to promote the use of Pull-Tape coffee cans.

The most expensive mailing you can make...

... is the one that ends up in the gutter. So when you have something to say, something to sell, be sure you select the paper that commands respect. An OXFORD PAPER. Why take a chance with anything less than the best? LASTING IMPRESSIONS BEGIN WITH **OXFORD PAPERS**

This picture appeared in space and direct mail ads for the Oxford Paper Company. The Direct Mail Advertisers Association awarded it first prize for the most spectacular direct mail campaign.

Indicating how the selection of specific pieces for a dealer promotional campaign requires constant study, continuing experimentation, and occasional change, Servel tentatively added a pocket-size magazine, *The Homemaker's Digest,* to its already established program of standard envelope stuffers, line folders, and broadsides. It was made available to sales outlets for mailing to customers and prospects and, as a starter, 100,000 copies were ordered. Published quarterly, the magazine contained articles digested from leading women's magazines and original articles on gas service and gas appliances presented in a colorful modern format. Dealers immediately found the magazine the answer to their needs. At the time of the *Digest's* introduction there were serious gas shortages in various parts of the country and the magazine gave dealers something to send out during a period when out-and-out product promotion might not have been welcomed. According to Mr. Hewson, it won them good will and friendship, and helped to establish and hold consumers' preference for Servel refrigerators and other gas appliances until the time when they, the dealers, could actively promote them. Orders for the magazine started coming in at such a rate that the company had to double and redouble its paper and printing orders. Within a year dealers were using 1,500,000 copies. The new piece supplemented other promotional literature.

How Promotional Costs Are Shared with Dealers

Every program involving dealers' use of literature prepared and furnished by manufacturers gives rise to the problem of how the costs shall be apportioned between them. While there are some cases in which the manufacturer assumes the whole burden, and others in which the dealer pays practically the entire freight, the usual present-day practice is for them to work out some equitable basis of sharing the costs.

In considering this subject, the *how* is less difficult to describe than the *when*. A manufacturer may find that his dealers will gladly cooperate in some types of promotions and not in others; the market —or general economic conditions—change, and they do a complete flipflop. Now they will accept a cost-sharing plan for what they rejected before, and reject what they previously accepted.

Such fluctuations in willingness to accept a share of promotional costs are as impossible to prognosticate as the general economy is; more than one company has gained acceptance of a promotion-cost-sharing plan, only to find that a swing in the local or national economy has frustrated the plans completely.

Nevertheless, there is some profit in studying what other companies have done—provided the reader will remember that the when is as important as the how in getting dealer cost-sharing promotions under way.

A Plan Used by an Oil Chain

One of the major oil companies, knowing that there is less waste of promotional literature when each piece costs the dealer a little something than when it is all provided by the company, has experimented with various plans for securing dealer-cost-sharing cooperation.

After considerable experimentation, it was found that the best results were obtained, under normal economic conditions, when the oil company carried 50% of the cost and the dealer the other half. Under this plan, the company would secure the dealer's agreement to the promotion before work was started on it. Unless a sufficient number of dealers to make the promotion worth while were signed up, the promotion was not produced.

Promotion plans were presented to the dealers, by the company's representatives, in rough-draft form, and low-pressure selling was used to gain dealer acceptance and participation. If the dealer didn't come along enthusiastically, the company representative gave him an easy out, and moved on to the next man. In this way, what promotions were produced were promoted by the dealer with greater willingness and confidence than if he felt he had been pressured into agreeing to the plan. Each company salesman was given careful instructions prior to his call on the dealers with his promotion kit.

Iron Fireman's "Credit Balance" Plan

A plan which was used successfully by the Iron Fireman Manufacturing Company was based on unit sales. Dale Wylie, Iron Fireman director of advertising and sales promotion, described the plan as follows:

"Every time the company forwards to a dealer a unit of domestic equipment like a home stoker, gas or oil burner, coal furnace, etc., it adds at the bottom of the invoice the net sum of $1.25 which is marked 'direct-mail charge;' if it is a commercial or industrial unit, the charge is $2.50. This direct-mail charge gives the dealer a credit balance entitling him to five complete three-piece direct-mail campaigns which will be mailed to any five prospects whose names and addresses he supplies. From there on the company handles all the details of the mailings and, as long as the dealer keeps on sending in his lists according to the number of units he sells, his campaign continues and increases automatically, the company is compensated in part for the preparation and distribution of the pieces, and the special direct-mail account set up for each dealer at the factory makes possible a broad and continuous sales promotional program.

"This service for dealers is an outgrowth of the procedure begun by the Iron Fireman company as far back as 1930. At that time it was supplying dealers with a wide assortment of sales literature, catalogs and folders, together with a series of sales letters signed by the dealer to accompany them in the mails. The various campaigns were collated in the home office, enclosed in stamped envelopes, and sent to the dealers for them to address and put in the mails. The only fault with the plan was that, as field men called on the dealers, they noticed that a large part of the campaign materials was under the dealers' counters gathering dust or that the envelopes had been opened and the literature used for purposes other than mailing according to schedule. Consequently, the company adopted its present policy of having the dealers write the names on prospect mailing list blanks and send them in, and then of doing the rest itself.

"In the case of a new dealer, there is, of course, no credit balance for mailings and he usually pays for the first mailings at the same rate of $1.25 for each five domestic names and $2.50 for each five industrial or commercial names. In other words, if he wants to start out with a list of, say, 100 names of each classification, he would pay $25.00 for one classification and $50.00 for the other. After he begins selling and as his sales build up, his promotional allowances accumulate and the volume of his mailings increases. The program is operated a little like an American plan hotel. We make no credit for 'meals missed.' The money is collected, and if the dealer doesn't use it, he loses the benefit of it. Many dealers have unused name balances that we work with them to put to use. Since the plan was put into operation, more than a million individual campaigns have been mailed out for dealers, which is considered remarkably high in such a specialized field."

Other Types of "Dealer" Promotion Plans

As noted above, dealer promotions are subject to enthusiastic acceptance, vehement disapproval, or reactions somewhere between these extremes to an extent which varies with changing conditions. However, consideration of a few additional plans may reveal adaptable elements.

While it often is not possible to determine definitely what such promotion plans produce in comparison with others, it has generally been observed that the dealers who are the largest users of the campaigns also sell the greatest volume—which may, of course, be due to the fact that such dealers are more aggressive merchants in the first place.

As a further example, the sales promotion department of a national radio network helps its "dealers" (the local independent radio stations), in promoting network programs at the local level by posters, mats, and other literature of uniform high quality; and of producing direct-mail promotional pieces to sell advertising time for stations owned by the network and, to a lesser degree, for independent station affiliates.

The reasons for this policy, according to the sales promotion manager, are: "Since a large part of our audience is made up of advertising men, we must plan our promotion to be as different from the average run of advertising as is possible. We find that direct mail offers the following advantages in achieving this end: (1) Complete flexibility as to size and shape; (2) control over printing processes, paper stocks, and colors; and (3) choice of the time of impression."

Likewise, one of the major airlines keeps travel agents all over the country and in many foreign countries well supplied with descriptive literature and factual information about places of interest. The sales promotion manager has enumerated the special kinds of literature useful for this purpose:

"New timetables are distributed each month to keep our 'dealers,' the travel agents, posted on current flight schedules; descriptive folders to point up the attractions of various interesting places and to show how easy and convenient it is to get there by our lines; brochures to tell of the advantages of various services to speed delivery, reduce inventory stock, widen market area for perishable products. Travel agents are very important to us, and we treat them as any manufacturer would treat his dealers."

LITERATURE TO ACCENT THE ADVERTISING

At almost every stage in the operation of an advertising campaign results can be strengthened by the proper application of sales promotional literature. Advertisers who use newspapers, magazines, radio, TV, or outdoor advertising to reach consumers, and business papers to reach the trade, supplement them with printed pieces to increase the effectiveness of both. Sales promotion is the force that brings buyer and seller together. A few of the types of pieces regularly used to tie in with the following advertising media are:

Magazine Advertising: Reprints of advertisements for store display; merchandising portfolios for salesmen; local direct-mail tie-ups for dealers; booklets for answering inquiries; letters to jobbers and chain stores.

Newspaper Advertising: Localized direct-mail campaigns for simultaneous mailing; blow-ups of advertisements; books of newspaper cuts and mats for dealer use; letters to retail outlets preceding appearance of advertisments.

Radio and TV Advertising: Post card campaigns to reach dealers on program dates; printed photographs and other paper premiums for inquiries; folders for salesmen and jobbers showing station coverage; display tie-ups with programs.

Outdoor Advertising: Envelope stuffers and miniature reproductions of posters on blotters and poster stamps; letters soliciting merchandising cooperation of local poster plants; "road maps" spotting poster showings in different localities.

Car Card Advertising: Special letterheads and printed specialties featuring car card designs; miniature blotter car cards; combination broadsides-and-posters for store display; four-page letters with cards reproduced on inside spreads.

Display Advertising: Package enclosures with merchandising tie-up; letter campaigns enlisting the support of jobbers' salesmen; broadsides promoting display contests; instruction literature on setting up store and window displays.

Business Paper Advertising: Reprints of advertisements for follow-up mailings; product and departmental letterheads for answering inquiries; booklets to be offered in advertisements; special packages for sampling; inserts for salesmen's portfolios.

How Western Electric Has Merchandised Buyer Advertising

One of the many national advertising campaigns of Western Electric affords an enlightening example of the sort of merchandising program that produces the fullest measure of sales results from inquiries that are developed.

In this campaign, for a hearing aid, advertisements appeared in a long list of general magazines including *Life, This Week, Better Homes & Gardens,* and many others. They were inserted in general magazines—although only 10% of the population is hard of hearing and only 5% actually needs hearing aids—because friends and the members of the families of hard-of-hearing persons are anxious to help them. Almost as many inquiries develop from helpful friends and relatives as from the patients themselves.

The program was described by a Western Electric promotion executive as follows:

"As soon as an inquiry from a magazine advertisement is received, a booklet and letter are sent out from Western Electric's head office in New York. The name of the inquirer is next forwarded to the local dealer who makes a personal call and then is placed on the dealer list for follow-up by mail. For this purpose the company furnishes its dealers a series of three folders and an 8-page booklet with accompanying letter. These pieces cost the dealer $1.50 per thousand, with reply cards and envelopes being furnished free. The printed pieces are imprinted with the dealer's name and address but the letters must be processed by the local dealer on his own letterhead.

"Related steps in the tie-up campaign are: (1) Two suggested letters to local otologists and other physicians to tie up with regular advertising schedules in the general and specialists' medical journals; (2) free series of blotters and reply cards to be used both in these professional mailings and to consumers; (3) three suggested speeches for dealers to make at civic and social meetings; (4) displays for store counters and windows, ranging in cost from colorful plastic stands at $6 each to paper decalcomanias at three for 25 cents; (5) a newspaper mat service for local newspaper advertising, the dealer receiving actual mats and ad proofs in a portfolio so that all he needs to do is contract for the space."

With variations according to kind of product, its cost, the number of dealers, the extent of the advertising campaign, and other factors, this is a program for intensifying the effect of consumer advertising that is followed by most successful advertisers. They leave no stones unturned in their efforts to get full value from their appropriations.

How SKF Industries Merchandised Trade Advertising

In launching a new industrial advertising campaign in a group of 62 trade publications serving a score of different fields, SKF Industries, Philadelphia manufacturer of ball bearings, simultaneously launched a new merchandising campaign to back up the advertising among its salesmen, distributors, and distributors' salesmen. Because the copy in the new advertisements not only provided information for purchasing engineers but also utilized diagrams, drawings, photographs, and the names of manufacturers who are SKF customers, the series formed the basis for excellent sales presentations as well as excellent advertising copy.

Accordingly, provisions were made for getting the new material to the sales organization as quickly as possible in the form of more than 100 sixty-page portfolios and 3,000 blow-ups of the advertisements. The jumbo reprints were mailed to the homes of company salesmen and distributors' salesmen, and were also posted on the bulletin boards of SKF factory buildings for employee information. The portfolios stressed the company slogan, "Engineered by SKF," which appeared on all literature, and the advertisement reprints themselves were enclosed in acetate envelopes for greater impressiveness and greater usefulness for salesmen. Since each advertisement includes photographs of customers' equipment, with copy giving a case history of the equipment and the part SKF ball bearings play in it, the series actually constitutes an emphatic body of evidence and testimony which salesmen find of value above and beyond its tie-up with the trade paper advertising.

LITERATURE THAT HOLDS OLD CUSTOMERS

The pieces of sales promotional literature which do not have the holding of old customers as one of their objectives, subordinated though it may be, are few indeed. Some serve this purpose directly, as with the uses for the various classifications of promotional pieces charted on page 285. Others serve it indirectly, but it is difficult to conceive of a well-planned vehicle of sales promotion which would have the opposite effect. It will be noted that the classifications almost universally acceptable in sales promotional problems having to do with customer relations are the post card, the letter and enclosure mailing, the catalog or price list, and the house organ or bulletin. These constitute the great bulk of mail-order pieces, and it is the good will and continued patronage of old customers that is more indispensable in mail-order merchandising than in almost any other promotional activity. Customers lists are invariably many times more productive than prospect lists obtained from any other source, and one of the secrets of mail-order success is to keep working customer lists with new product offerings, or with the same offerings of products which are purchased frequently.

A Customer List That Grew Into a Mail-Order Business

Typical of the start of many successful mail-order businesses is the experience of Webb Young, Trader, which became a mail-order house when its founder sent out a small catalog to the out-of-town customers who had visited his Curio Shop in Santa Fe, New Mexico, and left their names in the guest book. These people had originally bought Indian silver; pottery; blankets; and native-woven, mountain-made neckties, if they bought anything at all; some of them had browsed around only as shoppers. Nevertheless, when Webb Young sent out his first mailing to this list it pulled surprisingly well—or at least the necktie line did—to an extent, in fact, that paid for the entire cost of the catalog. Thereafter the success of the venture was assured even though the other lines were soon dropped and it concentrated on the sale of neckties. Mailings are made regularly in March, April, September, and October, centering around special illustrated letters of both timely and topical interest and an October "Round-Up" catalog. In a little more than 10 years the volume grew from 5,000 neckties to over 200,000. Samples of materials are enclosed and the copy stresses their richness of pattern and color.

The same promotional techniques that have proved so successful in this and countless other mail-order businesses are equally effective in the customer relations programs of retail stores and, at the consumer level, of manufacturers of many different kinds of products. In addition, they are useful in reviving inactive accounts by determining the cause of the inactivity, reclassifying those accounts into prospect groups, and instituting special campaigns for restoring them to active status.

LITERATURE FOR WINNING NEW CUSTOMERS

As in the case of literature for holding old customers, most literature is also designed with the objective in mind of winning new customers either directly or indirectly, for after all the only ways of increasing business are to make more sales to present customers on the one hand, or to enlarge the number of customers on the other. Sales promotional measures which exert pressure through salesmen, through retailers, or through merchandise advertising still operate in one of these two directions. Certain types of literature, however, are better adapted than others to the task of selling direct or influencing sales to new customers.

How "Stop-It" Literature Got Fast Action

In introducing a new type of deodorant, the manufacturer of Stop-It revealed a remarkable example of the flexibility of printed promotion for capitalizing quickly on a merchandising opportunity. The revolutionary feature of Stop-It was a new squeezable thermoplastic bottle with built-in atomizer. It was first offered with a sale of 1,200 bottles at a Chicago department store which announced it inconspicuously in its regular newspaper space. When the 1,200 bottles were sold in 3 days, its manufacturers realized that they had a winner on their hands. What they did, consequently, was to prepare a broadside entitled, "Here's how Chicago department stores and newspapers launched a new and revolutionary atomizer," and sent it out while the news was still hot with a personalized letter and a sample to every department store buyer and merchandise manager in the country. Summer mailings were then sent to the women's page editors of every daily newspaper, and to consumer and business magazines of every type which might conceivably be interested in the news. Next there were mailings to all drug store buying headquarters, to 20,000 independent drug stores, to men's stores, and beauty shop supply departments. Within a few weeks, through the medium of fast-action promotional pieces, word of Stop-It had penetrated the country's merchandising outlets to such an extent that more than 1 million bottles were sold the first year.

Selling Custom-Built Parts Without Benefit of Salesmen

The custom-fabrication of machine parts by a concern which makes nothing except on special order and obtains all its business by bidding on jobs would seem to make salesmen indispensable. Yet the firm of Kramer and Kramer in Los Angeles locates all its new business as a result of promotional mailings and handles all details by subsequent correspondence.

"What Can We Make for You?" is the standard heading on all the mailing pieces, and with spot drawings and short copy they proceed to give a complete picture of the company's ability to produce whatever new parts its prospects require. The literature goes to a list compiled from classified telephone directories, manufacturers' directories, chamber of commerce membership rosters, and lists of previous customers. It is addressed to design engineers, or to the men technically concerned with the purchase of machine parts who may be looking for bids on new parts, who may have new products in the planning stage, or may not be sure that a certain part can be machined to their own particular needs or specifications.

Following the success of the first experimental west coast mailing, national mailing pieces were prepared to show the range of parts made by Kramer and Kramer for different classifications of customers. As a result of the program, the plant has been kept operating at capacity in spite of the fact that no two jobs are ever exactly alike and seldom are even similar. Reply cards are frequently received over a period of many months after the mailings go out, indicating that many prospective customers keep the firm's literature on file until they have a production problem to solve.

Envelope Practices of Representative Businesses

Per Cent of Totals

BUSINESS CLASSIFICATION	Size			Number of Colors		Area Imprinted			Special Features		
	No. 6¾	No. 10	Other	One	Two	Front	Back	Both	Window	Return	Copy Besides Address
Totals	14	80	6	84	16	89	3	8	29	18	25
Advertising Agencies	13	80	7	83	17	88	10	2	11	2	25
Airplanes and Accessories	....	96	4	79	21	100	....	....	37	1	20
Art and Photographic Supplies	25	67	8	100	....	84	8	8	41	8	25
Automobiles and Trucks	7	93	....	92	8	90	....	10	7	5	23
Automotive Accessories	16	80	4	88	12	88	....	12	36	8	4
Banks and Investments	13	87	....	100	....	100	....	....	6	20	6
Beer, Ale, Soft Drinks	23	77	....	85	15	91	....	9	6	15	23
Building Construction and Materials	7	93	....	86	14	79	....	21	23	9	24
Chemicals and Synthetics	11	86	3	83	17	88	2	10	13	3	27
Cleansers	18	82	....	91	9	100	....	....	36	18	27
Clothing	32	68	....	92	8	76	8	16	26	24	24
Coffee and Tea	17	75	8	75	25	76	8	16	25	16	25
Communications	34	52	14	92	8	78	8	14	39	21	43
Drugs and Proprietary Medicines	9	81	10	91	9	73	9	18	40	9	34
Engineering	15	85	....	94	6	100	....	....	21	15	31
Farm Equipment	8	76	16	58	42	66	8	26	16	8	41
Flour and Cereals	10	90	....	60	40	70	....	30	10	20	20
Food and Dairy Products	20	77	3	81	19	78	2	20	20	16	32
Furniture and Rugs	18	78	4	92	8	92	....	8	42	32	28
Games, Toys, Music	12	88	....	100	....	100	....	....	44	22	22
Gasoline and Lubricants	9	82	9	87	13	94	....	6	31	34	22
Glass	17	83	....	100	....	92	....	8	33	16	25
Hardware	24	66	10	82	18	83	3	14	35	24	54
Heating, Fuel	8	88	4	88	12	88	6	6	23	15	23
Hotels, Real Estate	44	56	....	77	23	87	....	13	11	11	44
Household Appliances	6	88	6	76	24	92	4	4	36	6	10
Insurance Brokers, Accountants, Lawyers	30	64	6	96	4	88	10	2	1	16	22
Jewelry, Silverware, Optical Goods	7	86	7	100	....	100	....	....	46	7	14
Lighting, Utilities	13	75	12	88	12	81	2	17	30	22	23
Machinery, Manufacturing	10	89	1	86	14	95	1	4	32	20	19
Miscellaneous	15	78	7	86	14	90	9	1	28	20	13
National Associations	4	94	2	65	35	98	2	....	2	11	19
Office Equipment	16	78	6	94	6	96	....	4	37	12	25
Paints	12	84	4	84	16	92	....	8	24	32	36
Printing and Paper	2	92	6	76	24	90	3	7	27	7	33
Publishers	33	60	7	82	18	90	6	4	17	15	26
Research Associations	6	94	....	87	13	89	4	7	6	6	20
Retailers	37	48	15	93	7	94	2	4	37	13	18
Schools	21	73	6	100	....	100	....	....	25	12	10
Seeds and Plants	17	83	....	100	....	84	....	16	16	33	16
Shoes	20	80	....	100	....	100	....	....	20	....	50
Smoking Requisites	14	86	....	85	14	100	....	....	28	28	40
Stationery	10	90	....	90	10	100	....	....	60	10	85
Sweets	....	100	....	60	40	80	....	20	20	30	50
Textiles, Leather	21	73	6	87	13	83	....	17	13	37	27
Tires, Rubber	24	72	4	96	4	96	....	4	48	40	12
Travel and Transportation	6	88	6	80	20	97	....	3	25	22	12
Wines and Liquors	....	90	10	82	18	82	....	18	36	9	27
Warehouses	....	100	....	100	....	67	....	33	....	66	50

Chapter 11

SALES PROMOTION LITERATURE

II—Creation

THE creative phase of a sales promotion program begins with the product. Marketing, sales and promotion people are usually assembled for a presentation of the product and its features by its designers, engineers or production people, as the case may be. The designers present the features, point out the advantages they offer to the consumer and answer any technical questions which may arise. Often, they compare the features with those of competitive products or refer to surveys reflecting potential market demand.

Then it is up to the promotion people to build a "copy platform" in which they interpret the features, give them impressive names or slogans and stress their "consumer benefits." If an advertising agency is represented, it may later submit a list of names, title or slogans for selection and approval; otherwise the advertising and sales promotion department carries the creative burden.

In conjunction with the marketing and sales departments, the overall program is developed in two main channels; presentation to the trade and presentation to the public and this, in turn, determines the nature and number of the individual items needed, including not only printed material but other units as well, such as films, store displays, or radio and TV spot announcements.

The Two Primary Creative Functions

How far a sales promotion department can go toward a division of labor within its creative staff depends, of course, on the size of the company, the status of the department, and the volume of sales promotional literature it is responsible for preparing. Some departments consist of a single person, with or without a secretary or an assistant, who performs the duties of sales promotion manager in his organization even though that may not be his title and he may be doubling in brass as sales manager, advertising manager, or something else. Other departments contain as many as 40 to 50 people and compare in size and specialized personnel with a medium-sized advertising agency; they are self-contained units maintaining a full staff of writers, editors, librarians, artists, photographers, production people, operators of office printing and addressing equipment, mailing room workers, etc., under the direction of a fully qualified sales promotion manager.

Regardless of the number of people in the department or the titles they may hold, however, there are two functions of creative sales promotional work which require the professional attention of talented experts. One is the function of originating the material that goes into a piece of literature; the other is the function of presenting that material in graphic form. The former generally comes under the direction of a copy chief; the latter under the direction of an art director. Sometimes one or the other of these two offices is assumed by the sales promotion manager himself; sometimes both of them are centered in the same individual, but even a one-man sales promotion department must possess both the ability to originate and the talent to present it if it is to operate as a creative entity.

What Sales Promotional Copy Includes

The old conception of "copy" as being limited strictly to the text of a piece is now replaced by a broader interpretation which considers as copy all the other ingredients of the piece from the original idea to the subjects for illustrations and, in fact, the complete organization of materials. Copy chiefs and copywriters, consequently, may more properly be defined as idea-and-copy men and women because their contributions toward the finished piece go much further than simply setting down the words; they originate the basic ideas and carry them all the way through to the point where they are ready for the art director to take over. Even when the idea is suggested to a copywriter by the sales promotion manager or copy chief, it is his responsibility to elaborate on it in pictures and captions, headings and subheadings, charts, graphs, tables, summaries, and other devices, as well as in text. It is only when handed a lay-out complete with idea, headline, illustrations, and supporting elements and instructed to fill in the space indicated for copy that he remains simply a copywriter.

Distinction Between Advertising and Editorial Copy

Of the 10 principal classifications of sales promotional literature outlined in the preceding section, the 3 devoted to booklets and brochures, house organs and bulletins, and publicity releases and reprints are better adapted to the editorial than to the advertising treatment. Editorial technique calls for a sustained style of writing and a restrained style of design, as contrasted with the condensed brevity of advertising copy and the frequent flamboyance of advertising display. The editorial approach, however, need not signify any lack of sales effectiveness or any justification for long, dull copy or drab, uninspired art. It gets its results by means of more completeness of detail and less pressure and emphasis, but it gets them just as surely. Both editorial and advertising techniques have their places in sales promotional literature, and company books, company magazines, and company news which take the form of booklets, house organs, and news stories and which follow the general style of standard books, magazines, and newspapers, provide the place for editorial expression. In fact, the usual reason for selecting these sales promotional media in the first place is because their jobs are those that cannot be satisfactorily handled through strictly advertising devices.

Modern editorial practice tends more and more toward visual presentation. Wherever information can be more clearly imparted by a picture or a graph or a diagram than by words alone, pictorial treatment is employed. Solid type pages or large blocks of straight text are just as objectionable in a sales promotional piece as in a general magazine—probably more so because most people must be intrigued into reading commercial literature, while they turn voluntarily to the popular periodicals. Competition for readers' time and attention demands that the presentation of any subject be interesting as well as informative, entertaining as well as educational.

While a few talented writers are equally proficient at either advertising or editorial writing, generally the two do not mix. Few advertising agencies, for instance, turn out acceptable publicity releases for their clients unless they have set up special departments for the purpose manned by newspaper and magazine writers who know how to take the advertising flavor out of editorial material. Good advertising-copywriters' whole training has been to use words as selling instruments, to inject sales appeal into their messages; with rare exceptions, they are unable to write from the objective viewpoint necessary to keep editorial copy free from the coloring and editorializing which make it objectionable to editors and readers alike. By the same token, the best house organ editors and publicity writers aren't ordinarily the best advertising copywriters because they haven't been specially trained in the necessity of putting their points across with brevity or in writing to sell; their copy is more informative than persuasive and sells more subtly than directly.

A Third Type of Sales Promotional Writing

In addition to the advertising and the editorial-writing talent needed in a well-rounded sales promotional department, there is a corresponding need for another specialized talent— that of letter writing. While a person who possesses writing ability of any kind can usually write a pretty good letter, for the kind of resultful sales letters demanded in sales promotional work only skilled letter writers with a natural knack for the medium or with a broad background of practice and experience can qualify.

If the department is large enough, then, its creative staff should include specialists in all three forms of sales promotional writing: Advertising, editorial, and letter writing. If it is a small department and most of the writing assignments fall on one person, he should be a versatile writer with a flexible style adaptable to each of the three mediums of expression.

What Constitutes Good Sales Promotional Writing?

There have been almost as many definitions of good copy and what it is expected to accomplish as there have been good copywriters. Different kinds of pieces require different styles of writing, as has been noted in the cases of letters and house organs, booklets, and publicity releases. It makes a further difference in the copy approach whether a catalog or price list, a folder or broadside, a post card or self-mailer is a mail-order piece intended to produce actual orders or a direct-mail advertising piece intended to supply further information, get interviews for salesmen, or accomplish some other more indirect form of selling.

Good copy for one purpose, consequently, might be very poor copy for another, and even writers specializing in advertising, editorial, or letter copy need to have many variations of style and changes of pace. The best copy, obviously, is that which best performs the specific sales promotional job it sets out to do. Whether its purpose is to sell seeds or overalls by mail to people on farms and in small towns, or to acquaint a group of big-city allergists with a new method of therapy in cases of atropic dermatitis, good copy carries just the right degree of sales power—high- or low-pressure—to influence the recipient to do what the sales promotion writer wants him to do. Few generalities apply universally to all sales promotional writing, but the experiences of successful practitioners of the sales promotional art are helpful in sorting out those basic fundamentals which have the widest application.

How Time Has Used Special Copy for Special Groups

In selling subscriptions by mail to *Time, Life,* and *Fortune,* the experience of the circulation and advertising promotion departments of these publications emphasizes the importance of addressing individuals according to their particular interests. One circulation man once wrote a successful letter to nurses which began, quite truthfully: "My wife trained at Brooklyn Hospital." The same writer, again quite truthfully, began a letter to clergymen: "Reverend Sir— *Time's* Editor, *Time's* Managing Editor, *Time's* Religion Editor, and *Time's* Business Manager are all sons of ministers. And so am I."

Speaking before the Hundred Million Club of New York, some time ago, the then circulation promotion manager of the news magazine explained why this policy has proved effective. "We try to ask ourselves questions like these: 'What do the people who are getting this letter and our company have in common? What are our mutual interests? What are our mutual dislikes? What do we agree should and should not be done?' And we find, if we can answer these questions, it is not so hard to write a beginning for our letter that will immediately establish a common bond between our company and the people to whom we are writing. Of course, these are examples of letters in which you try to find your bond with the reader in his business or profession, and in advertising as well as circulation promotion we sometimes use this technique when we are using direct-mail advertising. For example, a mailing the advertising promotion department of *Time* sent recently to insurance men had the title: 'Some Names We Have in Common.' Through the die-cut in the cover the insurance man sees something with which he is very familiar—the Life Insurance Agency Management Association's own persistency rating chart showing the people on whom it is most profitable for insurance salesmen to focus most of their sales effort. We go on to show that this market it almost identical with *Time's* readership." Friendly relations are most quickly established by mention of interests held in common.

The speaker also points out that, while this formula doesn't invariably work out so successfully, it does in a large enough number of cases to make it worth trying. "Sometimes you can find a successful opening sentence in a reference to the geographic section where certain prospects live," he added. "We write, when we are inviting Canadians to subscribe: 'You have been helping to make NEWS one of the Dominion's biggest exports.' This letter pulled exceptionally well for us—so well that we wondered if an adaptation of it might work as well in this country. We tried such a letter in the great state of California: 'You have been helping to make NEWS one of your state's biggest exports.' The letter did all right—that is, it brought in exactly one more subscription than the best general letter we were using in California at that time. Our conclusion is that when a specialized letter works, it works exceptionally well— but that we can often waste our energies in trying to get too specialized and that we can sometimes do just as well by writing a more general letter, one in which we try to find our common bond with the reader in the current news itself."

Organization and Word Selection

Earle A. Buckley of Ramsdell, Buckley & Co., Inc., once outlined what he regarded as the principal points of a writing assignment before a meeting of the Direct Mail Advertising Association as follows:

Keep it simple. You won't sell many canoes if you say, "Choose from impregnated plywood, anodized aluminum alloy, or resorcin-formaldehyde plastic."

Keep it sane. A hosiery ad in the New York *Times* recently contained this copy—"Seductive whispers of eye-flagging color, in twenty dramatic shades, from silver blue to a wicked brown called Stinky Mink." Somebody forgot to be sane.

Keep it clear and understandable. "Brown, the furrier, begs to announce that he will make up coats, capes, etc., for ladies out of their own skins." That isn't what he intended to say at all.

Keep it specific. "Young man who gets paid on Monday and is broke on Wednesday would like to exchange small loans with a young man who gets paid on Wednesday and is broke on Monday." That is specific. He didn't say Friday or Thursday or any other day in the week—he said Monday. If you are talking about a saving, don't say you have a saving for someone— tell him how much you can save him. If you want to say that something is better, tell him how much better it is. If it is cheaper, tell him how much cheaper.

Keep it believable. On the front of a sloppy looking restaurant in one of the worst sections of Philadelphia is a sign which reads, "The finest dinner in America—25 cents." That is obviously so unbelievable that there is no point in even discussing it, but you will find equally unbelievable statements in advertising every day in the week.

Keep it appropriate. A mortician shouldn't use copy like this—"You are invited to see our exciting new collection of caskets." For every situation there are some words that apply, and some words that don't.

Keep it informative, but remember always the reader approach. The reader doesn't want an adding machine, he wants to get home early. She doesn't want soap, she wants the "skin you love to touch."

Mr. Buckley concluded by quoting a poem of Orville Reed's to illustrate his point that the necessity of informing also includes the necessity of doing so in terms of simplicity and quickly understandable ideas:

> Copy that lilts like the song of a bird,
>   Or flows like a brook in the spring,
> Syntax that sings—a joy to be heard—
>   I've found may not sell a darn thing.
>
> But stuff that informs is simple and plain,
>   That says what it says and then stops,
> Is often the reason that sales show the gain
>   That pays for the fine-written flops.

In similar vein William A. Temple wrote an article on "The Art of Using Words" for the house magazine of the International Business Machines Corporation, in which he said:

> The majority of our English words as now spoken are of Anglo-Saxon origin. Generally they are our shorter, simpler words and have to do with everyday matters such as home, food, love, dare, like, hate, fear, etc. They express feelings and personal comfort, while our longer words, of Latin or Norman origin, are more apt to deal with matters of cold reason. Hence, to express oneself vividly, the Anglo-Saxon words are best. They evoke response more effectively. The longer words give rise to thought and call upon the reasoning powers, but they are less apt to move the hearer emotionally.

Postal Life's Successful Writing Formula

Howard Dana Shaw—the same "H. D. Shaw" whose signature has appeared on hundreds of thousands of mail-order letters from the Postal Life Insurance Company over a great number of years—undertook to construct what he called "a brief introductory set of rules for writing language of the result-getting kind instead of the information-conveying kind." Based on his own experience of more than 20 years, together with the tests and conclusions of many others, he incorporated it in these "Six Checking Points for Writing That Gets People to Do Things":

> 1. *Be Natural Instead of Literary.* Don't talk like a book; talk like a human. Watch out about being too pompous, too formal, too abstract, too preachy—too anything that makes people think you're a stiff-neck stuffy sort of a goon instead of a nice human kind of a guy. Don't strain to be grammatical. Shun the bookish words. We know that correct English is *not* important—ordinarily. We know that if you are writing to a professor of English good grammar is much more useful to getting your effect than if you are writing to a plumber. And we know that if you can be correct, and still follow other rules and sound human, it's best to be correct. The point is: Don't work at it too hard. If you sound stiff and literary, if your style seems strained in its attempt to be correct, if you write too many *to-whiches* and *to-whoms* instead of using prepositions to end sentences with, it's very bad. To quote Claude Hopkins, eminent merchandising authority of another generation: "To many, language and style are considered important. They are not. If fine writing is effective in any way, it is a detriment. It suggests an effort to sell. And every effort to sell creates corresponding resistance."
>
> At the same time I would like to disagree with the experts who insist you

should write as you speak. Writing and talking are practically two different tongues, as Mark Twain and numerous others have observed. The spoken language—whether conversation or speech—is necessarily full of chaff and repetitions.

2. *Simplify Your Sentences* is the second rule of language that's supposed to get something done. People outside the campus just won't bother to unravel a complex sentence structure. Make your sentences short, but don't make 'em too short, or all the same length. Effective style requires variety. After a couple longish sentences, stick in a real short one—it makes the reader prick up his ears. And write your sentences in a simple, straightforward, active style. Put the subject first and then the predicate. Don't write backwards, like a well-known weekly news magazine. Avoid reflexives and inversions. And shun too many dependent phrases. If the sentence gets the least bit involved or lengthy, put the considerations in a separate sentence. The lawyer won't like it, but the customers will read it.

3. *Write in Pictures.* When I was on the copy desk of a daily newspaper years ago, I sat beside a guy who was forever saying "Put a picture in every headline." Since then I have learned that nearly every effective writer, whether writing a letter or a text on ancient history, employs the principle of imagery. He has the knack of using concrete words that picture something to the eye or bring something to life through other senses. Which word paints the vividest picture: *fainted* or *swooned, swallow* or *gulp?* Practice by describing the things you see, hear, taste, smell, and feel—then see how many of the same words you can carry over into your writing language. It will do wonders in putting flesh and blood into your copy. If you have written "This plan provides protection for your beneficiary," scratch it out and write "This plan promises to pay money to your wife so she can buy clothes and set the table."

4. *Make Things Move.* The only thing better than a picture is a moving picture. Writing should always have a sense of direction, of going somewhere. And the individual sentences and words should be sentences and words of action. The most elemental way to do this, of course, is to *use more verbs.* The English language is overloaded with adjectives and poverty-stricken in verbs, but there are plenty of them ready to work for you if you make friends with them, collect them, learn to enjoy them, and use them. Just be verb-conscious. Remember when it moves, it gets attention. It flags the eye and hooks the interest. But don't overwork the auxiliary verbs—they have no motion in them. Don't *hold a meeting* or *have a discussion;* instead, just *meet,* or *discuss.*

5. *Use Personal Pronouns.* Rudolph Flesch in his famous *Art of Plain Talk* (which you must read if you want to write English) shows how "personal references" broaden the audience and intensify the readability of the written word. The mail-order man will usually insist, if he can't prove it by test, that lots of capital I's in a letter make it more resultful. So if you mean *I,* say *I.* Don't try to escape the realities of life and perpetrate things like *the writer, the undersigned.*

And by the same token, when you mean *you,* say it. It greatly improves meaning and readability to put the first and second person pronouns right where they belong. Many times you can spruce up a sentence or paragraph unbelievably by getting rid of the formal circumlocutions and speaking in plain me-to-you English.

6. *Don't Inflate.* When you lean on adjectives, you give away your inferiority complex. And there is a similar weakening effect when you try too hard to be enthusiastic. When you know your business and have confidence in yourself and your product, you write with strength and character. At least, that's what the reader feels as a sort of sixth sense. When you sound bombastic or over-exuberant, he discounts you plenty. Tests prove it. Tone down your claims and temper your superlatives.

And learn to pick the right word that will stand on its feet without crutches. Many adjectives, if not most of them, represent an attempt to bolster up the word or idea you're not quite confident of. As a drill, try crossing out all the adjectives in a piece of writing. You'll find few in good writing.

O. M. Scott & Sons' "Three R's" in Copy

Putting the fundamental rules of effective sales promotional copy into practice usually means extending the definition of copy to include not only the actual writing but the accompanying illustrative material and, in fact, the whole manner of presentation. The practical application of the O. M. Scott & Sons' copy policy has been summed up by President C. B. Mills as "The Three R's of Romance, Readability and Returns." Each of them requires good sales promotional writing but, more than that, the additional support of good sales promotional presentation. Mr. Mills explains the technique as follows:

ROMANCE:

The Frank E. Davis fish mailings paint a thrilling picture of the sea and its treasure of fish. *Time, Newsweek,* and other magazines have put romance into the news and into their letters designed to get new subscriptions.

We sell something which isn't particularly romantic—grass seed—and yet occasionally a good story possibility comes along. One year we had a shipment of seed en route from New Zealand and about the time it took off, another freighter bringing a same variety ran into a typhoon and became disabled. Another was prevented from taking off at all. On the disabled ship, most of the seed was damaged and all of it delayed to the extent that it got into this country far behind the seeding schedule. We had good luck; our ship came through and it seemed like a news story, so we got out a special mailing piece using pictures of the crop being harvested and bagged in New Zealand, pictures which we had around for years with no excuse to use. We showed how this variety was used and, of course, a little description and details of the ship in connection with its safe arrival. It didn't make as exciting a story as *Mutiny on the Bounty* but better than a mere recital of what we sell, and how much it is. We sold an immense amount of fescue from that single mailing; it did much better than an ordinary mailing that simply says, "How much is it?" We have put into our selling copy, an account of how seed is cleaned. We quoted figures, worked it out on a mathematical basis, and we never got to first base. With no reference to intrinsic value at all, we tested against that mathematical equation a letter which talked solely of results, of what significance a sparkling lawn really is, how the whole family will enjoy it, the neighbors envy it, the passersby glow with excitement as they exclaim: "Now there's a lawn!" We find it better to interpret our products into people's lives, and show them how much richer their everyday living will become.

Selling gold-filled pen and pencil sets at $15 requires the projection of a quality image and customer-satisfaction. A. T. Cross Company not only stressed the word, "reputation," on a parchment-scroll illustration against a background of quality-store names, but used French-fold parchment-type paper. The interior spread contained reproductions of actual letters from satisfied users.

The composer of music does something similar to writing good sales copy. He puts a definite theme into the composition; then, at frequent intervals, the same theme reappears until finally a climax is reached. We substitute pretty pictures for pretty music, and then invite the prospect to get more enjoyment from his own lawn by coming over into our corner. Copy needed to convert prospects into customers involves a slow take-off followed by a rising tempo of sales effort. When you have aspects that the prospect's interest is aroused, you bear down harder. Some copy reads hard. It doesn't seem to have any swing to it, no rhapsody. It's tedious and tiresome. The first thing you know, you drop the letter without feeling the least impressed. I like to think that we can visualize our typical prospect as a man or woman in a given income bracket with certain objectives in life and wants which we feel ourselves qualified to satisfy. Thus we attempt to write copy directed point blank at such people. I think I know hundreds of folks who are just like the prospects whom we picture as specifically belonging to us.

How Warner & Swasey Use Case History Copy

J. E. Craig, manager of advertising for The Warner & Swasey Company in Cleveland, has reported that the questions usually asked among sales promotion men regarding the advisability of using case histories in their copy are as follows:

1. Can you get as much variety into literature based on case histories as in other methods of presentation?

2. Aren't case histories very difficult to obtain?

3. How does one know where good performance stories exist, and what are all the particulars of securing complete data?

4. What about new products? Many concerns are now manufacturing postwar models or products new to industry. Can case histories be applied in these instances?

5. What about results from this type of direct mail?

6. How do customers feel about the use of their name in your advertising literature?

From his company's experience in using a great deal of this sort of material over a period of many years, he is convinced that favorable answers may be given to each of the six questions by any company which seriously goes about the problem of collecting material. He has found that they give greater rather than less variety to the campaign; that, while not easy to obtain, they are no harder than comparable good material obtained from other sources; and that results from both the company's and its customers' standpoints are highly favorable.

Related Problems of Editing and Proofreading

In business writing, as in every other form of writing, an essential requirement is the development of a standard, consistent style. Style consists of a lot of little things: How to punctuate; what rules to follow for capitalizing and abbreviating; when to spell out numbers and when to use numerals; how to handle such matters as titles, dates, geographical and political names, ages, etc. In short, under the heading of style come grammar, spelling, construction, and all-around good taste.

In the development of style, sales promotional writing has struck a medium between the informality of the daily newspaper and the formality of literary and scientific writing. Consisting of advertising copy, editorial writing for house organs and booklets, and letter writing, business literature has developed a style of its own; and an acceptable style for letter writing can serve equally well for the other forms. (For detailed rules of style, see *U.S. Government Printing Office Style Manual.*) Regardless of which of several alternatives may be selected as the style to follow in certain specific cases, the one basic qualification of any style guide is consistency.

A copyreader, who edits copy before it is set in type, and a proof-reader, who reads copy after it is set in type and checks the proof against the original, both need to acquire close familiarity with the rules of style as adopted for their particular purposes. Standard equipment for both jobs is an authoritative unabridged dictionary such as *Webster's New International,* and an accepted style guide such as *A Manual of Style,* published by the University Press of the University of Chicago. The dictionary proves indispensable for deciding questions about compounding and hyphenating words, dividing words at the end of type lines, checking spelling, and capitalizing. For arbitrary distinctions which need, nevertheless, authoritative verification, the style manual will supply a good supplementary reference.

Brief explanations of the importance of proper editing and proof-reading are given on the following pages, together with the standard symbols for editing copy and reading proof. In some sales promotional departments, both jobs must of necessity be combined in a single person, and it is especially important for such a person to recognize the points of similarity and difference between the two.

Style is a qualification of make-up as well as of writing, especially in booklet, catalog, or house organ work where there are certain inviolable rules—such as, for instance, the dictate that all right-hand pages be odd-numbered and all left hand pages even-numbered —which come within the province of the copyreader, proofreader, and makeup man or woman to check.

EDITING COPY:

In marking corrections on the typewritten copy that goes to the printers, the symbols are placed in the copy itself rather than in the margins as in marking proofs. This is to make it just as easy as possible for the compositor or the typesetting machine operator to follow along, word after word and line after line, without having to pause and, as they say, "chase the copy all over the page." Good editing considers the speed and accuracy of the typesetting.

The symbols for editing copy used in the specimen page (see page 331) speak a universal language in the printing trades. All compositors understand them, and their use saves time and eliminates misunderstandings. A wavy line under a word or phrase, for instance, always means to set that copy in bold-faced type. A straight line means to set it in italic type. Two lines mean small capitals; and three lines, regular capitals. In addition to editing the copy for spelling, grammar, punctuation, factual accuracy, and accepted style in such things as abbreviations, capitalization, use of numerals, etc., also mark clearly on each piece of copy the exact type specifications: The kind of type, the size, the amount of line spacing, and the width of the line. A typical type specification for a booklet page might be: "Set in Bodoni Book, 8 pt. on 10, 21 picas wide." That means, of course, that Bodoni Book has been decided on as the most suitable type face for the job, that it is to be set in the 8-pt. size with 2-pt. spacing between lines, and that the column width is 21 picas or 3½ inches.

In editing, failure to make all the necessary corrections in the copy or to give all the necessary instructions to the printers will only result in resetting and needless alterations, which waste both time and money. A little extra care and attention to the copy make a big difference in speeding up deliveries and in keeping down costs. In case of doubt, don't hesitate to consult your dictionary or style book. It's a whole lot easier to correct the copy than to correct the type.

READING PROOF:

In marking corrections on the type proofs, the symbols are placed in the margins with connecting lines showing exactly the place in the type where the corrections need to be made. And again the reason for doing it that way is for the convenience of the typesetter. He doesn't need to follow the proofs word for word and line for line the way he does the original copy. He is looking only for the alterations, and it is economical to make it as clear and as easy as possible for him to find them.

Assuming that the copy was well edited beforehand, what a proofreader is concerned with are the strictly mechanical errors: Misspellings, transpositions, wrong fonts, bad spacing, omissions, etc. Proofreading, though, gives a final chance to correct any errors that may have slipped through the copyreading. Mechanical errors are the typesetter's fault; errors in sense or in construction belong to whomever edited the copy.

Proofs are best read by a team of two: A proofreader and a copyholder. The latter reads the copy aloud, including punctuation and all other style specifications, while the former marks the corrections. If no copyholder is available it is important to refer to the original copy. Otherwise the proofreader might easily overlook omissions of words, sentences, or even complete paragraphs.

COPYREADING MARKS

Symbols for editing copy according to the rules of style accepted for business writing. Correct editing reduces average costly alteration changes by more than half, and alterations account for 10 to 50% of most jobs.

ONE WORD	If our only yard stick of business profits is dollars,
BOLD FACE	and we measure our every activity by the noise
APOSTROPHE	it makes on the cash register, then I say, dont join
SEMICOLON	anything. Keep out of your trade associations; fight
LOWER CASE	shy of the local service clubs; have nothing to do
PERIOD	with executives organized on functional lines. In the
COMMA	first place, with such a philosophy, you probably won't
RESTORE	put much into these associations and you may be per-
RUN IN	fectly certain you won't take much out.
INSERT LETTER	It takes more than dues to make a succesful associa-
TRANSPOSE LETTER	tion. And you probably won't make many friends, for
OMIT WORD	people haven't much use for the man who joins in for
HYPHEN	business first purposes. If you are that sort of bird,
INSERT WORD	stay at your desk. Keep your head buried in your papers.
ITALICS	But don't blame anyone but yourself if you and your
EXCLAMATION POINT	business soon die of hardening of the arteries!
PARAGRAPH	If, however, you measure profits by the friends you
OMIT LETTER	make as well as the money you bank; if you agree with
SMALL CAPS	Theodore Roosevelt that "every man owes something to
QUOTES	his profession and are not satisfied to go through
DASH	life, taking all you can get—but giving nothing in re-
TWO WORDS	turn--then join at least one of your hometown's fel-
CAPITALIZE	lowship groups. after all, you know we are only on
SPELL OUT	this earth a few years. Most of us have but 20 years
NUMERAL	at best in the harness. Why not spend one per cent of
TRANSPOSE WORDS	those remaining years doing what we to can make this
QUESTION MARK	world a better place in which to live.

PROOFREADING MARKS

Symbols for correcting copy after it has been set in type, not to be confused with copyreading marks. Good proofreading checks the finished composition for three factors: Sense, typographical errors, faithful following of copy.

♂	Dele, or delete: take ℵ out.
◎	Letter reve‿sed — turn.
✳	Put in‿space.
◡	Clo͡se up — no space.
eq#	Bad ⌐spacing:‿space more ⌐evenly.
wf	Wrong font: character of wrong size or style.
tr	Transpoe͡s‿
¶	‿Make a new paragraph.
□	‿Indent; or, put in an em-quad space.
L	L Carry to the left.
⌐	Ca‿ry to the right.
⌐	Ele‿vate.
⌐	Depre‿ss.
×	Imperfect type — correct.
↓	Space‿shows between words — push down.
‖ =	‖Straighten ⌐alignme͡nt.
stet	Restore or ~~retain~~ words crossed out.
⁀/⁀	Print (a͡e, f͡i, etc.) as a ligature.
out, see copy	Words are omitted from, or in,‿copy
⑦	Query to author: <u>Is this correct‿?</u>
caps	Put in <u>capitals.</u>
sc	Put in <u>SMALL CAPITALS.</u>
lc	Put in <u>LOWER CASE.</u>
rom	Put in <u>roman</u> type.
ital	Put in <u>italic</u> type.
bf.	Put in <u>bold face</u> type.
⊙	Insert period‿
⌄	Insert an apostrophe in proof reade‿rs marks.
ᵌ/	Insert hyphen in printing‿office efficiency.
en-/	Insert en dash between 1918‿20.
em—/	Insert em dash‿

Another important thing to look for which can't be anticipated in the copyreading is the way words are divided at the ends of lines. Ligatures constitute another pitfall for proofreaders. For greater legibility and better letter-spacing where thin characters like "i's" and "l's" and "f's" are concerned, typographic usage dictates that certain combinations should be run together in a single type character rather than be set individually. Thus, such combinations as "fi," "fl," "ffi," "ffl," etc., from single condensed characters, and the proofreader has to be careful that they don't appear as widely spaced individual characters.

COPY FITTING

One of the important items in the cost of producing sales promotional literature is "alterations." It is not uncommon, when copy has been so poorly prepared for the printer that considerable changes must be made after the copy has been set in type, for the cost of the alterations to be as much as it cost to set the copy in the first place. Since alterations, or author's corrections as they are sometimes called, are usually charged on a time basis and billed as an extra, it is important that copy be written to fit the space it is to fill.

TABLE I
Characters per pica

Type Size	Average Characters Per Pica
4 point	5
5 point	4
6 point	3.5
8 point	3
10 point	2.5
12 point	2
14 point	1.5
18 point	1

TABLE II
Average characters per one square pica with corresponding average type face required to fill space

TABLE II *(Cont.)*

Size of Average Type Face Required To Fill	Characters Per One Square Pica
4 point solid	15
4 point on 5 point	12
5 point solid	9.6
5 point on 6 point	8
6 point solid	7
6 point on 7 point	6
6 point on 8 point	5.3
8 point solid	4.5
8 point on 9 point	4
8 point on 10 point	3.6
10 point solid	3
10 point on 11 point	2.7
10 point on 12 point	2.5
12 point solid	2
12 point on 13 point	1.8
12 point on 14 point	1.7
14 point solid	1.4
14 point on 15 point	1.3
14 point on 16 point	1.2

Straight Copy

While there are a number of methods used in copy fitting, the one most commonly employed is to first make a to-size layout of the piece, with the type sizes and measurements indicated. With that information before him the copywriter can easily compute the number of characters it will take to fill each line, and then set his typewriter accordingly. For example, if a space 13 picas wide is to be filled with 10-point body type, cast on a 12-point linotype slug (10-point leaded), reference to the table on this page indicates there are 2.5 ten-point characters to each pica of column width. Thus there will be 32.5 characters to the line. In writing copy to fit, set the typewriter to start at 0 and stop at 32 on the scale. Some copywriters hold down the period key at the stop point and give the carriage a few quick turns, which leaves a faint vertical line on the copy paper. They then type until the typing reaches the stop line, or nearly so, and then write the next line. The number of lines required is determined by measuring the up and down space with a line gauge, which gives the number of 8-, 10-, or 12-point lines required to fill. In fitting copy for house organs, a ruled layout sheet divided into picas and columns is generally used. This makes it easy for the editor to measure the amount of copy required to fill a certain space on the page.

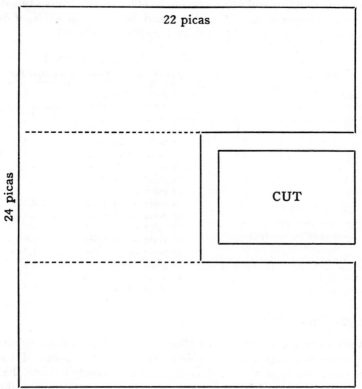

Run Arounds

How many characters will it take to fill the space, 22 by 24 picas, allowing for a cut 9 by 6 picas and a 1-pica border for three sides, if you want to use 8 point Bodoni? By measuring with a gauge, you will know that you want 12 lines 22 picas long, 12 lines 12 picas long, and 12 lines 22 picas long of 8 point Bodoni to fill this space. The table shows that each pica will use 3 characters, so set your typewriter to 66 characters and type 12 lines, then type 12 lines 36 (3 by 12) characters long, and finally type 12 lines 66 characters long, and your copy will run practically line for line when set in this type.

Suppose you have this manuscript typed as above: 12 lines of 66 characters (792), 12 lines of 36 characters (432), and 12 more lines of 66 characters (792), or 792+432+792=2016 characters. Find the area of this space: 22×8 (176 square picas) plus 8×12 (96 square picas) plus 22×8 (176 square picas)=448 square picas. Divide 2016 (total number of characters) by 448 (total number of square picas)=4.5. Find this factor in the "square pica" table and read to the left and you find you must use 8 point solid.

OTHER COPY-FITTING SYSTEMS

The Roto-Typometer and the Copy Scale

A calculating device which enables the novice as well as the expert to cast up copy quickly and easily, and to determine the proper size and face of type in which to set a given job. The Copy Scale, a durable celluloid companion piece to the Roto-Typometer, simplifies counting the amount of copy in a page of typewritten matter.

PDQ Copymeter and PDQ Printometer

With these two calculators, which work on the order of a slide rule, the measuring of type, copy, and photographs may be done automatically. They may also be used in fitting body type.

Hopper's Type Tables

This book includes five type tables, so arranged as to provide a quick solution, without calculation, of practically every copy-fitting problem. Table I gives pica width of 100 characters in any face or size of type; Table II gives the type faces of all sizes having the same "set," grouped together; Table III shows the number of characters that will set in a line of 100 picas; Table IV gives the average number of characters per line of any pica-width, for any "set"; and Table V is a reference table of half a thousand type faces.

Clason's Rapid Copy Fitter

This four-page copy fitter multiplies and divides and gives the answer in a few seconds. A celluloid rule is used in conjunction with the tables to show at a glance the measurement of a given piece of typewritten copy (elite or pica) or of type itself.

The Printers' Calculat

The Calculat consists of a broadside of Tables of Set Sizes, giving the body sizes of most of the type faces in ordinary use and a card-

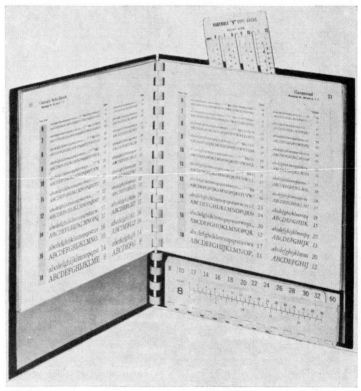

(Courtesy Haberule Company)

The space required for setting sales promotion copy in type may be determined accurately through the use of copy-fitting tools such as this. It includes specimen type faces, character-count scales and plastic type gauge.

board scale to be used with these tables containing the "set size," "pica measure," and "character."

Copy Fitting with the Slide Rule

The slide rule may also be used effectively as a tool in copy fitting. With it, a fairly accurate count of the average number of type characters in pica measures may be obtained, or copy may be converted into lines of type, or type lines into pica depth, and so on.

Copy Fitting Around Illustrations

Copy fitting is often affected by illustration sizes which must be determined in advance. A guide for doing this is shown in the photo-engraving section in the following chapter (Page 383). Everyone is familiar with magnifying glasses, but reducing glasses are also available to determine the reduced dimensions of photos or artwork.

Reductions may also be found algebraically. For instance, should one wish to reduce an eight by 10 photo to three inches wide, how high will it be? Here's the equation:

$$\text{Width : } 8 \text{ inches}$$
$$\text{Height: } 10 \text{ inches}$$

$$\text{New width : } 3 \text{ inches}$$
$$\text{New height : } \times$$

$$8 : 3 = 10 : \times$$
$$8\times = 30$$
$$\times = 3\tfrac{3}{4}$$

Complete Table of Characters Per Square Pica

Characters Per Pica	4 Point		4½ Pt.	5 Point		6 Point			7 Point			8 Point		
	Solid	1 Pt. Lead	Solid	Solid	1 Pt. Lead	Solid	1 Pt. Lead	2 Pt. Lead	Solid	1 Pt. Lead	2 Pt. Lead	Solid	1 Pt. Lead	2 Pt. Lead
5.1	15.3	12.2												
5.0	15.0	12.0												
4.9	14.7	11.8	11.8											
4.8	14.4	11.5	11.5	11.5	9.6									
4.7	14.1	11.3	11.3	11.3	9.4									
4.6	13.8	11.0	11.0	11.0	9.2									
4.5	13.5	10.8	10.8	10.8	9.0	9.0	7.70	6.75						
4.4				10.5	8.8	8.8	7.52	6.60						
4.3				10.3	8.6	8.6	7.35	6.45						
4.2				10.1	8.4	8.4	7.18	6.30	7.18	6.30	5.61			
4.1				9.8	8.2	8.2	7.01	6.15	7.01	6.15	5.47			
4.0				9.6	8.0	8.0	6.84	6.00	6.84	6.00	5.34			
3.9				9.4	7.8	7.8	6.67	5.85	6.67	5.85	5.21	5.85	5.19	4.68
3.8				9.1	7.6	7.6	6.50	5.70	6.50	5.70	5.07	5.70	5.05	4.56
3.7				8.9	7.4	7.4	6.33	5.55	6.33	5.55	4.94	5.55	4.92	4.44
3.6				8.6	7.2	7.2	6.16	5.40	6.16	5.40	4.81	5.40	4.79	4.32
3.5				8.4	7.0	7.0	5.98	5.25	5.98	5.25	4.67	5.25	4.66	4.20
3.4						6.8	5.81	5.10	5.81	5.10	4.54	5.10	4.52	4.08
3.3						6.6	5.64	4.95	5.64	4.95	4.41	4.95	4.39	3.96
3.2						6.4	5.47	4.80	5.47	4.80	4.27	4.80	4.26	3.84
3.1						6.2	5.30	4.65	5.30	4.65	4.14	4.65	4.12	3.72
3.0						6.0	5.13	4.50	5.13	4.50	4.01	4.50	3.99	3.60
2.9						5.8	4.96	4.35	4.96	4.35	3.87	4.35	3.86	3.48
2.8						5.6	4.79	4.20	4.89	4.20	3.74	4.20	3.72	3.36
2.7									4.62	4.05	3.61	4.05	3.59	3.24
2.6									4.45	3.90	3.47	3.90	3.46	3.12
2.5												3.75	3.33	3.00
2.4												3.60	3.19	2.88
2.3												3.45	3.06	2.76
2.2														
2.1														
2.0														
1.9														
1.8														
1.7														
1.6														
1.5														
1.4														
1.3														
1.2														

Complete Table of Characters Per Square Pica

9 Point			10 Point			11 Point			12 Point			14 Point		Characters Per Pica
Solid	1 Pt. Lead	2 Pt. Lead	Solid	1 Pt. Lead	2 Pt. Lead	Solid	1 Pt. Lead	2 Pt. Lead	Solid	1 Pt. Lead	2 Pt. Lead	Solid	2 Pt. Lead	
														5.1
														5.0
														4.9
														4.8
														4.7
														4.6
														4.5
														4.4
														4.3
														4.2
														4.1
														4.0
														3.9
														3.8
														3.7
														3.6
4.66	4.20	3.82												3.5
4.52	4.08	3.71												3.4
4.39	3.96	3.60	3.96	3.60	3.30									3.3
4.26	3.84	3.49	3.84	3.49	3.20									3.2
4.12	3.72	3.38	3.72	3.38	3.10	3.38	3.10	2.85						3.1
3.99	3.60	3.27	3.60	3.27	3.00	3.27	3.00	2.76						3.0
3.86	3.48	3.16	3.48	3.16	2.90	3.16	2.90	2.67	2.90	2.67	2.47			2.9
3.72	3.36	3.05	3.36	3.05	2.80	3.05	2.80	2.58	2.80	2.58	2.38			2.8
3.59	3.24	2.94	3.24	2.94	2.70	2.94	2.70	2.48	2.70	2.48	2.30			2.7
3.46	3.12	2.83	3.12	2.83	2.60	2.83	2.60	2.39	2.60	2.39	2.21			2.6
3.33	3.00	2.73	3.00	2.73	2.50	2.73	2.50	2.30	2.50	2.30	2.12	2.12	1.88	2.5
3.19	2.88	2.62	2.88	2.62	2.40	2.62	2.40	2.21	2.40	2.21	2.04	2.04	1.80	2.4
3.06	2.76	2.51	2.76	2.51	2.30	2.51	2.30	2.12	2.30	2.12	1.96	1.96	1.73	2.3
2.93	2.64	2.40	2.64	2.40	2.20	2.40	2.20	2.02	2.20	2.02	1.87	1.87	1.65	2.2
2.79	2.52	2.29	2.52	2.29	2.10	2.29	2.10	1.93	2.10	1.93	1.79	1.79	1.58	2.1
2.66	2.40	2.18	2.40	2.18	2.00	2.18	2.00	1.84	2.00	1.84	1.70	1.70	1.50	2.0
			2.38	2.07	1.90	2.07	1.90	1.75	1.90	1.75	1.62	1.62	1.43	1.9
			2.26	1.96	1.80	1.96	1.80	1.66	1.80	1.66	1.53	1.53	1.35	1.8
						1.85	1.70	1.56	1.70	1.56	1.45	1.45	1.28	1.7
									1.60	1.47	1.36	1.36	1.20	1.6
									1.50	1.38	1.28	1.28	1.13	1.5
									1.40	1.29	1.19	1.19	1.05	1.4
												1.11	.98	1.3
												1.02	.90	1.2

STYLE CHART FOR SALES PROMOTION

Writing is not an exact science, and rigid rules to govern it are impractical. Most of the large publishing organizations and advertising agencies have their own style, and have developed their own rules for style. These are followed by their proofreaders. The most widely used style sheet (or book) is that of the United States Government Printing Office. Another popular style book is that of the University of Chicago Press. The following rules have been adapted from several such style books. The importance of clarity in expression and the need of facilitating the writing and handling of copy used in the promotion of sales is important since the use of a style sheet in preparing copy for the printer can save costly corrections after the copy has been set in type.

In advertising departments where a large volume of copy is produced and set into type, it is usual to furnish those engaged in production work with a mimeographed or planographed style sheet which can be inexpensively prepared. The Medill School of Journalism, Northwestern University, Chicago, has prepared a handy style book for the use of writers, which is offered for general distribution at 75 cents a copy. This will be found quite useful, as will the following Dartnell style sheet prepared by John L. Scott.

	Style:	Correct:	Not:
Addresses	Use numerals for all street addresses	1 Park Avenue	One Park Avenue
	Spell out and capitalize Street, Avenue, Place, Road, Boulevard, etc., when used as part of the name of a thoroughfare, and North, South, etc., in addresses. Abbreviate only when necessary to save space.	791 Oak Street 36 North Grand Avenue	791 Oak Street *or* 791 Oak St. 36 N. Grand Avenue
	Spell out numbered streets of one or two numbers. (There is an exception in the case of New York City where the general practice is to use numerals with the suffixes, *st, nd, rd* and *th*.) Use numerals for streets over one hundred	23 Second Avenue 105 Thirty-third Street 950 West 133rd Street	23 2nd Avenue 105 33rd Street 950 West One Hundred and Thirty-third Street
	Abbreviate names of states only in lists, signatures, and bibliographical matter, and only when preceded by the name of a city. Never abbreviate Idaho, Iowa, Ohio, Maine or Utah	Detroit, Mich. Des Moines, Iowa Columbus, Ohio	A citizen of Mich. Des Moines, Ia. Columbus, O.
	Set off names of states with commas	Detroit, Michigan, is the Motor City.	Detroit, Michigan is the Motor City.
	Punctuate lists of names, cities and states with commas and semicolons	Walter Miller, San Francisco, California; Russell B. Jones, Portland, Oregon; etc.	Walter Miller, San Francisco, California, Russell B. Jones, Portland, Oregon, etc.
	Use a comma before *of* in connection with residence	Harold H. Mason, of 284 Clark Street, Chicago.	Harold H. Mason of 284 Clark Street, Chicago

Style Chart for Sales Promotion

	Style:	Correct:	Not:
Ages	Always use figures to express age except at the beginning of sentences	He was 60 years old. Twelve-year-old Robert White lives in New York.	He was sixty years old. 12-year-old Robert White lives in New York.
	Ages may be spelled out when used informally in ordinary reading matter	Men between the ages of eighteen and thirty.	Men between the ages of 18 and 30.

	Style:	Correct:	
Compound and Hyphenated Words	Compound two or more words to express a unit idea or to avoid ambiguity	anyone · today · writeup forethought · tomorrow · makeup hearsay · tonight · textbook something · moreover · upstate onlooker · alongside · nowadays everybody · newsprint · childlike hereby · cannot	
	Compound two nouns when one of them functions as a prefix or suffix	bookcase · copyholder · brickmaker doorway · airship · birthplace landowner · penholder	
	Use a hyphen to join the elements of an improvised compound	T-shaped · know-it-all · quick-fire blue-pencil · know-nothing · saddle-stitch high-minded · bell-shape · short-change blue-green · one-two · shell-shock make-believe · pipe-line · milk-white	
	Use a hyphen in adjectives formed of two or more words when they precede the nouns they modify, but not when they follow the nouns they modify	well-known · house-to-house up-to-date · black-and-white so-called · twentieth-century sales-building · matter-of-fact first-class · above-mentioned widely-quoted · two-party	
	In general, use no hyphens with the following prefixes and suffixes:	*a, after, age, anti, auto, by, co, counter, de, demi, ever, ex, extra, fold, grand, hood, holder, in, inter, intra, less, mid, mis, off, non, on, over, post, pro, re, semi, ship, some, sub, super, trans, tri, ultra, un, under, up, ward*	
	In general, use hyphens with the following prefixes and suffixes:	*able-, brother-, cross-, -elect, ex- (former), father-great-, half-, -hand, mother-, open-, public-quarter-, -rate, self-*	

	Style:	Correct:	Not:
Contractions and Omissions	Use apostrophe, without period or capital, to denote omission of letter or letters; contractions are not abbreviations	ass'n (contraction) Assn. (abbreviated) I'm; don't	Ass'n.; assn.
	Use a series of periods (ellipses) to denote omission of part of a quotation	Date lines . . . are set at the left side of the page.	Date lines (etc.) are set at the left side of the page.
	Use comma to denote omission of words	Mr. Smith was elected president; Mr. Jones, vice president.	Mr. Smith was elected president—Mr. Jones vice president.
Display Matter	Omit the period after headlines, captions and subheads	MORRIS ELECTED NEW MANAGER OF MOTOR COMPANY	MORRIS ELECTED NEW MANAGER OF MOTOR COMPANY.
	Avoid abbreviations and excessive punctuation in display lines		MORRIS ELECTED MOTOR CO. MGR. *or* MORRIS PROMOTED— ELECTED MANAGER, AUTOMOBILE FIRM

Style Chart for Sales Promotion

	Style:	Correct:	Not:
Display Matter (Cont.)	Omit the comma at the end of display lines, such as headings, running heads, box-heads, date lines, etc., and between months and year	*The Printing Art Quarterly* Formerly Printed Salesmanship November 1935	*The Printing Art Quarterly* Formerly Printed Salesmanship, November, 1935
Figures	In general, spell out numbers from one to nine, use figures for numbers above nine	There were only eight people present. There were 63 people present.	There were only eight people present There were sixty-three people present.
	Abbreviate *number* before figures	No. 17	Number 17 *or* No. Seventeen
	Spell out round numbers	He asked for one thousand volunteers. Approximately two hundred	He asked for 1,000 volunteers. Approximately 200
	When beginning a sentence, spell out figures and abbreviations	One hundred and twenty-five books were sold. Number 18 was the winner.	125 books were sold. No. 18 was the winner.
	Use figures with *percent*, which is spelled as one word	10 percent	ten per cent, *or* 10 per cent.
	In sentences requiring more than one numeral, some below and some above nine, use figures for all	Sales amounted to 137 cars in April, 88 cars in May, and 225 cars in June. From 9 to 110	Sales amounted to 137 cars in April, eighty-eight cars in May, and 225 cars in June. From nine to 110
	When numerals, particularly capitalized Roman numerals, are preceded by nouns or abbreviations which indicate place in a sequence, use figures and capitals	Act II; Room 606; Part IV; Vol. III; Fig. 5	Act Two; room 606
	Use figures for scores, degrees of temperature, sums of money, telephone numbers, dimensions, weights, measures, etc., and do not abbreviate in regular reading matter	Iowa 19, Illinois 0 32 degrees $12.50; 25 cents; $10 Longbeach 4000 9 by 12 inches; 6 feet 1 inch 5 gallons, 3 quarts 2 pounds, 7 ounces	Iowa, 19; Illinois, nothing thirty-two degrees twelve dollars and fifty cents; 25c; $10.00 Longbeach four thousand 9 x 12''; 6' 1'' five gallons, three quarts 2 lbs., 7 oz.
	Spell out ordinal numerals of less than one hundred	second, sixtieth	2nd *or* 60th
	Use numerals with hyphens in unit modifiers	10-inch board; 5-gallon jug; 45-degree angle; 5-pound weight	ten inch board; five gallon jug; forty-five degree angle; five pound weight
	Spell out fractions in ordinary reading matter	two-thirds of a yard	2/3 of a yard
Foreign Words	Italicize foreign words and phrases appearing in English text except those words which, because of continued usage, are now incorporated in the English language, such as:	Alma Mater, apropos, attache, au revoir, bona fide, camouflage, clientele, consensus, debut, ensemble, fracas, motif, nom de plume, protocol, regime, subpoena, versus, vice versa	

Style Chart for Sales Promotion

	Style:	Correct:	Not:
Foreign Words (Cont.)	In translations, quote the English equivalent of foreign words and phrases	*caveat emptor,* "let the purchaser beware"	
	Capitalize both proper nouns and proper adjectives in Latin and Dutch text; proper nouns but not adjectives in French, Italian, Spanish, Norwegian and Swedish text; and all nouns, both common and proper, but not adjectives, in German and Danish text	Nederland; Nederlandsche France; francaise Italia; italiani Espana; espanola Norge; norsk Sverige; svenska Deutschland; deutsch	nederlandsche Francaise Italiani Espanola Norsk Svenska Deutsch
	Capitalize the particle in French names, except when they are preceded by the Christian name or title	De Maupassant Jean de la Fontaine	de Maupassant Jean De La Fontaine
Geographical Names	Capitalize geographical names and their distinguishing names, whether they precede or follow	Ohio River; River Nile Long Lake; Lake Erie	Ohio river Long lake; lake Erie
	Capitalize sections of the country, but not adjectives derived from them; do not capitalize points of the compass	The East; The Middle West the eastern seaboard; middle western farmers They traveled east.	The east; the middle west the Eastern seaboard; Middle Western farmers They traveled East.
	In general, do not abbreviate parts of geographical names except in tabular matter where space is limited	Fort Meyers Port Huron Mount Everett San Diego	Ft. Meyers Pt. Huron Mt. Everett S. Diego
	Always abbreviate *saint* or *saints*	St. Paul	Saint Paul
Names of Organizations Institutions Etc.	Capitalize and spell out the full names of companies, corporations, mills, clubs, societies, banks, universities, schools, etc.	Brown Manufacturing Company Standard Corporation Central Woolen Mills The Downtown Club City Trust Bank New York Central Lines Northeastern University	Brown Manufacturing company Standard corporation Central Woolen mills The Downtown club City Trust bank New York Central lines Northeastern university
	Capitalize the full names of hotels, theaters, stations, buildings, etc.	Grand Hotel, Hotel Grand Lyric Theater Tenth Street Station Securities Building	Grand hotel Lyric theater Tenth street station Securities building
	Do not capitalize general designations of companies, buildings, organizations, institutions, etc., except when they are used as well-known short forms of specific proper names	The library; the company; the hotel The Canal (Panama Canal) The Street (Wall Street)	
Proper Names	Do not abbreviate Christian names except in signatures when the form used by the signer is retained	Thomas Mitchell *or* T, B. Mitchell John Cromwell William Johnson G. Washington	Thos. Mitchell Jno. Cromwell Wm. Johnson Geo. Washington
	Use the full name the first time the person is referred to in the text, thereafter simply last name and title	Walter R. Green delivered the opening address . . . in conclusion, Mr. Green said	Mr. Green delivered the opening address . . . in conclusion Walter R. Green said
	Capitalize proper nouns but not words derived from proper nouns that have developed special meaning	Prussia; prussian blue Paris; paris green Bohemia; bohemian	Prussian blue Paris green Bohemian
	Capitalize nicknames of cities, states, teams, etc.	The Windy City The Buckeye State The Chicago Bears	The windy city The buckeye state The Chicago bears

Style Chart for Sales Promotion

	Style:	Correct:	Not:
Political Names	Capitalize the names of political parties and organizations	The Republican Party He is a Democrat. The Republic of France The British Empire	The Republican party He is a democrat. The republic of France The British empire
	Capitalize nouns referring to the United States but not adjectives	The Nation; the Union The union army The national government federal	The nation; the union The Union Army The National government Federal
	Capitalize the names of specific national and state legislative bodies, but not adjectives	The Senate; the House of Representatives; the General Assembly; Parliament senatorial investigation parliamentary law	The senate; the house of representatives; the general assembly; parliament Senatorial investigation Parliamentary law
	Do not capitalize the names of national, state and city boards, etc., unless used in full as proper names	legislature; city hall; senate The Department of Agriculture; the Chicago Post Office	Legislature; City Hall; Senate The department of agriculture; the Chicago post office
Questions	Do not use a question mark after indirect questions or polite requests	Please send me a copy. He asked what time it was.	Please send me a copy? He asked what time it was?
	Use question marks to indicate direct queries, to express more than one query in the same sentence and to express doubt	What is the time? Will it mean the same to the salesmen? the dealers? the consumers? She walked fifteen (?) miles every day.	What is the time. Will it mean the same to the salesmen—the dealers?—the consumers?
	In question-and-answer testimony use dashes and question marks; do not quote	Q.—Where do you live? A.—92 Sherman Avenue.	Q: "Where do you live?" A: "92 Sherman Avenue."
Quotations	Set prose quotations of five or more lines and poetry quotations of two or more lines in narrow measure without quotation marks. When poetry is quoted, start each verse with quotations and end with the last verse	Regarding job printing, Mr. Gress has this to say: Attractiveness is as necessary to the typography of printing as dignity and legibility are to a law brief, but, in trying to get attractiveness into their work, job printers often go astray. As Whittier said: Let the thick curtain fall; I better know than all How little I have gained How vast the unattained.	
	Periods and commas are always set inside the quotation marks	He said, "The goods have been shipped." "The goods," he said, "have been shipped."	He said, "The goods have been shipped". "The goods", he said, "have been shipped",

Style Chart for Sales Promotion

	Style:	Correct:	Not:
Quotations (Cont.)	Interrogation points and exclamation points are placed inside quotation marks only when they are part of the quoted matter	"Good for you!" he shouted. "Have the goods been shipped?" he asked. The question is, was the shipment marked "rush"?	"Good for you"! he shouted. "Have the goods been shipped"? he asked. The question is, was the shipment marked "rush?"
	Use quotation marks to set off a word of unusual meaning or an unfamiliar or coined word the first time it is used but not thereafter	It will be the "go-aheads" who will get the most business . . . probably the go-aheads will be the only ones to make sales.	
	Capitalize the first word of a quotation when introduced by a comma, colon or some other break in sentence thought	He said that "business is rapidly improving." He said, "Business is rapidly improving." He said that business was rapidly improving.	He said that "Business is rapidly improving." He said "business is rapidly improving." He said, "that business was rapidly improving."
Religious References	Capitalize all names for the Bible, books of the Bible and other sacred books, but not adjective derived from them	The Authorized Version of the Bible	Biblical Characters
	Capitalize all nouns and adjectives used to designate the Deity, and all pronouns except *who, whose* and *whom*	The Almighty Trust Him who rules all things.	The almighty Trust him Who rules all things.
	Capitalize the names of religious denominations	Members of the Presbyterian church	Members of the presbyterian church
	Use the colon between chapter and verse in scriptural references and dashes between verses	I Corinthians xiii:13 Luke 1:2-4	
Time Date Seasons Etc.	Use figures for dates and omit *st, nd, rd, th*	September 10, 1935	September tenth, 1935 September 19th, 1935
	Spell out names of months and days except in date lines, tables, etc., and never abbreviate May, June or July; never abbreviate when day or month stands alone	It happened in September; he is leaving Saturday. The meeting was held on Tuesday, September 10, 1935. July 4, 1776	It happened in Sept. he is leaving Sat. The meeting was held on Tues., Sept. 10, 1935. Jul. 4, 1776
	Capitalize names of holidays, etc.	Fourth of July New Year's Day Armistice Day	fourth of July New Year's day armistice day
	Set off the year with commas except when only the name of the month appears	It was on August 15, 1935, that the accident occurred. August 1935	It was on August 15, 1935 that the accident occurred. August, 1935
	Spell out references to particular decades; do not capitalize	In the nineties	In the 90's *or* In the Nineties
	In general, use figures for expressing time; use lower-case letters for the abbreviations, a.m. and p.m. Capitalize B.C. and A.D. which should be set without a space between; A.D. should precede the year	11:30 a.m. 46 B.C. A.D. 1900	11:30 A. M. *or* 11:30 A.M. 46 B. C. A. D. 1900 *or* 1900 A. D.
	Time of day and dates may be spelled out when given in ordinary reading matter	Lunch will be ready at noon. The meeting opens at half past two. About the fifteenth of March He left at four.	

Style Chart for Sales Promotion

	Style:	Correct:	Not:
Time **Dates** **Seasons** **Etc.** **(Cont.)**	In using figures, never let the hour stand alone. Use either o'clock, or a.m., p.m., or 12 o'clock noon or midnight	It was 10 o'clock in the morning. At 7:30 p.m.	It was 10 in the morning. Tonight at 7:30
	Do not capitalize seasons of the year	During the spring and summer	During the Spring and Summer
Titles	Always abbreviate the titles, *Mr.*, *Mrs.*, *Dr.*, and *St.*, preceding personal names	Mr. Henry C. Gordon Dr. H. K. Clark Mrs. H. K. Clark St. John	Mister Gordon Doctor Clark Mrs. Dr. Clark Saint John
	Abbreviate *Honorable* and *Reverend* unless preceded by *the* when they are spelled out and capitalized; being adjectives rather than titles they should be used only when followed by the first names, initial or title	Hon. Carter Glass; the Honorable Carter Glass; The Honorable Mr. Glass Rev. E. T. Nichols; the Reverend E. T. Nichols; Rev. Dr. Nichols	Hon. Glass; the Hon. Glass Rev. Nichols; the Reverend Nichols
	Capitalize all titles of honor or nobility when referring to specific persons and used in place of the proper name	The President (President of the United States); the Senator from Idaho	The president (President of the United States); the senator from Idaho
	Abbreviate *Esq.*, *Jr.* and *Sr.* and use Roman numerals, II, III, IV, etc., when used after a name; use commas with abbreviations but not with numerals	Robert C. Porter, Jr. Hanford Hicks, Esq. James R. Bower III George V	Robert C. Porter, junior Hanford Hicks Esq. James R. Bower, Third George, V
	Capitalize and spell out titles preceding personal names, but do not capitalize when following names	President George T. Bush; George T. Bush, president Professor Howard A. Cook, professor of English	president George T. Bush; George T. Bush, President professor Howard A. Cook; Howard A. Cook, Professor of English
	Capitalize abbreviations for degrees and titles and set without space between the letters	Thomas D. Owen, M.D.	Thomas D. Owen, M. D. or Dr. Thomas D. Owen, M.D.
	Do not hyphenate ordinary titles of two or more words	vice president; sales manager; assistant treasurer	vice-president; sales-manager; assistant-treasurer
	Italicize the titles of books and of plays, essays, poems, etc., of book size	*Treasure Island* *The Merchant of Venice*	Treasure Island "The Merchant of Venice"
	Quote the titles of short poems, essays or plays of less than book length	"To a Waterfowl"	To a Waterfowl
	Italicize the names of periodicals, journals, pamphlets, published documents, etc., but not the article *the*	the *Saturday Evening Post* the *Dental Journal* the *Report of the United States Department of Agriculture*	the Saturday Evening Post *the Dental Journal* "The Report of the United States Department of Agriculture"
	Italicize the distinguishing portions of the names of newspapers, but not the city names; abbreviate and inclose in parentheses the name of the state when needed	the New York *Times* the Cleveland *Plain Dealer* the Bloomington (Ill.) *Pantagraph*	*the New York Times* *the Cleveland Plain Dealer* "The Bloomington Pantagraph"
	Quote the subjects of lectures, sermons, magazine articles, etc., including the initial *A* or *The*	"The Prospects for Inflation" "The Ten Commandments"	The Prospects for Inflation The "Ten Commandments"
	Quote the names of ships, aircraft, titles of pictures and the names of art objects	U.S.S. "Virginia" Whistler's "Mother"	U.S.S. Virginia "Whistler's Mother"

Chapter 12

SALES PROMOTION LITERATURE

III—Production

THE graphic arts field is undergoing a dramatically-accelerating revolution, brought on in part by the needs of great, modern-day newspapers and press services for faster and more efficient operations; and by the high wage levels of the several well-established craft unions in the industry. Electronic applications have added greatly to the fast-changing pace.

With the advent and now widespread use of the offset process, most printers no longer need typesetting departments: they use specialized type houses who provide camera-ready copy and set headlines on film. In some newspaper offices, copy writing and editing is being done on television-like equipment. The wire services send photos and other illustrations across the continent and abroad, through an electronic scanning process, on a same-day basis.

Electronic Developments

Today the printing industry is becoming rapidly involved with electronics. The most dramatic change is taking place in the use of computers to set type, justify lines and hyphenate. Many companies now have computers which, combined with teletypesetters, enable printers to span time and distance barriers that long seemed insurmountable.

With Telstar, Early Bird and satellite communications approaching everyday use, no spot on earth will be too distant from which to send and receive copy.

Some newspapers already routinely use computers to set type amazingly fast. It takes a computer about a minute to set a full newspaper page.

Other examples of electronic applications in printing are in controls to regulate cutting, folding, and stacking. Scanners, working through analog computers, are simplifying the complicated steps in making color separations directly from transparencies without a camera and without a lens.

Another printing technique is the 3-D process. This creates a startling illusion of depth by coating a printed surface with optical plastic. All of these new developments are described for the layman in an interesting booklet published by the Tension Envelope Corporation in cooperation with the Printing Industries of America, Inc.

Electrostatic Printing

Another revolutionary development of great significance for the future is electrostatic printing. Among other things, electrostatic printing eliminates the need for pressure and uniformity of contact at the printing surface. This means that it may be used to print on irregular or pressure-sensitive surfaces. It will print articles that cannot be printed by conventional methods. In the Tension booklet these are listed as: vegetables, foam, burlap, pills, capsules and tablets, glass, rock, ceramics, wood and plastic, among many other raw or processed materials.

Also of importance in the production of literature is the process for making engravings. Costs have been more than halved by use of a photoelectric process which cuts the engraving on plastic instead of the traditional copper and zinc base.

While not all these recent developments in the graphic arts apply directly to producing sales promotional literature, many do. It is therefore important in view of the prevailing high wage rates and resulting costs in the industry, that those responsible for the production of advertising and sales literature not only know about these cost-cutting developments, but that they take advantage of facilities where the use of advanced processes and high-speed equipment make for lower prices.

The Production Department

If the appropriation for printed and lithographic materials is sizable, as in the case of a national advertiser or an advertising agency, the responsibility for producing and purchasing it might profitably be delegated to someone who has specialized in that branch of sales promotion. There are so many ways for effecting savings in producing sales literature by better planning and alert buymanship, that an experienced production man who knows his way around should save his salary, and that of his assistants, many times over.

Then, too, there is the matter of giving "character" to the sales promotional materials used by a company. This involves a knowledge of lay-out, typography, and the printing processes seldom possessed by those who have not specialized in production. A good lay-out man, who knows type and how to use it to get desired effects, can save the company large sums of money. If the printer or lithographer is required to produce a piece of literature without a workmanlike layout, he must use his own judgment; which usually means resetting and costly alterations. At present wage rates alterations are a very expensive luxury. There are cases where the alterations on a direct-mail piece have exceeded the cost of the composition. A good production man can also save on the cost of sales promotional literature by making full use of types which can be machine set, avoiding the higher cost of hand composition. But he must know type. Year after year, many new faces have been cut for machine composition. At one time, fewer than 10 standard type faces accounted for more than 95% of commercial typography; then in a rush came the sans serif faces, the square serif faces, the newer script and cursives, and finally the modern revivals of nineteenth-century novelty faces, until only a specialist could keep abreast of typographic developments. Binding methods, too, had remained substantially the same for decades until the new mechanical bindings came into vogue and soon multiplied to the point where a printing buyer had not two or three bindings from which to choose but 20 or 30!

Higher prices imposed upon production men the necessity of utilizing the new methods and materials at their disposal, but of doing so with maximum economy. It compelled them to find short-cuts that would reduce costs without destroying effectiveness. It taught them to get modern effects at old-fashioned prices. It developed their resourcefulness, ingenuity, and buying acumen. They learned how to make blow-ups of type proofs take the place of hand-lettering; how to substitute flat colors for process plates; how to use type ornaments instead of art work and engravings; how to take full advantage of the most economical of the new processes.

In the face of paper shortages production men had to adapt their plates and printing to whatever paper they could get and still come up with creditable jobs. With priorities working against them on every side they had to simplify the specifications of each job to the barest necessities in order to get them produced at all. In a sellers' market they had to marshall all their sources of supply diplomatically enough to obtain reasonable quality and service without getting too far out of line on price. It was during those hectic days that production men proved themselves indispensable in sales promotion. In fact, many concerns which in the past had managed to get along without qualified production assistance, set up production departments during the war that they have kept in operation ever since.

Producer and Supplier Contacts

The maintenance and broadening of contacts with producers and suppliers, as a matter of fact, governs all the production department's other activities. Whether the department consists of one person or twenty, it does not possess within itself the ability to produce. It is dependent upon a myriad of outside agencies, all of which are in turn interdependent. A piece of sales promotion literature, consequently, may seldom if ever be considered as a single job entrusted solely to a single source of supply; rather it must be considered as a series of related jobs, and each job must be produced to meet (a) the required time schedule, (b) the required budget limitations, and (c) the required standards of quality. To achieve such objectives, efficient production departments are geared to operate according to systematic procedures which include, at a very minimum performance level, these four steps:

1. A thorough knowledge of the problems involved in each part of each piece of literature, based on a close study of all possible alternatives.
2. A wide enough choice of sources of supply to permit careful selection for each job.
3. Full instructions to each supplier and a complete understanding of delivery dates, prices and quality standards.
4. Regular and relentless follow-up of each supplier at each stage of the operation.

Whenever there is a break-down in a production system, it occurs at one of these four points. If the problem was correctly analyzed at the beginning, if the right supplier was selected to handle it, if he was fully acquainted with what was expected of him, and if he was followed up on regular schedule, then everything could be depended upon to run smoothly. But multiply one supplier by possibly a dozen, and the difficulties besetting a production department become more apparent. A slip-up in the negotiations with any one of the twelve might easily disrupt all the efforts of the other eleven and the job might come out late, might be of inferior quality, and might cost more than anyone ever suspected. When the great number of different individuals and firms accountable to the production department's direction is taken into consideration, the wonder is that slip-ups occur as rarely as they do. Even the following list is not necessarily complete, but it represents most of the craftsmen with whom the average production department does business:

Printers	Layout and Lettering artists
Photoengravers	Typesetters
Color-separation firms	Electrotypers
Steel- and copper-plate engravers	Bookbinders
Paper merchants	Finishers
Envelope manufacturers	Mailing list houses
Photographers	Letter shops
Illustrators	Display producers

A useful aid to sales promotion men is the "Creative Black Book" published annually by Strauss Publications, Inc., New York. It lists over 6,000 suppliers classified by services and location in New York, Boston, Philadelphia, Chicago, Los Angeles and San Francisco, to meet the needs of sales promotion, graphic arts, advertising and film production managers.

Where the Production Operation Begins

The production manager and his assistants are the point of contact between all these producers and suppliers on the outside and his own sales and advertising associates on the inside. In the case of advertising agencies, as pointed out in Chapter 19, he works directly with the art director and copy chief. In companies doing sales promotion, he gets his assignments from the sales promotion manager, the sales manager, or the advertising manager, depending on the setup of his organization.

Usually a piece of sales promotion literature reaches the production manager in the form of okayed copy and finished art and layout. Sometimes, especially in the case of companies which do not maintain their own art staffs, he gets only a rough dummy and is responsible for getting the necessary photographs made, for commissioning an illustrator to do the finished drawings and paintings, and for turning the whole thing over to a layout artist or designer to make up the final working dummy. The layout artist may either do whatever lettering is required himself or turn it over to a lettering specialist. He may also specify the type faces in which the job is to be set and, in consultation with the production manager, select color combinations, decide on printing techniques, and specify the paper.

Frequently, of course, the production manager or one of his assistants is qualified by talent or training or both to perform the functions of a layout artist himself and handle the working dummies. type and paper specifications, and other details. It is seldom, however, that a production department includes professional artists capable of doing finished work; in that event it becomes an art department doing production work only incidentally, instead of vice versa.

Neither does a production department often assume any responsibility for copy other than to set it legibly and correctly in type. It may do its own proofreading but not its own editing or rewriting, even when necessary to cut or fill to make the copy fit. That's a copywriting job; the production department has enough on its hands already.

OVERLAP, WAVE, SLANT, EXPAND, CONDENSE, & ITALICIZE.

Letters and words may be controlled in shape, style or form through the photo-film process, as shown in this illustration.

These procedures, obviously, are typical rather than universal. They apply principally to organizations doing a large enough volume of sales promotion work to warrant a good-sized production department. They do not apply to smaller operations in which the sales promotion or advertising manager may be his own idea man, copywriter, art director, and production man combined. There are such versatile promotion men and, within the limits of their available time, some of them are doing outstanding jobs. Creative and technical talents do not ordinarily mix, however, and good writers or artists rarely possess the organizing ability characteristic of a good production man who, similarly, is too methodical ever to catch the spirit of doing inspired writing or imaginative art. The nature of his work demands that he be an executive rather than a craftsman.

Which Printing Process to Select

The first question to be settled right at the beginning of production is how the job shall be printed. So many things hinge on this decision straight down the production line that it must be made before most of the other operations can start. Whether the job is to be printed by letterpress, offset, or gravure determines (a) what form the finished art work will take, (b) whether the type will be made up for printing or electrotyping or will be phototypeset for photographic reproduction, (c) whether engravings will be required or photostats will be made for key-line drawings, (d) what kind of paper will be used, (e) what size envelopes will be needed to accommodate the weight and bulk of the paper, (f) how much the job will cost to mail and the effect of those costs on the press run, and so on through almost every ramification of the piece. The time as well as the cost element must be weighed, and there are, in addition, such other considerations as the nature of the illustrations, the number of colors, the length of the press run, the size of the finished piece, and many more.

Because the selection of the printing process for an individual sales promotion piece is of such far-reaching importance, a thorough knowledge of the advantages and disadvantages, the possibilities and limitations of the various processes is indispensable to people in production work. Of all the methods of reproducing copy, design, and illustrations, probably more than 95 out of every 100 pieces of sales promotion literature are produced by the three major processes: Letterpress, offset lithography, and gravure. And the essential differences between the three processes are briefly as follows:

In letterpress or "relief" printing, ink is transferred to paper by means of *raised* surfaces.

In gravure or "intaglio" printing, ink is transferred to paper by means of *depressed* surfaces.

In lithography or "offset" printing, ink is transferred to paper by means of *flat* surfaces.

Each process differs from the other two not only in basic principles but in physical appearance. Experienced production men can identify each process at a glance; usually they also recognize whether it was employed wisely or unwisely for the specific job at hand. The factors on which they base their judgments are revealed in the detailed descriptions of each process.

RELIEF PRINTING—LETTERPRESS PROCESS

The letterpress process was the first major method of mass reproduction and is still widely used today. The ink is applied to the printing surface of raised type or engravings and the impression is transferred to paper by the application of slight pressure. Small jobs are printed either on platen presses, such as the Gordon, which handles sheet sizes of 10 by 15 inches, or on job cylinder presses such as the Miehle Vertical and Horizontal, Kelly, or Miller, which print on sheets up to 17 by 22 inches. Larger jobs are printed on cylinder presses of the flat-bed type which range in size from a sheet capacity of 17 by 22 inches up to 50 by 73½ inches. Newspapers, big circulation magazines, mail-order catalogs, etc., are printed on rotary presses using continuous rolls of paper instead of sheets, or on sheet-fed or magazine web rotary presses using flat sheets instead of rolls.

On platen presses, the impressions are made by a flat, even pressure of the paper against a flat area of type or plate. On flat-bed cylinder presses, the impressions are made by the pressure of a cylinder rolling across a flat area of type or plate. On rotary presses, the impression is made by having the flat printing area put into curved form by means of stereotyping or electrotyping against which another cylinder revolves with the paper. Among the advantages claimed for letterpress printing over other processes, are the following:

Sharpness and Clarity. This is the only process in which printing is done directly from type and photoengravings. However, the quality of the printed piece is largely dependent upon the "makeready" skills of the pressman. To do fine-screen halftone work, only coated papers should be used in letterpress.

Flexibility. All the ingredients of a letterpress printing job—type, zinc and halftone engravings, electrotypes, etc.—may be made up together and printed in the same form. The same form may be broken down and the various ingredients rearranged or placed in different forms and printed over and over again. For jobs which involve typesetting anyway, which have small press runs, and which contain illustrations or type blocks that may be re-used in other pieces, no other process has the flexibility of letterpress. But these advantages are not necessarily held when the runs get long enough to require electrotypes or when there is the possibility of later long-run reprints. When composition is on machine-cast slugs, it is possible to cast two slugs for each line at the same time, so that the second set of slugs can be used when the first set shows wear.

Developments in Letterpress Printing

The principal advance in the letterpress process in recent years has been the perfection and adoption on a large scale of so-called wet printing for the production of long-run magazine and catalog jobs at high speeds. By means of wet printing four or five colors may be printed almost simultaneously at speeds up to 12,000 revolutions per hour. Wet printing differs in many material respects from dry printing and requires special plates, special inks, and special papers, but it has solved the problem of producing the greatly increased number of full-color advertising pages for the weekly magazines with circulations well up in the millions. Instead of having an impression cylinder for each plate cylinder, as is the case with conventional rotary presses, in four-color wet printing a much larger impression cylinder is used to accommodate five press cylinders. As the paper web travels around this large impression cylinder, the various plate cylinders successively transfer layers of yellow, red, blue, black, and, when desired, an additional color to the paper, one on top of another. The process has its limitations so far as exactly matching the colors of the original color drawing, painting, or photograph is concerned; yet for the purposes for which it is used the quality has been developed to a surprisingly high point. The sales promotion jobs for which wet printing is adaptable are exceedingly few, but it adds one more tool to the resources of companies which occasionally have large runs of full-color jobs in which speed and economy are factors.

INTAGLIO PRINTING—GRAVURE PROCESS

The principle of gravure printing is exactly the reverse of letterpress printing. Instead of obtaining the impression from the top of the plate, it is made from minute recesses or "wells" etched into the surface of the plate which hold the ink and transfer it to the paper. The earliest form of intaglio printing was the etching, which was discovered by Tommaso Finiguerra, an Italian goldsmith, in the early part of the fifteenth century. The etching process, fundamentally, is that of scratching out an image in the surface of a sheet of metal either by hand tooling or by acids, then covering it with ink, wiping the ink off the surface, and finally picking up on a sheet of paper the ink remaining below the surface of the metal.

Steel or copperplate engraving is a form of intaglio printing, as are the various types of gravure: Hand gravure, which is known as photogravure; sheet-fed gravure; and cylinder or rotary gravure, familiarly known as rotogravure. An advantage of the gravure printing process is that much finer screens can be printed than by the letterpress process. For average fine printing, the photoengraved halftone uses a screen of 133 lines to the square inch. In gravure, the coarsest screen generally used has 150 lines to the square inch and they range up as high as 300 lines. A 150-line screen gravure plate, then, has 22,500 dots to the square inch and can be printed on the coarsest kind of paper stock. For a photoengraving halftone to print satisfactorily on the same coarse stock requires a 65-line screen halftone, or one having only 4,255 dots to the square inch. A gravure plate, in other words, has more than 5 times as many dots per square inch as a comparable halftone, accounting for its greater detail, the absence of visible screen, and the softness of its tone.

The rotogravure sections of newspapers are printed by rotary gravure presses on continuous rolls of paper. Pictorial house organs, catalogs, and long-run folders are frequently done by rotogravure. The fine reproductions of photographs, paintings and drawings used in the higher-quality sales promotion literature are printed by sheet-fed gravure presses on single sheets of paper, usually of a much heavier weight and fancier finish. Rotogravure is practical only for runs of upward of 100,000 impressions; sheet-fed gravure is practical for shorter runs even as small as a few thousand impressions.

While the dots in a halftone plate for letterpress or offset, as will be shown, vary in size to determine relative light and dark areas, in a gravure plate all dots are of the same size, shape, and number per square inch in both highlight and shadow areas. The tone is controlled by varying the depth of the ink wells. The deeper wells hold more ink and consequently print more darkly. Another requirement exclusive to gravure is that everything to be reproduced—type, illustrations, hand-lettering, and even solids—must be screened.

Gravure's gradual growth in popularity is indicated by the fact that there are now more than 50 national magazines printed entirely or in part by this process. Books, calendars, greeting cards, and such widely varied merchandise as wallpaper, textiles, wrapping paper, linoleum, labels, box covers, cellophane, glassine, and tissue are also being done in gravure. It is a versatile process of wide usefulness with which well-rounded production people need to be entirely familiar.

OFFSET LITHOGRAPHY

Lithography is the process of printing from a plane or flat surface, a technique which is neither intaglio nor relief. The image to be printed is in the same plane with the non-printing area. The differences between offset printing and other processes are, basically, the application of the principle that oil (ink) and water do not mix; and the method of placing ink on paper by offsetting it first from plate to rubber blanket, then to paper.

At first, lithography used smooth stone tables. Later, zinc or aluminum plates were developed, and the fact that they could be made to curve around a press cylinder made possible the high-speed offset lithography of today.

The offset process also differs in another way from letterpress printing. Instead of assembling heavy type and plates, photographic negatives or positives of illustrations, "repro" proofs of type matter or phototypeset copy, may be more conveniently used.

Essential to the modern offset process is the art of photography, which is used in photocomposing the printing plate. All the copy to be reproduced—type, lettering, illustrations, etc.—is photographed onto a coated plate, and the light-hardened portions which make up the image become the sections that attract the ink and repel water, while the balance of the plate attracts water and repels ink. Offset plates now may be deep-etched after the manner of intaglio plates so that more ink may be carried on the plate and thus a stronger color printed on the halftone sections of the image.

Among the advantages that offset offers to sales promotion production are the following:

More economical printing plates. While there may not be a great deal of difference in the cost of original halftones for letterpress or for offset, there is considerable difference between the cost of electrotypes and offset printing plates. By the use of step-and-repeat photography, the same image may be duplicated on an offset plate rapidly and at little cost. Thus the process is particularly well adapted to the printing of letterheads, labels, small folders, and other pieces where anywhere from four to a hundred of the same subject are printed on the same sheet. Further, line-engraving costs may be eliminated if the drawings are made to scale and are photographed on the same negative with the type proofs and lettering. Offset printing also permits the use of screened tint blocks and halftones on uncoated papers, producing soft, pleasing effects.

Lower cost of reprints. For jobs which are reprinted at intervals, the comparatively greater ease of storing offset plates and getting them back on the press and ready to run quickly are other factors in favor of the process. This advantage may be lost, however, if many corrections or revisions are made in the reprinting.

Easier to handle large-size work. The limitations in the size of photoengraving equipment plus the high cost of large engravings gives offset the edge when it comes to the reproduction of such large pieces as posters, displays, and fine art reproductions. Offset presses can handle sheet sizes as large as 52 by 74 inches, and printed images 42 by 58½ inches are standard in poster work.

Wider variety of papers available. By the offset process, fine screen halftones can be printed on any grade of paper from soft uncoated stock to enamel papers sized for offset.

Conversion of letterpress plates. Conversions may be made in the following ways: (1) by pulling inked reproduction proofs, (2) by direct transfer of the image, (3) photographically, and (4) by a combination of chemical and mechanical methods.

Reproduction proofs (repros) are pulled on a proof press, usually on 80 lb. or 100 lb. No. 1 enamel such as Kromekote by Champion Papers or Lusterkote by the S. D. Warren Co. A number of special materials have also been developed for this purpose. *Scotchprint* is a highly-ink-receptive, plastic material which can be made into a negative by contact or by camera. *Converkal* becomes a film negative instantly on contact with warmed type. *Brightype* is a photographic image conversion whereby the type form or plate is first sprayed with a nonreflecting black lacquer. The printing surface is then made reflective by burnishing with a rubber pad. A series of lights illuminate the polished surface which is then photographed.

Image conversion by a combination of chemical and mechanical methods requires neither ink nor camera. *Cronapress* is a nonphotosensitive film with a white, pressure-sensitive coating. After vacuum drawdown, thousands of small lead or steel balls are bounced at random over the film, the end result being a right-reading negative of the form.

With the proliferation of phototypesetting in recent years, the need for conversions has decreased dramatically.

OTHER PRINTING PROCESSES

Continuous tone printing. Both collotype, which permits continuous-tone printing by using a gelatin base without screen, and aquatone, which also uses a gelatin base but carries screens up to 400-line, are associated with the offset process. Collotype is planographic printing using a gelatin-coated glass or metal plate as the printing surface—glass for flat-bed presses and grained zinc or aluminum for rotary or offset presses. The basis of the process is the fact that when a bichromate is added to gelatin and exposed to light, the portion so exposed becomes hard and waterproof while the remaining gelatin is swelled by moisture, leaving the design slightly below the surface. After treatment, the lighthardened and dried portions of the gelatin take the ink and the unhardened and soluble portions repel it. No screen is used and the resulting true photographic gradation is unbroken by any line or screen. It is called continuous tone printing as distinguished from halftone printing, and is also known under the names of albertype, artotype, heliotype, and lichtdruck.

Letterpress embossing is basically the same process as letterpress printing, the chief difference being that, in embossing, the impression is made by male (raised) and female (depressed) dies, while in printing the impression is made by type and plates. Embossing produces the image in relief, either raising it above the surrounding surface or depressing it below the surface. In hot embossing, the female die is electrically heated to give a sharper and deeper impression. In so-called blind embossing, the impression is made, without ink, on the plain stock. Letterpress embossing is responsible for the distinctive relief effects noticeable in so many present-day labels and seals. The process also has wide application for booklet and catalog covers, letterheads, display cards, calendars, and printed specialties of various kinds.

Water-color printing is a regular letterpress process which makes use of special inks, plates and rollers. Introduced in America as the Jean Berté process in 1927, its principal advantage has been to make possible the printing of pure water colors on standard letterpress equipment. Specially prepared rubber plates, more resilient than those commonly used, lay the colors evenly on any stock without crushing even the most fancy finishes. By overlapping transparent water-color inks, many brilliant color combinations are obtainable without showing any sheen where they overlap. Through the introduction of new flat oil inks and special varnishes for making water-color pigments insoluble, the development of new coatings for ink rollers and the application of regular printing plates to water-color uses, several alternatives to the Jean Berté process have now been developed which are practically indistinguishable from it.

Silk screen printing. For many years exclusively a hand process, silk screen printing has recently advanced to a point where it can be done automatically on either of two presses designed for the purpose, and part of the work of affixing the image to the screen can now be done photographically. Basically, silk screen printing is the process of forcing a paint through a fine screen or silk, organdy, or wire cloth onto a printing surface of paper, glass, metal, cloth or, in fact, any material that can be printed or painted. Because of the ease and economy of preparing screens for as many different color impressions as are required, it is ideal for short runs of colorful solid color effects or for longer runs, up to 5,000 pieces, which call for more than the customary 3 or 4 colors; some subjects have as many as 40 or 50 different shades. By the use of a photographic emulsion which is light-hardened to the screen for non-printing portions, paint is permitted to go through the screen when the excess emulsion is washed out to open up the printing areas. By this method fine line cuts and even half-tones may be reproduced, as well as type.

OFFICE DUPLICATING PROCESSES

A few years ago, a wonderful cartoon appeared in one of our national magazines. It showed a high-ranking Army officer dictating to his clerk. The caption read something like this:

> " '. . . and because this excessive paper work is extremely inefficient and costly, it must be eliminated.' Now, Jenkins, get me 100 copies of that."

Every office manager in America could probably recite—with more rancor than humor—some similar experience. And usually, when the command "make a hundred copies!" is flung at the office manager, there is this added injunction: "And do it right away."

At that point, the office manager is confronted with the problem of finding the easiest, fastest, and least costly way of carrying out his orders. And this thrusts him into the field of office duplicating.

Time was when the office duplicating equipment of most offices consisted of a worn-out, dusty machine off in an obscure corner of the premises, which was occasionally operated by the office boy. But times have changed. And with them have changed the demands of business for copies of letters, forms, memos, reports, and brochures. This enormous diet of paper upon which modern business feeds has prompted the manufacturers of duplicating equipment to literally outdo themselves in developing new reproduction methods and machines. Today, the duplicating equipment field offers to the office manager a score of more different machines to obtain multiple copies of a page.

Principal Duplicating Methods

At the outset, it might be well to list and give a thumbnail description of the principal office duplicating methods.

Mimeographing

To produce office bulletins on mimeograph equipment, the operator types or draws directly on the stencil. This operation is the crucial step in obtaining quality copy results. For added effectiveness, however, it is possible to patch prepared cartoons and illustrations onto the stencil.

The mimeograph process is suited for short, medium, and long runs. It is fast and it is economical. Stencil duplicator prices cover a wide range.

The electronic stencil process has been developed to help the mimeograph attain copy quality results previously reserved for the offset process. These stencils make it possible to reproduce linework, solids, and remarkable halftone facsimiles. From 5,000 to 10,000 copies can be reproduced from one electronic stencil.

Photocopy

The photocopy process provides a quick way to obtain from one to any number of copies of an original document, such as reports, letters, invoices, etc. Some photocopiers will even copy pages in bound volumes, photographs, and blueprints. Generally, it takes only seconds and costs but a few cents to make a photocopy. Recent developments include two-side printing, additional color and collating.

Offset Duplicating

Compared to the cost of other office duplicating equipment, the initial cost of offset equipment is comparatively high. However, only the offset process can produce bulletins with print-like copy quality at a real saving of printing costs—including the reproduction of linework, solid areas, and halftones.

There are three configurations of offset duplicators: tabletop, standard consoles and fully automatic models. The first two are also available in manual or semi-automatic versions. Tabletop models run at speeds varying from 3,500 to 8,000 copies per hour, using paper sizes from 3"x5" to 11"x17". Console models are heavy-duty machines that can produce over 10,000 copies per hour. Fully automatic offset units incorporate a device which automatically produces a master and loads it onto the press.

Paper masters may economically be used for the production of a few hundred copies. Metal plates are required when thousands of copies are needed.

A. B. Dick Co. Model 310 Offset Duplicator

Quantitative Decisions Needed

How shall an office executive choose the equipment required? There are a half dozen basic factors which must be considered and evaluated before a choice is made.

First, something must be known about the load factor, which involves not only the total amount of work to be done each day, but also the number and type of specific jobs to be done. Duplicating processes that are economically sound must provide for long-, medium-, or short-run reproduction or any combination of the three. (A short run is 20 copies or less; a medium run from 20 to 500 copies; and a long run above 500 copies.) The method that is best suited to reproducing 5,000 copies of a form is not the most economical for obtaining 10 copies of engineering drawings, for example. Long-run work should be done by either stencil duplicating or by offset; short-run work can best be done by whiteprint duplicating, or photocopy equipment. When it comes to medium-run work, usually letters, price lists, or bulletins—hectograph, stencil duplicating, photocopiers and offset all offer good possibilities for practical, economical reproduction.

TYPESETTING

There are four basic methods of producing type: hand (foundry type), cast metal (hot type), typewriter (direct impression, also referred to as cold type or strike-on composition) and phototypesetting. Of these four methods, phototypesetting has become the most-widely-accepted method.

Hand Composition

Hand composition is produced with foundry type (individual metal characters) which are assembled by selecting the characters from a case and inserting them one at a time into a composing "stick" until reaching the desired line length. Lines are justified by adding spaces between the words. After the type has been set and printed, the type is returned to the case, a process called "distribution." At best a slow, tedious process, hand composition is rarely used today.

Machine Composition (Hot Type)

Machine-set copy can be produced on any of four machines. The Linotype and Intertype machines cast a line of type at a time; the Monotype produces individual characters; and the Ludlow, which also casts one line at a time but is mainly used for display type or headlines.

Linotype and Intertype

These machines cast a one-piece line of type to the desired length. The operator sits at a typewriter-like keyboard and, at the touch of a key, a brass matrix is released from a "magazine" (storage case). When the "mats" for one line have been assembled, the line is automatically justified by the use of space bands. The operator then sends the line though the machine which automatically casts the line and returns the matrices to the magazine.

Some linecasting machines have been equipped for semi-automatic operation from perforated tape. These tapes, which can be produced on off-line perforators or received over wire services, allow one operator to handle the production of several linecasters.

Monotype

This method of typesetting consists of two machines: a keyboard and a caster. The keyboard produces perforated paper tape used to drive the caster which produces metal type one letter at a time. To justify the line, a counting mechanism registers the widths of the characters as they are keyboarded. When the line is within justification range, a bell rings, alerting the operator, who strikes a series of keys to determine the amount of spacing necessary for justification of the line. The paper tape is then fed into the caster.

In limited use today, the Monotype is ideally suited for setting complicated tabular matter such as financial statements and charts.

Ludlow

This is a semi-automatic method of typesetting, combining hand and machine composition. Individual brass matrices are assembled by hand in a special composing stick. The justified line is then inserted into the Ludlow machine which casts the line into a metal "slug." While similar to hand composition, the advantage is that a new slug is made for each line of type, giving the printer the advantage of having a limitless supply of type from a single set of matrices.

Typewriter (Direct Impression)

This method is usually referred to as "strike-on" or "cold" composition as opposed to the metal, or "hot type" composition. While ordinary typewriters may be said to produce composition, they are rudimentary at best. There are several machines capable of producing print-quality composition. They are the Varitype, the Justowriter and the IBM Selectric Composer. All have proportionally designed typefaces and produce justified composition.

Varityper machines require double typing in order to produce justified copy and can mix two fonts on a line. The Justowriter generates a paper tape with line endings in justification range and a hard copy print-out. The tape is then inserted into a reproducing unit containing two readers. The tape is read and strike-on copy is automatically produced, in justified form, on reproduction type paper.

The IBM Selectric Composer, like the Varityper, requires double typing for justified composition. Fonts may be mixed on a single line by merely changing the ball fonts. A more sophisticated system, the MT/SC (Magnetic Tape/Selectric Composer) consists of one or more recorders that produce unjustified hard copy and coded magnetic tape. If the input is correct, the tape is processed and the Composer sets justified composition. Corrections can be made on another tape which is then merged with the original to produce final composition.

Word Processors

The IBM MT/ST (Magnetic Tape/Selectric Typewriter) was the first of many word processors on the market today. Essentially, it is a typewriter that produces hard copy along with a magnetic tape cartridge or magnetic disc that permits the operator to change or update input copy during or after typing.

Phototypesetting

In recent years, hot metal composition has gradually given way to phototypesetting so that today phototypesetting is the most-widely-used method of setting type. Even letterpress is using this process for the production of photopolymer or other photo-mechanical plates.

There are three elements required for this process: a light source, a master character image and photo- or light-sensitive material. Hence the name.

First generation units were simply adaptations of machine-set typesetting wherein a negative of the character was carried on the matrix and photographed rather than cast. While still a comparatively slow

A second-generation phototypesetter, the Mergenthaler VIP/T is a precision text and display typesetting system with 65 on-line point sizes.

method, the output was suitable for camera reproduction, thereby eliminating the necessity of pulling repro proofs.

Second generation units are electro-mechanical in nature and vary in sophistication, automation, speed and versatility. Input is usually in the form of perforated paper tape generated on a typewriter-like keyboard. Input may also be in the form of magnetic tape or by direct entry from the keyboard to the typesetter.

Containing mini-computers, phototypesetters will automatically hyphenate and justify lines, thereby freeing the keyboard operator from making line-end decisions. With simple tape commands, these units will mix fonts, change point sizes, line lengths and leading. Ragged left, right or center can be set from unjustified output by tape command, as can automatic quadding, right, left or center. Twenty or more columns may be automatically tabbed via tape command.

Third generation units employ cathode ray tube (CRT) technology and are completely electronic. Characters are stored on magnetic discs and are formed on the tube via a series of fine lines or dots. The resultant image is then transferred to photosensitive material. Because CRT typesetters set type with a beam of light, extremely high speeds are commonplace. Mergenthaler's Linotron 606 stores 2,000 fonts on a single disc and can set newspaper text (11-pica lines in 8-point type) at the rate of 1,850 lines per minute, for example. Output can be complete pages of text and headline copy in position. CRT typesetting is normally used for large-volume production such as newspapers, magazines, books, timetables and statistical material.

Optical Character Recognition (OCR)

This technology has the ability to take typewritten manuscript copy and scan it to produce input to a computer-driven typesetter thus avoiding redundant typesetting. Special typewriter fonts are usually required in order for the OCR unit to "read" the copy. Latest developments include the ability to read input from almost any form of copy, including substandard print, hard- and soft-cover books, magazines, newspapers, telephone directories and photocopies as well as typewritten pages.

Visual Display Terminals (VDT)

These units employ CRTs and allow the operator to view the contents of the input tape and then make corrections, changes, additions or deletions as required. A new, corrected input tape is generated. Originally manufactured as an editing device. VDTs have now become part of the typesetting function, permitting the operator to read and edit typeset copy before perforating tape for the phototypesetter. VDTs

OCR units, such as the ECRM Autoreader, scan original typewritten copy and produce tape input for phototypesetters. An on-line keyboard and display terminal, used for editing and function commands, is also displayed in this illustration.

have become commonplace in newsrooms, allowing reporters or feature writers to keyboard their articles into a VDT where they can see their article as it will appear in print. At the touch of a button, the copy is sent to a mass storage device, usually a magnetic disc, for subsequent retrieval for editing. The copy may then be sent directly to an on-line phototypesetter, thus eliminating rekeyboarding.

Photolettering

Photolettering or photo display type is produced on relatively small machines specifically oriented to that purpose, utilizing master film strips. By means of special lenses, characters may be expanded, condensed, italicised and backslanted. Lines may be waved or even set in a complete circle. Output may be a film negative or paper positive.

Photo courtesy of Visual Graphics Corporation

Other advantages offered by these units is the ability to enlarge or reduce any type in perfect proportion without losing fine lines or serifs. Faces may be enlarged 200% (2X up) or reduced 25% (4X down). Spacing between letters may be determined mechanically or visually, permitting the operator to space loose or tight to obtain the best typographic results.

TYPOGRAPHY

From a production man's standpoint, much more important than the manner in which type is set is a knowledge of which type faces to specify for a given sales promotion piece. And in the specification of type faces, an understanding of the distinction between text type and display type is fundamental. Text types are those used for the body of the message—the large blocks of copy that make up the bulk of the reading matter. Display types are used for headlines, subheads, and captions, and frequently for charts and boxes; they give the emphasis and the eye appeal to the typography. Text types are almost always machine-set. Display types are usually set on photo-lettering or photo-display devices which are capable of setting in sizes up to 144 point.

Factors Influencing Type Selection

Whether a given type is a text face or a display face is determined by its relative weight or boldness, its conformity to conventional letter forms, and its proportions—i.e., its width in relation to its height. Types which are unusually condensed or unusually expanded, which are relatively bold or relatively light, are seldom good text faces. On the other hand, the very neutrality of the good text faces makes them unsuitable for sales promotion display.

Classification of Type Faces

In its most simplified form, type face classification consists of only two divisions: *Old Style* and *Modern*. The Old Style letter forms are curved and rounded with pointed serifs that make a pleasing contrast between the bold and light strokes. Bookman, Century, Garamond and Caslon are examples.

The term "Modern" does not refer to a time period, but to a style of type designed almost 200 years ago. These faces are distinguished by great contrast between the thick and thin strokes. Times Roman and Caledonia are examples.

Faces having square serifs are contemporary type styles used mainly for display or small amounts of reading matter. The letters are characterized by relatively uniform strokes with little contrast. Cairo and Clarendon are examples.

Sans serif letters have no serifs and are generally uniform in appearance with little contrast between strokes. Helvetica, Universe, News Gothic and Avant Garde are examples.

Script letters are designed to simulate handwriting and are used for announcements and formal invitations. Examples are Bank Script and Trafton Script.

Text letters are designed to resemble the hand-drawn letters of early scribes and are normally used for wedding invitations, certificates and diplomas. Old English and American Text are examples.

Decorative types are contemporary faces that are designed to capture the eye and are unusual in appearance. Styles are only limited by the imagination of the designer and run the gamut from "Abramesque" to "Zebra."

With the advent of phototypesetting and photo display, where production of type designs and fonts have become a relatively simple procedure, some 2,000 display faces, as well as hundreds of text faces, are available today.

Factors Influencing Type Selection

Practically every piece of printed matter involves a combination of text and display types. The problem is to select types that will complement each oeher.

The bolder, blacker and more geometrical faces are generally considered most suitable for sales promotion literature directed to men and for featuring products like machinery, and business and industrial products. The lighter, more graceful and decorative faces are generally regarded as appropriate for women's fashions, household supplies, toiletries, cosmetics and other things that women buy. The dangers of combining a so-called masculine text face with a so-called feminine display face are obvious. A Script headline, for example, isn't used with Helvetica Bold.

Many type faces, moreover, are most effective when used sparingly. A few words of a script or cursive type or of a novelty type usually prove sufficient, so the specifications also depend on how much display material there is to set. If there is a great deal of it, the more or less conventional display faces like Futura or Stymie are decided upon. But if the amount is small and that little is expected to stand out decoratively and emphatically, something like Legend or Huxley or Cartoon or Onyx may be preferred.

The masculine-style types call for hard, smooth papers; soft colors; and plain, geometric lay-outs. The feminine-style types require softer antique finishes, daintier pastel colors, and a more informal and elegant style of lay-out.

Copy Preparation for Typesetting

Good copy preparation ensures good typesetting of manuscript copy. Careful checking and editing of copy before it is set is a must. Remember, it is incumbent upon the operator to set type exactly as it is furnished, even though he may suspect errors. Therefore, it is of utmost importance that spelling, punctuation and capitalization are checked before submitting the copy to the typesetter.

It is of equal importance to edit your copy carefully before it is set in type. Changes, alterations and deletions can prove to be very expensive.

The following guidelines will help ensure faster service, lower cost, greater accuracy and improved quality:

1. Typewrite your copy, double spaced, on one side of uniform sheets of paper, preferably 8½"x11". Allow at least one-inch margins all around.

2. If clippings, etc., are a part of your copy, paste them on the same size sheets. Do not pin them in place.

3. Check carefully for uniform style of punctuation, spelling, capitalization, figures such as dates, amounts of money, statistics, etc.

4. Number all pages consecutively. Mark "end' on the last sheet.

5. If many handwritten changes are required, retype the entire sheet.

6. When the first proof is received, mark all subsequent changes, thereon, *not* on the original copy. You should read all proofs. According to trade customs, a typesetter cannot assume any financial responsibility for typographical errors other than resetting them without charge. Changes or alterations that you make are, of course, chargeable.

7. When proofreading, read the letters separately rather than visualizing the entire word.

8. All marks should be made in the margin and on the typeset. Indicating them on the typeset only may result in their being overlooked. Always make sure that your mark is directly opposite the line in which the error occurs.

9. Whenever extensive additions are to be made to text in proof form, type them on 8½"x11" sheets indicating on both the new copy sheets and the proof where the added copy goes.

10. If no changes are made on the proof, merely write "OK," initial it and return to the typesetter. When changes are required, mark them, write "OK as corrected" or "Send new proof" as the case may be, initial it and return to the typesetter.

11. When checking revised proofs, the entire line containing the correction should be read.

Proofreaders' Marks

MARK	EXPLANATION and/or EXAMPLE	MARK	EXPLANATION and/or EXAMPLE
⊙	Insert period ∧	lf.	Set in (lightface) type
⌃ or ,/	Insert comma ∧	bf.	Set in (boldface) type
⊙ or :/	Insert colon ∧	bf. italic	Boldface _italic_
;/	Insert semicolon ∧	lf. caps	BOLDFACE (capitals) or
✌ or ℰ/	Apostrophe, boys	b	Superior letter[b] or figure ∧
❝❞ / ❝❞	Insert quotation marks ∧	2	Inferior letter or figure, HO
?/	Insert question mark ∧	⁋	Begin a paragraph
!/	Insert exclamation point ∧	no ⁋	No paragraph ⌐
=/	Insert hyphen =	run in	Run in or run on
1/en	En dash ∧	□ ⁋	Indent the number of em quads shown
1/em	One-em dash ∧	flush	No indention
3/em	Three-em dash ∧	hanging indent	Hanging indention. Mark all lines to desired indention.
(/)	Insert parentheses ∧1∧		
[/]	Insert brackets ∧ one ∧	O C or out copy	Insert matter omitted: refer to copy (Mark copy Out, see proof, galley 00)
′	Set pri∧mar′y accent		
″	Set sec′ on dar∧y accent	che /	Caret. Insert marginal addition
⁀ or lig	Use ligature (oͤe, aͤe, fi, etc.)	℈ or ℈	Dele. Take out (delete) ℰ
/	Virgule, slash; and or	℈	Delete and close up
○□○□○	Leaders (6 unit spacing)	e/	Correct latter or word marked
. . . . . .	Leaders (3 dot, tight space)	stet	Let it stand—(all matter above dots)
○□○□⊙	Ellipsis (6 unit spacing) . . .	] points	Move to right (How many points?)
⊗ or X	Replace broken or marred type	[points	Move to left (How many points?)
℃	Reverse (turn type or cut)	⌊___⌋	Lower (letters or, words)
(SP)	Spell out (twenty (gr)) grain	⌐⌐	Elevate (letters or words)
(Q? Ed)	Query to editor	⫽	Straighten line (horizontally)
_⌐	Mark-off or break; start new line	‖ or ⧚	Align type (vertically)
wf	Wrong font	tr	Transpose space
wfs	wrong font (size)	tr	Transpose enclosed in ring (matter)
lc	Lower Case or LOWER CASE	tr	Transpose (order (letters of) or words)
C	capital letter	tr	Rearrange words of order numbers in
caps	SET IN capitals	center	Put in center of line or page (ctr)
initial c & lc	Lower Case with Initial Capitals	⌐ ⌐	Center line for line
sm caps	SET IN small capitals	⌐ ‖ ⌐	Center chunk, square off on left
caps + s.c	SMALL CAPITALS WITH INITIAL CAPITALS	bring down	Run over to next line. (A two-letter di-vision should be avoided)
rom.	Set in (roman) type		
ital.	Set in _italic_ type	run back	Run back to preceding line. (Such a div-ision is improper)
ital caps	ITALIC Capitals or		

Proofreaders' Marks

MARK	EXPLANATION and/or EXAMPLE	MARK	EXPLANATION and/or EXAMPLE
reset 12 picas up up up	A syllable or short word standing alone on a line is called a "widow"; it should be eliminated	en quad	½-em quad (nut, en) space or indent
		☐	Em quad (mutton) space or indent
		☐☐	Indent number of em quads shown
◡	Close up entirely; take out space	ealed	Means "not leaded"
#	Close up partly; leave some space	ld in	Insert lead (specify base to base).
∨ or ◡	Less space between words	ℐ ld	Take out lead
∧ or ∨#	Equalize space between words	18 66 -	Base to base between any two lines.
l / s	LETTER-SPACE (Usually 1 unit extra)		Specify vertical spacing base to base
#̇	Insert space (or more space)	24 pts !	Specify horizontal spacing by points.
space out	Morespacebetweenwords		

Examples of Type Faces for Sales Promotion Literature

Futura Light (B) *6-84 point*—Not very legible for text. Fine for elite display in the larger sizes. Suitable for any subject. Still modern and a sparkling letter for advertising typography. (with oblique)

Futura Bold (B) *8-84 point*—Fine for display as companion to Futura Light, especially in larger sizes. Suitable for short captions, subheadings, etc. Never use for text. (with oblique)

Kaufmann Bold (A) *18-96 point*—A very suitable elite script letter for combination with the sans-serif family. Most practical for medium weight display purposes in the smaller sizes.

Franklin Gothic (A) *4-96 point*—A fine display letter of better than medium weight for combination with sans-serif faces or other Gothics. Needed for duplicating old jobs. (with italic)

Franklin Gothic Condensed (A) *6-72 point*—A ranking display letter, very well designed. Fine for newspaper ads, catalog use, and for general advertising display purposes. Companion to Franklin Gothic.

Examples of Type Faces for Sales Promotion Literature

Bodoni Bold *(A) 6-144 point*—Companion bold-face to the Bodoni Book. Fine for small captions. An excellent display face in any size above 12 point. Use for heads and subheads. (with italic)

Ultra Bodoni *(A) 6-120 point*—The heaviest Bodoni face. Fine for ultramodern captions. A versatile and readable display face in any size, but not too readable or printable. (with italic)

Onyx *(A) 30-96 point*—The finest condensed version of Ultra Bodoni. Entirely a display face but with a variety of uses. Use in caps and lower case wherever possible.

Bodoni Bold Shaded *(A) 10-48 point*—A fine decorative companion letter to the Bodoni series. Intended entirely for display purposes. Useful for initials. Most effective in all caps.

Corvinus Medium *(B) 8-60 point*—Another flat serif letter combining well as display with Bodoni as text matter. Never use for text matter itself. Slightly condensed. (with oblique)

Corvinus Skyline *(B) 10-84 point*—The super-condensed version of the Corvinus face. Particularly adapted to display in tall, vertical ads. Combines best with Bodoni Text.

Caslon Oldstyle No. 471 *(A) 6-72 point*—Our closest simulation of the original Caslon face. Without doubt the most versatile of the current type faces. Suitable for nearly any subject in text or display. (with italic)

Caslon Bold Condensed *(A) 6-120 point*—A suitable condensed face for modern display purposes in combination with any of the Caslon faces. Very readable, especially in its lower case.

Caslon Openface *(A) 8-48 point*—A companion, decorative Caslon letter. Suitable for decorative display in combination with any of the Caslon faces. Most effective in caps only.

Examples of Type Faces for Sales Promotion Literature

Stymie Black Italic (A) *12-72 point*—Companion italic to the Stymie Black. Another very powerful and important modern display letter. Swift moving and suitable for a diversity of subjects.

BETON OPEN★ (B) *20-84 point*—A fine decorative display letter suitable for combination with any of the square serif faces. Use only for a word or two in display, never for text purposes.

STENCIL ★ (A) *18-60 point*—A freak, novel, special-purpose display letter. Still quite modern and adaptable to a variety of display purposes. Never use more than a word or two.

Cheltenham Oldstyle (A) *6-72 point*—A much antedated but still possibly useful letter. Well designed and suited to a variety of purposes. Needed for the resetting of old jobs for reruns. (with italic)

Typewriter (M) *8-12 point*—A light-face typewriter type duplication. Identical to typing through a carbon and without a ribbon. Use it for reproduction purposes or where light-face is needed.

Barnum (A) *6-36 point*—A type face reminiscent of the gay '90's. Use it for effect only, in combination with sans-serif or square-serif text. A word or two is O.K. with sharp serif.

Bookman (M) *6-36 point*—A versatile and very legible and printable face for text purposes. Suited particularly to children's books in 14- and 18-point sizes. Suitable for display. (with italic)

Century Expanded No. 20A (A) *4-72 point*—One of the most legible and readable type faces extant. Use it for any subject. Particularly useful as regards printability on a poor grade of paper. (with italic)

Bodoni Book (A) *6-48 point*—One of the most legible and characterful of book and advertising text faces. Can be either masculine or feminine, mechanical or frilly. Printable and durable. (with italic)

Examples of Type Faces for Sales Promotion Literature

Typo Script (A) *12-60 point*—A beautiful light-face script of the old pattern for combination with any old-style type face. Fast moving. Elite and classical in effect. Very delicate.

Bank Script (A) *14-48 point*—Really a bold version of Typo Script with slightly more slant. The fastest moving of the script faces. Use for engraved effects. Combines with old-style characters.

Goudy Oldstyle (A) *6-72 point*—A classic face for classic purposes. Legible and readable. Useful for elite advertising purposes. Combines well as display with old-style faces. (with italic)

Traflou Script (B) *14-84 point*—Probably the most beautiful script face ever produced. Can be used in combination with any sharp serif, old-style face. Definitely elite in effect. Really a cursive.

Garamond (A) *6-72 point*—A classic text face suitable for a wide variety of purposes. Mainly feminine in character. Legible and readable. Larger sizes effective for light display. (with italic)

Garamond Bold (A) *6-120 point*—A versatile display face in all its larger sizes. Combines well with the Garamond Light, of course. Also useful for bold captions, headings, and subheadings. (with italic)

Deepdene (M) *6-60 point*—A classic Roman letter harmonizing well with all old-style characters. A neat letter for modern advertising text matter. Combines well with Garamond.

Deepdene Italic (M) *6-60 point*—A sparkling staccato letter, companion italic to Deepdene. Here is one of the finest italics in current use. Particularly adapted to modern advertising display.

Weiss Roman (B) *8-60 point*—Here is a modern letter with a far older feeling. Combines the good characteristics of many fine Romans. A fine character for book work.

Examples of Type Faces for Sales Promotion Literature

Weiss Italic (B) *8-36 point*—Companion italic to Weiss Roman. This italic approaches a cursive letter in its feeling. Use it mainly for decorative or caption. Not too readable.

Legend ★ (B) *18-72 point*—A fine occasional display letter with an Italian minuscule feeling. Harks to the Renaissance. Also slightly Oriental in feeling. Simulates manuscript writing.

Bernhard Cursive (B) *12-84 point*—A fine light-face cursive letter with a fancy feeling. Very delicate, but useful for most feminine subjects. A face for jewelry stores, announcements, cards, etc.

FORUM (M) *10-48 point*—Preserves the best in classic Roman capital design. Use this letter for bank announcements, classic programs, etc. Comes in caps only.

𝔈ngravers 𝔒ld 𝔈nglish ★ (A) *6-72 point*—Obviously one of the best of the Old English or Gothic letter designs. Mainly ecclesiastical in feeling. Has an engraved touch. Use for Christmas, etc.

American Text ★ (A) *18-72 point*—A staccato version of Old English. Here is a modern Gothic face that can be readily adapted to the best of advertising typography. Use it sparingly.

Baskerville (M) *8-36 point*—A classical text type which, in the larger sizes, is sometimes used for display when an impression of dignified elegance is sought. It is not used often but is indispensable when needed. (with italic)

Scotch Roman (M) *6-36 point*—One of the first of the so-called modern faces of the Bodoni tradition, Scotch Roman is an exceedingly readable body type which accounts for its wide use in magazines, house organs, and booklets. (with italic)

Lydian (A) *10-96 point*—A comparatively new face unlike any other in current popular usage. With the Bold and the Cursive, the Lydian family has accounted for one of the few outstanding typographic innovations of recent years.

HALFTONES AND LINE COPY

There are two basic kinds of original images: *line* and *continuous tone*. Line copy refers to type matter, pen and ink drawings and diagrams. Continuous tone refers to photographs, wash drawings and other images having a variety of tones.

To reproduce the wide range of tone values in photographs, most printing processes require that the image be converted into dot patterns, called halftones, accomplished by photographing the subject through a halftone "screen" containing a specified number of dots to the inch. A 133-line screen, for example, contains 133 dots horizontally and 133 dots vertically per inch. These dots are uniformly spaced but vary in size, according to the gradations of tones. The result is an optical illusion, making the printed halftone image appear as continuous degrees of shading.

Halftone screens range from 55-line to 300-line. The finer the screen, the sharper the detail in reproduction. Newspapers, which are printed letterpress, use 55- to 85-line screens, depending upon the type of equipment and paper used. Commercial printing and magazines use 100- to 150-line screens. Halftones to be gravure printed may run as high as 300-line.

Examples of Halftone Screens

65-LINE	85-LINE

110-LINE

120-LINE

133-LINE

150-LINE

Remember, lithographers can reproduce halftones and screens on both rough and smooth paper surfaces. Coated papers are, of course, the most desirable but halftones of excellent quality can be printed on antique surfaces ranging from offset paper smoothness to the roughest text papers. Letterpress printers, on the other hand, require smooth surfaces for good halftone reproduction, such as coated or English finish papers.

In general, the smoother or more even the printing surface, the finer the screen it will effectively reproduce,

Some screens, called "Special Effects" convert continuous tone into line copy employing varying patterns to create special moods. Patterns include concentric circles, wavy lines, straight lines, cross lines, mezzotints, brush, contour, pebble, steel engraving and posturized. It is important to remember that not every photograph lends itself to Special Effects treatment.

Duotones

A duotone is a halftone reproduction of a black and white photograph in two colors. The copy is photographed twice, at different screen angles. The black image is customarily a halftone processed slightly lighter than full scale, while the color image can be varied to achieve the best highlight and shadow control.

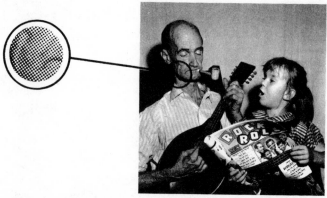

The magnification illustrated above shows the halftone screen pattern that creates the impression of an intermediate tone.

CONCENTRIC CIRCLE

MEZZOTINT

Gradation and Magnification of Tones

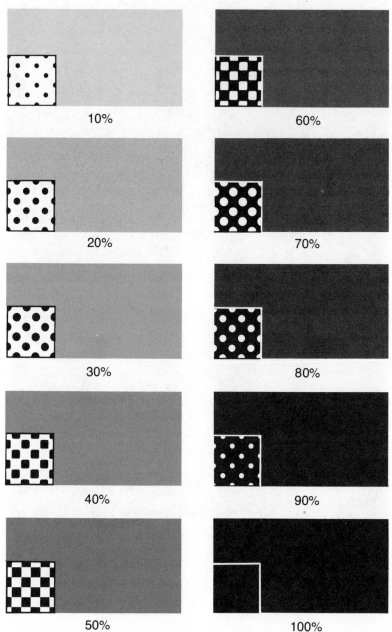

10%

20%

30%

40%

50%

60%

70%

80%

90%

100%

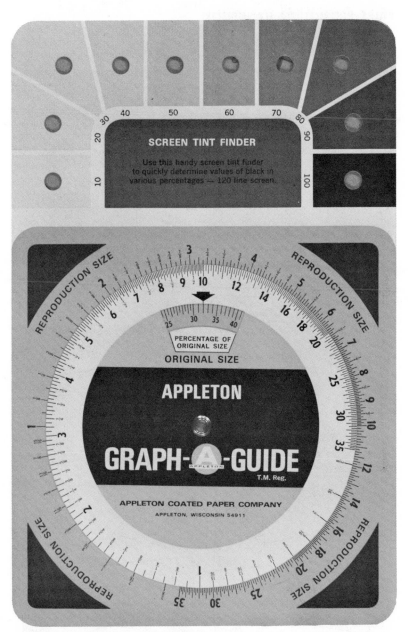

At the production stage, camera reductions for photos and other illustrations are reduced to required dimensions according to percentages. Appleton Papers, Inc., provides a highly useful and widely-acclaimed Graph-A-Guide as an aid to graphic arts personnel. An added value, at the top of the Guide, is a screen tint finder. The reverse side provides pica, agate and inch rules.

Ben Day Screens

The chief purpose of Ben Day screens is to relieve the monotony of line copy by providing backgrounds and shaded effects and to provide tint plates for the printing of colors in various patterns. Patterns include straight line, cross line, herringbone, pebble, etc. Unlike a halftone screen, in which gradations of tone are produced by dots of varying size, the dots or lines in Ben Day screens are of uniform thickness and produce uniformly flat tints.

Usually the shade patterns are limited to certain areas of the copy, and in order to protect the areas where no pattern is to show, they are painted out and only the areas to be shaded are left bare to come into contact with the film.

TWO WAYS OF DEPICTING THE SAME SUBJECT

Line cut of pen-and-ink drawing for sales bulletin, without Ben Day.

Line cut of same drawing with Ben Day added to give shaded effect.

Ben Day
Screens

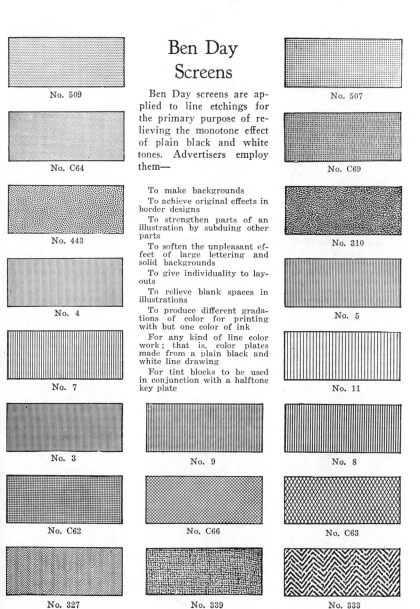

Ben Day screens are applied to line etchings for the primary purpose of relieving the monotone effect of plain black and white tones. Advertisers employ them—

To make backgrounds

To achieve original effects in border designs

To strengthen parts of an illustration by subduing other parts

To soften the unpleasant effect of large lettering and solid backgrounds

To give individuality to layouts

To relieve blank spaces in illustrations

To produce different gradations of color for printing with but one color of ink

For any kind of line color work; that is, color plates made from a plain black and white line drawing

For tint blocks to be used in conjunction with a halftone key plate

Hints on Ordering Halftones

1. *Mark Instructions Clearly.* Somewhere on each piece of copy you must include the following information: The exact size, the kind (square halftone, outline halftone, circular halftone, etc.), and the proper halftone screen.

2. *Scale Up Copy Accurately.* Usually you'll indicate the size in width, expressed either in inches or in picas, and frequently you'll find it necessary to figure the depth as well so that the photograph will fit properly into the layout. There are several ways of determining what the depth will be in proportion to the width: (a) Geometrically, by drawing a diagonal across the back of the original copy and then projecting the amount of the reduction or enlargement, as the case may be; (b) arithmetically, by using the simple formula—Copy Width : Copy Depth : Specified Width : X—with "X" representing, of course, the proportionate depth; (c) by means of a slide rule or other special mechanical device.

3. *How to Use Crop Marks.* Most photographs you use contain unnecessary backgrounds, foregrounds, and other irrelevant material which you'll want to eliminate. To do so, you'll indicate only the areas to be included. When possible, place your crop marks with a grease pencil on the white border around the photo.

4. *Avoid Marking on Face of Photo.* If the photograph has no white border, don't mark on the print itself. Either put your marks on the back—holding the photograph against the window or up to a strong light for the purpose —or mount it on a piece of board and put your crop marks on that. If you mark on the back, be careful not to use a hard pencil or to bear down too heavily, or the impression will show through and mar the photograph.

5. *Protect the Original Copy.* Every once in a while you'll get a photograph that has to be returned in perfect condition, so you'll want to take every safeguard to protect it. Since no crop marks must show, you may cut out a paper mask to indicate the area to be reproduced. In such cases, be sure that your corners are exactly square and the mask is accurately held in place over exactly the proper area of the photograph. Another device is to place a tissue flap over the entire photograph and indicate your dimensions on that.

When there are a number of illustrations to be made for a piece of sales promotion literature, it is usually a good idea to call in a reliable engraver or lithographer and secure his help in deciding how the engravings should be made, and the best process to use. A photo-engraver is often able to save an advertiser considerable money by avoiding the many extras which are involved in reproducing some illustrations; as, for example, making a large halftone in sections rather than in one piece, pasting up small illustrations so that they may be made in one reduction, etc.

The reproduction of photographs is largely a matter of determining the proper size, screen, and finish of halftones. There is no such simple, automatic rule to follow, however, when it comes to the reproduction of all the other various styles of illustrative and decorative material which come within the realm of printing production. Some of them require halftones, some line etchings, and some combinations of the two. The kinds of plates to order when confronted with different art techniques, for purposes of ready reference can be charted about as follows:

Art Technique	*Kind of Photoengraving*
Pen-and-Ink Drawing	Line
Pencil Drawing	Highlight Halftone
Scratch-Board Drawing	Line
Woodcut	Line
Dry-Brush Drawing	Line
Oil Painting	Halftone (usually vignette finish)
Wash Drawing	Halftone (usually outline)
Charcoal Drawing	Highlight Halftone
Hand-Lettering	Line
Combination Crayon and Pen-and-Ink Drawing	Line
Type and Photograph	Combination Halftone and Line

The use of three- and four-color reproductions of oil and water-color paintings in sales promotional work has been sharply reduced as a result of the increased cost of both making plates and printing them. "Process" plates are principally used in magazine advertising. Some of the larger magazines have installed special high-speed presses for four-color printing. Since a number of advertisements in the same form can be printed at the same time, the cost is not prohibitive. Savings are also made by furnishing each publisher with a duplicate set of plates or negatives.

Further savings can be made by rotating printing plates among several publications comprising the media to be used in a promotional undertaking. Thus, a set of printing plates for Advertisement A will be sent to the first publication on the list for insertion in the January issue, and to the second publication on the list for insertion in its February issue, etc.

LETTERPRESS PLATES

Photoengraving

The oldest of all photomechanical processes, photoengraving pertains to the production of relief printing plates for letterpress. Line drawings and photographs require the use of photoengraved plates for reproduction.

Original (Direct) Plates

Plates are made by placing the original copy on a sheet of precoated zinc, magnesium or copper Exposure to light hardens the image areas. The unexposed areas are then etched away chemically, leaving a relief printing surface. Line copy and halftones up to 110-line may be etched on zinc or magnesium. Copper is required for halftones over 110-line. If the plates are used for printing, they are called *direct* plates. They are referred to as *original* if duplicates are made from them.

Duplicate Plates

Original plates and forms are sometimes used to make duplicates for the actual printing. This is desirable for a number of reasons. They are necessary when printing plates need to be curved for mounting on the cylinders of rotary presses. They are used to furnish publishers with complete advertisements. They are used as a precaution against type being smashed and they save resetting should the type become worn down on long runs.

Stereotypes

These are used almost exclusively for letterpress newspaper printing. A matrix is made from the original plate by using a special papier-mache and the plate is made by pouring molten metal into the curved mold.

Electrotypes

Electrotypes are used for high quality letterpress, book, magazine and commercial printing. A mold of the original plate or form is made in plastic, soft metal or wax. The mold is then treated with a film of silver to make it conductive, after which a thin shell of copper or nickel is plated through an electrolytic process. The shell is backed up with molten metal and finished for use on a flatbed press or curved for use on a rotary press. Plastic molds are often made as insurance should the original become damaged or worn. Duplicate electros can then be made from the plastic mold.

Photopolymer Plates

Photopolymer plates are made from precoated plastics from which the unexposed areas are chemically dissolved. They may be used as original (direct) and wraparound plates. Duplicates are easily made, eliminating the need for electrotypes. DuPont *Dycril* and BASF *Nyloprint* are examples. Photopolymer plates are backed with metal and mounted on magnetic cylinders and are the most popular plates used in letterpress for magazine and commercial printing. *Letterflex* and *Dynaflex,* manufactured by Grace Chemical, are used extensively in newspaper printing. The Letterflex plate is also used on the Cameron Belt Press which prints complete books in one pass through the press.

Plastic Plates

Plastic plates are made by molding and baking thermoplastic materials under pressure. They are lightweight, economical and resist wear.

Rubber Plates

Rubber plates are molded from either natural or synthetic rubber or combinations of both. They are used exclusively in flexography for printing on rough surfaces such as cartons, bags, tags, corrugated boxes as well as on films for flexible packaging. Paperback books are also printed from rubber plates, but the process used is letterpress instead of flexography.

LITHOGRAPHIC PLATES

Offset lithography is based on the principle that grease and water do not mix. Since both the image and nonimage areas are on the same plane, separation is maintained chemically. The image areas must be ink-receptive, the non-image areas must be water-receptive. Offset plates are made from thin sheets of metal, plastic or paper that are wrapped around the plate cylinder of the press. The ink, which adheres only to the image areas, is transferred to the blanket cylinder which, in turn, transfers the image onto the paper.

There are three types of lithographic plates: surface, deep-etch and bi-metal.

Surface Plates

Surface plates, usually having an aluminum base, are made from film negatives and have a light-sensitive coating which becomes the ink-receptive image area of the plate. There are two classifications of surface plates: *additive* and *subtractive*. On the additive plate, the ink-receptive material is added to the plate during processing. On the subtractive plate, which has been precoated with an ink-receptive lacquer, nonprinting areas are removed during processing. Subtractive plates are used for long press runs.

Deep-Etch Plates

Deep-etch plates, like surface plates, usually have an aluminum base, are made from film positives and are intaglio in nature. After the coating in the image area is removed, these areas are chemically coppered and/or lacquered and inked so that they become ink-receptive. Some deep-etch plates are made presensitized and precoated and some are made on anodized aluminum. Deep-etch plates are used for long-run color reproduction.

Bi-Metal Plates

Bi-metal plates are the most hardy and most expensive of all lithographic plates but are capable of runs into the millions of press impressions. Materials and processing are similar to the deep-etch process in that the coating is removed from the image areas which consist of copper or brass. There are two types of bi-metal plates: copper plated on aluminum or stainless steel and chromium plated on copper or brass. Sometimes the copper is plated on a third metal which then becomes the base and is referred to as a tri-metal plate.

SELECTION OF PAPERS FOR SALES PROMOTION

Sales promotion production men, while relying on their printers and paper merchants for assistance in selecting the best paper for the job, almost always have a good working knowledge of paper themselves. It is their responsibility to produce the best possible piece of printing for the money and, within the limits of suitability, availability and cost, paper is of prime importance in achieving the best printing results. In general, paper represents 30%-50% of the cost of a printed job. Besides the cost, the paper's characteristics can have a large bearing on the appearance of the printed piece and on the printer's ability to print it.

Characteristics of Paper

Factors to be considered in selecting papers are weight, bulk and caliper, grain direction, color, opacity, surface texture, coatings, and strength as well as printability.

Basis Weight

Papers are manufactured and identified by their basis weight, the weight in pounds of a ream (500 sheets) of paper in the basic size for that grade. For example, the basic size and weight of book papers is 25″x38″ and weighs 70 pounds per ream, expressed as 25x38-70. Not all paper grades have the same basic size. Bond (writing) papers are 17x22, cover papers are 20x26, index is 25½x30½, etc.

While paper is referred to in terms of its ream weight, such as 20-pound bond, 70-pound book, paper houses usually list their prices on a per thousand sheet basis for any given size and weight, so that 25x38-70 book paper would be listed as 25x38-140M.

Paper Grades

Papers are generally classified and defined in terms of their end use, as suggested by grade names. Each grade serves a purpose. Some of the standard grades used in commercial printing are: bond, book, offset, text, coated, cover, bristol, index, tag and newsprint. In the following descriptions, the basic size for that particular grade is shown in parentheses.

Bond (17 x 22)

Papers commonly used for leeterheads and business forms. The surfaces readily accept typewriter and writing inks which can easily be erased. Since most letterheads are 8½″x11″ in size, four of these can be cut out of a standard 17″x22″ sheet without waste. There are two types of bonds: sulphite and cotton fiber (rag content).

Sulphite bond papers are made of bleached chemical pulps, hard sized, and usually have a fairly smooth finish. Some bonds are available in linen, ripple, and other finishes, and often in 10 to 12 colors.

Rag bonds contain from 25% to 100% rag fibers and are hard sized. All grades are usually watermarked. The outstanding characteristics are appearance, "crackle," permanence and strength. They are used in fine stationery and for better grades of commercial letterheads and envelopes.

Book (25 x 38)

Book papers, as the name implies, are primarily used for trade and textbooks. They have a wide range of weights and come in several finishes, such as M. F. (Machine Finish), E. F. (English Finish), antique, smooth, vellum and S. and S.C. (Sized and Super Calendered).

Machine Finish is the lowest grade of book paper, having a medium finish and is used for printing low-quality books, catalogs and circulars. *English Finish* has a smoother, more even finish than M.F. and is loaded with mineral fillers. The cheaper grades are widely used for package inserts, publications and catalogs. *S&SC* has a higher, glossier finish, has less bulk and is more transparent than E.F. Usually used in catalogs and pamphlets that have halftone illustrations.

Offset (25 x 38)

These are similar to coated and uncoated book papers but are sized to resist the slight moisture in offset printing and the surface is also treated to prevent picking. Generally available in three grades and, besides white, can be obtained in several pastel colors and a variety of finishes such as linen, crash, handmade, etc. Most offset papers can be printed letterpress but few letterpress papers can be printed offset.

Text (25 x 38)

These papers are characterized by a wide range of surface textures and colors and are commonly used for announcements, brochures, mailing pieces, etc. Many are available with matching cover weights and envelopes.

Coated (25 x 38)

Coated or Enamel paper comes in a number of grades of "folding" and "printing" qualities. Some are available in pastel colors. Coated book can be had in gloss or dull finish. To provide a smooth, glossy finish, the base paper is coated with clay and other materials for quality printing. The smoother and more even the surface, the finer the screen halftone that can be reproduced upon it. Coated-one-side (C1S) is used for labels, box-wraps, window displays, etc.

Cover (20 x 26)

Many grades of book, text and coated papers are made in heavier weights with matching colors for use as covers on booklets and magazines. Many are made with a variety of coatings, textures and finishes.

Bristol (22½ x 28½)

Printing Bristols are generally stiffer than Index and are made in antique, vellum, smooth and plate finishes. They print equally as well on either offset or letterpress.

Index (25½ x 30½)

Available in both smooth and antique finishes, index paper is used whenever a stiff, inexpensive paper is required. It is readily receptive to writing ink.

Tag (24 x 36)

Tag is a heavy sheet made from sulphite, pulp and various kinds of waste papers. Sometimes tinted or colored on one or both sides, tag has good folding qualities, tensile strength, good tearing and water resistance and a surface that accepts printing, stamping or writing.

Newsprint (24 x 36)

Used for printing newspapers, this stock is chiefly made from groundwood pulp with some chemical pulp. Ranging in basic weight from 28 to 35 pound, 30 pound is most commonly used for newspaper production.

Printing Promotion Pieces in Gangs

Standardizing the size of enclosures, folders, booklets, letterheads, and other printed matter has another decided advantage. It permits printing several small pieces in the same form, thus saving costly presswork. Gang printing also makes possible a paper saving as well. It is especially good for forms 5½ by 8½ inches or 8½ by 11 inches in size.

Pocket Pal

A gold mine of information covering every aspect of the graphic arts, is contained in a book published by International Paper Company, entitled "Pocket Pal," probably because of its paperback size. Now in its eleventh edition, its 192 pages, amply illustrated, cover the printing processes, art and copy preparation, photography, plate-making, binding, paper, inks and other production topics of interest to advertising, sales promotion and production managers. "Pocket Pal" is available from International Paper Company, 220 East 42nd Street, New York, N. Y. 10017 at a price of two dollars.

Stock-Estimating Table

Explanation: Determine the number of pieces that cut out of the size of stock selected, then find that number in the left-hand column. To know the number of sheets required for a given run, locate the run figure at top of column, and the number in that column opposite the number of pieces that will cut out of one sheet will give you the number of sheets required. No waste is figured.

Number out of Sheet	500	1000	1500	2000	2500	3000	3500	4000	4500	5000
1	500	1000	1500	2000	2500	3000	3500	4000	4500	5000
2	250	500	750	1000	1250	1500	1750	2000	2250	2500
3	167	334	500	667	834	1000	1167	1334	1500	1667
4	125	250	375	500	625	750	875	1000	1125	1250
5	100	200	300	400	500	600	700	800	900	1000
6	84	167	250	334	417	500	584	667	750	834
7	72	143	215	286	358	429	500	572	643	715
8	63	125	188	250	313	375	438	500	563	625
9	56	112	167	223	278	334	389	445	500	556
10	50	100	150	200	250	300	350	400	450	500
11	46	91	137	182	228	273	319	364	410	455
12	42	84	126	168	209	250	292	334	375	417
13	39	77	116	154	193	231	270	308	347	385
14	36	72	108	144	179	215	250	286	322	358
15	34	67	100	134	167	200	234	267	300	334
16	32	63	94	125	157	188	219	250	282	313
17	30	59	89	118	148	177	206	236	265	295
18	28	56	84	112	139	167	195	223	250	279
19	27	53	79	106	132	158	185	211	237	264
20	25	50	75	100	125	150	175	200	225	250
21	24	48	72	96	120	143	167	191	215	239
22	23	46	69	91	114	137	160	182	205	228
23	22	44	66	87	109	131	153	174	196	218
24	21	42	63	84	105	125	146	167	188	209
25	20	40	60	80	100	120	140	160	180	200
26	20	39	58	77	97	116	135	154	174	193
27	19	38	56	75	93	112	130	149	167	186
28	18	36	54	72	90	108	125	143	161	179
29	18	36	54	72	87	103	121	138	156	173
30	17	34	51	67	84	100	117	134	150	167
31	17	33	49	65	81	97	113	130	146	162
32	16	32	47	63	79	94	110	125	141	157
33	16	31	46	61	76	91	107	122	137	152
34	15	30	45	59	74	89	103	118	133	148
35	15	29	43	58	72	86	100	115	129	143
36	14	28	42	56	70	84	98	112	125	139
37	14	28	41	55	68	82	95	109	122	136
38	14	27	40	53	66	79	93	106	119	132
39	13	26	39	52	65	77	90	103	116	131
40	13	25	38	50	63	75	88	100	113	125

Standard Page Sizes

This chart shows the number of standard page size booklets, pamphlets, etc. that can be cut from stock size papers.

SIZE OF PAGE	NO. OF PAGES	SIZE OF PAPER	NO. OUT OF SHEET	SIZE OF PAGE	NO. OF PAGES	SIZE OF PAPER	NO. OUT OF SHEET
3 x 6	4	25 x 38	24	5 x 7	16	32 x 44	4
	8	25 x 38	12		24	28 x 42	2
	12	25 x 38	8		32	32 x 44	2
	16	25 x 38	6	5 x 8	4	35 x 45	16
	24	25 x 38	4		8	35 x 45	8
3½ x 6¼	4	28 x 44	24		12	28 x 42	4
	8	28 x 44	12		16	35 x 45	4
	12	28 x 44	8		24	28 x 42	2
	16	28 x 44	6		32	35 x 45	2
3¾ x 6⅞	4	32 x 44	24	5½ x 7½	4	35 x 45	16
	8	32 x 44	12		8	35 x 45	8
	12	32 x 44	8		12	38 x 50	6
	16	32 x 44	6		16	35 x 45	4
	24	32 x 44	4		32	35 x 45	2
4 x 5½	4	25 x 38	16	5½ x 8½	4	35 x 45	16
	8	25 x 38	8		8	35 x 45	8
	12	38 x 50	12		16	35 x 45	4
	16	25 x 38	4		32	35 x 45	2
	24	38 x 50	6	6 x 9	4	25 x 38	8
	32	25 x 38	2		8	25 x 38	4
4 x 6	4	25 x 38	18		16	25 x 38	2
	8	38 x 50	18		32	38 x 50	2
	12	38 x 50	12	7 x 10	4	32 x 44	8
	16	25 x 38	4		8	32 x 44	4
	24	38 x 50	6		16	32 x 44	2
	32	25 x 38	2	7½ x 10	4	32 x 44	8
4 x 9	4	25 x 38	12		8	32 x 44	4
	8	38 x 50	12		16	32 x 44	2
	12	25 x 38	4	8 x 10	4	35 x 45	8
	16	38 x 50	6		8	35 x 45	4
	24	25 x 38	2		16	35 x 45	2
	32	35 x 45	2	8½ x 11	4	35 x 45	8
4¾ x 6¼	4	28 x 42	16		8	35 x 45	4
	8	28 x 42	8		12	35 x 45	2
	12	32 x 44	6		16	35 x 45	2
	16	28 x 42	4	9 x 12	4	25 x 38	4
	32	28 x 42	2		8	25 x 38	2
5 x 7	4	32 x 44	18		16	38 x 50	2
	8	32 x 44	8				
	12	32 x 44	6				

Equivalent Weights

For easy comparison of paper weights, this chart shows the equivalent weights of various types of paper in reams of 500 sheets. The basic weights are shown in bold figures.

	Book 25 x 38	Bond and Ledger 17 x 22	Cover 20 x 26	Printing Bristol 22½ x 28½	Index 25½ x 30½	Tag 24 x 36
BOOK	**30**	12	16	20	25	27
	40	16	22	27	33	36
	45	18	25	30	37	41
	50	20	27	34	41	45
	60	24	33	40	49	55
	70	28	38	47	57	64
	80	31	44	54	65	73
	90	35	49	60	74	82
	100	39	55	67	82	91
	120	47	66	80	98	109
BOND and LEDGER	33	**13**	18	22	27	30
	41	**16**	22	27	33	37
	51	**20**	28	34	42	46
	61	**24**	33	41	50	56
	71	**28**	39	48	58	64
	81	**32**	45	55	67	74
	91	**36**	50	62	75	83
	102	**40**	56	69	83	93
COVER	91	36	**50**	62	75	82
	110	43	**60**	74	90	100
	119	47	**65**	80	97	108
	146	58	**80**	99	120	134
	164	65	**90**	111	135	149
	183	72	**100**	124	150	166
	201	79	**110**	136	165	183
	219	86	**120**	148	179	199
PRINTING BRISTOL	100	39	54	**67**	81	91
	120	47	65	**80**	98	109
	148	58	81	**100**	121	135
	176	70	97	**120**	146	162
	207	82	114	**140**	170	189
	237	93	130	**160**	194	216
INDEX	110	43	60	74	**90**	100
	135	53	74	91	**110**	122
	170	67	93	115	**140**	156
	208	82	114	140	**170**	189
TAG	110	43	60	74	90	**100**
	137	54	75	93	113	**125**
	165	65	90	111	135	**150**
	192	76	105	130	158	**175**
	220	87	120	148	180	**200**
	275	109	151	186	225	**250**

Comparative Weights Of Paper Sheets

Figured to nearest half-pound of standard sizes.

BOND, LEDGER, MIMEOGRAPH, DUPLICATOR

Sizes   **Weights Per 500 Sheets**

17 x22	13	16	20	24	28	32	36
8½x11	3¼	4	5	6	7	8	9
16 x21	11½	14½	18	21½	25	28½	32½
17 x28	16½	20½	15½	30½	35½	40½	46
17½x22½	13½	16½	21	25½	29½	33½	38
19 x24	16	19½	24½	29½	34	39	44
19 x28	18½	23	28½	34	40	45½	51
19 x48	32	39	49	59	68	78	88
22 x34	26	32	40	48	56	64	72
22½x28½	22½	27½	39½	41	48	55	61½
22½x35	28	34	42	50½	59	67½	76
24 x38	32	39	49	59	68	78	88
28 x34	33	41	51	61	71	81	91
28 x38	37	46	57	68	80	91	102
34 x44	52	64	80	96	112	128	144
35 x45	56	68	84	101	118	135	152

COATED BOOK

Sizes   **Weights Per 500 Sheets**

25 x38	50	60	70	80	100	120
17½x22½	—	—	29	33	41½	99
19 x25	25	30	35	40	50	49½
23 x29	—	42	49	56	70	84½
22½x35	41½	49½	58	66½	83	99½
23 x35	—	51	59	68	—	—
24 x36	45	55	64	73	91	109
26 x40	55	66	77	88	109	131
28 x42	62	74	87	99	124	149
28 x44	65	78	91	104	130	156
32 x44	74	89	104	119	148	178
34 x45	83	99	116	133	166	199
36 x48	90	110	128	146	182	218
38 x50	100	120	140	160	200	240
41 x54	117	154	163	186	233	280

Comparative Weights Of Paper Sheets

Figured to nearest half-pound of standard sizes.

UNCOATED BOOK

Sizes							Weights Per 500 Sheets
25 x38	30	35	40	45	50	60	70
22½x35	25	29	33	37½	41½	49½	58
24 x36	27	32	36	41	45	55	64
28 x42	37	43	50	56	62	74	87
28 x44	39	45	52	58	65	78	91
30½x41	39	46	53	59	66	79	92
32 x44	44	52	59	67	74	89	104
33 x44	46	53	61	69	76	92	107
35 x45	50	58	66	75	83	99	116
36 x48	55	64	73	82	91	109	127
38 x50	60	70	80	90	100	120	140

UNCOATED OFFSET

Sizes							Weights Per 500 Sheets
25 x38	50	60	70	80	100	120	150
17½x22½	20½	25	29	33	41½	50	62
19 x25	25	30	35	40	50	60	75
22½x29	34	41	48	55	68½	82	89
23 x29	36½	44	51½	59	73	88	110
22½x35	41½	50	58	66	83	100	124
23 x35	44	53	62	71	88	106	133
28 x42	62	74	87	99	124	149	186
28 x44	65	78	91	104	130	156	195
32 x44	74	89	104	119	148	178	222
35 x45	83	99	116	133	166	199	249
36 x48	90	110	128	146	182	218	272
38 x50	100	120	140	160	200	240	300
38 x52	104	125	146	166	208	250	312
41 x54	117	140	163	186	233	280	350
42 x58	128	154	179	205	256	308	385
44 x64	148	178	208	238	296	356	440

Comparative Weights Of Paper Sheets

Figured to nearest half-pound of standard sizes.

COATED COVER

Sizes				Weights Per 500 Sheets	
20 x26	**50**	**60**	**65**	**80**	**100**
23 x29	64	75	83½	102½	128½
23 x35	77½	93	100½	124	155
26 x40	100	120	130	160	200
35 x46	155	186	201	248	310

UNCOATED COVER

Sizes					Weights Per 500 Sheets		
20 x26	**40**	**50**	**65**	**80**	**90**	**100**	**130**
23 x29	51	64	83½	102½	—	128½	—
23 x35	62	77½	100½	124	139½	155	201
26 x40	80	100	130	160	180	200	260
35 x46	124	155	201	248	279	310	402

PRINTING BRISTOL

Sizes					Weights Per 500 Sheets		
22½x28½	**67**	**90**	**100**	**120**	**140**	**160**	**180**
22½x35	82	—	125	150	175	200	—
23 x35	84	—	125½	151	—	—	—
26 x40	—	—	165	198	—	—	—

INDEX BRISTOL

Sizes		Weights Per 500 Sheets		
25½x30½	**90**	**110**	**140**	**170**
17½x22½	45½	55½	—	—
20½x24¾	58½	72	91	111
22½x28½	74	91	115	140
22½x35	91	111	142	—

BINDING AND FINISHING OPERATIONS

While the binding of a book, booklet, catalog, house organ, or brochure is the last production operation to be performed, the method of its binding is one of the first things to be decided upon because it affects the paper size selected and the way the forms are laid out for printing. For the pieces mentioned, bindery operations include *folding* the flat sheets, *gathering* the various forms, signatures, or single sheets in proper sequence, *binding* them together by stitching, sewing, or one of the mechanical binding devices, *trimming*, and *covering*. These steps are not always followed in exactly that order, because in certain cases a book may have to be covered before it is trimmed or even trimmed before it is bound, but each step must be accounted for in the bindery. In the case of simpler pieces like folders and broadsides, bindery operations include only folding, trimming, and packing.

There are three principal styles of booklet or pamphlet binding: Saddle-wire stitching, side-wire stitching, and sewing. Saddle-wire stitching is most widely used because it is the fastest, the least expensive, and the most inconspicuous. The piece is gathered so that all pages open down the center or backbone; it is opened out and placed under the stitcher heads and staples are inserted. Another advantage of saddle-stitching is that as many as six booklets can be bound simultaneously on big stitching machines, then cut apart and trimmed afterward. Disadvantages are the fact that books smaller than $3\frac{1}{2}$ inches along the backbone can be stitched only with a single staple and that saddle-stitching is not practical for booklets more than $\frac{1}{2}$ inch thick; when staples hold more than $\frac{1}{4}$-inch thickness of paper they tend to pull through the covers and, in addition, are difficult to trim.

Side-wire stitching is used when the bulk is too great for saddle-stitching. Here the book is assembled in individual signatures, then stitched flat and the cover finally glued on to the square backbone. Side-wire stitched books obviously cannot open as flat as saddle-stitched books since the staples must be inserted at least $\frac{1}{8}$ inch from the binding edge.

The most common type of sewed book is thicker than either of the stitched types and has a glued cover. The various signatures are gathered and fed to a sewing machine which binds each signature to a cloth strip over which the cover is glued. The finished result is a neater-appearing book, a less conspicuous binding, and a flat-opening construction which makes it easier to handle and to read. It is also considerably more expensive.

NEW TECHNIQUES AND APPLICATIONS

Although marketing and sales considerations must always remain uppermost in promotional programs, new mechanical devices, equipment and processes are always of interest and value as a means of stimulating interest and obtaining attention.

Some of these include the reproduction on paper of scents by the 3M Company for food and cosmetic literature, pop-ups such as that used by Apeco for its copier models, the People-Finder Box for Motorola's Pageboy II and the seven-foot-long publicity streamer, in film-strip style and rolled into a paper-and-tin canister, issued by the Selby Shoe Company.

In the audio field are the cassettes for recording and reproduction for television-type or standard projection and the paper-thin, mailable records which are also used as inserts in business publications.

A Dial Soap "Singalong" recording was contained in a brochure produced by Armour-Dial Incorporated. The brochure was a prize-winner in the P-O-P Advertising Institute's Merchandising Awards Contest.

STANDARD U.S.E. ENVELOPE STYLES RECOMMENDED FOR MAIL ROOM EQUIPMENT

In Addition to the Sizes Listed, All Styles Are Available in Special Sizes to Meet Individual Requirements.

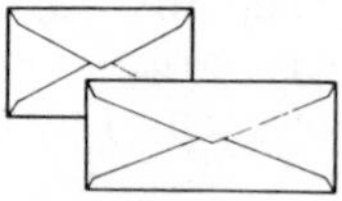

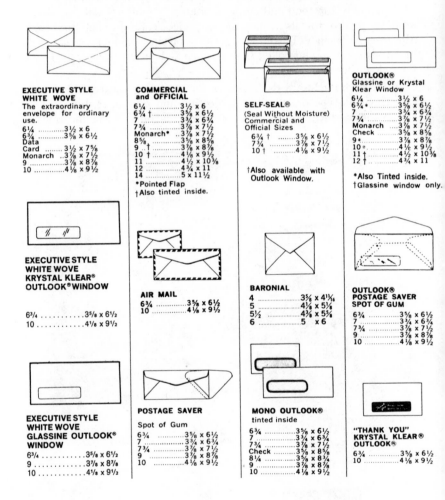

EXECUTIVE STYLE WHITE WOVE

The extraordinary envelope for ordinary use.

6¼ .... 3½ x 6
6¾ .... 3⅝ x 6½
Data Card .... 3½ x 7⅝
Monarch .... 3⅞ x 7½
9 .... 3⅞ x 8⅞
10 .... 4⅛ x 9½

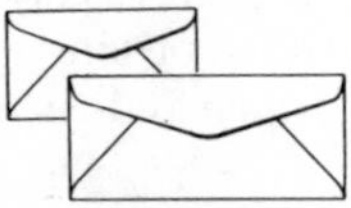

COMMERCIAL and OFFICIAL

6¼ .... 3½ x 6
6¾ † .... 3⅝ x 6½
7 .... 3¾ x 6¾
7¾ .... 3⅞ x 7½
Monarch* .... 3⅞ x 7½
8⅝ .... 3⅝ x 8⅝
9 † .... 3⅞ x 8⅞
10 † .... 4⅛ x 9½
11 .... 4½ x 10⅜
12 .... 4¾ x 11
14 .... 5 x 11½

*Pointed Flap
†Also tinted inside.

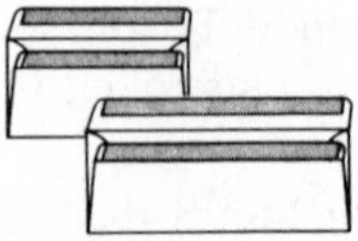

SELF-SEAL®

(Seal Without Moisture) Commercial and Official Sizes

6¾ † .... 3⅝ x 6½
7¾ .... 3⅞ x 7½
10 † .... 4⅛ x 9½

†Also available with Outlook Window.

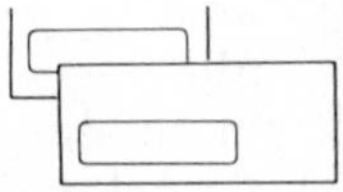

OUTLOOK®
Glassine or Krystal Klear Window

6¼ .... 3½ x 6
6¾* .... 3⅝ x 6½
7 .... 3¾ x 6¾
7¾ .... 3⅞ x 7½
Monarch .... 3⅞ x 7½
Check .... 3⅝ x 8⅝
9* .... 3⅞ x 8⅞
10* .... 4⅛ x 9½
11 † .... 4½ x 10⅜
12 † .... 4¾ x 11

*Also Tinted inside.
†Glassine window only.

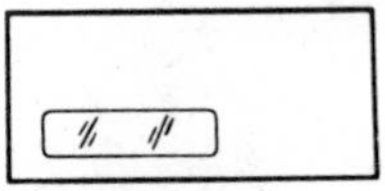

EXECUTIVE STYLE WHITE WOVE KRYSTAL KLEAR® OUTLOOK® WINDOW

6¾ .... 3⅝ x 6½
10 .... 4⅛ x 9½

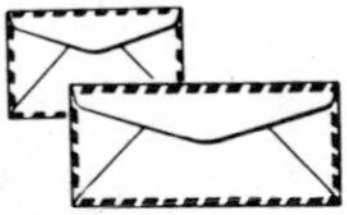

AIR MAIL

6¾ .... 3⅝ x 6½
10 .... 4⅛ x 9½

BARONIAL

4 .... 3⅝ x 4 11/16
5 .... 4⅛ x 5⅛
5½ .... 4⅜ x 5⅝
6 .... 5 x 6

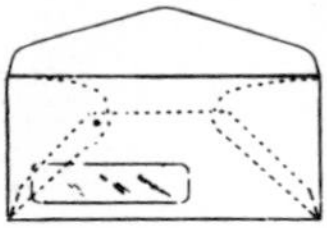

OUTLOOK® POSTAGE SAVER SPOT OF GUM

6¾ .... 3⅝ x 6½
7 .... 3¾ x 6¾
7¾ .... 3⅞ x 7½
9 .... 3⅞ x 8⅞
10 .... 4⅛ x 9½

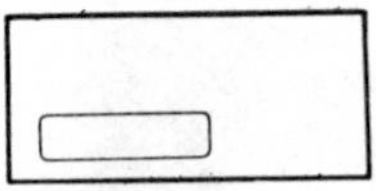

EXECUTIVE STYLE WHITE WOVE GLASSINE OUTLOOK® WINDOW

6¾ .... 3⅝ x 6½
9 .... 3⅞ x 8⅞
10 .... 4⅛ x 9½

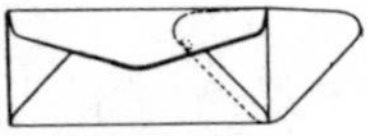

POSTAGE SAVER

Spot of Gum

6¾ .... 3⅝ x 6½
7 .... 3¾ x 6¾
7¾ .... 3⅞ x 7½
9 .... 3⅞ x 8⅞
10 .... 4⅛ x 9½

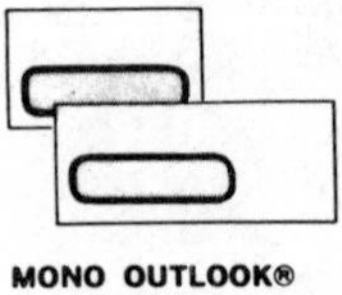

MONO OUTLOOK®
tinted inside

6¾ .... 3⅝ x 6½
7 .... 3¾ x 6¾
7¾ .... 3⅞ x 7½
Check .... 3⅝ x 8⅝
8¼ .... 3⅝ x 8¾
9 .... 3⅞ x 8⅞
10 .... 4⅛ x 9½

"THANK YOU" KRYSTAL KLEAR® OUTLOOK®

6¾ .... 3⅝ x 6½
10 .... 4⅛ x 9½

Courtesy: United States Envelope

STANDARD U.S.E. ENVELOPE STYLES
RECOMMENDED FOR MAIL ROOM EQUIPMENT

In Addition to the Sizes Listed, All Styles Are Available in Special Sizes to Meet Individual Requirements.

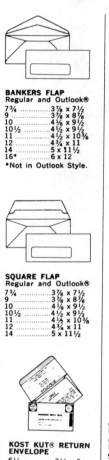

BANKERS FLAP
Regular and Outlook®

7¾	3⅞ x 7½
9	3⅞ x 8⅞
10	4⅛ x 9½
10½	4½ x 9½
11	4½ x 10⅜
12	4¾ x 11
14	5 x 11½
16*	6 x 12

*Not in Outlook Style.

SQUARE FLAP
Regular and Outlook®

7¾	3⅞ x 7½
9	3⅞ x 8⅞
10	4⅛ x 9½
10½	4½ x 9½
11	4½ x 10⅜
12	4¾ x 11
14	5 x 11½

KOST KUT® RETURN ENVELOPE

6¼	3½ x 6
6¾	3⅝ x 6½

**COLUMBIAN®
FLAT MAILER**

6½ x 9½
7½ x 10½
9 x 12
9½ x 12½
10 x 13
10 x 15

**COLUMBIAN®
AIR MAILER**

Red and Blue Border
9½ x 12½

**COLUMBIAN®
FIRST CLASS MAILER**

Green "Diamond"
Border
9 x 12
9½ x 12½
10 x 13

COLUMBIAN® CLASP

0	2½ x 4¼
5	3⅛ x 5½
10	3⅜ x 6
15	4 x 6⅜
11	4½ x 10⅜
25	4⅝ x 6¾
35	5 x 7½
14	5 x 11½
50	5½ x 8¼
55	6 x 9
63	6½ x 9½
68	7 x 10
75	7½ x 10½
80	8 x 11
83	8½ x 11½
87	8¾ x 11¼
90	9 x 12
93	9½ x 12½
94	9¼ x 14½
95	10 x 12
97	10 x 13
98	10 x 15
105	11½ x 14½
110	12 x 15½

BOOKLET ENVELOPES

5	5½ x 8⅛
6	5¾ x 8⅞
6½	6 x 9
7	6¼ x 9⅝
7½	7½ x 10½
9	8¾ x 11½
9½	9 x 12

**DUBL-GRIP®
SELF-SEAL®**
(Seal Without Moisture)
Open Side

5 x 11½
9½ x 12½*†
10 x 13°
10½ x 15*

*Available with green "diamond" border.
†Available with Air Mail border.

OPEN END, GUMMED

8 Glove	3⅞ x 7½
7 Glove	4 x 6⅜
10 Policy	4⅛ x 9½
11 Policy	4½ x 10⅜
1 Scarf	4⅝ x 6¾
3 Scarf	5 x 7½
14 Policy	5 x 11½
4¼ Scarf	5½ x 7½
6 Scarf	5½ x 8¼
1 Catalog	6 x 9
1¾ Catalog	6½ x 9½
3 Catalog	7 x 10
6 Catalog	7½ x 10½
8 Catalog	8¼ x 11¼
9¾ Catalog	8¾ x 11¼
10½ Catalog	9 x 12
12½ Catalog	9½ x 12½
13½ Catalog	10 x 13
14½ Catalog	11½ x 14½

Courtesy: United States Envelope

Standard Sizes of Envelopes

PAY

No. 2	2½x4¼
No. 1½	2 9/16x4

COMMERCIAL

No. 5	3 1/16x5½
No. 6	3⅜x6
No. 6¼	3½x6
No. 6¾	3⅝x6½

OFFICIAL

No. 7	3¾x 6¾
No. 7½	3⅞x 7½
No. 8½	3⅝x 8⅜
No. 9	3⅞x 8⅞
No. 10	4⅛x 9½
No. 11	4½x10⅜
No. 12	4¾x11
No. 14	5 x11½

BARONIAL

No. 4	3⅝x4 11/16
No. 5	4⅛x5⅛
No. 5½	4⅜x5⅝
No. 6	5 x6

POLICY (Open and Official)

No. 9	4 x 9
No. 10	4⅛x 9½
No. 11	4½x10⅜

CATALOG

No. 0	2½x 4¼
No. 3	3 x 4½
No. 5	3⅛x 5½
No. 9	4 x 9
No. 9½	4⅛x 9½
No. 10	3⅜x 6
No. 11	4½x10⅜
No. 12	4¾x10⅞
No. 14	5 x11½
No. 15	4 x 6⅜
No. 20	3⅞x 7½
No. 25	4⅝x 6¾
No. 30	4⅞x 7¼
No. 35	5 x 7½
No. 40	5⅜x 7½
No. 45	5¼x 8
No. 50	5½x 8¼
No. 55	6 x 9
No. 60	6¼x 9½
No. 63	6½x 9½
No. 65	6½x10
No. 68	7 x10
No. 70	7 x10½
No. 75	7½x10½
No. 80	8 x11
No. 83	8½x11½
No. 90	9 x12
No. 93	9½x12½
No. 95	10 x12
No. 97	10 x13
No. 105	11½x14½

On the horizon, too, are new opportunities through CATV and, already here, the AT&T Picturephone service now available in a few of the major cities.

GLOSSARY OF PRINTING TERMS

A.A.: Printer's or proofreader's abbreviation for author's alteration/s.

A.A.A.A.: Abbreviation for the American Association of Advertising Agencies; also called "the 4 A's."

ADDRESSOGRAPH: A method of addressing mailings through the use of metal plates with embossed letters.

AIA: Acronym for Association of Industrial Advertisers.

AIDA: The most popular formula for the preparation of direct mail copy. The letters stand for Get Attention, Arouse Interest, Stimulate Desire, Ask for Action.

AIR: Artists' slang for the white space within a layout.

AIR BRUSH: An instrument operating by compressed air, for spraying ink or liquid colors onto photographs or other illustrations.

AIRMAIL ENVELOPES: While any envelope may be used for airmail if endorsed "Via Airmail," most regular users of this class of postal service adopt special envelopes for the purpose. Designs for printed airmail envelopes are of two types: "A," a border consisting of alternating red and blue oblique parallelograms which must be printed on white paper and thus produce a red, white, and blue design 5/32 of an inch wide around the edges of both the address side and the back of the envelope; and "B," two ¼-inch stripes, one of red and the other of blue, extending horizontally across the center of the envelope with a ¼-inch band of white between. Both envelopes should be imprinted "Via Airmail."

AMPERSAND: The technical name of the symbol (&) used for "and" in company names, etc. Also called "short and."

ANIMAL SIZE: Gelatin employed for sizing surface of rag-content grades of paper.

ANNOUNCEMENT: A printed piece giving notice of special events, change of address, appointments of personnel, etc.

ANNOUNCEMENT PAPER: Papers intended for announcement (advertising or social). Usually supplied with matching envelopes.

ANPA-AAAA: Abbreviation for American Newspaper Publishers' Association-American Association of Advertising Agencies.

ANSA-LETTER: A patented mailing device used to facilitate replies to direct mail promotion letters.

ANTIQUE FINISH: Paper with slightly rough finish. Similar to eggshell finish.

ASCENDER: That part of the type which projects above the upper shoulder of the type.

ATCMU: Acronym for Associated Third-Class Mail Users.

AUTHOR'S ALTERATIONS: Changes marked in a proof by the author (or editor), as contrasted with corrections made by a proofreader.

AUTHOR'S PROOF: The proofs which are to be or have been sent to the author or editor.

AUTOPEN: A device which individually signs letters or other documents with a pen activated by a master disc created for any individual signature.

AUTO-TYPIST: Trade name of an electric typewriter used especially for facsimile letters.

BACKBONE: The back edge of a bound book.

BACKING UP: Printing one side of a sheet after the other side has been printed.

BACK LINING: A paper cemented to the backbone of sewed books to bind the signatures and to allow space between the backbone of the book and the backbone of the cover.

BAD BREAK: A difficulty occurring in printing makeup, as when a break line falls at the bottom or top of a page or when an illustration falls above or below a break line or in a space too small for it, etc. Also refers to words incorrectly divided.

BAD COPY: Manuscript or illustration copy that is indistinct, illegible, weak (as with poor photographs), or otherwise difficult to read or to reproduce.

BAD LETTER: A letter that does not print clearly or fully.

BALLOON: A circular, oblong, or other space indicated as emerging from the mouth of a speaker and conventionally used in comic strips to show speech.

BARONIAL ENVELOPES: An envelope for formal-appearing mailings; generally more nearly square than commercial types of covers.

BASE: Wood or metal upon which printing plates are mounted to hold securely at type height. Also called "block."

BASIC WEIGHT: Standard weights for basic size of a known classification. Weight generally applies to a ream this size.

BASTARD: Referring to size or form, one which is not standard and must be specially prepared and handled. Referring to a book title, a short title appearing alone on a separate page preceding the title page.

BEARERS: Strips of metal or wood placed around a form, or the "dead metal" left on an engraving, type high, to protect the material during electrotyping.

BEN DAY: (From the name of the inventor.) Sheets of transparent shadings, screens, dots, lines, and other designs which can be pasted on an illustration, either to fill in or to form a background. The use of ben day saves many hours of artists' time.

BIBLE PAPER: A strong, opaque, thin book paper, used to reduce the bulk of a book.

BILLHEAD: Printed form used for bills or statements.

BINDER BOARD: A paper board usually covered with cloth and used for the cover of books. Thickness generally ranges from 3/10 to 3/1,000 of an inch.

BINDING: The method in which a booklet, book, catalog, or brochure is fastened together. The method varies with the job and may consist of simple wire staples, a patented wire or plastic binding in more elaborate jobs, or a sewed binding in the base of permanent books.

BINGO CARD: A reply card inserted in a publication and used by readers to request literature and samples from companies whose products and services are either advertised or mentioned in the editorial columns.

BLACK-AND-WHITE LINE EDGE: An illustration framed with an outer black line inside of which is a white line of the same thickness.

BLEED: To trim into the matter of a page, usually in illustrations or rules.

BLOCK: The wood or metal base on which is mounted a printing plate. Also called "base."

BLOCKING OUT: Obscuring part of an illustration.

BLOTTING PAPER: Absorbent, unsized stock used for blotters. One side may be coated for printing.

BLOWUP: Any type matter or illustration which has been enlarged, usually several sizes, from the original. Also the process of enlarging.

BLURB: A short, concise summary used to introduce an article or story in the issue in which it appears or in a forthcoming issue. Also the type matter describing book and/or author on the dust jacket.

BMF: Acronym for Business Mail Foundation.

BODY STOCK: Foundation stock for any coated board or paper.

BODY TYPE: Type used for the main body of a job.

BOILER PLATE: Features and illustrations made up in advance of other material to be used as filler in newspapers, magazines, and similar publications.

BOLDFACE: Heavy-faced type, in contradistinction to light-faced type.

BOND PAPER: Originally, paper made entirely from rags and coated, for use in printing bonds and stock certificates.

BOOK JACKET: A paper cover placed over the board covers of a book, usually printed in a fashion to attract readers. Also called "Dust Jacket."

BOOKLET: Any small book, but especially one with a self-cover.

BOOKLET ENVELOPES: Special envelopes to fit any size of booklet; available in either regular or postage-saver style, usually with open sides or diagonal seams. In selection of envelopes for booklets it is wise to consider durability and folding qualities of booklet stock before ordering envelopes to match. Frequently paper used for booklet is not suitable for envelopes. In many cases contrasting or harmonizing color is preferable to matching color, particularly when matching color would involve unsuitable paper stock.

BREAK LINE: A line of type which is shorter than the full measure.

BRIGHTNESS: Term designating the color factor of paper.

BRISTOL BOARD: Heavy or extra-heavy index or announcement paper.

BROADSIDE: A single full sheet or half sheet of paper, printed on one side or two, folded for mailing or direct distribution, and opening into a single, large advertisement. Especially used for door-to-door distribution.

BROCHURE: Strictly a high-quality pamphlet, with especially planned layout, typography, and illustrations. The term is also used loosely for any promotional pamphlet or booklet.

BRONZING: Printing with a sizing ink and applying bronze powder while still wet to secure the effect of metallic inks.

BULK: A term which refers to sheet thickness.

BULLETIN: (1) News or announcements published periodically. (2) A statement of policy, an instruction, or a news item for posting on a bulletin board and/or for distribution.

BUNDLING: The typing up of signatures of a book.

BURNISHED: A plate on which some area has been rubbed with a burnishing tool to make it darker when printed.

BUSINESS FORMS: Special printed forms such as billheads, interoffice message forms, and other more or less standardized forms.

BUSINESS REPLY ENVELOPES: Concerns which have obtained permits from their postmasters are privileged to use business reply cards and business reply envelopes. The address side of such envelopes bears the following information: permit number; name of post office issuing the permit; the words, "Busines Reply Envelope"; the inscription, "No postage stamp necessary if mailed in the United States"; the words, "Postage will be paid by addressee" (whose name may be inserted if desired) over the name and complete address of the person or concern to whom the envelopes are to be returned. A space of at least 1⅛ inches shall be left for postmarking at the top of the envelope on the left of the indicia in the upper right corner. Such indicia shall be prominently printed and not obstructed or surrounded by any other matter. All the foregoing shall be arranged in one of the standard forms provided by the post office. No extraneous matter may appear on the address side. Applications for permits should be addressed to the postmaster on Form No. 3614. No deposit is necessary.

BY-LINE: A line giving the name of the author of an article, book, etc.

CABOT LETTER: A patented type of reply letter used in direct mail advertising and promotion.

C. & S.C.: Abbreviation for capital letters and small capital letters.

CALENDARS: Printed cardboard backs to which calendar pads are to be attached; also the calendars themselves. (Note difference in spelling between "calendar" and "calender.")

CALENDER: (Verb) To press between rollers for the purpose of obtaining a smooth, glossy surface. (Noun) The machine used for calendering.

CALENDERED PAPER: Any paper which has been smoothed in manufacture; there are various degrees of calendering.

CAPTION: The title or description at top of an article or illustration. Ordinarily a caption does not take a period; other punctuation is usually as elsewhere. Improperly but often misused to mean "legend."

CAPTIVE PLANT: A printing and/or duplicating facility operated by a company whose major business is in an unrelated field.

CARBRO: A lamination of thin color separation positives mounted on a reflective white surface.

CAR CARDS: Sheets of cardboard intended for advertising in buses, subway cars, etc.

CASE: A wooden tray with a number of small compartments wherein type is laid.

CASE BOUND: A book with a stiff cover which is made separately, the sewed book being inserted.

CATALOG: A book or booklet showing merchandise, with descriptive details.

CATALOG ENVELOPES: The same considerations which govern the selection of booklet envelopes also apply to those for catalogs except that catalogs, being usually larger and heavier, generally call for a stronger and heavier paper stock. Most catalog envelopes are made in the open-end style with a center seam, giving strength and durability. They are available in all sizes, with gummed or ungummed flaps.

CATHODE RAY TUBE (CRT): A television-like unit having a memory section which translates information and characters stored on paper or magnetic tape or discs into images which are then displayed on the screen.

CATTIE: Printer's slang for an ink smudge on a printed page.

CENTER SPREAD: A double spread appearing in the exact center of a bound or stapled book or booklet.

CHASE: The metal frame in which type is locked for printing.

CHECK BINDING: A book side stitched with board sides, covered with marble paper, cloth back, cut flush.

CHUNKS: Various elements—illustrations, borders, initials, etc.—proofed up together without being organized into proper order.

CIRCLES OF CONVENIENCE: A method of charting areas from which the bulk of customers is drawn for a store or institution.

CIRCULARS: General term for printed advertising in any form, including printed matter sent out by direct mail.

CLASP ENVELOPES: An envelope with a metal fastener.

CLASS MAGAZINES: Magazines which through their editorial appeal are designed to reach distinct classes of people. In the case of some magazines the class is very comprehensive, such as women's magazines or farm papers. In the case of others, such as trade papers, sporting publications, etc., the group is more limited.

CLOSE PUNCTUATION: Type matter containing an excessive amount of punctuation.

CLOSE UP: Instruction to printer to bring type matter or illustrations closer together.

COATED PAPERS: Any paper to which a surface coating has been applied by the manufacturer or converter.

COLD CANVASS: To solicit business from a general group of suspects without qualifying them as prospects, as in house-to-house canvassing.

COLLOTYPE: A photographic printing process which utilizes a lithography process from a heavy glass plate.

COLOR BARS: A conventional method of showing color depth and color control for the printer's operation.

COLOR CHART: A paper, booklet, or book showing various colors of ink for selection in color printing. Also called "tint chart."

COLOR FLAP: A transparent or translucent sheet placed over illustration copy to show color separation or other layout details.

COLOR PROOFS: Proofs showing the finished reproduction of a color illustration.

COLUMN RULE: A vertical rule used to separate columns of types or other matter, as in bill forms and tabular work.

COMBINATION PLATE: A printing plate which includes both halftone and line illustrations.

COMPOSING ROOM: The department in which all activities from the first setting of type to the final preparation of forms for the press are carried on.

COMPOSITION: Material set in type, or the art of setting type.

CONDENSED TYPE: Typefaces that are narrow or slender.

CONTROLLED CIRCULATION: Publications of any kind which are sent regularly to a list of persons who do not pay any direct subscription price. The term applies especially to association magazines, to which the subscription price is included in the membership fee.

COPY: Matter (manuscript, typewritten, artwork, or photography) to be reproduced in printed form.

CORNER CARDS: Originally conceived to meet postal requirements of a return address, the term "corner card" has come to embrace all the various types of design employed by advertisers and others to register an advertising impression on the recipient before he even opens the envelope. Good typography, artistic designs, the use of color all contribute to effectiveness. Care should be taken to observe postal regulations concerning the amount of space which should be left for addressing and stamping, and to include all pertinent information.

COST PER INQUIRY: A simple arithmetical formula—total cost of mailing or advertisement divided by number of inquiries received; of limited usefulness, since it excludes overhead and other cost factors and cannot anticipate delayed or indirect effects.

COST PER ORDER: Similar to Cost Per Inquiry.

COUNTER CARD: Advertising cards intended for display on the counters of stores.

COUNTER AND PACKAGE ENVELOPES: These come in a wide variety of special sizes and styles, depending upon the nature of the product to be packaged. Some are designed for their display value in retail stores; some for customers' convenience in carrying merchandise away. In either case, such envelopes are styled for packaging rather than for mailing purposes.

COUPON: A portion of a promotion piece or advertisement intended to be filled out by inquirer and returned to advertiser.

COVER: Synonym for envelope; also refers to any type of outside wrapping for mailing.

CRASH FINISH: A finish which gives paper the appearance of linen.

CREDIT LINE: A line accompanying an article or illustration giving credit to the originator or copyright holder.

CRIMPING: Creasing the binding edge of ledger sheets so that book will open freely.

CRISSCROSS DIRECTORIES: Special publications issued by telephone companies in which names are listed by street address rather than alphabetically.

CROP: To cut off or trim the parts of an illustration which are not to be included in the finished printing. Cropping of photographs is usually done by lines made with a grease pencil or with a cut-out paper mask overlay.

CUT-IN: An illustration, note, or heading printed within the text matter of a page or form, as when small type or a small cut is placed in a space between words of a regular text.

CUTOUTS: Printed pieces cut into irregular shapes by steel dies.

CYAN: The color sensation produced by the simultaneous reception of blue and green light. Often called "process blue."

CYLINDER PRESS: A press in which the type form is flat but the printing is done against a revolving cylinder.

DEALER-IDENTIFIED: Advertising prepared by a manufacturer but mailed over the name of a retailer or other selling unit.

DECKLE EDGE: Paper with one or more feathery edges.

DEEP ETCHING: Etching a printing plate extra deeply to give more contrast to the lights and shadows.

DENSITY: Percentage value in terms of black; for example, 50% density refers to a 50% tint of solid black.

DESCENDER: That part of the type which extends below the shoulder of the type.

DIE CUT: A sheet, cover, or other printed piece which has been specially cut into other than standard forms or shapes.

DIRECT ADVERTISING: A broad term encompassing all the diversified forms of advertising directed to specific audiences selected by the advertiser.

DIRECT MAIL AGENCY: A business organization which specializes in the creation of direct mail material for advertisers.

DISPLAY FACE: Type composition in which various sizes and faces of type are used to attract attention, as in cover and title pages, catalogs, and various kinds of advertising.

DMMA: Acronym for the Direct Mail/Marketing Association.

DODGER: A small sheet of advertising matter for enclosure with letters or for hand distribution. Also called "handbill."

DOUBLE LEADING: Matter with two leads, or strips of metal, inserted between the type lines.

DOUBLE-PAGE SPREAD: A display—usually an ad—which covers two facing pages. Also called "double spread." If in center of book, called "center spread."

DOUBLE PRINT: Superimposing a line negative on a halftone background.

DOWN STYLE: Style preference which uses a minimum of capital letters. Most newspapers prefer down style.

DROP FOLIO: A folio placed at the bottom of a page, usually centered.

DROPOUT: Creating white areas in the reproduction of a halftone by eliminating part or all of the screen on the plate.

DRY FINISH PAPER: Paper with a high finish which has been surfaced without moistening.

DULL COAT: A smooth-finish, enameled paper; contrasted to glossy.

DUMMY: A mock-up giving a preview of a sheet, booklet, book, or other unit intended for production, showing the placement and nature of the various elements as a guide for the artist, printer, or others concerned.

DUOTONE INK: An ink which, after drying, gives the job an appearance of having been printed in two different tones of the same color.

DYETONE: A process in which a black photo image is printed in modulated color.

DYE TRANSFER: A colored print made from a color transparency.

E.F.: Abbreviation for English finish paper.

EGGSHELL FINISH: A smooth, antique finish with a pitted effect, similar to an eggshell.

ELECTROTYPE: General term used for a metal plate employed in printing. Frequently called merely "electro."

ELEPHANT: Printer's slang for a sheet measuring 23 by 28 inches.

ELLIOTT: A method of addressing mailings through the use of cards containing an imbedded fiber stencil. Addresses are typed with a regular typewriter on the stencil and ink is forced through the stencil to create the address on mailing pieces.

EM: The square of a body of any given typeface.

EMBOSSING: Relief printing by means of dies after color printing is done by letterpress. When no printing is done on the area to be embossed, it is called "blind embossing."

EN: One-half the width of an em.

ENAMELED STOCK: Coated blanks, book paper, and other papers with a smooth, calendered finish. Used for fine printing, especially of color illustrations.

END PAPERS: Paper used for covering the inside of book covers.

ENGLISH FINISH: A book paper surface which is smoother than machine finish and not as smooth as supercalendered.

ENVELOPE PAPER: A general term descriptive of paper suitable for making envelopes for mailing. It should be strong and opaque for commercial uses, with good folding qualities and writing surface, and should lie flat without curling. While papers of nearly all types have been used for envelopes, the best are white wove writings, bonds, ledgers, manilas, ropes, krafts, and colored papers.

ENVELOPE STUFFER: Any advertising or promotional material enclosed in an envelope with business letters, statements, or invoices.

ETCH PROOFS: Black proofs made from a form which has been locked up in a chase with bearers.

EVEN PAGE: The left-hand pages of a book or booklet, which carry even numbers (2, 4, 6, etc.). Also called "verso."

EXPANDED TYPE: An extra-wide face of type.

EXPIRE: A former customer who is no longer an active buyer.

EXTERNAL: A publication for customers of a company.

FACSIMILE: The exact reproduction of a letter, document, or signature; also printed letters simulating typewritten letters.

FASTENERS: There are four principal styles of fasteners for open-end, catalog, booklet, and other styles of envelopes: (1) gummed flaps; (2) ungummed flaps, to be tucked in; (3) metal clasps; and (4) string and button.

FILING AND EXPANSION ENVELOPES: These range from plain, open-side envelopes with thumb cuts to accordion-pleated expansion envelopes of great strength and durability. Ordinary filing envelopes are made to contain standard 8½- by 11-inch material, although many are made in smaller sizes for other types of filing equipment.

FILLER: Minerals used to improve the printing quality of paper.

FILL-IN: A name, address, or other words added to a form letter. A fill-in is generally typed manually in automatic-typed letters, although in some operations mailing plates may be used to individualize form letters.

FILLED-IN: A term used to describe the result when too much ink is used in printing an illustration, resulting in areas which are printed too heavily. When the dots in a halftone screen are too close together for the quality of paper on which the cut is printed, there is danger that the illustration will be filled in.

FINAL COPY: When copy is sent to the printer in several installments, final copy is the last installment sent. Final copy should be plainly marked as such, in order that the printer may know when to proceed with makeup.

FINISH: The surface of any grade of paper, such as low finish (meaning dull), and high finish (meaning glossy).

FLAPS: In general, flaps of envelopes are of four styles: (1) The regular flap which is most popular but which, for reasons of extra strength or unusual appearance, is not always suitable; (2) the pointed flap, which imparts an air of distinction to the envelope and also provides a slightly larger gumming surface, frequently being used for executive correspondence; (3) the wallet flap, which is extremely strong, extending well down below the center of the envelope, with a very large gumming surface; and (4) the bankers flap, which is extremely deep.

FLATBED PRESS: A press which prints from a flat, horizontal type form.

FLAT TINT: A continuous tone resulting from the use of positive or negative dots of regular spacing and size.

FLEXOWRITER: A special typewriter which can be operated by punched paper tape. It is frequently used to prepare letters which appear to be individually typed but have a common message. The address and salutation are typed mechanically and then the machine takes over and automatically types the remainder of the letter.

FLOP: To reverse an illustration so that the right side of the original becomes the left side in the final printing, and vice versa.

FLUSH BLOCKING: Trimming a plate so that the printing surface comes flush with one or more edges of the block on which the plate is mounted.

FLUSH COVER: A cover that has been trimmed to the same size as the text pages.

FLUSH PARAGRAPHS: Paragraphs having no indentation.

FLYER: A small advertising circular.

FOLDER: A printed piece with one or more folds in which, when folded, each panel constitutes a separate page.

FOLIO: (1) The figure or numeral placed on a page to denote its sequence, (2) a sheet of paper size 17 by 22 inches.

FONT: Complete assortment of all the different characters of a particular style and size of type.

FOOTNOTE: A note of explanation or reference at the bottom of a page, apart from the regular body type. Footnotes are usually set in smaller type than the text matter.

FORM: Type and material locked in a chase and ready for the press or electrotyping.

FORM LETTER: Any letter, whether produced in quantity or individually, used to fit a specific situation likely to be encountered frequently. *See also* Guide Letter.

FORMAT: Strictly, the size, shape, and general makeup of a publication; loosely applied to the appearance of any printed material.

FOTOSETTER: A typesetting machine which uses matrices carrying an imbedded negative from which lines of type can be prepared photographically.

FOUNDRY PROOF: A proof made of a locked form intended for plating, but before making it into a plate.

FRENCH-FOLD: A type of fold for pieces printed on only one side, thereby doubling their bulk. Usually makes an eight-page mailing piece, only four of which are printed.

FRENCH FOLIO: A thin paper with an even finish, used for lightweight circulars, printing proofs, etc.

FULL BOUND: A binding completely covered with leather.

FURNITURE: Pieces of wood or metal used to fill out the blank spaces in a printing form.

GADGET LETTER: A letter containing an item fastened to or enclosed with the letterhead; such items, called gadgets, may be bits of string, miniature tools, coins, etc.

GALLEY: A long tray for holding type after it has been set.

GALLEY PROOF: A proof pulled after type has been composed or set and before it has been compiled or made up into pages.

GANG RUN: Printing from a form containing a group of typed pages or plates to be run at one printing. Applied, for example, to several different letterheads or bill forms printed simultaneously, to be cut apart later.

GATHERING: The operation of collating folded signatures in consecutive order.

GIANT LETTERS: A letter blown up to larger than standard 8½- by 11-inch size. Giant letters generally measure 11 by 17 inches or 17 by 22 inches.

GLARE: High reflection from a glossy, enameled, or polished paper surface.

GOTHIC: A synonym for sans serif type.

GRAIN: Grain, as applied to paper, refers to the parallel lay of fibers in machine-made paper. It runs in the direction the paper moves through the Fourdrinier machine.

GRAPHOTYPE: A machine for preparing Addressograph and Speedaumat address plates.

GUIDE LETTER: A form letter in which one or more sentences or paragraphs change to meet individual circumstances, but in which most of the form is the same for all recipients.

GUTTER: The division between two facing pages.

GUTTER MARGIN: The page margin at the binding edge of a book or pamphlet.

HACKER PROOF: A proof pulled carefully on enamel stock or transparent acetate, suitable for reproduction. (Also called "reproduction proof.")

HAIRLINE: A very fine line used in engraving or printing.

HALF-BOUND: A binding of which only the back and corners are covered with leather.

HALFTONE: A reproduction (usually of continuous tone copy) made by photographing through a halftone screen. The term also is applied to the plate or to the printed impression made from such a plate.

HALFTONE SCREEN: A lined screen used in a camera to break up a continuous-tone image into dots. The screen may be fine or coarse depending upon the paper upon which the completed halftone will be printed. (*See* Screen.)

HANDBILL: *See* Dodger.

HAND-SET TYPE: Type matter set by hand; contrasted to machine-set type, as with the Linotype, Monotype, Ludlow, etc.

HEADINGS: Headlines as distinguished from body type.

HIGHLIGHT HALFTONE: Eliminating the screen from portion of a halftone.

HIGH KEY PHOTOGRAPHS: Photographs in color or black and white made under brilliant illumination.

HOOVEN: Trade name of automatic electric typewriters, used in tandem, for making multiple copies of facsimile letters.

HOUSE ORGAN: A periodical published by a company for its employees and/or customers.

IMITATION PARCHMENT: Paper resembling parchment but generally made from hydrated sulfite pulp.

IMPOSITION: The process of arranging the pages in a form so that when printed and folded they will fall in proper numerical order.

IMPRESSION: The pressure, or effect of pressure, between the printing surface and the paper surface.

IMPRINT: The name of the publisher or the printer of a publication. The publisher's imprint is usually at the bottom of the title page and at the bottom of the backbone on bound books. The printer's imprint, if on a book, is generally at the bottom of the page backing the title page or on the last page of the book.

INDENTION: (1) The setting of a line or lines in from the margin, (2) the resulting blank space.

INDIA PAPER: A very thin bible paper used principally for books.

INITIAL: A large single type, often ornamented, used at the beginning of a chapter. An initial is always several times as large as the body type.

INSERTS: Illustrations or type matter not printed in the regular signatures of a book but tipped in between pages.

INSET: The pages cut off in folding and placed in the middle of the sheet.

INTAGLIO: A process of printing from lines or dots recessed into the surface of a metal plate. Gravure, an intaglio process, is printed from cells recessed into the surface of a metal cylinder.

INTERLEAVING: The placing of flat sheets together before binding.

INTERNAL: A publication for employees of a company.

INTERNAL-EXTERNAL: A publication for both employees and customers of a company.

INTERTYPE: A typesetting machine similar to the Linotype but differing in some details.

ITALIC: A style of letter that is slanted, in distinction from upright Roman.

JACKET: An extra protective cover of a book. Also called "book jacket" or "dust jacket."

JUSTIFY: (1) To write the exact number of words or letters to fill a given space. (2) To set one line or more of type to fill a given space.

JUTE MANILA: A wrapping paper suitable for cards, envelopes, tags, etc.

KERN: That part of certain letters or types which projects beyond the body, as in italic j or f.

KEYLINE: A mechanical diagram of reproduction copy for the guidance of the platemaker.

KEY PLATE: The plate of a set of plates which carries the most detail and to which the other plates are registered.

KEYED: Advertising is said to be keyed when an identifying letter or number is so used as to show the advertiser which mailing or publication brought a given response. Thus a coupon, order, or inquiry addressed to "Department A" indicates that a certain magazine or list pulled this reply.

KILL: To strike out words from copy or on proofs; also to destroy type or cuts.

KRAFT PAPER: A high-strength wrapping paper made from sulfate pulp. It is usually brown but may be dyed to other colors.

LABEL PAPER: Paper specially sized for printing labels; may be coated or uncoated.

LACQUERING: Applying transparent coating to protect the surface of a cover or page or to give a glossy finish. Also called "varnishing."

LAID PAPER: A paper which shows a pattern of finely spaced parallel lines and widely spaced cross lines when held up to the light; contrasted to woven paper.

LAMINATING: The process of uniting two materials, such as foil and paper, with an adhesive, using pressure, heat, or both.

LEAD (pronounced "led"): A less-than-type-high strip of metal used primarily to space between lines of type. Standard widths are one pt., two pt., and three pt., but they may be even wider.

LEAD (pronounced "leed"): A suggestion from any source that an individual, company, or group may be prospective buyers.

LEADERS (pronounced "leeders"): Rows of dots or dashes, such as used on contents pages between words and page numbers.

LEADING (pronounced "ledding"): The white space between printed lines.

LEAF: In books, generally considered as two pages, front and back, as, for example, pages 3 and 4. Pages 2 and 3 would be on separate leaves.

LEGEND: Descriptive matter under or beside a cut as distinguished from caption (title above cut). Often mistakenly called "Caption."

LETTER PAPER: Paper cut and finished for correspondence use.

LETTERPRESS: Any printing which is done direct from type. The term is used in contrast to printing done by the offset process.

LETTERSHOP: A business organization which handles the mechanical details of mailings such as addressing, imprinting, collating, etc. Most lettershops offer printing facilities and many offer some degree of creative direct mail services.

LIFT: The maximum number of sheets of paper stock that can be placed under the knife of the cutting machine at one time for efficient cutting.

LIGATURE: Two or more letters joined together and cast on the same body of type, like fi, ff, ffl, etc.

LIGHTFACE: A description given to type having a face with thin lines which prints a light tone, in contrast to bold or black-face type.

LINE COPY: Copy which is solid color throughout and obtains tonal variations by changing the size and spacing of areas of color with lines, stipple, etc.

LINE CORRECTION: Corrections made or to be made within a line of type, involving changes in characters or resetting the type.

LINE CUT: Engraving made from line copy in which the tonal variations, if any, result from the size or spacing of solid areas of color and not from the use of a halftone screen. Also called "Line Engraving."

LINEN FINISH: A finish applied to paper to give the appearance of linen.

LINOTYPE: A typesetting machine in which the letters set from a keyboard somewhat similar to that of a typewriter emerge on lead slugs of various lengths. Term used in contrast to Monotype and hand-set type, in which each letter is separate from the rest.

LIST BROKER: A business organization which arranges the rental of mailing lists compiled by others.

LIST CLEANER: A mailing to ask help of recipients in keeping a list up to date.

LIST COMPILER: A business organization which compiles special mailing lists for sale or rental to direct mail advertisers.

LITHOGRAPHY: In contrast to letterpress printing, a printing process which does not print from type but by offsetting the impression from the press plate to a blanket cylinder and then onto paper. Offset lithography is usually called simply "Offset."

LOCATION (type): Term applied to the galley on which type is stored before use or reuse; galleys are numbered for storage and corresponding numbers are placed on proofs to show location.

LOCKUP: Tightening a form securely in a chase by means of quoins or clips to prepare it for the press or the foundry.

LOGOTYPE: Originally meant to describe a word on a single type body. Now used to designate the characteristic signature of a firm or product. Also two or more letters cast together as ligatures.

LOWER CASE: Small letters, as distinct from capitals (upper case) and small capitals.

LUDLOW: A patented typesetting process, generally used for larger sizes and special faces of type.

MACHINE-COATED PAPER: A type of coated paper generally used in magazines and other media.

M.F.: Abbreviation for machine finish (paper).

MAGENTA: The color sensation produced by the simultaneous reception of red and blue light. Often called "Process Red."

MAKEREADY: Material used on a printing press to bring all type matter and illustrations to exactly the same height so that the printed impression will be even. Also the process of preparing material on the press.

MAKEUP: The arranging of type lines and illustrations into page form.

MANILA ENVELOPE PAPER: A finished paper especially made for envelopes.

MARBLED PAPER: Stock which has been decorated with a marble finish.

MARGIN: The space between pages or plates or between the edge of the printed matter and the edge of the paper.

MASA: Acronym for Mail Advertising Service Association, International.

MATCH: A direct mail term used to refer to the typing of addresses and salutations onto letters with a printed body.

MATRICES: The molds on Monotype, Linotype, Intertype, or Ludlow machinery which are filled with molten lead to form the letters of type.

MEASURE (type): The length, usually expressed in picas or ems, of a single line of type.

MECHANICAL SCREEN: Any dot or line pattern used by the photoengraver for reproducing an illustration.

MERCHANDISING: A method of increasing the effectiveness of advertising by (1) translating it into terms of advantages for dealers, retailers, salesmen, etc.; and (2) by projecting the advertiser's message beyond the audience of the media in which it originally appeared.

METALLIC PAPER: Paper with a coating giving the effect of metal. Also special coated paper which can be marked with metal letters or designs.

MIMEOGRAPH: Originally the trade name of a duplicating machine for reproducing bulletins, form letters, etc., by means of a typed stencil; now loosely applies to any of several stencil-operated reproduction machines.

MIMEOGRAPH PAPER: Paper specially made for mimeograph reproduction.

MINIATURE LETTERS: Letters which have been reduced photographically so that both the size of the sheet or letterhead and the printing or typing are smaller than normal. Miniature letters are usually $4\frac{1}{4}$ by $5\frac{1}{2}$ inches in size.

MITERING: The cutting of a rule at an angle so as to make perfect corners.

MOIRE: Undesirable pattern which results when a cut is made from the print of a halftone or certain other types of printed illustrations; i.e., by photographing a printed illustration.

MONOTYPE: A typesetting machine on which words and sentences are formed from individual type letters. *See also* Hand-set and Linotype.

MORGUE: Printer's designation for place where cuts or copy are stored after use or pending future use.

MORTISE: A hole or other space cut in the surface of a plate or in a printing block to accommodate type. Also the process of making such holes.

MULTIGRAPH: Trade name of a small printing press, used especially for multiple copies of printed letters, bulletins, circulars, etc.

MULTIGRAPH PAPER: Paper especially suited for use on the Multigraph machine.

NEWSLETTER: A publication which contains newsworthy material in the form of a letter. Most newsletters are $8\frac{1}{2}$ by 11 inches in page size with copy in typewritten form. Generally just one or two paragraphs are devoted to any single news item.

NEWSPRINT: Paper of the kind generally used for newspapers and comic books.

NIXIE: Mailing returned by the Post Office as undeliverable as addressed.

NONPAREIL: A unit of measure: $\frac{1}{2}$ of a pica (six points).

NOTEPAPER: Folded writing papers in standard sizes, finishes, and weights.

OBLONG: A book bound on the shorter dimension.

OCCUPANT LIST: Mailing lists which contain only addresses (eliminating names of individuals and/or companies).

ODD PAGE: Right-hand pages, which carry odd folios (3, 5, 7, etc.).

OFFSET: A smudge resulting from ink on one page smearing onto another. (Not to be confused with "Offset," referring to offset printing.)

OFFSET PAPER: Paper which can be used for offset lithography.

OFFSET PRINTING: A term used in contrast to letterpress. In offset printing the impression is made from the surface of a roll (usually rubber) to which an image has ben transferred from a photographic plate.

ONIONSKIN: A thin paper, generally translucent, with characteristics of bond paper.

OPAQUE: Referring to paper, not permitting passage of light, in contrast to translucent or transparent. In photoengraving, to paint out areas not wanted in the final illustration.

OPAQUE WHITE: A pigment used to white out areas on original illustration copy.

OPEN PUNCTUATION: Type matter containing the minimum of necessary punctuation.

OPTICAL BLUE: A shade of blue which will not be picked up in photographing illustration copy unless a special filter is used.

OPTICAL CHARACTER RECOGNITION (OCR): An OCR machine scans typewritten manuscript copy and then produces a paper tape or other form of input to a computer-driven typesetter.

ORDER-BLANK ENVELOPES: Various types of business reply envelopes have been developed to carry order forms on the inside. The order form is printed on one side of the sheet and the address and reply form on the other; the recipient simply fills in the order, folds and seals the envelope and mails it in.

ORDER CARD: A return card similar to a coupon in effect, to be filled out, checked, or initialed by the inquirer or customer and mailed back to the advertiser. Order cards are often self-mailers.

ORDER FORM: Similar to an order card except that it is printed on paper rather than on card stock; may require being sent in an envelope or may be sealed to form a self-mailer.

OVERHANG COVER: A cover larger in size than the enclosed pages.

OVERPRINTING: Printing over an area which has already been printed on.

PAGE PROOF: A proof of type matter which has been made up from galleys into pages.

PASTEUP TYPE: Preprinted letters which can be cut apart and then pasted onto layouts for use in preparing printed pieces.

PATENT BASE: A metal base, sometimes used to take the place of wood for mounting electrotypes.

PATTERN: A pattern plate consists of all printing elements of any one color soldered together in relationship to one another so that when molded they will provide a complete press plate of that color. Elements may consist of original engravings and/or electrotypes of halftones, zincs, type portions, etc. Example: The blue plate of a four-color set would contain all printing elements to appear in the blue press plate, all being so placed that they will register with similar press plates made from patterns of the black, red, and yellow.

PAYROLL ENVELOPES: Small containers for coins and bills which are bought in bulk by banks for distribution among their customers or by individual companies. Sizes range from 3 by 4½ inches upward. Sometimes used as enclosures for gadgets in gadget letters.

PENSCRIPT: Letters written in script, either by hand, processed, or printed.

PERFECTING: A sheet printed on the second side is said to be perfected or completed. A rotary press that delivers a signature printed on both sides of the sheet is said to be a perfecting press. There are also flatbed presses with two cylinders and two beds that print on both sides of the sheet. These are known as "flatbed perfectors."

PERFECTING PRESS: A press which prints both sides of the paper at one passage through the machine.

PERFORATING RULE: Sharp, dotted steel rule, slightly higher than type, and used in conjunction with type forms to perforate the sheet when printing.

PERSONALIZING: The individualizing of direct mail pieces by adding the name of the recipient.

PHOTO DISPLAY (also Photolettering): Display type produced on machines specifically oriented to that purpose, utilizing master film strips.

PHOTOGRAVURE: Printing done from large copper plates or copper-covered cylinders. Also called "gravure" or "rotogravure."

PHOTOTYPESETTER: A computer-driven typesetter of varying electronic sophistication, imaging speed, and typographic versatility, producing composition from simple straight matter to multicolumn formats, on photographic paper or film.

PICA: The standard for measuring type matter width or depth—⅙ of an inch, or 12 points.

PICKING: Removing foreign material or other paper elements from the paper surface.

PICKUP: A standing page or part of a page picked up to be worked on and used again.

PICTURE WINDOW ENVELOPES: Envelopes which have an opening through which a portion of the contents can be seen before the envelope is opened.

PINPOINT DOT: The finest halftone dot used in photoengravings.

POINT: The unit of type measurement—0.0138 of an inch, 12 points to the pica.

POLLARD-ALLING: A method of addressing mailings through the use of aluminum plates which are linked together into reels of up to 2,500 addresses. The system is normally used for large mailing lists.

POSTAGE SAVER ENVELOPES: Like regular envelopes in appearance and construction, the only difference being that they have a loose flap at one end which is simply tucked in without being sealed. In another style of postage saver envelope, one end is stuck with a spot of gum instead of being sealed full length and the words, "Pull out for postal inspection," are printed on or adjacent to the loose flap. Postage saver envelopes enable the advertiser to send out a third-class mailing in keeping with post-office regulations with the back flap of the envelope sealed in the same way as first-class mail.

PRESS PROOF: A proof which has been printed on a regular press (not a proof press) after makeready.

PROCESS PLATES: Color plates, two or more, used in combination with each other to produce other colors and shades. Usually involves the application of the primary pigments of yellow, magenta, cyan, and black.

PROGRESSIVE PROOFS: A set of proofs showing each of the color plates to be used in a multicolor illustration.

PROOF PRESS: A small printing press, usually hand operated, for pulling proofs.

PULLING A PROOF: Printer's term for making a copy of a cut or type matter on a proof press.

QUAD: A piece of type metal less than type high used in filling out lines.

QUERY: A small q. or an interrogation mark (?) made by proofreader to call author's attention to possible error. Question of spelling: ?sp.; question of fact: ?F.; question of grammar: ?G.; illegible: ?C.

QUIRE: 1/20 of a ream. A quire of fine paper consists of 25 sheets; of coarse paper, 24 sheets.

QUOIN: An expanding device (usually matching, toothed iron wedges) used to lock a form in a chase.

RAG CONTENT PAPER: Bond and ledger papers containing from 25% to 100% rag fibers.

REAM: Conventional unit for quantity of sheets of paper. Fine and printing papers run 500 sheets to a ream; coarse, tissue, and wrapping papers run 480 sheets to a ream.

REAM WEIGHT: The weight of one ream of any given paper.

RECTO: The right-hand page of a book or booklet, as opposed to verso, the left-hand page. Recto pages are always odd numbered (1, 3, 5 etc.).

REFLECTION COPY: Original copy which is viewed and must be photographed by light reflected from its surface.

REGISTER: A term referring to the accuracy of placement of printing; printed lines which do not fall exactly where they should are "out of register."

REGISTER MARKS: Small marks for guiding engravers in obtaining proper register in color separation printing.

RELIEFOGRAPH: A machine for preparing address plates for the Pollard-Alling address system.

REPLY-O-LETTER: One of a number of patented direct mail forms for facilitating replies from prospects.

REPRODUCTION PROOF: A proof of illustration or type matter, pulled on a special proof press, which can be photographed for offset reproduction or engraving. Abbr.: Repro. (Also called "Hacker Proof.")

RETURN ENVELOPES: Self-addressed envelopes, either stamped or unstamped, as distinguished from business reply envelopes, which bear a printed insignia and permit number obligating the mailer to pay the postage on their return.

REVERSED POSITION: A plate which has been reproduced facing one way is "reversed" when reproduced facing the opposite. For example, a portrait which has been facing "out" (toward the edge of page) is reproduced to face "in" (toward the gutter). Also called "flopping."

RFMR: Acronym for Recency-Frequency-Monetary Ratio, a formula used to evaluate sales potential of names on a mail order mailing list.

RIVER: In typesetting, a river is a white channel in a block of body type caused by wide word spacing near the same point in each of several succeeding lines.

ROBOTYPER: An automatic typewriter used for the preparation of letters in quantity.

ROMAN: Generic name for the type commonly used in all ordinary reading matter.

ROTOGRAVURE: A printing method in which inkwells are etched into copper cylinders. Ink from these wells is then deposited on paper or other printing surfaces to create an image. Especially suitable for fine color reproduction.

ROTOGRAVURE PAPER: A specially finished paper used for rotogravure newspaper supplements, catalogs, etc.

ROUTING: (rhymes with "outing.") Cutting away any metal from the surface of a printing plate. Applied both to printing surface and nonprinting areas.

ROYALTYPER: An automatic typewriter which permits the punching of a control stencil and use of that stencil to duplicate letters in quantity.

RUNAROUND: Type matter which is set in narrow measure to pass along the side of a cut.

RUNNING HEAD: Title repeated at the top of consecutive pages in a book.

RUN OF PAPER: A term applied to color printing on regular paper and presses as distinct from separately printed sections made on special color presses. Abbr.: R.O.P.

SADDLE STITCHING: Wire staples driven through the back fold of a booklet and clinched in the middle, enabling it to open out flat.

SALES PROMOTION: Techniques used by a company to promote the movement of its products and services toward the customer (as contrasted to advertising which is aimed at moving the customer toward the products and services). Sales promotion media are usually distinguished by the fact an advertiser controls the format and the audience, rather than working within the limitations imposed by a publisher or broadcaster.

SALES PROMOTION AGENCY: A business organization which specializes in the creation of all types of promotion material except magazine, newspaper, radio and television advertising.

SANS SERIF: Letters without serifs. Gothic styles of type are sans serif.

SATIN FINISH: Paper with a special smooth finish suggesting satin.

SCANNING: A new electronic process used in the making of color separations.

SCREEN: A term used to indicate the number of dots per inch in a halftone. Coarse screens (60-line, 65-line, 80-line or 85-line) are used for newsprint and other soft-finish paper; screens of 100, 110, 120, 133, 150, and 175 lines and finer are used for smoother and enameled papers. The term "screen" is also used for ben day, according to a special numbering code.

SCRIPT: Type similar in appearance to handwriting.

SCRIPTOMATIC: A method of addressing based on the spirit-duplicating principle. Addresses are typed directly onto cards with a special carbon. The system is most frequently used in conjunction with electronic sorting systems such as IBM, Remington Rand and McBee.

SELECTRIC: Trade name for a typewriter for which many different kinds of type can be used interchangeably.

SELF-COVER: A cover of the same paper as the inside text pages.

SELF-MAILER: A direct mail piece mailed without an envelope or special binding. Advertising post cards, for example, are self-mailers.

SELF-SEAL: An envelope with special adhesive requiring no moisture for sealing.

SEPARATION NEGATIVE: A negative made from any single color of a multicolor illustration.

SERIF: The fine lines at the end of a type letter, particularly the corners at top and bottom.

423

SHEET: Cut size or trimmed size of a finished paper.

SHEET FED: Printing produced on separate sheets of paper (in contrast to roto-gravure which is done on a continuous web, or roll, of paper).

SHEETWISE: A sheetwise form is one of two forms which lock up separately and run separately on opposite sides of a sheet. Example: A four-page fold printed from two forms of two pages each, pages 1 and 4 (outside form) being printed from one form, and pages 2 and 3 (inside form) being printed on the opposite side of the sheet. Each sheet makes one complete copy, and 2,000 impressions are required to make 1,000 copies. (*See:* Work and Flop, Work and Turn, and Work and Twist.)

SHORT AND: Proofreader's term for the ampersand. (&)

SHORT FOLD: A method of folding a piece so one or more pages are shorter than other pages.

SIDEHEAD: A headline placed in the margin instead of within the type body.

SIDE STITCHING: Wire staples driven through the side of a book, or a number of signatures, as they lie flat.

SIGNATURE: A section of a book, ordinarily obtained by the folding of a single sheet into 8, 12, 16, or more pages.

SILHOUETTE: An illustration from which the background of the image has been cut or etched away.

SIZING: Rosin or other material incorporated into paper to give water-resisting properties.

SLIP SHEETS: Paper sheets fed between sheets being printed to prevent ink from smearing.

SMALL CAPS: Printers' language for smaller capital letters of the same font as the regular capital letters of the font.

SOFT PAPER: Antique; egg shell; and other low-finish, lightly sized papers of soft body.

SOLID (TYPE): Type matter is said to be set solid when no leading has been added.

SPACES: Small pieces of type metal, less than type high, used for spacing between letters and words.

SPEA: Acronym for Sales Promotion Executives Association.

SPECIAL-DELIVERY ENVELOPES: Envelopes embodying a special design and special colors. Around the borders of special-delivery envelopes appear alternating yellow and green dots. On the right side—1$\frac{3}{8}$ inches from the top of a No. 10 envelope, for example, $\frac{1}{4}$ inch from the right-hand side, and 1$\frac{7}{8}$ inches from the bottom—are two yellow horizontal rules enclosing the words, "Special Delivery," which are printed in green. The design of smaller special-delivery envelopes is reduced in proportion.

SPEEDAUMAT: A variation of the Addressograph which uses a smaller metal plate.

SPLIT FOUNTAIN: Color printing of two different colors simultaneously.

SPLIT RUN: Division of a generally similar promotion piece into two or more variations, enabling the advertiser to test different copy appeals.

SPONSOR SYSTEM: A method of controlling names on a mailing list by assigning each name and address to a sponsor who is responsible for keeping that listing up to date.

SQUARE HALFTONE: A finishing style in which the halftone screen runs to the edge of the printing plate, which is trimmed straight both vertically and horizontally.

STAGING: Application of acid-resisting varnish or staging solution to local areas of line or halftone etchings so as to permit further etching of the untreated surface of the plate.

STANDING AD: One which runs in several issues without change.

STANDING TYPE: Type which has been set and is ready for use, or which has been used and is stored for possible future use.

STAT: Printer's slang for a Photostat.

STEREOTYPE: Reproduction plates made by impressing a form into a pliant mold or matrix and then making a cast of this with type metal.

STET: A proofreader's term meaning "let it stand." Used when a word or sentence has been marked out (deleted) and then the decision is made not to delete it, after all. The material marked for deletion is underlined by a series of dots and the word "stet" is written in the margin, to instruct the printer to disregard the deletion marks.

STOCK CUT: Printing engravings kept in stock by the printer or publisher for occasional use (in contrast to exclusive use).

STOPPER: Advertising slang for a striking headline or illustration intended to attract immediate attention.

STRIP: To combine two or more negatives into one illustration.

STYLE: Rules of uniform usage in a printing plant or publishing house. Style refers to such details as capitalization, compounding, punctuation, preferred spelling, etc. See Down Style and Up Style.

SUBSTANCE: Basic weights adopted to designate regular sizes of various kinds of papers; may refer to a ream or to 1,000 sheets.

SUPERCALENDERED PAPER: Paper with a high, glossy surface.

TABULAR WORK: Composition involving columns with vertical lines and horizontal rules.

TAG ENVELOPE: An envelope punched to serve also as a tag.

TEAR SHEET: A page torn from a book or magazine and sent to an advertiser, inquirer, or other person.

TEASER: An advertisement or promotion planned to excite curiosity about a later advertisement or promotion.

TESTING: A preliminary mailing or distribution intended as a preview or pilot before a major campaign. Test mailings are used to determine probable acceptance of a product or service and are usually made to a specially selected list.

THROWAWAY: An advertisement or promotional piece intended for widespread free distribution. Throwaways are usually printed on cheap stock and delivered by hand, either to passersby or house to house. Broadsides are sometimes referred to as throwaways.

TINT BLOCK: A solid plate, without etching or engraving on it, used for printing a color. The density of the color is described in percentages: a 25% tint would be ¼ as strong as the full color, and a 50% tint would be ½ as strong as the full color, etc.

TINT CHART: A paper, booklet, or book showing various colors of ink for selection in color printing. Also called "color chart."

TIP-IN: To paste or glue one or more pages into a bound or stapled book or booklet. Color plates of less than page size may be tipped in by pasting them onto bound pages. The item tipped in is called a "tip-in."

TRANSPARENCY: A transparent positive photograph in color or black and white, in contrast to a negative.

TRIM: To cut the edges of a book or other job. Folded forms are trimmed to open the pages.

TWO COMPARTMENT ENVELOPES: Any envelopes which carry first-class mail in one compartment and third- or fourth-class mail in another, with the resultant saving in postage and the assurance that both the letter and the literature arrive together. (Envelopes of this type are handled in the mail as matter of the third or fourth class, depending on the nature of the contents of the lower class compartment.)

TYPE C PRINT: A color print made directly from a color negative.

TYPE HIGH: A plate which has been mounted to exactly the same height as the printing surface of type, 0.918 of an inch.

TYPE METAL: Usually an alloy of lead, antimony, tin, and brass used in typemaking.

UNDERLAY: Pieces of paper pasted under type or cut to bring it to the proper level for printing.

UPPER CASE: Capital letters, as distinct from lower case and small caps.

UPRIGHT: A book bound on the longer dimension.

UP STYLE: Printing style which prefers maximum use of capital letters.

VANDYKE: A proof in the form of a positive print made from a film negative.

VARITYPER: Trade name for typewriter for which many different kinds of type can be used interchangeably.

VARNISHING: *See* Lacquering.

VELOX: A halftone print, made by an engraver, of a photograph. Retouching may thus be done without defacing the original photograph.

VELLUM PAPER: A high-grade ledger paper which imitates parchment.

VERSO: The left-hand pages of a book or booklet, as opposed to recto, the right-hand page. Verso pages are always even numbered (2, 4, 6, etc.).

VERTICAL PRESS: A printing press on which the type forms are locked vertically, in contradistinction to a flatbed press.

VIGNETTE: An illustration in which the background gradually fades away, in contrast to a silhouette or an illustration with a full background.

VISUAL DISPLAY TERMINAL (VDT): Originally designed as an editing device, these units employ CRTs to display contents of an input tape, allowing an operator to add, delete or change copy at will.

WATERMARK: A marking pressed into paper in the manufacture; consists of letters, words, or designs.

WEB: Printing paper which comes in rolls.

WEB PRESS: A rotary printing press which prints on rolls of paper.

WEIGHT: May refer to the unit weight of a ream, or of 1,000 sheets, or of a specified quantity or substance number of sheet.

WIDOW: A short line ending a paragraph and appearing at the top of the next column of type. By extension, any short line which ends a paragraph.

WINDOW ENVELOPES: So called because they permit the name and address typed on the enclosure to be read through the envelope itself. They are of three main types: (1) open-face, consisting of a plain, uncovered, die-cut opening; (2) one-piece, in which the window is made in the body of the envelope by impregnating that portion of the paper with a suitable oily material; and (3) two-piece type, with a piece of glassine, cellophane, or some other transparent material affixed over the panel. To be mailable, any type of window envelope must have a panel running parallel to the length of the envelope, and windows must not be closer than 1⅜ inches from the top, or closer to the bottom or either side than ⅜ inch. No "border" around this "window" portion may exceed 5/32 inch in width. Window envelopes are covered by particular restrictions as to printing. These envelopes must bear the return card of the sender, which must consist of the name and address, or post office box number, and city from which mailed. The name of a building will not suffice unless the mailer occupies that building in its entirety.

WIRE STITCHING: The fastening of pages together with wire staples. See Saddle Stitch and Side-Wire Stitch.

WORK AND FLOP: Work-and-flop forms are identical to work-and-turn forms except the sheet is turned toward the tripper (or lower) guides. Work-and-flop forms are used when the number of pages, lengthwise of the cylinder, is an uneven number. For example, a 16-page form could be printed work and turn, while a 20-page form would be printed work and flop. If a 20-page form should be run work and turn, the middle pages would back themselves.

WORK AND TURN: Work-and-turn forms are those which, when run on one side, back themselves up after the sheet has been turned over, so that the original side guide edge is on the opposite side of the press. Example: In place of printing two forms of two pages each (as described under sheetwise form), the four pages are arranged in one form and printed. The sheets are then turned end for end and printed on the opposite side. If 1,000 folders are to be printed work and turn, the same size as described under sheetwise, a sheet twice the size will be used and 500 sheets printed on both sides, or 1,000 impressions. This will make 1,000 folders, as each sheet when cut will make two folders.

WORK AND TWIST: Work-and-twist forms are those that require two impressions on each half of the sheet to complete the sheet. The second impression is made after twisting the sheets so that new edges are at both the side and gripper (or lower) guides. Used principally in printing double-blank or cross-rule forms.

W.F.: Proofreader's abbreviation for wrong font.

WRONG FONT: Letters of one series (or font) mixed with those of another. In proofreading, indicated by w.f.

ZINC: Synonym for a line cut, in contrast to a halftone.

Chapter 13

SALES MANUALS

ASIDE from its content, one of the important factors contributing to the value of a manual is "selling" it to the sales organization so that the salesmen will have a proper appreciation of the research involved and how the manual may be used to help them to do a better selling job. To do this right, the manual should be given a "build up." It should not just be mailed to the men with a note from the sales manager recommending its use. A well-planned sales manual is a tool. Just as with any tool, the person who is to use it must understand what it is for and what it will do. It should be presented following some sort of dramatized skit built around the life of the salesman. All his many troubles faded into thin air when he began to *use* the sales manual which he had supposed was just another piece of advertising literature. Sometimes a charge is made against the salesman's account, covering the manual. It is written off when and if the manual is returned. Sometimes the president of the company calls the men together and personally presents a manual to each man, with a talk on what the company spent to produce the copy he is about to hand each salesman, and how much it should be worth to the salesman in increased production. One of the reasons the original National Cash Register primer for salesmen proved so effective in the early days of that company, was the way John H. Patterson dramatized what was in the primer. A year's promotional program was built around the little book, just to make sure that every man would use it. And they did. To make sure they did, Mr. Patterson would "pop" questions at them and woe to the salesman who did not know the answers. He was quickly told where to get them.

Even the Title Is Important

The first impression a salesman or dealer gets of a manual is from its cover, The title should neither be too corny nor too clever. It should be dignified, keeping in mind that many of those who will use the book like to think of it as something the president of the company

Your Job AS AN EASY DISTRICT REPRESENTATIVE OR WHOLESALE SALESMAN

To make any good organization function properly it is well to analyze the individual's responsibilities to his job. It develops personal efficiency and brings more sales at less cost. It promotes a clear understanding of the problems of selling. And it ensures favorable relations between you and your supervisor. Therefore, let's consider WHAT EASY OR YOUR SALES MANAGER EXPECTS FROM YOU.

1. Proper Conduct and Personal Appearance.

It goes without saying that your personal appearance, your good grooming should at all times be free from criticism. Look the part of success—and you're well on the road to success. Your conduct should inspire the dealer's full respect and confidence.

2. Full cooperation with all company policies.

Because of EASY'S national distribution setup, the company's sales policies must naturally encompass a broad approach to any selling problems.

Company policy, you will find, is always designed to promote group efficiency and to insure the best interests of all who participate in the sale of EASY'S products.

Therefore, it is of utmost importance that even though you sometimes don't entirely subscribe to the company's long range policies, you will cooperate with EASY sales management in every way.

3. Be on the job.

You owe it to yourself—your family to make your job the most important thing in your life. Give the job all you've got. Put in a good honest day of work—and your perspiration will pay off in personal progress.

4. File all essential factory reports.

With postwar selling facing the biggest challenge it ever had for the consumer's dollar, it is more vital than ever that field reports, market and merchandising studies be given your immediate and complete attention. Every effort will be made by the factory to simplify the procedure of reporting. Only the most essential information will be requested in report form. You'll be instructed as to just what special reports are required from you.

5. Franchising a new dealer.

In connection with developing balanced dealer coverage in your territory (other all production restrictions have been lifted) don't permit your enthusiasm to "take on another dealer" put you in a position where you are selling one or two washers as an account opener.

When franchising a dealer, his initial pur-

You ARE THE COMPANY

As a salesman of EASY home laundry equipment—you represent the EASY corporation in your territory. You are the company. Your rate of earning power progress depends solely on how well you sell the company, its product and its programs. You've got the national acceptance—the long years of EASY leadership to maintain in your territory. The priceless asset of EASY's good name is in your hands—in trust. Make the most of this great opportunity by going out, and—

GET THE BUSINESS

This means exactly what it says. "Getting the business" is your foremost and principal job.

In carrying out your plan of "getting the business" your first step is to—

1. Establish and Develop Quality Dealers.

With the prospect of a boom market in washers (following the war, there will be a great temptation to "coast" on EASY'S current retail distribution outlets. All-out production of washers may be some time off—and a program of merchandise allocation cramping the natural development of new, quality dealers may further the feeling that "why put on new dealers—why change my distribution set-up—when I can't get enough units to satisfy my present outlets?"

While this may be temporarily the case, there is still a lot of spade work that can be done in—

Reviewing the present dealer set up in your territory with the long range purpose of

1. Building a stronger dealer organization.
2. Developing a balanced organization in metropolitan markets (proper EASY representation in the major classifications of—appliance dealers—department stores—public utilities—and furniture stores).
3. Improvement of the quality of your dealers in small towns already covered.
4. Coverage of all open towns.

Remember; you can't stand still in business even though wartime reconversion problems seem to dictate a "stand pat" policy. Either your territory will go forward, and will secure a larger share of the industry business in 19XX, or your markets will slip backward, the recovery of which may prove to be very difficult as sales competition gets keener.

II. General Supervision of Easy Dealer's Merchandising Program.

As you will know, a product is not sold when it leaves a manufacturing plant to fill a dealer order. This is a truism that quite often fails to impress an enthusiastic District representative or a Wholesale salesman who considers his duty done when he sends in his order. But he is only half a salesman. That kind of salesman won't prosper unless he helps his dealers make a decent profit. The problem is to make salesmen merchandising-conscious.

Actually your job is twofold:

1. Sell to dealers.
2. Then help dealers sell to the public.

You are both a merchant and a salesman. In other words, you are a MERCHANDISER.
As a MERCHANDISER you are to—

had a hand in creating. Sometimes all that is necessary in the way of a title is the company trade-mark with the salesman's name gold-stamped on the cover below it. This suggests it is his book and that it is about the company. There is no need of labeling it "Sales Manual" for it is obviously that. However, some companies run a line such as "My Sales Manual" on the cover. Others call their manuals "How Books." Still others go all the way and give it a tricky title such as "The Hotpoint Book of Knowledge," or "The Globe More-Sales Manual." One reason some companies don't stamp "Sales Manual" on the cover is that in case it is misplaced or left on a counter, it will not excite curiosity. Sales managers have a dread of competitors learning too much about how they sell a product.

Quizzes for Manual Users

The story has often been told of the sales manager who slipped a crisp $1 bill between certain pages of a newly issued manual, and then at the next sales meeting asked those who had found the dollar bill to hold up their hands. Those who didn't felt rather foolish. They were requested to go home, find the dollar, and mail it back. Since they hadn't read the manual, they couldn't keep the dollar bill.

An old practice is to hold impromptu examinations of salesman. One sales manager listed 100 questions, the answers to which any salesman who had really studied his manual would know. Then he rigged up a big pinwheel on the platform at a sales meeting, and had one man after another come up to the platform and spin the wheel. It stopped at a number. The number corresponded to the number of one of the 100 questions listed on a sheet of paper. The salesman was then required to face the audience and answer the question. The men were quite keen about it, even the ones who got stumped and had to do some silly thing such as taking everything out of their pockets and placing it all on the table.

Some sales managers prefer to conduct quizzes by mail. If that is done, it is important that the letter accompanying the questionnaire explain the value of the examination. Make the man feel that you are doing it to help him make more money. Here are a few of the questions used by the Victor Adding Machine Company for this purpose:

(ILLUSTRATION PAGE 429.) *Sample pages from a former manual for Easy washing machines which does a good job of getting over some facts about sales jobs, and what a sales manager expects of a salesman. The thumbnail illustrations "pep" up the page and invite reading.*

1. After reading Section One of the Sales Manual, what point or points impress you the most from the standpoint of your sales practice? Tell why.

2. What personal qualifications seemed most important to you from the standpoint of your past selling experience?

3. As a result of your study of this section and your self-rating analysis, are you planning on any special effort to increase your sales effectuality? If so, what?

Some concerns find the plan of charging for the manual effective in making salesmen appreciate its value. Others hold "round robin" meetings at which the salesmen quiz each other about the contents of sales manuals. This plan is employed by the Procter & Gamble Company which ensures full use of manuals by the following methods:

1. In the first place, the manual is used as the basis for each salesman's training which consists, in most cases, of 3 weeks of special instruction on the job by a trained sales instructor. There is a lapse of from 6 weeks to 2 or 3 months between each of these 3-week periods of training.

2. In addition, quizzes are given following assignments made the salesmen covering the manual. These quizzes check the knowledge gained.

3. Each manual has a thorough index, which makes it very convenient for reference purposes after the initial training period is completed.

4. If salesmen ask their supervisors or the office for information which they can find in their sales manual, they are referred to it for answer.

5. Continuous training with reading assignments.

From the foregoing it may be concluded that successful sales manuals will:

1. Leave out a lot of the dull material designed to tell salesmen about the wonderful company they are working for, and what a privilege it is to be associated with such a fine organization. A few well-placed pictures will do that job without putting the reader to sleep.

2. Include more pictures, charts, boxes, and "flash" material, so that the salesman who runs can read. Sales managers have quit kidding themselves about salesmen taking time out to read page upon page of small print. If they do read it, they don't remember it.

3. Boil down the "how to do this and how to do that" type of materials to a few pithy paragraphs. Attempting to make salesmen sell the way you sell is hopeless and unwise.

4. Include fewer generalities and more concrete examples; less sermonizing and more suggesting; less talking down to the salesman, more talking with him. Most salesmen are eager to know how other salesmen meet common problems, but they are just a bit fed up on being told what to do by somebody in whom they may not have too much confidence.

5. Above all, if it is to earn its keep, be designed for use. That means material must be presented and arranged so that a salesman can put his finger on it when needed. If he has to dig the facts out of a hundred pages of small type, he won't.

Because of the number of government regulations which will affect a salesman's relations with his customers, the successful manual will provide a salesman with a digest of such information as well as with the policies of the company, in a form he can use as well as read. They will have to be treated so that the salesman can lay the page down before the customer and show him, "by cracky," that there it is, black on white. Most company policies, and especially those that are not too rigidly followed, can be boiled down to one sentence instead of taking a page or more to explain. They should be set off with sideheads for quick reference, and, if possible, a cross index should be included.

Manuals for Managers

In large operations, such as selling house to house through commission salesmen, the company concentrates on training the trainers, and leaves it pretty much up to the trainer or district manager as the case may be, to impart the information to the salesmen in his unit. Manuals for managers tend to become bulky and long-winded. There are so many things that somebody thinks should go in, and so few things anyone will agree could be left out. But experience proves that best results are obtained when the manual is condensed and the salient points presented with almost telegraphic brevity. The Hoover Company, making suction sweepers for sale direct to housewives, came up with a manual of 96 pages. It was judged to be too long to ensure reading and maximum use, so it was cut to 11 pages. W. W. Powell, Hoover's director of sales education, writing in *Sales Management,* said:

> Our 8-page booklet titled *Supervision on the Job* is an example, too. It is $3\frac{1}{4}$ by $4\frac{1}{4}$ inches and fits into most any pocket or billfold. Thus, a district manager need not be without a handy reference for nearly any problem he is likely to meet on the job.
>
> Page 2, for instance, has 10 short rules for field training, such as: "In the first half of initial field training do about two-thirds of the work; in later training, have salesmen do two-thirds."
>
> The next page lists five major steps in training and ends with this statement: "If the salesman hasn't learned, the supervisor hasn't taught." The next two pages deal with curb conferences and curb conference procedure, with such simple rules as "The curb conference is an explanatory or corrective conference held by the supervisor with an individual salesman":
>
> 1. It should cover only one idea or related ideas.
>
> 2. It should be held immediately before or after performance of an activity.
>
> The manual on training salesmen starts out with this remark: "You've been in this business long enough to know that nobody knows all the answers on training." This places the author and the reader on the same level and

prepares the reader to absorb a concise group of training ideas. These ideas are condensed into 20 pages. They are based on Hoover experience, the experience of teachers in the Armed Forces, etc.

There are no long, involved sentences. Instead, there are sections such as this:

> There are three things that make a salesman tick: (1) His attitude; (2) his knowledge; (3) his work habits.
>
> A good job of training covers each of these points.
>
> Again, whole books have been written on the various steps in training.
>
> But we have set them off as follows: (1) Prepare, (2) tell, (3) show, (4) have them do it, (5) check.

Again and again we highlight those five steps. Our meeting guides, sales schools, and much of our sound-slidefilm material is designed to stress these points and to teach district managers how to put them to work for them.

Johnson & Johnson Manuals

The finest standards and concepts, both graphically and in content, are embodied in a series of sales manuals produced by Johnson & Johnson, New Brunswick, N. J., based on continuous research over a period of many years.

Volume 1 in the current series is dedicated to the modernization of pharmacy management with emphasis on the principles of selling —advertising, sales promotion and personal salesmanship. Its thorough analysis of retail sales management is indicated by its table of contents, which includes the following subjects:

SECTION A—ADVERTISING & SALES PROMOTION

SECTION B—PERSONAL SALESMANSHIP

Another volume in the Johnson & Johnson series of manuals covers the vast field of supermarkets, most if not all of which have Health & Beauty Aids Departments. It begins with a letter from President D. R. Clare, which reads:

A NEW OPPORTUNITY FOR MANAGEMENT

The Health & Beauty Aids Department yields more net profit than produce, meat, dairy or packaged goods; and, consequently, has become a major contributor to the financial well-being of most supermarkets.

For this reason, it has become increasingly competitive, and requires the same kind of management attention as the Food Departments.

This manual outlines an approach to the strategy, management and procedures necessary to "work" the HBA department with the same professionalism that you routinely give other departments.

While it attempts to cover the major factors influencing HBA Department performance, this manual does not pretend to include all of the answers. Rather, it seeks only to summarize 16 years of research among the leading firms in the industry.

Strictly objective, it contains no brand names . . . no untested opinions. However, it does include practical, store-tested ideas for the HBA Department Manager who is the keystone to successful implementation of management's objectives.

D. R. Clare

In this manual, the subjects discussed are:

The Mini-Manual intended especially for department managers is a smaller-size 24-page booklet neatly contained in the pocket of the inside back cover.

The third manual, "Service Merchandising of Health & Beauty Aids," covers the role of the retail specialist; how he functions as a management aid; and discusses operational, merchandising and promotional factors which build sales and profits.

From a graphic arts standpoint, all three volumes are superbly reproduced. The covers are in simulated wood-grain stock, with the titles in gold. The text is printed in brown, with blue headings and sub-headings. The typography, layout and use of color and white space reflect the highest standards of graphic design and production. In addition to their highly informative values, the booklets are pleasantly easy to read.

Question Box Method of Compiling Manual

In order to overcome the skepticism of salesmen toward sales manuals which emanate from swivel chair executives, some companies let the salesmen write their own sales manual. This applies to dealer manuals as well as those issued for use in the field.

First, outline the subjects which the manual is to cover, and then assign certain subjects to those members of the organization best qualified by experience to handle that subject. For example, determine the 20 most commonly encountered objections, then give one objection to each of 20 salesmen and have each one tell how he

CHECKLISTS FOR FOLLOW UP EVALUATION

Many crucial operating standards defy expression in the kinds of figures which a Profit Performance Control Form presents. That form serves the same purpose as a medical doctor's stethoscope, disclosing some of the basic indicators of ill health in the operation.

The factors which hold together a successful HBA department include scores of other considerations which can be checked by observation only. The following check lists have proved extremely valuable in upgrading a department's performance.

RETAIL OPERATIONS CHECKLIST —
Management

1. Has the HBA Department responsibility been assigned to a specific individual as his (or her) primary duty?

2. Has the HBA Department manager been oriented concerning the vital importance of the job to store profits?

3. Has the HBA Department manager completed a comprehensive training program in both maintenance and merchandising aspects of the job?

4. Has an alternate, or assistant, to the HBA Department manager been designated, so that HBA is not neglected when the manager is ill or vacationing, and has this back-up person been given the same training?

5. Is the HBA Profit Performance Control Program being followed each period?

RETAIL OPERATIONS CHECKLIST —
Facilities

1. Is the HBA department located in one of the highest traffic areas of the store, and not segregated in an alcove frequented by only a few customers?

2. Is the HBA department well identified with a striking departmental sign or banner?

3. Are there at least 150 footcandles of lighting in the HBA area supported by spotlights for feature displays?

4. Does your HBA department have at least 40 linear floor feet based on a weekly store-wide volume of $50,000?

5. Has shelving been made adjustable and are shelf section adjustments made to ensure that the cubic area is fully utilized at all times?

6. Do prominent identification signs, placards or murals make each product category stand out?

7. Are all display areas within easy reach for the customers?

8. Have portable display units been provided displays to feature HBA items in other departments?

9. Does the HBA department manager have a locked drawer in the backroom, or an assigned area in the store office where departmental records and order forms can be stored safely?

10. Is the HBA department under the close surveillance of the HBA department manager or other store personnel to minimize pilferage?

Throughout the series of Johnson & Johnson manuals, the layout and typography are outstanding as shown by this page, without illustrations, from the manual on the Health & Beauty Aids Department, specially written and produced for supermarket managers.

answers that objection. Or if time permits, send one objection a week and ask salesmen to tell you how they overcome it in their sales practice.

CHAPTER XV	TRAINING FOR ALL EMPLOYEES

The "Working Hours" Method

Put teamwork in your training . . . The best example of teamwork is carried out by your own staff to whom you should assign the major responsibility for on-the-job training of your new employee. If they all share in orientating your new man on store operations and selling policies, they also benefit. Being forced to review the techniques they have learned to do automatically often alerts them to new ideas and better performance.

Begin by selling your good salespeople the job of helping new employees learn these basics of successful salesmanship.

1. Merchandise "know how" . . . the importance of knowing merchandise features . . . and knowing the reasons why brand name integrity breaks down sales resistance.

2. Sales "know how" . . . knowing how to approach customers . . . how to hold interest . . . how to sell product benefits . . . and how to suggest sales for that extra profit that pays the salesman's way.

3. Merchandise display . . . the "show-how" of making each product display a silent salesman . . . eye-catching set-ups that stop traffic on the street and invite shopping.

4. Store systems . . . cash register "know-how" — simple money safeguards such as leaving a big bill out of the register until change-making is complete . . . check cashing precautions . . . maintenance procedures . . . security techniques . . . returned goods policies

5. Housekeeping . . . keeping the store neat . . . cleaning, rotating and protecting the merchandise . . . how to open and close the pharmacy . . . protection of utilities and appliances . . . illumination of displays . . . operating the heating and cooling system.

6. Customer good will . . . handling complaints . . . procedures for maintaining professional image and friendly atmosphere . . . doctor detailing . . . featuring new products . . . special customer services, i.e., gift wrapping, credit extension, emergency deliveries, etc. . . . emphasize the fact that the satisfied customer will be the regular customer.

The "After Hours" Meeting

It is a fact that taking the boredom out of your training meetings is your biggest selling job. So prepare your meetings carefully. Encourage your salespeople to demonstrate their particular sales skills or knowledge of particular lines. Make it the sort of informal discussion meeting that will encourage your new salesmen to participate.

When possible, concentrate on one point. Some of the subjects you might cover are: (1) How to approach a customer (2) Basic counter selling techniques (3) How to demonstrate specialty items (4) Counter displays and their rotation (5) How to build store promotions which tie in with national advertising campaigns.

When you run out of ideas . . . call on your major suppliers to help you! They can best serve you by adapting the basic selling principles you teach to the particular merchandise they supply.

A sample page from the Johnson & Johnson Sales Management Manual: two colors, line illustrations, good layout and typography combine to produce a pleasant, easy-to-read book.

SUBJECTS TO BE COVERED IN A COMPANY SALES MANUAL

1. Advertising
2. Aftersale
3. Allowances
4. Application of salesmanship
5. Applications (uses) of product
6. Approach
7. Basic knowledge for selling product
8. Catalogs
9. Claims
10. Classes of trade
11. Close
12. Company, History of
13. Company outlook
14. Company policies
15. Conclusions
16. Correspondence with home office
17. Credit policies
18. Customers' buying motives
19. Dealer helps
20. Demonstrating
21. Design features
22. Dictionary of trade terms
23. Direct-mail literature
24. Discounts
25. Executives
26. Expenses
27. Field organization setup
28. Fundamentals of successful salesmanship
29. General instructions to sales personnel
30. General sales meetings
31. Helps for salesmen
32. Home office, Relations with
33. House literature
34. Information and duties of salesmen
35. Introduction
36. Invoicing
37. Lost orders
38. Management-employee relations
39. Manufacturing methods
40. Market study by graphic analysis
41. Merchandising
42. Miscellaneous selling suggestions
43. Missionary work
44. Objections, Handling
45. Organization chart
46. Organization, training, and supervision
47. Outselling competition
48. Personal development and personality
49. Planning and controlling work
50. Preapproach information
51. Presentation
52. Price lists
53. Product, Advantages of
54. Product, Classification of
55. Product, Companies using
56. Product, History of
57. Product, How to sell
58. Product, Market for
59. Product, Use of
60. Prospecting
61. Purpose of the manual
62. Quotations
63. Remittances, reports, and commissions
64. Report forms
65. Returned goods
66. Rural selling
67. Sales equipment
68. Sales techniques
69. Sales training, Field
70. Sales training, General
71. Sales training, Need and benefits of
72. Sales points
73. Sales policies
74. Self-analysis and self-improvement
75. Service and repair parts
76. Services offered
77. Shipping
78. Spoilage
79. Technical information
80. Territory analysis
81. Testimonal letters
82. Trade-ins
83. Typical installations
84. Visual selling

Chapter 14

PORTFOLIOS AND VISUALIZERS

THE production of the formal business presentation of the product, its features and customer benefits, whether for industrial or retail purposes, usually takes graphic arts forms, with printed or hand-lettered pages plus photographs, line drawing or graphs. Often, the pages are over-sized, hence the term "portfolio;" or spiral-bound into "flip charts."

With the development of audio-visual equipment, sound and motion have been added through the use of 16 or 35mm films, film strips and records, giving product presentations and training programs greater impact. Today's sophisticated audio-visual equipment combines picture and sound in a single portable case and may be used under ordinary lighting conditions in store or office.

The printed portfolio, however, still occupies top position. First of all, it is aided by the personality and voice of the salesman who reads and ad-libs from the material. The presentation may be made at any desired pace; previous pages may be easily referred to and each subject or section may be discussed before proceding to the next. Too, it is less expensive than sound-on-film and pages or whole sections may be replaced or added if necessary. Requiring no mechanical equipment, it can be used anywhere at any time.

Another growing use for sales portfolios is on the dealer's counter. Some of these are quite elaborate. Dealers like them because they save them from having to carry a large stock. They also help them to do a better selling job for a line of products which clerks may not know too much about. They are usually large enough to be impressive and to permit colorful illustrations which do the product full credit. Yet they should not be too large. If they take up too much counter room, the dealer is likely to store them behind the counter, and "out of sight is out of mind." Some companies furnish dealers with a low stand for holding their counter portfolios, which induces the dealer to make a place on his counter for the portfolio and to keep it there. Portfolios for use on the dealer's counter should depend upon illustrations more than text, and such text as is used should be set in large type so that it can be read by customers with poor eyesight. It is usual to bind this type of promotional piece with plastic ring-backs. This permits the portfolio to lie flat on the counter, and facilitates its use by the dealer or his clerk.

Dramatizing the Sales Points

When the product is sold to executives, it is now common practice to supply salesmen with "visualizers" they can use in developing their presentation. These visualizers are of several types. Some of them are quite elaborate and represent a considerable investment. Others are merely a sheaf of printed pages which the salesman carries in his brief case, and hands to the prospect one at a time as he talks. One effective presentation of this sort was a pack of 5- by 8-inch cards, with each card serially numbered. As the salesman talked, he stood the cards, one at a time, against any object on the prospect's desk. The advantage of the loose cards was that they permitted the salesman to change their order according to the nature of the presentation he intended to make. The most popular type of visualizer is the 8½- by 11-inch ring binder, in which the presentation material is organized under quick reference tabs. This type of visualizer is recommended when the salesman must demonstrate or drive home certain points in his sales presentation and may not always desire to page through the entire book.

When salesmen sell from samples, if the line is long, portfolios containing full colored illustrations of the various numbers in the line are often used instead of actual samples. In selling shoes, for example, the salesman carries a few numbers to show the quality of workmanship, and depends upon colored illustrations to show the complete line. This saves the salesman a lot of work and the company a lot of money. Usually the portfolio is built up from photographic prints, tinted to show coloring. The photographs are arranged, loose-leaf fashion, in a portfolio type binder which the salesman can use over and over, simply by rearranging the contents.

Planning the Portfolio

A promotional portfolio, like any good sales tool, should have a plan behind it, and not comprise a lot of unrelated sheets or illustra-tions as is so often the case. The aim should be to help the prospect solve a specific problem. The desire to sell should be subordinated to a desire to serve. A portfolio should be so organized that it will support a salesman, and not attempt to do the entire selling job for him. An exception to this is the "silent salesman" type of portfolio used to ship from one customer to another to get direct orders.

An examination of a number of sales portfolios, used to support the salesman in making a presentation, shows the following general arrangement:

1. Pointing up the problem to get attention.
2. Dramatizing needs to focus interest.
3. Describing the product to win confidence.
4. Proving values to create desire.
5. Showing profits (or savings) to get action.

One of a new breed of visual sales tools, produced by Taylor-Merchant, that are versatile, lightweight, flat-folding, and employing real-as-life color strips to get the sales message across and leave a lasting visual impression. Some of the ways these viewer kits may be used are to introduce new products; demonstrate nonportable products; preview new ad campaigns; preview TV commercials; show facilities and services; "kick-off" new marketing programs.

However, not all sales portfolios are designed to serve as a track for a sales talk. For companies selling a "horizontal" service or a product used in different ways by different classifications of businesses (for example, visual card index systems), the sales portfolio is arranged according to specific applications. This arrangement permits a salesman calling on a prospect in, say, the publishing business to turn to the section of his presentation book covering the application of his product to a publisher's problems. Similarly, insurance companies usually arrange portfolios according to the problem the agent is discussing with his prospect.

An East Coast life insurance company, for example, keys each page or exhibit in its visual demonstration portfolio, and furnishes agents with a list of pages covering: (1) Business insurance, (2) endowment insurance, (3) estate preservation insurance, (4) family protection, (5) monthly income insurance, (6) child education insurance, etc. The salesman puts markers in the pages he wishes to use, according to the type of insurance of interest to the prospect upon whom he intends to call.

In general, however, arrange visual pages so as to guide the salesmen through the psychological steps to the order. Thus the first few pages, or introduction, focus attention on the prospect's problem. This approach assures prospect interest and attention. If the first several pages are devoted to glorifying the product and the house, the task of getting the prospect's favorable consideration is more difficult. He is interested in his problem and not yours. Some sales presentations lead off with a picture of the factory and the various departments in which the products are made. Such treatment may impress the owner of the business, but it leaves the prospect cold.

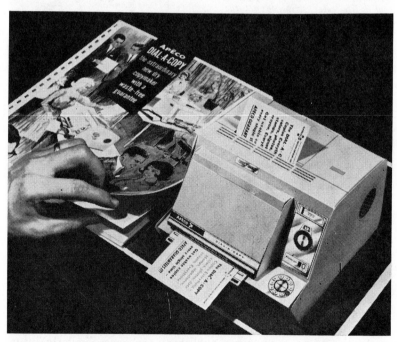

A miniature cardboard replica of the Apeco "Dial-A-Copy" machine is a vital part of a sales presentation portfolio kit used for first calls. The pop-up model has proved to be a valuable asset for the salesman.

Paint companies have long recognized that color chip display units provide the best visual aid a retailer can have. This counter display is used by The Lowe Brothers Co.

Courtesy Point-of-Purchase Advertising Institute, Inc.

It is hard to understand why sales managers who would not think of permitting their salesmen to talk about how their products are made, in opening a sales solicitation, sanction that treatment in a portfolio which supposedly their salesmen will use as a guide in telling their sales story.

Presenting proof is, perhaps, the most important job a sales portfolio or visualizer has to do. It is the step in the sale which stops most salesmen. They need something more than words to turn the interest and desire they have created into conviction and action. The proof given in the presentation book supplements the verbal statements made by the salesman, and removes any lingering doubt from the prospect's mind. So long as those doubts remain, the chances for a close are thin indeed. The proof may take the form of photographs showing a piece of equipment at work; it may consist of certified statements from experts who have tested it in their laboratories; it may be reports from satisfied customers; it may be a sheaf of repeat orders from companies known in the industry to be smart buyers; or it may be copies of *unsolicited* testimonial letters. The nature of the proof will naturally vary according to the nature of the selling, but the value of the proof in completing the sale, no matter what the product might be, depends upon presenting it clearly and dramatically. For example, if testimonials are used, portions of the letter bearing a certain sales point should be set off by the use of colored marks, so the prospect will not let his mind wander while the salesman reads through long-winded letters. Most salesmen read poorly. Another way to prove acceptance for a product or a service is to bind into the portfolio a sheaf of photostatic copies of orders received from well-known companies, arranged by industries.

A Pop-Up Visualizer

A very interesting and effective visualizer has been developed by Apeco Corporation, Evanston, Illinois, for its Systematic Copier. A horizontal folder, 11¾- by 17 inches in size, indicating the large-size applications of the Copier, opens up with dramatic effect when a miniature cardboard replica of the model automatically springs into four-dimensional shape with only the aid of two rubber bands. The pop-up shows three sides of the copier and the top, which folds over into place when not in use. At the bottom of the folder are six "reasons why" the copier is beneficial to the customer. The visualizer is a real attention-getter, provides a four-dimension miniature of the copier and summarizes the consumer benefits flowing from its use.

ORGANIZING THE MATERIAL

The well-organized portfolio will likewise help the salesman when it is time to close by summing up the reasons for buying in a simple chart, which the salesman can use to artfully bring his presentation to a close. If the technique is to close by giving the buyer a choice, then that choice would be made the closing feature of the book. Too many sales portfolios, supposed to carry the prospect through all the five stages of making the sale, fall down in handling the close. They leave the prospect hanging in mid-air. They should bring him back to his problem, and pave the way for the salesman to ask for the order.

The closing device used in the Coleman portfolio, previously mentioned, is a page showing, in relative size, pictures of the three sizes of Coleman heaters available. When the salesman comes to this page of his visualizer, he stops for the prospect's reaction. If he senses the prospect is pretty well sold, he tries for a close by inquiring how much hot water the prospect uses in his home. He then suggests which of the three sizes the prospect should have. Another popular closing device, used when there is a choice of colors, is a color chart toward the end of the presentation. This gives the salesman a chance to try for a trial close on color section. If he misses, he then proceeds with the remaining pages in the portfolio which are usually planned to lead up to a second, and even a third, trial close.

Some of the most effective portfolios used in selling magazine subscriptions close with a summarization followed by a pocket with an exposed order blank. When the salesman has finished turning each page of his portfolio, he stops talking when he comes to the order blank. If he has made his sale, the chances are nine to one that the suggestion will work, and the prospect will ask some question which indicates to the salesman that he is ready to sign on the dotted line. On the other hand, if the salesman has not sold his prospect, the suggestion of the order blank will usually cause him to mention some reason why he is not ready to buy, so that the salesman can proceed to his second closing tactic.

The "Canned" Sales Talk

How far to go in providing those who use visualizers with a "word-by-word" selling talk for each page is a moot question. Some sales managers, with sound reason, insist that it is better to list the points to be covered before turning the page, and let the salesman use his own words to drive the points home. These sales managers contend that when you try to put *your* words into the salesman's mouth, they rob him of *his* individuality and cramp his style. Another group of sales managers hold that a sales talk should be spelled out, word for word. They contend that the average salesman will adapt a canned sales talk to suit his method of selling, so you are better off to give it to him word for word. Doing it that way, they insist, reduces the risk of important points being underemphasized, and relatively unimportant points being overemphasized.

Thus, a number of the larger life insurance companies provide salesmen with a training manual to help them use the company's visualizer to best advantage, reproducing each page of the visualizer, and on a facing page (in the manual, not in the visualizer itself) printing the recommended talk to be used with that particular chart. For example, in selling life insurance it is important to dramatize the relatively few people who are financially independent when they reach age 65. To do this the New England Mutual used the chart on page 446 to get the point across to the prospective applicant. The following sales talk was suggested.

When You Reach Age 65 Don't Be In The Majority

STATISTICS from *Fortune* magazine show that 91 people out of 100 who reach 65 are dependent upon charity or are still working for a living. Only 9 out of 100 have been able to retire on their savings.

When you reach age 65 you'll want to be one of the 9 who are financially able to retire. To assure your place with this successful minority invest in a New England Mutual Retirement Income Plan.

39 are living on charity

34 are still working for a living

18 are living on public or private pensions

9 are financially successful

A good portfolio "spells out" each point in a way that even a 12-year-old can understand. This chart dramatizes the well-publicized fact used by life underwriters that at age 65, 91 out of every 100 people are dependent upon others.

A survey by *Fortune* magazine helps to back up Mr. Kennedy's statement showing that 91 out of 100 people who reach age 65 are dependent upon charity or are still working for a living. Only 9 out of 100 have been able to retire on their savings.

I asume, Mr. Prospect, that like most men you're thinking of retirement some day. Isn't that so?

And I also assume, Mr. Prospect, that when you reach age 65 you'll want to be one of the 9 who are financially able to retire. Isn't that so, Mr. Prospect?

About how much money would you think it would be necessary for you to have to retire comfortably at age 65?

As Mr. Kennedy has said, a young man in business today can hardly meet living costs, much less accumulate any substantial amount of capital. Do you realize, Mr. Prospect, that for every $100 a month income you wish at retirement you'll have to have $48,000 invested at $2\frac{1}{2}\%$ interest? That's probably more than you will be able to save in the next 30 years, isn't it?

If I could show you a plan which would provide this $100 a month at about one-third of $48,000 you'd be interested, wouldn't you? Let me show you what I mean.

Types of Portfolios

The philosophy of the sales portfolio or visual presentation is that it provides the salesman with a track upon which to run. It is not intended (except in the case of "silent salesmen") to do the talking for the salesman. It is here most sales presentations, whether they are in portfolio or some other form, fall down. The most effective presentations are those which "high spot" a sales talk, but carefully avoid endeavoring to make a messenger boy out of the salesman. An examination of more than a hundred sales portfolios furnished salesmen as part of their sales kits showed the following types most popular:

THE ZIPPER CASE PORTFOLIO:

At present this is the most popular method for the visual presentation of a sales story. The secret of building this type of portfolio is to organize the material under finding tabs, so that salesmen can turn to needed data quickly without fumbling. Several of the portfolios sent to us carried cellophane envelopes, punched to fit the rings on the portfolio, in which original testimonial letters are placed (back to back so two letters were exposed in each envelope). Photographs mounted on muslin, punched for the rings, with printed data on the back, were also widely used.

EASEL TYPE PORTFOLIO:

This had a "run" several years ago and was very widely used by salesmen calling on customers, and some of them are still used in that way. However, salesmen object to carrying this type of equipment and since the development of the zipper case, its use has declined. It is still favored as a counter demonstration portfolio by clerks. Most of the portfolios of this type which we examined were too slow in starting. Too large a proportion of the pages was given over to "the build up." Our recommendations are that in developing these portfolios, especially for counter use, the presentation be speeded up. Another criticism is that most of those examined did not make the best use of color. In order to hold interest and attention there should be plenty of "flash" and color. One-color presentation charts and pages are too drab to be effective.

SPIRAL BOUND PORTFOLIO:

Several different types of these were submitted. They were used principally for counter books and supplementary pieces for salesmen to use with customers. They were of two kinds: The wire spiral binding, and the flat celluloid, plastic binding. Some were very well done. Effective results are obtained when the leaves of these portfolios are of paper heavy enough to turn easily in the book. Large, striking photographs predominated in most of the portfolios we examined, the idea being to get the prospect or customer into the picture. In order to keep this type of equipment from becoming too quickly soiled, the pages may be "laminated" with cellophane or treated with a varnish preparation on the press. This treatment gives luster and depth of color to the illustrations, as well as prolonging the life of the portfolio.

TIMETABLE FOLDER PORTFOLIO:

A type of presentation book popular with companies which require a variety of presentations for different types of buyers. These are usually six and eight folds, with reinforced joints, so they may be carried conveniently in a brief case and opened up quickly and placed before a buyer. They are the least expensive of the various portfolios submitted. Pocket-size portfolios are used by book salesmen and others who require equipment which can be carried out of sight. These are usually made up in the timetable folder form.

SALESMASTER PORTFOLIO:

This kind differs from the conventional zipper type in having a series of Kardex pockets attached to one or both covers. These pockets hold cards which carry a connected story of the principal sales points arranged in logical fashion. These cards may be photographs, line drawings, or a combination of either with limited amounts of texts. Captions on the visible margin are arranged to flash the major sales points made on the body of the cards in sequence. Salesmen weave their story around the text or illustration on the cards. These portfolios are of lightweight and compact construction. There is space for testimonials, letters, order blanks, and other material under a concealed flap.

Regardless of which type of portfolio is used, however, it is most important that it be developed and laid out so that it will follow the presentation as used by a salesman in actual practice, rather than to endeavor to make a salesman's talk conform to a more or less theoretical arrangement.

"SELLING" THE PORTFOLIO TO THE SALES FORCE

As in the case of the sales manual, a presentation portfolio's value to the company depends upon getting it used. Some salesmen, unless they are "sold" on its worth, want no part of what they consider a "canned" presentation. They insist that it cramps their style, and that they can do a better job just talking informally with the prospect about his problems. They think pulling a portfolio on a prospect is a sure way to "freeze him." This view is understandable since salesmen are inclined to overrate their ability to present a sales proposition. While some salesmen can do a better job without "props," experience has shown a sales organization as a whole will produce more business with good tools than it will without them. And in sales management we must deal with averages and not isolated cases.

To convince these skeptical salesmen that they can get more business with a presentation portfolio than they can without one, the best plan is to select a "guinea pig" territory, and if time permits, give a hand-tooled copy to some salesman who can be depended upon to make the very best use of it. It should be an average territory and the salesman should be neither in the top nor the bottom earnings' bracket. At the end of a 2-month test period, assuming results have been good (and it is up to the sales executive to make sure they are good), call the salesmen in and let the "test pilot" tell his story. Point out, as dramatically as possible, how the use of the visualizer helped the salesman to produce more closed business, saved call-backs and lost time, and made a definite contribution to his earnings. But don't let it die there. After the men return to their territories, a barrage of "experiences" should be kept going to them. Once the men have formed the habit of carrying their visualizers with them, and using them at every opportunity, they will consider them standard equipment in the same category with their order books or fountain pens.

If it is not practical to call the salesmen together to "sell" them on using the new visualizer, you will have to depend upon a letter, and it had better be good. Here is a letter that was used by the Squibb organization to promote the use of a portfolio designed to help Squibb salesmen show retail druggists how they could have more time for fishing:

Gentlemen:

"More Time for Fishing"--There are 42 pages in that portfolio--big fellow, isn't it? You can't catch Mr. Druggist on the fly between the fountain and the prescription department and expect to tell him this story.

No Sir. You have a real PLAN that is going to save the druggist many hours, create more sales, and provide him with a PROTECTED PROFIT. A profit that averages 44.1 per cent on Home Necessities and Merchandising Vitamin products when bought under the terms of this PLAN, not including Squibb Plan Promotional Earnings.

The first thing to do is to get a half hour alone with the dealer WHERE YOU WON'T BE DISTURBED. It is almost better not to open the book at all if you cannot get his uninterrupted attention.

Swell--you have the druggist alone--you are ready to start. We are not going to try to tell your story for you. But we have worked quite a bit with the portfolio and perhaps there are a few suggestions we might make that will improve your own presentation and help the continuity. So let's take it page by page--where the page doesn't require any additional comments, we have not made any.

Practice telling your story perfectly until you get it smoothed out so that it is presented as a COMPREHENSIVE PLAN which is flexible and adaptable to the merchandising requirements of your dealers.

Got your portfolio in front of you? Turn to Page 1. You are sitting down with the druggist now. Let's go:

PAGE 1--"'More Time for Fishing'--Bill, how would you like to get away from the store more often--go fishing, relax and enjoy yourself? I believe I know the answer to that question, and it's YES. To let you do this, we have developed a plan which will help you maintain sales and profits and, at the same time, provide you with more time for yourself, and perhaps to go fishing if you like that great sport."

PAGE 2--"All signs point to some big changes in the drug business in the years just ahead. For example, several of my accounts are enlarging their prescription departments, and when I attended our Summer Sales Conference, I saw a couple of beautifully arranged stores. What impressed me was the large floor space, indirect lighting, open display and the new arrangement of windows which display the whole store.

"Yes, things are going to be different.

"Of course, I know that you are anxious to keep your volume at the 19-- level which averaged $25.89 per capita for the country. You have to keep it high if you are to meet increasing costs of operation. That's another reason for our PLAN since it provides you with an over-all profit of 44.1 per cent on Squibb over-the-counter products. Besides that it gives you more time for yourself and more time for servicing your doctors and customers. When you select profitable products to sell, you are bound to make more money."

PAGE 3--"As I said before, this is a complete PLAN and we can map your whole Fall Sales program from now right through December. When we get through, you'll know WHAT you're going to do and WHEN you are going to do it. I won't be bothering you every other week with this or that--you are going to save lots of time and things will run more smoothly because we will both know what we are doing. You and I will be partners in this department of your store. We will have a plan that works.

"I want to show you this plan in broad detail; show you the things we are prepared to do to help you sell more merchandise more profitably. I want to go through this fairly fast so you will get the complete picture. We can come back and dig into details later. Of course, I'll discuss any part you want as we go along, but let's look at it all first. Among other things this plan includes:"

Why Sales Portfolios Go Wrong

Richard Borden, of Borden and Busse fame, checked 1,000 sales executives attending a conference of the American Management Association to determine why the money annually invested in sales "props" and "presentation portfolios" sometimes produced such poor results. The audience was checked first of all from the salesman's point of view. Those at the meeting were asked to consider themselves salesmen, rather than sales executives, and to check a list of objections gathered from salesmen who had been furnished sales "props" by the company. Then they were asked to consider themselves prospects for some product, and think back over the sales presentations to which they had been exposed, and answer another set of objections from the point of view of the prospect.

The result of the autopsy was as follows, the most common objections being listed with those having the highest number of mentions at the top of the list, and those with the least mentions at the bottom. It will be noted that the most mentioned objection from the salesman's standpoint was "bulk and weight."

FROM THE SALESMAN'S POINT OF VIEW:

1. It was too long and bulky. The prospect took one look at its "Gone-with-the-Wind" dimensions, and then started to figure out how he could cut me off before I got too far into it.

2. Each page of the presentation contained too much copy, which made for confusion. The printed page talked while I talked, so the prospect didn't really get either message.

3. The presentation was an advertising man's dream and gave everything except the brass-tacks dope which the customer wanted.

4. The presentation was difficult to manipulate physically, so there were awkward stages in setting up and turning its pages.

5. The damn presentation kept falling down.

6. The presentation was so complete in itself that it made me feel like an unnecessary dope—or a Western Union messenger boy.

7. The presentation was so bulky it made me feel like a safari every time I went out with it. A week after I got it, I dropped it behind the piano.

8. The presentation didn't talk my customer's language, confining itself to bragging about how good my company was, and what smart guys we had in our factory.

9. The presentation was so circusy in its whole makeup that it made me feel self-conscious and insincere.

10. The presentation didn't climax in material which would be helpful in closing the sale and getting the signature on the dotted line.

11. The presentation was foisted on me without any effort to train me in its use or sell me on its value.

12. The presentation was too dull, statistical, and "catalogy." It merely made my prospect say "Ho hum!"

1. The presentation was obviously prepared for consumption by a low-grade moron. This is a cat. The cat is being chased by a dog. ABC kindergarten stuff that insulted my intelligence.

2. The salesman read off all the captions on each presentation page, much to my disgust. After all, I can read.

3. The salesman wasn't familiar with the presentation, and displayed his unfamiliarity.

4. The presentation was too long-winded, going into unnecessary detail about company history and manufacturing procedure.

5. The sales presentation overclaimed and underproved. It assumed that because a statement was in print, I ought to believe it without further evidence.

6. The sales presentation alarmed me by its length and bulk.

7. The presentation was poorly sequenced and loosely organized. It served up its points in the form of goulash instead of a course dinner.

8. The salesman irritated me by the liberties he took with my desk, setting up some easel contraption.

9. The salesman turned to the next page before I could read what was on the first one.

10. The sales presentation had too much copy on each page, much of it printed in type so fine I couldn't read it easily.

The Instruction Sheet

Some of the best planned sales presentations go wrong because the salesmen don't know how to effectively use them. Executives experienced in developing visualizers and related sales tools find it is most important that those who are expected to use them are not only sold on their value as a sales aid, but *thoroughly* understand how to use them. This information is usually imparted at the time the portfolio is presented, but in addition an instruction or suggestion sheet should be enclosed so that the person who is supposed to use it can study it leisurely after leaving the meeting. The following instructions accompanied a visualizer prepared for the use of agents by Reliance Life Insurance Company of Pittsburgh:

IMPRESSIONS BY EYE, AS WELL AS BY EAR

When you use this presentation, what your prospect hears will be reinforced by what he sees. Pictures illustrating your selling story give at a glance more vivid impressions than hundreds of spoken words.

Unfortunately, insurance policies and insurance service are prosaic, sometimes a pretty dull subject to a layman; life, drama, color, and action may be added to your important message when you use a visual portfolio like this.

Particularly if you have not organized your sales presentation on analysis-survey service—the modern, proved agency approach—this graphic presentation of the subject will help you get across the most important points. Your complete analysis-survey story can be told far more briefly this way.

Visual presentation is particularly adapted for getting across a new idea—and in spite of years of talking about it within insurance, only a very small percentage of buyers have ever had the analysis-survey idea well presented to them.

Sequence of ideas is tremendously important in selling. This book makes the selling points in logical sequence, and interruptions will not throw you off the track. Remember that selling is the process of guiding a prospect's mind from something of interest to him to your interest: Rendering analysis-survey service. This book can be *your* guide in guiding him.

You can hold the attention of two or three men much more easily with a presentation like this than you could without something to hold the attention of their eyes as well as their ears.

The experience of thousands of businesses shows that a standardized presentation—not a memorized "canned" sales talk but a methodical, point-by-point selling procedure—saves time and makes more sales.

When you put this closed book in front of your prospect, *turn the pages yourself,* and keep a hand lightly on the book. Watch his eyes and turn when he's ready. Repeat the words as he reads. When you get to the "First," "Second," "Third," and "Fourth" points—the meat of the presentation—give examples of each point from your own experience, and preferably from insurance situations similar to his.

Used correctly, and properly salted with actual examples you know about, the end of this book puts you in a position to start asking the questions on one of the questionnaires in the back pocket—it leaves you right where you want to be: Getting the information necessary for an analysis-survey.

It should be remembered that sales portfolios, whether of the visual or nonvisual type, deteriorate with use. It is therefore a good plan, since the run-on cost of producing this type of sales tool, after once on the press, is not great, to print enough copies to provide each man with a replacement if and when needed. If the portfolio is of the loose-leaf type, it is possible to make changes in the material from time to time, so that when replacement copies are sent to salesmen requisitioning them, they will be up to date as well as clean. Nothing so undermines the effectiveness of a sales presentation as a portfolio that is dog-eared and dirty.

In general, there are three broad classifications of portfolios and presentations, designed to do three different kinds of selling jobs:

1. *Standardized Forms,* which enable salesmen to give substantially the same story in the same logical sequence to many different buyers. This is the customary style of piece and its advantages and limitations are enumerated elsewhere. Usually it is big in size to give it impressiveness and to make the type readable at a distance,

and is more suitable for use before groups than before individuals. Salesmen do not mind "putting on a show" before an audience, but an "audience" of only one more often than not results in self-consciousness and a feeling of pretentiousness on the part of both the salesman and his listener. To avoid this difficulty, as well as the confusion of setting up large, complicated display pieces on a buyer's desk, it is advisable to make up presentations for showing to individuals in more modest form, preferably in such quantities that they can be left with the buyer after the showing for his later study and reference. "A small presentation for each buyer" may be a more profitable policy than "a large portfolio for each salesman," and it may not cost any more— if as much.

2. *Individualized Forms*, which are standardized to the extent of supplying an orderly framework of the basic sales story for the salesman to embellish with specific facts, figures, and exhibits relating to his prospect's individual case. This style is not ordinarily as elaborate as the regular standardized form because it is made up for leaving with the prospect rather than being part of the salesman's permanent equipment, but here again results are greater because of the individualization. And it is just as useful as a means of organizing the sales talk and visually emphasizing the important points. Addressograph and Multigraph salesmen are specially trained in the preparation of impressive-looking individualized presentations.

3. *Exhibit Forms*, which make an ideal way of showing actual physical exhibits when they are the basis of the presentation. Some compact, well-organized, impressive sales instrument is almost a necessity for properly showing collections of photographs of typical installations; different styles and models or pertinent manufacturing processes; series of advertisements, direct-mail pieces, displays or other dealer helps; actual samples of products, materials used in products, color swatches and combinations, and other tangible merchandise when it is of such size or shape that it can be put up in portfolio form. Especially when the physical objects can be suitably combined with brief text and graphic illustration to develop a coordinated sales story, are exhibit portfolios and presentations of great value.

Literature of this classification is closely related in use to the small hand projectors which some companies furnish their salesmen for showing the familiar 35mm. 2- by 2-inch slides or, as a comparatively recent development, the new full-color stereopticon slides. Printed materials, however, can be designed to lead more smoothly from one sales point to another; to employ a greater and more flexible number of attention-getters in the way of display type and lettering, cartoons, drawings, and illustrative matter of all kinds; and to build up more swiftly and dramatically to a climactic peak.

Chapter 15

MAILING LISTS

THE computer has dramatically improved efficiencies in the use of mailing lists. It has made it possible to select, classify, record, cross-reference and eliminate duplications of names and addresses. It has also greatly simplified the testing of both mailings and lists. Computer-compiled lists find their greatest application in the direct-marketing, or direct-response, field, especially in testing huge lists.

Thanks to the computer, one can specify an "Nth" name selection in testing a list. The reason for this is that most lists are maintained in zip code sequence; you might find yourself mailing to Massachusetts and Rhode Island exclusively.

Carl Bender, Vice President, List Management, Golden Fifty Pharmaceutical Company, states in "The Truth About Business Mailing Lists":

1. There's nothing magic or mysterious about names on a computer. It depends on the sources from which the names were compiled.

2. Duplications can cost from three to twenty dollars per thousand or more.

3. Business mail can be fully deliverable and still be deadwood to you.

4. If you want your mail to reach the right man, mail by job title, not by individual name. He quotes Paul Bringe, direct mail consultant, as saying: "I have seen a study which shows that of every 1,000 purchasing agents on the job today, 400 will not be on the same job a year from now."

Because the mailing list is important to the profitable operation of nearly every business, and because of these constant and continual changes in the list, there is a trend toward the simplification of mailing lists. In fact, some companies find it more profitable not to maintain any permanent mailing lists, outside of current buyers, but rent or purchase lists as needed from reliable sources, or to address directly from current directories and similar reference books. Impetus has been given to this trend by the advent of the mailing-list broker, who specializes on renting up-to-date lists of people with known buying habits, or buying preferences.

Then too, businessmen have come to depend more and more on the publishers of business and other periodicals for mailing-list service. Such lists, of necessity, are kept up to date by the publisher for his own use, and they include names of especially desirable prospective customers. For example, every year thousands of people start in business. About the first thing they do is to subscribe to a trade publication which covers the field of special interest to them. It might take a manufacturer of equipment or merchandise in that field a year or more to make contact with these newcomers were he to depend upon his own sources of information. By purchasing or renting lists as needed from publishers of business papers circulated in that field, the seller can reach these newcomers quickly and at a time when they are first coming into the market for the things he wishes to sell them.

Types of Mailing Lists

In the case of a company doing business with established customers, the mailing list is, of course, the backbone of the business. If you capitalize the profit earned on purchases by these names over the years they have been on the list, some idea as to the balance sheet value of such names may be determined. A mail-order house in Chicago, for example, found by this method that each name on its active customer list had a good-will value of $350 to the business. A new name may be worth only a dollar or so, but as money is invested in circularizing that name and building up in the mind of that person acceptance for what the company is selling, the value of the name multiplies rapidly. Mailing lists can be divided, grouped, or tabbed as follows:

1. *Customers with whom you are now doing business*—The customer's mailing list should be maintained in the sales department on card index address plates or stencils and not, as is often the case, kept only in the accounting department. It should be arranged geographically, with selector tabs or signals indicating the interests of the customer or, in the case of a company selling to a horizontal market, the customers should be tabbed according to their lines of business. Such classification permits the effective use of specialized follow-ups and enables a seller to select groups of customers for special orders.

It is a good practice to segregate the best customers into a "blue" list, identified by tabs or blue cards on the address plates; the next best customers in a "white" list with white cards; and so on. This arrangement permits closer working of the most profitable accounts and less frequent mailings to the occasional buyer. Too often it is the practice to lump all customers together, regardless of their importance, with the result that too large a proportion of the sales budget is spent on the least important customers. Experience shows that about 20% of the names on the average customers' list yield 80% of the sales. It is upon this 20%, then, that attention should be concentrated. Modern addressing equipment permits the centralization of lists, and selecting devices make it possible to pick out automatically names in any desired classification as the plates or stencils pass through the addressing machine.

Department stores make good use of their customer lists. It has long been a practice to include product leaflets or folders with statements but department stores also make special mailings to established customers. As a typical example, Lits, a Philadelphia department store, offered a stereo radio-phono-tape system in a mailing which included a four-page letter, a full-color broadside, an order card and return envelope.

2. *Customers with whom you once did business*—It is usually better to keep these names separate from the current customers' list. They should not be worked as intensively as active customers, especially when the account turnover is large and there are more names on the inactive list than on the active list.

Arrangements should be made with the accounting department to report monthly, when the statements are run off, all inactive accounts. In most businesses where loose-leaf ledgers are used, inactive ledger accounts are periodically transferred to a reserve ledger to facilitate posting. That is also a good time to transfer the address plate. When a name is transferred to the inactive customers' list, it should be dated with a rubber stamp. The list should be checked regularly, and all inactive customers more than 2 years old should be either discarded or transferred to a general prospect list.

The same method of classification and selection used for the customers' list should be followed on the inactive list. Since the mortality in a customers' list is due largely to individuals going out of business or changing their field of activity, it is important that mail returned by the post office should be watched carefully and other means taken to make sure that the former customer is still a prospect. Do not, however, put too much confidence in a salesman's recommendation that certain names on the inactive list be killed. Often accounts that a salesman thinks are dead will respond to mail treatment. Moreover, the fact that the salesman has probably stopped calling on the account makes it particularly important to keep contact.

3. *Prospects with whom you hope someday to do business*— Great strides have been made in this area. List brokers, computers and trade and consumer magazines'-services have brought lists in this category to new high levels of effectiveness. Time was when advertisers compiled lists, on pretty much of a hit or miss basis, from directories, credit rating books or classified telephone directories. Classifying, selecting, tabbing, was all done manually.

Many reputable and well-known mailing list companies offer computer-compiled, tested, zip-coded lists with *guaranteed* rates of delivery. National Business Lists, for instance, guarantees 97½% deliverability on first class mailings; 94% on third class.

Computers have turned mailing lists into valuable marketing tools. An advertisement by Advertising Distributors of America, Incorporated, reads, in part, as follows:

"AD of A's computers can store a wealth of information about each person on your list. For example, include a man's height, his wife's first name, his children's names, his birthday, his alma mater, his clothing sizes, his club affiliations, his hobbies . . . his anything!

"Then you can instantly refer to any of this information to remind him of policy renewals, seasonal sales, opportunities for his children, birthdays, anniversaries, alumni meetings . . . anything.

"It's all done with AD of A's computer lists, computer letters, automated addressing and mailing services."

Industrial Lists

List brokers and publications in the business, trade and professional fields are the chief sources for up-to-date, reliable, lists of people in these specialized markets. Some lists are classified according to the government-sponsored Standard Industrial Classification System (S.I.C.) which provides a four-digit number to identify the functions of the entire field of economic activity. This makes it possible to select and retrieve names in up to 1,000 different classifications.

Business, professional and trade magazines are an excellent source of prospect lists since their subscribers fall in the field served by each publication. Some magazines offer additional list services. *Chemical Engineering,* for instance, has developed its lists into a direct marketing program with a choice of five services: its all-paid subscriber list, a census list of plants in the chemical process industries, a list of OEM suppliers, a product-directed list and a postcard mailing service.

Write your prospects' names on this stub for your own reference	PAINT PROSPECTS Town _____ State _____ , ___		
	Date _____ _____ Agent		
	Use this Card for the Names of Property Owners whose homes actually need painting		
			INTERESTED IN
	NAME	ADDRESS	NEW HOME / Remodeling TOWN / Remodeling FARM
	The More Good Worth-While Names You Send In The Greater Your Sales Will Be		

A simple form furnished dealers to send in names of "hot" paint prospects to the Lowe sales promotion department. The dealer is asked to send in only names of property owners whose homes actually need painting. The form classifies each name according to what the prospect is going to paint, so that appropriate promotional literature may be mailed to him.

Ways in Which Lists May Be Checked

1. One manufacturer checks the ratings of all retailers on its lists at specified intervals. Dun & Bradstreet and the services of the National Association of Credit Men are used in making the check. Only retailers whose ratings are maintained may remain on the list.

2. Another firm divides lists by territories and sends each section to the salesman covering that territory. The salesman goes over the list and makes necessary changes. As the salesman sends in many of the names, he readily recognizes "deadwood."

3. A manufacturer of ladies' wearing apparel sets a definite time limit after the last order, following which names are dropped from the mailing list. This keeps the list down to live names only. The inactive names are placed on a reserve list.

4. Many concerns subscribe to a clipping service which promptly informs them of firms that go out of business, burn out, are newly incorporated, consolidate, reorganize, and so on.

5. A manufacturer of machinery and supplies always precedes every important direct advertising campaign with a letter sent under *first-class* postage to every name on his mailing list. When letters are returned by the post office, those plates are removed.

6. Every year or so a manufacturer of office devices writes a letter frankly telling each one who has not responded the actual cost

of keeping his name on the mailing list and asking the recipient to please reply if he desires to be kept on the list.

7. The Post Office Department will help you check mailing lists. Certain rules and regulations govern the charge for this service and the work that a postmaster is permitted to do for business firms. Check with your local postmaster for details.

Organization of Mailing List

A great deal of money is lost every year by loose control of mailing-list costs. There is, for example, the way lists are organized or arranged. Prevailing practice in most business establishments, which do only occasional direct-mail work, is to have different lists for different purposes. Thus there may be 20 lists for buyers of 20 types of products; for prospect groups engaged in various lines of business, etc. While there is considerable value to a business in having its lists so arranged, a multiplicity of mailing lists requires a multiplicity of checking to find the list in which a name is filed. Then, too, the increasing cost of addressing plates and stencils makes the duplication between names on these lists a matter of consequence. Modern practice is to maintain two over-all mailing lists, an active list and an inactive list. Different lists are then consolidated under each of these two main divisions into one general list using a selector on the addressing machine to pick out names on any component list. The only reason for maintaining two lists, instead of throwing all names into one big list, is the saving of time in running the list.

No matter what arrangement is used, it is important that names which have been on the list for some time without results should be transferred to an inactive list. One way to do this is to use a different color stencil or address plate card for each year. Suppose all names added during a certain year were put on plates with red cards. When it might be desired to weed out the list, all blue-carded address plates could be removed from the drawers for checking and comparing with the sales records.

Another way to accomplish the same result is to emboss the month and year the plate was put in file on the right-hand side of the plate, and then use a cut-off device to blank out the date when addressing. Advantage of this method is that it permits running off the entire mailing list on paper strips which can be checked from time to time. After checking, these strips may be stored outside of the building for fire records. They would thus provide information which might be destroyed on the address plate record in case of fire, flood, or heat damage.

There are several different addressing systems on the market. Common practice is that when names must be written four or more times, it pays to put them on an inexpensive metal plate or fiber stencil. The fiber stencil has the advantage that it can be cut on any typewriter and does not require the purchase of a special embossing machine. Less storage space is required for mailing lists on fiber stencils than on card index metal plates. However, there are systems using one-piece metal plates which are inexpensive and take up no more floor space than fiber ones.

For all-round use, however, the preference seems to be for the 3-piece embossed metal plate, with 12 tab positions. While the first cost of this plate is considerably higher, this is offset by a lower maintenance cost. Most of the cost of maintaining a mailing list is the time spent looking up names, making corrections, and reading plates or stencils as the case may be. Even a small daily saving in time spent justifies a higher first cost. Where lists run into the millions, as in the case of certain mail-order houses, fiber stencils seem to have the call.

The important thing when putting a mailing list on plates or stencils is to be sure the system adopted is capable of expansion. Mailing lists have a habit of growing, and unless the direction of growth is foreseen and provided for at the outset, unsuitable equipment, involving the remaking of thousands of address plates, can be very expensive. (See also Chapter 41, "Sales Promotion Equipment.")

The National Cash Register Company,* which won the Henry Hoke Award of the magazine *Direct Advertising*, centralizes its direct-mail operations at headquarters.

Mailing lists are maintained at Dayton on Speedaumat plates and new lists are compiled daily. Branch offices have only to specify the type of campaign wanted by classification number but headquarters will also mail to addresses supplied by the branch office.

The company aims for an inquiry rate per campaign of 5%. Inquiries are followed up by salesmen, and Dayton keeps a check on when the sales call is made, what happened and what is planned for each inquirer. One particular letter campaign, mailed to 45,982 bar owners, pulled at the rate of 12.3%.

Helping Dealers to Get Good Names

Most dealers, especially if located in a rural territory, are awake to the importance of not only building a live list of customers and possible customers, but keeping it up to date. It is to the interest of

*Now NCR Corp.

the manufacturer depending upon these dealers for sales promotional cooperation to help them develop a list which will yield maximum returns. Naturally, a dealer will soon taper off mailing manufacturer's promotional literature to his list unless he feels it is profitable. Too many lists used by dealers are woefully obsolete and cluttered up with "dead" names.

One national advertiser who has invested heavily in direct-mail promotions to lists furnished by dealers is Lowe Brothers Company, Dayton paint manufacturer. The company is convinced this is just about the most profitable type of promotion it can do, especially when filled in with the recipient's name in long-hand (Mr. Jones). There are four series of these letters, each series requiring a different type of list. These series include: (1) General city series; (2) general farm series; (3) exterior product series; (4) interior product series.

DEALER NAME ....

TRADE NAME (*If different*)..

STREET ADDRESS ....

CITY...COUNTY.............................

STATE...ACCOUNT NO............................
Leave this space blank

BUSINESS CLASSIFICATION...
Mention principal classes of goods sold which give your store or business its recognition in your city or town

ADDITIONAL REMARKS...

....

Please write plainly so that details furnished will be correctly recorded

---

This card is enclosed with the letter qualifying the customer. It is printed on ledger stock, and is 3½ by 5½ inches in size. This size is used so that the cards will fit into the regular mailing list files. The card is self-addressed and stamped.

In using these letters, Lowe dealers are urged to take great care to make sure the lists they send in are all good prospects for the sale of paints, and the company requires that the mailing list submitted by the dealer specify their interest, so they can be placed on the proper list. To make sure the names are good, dealers are given six specific suggestions as to how they may obtain them:

1. By securing the names of people who come into your store for estimates.
2. By following new building permits.
3. By looking for houses needing paint.
4. By recording information on prospective work, secured from painters.
5. By following up old customers who should be ready for repairing and redecorating.

6. By having delivery man turn in names of people whose homes need paint —names secured in the course of his regular work.

Each of these cards may be made a special salesman for your store. Fill out the cards, mail to us, and we will have you close the business. Special promotion will begin as soon as the card reaches our Advertising Department.

Cleaning Up Old Mailing Lists

If a list is more than 4 years old, and has not been systematically kept up, it is usually just as well to scrap it and build an entirely new list. In building the new list, you can use, as a foundation, names which are definitely known to you to be good.

In the absence of any definite information about these names, and assuming that the probable percentage of good names among them is large, these questionable names should be worked with a special letter or mailing card and only those who reply put back on the list. Those who show no interest can be dropped entirely or put on a secondary list for occasional working. The cost of such a check-up may be reduced by enclosing with such letters a special-offer circular or inquiry-getting enclosure. In fact, this plan can profitably be used even where a list is periodically checked against returned mail. A suggested letter for checking a mailing list is shown below:

Dear Sir:

We have been glad to send you our catalogs and other literature in the past, but we have run into a problem which we sincerely hope you will understand.

The fast-growing demand for the catalog has made it necessary to review our mailing list from a cost standpoint.

We would be glad to continue sending the catalogs and literature to you were it not for the fact that the abnormal increase in the cost of publishing them compels us to limit the number of catalogs issued.

Accordingly, we are limiting the list to the names of customers from whom we receive an order each season.

We respectfully suggest that you send us an order for an article illustrated in the attached circular, or from the catalogs already in your possession. This will insure that your name is retained on our permanent mailing list.

Cordially,

Careful checking, at least every 2 years, is especially necessary on mailing lists of consumers furnished by dealers. Such lists should be run off by territories at least once a year and sent to salesmen to check. While too much dependence should not be placed on the checking done by salesmen, especially so far as adding new names is concerned, this method saves a great deal of money, and at the same time familiarizes the salesman with the support he is receiving from the advertising department. The best time to check a mailing list is just prior to issuing a new catalog, or any piece of sales literature which the prospect especially needs.

The use of the card in this way is a great attention-getter and in nearly every instance where this plan has been used it has produced very good results. A development of this same idea, showing its adaptable possibilities, is to print the cut of an address plate at the head of a letter and Addressograph the prospect's name and address on the illustration. It thus serves as a fill-in for personalizing the letter. The letter in this case starts out by referring to the fact that the address plate that is shown above has been in the files for 3 years, that 25 pieces of advertising have been sent to the person whose name appears on the plate but no letters or orders have been received.

An Effective Clean-Up Letter

There are, of course, any number of ways that can be used to eliminate dead names. One good plan is to date each card with a small dater showing the month and year the name went into the file. These names should be checked with the sales ledgers every year and if no interest is shown within 2 years, the plate should be taken out and transferred to a suspended list. But before doing so, a personal letter—preferably an individually typed letter—should be sent to each name to be sure that you are not killing a prospect who is on the verge of buying. A large paper company which uses this plan finds that by mailing out a letter and Business Reply card about once a year, it can keep its mailing list free of dead names. In addition, mistakes growing out of wrong trade names, inaccurate addresses, and other misinformation are largely eliminated. This results in less delay in handling its sales records and fewer misunderstandings with its trade.

Another company cleans up its mailing lists every year by sending each name a two-way reply card. One card carries the word "NO" in big red letters—"Take us off your list, we are not interested because . . ." The other card, separated from the "NO" card by perforations, carries an equally big "YES—Keep us on your list to receive your bargain announcements."

When No R.F.D. Mailing List Is Available

Postal regulations permit mailing circular letters and sales literature to box holders on rural routes without the name of the addressee. Under the postal regulation, it is necessary to secure a list of the routes and route numbers and the numbers of boxes on each route for bulk mailings to R.F.D. box holders. The following letter is used as the first step in this plan, for securing this information. It is addressed to the postmaster in each town and is accompanied by a self-addressed, stamped envelope.

Dear Sir:

Will you kindly do us a favor by giving us, at the bottom of this sheet, the numbers of the rural routes running out of your office and also, if possible, the number of boxes occupied during the winter on each of these routes?

This request is in accordance with a ruling by the Post Office Department at Washington.

We enclosed a stamped, addressed envelope and shall appreciate your honoring this request at an early date.

Very truly yours,

The postmaster gives the information requested on the bottom of this letter and returns it to the writer. By calling attention to the fact that the request is in accordance with postal regulations, any objection from the postmaster due to ignorance of department rulings is forestalled.

When the list is received at the home office, the envelopes are addressed mechanically by means of the Addressograph, Multigraph, or other forms of printing or addressing devices. A typical address is as follows: Box Holder, Route No. 6, Woodstock, Illinois.

No..............	No..............
For Distribution to Box Holders	Route
	P.O.
Route..............	State
	Section
P.O..............	Quantity
Mailed.............. State..............	Addressed
Number of Bundles for Route..........	Mailed

This form is used to identify bundles of mail for each rural route for each post office. The coupon at the right is detached for office record and is numbered to correspond with the portion which goes to the post office.

A sufficient number of envelopes for each route number is printed without changing the address, then a change is made and another lot is printed for the next route number and post office.

The mail is sorted and tied into bundles, one for each route, after addressing and inserting. Each bundle is identified by means of a printed slip as is shown on page 466. The coupon on the end of this slip is detached before mailing and is used as a record of the date of mailing, number of pieces, postage cost, etc.

Using the U.S. Postal Service Check Lists

The U.S. Postal Service will help you check mailing lists. Certain rules and regulations govern the charge for this service, and the work which a postmaster is permitted to do for business firms. A phone call to your local postmaster, or to the nearest post office branch (if you are in a large city), will bring you the current information on costs for this service.

One of the requirements is that names be submitted to the post office on cards rather than on lists. The reason that the department requests list owners to submit them in card form, approximately the size and quality of ordinary post cards, one name to a card, with the owner's name stamped or printed in the upper left corner, can readily be seen when it is understood that in this form the employees in charge of the work are enabled to distribute them to the carriers, the same as mail for correction, instead of being corrected by the directory section.

Where concerns entitled to correction service under the provisions of the regulation mentioned above maintain mailing lists by various classifications, postmasters are authorized to correct each separate classified list, or portion of the list, not more frequently than twice a year. Such concerns, when asking for correction service should indicate the particular list to which the desired corrections apply so that suitable notation may be made of the dates when such separate lists, or portions, are corrected in order that the frequency with which corrections are authorized may be tabulated by the post office.

Through the use of the various postmaster notices permitted by the department for second-, third-, and fourth-class mail it is possible not only to obtain the new address in case of a change but to direct the postmaster as to whether your mailing piece is to be returned to you, forwarded to the addressee, or destroyed; and whether the forwarding postage is to be paid by you or collected from the addressee.

In connection with first-class mail, while theoretically there should be a 100% return of undeliverable first-class mail, it should be remembered that many pieces are forwarded from one place to another until they finally reach the addressee or his heirs. Consequently, the mailer frequently never gets the change of address or hears of the death of the addressee.

In recent years a new development in special mailing list sources has taken place. Formerly trade-paper publishers refused point-blank to furnish advertisers or advertising prospects with mailing lists for their industry. Their point of view was that to do so would compete with their own advertising space. But lately trade-paper publishing policies have changed. The better publications now confine their circulation effort to the 20% of important buying units in their field which purchase 80% of the equipment and supplies. This leaves a large fringe which cannot be covered through advertising in business papers. Most manufacturers prefer to spend only a small part of their appropriations to reach these small buyers. They concentrate their main efforts on the important "top" group through advertising in business publications covering it.

To provide advertisers with a means of reaching this fringe trade once or twice a year, publishers now sell mailing list service as well as advertising space service. Their central position enables them to secure and maintain lists for their field properly, better than an individual manufacturer could do it. By making a reasonable charge for the use of such lists, the publishers not only maintain their own mailing lists without cost, but are able to make a profit on the lists besides.

List Service You Can Get from Business Papers

Some of the ways in which special lists obtainable from business paper publishers may be used are mentioned in the promotion literature of one such publisher, The Chilton Company, Philadelphia, Pa. 19139.

1. ANALYZING YOUR MARKETS: With the name and address of every desirable wholesale and trade outlet in the country, you have the material for any kind of market analysis you wish to make. You can compare your list of customers with the total names. You can take any individual state, county, or even town, and do likewise.

2. DETERMINING SALES QUOTAS: If you wish to set a sales quota for your own sales staff or any of your wholesalers in any particular section, you can do so by the use of the trade names together with car registration, population, and wealth factors obtainable in these lists.

3. MAKING UP SALESMEN'S ROUTES: Knowing the number and location of both wholesale and retail outlets, salesmen may be routed so that the territory may be thoroughly covered with the least traveling expense. The classification

of outlets permits you to select those that should be most receptive to your sales message.

4. REACHING THE RIGHT MAN: Chilton Trade List, in most cases, gives the name of the proprietor of retail service outlets. It contains the names of the owners, buyers, and managers of all wholesale concerns. Knowing these keymen helps your salesmen produce more quickly and assures your mailing efforts reaching the individuals who really count.

5. DECIDING WHO GETS DISCOUNTS: Not only the wholesalers, but the retailers sometimes want jobbers discounts. With Chilton Trade List it is easy to determine who are wholesalers and who are retailers. All outlets are classified and grouped.

6. EXTENDING CREDITS: Chilton Trade List tells you the value of the stock carried by wholesalers, the size of territory they cover and number of men traveled. The size of retail and service establishments is indicated, to an extent in the retail section, by the number of departments operated and the cars or trucks handled, if any. Whenever you receive an order from a concern not rated by the usual credit sources, this information will be of assistance until you obtain definite credit information.

7. ANALYZING DIFFERENT CLASSES AS CUSTOMERS: If you sell through jobbers alone, you can quickly learn which classes are your best customers. Maybe those specializing in tools. With the information in the Wholesale List, you can quickly make this analysis. If one class is better than another—Why? Maybe you have done more work with it or perhaps you have neglected the other classes. The same analysis can be made with the retail units in case you sell direct. Perhaps the car dealer is your best customer; maybe the independent repair shop. If you know this, you can make your plans accordingly.

8. FOLLOWING NEW COMPANIES: They should be your best prospects. Normally 25,000 new concerns enter the automotive field every year. They must buy supplies and equipment. The time to reach them is when they are new. The New Name Bulletins—monthly supplementary service of the Chilton Trade List—report these additions. There are in the neighborhood of 2,000 new prospects every month for the user of the list.

9. DROPPING CONCERNS OUT OF BUSINESS: No need of wasting time and postage on the dead ones. The Dropped Name Bulletins—which are a part of the monthly service—give you the names of all such outfits disappearing as customers or prospects.

10. CIRCULARIZING: To reach all the trade with comparatively little waste, it is necessary to use Chilton Trade List. It is kept up to date with additions and corrections.

11. CIRCULARIZING SELECTED GROUPS: With the Chilton Trade List it is easy. Your company can select any one of several groups for special mail work. There are many ways in which selection can be made according to state, county, population figures, vehicles handled, service rendered, or supplies sold.

The cost for mailing service, as furnished by publishers, is not as cheap as buying prepared lists from mailing list houses. But it must be borne in mind that a publisher spends a great deal of money to maintain his list, usually far more than a mailing list house could afford to spend.

Mailing List Information

There are almost as many different ways of getting names of persons who are prospects for what you sell as there are kinds of business. Some of these have already been mentioned in Chapter 6, "Sales Leads and Inquiries." A commonly used method of building mailing lists is to employ the services of some organization which specializes in their preparation. Such lists are usually compiled by

```
-----------------------------------------------------------------
|                      LIST MAINTENANCE                          |
|       American Marketing Services Inc.   | List:               |
|                                          |                     |
|  [>]                                     | Name Change         |
| Plate Now                                |---------------------|
|   Reads                                  | Address Change      |
|                                          |---------------------|
|                                          | New Listing         |
|                                          |---------------------|
|  [>]                                     | Change Notch Code   |
| Plate Should                             | Volume     Returned |
|   Read                                   | Remove From List    |
|                                          |---------------------|
|                                          | Bad Credit Risk     |
|                                          |                     |
|  Ordered by:_____   Date:_____   |
|                                                                |
|  List Maintenance by:_____  Date:_____    |
-----------------------------------------------------------------
```

Example of list maintenance card used by American Marketing Services, Inc.
From the Dartnell Direct Mail and Mail Order Handbook

checking trade and city directories with other reference books to get ratings, street addresses, and other needed information seldom collected in any single directory. When such lists are compiled, several carbon copies are made and kept on file for sale to others who might be interested in the same list of names. These mailing list houses publish printed lists of mailing lists available. Dun & Bradstreet offers a mailing list service with names of business establishments classified by number of employees, line of business, and so on.

Another good source for names is trade and special directories, of which there are several thousand. Many are kept up to date by revisions occurring annually or even oftener, especially when compiled by publishers of magazines in the same field.

A list of directories, with prices, publishers' names and addresses, and other available data, follows.

PRINCIPAL BUSINESS DIRECTORIES

AB FUN RIDE SURVEY. Lists U.S. ride manufacturers showing type of unit, capacity, and price. Also includes importers and foreign manufacturers of the equipment. Arranged alphabetically. 40 pp. AMUSEMENT BUSINESS, 2160 Patterson St., Cincinnati, Ohio 45214.

ACCOUNTING INFORMATION SOURCES. Complete listing of current accounting literature. Three sections: background of modern accounting; associations which represent the entire profession; literature covering the regulation of accounting and auditing practices by U.S. Federal agencies. Alphabetically arranged by entry. Includes listing of Basic Accounting Library. Appendixes. Author and subject indexes. 420 pp. GALE RESEARCH CO., Book Tower, Detroit, Mich. 48226.

AD CHANGE. Designed to give subscribers up-to-the-minute news of changes in the national advertising field. Issued weekly giving agency appointments and changes in personnel in the field. NATIONAL REGISTER PUBLISHING CO. INC., 5201 Old Orchard Rd., Skokie, Ill. 60076.

ADVERTISERS ANNUAL. An alphabetical list of all British Firms engaged in advertising and selling, covering newspapers and magazines, outdoor publicity and posters, commercial television, radio, and cinema, advertising agents, consultants and public relations; direct mail agents; marketing specialist; etc., 1,260 pp. Annually. INTERNATIONAL PUBLICATIONS SERVICE, 114 E. 32 St., New York, N.Y. 10016.

ADVERTISING, EDITORIAL, AND TELEVISION ART AND DESIGN ANNUAL. Contains an alphabetically classified directory of products and services in the graphic field. Also other illustrated information is included. 576 pp. Annual. WATSON-GUPTILL PUBLICATIONS, One Astor Plaza, New York, N.Y. 10036.

ADVERTISING SPECIALTY REGISTER. Directory contains entries of approximately 1,000 names and addresses of firms selling through advertising specialty distributors and jobbers—names of executives, products, and trade names. Published by ADVERTISING SPECIALTY INSTITUTE, 4730 Chestnut St., Philadelphia, Penn. 19139. Available to trade members only.

AERONAUTICAL ENGINEERING—A SPECIAL BIBLIOGRAPHY. A selected bibliography on aeronautical engineering. 132 pp. NATIONAL TECHNICAL INFORMATION SERVICE, Springfield, Va. 22151.

AGENT, THE. Lists suppliers of fabrics, trimmings, services and equipment used in the garment manufacturing industry. Semi-Annual. HALPER PUBLISHING CO., 300 W. Adams St., Chicago, Ill. 60606.

AGING, DIRECTORY OF NATIONAL ORGANIZATIONS WITH PROGRAMS IN THE FIELD OF. An alphabetical listing of 300 private, nongovernmental agencies representing a broad spectrum of organizations—social welfare, unions, professional groups, churches—whose programs directly or tangentially serve the interests of older people. 95 pp. NATIONAL COUNCIL OF THE AGING, INC., 1828 L St., N.W., Washington, D.C. 20036.

AGRICULTURE HANDBOOK 305. PROFESSIONAL WORKERS AND STATE AGRICULTURE EXPERIMENT STATIONS AND OTHER COOPERATING STATE INSTITUTIONS. Published by the UNITED STATES GOVERNMENT PRINTING OFFICE, Supt. of Documents, Washington, D.C. 20402.

AIA GUIDE TO NEW YORK CITY. Describes thousands of architecturally interesting buildings in New York City. Produced by the American Institute of Architects. 464 pp. MACMILLAN & CO., 866-3rd Ave., New York, N.Y. 10022.

AIR CARGO GUIDE. An index of all cargo airlines, their routes, flights, freight charges, etc. 186 pp. Monthly. REUBEN H. DONNELLEY CORP., 2000 Clearwater Dr., Oak Brook, Ill. 60521.

AIR-CONDITIONING & REFRIGERATION WHOLESALERS DIRECTORY. A list of 740 member air-conditioning and refrigeration wholesalers with their addresses, telephone numbers, and official representatives. Arranged alphabetically by region, state, and city. 52 pp. Annually. AIR-CONDITIONING & REFRIGERATION WHOLESALERS, 22371 Newman Ave., Dearborn, Mich. 48124.

AIR FORWARDER. A listing of air freight forwarders and cargo agents. Annual. REUBEN H. DONNELLEY CORP., 711 W. 3rd Ave., New York, N.Y. 10017.

AIRLINE INDUSTRY DIRECTORY OF PUBLICATIONS. Lists members of the Air Transport Association of America, and bibliography of Association publications. 20 pp. Published by the AIR TRANSPORT ASSOCIATION OF AMERICA, 1000 Connecticut Ave., N.W., Washington, D.C. 20036.

ANIMALS NEXT DOOR. THE. A guide to over 400 zoos and aquariums of the Americas published in cooperation with the National Recreation and Park Assoc., Washington, D.C. Describes the contents of each, visiting hours, fees, etc. Also describes factual material about zoos, endangered species and other important information. 170 pp. FLEET ACADEMIC EDITIONS INC., 160 Fifth Ave., New York, N.Y. 10010.

A.O.P.A. AIRPORT DIRECTORY. Lists 11,500 airports, seaplane bases, heliports in the U.S. geographically and alphabetically. 475 pp. Annual. AIRCRAFT OWNERS AND PILOTS ASS'N., Air Rights Bldg., 7315 Wisconsin Ave., Washington, D.C. 20014.

APPAREL TRADES BOOK. Publication contains a grouping of entries providing a listing of approximately 110,000 retail and wholesale apparel enterprises, with financial ratings noted for each. Published by CREDIT CLEARING HOUSE DIVISION of DUN AND BRADSTREET, INC., 99 Church St., New York, N.Y. 10007.

ARCHITECTURE, MEMBER AND ASSOCIATE MEMBER SCHOOLS OF THE ASSOCIATION OF COLLEGIATE SCHOOLS OF. Directory provides material on 95 American and Canadian schools that are members and associate members of the Association of Collegiate Schools of Architecture, noting name of school, address, and name of head or dean of each. ASSOCIATION OF COLLEGIATE SCHOOLS OF ARCHITECTURE, INC., 1735 New York Ave., N.W., Washington, D.C. 20006.

ART BIBLIOGRAPHIES. A new international reference service covering the literature published in Art and Design and comprised of three bibliographical series: Art bibliographies Modern: Art bibliographies Current Titles: are Art bibliographies Historical. Consult publisher for further information. ABC-CLIO INC., 2040 A.P.S., Santa Barbara, Calif. 93103.

ASSOCIATION OF DIESEL SPECIALISTS MEMBERSHIP DIRECTORY. A list of over 200 service and supply specialists in diesel parts. Listed alpha-geographically. Published in the September issue of FLEET MANAGEMENT NEWS, 300 W. Lake St., Chicago, Ill. 60606.

AUDIO-VISUAL CATALOG DIRECTORY. Information on motion pictures, film strips, slides, sound recordings and video tapes that the federal government produces and either sells or loans for educational purposes. NATIONAL AUDIO-VISUAL CENTER, National Archives and Records Service, General Services Administration, Washington, D.C. 20409.

AUDIO-VISUAL COMMUNICATIONS ANNUAL BUYING GUIDE TO AV EQUIPMENT AND SERVICES. An alphabetical listing of products and services to the audio-visual communications industry. Listed are still projects, silent and sound, motion picture supplies and equipment, color labs, etc. 118 pp. Annual. UNITED BUSINESS PUBLICATIONS INC., 750 Third Ave., New York, N.Y. 10017.

AUDIO-VISUAL EQUIPMENT DIRECTORY. A list of 2,200 items of audio-visual equipment, alphabetically by company within 67 categories. 512 pp. Annually. NATIONAL AUDIO-VISUAL ASSOCIATION, INC., 3150 Spring St., Fairfax, Va. 22030.

AUDIO-VISUAL MARKET PLACE. Provides company names, addresses and key personnel and product lines for all active producers, distributors and other sources of AV learning materials. Also includes: national, professional and trade organizations concerned with AV; educational TV and radio stations; manufacturers of AV hardware, with full address, key personnel, etc.; AV dealers, contract production services; a bibliography of reference works on AV materials; etc. 293 pp. R. R. BOWKER CO. 1180 Avenue of the Americas, New York, N.Y. 10036.

AUDIO-VISUAL RESOURCE GUIDE. THE. Designed for use in religious education, this cumulative edition includes classified evaluations of more than 2,500 current church-related audio-visual materials. Materials include under such headings as The Bible-Old Testament background, history of the Scriptures, contents of the Old Testament, concepts of God, historical and narrative literature, ethics, mental health, parent training, intergroup relations, problems of war and peace. FRIENDSHIP PRESS, P.O. Box 37844, Cincinnati, Ohio 45237.

AUTO SUPPLIES AND HARDWARE CHAINS. Publication names approximately 1,900 chain stores operating over 38,000 stores in the United States; includes listings of buyers' names, products handled, number of stores operated, and executive personnel. Annually. CHAIN STORE GUIDE, 425 Park Ave., New York, N.Y. 10022.

AUTO TRIM NEWS DIRECTORY OF PRODUCT SOURCES. Lists manufacturers and their products servicing the auto trim industry. Annual. NATIONAL ASSOC. OF AUTO TRIM SHOPS, 129 Broadway, Lynbrook, N.Y. 11563.

AUTOMOTIVE YEARBOOK, WARD'S. Contains 600 automotive equipment and accessory industry executives listed alphabetically by company. Included are company and product listings and other statistical information. 284 pp. Annually. WARD'S COMMUNICATIONS, INC., 28 West Adams St., Detroit, Mich. 48226. Free to subscribers to "Ward's Automotive Reports."

BANK DIRECTORY, AMERICAN. Consists of an alphabetically arranged list of 14,000 national, state, savings, private banks and trust companies—telephone number, address, date established, transit number, officers, directors, principal correspondents, condensed statement of condition, and out-of-city branches. Semiannually. McFADDEN BUSINESS PUBLICATIONS, 6364 Warren Dr., Norcross, Ga. 30071. National edition.

BANK MARKETING BIBLIOGRAPHY. A selected bibliography of books and other materials to aid those in bank marketing. Listings are annotated with pertinent information. THE AMERICAN BANKERS ASSN., Marketing Division, 1120 Connecticut Ave., N.W., Washington, D.C. 20036. 125 pp.

BASIC BOOKS IN THE MASS MEDIA. Contains an annotated by subject booklist of 665 publications covering publishing, general communications, broadcasting, film, magazines, newspapers, advertising, indexes, scholarly and professional periodicals. 252 pp. UNIVERSITY OF ILLINOIS PRESS, Urbana, Ill. 61801.

BEAUTY AND BARBER BUYING GUIDE. A directory of manufacturers, their products and brand names, alphabetically according to categories. Also includes beauty and barber supply dealers and schools. Over 5,000 listings included. 186 pp. Annual. SERVICE PUBLICATIONS INC., 100 Park Ave., New York, N.Y. 10017.

BEAUTY AND BARBER SUPPLY DEALERS, DIRECTORY OF. Contains listings of approximately 1,600 beauty and barber shop suppliers—owners' names, number of salesmen, territory covered and type of customers. Maintained in current condition by issuance of Supplements every 3 to 4 months. NATIONAL BEAUTY AND BARBER MANUFACTURERS' ASSOCIATION, 100 Park Ave., New York, N.Y. 10017.

BEST REFERENCE BOOKS. Contains a selected 818 substantial reference titles from over 12,000 reviews in the seven volumes of ARBA. 448 pp. LIBRARIES UNLIMITED, P.O. Box 263, Littleton, Colo. 80160.

BIBLIOGRAPHIC GUIDE TO BUSINESS AND ECONOMICS. Includes comprehensive cataloging and bibliographic information for Business and Economics including Economic theory, population, demography, economic history, land, agriculture, transportation and communication, commerce, business administration, finance, etc. 1,935 pages, 3 volumes. G. K. HALL & CO., 70 Lincoln St., Boston, Mass. 02111.

BIBLIOGRAPHIC GUIDE TO CONFERENCE PUBLICATIONS. A comprehensive guide for acquisitions, cataloging and research for locating proceedings, reports and summaries of conferences, meetings, and symposia, as well as collections or partial collections of papers presented at conferences in all languages and subjects. G. K. HALL & CO., 70 Lincoln St., Boston, Mass. 02111.

BIBLIOGRAPHIC GUIDE TO LAW. Reference source for new publications in the legal field including United States Law, International law, International arbitration, Treaties and foreign law, etc. 1,254 pp. 2 volumes. G. K. HALL & CO., 70 Lincoln St., Boston, Mass. 02111.

BIBLIOGRAPHIC INDEX. Bibliographies in English and foreign languages, including those published separately as books of pamphlets and those appearing as parts of books or pamphlets are covered. In addition over 2,200 periodicals are regularly examined for bibliographical material. Material is listed by name of author under subject headings. H. W. WILSON CO., 950 University Ave., Bronx, N.Y. 10452.

BIBLIOGRAPHY OF PUBLICATIONS OF UNIVERSITY BUREAUS OF BUSINESS AND ECONOMIC RESEARCH. A reference guide to those publications of schools of business and economics which do not appear in traditional library indexes. Lists books, bulletins, monographs, working papers and periodicals covering a wide range of subjects—from economics, pollution and environment, business management, etc. UNIVERSITY OF COLORADO, Business Research Division, Boulder, Colo. 80302. Annual. 200 pp.

BIBLIOGRAPHY ON PHYSICAL DISTRIBUTION MANAGEMENT. An annual publication supplementing the 1967 bibliography with entries in nine categories such as physical distribution concept, legal and public policy sources, handbooks and general reference, etc. NATIONAL COUNCIL ON PHYSICAL DISTRIBUTION MGT., 222 W. Adams St., Chicago, Ill. 60606.

BIOGRAPHICAL DICTIONARIES AND RELATED WORKS. Entries of 4,829 who's who's, directories, encyclopedias, rosters, histories, professional guides, portrait and biography indexes and catalogs, registers, dictionaries of anonyms and pseudonyms and other sources of biographical information about persons of note throughout the world. Includes title, subject and occupational indexes. 1056 pp. Published by GALE RESEARCH CO., Book Tower, Detroit, Mich. 48226.

BLACK ENTERPRISE—LEADING BLACK BUSINESSES ISSUE. Contains a listing ranked by financial size of 100 Black-owned or Black-controlled businesses with sales of $2 million or above, 49 banks with total assets of $2 million or more, 41 savings and loan associations with total assets of $100,000 or more, and 41 insurance companies with total assets of about $200,000 or more, includes company name, city and state, name of chief executive, year founded, financial data, etc. EARL G. GRAVE PUBLISHING CO., 295 Madison Ave., New York, N.Y. 10017.

CEMETERY DIRECTORY, INTERNATIONAL. A geographic listing of approximately 10,000 cemeteries including telephone numbers, type of corporations and style of cemetery. Buyers' Guide section lists cemetery suppliers and type of merchandise handled. 260 pp. Published every six to eight years by the AMERICAN CEMETERY ASSOCIATION, 250 E. Broad St., Columbus, Ohio 43215.

CERAMIC COMPANY DIRECTORY. Publication presents alphabetical listings of approximately 1,600 companies in or allied to the ceramic field. Listings detail name, address, telephone number, TWX, Telex and cable numbers, company description, names of officials and their titles, and number of employees. 150 pp. Annually. American Ceramic Society "Bulletin" by THE AMERICAN CERAMIC SOCIETY, 65 Ceramic Dr., Columbus, Ohio 43214.

CERAMIC DATA BOOK. Contains a list of approximately 3,000 ceramic equipment and raw materials manufacturers and supplies. Annually. CAHNERS PUBLISHING CO., 89 Franklin St., Boston, Mass. 02110.

CHEMICAL GUIDE TO THE UNITED STATES. Directory consists of listings of approximately 600 major American chemical concerns, providing name, address, principal officers, representative annual sales figures, plant locations and products; foreign subsidiaries and affiliates are noted, as well. Biennially. NOYES DATA CORP., Noyes Bldg., Park Ridge, N.Y. 07656.

CHEMICAL INDUSTRY HANDBOOK. A guide to the chemical industry in the United Kingdom and European industries such as paint, oil, plastics, pharmaceuticals, etc., with information on each firm listed. 390 pp. INTERNATIONAL PUBLICATIONS SERVICE, 114 East 32 St., New York, N.Y. 10016.

CHEMICAL MARKET ABSTRACTS. Provides in-depth coverage of all domestic and foreign information significant for the chemical, plastics, paper, metals, fibers, rubber, petroleum and other process industries. Over 14,000 digests annually are obtained from more than 100 key foreign and domestic sources. Monthly. PREDICASTS, INC., 200 University Circle Research Center, 11001 Cedar Ave., Cleveland, Ohio 44106.

CHEMICAL WEEK BUYERS' GUIDE ISSUE. The complete guide to sources for chemicals and packaging. This Guide lists 1,600 manufacturers and distributors; home branch and district offices; telephone numbers; 6,500 office listings. It is made up of a Catalog Section; Chemicals, Raw Materials and Specialties Directory with over 6,000 product listings and 50,000 individual listings of major producers with distributors. There is also included a Tradenames Directory of over 6,500 names. In the Packaging Area there is a Company Directory of manufacturers of all types of packaging containers, accessories and bulk shipping equipment; also a Packaging Catalog Section. Included are 400 different categories of packaging items with 4,000 listings of all major suppliers. In addition there is a Packaging/Shipping Trade names directory of over 300 names. Published annually in October by CHEMICAL WEEK, McGRAW-HILL, INC., 1221 Avenue of the Americas, New York, N.Y. 10021. Available only to subscribers of *Chemical Week* magazine.

CITIZEN'S ENERGY DIRECTORY—A GUIDE TO ALTERNATIVE ENERGY RESOURCES. Provides a geographical listing of 500+ citizen groups, manufacturers, gov't agencies, researchers and private individuals with expertise on alternative energy technologies. 150 pp. Annual. CITIZEN'S ENERGY PROJECT, 1518 R St., N.W., Washington, D.C. 20009.

CITY DIRECTORY CATALOG. Presents a listing of every city directory in North America. Contains a census, county list, listings of auto owners, farmers, householders, property owners, telephone numbers, rural routes, taxpapers; wives' names detailed in each listing. Annually. ASSOCIATION OF NORTH AMERICAN DIRECTORY PUBLISHERS, 270 Orange Street, New Haven, Conn. 06509.

CIVIL RIGHTS: A GUIDE TO THE PEOPLE, ORGANIZATIONS AND EVENTS. An alphabetical guide to names of individuals and organizations prominent in the civil rights movement between 1954 and the present. Also a list of states with civil rights legislation and state agencies with civil rights responsibilities, and a list of black elected officials in the United States, 194 pp. Published by R. R. BOWKER CO., 1180 Avenue of the Americas, New York, N.Y. 10036.

CIVIL SERVICE HANDBOOK. A complete guide to federal, state and local positions in the U.S. Civil Service. It tells you how to apply and includes other information on jobs available. 128 pp. ARCO PUBLISHING CO., INC., 219 Park Ave. South, New York, N.Y. 10003.

COLLECTION AGENCIES, AMERICAN DIRECTORY OF. Lists professional collection agencies and collectors throughout the U.S., Canada and parts of Europe. 255 pp. Annual. THE SERVICE PUBLISHING CO., 168 Washington Blvd., 15th & New York Ave., N.W., Washington, D.C. 20005.

COMPUTER DISPLAY REVIEW. Contains in four volumes information on cost, availability and application of all types of Display terminal equipment. 2,000 pp. Annual with supplements. G. L. M. CORPORATION, 594 Marrett Rd., Lexington, Mass. 02173.

COMPUTERS AND DATA PROCESSING INFORMATION SOURCES. Twelve sections covered: General Orientation, Planning and Organization, Personnel (staffing), Equipment, Supplies, Facilities, Communication and Records, Comptrollership, Operating, Directing, Front Office References, The Future, broken down into 79 subheads. Appendixes. Author and Title index. Subject index. 275 pp. Published by GALE RESEARCH COMPANY, Book Tower, Detroit, Mich. 48226.

COMPUTER YEARBOOK AND DIRECTORY. Publication contains entries on manufacturers of data processing equipment and services, colleges and universities offering data processing courses, private business schools, private and public institutes, associations with interest in data processing, computer-user organizations, audiovisual aids. Also provides information on flow charting symbols and techniques, computer manufacturers, computer and computer systems, insurance companies' data processing usage, federal government ADP installations inventory and a list of data processing abbreviations. Annually. AMERICAN DATA PROCESSING, INC., 401 N. Broad Street, Philadelphia, Pa. 19107.

CONCISE HANDBOOK OF OCCUPATIONS. Describes the different occupations, and job and career opportunities in each. 320 pp. J. G. FERGUSON PUBLISHING CO., 111 E. Wacker Dr., Chicago, Ill. 60601.

CONCRETE INSTITUTE DIRECTORY, AMERICAN. Directory's approximately 15,000 listings provide a complete membership roster of the American Concrete Institute. Biennially. AMERICAN CONCRETE INSTITUTE, P.O. Box 19150, Detroit, Mich. 48219.

CONCRETE INSTITUTE—MEMBERSHIP DIRECTORY, PRESTRESSED. Directory contains information on approximately 2,100 company members (producers), associate company members (suppliers), and affiliate members (non-register personnel), and professionals and students (architects and engineers) in the field, affiliated with the Prestressed Concrete Institute. All technical and other committee personnel listed by committee. Annually. 96 pp. PRESTRESSED CONCRETE INSTITUTE, 20 N. Wacker Dr., Chicago, Ill. 60606.

CONSUMER DISCOUNT PRICE GUIDE. Information on over 10,000 products; automobiles, appliances, hi-fi stereo equipment, televisions, air conditioners, etc. 386 pp. Annually. PUBLICATIONS INTERNATIONAL, LTD., 3841 W. Oakton, Skokie, Ill. 60076.

CONSUMER EDUCATION BIBLIOGRAPHY. Lists with brief annotation, 2,000 books, booklets, pamphlets, films, filmstrips, etc., designed as a guide to the knowledge and information necessary to make intelligent choices in the marketplace. 170 pp. SUPT. OF DOCUMENTS, U.S. GOVERNMENT PRINTING OFFICE, Washington, D.C. 20402.

CONSUMER HELP. Lists the names, addresses and phone numbers of City, County, State and Federal agencies, as well as important business organizations. Including information regarding consumer rights in mobile homes, condominiums, auto repairs, auto sales, landlord/tenant problems, television repairs, food, retirement and other facets of everyday concern. THE BROWARD COUNTY DIVISION OF CONSUMER AFFAIRS, 200 S.E. Sixth St., Fort Lauderdale, Fla.

CONSUMERISM, CAPITAL CONTACTS IN. Provides information needed for contacts to solve consumer problems, including every government consumer affairs office with address and phone number and a description of each of the offices, etc. FRASER/RUDER & FINN, 1701 K Street, N.W., Suite 906, Washington, D.C. 20006.

CONSUMER INDEX TO PRODUCT EVALUATIONS AND INFORMATION SOURCES. Provides a listing of product tests and evaluations from more than 110 sources—tests refer to general consumer, business, educational and library products—grouped into 121 categories—includes alphabetical index with subject index to categories. 263 pp. Quarterly with annual cumulation. PIERIAN PRESS, P.O. Box 1808, Ann Arbor, Mich. 48106.

CONSUMER PRODUCT INFORMATION. Lists federal publications aimed at assisting the consumer in the purchasing, usage and care of products. Areas covered include appliances, automobiles, child care, health, food, housing, etc. 16 pp. PUBLIC DOCUMENTS DISTRIBUTION CENTER, Pueblo, Colo. 81009.

CONSUMER PROTECTION DIRECTORY. Contains a listing of national, state and local governmental and private organizations offering information, protection, or assistance on consumer problems. 466 pp. MARQUIS ACADEMIC MEDIA, 200 E. Ohio St., Chicago, Ill. 60611.

CONSUMER'S REGISTER OF AMERICAN BUSINESS. Provides a listing of 51 business classifications alphabetically with trade names including 12,500 advertisers along with the products they produce. 1,100+ pp. Yearly. NATIONAL REGISTER PUBLISHING CO., 5201 Old Orchard Rd., Skokie, Ill. 60076.

CONSTRUCTION DIRECTORY. Lists 8,000 contractors, sub-contractors and services connected with the construction industry in Texas, Louisiana, Oklahoma, Arkansas and New Mexico. 224 pp. Annual. CAPS OF THE SOUTHWEST, 3108 W. 6th, Ft. Worth, Texas 76107.

CONSTRUCTION EQUIPMENT BUYERS GUIDE. Lists 10,000 makers and local distributors of construction equipment; includes complete product and trade names listings. 400 pp. Annually. CAHNERS BOOKS, 221 Columbus Ave., Boston, Mass. 02116.

CONSTRUCTIONEER DIRECTORY. Lists manufacturers and distributors serving the construction industry. 330 pp. Annual. REPORTS CORP., 1 Bond St., Chatham, N.J. 07928.

CONSTRUCTOR—DIRECTORY ISSUE. Provides an alphabetical listing by company name of more than 8,000 member firms engaged in building, highway, heavy, industrial, municipal utilities, and railroad construction. 330 pp. Annually in July. ASSOCIATED GENERAL CONTRACTORS OF AMERICA, 1957 E. St., N.W., Washington, D.C. 20006.

CONTRACTORS REGISTER. Publication contains listings of 10,000 architects, general contractors, subcontractors, construction material and equipment suppliers and dealers. 90 pp. Biennially. SERINA PRESS, 70 Kennedy St., Alexandria, Va. 22305.

CONVENTIONS, DIRECTORY OF. Provides a geographical and industrial listing of 18,000 association conventions, trade/industrial and public shows. 360 pp. Semiannual. SUCCESSFUL MEETINGS MAGAZINE, 1422 Chestnut St., Philadelphia, Pa. 19102.

CRUSADE FOR EDUCATION. Published nine times per year, "Crusade for Education" describes professional openings in the United States and abroad for teachers, librarians, administrators and scientists; information on undergraduate scholarships, current graduate awards, summer opportunities, teachers' discount services; educator's bookshelf, writing, and part-time work. Published by ADVANCEMENT AND PLACEMENT INSTITUTE, 169 N. 9th St., Brooklyn, N.Y. 11211. Subscription included in annual membership fee.

DECISION JOB DIRECTORY. Contains a listing of 1,500 American companies offering engineering or scientific employment opportunities to technical personnel, and 7,500 key executive and engineering contacts. Entries detail company name, address, phone number, industry and/or products; year established, sales, total number of professional and non-professional employees; name of president, director of engineering, directory of research, name of technical employment manager, listed alphabetically and cross-indexed. Revised and published annually. DECISION, INC., 4500 Summerside Rd., Cincinnati, Ohio 45244.

DICTIONARY OF PERSONNEL AND GUIDANCE TERMS. An alphabetical listing of terms for the personnel and guidance worker. Also includes associations, agencies and professional organizations in the U.S. and Canada. J. G. FERGUSON PUBLISHING CO., 111 E. Wacker Dr., Chicago, Ill. 60601.

DIRECTORY OF CAREER PLANNING AND PLACEMENT OFFICES. Contains information on placement personnel and interview dates on 1,900 four-year and two-year campuses. 228 pp. COLLEGE PLACEMENT COUNCIL, INC., P.O. Box 2263, Bethlehem, Pa. 18001.

DIRECTORY OF DIRECTORS. An alphabetical list of over 13,000 key executives with their titles, directorships, business and home addresses plus a list of over 2,400 leading Canadian companies with head office addresses and the names of officers and directors. 770 pp. Annually. FINANCIAL POST DIVISION, MACLEAN-HUNTER LTD., 481 University Ave., Toronto M5W 1A7, Ontario, Canada.

DIRECTORY OF DIRECTORS IN THE CITY OF NEW YORK. Contains a listing of approximately 15,000 executives and directors of 3,000 New York corporations, and a cross-index of companies by executives and firm names. Annually. DIRECTORY OF DIRECTORS CO., 350 Fifth Ave., New York, N.Y. 10001.

DIRECTORY OF GOVERNMENT AGENCIES SAFEGUARDING CONSUMER AND ENVIRONMENT. Contains state-by-state listings of federal and/or state officials with jurisdiction in each state over food and drugs, meat and poultry, pesticides, air pollution control, water pollution control, consumer protection: Fraud and deceptive practices, weights and measures, environment and narcotics control, etc. Also includes local officials. 90 pp. Biennially. SERINA PRESS, 70 Kennedy St., Alexandria, Va. 22305.

DUN AND BRADSTREET REFERENCE BOOK OF CORPORATE MANAGEMENTS. Contains a biographical sketch of each officer and identifies all directors in the 2,400 companies of greatest investor interest in the United States. Each biographical sketch includes the following: name, marital status, age, education and career description. Contains approximately 30,000 listings. 1,400 pp. Annually. DUN AND BRADSTREET, INC., 99 Church St., New York, N.Y. 10007.

ECOL: BOOK CATALOG OF THE ENVIRONMENTAL CONSERVATION LIBRARY. A bibliography of books, documents, papers and related materials from all subjects which have a bearing upon the physical environment and man's impact on it. Includes subjects as resource management, pollution, environmental policy and law, conservation, population and many more. 208 pp. AMERICAN LIBRARY ASSOC., 50 E. Huron St., Chicago, Ill. 60611.

ECOTECHNICS: AN INTERNATIONAL ECOLOGY DIRECTORY. Contains information on 900 product categories and provides manufacturers and service organizations in the U.S., Canada, Japan, and Western and Eastern Europe, lists more than 35,000 sources: names, addresses, telephone, and telex numbers on major areas of environmental concern. 480 pp. FAIRCHILD BOOKS AND VISUALS, 7 E. 12th St., New York, N.Y. 10003.

EDITOR AND PUBLISHER INTERNATIONAL YEARBOOK. Consists of alpha-geographically arranged entries of approximately 250,000 international daily and weekly executive newspaper personnel; detailed information on all American and Canadian daily and weekly newspapers—giving circulation, advertising, rates; also contains material on equipment, syndicates, schools of journalism, and press galleries. Annually. 626 pp. EDITOR AND PUBLISHER CO., INC., 575 Lexington Ave., New York, N.Y. 10022.

EDITOR AND PUBLISHER MARKET GUIDE. Entries on approximately 1,500 newspaper market areas, including data on population, income, sales, transportation, housing and banking, etc. List of newspapers in each area giving circulation data and name of advertising representative or contact personnel. 540 pp. Annually. EDITOR AND PUBLISHER CO., INC., 575 Lexington Ave., New York, N.Y. 10022.

EDUCATION INDEX. A cumulative author subject index to 241 educational publications in the English language. Although primarily a periodical index, proceedings, yearbooks, bulletins, monographs and material printed by the United States Government are included. Subject areas indexed include administration; pre-school elementary, secondary, higher and adult education; teacher education, counseling and guidance; curriculum and curriculum materials. Subject fields indexed include the arts, applied science and technology, audio-visual education, business education, comparative and international education, exceptional children and special education, health and physical education, languages and linguistics, mathematics, psychology and mental health, religious education, social studies and educational research relative to areas and fields indexed. Published monthly (except July and August) with annual cumulations by THE H. W. WILSON CO., 950 University Ave., Bronx, N.Y. 10452. Specific service basis rates available on request from publisher.

E.I.A. GUIDE, THE. Publication provides entries on where to buy for approximately 25,000 national manufacturers of electronic, industrial and aerospace equipment and supplies and their western representatives. Classified product and service section included. 580 pp. Annually. DIRECTORIES OF INDUSTRY, INC., 9371 Kramer-Unit I, Westminster, Calif. 92683.

EEM-ELECTRONIC ENGINEERS MASTER. Contains entries of approximately 6,300 electronics manufacturers—with names, addresses, telephone numbers, sales managers, plus sales office locations; 3,000 product headings with manufacturers' names, addresses and 6,000 trade names. Catalog section of 661 manufacturers included. 1,500 pp. Annually. UNITED TECHNICAL PUBLICATIONS, 645 Stewart Ave., Garden City, N.Y. 11530.

ELECTRONIC MARKET DATA BOOK. Lists electronic products and information on their sales and production. 110 pp. Annually. Published by ELECTRONIC INDUSTRIES ASSOCIATION, 2001 Eye St., N.W., Washington, D.C. 20006.

EMERITI FOR EMPLOYMENT. Provides information on approximately 500 recently or soon-to-be retired professors emeriti available for teaching, consultation and research appointments, listing for each the degrees held, institutional affiliations, and year of retirement; field or specialty of each included. Published by THE NATIONAL COMMITTEE ON THE EMERITI, P.O. Box 24451, Los Angeles, Calif. 90024.

ENERGY ATLAS. Listing of 52 Federal Departments and agencies including Regional Offices and Laboratories, 100 Congressional committees, subcommittees and organizations, 500 State energy related agencies. Legislative organizations and city energy office, 150 Federal, Regional and National non-Government organizations at the State and local level, and 600 energy publications, periodicals, guide-books and directories and government publications, etc. FRASER/RUDER AND FINN, 1701 "K" St., N.W., Washington, D.C. 20006.

ENERGY DIRECTORY, THE. Provides information on thousands of energy organizations, trade associations, professional societies, state governments, or corporations, etc. Including 12,000 officials and executives, their addresses and phone numbers. 500 pp. EIC ENVIRONMENT INFORMATION CENTER, INC., 292 Madison Ave., New York, N.Y. 10017.

ENERGY INDEX. Contains 12,000 abstracts of key articles, documents and reports on all aspects of the energy crisis and power technology since 1970. Covers consumption, usage, energy resources, plant sitings and other information. 400 pp. Annual. ENVIRONMENT INFORMATION CENTER, INC., 292 Madison Ave., New York, N.Y. 10017.

ENGINEERING AND MINING JOURNAL, MARKETING DIRECTORY GUIDEBOOK. Classified listing by product of companies supplying machinery, equipment and supplies used in the industry. Annual. McGRAW HILL, INC., 1221 Ave. of the Americas, New York, N.Y. 10020.

ENGINEERING EDUCATION IN THE U.S. A guide for foreign students to engineering institutions in the United States. 60 pp. IIE, 809 United Nations Plaza, New York, N.Y. 10017.

ENGINEERING INDEX ANNUAL. Annual volume consists of an annotated bibliography of articles involving engineering concepts and methods abstracted, listed alphabetically, cross referenced and indexed by subject and author from periodicals and society transactions, bulletins and reports of government agencies, universities, institutes and research organizations. Indexed by subject, giving title, author of the article; listed by author, listing all the authors and co-authors of the articles listed in the subject index. Published annually by ENGINEERING INDEX, INC., 345 E. 47th St., New York, N.Y. 10017.

ENVIRONMENT INDEX, THE. Lists 60,000 entries representing coverage from scientific, technical trade and general magazines, government reports, conference papers and proceedings, nationally-read newspapers, books and films. Also listed are environmental control patents, major legislation introduced and names and addresses of state and federal pollution control officers. 800 pp. Published by ENVIRONMENTAL INFORMATION CENTER, INC., 292 Madison Ave., New York, N.Y. 10017.

ENVIRONMENTAL DIRECTORY WORLD. Provides an alphabetical listing by country of 30,000 companies, organizations, personnel involved in environmental activities throughout the world. 1,600 pp. Biennially. BUSINESS PUBLISHERS, INC., P.O. Box 1067, Blair Station, Silver Spring, Md. 20910.

ENVIRONMENT U.S.A. A guide to 5,400 agencies, people and material concerned with environmental activities in the U.S. with descriptions and information on each. Over 1,500 sources listed: agencies, consultants, libraries, conferences and meetings in the field, newspapers, periodicals, etc., including a comprehensive bibliography of 1,500 publications and books. 451 pp. R. R. BOWKER CO., P.O. Box 1807, Ann Arbor, Mich. 48106.

ENVIRONMENTAL PROTECTION DIRECTORY. Provides a listing of national, state, and local government and private organizations where users can seek information about current programs or receive assistance on solving current problems. 526 pp. MARQUIS ACADEMIC MEDIA, 200 E. Ohio St., Chicago, Ill. 60611.

EQUIPMENT GUIDE BOOKS. 18 volumes of information on construction equipment. 5 books are guides to new and used values for construction equipment, and to rental rates. 13 volumes contain current specifications for one type or class of construction equipment. Approximately 75,000 listings. 25,000 pp. Published by EQUIPMENT GUIDE BOOK CO., 3980 Fabian Way, Palo Alto, Calif. 94303.

EXECUTIVE DEVELOPMENT PROGRAMS IN UNIVERSITIES. Lists executive development programs conducted by 50 U.S. universities. Detailed information is given on each program. An annotated bibliography is also included. 100 pp. NATIONAL INDUSTRIAL CONFERENCE BD., INC., 845 Third Ave., New York, N.Y. 10022.

EXHIBITS SCHEDULE. An alphabetical listing of events for selection of exhibit opportunities for your products or services. Included are location and dates of exhibits. Approximately 12,000 trade and industrial shows, fairs, and expositions are listed. Annually. SUCCESSFUL MEETINGS, Directory Dept., 1422 Chestnut St., Philadelphia, Pa. 19102.

EXPORT DIRECTORY OF THE BLUE BOOK OF EUROPE. Lists over 90,000 European companies alphabetically by product, country and name, giving name, address and phone number for each. 1,850 pp. INTERNATIONAL PUBLICATIONS SERVICE, 114 E. 32nd St., New York, N.Y. 10016.

EXPORTERS DIRECTORY AND U.S. BUYING GUIDE. Lists 30,000 U.S. manufacturers, exporters, export managers, and export merchants involved in the majority of domestic products and commodities sold in world markets. Included are names, addresses, titles, and phone numbers. 800 pp. JOURNAL OF COMMERCE, 445 Marshall St., Phillipsburg, N.J. 08865.

EXTENSION FACILITIES GUIDE. Describes private degree-granting correspondence colleges in the U.S. and several countries abroad. AUREA PUBLICATIONS, Aurea House, Allenhurst, N.J. 07711.

FACT FILES. Provides key data on trends in the U.S. economy including consumer income and expenditures, population, employment, prices, retail sales, education levels, etc. Included are department store sales, fashion accessories, floor coverings, home electronics, home textiles, major appliances, beauty aids, etc. FAIRCHILD BOOKS, Dept. NFF, 7 E. 12th St., New York, N.Y. 10003.

THE FEATURE WRITER AND SYNDICATE DIRECTORY. Presents a listing of over 900 entries of free lance writers and photographers, fully indexed and cross-referenced. Includes alphabetical listings of the nation's leading free-lance writers, including mailing address and zip code. Principal subjects in which writer specializes are given. Alphabetical listing of the subject matter in which writers specialize, listing writers so occupied under each. Lists publications served by these free lance writers ; special section containing detailed explanations submitted by leading magazine editors outlining type of articles they are seeking ; sources of historical photographs, drawings, sketches and old prints ; alphabetical listing of leading free-lance photographers ; special interest listing under which the free-lance photographers are cross-referenced, and feature syndicates and their personnel, cross-referenced by subject matter. 320 pp. Annually. THE NATIONAL RESEARCH BUREAU, INC., 424 N. Third St., Burlington, Iowa 52601.

FEDERAL EDUCATION PROGRAM GUIDE. Lists more than 300 federal programs in more than eight departments and agencies. Included are complete mailing address and telephone numbers. Provides aid to securing all kinds of institutional and program assistance from the federal government. ACROPOLIS BOOKS, 2400-17th St., N.W., Washington, D.C. 20009.

FILMGOERS COMPANION, THE. An international encyclopedia of over 10,000 actors, producers, directors, writers, camera men, film-makers, art directors and composers, each entry contains a biographical note and a listing of principal credits, 1,070 pp. HILL AND WANG, INC., 19 Union Square West, New York, N.Y. 10003.

FINANCE DIRECTORY—SHOPPING CENTER WORLD. ANNUAL. An alphabetical listing of 500+ firms and organizations which finance or invest in shopping centers as follows: long term lenders, construction lenders, equity investors, mortgage brokers/bankers, etc. 8-12 pp. COMMUNICATION CHANNELS, INC., 461 8th Ave., New York, N.Y. 10001.

FINANCE-INVESTORS ISSUE. Lists alphabetically by company name the top 400 security dealers in the U.S., includes type of ownership, address, phone, teletype and telex numbers, underwriting and syndication of corporate issues in previous year by number, type and dollar volume, etc. FINANCE PUBLISHING CO., 5 E. 75th St., New York, N.Y. 10021.

FINANCIAL ANALYSTS FEDERATION—MEMBERSHIP DIRECTORY. Provides a geographical listing by constituent local or state societies of 14,000 security and financial analysts who practice investment analysis. 380 pp. FINANCIAL ANALYSTS FEDERATION, Tower Suite, 219 E. 42nd St., New York, N.Y. 10017.

FOREIGN COMMERCE HANDBOOK. Presents a grouping of listings providing sources of information for exporters and importers, giving names and addresses of sources and procedure for procurement. Published by the CHAMBER OF COMMERCE OF THE UNITED STATES, 1615 H St., N.W., Washington, D.C. 20006.

FOREIGN TRADE DEPARTMENTS AND/OR BUREAUS IN CHAMBERS OF COMMERCE THROUGHOUT THE UNITED STATES. Publication presents an alphageographically arranged roster of local chambers of commerce, foreign trade departments and/or bureaus in the United States which maintain foreign trade services. Gives name of director of foreign trade matters for each chamber of commerce. CHAMBER OF COMMERCE OF THE UNITED STATES, 1615 H St., N.W., Washington, D.C. 20006.

FOREST GUIDE NATIONAL. A guide to the National forest arranged geographically, including a catalog of other national recreational facilities. Maps showing the location of National Forests. 224 pp. RAND McNALLY, P.O. Box 7600, Chicago, Ill. 60680.

GROVE'S DICTIONARY OF MUSIC AND MUSICIANS. Consisting of ten volumes, this edition contains more than 12,000 entries written by over 600 expert contributors, 76 plates, thousands of musical examples, line drawings and diagrams, more than 2,000 extensive bibliographies, a calendar of operas produced between 1600 and 1959, and articles on the folk music of more than 40 countries. It defines all musical terms, describes in detail most musical instruments and lists every composition of the great composers. 8,900 pp. Published by ST. MARTIN'S PRESS, 176 Fifth Ave., New York, N.Y. 10010.

HISTORY: REFERENCE HANDBOOK. Over 700 historical publications including encyclopedias, dictionaries, abstracts, bibliographies and booklists, atlases and guides to records offices and libraries containing the political and constitutional history of the English people from the earliest times onward. 354 pp. THE SHOE STRING PRESS, INC., P.O. Box 1327, 995 Sherman Ave., Hamden, Conn. 06514.

HISTORIC AMERICA GUIDE. Listing of all 50 states including their historic shrines, monuments, battlefields, museums, and residences, covering 400 years. Includes prices, hours and how to get there. 50 full-color maps and 175 illustrations in color and black and white. 292 pp. RAND McNALLY, P.O. Box 7600, Chicago, Ill. 60680.

HISTORIC DOCUMENTS. Provides a listing of speeches, treaties, debates, proclamations, court decisions that have documented historic events. 1,050 pp. CONGRESSIONAL QUARTERLY, INC., 1414 22nd St., N.W., Washington, D.C. 20037.

HOW AND WHERE TO RAISE VENTURE CAPITAL TO FINANCE A BUSINESS. Included are 227 sources of venture capital, classified by name, address, telephone number and individual to contact. Also information as to how to approach a capital source, and many of the author's personal experiences. ENTERPRISE PUBLISHING CO., 1300 Market St., Wilmington, Dela. 19801.

INSTITUTIONAL INVESTOR—ANNUAL FINANCING. Describes alphabetically domestic and foreign firms: 85 major U.S. investment bankers and 85 abroad who handle the bulk of corporate financing during the previous year and for foreign firms, the bulk of government financing. Annually in May. INSTITUTIONAL INVESTOR SYSTEMS, INC., 488 Madison Ave., New York, N.Y. 10022.

INSTITUTIONS. Provides a listing of approximately 700 portfolio managers, analysts and traders of financial institutions in North America. Gives complete organization structures for the largest bank trust departments, mutual fund management companies, insurance group investment departments and the major investment counseling firms. Three issues per year. TECHNIMETRICS, INC., 919 Third Ave., New York, N.Y. 10022.

INSTRUMENTALIST BUYERS' GUIDE. Arranged alphabetically by category, publication provides information on several hundred instrument manufacturers, uniform manufacturers, manufacturers of musical equipment and supplies, music publishers, and other categories serving the music world. "Instrumentalist" Magazine by THE INSTRUMENTALIST CO., 1418 Lake St., Evanston, Ill. 60204.

INSTRUMENTATION REFERENCE ISSUE. Contains an alphabetical listing by product of 7,200 manufacturers and suppliers. 3-8 pp. Annually. SOUND AND VIBRATION, 27101 E. Oviatt Rd., Bay Village, Ohio 44140.

INTERNATIONAL DIRECTORY OF MUSIC EDUCATION INSTITUTIONS. Gives information on institutions offering music education training throughout the world. 115 pp. UNESCO PUBLICATIONS CENTER, P.O. Box 433, New York, N.Y. 10016.

INTERNATIONAL DIRECTORY OF SPECIALIZED CANCER RESEARCH AND TREATMENT ESTABLISHMENTS. Provides a geographical listing of 500 cancer research and treatment institutes. Includes names of directors and department heads. Description of research and treatment facilities and activities. 521 pp. Every four years. INTERNATIONAL UNION AGAINST CANCER, 3 rue du Conseil-general, 1205 Geneva, Switzerland.

INTERNATIONAL FILM GUIDE. Contains reports from fifty countries, including every aspect of the cinema, including film festivals, film books, film schools, film archives, educational films, etc. 608 pp. A. S. BARNES AND COMPANY, Cranbury, N.J. 08512.

INTERNATIONAL INTERTRADE INDEX. Directory presents a descriptive listing of 1,000 foreign manufacturers' products offered to importers, with complete information on each product as to size, price and use. Gives names and addresses of manufacturers; includes a complete listing of new products released by the United States Department of Commerce and other international agencies and firms. Also lists sources of supply. Monthly. "INTERNATIONAL INTERTRADE INDEX," Box 636, Federal Square, Newark, N.J. 07101.

INTERNATIONAL REFERENCE HANDBOOK. Lists 120 nations and provides information on each, such as: publications and cultural institutions, advertising organizations, marketing research organizations, trade and investment organizations. American firms operating in the country, business directories of the country, selected bibliographical references. 600 pp. SIMON & SCHUSTER, 1 W. 39th St., New York, N.Y. 10018.

INTERNATIONAL STOCK AND COMMODITY EXCHANGE DIRECTORY. Lists more than 100 exchanges in over 50 countries, including 60 additional exchanges for which detailed data are not currently available. 350 pp. PHOENIX PUBLISHING, Canaan, N.H. 03741.

JAZZ PUBLICITY II. Provides a listing of over 200 jazz critics and jazz periodicals which are worldwide. 25 pp. REESE MARKEWICH, M.D., 39 Gramercy Park North, New York, N.Y. 10010.

JAZZ—THE LITERATURE OF. Lists and annotates books on every aspect of Jazz. Published by the AMERICAN LIBRARY ASSOCIATION, 50 E. Huron St., Chicago, Ill. 60611.

JOURNAL OF MUSIC THERAPY. Includes articles and research reports by music therapists, physicians, psychologists, psychiatrists and educators on use of music in therapy. Published quarterly by the NATIONAL ASSOCIATION FOR MUSIC THERAPY, P.O. Box 640, Lawrence, Kan. 66044.

KEMP'S MUSIC AND RECORDING INDUSTRY YEARBOOK. Contains British record companies, sound studios, sound equipment, record distributors, television and sound broadcasting companies, music publishers, music libraries, agents and managers, and other allied services and facilities. Includes selected international addresses. 150 pp. NICHOLS PUBLISHING COMPANY, 175 West 79th St., New York, N.Y. 10024.

MATERIALS REFERENCE ISSUE. An alphabetical index of 1,000 manufacturers and producers, and lists suppliers of specific types of wrought ferrous mill forms and shapes, wrought nonferrous castings and formed and shaped parts. 250 pp. Annually. PENTON PUBLISHING CO., Penton Bldg., 614 Superior Ave. West, Cleveland, Ohio 44113.

MEDIA GUIDE INTERNATIONAL: NEWSPAPER, NEWS MAGAZINE EDITION. Provides data of the 800 leading foreign newspapers and new weeklies in the world. Only those papers and magazines with national or near-national circulation and influence in their respective countries, read by top management executives, government officials and other opinion leaders. 243 pp. DIRECTORIES INTERNATIONAL, INC., 1718 Sherman Ave., Evanston, Ill. 60201.

MEDICAL DIRECTORY—U.S. Contains a listing of medical doctors, hospitals, nursing facilities, laboratories, medical information sources, poison control centers, U.S. Medical Schools and Health Care Buyers Guide. U.S. DIRECTORY SERVICE, 121 S.E. 1st Street, P.O. Box 011565-K, Miami, Fla. 33101, telephone orders (305) 371-8881.

MENTAL HEALTH AND FAMILY LIFE EDUCATION. A guide to films, recordings, pamphlets, books, programs, plays, research studies, film strips, covering all aspects of mental health and family life. 840 pp. PERENNIAL EDUCATION, INC., P.O. Box 236, 1825 Willow Rd., Northfield, Ill. 60093.

MENTAL HEALTH DIRECTORY. Listings of personnel of the National Institute of Mental Health, and its regional offices; geographical entries of state institutions and services, with varied data on each as to status and age limitations, programs and services offered, etc. United States Government Printing Office, Division of Public Document, Washington, D.C. 20402.

METALS SOURCEBOOK. Activity reports of the major world-wide producers of metal, mines, smelters and refineries. Twice monthly. McGRAW-HILL, 1221 Ave. of the Americas, New York, N.Y. 10020.

MILITARY INSTITUTIONS AND THE SOCIOLOGY OF WAR: AN ANNOTATED BIBLIOGRAPHY. Provides text and a bibliography of books and other material divided by subject area on Miliary Institutions and the Sociology of War. 338 pp. SAGE PUBLICATIONS, 275 S. Beverly Dr., Beverly Hills, Calif. 90212.

MINER: HIS JOB AND HIS ENVIRONMENT, THE. A review and bibliography of selected recent material and research on his human performance. 206 pp. NATIONAL TECHNICAL INFORMATION SERVICE, Springfield, Va. 22151.

MOTION PICTURE, TV & THEATRE DIRECTORY. Contains 7,500 entries listed alphabetically within over 130 classified headings. Listings range from Advertising Agencies through Video Tape and include Editing Services, Laboratories, Producers and others used in the fields of motion pictures, television and theatre. 152 pp. Semiannually. MOTION PICTURE ENTERPRISES PUBLICATIONS, INC., Tarrytown, N.Y. 10591.

MUSEUM GUIDE. Lists over 100 federal programs and bills in Congress which affect museums. Including the purpose of the program and eligibility requirements, type of assistance available, application tips, financial information on program budget and number of grants awarded, and who's in charge and where to write. ASSOCIATION OF SCIENCE-TECHNOLOGY CENTERS, 2100 Penn Ave. N.W., Washington, D.C. 20037.

MUSEUM MEDIA. A directory and index of publications and audio-visuals available from U.S. and Canadian museums, galleries, art institutes and similar institutions. Listed are books, monographs, catalogs of exhibits, collections, showings, pamphlets, booklets, etc. Excluded are regularly issued magazines, journals and newsletters. Includes several indexes. 456 pp. GALE RESEARCH CO., Book Tower, Detroit, Mich. 48226.

MUSIC INDEX, THE. Alphabetical entries providing a subject and author guide to material in music periodicals from all parts of the world. Published monthly and cumulated annually by INFORMATION COORDINATORS, INC., 1435-37 Randolph St., Detroit, Mich. 48226.

MUSICIAN'S GUIDE, THE. Contains data covering 1,197 colleges, conservatories, junior colleges and schools with courses and degrees offered in music, music department chairmen, and scholarships and fellowships available; over 800 music periodicals; 1,625 recent books on music; 263 competitions and awards; 634 opera companies; 814 symphony orchestras, with names of conductor, business manager and concertmaster; 572 summer camps and workshops; 412 music libraries; 5,000 music publishers; 440 newspapers and periodicals, with names of editors, critics and record reviewers; basic classical, jazz and rock record libraries; 882 music festivals. Also associations, arts councils, awards statistics, certified music teachers and registered piano tuners, many other lists. Careers chart. 1,025 pp. Published triennially by MUSIC INFORMATION SERVICE, INC., 310 Madison Ave., New York, N.Y. 10017.

NATIONAL DIRECTORY OF FREE TOURIST ATTRACTIONS. Provides a listing of free gardens, restored villages, ships, museums and other interesting presentations of history, science, folk and fine art throughout the United States. PILOT BOOKS, 347 Fifth Ave., New York, N.Y. 10016.

NATIONAL FEDERATION HANDBOOK. Presents entries of approximately 50 public high school associations, members of the Federation of State High School Associations. Biennially. NATIONAL FEDERATION OF STATE HIGH SCHOOL ASSOCIATIONS, P.O. Box 98, Elgin, Ill. 60120.

NATIONAL INDUSTRIAL RECREATION ASSOCIATION MEMBERSHIP DIRECTORY. Contains an Alpha-Geographic listing of all business, industry and military members of the National Industrial Recreation Association. Provides names and addresses of members of the association and is available at no cost to business and industry members as well as associate members. Associate members are defined as suppliers of recreation-leisure time products services. Published yearly by the NATIONAL INDUSTRIAL RECREATION ASSOCIATION, 20 N. Wacker Drive, Chicago, Ill. 60606.

NATIONAL MUSIC COUNCIL BULLETIN. Presents listings of 60 American music organizations, members of the National Music Council—membership of the 60 organizations exceeds two million persons. Entries on organization executives included. Published semi-annually by the NATIONAL MUSIC COUNCIL, 250 West 57th St., Suite 626, New York, N.Y. 10019.

NATIONAL OPERA ASSOCIATION—MEMBERSHIP DIRECTORY. Alphabetical listing within membership divisions of 750 opera companies, composers, directors, publishers, teachers, translators, and other interested persons in the National Opera Association. Annually in January. NATIONAL OPERA ASSOCIATION, c/o Mary Elaine Wallace, School of Music, Southern Illinois University, Carbondale, Ill. 62901.

NATIONAL REAL ESTATE INVESTOR DIRECTORY. An alphabetical listing of appraisers, associates, builders, contractors, developers, corporate real estate managers, economic and industrial development authorities, equity investors and investment companies, housing and urban renewal authorities, etc. 210 pp. Annual. COMMUNICATION CHANNELS, INC., 461 Eighth Ave., New York, N.Y. 10001.

NATIONAL ROSTER OF REALTORS DIRECTORY. Alpha-geographic listing of names and addresses of 110,000 members of the National Association of Realtors. Annually. STAMATS PUBLISHING CO., 427 6th Ave., S.E., Cedar Rapids, Iowa 52406.

NATIONAL SECURITY AFFAIRS. Describes key sources of information on national security affairs by subject categories. Listed are books, periodicals, research and educational organizations, libraries, etc. 400 pp. GALE RESEARCH CO., Book Tower, Detroit, Mich. 48226.

NATIONAL SOURCE AND OPPORTUNITY DIRECTORY, THE. Contains information regarding business contacts, sources, unique opportunities, financial news, mortgage and finance journal, real estate, etc. NDF, Box 703, Freeport, Ill. 61032.

NEED A LIFT. Contains source of career, scholarship and loan information for not only children of veterans, but for all children. Includes fellowships, loans and part-time jobs to help finance their education, lists information relative to state laws offering educational benefits. Serves as an excellent guide for teachers and parents in planning with students to further their education beyond high school. 132 pp. THE AMERICAN LEGION, Dept. S., P.O. Box 1055, Indianapolis, Ind. 46206.

NEW CODE NAMES DICTIONARY. A dictionary of 2,500 code names, cover words, slang terms, and nicknames. Four softbound issues. GALE RESEARCH CO., Book Tower, Detroit, Mich. 48226.

NEW YORK TIMES POLITICAL MARKETPLACE. A who's who of politics, national, state and local. Lists over 20,000 officials: U.S. Senators and Representatives, governors and all other statewide elected officials of the 50 United States. Also lists all members of every state legislature, mayors of the 10 largest cities of each state and thousands of officials of all major political parties. Also national committees, fund raising committees, etc. 800 pp. QUADRANGLE BOOKS, 3 Park Ave., New York, N.Y. 10016.

NEWS BUREAUS IN THE U.S. Contains a listing of more than 500 newspapers, magazines, business publications, wire services and syndicates. Features the addresses, phone numbers, names of editorial personnel and other information including state capital, suburban and regional news bureaus, plus Washington, D.C., and all bureaus in every state. RICHARD WEINER, INC., 888 Seventh Ave., New York, N.Y. 10019.

NEWSPAPER DIRECTORY, THE. Contains over 1,800 influential weekly newspapers, the labor press, ethnic group publications, etc. NATIONAL RESEARCH BUREAU, Burlington, Iowa, 52601. Volume 1 of five volumes.

NEWSPAPER INDEXES: A LOCATION AND SUBJECT GUIDE FOR RESEARCHERS. Identifies hundreds of newspaper indexes available in 300 locations—libraries, historical and genealogical societies, as well as indexes in the possession of individuals. Indexed into two parts, the first part is a listing of the newspapers indexed, arranged by state, county and town in which the paper was published with dates of the index coverage and a letter symbol designating the index location. Included are some listings for church publications, American foreign language newspapers, specialized subjects and other miscellaneous newspapers. 210 pp. SCARECROW PRESS, INC., P.O. Box 656, Metuchen, N.J. 08840.

NEWSPAPER PRESS DIRECTORY. Lists newspapers, periodicals, trade and technical journals, house organs and directories published in the British Isles. Also includes British Commonwealth newspapers as well as publications of other principal overseas countries. 1,062 pp. INTERNATIONAL PUBLICATIONS SERVICE, 114 E. 32nd St., New York, N.Y. 10016.

NIH FACTBOOK. A guide to programs and activities of the National Institute of Health. Including a chronological history of the growth of this powerful federal agency which accounts for nearly 40% of all expenditures for medical research in the United States. Annually. 597 pp. MARQUIS WHO'S WHO, INC., 200 East Ohio St., Chicago, Ill. 60611.

NORTH AMERICAN FILM AND VIDEO DIRECTORY: A GUIDE TO MEDIA COLLECTIONS AND SERVICES. Lists some 2,000 college, public, special museum and archival libraries and media centers with 16 mm and/or video collections and programs are listed by state and city. Also includes loan and rental policies, publications, production facilities budgets, equipment on hand, special collections, selection policies, etc. 284 pp. STECHERT MACMILLAN, INC., 866 Third Ave., New York, N.Y. 10022.

OFFICIAL BASEBALL REGISTER. Lists season-by-season records and personal data of more than 1,100 active major league players, managers, coaches, umpires, and former stars, arranged alphabetically. 528 pp. Annually. THE SPORTING NEWS, P.O. Box 56, St. Louis, Mo. 63166.

OFFICIAL NATIONAL BASKETBALL ASSOCIATION GUIDE. Guide arranged alphabetically by sports, contains a listing of all National Basketball Association records since 1946, including playoffs, championship, team and individual records. Contains a complete listing of active players and their playing statistics plus a directory of club officials. Also contains a comparison of last season team records against each other, and current season schedules. 512 pp. Annually. THE SPORTING NEWS, P.O. Box 56, St. Louis, Mo. 63166.

PACKAGING INFORMATION SOURCES. An annotated bibliography covering the literature that deals with the various aspects of the packaging industry. General subjects covered are planning and development, merchandising, management and operations, materials, adhesives, closures, retail unit packages, shipping containers, testing machinery, and special packaging problems. 225 pp. Published by GALE RESEARCH CO., Book Tower, Detroit, Mich. 48226.

PHOTOGRAPHER'S MARKET. Lists 1,616 buyers and users of free lance photography in categories such as ad agencies, PR firms, periodicals, book publishers, architectural firms, audiovisual firms, etc., as well as other firms and services of use to photographers such as galleries, clubs, technical services, competitions and foundations. Most are listed alphabetically according to category, some geographically (clubs and technical services). 432 pp. Annual. WRITER'S DIGEST, 9933 Alliance Rd., Cincinnati, Ohio 45242.

PHOTOGRAPHIC LITERATURE VOLUMES I AND II. Consists of a bibliography of approximately 12,000 basic books, journals, magazines, articles and technical papers on photography arranged under 1,200 subject headings. 335 pp. MORGAN AND MORGAN, INC., 145 Palisades St., Dobbs Ferry, N.Y. 10522.

PRICE LIST AND GUIDE TO MEDICAL PERIODICALS. An alphabetical price list and guide to 1,350 periodicals. 28 pp. Annually. Seaboard Subscription Agency, P.O. Box 1482, 44 Fulton St., Allentown, Pa. 18105.

PRINTERS BUYING GUIDE. Lists all suppliers of the printing industry located in the New York metropolitan area. Published by PRINTING INDUSTRIES OF METRO-POLITAN NEW YORK INC., 461 8th Ave., New York, N.Y. 10001.

PUBLISHERS' INTERNATIONAL DIRECTORY. Names and addresses of over 30,000 active publishers in 145 countries—geographically arranged and coded to indicate the firms' specialties in 53 different publishing areas. Includes an index listing publishers by subject interests with 60,000 cross references; a guide to publishers' and booksellers' associations in 50 countries; an international bibliography of publishers' directory and index terms. Two volumes. 1,100 pp. R. R. BOWKER CO., 1180 Avenue of the Americas, New York, N.Y. 10036.

PUBLISHERS' TRADE LIST ANNUAL. Binds the trade order list of about 2,550 publishers into seven large volumes. It includes the International Standard Book Numbers. 10,000 pp. Annually. R R. BOWKER CO., 1180 Avenue of the Americas, New York, N.Y. 10036.

RAILROADS. Contains a collection of 259 books on North American railroads, locomotives, rolling stock, stations, railroads by region, tourist and industrial streetcars and interurbans, museums and collecting. 152 pp. LIBRARIES UNLIMITED, INC. P.O. Box 263, Littleton, Colo. 80160.

REFERENCE ISSUE. Categorically describes 6,000 facilities for the deaf and hard of hearing—residential schools, public day schools and classes, denominational and private schools in the United States and Canada. Gives names of religious personnel for the deaf in the U.S., camps for the deaf and hard of hearing, organizations for the deaf in the U.S., list of homes for the aged deaf, speech and hearing centers, and information about training of the deaf. 280 pp. Annually. "AMERICAN ANNALS OF THE DEAF," 5034 Wisconsin Ave., N.W., Washington, D.C. 20014.

RESEARCH CENTERS DIRECTORY. Contains information on the existence, location, activities, and fields of interest of the nearby 5,500 university-related and independent non-profit research units. Subject index included. 1,056 pp. Published by GALE RESEARCH CO., Book Tower, Detroit, Mich. 48226.

RESEARCH AND DEVELOPMENT DIRECTORY. Provides a listing of firms involved in R&D activities, classified by type. Economic Research Bureau of the San Diego Chamber of Commerce, 233 A Street, Suite 300, San Diego, Calif. 92101.

SAFETY JOURNAL DIRECTORY. Provides entries of 2,000 American and foreign associations and trade groups in the accident and fire prevention field; includes a list of safety product manufacturers. Annually. "THE SAFETY JOURNAL," Wilmary Building, Anderson, S.C. 29621.

SAFETY MAGAZINE—ROSTER ISSUE. Contains an alphabetical listing of 1,000 members of the Metropolitan Chapter of the American Society of Safety Engineers and of the Commercial Vehicle Section of the Greater New York Safety Council; includes other members of traffic engineers and others interested in safety precautions. 20 pp. Annually. GREATER NEW YORK SAFETY COUNCIL, 302 Fifth Ave., New York, N.Y. 10016.

SAFETY MATERIALS DIRECTORY. Listed are safety aids available to the private boating industry. Arranged by categories such as: boating guides and pamphlets; courses; films; navigation; rules and regulations; safety equipment. 45 pp. THE BOATING INDUSTRY, 205 East 42nd St., New York, N.Y. 10017.

SALES AND MARKETING EXECUTIVES INTERNATIONAL—ANNUAL REPORT AND DIRECTORY. Publication contains names of approximately 800 officers, directors, national committeemen and officers of affiliated clubs of Sales and Marketing Executives International. Annual. SALES AND MARKETING EXECUTIVES INTER-NATIONAL, 380 Lexington Ave., New York, N.Y. 10017.

SECURITY SYSTEMS. The market for purchased private security systems is analyzed. The structure of the industry is examined and the products-protective services, deterrent equipment, monitoring and detection systems and fire control are described. An overview of the market is presented with a list of selected companies that manufacture security equipment or provide some security service. 60 pp. PREDICASTS, INC., 200 University Center, Research Center, 11001 Cedar Ave., Cleveland, Ohio 44106.

SOCIETY OF THE PLASTICS INDUSTRY DIRECTORY AND BUYERS' GUIDE OF MEMBERS. Directory consists of an alpha-geographic listing of 1,200 plastics industry companies, giving firm name, address, key personnel, products and processes; included is a who's who of The Society of the Plastics Industry. 407 pp. Annual. SOCIETY OF THE PLASTICS INDUSTRY, INC., 355 Lexington Ave., New York, N.Y. 10017.

PRINCIPAL BUSINESS DIRECTORIES

SOURCES OF STATISTICS. This guide provides the principal sources of statistics in the United Kingdom, the United States and various international organizations. Grouped under ten headings are those publications covering demographics, sociology, education, labor, production, trade, finance, prices, transport and tourism. 126 pp. THE SHOE STRING PRESS, INC., 995 Sherman Ave., Hamden, Conn. 06514.

STATISTICAL ABSTRACT OF THE UNITED STATES. This guide to sources list over 800 statistical publications on 50 major subjects, including population, government, health, education, agriculture, industry, construction, etc. 1,300 tables and charts are also included. 1,024 pp. Annually. Superintendent of Documents, U.S. GOVERNMENT PRINTING OFFICE, Washington, D.C. 20402.

THE TRADEMARK REGISTER OF THE UNITED STATES—1977 EDITION. Alphabetically arranged, classified entries of approximately 450,000 currently registered trademarks in the United States Patent Office since 1881, with date of registration number. 1,000 pp. Annually. THE TRADEMARK REGISTER, 422 Washington Bldg., Washington, D.C. 20005.

TRADE NAMES DICTIONARY. A guide to trade names of food, beverages, apparel, household appliances, sports equipment and other consumer products. 100,000 entries listed. Two Volumes - 666 pp. GALE RESEARCH CO., Book Tower, Detroit, Mich. 48226.

UNESCO HANDBOOK OF INTERNATIONAL EXCHANGES. A reference on international activities and exchanges in the fields of education, science, culture and mass communication. Covers the aims, programs and activities of 295 international organizations and more than 5,000 governmental and nongovernmental agencies and institutions in 130 countries and territories. 1,102 pp. Published by UNIPUB, INC., P.O. Box 433, New York, N.Y. 10016.

UNITED NATIONS LIBRARY, THE. A bibliography containing all items relating to the Library and to the documents of the United Nations Library in New York. Also a description of the historical evolution of the Library. 250 pp. AMERICAN LIBRARY ASSOCIATION, 59 E. Huron St., Chicago, Ill. 60611.

URBAN REAL ESTATE RESEARCH. Publication contains an annotated list of 951 publications and research in process related to urban land use and urban planning, including central business district, economic base, finance, housing, industry, land planning, land use, zoning, real estate, redevelopment, shopping center, taxation, transportation, and urban renewal studies. Systematic topics include bibliographies, textbooks, reference works, metropolitan area studies, regional studies, urban research, and urbanism. Entries arranged by subject, with author and geographic indexes. 90 pp. ULI-THE URBAN LAND INSTITUTE, Ring Building., 1200 18th St., N.W., Washington, D.C. 20036.

U.S. NON-PROFIT ORGANIZATIONS IN DEVELOPMENT ASSISTANCE ABROAD—1971. Lists 499 non-profit organizations and their programs in 124 countries around the world (excluding Europe). 1,038 pp. TECHNICAL ASSISTANCE INFORMATION CLEARING HOUSE OF THE AMERICAN COUNCIL OF VOLUNTARY AGENCIES FOR FOREIGN SERVICE, INC., 200 Park Ave., S., New York, N.Y. 10003.

U.S. OBSERVATORIES: A DIRECTORY AND TRAVEL GUIDE. Geographical listing of approximately 300 optical and radio observatories and planetariums, including address, description of the facility, admission charges, brief history, etc. 175 pp. VAN NOSTRAND REINHOLD CO., Division of Litton Educational Publishing, Inc., New York, N.Y. 10001.

U.S. ZIP CODE BUSINESS MARKETING MAP ATLAS. Provides over 465 U.S. cities and metropolitan markets, five digit county maps, U.S. sectional center wall map, postal region state maps, income, age and occupation information, complete zip code marketing and advertising applications, full color demographic maps, complete postal marketing data, both as numeric and alphabetic U.S. post office directory. 1,000 pp. plus. NATIONAL DEMOGRAPHIC RESEARCH, 24 East Wesley Street, South Hackensack, N.J. 07606.

U.S. ZIP CODE DIRECTORY. Lists all cities and their zip codes in the U.S. U.S. ZIP CODE SERVICE, P.O. Box 2808, Main Post Office, Washington, D.C. 20013. (Not a U.S. Government publication.)

WALLCOVERINGS—ANNUAL DIRECTORY. Directory contains a master resources list, an alphabetically arranged list of 1,000 manufacturers, wholesalers and suppliers, wallpaper mills, specialty wallcoverings, machine print lines, hand prints, scenics and murals, etc. Also included is a list of accessory and equipment manufacturers. Annually. 172 pp. WALL COVERINGS, 209 Dunn Ave., Stamford, Conn. 06905.

WHAT'S HAPPENING, WHEN. Lists all the special promotion days, weeks, months plus many important dates. Designed to assist in the coordination of advertising and marketing plans with established observances during the year. Includes names and addresses of sponsors and other pertinent data. 28 pp. Annual. NATIONAL RESEARCH BUREAU, INC., 424 N. 3rd St., Burlington, Iowa 52601.

WHO WAS WHO IN AMERICAN HISTORY—SCIENCE AND TECHNOLOGY. Listing of 10,000 scientists, engineers, and inventors of American History. Covers more than 350 years of American History. 688 pp. MARQUIS WHO'S WHO INC., 200 East Ohio St., Chicago, Ill. 60611.

WHO'S WHO IN ADVERTISING. Lists 6,500 executives in all areas of advertising in the U.S. and Canada plus professors of advertising and marketing. 764 pp. Biennially. REDFIELD PUBLISHING CO., INC., P.O. Box 556, Rye, New York 10580.

WHO'S WHO IN BOOK MANUFACTURING. A list of firms and people who produce books. Included are their suppliers, bookbinders, and the manufacturers of bookbinding equipment. Each manufacturer will have their products and specialties, their major capital equipment and back-up facilities. Their number of employees, addresses, and other company data. Published by NORTH AMERICAN PUBLISHING CO., 401 N. Broad St., Philadelphia, Pa. 19108.

WHO'S WHO IN PUBLIC RELATIONS. An alpha-geographic list of 5,000 public relation leaders in 59 countries, including full biographical sketches of each. 474 pp. Published every four or five years. PR PUBLISHING CO., INC., P.O. Box 600, Dudley House, Exeter, New Hampshire 03833.

WHO'S WHO IN PUBLISHING. An alphabetical list of over 2,000 biographical sketches for men and women throughout the world prominent and active in the world of publishing. 225 pp. Published every five years by ALEXANDER P. WALES, 18 Charing Cross, London, England.

WHO'S WHO IN RELIGION. Contains more than 18,500 sketches of outstanding men and women from America's religious community. Including church officials (both lay and clergy), religious educators, founders and directors of religious charities and other religious organizations, editors and writers for major religious publications, plus leading priests, rabbis, ministers, and other clergy. 736 pp. MARQUIS PUBLICATIONS, 200 East Ohio St., Room 5605, Chicago, Ill. 60611.

WORLD DIRECTORY OF MAP COLLECTIONS. Data on 285 map and chart collections held in national libraries, scientific and historic societies, and military departments of 46 countries. Including printed and manuscript maps, atlases, globes, relief models, aerial photographs, reference books, serials. 326 pp. UNIPUB, Box 433, Murray Hill Station, New York, N.Y. 10016.

WORLD DIRECTORY OF ORGANIZATIONS. Comprehensive guide to organizations in all parts of the world that are concerned with the pressing problems of the human environment. Describes over 3,200 organizations in nearly 200 countries. 288 pp. CENTER FOR CALIFORNIA PUBLIC AFFAIRS, P.O. Box 30, Claremont, Calif. 91711.

WORLD DIRECTORY OF RESEARCH CENTERS. Lists 4,800 American organizations and many others throughout the world engaged in research on the environment. Includes research institutes, laboratories, industrial organizations and private foundations and federal, state and local governmental organizations. Material is divided into subject categories. 330 pp. R. R. BOWKER CO., P.O. Box 1807, Ann Arbor, Mich. 48106.

WORLD GUIDE TO ABBREVIATIONS OF ASSOCIATION AND INSTITUTIONS. This two-volume edition lists 50,000 nationally and internationally accepted Roman alphabet acronyms used by more than 120 governmental, commercial, cultural, religious, and other institutions. An alphabetical index of acronyms by country is also included. 1,295 pp. R. R. BOWKER CO., 1180 Avenue of the Americas, New York, N.Y. 10036.

WORLD GUIDE TO SCIENTIFIC ASSOCIATIONS. Describes 10,000 scientific associations, organizations and academies in more than 134 countries. Covers all scientific disciplines plus medically oriented groups. Nams are arranged by countries with an index to field of endeavor. 700 pp. R. R. BOWKER CO., P.O. Box 1807, Ann Arbor, Mich. 48106.

ZIPCODER. Provides over 2,500 9-⅞" quality bond loose-leaf pages of current zip code listings with county identification and all single coded cities and over 60,000 place name listings alphabetically by state on white bond paper, etc. ZIPCO, INC., 40 Guernsey St., Stamford, Conn. 06904.

COMPILED LISTS

There are many sources from which lists can be compiled—directories being the most common, but by no means the only source. Only the more common sources are included in the basic list.

Labor Organizations

One way to pinpoint a list of people with common occupations is to use a list compiled from members of labor organizations.

Religious Organizations

While the availability of church and synagogue membership lists varies, this is a frequently used source for fund-raising membership lists. To obtain the use of such lists, direct mail advertisers often work some kind of contribution arrangement with their sources.

School Lists

Many advertisers pay special attention to lists of both students and teachers. Particularly in demand for special promotions are lists of students about to graduate. Many schools make such lists available without charge and several list compilers offer lists to cover all schools in a given area.

Convention Registration Lists

Groups sponsoring conventions often make it a regular practice to publish lists of all registrants. These are not only used for special promotions during the conventions, but also are frequently used both for pre-convention and post-convention mailings. Such lists are frequently available only to members of the sponsor group and/or exhibitors at trade shows held in conjunction with the conventions.

Just as association membership lists are often considered choice sources for the development of mailing lists, those who attend conventions are also often considered to represent a particularly good audience for direct mail of many types.

Cultural Interests

Many direct mail advertisers have a special interest in lists of those who purchase theater, concert, or opera tickets; patrons of art galleries and museums; subscribers to literary and other cultural magazines; purchasers of records, music, and musical instruments;

book buyers; and similar groups. Such lists obviously have a high potential for those who are promoting similar products, services or events and are often considered to have better-than-average potential for many other products and services promoted through direct mail.

Birth Lists

Birth lists are followed with special interest by many direct mail advertisers. New parents have been found to be highly responsive to many direct mail promotions. While makers of such items as baby foods, diaper services, and photographs are obvious users of such lists, many other direct mail advertisers consider new parents logical prospects. For example, one firm which compiles a national birth list reports that the majority of users of this list want to promote products and services far removed from the babies' needs. For example, companies which market through door-to-door sales have found new mothers and fathers particularly receptive to offers which promise them a source of additional income. Another frequent user of such lists are correspondent schools.

Birth lists are compiled in a number of different ways. Birth registration records are often available. In many communities, newspapers regularly publish lists of all new parents. In other cases, hospitals make available such information. Most direct mail advertisers, however, turn to the professionals who compile such lists and then rent or sell them to interested users.

Alumni Lists

Another excellent source for lists with high potential are alumni groups—particularly those associated with colleges and universities. Some lists are available broken down not only by school and year graduated but also by degrees awarded and other more specialized information. The availability of such lists varies greatly so it is well to check with a list compiler or broker before making plans to use any specific list.

Voter Registration Lists

Local lists are often compiled from the official voter registration lists. Obtaining such lists for direct mail use varies from simple to highly complicated. As one list expert puts it, "Occasionally they're free; sometimes there's a regular charge, and frequently you have to know someone."

Contributors

Those who have contributed to one cause or another often represent good potential for other mailers. They are, of course, particularly valuable names for those seeking a contribution for a similar cause. Most often they are obtained on an exchange basis, although many lists of this nature are available for rental and a number of list brokers specialize in making arrangements for use of such lists. Unfortunately, many contributors' lists are badly out of date and/or compiled with little attention to accuracy.

Mail Order Buyers

The best list for anyone seeking to sell a product by mail order is a list of known mail order *buyers*. Successful mail order advertisers recognize that any group of people contains only a certain percentage who can be described as "mail oriented"—those who readily respond to offers to purchase products or services by mail.

The very best list, of course, is one composed of those who have previously bought a similar product from you *by mail*. Next best is probably a list of those who have bought an unrelated product from you by mail. The reason why such lists are particularly important is that these buyers have already been convinced that you represent a reliable—and desirable—source (unless, of course, you have failed to serve them satisfactorily in the past).

In "Successful Direct Mail Advertising and Selling," mail order expert Bob Stone comments[1]:

> At National Research Bureau, we consider our customer list the most valuable asset we have. No list we buy or rent comes close to it in pull. For instance, when we launched *Sparks,* a service for small businesses, outside lists averaged a little less than 4% on a $1 offer. Our customer list pulled 14%!
>
> Why the tremendous pulling power of a customer list? There are two reasons: (1) everyone on the list has previously bought by mail; (2) every customer receiving the mail knows the firm as a result of previous purchase. Point two makes the difference. When you use an outside list of known mail order buyers, the list qualifies on the basis of mail-buying habits. When you use your own customer list you have mail-buying habits *plus* familiarity with your organization too. It's an unbeatable combination.

To supplement your own mail order customer lists, the next best source is those who have purchased similar products from others *by mail*. While many mail order companies will not rent their customer lists for use in promoting products competitive

---

[1]Copyright Prentice-Hall, Inc.

with their own, it is frequently possible to arrange an exchange of customer lists.

Don't underestimate the importance of "mail oriented" prospects. Many a great mail order idea has fallen flat because the promoter was unable to find enough available lists of mail order buyers within the fields of interest in the product or service he was offering. It is not uncommon to find that lists of mail order buyers will pull 10, 20, or 30 times the number of orders as can be obtained through lists of people with basically the same characteristics but who have not necessarily identified themselves as being "mail oriented." An additional advantage is that most mail order buyer lists have been screened for deadbeats and slow payers.

Expires

Many companies who solicit business by mail order may not rent their active customer lists but will offer lists of previous buyers. These lists are usually classified by year of last purchase and often by other characteristics such as amount of purchases. This is particularly true in the subscription field, where lists of active subscribers are often unavailable while lists of those who have let subscriptions expire are readily available.

In using lists of expires it is important to recognize two points: (1) such lists are often poorly maintained and may easily contain a high percentage of "nixies" (undeliverable mail); and (2) if you are trying to sell by mail order, make sure that the expires list contains a high percentage of names which were originally obtained through mail order selling.

Inquiry Lists

Another type of compiled list which is available from many direct mail advertisers—particularly those who sell by mail order—is the inquiry list. Such lists consist of those who have made inquiries —usually by mail—about a specific product or service. Such lists may or may not include inquirers who have been converted to customers.

Such lists are of questionable value for most direct mail advertisers, although there are times when inquiry lists represent the only compiled list readily available to cover some specific interest area.

Automobile Lists

The basic list source for many direct mail advertisers is automobile and truck registrations. Nationwide, state, and local vehicle registration lists are available and can be broken down in a variety of ways including by make and model of vehicle, multiple vehicle ownership, and so forth.

Manufacturers of automobiles, automotive accessories, and supplies such as gas and oil are obvious users of such lists. But vehicle registration lists are also used by direct mail advertisers in many other fields. It has generally been found that ownership of certain makes and models of automobiles is compatible with other specific interests.

Frequently, direct mail advertisers will combine vehicle registration information with other factors to isolate a particular prospect audience. For example, an advertiser might select a group of census tracts where the average income level is high. And then to further refine the list and eliminate names of individuals with low incomes who may live within these areas, the advertiser may select only families with newer models of more expensive automobiles or just families owning two or more automobiles. While this doesn't necessarily yield a 100% accurate rate, it usually produces a very high percentage of names which meet the established qualifications.

While it is possible in certain areas to obtain vehicle registration lists directly from government sources, the more common practice is to deal through compilers who have converted the registration records to coded mailing lists for rental purposes.

Homeowner Lists

Along with automobile registration lists, homeowner lists are favorites of direct mail advertisers in many fields. One problem that frequently arises in the use of such lists is that the registered owner of a given home is not necessarily the resident of that home. Therefore, such lists should be approached with caution unless your primary purpose is to reach people who own homes—regardless of whether or not they actually reside in the area you have selected for promotion.

OTHER DIRECT MAIL LIST SOURCES

Even though we have already discussed 57 different list sources, there are still at least nine other sources for mailing lists—including the three most important of all which we have left for last.

Trade and Consumer Publications

Many publications make their subscription lists or other specially compiled lists available for rental. In many cases, however, use is limited to advertisers. Generally, it can be assumed that publication lists are as up to date as any lists available.

Quite frequently subscription lists are used for direct mail which directly ties in with space advertising. Such a technique, for example, makes sampling possible and gives the advertiser an opportunity to use more copy than is practical or economical in space advertising.

Federal Government Sources

While the Federal Government is not in the direct-mail-list-compiling business, it still represents an excellent source for many kinds of lists. For example, hundreds of business and institutional directories are published by government agencies and are available at low cost from the Superintendent of Documents, Washington, D.C. 20402. You can obtain a catalog of all available government publications but the best starting point is your nearest field office of the Department of Commerce.

Other Government Sources

State and local governments are also good list sources for many direct mail advertisers. Among the lists which can frequently be obtained are taxpayers, voting lists, birth names, marriage license applicants, automobile and truck registration lists, boat registrations, hunting and fishing licenses, and so forth. The availability of any particular kind of list varies from place to place so no general "rules" can be offered. In most cases, local lettershops have a working knowledge of just what types of lists are available and can arrange to get them for you.

Local Post Offices

While postmasters are not list compilers, they can assist you with information which makes it possible to mail to certain areas without lists. For example, you can mail to all rural route boxholders without addressing by name or address. Postmasters will provide information as to how many boxholders are on each of the rural routes they supervise and all you need to do is to prepare bundles of mailing pieces for each route you wish to cover and request full boxholder distribution.

Business Services and Construction Reports

Many direct mail advertisers make regular use of special services which provide information useful for compilation of mailing lists. For example, you can subscribe to reports which list all new construction in a given area. Other services cover personnel changes, major business activity, and so forth.

List Exchanges

We have already mentioned several cases where lists are available on an exchange basis. A direct exchange on a name-for-a-name basis is often the working arrangement between mail order companies. Similar arrangements are made in other direct mail areas. List brokers frequently handle exchange arrangements and maintain the necessary records.

While a name-for-name exchange sounds quite simple on the surface, it is not an arrangement to enter without a thorough consideration of all the facts. All lists, even though they represent mail order buyers for similar products, do not necessarily balance out one another. It is not uncommon for some mail order companies to hold back their best buyers when making an exchange and offer only lists with limited potential.

It is also important to make sure that *the offers* which will be made balance out one another. Some mail order advertisers will use exchange lists to offer free samples, catalogs, or low-priced come-ons. Since such offers usually bring a particularly heavy response, they can quickly skim the cream off competitors' lists and convert the names of respondents to the mailer's own list, eliminating the need for further exchanges. There is nothing wrong with this procedure *if both parties* to the exchange are making similar offers. But if one party makes a cream-skimming offer while the other makes a direct full-price offer, the exchange quickly becomes inequitable.

List Compilers

In many cases there is no good reason why you should compile your own lists for there are many specialists ready and able to do the job for you. In fact, a list compiler quite probably has already compiled the list you need and will either rent or sell it to you for less than it will cost you to compile it.

Many list compilers have extensive catalogs of pre-compiled lists. A representative sample of the kind of lists you can obtain starts at the bottom. Most pre-compiled lists are available at between $25 and $50 per thousand names, although some of the more-difficult-to-compile lists or those with limited markets will cost as much as $100 per thousand names.

List compilers use many sources, including most of those we have listed. Some list compilers specialize in compiling a specific kind of list such as industrial lists, birth lists, retail merchants, automobile registration lists, and so forth. Others are in business to compile every possible kind of mailing list for which there is a market. You will generally find that a vertical specialist will provide the best list if you have a vertical need.

TYPICAL COMPILED MAILING LISTS

There is almost no limitation to the types of people you can reach through compiled mailing lists. The following examples show the quantity and titles of typical lists among the thousands offered by a single list compiler.

4,782	Abattoirs and Slaughterhouses	70,108	Barbershops
109	Abdominal Belt Manufacturers	507	Bargain Basements in Department Stores
1,441	Accordion Players (Professional)	806	Basket Makers
		559	Baths, Turkish
48,622	Accountants (CPA)	132,023	Beauty Salons
9,404	Advertising Agencies	62	Beeswax Manufacturers and Distributors
21	Agar Manufacturers	40	Bellfounders
55,822	Aircraft Owners (Private)	10	Best-dressed Ladies
150,090	Aircraft Pilots (Commercial)	132	Better Business Bureaus
		34	Bird Cage Manufacturers
721	Alcoholism Clinics	606	Blacksmiths
101	Animals (Stuffed) Manufacturers	3,586	Blood Banks (in hospitals)
32	Anvil Manufacturers	2,500,000	Blue-Collar Workers
652	Archaeologists	15,375	Boards of Education
30	Aspirin Manufacturers	1,912,301	Boat Owners
253,114	Attorneys	7,399	Bowling Alleys
19,100	Bakers	490	Brassiere Manufacturers

TYPICAL COMPILED MAILING LISTS (cont.)

5,900	Brown (firms trading under the name of)
74,567	Builders and General Contractors
67	Bulldozer Manufacturers
1,933	Business Brokers
2,500,000	Businesses, One-man
532	Button Manufacturers
186	Calico Printers
811	Camera Clubs
170	Candlemakers
83,737	Carpenters and Builders
278	Cartoonists
13	Cascara Sagrada Manufacturers
376	Cathedrals
17,820	Churches, Catholic
107	Catsup Manufacturers
3,000	Celebrities
9,524	Cemeteries
3,821	Chambers of Commerce
13,539	Charitable Organizations
1,310	Cheese Factories
23	Chess and Chessboard Manufacturers
4,000	Chinese Laundries
54	Chintz Manufacturers
23,482	Cigar and Tobacco Stores
74	Circuses
262,211	Clergymen
300,000	Clubs and Associations
388	Coffin and Casket Manufacturers
9,935	College Coaches
444,000	College Professors and Instructors
9,000	Country Stores
199	Crow Bar Manufacturers
1,823	Daily Newspapers
97	Dams
29	Date Packers
10,971	Day Nurseries
16,878	Decorators (Interior)

13	Degasser Manufacturers
10,600	Delicatessen Stores
136	Demolishers (factory)
103,424	Dentists
11,580	Department Stores
522	Diamond Cutters
92	Diaper Manufacturers
269	Dietitians' Schools
35	Dining Car Supervisors
38	Dishcloth Manufacturers
212	Divers (Water—Professional
279,774	Doctors
18	Dog Biscuit Manufacturers
11,212	Dog Breeders and Kennels
217	Doll Manufacturers
41	Door Bell Manufacturers
4,932	Doughnut Bakers
14,566	Drive-in Restaurants
48,869	Drugstores
56,102	Drycleaners
104	Dumbwaiter Manufacturers
5,536	Ear, Nose and Throat Specialists
25	Eau de Cologne Manufacturers
13,000	Economists
35,000	Editors
714	Efficiency Engineers
3,151	Electric Light and Power Companies
74,899	Elementary Schools
781,000	Elementary Schoolteachers
1,512	Elks Lodges
1,823	Embroiderers
259	Emerald Dealers
23,189	Engineers, Aeronautical
292,517	Factories
8,090	Farmers' Co-operatives
23,928	Finance Companies
18,881	Fire Brigades (Volunteer)
4,789	Firearms Dealers

TYPICAL COMPILED MAILING LISTS (cont.)

489	Fishing Clubs	13,708	Implement Dealers
25,234	Florists	111,522	Insurance Brokers
89	Fox Hunt Clubs	16,878	Interior Decorators
1,402	Fruit Canners	11,278	Investment Analysts
25,054	Funeral Directors	102	Ironing Board Manufacturers
35,219	Furniture Dealers		
5,542	Garbage Collecting Firms	18	Jet Plane Manufacturers
43	Geiger Counter Manufacturers	31,069	Jewelers (Retail)
		16	Jigsaw Puzzle Manufacturers
8,500	Geophysicists		
26,134	Gift Shops	8,919	Judges
8,532	Golf Clubs	9,212	Junk Dealers
27,904	Grain Dealers	356	Keg and Barrel Manufacturers
31,885	Greenhouses and Nurserymen		
		10,971	Kindergartens (Private)
220,000	Grocers	24	Kite Manufacturers
170	Guided Missile Contractors	5,724	Kiwanis Clubs
77	Harbor Masters	20,000	Labor Unions
28,297	Hardware Retailers	188	Lathe Manufacturers
95	Harrow Manufacturers	24,807	Librarians
4,181	Health Officers	34,234	Liquor Stores
922	Helicopter Owners	1,453	Livery Stables
31,254	High Schools	4,955	Logging Camps and Loggers
485,000	High-School Teachers		
151	Hinge Manufacturers	22,004	Lumber Retailers
8	Hobby Horse Manufacturers	22,736	Machine Shops
4,348	Hobby Shops	2,734	Magazines (Business & Trade)
16,010	Home Builders		
3,726	Home Demonstration Agents	675	Mail Order Houses
		4,806	Management Consultants
6,500,000	Home Owners (in rural and small towns)	292,517	Manufacturers
		53	Marquee Manufacturers
1,067	Horse Breeders	3,000	Marriage Counselors
24	Horse Blanket Manufacturers	3,281	Mayors
		210	Midwives
7,318	Hospitals	2,563	Monasteries and Convents
6,458	Hotel and Motel Managers	48,828	Motels and Tourist Courts
16,142	Hotels	70	Muff Manufacturers
76	Hurricane Warning Stations	8,046	Movie Theaters (Indoor)
4	Hypnotism Schools	839	Museums
44	Ice-making Machinery Manufacturers	4,200	National Associations
		12	Naval Yards

TYPICAL COMPILED MAILING LISTS (cont.)

4,894	Newsdealers, Retail		350,000	Sportsmen
79,749	Nurses		17,100	Stamp Collectors
			8,055	Stationers
25	Oar Manufacturers		725	Steel Plants
52	Onion Ring Manufacturers		8,273	Stenographers (Court)
295	Opera (Metropolitan)		355	Stockyards
	Boxholders		83	Straw Hat Manufacturers
6,453	Outboard Motor Dealers		1,067	Stud Farm Managers
17,881	Paint Manufacturers		2,579	Tailors (Ladies')
35,942	Paint Dealers		61,572	Taverns
256	Pajama Manufacturers		11,204	Taxicab Companies
51,653	Parent-Teacher Associations		820	Television Stations
8,167	Patent Attorneys		2,578	Tennis Clubs
17,722	Pediatricians		40,017	Tire Dealers
135	Pencil Manufacturers		5	Titanium Producers
5,000	Pharmacists (Hospital)		214	Toll Bridges and Highways
13,006	Photographers (Commercial)		10,042	Tourist Agents
			1,649	Toy Manufacturers
14,176	Pizzerias		41,152	Truckers
46,063	Plumbers			
24,052	Post Offices		127	Umbrella Manufacturers
25,191	Printers		3	Umpires' Schools
19,472	Psychiatrists		7,127	University Deans
78,000	Purchasing Agents		18,200	Upholsterers
186	Putty Manufacturers			
			10,342	Vermin Exterminators
6,000	Quarries & Pits		110	Vest Manufacturers
18	Quebracho Extract Manufacturers		2,900	Violinists (Professional)
95	Racetracks		7,534	Weekly Newspapers
283,996	Radio Amateurs		96	Whiskey Distilleries
5,059	Radio Broadcasting Stations		16	Wind Tunnels
441	Railroads		370	Worm Farms
101,000	Real Estate Agents and Dealers		674	X-ray Laboratories and Technicians
2,340	Reducing Salons			
229	Rehabilitation Centers		18	Xylol Manufacturers and Distributors
198,517	Restaurants		17	Xylophone Manufacturers
70,000	Sales Executives			
54	Sardine Canners		1,280	Yacht Clubs
6,090	Savings and Loan Associations		9,972	Yacht Owners
			9	Yohimbine Hydrochloride Manufacturers
150,000	Schools and Colleges			
858	Secondhand Booksellers		10	Yo-Yo Manufacturers
26,347	Shoe Retailers			
10,633	Shopping Centers		122	Zipper Manufacturers
588	Silk Mills		163	Zoological Parks
511	Ski Clubs		24	Zwieback Manufacturers

An indication of how important it is to use current lists can be seen by some of the changes in the list quantities shown above. The catalog of the same compiler ten years earlier compared with the 1972 edition used in compiling the above examples showed such changes as:

Aircraft Pilots (Commercial) from 44,200 to 150,090

Barbershops from 24,472 to 70,108

Boards of Education from 9,691 to 15,375

Brassiere Manufacturers from 279 to 490

Cartoonists from 402 to 278

Charitable Organizations from 7,700 to 13,539

Cheese Factories from 2,669 to 1,310

Chintz Manufacturers from 25 to 54

Circuses from 14 to 74

College Professors from 105,000 to 444,000

Crowbar Manufacturers from 45 to 199

Day Nurseries from 3,499 to 10,971

Diamond Cutters from 285 to 522

Dining Car Supervisors from 56 to 35

Professional Water Divers from 55 to 212

Doll Manufacturers from 170 to 217

Doughnut Bakers from 2,786 to 4,932

Economists from 7,570 to 13,000

Finance Companies from 10,724 to 23,928

Garbage Collecting Firms from 2,765 to 5,542

Geiger Counter Manufacturers from 23 to 43

Gift Shops from 17,600 to 26,134

Harbor Masters from 122 to 77

Horse Blanket Manufacturers from 35 to 24

Hotels from 30,725 to 16,142

Implement Dealers from 22,176 to 13,708

Interior Decorators from 11,925 to 16,878

Investment Analysts from 6,150 to 11,278

Private Kindergartens from 3,499 to 10,971

Logging Camps and Loggers from 9,800 to 4,955

Management Consultants from 820 to 4,806

Marriage Counselors from 463 to 3,000

Oar Manufacturers from 16 to 25

Onion Ring Manufacturers from 100 to 52

Commercial Photographers from 6,817 to 13,006

Pizzerias from 1,800 to 14,176

Psychiatrists from 11,364 to 18,472

Railroads from 566 to 441

Secondhand Booksellers from 317 to 858

Shopping Centers from 3,974 to 10,633

Stationers from 14,200 to 8,055

Steel Plants from 377 to 725

Straw Hat Manufacturers from 165 to 83

Taverns from 31,600 to 61,572

Tire Dealers from 126,800 to 40,017

Tourist Agents from 4,848 to 10,042

Toy Manufacturers from 2,012 to 1,649

University Deans from 2,028 to 7,127

Wind Tunnels from 8 to 16

Worm Farms from 1,188 to 370

The advantage of using a list compiler's service rather than doing the job yourself—in addition to the fact you will probably save money in the process—is that experienced compilers are well acquainted with the limitations of various sources and have developed techniques for interfiling names from various sources to make their lists as accurate and complete as possible.

There is a great variety of sources for compiled lists. Most every large lettershop, for example, offers a list compilation service. (If you want information about lists available through lettershops in any community, we suggest you contact the Mail Advertising Service Association, 425 13th St. N.W., Washington, D.C. 20004.) For compiled lists which are national in scope, a good starting point in locating what you need is the "Direct Mail Directory" section found in every issue of *Direct Marketing* (224 Seventh St., Garden City, N.Y. 11530).

Occupant Lists

One type of compiled list requires special discussion. This is the so-called occupant list. These are lists of just addresses, no names. They are often used when saturation mailings are desired and the direct mail message is not of a personal nature. They have the advantage of being delivered to whomever lives at a given address, with no problem of non-deliveries if someone has moved.

The cost of such lists, of course, is far less than for lists with names. Most compilers of occupant lists permit you to be highly selective in the areas you pick for mailing.

Analyzing Mass Lists

A guide to assist direct mail advertisers in analyzing mass mailing lists has been prepared by R. L. Polk & Co.:

> The most important elements affecting success with mail are the *offer,* the *mailing piece* and the *list.* While you may have only one basic proposition for the consumer, there are many ways of offering it. And there are an endless number of mailing pieces with which to present the offer. But there are only a *few* mass lists to which it can be sent.
>
> Finding the *best* offer and mailing piece can only be accomplished by properly testing several approaches. And improvements can be made *only* through testing.
>
> Finding the best mass list can, to a very large degree, be determined from a careful analysis of the nature of available lists and how they relate to your requirements. Learning to use any list with maximum effectiveness also involves a good deal of testing.
>
> Fortunately, direct mail is more susceptible to scientific testing than any other advertising medium because conditions can be controlled quite precisely.
>
> The most important factors to consider about a list are *coverage, deliverability,* and *selectivity.* And price too, of course, in terms of value delivered.
>
> A. *Coverage*
>
> 1. *Who?*
>
> Whom does the list cover—and fail to cover? For example, lists compiled from telephone directories do not include phone owners with unlisted numbers or, of course, non-phone owning households. The

auto list excludes owners who register their cars at their business and all non-car owners.

2. Where?

Is coverage available in all post offices in the United States? Some of them?

3. How Many?

There are about 60,000,000 households in the United States. How many does a given list cover?

4. How Many Twice?

How much duplication is there within a list?

B. Deliverability

Deliverability depends upon the accuracy of the *source,* the length of *time since the list was compiled,* the accuracy of *"atlasing"* and the *mode of addressing.*

1. Accuracy of Source

Obviously, a list is only as accurate as its source. The sources vary. Minor inaccuracies don't necessarily affect deliverability or effectiveness.

2. Length of Time Since the List was Compiled

The mobility rate of households in this country is about 20% per year. It is highest among low income and young families. *No list* is absolutely current. Each national list is really a mixture of lists compiled at different times. The phone list is compiled from more than 5,000 directories which are issued throughout the year. The auto list is compiled from registration data available throughout the year from the 50 states and Washington, D. C. Therefore, the length of time since compilation of a given block of names and addresses varies *within* every list. It might be three months in one city and eleven months in another.

3. Accuracy of Atlasing

Every third class mailing piece must have a correct post office address and ZIP number. There are some 34,000 post offices in the U.S. but there are more than 120,000 communities. Community names won't do for third class mail. Atlasing refers to the business of getting the right post office or branch name on each address, the correct ZIP number and the correct street spelling along with proper directionals (NW, South, etc.). Doing the job properly is a daily and endless task.

4. Mode of Addressing

In post offices having foot carrier delivery service, it is permissible to address mail "occupant" or "resident." As long as the dwelling unit is occupied, the mail will be delivered. Since the "mobility" of dwellings is nowhere near as great as the mobility of families and since the post office is not obliged to forward third class mail, "resident" addressing will get better *delivery* than name addressing. In multiple dwelling units, apartment numbers must appear to ensure deliverability.

C. *Selectivity*

There are three methods available to rationally prune coverage: deletions based on the inherent selectivity of the list used; exclusions based on geographical segments; and selectivity on a household-by-household basis.

1. *Inherent Selectivity*

This is in the *nature* of the list. The phone list has inherent selectivity because it selects only listed phone owners. The auto list has it too. The "occupant" list does *not* have it since it covers all households.

2. *Geographical Selectivity*

Geographic eliminations can be made by county, post office and postal zone from all mass lists. These selections are very gross indeed from a socio-economic standpoint since units of this size invariably include a cross section of demographic groups. Some lists offer smaller geographic selection units, such as census tracts, which are rated socio-economically from time to time and are good selection units— but with very definite limitations.

3. *Household-by-Household Selectivity*

This is based on some fact known about each household on a list such as sex, number of persons in the household, year model of car owned, etc. If the factor known is *relevant to your interests,* it is by far the best selection technique. These kinds of factors possess some relevance in nearly all cases and in many cases they can be of very great importance. The latter are not always obvious before a test discloses them.

FACTORS IDENTIFIABLE IN A MASS LIST

While the R. L. Polk auto registration list is primarily a list of automobile owners, there are a number of other selectivity factors built into the list. Such multiple factors are typical of those found in major mass mailing lists.

1. Current market value of cars owned
2. Number of cars owned
3. Make of newest car
4. Series of newest car
5. Price class of newest car
6. Year model of newest car
7. Body style of newest car
8. Number of doors in newest car
9. Number of cylinders in newest car
10. Make of other car

11. Series of other car
12. Price class of other car
13. Year model of other car
14. Body style of other car
15. Number of doors in other car
16. Number of cylinders in other car
17. Sex of head of household
18. Type of dwelling unit
19. Proximity to known customer
20. Degree of metropolitanization
21. Geographic region
22. Census tract characteristics

   A. Median income
   B. Median years of school completed
   C. Percent homeowners
   D. Percent non-whites
   E. Percent "young families"
   F. Percent with children under 6
   G. Percent of dwelling units built between 1960 & 1970
   H. Growth index
   I. Percent in large apartments

List Brokers

One of the most important specialists in the direct mail field is the list broker. A competent specialist in mailing lists, the list broker can save you time, work ... and frequently money. Whether you are a list owner or a list user, you will find it profitable to work with a list broker. A DMMA Research Report[2] explains:

> List brokers can be defined as independent agents whose primary function is to arrange rental and addressing transactions between list users and list owners. Brokers represent the list owners, and the commission that they receive from them for their services usually is 20% of the amount the mailer pays. The commission is deducted by the broker before payment is forwarded to the list owner.
>
> Here it should be pointed out that often there is an overlapping of activity in the list business. Some brokers not only arrange for the rental of lists that are owned by other companies, but they also either do compilation work or buy outright certain lists which they can make available for rental.

---

[2]"How to Work With Mailing List Brokers," by members of the National Council of Mailing List Brokers. A DMMA Research Report. 1959. Direct Mail Marketing Assn.

Although this may seem confusing, in the course of working with list organizations you are likely to find that each has its own particular specialty. And very often you may decide that it is wise to deal with certain organizations for specific types of lists.

It is the list broker's job to keep abreast of all developments in the list field. Most brokers have an experienced staff which is always searching for "new" lists, more detailed information about known lists, ideas which will help mailers use their lists more profitably, and anything else which will help improve the effectiveness of direct mail.

A list broker can help direct mail advertisers in many ways other than just helping to arrange list rentals. He is a particularly good source for information on list maintenance; keeping direct mail records; testing; and he often provides valuable counsel on copy, art, mailing methods, and so forth.

Functions of List Brokers

The DMMA Research Report lists the following services performed by list brokers:

Finds New Lists—The broker is constantly seeking new lists and selecting for your consideration ones which will be of particular interest. In fact, brokers spend a great deal of their time encouraging list owners to enter the list rental field.

Acts as Clearance House for Data—The broker saves you valuable time because you can go to one source for a considerable amount of information, rather than to many sources which may or may not be readily available.

Screens Information—The broker carefully screens the list information provided by the list owner. Where possible he or one of his representatives personally verifies the information provided by the list owner. In addition, brokers in the National Council of Mailing List Brokers have available to them a wealth of information resulting from the combined efforts of the members.

Reports on Performance—The broker knows the past history of many lists and usually knows the performance of ones which have previously been used by other mailers.

Advises on Testing—The broker's knowledge of the makeup of a list is often valuable in determining what will constitute a representative cross section of the list. Obviously, an error in selecting a cross section will invalidate the results of the test and possibly eliminate from your schedule a group of names that could be responsive.

Checks Instructions—When you place an order with a list owner through a broker, he and his staff doublecheck the accuracy and completeness of your instructions, thus often avoiding unnecessary misunderstandings and loss of time.

Clears Offer—The broker clears for you in advance the mailing you wish to make. He supplies the list owner either with a sample of your piece or a description of it, and by getting prior approval minimizes the chance of any later disappointments.

Checks Mechanics—The broker clears with the list owner the particular type of envelope, order card, or other material which is to be addressed.

Clears Mailing Date—When contacting the list owner, the broker checks on the mailing date which you have requested and asks that it be held open as a protected time for you.

Works Out Timing—The broker arranges either for material to be addressed or labels to be sent to you at a specified time, thus enabling you to maintain your schedule of inserting and mailing.

Working With Brokers

An up-dated DMMA publication[3] provides a guide to most effective mailer-broker list owner relations:

WORKING WITH BROKERS

How to Get the Most Out of Your Lists Brokers—Whether you are a list owner or a mailer, your dealings with the list broker will be most efficient and profitable if you have confidence in him and treat him as a trusted aide.

Mutual confidence is essential if broker-client relations are to yield maximum results.

MAILER-BROKER RELATIONS

Give Background—Discuss frankly and fully your aims and purposes as well as any past mailing experience you may have had. In that way the broker will have the clearest possible picture of your operation and be able to help you avoid many pitfalls.

Outline Goals—Discuss your goals and ambitions with your broker so he may have a full understanding of the complexity and magnitude of the job he is sharing with you.

Policies—Formulate policies based on fairness and equity so when dealing with brokers, you may minimize or completely eliminate friction. Although you will find a broker may at times call you on the phone to discuss various newly released lists he most often will mail data cards to you.

On occasion if you are working with several brokers, three or four cards covering the same lists will arrive in the same mail. You should have a policy which will enable you to decide on which presentation you will consider.

---

[3]"How to Work With A List Broker," Direct Mail/Marketing Assn., 6 East 43rd St., New York, N.Y. 10017.

Have Confidence—It will come to the point where you have such confidence in your brokers that you will use them as sounding boards for your mailing ideas. Since they are specialists in direct marketing techniques, use their knowledge and experience to assist you in selling your product or services. This knowledge is given, "freely" to you.

Request Newest Information—In the planning stages of your campaign, request up-to-date information on the lists you are using from your broker. At that time, request new recommendations for your current offer.

This will save much time in going through your out-of-date data cards and in fighting the losing battle of daily filing data cards.

Keep Brokers Posted—Keep your broker posted on your mailing schedules so he may properly time his efforts in your behalf. He will appreciate this consideration, and you will benefit.

State Objections—The broker's primary concern is rendering efficient service to you, but he is not a mind reader. If you object to anything he does, state your objections fully and promptly. Each broker wants and tries to keep you as a client, but misunderstandings do develop. And they can hurt you as well as the broker unless they are resolved without delay.

Consider Priority—Generally it is accepted practice that if you test a list through one broker, you should continue using it through him so long as you are satisfied with the service he renders.

LIST OWNER-BROKER RELATIONS

Get List Maintenance Advice—Consult with the list broker when deciding how to maintain your list so you may set it up the most practical, economical and rentable way.

Discuss Rates—Discuss with your broker the price you will charge for rentals and decide on a price schedule that will bring you the greatest volume of profitable business.

Supply Accurate Data—Be sure the list information you furnish is accurate.

If the addresses in a list have not been corrected within a reasonable period of time, tell the broker.

If a list contains a percentage of names of people who bought on open account and failed to pay, give this information to the broker.

If you represent your list as made up entirely of buyers, be sure it does not include any inquiry or prospect names.

If you have bought out a competitor and have included some of his names in your customer list, be sure to state this fact.

Aside from obvious aspects of misrepresentation, you will be the one who suffers when you mislead a broker.

Address on Schedule—Establish a reputation for addressing on time as promised. If you accept orders and fail to fulfill them on schedule, brokers become aware of this and find they cannot conscientiously suggest your list to potential users. If, for some reason, you forsee a delay, advise the broker immediately so he can advise the mailer.

Furnish Latest Counts—Keep the broker posted on current list counts, rates, changes in the sources of the names and the like. When the composition of a list changes, it may very well become more interesting to a user who had previously felt that it was not suitable for his purpose. In addition, when current information is offered to a potential user through the broker, it is more likely to develop activity than is an out-dated description.

Choose Brokers Wisely—Consider carefully whether to make your list available to a number of list brokers or just to one broker. There are many things to be said in favor of working with several brokers. And at times there are also good reasons for working exclusively with one broker. While the decision is yours, you should keep in mind this fact—brokers are people and each one has his own particular personality, following and sphere of influence. Therefore, as a list owner, you will be well advised not to narrow the field unless your facilities for addressing are so limited the orders one broker can develop for you will be more than sufficient to take up all available addressing time.

Protect Brokers—It takes a lot of time and effort on the part of a broker to interest a mailer in testing your list. Therefore, continuation runs should be scheduled through the original broker so long as he continues to render satisfactory service to his client. The broker is a member of your sales force, and he can only continue to do an effective job so long as you protect him on the accounts he develops for you.

WHAT YOU SHOULD KNOW ABOUT LISTS

How to Locate Lists—Well qualified and up-to-date mailing lists are the lifeblood of any direct mail business. Without them there can be no profitable business. The importance of selecting and using the best available lists is therefore obvious. For no matter how potent and effective the selling effort, no matter how well the promotion is timed, it's all to no avail if the lists are so poorly selected that the mailing fails to reach eligible prospects. Throughout the history of direct mail the problem facing mailers has been the location and selection of lists of people who are ready, willing and able to buy specific products or services. In most organizations large or small, the job of gathering information and making selections is directed by an executive who must shoulder many other responsibilities. Usually he and his staff are limited in the amount of time they can spend on list matters.

Few large companies have separate departments staffed by list specialists, whose job it is to assemble all of the list data submitted to them, to appraise it and keep it filed for ready reference and use. *The Mailing List Brokers Professional Association* has prepared this booklet with two main purposes. One is to help mailers in organizations of all sizes determine how brokers can render the most efficient, effective service to them. The other is to help list owners determine how the services of list brokers can help them build extra profits.

Specialists—The essence of direct mail is its selectivity. Where a magazine advertisement can be selective only in a broad sense, depending on such factors as the publication in which it appears and the headline which is designed to catch the prospect's eye, direct mail can be selective to a much higher degree. It is possible for brokers to secure lists of almost every type of person, but the main function of a broker is to make recommendations of markets which in his experience are most appropriate. The broker usually has a wider experience of which types of lists do best for each type of product or service than any single mailer has.

Where to Start—There is no one best way to begin learning about list procurement, selection, maintenance or rental. There are two principal alternatives—either you can do your own research job or you can call in one or more brokers. If you decide that your first move will be to get as well acquainted with the subject as possible, you can refer to the books available in the library and select those which contain specific information about the use and renting of mailing lists. Or you can start from scratch with the brokers, if you cannot spare the time to do any of your preliminary research. And as you work with them, you will find you can add rapidly to your store of knowledge on the subject of mailing lists.

Commissions—List brokers are specialists whose primary function is to find a direct mail market for a product or service and to arrange a transaction between list users and list owners. The knowledge and experience of a list broker costs the mailer nothing. He is paid by the list owner for whom he is acting as a sales representative. The standard commission he receives for his services is 20% of the rental amount the mailer pays. This commission is deducted by the broker before payment is forwarded to the list owner.

One-Time Rentals—Most lists available through brokers are "rented" rather than sold. When a rental transaction is arranged, it is with the understanding that names will be used for one specified mailing and for no other purpose. If a mailer wants to make additional uses of the same names he must arrange for it in advance. Frequently the list owner will allow a reduction in rate for double or triple uses.

Classifications—Most lists fall into the following classifications:

Customer lists are just what the term implies. A list of customers can be graded in various ways, such as media used to secure them, age of list, percentage of repeat sales, amount of money paid, method of list maintenance, etc. Customers, of course, include active subscribers to publication and services.

Inactive Customers or expires are best kept by years.

Inquiries are also best kept by years.

Prospects are compiled names, secured from directories, friends' recommendations, trade show attendance, newspaper clippings, etc.

In the case of magazines as well as clubs offering books, records and a variety of other items the active names are called *subscribers* and they are not grouped by years, since in these cases there is continuing activity. The inactive names which such companies maintain are called *expires* or *former subscribers,* and they are usually grouped by years. Inquiry lists are made up of names of people who have actually asked for information about specific products or services. They are usually grouped accordingly to the dates they inquired.

Prospect lists are names of people likely to be interested in certain types of offers. The value of such lists relies largely upon the extent of the care, discretion and accuracy with which the selection of names is made.

Compiled lists are in many respects similar to prospect lists. Many of them are culled from directories. Some are taken from membership lists, association rosters, trade show attendance records, salesmen's reports, newspaper clippings and a variety of other sources, in each case they offer the compiler an opportunity to select names on the basis of some particular interest, background, physical or intellectual standard. Descriptions of these lists also include the dates of the source material.

Assembling List Information—Whether you want to locate lists to mail your offer to or you are a list owner interested in renting your list, it is essential that your list brokers have specific information which clearly defines the lists concerned.

BROKERS SERVICES

Whether you are a list owner or a mailer, your dealings with the list broker will be most efficient and profitable if you have confidence in him and treat him as a trusted aide.

How Brokers Work With List Users—The broker performs a vital function in locating lists for the mailer. Through knowledge and experience, the list broker helps you select the markets you desire and can suggest peripheral fields that will prove lucrative. In performing this service, he does a great deal of work which would be costly, time consuming and tedious for the mailer. Were the mailer to try to do the job himself, he would get involved in a lot of extra work ... phone calls and other contacts with various list owners. Even then he would not be able to cover more than a fraction of the ground that is explored by brokers. Nor would he be in a position to make the performance studies which are so necessary a part of list selection work.

VITAL SERVICES PERFORMED BY THE BROKER

Finds New Lists—The broker is constantly seeking new lists and selecting for your consideration lists which will be of particular interest. In fact, brokers spend a great deal of their time encouraging list owners to enter the list rental field.

Verifies Information—The broker carefully verifies the list information provided by the list owner. In addition, brokers in the MLBPA have available to them a wealth of information resulting from their combined efforts. The MLBPA will be discussed in more detail later on.

Reports on Performance—The broker is qualified to check past performances of many lists.

Checks Instructions—When you place an order with a list owner through a broker, he and his staff double check the accuracy and completeness of your instructions, thus often avoiding unnecessary misunderstandings and loss of time.

Clears Offer—The broker will clear in advance the mailing you wish to make. A sample of the literature to be mailed or a description of the offer will be sent for clearance. The broker can also advise the list owner on the best rental rate to produce the greatest profit. A too high rate will discourage rentals. A too low rate might make rental unprofitable.

Checks Mechanics—The broker clears with the list owner the particular type of envelope, order card or other material which is to be addressed.

Clears Mailing Date—When contacting the list owner, the broker checks on the mailing date which you have requested and asks that it be held open as a protected time for you.

Works Out Timing—The broker arranges for material to be sent to you at a specified time, enabling you to maintain your schedule.

Delivery Date—The broker checks the date when the list user would like his material returned to his letter shop and follows up to insure meeting the mail date.

How Brokers Work With List Owners—When you work through a broker, you are dealing with a specialist who is in close touch with national list users and is well acquainted with their needs. While you must concentrate on your business and have little time to devote to your list matters, the broker and his experienced staff will spend all of their time performing services for you whether you are a list user or a list owner.

Maintenance—The broker can give advice on the most practical method of maintaining your list.

Payment—A broker usually accepts only those mailers who have established proper credit references. If there is any doubt, the list owner makes the final decision. When the broker collects payment, he promptly sends a check to the list owner.

MOST IMPORTANT THINGS TO KNOW
ABOUT LISTS

NAME

1. All of the names by which lists can be identified (including any trade styles that are used for advertising purposes).

2. The name of the list owner.

TYPE

Whether the list is:

1. A customer or subscriber list

2. An inquiry or expire list

3. A prospect list

4. A compiled list

5. A combination of any of the first four

For a most helpful booklet on list brokers, send for "How to Work With a List Broker," Direct Mail/Marketing Assn., 6 E. 43rd St., New York, NY 10017.

How to Rent Lists

It is important to remember that all lists are rented for one-time use only. If a direct mail advertiser wishes to make a second mailing to a list, he must again pay the established rental fee. While the amount charged for rental of lists varies greatly, the average list of active buyers rents for between $45 and $55 per thousand names. Lists of prospects, expires, or other less active names average between $35 and $45 per thousand. Prices include addressing, but any other mailing costs are additional. Most list owners will provide a magnetic tape for computer addressing or labels to attach to your mailings. A number of list owners, however, insist on handling the complete mailing themselves. In such cases, you must send all material to the list owner's mailing service and pay inserting and mailing costs in addition to the rental fee. When preparing material for mailing by a list owner, make sure that your printed indicia are correct.

The mail order list expert, Lewis Kleid *(The Reporter of Direct Mail Advertising,* February 1963), offers the following suggestions:

Identification—Indicate exactly which names you want (buyers, inquiries, prospects, etc.) and which years are to be used.

Test Sample—Indicate specific areas if geographical, years if chronological, and sections if alphabetical.

Addressing Position—If the address must appear precisely on the order card or envelope, find out if it can be done. If samples are not ready, give precise measurements or make up "dummies" for each list owner.

Omissions—If you wish to omit names used previously, specify this in your instructions.

Mail Date—This should be realistic, based upon your ability to deliver material to be addressed, the ability of the printers to supply the material to the lettershop, and for your lettershop to mail. The dates should not be vague as, for example, "will mail on receipt."

Confirmation—Before you ship material to be addressed, request confirmation of all details pertaining to the order: price, latest quantities available, and shipping point for addressing.

How Shipment Is to Be Returned—If you say "Rush," the list owner may return addressed material by airmail or railway express, both of which are costly. If time is abundant, specify "Ship Cheapest Way."

Packing—Instruct the list owners to return the addressed material (a) in the original cartons, (b) in the same order as list is maintained, (c) do not crush or squeeze material, (d) face material all in one direction, (e) identify each carton and package in the shipment with the name of the list, quantity, and key numbers.

Helping Dealers to Build Better Lists

On the theory that the mailing lists maintained by distributors and dealers are just as important in promoting the sale of a product as those maintained at the factory, some companies make a special effort to assist dealers to build and profitably use prospect and customer lists. This is especially true in promoting "big ticket" merchandise, such as equipment, building materials, and products with a large unit of sale. The Culligan Corporation, for one example, goes to some length to assist dealers to compile mailing lists which will really do a job. The following is taken from a dealer help-piece distributed by that company to its dealers:

GENERAL LISTS

The important thing to remember in compiling general lists for direct mail advertising is to look for prospects, rather than "suspects." One source of names may be far more valuable to you than another. For example, actual location of the home in its relationship to neighborhood routing is important in your service business. Consequently, lists that are arranged by streets should be more desirable than those arranged alphabetically.

The nine general sources most commonly used are listed below. You may want to use one or several of these sources, depending on their availability in your community.

Duplication may be found, since some of these sources are offered as alternates.

1. *Telephone Directories.* Most of the people you want to reach are listed in the local telephone book. It can be used for checking correct spelling of names, individual's initials, and the street address of names you secure from other sources. In smaller cities, the telephone book may be your main source of names. (A disadvantage of this listing is that it is in alphabetical, rather than street order.)

2. *City Directories:* Lists of all residents and business organizations are available in many cities, usually in both alphabetical name sequence and numerical street order. A city directory is ideal for making up lists on a street or area basis, and also can be used very effectively to obtain individual names where only the house number is known. (According to the U.S. Census Bureau about half the people change homes in 7 years, so be sure the directory is up to date.)

3. *Cross-Indexed Telephone Directories:* In larger cities, organizations independent of the telephone company sometimes compile a list of all telephone subscribers in numerical street order. It is usually published each time a new telephone directory is issued and for this reason is more up to date than a city directory.

4. *School Enrollments:* Schools usually maintain an alphabetical list of all parents of pupils in attendance. This can be a valuable list, because it represents homes with children.

5. *Voting Lists:* Usually available in all states where permanent registration is required. They are maintained by precincts, in numerical street order, at the county clerk's office.

6. *Rural Lists:* Members of Farmers' Co-Operatives and Rural Electrical subscribers offer a very fine potential in some territories. Check with your local co-operatives in R.E.A. office for these lists.

7. *Public Utilities:* Local gas, electric, and water companies maintain lists of subscribers in numerical street sequence. It is worth considerable effort to obtain one of these lists, as they are accurate and up to date.

8. *Names from Other Merchants:* Noncompetitive businessmen often maintain mailing lists. An appliance dealer's list is an excellent example, for all automatic washer users should have soft water. You may trade direct mail lists with most any merchant in town, but *you are cautioned against making your own customer list available to any outsiders.*

9. *R. F. D. Boxholders:* You can have the postman deliver direct mail literature to all boxholders. In this case, you do not need actual names, yet you do have a means of sending literature to all the people on a given postal route.

SELECTED LISTS

In addition to general lists of householders (which may include many "suspects"), dealers will be able to develop special lists that contain the names of genuine *prospects.*

These are people who have at some time or another heard about the advantages of soft water or are in immediate need of soft water service.

The names obtained from the following sources may be sent regular direct mailings, the same as those on the general list, or they may have special "call-for-action" mailings sent to them at regular intervals. In any case, the direct mail activity must be followed by personal solicitation.

1. Personal Contacts
2. New Homes
3. Business and Professional Men
4. Commercial Accounts
5. Names from Group Film Showings

6. Home Shows, Cooking Schools, Fairs
7. Club Membership Lists
8. Neighbors of Customers
9. Customers
10. Newspaper Items

If the intent is to produce an inquiry, why not feature the reply card? This is the technique employed by Suppli-Care in placing it at the very top of its self-mailer. Below, name and address of recipient are revealed on the opposite side of mailer.

MAILING TIPS FROM PITNEY-BOWES INC.

A very helpful 14-page booklet has been issued by Pitney-Bowes Inc., leading manufacturer of postage meters and other mailing room equipment, entitled "29 Mailing Tips." Just a few of the "tips" are:

REGULAR DAILY MAIL

Your outgoing mail will skip one sorting operation at the post office—and be on its way sooner—if you'll bundle separately and label it for "LOCAL" and "OUT-OF-TOWN" delivery.

Most post offices receive 75% of the day's mail in late afternoon or early evening. You can avoid this 5 o'clock rush by mailing at least once earlier in the day—at noon, for example..

You'd be surprised how you benefit when your mail can catch earlier planes and trains. By mailing an hour earlier, for instance, you may save as much as 24 hours or more in delivery time.

Make sure your addressing is clear, complete, and correct. Include street and number. Include the postal delivery zone number.

Certified mail is a service for mail that has no tangible money value, but that nevertheless is important enough to warrant a record of mailing and delivery. The fee—35 cents—is cheaper than registered mail.

PARCEL POST

A good way to start is to ask your post office for the free pamphlet (an excerpt from the U.S. Postal Manual) entitled: "Packaging and Wrapping Parcels for Mailing."

Probably the greatest single cause of trouble is unnecessary empty space in a carton. Contents "float" free and are easily damaged.

Excelsior, flexible corrugated fiberboard, or felt are commonly used to cushion heavy articles. Cellulose materials, cotton, clothing, shredded paper, or tissue paper are used for lighter items.

If you use gummed tape, make sure it is wide enough and heavy enough for the job. Seal all seams—center and edge seams—securely.

Some things can't be mailed, and the law provides stiff penalties for offenders. In general, nonmailable items fall under the headings of "Harmful, Obscene and Indecent Matter" and "Lotteries, Frauds and Libelous Matter."

VOLUME MAILING

Postal regulations for third class mail, when large quantities are involved, now make it possible for mailers to sack their own mail on their own premises, thereby providing for faster postal handling.

To "police" your list, print "Return Requested" on outgoing envelopes at regular intervals. Through this method, the post office advises you of address changes or reasons for nondelivery, keeping your list free of waste.

If you wish, you may submit your list (no cards) to destination post offices for correction. The charge is 5 cents per name, with a minimum of $1 for lists of less than 20 names. It's excellent insurance at this low cost.

METERED MAIL

Postage in the meter is theftproof, wasteproof, can't be borrowed. The postage meter does postage bookkeeping automatically.

Needs no post office facing or canceling. Often catches earlier mail trains or planes.

Prints date on mail and parcel post. Ordinary parcel post carries no mailing date.

"Meter Ads" are printed simultaneously with the meter stamps, at no extra cost except for printing plates.

Free assistance with postal and mailing problems through PB's special postal consulting service.

At the bottom of many pages are several suggestions under the heading of "Did You Know That?" which are also very helpful to anyone in any way responsible for mailings.

Chapter 16

CUSTOMER SERVICE PROGRAMS

TODAY, no business can long progress or succeed without adequate customer service policies. The realization of this need by top management is reflected in the extreme cases of the recall of thousands of cars for repairs by the major automobile companies, the attempt to improve the effectiveness of Better Business Bureaus throughout the country and in greater response to the warnings and edicts of government departments, such as the Food and Drug Administration, arising from pressures from consumer-protection organizations.

Customer service has tremendous sales values. It is well-known, for instance, that housewives prefer to shop in department stores because of the return privileges they offer customers. Technical service is an important factor in the television industry. Banks, formerly considered as laggards in promotion and merchandising, compete fiercely with new services, on a wide scale, for customers and prospects.

Retailers also benefit from more progressive management policies; some major manufacturers offer their distributors and dealers financial advice and training programs which go beyond (though not neglecting) product emphasis. They tell their retailers how to manage their businesses to assure profitable operations.

It is a maxim of marketing that increased sales can only come in two ways: (1) From securing new customers who have never been on the books before, and (2) from persuading customers already on the books to buy *more*. There seems to be a tendency on the part of marketing men, and especially sales managers, to devote most of their thought and effort to getting new customers, when, in fact, the best opportunity the business has to build sales profitably is by doing a better sales promotional job on present customers. They are indeed the unseen "acre of diamonds" right under our noses.

The techniques used in promotion programs aimed at getting new business are naturally different from those which produce results in getting old customers to give you a larger share of their business. In getting new business emphasis must be placed on salesmanship. The prospect must be interested. He must be convinced that he is dealing with a good house. He must be motivated to act, even though the tendency of people to put off buying from you for the first time is tremendous. On the other hand, getting a customer who is buying from you regularly, who knows the kind of service you give and the values you offer, does not need to be convinced of those facts. What he wants to know is *how* he can make *better* use of whatever it is that you sell to him. In other words, he needs to be serviced rather than sold, although both add up to the same thing. When you make it possible for a customer to use more of what you are selling to him, at a satisfactory profit, the repeat orders come naturally. By making him a better customer you make him a bigger buyer.

The growth of the consumer movement is largely due to three causes: quality, price and service. In an address before the Young Presidents' Organization, meeting in Acapulco, Mexico, Morris B. Rotman, of Harsh-Rotman & Druck, Chicago, said: "Consumerism is now a fundamental in competing for share of market."

He cited a number of examples of companies that have made consumerism work for their benefit:

Giant Food Stores, Washington, D. C., dated shelf life of perishable items, instituted unit pricing, posted nutritional values on food packages, and rejected packages considered unsafe or unfair. Over the same period, sales and profits both reached record levels.

Jewel Tea, Chicago, the first large supermarket chain to use unit pricing, expanded it from an experiment with items like soap and canned goods to cover a wide range of items.

Motorola calls everyone who buys a Motorola receiver within the first six months of ownership and, if there is a problem, arranges to have the set repaired if necessary. Then the company follows up with another call to check the results.

The Ford Program

In its annual report, Ford Motor Company recognized the importance of customer service by including a section reading: "To meet the growing need for better automotive service, Ford established a new Customer Service Division in 1971. First of its kind in the U.S. automotive industry, the 1,700-employee division's objective is to help Ford and Lincoln-Mercury dealers upgrade car and truck service to the highest possible level of customer satisfaction.

"The new division opened field offices in 34 cities and announced new programs in dealer-owner relations, service merchandising, service department analysis and technician training via video tapes. The division also instituted a system for faster handling of customer complaints.

"Ford Listens": A few years ago, the company's consumer relations program, "Ford Motor Company Listens," expanded its efforts from TV to print media, with a series of nationwide advertisements discussing automotive industry problems and Ford's efforts to solve them. In the fall, "Ford Listens" also published a 144-page book, "Car Buying Made Easier," including helpful consumer information on selecting a new car."

Experience of Scott Paper Company

An outstanding example of using customer's service to break down sales resistance and attain leadership in a hard-fought field is reported by the Scott Paper Company, the Philadelphia-based manufacturer of tissues for home use and other paper products. The Scott Paper Company is one of a number of successfully managed enterprises which have won acclaim as "trend buckers"—that is to say, increasing sales and profits at a time most paper products manufacturers cut back sales promotional expenditures and reefed sail. Going contrary to the trend, Scott Paper Company adopted the policy of spending more for sales promotion and advertising, on the theory that the time to advertise is when you need business the most. As a result, sales climbed during a recession year from $73 million to $80 million. At the same time profits on operations rose from $3,839,179 to about $5 million. In other words, a sales increase of 17% produced an increase in net profits of 44%. The increase in net profits for that period, interestingly enough, more than compensated the company for the additional money spent for market cultivation and expansion.

It would be straining the facts to say that this increase in sales and profits was due to the company's enterprising sales promotional policy, but its free service to customers and retailers in connection with the company's long-range sales development program tops the list of reasons which the management credits with this achievement. These were as follows:

> Free service to customers and retailers in connection with the company's sales program.
> Advertising and promotion programs directed at the housewife.
> A line of products that is practically "depression-proof."
> Development of new machinery to make goods better, faster and cheaper.
> A constant search for new and better products.

Good employee and stockholder relations.

An important free Scott service is its corps of washroom advisory consultants. On request, a technician will make a detailed survey of washroom facilities in industrial or public buildings. In nine out of ten cases, the suggestions are adopted and often Scott adds a new customer.

The advisory corps has surveyed more than 400,000 washrooms. It has found that attention to their design and facilities pays off in better employee morale.

In connection with this free washroom service the company issues a variety of sales promotional material slanted at different types of operations. For example, there is one portfolio dealing with the problems of service stations, another covers industrial applications, there is a service for architects, etc. These booklets give detailed information about washroom lay-out and equipment, suggested floor

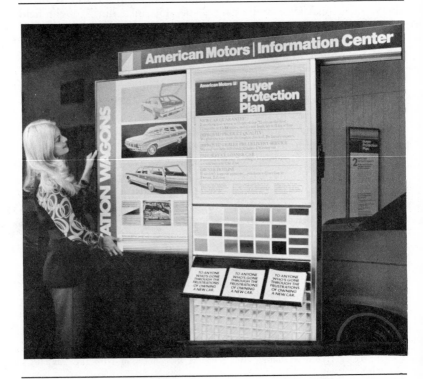

The company's Buyer Protection Plan is emphasized in this Information Center, described as a new point-of-purchase concept, for use in American Motors dealers' showrooms. Behind the front are separate sliding panels for each model series.

plans for plants of various sizes, together with a description of the cabinets available from the Scott Company for dispensing its products. A much appreciated feature of this service is a wide selection of posters and stickers available upon request from the company's sales promotion department for use in the washroom.

The Scott service program does not overlook the retailer. The company has established a Store Advisory Service to improve selling practices and bring more money into tills.

Using 10 large stores in the Philadelphia-Chester-Wilmington area as guinea pigs, this service developed better lighting, more attractive color schemes, intriguing store fronts, and lay-outs.

The service for retail stores is a separate operation from the washroom service which is beamed at industry. As in the washroom service, a wide variety of promotional literature is used to supplement personal contacts by field representatives. These include a brochure on "Color in Store Merchandising," "Use of Light in Tomorrow's Store," "Success Formula for Food Stores," "Fire Prevention for Food Store Operators," "Modern Fronts for Food Stores," etc. There is also a packet of profit-building ideas for food stores, together with a wealth of material on display and sale of Scott's own products. However, most Scott material is intended to help the storekeeper develop a successful business, with the thought that as the traffic increases he will automatically sell more Scott products.

Not all manufacturers have a product which repeats fast enough, and yields a margin of profit adequate enough, to justify a service operation as extensive as that maintained by Scott Paper Company. The next best thing is to do the job by means of some other form of communications, such as periodical publications.

Appleton's Metric Folder

It has always been a puzzle as to why paper manufacturers and processors don't use the great amount of blank space available on their sample sheets and paper samples to provide useful information to their customers and prospects. A refreshing exception is Appleton's folder entitled "Paper is a Measurement," one whole side of which is devoted to the "Appleton Woodbine Guide to Decimal and Metric Systems." It gives the metric equivalents of the standard English measurements, bordered by centimeter and pica rules. The United States was the last remaining country to take the steps to conversion to the metric system (Britain is now in the process of change) and American manufacturers must inevitably follow the

DECIMAL SYSTEM

Decimal Equivalents of Common Fractions

1/64	.0156
1/32	.0313
3/64	.0469
1/16	.0625
1/12	.0833
1/11	.0909
3/32	.0938
1/10	.1000
7/64	.1094
1/9	.1111
1/8	.1250
9/64	.1406
1/7	.1429
1/6	.1667
11/64	.1719
2/11	.1818
3/16	.1875
1/5	.2000
13/64	.2031
7/32	.2188
2/9	.2222
15/64	.2344
1/4	.2500
3/11	.2727
9/32	.2813
2/7	.2857
19/64	.2969
3/10	.3000
1/3	.3333
11/32	.3438
4/11	.3636
3/8	.3750
2/5	.4000
13/32	.4063
5/12	.4167
3/7	.4286
4/9	.4444
5/11	.4545
15/32	.4688
1/2	.5000
17/32	.5313
6/11	.5455
5/9	.5556
9/16	.5625
4/7	.5714
7/12	.5833
3/5	.6000
5/8	.6250
7/11	.6364
2/3	.6667
11/16	.6875
7/10	.7000
45/64	.7031
5/7	.7143
8/11	.7273
47/64	.7344
3/4	.7500
7/9	.7778
51/64	.7969
4/5	.8000
13/16	.8125
9/11	.8182
5/6	.8333
6/7	.8571
55/64	.8594
7/8	.8750
8/9	.8889
9/10	.9000
10/11	.9091
11/12	.9167
59/64	.9219
15/16	.9375
61/64	.9531
63/64	.9844
1"	1.0000

To convert to percentage, carry the decimal point two places to the right. Thus, 63/64, or .9844, equals 98.44%.

METRIC SYSTEM

LENGTH

Millimeter (mm) ..... = Meter ÷ 1,000
Centimeter (cm) ...... = Meter ÷ 100
Decimeter (dm) ...... = Meter ÷ 10

Basic Unit .... Meter (m)

Decameter (dkm) .... = Meter x 10
Hektometer (hm) .... = Meter x 100
Kilometer (km) .... = Meter x 1,000
Myriameter (mym) ... = Meter x 10,000

1 mm	.0394 in.
1 cm	.3937 in.
1 dm	3.937 in.
1 m	39.37 in.
1 m	32.81 ft.
1 dkm	328 ft. 1 in.
1 hm	or 109 yd. 13 in.
1 km	**3,280 ft. 1 in.**
	or .62 mi.
1 mym	6.2 mi.

2.540 cm	1 in.
30.480 cm	1 ft.
.914 m	1 yd.
1.609 km	1 mi.

CAPACITY

Milliliter (ml) .... = Liter ÷ 1,000
Centiliter (cl) .... = Liter ÷ 100
Deciliter (dl) .... = Liter ÷ 10

Basic Unit .... Liter* (l)

Decaliter (dkl) .... = Liter x 10
Hektoliter (hl) .... = Liter x 100
Kiloliter (kl) .... = Liter x 1,000

*Liter = 1000 cu cm (approximately 1 qt.). Liter implies cubic capacity, so is *not* prefixed by *cubic*. In metric system, dry and liquid measures are identical.

Cubic Capacity

1 ml	.06 cu. in.
1 cl	.6 cu. in.
1 dl	6.1 cu. in.
1 l	61.02 cu. in.
1 dkl	.35 cu. ft.
1 hl	3.53 cu. ft.
1 kl	1.31 cu. yd.

1.67 cl	1 cu. in.
2.85 dkl	1 cu. ft.
.76 kl	1 cu. yd.

Liquid Capacity

1 ml	.27 fluidram
	or .0338 fl. oz.
1 cl	.338 fl. oz.
1 dl	3.3815 fl. oz.
	or .21 pt.
1 l	2.1134 pt.
	or 1.0567 qt.
	or .2642 gal.
1 dkl	9.081 qt.
	or 2.64 gal.

.02957 l	1 oz.
.473 l	1 pt.
.946 l	1 qt.
3.785 l	1 gal.

Dry Capacity

1 dl	.18 pt.
1 l	1.816 pt.
	or .9081 qt.
	or .1135 pk.
	or .028 bu.
1 dkl	18.162 pt.
	or 9.0810 qt.
	or .14 pk.
	or .28378 bu.
1 hl	2.84 bu.

.550 l	1 pt.
1.101 l	1 qt.
8.809 l	1 pk.
35.238 l	1 bu.

AREA

Sq. centimeter (sq cm) ... = .0001 centare (ca)
or 1 ca ÷ 10,000

Basic Unit ... Centare (ca)
which is 1 Square Meter (sq m)

Are (a) .... = 1 ca x 100
Hectare (ha) .... = 1 ca x 10,000
Sq. kilometer (sq km) ... = 1 ca x 1,000,000

1 sq mm	.00155 sq. in.
1 sq cm	.155 sq. in.
1 sq m or ca	10.764 sq. ft.
	or 1.196 sq. yd.
1 a	119.60 sq. yd.
1 ha	2.47 acres
1 sq km	.3861 sq. mi.

6.451 sq cm	1 sq. in.
.093 sq m	1 sq. ft.
.836 sq m	1 sq. yd.
4047 sq m	1 acre
2.590 sq m	1 sq. mi.
	or 640 acres

VOLUME

Cu. Centimeter (cu cm) = .000001 cu m
or 1 cu m ÷ 1,000,000
Decistere (ds) ...... = .10 cu m or cu m ÷ 10

Basic Unit ... Stere (s)
which is 1 Cubic Meter (cu m)

Decastere (dks) ... = 10 steres or 1 cu m x 10

1 cu mm	.000061 cu. in.
1 cu cm	.0610 cu. in.
1 cu dm	61.02 cu. in.
	or .035 cu. ft.
1 ds	3.53 cu. ft.
1 cu m or 1 s	35.31 cu. ft.
	or 1.31 cu. yd.
1 dks or 10 cu m	353.1 cu. ft.
	or 13.10 cu. yd.

16.387 cu cm	1 cu. in.
.028 cu m	1 cu. ft.
.765 cu m	1 cu. yd.

WEIGHT & MASS

Milligram (mg) .... = Gram ÷ 1,000
Centigram (cg) .... = Gram ÷ 100
Decigram (dm) .... = Gram ÷ 10

Basic Unit ... Gram (g)

Decagram (dkg) .... = Gram x 10
Hectogram (hg) .... = Gram x 100
Kilogram (kg) .... = Gram x 1,000
Quintal (q) .... = Gram x 100,000
Metric Ton (MT) .... = Quintal x 10

1 mg	.015 grains
1 cg	.154 grains
1 dg	1.543 grains
1 g	.035 oz.
1 dkg	.353 oz.
1 hg	3.527 oz.
1 kg or 1,000 g	35.274 oz.
	or 2.2046 lb.
1 q or 100,000 g	220.46 lb.
Ton	
.907 MT	1 short ton
	2,000 lb.
1.016 MT	1 long ton
	2,240 lb.

Hundredweight (cwt)
45.359 kg	1 short cwt
	100 lb.
50.802 kg	1 long cwt
	112 lb.

28.349 g	1 oz.
453.00 g	1 lb.
.453 kg	1 lb.
.907 MT	1 short ton
1.016 MT	1 long ton

Appleton Papers, Inc. constructively used one side of its Woodbine Colored Cover Paper folder to list a guide to decimal and metric systems in use in most countries around the world.

worldwide system. The folder thus serves a highly useful informative purpose.

As reported by Robert D. Suess, Manager, Marketing Services, "Response to 'Paper is a Measurement' has been highly favorable from specifiers (of paper). Merchants have requested hundreds to use for promotional calls and for their own mailings . . . one of the world's largest retail chains requested several hundred copies to supply its purchasing departments."

Determining the Need

As a rule it does not pay to get out service promotions to customers unless they really need help and ask for it. In most fields there are business papers which provide a forum for the exchange of business-building ideas. These papers are well edited, and are available to your customers at small cost. Obviously there would be little advantage for an individual manufacturer to undertake a program which would overlap the service these publications render. It would be better and far less expensive to contract for a series of "reader advertisements" to be included in each issue of these publications. These advertisements would, of course, feature ideas and suggestions for increasing the use of your particular product, thus tying in with the editorial purpose of the publication. On the other hand, if the business papers in the field have spotty coverage of your customers, or if they are not read by the right men in customers' establishments, or perhaps not read at all, then there is an opportunity to supply customers with ideas and suggestions, used successfully by others, which they can adapt to promoting their businesses.

For example, take the case of a manufacturer of a new type of sausage casing. When put on the market there arose the problem of helping packers who used these casings to publicize them and develop new markets. Even though there were several well-edited papers in the field, they could hardly devote much editorial space to a product which, to most readers of the publication, was not especially important. But it was very important to the department which had the responsibility for creating a market for sausage. So to provide this group with information useful in merchandising "skinless frankfurters" and other sausages, the firm undertook to send its customers and prospective customers, in loose-leaf bulletin form, "how to" information. It was strictly a "service" feature, with little or no direct effort to sell anything. And it worked out very well. There was a need for it.

In the same way a manufacturer of a well-known duplicating machine discovered that some purchasers of his equipment used it only a few days a month. This raised several problems. Partial use of the equipment limited the supplies required by these users. The company depended upon supply sales for most of its profits. Then the opportunity to sell these users additional equipment was slim. But most important of all, the user who had his money invested in the appliance was not getting the returns he should be getting and was not too enthusiastic about it. Investigation showed that the reason the equipment was not fully used was because the management was not informed as to other ways it could be put to work making profits. The salesman who sold the equipment, perhaps, was not able to contact policy-making executives, or possibly his recommendations fell on deaf ears because they meant extra work for somebody. This was especially true of the small business, which did not usually have anyone in the organization who was promotion-minded and who had a flair for writing sales letters. So a "User's Service Bureau" was set up in the home office under the sales promotion department. A news bulletin, telling how users of the equipment were finding "plus" jobs for it, was issued once a month. Actual letters, with the results obtained, were published and an authority on writing promotional letters was employed to help users develop a series of "follow up" sales letters which they could process on their duplicating equipment with very little cost. This sort of free service created some problems for the manufacturer, but it did help to get the company's equipment fully used. It also gave salesmen a powerful talking point—they were able to assure prospects who had a rather limited apparent use for the equipment (it cost well over $1,000) that when they had their duplicator installed, the User's Service Bureau would help them to prepare follow-up letters which would bring in enough "velvet" business to more than repay the investment! Unfortunately some salesmen "oversold" the service. Eventually it was discontinued in favor of periodical service bulletins. It effectively promoted the use of the equipment, but it became burdensome costwise.

Then there is the small merchant who would be a better customer if he had a modern store with up-to-date fixtures and displays. In spite of all that is published in print about modernizing stores, the average storekeeper has to be taken by the arm and led into spending money. So wholesalers and others, whose sales volume depends upon making their customers more successful, usually have some sort of customer merchandising service operation. The service not only includes sketches and plans for modernizing the store, but advertising and promotion service after it is modernized. Thus it is possible to show a skeptical merchant that by spending x dollars for store modernization, and x dollars a month for the merchandising service

Joyce Brothers, nationally known woman psychologist, instructs salespeople in "How to Succeed in the People Business," a customer-contact movie produced by The Dartnell Corporation. Such v i s u a l aids, which tend to help dealer sales personnel increase sales and build loyal customers, make good indirect promotional material for any firm.

available to the wholesalers' customers who are equipped to put the promotions into effect, a return of x dollars a month is reasonable to expect. When this estimate is supported by earnings of other merchants using the service, even the tight-fisted customer loosens up.

Types of Bulletins

The format in which service material is sent to customers depends upon the nature of the material, the number of customers to receive it, and the appropriation. The most popular form is duplicated sheets, stitched together. If illustrations are not important, or if they are line drawings which can easily be traced onto a stencil, these sheets can be produced on a mimeograph type of duplicator, inexpensively. While such sheets may not look as nice as if produced by some other form of printing, they have the advantage of seeming important. On the other hand, if the nature of the information to be circulated calls for halftone and detailed illustrations, or if it is necessary to "squeeze" a lot of copy into a few sheets of paper, the multilith or offset process should be used. "Copy" can be prepared on changeable face typewriters, some of which "justify" the right-hand type margin so that it looks very much like letterpress printing. Offset printing, while more expensive than the mimeograph type, costs less than letterpress. Again, if there is a lot of copy and a variety of illustrations, and perhaps color to be used, then the most satisfactory process for producing the material is by offset—that is to say, printing from lithographic plates and on practically any grade of paper.

No matter what process is used to produce the bulletins, it is important that they have the appearance of service material and not advertising material. The more you can make the customer feel he is participating in information which is distributed to a limited number of select customers, the more value he will attach to it and the more good he will derive from it.

One of the most successful customer services consists of several loose-leaf sheets of various sorts, on different colors of paper, en-

Owens-Illinois promotes Libbey Glassware for food service operations with a helpful Merchandising Guide. The contents include useful information on costs, minimizing breakage, bar service and a bar glassware guide.

closed loosely in a four-page folder. Some of these sheets are just simple mimeographed affairs high-spotting a single idea the customer can adapt to his needs. Others may be more detailed, illustrated, and comprise a four- or eight-page saddle-stitched piece. Still others may be suggested advertisements or pass-out literature which the customer can change to suit his needs and use to promote his business. A small "Suggestion Slip" is clipped to each piece telling how it can be used. The inside cover, which contains the material, has a promotion calendar, with space so that the customer can use it to plan his promotional program for the month. The outside front cover features a single idea included with the service material which might appeal to him. This serves to get the folder opened and used. The back cover carries a reproduction of the company's current advertisement in the trade papers. The whole release is relatively inexpensive and it is highly valued by hundreds of the company's best customers. The same information could be condensed into a few sheets and mailed out for a few cents, but it would not be nearly so effective.

To ensure maximum use, bulletins are usually punched for a standard ring binder, which carries the name of the company providing the service and the name of the customer individually stamped on it. This adds to its personalized appeal. These binders cost, in quantities, about a dollar each. They are shipped with the initial release of back material and have paper indexes so that subsequent sheets can be filed according to the index number printed on each piece.

Another type of service bulletin, used by one of the automobile companies to help dealers promote their business, is what is called "Idea of the Week" post cards. Each week the executive responsible for dealer sales selects a merchandising idea successfully used by some dealer and runs a thumbnail description of the idea under a small cut of the dealer who submitted it. These cards are mailed to a special list which the sales promotion department maintains for that purpose. The theory is that dealers are too busy to read lengthy descriptions of selling plans, but that they will read a post card. The aim is to stimulate dealers to think creatively about their problems and to motivate them if possible. They have as their approach: "What this dealer did, you can do." The success of this type of bulletin depends upon getting dealers to share their best ideas with others. That is the reason for printing their pictures. The sales manager of this company says he has no trouble getting dealers to cooperate, because they get a bang out of the publicity. Since the best ideas usually are contributed by a relatively few wide-awake dealers, the cuts are saved and used over and over again. In order to get on this special mailing list a dealer must ask to get the post cards.

Some of the larger companies, like General Electric, issue elaborate magazines or house organs filled with all sorts of helpful ideas for those who sell their products. These are attractively printed and well illustrated. That they are effective there is little doubt. However, it is not necessary to spend that kind of money if money is a problem. A four-page news letter, mailed every fortnight or even every month costs but little and, if well done, can do a real job for a smaller company.

Giving Copy a Service Slant

Bulletins, service sheets, or other material used to implement a customer's service program should be prepared by someone who understands the problems of the customer. The more experience the copy writer has had in personally solving the customer's problems, the more effective the program will be. Customers, no matter what their line of business may be, are quick to sense lack of practical experience on the part of whoever wrote the bulletin or booklet, and if it does not talk his language, the customer heavily discounts it. For that reason it is usually not advisable to have this type of promotional material, or this sort of a program, developed and prepared by an advertising writer, or the company's advertising agency. Advertising writers are inclined to depend too much on generalities and overstatement. On the other hand, customer service material prepared by the engineering department, or by some recognized authority in a particular field, is usually factual and gets greater acceptance.

Customer service copy, unlike general advertising copy, should be slanted to serve rather than sell. A too-evident desire to sell puts the customer on guard against any subsequent suggestions you offer. The name of the product and the company, usually played up in selling copy, should be played down in service copy. The attitude of whoever is preparing the material should be objective. He should approach the project in the capacity of a trusted adviser of the customer. If the product or the company is mentioned, it should only be where it is obviously necessary to do so. Then it should be done deftly, not printed in capital letters, or set off in a way to suggest the only purpose of the piece is to "plug" the company.

The most effective service pieces talk with the customer rather than *at* him. Young promotion men have a tendency to get up on a mental soap box and talk down to the customer. They love to tell him what he "must do" rather than what others have done. The very tone of what they write suggests that they consider themselves "big shots" and the customer doesn't know what it is all about. There are times when an authority on some subject is justified in telling a customer what to do and what not to do, and the customer will like it. But for some reason, those who have had long experience in a certain field are usually the first to admit that they have a lot to learn, and are not inclined to assume they know all the answers. They seem to prefer to write out of their experience, and create the impression that they want to share their experience and knowledge with you. They don't pontificate.

Service copy, as well as evidencing a sincere desire to serve, should also be easy to understand. It is natural for engineers and others well grounded in their subject to use technical words and terms which the average reader does not quickly grasp. Some folks can't understand that because a thing is clear to them, that it may not mean a thing to others less conversant with technical jargon. The value of any service material is measured by the good it does the greatest number of customers, and it should not be written to please the president's wife or the board of directors. Simple, Anglo-Saxon words are best—"see" rather than "perceive," "get" rather than "procure," "guts" rather than 'intestinal fortitude." Short words, for some reason, dig in and take hold; whereas the $10 words so many businessmen love to use just don't register.

The captions and headings used in service material should be selected with great care. They should be interesting, so as to get attention; they should be instructive, so as to give the impression of helpfulness; and they should be authoritative, to emphasize their importance. The most favored type of heading is the "how to" caption, but it should not be overdone. There are several variations of the "how to" head which may be used to avoid montotony. For example, suppose the caption was for a plan to increase store traffic. The obvious head would be "How One Merchant Increased Store Traffic." Variations of the head might be: "Uses Give-Aways to Increase Store Traffic," or "A Tested Plan to Get More People Into the Store." These are all "how to" heads but they offer a change of pace.

Give the Customer Information

Instruction sheets, service notes, care-and-use booklets should be an integral part of a customer service program, and this is especially true for mechanical products, i.e. typewriters; electronic products, i.e. TV sets; and other devices of a technical nature. Also, some products are delivered to the customer in separate parts that are ready to assemble; instructions should be clear, complete and easy to follow.

Hamilton Beach provided an eight-page, accordion-type instruction folder for its 16-speed blender, with sections headed Know Your Blender, How to Use the Blender, Special Conveniences, Care of Your Blender, Cleaning Containers and, highly useful, What Won't a Blender Do. It reads: "Don't expect the Blender to do everything; it does have some limitations, although it is a very versatile appliance. The Blender will not beat egg whites alone. The Blender will mix unbeaten egg whites with other ingredients in custards but will not give volume in whites alone. It will not crush ice cubes. One ice cube at a time may be added to at least 2 cups liquid in the Blender container to chill and dilute a drink; otherwise always crush ice before putting in Blender container. It won't make fluffy mashed potatoes, but it will puree them for a soup. It won't chop or grind raw meat, but will chop small quantities of cubed, cooked meat for baby foods, diet foods or sandwich spreads."

Sunbeam Corporation products include a folder with instructions on "How to Get Quick Service" to the extent of how to pack and ship the product to meet postal requirements. Service stations in every state are listed on the back page of the folder. Enclosed with the folder is a guarantee register card.

Frequency of Publication

A majority of companies which prepare and distribute service material to customers issue it at regular intervals. Some send it out once a week, others once a month, and some quarterly. The frequency of issue depends, of course, on the nature of the material and the needs of the customer. Generally speaking, however, weekly mailings accumulate too fast if the customer does not read the material when it comes in, and few of them do. Monthly mailings are better, but it may be more desirable to mail every 6 weeks and send more material. It makes a better impression. Quarterly mailings are too far apart to be effective so far as keeping the company and its products before customers.

Getting the Material Used

It is one thing to get out service material for customers, but it is something else to get customers to put the ideas to work. Unless the ideas you develop are used, they are of little value to the customer or the company. Before putting any name on a special mailing list it is well to make sure the customer understands the importance to *him* of the proposed program. An excellent plan is to test it out in a small way on a select group, before making any large mailing; carefully check results and obtain, if possible, statements from those "test" customers which will be helpful in "selling" the program to the full list. These statements can then be made the basis of a "selling" campaign to precede the first release of service material. Some companies require that a customer first send in a card asking to be put on the list. However, it is not always wise to to be too insistent on that point, as some of your best customers, as well as those who need your help the most, may for one reason or another overlook returning your card.

When the mailings begin to go out, a special label or container should be used which carries a reference to the material inside. This tends to flag the attention and interest of the recipient who otherwise might lay it aside unread. Then there should be some way to induce customer participation in the interchange of experience. Offer a useful gadget to those who send in a business-building idea which is used in a subsequent service release. This has the effect of underscoring the "idea exchange" angle and gives customers a "top to spin." At the end of a year, a letter is usually written to all those on the list, so that they can "vote" whether or not they wish the service continued.

On the theory that people value lightly that which they get for nothing, and value more highly something for which they pay, some companies find it expedient to send customers the service without charge, provided the customer agrees to pay the postage—a matter of a dollar a year. However, the cost of preparing the material and getting it ready for the press is such a large part of the total appropriation, that it may not be to the advantage of the company to restrict the distribution of the material. The more customers who benefit from the program, and increase their sales as a result of the cooperation, the more profitable the promotion will be to the company. A few hundred dollars of "plus" business from a customer would be worth far more than the dollar postage money. If the material rings the bell, and really helps a customer to solve bothersome problems, there is little danger of his laying it aside unread.

FIDELITY BULLETIN

AN INFORMATION SERVICE FOR CUSTOMERS AND FRIENDS

VOL. 19 NO. 5   1972

Enthusiasm

*E*nthusiasm is the greatest business asset in the world. It beats money and power and influence. Single-handed the enthusiast convinces and dominates where a small army of workers would scarcely raise a tremor of interest.

Enthusiasm tramples over prejudice and opposition, spurns inaction, storms the citadel of its object, and like an avalanche overwhelms and engulfs all obstacles.

Enthusiasm is faith in action; and faith and initiative rightly combined remove mountainous barriers and achieve the unheard of and miraculous.

Set the germ of enthusiasm afloat in your business; carry it in your attitude and manner; it spreads like a contagion and influences every fiber of your industry; it begets and inspires effects you did not dream of; it means increase in production and decrease in costs; it means joy and pleasure and satisfaction to your workers; it means life real and virile; it means spontaneous bedrock results—the vital things that pay dividends.

—AUTHOR UNKNOWN

An informative bulletin is distributed by the Fidelity Bank as a means of winning new customers. The folder contains items of general interest as well as bank "plugs."

Chapter 17

STORE DISPLAYS AND PROMOTIONS

A GOOD retail display, in an appropriate location, helps lower selling costs, increase sales and produces a higher profit per square foot of floor or counter space.

Sales-stimulating, productive displays are not simply a matter of graphic design, clever ideas or pretty girl pictures. Yes, those elements are attention- getters but there are other factors to be considered of equal or greater importance. They include:

Store traffic patterns

Profit contribution (to space used)

Merchandising values

Evaluation of effectiveness

Motion or lighting costs

Versatility

Integration with package design

Correlation with advertising

Ease of shipping and assembly

Stimulus to impulse buying.

There is no question that displays stimulate impulse buying and some studies indicate that about 51% of the merchandise in supermarkets is bought on impulse. Regardless of shape, form or size, displays play a vital role in retail sales promotion.

That being the case, why are the design, production and distribution of displays subject to criticism by dealers? (See, also, Chapter 18.) Kirk W. Goines, Director of Sales, People's Drug Stores, Incorporated, made the following statements in a talk before the Point-of-Purchase Advertising Institute's 22nd Annual Symposium in New York:

"We cannot use all of the point-of-purchase material offered to us. We try to separate the wheat from the chaff, select that which we feel will do the most for us . . . is most practical for our operation.

1. We prefer the less expensive, expandable material—material that can be discarded in two to four weeks. Our customers average two and a half visits to our stores each week. We feel that it is important to keep changing point-of-purchase material.

2. For us, display merchandisers must be simple, easy and quick to put together. We have had units which even the manufacturer's salesmen couldn't assemble.

3. When practical for the manufacturer to do so, we prefer merchandise and display unit to be packed all in one carton. It simplifies our distribution and increases the probability of merchandise and display being used together.

4. When it is not practical to do so (as above), we insist that the empty display units be packed singularly. If we have to repack them for distribution, we don't want them; we can't afford them!

5. Empty display units usually come to us direct from the display manufacturer rather than from the product manufacturer. When such is the case, these units all too often fail to carry product identification on the outside. We receive much unsolicited point-of-purchase material. Most of it is promptly discarded. On the other hand, even if it has been requested and if it is not readily recognizable, it stands a good chance of being overlooked either in our warehouses or in our stores.

6. Here's something to consider, too. Why not print sales tips on the back of counter displays and selling messages on the back of floorstands? Quite often, floorstands are used free-standing in our big double-entrance shopping mall locations. They would stop the customer who approaches from the rear and who might walk right by.

7. Naturally, we like motion displays . . . motion when used toward visual demonstration best of all. We're not psychedelic, so we don't want all motion displays, but there are products and times when a clever motion display really cuts the mustard.

8. We're not as spacious as the food stores or the variety stores. We want our display merchandisers to be less towering, less overpowering. Until recently we drew the line at 54 inches height. Now, to help achieve an impression of openness in our new, larger stores, and to retard pilferage, we are leaning toward 48 inch height.

9. Rising costs of doing business are forcing the drugstores of America to remove showcases and wrapping counters and to go more self-service. As this becomes prevalent, there will be less use for counter displays—everybody can't get on the checkout stand—but, correspondingly, there will be increased acceptance by the chains of good floor-stands.

10. If your display merchandiser contains contest entry or premium order blanks, please put in a couple of extra pads so that we can stay in business on the promotion. And, be sure to print in the required particulars right on the display under the last mail-in coupon.

11. While we're talking about mail-ins, let me tell you that some buyers are now refusing display merchandisers which feature mail-in premium offers because of the aggravation created for them and for store managers by irate customers. Please try to get better service from your redemption houses.

12. Another thing we'd like to see is better velocity ratios in display merchandisers. Don't pack equal or disproportionate amounts of slow and fast items, or slow and fast sizes, in a unit. You may get some distribution on a weak item, but with the cost of money being what it is today, I think the drug chains will forego your deal rather than tie up working capital. Remember, with us turnover is the new name of the game.

13. Colorful, eye-catching, *exciting* point-of-purchase material really moves merchandise for us, really makes our cash registers ring. We like it. We need it. We want more of it. We ask, though, that you make certain that every sign gives at least one big feature selling point . . . some statement that will excite the consumer, make her want to buy that item, and buy it now.

It certainly won't be easy for you to implement, but, in your thinking and planning, please bear in mind that in the market place today the great American consumer buys far more of the seller's excitement than either the consumer or the seller realize."

Scientific evaluation of shopping habits in the modern self-service store indicate that a product has less than seconds to catch a customer today. Add to this the fact that during the past 20 years some one and one-half million retail clerks have vanished from the scene. It's no wonder, then, that the theme of a recent Point-of-Purchase Advertising Institute annual symposium was "Who's Minding the Store?"

The point is that producers of the merchandise sold in these outlets must rely on their own ingenuity to make the sale. Packaging, display and promotion are the tools available, and many are making good use of these aids.

The meteoric rise in sales of Chun King Corporation products stands as an example of marketing drive. As most know, the company was formed in the early 1950's to sell prepared Oriental foods in supermarkets. There was no great known demand for the

An action display: "Watch your customer shave himself into a sale." At the top is a mirror; below is the Ronson shaver ready for customer demonstration.

foods, but this didn't deter the company from its decision to rely on dramatic promotion and packaging to create a demand. The result—annual sales now reportedly top $50 million. The company is setting its sights on new buying groups and has an unabashed goal to make all Americans consumers of prepared Oriental foods.

Today, manufacturers rely on wood and wire merchandisers, posters, illuminated signs, motion displays, corrugated bins and other forms of point-of-purchase designs to bring attention to a product which is normally very close at hand. Obviously when several hundred (or thousand) products are placed in the close confines of a few hundred or thousand square feet, the battle for attention is heightened. Large posters or elaborate displays cannot be set up for every item on sale. Retailers must make decisions, and manufacturers must be alert enough to produce displays that will be acceptable to the retailer and still attract the customer.

Packaging is the first element available to the manufacturer. A good package must be easy to recognize, easy to place on the shelf, easy to pick up and attractive enough to catch the customer's eye. A display unit is a valuable asset if it is easy to set up, takes only enough space to do its job and proves itself as a sales builder.

Retail space is being limited by cost of construction and the growing number of new products. In some cases, now, computers are determining the life of a product. If it doesn't move according to a predetermined rate, it moves off the shelf completely. There is always something to take its place.

Sales of candies, garden tools, and a thousand other consumer products have likewise been increased by skillfully designed and strategically located store displays and fixtures.

Counter Units Win

"Try it yourself" demonstration units placed strategically on counters with high traffic are sure-fire sales builders for impulse buying. The curious customer who takes advantage of an offer to use a product may quickly be converted to a potential buyer, ready for the dealer to close the sale. This is point-of-purchase merchandising that helps the retailer find a prospect he didn't know was in a buying mood for the product.

By the same token the sale of thousands of products has been held back because the manufacturer left it to the distributor or dealer to decide what, if any, display should be made of his products in stores. In too many cases, the product was put on a shelf or under a counter and only shown when someone asked for it! A national survey of jewelry stores, made by an independent research organization for the jewelers' trade assocation, brought out the significant fact that of all the people entering a jewelry store without a definite purchase in mind, 60% said they saw nothing they might like to buy for themselves and 73% said they saw nothing they might like to buy for a friend! Yet two-thirds of the people who go into a jewelry store have no specific purchase in mind. And the same is true of many other stores. Millions of persons with money to buy what they want come out of a store without buying because they did not *see* anything they wanted.

The Store as a Display Case

In working with Goodyear dealers to help them do a better job of displaying merchandise, the company's merchandising manager likens a modern store to a merchandise dispensary, with a "Come and Get It, We Have It" sign in the window. To that end the Goodyear people recommend that dealers conduct a survey to determine what to promote and when; then plan coordinated display and promotions to play the winners. With the maximum number of different items exposed and offered for sale the first long step toward successful merchandising has been taken. However, operating conditions in any store change from day to day. It is necessary to shift the promotional plan to meet these changing conditions, which can be determined by a merchandising analysis at the point of sale. Such an analysis should cover the following points:

1. A sales and space analysis is necessary to constantly guide sales planning activities. What products are moving well? What space is available to further promote them?

2. What is the value of space by department in terms of expense per square foot? (Keep in mind the value of different department locations.)

3. Does each department stand on its own feet? What about lines? What about items?

4. How do sales and space for each department compare in percent to total store sales and space?

5. How do sales and space for each line compare in percent to total department sales and space?

6. How do sales and space for each item compare in percent to total line sales and space?

7. What items attract more customers? (Highest unit sale items.)

"Selling" the Promotion to Customers

Data gathered in field studies to determine what displays customers prefer, and will therefore be most likely to accept, are important in getting over the idea a promotion is tailor-made to fit customers' needs, and not the brain child of some "smart" advertising man. If adroitly handled, this information can be used to set the stage, not only for the promotion, but for the product itself. When Gerber Products Company, manufacturer of baby foods, desired to step up over-the-counter sales of its products it launched, after a careful study of dealers' needs, a store modernization program, with the baby food department well in the foreground. Both self-service and clerk-service stores were covered with separate promotional literature. In presenting the modernization idea to the owners of self-service stores, the research work done by the company served as a peg on which to hang the promotion, and was presented to the trade as follows:

FASTER RESTOCKING AND MAINTENANCE

Smart self-service operators report that departments not fully stocked mean lost sales and profits. As a result, they insist on a department that can be restocked and maintained with the least possible expenditure of time and effort. Economies in time and effort make a favorable impression on net profits, for an hour saved can always be put to profitable use in many jobs in today's busy food store. Alert merchants know that good self-service equipment is the first step to higher sales and easier maintenance in baby foods.

VARIETY ADEQUATE TO SATISFY ALL CUSTOMERS

With the steady and sensational increases in demand for prepared baby foods, every aggressive operator has become aware of the importance of full variety selections. He knows that there are almost as many kinds of baby diets as there are babies. For instance, some doctors favor fruits as an early food—others soups. Then little by little new foods are added. In addition to meeting the demand for many varieties, a complete department wins extra impulse sales.

CLEAR IDENTIFICATION OF EACH VARIETY AND BRAND

Hardly a self-service store employee is now alive who hasn't heard in harassed tones from a customer, "I can't seem to find the beans. There's a sign saying they should be right here, but I can't find them." Confusion and irritation on the part of customers and employees are needless and easily eliminated by keeping variety markers in their right place. It wins the continued baby food patronage of these valued customers you wish to cultivate and saves considerable time for the employees who are on the floor.

A DEPARTMENT THAT CAN BE SHOPPED QUICKLY

Successful self-service merchants also know that mothers of small children are perhaps their busiest customers. Their household and social duties leave little time to spare. The baby food department that can be shopped quickly makes it a certainty that these customers will not cut their shopping tour short, but will have plenty of time to shop every part of the store in leisurely fashion. Baby food, a famous multiple purchase item, sells better and faster when customers buy from a properly planned, complete self-service department.

CONTROLLED MASS DISPLAY

Mass has a magic effect on sales, but no store can afford to devote unreasonable space to any single product because of the great number of items that must be handled. As a result, controlled mass display, the display that makes a definite impression yet does not extend beyond its rightful limits, is welcome in today's food store. This applies to baby foods and the department which is easily visible and so constructed that big stocks are housed in a limited area, assured fast turnover at substantial margins.

Some companies attach so much importance to "selling" a display idea that they employ well-known research organizations, with national acceptance, to make the preliminary study, and then play up the name for all it is worth in their covering letter or introductory copy. Another way is to pave the way for a promotion with a letter preceding the mailing of the promotion by 3 weeks, soliciting the dealer's ideas. This tends to make him feel he had a part in planning it.

Where Good Display Begins

Store promotions, whether conducted by a manufacturer or a distributor on behalf of a dealer, or by the merchant on his own, have a three-fold job in modern merchandising:

1. People who otherwise might not go into the store, such as passers-by out window-shopping must be stopped and induced to come inside by an attention-arresting window display or store front.

2. After they are inside the store, whether they came in to buy or just to look, these people must be exposed to buying suggestions by strategically located floor and counter displays, and, if possible, want-creating signs and counter literature.

3. Those who come in to buy something, say a Mazda lamp, can be induced to buy a larger supply by smart packaging and smart display at the point where the purchase will be made. This is especially true with food, now that so many families have freezers.

Some sales promotional programs cover all of these objectives. Thus at Eastertime, when most meat merchants are eager to sell hams, the packers offer them a "packaged" promotion which usually includes: (1) Dummy hams for trimming their window, along with the necessary window streamers, window cards, and some sort of cut-out for the background; (2) wall hangers and counter displays suggesting a baked ham for the Easter feast, together with the usual mats and electros for newspaper ads and local publicity; (3) recipe books for handing out to customers, telling the many ways to prepare a ham, the best way to bake it, and a score of ways to serve left-overs. The purpose of the booklets, of course, is not only to help the housewife in her ever-present problem of what to give the family to eat, but to demonstrate how economical it is to buy a *whole* ham.

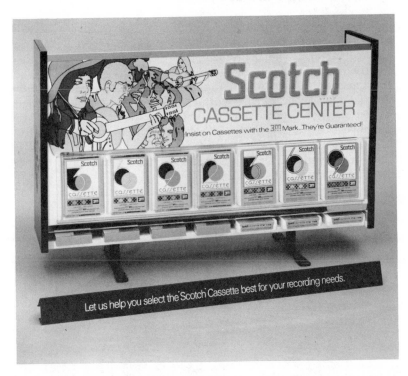

"Scotch Cassette Center" designed and produced for the 3M Company by Advertising Metal Display Company, Chicago, allows the retailer to choose between self-service and pilfer-proof merchandising. For self-service, the top-loaded cassettes kick out at the bottom front, so a customer may help himself to his choice. To switch to a pilfer-proof display, a metal "pilfer bar" screws across the bottom; the cassettes then feed out of the bottom rear for clerk access only.

Motion in the Window

The best window displays supplied by national advertisers for the use of those who sell their products usually depend upon motion to get attention and interest. Typical of this type of display is the head of "Elsie," the famous Borden Company cow. A large papier-mache head, featuring Elsie calmly chewing her cud, makes a dramatic tie-in with the Borden magazine, newspaper, and outdoor advertising publicizing the famous animal. Children especially are intrigued by motion displays, thus helping to create local word-of-mouth publicity for the product. Contrary to the opinion of many advertising men, who regarded the Elsie advertising of Borden as a bit silly, this device proved tremendously popular. It also proved effective as a sales producer. "People," said the man who conceived the idea, "are pretty well fed up with stuffy advertising and relish something humorous and folksy. Farm people especially are interested in farm animals. When we started shipping Elsie around the country in a chartered plane, to participate in state fairs, we got thousands of columns of publicity for Elsie which laid the foundation for one of the most extensive promotional campaigns Borden has ever undertaken." While the animated display lacks the appeal of the real Elsie, it enables the company to put a lifelike replica of the famous bovine's intriguing head in thousands of food store windows. Dealers wait in turn to get the display, because of its attention-getting qualities.

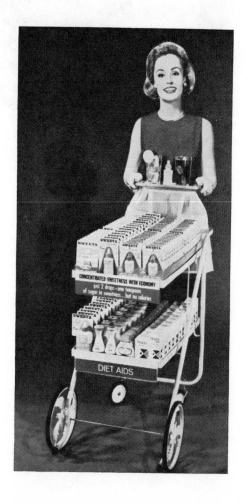

Almost lifelike in appearance, this award-winning Sweeta Tea Cart store display effectively drew attention to Squibbs diet aids.

Courtesy Point-of-Purchase Advertising Institute.

A massive supermarket display of soups served as an impressive base for a free-spoon premium offer by Campbell Soup Company.

When appropriations do not permit animated displays such as the Borden cow, motion may be secured by such simple means as attaching crepe-paper streamers to a cut-out display, and placing a small electric fan in the window to keep the streamers flying. Still another popular animated display is seen in bank windows where illustrated cards are used to "get over" a sales promotional message. The cards are automatically changed at 15-second intervals. These displays are purchased in quantities by a national advertiser and loaned to customers upon the recommendation of the territorial salesman. They are electrically lighted.

New Display Animation

Light and motion have long been utilized to give displays added attention values. Small motors, simple spring mechanisms, turn-tables, are used effectively to inject life and force to conventional display forms. The merchandiser-display cabinet, with its rotating shelves, used in the watch industry, is well-known.

A new form of display animation has recently been developed by Ashley-Butler, Incorporated, New York, utilizing nematic liquid crystals, which turn from clear to milky white when small amounts of electricity are passed through them. The crystals revert to the clear state when the current is stopped.

By patterning areas where an image is desired, and "sequencing" the current, animated displays are created in a clear pane of glass.

Because the liquid crystal material is light-reflexive (the brighter the light, the brighter the picture), and uses extremely small amounts of current, the display may be under the bright lights of retail stores.

Life-Size Store Cut-Outs

The trend in some sections of the country, notably California and Florida, toward show-windowless stores, has brought about the development of a type of inside-the-store display, of such a size that it attracts the attention of the passer-by on the street as well as the customer within the store. Typical of this type of dealer help was that of Youngstown Kitchens, the manufacturer of which furnished dealers with life-size cut-outs of the woman of the house, and another of the man of the house. The dealer set them up in the front of the store in such a way that it would center attention on the product. The store display was supported by magazine advertising and pass-out literature built around the idea of the husband chasing the wife out of her electrically operated kitchen so that he could have the fun of washing the dishes in the new dishwasher.

This display worked out so well that the company embarked upon a series of promotions using life-size cut-outs of the figures appearing in the company's current magazine advertising. Dealers who wished to do so could reproduce in the store the kitchen scene featured in the magazine advertisement. At the same time, dealers were furnished mats for local newspaper advertising featuring the store display. Six of these promotions were used, and according to the sales promotion manager for the kitchens, 3,000 home equipment dealers used them. Each promotion lasted 2 months. Half the magazine list was used for one month and half for the next.

Similarly, an electrical refrigerator manufacturer, also selling through home appliance dealers, developed a mechanism which kept opening and closing the door of an electrically lighted refrigerator. A sign on the inside of the moving door called attention to the features of the refrigerator. It also proved to be a great attention-getter.

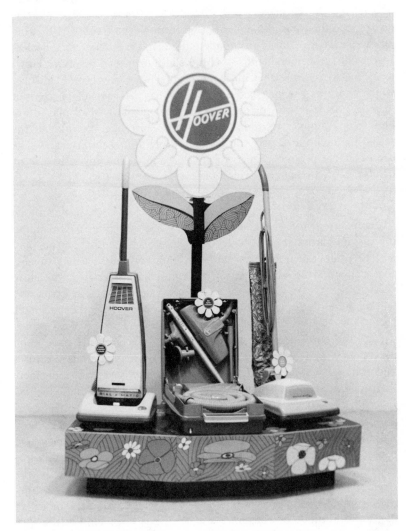

Parts and attachments are sometimes difficult to display attractively but in this Hoover display stand they form an integral part of a unified unit. The floral theme nicely tops the display and is repeated to suggest a "fresh-as-a-daisy" appeal.

Displays Showing the Actual Product

Another type of store display which has a high acceptance with merchants, and which is especially adapted to promoting the sale of package goods, has an opening cut in the design, into which a can or package of the product can be placed. Some argue that there is no point to this, that dealers won't go through the trouble of hunting up the package required to complete the display, or that some dealers just won't take merchandise off the shelf to use in displays. However, checks indicate that most merchants favor any type of display which features the product itself. This may be psychological, or it may fit into the store owners' theory that goods well displayed are half sold. At any rate, the average storekeeper likes the idea of the actual package on display, rather than a picture of the package. The use of actual product displays is two-to-one compared to the use of display cards or hangers which merely picture the package.

Counter Cards and Displays

Competition for space on a dealer's store counter is becoming increasingly keen. Some dealers are dead set against putting any sort of promotional material on their counters, unless it has suggestive value to the customer or contributes in some way to store service. As a result, there is a heavy waste of counter cards and run-of-the-mill displays. The dealers just won't give them counter room. On the other hand, neat counter cards or displays which "plug" the store's service and "soft pedal" the product have good acceptance. This is especially true if the product is a fast repeater and carries a margin of profits which the merchant considers "adequate," and toward which he therefore has a friendly feeling.

In these days of big appropriations for national advertising it is a mistake to think dealers will get excited about "tying-in with national advertising" to get local prestige for stores. That argument used to be effective, and it still is with such well-entrenched lines as Hart Schaffner & Marx clothes, Timex watches, Stetson hats, Swift's Premium meats, etc. But there are many years of advertising behind these products. Where a product is a newcomer to the field, or where the appropriation for consumer advertising is large only in the eyes of the company that is footing the bill, dealer helps must stand on their own feet. Whether they will be used, or laid aside, and how long they will be used, depends upon the value the merchant places upon them as *sales makers*.

Double-Duty Displays

The Adgrow Mandeville Company, Incorporated, increased exposure for its seed products at the point-of-purchase by developing a new type display. In the past, seed packets were displayed in wooden, metal or wire racks owned by the seed company. The new unit served both as a shipper-carton and display which did not require placing the packets and was disposable at the end of the season. The unit expedited shipments and eliminated the effort and labor to return the traditional racks.

Owens-Illinois got extra mileage out of one of its dealer announcements by utilizing the reverse side as a point-of-sale poster. Announcing three new iced tea glasses with illustrations and copy printed on a colored sheet 11 by 13 inches in size, a note at the bottom read: "Save this sheet! Use the reverse side as an attention-getting point-of-sale aid. Mount it above your display of Libbey merchandise. Hang it on your door or front window. Its bright color attracts attention . . . invites impulse sales." The reverse side showed a cartoon illustration of a polar bear holding a "Giant 25-Ounce Jumbo Cooler" glass with the heading: "Sale! Warm Weather Special." Space at the bottom was left for the price.

Related Displays

Some dealers are averse to using a display which features the product of a single manufacturer, but will gladly install a display of related products. For example, the Bristol-Myers Company cooperated with dealers in a "Going Away" display which included a variety of products sold in drug stores. A questionnaire mailed to 250 retail druggists by the Point-of-Purchase Advertising Institute for Bristol-Myers, brought responses from 105 dealers, of whom 96 preferred the related item display to single product displays. A majority favored a 2 weeks' period for such displays; 20 favored 3 weeks. Of those replying, 88% thought the material provided for such displays was good enough to use again next year; 62% said that this type of display definitely resulted in a sales increase on the items included. Only 3% said they did not notice any increased demand for the featured products.

This idea of furnishing display material which a dealer can use for a display of related items is not new, but it has a strong appeal. It permits a merchant to include in the display a variety of profitable items which he has in good supply. Most of the display ideas submitted by manufacturers, or wholesalers, are designed to sell a product which the dealer would soon have to reorder. While he may have no objection to doing that, he is still more interested in getting his money out of merchandise which he has previously overbought and thus increase his working capital.

"Merchandising the Advertising" Promotion

The decline in magazine lineage which followed the boom caused publishers of advertising media to step up their syndicated store promotions of nationally advertised products. This type of "related" display has proved popular with dealers. They like its "prestige" value. Such displays are usually built around a central theme, such as "Goods Especially Selected for Men of Attainment," used successfully by *Time*. The *Time* display neatly gets over the idea that the stores' customers and *Time* readers are one and the same. This type of promotion was pioneered by *Vogue* about 25 years ago, and has now become standard practice by "class" magazines. More than 1,350 stores used *Holiday* display materials—brightly colored streamers, pennants, and window cards—in one year. A Texas retailer wrote that a *Holiday* sale he put on doubled the store's sales. An Indiana men's store credited a Father's Day promotion, using *Esquire* tie-in promotional material, with a 20% increase in business. Many dealers have reported that they feel the magazine tie-up helps the display, and they like the idea of publicizing their store as headquarters for well-known quality products.

Teaching Store Owners Display Techniques

While most dealers readily admit that "goods well displayed are half sold," only a relatively few understand the principles of good display. Most of them evaluate a display by the number of items which can be crowded into it, with the result that their stores, windows, and counters have a decidedly "junky" look. To help its dealers utilize tested display principles, the Mirro Aluminum Company, like many other astute national advertisers, conducts a continuing program of display education for its dealers.

It makes suggestions for window displays of aluminum cooking utensils, wall displays, counter displays, and especially floor displays. This "how-to-do-it" promotional literature not only shows the dealer how to make the display, but (and this is important) it explains the principles of display involved, so that over a period of time the dealer becomes display-conscious, and acquires an appreciation for the techniques used in modern merchandising display. In the same way, Westinghouse Electric Corporation uses cartoons in its trade-paper advertising to get over to its distributing organization display ideas for promoting "point-of-purchase" sale of electric lamp bulbs. Cartoons are used, rather than heavy educational text, on the theory that electrical goods dealers, like most people, will read "funnies" when they might skip over a conventional advertisement. The light-hearted message often works best.

STANDARD STORE DISPLAY MATERIALS

Before deciding what kind of displays to prepare as a part of a sales promotional campaign, it is advisable to have the use of previous materials checked by an outside organization. Most advertisers depend upon salesmen to get this information for them. That is better than no check at all, but salesmen, like advertising men, often have preconceived ideas as to what displays are best for a company to use. Customers preferences change from time to time, and advertisers find it pays to use some of their appropriation for spot dealer checks before contracting for new dealer helps. Not only should the use made of previously furnished material be checked, but a check should be made to determine what type of displays dealers are currently using. Some advertisers go so far as to ask them what they would like to have, but most dealers would like to have the moon.

There are a hundred different types of display materials currently being supplied to dealers, agents, and distributors by national advertisers. Those most favored are:

"Packaged" Window Displays

These are provided upon request (usually the dealer pays some of the cost), for the purpose of dressing an exclusive window. The best practice is to have the display installed by a national window display service, or by a traveling representative of the sales promotion department. The average dealer puts off window trimming as long as possible, and usually ends up filling his window with a conglomeration of signs and products without any central idea.

Window Streamers

Used mostly by food and other stores that like to make billboards out of their windows. Inexpensive, and if striking in design, can be very effective. To get maximum use of such dealer helps, the streamers should be self-sticking.

WONDERFUL WHITE!
WHAT WORKS: One large and several smaller pieces of spring materials in different colors and prints. Assortment of boxes. White shoes.
HOW TO: Use the large piece of material as the backdrop and floor covering. Cover the different sized boxes with the smaller pieces of material. Stack the boxes at various heights and arrange them for shoe props. Display your white shoe collection on and around the arrangement.

BEAUTIFUL-DUTIFUL SHOES
WHAT WORKS: Different sized shoe boxes. Magazine clips of active women and working-situation scenes. Duty shoes.
HOW TO: Glue magazine clips of women in white and related careers to the boxes. Arrange the boxes in a "stair-step" pattern. Display your complete collection of Joyce's fashion-right and comfort duty shoes on the "stair steps."

FRESH CASUALS
WHAT WORKS: Fruit poster. Baskets. Artificial fruit. Tree branch. Grass mat. Fishing line. Fun casuals. Dress casuals.
HOW TO: Pin-up the poster for a backdrop. Suspend the tree branch from the ceiling with fishing line and cuphooks. From the branch hang lightweight fruit baskets filled with artificial fruit and several pairs of shoes. Use the grass mat for the display floor, with overturned baskets and pieces of artificial fruit as shoe display props.

SOFT SENSATIONS!
WHAT WORKS: No-seam paper. Various sized cardboard cylinders. Cut-out cloud shapes. Cotton fluffs. Soft-looking shoes. Soft-feeling shoes.
HOW TO: Hang soft-colored, no-seam paper for the background and extend it down across the display floor. Attach the cloud shapes to the cylinders. Put cotton on cylinder tops, and let some of it drape over the sides and onto the floor. Set your soft shoes on the cotton and cylinders.

PRETTY SHOE APPEAL!
WHAT WORKS: Lots of clay flower pots. Artificial flowers. Grass mat. Potted plants. Lattice work. Pretty shoes.
HOW TO: Using the grass mat as the floor covering and the lattice work as the background, stack and arrange the clay flower pots for the shoe display props. Also, put shoes on the lattice work, along with artificial flowers. Then, add the potted plants for a pretty and feminine looking display.

IT'S AN OPEN, LIGHT, SANDAL SEASON!
WHAT WORKS: Picnic baskets. Balloons. String. Sun sandals. City sandals. Dress sandals.
HOW TO: Attach helium balloons to picnic baskets. Open the baskets and display the sandals on, in and around them.

Many manufacturers offer their dealers complete window displays. In the promotion book for Joyce Shoes, the company suggests some general backgrounds with instructions as to the materials needed and how to assemble them.

Such streamers are usually furnished free to customers who like to have something novel to "stick in the window." Best results from such displays are secured when the piece calls for an accompanying in-store floor display of the advertised product.

Window and Door Stickers

Usually printed on self-sticking papers. All the storekeeper has to do is to peel off the protective covering and stick it up. When he wants to take it down, he just peels it off the glass. These stickers are usually suggestive. General Electric has used stickers reminding the person opening the store door she might need electric lamps; Canada Dry furnished stickers for the shopping carts used in chain food stores; Campbell Soup Co. supplied dealers with books of shelf markers for merchants to stick on the shelf to mark the kind of soup to go there. While such stickers feature the advertised product, they are one of the kinds of dealer helps self-service stores will use because they help buying in general.

Wall Posters and Hangers

Not so popular as they once were. To get preferred position they must be unusually attractive. They should also do a sales job, and not merely feature the advertiser's product. One of the most popular and widely used wall posters was "The Country Doctor" which thousands of rural drug stores hung on their walls for years. Coca-Cola has been successful in popularizing wall hangers in Coke bars and taverns; they feature glamorous girls. Coca-Cola drivers are alert to put them up at every opportunity.

Floor Displays

Expensive but effective when properly done. Can be used in connection with attracting attention to "big ticket" products like furniture, home appliances, garden tools, etc. Usually cut-outs with easel backs so they can be stood about the store in strategic locations, or racks for holding quantities of the product.

Counter Cards

Should not be too large and must be sufficiently attractive so that they add to the store's appearance. Usually suggestive. If the merchant will give them space on the counter where the product is sold, these cards and signs are most effective point-of-sale promotion. The backs of such cards make a good place to print the principal selling points of the product. This helps the clerks behind the counter who may not be too familiar with the product.

Counter Displays

Store owners are well aware that the best way to increase sales is to improve their display methods. They are usually receptive to any fixture, case, or rack which enables them to make a good point-of-sale display, and if the manufacturer does not plaster his name all over it, merchants will often pay for such fixtures, or they can be offered with assortments of merchandise. They should not take up too much' counter space.

Gerber Products Co. provides dealers with store lay-out plans (shown opposite) which aid them in arranging their stores, and at the same time suggest where to locate and organize a baby food display.

"Dummy" Cartons

Package goods manufacturers, as well as those making such products as hams and bacon, find dealers like to have giant-sized replicas of the product or package which they can put around the store and in show windows. They are most effective when the package itself has good design and makes a pleasing appearance.

Dealers and Displays

The waste of costly litho-

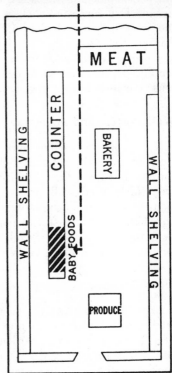

In counter-service stores use of a special self-service fixture on top of the counter is an excellent way to achieve partial self-service. A gondola unit in center of store is also very practical. The "necessity" merchandise is displayed and sold in the rear of the store.

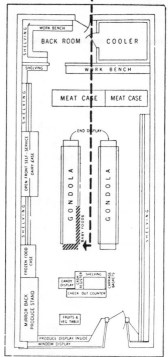

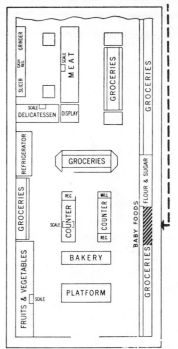

In self-service stores a preferred location is one immediately seen by incoming customers, yet out of high traffic lane at the right. Location meets both of these requirements. Displays should be built high enough to permit sign to appear at eye level.

In semi-self-service stores a wall location usually brings high sales. It is not in the busy zone of produce or meat departments. So, mothers shop for baby food without being crowded. A location opposite a cross aisle is preferred to a dead-end position.

graphed signs, window trims, counter cards, banners, and streamers supplied to dealers by manufacturers can be reduced by showing dealers how to use them more advantageously. This problem was acute in the paint field. Owners of stores selling painters' supplies are usually tradesmen who have saved a few thousand dollars and gone into business. They are not promotion-minded. When some display card which they especially like comes in, they try it for size in a few empty spots on the wall, and if there is a likely spot, up it goes. To make paint dealers more sales-promotion-conscious and to help them do a better promotion job, the National Paint, Varnish and Lacquer Association, Inc., prepared and published a 350-page promotional manual for the trade called *Paint Power*. The following suggestions were included on display materials, which the manual referred to as "silent salesmen":

1. When the display features a general idea, place it in a prominent location where it will be seen by all customers. The space opposite the front door is, incidentally, the preferred position in the whole store.

2. A specific item, or specific line display, should be placed as near as possible to the merchandise described.

3. A display offering merchandise for the customer to examine should be placed where the customer can touch it.

4. All displays should be placed where they can be seen and read by the customer.

5. Displays designed to be hung from the ceiling should be hung low enough for the customer to read and look over easily.

6. All displays should be placed where they will not conceal merchandise.

7. Never place displays where they will have to be moved back and forth by salesmen when taking care of customers.

8. Always place displays in a well-lighted position.

Getting Display Material Used

There is no ready-to-wear formula for making sure that after you have spent good money to produce store displays that they will be adequately used, in fact that they will be used at all. While the percentage of waste in this type of promotion is high, it can be held down quite materially by making the material important in the eyes of those who are supposed to use it. Here, for example, are a few suggestions offered by Einson-Freeman, well-known producer of display material:

1. *Free Goods for Photographs.* Simply offer two or three packages free for receipt of a snapshot showing the display in use. It helps to put a sticker, repeating this offer, on the outside of the container in which the display is shipped. The photographs received provide interesting pictures for trade advertising.

2. *Contest for Best Windows.* This always stimulates the use of material, and, like the plan above, provides good trade pictures, but the objection is cost. There have been so many window-display contests that it takes real money to excite dealers, these days. And, there is always the "sorehead" who thinks he should have won.

3. *Display Checker.* Here the trade and dealer advertising features the "checker" who shops stores and awards $5 to each dealer using the display during the period of the drive.

It has a mail variation for smaller towns, wherein displays are numbered and a sticker, like a raffle slip, is mailed in by the dealer, attesting also to the fact that his store is prominently showing the display. A drawing takes place, and the winners are notified as in any other contest. The value to the advertiser is that the dealer must actually use the display to get in on the drawing.

4. *Free Goods Via Jobbers' Salesmen.* Here the manufacturer agrees to give the retailer, say, two packages, for a week's showing, but the retailer must get his free goods certificate signed by the wholesaler's salesman as a witness to the fact that the display was used.

The usual friendships between dealer and salesman make this plan of doubtful value, but it is frequently used because it is much less trouble than taking a photograph, and it also reminds salesmen to check stocks.

5. *Press Advertising.* It is axiomatic that broadsides and trade-paper advertising should feature window and counter displays and also that it will be more resultful if it pounds one of the reward plans described here, or some other that will do the same job.

6. *Display Packing.* If you can ship goods in a counter display, all ready to set up, by all means do it. The factor of inertia may be made to work for you. When it is more trouble to take out the goods and put it away than to use the display on the counter, a big percentage of dealers will choose the easiest way.

Pack counter displays for salesmen in convenient cartons of 25 units that can be handled easily in a small car. A mass display, like a counter basket, can be used to inventory a dealer's stock, and salesmen can be prompted by a reminder printed on the outside of each carton of displays.

There is one more factor in distributing display material through the chains: Display units are most frequently sent direct by the manufacturer to each store in the chain. Very rarely, only where tie-up is being made with the chain's own promotion, does the chain care to do the distribution. The displays can be shipped with merchandise, particularly advisable if they fit into the merchandise containers or packages, or they can be shipped individually and separately.

In any case, the display material should be wrapped and taped up so that it arrives in good usable condition. Watch the corners of your packages, if they hold display cards. Stores don't like to put banged-up, shabby-looking cards on display. Be sure a large label brings attention to the contents of the package. This should be addressed to the store manager or the floor girl in charge of the section where the display is scheduled to be posted. If the package contains several displays, itemize the contents.

For example, a label or sticker may say: "This package contains two 11 x 14 signs for your Back-to-School Stationery Counter, two 5¾ x 7 cards for your sign-holders, two 6 x 36 paper streamers for your windows. Use without delay!" It isn't a bad idea to have an explanatory display sheet inside the package, particularly if it contains an illustration of the display material in use. Die-cut displays, cylinders that have to be rolled, displays that have to have months affixed should have instructions clearly pasted on the back.

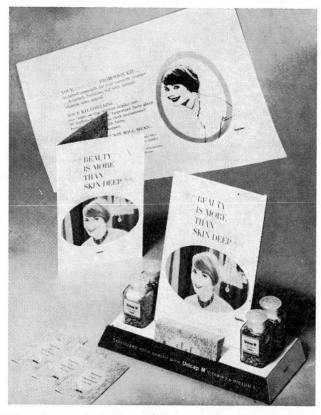

This Upjohn "Unicap M" promotion was designed to serve three tasks: (1) to train the cosmetic clerk on the subject of vitamins; (2) to relate the sales of cosmetics and vitamins; (3) to display vitamins in an unusual and different part of the store—the cosmetic counter.

PROMOTIONS THAT BUILD STORE TRAFFIC

The type of promotional activity most popular with dealers or distributors of any good product is one which brings people into the store to look and to buy. While the merchant is mildly interested in promotions which increase the unit of sale, or suggest purchases of products the customer otherwise might not buy, the problem of building store traffic is basic. For that purpose he belongs to the Main Street Association, which puts on the annual street festival; he spends his money for newspaper advertising, featuring specials; he builds a new store front and puts up a better sign. He knows, only too well, until he can get Mrs. John Doakes into his store, his chances of selling her are slim indeed. She might buy by telephone, but then again she might not.

One of the earliest promotions to build store traffic was "give-aways" for the youngsters. Manufacturers supplied dealers with kites, rubber balloons, paper caps, and what have you, imprinted with the name of the product for this purpose. Before the era of "plenty," when youngsters no longer walk a mile for a kite, these traffic builders were quite effective. Indeed, they are still used by many small-town merchants to build parent good will. But times have changed, and the merchant of today is more interested in getting the parents to come and leave the kiddies at home.

The Birthday Party Idea

A shirt company capitalized on its thirtieth anniversary by furnishing dealers with materials needed to put on local birthday parties, to which the store's customers were invited. They were urged to come and share the big birthday cake and in the equally big birthday bargains the store was offering. A promotional campaign to dealers was built around the making of a birthday cake, with an actual piece of cake carefully packed and wrapped in cellophane. Another promotion, which panned out for a druggist, was a "prize" window in which a variety of items were displayed and a prize awarded to the customer able to list the most products whose names began with those letters of the alphabet which formed the name of the store. Then there is the clothing merchant who sends a letter of welcome, with a crisp new dollar bill, to every new baby which arrives in town.

Other promotions successfully used by merchants in the past to build store traffic and increase sales are reported following:

LUCKY TICKETS

A refrigerator dealer sent out letters to selected prospects within his sales area, inviting them to visit his store on a certain date at a certain time for a demonstration of appliances. Enclosed in the letter were two lucky tickets which were to be deposited in a box at the demonstration. The winner took home free any appliance she wanted.

This stunt was used by dealers in over 100 cities. It proved to be a good traffic builder. One Florida retailer pulled 550 customers into his store for the demonstration and drawing. A Salem, Oregon, retailer lured 450 prospects into his store with the invitation. In some cases retailers reported the promotion brought in more traffic in one day than they normally have in two weeks or more.

FREE TRIP TO DETROIT

A distributor of automobiles for the Denver, Colorado, trading area, offered everyone buying a new car from one of the seven local Denver dealers during a stated period a free trip on a chartered plane to Detroit. The first group numbered 29. They were shown through the automobile plant, given dinner at an exclusive club, and then presented with their new cars to drive back to Denver. This plan brought sales of this car from third to second place in Denver.

The dealers bought newspaper space and radio time to advertise their sales promotion plan. They also gave away six new sedans and a convertible in a contest at a chain of local theaters, in exchange for the theater advertising and endorsing the plan.

PHOTOGRAPHS DRAW CROWDS

In order to move its higher-priced shoes, a Kansas City shoe merchant made arrangements with a local photographer to give each purchaser a free photograph with each pair of shoes. In order to make such an offer apply to children's shoes, the dealer had to have an understanding with a photographer and furnish one picture on the dealer's order. One successful shoe dealer watched the birth records and wrote the parents a letter of congratulation, offering to present the baby with a photograph with the first pair of shoes purchased in the store. Pictures of babies are of special interest to mothers and this method affords an opportunity to get on a firm and friendly basis with the family that will mean much increased business.

TALKS ON TABLE ETIQUETTE

A Boston department store secured a notable increase in silverware sales through a unique method of stimulating interest. The company engaged a locally famed authority on table arrangements to give a series of four lectures on "The Etiquette of Table Appointments," at 3:30 daily each afternoon in the assembly hall. The subjects were: "The Luncheon Table," "The Breakfast and Afternoon Tea Table," "The Dinner Table and the Supper Table," and "The Bridge Luncheon." Admission to the lecture was free, but by ticket issued by the company. Every session filled the hall.

Tied up with the lecture was a display of the "Pieces of Eight," featured by the company's advertising, the displays included a window showing a "Pirate's chest" filled with silverware, and a table display, with counter displays in the silverware section inside. Coupled with advertising of the store was display advertising prepaid by the manufacturers.

STORE DISPLAYS AND PROMOTIONS

Valentine-Making Contest

This plan, successfully used by a Michigan dealer, involved a contest of boys and girls under fourteen. The retailer advertised in his local paper announcing a prize to be awarded the boy or girl making the prettiest valentine and writing the best verse for it. One of the requirements was that those entering the contest should come to the store with one of their parents. These parents signed their names and addresses on cards which became a part of the store's mailing list. Two of the teachers were selected as judges, and the prizes were awarded Valentine Day. There were also second, third, and fourth prizes offered.

"Gone But Not Forgotten" Customers

Old customers of a shoe store in Los Angeles are reminded by a folder of the fact that they have not called for some time. On the top flap of this folder is a cartooned funeral wreath surrounded by the words, "Gone but not forgotten." The underflap bears a letter which suggests that if the customer is dissatisfied, he should come in for an adjustment.

"Look for the Number" Idea

A retailer in West Virginia sent out a notice of a mark-down sale. This called attention to a number printed in the corner and invited the customer to come to the store and look around. If he found an article to which that number was pinned, he could have it with the store's compliments. Many who came to look for numbers, remained to buy.

Mating Contests (Gloves)

In order to induce farmers to come to town on special sales days, a Kansas store mailed a right-hand cotton glove to a number of customers, who were asked to come in and receive the mate. They came.

Overinflated Inner Tube

Here is a simple stunt that, although costing practically nothing, resulted in attracting a large number of new customers as well as old customers to this tire shop. An inner tube was inflated until it stretched to a total diameter of 7 feet. When it reached this size, the tube was hung on a line across the service court. A sign gave the size and kind of tube. More than 300 persons stopped in to inquire about the tube within 3 days.

Nonstart Donkey Sells Batteries

A donkey and rig proved to be a good crowd-gathering stunt for a South Carolina battery dealer. Every time the donkey became stubborn and refused to move, the driver climbed out, gazed over his specs at the Exide slogan, "When It's an Exide, You Start," and then climbed back into the rig. The donkey would then start with a flourish on his hind feet. The crowds chuckled and applauded.

"Believe-It-or-Not" Window

This idea is adaptable to practically any line of business. A giant book forms the centerpiece. Its heading is "Furniture Believe-It-or-Nots." Streamers carry the eye of exhibits commented on. For example, an open can of paint has a streamer running to a paragraph in the giant book, which says, "Linoleum was discovered in a paint can. The film of oil that forms on the top of paint exposed to air furnished the idea from which originated our modern linoleum." This statement also tied in with patterns of Armstrong's Linoleum shown in the background of the window.

SHOW WINDOW ON WHEELS

Beech-Nut advertising was brought to life by a moving exhibit on a display truck. Twenty different features in the circus were exhibited in action in this impressive display. The display was the pivot point of an outstandingly effective sampling campaign which was given high praise by local dealers. The troupe which appeared in circus costume started a sampling and promotion campaign in Miami and then moved north covering many cities. Not only did the stunt attract large crowds wherever it was staged, but it brought about a considerable amount of local newspaper publicity and general comment that multiplied the effectiveness of the sampling activity.

MINIATURE RACING CAR

An effective way to attract crowds and stimulate sales was used by a Maytag dealer. The focal point of interest was a sleek miniature racing car with the Maytag trade-mark displayed on the hood. A conspicuous sign announced a "give-away" which resulted in bringing children and adults clamoring for details. The dealer, also a hardware store operator, worked out the plan to include other items by giving a chance on the car for each dollar of a purchase. The combination of the raffle idea with the novel prize, it is reported, brought a substantial increase in sales and also stimulated payment of many old accounts. The use of this kind of stunt to attract youngsters has proved effective in bringing crowds of grown-ups to the stores, according to several manufacturers.

ADVERTISING TRAILER

Although trailers have been used effectively in a great variety of ways, the Hotpoint advertising trailer used by a public utilities company in the South introduced an entirely different idea that was recommended to dealers throughout the country. The trailer has a low slung platform just large enough to display one range. It is inexpensive to produce. Being open, it has some important advantages from an exhibit and advertising standpoint. It not only takes the product to the prospect, but it attracts the interest of others and helps to make prospects.

TALKING OUTDOOR DISPLAYS

At frequent intervals, dealers should be given ideas for floats and rolling displays, according to a manufacturer in the electric household appliance field. Many dealers use rolling outdoor displays as a feature of their local advertising, but ideas of this nature passed along at intervals also prompt dealers to take advantage of civic parades, festivals, and other local events that draw crowds. Usually they are equipped with loud-speakers. Large placards carry the simple slogan, "At Your Service."

POSTING NAMES OF SATISFIED CUSTOMERS

Most dealers and dealer salesmen frequently refer to "the lady down the street who just bought," and many dealers publish periodically a list of users in the local newspapers. A Maytag dealer in Hartford City, Indiana, went a step further, listing names of local buyers on a large blackboard in the rear of his store. The very size of the list is impressive, and rarely misses getting the attention of any prospect coming into the store.

STORE DISPLAYS AND PROMOTIONS

Mower Demonstrator Plan

In order to bring the merits of the Yardman lawn mower to the attention of a prospective purchaser, the manufacturer has established an attractive sales plan. Under it, if the dealer purchases two machines at the regular wholesale cost, he is offered the opportunity of purchasing a third "demonstrator machine" at an additional discount. This machine is used on a loan basis to any interested prospects. When the question of price arises, as it often does, the dealer suggests that the prospect ascertain for himself the many advantages of this mower.

Plumb's Woodchopping Exhibition

Fayette R. Plumb, Inc., is a trade name long connected with quality wood-cutting tools. This organization has a keen sense for cooperating with the independent retailer. One of the features which this manufacturer uses to focus attention on his product and on the dealer's store is a woodchopping contest and master woodcutter demonstration. A well-known master wood-cutter is scheduled to appear at the dealer's store on an established date. For local publicity the dealer advertises a local woodchopping contest with prizes for the best local chopper. This is done on a timing basis, chopping through a log with an ax. A Plumb ax is, of course, selected as one of the awards.

Door-Opener Plan Sells Oil Burners

The manufacturer of the Delco Oil Burner prepared for the use of its dealers' outside salesmen a "door opener" known as the Heat Guide. It consists of a card bearing a standard thermometer tube and bulb. But instead of having the customary temperature degrees, it is marked off into three zones, as follows: "Too Hot," "Too Cold," and "The Zone of Health." Alongside of each zone appear explanations of that zone. Of course, for the first two, the prospect is shown why each is not healthful and not economical. At the bottom there are blank spaces in which the prospect can check and record if the home temperature is either "in" or "out" of the third zone—that of health and economy.

Moderate-Priced Saw Display Wins Sales

In order to permit retail hardware dealers to compete favorably with catalog houses and other sources of low- and moderate-priced merchandise, Henry Disston & Sons, Inc., presented the Keystone brand of handsaws in a popular-priced assortment, including a walnut-stained display rack for counter use. This display rack, when filled, contains five differently named Keystone-brand saws.

Empty-Can Display Sells More Oil

A dealer took on the local sale of Texaco Motor Oil, packaged in sealed 2-gallon cans. He had sold only bulk motor oil prior to this time, and as garages with their free-oil-change service were taking most of the bulk oil sales he was naturally somewhat skeptical as to what he could do with even such a popular-priced article. It seems that some of the very simplest merchandising principles bring marvelous results, providing the dealer applies them to an item of extensive and continuous demand. This dealer sold dozens and scores of these 2-gallon cans of oil—in fact, it would be more nearly correct to state that they sold themselves. The sales method used was merely to set a stack of them each day in front of the store, together with a large-type printed sign giving the brand name and price.

SALES PROMOTION HANDBOOK

APPEAL TO YOUNGSTERS BRINGS NEW BUSINESS

A sales plan devised by a manufacturer for the purpose of focusing the attention of boys and girls on traffic regulation and highway safety, coupled with the use of handy cans of the product, was the 3-in-1 Oil Safety League. To secure membership the youngsters had to fill out a printed questionnaire on simple rules governing general traffic designed to make each entrant more careful when roller skating on town and city streets. The questions and explanations were so easy that any average youngster could answer enough of them with sufficient correctness to win the award of a Safety League badge or chevron. Naturally, it suggested keeping roller skates in good condition with 3-in-1 Oil.

LOCK AND KEY PLAN

In this plan, dealers are encouraged to have a master lock, a number of master keys fitting the lock, and a quantity of dummy keys attached to printed cards. The keys are distributed and the urge to "get something for nothing" brings prospective buyers to the store to try their luck in opening the lock. The plan is controllable because any percentage of master keys can be included in the lot distributed. The key-cards are distributed door to door, handed out by salesmen, or displayed in windows having a card inviting the public to step in, choose a key, and try their luck. All prospects who come in are given a demonstration and followed up carefully with a view toward selling them.

DAILY SUGGESTION

Each morning, one dealer decides on a daily Suggestion Item. Make a regular contest to see who can sell most of that item each day by suggesting after each sale. Added fun, incentive, when small prize is offered for largest daily sales of item. Try: (1) Package of dozen wash cloths, 59 cents; (2) five small hand towels for kitchen, 5 for $1; (3) half dozen dish towels, $1; (4) 3-piece set, $1.

CARDBOARD PENNIES FOR REAL ONES

Fifty thousand sham pennies were distributed all over N. W. London for 3 days prior to the opening of a new store. They were put on the doorsteps of houses, on the running boards of parked cars, and many other places where they would be easily noticed.

The coins were really little cardboard discs, the size of a penny, and with the reproduction of the "heads" side of a penny on one side. On the other was a note to say that one (and no more) of the discs could be spent as a real penny on the opening day of the store.

SELLING NUTS BY MAGIC

Free distribution of peanuts for children during suburban theater matinees is being used by an Australian nut food manufacturer to popularize his product.

Children in the audience are given bags of peanuts by a stage magician, with membership badges for a Magicians' Club and coupons securing a conjuring book. Children are urged to become master magicians and to save all the tricks offered by coupon.

Tying up with the scheme are slides shown in smaller towns, and newspaper and radio advertising is also being used. Schools are to be supplied with tie-up blotters, and retailers are being included by advertising.

COUPON DAYS

Here is an idea for a good clearance sale. The shopper had to clip a coupon and bring it to the store in order to take advantage of the price quoted in the announcement. In some cases, purchases were limited, one to a customer.

The items included some that were priced low, as leaders. Most, however, were items that were marked down for the sole purpose of getting rid of them.

Under the main head in the ad, the copy reads, "We must clear our shelves of all winter merchandise to make room for spring goods arriving daily. We intend to sell out our winter stock in these 3 days. We realize this is a tremendous undertaking, but the prices we are offering in the coupons below will make this stock go like hot cakes! Ready every item and judge for yourself! We are out to set a record on these 3 great coupon days. See dates above!

"Remember, you must clip out the coupons of the items you want and bring them with you to the store. No goods advertised on the coupons will be sold unless the coupon is presented!"

MYSTERY LETTERS

These create interest among the salespeople for one group of affiliated stores. They are sent out from headquarters, but the idea is just as applicable to single stores, where the mystery letters could be posted by the store owner, who would be the only one to know exactly what they stood for . . . just as the Chicago office is the only group that knows exactly what they stand for in this case.

Each store in this group receives a card measuring about 4 inches by 10 inches. At the time of this editor's visit, four letters were printed on the card (new ones are sent at regular intervals) and every member of the sales force is invited to write a letter to the Chicago office with his deduction as to just what the four letters stand for.

In this case, the four letters were "O M R C" and they stood for "One More Regular Customer." If no one sends in the exact answer, the best of the entrants is given a cash award. It so happened that the best answer to this contest was "Our Motto—Repeat Customers," although it was not the correct answer.

"THRIFT WEDNESDAYS" PAY BIG

The "Thrift Wednesday" idea is simply this: A typical box advertisement in the shopping news edition of a daily newspaper announces that on Wednesday The Hollywood Typewriter Shop will clean, adjust, and place a new ribbon in any typewriter brought to the shop for the sum of $1. Ordinarily this happens two Wednesdays out of each month but occasionally only one Wednesday in the month. For a considerable time immediately after the idea was conceived the offer was made for every Wednesday in the month.

During the first 3 months the plan brought in an average of 100 typewriters per Wednesday. Naturally, the number began to drop down after 3 months but even today "Thrift Wednesday" never brings in fewer than 25 typewriters.

Prosperity Money Auctions

Home furnishings merchants of Tell City, Indiana, report excellent results from a cooperative promotion. The plan calls for a group of merchants, in different lines, putting up prizes which are sold at auction once a month in the local theater.

"Prosperity Money" is used to buy these various prizes at the auction. This prosperity money is accumulated by customers of the various participating merchants, who secure it by making cash purchases at their stores. It is printed in different denominations, and is issued by the merchants on a dollar-for-dollar basis. Note that the money is given only for cash payments and not for credit purchases.

A particularly effective feature of this plan is that every 2 weeks a different merchant puts on a special "event." The other merchants cooperate by sending their customers to the place where the special event is being held. The event lasts one day. Each merchant holds one of these special events.

The Busy Dollar Contest

This plan was developed in Nampa, Idaho. Cellophane envelopes containing dollar bills and a card for recording the transaction in which the bills participated were placed in circulation by 26 stores. In addition to the name of the firm which started the dollar on its busy way, the card contained these instructions:

"This Busy Dollar is never too busy to work for you. Keep it going. Sign your name on the back of this card and put it back into circulation."

Space was also provided on the card for each store to sign its name when a purchase was made. Prizes were offered to the persons which the records showed to have spent the most money in the 2 days of the contest, and individual prizes in each store to the person making the largest purchase using the bill which was marked with the particular store's name. The contest lasted 2 days. During the period of the contest each bill averaged $7 in value. Twenty of the dollar bills for which records were obtained were handled by 164 individuals.

Spring "Mystery" Plan

During the month of March a distributor made arrangements so that all electric meter readers who visited the homes of the city wired for electricity left at each home a mysterious envelope marked *Important.* Upon opening the envelope the housewife found a prize certificate which entitled her to participate in a big prize drawing for electric refrigerators. No obligation was entailed except that the housewife register her name and address with any electric refrigerator dealer in the town.

During the month a cryptic daily announcement over the radio urged housewives to watch for the electric meter reader. Each dealer also sent post cards to his prospects. The post cards were personalized by having the prospect's name on them. These cards urged the prospect to register at the dealer's store.

The dealer's salesmen also started an intensive follow-up trying to get housewives to register and to view prize refrigerators on display at every showroom. Announcement of the winners was made a week after the registration period closed. The other registrations provided a substantial list of prospects for dealers' salesmen to follow up.

The circus is an old stand-by that still pulls 'em in, especially in rural areas. When a number of manufacturers get together with a merchant for such a promotion, all benefit through increased traffic and the psychological stimulation of the urge to buy.

A "WOMEN'S DAY" PROMOTION

    A store promotion plan that has been used annually with outstanding success, is based on the idea of staging a Women's Day, to put over a day of history-making sales volume, under the planning and direction of the women in the store. A board of "Women's Day Directors" is formed. They direct the planning and staging of the big event. Women are appointed temporarily to take the place of men serving as merchandising managers. The event is publicized to women customers. Announcement is made that woman reigns for the day. All kinds of stunts and merchandising ideas are developed to put the management of the women in the foreground. Women's organizations are called on for their cooperation. Special events are introduced to entertain the women, and the prospect of having a good time as well as doing some shopping helps attract the crowds.

Promoting Sales by Telephone

A wide-open opportunity for improving promotions exists in helping dealers make better use of telephone selling.

In some communities, abuse, or clumsiness in use, of this type of selling has caused a bad consumer reaction. Some manufacturers, therefore, have now prepared suggestions for better telephone-promotion techniques.

By supplying telephone sales manuals for selling their products, which the dealer can turn over to his clerks to use, excellent results have been obtained. Stores depending upon counter trade must do the bulk of their business between 10 o'clock and noon, and between 3:00 and 6:00 in the afternoon. This leaves several hours of the day which can be given over to systematic telephone canvassing. Some stores secure as much as 60% of their business by telephone. While this method has been used in grocery and hardware stores for a long while, it can be effectively used by many other stores. An Indiana dry goods dealer informs his customers by telephone of his specials, and while he does not sell direct, the call brings the customers to the store.

A Cincinnati shoe dealer keeps a record of the sizes required by his clients, both men and women. He calls them at intervals offering to send the shoes to the home for fitting; also telling them about special sales. A card index keeps him informed when 6 months have elapsed since their last purchase.

A heater manufacturer in Cincinnati uses the telephone extensively in promoting the sales of his clothes drier direct to the user. Girls sit at the telephones all day, calling the home owners who would be logical prospects. The prospects thus secured are followed up by a personal salesman.

In New York, a piano company has been successful in soliciting piano business by telephone. The young lady using the phone first informs herself as to the model in which the prospect may possibly be interested; then she makes her sales talk, urging the prospect to come to the store. The telephone solicitor, in telling of her work, states:

> My first sales maxim is never to deceive a prospect. I tell the woman—in most instances it is a woman to whom I talk—that I represent the Blank Piano Company. The only time I deviate from this rule is when a maid answers the phone, in which case I tell her my name, and add that I represent the Blank Company. By leaving off the word "piano" I find that in instances like this it does help. But where the woman herself answers I always tell her who I am and whom I represent. Then . . . I begin to tell her about one specific piano, stressing the fact that the woman should come into the salesroom as soon as possible to see it.

A Missouri merchant gives a cash bonus to the clerk taking the greatest number of telephone orders each month. This stimulates the clerks to become telephone salesmen, and causes some friendly rivalry that is productive of added business. These are just a few of the many ways a live-wire dealer or merchant can get people into his store.

But no matter what the promotion may be, the measure of its success will depend largely upon how attractively the merchandise is displayed within the store, and the manner in which it is advertised. There is still a big selling job to be done *after* the buyer is in the store.

Displays for Chain and Variety Stores

Distributors and merchants primarily interested in selling branded merchandise which they control, are naturally wasteful of display material featuring nationally advertised brands. Manufacturers hesitate to provide this type of distributor with display material. However, chain stores which do handle nationally advertised brands, do so because they want to cater to public demand. In that case they want their store associated in the public's mind with prestige-building products. Joseph Reiss of New York, who has had considerable experience in preparing and distributing store display materials to variety and chain stores, prepared the following suggestions (see also Chapter 34—"Promoting Sales Through Chain Stores"):

1. Decide whether your line is a staple, with small promotional possibilities, or a specialty with good promotional potentials. In general, assay the display merits of your line. Too many manufacturers want the whole variety chain turned over to them on a line that, at best, can account for perhaps .001% of the chain's total volume. A line of packaged thumbtacks won't get the display cooperation of variety chains that will be given to a line

like Clopay. The manufacturer's display program, therefore, must strike a sensible compromise between his very natural ambitions and the actual display potential of his line.

2. Be liberal with your display budget. Here is one advertising agency man who cheerfully suggests running one less national ad, if necessary, to furnish display funds. National advertising on a line sold through chain stores simply cannot make a worth-while return on the investment if the line is not adequately tied up in display in the stores themselves!

3. Don't saddle the display budget with charges that don't belong in it. For example, while it is absolutely true that the package is an integral part of chain store display, the cost of packaging definitely is not part of the display charges.

4. Remember that if your package has not been designed for variety store bin display and for variety store retailing technique, your display program simply cannot click. *All variety store display starts with the merchandise.* If your merchandise is packaged, bagged, wrapped, tied, labeled, tagged, carded—put clever brains to work to make the most display potentials of the merchandise, itself.

5. The variety store bin is the basic element in variety store operation. The fact with regard to these bins that effects your merchandise design, your packaging design, the design of your displays, is merely this: Variety store bins are the variable building blocks out of which counter display arrangements are constructed. Bins are merchandise troughs made up of $\frac{1}{4}$-inch glass in 4-, 6-, 8,- 10-, and 12-inch sizes. These sizes are general, although a bin can be made to any size, depending upon the merchandise to be featured. Since every foot, nay, every square inch of counter space has to pay off an average dollar return quota set by the home office, it is advisable that your merchandise, display card, or package occupy as little space as possible. On the other hand, since the majority of people shop in variety stores in a hurried manner, it is important that the package be strongly relieved from the counter background—by color, art, etc.

6. Bear in mind that in addition to displays which the chain builds itself out of its own equipment, you can furnish the chain with counter display equipment for your merchandise. This can consist of a simple cross-counter display rack for a line of hot iron transfer designs for the art needle-goods counter, made in varying sizes to fit the various widths of chain store counters; it may be a more elaborate set-up display fixture for nail polish or paper doilies; it may be a wall rack for a backwall, for greeting cards. In developing display racks for the counter, you must bear in mind the fact that most 5- and 10-cent store counters are fully 90% "island" counters and fixtures placed thereon are visible from all sides. They must do a selling job from both sides of the counter. They should not be stepped-up so as to impede the free movement of the saleslady behind the counter. Whatever the display you want to develop, it should be checked, down to the last tier and tray, with the chains to which it will be furnished

7. Of course, as variety stores get further and further into higher price lines and bulkier merchandise, the bin counter arrangement must be dropped in some departments. It has already been eliminated in some departments. Where the bin is not used, there is greater room for display flexibility. It is important, therefore, to know whether your line is being displayed or arranged on the counter in some manner other than through bins.

8. Remember, too, that a line may be displayed both in bins or counter boxes and in some other manner. This is particularly true of important lines. The variety chains are becoming increasingly flexible in their counter setups.

9. Other display opportunities at the counter revolve around the so-called overhead display. This may be merely several wood uprights with a connecting horizontal arch—or it may be an elaborate contraption. The variety chains favor overhead displays only for major lines of important novelties. Where merchandise lends itself to colorful display, one of the uprights can be made to carry a tack-on of the merchandise up the length of the upright. For example, sun glasses can be mounted to run right from the counter to the arch itself, which might be from 30 to 36 inches above the counter.

10. Then there is the wall display. The variety chains make excellent use of their walls. They use ledge trims, wall racks, etc. Manufacturers can tie up with these vantage points of display provided their merchandise is displayed nearby to the wall or ledge of the store. Since ledge trims, wall panels, etc., are special displays that have to be built to fit into the store scheme, it is important that they be approved in blueprint form before shipping them to stores.

11. The variety chains are also willing to use streamer displays—displays placed over the counter, perhaps 1 foot high and 24 feet long. Such signs must be made out of wallboard or some other rigid material and supported by thin wires strung to hooks in the ceiling.

12. In addition to these interior display angles, there is also the special booth— which is a hugely important display factor. Naturally, it is given only to a line with important potentials. Lines that are demonstrator-sold are very often given special booth display. The supporting posts and canopy of the booth can be treated colorfully, creating a "specialty shoppe" atmosphere for the line.

13. Of course, there are also a number of miscellaneous display opportunities inside the store. Salesgirls may be furnished special badges or pennons. Corner posts may be decorated. Turntables may be supplied, provided they're foolproof.

14. While the chains have rules and regulations concerning display, these are more for basic guidance and frequently can be modified, with the chain's help, to accomplish a specific job at hand. I've had more than one manufacturer tell me that the chains just won't do thus and so with regard to interior display—and I've taken the manufacturer by the hand on a tour of certain variety stores and showed him displays of the very kind he was positive the chains would not use. The point is that rules and regulations can be flouted only with good reason; they can't be simply ignored.

15. I have been asked whether self-service will become important in the variety chains and thus affect display policies. My belief is that chains did considerable work with self-service during the war years, when personnel was their Number One Headache. I think those chains will have to be tackled separately from an interior display point of view. These stores, in the chains which are completely or semi-self-service, will have to receive special display consideration and treatment. The self-service operation will have to be more heavily "signed" than the full service store.

16. I have also been asked whether radical new types of display will be necessitated by radical innovations in the future appearance of variety chain interiors. I think the answer is an emphatic "no."

17. Of course, it is always important to bear in mind, when working with the variety chains, that they have stores of different types—that is, Class A stores, Class B stores, etc. Display policies vary with the different types of units. The sensible manufacturer therefore has a separate display program for each type of store unit insofar as that is made necessary by the scope of his display program.

18. Of course, contact should be established and maintained with the chain's display department. Obviously, the chain's display department can't see a representative from every resource—time wouldn't permit. But where a line is of sufficient display importance, contact with the chain's display department should be sought, usually with the buyer's knowledge. In addition to personal contact, mail contact is also an obviously sensible procedure.

19. Where feasible, there should be a tie-up between the display material offered to variety chains and the manufacturer's national advertising. In fact, good judgment suggests the advisability of at least occasionally planning the national advertising with its variety store display potentials to the fore.

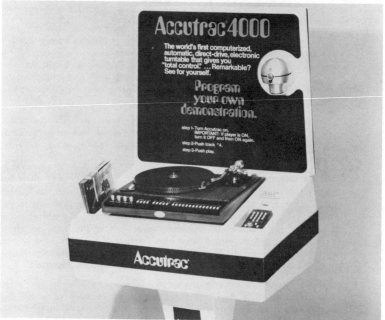

The BSR Accutrac Merchandiser invites prospects to program their own demonstrations. The "space-age" base holds an actual unit which is featured as the world's first computerized electronic turntable; and the programming computer. The unit is theft-proof.

Chapter 18

DISTRIBUTING PROMOTIONAL MATERIALS

IT IS STRANGE that so much time, effort and money is spent on the planning, creation and production of promotional material and, in so many cases, so little on its use, or, rather, on its *lack of use* because of inefficient distribution and follow-up. The creation of promotion campaigns and their components involves the manufacturer's marketing, sales and advertising and promotion managements; the advertising agency, sometimes special consultants; and, finally, the suppliers. Each of these sources follows definite procedures, with reports, follow-ups, schedules, deadline dates and, yes, a lot of other "red tape."

Once the material is produced, what happens? First an announcement goes out to the sales force, the distributors and dealers, with descriptive illustrated brochures. Then everybody sits back and waits for orders from the field with follow-ups by the salesmen, if, as, and when they have time.

But salesmen have other things in mind; they must produce orders for merchandise. If the dealer says "no", they will not press for orders for displays and literature; once they have a sales order, their interest quickly subsides. Their salary or commissions do not depend on advertising and sales promotion material except in a vague, indeterminate way. Could that be a clue?

Why don't dealers make better use of promotional material? The reasons usually advanced are:

(a) The material does not apply to their market;
(b) They don't handle the units featured;
(c) Displays are too complicated and hard to set up;
(d) They want something different;
(e) They don't have the space;
(f) They simply don't like it!
(g) They won't pay for any part of it.

When these objections come from any great number of re-tailers, they indicate that salesmen are not adequately reflecting dealers' needs to the home office and that the manufacturer's sales promotion people and agency executives are not keeping in close enough touch with the field. Every company should have a policy requiring its advertising and sales promotion people, its advertising agency creative personnel, and possibly even the sup-pliers, to visit the dealers and other outlets to learn what they want and need.

There is clearly a need for a formalized, regular procedure for the salesmen to follow to assure that the material is put to work where it counts—at the retail store. This may entail some system of rewards or incentives.

Nothing is more wasteful than having to pay for expensive sales promotion material which is not used. In view of the cost involved, that this situation should exist is perplexing because it is subject to measures of control. It is not enough to plan and produce sales promotion material, the sales department must see that it is put to work and made to contribute to the sales-producing process.

But the sales promotion department is not absolved of respon-sibility. In a recent survey by the writer, the comments received on the subject from advertising and sales promotion managers were not very promising. None had a planned or organized system of distributing materials and checking usage; many depended on sporadic reports from salesmen. Here are just a few of the com-ments received:

"The only method we have of determining usage is the rate of orders received from field sales."

"Costs are controlled, in some degree, by *reducing* quantities made available to the field organization, which generates pressure for additional amounts."

"We depend on our sales representatives to inform us."

"Through *occasional* visits to the field, we determine the use of our literature and window display materials."

"If (they) do not use it, the material stays on our shelves (sic) so we "know" what is used and what is not used. This is sometimes a painful but effective(?) control over what we produce."

To say the least, these comments are distressing.

An advertiser in the clothing field, who had been allowing his salesmen to order out sales promotional materials for their customers, began to wonder just how much of it was actually used, and how it was used. So he employed an independent research organization to make a spot check of customers in five cities. These investigators called upon the dealers to whom promotional materials had been shipped, determined what they had done with them, what they thought about them as sales helps, and just what kind of helps they would like to receive from the manufacturer next year.

The check brought out some interesting facts. While 70% of the customers checked had used some of the materials the salesmen had ordered sent to them, only 15% had used all that was shipped out. Most of them had used one piece only, a rather attractive counter cut-out. Others stated they had the material in their basement or warehouse and intended to use it one of these days. Others frankly admitted they didn't like it enough to use, so had thrown it out. Most of them said they were flooded with advertising display material, and only used the best. On the basis of this check about 60% of what this advertiser was currently spending for sales promotional materials to help dealers, was wasted. It was doubtful if the 40% that was used, produced enough additional sales or good will to justify the total expenditure. (See also Chapter 38—"Controlling Sales Promotion Expenditures.")

The experience is cited to underscore the importance of distributing materials intended to advertise a product at the point of sale. Since promotional material costs nearly twice what it did before the war, and competition for it is greater than ever, manufacturers are spending a little less for the materials and a little more to get them into the hands of their customers to best advantage. Obviously, the practice of sending a customer all the materials he thinks he will use, or permitting salesmen to decide what and how much to send, leaves a great deal to be desired.

Salesmen as Sales Promotion Advisers

Where salesmen must be depended upon to get distribution for promotional materials, it is important that they be trained in store promotional methods. All salesmen do not have a promotional flair. Many, in fact, regard helping the dealer move the merchandise, after it has been sold to him, as a waste of time. They think it interferes with their Number One job which is to close orders. Yet it is the experience of nearly every progressive company, that there are few more effective ways of increasing sales than by helping a customer to sell the merchandise he buys from you.

Chrysler Airtemp, for example, coaches salesmen to help their customers plan and carry through monthly promotions. The salesman sits down with each dealer, goes over his resale problems, and together they work out a sales plan for the ensuing month. Sales objectives are blocked out, a budget is set up, and a list of sales promotional materials, available from the company, is made up. This includes direct-mail literature, window signs, interior signs, floor displays, visualizers, literature and films for use in training the dealer's salespeople, letterheads, and other supplies. At the same time, the salesman advises the customer on the allocation of his total advertising budget, how much to spend in the newspapers, for outdoor bulletins, radio, direct mail, etc. This is all blueprinted on a special form which the salesman carries, so that a record can be made not only of how much was budgeted, but how much was actually spent and what results were accomplished.

Merchandising Surveys

Some of the larger companies, notably Westinghouse Electric Corporation, employ sales promotional men attached to district or division offices, to canvass the dealers in their territories and "blueprint" the stores. While the primary purpose of the survey is to uncover manpower shortages and other merchandising weaknesses in a merchant's operation, a check is made of the identifying signs which the dealer uses to publicize his Westinghouse franchise, his demonstration equipment, what sales promotional materials he can profitably use, and the nature and extent of his local advertising. Inquiry is also made as to what annual promotions, such as a cooking school, the dealer undertakes, the date and the manner of conducting them. This information, when carded and made available in the district office, gives the territorial promotion manager a good picture of the kind of store the dealer operates, what promotional materials he can profitably and effectively use, and when he needs merchandising help.

Surveys of this type, even though much more limited in the nature of information obtained, help tremendously to get advertising and other promotional materials efficiently distributed. Without some check a dealer might requisition, without too much thought, materials he cannot use. But he does not realize this until after the materials land in his receiving room. Dealers do not have too much imagination when considering promotional materials offered by a manufacturer; and even when they pay something for them, they order more than they need; or, worse than that, they order what they cannot use. This is especially

DEALER MERCHANDISE SURVEY

NEW **X**

RENEWAL

DATE

Town **Anytown**　　County **Dane**　　State **Illinois**　　Population **65,000**

Firm Name **Doe Appliance Shop**	PTC ☒	Wired Homes **15,000**
Street Address **114 E. Main Street**	STC ☐	Quota **200**
Manager **John Doe**	RT ☐	Excl. W ☒ **Yes**
Type of Business **Specialty Appliances**	Class DS ☐　M ☒　Sp. ☐　L. ☐	
Territory Description: **Dane County**		

MAN-POWER: Dealer Employs: Sales Supervisor **Fred Hamilton**

Salesmen: H. H. **4**　　Inside　　Outside　　Part Time **None**　　Commercial **0**

Recommended **6**

Remarks **Need more manpower to do quota job.**

IDENTIFICATION:

Outdoor Signs ☒　　Indoor Signs ☒　　Painted Billboards ☐

Trucks Painted ☒　　Painted Window Signs ☒　　Decalcomanias ☒

MERCHANDISING JOB: Specialties Sold: Refrig. ☐　Electric Range ☐　Gas Range ☐　Washer ☐

Ironer ☐　Vac. Cleaner ☐　Radio ☐　Stoker ☐　Oil Burner ☐　Water Heater ☐

Display: Models **ED-50, 60, 70; EDX-78**

Location **Front of store.**　　Using Buffet Top ☒

Model Operating ☒　Ice Frozen ☒　Artificial Food ☒　Display in Window ☒　W. D. S. Year ☒　Month ☐

Remarks **Store needs rearrangement. No chairs for prospect to sit down.**

DEMONSTRATION HELPS: Dr. Dem. Kit ☒　　Sp. Disc Demo. ☒　　Consumer Films ☐

Cutaway Cabinet ☐　Cutaway Unit ☒　Cabinet Section ☒　Froster ☐　Hell's Kitchen ☐

SALES PROMOTION: Selling Book ☒　　Spec. Sheets ☒　　Line Folders ☒　　Cold Cooking ☒

Current Literature ☒　Food Budg. Pl. ☒　Family Album ☐　User's Plan ☒

SALES EDUCATIONAL: Q. Cl. F. Educ. ☒　　Q. Cl. Weekly ☒　　Specialist ☒

Handbook ☒　　Cycle Chart ☒　　Scrapbook ☒

SALES STIMULATION: Prospect File ☒　　Quota Buster Club ☒　　Cold Selling Talk ☒

(Needs more organized prospect file follow-up)

ADVERTISING:

1. Direct by Mail ☒ :

2. Newspaper **News-Dispatch - Evening Times**

Nat'l. Rate **.75 - Times .60**	Local rate **.60 - Times .50**
Movie Trailers **Yes, Palace Theatre**	Rate **$2.40 per 1000**
Radio Spot announcement, tri-weekly	Rate **$60.00 per week**
Outdoor Adv. **Yes**	Type Showing
Shows and Exhibit ☒ : **Home Show, F.H.A.**	Cooking Schools ☒ : **Newspaper school**

COMMERCIAL: Franchise ☐　Eng. Data Book ☐　Installation Manual ☐　Survey Sh. ☐　Literature ☐

(None)

SERVICE:

Mgr. **A. J. Johnson**　　Men **None**　　Trained for Com'l. ☐ **None**

SUPERVISOR M. A. Miller　　　DISTRIBUTOR **Hawkeye Appliance Co.**

Efficient distribution of promotional materials depends a great deal on the dealer information on file in the sales promotion department. This form is used by Westinghouse to evaluate dealer's need for promotional help. Some dealers have a very hazy idea as to the number of pieces of direct mail they will use, or the number and size of displays they need. They ask for twice as much material as they will actually put to work.

true in the case of sales literature to be mailed out to customer lists. If they maintain a list of their own, it is usually cluttered up with dead names. A waste of as high as 30% of such literature is not unusual. If they have an arrangement with the local newspaper, utility company, or some addressing concern to use their lists of local residents, there is often a costly duplication in the names. A survey card on each dealer, with a count of the number of wired homes in the trading area in the case of Westinghouse, gives some check on the actual requirements of a dealer or customer.

Subsidiary Dealer Service Companies

To facilitate the distribution of sales promotional material used by dealers and distributors some national advertisers set up separate companies for this purpose. These companies function in relation to the dealers much as an advertising agency functions in relation to the advertiser. The subsidiary company creates, produces, and distributes all advertising and promotional materials, usually on a share-the-cost basis, which permits a close control of expenditures as well as better service to the customer.

Some of these affiliates render a complete advertising and merchandising service on a monthly fee basis. Others are financed by a direct appropriation from the parent company, but charge some part of the cost of the materials and the service to the dealer. A pioneer in this type of activity was the United States Tire Company, which successfully operated the U.S. Tire Mutual Corporation with headquarters in New York City, and strategically located offices from which contact was maintained with customers. One of the advantages of the plan is that it placed merchandising cooperation on a self-supporting basis. Any sales promotional contract made with the dealer by the advertising company had nothing to do with the franchise arrangement between the parent company and the dealer.

One interesting angle on the operations of the United States Tire Mutual Corporation was that it enabled the merchandising subsidiary to concern itself with a wide range of dealers' problems, such as batteries and accessories, other than tires. In order to really help a dealer to become more successful, it is usually necessary to do an over-all counseling job. Dealers prefer to pay for a service which is not just concerned with promoting the sale of one brand of tires and the accessories made by one manufacturer.

While the operating methods of mutual advertising companies

vary according to the industry, best results are obtained when the promotions are packaged—that is to say, when there are three or four "campaigns" during the year each complete with window displays, direct-mail literature, streamers, store cards, newspaper electros, etc. These packaged promotions are shipped to subscribers about 60 days prior to the scheduled start of the drive. The packaged promotions get almost twice the acceptance from dealers as the piecemeal promotions which so many advertisers offer their customers.

Some of the wholesale houses have used the independently operated merchandising service company to effectively help dealers to meet chain store and mass distributor competition. In addition to a year-around advertising service, sold on a subscription basis to customers, these merchant service organizations offer accounting service, stock control service, window and store display service, etc. Sometimes the service is restricted to merchants who are customers of the wholesale house; a few offer the service to any company who pays for it. In any case, however, the purpose is to supply a rounded merchandising service to customers who concentrate their purchases with the company sponsoring the operation.

In this type of operation the dealer's service contact man not only makes a periodical check of what the store needs in the way of merchandising helps, but assists the store owner to make the best possible use of the material. Since the merchant is paying for the service, he is more inclined to make full use of the suggestions passed along to him by the field man.

Another way of distributing sales promotional material, especially store displays, is through the companies which regularly contact noncompetitive dealers in a locality. They put up advertisers' signs, and store displays. They have an arrangement with the cooperating merchants, and compensate them for store and wall space. The distributor is compensated directly by the advertiser, on the basis of so much a dealer. The work usually is done on a most professional basis.

Some of these services operate advertising card racks in good store locations. The clients' regular streetcar cards are placed in these racks on a fee basis, and changed monthly. Others specialize in window displays. They lease the windows from merchants, and in turn "rent" them to clients. Another type of service puts up store displays for national advertisers. A wagon serviceman, working for a number of different advertisers, carries store fixtures and displays in his truck, takes them into the store, gets the merchant's permission to put the display up and actually does it. This type of distributing service is on an hourly charge basis, the display or fixture itself being furnished by the advertiser. Then, of course, there are in nearly every community, individuals who have "spots" under contract where they post advertising signs and wall bulletins.

DISTRIBUTING THROUGH SALESMEN

Next to maintaining an advertising distribution service, such as the packers operate, salesmen traveling in their own cars are in the best position to make sure that promotional materials and displays are used to best advantage. Salesmen are furnished a supply of timely promotional material to show to customers, and ask permission to display it in their places of business. An alternate plan is to furnish each salesman with an advertising portfolio. It describes the materials available. The salesman goes over the portfolio with the customer, who orders such helps as he fancies. The salesman writes up the requisition and turns it in with his day's orders, and usually gets credit for doing so. Some companies give salesmen who get their customers to use dealer helps a certain number of credits for each requisition sent in. These credits or points are good for prizes of the salesman's own selection from a syndicated prize catalog.

A handy sheet used by Airtemp to correlate sales promotional material requirements and determine monthly allocation of promotional expense against budget.

To ensure the use of promotional material in the field, it is desirable to require distributors and dealers to place definite orders, whether the items are free or not. When new models are introduced, dealer promotion kits usually include samples and illustrations of literature and displays together with order forms to be sent in to the factory. This controls distribution and helps to reduce waste by specifying quantities.

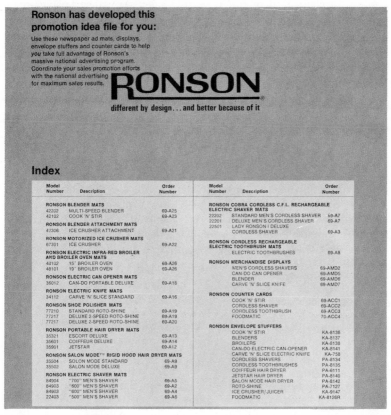

All the sales promotion material available to its dealers is illustrated and listed in the Ronson promotion book. Dealers must order what they want—by order number. This helps to control distribution.

The Advertising Portfolio

One of the problems in getting salesmen to "sell" sales promotional materials (even if no charge is made for them) is the difficulty of getting businessmen to take time to decide what materials to order. If he knows the salesman, he is very likely to say: "Look, John, I'm too busy right now to talk advertising, you send me what you think I need, and I'll use it as you suggest." Obviously, the reason he "hasn't time" is because the presentation made by the salesman didn't seem important. It just didn't have any cash register jingle.

To be effective, an advertising or trade promotional presentation, however it is made, must be exciting. It must start the customer thinking, not about a lot of assorted promotional materials, but about a "packaged" plan for increasing sales. Any alert businessman will *make time* to consider a plan for increasing sales. So the presentation book, or portfolio, must not only look important, but it must stress what the promotion will do, rather than what it is. Yet care must be used not to make the portfolio so big and bulky that the salesman will leave it behind in his car when he goes into the customer's store or office. There is such a thing as making presentation books too big to be practical.

There should be a pocket in the portfolio, preferably in the back cover, where actual samples of some of the pieces can be carried. The larger pieces should be colorfully illustrated. There should be a chart, making it easy for the salesman to go over the plan, point by point, with a customer. An order blank, with specifications for each piece, is provided for the salesman to use in making up the "order." This blank should state prices, if the customer is to pay some of the cost, and specifications given for each piece. A copy of the order blank is left with the customer, together with a brief outline of the over-all plan.

The Jobber's Salesmen

When a product is distributed through wholesalers, it is more difficult for a manufacturer to get his trade promotional materials used to advantage. Some companies employ window trimmers to travel from store to store and, where a merchant handles the product, arrange for a store or window display. But that is costly. The next best way is to pack a circular in every dealer carton, playing up the helps available and offering to send them upon request, or at a stated price, if the dealer returns the coupon attached to the circular. An addressed envelope for that purpose is attached to the circular. Not many will take that much interest, but some will. Gradually, a mailing list of promotion-minded dealers handling the product will be built up, which may be worked from time to time with announcements of new pieces. Some national advertisers endeavor to get the wholesaler to supply lists for the purpose of sending dealer helps, but usually they just won't take the time. Neither will their salesmen.

One hardware manufacturer built a rather complete list of dealers handling his product, together with the name of the jobber from whom they purchased this particular product. He first got a list of the jobber's salesmen in return for mailing them a monthly expense account book; and then in turn offered each salesman an automobile key container, which held a driver's license, in return for the names of 10 hardware merchants in the salesman's territory who carried the line and who, in the salesman's opinion, would be most likely to make the best use of advertising helps from a manufacturer. Any plan of this sort, however, should be carried out with the knowledge and approval of the wholesaler. Some wholesalers don't like to have manufacturers writing to their salesmen. Others, appreciating such a program will help them as well as the dealer, are glad to cooperate so long as they don't have to do any work.

It is not unusual in the more highly specialized fields for manufacturers of nationally advertised products to take space in the trade papers to advertise new dealer helps. The advertisement illustrates the display piece, or the plan, and suggests writing for it. The coupon requests the name of the wholesale house from whom the retailer buys the advertised product. While inquiries obtained in this way are costly, there is a certain prestige value to such trade advertising. At least, the retailers who see the advertisement know the manufacturer is on his toes, and getting out advertising helps for retailers. Even though the retailer may not sit down and fill out the coupon, he may remember the advertisement the next time the manufacturer's salesman calls.

"Pull 'Em In" Contest

The success any firm has in getting salesmen, either their own or their wholesaler's men, to get dealer promotional materials distributed and used, depends upon the appreciation which the salesman has of their value to him, as well as their value to the company and to his customer. That is why so much attention is paid in sales conventions, and meetings of jobber's salesmen, to the company's advertising, and especially its sales promotional program. That is why most companies spending any large sum on dealer helps, constantly hammer away at their importance as a sort of "work while you sleep" proposition. Not many salesmen have as much appreciation as they should have, of the power of good advertising. Like so many things that are done to help them, they take advertising pretty much for granted. They admit it pays to advertise, but they seldom stop to think how it pays them to go out of their way to get their customers to advertise. They overlook the very important fact that anything that increases a customer's sales of the products he buys from them, helps them.

As a part of an educational program designed to make General Electric lamp salesmen display-conscious, the lamp division at one time conducted a contest to get salesmen to "sell" more GE lamp sales agents on putting in window and store displays featuring the carton of lamps GE was then pushing. The symbol of the contest was a shepherd's crook. Prizes were awarded to those salesmen who "pulled in" the most lamp displays. Different points were awarded for different kinds of displays. Thus a salesman got so many points for a window display, so many for a counter display, and so many for both. Interest in the contest was maintained by weekly mailings. In these mailings the shepherd's crook theme was worked hard, standings of top salesmen in various offices shown, and names of the salesmen doing the best job of cooperating with the sales promotional department were publicized. One of the reasons for the success of this particular activity was the emphasis placed on the ways to get more dealers to put in displays. Another contributing cause to the way the contest went over was telling the salesmen every week what they could say to agents to get them to put in a GE lamp display.

Paying Salesmen for Selling Dealer Helps

A common argument against charging customers for advertising helps is that it limits the distribution of the material. The reasoning is that since it costs but little more to produce twice as many displays or signs, it is good business to get twice as many used. And the best way to get twice as many used is to give them to any dealer who will promise to use them.

In actual practice it does not always work out that way. It is next to impossible to get customers to ask for free dealer materials. They have to see the actual material before they will agree to use it, and they are hesitant to buy from pictures. An alternate plan, therefore, is to provide salesmen with samples of the actual material to be supplied, make a small charge for it, and then pay salesmen the same commission on orders they take for advertising materials as they are paid on the sale of the product itself. In the case of salaried salesmen, bonus points are awarded. Under such a plan salesmen will really go down the line for a promotional campaign, because it pays them *double*—(1) the commission or bonus points *and* (2) the extra business which the use of the advertising materials by the merchant should create for them.

Sales and Demonstration Rooms

Salesmen who are called upon to make office demonstrations of equipment or products depend a great deal on supporting sales literature. Office appliance manufacturers such as Addressograph-Multigraph Corporation distribute a considerable amount of this type of sales promotional material *at the point of demonstration.* It is unquestionably the most effective way of placing such literature in the hands of prospective buyers. Yet there are relatively few salesrooms, or demonstration rooms, which provide for the proper storing of sales helps. It is not uncommon to go into a demonstration room or a sample room and find the sales literature dumped into a drawer or cabinet, helter-skelter. It is a 10-minute job to find some particular piece. While the salesman is looking, the customer's mind wanders off into other channels. After a few such experiences salesmen skip using sales literature at all. They are fearful that if they mull through the pile over in the cabinet, they might lose the sale.

Similarly, in places where salesmen report for work in the morning, provision is seldom made to organize and arrange promotional material they need in making their calls. It is scattered about through desk drawers and cabinets, piled on radiators, or dumped in some out-of-the way place where it is soon out of mind. The average salesman just won't take the time to try to find the piece he needs. He will get along without it. As a result, salesmen are deprived of valuable tools they could use to get orders. Time soon renders most of the unused material obsolete, and hundreds of dollars' worth of dirty, dusty, outdated literature accumulates. It finally ends up in the baling machine.

Another mistake in arranging salesrooms is to place assorted booklets, folders, and catalogs on a big table in neat little piles. The theory is that by putting them out where they will be seen, they will be used. This may be good practice so far as distributing the literature is concerned, but it is bad sales strategy. It excites the curiosity of the prospective buyer and, at the first glance, he is certain to stroll over to the table and leaf through pieces that intrigue him. It makes the salesman's job of keeping the prospect on the beam just that much more difficult.

It is good practice, and good economy, to equip a salesroom with a closed cabinet having shelves as in a bookcase. The shelves should be 11 inches deep. The various pieces of sales literature required by the salesmen, either in making demonstrations or in outside calling, are neatly stacked on these shelves and the doors kept closed. It should be the job of someone in the office to check the literature cabinet every Monday and replenish any material that is low, put in new literature, throw away obsolete materials, and make sure the right pieces are in the right piles.

Distributing Heavy Materials

There are certain materials and certain promotion programs which simply cannot be carried around to the buyer. For instance, a company which is trying to get a merchandiser or a standard display case installed in retail outlets can hardly expect to show an actual sample; in the same way, the salesman for a company making heavy machinery cannot lug a three-ton air-conditioning unit into prospects' offices.

One way around this problem is by the use of scale models. These are particularly helpful in such promotions as an attempt to get uniform buildings and arrangements for retail outlets. Either paper templates or actual toy-size models of needed equipment are carried by the salesman in a small case which also includes a piece of paper or wood scaled in the same proportion for use in trying out various possible arrangements.

Another method is to equip the salesman with a paper template which occupies the same amount of floor space as the unit he is trying to sell. Salesmen for the Seven-Up Co. are equipped with such aids for opening new accounts. The template is on blueprint paper the size of a Seven-Up case. The salesman simply finds a blank place on the floor and drops the blueprint. When the curious dealer investigates, he reads this copy:

> Dealer's profit floor plan:
>
> This space devoted to Seven-Up case display will return 20 to 33⅓% profit.
>
> Same space devoted to other items will return following profits:
>
> > Butter, coffee, and sugar—9% or less.
> > Canned milk, soap flakes—10 to 15%.
> > Baby foods, flour mixes, cocoa—16 to 20%.
>
> Seven-Up turnover 52 to 104 times per year.
>
> Average grocery item—12 turnovers.

A similar plan was used very successfully by the Coca-Cola Company in getting dealers to install soft-drink coolers.

Still a third way is by use of color slides. Salesmen for O'Cedar Corporation, in a campaign to get self-service merchandisers into stores, were given a small viewer and color slides of actual installations of the display in hardware, paint, grocery, and supermarket locations. The salesman could insert the appropriate slide before calling on any one of these types of accounts.

DISTRIBUTING BY MAIL

Getting requests for attractive promotional materials from dealers by mail is easy enough, but to get advertising helps into the hands of customers who will make good use of them is another matter. The usual practice is to prepare a rather elaborate prospectus showing the various pieces which have been prepared, together with suggestions for using them, and mailing it to select lists. The prospectus is sent only to dealers who have purchased a certain amount of merchandise during the preceding year, or who are on a special "blue" list. This eliminates some waste. At least it shuts out the fringe dealers who will ask for anything they can get for nothing. But this method, while better than most, leaves two important things undone:

1. There are certain newcomers to the field, who may not be large buyers at the moment, but who have good stores, are live-wires, and will usually use store displays, signs, and special promotional material to good advantage. These are good bets for the future, and it is important that a manufacturer of branded goods make some effort to contact these customers and get them to tie-in with his national advertising. If it is not possible to use salesmen for this purpose, then the job should be done with personalized letters. It is too important to trust to a general mailing. Dealers are constantly dying, retiring, or just naturally "dying on the vine." As they do, new advertising-minded dealers must be found to replace them. Too many companies just keep on mailing the same dealers year after year, with little or no thought to this problem of new blood.

2. As a rule no provision is made, in distributing by mail, to make sure that the material is used. This involves two things: A letter "selling" the merchant on the sales value of the material. This letter or presentation should explain that the material is expensive and ask the customer's cooperation in making the expenditure mutually profitable. Secondly, after sufficient time has elapsed to permit the merchant to put the material to use, he should receive another letter asking him how he likes it, and quoting others who liked it well enough to say so voluntarily. This is in the nature of a reminder. The aim is to get the dealer to express himself as to the value of the help so far as he is concerned. Such comments often come in handy where it is necessary to sell a board of direc-

tors, or a skeptical top management, on the importance of sales promotional helps for the dealer.

Mail Questionnaires

Some companies follow the plan of making an annual check-up, usually just before a new sales promotional campaign is ready to be distributed, to ascertain to what extent dealers used material furnished them by the manufacturer. One method of doing this is to use a brief friendly letter, and then list on the back of the letter a few questions about the use of the material. The following letter, designed to secure information regarding the use of a rather expensive catalog, was successfully used a few years ago by the Johns-Manville Corporation. It was sent to architects:

```
Dear Mr. Doe:
    I wonder if you will help me out of a little difficulty?
    About a year ago I persuaded our company that one of the things
architects most needed was a catalog that would give them the whole
story about all J-M building materials and their part in building and
remodeling homes.
    The attached catalog resulted--the first of its kind.
    But now our stock is getting low, and when I mentioned it to our
president he said (as presidents will) that he would have no objec-
tion to another edition provided I furnished satisfactory evidence
that the catalog had done the job for which it was designed.
    Naturally I must come to you for help, and I am therefore taking
the liberty of asking you and a few other top-flight architects whose
opinions we value, to be the jury.
    To make it easy I have written a few simple questions on the back
of this letter. I will regard it as a personal favor if you will
check the answers, add any comments that you wish to make, and then
slip this letter into the enclosed stamped envelope.
    Needless to say, this won't obligate you in any way, and I now
leave it to you, the jury, to say whether this catalog shall be dis-
continued or reprinted with improvements based on your experience
and advice.
    In any event, rest assured we appreciate your cooperation very
much. Thank you!
```

This letter breaks a good many of the rules, especially the one which says a good sales letter must talk about the buyer and his interests and not expect a buyer to act because the seller wants him to act. It is pretty much a "we" sort of letter. But it did the job, possibly because, as one commentator suggested, it: (1) Appealed to the customer's sense of importance by asking his advice; (2) made the need for help urgent; (3) expressed appreciation; (4) made it easy for the customer to reply.

Requiring Dealers to Pay Express Charges

As a compromise between giving customers what sales promotion materials they think they will use free, and requiring them to pay all or part of the cost, some sales executives have adopted the plan of sending the material without charge, but require the dealer to pay the expressage. One sales manager reports: "This policy permits us to send out small lots of advertising and sales helps at frequent intervals, rather than a big batch at one time. Obviously, a customer will not order more than he needs, when he knows the materials will be sent express collect.

"Out of some 800 dealers to whom we sent literature on an express-collect basis, only one to date has expressed disapproval. By explaining that this plan makes it possible for us to give better helps, through the reduction of nonused materials, our customers usually agree with the policy."

Postal Laws and Regulations

Although about the last thing done with a piece of printing is to mail it, the manner of its mailing isn't something safely left until the last minute to decide. At several points along the trail of its production, the question of how it will be mailed has had to be anticipated.

For one thing, whether the mailing was to go out first-class or third-class probably had something to do with the number and kind of enclosures used, because you mail 3.809 ounces under minimum third-class rates but only one ounce under minimum first-class rates. The matter of weight may also have come up in selecting the paper stock, and the class of mail to be used was certainly a deciding factor in buying the style of envelope you did.

It goes almost without saying that no one intending to do mail promotion should be without the U.S. Government *Postal Manual,* which gives the details of the what, how, and how much of the various types of postage; since these are subject to frequent revision, it is also well to enter a subscription to the *Supplements,* which keep the information up to date.

Further details on this subject should be obtained from one's local postmaster.

U.S. POST OFFICE PUBLICATIONS FOR MAILING DEPARTMENTS

	Price
Domestic Postage Rates, Fees and Information	Free
Mailing Permits	Free
How to Address Mail	Free
Packaging for Mailing	Free
Instructions for Mailers	$12.05
International Postage Rates and Fees	Free
International Mail Manual	N.A.
Neither Snow Nor Rain, A History	$ 3.25
National Zip Code Directory	$ 8.00
Postal Laws, Transmittal Letter #24	$ 3.25
Combination Mailings (Letters-and-Package)	Free
Directory of Post Offices (Includes numerical list of ZIP Codes)	$ 5.55
Postal Service Manual (Chapters 1 thru 6) (Services, Rates and Fees)	$33.00
Postal Bulletin (Weekly advance information) ....Year	$60.00
Domestic Mail Manual	$25.00

Chapter 19

CONSUMER ADVERTISING

ADVERTISING has come under greatly increased regulation, many say attack, by various government agencies, including the Federal Trade Commission, the Food and Drug Administration, the Federal Communications Commission; and by state and city legislative groups, prodded by what has come to be known as the consumer movement.

"Consumerism is a look at business from the buyer's point of view, a social movement which places the rights and powers of the buyer above those of sellers," stated Jerome B. Gray, Chairman of the Board of Gray & Rogers, Philadelphia, in an address before the Lehigh Valley Advertising Club.

"Many factors are contributing to the rise of consumerism. Among these are inflation, war, race, pollution, dishonesty, consumer organizations. Peter F. Drucker, business philosopher, says that consumerism should be and must be the opportunity of total marketing just as it is the shame of total marketing when it is ignored.

"If we accept marketing as the complete orientation of the consumer to all aspects of a business having any bearing whatever on making sales at a profit, let us regard consumerism as the key to marketing's success.

"Effectual marketing, an economist said, is consumerism. It must fit the reality of the consumer and not the sales egotism of the advertiser. The businessman who insists that he knows better than his customers how his product or service fulfill their needs and fit into their life styles is headed for trouble.

"In the early days of advertising, the philosophy of consumerism had not been set aside and labelled. But a philosophy with a singular similarity existed and was practiced. It was known as the philosophy of consumer benefit . . . and woe be to the personal salesman or advertising writer who didn't present his wares in terms of their advantages and benefits to potential buyers."

That the consumer movement has had considerable impact is unquestionable. Grey Advertising, Incorporated, conducted a survey among the 13,000 readers of its newsletter *Grey Matter* and found that 94% of the advertising-marketing executives favor some form of consumer protection; 66% think that more needs to be done in this area. The agency reported that most of the respondents to its questionnaire felt that the consumer protection movement will be beneficial in improving standards of product and service or will at least prevent lowering of standards.

One definition of advertising is "mass, paid communication, the ultimate purpose of which is to impart information, develop attitude, and induce action beneficial to the advertiser." (Association of National Advertisers.) A corollary of this is that it is also beneficial to the consumer and valuable in areas such as public service, medicine, politics and international relations. In the field of mass entertainment, advertising pays the huge bill for the unequalled television programs in the United States, eliminating the viewer licenses, taxes or fees common in some other countries.

Advertising is a powerful force in many ways. It improves and expands the channels of communication to and from the public. How else could the New York News produce a top Sunday issue of 972 pages? Or the Sunday magazine supplement, *Family Weekly,* provide informative, educational, entertaining material to more than nine million readers every week?

In a typical year, of the money spent in the United States for advertising, about 30% went for newspaper advertising; 16% for direct mail; 18% for television advertising; 7% for consumer magazine advertising; 6.5% for radio broadcasts; 4% for business paper (trade and technical) advertising; 1% for outdoor advertising; 1% for farm paper advertising; and the balance for miscellaneous advertising. Most of this was used to reach the consumers.

In a sales promotional sense mass advertising creates public acceptance for a product or a service.

It is, of course, possible to successfully promote a business without consumer advertising. In fact there are a number of companies which have succeeded without national advertising. They have depended upon word-of-mouth advertising to do the job. But it takes too long for the average business to attain leadership that way, so businessmen employ, along with other sales promotional devices, general advertising to bring the merit of a product or a service to the favorable attention of the public. And having won public acceptance for the product, they continue advertising to keep the product before the public. National advertising, once leadership has been attained, protects the advertiser from the raids of competitors and is an inexpensive form of market insurance.

To function with utmost effectiveness consumer advertising should be subordinated to the total sales promotional objectives of the business, and used for a definite and well-defined purpose. That is why in the last 25 years there has been a steady trend toward making the sales executive responsible for advertising, both to the consumer and to the trade. The old idea that advertising was paid publicity, and a thing apart from selling, has long since been repudiated by the most successful companies. It is now regarded as a sales promotional tool.

The future plans of large national advertisers call for a further coordination of sales and advertising under the direction of an executive who functions as the director of distribution. He will determine the advertising appropriation, have the deciding vote in the selection of advertising mediums, and approve or disapprove advertising plans and copy prepared by either the advertising agency or the advertising department.

The administration of the advertising program is usually in the hands of an advertising manager, who may or may not be responsible for the production of sales promotional materials required in the over-all sales plan. He works closely with the advertising agency. Usually he is selected because of his knowledge of markets, advertising techniques and, above all, the motives which make people buy. He should be able to judge, if not to actually write, good advertising copy. In addition he should know where to buy to advantage the art work, printing, displays, and other materials needed in carrying through a modern advertising and sales promotional program.

In smaller organizations, where it may not be feasible to have an executive devote his full time to sales planning, that responsibility is usually assumed by one of the officers of the company—either the chief executive himself or a vice president. His title is not important, but his function of coordinating advertising with sales is most important. It is his job to determine first the markets which are to be covered in a sales promotion program, and then in cooperation with the advertising manager decide upon the best methods of covering them. The advertising manager and the advertising agency then arrange for the media and the copy best suited to carry out the program as planned. Such a procedure assures full cooperation between sales and advertising with correspondingly greater results.

The Advertising Appropriation

Branded products sold to the consumer through established channels of trade are usually supported by an advertising appropriation based on the total sales for the previous year. The figure ranges from 1% to 25%, and are lowest in the case of established products in less competitive fields and highest in the case of new products being introduced in highly competitive fields, such as a patent medicine. Among the factors which should be considered in setting budgets for national advertising are: The margin of profit available for advertising; the company's changed competitive position; the attitude of consumers and the trade toward the company's advertised brands; whether the dominant theme of the advertising is simple or complex; the sales increase it is desired to attain, and how quickly it must be accomplished. Still another factor is taxes. Under a tax program which takes a large portion of a company's earnings, it is sometimes desirable to consider the total budget in the light of its effect on the company's net profit position. Some companies make a fourth quarter adjustment.

A Dartnell survey of appropriations for consumer and supporting advertising, based on a percentage of sales for a normal year in 28 lines of business, showed the following expenditures:

Automobile Accessories	4.625%
Automobiles and Motor Trucks	2.41%
Building Materials and Supplies	3.54%
Cereal Feed and Flour Milling	1.79%
Cigar Manufacturing	5.76%
Clothing, Men's and Boys'	2.46%
Clothing, Women's	3.53%
Confectionery	3.24%
Electrical Household Appliances	5.87%
Farm Implements and Equipment	3.67%
Foods and Beverages	7.35%
Furniture and Furnishings	4.01%
Household Specialties	5.57%
Insurance (All Kinds)	1.03%
Machinery and Supplies	3.67%
Musical Instruments	5.49%
Office Appliances	4.23%
Oil and Petroleum (Specialties)	6.56%
Paint and Varnish	2.97%
Pens and Pencils	8.75%
Proprietary Medicines	25.36%
Publishers, Books and Magazines	10.82%
Radio Apparatus	9.50%
Refrigerator Manufacturing	5.56%
Rubber Specialties	2.03%
Seeds and Nursery Stock	11.81%
Shoes and Boots	2.23%
Sporting Goods	7.75%
Stoves and Furnaces	5.47%
Toilet Requisites	8.53%

FROM THE PEOPLE WHO GAVE YOU CHRISTOPHER COLUMBUS.

72 NEW ATLANTIC CROSSINGS.

We Italians have been crossing the Atlantic since 1492.

So it shouldn't be any big surprise that we're making more crossings this year than anybody else in the business.

All told, Italian Line has 72 transatlantic crossings in 1972. Stopping by places like Lisbon, Gibraltar, Malaga, Cannes, Naples, Genoa, Algeciras, Trieste, Palermo, Palma de Majorca, Piraeus, Messina and Venice.

You can book your clients on the Michelangelo, the Raffaello, the Leonardo da Vinci, and—appropriately enough—the Cristoforo Colombo.

And you can give your clients the widest choice of sailing dates imaginable. From New York, they can leave March 14, 25, April 7, 22, 27, May 7, 13, 17, 28, 31, June 8, 13, 23, July 2, 10, 24, August 5, 11, 23, 26, September 1, 6, 19, 22, October 7, 13, 22, November 8, 14, and December 2, 10, and 15.

(Check our sailing guide for dates leaving from the other side, and for particular ships and ports.)

But we Italians don't just give your clients a crossing. We offer them something much more important: a new way of living, of relaxing and having fun. Of being, for a little while, *Italian.*

Right about now, your clients deserve a vacation. But most of all, they deserve to be Italian. At least once a year.

Italian Line
EVERYBODY SHOULD BE ITALIAN AT LEAST ONCE A YEAR.

All-year-round transatlantic voyages, Caribbean cruises, Mediterranean tours. ss Michelangelo, ss Raffaello, ss Leonardo da Vinci, ss Cristoforo Colombo. Country of registry: Italy.

Many consumer advertisements rely on illustrations to attract attention to the message. Here, the headline does the job.

The foregoing percentages are an average of percentages reported by five leading national advertisers in each classification. They do not represent the percentage spent for national and supporting advertising by the industry as a whole. However, they indicate, if somewhat generally, the practice of these groups. If nonadvertisers were included, the percentages would, of course, be greatly reduced.

Some national advertisers have discontinued the practice of annual appropriations for advertising, and are using quarterly appropriations instead. While this plan has many desirable features, it complicates the purchase of advertising space and works a hardship on those who must make plans which often require several months to get under way. One method of setting advertising budgets is to base them on the sales expectancy for the coming year, and then make quarterly adjustments to cover sales fluctuations. This method, however, calls for a dependable system of estimating future demand and the willingness of top management to back those estimates with money.

Checking the Appropriation

As an aid to sales executives who have not had a great deal of experience in laying out advertising programs, and in determining the amount required to carry these programs through, we give five questions which may help them to avoid inadequate and unwise advertising budgeting:

1. *What do you mean when you speak of advertising?*

   Does it cover only advertising in magazines and newspapers, direct-mail, billboards, streetcar advertising, and the other commonly accepted avenues for publicity?

   Does it include exhibitions at conventions, business shows, fairs, etc.?

   Does it include all the printed matter used by the concern?

   Does it include entertainment?

   There are certain things which are properly chargeable to advertising and certain other things which are not. How broad the term will be is usually determined by how well the business is departmentalized. The large corporation has, in addition to an advertising department, a sales department, a sales promotion department and various other divisions that take care of matters which, in the small business, are perhaps best included under the advertising department.

   To simplify matters, suppose the advertising department has charge of all publicity and sales helps for use by salesmen and dealers.

2. *What should advertising, as defined, be expected to do?*

   A list of some of the principal conditions to be faced by the business during the period under consideration should be named. For example:

Probable increase and decrease in selling resistance experienced by salesmen and by dealers.

The introduction of new products to the line which must be advertised.

Stimulus that needs to be given to the sale of certain products.

The necessity for offsetting the influence of increased advertising on the part of competitors.

After thought has been given to the listing of these conditions which will probably have to be met, the next thing is to formulate certain definite tasks for the advertising to accomplish. It is best to keep these tasks modest in scope, rather than to expect advertising to work revolutionary changes within a year.

3. *How can advertising best do the tasks set, and meet the conditions likely to be confronted?*

Will magazine advertising do it or should newspapers be used?

How about direct mail?

Should billboards be given a trial?

Many firms have used streetcar cards with great success.

Should all these mediums be used, or only one, or two, or three?

This is one of the most important questions to be answered in determining an advertising appropriation. Probably no firm ever answers it in a manner satisfactory even to itself. Experience, the experience of others, the counsel of a good advertising agency, coupled with sound judgment, must be relied on to define the course of action that should be followed.

4. *What is the relative importance of each type of publicity and how much money should be spent on it?*

In every advertising department there are certain fixed expenses, such as salaries, supplies, telephone and telegrams, postage for correspondence, traveling expenses, and so on. These expenses should be estimated for the period, based on past experience.

In addition to these fixed charges there are certain other expenses which are practically unavoidable; there are certain sales helps and working tools for the sales organization and for dealers that are standard and which must be kept in stock.

There are certain other items which judgment plainly indicates are absolutely essential—items which the selling organization expects and needs.

By adding the estimated cost of these expenditures to the fixed charges already determined, you will then have a sum which must be appropriated if there is to be an advertising department which functions in a measure at least, and gives some evidence of its existence.

5. *How much money should be appropriated for meeting the remaining conditions and for accomplishing the task set?*

There are two principal ways of determining advertising appropriations:

A. Taking a percentage of sales quota, or of sales volume. This may be for the past year, the current year, or the year to come. It can be figured either as a percentage of the gross sales or as a fixed sum per unit of the product.

B. Appropriating a fixed sum. Some firms appropriate a fixed sum for the entire year—others for a half year, or even for a quarter. As each of these periods draws to a close, appropriations are made for the succeeding half year or quarter. This is not to be recommended as a general rule, however, because advertising programs figured in such a way are apt to lack continuity. It often takes a long time to get printed matter under way and to catch certain magazine schedules.

A far better way is to lay a plan for 3 years based on anticipated sales.

It is never easy to fix an advertising appropriation. The factors one has to work with are, at best, indefinite and vague. Oftentimes they are unknown. Advertising is very susceptible to changes in business conditions and in company policy. *Sometimes* it is advisable to discard the most carefully laid advertising appropriation plans after a few months of operation in order to take advantage of changed conditions. Ninety-nine times out of a hundred, however, it is far better to make a plan and then stick to it.

The concern that has a definite advertising plan has a chart by which to steer. Adverse currents and storms may force it to leave the course for a time, but if it has an appropriation and plan written out, it can at least make an attempt to get back on the main course.

Perhaps the most important things to keep in mind in making an advertising appropriation are the following:

A. Decide that you will advertise.

B. Set certain objectives for your advertising to reach.

C. Determine how these objectives can best be reached.

D. Stick to the plan which your judgment has told you is the right one.

Spreading the Appropriation

Some companies, especially those selling through agents and distributors compensated by a share of the profit, prorate a portion, sometimes all, of the advertising appropriation among such distributors. This practice is not recommended. It usually leads to dissatisfaction, since it is an expense which the distributor cannot control. When such a plan is followed it is the wise policy to give each distributor or agent the right to approve *in advance* the maximum amount that will be charged against his operations. This is better than the customary practice which is to determine upon some arbitrary percentage figure which each distributor must pay. Very often the introduction of a new product, or an unexpected competitive development, makes it expedient to greatly increase advertising expenditures during the budget year. In such cases the expense is likely to upset the calculations of the distributor and cause bad feelings. It is one of those arbitrary charges, sometimes levied against a profit-participation plan, that is apt to defeat its purpose.

The more successful advertisers adjust the compensation plan so that all advertising and a great deal of the sales promotion, excepting direct mail, will be absorbed into the general cost of doing business rather than treating it as a direct selling expense. Since its benefits will accrue to the business over a period of time, usually considerably in excess of any one operating year, this plan is to be recommended as fair both to the company and to the independent contractor.

ADVERTISING AGENCY RELATIONS

A question frequently asked by sales managers about to advertise is: "Is the amount of money we will spend large enough to make it worth while to have an advertising agent?" The question is prompted by the widely held belief that unless a manufacturer spends upward of $50,000 a year for advertising, his account is not profitable to an advertising agency. In a measure this is true. But in a larger sense it is not true, because an advertising agency, like any other business, is willing and even glad to lose money for a time on a small account if there is a possibility that it can be developed into a large account. The ethics of the industry prevent agencies from soliciting each other's accounts. And while there will probably always be a certain amount of account stealing, the more reputable agents create their new business. The obvious way to do that is to build up small accounts into profitable advertisers.

So do not feel that just because you are not spending a large sum of money for advertising you should not avail yourself of the services of an advertising agency. The right sort of agent will be glad to handle an account where the appropriation is as low as $15,000, if it offers possibilities for growth. As a matter of fact, the counsel of a skilled advertising expert is more valuable to the small advertiser than to the large advertiser, because the small company starting out in advertising needs the benefit of advice.

The average advertiser is too close to his own business to be able to single out a dominant selling idea around which to build a successful advertising plan. The things that interest you about your business seldom interest the public. A capable advertising man brings to bear upon your selling problem ability to interpret those things about your business which will catch the imagination and quicken the interest of the public.

Cost of Agency Service

One of the erroneous ideas connected with the employment of advertising counsel is that it costs the advertiser nothing. It is true that the publisher pays the recognized agency a commission on all the advertising he places in his publications. Agencies also usually collect a commission on the materials used in the production of an advertising campaign. But, except in a few cases, these commissions alone are insufficient to cover all the expense connected with launching an advertiser on the road to leadership. Before undertaking a campaign the right sort of agency will usually recommend a market survey to determine the best approach to the problem. If this survey is conducted by the agency, an extra charge will be made to cover its cost unless the appropriation is unusually large. Even in the actual execution of the campaign, the agent's commissions are seldom sufficient to cover all the expense. It would be shortsighted economy on the advertiser's part to insist that the agent look to the publisher for his entire remuneration under such conditions. That is why the majority of advertisers today employ their agents on some basis which provides extra compensation if the nature of the account requires it. The three most commonly used plans of agency compensation follow:

1—AGENT RETAINED ON A FIXED FEE BASIS: There is a growing sentiment in favor of employing advertising counsel on a fixed annual fee. Under this plan all commissions, allowances, and discounts belong to the advertiser. Advertising counsel acts as the agent of the advertiser and has no interest in the amount of money spent for advertising.

The objection to this plan is that the most capable advertising men are not usually able to secure fees large enough to compensate them adequately. The plan, however, is preferable when the servicing of the account requires a disproportionate amount of work. It is the most desirable plan for concerns spending large amounts in direct-mail advertising or in technical and trade publications, where the commission paid by the publisher makes it necessary for the agent to do either a superficial job or lose money on the account.

2—AGENT RETAINED ON A PERCENTAGE OVER COST BASIS: When the account exceeds $50,000 annually, or where it is difficult to determine in advance the amount of work to be done in servicing the account, the most satisfactory plan of compensation for the advertising counsel is to pay him a retaining fee, which covers the services of the principal in an advisory capacity, plus a fluctuating fee based upon the amount spent for advertising.

Under this method of operating the advertiser is billed at the net charge to the agent and a flat service charge (usually 15%) is added to that net figure. The advantages of this plan are that the services of counsel are retained regardless of the amount of advertising that is done, and the advertiser need feel no hesitancy in putting problems up to his advertising counsel or requesting special service.

This plan also reduces the possibility of an advertising agent or counsel favoring one medium or one form of advertising over another in order to make money. He gets the same compensation in all cases. The objection to this plan is that from the standpoint of what is paid the agent it is more costly to the advertiser, but from the standpoint of the ultimate cost of the advertising, judged by results, it is usually far and away the most economical.

3—Agent Paid Out of Commissions Earned: Under this plan of operation the services of the agent are paid by the seller. He must operate within the publisher's 15% commission allowed to advertising agents, or the 5 to 10% which printers and engravers grant him. With the growing competition among advertising agencies and counselors this method is becoming less and less satisfactory to the advertiser. It has a tendency to influence advertising into those publications and those mediums offering the largest commissions, and obviously the publications paying high commissions and printers willing to allow large discounts are usually the most urgently in need of business.

True, advertising discounts have been standardized to a large extent, but there are so many ways by which a seller of advertising can make it advantageous for an agent to favor him in competition with other mediums, that temptation is very great. While this plan appeals to many advertisers as being a good way to pass the cost of advertising service on to the seller, it usually happens that he pays dearly in the long run. Moreover agents who are able to operate under the less speculative plans mentioned above usually do so. If an advertiser elects to place his advertising and to employ his advertising counsel under this last-mentioned plan, he must realize that he is dealing with the agent of the publisher and the printer, whose remuneration is directly related to the *amount of* advertising he can sell and the mediums which he can persuade his client to use.

SELECTING AN ADVERTISING AGENCY

Some time back, the Dartnell editorial staff made a rather searching inquiry among advertisers and advertising agencies in an endeavor to lay down certain definite tests which could be used by an advertiser in selecting an advertising agent.

In again presenting these tests to the Dartnell clientele we have modified some of them to conform to new conditions which have developed since their conception. They are recommended as a means of narrowing the field down to a possible three or four agents, who can then be personally interviewed.

Test No. 1. Success in Advertising a Product Similar to Yours

When a manufacturer contemplating advertising sets out to employ an agent, he invariably goes at it as though he were hiring a sales manager. He feels that the more experience the agent has had in his line, the less risk he will take. Yet some of the worst advertising failures can be traced to the fact that an advertising agent knew too much about the line of business, with the result that he was not able to free his thinking from the customs of the trade concerned.

Test No. 2. How the Agency Is Regarded by Other Advertising Agencies

Fortunately there is an easy way to determine this point. Advertising agents, like other industries, have an organization known as the American Association of Advertising Agencies. The qualifications for membership are, briefly, as follows:

1. Size or volume of business is not an influential factor in determining the agency's qualifications.

2. Geographical location has no bearing but does determine the council in which the application is to be voted upon.

3. The applicant must have been doing business as a going concern.

4. So-called "house agencies," established by one or more advertisers, are not eligible for membership, nor is an agency which is owned by any publishing, printing, engraving, or any other business from which the agency purchases in the interests of its clients.

5. Experience counts: An applicant must be able to furnish references as to both business and advertising experience.

6. The factors of character, ability, and financial responsibility are considered extremely important.

7. It is desirable that an applicant shall have obtained satisfactory recognition within each of the four principal publishing groups.

8. No agency is admitted that handles business at less than card rates, or makes rebates of any kind.

9. There are strict requirements as to business methods.

While it is true that there are members of this association who do not live up to the full letter of these standards, it is a fact that the association requires strict adherence to the code from its members and will not admit into membership any agent who does not meet these tests or who is not acceptable to the present membership. It also does everything possible to assure its members living up to its standards and disciplines those who are found guilty of any unethical practices. An agency that is a member of this association, therefore, has much in its favor, although there are many worthy agents, with principles as high as those defined under the Four A code, who are not members.

Since an advertiser may be sued by a publisher for any bills contracted by *his* advertising agency, even though he has given the agent the money with which to pay the bill, be reasonably sure that the agency has sufficient capital of its own, or at least the means of getting it, so that there will be no temptation to use yours for operating expenses.

Test No. 3. Size of Agency

If the account is one which calls for a full use of all types of mediums, with field cooperation, checking, and research work, it is obviously wise to engage an agency which has these facilities. On the other hand, if the campaign is to be confined to advertising in industrial papers, with little or no consumer advertising, it is well to employ an agency which specializes in industrial advertising. And by the same reasoning if the nature of the advertising is to be direct-by-mail or radio, and you wish to shift the responsibility for the execution of such a campaign onto other shoulders, it is wise to consider employing the services of an organization specializing in those kinds of advertising.

It is only fair to add, however, that in late years the larger advertising agencies have developed within their own organizations special departments for handling practically every form of advertising, including television, direct-mail, and industrial accounts.

It must be realized that a large agency, in the last analysis, is a group of small agencies welded together under one personality. Thus the matter of size, provided the agency is adequately staffed to handle your account properly in addition to its present accounts, is of secondary importance. Generally speaking, however, if your account is a large one, best results will probably be secured from a large agency; and contrariwise the smaller advertiser is likely to get the best results from a smaller agency.

Test No. 4. Attitude Toward Direct-Mail and Business Paper Advertising

To the credit of the American advertising agents, they seldom permit the amount of work necessary to use any one form of advertising to influence their recommendations. There was a time when shortsighted agencies would not recommend the use of publications of low advertising rates because it took too much time to prepare copy. In the same way they did their utmost to discourage clients from spending money for direct-mail advertising because it involved more work than space advertising. But with standardization of the type page size and the development of printers' service departments able to assume the burden of preparing direct advertising under the advertising agent's supervision, these difficulties have largely passed. Nevertheless, it is an excellent test when selecting an advertising agent to check him on that point.

Test No. 5. Reputation of Agency for Holding Accounts

An advertising agency that is rendering satisfactory service to the clients has a smaller turnover in accounts, as a rule, than an agency that is interested in accounts merely for the commissions it can get out of them. That is obvious. By asking an agent to give you a list of his accounts and to tell you how long each has been with him, you can get a very good idea of his ability to serve you satisfactorily. By getting in touch with the advertisers whom he has been serving over a period of years you can also get from them valuable information about the agency's ability to satisfy its clients.

Test No. 6. Special Inducements or Secret Rebates

We have no bone to pick with the advertiser who wants to get every possible value out of his advertising dollar. On the contrary, we admire the man who is a good buyer. But one of the first rules for being a good buyer is to buy only the best when it comes to brains—because the highest priced brains are usually the least expensive.

You can get advertising counsel at any price you wish to pay, just as you can get coal for any price you wish to pay. But all coal is not just coal, and all advertising agents are not just advertising agents. There are degrees. You can choose, if you wish, an agent who will handle your advertising on a brokerage basis and rebate the commissions. There are still a few agencies who will do this. You might compare them to "yard sweepings" in the coal business. Or you can find an agency which will agree to handle your advertising with certain kinds of plus-service thrown in— it might be willing to let you put your advertising man on its payroll or give a job to one of your wife's poor relations. There are unprincipled men in the advertising agency business, too.

There is a world of wisdom in that saying of Plutarch: "If you live with a lame man, you will learn to halt." An advertising agent who is so weak that he has to offer trick inducements to get business is usually a lame duck.

Test No. 7. Age of Agency

While the age of an agency is important, it means nothing until all the factors relating to its age are taken into consideration. There are agencies in this country 40 years old that still live in the dark ages of advertising. They have completely failed to keep step with progress. They continue to place the same patent medicine accounts that they placed in George Rowell's time; they have no conception of research work, no sense of obligation for the results of their copy, no aim in life other than the grubbing of a few commissions. If age alone meant anthing—these agencies would rank very near the top.

But when you find an agency that has been established for some years, whose record shows that it has been one of the leaders in advertising progress, and which is just as up-to-date as its youngest competitor, that agency is entitled to more than passing consideration. It is logical to assume that during the years it has been in business, it has gathered a great deal of advertising wisdom and experience that should be of value to you. We must remember that important as brilliant copy and attractive lay-outs in advertising are, sound judgment based on experience is just as important. This seasoned judgment is most likely to be found in an older agency.

Test No. 8. Policy in Charging for Cuts and Supplementary Material

A large part of the difficulties which advertisers get into with their agencies arises over charges for art work, engravings, printing, and the other supplementary materials that are involved in a complete advertising program. There are agencies which will take an advertising account on a basis that offers them little or no profit on the space, figuring to get their entire profit out of "extras." If it is the policy of the agency to bill you whatever it wishes for these extras, trouble is sure to follow.

So one of the first things to find out is how the agent proposes to handle his charge for this sort of work. He is entitled to a fair compensation, and you should expect to pay for whatever work is done on your account. But the time to find out what his basis of charge will be is before you appoint him and not after.

Test No. 9. Contract Requirements

At first thought, it would seem that an advertising agency which believes in itself should be willing to take your advertising account on a basis that would permit severing the relationship on short notice.

It is debatable, however, if this is the best arrangement to make with your agent—for several reasons. First, before an advertising agent can give you the service to which you are entitled, he has to spend considerable time and money in studying your problems. If he does not do this thoroughly, it is difficult to conceive how he can spend your money most advantageously. If your arrangement with your agent is subject to termination at short notice, the agent cannot afford to make the thorough study of your advertising problem he should. On the other hand, if you have an agreement with him, assuring him of your business for a definite period, he can afford to spend more for preliminary work.

A second reason in favor of a time contract is that you protect yourself against yourself. It is a well-known fact that few advertising undertakings show immediate results. Advertising success is a plant of slow growth. It takes time to develop. Very often an advertiser starts his advertising in high hopes and sits back to wait for a deluge of business. But the avalanche of orders does not come. He gets cold feet and cancels his advertising. Had he the courage to hang on for a few months longer, the orders would come and he would reap a full measure of success. But he stops too soon and pays dearly for his lack of courage. A time contract covering one, two, or even five years' advertising might save him that loss.

Recognized Advertising Agencies

While there are 7,500 concerns in the United States which call themselves advertising agencies, many of them are individuals who have, for one reason or another, never secured recognition from any publisher's association. Lack of such recognition may merely mean that the advertising firm has never applied for it; or, what is more likely, it has applied and has not been granted recognition for one of the following reasons:

1. Lack of sufficient capital to finance advertising placed with a publisher in the event the agent's client should fail.

2. Lack of sufficient experience in the practice of advertising, especially the preparation of advertising copy. Since a part of the commission paid agents by publishers is for the preparation of result-getting copy, it is required that they must be able to satisfy the publisher's committee on that point.

3. The nature of the agent's billing is such that it would indicate he is functioning as a service agency for one or two accounts and would therefore not be likely to spend any time in developing new business or new accounts for the publisher.

The publisher's association which is most painstaking in the granting of recognition is the National Magazine Publishers Association. Next in order comes the American Newspaper Publishers

Association (A.N.P.A.) Then the Agricultural Publishers Association (A.P.A.). Recognition by the Associated Business Press simply indicates a satisfactory financial status to warrant members of that group extending credit.

ADVERTISING COPY AND MEDIA

Advertising Copy

The simplest definition of good advertising copy is that it must be good salesmanship. It must also have the added virtue of accomplishing in a few words what a salesman can take an hour to explain. It must command attention. It must be dignified to win respect. It must be interesting. And above all, it must be sufficiently convincing to get action. Robert Ruxton holds that there are four kinds of copy and only four. "It may seem difficult," he suggests, "to write copy that sells goods at a profit, and the preliminary study necessary may seem infinitely complex, but students of the subject will find much of the seemingly difficult disappear if they will recollect that there are really only four physical forms of 'copy': (1) Description, (2) Narration, (3) Exposition, (4) Argumentation. All rhetorical works describe the characteristics of these four forms and the methods by which those characteristics are obtained. In any event, the terms are largely self-explanatory. We all know what it is to describe a person or an article. Nearly everyone is familiar with the process of telling a tale (narration). Exposition is the art of making clear; argumentation is the art of convincing."

Out of the four physical forms comes, phoenixlike, a fifth, persuasion. Persuasion induces action. Action is the cracker of the whip in all business presentation. Be sure it is there. If it isn't, you have in all that you have written (however ornate, however elaborate) a fishhook without a barb.

In writing advertising copy, *don't argue—explain.* In the rhetorical sense "argument" may be defined as "proof of arguments based on laws or reliable authorities." In the sense that argument is contention all salesmen dread it, and all salesmen avoid it, though ready to meet it should the necessity develop. What salesmen seek to do is to get their presentation accepted as manifestly clear and right without argument. That process is termed exposition. Do not challenge the reader by a "leading" question such as "That's as plain as daylight, isn't it?" But make it plain as daylight. One treatment is expository, while the other is argumentative. It is

The Cost of Advertising Space

Rate	1 Inch 14 Lines	2 Inch 28 Lines	3 Inch 42 Lines	4 Inch 56 Lines	5 Inch 70 Lines	6 Inch 84 Lines	7 Inch 98 Lines	8 Inch 112 Lines	9 Inch 126 Lines	10 Inch 140 Lines	15 Inch 210 Lines	25 Inch 350 Lines	1 Col. 294 Lines
$0.01	$0.14	$0.28	$0.42	$0.56	$0.70	$0.84	$0.98	$1.12	$1.26	$1.40	$2.10	$3.50	$2.94
.02	.28	.56	.84	1.12	1.40	1.68	1.96	2.24	2.52	2.80	4.20	7.00	5.88
.03	.42	.84	1.26	1.68	2.10	2.52	2.94	3.36	3.78	4.20	6.30	10.50	8.82
04	.56	1.12	1.68	2.24	2.80	3.36	3.92	4.48	5.04	5.60	8.40	14.00	11.76
.05	.70	1.40	2.10	2.80	3.50	4.20	4.90	5.60	6.30	7.00	10.50	17.50	14.70
06	.84	1.68	2.52	3.36	4.20	5.04	5.88	6.72	7.56	8.40	12.60	21.00	17.64
.07	.98	1.96	2.94	3.92	4.90	5.88	6.86	7.84	8.82	9.80	14.70	24.50	20.58
.08	1.12	2.24	3.36	4.48	5.60	6.72	7.84	8.96	10.08	11.20	16.80	28.00	23.52
.09	1.26	2.52	3.78	5.04	6.30	7.56	8.82	10.08	11.34	12.60	18.90	31.50	26.46
.10	1.40	2.80	4.20	5.60	7.00	8.40	9.80	11.20	12.60	14.00	21.00	35.00	29.40
.11	1.54	3.08	4.62	6.16	7.70	9.24	10.78	12.32	13.86	15.40	23.10	38.50	32.34
.12	1.68	3.36	5.04	6.72	8.40	10.08	11.76	13.44	15.12	16.80	25.20	42.00	35.28
.13	1.82	3.64	5.46	7.28	9.10	10.92	12.74	14.56	16.38	18.20	27.30	45.50	38.22
.14	1.96	3.92	5.88	7.84	9.80	11.76	13.72	15.68	17.64	19.60	29.40	49.00	41.16
.15	2.10	4.20	6.30	8.40	10.50	12.60	14.70	16.80	18.90	21.00	31.50	52.50	44.10
.16	2.24	4.48	6.72	8.96	11.20	13.44	15.68	17.92	20.16	22.40	33.60	56.00	47.04
.17	2.38	4.76	7.14	9.52	11.90	14.28	16.66	19.04	21.42	23.80	35.70	59.50	49.98
18	2.52	5.04	7.56	10.08	12.60	15.12	17.64	20.16	22.68	25.20	37.80	63.00	52.92
.19	2.66	5.32	7.98	10.64	13.30	15.96	18.62	21.28	23.94	26.60	39.90	66.50	55.86
.20	2.80	5.60	8.40	11.20	14.00	16.80	19.60	22.40	25.20	28.00	42.00	70.00	58.80
.21	2.94	5.88	8.82	11.76	14.70	17.64	20.58	23.52	26.46	29.40	44.10	73.50	61.74
.22	3.08	6.16	9.24	12.32	15.40	18.48	21.56	24.64	27.72	30.80	46.20	77.00	64.68
.23	3.22	6.44	9.66	12.88	16.10	19.32	22.54	25.76	28.98	32.20	48.30	80.50	67.62
.24	3.36	6.72	10.08	13.44	16.80	20.16	23.52	26.88	30.24	33.60	50.40	84.00	70.56
.25	3.50	7.00	10.50	14.00	17.50	21.00	24.50	28.00	31.50	35.00	52.50	87.50	73.50
.26	3.64	7.28	10.92	14.56	18.20	21.84	25.48	29.12	32.76	36.40	54.60	91.00	76.44
.27	3.78	7.56	11.34	15.12	18.90	22.68	26.46	30.24	34.02	37.80	56.70	94.50	79.38
28	3.92	7.84	11.76	15.68	19.60	23.52	27.44	31.36	35.28	39.20	58.80	98.00	82.32
29	4.06	8.12	12.18	16.24	20.30	24.36	28.42	32.48	36.54	40.60	60.90	101.50	85.26
30	4.20	8.40	12.60	16.80	21.00	25.20	29.40	33.60	37.80	42.00	63.00	105.00	88.20
.31	4.34	8.68	13.02	17.36	21.70	26.04	30.38	34.72	39.06	43.40	65.10	108.50	91.14
.32	4.48	8.96	13.44	17.92	22.40	26.88	31.36	35.84	40.32	44.80	67.20	112.00	94.08
.33	4.62	9.24	13.86	18.48	23.10	27.72	32.34	36.96	41.58	46.20	69.30	115.50	97.02
.34	4.76	9.52	14.28	19.04	23.80	28.56	33.32	38.08	42.84	47.60	71.40	119.00	99.96
.35	4.90	9.80	14.70	19.60	24.50	29.40	34.30	39.20	44.10	49.00	73.50	122.50	102.90
.36	5.04	10.08	15.12	20.16	25.20	30.24	35.28	40.32	45.36	50.40	75.60	126.00	105.84
.37	5.18	10.36	15.54	20.72	25.90	31.08	36.26	41.44	46.62	51.80	77.70	129.50	108.78
38	5.32	10.64	15.96	21.28	26.60	31.92	37.24	42.56	47.88	53.20	79.80	133.00	111.72
.39	5.46	10.92	16.38	21.84	27.30	32.76	38.22	43.68	49.14	54.60	81.90	136.50	114.66
.40	5.60	11.20	16.80	22.40	28.00	33.60	39.20	44.80	50.40	56.00	84.00	140.00	117.60
.41	5.74	11.48	17.22	22.96	28.70	34.44	40.18	45.92	51.66	57.40	86.10	143.50	120.54
.42	5.88	11.76	17.64	23.52	29.40	35.28	41.16	47.04	52.92	58.80	88.20	147.00	123.48
.43	6.02	12.04	18.06	24.08	30.10	36.12	42.14	48.16	54.18	60.20	90.30	150.50	126.42
.44	6.16	12.32	18.48	24.64	30.80	36.96	43.12	49.28	55.44	61.60	92.40	154.00	129.36
.45	6.30	12.60	18.90	25.20	31.50	37.80	44.10	50.40	56.70	63.00	94.50	157.50	132.30
.46	6.44	12.88	19.32	25.76	32.20	38.64	45.08	51.52	57.96	64.40	96.60	161.00	135.24
.47	6.58	13.16	19.74	26.32	32.90	39.48	46.06	52.64	59.22	65.80	98.70	164.50	138.18
.48	6.72	13.44	20.16	26.88	33.60	40.32	47.04	53.76	60.48	67.20	100.80	168.00	141.12
.49	6.86	13.72	20.58	27.44	34.30	41.16	48.02	54.88	61.74	68.60	102.90	171.50	144.06
.50	7.00	14.00	21.00	28.00	35.00	42.00	49.00	56.00	63.00	70.00	105.00	175.00	147.00
.60	8.40	16.80	25.20	33.60	42.00	50.40	58.80	67.20	75.60	84.00	126.00	210.00	176.40
.70	9.80	19.60	29.40	39.20	49.00	58.80	68.60	78.40	88.20	98.00	147.00	245.00	205.80
.80	11.20	22.40	33.60	44.80	56.00	67.20	78.40	89.60	100.80	112.00	168.00	280.00	235.20
.90	12.60	25.20	37.80	50.40	63.00	75.60	88.20	100.80	113.40	126.00	189.00	315.00	264.60
1.00	14.00	28.00	42.00	56.00	70.00	84.00	98.00	112.00	126.00	140.00	210.00	350.00	294.00

Courtesy Brooke, Smith, French & Dorrance, Inc.

as much human nature to rise to a challenge as it is to accept a satisfactory explanation.

The impulse that an advertisement should arouse is the desire for possession. Approval, praise, commendation, admiration are static qualities that stand still and get the public no nearer the advertiser or the advertiser no nearer the public.

The chink of dollars falling in the till or the glint of color in the form of checks is the primary form of applause that business wants. Like the box office of a theater, it can be both pleased and gratified to hear the secondary form of applause ringing out from box and orchestra, but it doesn't want the form of business that admires the posters but forgets to buy tickets of admission. (See also Chapters 10, 11, 12—"Sales Promotional Literature.")

The Selection of Media

Great confusion exists in the minds of most sales managers today as to just what are the best media to use in marketing their products. Newspapers seem to be leading in favor because of the opportunity they offer to handpick markets and to concentrate the bulk of the advertising effort on territories where the advertiser is well equipped to follow through on the advertising. It is natural that people should depend upon newspapers to a greater extent for their reading. A family which has had to curtail its expenditures will cut off practically everything else before it stops buying daily newspapers.

Then, too, the daily newspaper enables an advertiser to take advantage of timely situations. It is essentially a quick action medium. While it takes from 2 to 4 weeks to plan and execute an advertising campaign in the magazines, a campaign can be launched and completed in the newspapers in 4 days.

Against these advantages the newspaper has a relatively short life and offers little opportunity for class selection. With the exception of a few newspapers which appeal to the carriage trade, the newspaper offers the manufacturer of the class product little opportunity to call his shots. The magazines do. And as the gap between the consumer's income and expenditures for necessities of life widens, a correspondingly increased use of magazine advertising is bound to grow.

The problem of media is primarily and essentially a problem of markets. It is the market influence of the medium that the advertiser is buying, and the test of the value of a medium is the character and extent of its market influence. It is the job of the sales manager, or his advertising assistant, to draw up his list of media very much as the chess player ranges his pieces on the board, combining his various values in such a way as to "cover" strategic points and at the same time avoid leaving anything unprotected.

The sales executive who approaches the problem from this standpoint will often find it simplified. It is the adaptability of the medium to his own particular situation that he is solely concerned with. Let him visualize clearly the particular market that it is desired to cover. That, for the time being, is all that matters. What medium or group media can be employed to reach this particular market most effectually? That is the main question, and by keeping it clearly in focus the advertiser may avoid getting himself involved in a morass of competitive arguments and statistics which have no practical bearing upon the problem.

The Foundation Media

Most advertising media are developed with the requirements of more or less definite markets in mind. These markets may be bounded by geographical or territorial limits; they may consist merely of persons who occupy a certain position with respect to social standing or income; they may be based upon a general community of interest in some business or social or religious activity; they may be concentrated in some definite locality; or they may be scattered across the length and breadth of the continent. But in most cases they are aimed to meet the interests of a clientele that is visualized with more or less definiteness, and which, from the advertiser's point of view, may constitute a market. Thus, it is entirely logical to treat the problem of mediums from this standpoint.

Now in discussing the various groups or types of media separately, we should not be understood as implying that the advertiser should consider them after that fashion. Seldom can the best results be obtained by relying upon a single type of appeal. Generally speaking, in a national campaign to the consumer, or in a campaign that is designed to become national, the advertiser will use one type to support and reinforce another. Thus the value of a given medium to the advertiser will depend not merely upon its direct effect upon the market, as standing alone, but also upon the service it may render as an auxiliary to other media.

Publication media are generally classified in four main divisions: Newspapers, magazines, farm papers, and business papers. Each of these groups is further subdivided extensively, and the divisions to a certain extent overlap. As a matter of fact, however, the foregoing classification is logical, because there are certain characteristics that belong peculiarly to each group.

Treating the subject wholly from the standpoint of the market influence that is exercised by the various groups of media, it is possible to illustrate these different characteristics by means of an imaginary graphic chart.

As a basis we assume that the sum-total buying power of the national market may be represented by a rectangle of approximately such shape as would just contain a map of the United States. This represents, in other words, the 130,000,000 people who make up what is generally referred to as the "buying public," and is the ultimate potential or possible market for any product.

Territorial Boundaries of Newspaper Markets

Buying power can be definitely graded and classified. From left to right in the diagram it is classified strictly according to geographical or territorial divisions, so that every individual buyer in Cleveland, Ohio, for example, would be in the same vertical column. From top to bottom, the classification runs according to a purely mythical system based upon wealth, intelligence, social position, etc., so that theoretically all the people with common activities and interests will be found at the same horizontal level. On such an imaginary chart of buying power the market influence of the various groups of mediums can be laid out in visible zones.

Taking up the newspapers as a class, we find that their market influence is ordinarily bounded very definitely by territorial lines. The essential characteristic of the newspaper is its service to a community that is more or less self-contained and self-conscious. We find, moreover, that the newspaper in general reaches almost all classes in the social scale. There are many individual newspapers, of course, that appeal mainly to people of wealth and refinement, or to what are vaguely denominated the masses, but the newspaper in general serves the whole local group rather than any one social group. The market influence or coverage of the newspapers would be indicated on the chart by vertical stripes or bands, relatively narrow and sharply defined, and relatively deep in color to indicate per capita density of circulation.

Class Influences of Periodicals

Turning to the magazines we find that their market influence is affected very little, if at all, by territorial or geographical boundaries. Generally speaking, they serve the social group rather than the local group, and magazine circulation may be defined as a selection of people who act and think alike, wherever they may happen to be located. Magazine coverage would therefore be represented in our chart in horizontal zones, broader and less sharply defined than the vertical columns and relatively lighter in color.

We have now produced a sort of sublimated checkerboard, with dense areas of color where the vertical and horizontal stripes cross, and irregular spaces between where the color shades off into the background. These irregular spaces represent, obviously enough, the rural and small-town markets, where the circulation of both magazines and metropolitan newspapers is relatively thin. This is the field that is covered by the farm papers, and the special group of publications that are generally known as "mail-order papers." These media definitely serve, in the main, the interests of the rural and small-town markets, though both farm and mail-order media overlap, to some extent, the territory covered by newspapers and magazines.

The fourth great class of publication media—the business papers —reach highly specialized markets that are bounded neither by territorial lines, nor by lines of general interest. Their influence is very largely concentrated in industrial and mercantile centers and is directed at the industrial consumer or the mercantile unit rather than the private or individual consuming unit. They render a highly important service in connection with national advertising to the consumer, but it is a service that is almost wholly supplementary and auxiliary. They influence in one way or another pretty much the whole field of media.

In recent years, newspapers have developed the use of magazine-size advertising supplements which are becoming increasingly popular with manufacturers, industries, retailers, and governments.

Diamond & Co., a large Philadelphia haberdasher, used a handsome four-color supplement in the *Evening Bulletin* during the Christmas season and included a coupon for mail orders. Thus, the customer was given the choice of ordering in person, by telephone, or by mail.

Form of Advertising Order

In placing orders with publications or broadcasting companies it is recommended that the standard order form as drafted by a special committee of the American Association of Advertising Agencies be used, as it covers a variety of contingencies which can arise in connection with carrying out an advertising program. A sample of this form will be sent by the AAAA on request.

Used by all advertising agencies which are members of the association, its use is by no means limited only to those agencies. Advertisers would do well to insist that their advertising agency, if not a member of the Four A organization, adopt and use this form of contract for all advertising orders placed on their account. There are two forms, one for publications and the other for spot broadcasting. In the main they are similar, but both forms contain a number of special provisions to cover the different needs of their respective fields. The advantages to the advertiser in demanding the use of this form of advertising contract are as follows:

1. Both blanks make the agency solely liable for payment of medium bills, thus protecting the advertiser against contingent double liability in case of agency failure to pay after the advertiser has paid the agency.

2. The rate paragraphs afford the advertiser maximum protection. Secret rates, rebates, or agreements affecting rates are prohibited. The advertiser is safeguarded against a competitor getting a secret advantage.

3. The paragraph forbidding rebating by the agency assures the client that he is getting a square deal from his agency and the same terms as any other advertiser.

4. In general, advertising covered by the uniform conditions of the Standard Order Blanks is placed with assurance to the advertiser that, should any dispute arise, his rights are protected by definite provisions in respects which experience has proved to be most needed.

PUBLICATION BLANK

1. The 60-day limitation on short-rate bills is a protection to the advertiser against annoying claims bobbing up at a later date, after he has assumed that the contract had been completed and all charges paid for.

2. The circulation paragraph is another safeguard. It entitles the agency, in case the publisher is not a member of the Audit Bureau of Circulations, to a statement of net paid circulation verified by a certified public accountant, or in lieu thereof to examine the publisher's circulation books.

RADIO AND TELEVISION BLANK

1. In the broadcasting blank, reasonable and fair settlement of such knotty problems as program interruptions and the substitution of sustaining programs is provided.

2. In this blank, there is also a clear statement of the duties and rights of parties in connection with copyrighted material.

Importance of Verified Circulation Statements

For a good many years one of our major problems in the advertising business was the establishment of some generally accepted standard of measurement for circulation.

Advertisers, advertising agents, and leading publishers struggled for many years to bring about the adoption of some system by which circulation claims could be intelligently compared. The effort finally bore fruit in the Audit Bureau of Circulations, which establishes a standard definition of circulation and measures all publications by the same yardstick.

The adoption of this system has been of incalculable benefit to the buyer of advertising space and has vastly simplified the problems of the agent and the publisher.

For the first time in the history of advertising it provided a sound basis of comparison and gave every advertiser the assurance that when two or more publishers talked about circulation they were talking about the same thing.

Paid vs. Controlled Circulations

The demand from advertisers for media which "blanket" a territory or a market gave rise to what is known as "controlled" circulation mediums. These are usually called "Shopping News." Copies are left at the doors of selected families throughout a residential district. They contain mostly all advertising and are therefore read, if read at all, for their advertising. Similarly class and trade publications are distributed to "controlled" lists in an effort to get full coverage of a specialized market. A paid circulation publication requires what is called "turning room" and seldom gives more than 50% coverage of a market. The other 50% is required for securing replacement subscriptions. An association has been organized to check the distribution of these controlled papers and issues statements certifying the number of copies mailed.

While advertising media which are given away, rather than sold, have a certain value and often produce inquiries at a very low cost because of a lower advertising rate, it can be concluded that media which the reader pays to get, and which come at his request, have a greater reader interest than those which he gets for nothing. In other words, a publication which is not worth paying for, usually is not worth reading. There has been, in some areas, a tendency for controlled and distributed publications to convert to paid circulation.

Broadcasting

Television is the most rapidly growing entertainment and promotional medium in the U.S. today. With families watching TV over six hours a day in more than 62 million homes, it has tremendous power as a marketing force. Three great developments have given it even greater impact. These are color TV, UHF reception, and Community Antenna TV.

What is the significance and value of this great penetrational medium from a sales promotion standpoint?

First, consider that TV station and network billings totalled nearly three billion dollars in 1970, according to an FCC report.

Add to this the fact that some national advertisers spend as much on TV advertising as on all other media combined.

Television lends itself to all types of promotion; alone, or in conjunction with other media. Its limitations are based on product restrictions, i.e., liquor, rather than any promotional considerations.

Television

* "Television's coverage pattern, often 100 miles or more in diameter, crosses political lines, and has led to sales areas defined by TV's contour. The advertiser has a map on which he has areas in which he knows his advertising pressure and can measure his sales results. TV contour maps have redesigned many companies' sales maps." So wrote a top executive of the Television Bureau of Advertising.

It has been fairly well established that the average family spends six hours and 20 minutes daily watching television. One authority points out that "the family spends more time before the TV set than in any other human activity, apart from working and sleeping."

Television advertising combines the elements of personal salesmanship: sight, sound, motion, and demonstration.

Its effectiveness, in addition to the size of the audience, is reflected in the fact that the 100 largest advertisers in the nation spend more on television than on all other advertising media combined!

The executive vice president of the second largest user of TV advertising says "television is obviously the most efficient way of reaching the most people at the lowest cost."

Many people think of television broadcasting chiefly in terms of network programs, but the fact is that spot sales are almost equal in volume.

Television is now divided into several classifications.

The "all-channel law" which went into effect in May, 1964, made it illegal to manufacture sets which could not tune to all

82 channels—70 UHF and 12 VHF channels. This was done to meet the need for more stations, which could only find room on the UHF band.

In some markets, UHF is the basic form of television. In others, VHF has come in as competition to established VHF stations. Still other markets have no UHF at all. The advertiser would do well, therefore, to avoid artificial classifications based on the TV spectrum and to concentrate on television as a medium for market coverage.

Another rapidly growing field is Community Antenna television, better known as CATV, which receives programs and distributes them to homes by wire on a subscription basis.

The number of homes on cable TV is expanding by 16% a year and by 1985, it is expected that, if this rate continues, more than one half of all U.S. homes will have CATV.

What CATV viewers see is "monitor" quality reproduction on TV screens in homes, apartments, and business offices subscribing to one of the wire-TV services.

CATV early growth was in areas beyond the reach of normal TV broadcasts. There were two million such CATV homes that had to be cable-fed. However, a wired-TV development in New York is different in that it is designed to give better reception in homes that already get TV. There is the possibility of other TV services becoming available. For example, since the wires can carry all kinds of data, they could provide a direct line for ordering merchandise which would be exhibited on the TV screen. The system could be a means of exhibiting credit cards by remote control in making actual purchases.

A wired home could become a subscriber to a pay-TV system which broadcasts unsponsored shows.

In an address at a meeting of the Television Bureau in Chicago, James Landon, Director of Research, Cox Broadcasting Company, said:

"Cable television has hardly scratched the surface, with about 14 million U.S. homes currently wired, representing $33\frac{1}{3}\%$ of all TV households. The impact of cable on the broadcasting business in the 80's will depend on the extent of CATV growth, and CATV growth in turn will depend primarily on government regulation. If the government opens the door for cable, it will expand rapidly, because the affluent consumer will seek quality reception and program variety.

"If government continues to control the growth of cable in the 80's, CATV will not offer significant competition to the broadcaster. The cable operator will not be able to afford attractive programming, circulation will be low and he will sell his advertising to specialized segments.

"If cable is free to expand rapidly, and begins to exceed 50% penetration in metropolitan areas, local TV stations might find a new competitor in the arena. The cable operator enjoying 50% or better penetration in a major market could be in a position to buy the same film packages, syndicated and sporting events as the local stations and conceivably could run an independent TV station on his local origination channel, pulling substantial revenue from both subscribers and advertisers.

"UHF on the TV side and FM on the radio side will no doubt enjoy significant growth in the 80's. Since FM is a superior service to AM, as more FM stations go on the air and more FM sets are purchased, the majority of listening is likely to swing to the FM side, possibly driving the weaker AM stations off the air."

Radio

It was estimated that the total number of homes with one or more radio sets totalled more than 150 million in 1980. In addition, very few cars or trucks are sold without radio equipment. Considering how people use portables on the street, at work, on the beach and in boats, it may truly be said that radio follows the listener.

Retailers make good use of radio commercials, whether FM or AM. Many FM stations, particularly, rely largely on retail advertising and many dealers use FM broadcasting because they have found that, with lower rates and local coverage, they obtain results.

Transit Advertising

Many companies have found transit advertising to be an effective, low-cost medium, particularly in metropolitan areas. The Transit Advertising Association emphasizes that transit ads reach a mass audience, have high repetitive value, offer maximum flexibility, geographic selectivity, and unlimited use of color.

Transit advertising is carried by more than 66,000 vehicles (buses, subways, elevated and commuter trains) throughout U.S. urban areas. According to a Sindlinger & Company survey, nearly 14 million persons ride transit in a single day. Transit advertising builds its mass audience fast, because by the end of the month, 400 million different people have used public transportation.

Four groups of national advertisers—producers of alcoholic beverages, foods and confections, tobacco, and pharmaceuticals —dominate the transit medium's top 50 advertisers. The five largest advertisers account for 18.6% of the medium's total revenue. They are: Wm. Wrigley Jr. Co., American Home Products, Schieffelin & Co., General Motors Corporation, and Joseph E. Seagram & Sons. Completing the top ten, in descending order by expenditure, are: Liggett & Myers Tobacco Company, R. J. Reynolds Tobacco Company, Pepsi-Cola Company, Bristol-Myers Company, and P. Lorillard Company.

Aside from the 36 advertisers in the four dominant groups, the 14 other corporate advertisers in the top 50 come from these categories: three in theatrical enterprises, two each in automotive products and toiletries, and one each in packaging, utilities, insurance, home instruction, insecticides, cosmetics, and financial institutions.

A market study by the Alfred Politz organization for O'Ryan & Batchelder, a member firm of the Transit Advertising Association, found that in Chicago an advertisement placed on 300 king-size bus posters produced 33.9 million exposures each month, at a cost of 33 cents per thousand. These posters (2½ by 12 feet) placed on Chicago Transit Authority buses deliver 1,130,000 exposures an average day.

Another measure of transit ads on the *outside* of buses by A. C. Nielsen Company was supplied by a pilot study in Los Angeles. The study indicated that, over seven consecutive days, 93% of adults encountered an average of 29 buses and could see 51 sides of advertising on the buses with proper visibility. A showing on the 1,300 buses in the area offers a potential seven-day cumulative reach of 93% and a frequency potential of 29 times.

Some years ago, the Johnson & Lewis Advertising Agency of San Francisco mapped out a campaign for River Valley Frozen Foods based on market data supplied by Fielder, Sorensen & Davis, transit advertising company for the area.

Two factors led to the choice of transit as the sole medium for the campaign. First, market statistics indicated that a high percentage of San Francisco's population used the transit system. (The Sindlinger Study confirmed this by showing that 25% of the Bay Area population used transit.) Second, River Valley's distributor, the Langfield Co., had only a small amount of money to devote to promotion.

The FS&D survey revealed that the average rider notices five cards on each trip and that he spends from a minute to a minute and a half reading each of them. It was this bit of information that led to a distinctive and successful all-copy campaign—a complete departure from the theory that car-card advertising—like billboards—must be in poster form. Since no other medium was used, a six-fold sales increase certainly was evidence of the effectiveness of transit advertising.

Outdoor Bulletins and Displays

The advantage of outdoor advertising is that it permits a strategic use of the appropriation. By picking outdoor locations in the vicinity of important stores it is often possible to bring sufficient pressure to bear upon a merchant to force him to carry the advertiser's products. Similarly, a painted bulletin on the side of a store handling the advertised product has a long life and assures a demand for that product at the point of purchase. An excellent example of what can be done by the use of outdoor advertising, particularly well-placed, painted and lithographed bulletins, is seen in the amazing growth of Coca-Cola, whose sales have steadily increased during the depression and even after the repeal of prohibition. This advertiser, like Wrigley, is also a large user of transit advertising.

Outdoor advertising lends itself especially well to products for home use since the bulletins are read by all members of the family. Soap manufacturers spend a large share of their appropriations for outdoor bulletins because, in addition to reaching the woman of the home as she drives by in her car, they also reach the no less important domestic help whose likes and dislikes influence many a soap order. Outdoor advertising is less expensive than most other forms of advertising, due to its long life. It has proved particularly effective in securing zone distribution for automotive products. A single painted bulletin or poster well placed on an automobile highway will, in the course of a year, be read by practically every motorist in a locality.

Point of Purchase

Akin in importance to outdoor bulletins are window displays, store signs, counter displays, and hangers which manufacturers furnish to dealers. There is a tendency to appropriate an increasingly large percentage of the total appropriation for this sort of advertising, because it puts the advertising pressure at the point of purchase. They suggest other needs to the person coming into the store to make a casual purchase. They also tie up the acceptance which national advertising has created in the consumer's mind for the product.

A common criticism of point-of-purchase advertising is that much of it is wasted. This may be true of the mediocre displays which crudely shout the praises of products which dealers are not particularly interested in pushing, but it certainly does not apply to displays which are properly designed and painstakingly distributed. The most successful current displays are those which share their advertising with the dealer and do not try to hog all the space for the manufacturer. After all, it is the dealer's store and you cannot blame him if he would rather use his wall and counter space for advertising his store than your products.

Films for Promotion

As with radio and television, trends in the use of motion-picture films for sales promotion are too variable to pin down in a book. Advertising film trailers are acceptable, as this is being written, only in the smaller community theaters; yet the industry-wide promotional film is on the ascendancy.

The latter are films which carry no single-company identification, but tell the story—usually in a "from-earliest-times-to-present" treatment—of a certain product, as in the story of the discovery and development of paper, glass, steel, etc. Combined live action and artwork, in natural color, and as dramatic action as can be developed, are the usual pattern for these films, which are handled in a narrative-travelog fashion and made as "uncommercial" as possible.

Promotional films for free showings to clubs, societies, and schools are innumerable, as are commercials developed for special groups, as in the pharmaceutical industry for showing to medical meetings. It requires considerable skill to develop such films in such a way as to avoid either boredom, through a heavy-handed "product" story, or oversubtlety which loses all promotional impact. Therefore, until the promotion practitioner has had considerable experience in the preparation of such films, it is wise to secure the assistance of professional film experts.

Telephone and City Directories

The need of making nationally advertised products easily available to consumers, by telling them where the brand may be purchased *locally,* is most important. It is of little avail to create national acceptance for a product, and then lose a large share of the resulting demand by lack of dealer identification. While local newspaper advertising by the distributor or manufacturer, or both, bridges this gap to some extent, the life of such advertising is short. To provide a year-round reference, many national advertisers employ such media as the telephone Yellow Pages (which list local outlets for nationally advertised products), neighborhood telephone directories, and city directories. Such advertising is not expensive and it has a definite reference value when an advertised product is marketed selectively, or through exclusive dealers.

Advertising Specialties

While not one of the major media for creating consumer acceptance, the distribution of books of matches, playing cards, calendars, souvenir post cards, key rings, pencils, and similar specialties are important in building consumer good will. However, much of their value depends upon the manner in which they are distributed. Some companies, for example, find it profitable to pass specialties out at state and county fairs, trade shows, conventions, and similar affairs. Others furnish them in quantities to dealers and let the dealer's salespeople hand them to consumers. If the person passing out the novelty speaks a good word for the product or the company at the same time, this plan is especially effective. Another use for this type of consumer advertising is to mail it to select lists, either directly from the manufacturer or pay the dealer to mail it to his lists. Style books, recipe books, and similar promotional materials are usually distributed in that way.

Some manufacturers require dealers to supply a list of their customers to whom such literature is to be mailed, and ask the dealer to pay the mailing costs or at least the postage. In such cases the literature is imprinted with the dealer's name and address. It establishes a local point of distribution. Celluloid pocket calendars, a popular advertising specialty, are sometimes mailed to stockholders with their January dividend checks. Swift & Company has followed this plan for many years and stockholders look forward to receiving these useful reminders each year. (See also Chapter 25, "Specialties for Increasing Sales.")

Agency's Experience with Media

Unless a sales manager has had wide experience with buying consumer advertising, it is best for him to confine himself to deciding upon the markets to be covered and to depend upon an advertising agency or advertising counsel to make specific recommendations as to media. Buying advertising space in consumer publications is a business in itself. While it has been greatly simplified and standardized since the formation of the Audit Bureau of Circulations, it still presents many pitfalls.

PPG glass reflects the beauty of saving energy.

Crowning jewel of the renaissance of downtown Los Angeles is the dramatic new Bonaventure Hotel, a vibrant architectural statement from an exciting city.

Its centerpiece is a gleaming 35-floor cylinder with four connecting towers. The entire structure wears a skin of 310,000 square feet of Solarcool® Bronze reflective glass, the largest application of this glass in the world.

But spectacular appearance is not the only reason for using

Solarcool Bronze glass. Its ability to reduce solar heat gain is the ingredient that makes such a lavish design statement so practical in the warm Southern California climate.

Making glass play more than its conventional role is PPG's way of doing business. We take the products we know best in chemicals, glass, fiber glass, coatings and resins and improve them through research and manufacturing so that their value and usefulness to our customers are increased.

For a multi-industry company, it's a great way to grow.

PPG Industries, Inc., One Gateway Center, Pittsburgh, Pa. 15222.

PPG: a Concern for the Future

PPG
INDUSTRIES

PPG Industries, Inc., a multi-industry company, tells its story to consumers in this attractive, attention-getting advertisement which appeared in TIME.

"Scented" Advertising: A brochure by the 3M Company includes samples of its Microfragrance products. They enable consumers actually to smell the scent of food and cosmetics in advertising and promotional literature.

Important Copyright Laws of the United States

¶102. Subject matter of copyright: In general

Copyright protection subsists, in accordance with this title, in original works of authorship fixed in any tangible medium of expression, now known or later developed, from which they can be perceived, reproduced or otherwise communicated, either directly or with the aid of a machine or device. Works of authorship include the following categories:

    (1) literary works;
    (2) musical works, including any accompanying words;
    (3) dramatic works, including any accompanying music;
    (4) pantomimes and choreographic works;
    (5) pictorial, graphic and sculptural works;
    (6) motion pictures and other audiovisual works; and
    (7) sound recordings.

¶302. Duration of copyright: Works created on or after January 1, 1978

(a) In General.—Copyright in a work created on or after January 1, 1978 subsists from its creation and, except as provided by the following subsections, endures for a term consisting of the life of the author and fifty years after the author's death.

(b) Joint Works.—In the case of a joint work prepared by two or more authors who did not work for hire, the copyright endures for a term consisting of the life of the last surviving author and fifty years after such last surviving author's death.

¶303. Duration of copyright: Works created but not published or copyrighted before January 1, 1978.

Copyright in a work created before January 1, 1978 but not theretofore in the public domain or copyrighted, subsists from January 1, 1978, and endures for the term provided by Section 302. In no case, however, shall the term copyright in such a work expire before December 31, 2002; and, if the work is published on or before December 31, 2002 the term of copyright shall not expire before December 31, 2027.

¶304. Duration of copyright: Subsisting copyrights

(a) Copyrights In their first term on January 1, 1978.—Any copyright, the first term of which is subsisting on January 1, 1978, shall endure for twenty-eight years from the date it was originally secured with certain limitations.

¶305. Duration of copyright: Terminal Date

All terms of copyright provided by Sections 302 through 304 run to the end of the calendar year in which they would otherwise expire.

¶401. Notice of copyright: Visually perceptible copies

(a) General Requirement.—Whenever a work protected under this title is published in the United States or elsewhere by authority of the copyright owner, a notice of copyright as provided by this section shall be placed on all publicly distributed copies from which the work can be visually perceived, either directly or with the aid of a machine or device.

(b) Form of Notice.—The notice appearing on all copies shall consist of the following three elements:

    (1) the symbol © (the letter C in a circle), or the word "Copyright," or the abbreviation "Copr."; and

    (2) the year of first publication of the work; in the case of compilations or derivative works incorporating previously published material, the year date of first publication of the compilation or derivative work is sufficient. The year date may be omitted where a pictorial, graphic or sculptural work, with accompanying text matter, if any, is reproduced in or on greet-

ing cards, postcards, stationery, jewelry, dolls, toys or any useful articles; and

(3) the name of the owner of copyright in the work, or an abbreviation by which the name can be recognized, or a generally known alternative designation of the owner.

(c) Position of Notice.—The notice shall be affixed to the copies in such manner and location as to give reasonable notice of the claim of copyright. The Register of Copyrights shall prescribe by regulation, as examples, specific methods of affixation and positions of the notice on various types of works that will satisfy this requirement, but these specifications shall not be considered exhaustive.

¶407. Deposit of copies or phonorecords for Library of Congress

(a) Except as provided by Subsection (c), and subject to the provisions of Subsection (e), the owner of copyright or of the exclusive right of publication in a work published with notice of copyright in the United States shall deposit, within three months after the date of such publication—

(1) two complete copies of the best edition: or

(2) if the work is a sound recording, two complete phonorecords of the best edition, together with any printed or other visually perceptible material published with such phonorecords.

Neither the deposit requirements of this Subsection nor the acquisition provisions of Subsection (e) are conditions of copyright protection.

(b) The required copies or phonorecords shall be deposited in the Copyright Office for the use or disposition of the Library of Congress. The Register of Copyrights shall, when requested by the depositor and upon payment of a fee, issue a receipt for the deposit.

¶409. Application for copyright registration

The application for copyright registration shall be made on a form prescribed by the Register of Copyrights and shall include—

(1) the name and address of the copyright claimant;

(2) in the case of a work other than an anonymous or pseudonymous work, the name and nationality or domicile of the author or authors, and, if one or more of the authors is dead, the dates of their deaths;

(3) if the work is anonymous or pseudonymous, the nationality or domicile of the author or authors;

(4) in the case of a work made for hire, a statement to this effect;

(5) if the copyright claimant is not the author, a brief statement of how the claimant obtained ownership of the copyright;

(6) the title of the work, together with any previous or alternative titles under which the work can be identified;

(7) the year in which creation of the work was completed;

(8) if published before, the date and nation of its first publication;

(9) in the case of a compilation or derivative work, an identification of any preexisting work or works that it is based on or incorporates, and a brief, general statement of the additional material covered by the copyright claim being registered;

(10) in the case of a published work containing material of which copies are required to be manufactured in the United States, the names of the persons or organizations who performed the processes specified by with respect to that material, and the places where those processes were performed; and

(11) any other information regarded by the Register of Copyrights as bearing upon the preparation or identification of the work or the existence, ownership or duration of the copyright.

Chapter 20

TRADE AND TECHNICAL
ADVERTISING/PROMOTION

SALES promotion depends upon trade and technical advertising to reach specialized markets with a specialized sales appeal. Its influence is very largely concentrated in industrial and mercantile centers and is directed at the individual buyer or an industrial or mercantile unit, rather than broad groups of consumers as is the case of consumer advertising. It renders a highly important service to national consumer advertising, but it is a service which is largely supplementary or auxiliary. The principal media used in connection with this kind of advertising are business papers (sometimes erroneously referred to as "trade papers"), direct-mail, trade directories, and general reference advertising.

Why do industrial producers of raw materials and industrial products spend so many millions of dollars in trade and technical advertising? The answer is that the cost of reaching prospective buyers is lessened by advertising. Many companies have tried to determine the cost of a salesman's call and several publishing and research organizations, including Dartnell, have tried to come up with dependable answers. The latest Dartnell estimate is that it costs approximately $106.91 for a sales rep to call on a prospective buyer. Thus, an advertisement may deliver a sales message to several thousand readers at the approximate cost of a single personal call. An added advantage is that advertising paves the way for the salesman by making the company and its products familiar to the buyer in advance and, if the advertising is scheduled on a more or less regular basis in leading industry magazines, builds a certain degree of confidence in the company in the mind of the buyer.

In selling to specialized markets, business magazines, including industrial and trade papers, constitute a main promotional channel. *Bacon's Publicity Checker* lists almost 4000 publications, not counting newspapers, and about half of them cover all the various segments of business and industry. The remainder consist of professional, farm and general-interest magazines.

Although trade and technical magazines are important to advertisers, one sometimes hears the opinion that they do not always receive the best attention of some advertising agencies. If true, the reason is purely economic. Although the category is large, individual business publications do not offer the wide circulation to support advertising rates and agency commissions comparable to those of the mass circulation magazines. Their circulation is concentrated on readers who are potential buyers of the products advertised in each publication.

Due to the selective nature of the circulation of the better business papers published in trade and technical fields, the advertising rate per page per thousand circulation is much higher than in the case of general publications, although the rate per page due to the limitations on the number of subscribers a business paper needs to cover its field is less. The average rate for a well-edited business paper, which conforms to the standards of practice of the Associated Business Press (furnishing advertisers with verified circulation audits) is a few dollars per page more per thousand subscribers than the average rate in general publications for the same space. This higher milline rate reflects the cost of maintaining coverage in the industry or field where the publication circulates.

The circulation problem of a business paper is entirely different from that of a general magazine or even a class publication, since the emphasis is on quality of subscribers rather than quantity. Out of some 3,500 business papers published in the United States and Canada only about 10% subscribe to and conform to the standards of practice of the Associated Business Press, which puts the interests of the subscriber ahead of the interests of the advertiser.

How to Evaluate Tradepapers

An advertising executive at PPG Industries, Incorporated, was asked: "How do you evaluate tradepapers?" His reply:

"More or less in descending order of importance, here are our general criteria:

1. "Editorial content—Is it extensive, thorough and accurate; offering real substance for the intended audience?

2. "Readership—Is the book read and believed by the majority

of the audience? This is based both on readership studies and inquiries (coupons, bingo cards, personal observation).

3. "Advertising lineage—Valuable insight is gained from three standpoints: Is the book currently financially healthy? Is it growing or dying? How do your peers regard it? The latter point is essentially more than "monkey see—monkey do." If a substantial percentage of logical "blue chip" advertisers aren't buying the book—there could be a reason.

4. "Demographics—This is not as critical under controlled circulation, but certainly still a necessary base to cover."

Many books that qualify according to these criteria never get bought, however, usually for budgetary or special reasons. There may be other situations, at the "tie-breaker" or "nitty-gritty" stages. These involve:

1. "The Space Rep—Is he knowledgeable about the industry and dedicated? Does he make calls; bring market data to the party; and report industry developments?

2. "Publication Services (The Rep's backup support)
   a. Newsletter—Regular periodical that delivers good marketing facts in a crisp, entertaining, telegraphic style.
   b. Direct Mail—Occasional mailings delivering good market data or statistics (with the media pitch low key). Chest thumping and "grandest tiger in the jungle mailings" may produce negative reactions.
   c. Personal liaison—Setting up conferences with editors and other staffers who may have information at their disposal of value to the advertiser.
   d. Merchandising Aids—Ideas and assistance that are fresh and pertinent."

Penetrating the Market

Getting a new account or making a large sale usually involves many people. There is the person who places the order, possibly the purchasing agent, upon whom the salesman calls. Then there is the person who requisitions the material or service. He may be one of several supervisors or department managers. There are, in the case of some plants, the persons who will use the material. And lastly, and very importantly, there is the executive who may have to O.K. the order before it can clear the purchasing department. To reach and influence all these people is a major problem in sales promotion. It is a job that business papers do especially well.

By checking the markets a sales promotional activity is designed to reach, with business papers which cover them to best advantage, it is often possible to greatly increase the results from a promotion. Advertising tying in with the promotion can be placed in business papers whose circulation is concentrated on these target groups, at a relatively low cost. Even though other ways may also be used to reach these groups, such as direct-mail, the double coverage

Which sealants give you more of what you're looking for?

Here are the facts:

Some Sealant Performance Characteristics

	Thiokol's Polysulfide	Competition A (1-part Silicone)	Competition B (1-part Acrylic Solvent Release)
Sealant movement capability	25%	20%	5%
Adhesion after water immersion to: Concrete Glass Aluminum	Excellent Excellent Excellent	Questionable Fair Questionable	Questionable Fair Questionable
Aging characteristics	None	None	Toughens
History of use in buildings	24 years	7 years	10 years
High temperature	Good	Excellent	Flows
Low temperature	Good	Excellent	Embrittles
Use where immersed in water	Yes	No	No
Dirt pickup after cure	None	Very bad	Very bad
Tear resistance	Good	Poor	Good

Compared with two leading competitive types of sealants, the Thiokol polysulfide entry wins in a breeze.

It's not surprising. Besides having a track record which includes the longest period of successful use, sealants based on Thiokol's LP polysulfide polymer are constantly tested to assure topnotch performance.

Under our exclusive Seal of Security program, polysulfide-based sealants are regularly checked to meet rigid specifications. In fact, our technicians and chemists check more than 200 samples every year.

The check consists of a series of tough tests, ranging from four to six weeks. Samples are tortured, twisted, stretched, heated and frozen to make sure they can survive what the ele-

ments dish out over long periods of time.

If the sealant passes each and every test, then it's entitled to bear Thiokol's Seal of Security. We're proud of this program. It's the first of its kind in the United States. And, since its inception in 1965, more than 300 sealants, produced by 20 manufacturers, have earned the right to carry the seal.

Insist on sealants with the Thiokol Seal of Security and you can't go wrong. For a more detailed comparison between polysulfide-based sealants and eight other types write: Thiokol Chemical Corporation, P.O. Box 1296, Trenton, N.J. 08607.

Thiokol

A widely-held view is that technical advertisements must give readers facts and figures to be effective. This ad by Thiokol Chemical Corporation presents the facts about its sealing products in a neat, orderly, easy-to-read style.

obtained through business paper advertising assures deeper penetration of the largest and most important companies, which as a rule buy about 70% of what is sold to an industry. A weakness in sales promotional planning is failure to spread the appropriation on the basis of buying importance. A one-shot promotional effort may be all right for the one-man plant, but it would hardly do a job on the General Electric Company or International Harvester.

This matter of adequate penetration is especially important in selling to industry. In a large industrial operation, where a company has several plants in various localities, it is difficult to maintain a reliable mailing list of the "men to see." Your own salesmen may not be seeing the right people. They may be calling on the purchasing agent, when the man who initiates the order is the refrigeration engineer or some other person not available to the salesman. Then, too, personnel changes are numerous these days. This is especially true of the larger companies. Technical papers going into these establishments, even though directed to a certain individual, have a way of circulating through the department or plant, so that your message finds its way into the hands of everyone who is interested enough in his job to keep posted on new developments.

Buying Influence of Trade Papers

Several years ago, E. I. du Pont de Nemours & Co., Inc., polled a list of 16,841 customers, suppliers, and selected industrial buyers to determine which type of sales promotion and advertising influenced purchases in their establishments.

Nearly all Du Pont customers and prospects look to some printed source, the survey disclosed, when attempting to locate general information about industrial supplies and equipment. Trade and technical publications were mentioned by 79%; manufacturers' catalogs, 60%; and direct mail, 50%. About 73% mentioned manufacturer's men as an important source of information.

As to reading of ads in trade and technical publications, only 4 of the 1,420 said they never read them and only 20 said they seldom read them. On a question of whether information contained in a manufacturer's advertising is valuable in the respondent's work, 89% said yes. Helpfulness of the manufacturer's advertising in discussing the advertised product with a salesman was affirmed by 86%.

On the degree of influence exerted on buying decisions, 52.5% classified themselves as a direct influence on purchase of materials or ingredients. Direct or indirect influence, or both, was asserted by 80.5% of all the respondents.

Direct influence on purchase of operating supplies was indicated by 46.7%, indirect influence by 25.8%. Direct influence on plant and production equipment purchases was reported by 39.5%, indirect influence by 32%.

The fact that 79% of those replying to the questionnaire stated they read trade and technical publications to obtain information about materials and products they were interested in purchasing, pretty well explodes any lingering, mistaken ideas businessmen may have about the buying influence of these media.

Picking a List of Business Papers

A well-edited business or technical publication has a definite place in the sales promotion plan because it helps to create acceptance for the products advertised in it. For example, most business papers publish articles which assist subscribers to reduce costs. It is for such articles that businessmen buy business papers. They do not buy them to be entertained or amused, but for ideas which help them to be more successful. Therefore the readers of a business paper read, and pass along to their associates, articles which bear upon current management problems. Since companies making equipment or accessories for use in the industry usually sell them on the basis of cost-cutting ability, those who advertise in business papers reap the benefit of the "spade work" done by the editor. The articles on cutting costs by modernizing the plant or office alert the reader to the advantages of better equipment and make him more receptive to the advertiser's message.

This plowing of the ground, which every business paper does to some extent, has an important relation to its value as an advertising medium. It is quite as important as coverage, the number of subscribers, or even the cost per page. It is conceivable that a business paper with 5,000 carefully picked, and well-conditioned subscribers might be a better buy at the same page rate, than a business paper with 10,000 subscribers who are not so carefully selected and only superficially conditioned.

The shrewd advertiser in business papers therefore judges a medium by the character of its editorial contents rather than by its circulation statement. Above all, he wants to place his advertising in publications which are helping him to promote the sale of the kind of products he sells. But at the same time, he turns thumbs down on papers which make it a practice to publish "puffs" about certain products in their editorial columns. A business paper which stoops to that method of attracting advertising soon loses the confidence of its readers, and any business paper which has not the reader's confidence is a poor advertising medium. It is like employing a salesman whom customers do not trust.

In this ad for Delco Bearings, the company offers to conduct in-plant seminars and a programmed learning course to help manufacturers solve bearing applications and engineering problems. The advertisement ran in such publications as Iron Age, Plant Engineering, Power Transmission Design and several others.

Courtesy: Campbell-Ewald Co.

Another good way to test the value of a business paper as an advertising medium is to carefully check the way it gets its circulation. The most responsive circulation is usually that which is sold by mail without any special inducements.

Advertising to Help Salesmen

The greatest returns from trade and technical advertising are the reductions effected in the cost of selling, especially the cost of employing salesmen. It requires less sales effort to obtain interviews and orders for a company or a product which is well and favorably known than one which is not well known or, perhaps, unfavorably known to the prospective buyer. The rising costs of utilizing salesmen make this a matter of growing concern in sales management. Among the ways well-planned trade and technical advertising help a salesman are:

1. Paving the way for salesmen's calls by educating the prospect in advance.
2. Obtaining direct inquiries for salesmen to follow up.
3. Confirming salesmen's verbal statements with printed statements from the company.
4. Multiplying a salesman's contacts.
5. Introducing and "building up" the salesman in advance of his calls.
6. Training salesmen in the most effective selling procedure.
7. Stimulating effort through special drives and contests.
8. Pre-establishing and ensuring the company's leadership.
9. Supplying selling ideas that make interviews more productive.
10. Facilitating the supervision of salesmen.
11. Providing regular sources of inspiration and instruction.
12. Promoting sales meetings and conventions.
13. Attracting the highest type of salesmen.
14. Assisting salesmen to concentrate on their best prospects and customers.

Advertising to Strengthen Dealer Relations

In the same way advertising in influential business papers, which reach all factors in the distribution of a product for resale, cuts the cost of maintaining the dealer organization. Such advertising is both informative and stimulative. While it is true not all dealers read business papers as faithfully as industrial executives, reader surveys show that most merchants and executives of mercantile establishments which do the bulk of the business, and are therefore all-important to the manufacturer, depend upon trade publications for new merchandising ideas and trade news. Some of the ways advertising in trade papers helps dealer relations are:

1. Obtaining new dealers.
2. Acquainting dealers with selling points of the product.
3. Providing dealers with merchandising plans and ideas.
4. Selling the advertising program to dealers.
5. Educating retail clerks in better selling methods.
6. Inquiries from national advertising for local dealers to follow up.
7. Explaining house policies which safeguard the dealers' interests.
8. Giving distributors' salesmen helpful facts and suggestions which they can pass along to dealers.
9. Furnishing ideas for windows and store displays.
10. Advisory assistance in matters of advertising, collection, financing, etc.
11. Promoting contests among dealers and clerks.
12. Promoting traveling exhibits, merchandise shows and other affairs in dealers' communities.

Promoting a Booklet on the Air

To stimulate store traffic for its dealers, RCA provided them with radio scripts for local broadcasting, featuring a free booklet on how and when to use batteries. To obtain the booklet, prospective buyers and interested listeners had to visit the dealers' stores. Following is one of the 60-second scripts:

"When you're spending money for batteries for your radio, tape recorder, camera, toy—or whatever—may we make a suggestion? Ask yourself this question. Which one is my best battery buy? The correct answer may save you money . . . and give you more satisfaction for your battery operated device.

"You see, there are a number of battery systems made today. Some work better in light-drain uses—others in high-drain uses. Some don't last too long in high temperatures (like on the beach), others excel in the cold. In short, there's a *right* battery for your *specific* application, need for convenience, amount of money you should spend.

"There's a useful booklet, prepared by RCA, which will give you an insight to the merits of the major battery systems. Why not drop in for a free copy or discuss your needs with us:
(dealer name and address)

"Ask the expert. We're strong in electronics! Like RCA and RCA Batteries."

TRADE AND TECHNICAL ADVERTISING/PROMOTION

Supporting Consumer Advertising

There is a growing practice on the part of national advertisers to spend a large proportion of their total appropriations for advertising in business papers and in mail campaigns to carefully selected lists. Prior to the war there was a theory, frequently voiced by advertising space salesmen, that if the appropriation in general mediums was large enough, supplementary advertising to the trade was unnecessary. The dealers would see the ads in the consumer publications anyway. This theory has been exploded. The success attained by general magazines, such as *Vogue*, which issued special "trade editions" designed to acquaint dealers with the national advertising support being given to products sold over their counters has been notable. It showed that national advertising to consumers could be made more effective when those responsible for the resale of the product were informed in advance about the consumer campaign. So today increasing attention is being given to "merchandising the advertising" through the use not only of trade papers, but direct mail to lists of dealers and prospective dealers. The importance of reaching down into large mercantile establishments is so great, that both mediums are required to obtain "saturation." The former practice of depending entirely upon salesmen to do that job has been found too costly. It can be done better and cheaper through advertising, and allowing salesmen to devote all their time to actual selling.

Among the ways which supplementary advertising of this sort increases the results of national consumer advertising are:

1. Republishing newspaper and magazine advertisements with suitable explanations.

2. Typing up local advertising with national advertising.

3. Giving radio advertising trade support.

4. Converting advertising inquiries into sales.

5. Teaching distributors how to merchandise the advertising in store displays.

6. Teaching dealers how to capitalize on the advertising through local direct-mail campaigns.

7. Stimulating trade inquiries by offering educational booklets and folders.

8. Engaging the merchandising cooperation of newspapers, magazines, radio stations, poster plants, etc.

9. Following up dealers about inquiries.

10. Gathering facts, testimonials, etc., to use in advertising.

Ask the Expert!

Ad Repro Sheet

1P1440

RCA
Batteries

Ask the Expert!

When you're spending money for batteries for your radio, tape recorder, camera, toy—or whatever—may we make a suggestion? Ask yourself this question. Which one is my best battery buy? The correct answer may save you money...and give you more satisfaction from your battery-operated device.

You see, there are a number of battery systems made today. Some work better in light-drain uses, others in high-drain uses. Some don't last too long in high temperatures (like on the beach), others excel in the cold. In short, there's a *right* battery for your *specific* application, need for convenience, amount of money you should spend.

There's a useful booklet, prepared by RCA, which will give you an insight to the merits of the major battery systems. Why not drop in for a free copy or discuss your needs with us:

(Dealer Name and Address)

Ask the Expert.
We're strong in Electronics!
Like RCA and
RCA Batteries.

1 Col. x 9"

which one is your best battery buy?

Ask the expert!

(Dealer Name and Address)

RCA
Batteries

2 Cols. x 5"

RCA
Batteries

Which one is your best buy?
Ask the Expert

(Dealer Name and Address)

1 Col. x 2"

RCA
Batteries

Ask the Expert!

Did you know there's a *right* battery for your *specific* battery-operated device ...the way you use it...the amount of money you should spend?

Ask us to help you select the proper battery system for your radio, tape recorder, camera, toys—whatever.

(Dealer Name and Address)

Ask the expert. **We're strong in electronics!** Like RCA and RCA Batteries.

(3 Col. x 4")

As part of its dealer-aid program, RCA supplies retailers with a variety of ad mats featuring the theme: "Ask the Expert."

Copy for Business Papers

One of the reasons that some advertisers are not getting better results from the money they invest in trade and technical advertising is poor copy. The specialized nature of business papers calls for the use of equally specialized advertising copy. It should be aimed specifically at the executives or individuals who subscribe to the paper to provide them with trade and technical information they cannot obtain in general magazines. It should, therefore, adhere to the editorial policy of each particular business paper the advertiser uses. It should be written by technicians who understand the problems of these readers. It should be specific and factual, taking up where the editorial content of the publication leaves off. In other words, the editor of a business paper plows the field for the sales seeds which the advertising sows. The editorial columning of the business paper conditions the reader to receive and act upon the buying suggestions he finds in the publication's advertising columns.

Many of the large advertisers, for that reason, prepare their own advertising copy for use in trade and technical publications, General Electric Company being a case in point. On the other hand, there has been a tendency for some of the better advertising agencies to install departments for the preparation of specialized advertising copy. Such commissions as the agency may receive from publishers are credited against a flat fee. Other advertisers find it advantageous to have their trade and technical advertising copy prepared by an agency specializing in mercantile and industrial fields. The relatively small billings from business papers, compared to general media make this service unattractive to most advertising agencies. Their profits in the main come from business placed with publications having rates substantially higher than those of most business and technical publications.

The most effective copy for use in trade and technical papers aims to establish the advertiser as headquarters for a specific product or service. It usually has a strong "how" or testimonial appeal. Its purpose is to condition the field or market covered by a particular publication to accept the advertiser's products; thus breaking down sales resistance for the advertiser's salesmen and reaching down into a buying unit to influence the various individuals who have a voice in getting the product specified. While the salesman may secure the actual order from the purchasing agent, it is highly important to reach all those in the field who initiate orders. For example, in marketing a machine tool if acceptance for a particular tool has been created throughout an industrial unit by well-planned advertising in publications read by the engineering, production, and purchasing personnel, as well as by top management, the salesman's work will be greatly reduced. Good advertising copy does that sort of market conditioning job. Inquiries, while important, are secondary to the value of the advertising from a prestige-building standpoint. That is why the practice of some advertisers, and of too many advertising agencies, of preparing one piece of copy and running it in a long list of assorted business papers is to be condemned. It is unfair to the agency preparing the copy, unfair to the advertiser, and unfair to the publications in which it is used.

The Amprobe Newsletter

Supplementing its trade paper advertising, Amprobe Instrument, Lynbrook, New York, issues a bi-monthly Newsletter, previously called "Sales Stimulator" to its electrical supply representatives and retailers. The Newsletter is published in the form of a four-page, two-color folder with an occasional insert when necessary. A feature of the Newsletter is the offer of $25 for "Application Tips" involving successful or unusual uses of Amprobe products. The folder includes product information, questions-and-answers and reproductions of company advertising. A recent issue contained an insert sheet with the heading "What's the Point in Point of Sale?" describing and illustrating its new poster frame and literature dispenser, incorporating a reply card for the sales aids. Periodically, the company also sends out inexpensively-produced, humorous memos with proofs of the latest Amprobe advertisements.

Modern-Age Opportunities

Developments in space-age technology, ecology and nuclear-power advances have created whole new fields for many industries and companies requiring far-seeing and immediate marketing strategies. While highly technical in basic concepts, companies in these fields require the full range of marketing and promotional skills with which to take advantage of current and future opportunities.

Nuclear power-generating facilities are spreading across the nation, government agencies and private organizations are focusing attention on ecological problems and integrated circuits have been given a tremendous boost toward their application to consumer products. Manufacturers, contractors, and related component suppliers may all benefit from these new services and products by their alertness to their marketing opportunities and their translation into promotional programs.

NUCLEAR POWER PLANTS IN THE U.S.

(Operating, under construction, planned)

SITE	PLANT NAME	CAPACITY (Net Kilowatts)	UTILITY	INITIAL DESIGN POWER
ALABAMA				
Decatur	Browns Ferry Nuclear Power Plant: Unit 1	1,065,000	Tennessee Valley Authority	1972
Decatur	Browns Ferry Nuclear Power Plant: Unit 2	1,065,000	Tennessee Valley Authority	1973
Decatur	Browns Ferry Nuclear Power Plant: Unit 3	1,065,000	Tennessee Valley Authority	1973
Dothan	Joseph M. Farley Nuclear Plant: Unit 1	829,000	Alabama Power Co.	1975
Dothan	Joseph M. Farley Nuclear Plant: Unit 2	829,000	Alabama Power Co.	1977
ARKANSAS				
Russellville	Arkansas Nuclear One: Unit 1	820,000	Arkansas Power & Light Co.	1973
Russellville	Arkansas Nuclear One: Unit 2	920,000	Arkansas Power & Light Co.	1975
CALIFORNIA				
Humboldt Bay	Humboldt Bay Power Plant: Unit 3	68,500	Pacific Gas and Electric Co.	1963
San Clemente	San Onofre Nuclear Generating Station: Unit 1	430,000	So. Calif. Ed. & San Diego Gas & El. Co.	1967
San Clemente	San Onofre Nuclear Generating Station: Unit 2	1,140,000	So. Calif. Ed. & San Diego Gas & El. Co.	—
San Clemente	San Onofre Nuclear Generating Station: Unit 3	1,140,000	So. Calif. Ed. & San Diego Gas & El. Co.	—
Diablo Canyon	Diablo Canyon Nuclear Power Plant: Unit 1	1,060,000	Pacific Gas and Electric Co.	1974
Diablo Canyon	Diablo Canyon Nuclear Power Plant: Unit 2	1,060,000	Pacific Gas and Electric Co.	1975
Clay Station	Rancho Seco Nuclear Generation Station	804,000	Sacramento Municipal Utility District	1973
Pt. Arena	Mendocino Power Plant: Unit 1	1,128,000	Pacific Gas & Electric Co.	1978
Pt. Arena	Mendocino Power Plant: Unit 2	1,128,000	Pacific Gas & Electric Co.	1979
COLORADO				
Platteville	Ft. St. Vrain Nuclear Generating Station	330,000	Public Service Co. of Colorado	1972
CONNECTICUT				
Haddam Neck	Haddam Neck Plant	575,000	Conn. Yankee Atomic Power Co.	1967
Waterford	Millstone Nuclear Power Station: Unit 1	652,100	Northeast Utilities	1970
Waterford	Millstone Nuclear Power Station: Unit 2	828,000	Northeast Utilities	1974
DELEWARE				
•	Delmarva Unit 1	770,000	Delmarva Power & Light Co.	1979
•	Delmarva Unit 2	770,000	Delmarva Power & Light Co.	1982
FLORIDA				
Turkey Point	Turkey Point Station: Unit 3	693,000	Florida Power & Light Co.	1971
Turkey Point	Turkey Point Station: Unit 4	693,000	Florida Power & Light Co.	1972
Red Level	Crystal River Plant: Unit 3	825,000	Florida Power Corp.	1973
Red Level	Crystal River Plant: Unit 4	897,000	Florida Power Corp.	1978
Ft. Pierce	Hutchinson Island: Unit 1	800,000	Florida Power and Light Co.	1974
GEORGIA				
Baxley	Edwin I. Hatch Nuclear Plant: Unit 1	786,000	Georgia Power Co.	1973
Baxley	Edwin I. Hatch Nuclear Plant: Unit 2	786,000	Georgia Power Co.	1976
Hancock Landing	Alvin W. Vogtle, Jr. Plant: Unit 1	1,100,000	Georgia Power Co.	1978
Hancock Landing	Alvin W. Vogtle, Jr. Plant: Unit 2	1,100,000	Georgia Power Co.	1979
ILLINOIS				
Morris	Dresden Nuclear Power Station: Unit 1	200,000	Commonwealth Edison Co.	1960
Morris	Dresden Nuclear Power Station: Unit 2	809,000	Commonwealth Edison Co.	1970
Morris	Dresden Nuclear Power Station: Unit 3	809,000	Commonwealth Edison Co.	1971
Zion	Zion Nuclear Plant: Unit 1	1,050,000	Commonwealth Edison Co.	1972
Zion	Zion Nuclear Plant: Unit 2	1,050,000	Commonwealth Edison Co.	1973
Cordova	Quad-Cities Station: Unit 1	809,000	Comm. Ed. Co.-Ia.-Ill. Gas & Elec. Co.	1971
Cordova	Quad-Cities Station: Unit 2	809,000	Comm. Ed. Co.-Ia.-Ill. Gas & Elec. Co.	1972
Seneca	LaSalle Co. Nuclear Station: Unit 1	1,078,000	Comm. Ed. Co.-Ia.	1975
Seneca	LaSallé Co. Nuclear Station: Unit 2	1,078,000	Comm. Ed. Co.-Ia.	1976
•	—	1,100,000	Comm. Edison Co.	1978
•	—	1,100,000	Comm. Edison Co.	1979
INDIANA				
Dune Acres	Bailly Generating Station	660,000	Northern Indiana Public Service Co.	1976
IOWA				
Cedar Rapids	Duane Arnold Energy Center: Unit 1	529,700	Iowa Electric Light and Power Co.	1973
LOUISIANA				
Taft	Waterford Generating Station: Unit 1	1,165,000	Louisiana Power & Light Co.	1976

NUCLEAR POWER PLANTS IN THE U.S.

(Operating, under construction, planned)

SITE	PLANT NAME	CAPACITY (Net Kilowatts)	UTILITY	INITIAL DESIGN POWER
MAINE				
Wiscasset	Maine Yankee Atomic Power Plant	790,000	Maine Yankee Atomic Power Co.	1972
MARYLAND				
Lusby	Calvert Cliffs Nuclear Power Plant: Unit 1	845,000	Baltimore Gas and Electric Co.	1973
Lusby	Calvert Cliffs Nuclear Power Plant: Unit 2	845,000	Baltimore Gas and Electric Co.	1974
MASSACHUSETTS				
Rowe	Yankee Nuclear Power Station	175,000	Yankee Atomic Electric Co.	1961
Plymouth	Pilgrim Station	655,000	Boston Edison Co.	1972
MICHIGAN				
Big Rock Point	Big Rock Point Nuclear Plant	70,300	Consumers Power Co.	1963
South Haven	Palisades Nuclear Power Station	700,000	Consumers Power Co.	1971
Lagoona Beach	Enrico Fermi Atomic Power Plant: Unit 1	60,900	Detroit Edison Co.	1970
Lagoona Beach	Enrico Fermi Atomic Power Plant: Unit 2	1,123,000	Detroit Edison Co.	1974
Bridgman	Donald C. Cook Plant: Unit 1	1,054,000	Indiana & Michigan Electric Co.	1973
Bridgman	Donald C. Cook Plant: Unit 2	1,060,000	Indiana & Michigan Electric Co.	1974
Midland	Midland Nuclear Power Plant: Unit 1	492,000	Consumers Power Co.	1976
Midland	Midland Nuclear Power Plant: Unit 2	818,000	Consumers Power Co.	1977
MINNESOTA				
Monticello	Monticello Nuclear Generating Plant	545,000	Northern States Power Cc.	1971
Red Wing	Prairie Island Nuclear Generating Plant: Unit 1	530,000	Northern States Power Co.	1972
Red Wing	Prairie Island Nuclear Generating Plant: Unit 2	530,000	Northern States Power Co.	1974
NEBRASKA				
Fort Calhoun	Ft. Calhoun Station: Unit 1	457,400	Omaha Public Power District	1973
Brownville	Cooper Nuclear Station	778,000	Nebraska Public Power District and Iowa Power and Light Co.	1973
NEW JERSEY				
Toms River	Oyster Creek Nuclear Power Plant: Unit 1	650,000	Jersey Central Power & Light Co.	1969
Forked River	Forked River Generating Station: Unit 1	1,140,000	Jersey Central Power & Light Co.	1977
Salem	Salem Nuclear Generating Station: Unit 1	1,090,000	Public Service Electric and Gas, N. J.	1973
Salem	Salem Nuclear Generating Station: Unit 2	1,115,000	Public Service Electric and Gas, N. J.	1974
Bordentown	Newbold Nuclear Generating Station: Unit 1	1,088,000	Public Service Electric and Gas, N. J.	1975
Bordentown	Newbold Nuclear Generating Station: Unit 2	1,088,000	Public Service Electric and Gas, N. J.	1977
NEW YORK				
Indian Point	Indian Point Station: Unit 1	265,000	Consolidated Edison Co.	1963
Indian Point	Indian Point Station: Unit 2	873,000	Consolidated Edison Co.	1972
Indian Point	Indian Point Station: Unit 3	965,000	Consolidated Edison Co.	1973
Scriba	Nine Mile Point Nuclear Station: Unit 1	625,000	Niagara Mohawk Power Co.	1970
Scriba	Nine Mile Point Nuclear Station: Unit 2	1,100,000	Niagara Mohawk Power Co.	1977
Rochester	R. E. Ginna Nuclear Power Plant: Unit 1	420,000	Rochester Gas & Electric Co.	1970
Brookhaven	Shoreham Nuclear Power Station	819,000	Long Island Lighting Co.	1975
Lansing	Bell Station	838,000	New York State Electric & Gas Co.	1978
Verplanck	Con. Ed. Nuclear $=4$	1,115,000	Consolidated Edison Co.	1977
Scriba	James A. Fitzpatrick Nuclear Power Plant	821,000	Power Authority of State of N. Y.	1973
NORTH CAROLINA				
Southport	Brunswick Steam Electric Plant: Unit 1	821,000	Carolina Power and Light Co.	1975
Southport	Brunswick Steam Electric Plant: Unit 2	821,000	Carolina Power and Light Co.	1974
Cowans Ford Dam	Wm. B. McGuire Nuclear Station: Unit 1	1,150,000	Duke Power Co.	1975
Cowans Ford Dam	Wm. B. McGuire Nuclear Station: Unit 2	1,150,000	Duke Power Co.	1977
Bonsal	Shearon Harris Plant: Unit 1	915,000	Carolina Power & Light Co.	1977
Bonsal	Shearon Harris Plant: Unit 2	915,000	Carolina Power & Light Co.	1978
Bonsal	Shearon Harris Plant: Unit 3	915,000	Carolina Power & Light Co.	1979
Bonsal	Shearon Harris Plant: Unit 4	915,000	Carolina Power & Light Co.	1980
OHIO				
Oak Harbor	Davis-Besse Nuclear Power Station	872,000	Toledo Edison-Cleveland Electric Illuminating Co.	1974
Moscow	Wm. H. Zimmer Nuclear Power Station: Unit 1	810,000	Cincinnati Gas & Electric Co.	1974
OREGON				
Prescott	Trojan Station	1,130,000	Portland General Electric Co.	1974
PENNSYLVANIA				
Peach Bottom	Peach Bottom Atomic Power Station: Unit 1	40,000	Philadelphia Electric Co.	1967
Peach Bottom	Peach Bottom Atomic Power Station: Unit 2	1,065,000	Philadelphia Electric Co.	1973
Peach Bottom	Peach Bottom Atomic Power Station: Unit 3	1,065,000	Philadelphia Electric Co.	1974
Pottstown	Limerick Generating Station: Unit 1	1,065,000	Philadelphia Electric Co.	1975
Pottstown	Limerick Generating Station: Unit 2	1,065,000	Philadelphia Electric Co.	1977
Shippingport	Shippingport Atomic Power Station: Unit 1	90,000	Duquesne Light Co.	1957
Shippingport	Beaver Valley Power Station: Unit 1	847,000	Duquesne Light Co.-Ohio Edison Co.	1973
Shippingport	Beaver Valley Power Station: Unit 2	847,000	Duquesne Light Co.-Ohio Edison Co.	1978

NUCLEAR POWER PLANTS IN THE U.S.

(Operating, under construction, planned)

SITE	PLANT NAME	CAPACITY (Net Kilowatts)	UTILITY	INITIAL DESIGN POWER
PENNSYLVANIA				
Middletown	Three Mile Island Nuclear Station: Unit 1	831,000	Metropolitan Edison Co.	1973
Middletown	Three Mile Island Nuclear Station: Unit 2	907,000	Jersey Central Power & Light Co.	1975
Berwick	Susquehanna Steam Electric Station: Unit 1	1,052,000	Pennsylvania Power and Light	1978
Berwick	Susquehanna Steam Electric Station: Unit 2	1,052,000	Pennsylvania Power and Light	1980
*	Philadelphia Electric Co.: HTGR No. 1	1,150,000	Philadelphia Electric Co.	1979
*	Philadelphia Electric Co.: HTGR No. 2	1,150,000	Philadelphia Electric Co.	1981
SOUTH CAROLINA				
Hartsville	H. B. Robinson S. E. Plant: Unit 2	700,000	Carolina Power & Light Co.	1971
Seneca	Oconne Nuclear Station: Unit 1	841,000	Duke Power Co.	1972
Seneca	Oconee Nuclear Station: Unit 2	886,000	Duke Power Co.	1972
Seneca	Oconee Nuclear Station: Unit 3	886,000	Duke Power Co.	1973
Parr	Virgil C.Summer Nuclear Station: Unit 1	900,000	South Carolina Electric & Gas Co.	1977
TENNESSEE				
Daisy	Sequoyah Nuclear Power Plant: Unit 1	1,124,000	Tennessee Valley Authority	1974
Daisy	Sequoyah Nuclear Power Plant: Unit 2	1,124,000	Tennessee Valley Authority	1974
Spring City	Watts Bar Nuclear Plant: Unit 1	1,169,000	Tennessee Valley Authority	1976
Spring City	Watts Bar Nuclear Plant: Unit 2	1,169,000	Tennessee Valley Authority	1977
VERMONT				
Vernon	Vermont Yankee Generating Station	513,900	Vermont Yankee Nuclear Power Corp.	1971
VIRGINIA				
Gravel Neck	Surry Power Station: Unit 1	788,000	Virginia Electric & Power Co.	1972
Gravel Neck	Surry Power Station: Unit 2	788,000	Virginia Electric & Power Co.	1972
Mineral	North Anna Power Station: Unit 1	845,000	Virginia Electric & Power Co.	1974
Mineral	North Anna Power Station: Unit 2	845,000	Virginia Electric & Power Co.	1975
Mineral	North Anna Power Station: Unit 3	900,000	Virginia Electric & Power Co.	1977
Mineral	North Anna Power Station: Unit 4	900,000	Virginia Electric & Power Co.	1978
WASHINGTON				
Richland	N-Reactor/WPPSS Steam	800,000	Atomic Energy Commission	1966
Richland	Hanford No. 2	1,110,000	Washington Public Power Supply System	1977
WISCONSIN				
Genoa	Genoa Nuclear Generating Station	50,000	Dairyland Power Cooperative	1969
Two Creeks	Point Beach Nuclear Plant: Unit 1	497,000	Wisconsin Michigan Power Co.	1971
Two Creeks	Point Beach Nuclear Plant: Unit 2	497,000	Wisconsin Michigan Power Co.	1971
Carlton	Kewaunee Nuclear Power Plant: Unit 1	541,000	Wisconsin Public Service Co.	1972
PUERTO RICO				
Puerto De Jobas	Aguirre Nuclear Power Plant	583,000	Puerto Rico Water Resources Authority	1975
* Site not selected.				
*	—	1,175,000	Tennessee Valley Authority	1977
*	—	1,175,000	Tennessee Valley Authority	1978

Courtesy: Industrial Distributor News

The strange, but true story of the ice cream pops that pooped.

During the summer, a leading ice cream company in Brooklyn turns out over ten thousand ice cream pops a day, over two shifts.

At least it did. Until one week last summer.

One day, the maintenance chief noticed that the huge turntable which molded the pops was only operating at 60% capacity. The next day, however, it went up to 100%. A couple of days later it was back down to 60%.

Big trouble. And particularly troublesome for the chief because the slowdown seemed to occur on the second shift when he was home. And he wasn't happy about the prospect of hanging around evening after evening to see if it occurred.

Recorders to the rescue! He hooked an Amprobe® voltmeter recorder into the line together with an Amprobe recording ammeter. Why? Because they do more than take electrical measurements. They write them down. An operator doesn't have to stand around to get measurements. He can set up a recorder. Go away. Come back hours, days later and look at a continuous record of measurements.

Which is what he did.

After a week, he had his pattern. On certain nights, current was being drained off the line to the turntable motor, causing it to labor under peak demand and overheat. Thus, production slowed. Pops pooped.

Then, he did the one thing that the Amprobes can't do. He tried to come up with a logical reason why the slowdown occurred on the second shift. Re-checking the charts gave him his first clue. The slowdowns occurred on extremely hot nights.

So the next extremely hot night he hung around.

And eventually found his culprits, some men working in a warm carton storage room adjacent to the plant's reserve freezer. They left the freezer door open for hours, in order to cool off their work space.

Naturally, this caused the thermostatically-operated freezer compressors to start up and run constantly in order to maintain correct temperature in the freezer. This in turn produced the heavy drain on the turntable motor.

The maintenance chief solved the workers' problem with an air conditioner in their work space.

And today, the plant is turning out over ten thousand pops a day. Every day. Day after day. And there isn't a pooped pop in the bunch.

Do you have problems that can only be solved by hanging around meters for a couple of hours or days?

Try it the Amprobe way. Let an Amprobe recorder write it down for you. It can save you time. And trouble. And money. Write for free catalog.

▲ AMPROBE INSTRUMENT®
Division of SOS Manufacturing Co., Lynbrook, N.Y. 11563

Advertisements for technical products customarily are serious, staid or simply factual—but need not be. Amprobe Instrument varies its approach with attention-getting headlines or illustrations in lighter vein, with favorable reactions from electrical supply dealers and buyers.

Seven variations on any theme

Contrast is a basic quality in a black-and-white print. It must be right for the subject. *Kodak Polycontrast* Papers and the seven filters in the *Kodak Polycontrast* Filter Kit give you the *right* contrast every time.

Polycontrast Papers render rich images warm or cool—highlights crisp, shadows deep.

A range of tones for a variety of tasks. An assortment of surface textures and sheen suitable for nearly all your printing.

They offer shades of grey—sparkling with highlights, offset by luminous shadows. At the same time, stocking is simpler and more economical, and printing is more profitable.

See your dealer in Kodak professional products for the lowdown on *Polycontrast* Paper—it's the seven-for-one buy. Professionally, you can't afford less.

Eastman Kodak Company
Rochester, N.Y.

Kodak

Kodak is a consistent advertiser in such trade publications as Photographic Business and Product News, The Professional Photographer, Photo Methods for Industry, Industrial Photographer. This ad features Kodak Polycontrast Papers and uses an attractive illustration as an attention-getter.

Chapter 21

STORE AND HOME
DEMONSTRATIONS

MRS. LESLIE, browsing through a department store, was attracted to a crowd listening to a smartly-dressed woman speaking from a platform which held a chair, a table and a display of Babe Cosmetics. As she approached, the speaker said:

"And now we will actually demonstrate what Babe Cosmetics will do for your facial appearance. Who would like a free make-up with absolutely no obligation to buy anything? We just want you to look refreshed and more attractive after your tiring shopping trip."

Looking around and seeing that no one else volunteered, Mrs. Leslie's hand tentatively went up and the demonstrator invited her to come up and sit in the chair. A make-up specialist stepped out and began to apply her magic touches and materials to Mrs. Leslie's face. When the task was completed, she stood up. The crowd applauded the results.

DEMONSTRATOR: (Holding up a mirror) Are you pleased with your new look? You certainly look charming and attractive.

MRS. LESLIE: Yes, I like it. Thanks.

DEMONSTRATOR: Well, for your fine cooperation, we're giving you this trial sample of Delirious Joy for your lips. I know you'll enjoy using it and you can always get more when you want it right here in this store. (Turning to the audience) Folks, don't you think she looks nice? Attractive? You see what Babe Cosmetics will do for a woman? (Murmurs of approval)

Now listen to this. Because of these demonstrations, we have arranged with this store to sell all Babe Cosmetic products at special introductory prices for this week only. They will be on sale at a remarkable 25% off; that's right 25% off. That's because we want everybody to try them. Folks, thanks very much for your attention. The cosmetic counters are right behind you.

At the present time the use of demonstrators is confined to certain specific fields—primarily food, cosmetics, small appliances and household specialties. Many manufacturers feel that the cost of demonstrators is too high; others avoid using them to escape entanglement with the union; still others feel that their use involves a danger of prosecution under the Robinson-Patman Act. There is some justice to all of these criticisms, but the fact remains that demonstrators are being employed, both by manufacturers and by aggressive retailers, with a good deal of success. The demonstration, like any other tool in the sales promotion man's kit, can be effective if it is properly employed.

Of course, the ideal situation is one in which the retail clerk, in the course of her regular duties on the sales floor, can give a complete and accurate demonstration. Most companies eventually develop training programs aimed at reaching this goal; examples will be given in this Chapter (see also Chapter 26, "Training Dealer Personnel"). However, even in the case of a well-known and generally accepted product, there is often psychological value in the appearance in the retail outlet of an "expert" who can demonstrate and give personal advice. In the case of a new product, the function of the demonstrator is in part to sell the dealer and the retail clerk, and in many companies it is a definite part of the demonstrator's responsibilities to train the regular personnel in each outlet.

The very word "demonstrator" means many different things in different companies. For the purpose of this chapter, the word has been taken to mean a person, on the payroll of manufacturer, distributor, or dealer, whose primary responsibility is promoting sales through face-to-face contacts for a limited group of products. The variety of activities included in this definition is indicated by the analysis of types of demonstrations which follows.

Demonstrations in Retail Outlets

The simplest type of demonstration is that in which a trained person travels from one retail store to another, spending a day or several days in each to acquaint consumers with the product. These demonstrations are of two types; in the heavy consumer appliance field the demonstrator ordinarily shows what the

This demonstration booth built by Functional Display, Inc., for Tricolator also affords attractive display space for other product lines.

product will do; in such fields as cosmetics and food the demonstration is actually sampling.

Geo. A. Hormel & Company is typical of the companies in the food field which use this technique. Demonstrations are not a continuous activity, but are used to introduce new products or to spark a special sales promotional event. When Hormel brought out its high-quality canned chili con carne, demonstrators were used because market research indicated that housewives were prejudiced against any product of this type, and it was necessary to convince them quickly that the new chili really was new and different from competing brands.

Hormel does not employ any permanent staff for this work. Ordinarily the location of a demonstration and the selection of the girl are left to the salesman in the territory, with the approval of his district sales manager. A demonstration is never put on by itself; it is always backed by advertising, store display, and the assistance of store personnel. Hormel demonstrators always begin the day's work by sampling the store clerks so that they will be convinced of the merit of the product.

Paradoxically, Hormel believes the best demonstration is one in which not many samples are given out. The one basic rule given to demonstrators is, "Don't feed 'em, sell 'em." The company's theory is that if the customer is sufficiently intrigued by a taste of the product to take a can home, she will be exposed twice. Girls are instructed that sampling is to be used when the demonstration is not going too well, when customers just aren't interested, but that ordinarily it is much better to try for an immediate sale.

In discussing this type of demonstration, a home economist who has had a good deal of personal experience in such activities remarked feelingly, "Don't let anyone get the idea that this is an easy job. It's darned hard for anyone to serve a good hot cup of fresh coffee. The demonstrator ordinarily has a limited space in which to work. She has to arrange for heat and water, and figure out something to do with the used cups so they won't clutter up her space or the store. In the meantime, she has to keep a constant supply of fresh coffee available, and at the same time keep her own person neat, tidy, and unflustered."

This is an important point which has been overlooked in many demonstrations of this kind. An exception is the booth developed by General Mills for sampling soups; the unit contains all the equipment, and all the space, which the demonstrator will need. The entire unit can be knocked down for shipment from store to store.

A second type of retail demonstration is that in which the demonstrator shows how to use a product rather than simply sampling customers. Such appliances as vacuum cleaners, irons, washing machines, and orthopedic shoes are currently sold by this technique.

Ordinarily, a demonstration of this kind is made a merchandising event by the retailer, with newspaper and perhaps radio advertising to announce to the community that the expert will be on hand on certain specified dates. Many of these demonstrators are on the permanent payroll of the manufacturer, and are trained to contact the woman's page editors of local papers and other publicity sources on arrival in a new town. A common setup for this kind of activity is to have a home economist at headquarters supervising the work of one demonstrator in each major geographical division of the country.

As the pressure for more sales mounts, more and more appliance manufacturers are testing, or are actively engaged in, house-to-house canvassing for the sale of their products. There are obvious advantages in demonstrating a vacuum cleaner, for instance on Mrs. Housewife's own living room rug; it may be that the trend in this type of activity will be more and more toward home demonstrations.

New-Product Dealer Demonstration

To assist in launching its new KitchenAid Hot-water Dispenser, Hobart Manufacturing Company developed a promotional campaign to inspire distributor salesmen to get existing KitchenAid dishwasher retailers to buy, display and sell the new appliance to consumers. This new product was designed to replace the inefficient heating of hot water on a range in preparation of standard and instant-convenience foods and for many other uses.

Following a decision to market the new kitchen appliance through the same channels of distribution as KitchenAid dishwashers, which already enjoyed good consumer and retailer preference; a complete package of demonstration and training tools was developed to make the introduction successful.

Since the supplemental hot-water source for the kitchen-sink area was a new concept unfamiliar to most distributor salesmen and retailers, a portable "live" demonstrator was designed to deliver a cup of 190° hot-water in the retailer's store.

A garden pressure water tank and hot-water dispenser, were installed and hooked-up in a luggage-type carrying case. The salesmen making the presentation could carry the demonstrator into the retailers and plug in the demonstrator to electric current. While he was presenting the benefits of the product and the advertising program associated with the introduction; the water in the demonstrator would be heating. After an approximate 15-minute presentation he could climax with the drawing of 190° water.

The components of the demonstrator were in full view so that the salesmen could describe the ease of installation and operation.

To involve the prospect further, the 190° water was drawn into a polystyrene cup which had a portion of instant coffee, soup or hot chocolate in the bottom. A supplier of these portion beverage cups incorporated 60 cups with an assortment of the beverages into an attractive, wood-grained, corrugated KitchenAid Hot-water Dispenser "Refreshment Center" which served as a carrying case for the distributor salesman. Where the retailer bought a hot-water dispenser for "live" hook-up demonstration in his own store, he could utilize the refreshment center and beverages in introducing the dispenser to his customers.

At the conclusion of the presentation the distributor salesman gave the retailer a specially designed and imprinted ceramic Hot-cup to remind him of the new KitchenAid appliance. At group meetings for retailers, distributors also used the distinctive Hot-cup as an attendance favor.

Since the hot-water dispenser was a new product, a decision was made to make the carton containing the dispenser a self-contained display and selling piece. Over a dozen uses for the dispenser were dramatized with colorful illustrations to attract consumers and train the retail salesmen.

Incentive programs were developed for the distributor sales-man, retailer principal and retail salesmen so that they could earn their own KitchenAid Hot-water Dispenser as a result of their sales of the product. This enabled them to sell the new product with confidence after seeing the convenience created in their own homes.

The "School" Demonstration

A second type of demonstration is that in which a utility or department store sponsors a "school" for some type of consumer group. These demonstrations are usually sold to the consumer on the basis of their educational value, and are not ordinarily intended to lead to immediate sales. Their effectiveness, however, is plainly indicated by, for example, the growing use of electric ranges; consumer resistance to this type of cooking has been overcome at least in part through these educational classes.

In demonstrations of this kind the consumer is invited to spend one or several periods at the dealership or a hall hired for the purpose. In order to assure turn-out, a variety of devices has been used. Some schools offer door prizes; others work through existing groups, offering some reward to a women's club or a ladies' aid society based upon the number of members who can be talked into attending.

Metropolitan Utilities District of Omaha has been particularly successful with a long-range promotion of this type; groups of Girl Scouts are invited to attend a series of five Saturday morning cooking classes. At the final session the mothers are invited for a dessert luncheon prepared by the youngsters, and certificates are awarded. Using materials prepared by manufacturers in the food and appliance fields, supplemented by inexpensive pieces of their own, Metropolitan's Home Service Department has trained more than 2,000 future prospects at a total cost of less than 15 cents each.

Demonstrating a Group of Products

In many cases the utility or the department store sets up its demonstration school in a somewhat different way from that just described. Instead of concentrating on any one product, the plan is to expose the audience to a variety of merchandise.

Goldblatt's in Chicago offers a full-day program for women's groups. During the morning they may see the latest developments in, for example, ironing techniques. They are then served a complimentary luncheon with credit lines to all the manufacturers whose products are served. In the afternoon there is another educational session, and the serving of tea closes the day.

Manufacturers interviewed in preparing this chapter expressed some doubt about the value of participation in such a general demonstration program. While the plan has the advantage of costing the manufacturer much less, it does not ordinarily result in the consumer's purchase of any one particular product immediately. Because of the difficulty of measuring effectiveness, and because of the number of products to which the audience is exposed, this type of demonstration is more popular with the retailer than with the manufacturers participating.

Club Demonstrations

The problem of getting an audience of sufficient size to visit a retail outlet has already been mentioned. In some cases the sponsors have avoided this difficulty by taking the demonstration to the club group's headquarters.

This kind of demonstration has proved popular enough to support commercial organizations which do nothing else. A company will arrange a succession of luncheons, for example, at which a manufacturer's product will be featured and discussed. Usually the manufacturer supplies the necessary amount of his product and pays a small fee in addition.

Perhaps because of the problem in getting the necessary "props" in and out, the club demonstration has not been used very much by manufacturers of heavy consumer durables. The popularity of such meetings, however, might offer a suggestion for a new type of sales promotion in these fields.

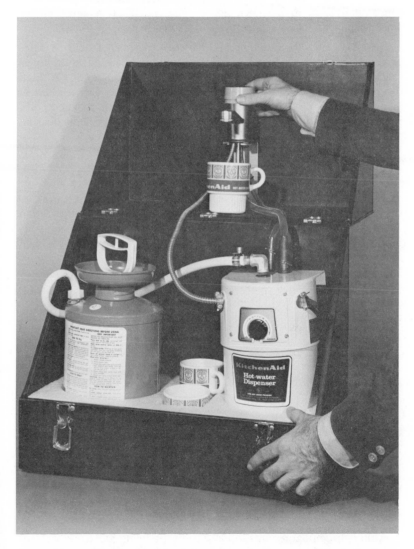

A portable working model, housed in a luggage-type case, helped distributor salesmen to demonstrate the new KitchenAid Hot-water Dispenser to retailers, simply by plugging in to the power supply.

SALES PROMOTION HANDBOOK

Door-to-Door Demonstrations

More and more manufacturers are getting their feet wet in
the field of house-to-house selling. The essential ingredient in this
type of selling is, of course, the demonstration; the housewife
can actually see, in her own home, why she needs a new Hoover
vacuum cleaner or another type of Fuller brush.

Demonstrating door to door is a highly specialized field of sales
promotion which should be entered only with tested techniques,
careful training of personnel, and provision to avoid the high
turnover of demonstrators which is a constant headache to most
manufacturers. This type of activity should be approached with
particular caution by the company which sells through dealers,
since the company's control is limited.

Training Salesmen to Demonstrate

Some promotional plans based upon demonstrations misfire because the salesman or sales clerk looks upon the demonstration
as a way of entertaining the buyer rather than as a means of
getting an order. Some time back the Hoover Company developed
a dirt meter for its salesmen to use in making home demonstrations.
It was a glass affair which showed a housewife the dirt the Hoover
got out of rugs which supposedly had been cleaned by some competitive cleaner. It went into the cleaner in place of the usual bag,
and proved of great interest to women who "couldn't believe there
was that much dirt in my rug."

Hoover's manager of sales education has often pointed out that
training salesmen to demonstrate is a psychological as well as a
technical matter. He has said:

"The first step is that of attitude—getting into the proper frame
of mind. The next is knowledge—imparting knowledge intelligently,
a simple, down-to-earth program. The third, is that of establishing
good work habits—the use of sales tools, practice sessions, and
supervision. It is a three-way proposition. They come in sequence,
one, two, three, as they have been presented."

Demonstrating for Key People

Although companies in a wide variety of fields are using demonstrators profitably, there is a large group of manufacturers who
do not feel that the expense of consumer demonstrations can be
justified for their products.

General Foods does no store sampling and does not take part in "schools" on any continuing basis, because the company feels the expense is disproportionate to results. Demonstrators at the retail level are used occasionally in selling a particular product in a particular territory, but these are purely local situations.

The company does, however, use demonstrations to introduce new products to such key people as radio commentators, newspaper columnists, and other publicity sources. When a new breakfast food was introduced recently, a series of breakfasts for the press was held across the country. The new product was discussed and then served.

Demonstrations by Retail Clerks

For most products, the eventual goal of the manufacturer is to have trained personnel at the point of purchase who can demonstrate the product in the course of their regular selling duties. Corning Glass Works, for instance, has a staff of seven trained home economists who do no demonstrating themselves, but instruct floor sales personnel in the important selling points of Pyrex cooking utensils.

A second method is the standardized presentation, typified by that used by Proctor Electric Company. The material is set up in parallel columns, headed "Do It," and "Say It." By simply following the outline of activities and saying the things she is supposed to, the clerk can give a competent demonstration.

A more elaborate version of this idea was a demonstration manual prepared for use by clerks in selling Speed Queen washers. The 40-page book, illustrated on every page, showed the clerk taking a prospect through a complete demonstration, right down to the opening of the order book.

A different approach, employed by a large number of manufacturers, is the preparation of a product tag which will guide the clerk through a demonstration of the special selling points for the item. The tag serves a double purpose, since it is still on the product when the customer gets it home, and can serve the important and often overlooked function of reassuring the customer after the sale.

Television Demonstrations

The TV commercial has made a definite place for itself in sales promotion. Subject to time limitations, it is second only to live, personal, demonstrations: the impact is such that it has come under the scrutiny of the Federal Trade Commission. The concern of the government is that the demonstrations, in some cases, represent simulations which do not conform to actual, real-life conditions.

From a legal standpoint, it is highly important that claims made during a demonstration be substantiated, if necessary, by proof and documentation. To avoid possible complications, the television and radio associations have established codes for the guidance of advertisers of products in controversial areas, from the standpoints of good taste, impact on children and exaggerated claims.

ADMINISTERING A DEMONSTRATION PROGRAM

While the number of persons involved in actual demonstrating as a full-time job is usually small, there are a number of headaches in administering the group's activities. For example, there is little agreement on the question of who in the company shall be responsible for the demonstrators; in some cases this is a full-time headquarters job and in others it is handled incidentally by each salesman in his own territory.

The Demonstrators' Union

When one executive was asked how he recruited demonstrators he replied, "That's no problem at all; we just call the union." The Demonstrators' Union, a part of the Retail Clerks, A. F. of L., is at present active in several metropolitan areas. The union trains demonstrators and makes them available to any manufacturer who requests them. The manufacturer is not required to accept the first candidate sent to him.

Demonstrators and the Law

Controlling legislation for the employment of demonstrators, like most other sales promotional activities, is the Robinson-Patman Act. Basically, the Act is intended to prevent a manufacturer from giving more help in any form to one retailer than to another. However, the Act is so loosely drawn that a wide variety of interpretations is possible on almost any specific case.

The major decision involving demonstrators was reached in Federal Trade Commission vs. Elizabeth Arden, Inc. (cosmetics manufacturer) F.T.C. Docket 3133. In this case the Commission held that the terms under which the company made demonstrators available disqualified 90% of the dealers from receiving such help, and ordered the system either abandoned or modified because it "failed to accord to competing purchasers of their products such services or facilities on proportionally equal terms."

The possibility of this type of prosecution is always possible unless the manufacturer offers in writing the same terms to all dealers, and unless the terms are such that a good many dealers are in a position to take advantage of them. The Commission has not committted itself to any rule-of-thumb which a manufacturer can use in determining "proportionally equal terms."

Recruiting Demonstrators

Newspaper advertising and recommendations of retail clerks by the company salesmen are the two most common recruiting techniques used by organizations outside the unionized fields.

Because the selection of a demonstrator is not a problem which arises frequently, little attention has been paid to an analysis of qualifications needed for success. Ordinarily they are hired, given brief training, and sent to the field on a "sink or swim" basis. Oddly enough, even trained home economists were in general agreement that the type of schooling which the candidate has had makes little difference in her prospects of success, except of course, in cases where the prestige of the expert is involved.

Here's a list of qualifications, only partly humorous, suggested by the director of a large staff of demonstrators:

Ability to sell her own personality.

Good stage presence.

Enthusiasm.

Tirelessness.

Even temper.

Good and appropriate grooming.

Perseverance.

Teaching and writing ability.

Ability to sell the product to individuals and groups.

The patience of Job.

Demonstrating is, after all, hard physical work. In view of the comparatively low incomes offered by a career in this field, perhaps the mere fact that a girl is interested in such work is in itself the answer to a good part of the selection problem.

Training Demonstrators

The low quality of demonstrators as a group, bemoaned by many manufacturers, is probably due in part to the informality with which they are trained in the majority of companies. The usual procedure is for the new demonstrator to be given a very brief training on the product by the company's salesman in the territory in which she is to work. This is often checked by having headquarters' personnel look in on her activities whenever the sales manager, the district manager, or the home economist happens to be in the city in which she is working. Some companies supplement this with a written demonstrators' manual. Generally, however, the training is pretty much hit or miss.

There are of course exceptions, in most cases among companies which rely heavily on demonstration. A manufacturer of shoes has each new demonstrator come to headquarters for 3 months of careful and detailed training; Thor Corporation brings all demonstrators to headquarters for individual instruction by the resident home economist.

Training is also done in some companies by having the new girl spend a week or so with an experienced demonstrator. This system is generally used in training personnel for door-to-door or home party demonstrations.

Demonstrations are also used to introduce a service. When the Illinois Bell Telephone Company changed over a unit to the dial system, it used a good-humored skit, which it sent from plant to plant, to instruct the subscribers' employees in the proper way to dial a number.

USING DEMONSTRATORS EFFECTIVELY

For some consumer hard goods, such as vacuum cleaners, the effectiveness of a demonstration can be measured immediately in terms of sales. However, this is not true of soft goods items which are bought on a repetitive basis, such as foodstuffs. In these cases, the value of the demonstration must be judged not only in terms of immediate sales, but consideration must also be given to the post-demonstration sales record for several weeks. If sales continue high it can be assumed that the demonstrator has satisfactorily introduced the product to a group of new buyers.

A manufacturer in the food field suggested a quick way to check on the work of a new demonstrator to make sure she is not overselling. In his company's experience, the housewife will take a package of the product from the demonstrator to avoid argument and then quietly deposit it on a shelf somewhere before she takes her purchases to the check-out counter. This happens so regularly that the company uses the number of discarded packages as its check on the demonstrator's selling ability.

Whether or not the demonstrator should sell is a debated point. Some companies instruct their demonstrators to turn every prospect over to a regular clerk as soon as she approaches the dotted line, on the theory that the store personnel will resent the demonstrator otherwise. Other organizations keep all demonstrators on straight salary and instruct them to do no direct selling at all, on the theory that the demonstration is intended to arouse eventual interest rather than to make an immediate sale. In the case of one heavy consumer durable, demonstrators are told to end the demonstration with a request to repeat it in the prospect's home when the husband can be present, because experience has shown that the head of the house resents being bypassed on the purchase of a big-ticket item. At the opposite extreme, some companies instruct their demonstrators to keep on closing right through the demonstration. One chain of stores has figured out the dollar volume per week per foot of shelf space which it must turn over to remain profitable; demonstrations are tested to see if they can attain this figure.

A campaign which depended heavily on getting prospects to dealers' stores so they could receive actual demonstrations was successfully executed by Harman-Kardon, Inc., of Philadelphia.

In outlining the campaign, Jay Morton Roberts, advertising and sales promotion manager of the company, said:

"Harman-Kardon's program was designed to increase sales of the company's high-fidelity components and compact music systems during the last three months of the year. This quarter is traditionally the major selling season of the year.

"While the component line was made up of existing products and models, the program helped to introduce the compact systems to the market. These compacts represent a new product idea. They are true high-fidelity components—AM-FM stereo receiver, automatic record turntable, and two separate speaker units—packaged together in easy-to-use and attractive cabinetry. They deliver component quality sound, take less space than consoles, and are more versatile than consoles because of having separate speakers. This was the sales message that had to reach dealers and consumers. And because demonstrations are so vital to selling good sound, getting the prospect to the dealer was an important feature of the program.

"Area meetings were held where possible so that live-vs.-recorded demonstrations could be made to dramatize the quality sound.

"Dealer mailings, trade advertising, and promotion material were also used extensively.

"A special merchandiser was developed for the compact unit.

"A sales incentive program was aimed primarily at dealer salesmen. They received points for each sale to earn prizes ranging from steak knives to washing machines. Upon reaching certain point levels, they also became eligible for grand-prize drawings. The prizes included motion-picture equipment, fur coat, color TV, and a sports car.

"Due to the nature of the product, advertisements were run in class publications. All ads were couponed to get requests for demonstrations and literature. The coupons received were relayed to dealers for followup.

"The results of the promotion may be judged by two facts: Some 50% of prospects who received demonstrations were converted into buyers. Harman-Kardon compact music systems sold in a volume which surpassed even the most optimistic estimates."

"Give 'em a Gimmick"

The essential function of a demonstration is to attract attention and arouse interest. An eye-stopping display to attract the passers-by and to dramatize the product is extremely helpful to the demonstrator. As one executive put it, "Give 'em a gimmick."

A manufacturer of industrial clothing had difficulty convincing the salespeople in dealers' stores that his garments were well worth the extra price because they wore longer. Similar claims were made by his competitors. To demonstrate that his garments would give greater customer satisfaction, and therefore had greater repeat qualities, his salesmen got the prospect to hold on to one leg while he held the other, then both pulled with all their might. The demonstration usually clinched the sale. This manufacturer built a 3-year promotion plan around that test.

A woman may balk at paying a few cents more for a cake flour than she pays for ordinary flour. The flour and mix look alike. She has always used regular flour and prides herself on the cakes she bakes with it. But when she is given an opportunity to see the cake mixed, then smells and tastes the result, she sells herself.

One of the purposes of this campaign by Harman-Kardon, Inc., was to bring prospects to dealers' stores for demonstrations, often dramatized with live-vs.-recorded musical selections. Window and store streamers, a merchandiser, and class-publication coupon ads were all forceful factors in the sales drive. Effective? 50% of the prospects who received demonstrations were converted into buyers!

One of the tire companies developed a new tread which was especially resistant to skidding. The grip of the tire on the road was played up in the company's advertising. Tire dealers and their sales personnel were coached to "talk up" the ground-gripping tread. But other tire manufacturers made similar claims so the public, as is often the case, discounted them all. Then a sales promotion man in Akron got an idea. He designed a machine, which a dealer could place in a strategic spot in his store, that measured the resistance to skidding of various treads. Tire segments were propelled down an evenly wet surface by equal force. The tire with the greatest ground-gripping, nonskid qualities won the test, and the order.

When introducing Zerone, a new antifreeze, salesmen supplied dealers with two rubber balls, one of which they can put into a glass of Zerone and the other into a glass containing a competitive product. The competitive antifreeze soon swells the rubber, whereas the Du Pont product does not. The dealer uses this demonstration to show the motorist what happens to his engine hose connections.

To display products, show services in action, or to sell ideas, this award-winning desk-top slide projector uses 35mm. slides.

Courtesy: Hudson Photographic Industries, Inc.

In view of the obvious advantages of demonstration, it is surprising that so little attention is currently paid to the subject. With the widening availability of television, if for no other reason, the sales promotion man should consider seriously whether or not a demonstration program should not be included in his plans for the competitive future.

Chapter 22

DEALER MEETINGS

WHEN planning to introduce new products through dealer or distributor meetings, three questions immediately confront company managements:

1. Should the meetings be national or regional?
2. Who pays what share of the cost?
3. How long should the meetings last?

Lasting from one to three days, programs have to be well organized so that they do not bore, tire, or wear out the listeners.

The bigger the meeting or dealer convention, the greater the need for professional-type presentation. To meet this need, specialized agencies now offer complete stage-production facilities, with actors, singers, music, copy-writing services, direction, and all necessary equipment for a lively business presentation.

The secret of making a dealers' meeting click is to give those who attend a "top to spin." Most dealer meetings bog down because they are stuffy, dull, and preachy. The sessions are too long. They lack a central theme. And they drag.

One sales manager with a reputation for putting on meetings which dealers like to attend, and never miss if they can help it, has a rule that no session may last over an hour. At each session he spells out an idea which the dealers can put to work in their business. Between each session there is a short intermission for the men to get together and talk over what they have heard, grab a "Coke," or otherwise break the monotony of the meeting.

Some companies, Standard Oil of Indiana, for example, maintain interest by putting on a sales show, and present the sales promotional program with well-planned skits and playlets. There are no set speeches. Portable stages with the required scenery and props are used. They can be taken down in a few hours, loaded into waiting trucks, and moved overnight to the next destination.

Similarly, Sunbeam Corporation, Chicago, Illinois, applies the principle of giving dealers who come to their breakfast meetings a "top to spin" by having them brew their own coffee in Sunbeam Coffeemasters, fix their toast on Toastmasters and, to put zip into the party, the dealers are asked to come to the breakfast unshaven, so they can enjoy a shave with Shavemasters supplied for their use.

Since the reason for getting dealers together in meetings is to afford them an opportunity to arouse enthusiasm in one another, any program which helps to get them better acquainted and ready to participate in the meeting is very much worthwhile.

How Dealer Meetings Are Used

The dealer meeting as a sales promotional device attained popularity in the early days of the automotive industry. Car makers urged dealers to attend the national shows to preview new models, and took advantage of the enthusiasm which usually attended the showing of the new line to get them to place orders for the year ahead. It was not unusual for a manufacturer to sell the factory's annual production at such meetings. A dealer who came to the meeting convinced he could only sell 100 cars that year, under the spell of the oratory of the manufacturer's sales manager, decided to up his order to 200 cars before leaving for home. Hugh Chalmers was one of the pioneers in this development.

While dealer meetings are best suited to promoting the sale of big-ticket merchandise which requires creative selling, they are successfully used to "trade up" dealers in nearly every field. Among the many ways they can be made profitable are:

1. Introducing a new product or model.
2. "Selling" a packaged merchandising plan.
3. Introducing "trade up" educational programs.
4. Winning dealer cooperation and support for national advertising.
5. Getting dealers to make better use of advertising helps.
6. Combating price cutting and promoting fair trading.
7. Launching regional contests for dealers and store personnel.
8. Getting acceptance for sales training programs.
9. Promoting store development and modernization.
10. Promoting product demonstrations.
11. Enlisting dealer participation in industry-wide or community-wide consumer educational activities.

Since the dealer is not directly on the manufacturer's payroll, and since the meeting in the great majority of cases will take him away from his place of business during working hours for anywhere from an hour to a couple of days, the meeting should be presold by the manufacturer to assure attendance. It should offer the dealer enough realistic nuts-and-bolts information so that he will be eager to come the next time.

WHERE TO HOLD THE MEETING

A meeting at the manufacturer's headquarters city has certain marked advantages in situations where it can be arranged. All the company's top brass can be on hand; dealers can actually tour the factory and be shown the scope of the company's operations; and the manufacturer can get the undivided attention of the audience for as long as necessary.

Two disadvantages make headquarters meetings impossible for many companies. In the first place, the dealer organization is often just too big to be handled at a single meeting; second, the expense of transportation makes such a meeting impractical. Headquarters meetings are used chiefly by companies with comparatively few dealers and with dealers who handle the company's lines on an exclusive territorial franchise. The usual arrangement is for the dealer to pay his own traveling, lodging, and incidental expenses, and for the company to supply meals and entertainment during the period.

Planning Assistance

Companies in the travel and transportation field offer assistance in planning meetings, selecting sites and arranging transportation. An advertisement by Eastern Airlines reads, in part, as follows:

"To plan a successful meeting could take you 3½ weeks. Eastern will do it in 72 hours. Free. We've got a whole department that does nothing but arrange custom-made meetings for companies who've got something better to do with their time. It's called 'Meetings Unlimited.'

"The size of the meeting doesn't matter. 10-25-100—as many people as you want. What we do is put an experienced representative to work for you. With the help of a computer, he recommends sites and accomodations best suited to your specific requirements. Then he gives you a complete cost analysis.

"He handles air and ground transportation, ticketing, programs, tours. You name it, he plans it—right down to the last detail. And fast. He even gets you better prices than you could get yourself.

He knows all the best buys in places like Miami, San Juan, Jamaica, and plenty of other great spots.

"Eastern's 'Meetings Unlimited' representative is ready to start working for you. Free."

In similar vein is the message from TWA, reading:

"If you're going to hold a business meeting, this is the only way to do it. Our new Getaway Conferences program is the most complete meeting-planning program in the business and is designed to give you meetings with more impact and excitement.

"TWA gives you more than 2,000 meeting locations to choose from, in the United States and around the world. It gives you the lowest prices. And it does more to help you actually set up the meeting than anyone's ever done. Here are some of the specifics.

"A meeting in Europe for the price of a meeting in the United States. TWA can give you a week in Europe for $50 a day per person. Including round-trip airfare from New York, first class hotel accommodations, breakfasts and dinners, conference rooms, sightseeing, and all tips."

Cambridge Tile's "Suntile Seminar"

The Cambridge Tile Manufacturing Company is among the companies which sponsor a headquarters meeting. One of their sessions was attended by more than 300 persons from 147 dealerships, all of whom paid their own transportation and hotel bills.

The preliminary invitation which brought this turn-out was sent months before the meeting; from then on printed stickers on every piece of dealer correspondence, letters on specific aspects of the program, and verbal reminders from company salesmen were all used to keep the meeting in the dealers' minds.

The meeting was held on a Friday and Saturday. The first day's program included a tour of the company's new plant and an afternoon business session, a cocktail hour and a banquet. On the second day several prominent outside speakers were on the program, which also included a round-table session on sales problems raised by the dealers themselves. Cocktails and another dinner concluded the day.

The retailers were invited to bring their wives, and the ladies attended the same sessions as their husbands. "By attending, wives of the dealers obtained a first-hand insight into their husbands' and the company's joint problems," according to R. L. Carlee, the company's advertising manager.

A company planning something radically new might find a headquarters session a dramatic way of kindling dealer enthusiasm. It should be remembered that such a meeting involves a lot of hard work; Cambridge's staff spent 2 hours a day for several weeks rehearsing their parts in the show.

Headquarters Meetings for Dealer Panels

Another method of communicating with the dealer organization which is spreading in use is the headquarters meeting attended not by all dealers but by representative retailers. In some companies this panel is selected by popular vote among the dealers themselves; in other organizations, such as Frigidaire Division of General Motors, the panel is made up on a scientific sampling basis so it will include representatives in the proper proportions from cities and rural areas, from large and small dealerships, and so on.

This panel system was pioneered by the automobile manufacturers, but it has been spreading in other consumer durable lines. One stove manufacturer has a panel which meets at headquarters after each representative has held a meeting with all the dealers in his area; by this means problems of all retailers are brought to the attention of company officials. Following a national panel meeting, each man holds another conference with the dealers he represents to pass on to them the decisions reached and the selling suggestions offered.

A panel of this sort has a number of advantages. It permits the manufacturer with a large dealer organization to keep in touch with what his dealers are thinking and the problems they are facing, without involving him in the often impossible task of trying to get all the retailers together.

What was said to be the first meeting of this type in the petroleum industry was sponsored by the Deep Rock Oil Corporation some years ago. Independent jobbers elected representatives who spent 4 days at Excelsior Springs, a Missouri resort town, in a conference with Deep Rock's top management from the chairman of the board on down. All salesmen were also in attendance.

"This is not a one-shot or one-time conference," B. L. Majewski, vice president for marketing, said in announcing the session. "It will be a continuing plan under which Deep Rock franchise distributors, through their chosen delegates, can discuss with Deep Rock's top management any and all problems that may arise at any time. Such discussions may be initiated either by the jobber delegates or the management."

Because of the repeated requirements of its several divisions, Celanese Marketing Fiber Company converted a meeting room into a theatre seating forty people for its business demonstration shows. Audio-visual equipment includes three rear-projection screens flanked by two front-projection screens angling toward the audience; six Carousel slide projectors and a stereo tape recorder. A push of a button and the programming machine starts the show. Shows have been so successful that they have been held over for extra weeks and some companies have copied the idea.

Reprinted with permission from SM/Sales Meetings Magazine

A company planning to sponsor such a panel should consider carefully how far it wishes to commit itself to following the panel's recommendations. In one organization, which promised to do something about every suggestion made, the panel one year was overwhelmingly in favor of a very inexpensive kit of sales promotional materials. Against the better judgment of the manufacturer it was produced; within a few months the dealers themselves admitted that they had been wrong and needed a lot more material. Meantime a selling season had been lost.

A "Road Show" by Company Executives

Another popular method of bringing headquarters personnel and dealers together is for a team of executives from the sponsoring company to take the meeting on the road, repeating their presentation in a series of strategic cities to as many dealers as possible. Williams Oil-O-Matic Division, of Eureka Williams Corp., for example, sent a team of 10 executives on such a tour, presenting a 2-hour dramatic skit to dealer audiences in the following cities:

Charlotte, N. C., Friday	Detroit, Mich., Monday
Philadelphia, Pa., Monday	Chicago, Ill., Wednesday
New York, N. Y., Wednesday	Cincinnati, Ohio, Friday
Boston, Mass., Friday	Des Moines, Iowa, Monday
	Minneapolis, Minn., Wednesday

There is the danger in this type of arrangement that the company executives will become somewhat tired or a little bored with the presentation before all of the meetings have been completed; this can be avoided, and travel expenses somwhat reduced, by exchanging personnel as the meetings proceed. The Eastern division manager, for example, will put on the show in Cleveland with the Middle Western manager in attendance; the latter will then take over his share of the program and carry it as far as Kansas City, where the Western man takes over.

Although it keeps the headquarters men away from their jobs a little longer, some companies always include enough time in such an itinerary for visits to the dealerships between meetings. This face-to-face contact, they feel, is of great value both to the company executives and to the dealer who can get his troubles off his chest directly to the top brass.

Regional Meetings

Probably the most common method of running dealer meetings is at the regional level, with a salesman or branch manager in charge of the actual session and with props and equipment supplied by headquarters. The problem in this type of meeting is, of course, that of achieving equally high quality in a group of sessions run by men of very different personalities, often quite inexperienced in this kind of work.

An adaptable idea was used by one big appliance company in connection with a series of dealer meetings designed to "kick off" a national sales contest. The entire program was set up in tentative form and tested in one city before general release. As a result of this actual test, a few rough spots were straightened out and the company was able to issue a comprehensive program to the field.

The difficulty in keeping control over local meetings can be at least partially overcome by putting the essential story in such form that the person running the meeting has no chance to make a mistake. A manufacturer of refrigeration equipment, for instance, planned nine meetings to introduce a new line. While much of the detail was left up to the individual sponsor, the story of the new line was put on sound-slidefilm; in this way a uniform presentation was assured.

The more material that headquarters can supply, the more control will be obtained. Proctor Electric Company planned a meeting which the company's district managers presented to 67 different audiences of distributors. The district manager was supplied with a time schedule for mailing invitations, copy to use in the invitations, a minute-by-minute schedule of the meeting itself, a checklist of everything which had to be done before the meeting, a blueprint of the ideal room arrangement for the meeting, "canned" presentations for speakers and charts to illustrate them, a supply of take-home broadsides which repeated the story.

The objection which is raised to any sort of "canned" material, that it may result in an unspontaneous affair, is of course valid. However, companies which have tried both ways are almost unanimous in their opinion that some degree of headquarters' control is necessary. If the time schedule permits, a factory representative can attend all of the meetings, to help out the local man with last-minute details and also to answer questions from the audience.

MEETINGS SPONSORED BY DISTRIBUTORS

In some fields where wholesalers or distributors are an active and aggressive group, the manufacturer is requested to appear on programs sponsored by the distributor. The problem in these meetings, where representatives of several companies are usually present, is somewhat different from that in a meeting devoted wholly to the products of one company.

The Sales Management Committee of the National Wholesale Druggists Association recently prepared a list of do's and don'ts for such meetings, both from the standpoint of the manufacturer and that of the wholesaler. Here is the list for the manufacturer:

1. Make definite arrangements in advance with the Sales Manager as to time and place of meeting and be there.

2. Prepare an outline of talk and submit to Sales Manager to ensure that he has complete knowledge of the subject matter.

3. Have samples of your product when presenting your story.

4. Tell the salesmen what the promotion consists of and break it down so the salesmen will have a complete picture of the program, in order to intelligently present it to the druggist.

5. Give a clear and concise sales story—something that the salesman can use when he is talking to a retailer. If possible, tell of a plan that has been used successfully.

6. Emphasize the important selling points . . . *Drive these home.*

7. Present the story in orderly fashion . . . be brief.

8. Put your point across fast, direct and hard.

9. Give one or more reasons why the retailer should buy.

10. Be sincere about wholesaler's accomplishment.

1. Don't ask to appear at the meeting unless you have a definite message.

2. Don't apologize for talk or preparation. Say what needs to be said without apologies. Excuses weaken a presentation.

3. Don't ask for questions from the audience.

4. Don't take advantage of the time allotted by running overtime. If you have only a 2-minute story, only take 2 minutes.

5. Don't brag about the number of deals you personally sold. Instead use the time to try and give the salesmen a story of how you did it.

6. Don't make comparisons between wholesalers on past accomplishments.

7. Don't give quotas to the salesmen at the meeting. Let the Sales Manager handle this phase of the program.

8. Don't offer bonuses or prizes to salesmen without clearing with the Sales Manager. Even then it is best to let the Sales Manager handle this part of the presentation. Don't tell the salesmen they will earn so much in commission.

9. Don't criticize salesmen about past performances. This is the Sales Manager's job.

10. Don't deal in statistics unless these are included on charts.

And here is the list for wholesalers:

1. Have a display of the manufacturer's item or line in the sales meeting room.

2. Be considerate of the representative . . . he may have traveled 200 miles to appear on your meeting program.

3. See that the representative goes on the program at the time assigned.

4. Give the representative a good introduction. Thank him for his cooperation.

5. Stress the importance of the manufacturer's line to the wholesaler's over-all business . . . make certain that the salesmen understand.

6 Make certain that the selling period immediately following the meeting features the item or line presented by the manufacturer's representative.

7. Review briefly the highlights of the talk before the representative leaves the room. Request the support and cooperation of all salesmen.

8. Make certain that the salesmen understand the importance of the item or line and its benefit to the druggists. Emphasize profit.

9. State that any points not clear will be discussed individually after the meeting.

10. Thank the representative for appearing on your program.

1. Don't say to the manufacturer's representative, "We are running behind schedule—perhaps you can cut your talk to 5 minutes."

2. Don't leave the impression with the representative that you are doing him a favor by having him appear on the program.

3. If you have questions about company policy matters, discuss this later, not in the sales meeting.

4. Don't make joking remarks about the lack of turnover orders.

5. Don't allow the impression to creep into the salesmen's minds that because a similar promotion was worked in a recent period that a constructive selling job cannot be accomplished on the line presented.

6. Don't have competing representatives on the same sales meeting program . . . if this can be avoided.

7. Don't schedule a promotion on any item at an unseasonable period.

8. Don't invite a manufacturer's representative to appear on your program simply to fill up time.

9. Don't, in opening remarks, ever give the impression that the line being presented is of secondary importance.

10. Don't permit questions about the manufacturer's selling policy in the meeting.

FORMAL MEETINGS

The formal presentation has certain marked advantages. The entire program can be rehearsed and timed; usually it is possible to cover a lot more ground in a brief period in this manner. By manipulation of visual aids and by presenting material in a variety of ways, the meeting can be given continuing change of pace to hold the interest of the audience. For a large group such a presentation is the only solution.

Of course the method has disadvantages as well. It is difficult for the sponsor of the meeting to know how much of the material has been absorbed. A big meeting of this kind, with a lot of props, will cost substantial money. If the men scheduled for speeches are not practiced orators, or if the amateurs in a skit are too amateurish, the audience will be bored, and the sponsor will lose rather than gain goodwill. The longer and more complicated the meeting is to be, the more time will be required for preparation and the more possibilities there will be for something to go wrong.

The Libbey-Owens-Ford campaign for store-front modernization featured the theme: "As big as you make it" as an indication of marketing possibilities. Company representatives and distributors were provided with a meeting manual to aid them in conducting area presentations.

Planning the Meeting

A folder on dealer meetings is usually kept permanently in the files of the sales promotion department. The day after a meeting has been held, collection of materials for the next session begins. This material may include lessons learned at the previous session, suggestions from dealers on topics they would like to have covered, sources of new meeting gadgets and props, and dozens of other details.

The meeting guide of the Automotive Advertisers Council, intended primarily for the wholesalers who are customers of members of the group, listed major areas of planning which are essential to a well-run meeting. The following outline is adapted from their publication:

1. General Plan:
   - Purpose of the meeting.
   - Time.
   - Size.
   - Participants.
   - Location.

2. Program Plan:
   - Subjects to be covered.
   - Demonstrations to be made.
   - Allotment of time.
   - Refreshments.
   - Entertainment.
   - Prizes.
   - Props.

3. Contact Participants:
   - Make assignments.
   - Give out copies of program.
   - Rehearse and time speeches and skits.

4. Advertise:
   - Direct mail.
   - Telephone.
   - Personal invitations by salesmen.
   - Admission cards.

In general, 2 months ahead is probably an absolute minimum for making detailed plans for a meeting of this nature. Companies which invest substantial sums in this type of sales promotion begin their planning as far as a year ahead.

Ordinarily, the success or failure of a formal meeting is pretty well determined before the first dealer is greeted at the door. Advance planning and detailed rehearsal are essential if the affair is to run smoothly. Should the meeting be planned to run in a

PLANNING AND ORGANIZATION CHECKLIST

Item to be Accomplished	Person Responsible—Name	Deadline Date	Done Check Off	Double Checked or Confirmed
1. Hold Planning Meeting with Sponsor				
2. Establish Date				
3. Establish Time				
4. Establish Place Arrange for				
5. Order "As Big As You Make It" Contractor Sales Kits from LOF				
6. Door Prizes Determined				
7. Agenda Set				
8. Invitation List				
9. Establish Budget				
10. Establish Menu				
11. Establish Promotion Plans				
12. "As Big As You Make It" Slide Film and Take Film on Hand and in Good Condition				

This is one of several checklists in the 30-page meeting manual of Libbey-Owens-Ford Company. Other checklists follow sections on Promotion, Room Arrangements and Day-of-Meeting.

number of cities, it is important to remember that the program must be readily adaptable to rooms of varied dimensions and facilities.

Getting Attendance

Teaser cards sent in advance of the program announcement can be effective in arousing curiosity about a forthcoming meeting. If they carry a line like, "Reserve the afternoon of June 25," it will be helpful in getting the dealers to avoid conflicting plans.

The type of mail promotion used to get attendance will depend upon the type and purpose of the meeting. If it is to be a dignified presentation of a new product, some of this dignity should be in the invitations. If, on the other hand, it is going to be used to announce the biggest sales contest in the company's history, the sales promotion man can let himself go.

The company's salesmen should be completely informed about the meeting before they make their last swing through their territories before the meeting date. The personal touch, backed by factual knowledge of just how the session will benefit the dealer, can help to bring out a lot of retailers who might otherwise be reluctant to spend the time.

Door prizes can be used to stimulate the largest attendance. A stunt employed by the Sales Executives Club of Chicago might be adapted. Persons who registered before a certain date were given ten stubs for the prize drawing; persons who registered after this date, but in advance of the meeting, got five; and those who registered at the meeting itself got only one.

An attempt to get advance registrations is very helpful. It commits the dealer to keeping his calendar clear on the meeting date. It also gives the sponsor of the meeting a good idea of the facilities that will be needed—size of meeting room, number of chairs, type of visual aids to be used, and so on. Advance registrations can be requested in the announcement.

Change of Pace Is Important

A formal meeting is essentially a show, and those in attendance will at least subconsciously compare it with professional performances they have seen. Recognition of this fact has led a number of companies recently to use professional actors for the skits in their dealer meetings.

Because of this attitude, change of pace is basic to a successful formal meeting. It can be obtained in a variety of ways; the important point to remember is that presentations should be as varied as possible. Here is a typical outline for a 1-day meeting:

Welcome Address. A formal speech.

Outlook for the Selling Season. Another speech, but with statistical data on charts or overhead projector slides.

How to Sell the Product. A panel of four outstandingly successful dealers.

Luncheon. A humorous talk by a professional speaker.

Advertising Plans. A skit.

Sales Training Plans. A sound-slidefilm.

Product Demonstration. Audience participation, with each man given a sample of the product to handle and work with.

Dinner. A short speech by the president of the company summarizing the day.

In planning a specific session, of course, the form of each presentation will be dictated by the kind of information the company wishes to put across. It is surprising, however, how many different methods of presentation can be employed if the session is deliberately planned with this angle in mind.

The director of training for a leading automobile company prepared the following quick checklist for use in selecting the most effective method of presentation.

MOTION PICTURES (silent or sound), FILM STRIPS OR SLIDES (silent or sound)
Use when over-all view or impression is needed, for group demonstrations of sales situations or methods, when noise of actual operation would prevent explanation, to show actual use or operation of product at distant points, when operation has to be slowed down or stopped for explanations, when viewing factory operation would hamper production, when it is safer to view from film instead of in person.

PROJECTIONS
Where all of group need to look at same drawing, chart, or photograph simultaneously and leader wants to focus all attention on one specific point.

ILLUSTRATIONS, CHARTS, DIAGRAMS, PHOTOGRAPHS
When trends need to be emphasized, when keeping sequence clear is important, for comparative statistics, for clarifying intangible points, when actual product or part is not available.

SAMPLES
To show real object.

CUTAWAYS
To show structure of opaque object, relative position.

MODELS, LARGE-SCALE
Large enough to permit handling, identifying small parts.

MODELS, SMALL-SCALE
Permit operation without using large quantities of material, make a whole operation visible.

BLACKBOARD
> For sketches, diagrams, outlines, definitions, directions, summaries, assignments.

BOOKS, MANUALS, PAMPHLETS, INSTRUCTION SHEETS
> For standard information and guides, manufacturer's information, reference background.

CARTOONS, POSTERS
> To arouse interest, attract attention.

The Meeting Timetable

A successful dealer meeting starts on time, runs on time, and finishes on time. There is nothing that detracts from the effectiveness of a meeting more than late starts, talks which run overtime, or holding the audience after the time the meeting is supposed to break up.

To avoid the possibility of bad timing, it is advisable to prepare a timetable stating the number of minutes allotted to each speaker or each presentation.

PROGRAM TIMING
Proctor "Lady Be Seated" Dealer Meetings

I. WELCOME—OG&E REPRESENTATIVE
Time: 1 Minute
> Ardmore—D. Anderson
> Enid—E. D. Dixon
> Muskogee—C. M. Smith
> Shawnee—Otto Crutchfield

II. INTRODUCTION OF PROCTOR PERSONNEL BY SOUTHWEST RADIO AND SUPPLY COMPANY DISTRICT SALES REPRESENTATIVE
Time: 1 Minute
> Ardmore—Mr. Fleming
> Enid—Mr. Williams
> Muskogee—Mr. Burrough
> Shawnee—Mr. Burrough

III. HISTORY OF "SIT-DOWN IRONING" AND THE DEVELOPMENT OF THE "LADY BE SEATED" PROGRAM
Time: 5 Minutes
> Bob Dewalt

IV. BRIEF PRODUCT STORY ON "NEVER LIFT IRON"
Time: 2 Minutes
> Bob Dewalt

V. "OLD VS. NEW" SKIT
Time: 2 Minutes
> Gus Nelson
> 1 girl

VI. "LADY BE SEATED" TECHNIQUE "HOW TO IRON A SHIRT IN LESS THAN 5 MINUTES"
Time: 5 Minutes
> Suzanne Patterson

VII. PREPARATION OF CLOTHES
Time: 5 Minutes
> E. Moore—Explaining
> Joe Wiggins—Preparing Clothes
> A. Sprinkle shirt once—Group watching
> B. Repeat—Group participating

VIII. EXPLANATION OF IRON
Time: 3 Minutes
> E. Moore
> A. Release
> B. Left- and right-hand ironing
> C. Balance

Program Timing (continued)

D. Temperature control
1. Set dial to light cotton.
E. Plugging in the iron
(Heat iron if possible)

IX. TECHNIQUE OF IRONING A SHIRT
Time: 15 Minutes
E. Moore—Explaining
Joe Wiggins—Ironing

A. Iron one shirt slow motion
B. Repeat—class ironing
C. Contest

1. Divide into groups

2. Explain contest
a. Time—stop when finished
b. Prize for women
c. Prize for men

3. Technique—75%
Appearance—12½%
Time—12½%

X. SOUTHWEST RADIO AND
EQUIPMENT PROMOTION PLANS
Time: 5 Minutes
Bob Dewalt

XI. OKLAHOMA GAS & ELECTRIC
PROMOTION OF "SIT-DOWN IRONING"
Time: 3 Minutes
D. Anderson
A. Introduce OG&E Local Home
Service Representative

XII. PROCTOR AND DISTRIBUTOR
FOLLOW-UP PLANS
Time: 5 Minutes
Bob Dewalt

XIII. PROFITS, DEALER ACTIVITIES
AND ORDERS
Gus Nelson

XIV. REFRESHMENTS

XV. DISCUSSION AND ADDITIONAL
TRAINING FOR THOSE WHO
WISH TO PARTICIPATE

Stunts for Meetings

Another method of getting change of pace in a meeting is by the use of brief but dramatic stunts to liven up the proceedings. These take a variety of forms; one simple but highly effective example is the "magic chart" used by The Kroger Company. For a graphic presentation, a board was prepared with staples tacked vertically at each point where the graph line turned up or down. A fine but strong white thread was passed through the staples; as the talk went on and the chart was needed, an assistant behind the board pulled the thread, bringing into view a tightly woven corded rope of the type upholsterers use for edging. From the audience's viewpoint the chart "filled itself in."

A somewhat different type of stunt is the "hopper." This was used effectively at a dealer meeting sponsored by Culligan, Inc. On stage was placed a huge hopper made of cardboard, and open at the top. Each speaker wrote the figures from his presentation on chart-sized paper which was thrown into the hopper. After advertising plans, promotion plans, and all the other material had been thrown in, the last speaker ground up the material and opened a drawer at the bottom. Out of the hopper came money—dollars for the dealers.

Stunts are particularly effective if they are used to highlight the major message of the meeting. If they are not employed with caution, they may prove a side show which distracts attention from the main tent.

Audience Participation

Even in formal presentations, there is a growing trend toward getting the audience into the act. As a minimum it may be suggested that after each presentation a few minutes should be allowed for questions. This gives a "cushion" to prevent the meeting from running overtime, since the question period can be shortened if need be; the nature of the questions asked gives the sponsor a good indication of how well his presentation has been absorbed by the listeners.

A second type of audience participation is based on radio programs of the "Information Please" type. In one version of these meetings, representatives of major departments in the sponsoring company—a man each from sales, production, service, advertising, and perhaps market research—are the "panel of experts," and the audience is invited to submit questions for one or more of them to answer. In another version, members of the audience form the panel and the other dealers present can submit questions on problems of retail operations.

In another audience participation technique, a competitive angle is added. Four volunteers, for instance, are timed while they erect a point-of-sale display; the man who finishes first wins an award and the audience is shown how easy it is to do the job. Another stunt of this type is for the master of ceremonies to light a match. While the match burns, the contestant demonstrates his sales talk; after all contestants have tried, the applause of the audience determines the winner.

For a company whose product lends itself to such treatment, a session in which each dealer is given a sample to handle can be valuable. Introducing a new meat-slicing machine, for instance, one company recently put a machine in front of each dealer at the meeting. As the talk on the new product proceeded the dealers actually dismantled the machines; when they had been put together again, each man was given a section of meat to slice. The sliced meat was then used for the cold buffet luncheon which followed.

Audience participation does break the monotony of a formal meeting, and it is helpful in making the dealer feel himself part of the show. The danger is that unless there is a firm hand on the helm during an audience participation session, the timing of the meeting will be thrown off. Some good-natured device like a clock which goes off at the end of the speaker's allotted time can be helpful in minimizing this problem.

Supplying Props for Regional Meetings

For a formal meeting at the regional level it is usually advisable for headquarters to develop a simple but comprehensive kit of materials to be used in the presentation and send copies of the kit to each man who is to run a session. With the kit a brief manual or outline is usually included, indicating to the man in charge what the meeting is intended to accomplish, the amount of time to be allotted to each subject, suggested arrangements for the meeting room, and instructions on how and when to use his props.

In planning regional meetings it is important to remember that they will be presented under a variety of physical conditions. For this reason, to take a single example, many companies prefer slide-film or overhead projector slides to material on charts, because the size of the image can be adjusted to suit the size of the audience and the shape of the room.

All props for such meetings should be kept as simple as possible and their use explained carefully. It is always advisable to run through the whole meeting in a "dress rehearsal" to make sure the participants are familiar with their parts. It is also handy to prepare a checklist of all the details which must be taken care of before the meeting starts.

Sales Meeting Checklist

A successful sales meeting is largely a matter of little things done right. A projector which doesn't work because somebody forgot to check the outlet and make sure it was close enough to the projector for the extension cord; lights which were supposed to go out, but no arrangements made to put them out; inadequate spot lighting; these and a hundred other things can "gum up" any meeting. Here are a few check questions from the Lily-Tulip Cup Corporation's manual, "Conducting Sales Meetings That Pay Off":

1. ☐ You—Are you prepared? Know your subject matter thoroughly?
2. ☐ The Wholesaler—Did you confirm meeting *date, time, place?*
3. ☐ The Room—Enough chairs for everyone? Wide center aisle to permit film showing? Enough air, light?
4. ☐ Equipment—Have you all the props, samples, easels, charts, manuals, etc., you will need?

5. ☐ If you plan to show "Paper, Guardian of Health," have you allowed sufficient time for shipment to you? Have you arranged for, and confirmed, the use of a movie projector and services of an operator if necessary?

6. ☐ Is your sound-slide projector in *good running condition?*

7. ☐ Is the *cord* of your projector *long enough* to reach the outlet?

8. ☐ Can the room light be switched off *without cutting off current* for the projector?

9. ☐ Is the screen placed so that *everyone can see it easily?*

10. ☐ Is the projector *correctly placed* and *focused* so that the picture *fills the whole screen* and the *image is sharp?*

11. ☐ Have you practiced running through each film and record in the meeting room, *testing for volume,* record *flaws, speed,* and *needle noise?*

12. ☐ Are the films *rewound* and *ready for showing* at the meeting?

13. ☐ Have you the *right film* and *record?*

CONFERENCE AND ROUND-TABLE MEETINGS

Conference meetings, in which all those in attendance are urged to contribute their thinking and their experience, are growing rapidly in popularity. The psychology of such meetings is that agreement reached after general discussion is apt to be more genuine, and action is more likely to follow from it. The fact that a dealer knows the company is interested in his viewpoint and eager to obtain his ideas can be helpful in building a loyal, hard-hitting organization.

Since the dealers are not directly on the manufacturer's payroll, the informality of a conference-type meeting is likely to appeal to them more than is the somewhat colder, formal speech-making type of session. In the course of the conference the leader can check continually on how much information is actually being absorbed. Finally, the conference method offers a system by which a manufacturer with a large and complex system of distribution can pass information all the way down the line. The U.S. Rubber Company, whose program will be described in detail a little later, planned its conferences to sift down through distributors and dealers to, eventually, 30,000 retail salespeople.

Conference method has certain disadvantages. It requires meetings for small groups; anything much over 40 begins to become unwieldy, although some companies have held conferences for as many as 100 dealers at a time. Ordinarily, it is difficult to get information to the whole organization rapidly with this kind of meeting. Unless conference leaders are trained in the technique of keeping their meetings on the beam, it is a very wasteful method of passing on information. This training of trainers becomes a very serious problem in organizations whose distributive setups are plagued by rapid turnover; however, it is certainly no more serious than the need for maintaining a supply of adequate public speakers for more formal sessions.

How to Run a Conference

The following brief outline was contributed by the former training director of one highly successful sales organization. It is taken from a booklet for dealers called "How to Conduct a Sales Conference."

GET READY

Define objective clearly—If there is no objective, don't hold a meeting. Decide what is specifically wrong and list points to cover in logical sequence to discuss.

Decide what methods or aids you will need such as: Exhibits, reports, diagrams, blackboard, samples, models, photographs, charts, film strips, etc.

Choose a suitable place to hold the meeting—a room that is large enough, where lighting and ventilation are adequate and chairs comfortable, where you will not be interrupted or disturbed by noises or visitors.

Set a time for the meeting—Consider reasons for having the meeting. Is it worth the collective time that will be spent on it? Are hours convenient for all? Do not make it any longer than necessary.

Notify those who will attend—Give them time to arrange to come. Do not make the interval so long the meeting is forgotten. Is a personal last minute check of expected attendance necessary?

Make a last minute check of facilities—The room, the methods, and aids.

OPEN THE MEETING

Start the meeting on time—If you habitually wait for stragglers you penalize yourself and those who are prompt. Put group at ease. Keep meeting informal.

State the objective clearly—State just what you are trying to accomplish. This is basic for concentrating attention on some specific subject which you want understood, accepted or opened up, corrected, improved, or prevented. Put your objective on the blackboard if necessary—stress its importance— refer to it—hold to it. Talk while you do board work and don't block the view.

Find out what the group already knows about the subject. Fill in the gaps.

GUIDE THE DISCUSSION

Provoke group thinking by using questioning technique. Be impersonal. Direct thought-provoking questions to individuals, not to the group. Do not "call on" a member or introduce the question by his name—use the name at the end of the question. Avoid questions that can be answered by "yes" or "no." Try to keep participation voluntary, but if some are reluctant, direct leading or obvious questions to them.

Keep participation moving—Don't let any one person monopolize the discussion. Be ready to break in with a "thank you"—and have a question ready for another member. Don't answer his questions directly. Get other members to answer them—but avoid arguments.

Define obstacles—Find out whether anything interferes with accomplishing the objective—and what it is. Guide the discussion toward concrete evidence and specific difficulties you can do something about.

Discuss possible solutions—If needed, list obstacles and solutions on board. Talk while you do board work. Do not block view of board. Summarize frequently.

Clinch ideas—With reports, samples, charts, and other materials. Use illustrations, motion pictures, film strips, diagrams, mockups, cutaways, exhibits, etc. Confine discussion to specific subject under consideration. Watch your schedule so you can close on time.

CLOSE THE MEETING

Summarize solutions—Get agreement. Each solution should be clearly understood by all. Majority rules. An effective plan should be developed to carry out the objective.

Assign responsibility for agreed action by making sure each understands "who's going to do what, and when." Forestall "buck-passing." Use the board if needed.

Compliment on participation—To make them realize they've had a part in solving the problem. Be genuine and appreciative so they'll want to help you solve other problems.

Finish on time—Close the meeting just once. When the objective has been reached, quit—even if it's ahead of time.

Record obstacles and agreements so an efficient follow-up can be carried on and results measured. It might be advisable to give each a written report on action decided or policy accepted.

How U.S. Rubber Uses Conference Method

The U.S. Rubber Company spent 3 years developing a conference meeting program which resulted in distributors paying for training materials and for personnel overtime and holding more than 5,000 meetings in a 6-month period. The activity may offer a few suggestions to other organizations.

Once the decision to use conference method was reached, seven trainers were hired and given a 3-months' course in conducting conferences. They were then assigned to various sections of the country to pass the technique along to company salesmen. These in turn carried the story to distributors, and the distributors reached the ultimate objective—the retail sales personnel.

Naturally, not all salesmen were either enthusiastic about or proficient at the conference technique. The men who got the idea began using it at once, while the trainers worked individually with the less successful men. Each trainer sat in on several conferences with each man, offering suggestions for improvement until the salesman could run a practically perfect meeting.

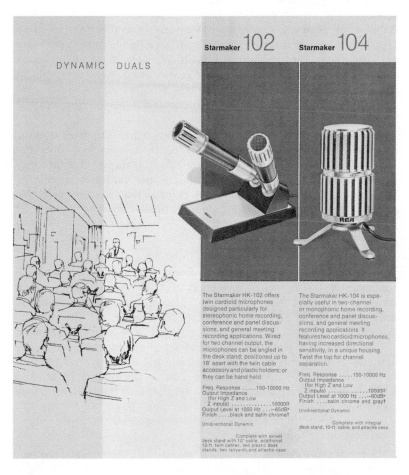

DYNAMIC DUALS

Starmaker 102   Starmaker 104

The Starmaker HK-102 offers twin cardioid microphones designed particularly for stereophonic home recording, conference and panel discussions, and general meeting recording applications. Wired for two channel output, the microphones can be angled in the desk stand; positioned up to 18' apart with the twin cable accessory and plastic holders; or they can be hand held.

Freq. Response . . . . .150-10000 Hz
Output Impedance
(for High Z and Low
Z inputs) 10000Ω
Output Level at 1000 Hz . . .—65dB*
Finish . . . . black and satin chrome†

Unidirectional Dynamic

Complete with swivel desk stand with 10' cable, additional 10-ft. twin cables, two plastic desk stands, two lanyards, and attache case.

The Starmaker HK-104 is especially useful in two-channel or monophonic home recording, conference and panel discussions, and general meeting recording applications. It features two cardioid microphones, having increased directional sensitivity, in a unique housing. Twist the top for channel separation.

Freq. Response . . . . .150-10000 Hz
Output Impedance
(for High Z and Low
Z inputs) 10000Ω
Output Level at 1000 Hz . . .—60dB*
Finish . . . .satin chrome and gray†

Unidirectional Dynamic

Complete with integral desk stand, 10-ft. cable, and attache case.

The RCA Microphone catalog features two models which are especially useful for meetings, conferences and panel discussions. One model has twin microphones which can be angled; the second model features two microphones with increased directional sensitivity in a unique housing.

To assure uniformity in the program, U.S. Rubber developed a very simple kit for sale to distributors. It contains two basic tools —the conference manual is a loose-leaf notebook with a trick cover which permits the leader to use it at about a 30-degree angle to guide his own presentation, or to stand it at about a 70-degree angle for use as a visualizer for the audience; an easel is also included which has flip-flop chart presentations on the right side and big sheets of blank paper for notemaking on the left.

With the purchase of the manual and easel the distributor receives sets of all the charts and course materials currently in stock. As new programs are developed they are mailed to participating distributors. Some of the materials, of course, become dated and are discarded, but the others remain available in a single handy package. As a result the program is elastic; a new development can be brought to the organization's attention quickly, and the individual distributor can arrange to repeat any part of the material as he thinks necessary.

One final point about this activity is quoted in the sales training director's own words: "The use of conference method does not imply at all that we ignore any of the aids to training. Our meetings vary a good deal—some include films, some stunts, some demonstrations, and so on. The important point is that we recognize aids as just that. Showing a film doesn't prove anything unless the audience actually learns from it."

Conferences at Formal Meetings

Situations will of course arise from time to time in which a combination of a formal presentation with individual or group conferences is necessary. Gunnison Homes uses this technique in conjunction with a 1-day headquarters meeting for dealers and prospective dealers. The major portion of the day is given over to a tour of the plant and speeches on the company's plans and activities. These end at about 4 o'clock, and the last hour is spent by the dealers discussing problems on an individual basis with whichever member of the headquarters staff is most immediately concerned.

The Telephone Conference

The telephone conference is a means of "bringing together" people from widely separated locations without moving them geographically.

According to the AT & T Booklet "How to Call a Conference," it allows up to 30 locations to conduct two-way conversations, where conferees at each point can discuss, listen and participate in a meeting. When the need is for one-way broadcast only—where the speakers are located at only one point to address all the others who only hear but not speak—then many more points can be added to the hook-up.

Each point, though, should not be thought of only in terms of a single individual. Through such equipment as the Portable Conference Telephone, a group of conferees can attend at each location and be in two-way communication with similar groups at other locations.

Conference service values can be maximized with sound planning, advance preparation, and an understanding of how to conduct the telephone conference.

As a general rule, the telephone conference should be even better planned and organized than a face-to-face meeting. The larger the group involved, the more necessary are the following suggestions:

1. All members should receive sufficient advance notice to be available for the conference.

2. All agenda and useful background material should be sent to each, well in advance. This permits the participants to prepare for the subjects to be discussed for maximum benefits.

3. Visual materials should be prepared and mailed in advance if such aids can be useful and will be an integral part of the discussion. Slides, flip charts, photographs, and posters add a vital dimension. They should be sent in proper sequence with instructions for use to each location included in the conference.

Sound is a strange, interesting phenomenon. Certain materials absorb sound. Others reflect and rebound it. This affects its clarity. It isn't mandatory to have custom-designed rooms for telephone conferences. But, here are some hints to help achieve pleasant, clear, satisfying sound reception.

1. Select telephone conference rooms where the outside noise level is minimal. Avoid rooms with many windows and which face a busy, noisy street.

2. New telephone conference equipment offers good reception, almost regardless of location. But, for the best possible reception, sound engineers recommend rooms furnished with sound absorbing materials. Carpeting, drapes, fabric-upholstered furniture, and acoustical ceilings can help to improve sound quality.

3. If visual materials are to be used, slide projectors, screens,

and other gear should be conveniently located with appropriate electrical power and outlets.

The newest, most versatile equipment now available is the specially-engineered Portable Conference Telephone. With a built-in microphone for someone near the unit, two hand mikes that can be passed around a table to a speaker, and a full-fidelity sound system so that all participants can hear, this push-button instrument is a useful tool for conducting effective group conferences. When not in use (it can even be used as a desk phone), it can be stored conveniently in its own carrying case.

HOW TO GET THE MOST OUT OF A MEETING

A basic rule for any type of sales promotional activity, so simple that it is occasionally overlooked, is that the sponsor must decide in advance exactly what it is he wishes to accomplish. If the meeting is intended to arouse enthusiasm for a new product, it will take an entirely different form and approach than will a session in which techniques for recruiting the best types of salesmen are to be presented.

Speaking of meetings for his own sales force, A. R. Kneibler, vice president in charge of marketing for Coopers, Inc., said recently, "The basic question which must be answered is: What is the purpose of a conference? Is it worth the expense of bringing our men to Wisconsin from all over the United States so the president can tell them we're a good company, the treasurer can tell them expenses are too high, and the sales manager can tell them to get out and sell?"

Modified to suit the situation, this critical approach is even more important in planning a dealer meeting. The sponsor is inviting a group of independent businessmen to spend an hour or a day listening to his pitch; if the meeting is to be a success, it had better offer them something.

It is usually not a good idea to schedule dealer meetings at a traditional time of year or on an annual or semiannual basis; there is always the possibility that the program will be planned because "We've got a meeting coming up," rather than because the manufacturer has some significant information for the group.

At the other extreme, there are companies which do not use meetings as often as would be advisable. Any time that the company has a story to tell the whole organization, a meeting should be at least considered. The basic question involved is whether it

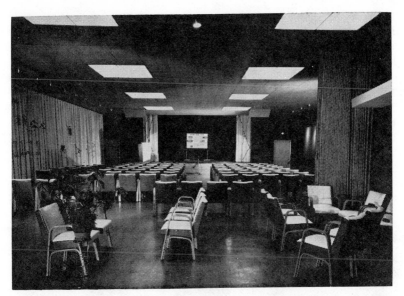

An attractive meeting place adds much to the success-potentials of sales meetings. This Kimberly-Clark Sales Center auditorium seats about 200 persons, and is provided with all facilities for use either as a conference room or a "theater" for skits, playlets, and films, for sales-training and sales-promotion meetings.

will be more economical to do it this way or to have the salesmen pass on the story to each dealer individually, cutting into his few precious hours of selling time and subject to the interruptions which are almost inevitable in a retail store.

Staging the Meeting

Much of the success of a conference depends upon arranging the room so the conferees will be comfortable and the speaker will be at ease. If the hotel has some comfortable armchairs, instead of the folding contraptions most of them provide, insist upon having them. If possible arrange for tables, putting them in rows, with not more than two men (facing the platform) to a table. It is nice to have a place to make notes and keep papers. If the men are strangers to one another, it costs but little to have a "place card," lettered large enough to read from a distance, for each man. It also establishes his right to the place, and makes him feel important. At the back of the room, post a list of those attending the conference, the number of their table, and their business connection. That facilitates visiting during a "seventh inning" stretch. It is also a nice gesture, to have an inexpensive binder containing the agenda and other material to be used during the meeting, with the dealer's name stamped on it. It is something in which he can keep his papers and memoranda, and can take home.

Another important detail about conference meetings is the seating arrangement. Unless pictures are to be shown, it is best not to have a wide aisle down the middle of the room to the platform. Space the chairs (or tables) far enough apart so conferees will not have to climb over one another, and have aisles on each side. Speaking

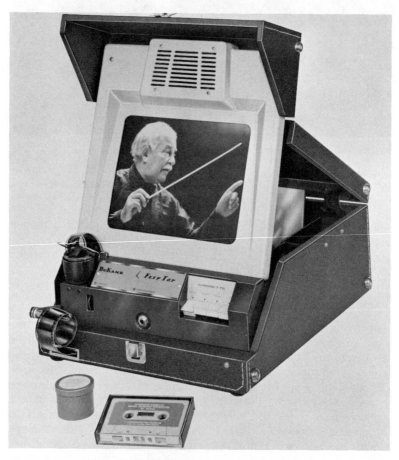

DuKane Cassette Flip-top Automatic Tape Sound Film Strip Viewer is designed for sales presentations, small-group instruction and individual instruction. Features: automatic operation, easy-loading cassettes, program hold control, sharp pictures, quality sound and light-weight carrying case.

to an empty aisle is hard on a speaker. He has to keep turning his head from one side to the other. If pictures or slides are to be used, try to arrange for an overhead projector, placed in the back of the room rather than in the aisle. A white board, instead of a blackboard, permits the use of colored crayons. It also is more easily lighted. The less furniture on the platform the better. Let those who are going to participate in the meeting sit in the front row, until called. The speaker should have the undivided attention of his audience.

Be Realistic

It is a good idea to have at least nominal responsibility for meeting arrangements placed with a high company official, because to be realistic means to be tough as well. If company personnel are to be used for skits, their dramatic ability is far more important than their titles in the organization, but this is not a matter for an assistant sales promotion man to explain to the president.

An account executive for an advertising agency, after attending a couple of the dealer meetings sponsored by a client, tactfully told the president of the client company that he had been bored stiff and suspected the audience had too. Asked for suggestions, he proposed formal training for company executives in public speaking. Ten top men, at the invitation of the president, took such a course—and interest in later meetings was much higher.

A critical approach to meeting content may make it necessary to step on a few toes in the interest of a good show. Many meetings are far longer than they need be because certain departments or personages have traditionally taken part in each program.

Being realistic involves accepting the facts of the company's situation and planning the meeting on the basis of those facts. Regional meetings, if half the company's branch managers are not good public speakers, should be planned so that the managers will have a minimum of speaking to do. Conference meetings are almost sure to flop if the men in charge have not been trained in conference method. Equipment which is new to the men who will have to use it should never be used in a meeting without drilling the users in its operation. And so on.

Re-Use Meeting Materials

Very often the meeting sponsored by the manufacturer is followed by similar meetings run by the distributors for dealers in their franchise areas. In this situation it is economical and practical to make at least part of the material from the first meeting available for the other meetings at very little cost.

At a meeting of the Venetian and Vertical Blind Association a "how-to-sell" skit was presented. The presentation was recorded on wire tape and made available to members for use at later meetings.

The Seven-Up Company produced a successful distributors' meeting at which 50 separate events were crowded into a 2-day session. Mimeographed copies of all the skits were offered to the distributors for use in their meetings. Because the program was planned to include this idea, all skits were kept very simple—short, with just a few characters, and using as few props as possible.

The Eureka Williams "Alibi Ike" meeting, mentioned earlier under traveling meetings, proved so successful with dealers that it was repeated to a wider audience some months later at the National Oil Heat Exposition.

Iron Fireman Mfg. Company set up a row of "tough guys" representing various kinds of sales resistance, and passed out baseballs for the audience to use in knocking them down. The idea was used over and over again.

Supply Take-Home Materials

Whether they be simple or elaborate, some kind of written summary sheets covering the material presented in the meeting should be given to those attending, at the end of the session. In the case of an extended meeting for big distributors, some companies go so far as to record and publish a transcript of the entire proceedings of the meeting.

Organizations which sponsor a dealer bulletin can of course use an issue of the publication to summarize the meeting and get a lot of dealers' pictures in print.

It is usually a good idea to preface any discussion which involves a mass of statistics with the statement that the figures will be made available after the meeting. Otherwise the conscientious note-taker will probably get lost along the way, and all of the audience is likely to lose the broad pattern in an attempt to keep the figures in mind.

Another organization used a readily adaptable idea for a conference meeting at which a number of graphs were employed. Instead of putting the graphs on big charts, the company mimeographed them on standard letterhead size paper. Each participant was given a complete set before the meeting began. He could follow the presentation from the sheets in front of him and take the whole collection along for reference afterward. However, the audience has a tendency to play with the papers during the meeting.

Follow-Up for Action

The meeting has ended; the compliments have been exchanged; the audience has gone home. It still isn't over for the sponsor who wishes to be sure he has put his story across, because a follow-up for action is necessary.

Sometimes it is possible to get a commitment from the audience at the time of the meeting and to simply check sales control records to see that the dealers are living up to their commitments. Ordinarily, however, this is not enough. The company's salesmen can often check in the course of their regular trips through their territories, and headquarters can help them by direct-mail pieces.

The more individualized the follow-up, the more effective it will be. Some distributor and dealer meetings, as has been mentioned before, are planned to allow 1 day at the end for individual conferences. In these conferences the dealers can outline their plans for adapting the manufacturer's program to their individual operation.

A company working through distributors, in a situation where the distributor runs the dealer meetings, has an even more complicated problem. U.S. Rubber has asked its distributors, on a purely voluntary basis, to report on each such meeting held and comment frankly on how successful it was. Although this will not give an accurate figure of the number of meetings held, it does at least establish a minimum.

Closed-Circuit Television Meetings (CCTV)

So far, the sports field has made good use of CCTV. Some companies have tentatively explored the medium as a means of reaching distributors and dealers across the country as a less expensive and perhaps novel alternative to bringing them in to a central assembly point. Companies such as Brown-Forman Distillers Corporation and Thomasville-Armstrong have used CCTV. In the case of Thomasville Furniture, one of the purposes of which was to announce the merger with Armstrong Cork Company, the ninety-minute program was viewed by approximately five thousand retail furniture salesmen and executives assembled in hotels in 32 cities. Videotape, live performers and speakers were mixed in a professional manner to produce a very effective program. The General Electric Command Performance network is capable of broadcasting color presentations to 20-foot screens in 25 cities. At the time, the cost of a one-hour buy was about $42,000 and $25,000 for each additional hour. There can be no doubt that CCTV, like Cable TV, has many advantages that will lead to further development and wider use year by year.

CHECKLIST FOR A SUCCESSFUL MEETING

1. ATTENDANCE

   Total number of members expected
   Method of transportation to hotel city
   Limousine service from airport

2. DATES

   Date group will arrive
   Date group will depart
   Date uncommitted guest rooms are to be released

3. ACCOMMODATIONS

   Approximate number needed:
   singles..............doubles..............suites..............
   Room rates for members
   Reservations confirmation: to delegate, copies to group chairman or secretary

4. COMPLIMENTARY ACCOMMODATIONS

   Number of hospitality suites needed
   Room rates
   Bars, snacks, service time and dates
   Names of contacts for suites
   Checkrooms, gratuities

5. GUESTS

   Invitations to local dignitaries
   Tickets
   Transportation
   Welcome at hotel
   Guest speakers

6. SPECIFIC EQUIPMENT AND FACILITIES

   Signs for registration desk and other points: program schedules, directional signs, welcome signs
   Complete list of available equipment and prices furnished
   Notes to be placed in guest boxes
   Lighting: spots, floods, operators
   Size of staging
   Blackboards, chart stands, easels
   Lighted lectern, gavel, block
   P.A. system: microphones, types, number
   Recording equipment, operator
   Projection equipment, blackout switch, operator
   Phonograph and records
   Piano, organ

6. SPECIFIC EQUIPMENT AND FACILITIES (Continued)

Printed services
Special flowers and plants
Decorations (must meet fire regulations)
Dressing rooms for entertainers
Garage and parking arrangements
Other equipment
Cost of extra equipment or services
Telephones, number
Flags, banners
Photographer, stenographer
Radio and TV broadcasting: closed-circuit TV
Live and engineering charges for radio, TV

7. MEETINGS

Times and dates of each
Room assignments and rentals
Complete floor plan furnished
Headquarters room
Seating plans for each meeting
Speakers' tables
Timing of meetings for speedy traffic flow
Staging required
Other equipment
Points to check just before each meeting:
 Checkroom operation
 Seating plan as specified
 Location of additional seats
 Room temperature
 Operation of P.A. system, mikes, recording equipment
 Lectern and light, gavel, block
 Water pitcher, water and glasses at lectern, at conferees' tables
 Table ashtrays, stands, matches, pencils, notepads, paper
 All audio-visual aids: charts, stands, easels, blackboards, etc.
 Projector, screen, stand, operator
 Piano, organ
 Lighting as specified
 Signs, flags and banners placed correctly
 Special flowers and plants
 Other special facilities
 Signs directing members and guests to rooms
 Stenographer, photographer present
Points to check after each meeting:
 Removal of organization property
 Check for forgotten property

8. ORGANIZATION OF EXHIBITS

Number of exhibits
Floor plans
Date of setup and dismantling
Room assignments and daily rentals
Name of display company
Directional signs

8. ORGANIZATION OF EXHIBITS (Continued)
   Labor charges: electrician and carpenter services
   Electrical power, steam, gas, water and waste lines
   Electrical charges
   Partitions, backdrops
   Storage of shipping cases
   Guard service

9. REGISTRATION
   Approximate time required
   Registration cards: number and size
   Personnel to handle
   Number of tables............., chairs.............
   Ashtrays
   Typewriters: number and type
   Paper, pencils, pens
   Signs
   Water pitchers, glasses
   Lighting
   Telephones
   Bulletin boards: number and size
   Cash drawers: number and size
   File boxes: number and size
   Safe deposit box
   Points to check just before opening:
      Personnel understanding of procedure
      Necessary information on registration cards, badges
      Location of programs, other material
      Hospitality desk
      Mimeograph registration lists
      Posting of instructions at convenient spots
      Location of tables
      Lighting at tables
      Wastebaskets
      Cards, pencils on tables
   Points to check during registration:
      Presence of administrator to make policy decisions
      Policy for registration of members after desk is closed
      Provision for checking funds at closing time

10. BANQUET FACILITIES
    Complete floor plans of banquet rooms
    Dates and times of each banquet or catered gathering
    Assignment and rental of banquet rooms
    Seating plan for each banquet, special menus, place cards
    Equipment for each banquet
    Other special requirements
    Points to check just before banquet:
       Menus and place cards as specified
       Ashtrays
       Audio-visual aids
    Points to check just after banquet:
       Removal of organization property
       Check for forgotten property

11. ENTERTAINMENT

For reception, banquet, special events
Entertainers and orchestra rehearsal for shows
Recorded or live entertainment
Music stands provided by orchestra or hotel
Variety of entertainment program

12. MISCELLANEOUS

Sightseeing trips arranged
Car rentals

13. PUBLICITY

Publicity committee
Press room, typewriters and telephones
Personal calls on city editors, radio and TV program directors
Press releases
Copies of speeches in advance
Arrangements for photographs, publicity

Courtesy: Hyatt House Hotels and Training in Business and Industry

A Complete Meeting Manual

In connection with its storefront modernization sales campaign, Libbey-Owens-Ford provided its sales representatives with an excellent, complete meeting manual for distributors and dealers involved in glazing or in supplying glass, metal and labor in the storefront remodelling market. The theme of the campaign was "As Big as You Make It." The meetings were built around a synchronized cassette and slide film presentation based on a successful selling system used by the Rhinelander Glass Company in Wisconsin.

The 30-page, spiral-bound meeting manual included the following sections:

Facts About the Program (Objectives)
How to Organize the Meeting
Promotion and Checklist
Invitation Letter and RSVP Card
Follow-Up
Sample Invitation Letter
Room Arrangements and Checklist
Refreshment Guide
Door Prizes
Special Instructions for Carousel Trays and Cassettes
Conducting the Meeting
Suggested Agenda
Day-of-Meeting Checklist
Follow-Up and Sample Letter

In summary, Richard Cavalier, professional meeting planner, offers, in *Advertising & Sales Promotion,* the following significant suggestions:

Meetings are a commitment to convey information, to communicate. Unless you measure, by written test or role simulation, you cannot legitimately claim success in communicating.

The biggest dog-and-pony show on earth cannot outperform educational values of competent, repeatable, training programs.

To get real mileage, create the entire meeting from the viewpoint of your audience.

Producers have countless packaging tricks . . . the most visible, but least intrinsically valuable.

You really need only a message, someone to deliver it properly and someone who will react because the message affects him.

Pep-Up the Meetings*

"Someone to deliver (the message) properly," said Mr. Cavalier. There is nothing so boring as a dull speaker who is monotonous and long-winded; he will put dealers to sleep. If the company president or other executives are tiresome, keep them off the program, except perhaps to say hello.

Next, there is a proliferation of audiovisuals, available from a variety of sources, produced specifically for sales-training purposes in a lively, interesting way. They offer welcome relief to a dealer audience which has been sitting and listening to talk after talk; but they contribute appropriately to the general purpose of the meeting, which is to inspire bigger and better salesmanship for a company's products.

---

*For more information see Dartnell's *How To Plan & Conduct Productive Business Meetings* by Donald L. Kirkpatrick.

Chapter 23

PROMOTIONAL CONTESTS

IN planning a contest of any kind, *the most important thing to consider is the law*. That cannot be emphasized too much. In many major corporations, some advertising and sales promotion managers moan about the requirement that ads and promotional pieces be submitted to the legal department for approval, but here is one area where it is *absolutely necessary*.

Contests and sweepstake promotions are subject to the disciplinary jurisdiction of the Federal Trade Commission and, equally important, to that of the United States Postal Service.

There are all kinds of contests, for the general public, for dealers and for salesmen; all must comply with government standards designed to prevent fraud, deception or favoritism. Violations can be costly even if only limited to revising and reprinting a ton of literature.

Today, most contests do not require the entrant to make any cash outlay whatever. He need not buy anything. If he doesn't have a box-top, a facsimile sketch, however rough, is often acceptable. All this is due to the need for compliance with government regulations and to the desire of the advertiser to bring his product to the attention of as many potential customers as possible.

Manufacturers selling through retailers try to channel this interest to dealers' stores to expose prospective buyers to the product and to give the dealers a chance to make a presentation. Some companies mail out numbered tickets, and the contestant has nothing more to do than enter a dealer's store to verify whether or not he won a prize! That's when the dealer receives the opportunity to do some selling.

While the nature of sales contests has changed considerably, the underlying principle of this form of promotion remains: *Get people to do something*. Any promotion which gets "audience participation" is good because it bridges the gap between indifference and action.

Whether it is mailing in box tops, sending a post card to your favorite radio station, guessing the names of famous people from partially concealed photographs, or writing 25 words to tell why you favor some advertised product over all others, the promotional principle is the same—audience participation. The more people you can get to participate, the more people you have on your side. Whether they buy or not is another matter. At least you have taken the first step—getting their interest and attention.

In some years, more money has been spent from the advertising appropriation to promote contests than to promote premiums; in other years, the trend has been in the other direction.

An analysis by *Premium Practice* magazine of 478 contests advertised in 10 leading publications showed that 150, or 31%, required no cash outlay on the part of respondents; 77 called for from 1 to 24 cents; 149 for 25 to 49 cents; 75 for 50 cents to $1; and 10 for over $1. Seventeen offers called for no evidence of purchase.

Out of 180 contests, 128 or 70% offered merchandise or merchandise-and-cash prizes; 52 offered cash only; 62 required the completion of a sentence; 32 the completion of a limerick, 19 the writing of a letter, and 7 the writing of a slogan; 60 contests were of different types.

CONSUMER CONTESTS

The promotional contest, as we are considering it here, differs from the competitive contest used to motivate salesmen. This type of contest is used in sales management and is covered in Chapter 45, "Sales Contests and Drives," of our *Sales Manager's Handbook*. It is based on the principle that men will put forth a greater effort when they are pitted against one another in friendly competition than when they have only a money incentive to induce them to work. There is an appeal to pride as well as to gain. While this principle is sometimes found in consumer contests, where costly prizes are offered to a few winners, the sales purpose of such contests is to get people to participate in the competition, by going to their dealers and asking for the product.

The effect of a number of customers asking for a product not in stock usually results in the dealer ordering from his supplier. This process lays the foundation for national distribution. This technique is particularly suited to spot radio broadcasts and television. However, its use is limited to fast-repeating, popular-priced products available through established channels of trade. Failure usually results if the product lacks repeat qualities, or involves too large an outlay on the dealer's part.

Examples of Consumer Contests

A $175,000 Win-a-Way contest featuring prizes for 3,000 people, grand prizes for two, was conducted by American Machine & Foundry Company, Bowling Products Group, Westbury, New York.

Ads announcing the contest appeared in 8½ million copies of *Life*. Each ad bore a "lucky number" which had to be matched on a prize winner list available only at AMF dealers. Since the magazine publishes a number of regional editions, only participating dealers in specified areas covered by the regional edition were listed.

If a reader's "lucky number" appeared on the prize sheet, he won his choice of an AMF bowling ball, bag, or shoe set pictured in the ad.

Entrants also had a chance to win an all-expense-paid trip for two to Europe, or a trip for a five-member bowling team to any authorized tournament anywhere in the U.S. during 1966. There were also 10 consolation prizes of $100.

Pillsbury Company annually conducts a widely promoted "Bake Off" contest in which 100 finalists bake their own recipes in a televised finale publicized in newspaper ads in 70 cities.

Other interesting contest plans are to be found in the publication field, where they are used to gain additional circulation.

In Philadelphia, two competing newspapers simultaneously were giving cash awards totaling $1,000 daily to owners of prize-winning social security numbers. The readers mailed in their own numbers, but this was not a requirement, as some numbers were drawn from official lists. All the contestant had to do was to read a paper every day to see if his number had "turned up."

A promotion covering a period of two months was conducted by Borden, Inc., for its cheeses with a tie-in campaign for General Electric's Toasters. Ads were run in *Progressive Grocer, Woman's Day* and *Reader's Digest*. During the period, purchasers of Toast-R-Ovens who sent in proof of purchases received coupons for 5 free packs of Borden cheese.

Highlighting the campaign was a Borden "Easy Living" sweepstakes featuring first prize of a GE Americana "dream" kitchen (refrigerator, range, dishwasher, disposal and trash compactor), plus a remodeling cost allowance of $3,000. Toast-R-Ovens were awarded to 250 second-prize winners.

The Nestlé Company started a "Ton of Groceries" sweepstakes to premote its Decaf instant coffee, supported by ads in women's magazines and on network radio.

Color pages in *Family Circle, Good Housekeeping, Ladies' Home Journal,* and *Woman's Day,* plus commercials on a popular radio show (CBS) told consumers that first prize in the sweepstakes was "a ton of groceries (we give you $5,000—you buy the groceries)" and second prize was "free dinner parties for one year (we give you $3,000—you buy the dinners)."

A prospective depositor looks over the selection of secondary prizes at Girard Bank's grand opening on Philadelphia's Girard Plaza. The Grand Prize was an all-expense, two-week trip for two to any three plazas in the world—London, Paris, Madrid—anywhere.

To enter, a consumer was required to send in the inner seal from the lid of a Decaf jar or "a piece of paper on which you have hand drawn the word 'Decaf' in plain block letters."

Philadelphia's Girard Bank moved an entire grand opening program out onto the sidewalks of center city.

Called Pick-A-Plaza, the opening promotion centered around a contest in which the grand prize was an all-expense, two-weeks trip to three cities—winner's choice—in London, Paris, Madrid, Rome, Lisbon, Amsterdam. There were also a number of secondary prizes and gifts for new accounts; items like bubble umbrellas, electric coffee-makers, luggage, etc.

To promote the contest, the bank, through its agency, Aitkin-Kynett Company, developed a complete plaza theme right on its own sidewalk. For the entire promotion week, the sidewalk featured an outdoor restaurant, a gazebo, strolling musicians, an organ grinder, a balloon vendor, a quick-portrait artist, real flowers, fake trees, and lots of people.

During the week-long opening period, the bank got more than 700 new accounts totalling more than $165,000. It was, according to Dick Park, the bank's V.P., Advertising and Public Relations, a highly successful opening.

Pointing to the success of the program was the fact that the bank had to "raid" some of its other locations for tellers during the opening. At some times during the opening the crowds were more than ten-deep at the teller stations.

The bank is considering more of such open-air promotions for future branch openings.

The Reuben H. Donnelley Corporation of Chicago, which has a department specializing in putting on and operating consumer and related contests for advertisers, lists the purposes for which promotional contests are used as follows:

1. To stimulate the immediate sale of an established product. Occasionally the sponsor may be interested simply in increasing total sales but it is more likely that he will have in mind one of the more specific reasons listed below.

2. Intensify distribution of old product. This would be to secure additional dealers in the territory where distribution is now spotty.

3. Open new territory by local contests.

4. Stimulate a product which has been slipping by reason of inadequate promotion or by the greater aggressiveness of competition.

5. To stimulate "full-line" purchase. Where the "leader" in a line of related items has received the major share of the promotion, it is usual to find the "trailers" running far behind the leader in volume; for example, Ivory Soap has such universal acceptance that anyone who wishes to enter the contest would be glad to buy it but the interest in Ivory Snow can be stimulated and the advertiser can cash in on the prestige of his leader by requiring proof of purchase of both items in order to qualify for the contest.

6. To level out a seasonal peak and valley condition. For example, all tomato soups, catsups, etc., are produced within a period of about 30 days as the tomatoes ripen, as it is, of course, impossible to store them. With an entire year's production of tomato products on hand the manufacturer has a terrific warehousing problem, not to mention the cost of having his capital thus tied up. He therefore undertakes to force the jobber to carry

maximum inventory. The jobber undertakes to load the retailer. And all concerned would like to load up the consumer who is the only one who does not have an insurance and warehousing cost. In this situation a contest requiring a sales slip or other proof of purchase of perhaps twelve cans of soup would be a powerful means of pushing this inventory down the line into the consumers' hands.

7. Train the public to increase the unit of purchase by asking for three wrappers to enter the contest.

8. Clear the retailers' shelves just before introducing a new package design or perhaps a new product to replace the old one which is going to be withdrawn entirely.

9. Introduce new product. Here we have the closest approach to the "sampling" process which has already been discussed under premiums in the Manual. In other words, instead of spending his money to do manual sampling or couponing and giving away a free sample or a discount on the full-size package—the advertiser frequently finds it cheaper to spend the money on a contest, thereby inducing the consumer to purchase the sample at the full price and in the full size where there is greater probability of her giving it a thorough trial.

10. Focus attention on certain features, or uses, of product. The manufacturer may have put so much emphasis on one use of his product that

	Top Choice	Second	Third
Type	Sweepstakes	Limerick or jingle	Naming
Prize	Cash	Autos	Choice of Mdse
Value of Prize	$10,000 to $19,999	$20,000 to $34,999	$35,000 or more
Number of Prizes	750 or more	350 to 749	200 to 349
Principal Audience	General	Women	—
Proof or Task Required	3 to 5 labels or Proof Purchase	1 label or Proof Purchase	2 labels or Proof Purchase
Value of Proof Required	Less than 25¢	25¢ to 49¢	50¢ to 99¢
Length of Contest Period	6 to 8 weeks	10 to 16 weeks	Less than 4 weeks
Number of Contest Periods	5 to 6	7 to 9	10 plus
Contest Opening Date	February	April	October

The Donnelley Study, on analysis of contest results, indicates that contests draw 25 million entries a year. The popularity of various types of contests is summarized in the chart above.

Courtesy: Incentive, Magazine of the Premium Industry

it has become "typed" and he finds it necessary to remind the consumer of its other uses. For example, Bon Ami has such universal acceptance for window cleaning and silver polishing that the manufacturer might find it desirable to run a contest on "I like Bon Ami for washing painted walls and woodwork because . . ."

11. Sampling an established product. The principle of using the contest as a sampling medium is not necessarily confined to new products as discussed under No. 9 above. The contest can be an effective sampling medium on an established product.

12. To find new uses for the product. Here again Bon Ami is a good example. They ran a contest in which contestants were invited to write about their preference for Bon Ami in any particular usage which they preferred. The result was to uncover a large list of uses which would not ordinarily be suspected.

13. Check consumer understanding of advertising copy. The manufacturer of a heavily advertised product may announce a contest and, contrary to the usual custom, not give the contestant much information about the product in the contest announcement. The entries will then reflect the effectiveness of advertising previously done—or the lack of such effectiveness.

14. The advertiser may have a genuine desire to get a new name or slogan for his product. In such a case, of course, he must use a tie-breaker statement since the best name or best slogan is apt to be duplicated many times.

15. Checking advertising media. By using a different post office box number in each publication ad, the advertiser can count the number of entries received from each publication and measure that against the rate for that publication thereby establishing some measure of the cost per reader. When the contest is announced on the radio, the entries can be sent to the station over which the announcement is heard. These stations are then permitted to forward such mail to the contest judges or to the sponsor himself at low cost by express provided that the mail is not opened at the station. It is hardly feasible to use a different post office box number for each station to have the entries come to one central city. Usually, there are too many stations involved and it is easier to say "Send your entry to the station to which you are listening."

16. As an attention getter. When a product has been advertised consistently and persistently, the reader is apt to pass over the ad very quickly unless some "stopper" is introduced. This is accomplished, of course, with such a caption as "$50,000 CASH." Most readers will stop to see what all of the shouting is about and will read the ad even though they may not enter the contest. This enhanced readership might very easily be worth the entire cost of the contest although, of course, there would never be any way of proving it.

The "guessing" competitions conducted by retailers are another type of consumer contest. A jar of beans, or something similar, is placed in the store window and a prize offered to whoever comes the closest to guessing how many beans are in the jar. Entry blanks are inside the store, of course.

STAGING THE CONTEST

Four things determine the success of a contest, in the opinion of a Donnelley executive: (1) The type of contest, (2) the prize schedule, (3) advertising and promotion of the contest, and (4) the availability, price popularity, etc., of the product itself.

For many years the 25-word essay type was the most popular. It was considered an easy type of contest to enter and advertisers felt that participants, in writing about the product, would sell themselves on it. Recently there has been a trend away from the essay in favor of jingle and limerick contests and some other kinds. There is a puzzle element in the jingle which attracts people and the entry can be composed without pencil and paper. Therefore jingle contests encourage heavy participation. The easiest contest to enter, however, is the naming contest—a name can be thought up in a moment. Advertisers are advised, however, to name something with human or emotional appeal.

Some contests are, from the judging angle, dangerous to conduct. Any contest which has a mathematical answer is an easy one in which to determine the winner, but it is sometimes difficult to prove that a contestant did not win. An example would be a contest to make the greatest number of 3-letter words from the letters in "America the Beautiful," the words to be limited to those found in a certain edition of a certain dictionary. Entries will vary from 1,000 to perhaps 10,000 words, and a participant will be sure that he can prove that each combination of letters on his list is actually a word. Here the authority is a book, rather than an opinion. Judging such a contest is so difficult that The Reuben H. Donnelley Corporation will not handle such contests.

Length of Contest. Duration of the contest depends on the advertising schedule. If the advertiser uses newspapers, magazines, and store displays without radio, he is almost limited to a single contest. If, on the other hand, he relies on radio, he can have a series of weekly contests rather than a single one. If his prize money must be small, a single contest is more attractive than a series with little first prizes. A single contest should run from 4 to 8 weeks; weekly contests from 4 to 6 consecutive weeks.

Prize Schedule. This is the "carrot" to attract participants. The most successful contests have had very large prizes—Old Gold's $100,000 first prize, Miss Hush with practically a store full of merchandise, Spic & Span's six new homes, etc. The main prize is the only one that contestants are interested in. There should be secondary prizes but the advertiser should concentrate his money in the first. It is not uncommon to drop from a first prize of an automobile to a second of a $10 bill.

Before World War II, cash was a popular prize. During and shortly after the war it was war bonds and hard-to-get merchandise. Now it is cash

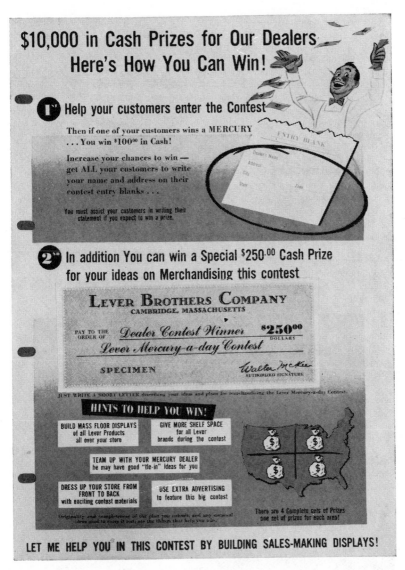

Page from a portfolio developed by Lever Brothers to promote a dealer contest for its products. Purpose of contest was to quicken dealer interest in the "Lever Mercury-a-day" contest. Actual size of this portfolio was 12 by 18 inches, large enough to look impressive. The portfolio is an important part of any consumer contest as it has the job of arousing dealer enthusiasm, not always too easy to accomplish.

Your Advertising
Allowance is: _____

LUX Regular _____
Large _____

LIFEBUOY Reg. _____
Bath Size _____

RINSO Regular _____
Large _____
Giant _____

LUX TOILET
SOAP Regular _____
Bath Size _____

SWAN FLOATING
SOAP Reg. _____
Lg. _____

BREEZE

Be sure to get your share
of increased business—
order sufficient stocks of
ALL Lever brands.

This is what you should sell!

$50,000 IN CASH

OVER 3000 PRIZES

"CONTEST OF A LIFETIME"

OXYDOL

TAKE ONE

The "CONTEST OF A LIFETIME"
$50,000 in Cash Prizes
1st Prize — $10,000.00

OXYDOL
MAKES CLOTHES SPARKLE

10 Prizes
$1,000 Each

3000 Prizes
$10.00 Each

Think of it—over 3,000 Winners!
ENTER AS OFTEN AS YOU LIKE

Just complete this sentence in 25 additional words or less:
"I like new 'Lifetime' Oxydol because

_____
_____
_____
_____
_____
_____
_____
_____

*Pocket in a promotional portfolio used
by Lever Brothers. The pocket carried
a filled-in form stating the advertising
allowance the dealer would receive on
purchases of quantities of merchandise.*

*Wall-hanger, with supply of entry
blanks, used by Procter & Gamble
to get dealer tie-in with national
radio contest for Oxydol. Entry
required mention of dealer's name.*

again but with intriguing twists. Instead of $25,000, it may be $5,000 a year for 5 years. In merchandise, novelty has a strong appeal—a motor scooter instead of a bicycle, a dish washer rather than a vacuum cleaner.

Advertising the Contest. No contest will succeed without advertising. Advertisers should use the kind of advertising to promote their contests that they regularly use to promote sale of the product. In general the larger the prizes, the less the need for advertising, but a balance must be struck. General advertising on a regular radio show usually brings more entries than other types of advertising. It is important that the contest itself be advertised; the contest must not be subordinated to product advertising. In the advertising, the prize schedule is, of course, the feature.

Grocers, druggists, and other merchants as a whole will not push contest promotions aggressively for the reason that they do not profit much from such activities. It is against the lottery laws to promote dealer interest by offering a prize to the one who happens to give out the entry form on which the winning entry is written. On the other hand, a dealer can participate in the prize money if he helps a participant to compose an entry.

Contest Judging. Judging contests is becoming more difficult and complex. Unscrupulous participants cause difficulties. The cheaters are not the so-called professionals who make a hobby of contests. The cheaters enter more than one entry in hope of winning more than one prize and use fictitious names. Some of them sell identical entries to anybody who will buy them. The judges must choose the winner on the basis of merit and merit consists of aptness and originality. A purchased entry may rate high under the Donnelley Objective Rating System on aptness, but if there are other identical entries, it would rate zero on originality.

Advertisers should incorporate a rule which says that all entries submitted must be the original work of the contestant, and require an affidavit to that effect of each winner before a prize is awarded. Advertisers, almost without exception, employ professional contest organizations to handle their contests for the following reasons: (1) No ill will, as on the part of losers, is directed toward the advertiser, (2) the advertiser cannot be accused of collusion or cheating, (3) the advertiser does not know how to handle and judge a contest and has not the facilities for the task.

Writing the Rules

Experience in the use of promotional contests shows that many of the headaches can be avoided if care is used in drawing the rules. The following points should be covered:

1. Closing date.
2. Provision for ties.
3. Entry requirements.
4. Where to send entries.
5. Who is eligible.
6. List of prizes in exact order of award.
7. How entries will be judged.
8. Who will judge them.
9. Judges' decisions will be final.

10. Entries become property of the sponsor.

11. None will be returned and no correspondence will be acknowledged.

12. How winners will be announced and when.

Merchandising a Consumer Contest

One of the particularly effective contests, planned to stimulate consumer sales through dealers was Meredith Publishing Company's promotion for its *Better Homes & Gardens Cook Book*. It produced a 45% increase in sales over the previous year, and had a marked effect on the interest which booksellers had in the book. The various steps taken in staging this contest, in a way to exert the greatest dealer influence, were outlined by a Meredith executive as follows:

> The first step to be taken, after the plan has been blueprinted, is to have it carefully checked, both legally and by contest authorities. Failure to do this is likely to prove costly. When checked the promotional material required to "put it over" is prepared and readied for mailing.
>
> Our first announcement of the contest came with a letter to book dealers of which we have several thousand. This letter announced the contest and made the point that 3 million copies of the *Better Homes & Gardens Cook Book* have been sold. With that letter we enclosed a copy of the dealer contest rules and the $3,000 recipe contest. In addition we enclosed an order card for ordering promotion material and a return envelope.
>
> This was followed up in approximately 30 days by another letter to the dealers showing the response, with a repeat enclosure on the rules and special order form for promotional material. A third follow-up letter went to the dealers which kept them up to date on what the dealer program was really doing. With this letter we enclosed an order card for not only the *Cook Book*, but for the *Baby Book*. While the *Baby Book* did not enter into the contest, it was a plus sales potential for the dealer while the promotion was going on. It received exceptionally fine response.
>
> The promotion included the following: Letters to dealers; advertising in trade magazines; advertising in *Better Homes & Gardens* magazine; special posters; contest rules, either handed out by book stores and dealers or mailed direct upon inquiry; a gold band placed on each and every *Cook Book* sent out during the contest; newspaper mats; as-seen-in cards; radio spot announcements; radio tie-ins with such programs as Don McNeill; windows placed by dealers in answer to the dealer contest; editorial support in *Better Homes & Gardens* magazine with full color spreads and reference to the recipe contest.
>
> Our final letter to the book dealer reviews the success of the contest. This letter indicates that we had thousands of entries in the contest and hundreds of dealers entered the window display contest. A follow-up was made by book dealers through store promotion and store promotion newspaper and radio tie-ins when a contest winner appeared in their city.

Product Tie-In Material

When the product is sold over the retail counter, in the form of a small package, for example, it is most important that dealers who are expected to tie-in with the contest be supplied with attention-arresting display material. The most effective displays for promoting contest entries are those which can be placed behind an actual package on the dealer's counter, with a pad of entry blanks tacked to it so people can tear one off and enter the contest. Another good way is to get dealers to put an entry blank with each delivery.

In addition to counter displays, it is usual to have salesmen, when calling on a dealer, explain the contest and its traffic-building values, and "sell" him the idea of spending some of his own money for tie-in newspaper advertising. Mats for this purpose, are, of course, provided. In addition, posters and window streamers announcing that entry blanks for the contest may be obtained in the store should be furnished to cooperating dealers. The less work involved in using these materials the better the results will be.

DEALER CONTESTS

While the principal use of promotional contests is to stimulate consumer interest and demand, they have proved to be effective as a means of speeding sales through dealers. There are two types of dealer contests: (1) Contests in which the dealers or their salespeople participate, and (2) contests which the dealers themselves put on to increase store traffic and move merchandise off the shelves into consumer channels. In both cases the contests are usually planned and promoted by the manufacturer, but with a varying degree of dealer participation.

A Westinghouse Incentive Program

"Easy Eight" was the theme of a retail salesmen's incentive program conducted by the Home Laundry Department of the Major Appliance Division of Westinghouse Electric Corporation. The company awarded all retail salesmen a prize for selling eight washers or dryers during an eight-week period.

In three different recent campaign periods, the prizes were a Minolta miniature camera, a decorative wall barometer and a 44-piece goldplated table service for eight. A company merchandising executive stated:

"We measure results by comparing similar sales periods and sales levels before and after each program. Our measurements are distributor sales to dealers and replenishment sales. Our success is

Westinghouse conducted a series of "Easy Eight" retail incentive programs in which salesmen won a prize for selling eight washers or dryers during an eight-week period. In successive campaigns, prizes were a miniature camera and a 44-piece table service for eight. Shown is the distributor announcement to the dealers and salesmen.

made apparent by the fact that we have sponsored nine "Easy Eight" programs during the past three and a half years."

Window Display Contests

This promotion has proved highly effective in securing window and store displays for nationally advertised merchandise. The Silex Company has made good use of interstore competitions to encourage dealers to put in window displays and quicken the interest of store personnel in pushing Silex products. Cash prizes were usually awarded, on the basis of $500 for the best department store window, $500 for the best hardware or appliance store window, with second and third prizes of $250 and $125 respectively. Honorable mentions received $25 each. The rules were as follows:

1. Any retail outlet selling Silex Coffee Makers, Silex Steam Irons, or Silex Lox-in Glass Filters is eligible to compete.

2. The window must feature one or more Silex products *exclusively,* and must be in for at least a 1-week period.

3. Contest begins September 15 and ends November 15. Any Silex window display installed during this period is eligible.

4. A photograph or snapshot of your window must be sent to: The Silex Company, Window Display Department, Hartford 2, Connecticut, postmarked on or before November 20. Send in as many entries as you wish. All prize winners will be announced by December 15.

5. On the back of your photograph or snapshot please print the following information:
   a. Name of person installing display.
   b. Name and address of the store.
   c. Date and length of time each display was in window.
   d. Type of store: Department, General, Hardware, or Appliance.
   All photos remain the property of the Silex Company.

6. The individual whose name accompanies the winning entry will receive the prize. If prize money is to be divided among two or more people in any store, the store's own management will determine divisions of such prizes.

7. Judges will be men well known in the field of display and advertising, and judges' decision will be final.

Elgin Dealer Contest

Elgin Watches conducted a campaign in which dealers were eligible for over $20,000 in prizes in the company's Guarantee Card Sweepstakes, plus a grand prize of an all-expense trip for a family of four to Walt Disney World in Florida. The rules for the dealers were simple: (1) Sell an Elgin; (2) Assist the customer in filling out the guarantee registration card; (3) Mail in the card and sweepstakes form. Each card entitled the dealer to another chance at winning a cash prize.

OVER $20,000 IN CASH PRIZES

Here's all you do:

1. Sell an Elgin—Elgin watches offer your customers more value and features for the money.

2. Assist your customer in filling out the Guarantee Registration Card. Tell the customer you'll send the card to Elgin for registration.

3. Fill out the Elgin Sweepstakes entry form...enclose the Guarantee Registration Card...and mail in the self-addressed Sweepstakes entry form envelope.

Every time you sell an Elgin you have another chance to win a cash prize.

"Every time you sell an Elgin you have another chance to win a cash prize" was the theme of an Elgin promotion to stimulate dealer sales. Note the simple rules.

Contests for Dealer Personnel

It is one thing to prepare material which will help a retail sales-person to do a better selling job, and another to get him to use it effectively. Westinghouse and others find contests help to promote interest in better salesmanship, and widen the use of educational material prepared by the sales promotion department. A typical contest of this type was used by Westinghouse to launch its "Select-O-Ray" heat and sun lamps. Twenty-five cash prizes were awarded for the best answers to a series of questions. In order to answer the questions the contestant had to study the sales material provided by the manufacturer. At the close of the contest the winning an-swers were distributed to all contestants so that they could compare them with the ones they submitted.

Contests for dealers and dealers' salespeople, where prizes are awarded on the basis of sales, have been successfully used, but Federal agencies look with disfavor on any attempt to "push" (for a consideration unbeknown to the buyer) one product at the expense of another. Then there is the danger of tangling with the U.S. Postal Service should the contest be construed as being a lottery. One com-pany, for example, used a "Winning Aces" contest where a card was drawn in the home office and sent to dealer's salesmen upon receipt of each order. This was held to be a lottery and the right to use the mails to send out the "winning" cards was denied the com-pany. Such a contest, of course, could be promoted locally provided the United States mails were not used.

Prize Incentives

Merchandise prizes have become popular as awards in contests for dealers and distribution salesmen, because the winners may choose their own prizes from suppliers' catalogs. Some large manufacturers produce special catalogs for this purpose, or even complete incentive campaigns.

An example of this is the Van Heusen Incentive Awards plan, which includes full-color preview sheets, prize certificates, a "Luxury Living" catalog, a special alpaca sweater brochure, and presenting envelopes.

Kodak's High-School Awards

Where it is important to build up interest in a product among teen agers, with the thought the interest once awakened will grow into a lifelong hobby, consumer contests through dealers, slanted at stu-dents, is a sure-fire promotion. The Eastman Kodak Company is

SPAIN IS YOUR DESTINATION IN OCTOBER—MADRID WILL BE YOUR HOME . . .

. . . If you are among the sixty qualifiers of Royal's 1972 SPANISH FIESTA HOLIDAY.

Between February 1 and July 28, 1972, your Royal Typewriter purchases can earn you a fabulous all-expense paid week for two in Madrid.

You'll experience all the delights that make Spain the magnificent kaleidoscope that it is. The colorful fountains, the narrow winding streets, the shops of every description, the Moorish architecture, the flavor of Spanish wines and foods, the rhythm of the Flamenco, and the excitement of a way of life that blends the best of today with the preserved beauty of yesterday.

Just follow the simple program rules below, and begin planning now for your Spanish Fiesta Holiday.

RULES: Dealers will be assigned to one of four groups—based on their annual sales quota-

ANNUAL SALES QUOTA	ASSIGNED GROUP
Under $25,000	Group A
$25,000 - $40,000	Group B
$40,000 - $70,000	Group C
Over $70,000	Group D

DEALER MINIMUM QUALIFIER: Dealers must purchase 135% or more of total typewriter quota for a six month period. (Winners will be selected based on highest percent of quota over 135% in each category. Others will participate in the Sweepstakes.)

DEALER SWEEPSTAKES: All Dealers purchasing 105% of total typewriter quota enter drawings for a SPANISH FIESTA HOLIDAY vacation. (Minimum dollar qualification—$15,000.)

DEALER AWARD CATEGORIES:
Group A   · 5 winners (plus 2 Sweepstakes Winners)
Group B   10 winners (plus 3 Sweepstakes Winners)
Group C   20 winners (plus 3 Sweepstakes Winners)
Group D   13 winners (plus 2 Sweepstakes Winners)

NOTE: Only billed deliveries will be used in determining final contest percentages. Retail orders billed by Royal will count toward contest.

All decisions as to winning dealers will be made by Royal Typewriter Company. All decisions are final.

The winning prize cannot be substituted or changed in any way. In the event the winner is unable to use his trip there will be no other reimbursement.

In the event of strikes or other causes beyond its control Royal Typewriter Company will not be responsible for orders not credited.

"THE HEART OF SPAIN"

Royal Typewriter Company promoted a dealer contest with a variety of mailings featuring free trips to Europe. The Spanish Fiesta Holiday mailing consisted of a die-cut circular the top half of which folded down to disclose an outline map of Spain. The interior fold listed the rules and regulations for the contest.

famous for its photographic competitions of that sort. Winners have had their prints publicized throughout the nation and impressive prizes have been awarded. Contestants must call at a Kodak dealer's store to obtain an entry blank, and entries are cleared through the same dealer. The purpose of this, of course, is to increase store traffic and win dealer commendation.

However, it is not always good practice to require the contestant to call at the retail outlet to secure a contest entry blank. It reduces the number of entries and creates the problem of keeping the retailer stocked with the entry blanks, being sure that he keeps them in sight. This is all very wasteful, but nevertheless in some cases it is desirable to do this, particularly when it is important that the prospect see a certain display of the product in order to be properly sold.

Force Demonstrations. This, of course, would be usually in connection with a durable goods item, such as an electric appliance. Such contests are usually tied up with a prize for the dealer. In other words, in order to become eligible for the contest, the woman must go to the dealer's store, witness a demonstration of the product, and then as proof of that fact she receives an entry blank carrying the dealer's name. It would seem that this might be applied to appliances sold on a house-to-house basis. For example, a vacuum cleaner manufacturer might advertise the fact that by returning a coupon or otherwise inviting a demonstration in the home, the salesman will call and at the completion of his demonstration present the prospect with an entry blank which permits her to enter the contest.

Secure Point-of-Sale Display. With some advertisers this is the main reason for holding a contest. There are 300,000 grocers in the United States. Let us assume that the sponsor is able to get 100,000 of these grocers to exhibit his sales display for a period of 2 weeks in connection with the contest. This might be a window display, counter display, aisle display, or back-bar display. It would be reasonable to value such advertising space at $5 per week or $10 for the period. This would mean $1 million worth of free advertising for the manufacturer at a cost of let us say $50,000 in prizes and $50,000 for judging. The manufacturer does not have any additional cost for announcing the contest because he announces it in advertising space which would otherwise be used for straight product advertising.

Getting Names of Prospects. On store demonstrations, of course, the list of prospects would be compiled and presumably followed up. However, the contest may be used to compile lists of prospects without a demonstration. For example, the contest might be "I need an electric ironer in my home because . . . " It might be asking too much of a salesman to call on the losers in such a contest and try to sell them an ironer but there is no reason why such prospects should not receive a very polite thank you letter followed by a series of two or three mailings to break down her resistance.

Previous to the Robinson-Patman Act, a number of companies used prize contests as an inducement to get a distributor to stock a line. For example, Sears Roebuck put in a line of pressure cookers with the understanding that the manufacturer would operate a contest among the employees of Sears' stores, and offer prizes to clerks who did an especially good sales job. This type of sales promotional activity is now regarded as price discrimination by the Federal Trade Commission. Any offer to dealers or distributors must be made to all alike. It cannot be limited.

The Chase Visa Shopping Spree Sweepstakes

To stimulate the use of its credit card, Chase Visa/BankAmericard announced its Shopping Spree Sweepstakes with a grand prize of $10,000, two first prizes of $2,500, 10 second prizes of $500 and 100 third prizes of $100; in credits, with *automatic* eligibility each and every time its credit card was used! There were no entry forms or sales slips to submit, the use of the credit card was the only requirement. The amounts credited to winners' accounts not used within 30 days would be forwarded to the winners by check.

The contest period was from June through September, 1978, with the winners selected in a random drawing conducted under the supervision of Promotion West, Inc., an independent, judging organization.

Further, no purchases were necessary. Entrants were eligible for the prizes simply by printing the words Chase Visa/BankAmericard and their account number on a 3" x 5" card and mailing it in.

An extra touch for the grand prize was the bank's statement that "for 24 hours a limousine and driver will take you on your shopping spree. Buy anything you wish up to $10,000 using your Chase Visa/BankAmericard."

Chapter 24

STATE FAIRS AND
TRADE SHOWS

THE purposes of a trade show are to give exhibitors the opportunity to develop sales leads, maintain distributor and dealer contacts, introduce new products and support public relations programs. Sales leads depend on visitors, but not all visitors are prospects. The industry has recognized the need for audited attendance figures as an aid to management in justifying exhibit costs.

Several associations are at work on the problem with the object of establishing formalized procedures to determine not only the quanity but the quality of trade show attendance. The Exhibit Designers and Producers Association conducted a survey among its 2000 members on such subjects as attendance, traffic, inquiries and sales leads. Sixty percent of the respondents stated that attendance figures were inflated and not always accurate.

Security problems and labor costs have also plagued the medium. In December, 1978, The National Trade Show Congress devoted attention to the development of standard exhibitors' contracts, exhibit hall contracts, codes of work rules for labor, codes for show management trade practices and a national trade show auditing bureau. From a sales promotion standpoint, the last is the most important.

Computerized Registration and Audits

To speed people into the exhibition, a new, computerized system of registration was inaugurated at the 4th annual National Printing Equipment Show at the New York Coliseum.

Silent, automatic equipment, activated from electronic keyboards, produced show visitors' identity badges and specially embossed inquiry-recording cards in a single operation taking only seconds.

As the equipment produces visitors' badges, it also stores the information in memory circuits so that a running total of show registration is produced by the computer at any time. The computer likewise furnishes breakdowns of numbers of show visitors by states, cities and other classifications.

Show Systems Limited, La Jolla, California, has developed a computerized system which provides exhibitors with detailed information about show visitors and gives them accurate sales leads.

Every registrant receives his own registration number and badge which is keyed to his registration card. The card includes his name, title, company address, phone number, area of main product interest and purchasing capability (which becomes a red dot on his badge to reflect buying influence). As the visitor makes the rounds of the show, the exhibitor merely notes the visitor's badge number and an "action code" on a master log for post-show follow-up. The eight action codes range from "send literature," "schedule sales call" to "arrange a demonstration."

Show Systems Limited personnel collect the completed forms on a daily basis and process the data on high-speed computers which provide the exhibitor with reports at no cost to him.

Today, practically every industry holds trade shows every year, and, in some cases, twice a year, in different cities. Often, association conventions are held simultaneously, to attract greater attendance to both events.

The value of trade shows is indicated by the fact that the Machine Tool Show, in Chicago, scored the amazing attendance record of more than 102,000 *paid* visitors!

Types of Promotional Shows

The most popular promotional show is the state (or in some cases a county) fair. There are hundreds of these held each year, and some companies maintain special units of the sales promotion department for the specific purpose of planning and operating these educational exhibits. In some instances, as in the case of a regionally distributed soft drink, the display can be made to pay its own way. In other cases, enough actual sales are closed to make it pay. All of the sales may not be closed at the fair, but the leads are followed up by local distributors and closed. The public relations value of these shows is usually considered important.

Next to state and county fairs, come national, regional, and even local trade shows. The Road Builders Show usually held in Cleveland, the Furniture Show in Chicago, the Automobile Show in New York are typical. Nearly every important industry now has its trade show, and in the case of the office equipment industry there are two or three national shows, a number of regional or local shows, as well as the exhibition held along with the annual convention of the National Stationery and Office Equipment Association.

The larger cities, with ample hotel facilities, have often been selected as permanent locations for such shows. Some of them, like the furniture show, are called "markets" and enjoy a large attendance. Merchants from all over the country attend them to look over the new lines and place orders for future delivery.

In some lines, like wearing apparel, it is the practice of a group of representatives of leading manufacturers to conduct "shows" which travel to the principal communities in an area and afford local merchants an opportunity to visit their sample rooms at the local hotel or hotels and place orders. These shows save both the salesmen's and the merchants' time. These traveling shows are well organized. Membership is elective. A promotion manager is employed by the group, who does the advance work for the shows and gets out the buyers. During the period when goods were scarce, it was not unusual for a member of one of these traveling shows to sell his entire allotment that way. They are still rated as one of the

An impressive view of the trade show held by the National Institute of Dry Cleaning in cooperation with the Institute of Laundering in Atlantic City's great Convention Hall.

best ways to sell related lines of merchandise, since the build-up the show is given attracts buyers from rural communities which the average territorial salesman would be unable to contact individually.

Then there is the traveling show used by individual manufacturers to promote the sale of specialized consumer equipment, such as the electric kitchen train which General Electric routed across the continent, and the special train used by American Type Founders Sales Corporation to demonstrate the cost-cutting possibilities of printing equipment the company distributes. The train made it possible to show the machinery under actual working conditions, an expensive undertaking if the display had to be taken down and then set up again in cities where the company had branch offices. A somewhat similar promotion was successfully conducted by General Motors, when it routed its "Cavalcade of Progress" through the country. This promotion comprised a fleet of panel body trucks, with let-down sides which could be quickly arranged into an exhibition hall. Millions of persons saw these shows. The idea was adapted by the Shell Oil Company, which used a fleet of trucks to entertain the public, and plug Shell products, in locations near Shell stations. Sound equipment furnished the music and made the announcements. Each truck carried a crew of six men, including a magician, a clown, and other personnel. This type of promotion, however, is limited by local ordinances restricting sound advertising.

Problems of Smaller Exhibitors

A manufacturer of printing equipment participates in four trade shows a year because they have proved productive. Some of the situations and problems encountered, however, are summarized by the president of the company as follows:

"We go to approximately four exhibits per year and we can safely say that the value of trade shows, as far as we are concerned, is extremely important. We spend approximately 70% of our advertising and sales promotion budget at trade shows because we feel that they are an essential part of explaining our capabilities to prospective customers.

"We have established a policy of not asking our existing customers to open their factory to prospective customers; hence we are faced with a demonstration problem; trade shows obviously meet this problem.

"Our basic goal is to attract people who have never heard of our company, those who have never seen our type of machinery and others who are there to get information.

"We definitely feel that the addressograph-type card, stamping the individual's name, address, company, etc., is the only practical way to follow leads. Attempts were made at one show to work with a computer follow-up system which, in my opinion, proved fruitless. I like to know the prospect's name, address, position, etc., rather than knowing him by a number.

"Our follow-up system consists of a personalized letter thanking visitors for coming to our booth. We try at this time to qualify the prospect, putting him into four categories; lookers; warm prospects; hot prospects and very serious buyers.

"Frankly, we cannot compete with the larger corporations with their greater expenditures; we try to keep the cost of our booths down to a minimum.

"We do not use any women in our booths because we are selling machinery, not women. We produce no magic or dramas at our shows—we merely show our machines in their actual condition. Nothing is chrome plated or out of the ordinary.

"We use people in our booth who are intelligently informed about the products and how they can help the customer. There is nothing worse than going into a booth where the personnel do not have an idea of exactly what is on the floor and what the company capability is.

"As far as installation is concerned, we have found that labor costs are almost prohibitive in some cities and in other cities, totally ridiculous. We have attempted to minimize our expenses at the show by having our own truck deliver the machinery. By delivering our machinery uncrated and on casters, we avoid the cost of riggers and, where there is a loading platform, our machinery can be rolled directly to the booth. This avoids the rigging costs that we have typically experienced at various shows for crating and uncrating and the constant debate between different work groups as to who should touch your machinery.

"Our equipment gets to the show in tiptop condition under the supervision of a qualified driver of our truck who is an employe of our company. This driver is capable of setting up the exhibit and properly checking the machinery to be sure that it is ready and operative for our sales staff.

"As far as furniture is concerned, it certainly doesn't pay, to rent a chair for a week at $20.00 when we can buy one for $18.00 and use it for 20 or 30 shows.

"The location of the show is extremely important to us as to whether or not we will be exhibitors. Exhibits in certain cities, assuming we bring in exactly the same equipment, will cost twice as much as in other locations, due to differences in labor situations. We flatly refuse to exhibit in certain cities mainly because the labor situation makes it prohibitive to even be in the show. I know that for a large corporation this doesn't seem to make much difference but it is very important to us to have minimal costs. I think this reflects the opinions of most of the smaller exhibitors."

Display Trailers

The cost of preparing a special exhibit, shipping and erecting it, and then taking it down after the show is over, is a problem for many advertisers.

The Western Union Telegraph Company solved the problem by a traveling telegraph office in a trailer. This is equipped with the latest apparatus for sending and receiving telegrams. When it is desired to exhibit at some affair, the trailer is hitched to a field man's car, taken to the fair grounds, parked, and is ready to go into action. It is used even for inside exhibitions such as The National Business Show in New York.

Trailers for such purposes should have two doors so that people can enter by one door and leave by the other. A common complaint against the use of trailers for fairs and shows is that they are usually one-door affairs which trap the crowd. Some exhibition trailers have hinged sides so that when opened up, the crowd can view the display without coming in.

The Singer Manufacturing Company likewise found trailers to be an effective method for promoting interest in home sewing. The demonstrations were planned in connection with dealers who conducted the demonstrations and underwrote the local advertising expense. They proved especially effective at county fairs. Trailers have been used to display Westinghouse Electric refrigerators. International Shoe Co. has used one to show 150 different shoe styles to store buyers.

Retailers also use traveling shows to "take the store to the customer." A department store in Greensboro, North Carolina, for example, used a trailer, wired for sound, to introduce new style merchandise to out-of-town customers of the store. These traveling "shows" were especially effective in connection with "Homecoming" weeks at the four colleges in the Greensboro area. While the actual sales were not sufficiently important to warrant indefinite use of the trailer, the promotion served to widen the trading area of the store. A large department store in San Francisco used a trailer to sell horseback-riding equipment to riding clubs and at horse shows.

Meetings at Trade Shows and Conventions

One way of getting together a company's most alert and progressive dealers is to hold a meeting in conjunction with the retailers' annual trade show or convention. When this is done, the manufacturer's meeting is usually scheduled for the day before or after, so as not to compete with the meeting the dealer came to attend. The Ampro Corporation, for example, has held such meetings in conjunction with the annual convention of the National Audio-Visual Association.

The Ampro plan has been to invite dealers to a full-day session the day before the Association's meeting begins. At one such meeting the morning program consisted of talks on the company's service setup and management's plans for the new selling season, together with an inspirational address by an outside speaker. At lunch the company's advertising plans were presented in the form of a skit. In the afternoon a skit was used to introduce a new product, and samples of the product were made available to all in attendance. The day ended with a cocktail party, a dinner, and over 1,000 orders for Ampro products.

Retailers' conventions are usually held in cities which offer additional facilities in the way of sights to see and things to do. There is the danger that dealers will prefer these distractions to spending their time at meetings, particularly if the session is scheduled for the day after they have just finished 2 solid days of listening to speeches and presentations. In such a meeting the problem of preselling the dealer is particularly acute.

When a display of merchandise is to be held in a hotel suite during a retailers' convention is is a good idea to send out some sort of an invitation to customers, announcing the showing of new merchandise and urging them to visit the room during the convention. The invitation, even if it is not used, is appreciated by customers, especially if it carries with it the suggestion that cocktails will be served. These invitations, of course, are mailed out well in advance of the convention and should include an admission card for the customer to present at the door. This keeps out the horde of drink collectors which are a problem at most conventions.

Motion Pictures at Trade Shows and Conventions

Many exhibition halls where trade shows are held have projection rooms in connection with them, where, at specified hours, exhibitors can show movies about their product and its uses. If the picture is really good, and is not too coldly commercial, this is an excellent way to promote interest in a product. If the movie is of sufficient interest to those attending the convention, it is also possible to have it shown at a luncheon meeting. In some instances the delegates are the guests of the company sponsoring the movie; in others the cost of the lunch is included in the registration fee.

It is not good practice, however, to show sound-slidefilms at trade shows, unless they are shown in connection with an instructional program. Action in sound-slidefilms is slow and they are apt to bore the audience. There are on the market, however, projectors which can be used in the exhibit, which are lighted from behind the picture. The pictures change automatically. It is not necessary to darken the room.

Exhibiting to Get Results

That's the name of one of a series of helpful, instructive booklets issued by Firks Exhibitions, Inc., Chicago, Ill., which provide highly informative suggestions to exhibitors. One page in the booklet reads:

Lessons to be Learned

1. Audiences are on their feet. Keep them there. Also keep staffers on their feet. Dealing with from dozens to hundreds of visitors per hour, efficiency and turnover are enhanced with a standing audience.

2. The presentation should be brief and to the point. Far-fetched, unrealistic or rambling, involved presentations take too long to reveal the user benefit and will dissipate the audience.

3. The presentation may be given by company personnel or by outside professionals. This decision must be carefully made, assessing the training capability and availability of staff personnel to perform this vital task—really the culmination of the trade show activity.

4. Presentations which attract the entire show actually hinder access to that segment of the total audience which is most interested in your product and its benefits. AVOID the broad appeal unless the need has been carefully calculated in advance.

5. Giveaways, for much the same reason, are of marginal value. They tend to attract the entire audience, which is seldom the goal.

6. Staff personnel in the exhibit should be identified for quick recognition. Blazers, or other items of wearing apparel tying in with the theme of the exhibit, are very effective.

The exhibitor who effectively ATTRACTS, TELLS and RE-CORDS at the trade show paves the way to sales at a lower cost than in any other way.

WHAT MAKES A GOOD EXHIBIT*

Many industries now organize shows in the big cities to present their products to the public. An example of a great crowd-attracting event is the annual Boat Show in New York City.

As reported in the *New York Times:*

"When the 56th National Boat Show ends its nine-day 'cruise,' an estimated 350,000 visitors will have discovered what's new in boating.

"As usual, the 550 boats, the motors, the bilge pumps, the radio direction finders, and the thousand and one other items that fill 181,612 square feet of display space contain the customary flock of firsts.

"There's an inflatable kayak that sells for $40, a diesel yacht that sells for $100,000, a folding outboard motor, a 19-foot runabout guaranteed to hit 60 miles an hour, a driverless boat that tows water skiers.

"More than 400 exhibitors, some of them for tabs of up to $25,000, are showing $2.5-million worth of merchandise."

Planning the Exhibit

First of all it should be in keeping with the theme and the character of the show. This is especially true if the over-all purpose of the show is to promote the industry as well as the exhibitor's products. The trouble with most trade shows is that they have no central theme, no outstanding feature to attract attendance to which exhibitors can tie their product. A good trade show, like a good advertisement, needs a central dominating theme, so that those who attend will carry away a favorable impression of the industry. For example, a show might be held to promote the idea that good paper is the foundation of good advertising. The central feature around which the publicity is built might be an actual paper-making operation. Buyers of direct mail who have never seen paper made, will flock to the show to see the central exhibit. Then if the exhibitors tie in with the theme of the show, and show how the particular kinds of paper they make and sell contribute to making direct-mail advertising more profitable and useful, those who attend will go away with a firm conviction that good paper is not an expense but an economy. The

*Dartnell has a comprehensive manual entitled *How To Participate Profitably In Trade Shows* by Robert B. Konikow.

Every product is easily displayed in this attractive 30-foot Ronson trade show exhibit. The louvered top and raised platform lend unity to the display of many small appliance models, in a tasteful and pleasing exhibit.

slightly higher cost is more than made up by increased benefits to the advertiser. What actually happens at most direct-mail advertising shows, is that each exhibitor contents himself with displaying samples of printing on his paper. These may be interesting to the exhibitor, but they don't get anyone else very excited. The average advertiser attending the show sees so many "samples" that they leave him cold.

Besides tying in with the character and purpose of the show, a good exhibit should have the following features:

1. It should be built around a simple idea.

2. It should stop traffic and attract attention preferably by the use of motion rather than sound.

3. It should be open to the traffic, so that interested persons have access to the exhibit, without jamming the booth.

4. It should have billboard value, so that even those in a hurry may read as they "run."

5. It should provide facilities for salesmen or others in attendance to talk at ease with interested prospects.

6. It should be well lighted, preferably with ceiling spots.

7. It should provide a place, not too prominent, for storing sales promotional literature.

8. It should register a definite sales impression that will stay with those who attend the show after they leave.

Most exhibits are too messy. They include too many "pin up" displays with type so small only those with perfect eyesight can read the print. If photographs are used they should be transparencies illuminated from behind, rather than black-and-white prints tacked on the walls, or wings, of the booth. More exhibits fail because they try to do too much. It is better to do a few things well.

Another desirable feature in any exhibit, even though it might seem as though the company would have no further use for it, is "shipability." As a rule exhibits must be set up quickly, sometimes overnight, before the opening of the show. If the exhibit is composed of relatively small, interlocking panels, which can be put together without a carpenter, it can be taken down and packed in crates ready to be shipped out on short notice to any other show where it is needed. There are companies which design and make displays or exhibits for use in fairs and shows. Their services, while not cheap, usually result in a far more satisfactory exhibit and, in the long run, real economy. Considering that on an average a display may be used as many as ten times a year, and that it will be seen by several thousand people, the cost per person is not much more than what it would cost to reach the same number of people with a well-done direct-mail campaign.

Names of the companies specializing in the planning, making, and installing of trade show displays can be found in the classified telephone directories of the larger cities ("the Yellow Pages"). They will be found listed under the heading "Displays—Convention, Window, Etc."

Not only the display itself, but the shipping case in which it travels, should be built of plywood or other lightweight material. This facilitates handling and saves transportation expense. Cases should be made to travel as baggage if necessary.

MAKING THE EXHIBIT PAY

The most effective advertising that a manufacturer can do in a trade show, or for that matter any time a crowd gathers, is to show the product *at work*. This is, of course, not always possible. Yet there are many instances where the product could be shown in action, but for some reason the exhibitor prefers to merely place it on display. An illustration of this is found in the many exhibits of honey at state and county fairs. Most honey producers think they have met all requirements of an effective advertising display when they arrange various sized containers of honey on a table or wall display. It makes a pretty display but it could hardly be called an "interesting" display. Certainly it would never stop the casual stroller. On the other hand, when a honey producer installs in his exhibit, as some do, an observation hive with glass sides, so those attending the fair can see the bees actually making honey, great crowds are attracted and, according to all reports, far more honey is sold. More important, the educational value of that type of display is tremendous. On the other hand, exhibitors who run puppet shows which indirectly plug the product get a crowd, but the crowd stays to be entertained rather than to learn.

Using Shows to Sample Opinion

Shows and fairs offer a convenient way to find out what customers, regardless of whether they may be users or consumers, think of your product, your package, your advertising, or whatever it might be. This information can be obtained by the usual polling techniques at your exhibit, or it may be obtained through competitive schemes where prizes are given for the best answers, or awarded to holders of "lucky number" questionnaire stubs. In order to answer the questionnaire properly it is necessary for the contestant to study the uses of the product, or at least understand its points of superiority. During the early days of television, Gimbel's Philadelphia store wanted to test the effectiveness of intrastore television. An arrangement was made with RCA to set up a television studio in the store, with twelve 10-minute telecasts daily. There was a show demonstrating hair styling, another called "Scarf Magic" showing how scarves can effect a change in the appearance of a dress, etc. The telecasts, of course, featured merchandise on sale in the various departments of the store. Television stations where patrons, unable to get into the studio, could view the show were established at strategic locations throughout the store. Eighty-eight percent of some 2,500 store patrons who filled out the questionnaire, handed to all those who attended the shows, stated they found "Shop by Television" an aid to purchasing. Forty percent said they expected to visit the department where the merchandise could be purchased after the show. The experiment demonstrated to the store management the possibilities of

Return To: National Association of Exposition Managers
1101 16th Street, N.W., Washington, D. C. 20036

CONFIDENTIAL REPORT

for

NAEM SITE INFORMATION BANK

City..Exhibit Facility..

Sponsor of Show..

Dates: Installation.....................Show.....................Move Out...............................

Gross Sq. Ft.............Net Sq. Ft............Charge for Exhibit Facility.......................

Special Charges from Exhibit Facility...

No. of Hall Meeting Rooms: Used.....Charge $..........Complimentary.....................

Headquarters Hotel..

Complimentary Suites and Sleeping Rooms...

....

No. of Hotel Meeting Rooms: Used.....Charge $.......... Complimentary..............

Exhibitor's Space Rental $............................. Based On..

Were Guards Required for Night Security: Yes ( )   No ( )

Guard Contractor Used..

No. Guard Hours..............................Total Guard Cost $...

Crate Storage Available: Yes ( )   No ( )   Free ( )

Cost for Crate Storage If Sponsor Pays $..

Show Hours...

No. Girls Used for Registration...............Average Paid Per Hour $.......................

No. Registration Girls Furnished Free..

Cartage Firm Used..

Rating of Cartage Firm: Excellent (   )   Fair (   )   Poor (   )

Comments...

Decorator Used..

Rating of Decorator: Excellent ( )   Fair ( )   Poor ( )

Comments...

Amount Paid Per Running Foot for Drapes $...per foot.

Electrician Used...

Rating of Electrician: Excellent ( )   Fair ( )   Poor ( )

Comments...

....

Union Problems: Yes ( )   No ( )

Please comment on the:

Cooperation of Convention Bureau...

Cooperation of Hotel Management...

Cooperation of Hall Management...

Cooperation of Local Fire Marshal...

Cooperation of Local Police...

Cooperation of Other Local Officials...

Special Insurance Needed...

Other Comments (Unusual Circumstances)...

....

....

Signed...

Title...

Association Name...

Date Submitted...

Following a trade show managed by one of its members, the National Association of Exposition Managers requests them to send in a report covering all aspects of the conditions encountered. The "site information" bank assists members in evaluating the facilities for future shows.

television as an advertising tool. From the experiments the following conclusions were reached:

1. Customers are willing to look at a straight merchandising presentation. We think that although 10 minutes is not too long while the medium is a novelty, a much shorter presentation would be more effective after the public becomes more accustomed to the device itself. Five minutes should be the longest—2 to 3 minutes would be best.

2. Only when it shows what the merchandise will do for the customer can the medium be used most effectively.

3. No enclosed areas are necessary. The television screen can be exposed in the midst of the general lighting of the store, but the location must be carefully selected so as not to interfere with selling. Some of the sales literature distributed by television manufacturing companies illustrates receivers on a fixture in back of a salesperson making a sale to a customer. This is a very unrealistic way to illustrate the use of intrastore television. It would hurt rather than help sales if done this way.

4. Color will be a dramatic advance.

The General Electric Company frequently polls visitors to its exhibits to determine if the display is effective from a sales promotional standpoint, or if there is sufficient interest to warrant coming into the show next year. Questionnaires for this purpose, however, should be very short and ask pertinent questions. Most persons attending a show are reluctant to take time to fill out a lengthy questionnaire. The key question should be: "What impressed you most favorably about the exhibit?" That usually brings out answers which help to evaluate the exhibit. In the case of General Electric, a few questions are usually included to help the sales and advertising department in the selection of markets and media. The back of the questionnaire is blank for more extended comment.

Give-Away Novelties and Literature

It is safe to say that about half the free souvenirs and booklets distributed at shows and fairs are wasted. They get into the hands of children, souvenir collectors, or persons who have not the slightest interest in your product. But even so a careful distribution of not-too-expensive good-will builders at meetings attended by persons whose friendship is valuable to the business can be a good investment. For example, it was the custom of Swift & Company to give away a packet of picture post cards on appropriate subjects, such as the importance of good roads, to those who visited the Swift exhibit at state fairs. The cards carried no Swift advertising, other than the name of the company, so those attending the show used them to "post card" friends pack home. If, during a season, 100,000 packets of six postal cards were passed out, and half of them were mailed,

300,000 families would get a good-roads message. While Swift & Company do not sell roads, they have a vital interest in road improvement. It facilitates the problem of getting livestock to market. Like all packers, Swift & Company are alert to any promotion which will bring down the price of meat, for the lower the price of meat the more meat will be eaten. These packets of postal cards were very popular and widely used.

Exhibitors who wish to get the names of persons attending a demonstration of their product for a subsequent direct-mail follow-up, find it advantageous to offer some sort of a souvenir to those who register. To avoid needless waste, however, blanks used for registering visitors to the exhibit should qualify the registrant to determine if he is a prospective buyer. In the case of a company making tractors, the qualifying question might be: "Do you plan to buy a tractor within the next year?" Or if the company makes trucks: "What kind of a truck are you using?" A sewing machine manufacturer, who wanted names of women who might be in the market for a new sewing machine, gave away a mending packet to those who attended a sewing demonstration and filled out registration cards. The big question was: "How old is your sewing machine?"

World Fairs

World fairs have been popular for centuries. In recent years, they followed each other so fast, in so many cities around the world, that it was necessary to organize an international association to schedule them officially.

Although the New York World's Fair allegedly lost money, it attracted 27,148,280 people in 1964 (at $2.00 each) and 24,458,000 in 1965 (at $2.50 each, except for the schoolchildren). Any loss, according to the fair administration, was more than offset by the fact that it contributed over half a billion dollars to the economy of greater New York.

The major business interests of the nation were represented, all eager to project an image of leadership in their respective fields. Their exhibits served as a gigantic showcase of what industry has already contributed to our lives and the wonders it envisions for the future. Thousands of products and services reflected the good life in American society today.

However, the industrial exhibits were more than a display of wares. A combination of the country's top creative talent and advanced technological knowledge produced tasteful promotions directed primarily towards an impact on good will. Exciting live products, unusual films, thrilling rides, fabulous art collections, audience participation games, and ingenious teaching techniques contributed to an extravagant variety of new exhibit concepts.

With rare exceptions, almost all of the business attractions were free of charge. The Pepsi-Cola Company provided an excellent example of good public relations by donating all revenue from its delightful, Disney-designed exhibit to the United Nations Children's Fund.

Among the industrial exhibitors at the fair were Formica, IBM, General Electric, Johnson's Wax, Ford, General Motors, RCA, National Cash Register, and many other leading companies. These company exhibits drew so many visitors that, at certain times, people waited in line for 2 hours or more for admission.

Convention Speakers

Trade conventions and promotional shows have become so important in some industries that the larger companies find it profitable to have an executive, qualified as a public speaker, on their staffs. He represents the company at conventions of customers and, if requested, appears on the program. While it is not in good taste to directly promote the business in such talks, it is possible to accomplish, indirectly, certain promotional objectives. For example, the Proctor Electric Company, which makes a quality iron, had a sales promotion man by the name of Sam Vining, who appeared upon request before convention groups and gave a talk on salesmanship. To demonstrate the principles he talked about, he used an electric iron. His talk was in great demand.

The Importance of Personnel Effectiveness

Pitney-Bowes, a consistent trade show exhibitor, gives its salesmen the following "Tips for manning a trade show booth":

1. Look alert; be enthusiastic.
2. Understand a machine thoroughly before you attempt to demonstrate.
3. Help keep the exhibit as neat as your personal appearance.
4. Stay on your feet; do not sit down while on duty.
5. Welcome newcomers who enter the booth.
6. Treat every visitor with equal respect.
7. Get that lead by offering to send literature to the prospect's business address.
8. Take your rest period away from the exhibit.
9. Eat before you report for duty.
10. Process the lead form promptly.
11. Never smoke or chew gum.
12. Keep the exhibit open to the last minute.
13. Don't knock competition.

Remember that Pitney-Bowes' "best foot" is yours—so put it forward.

Standardized display backgrounds are available from exhibit producers. Rappaport Exhibits, Inc., Cleveland, offers three styles: Easy-pac, Lite-pac and Roll-pac, (illustrated).

TRADE SHOWS AND FAIRS

Opportunity for exhibits are suggested in this list, under the months in which they are usually scheduled; however, time of show is subject to change from year to year and should therefore be verified before plans are made. (From U. S. Department of Commerce.)

JANUARY

Farm Store Merchandising Conf. & Trade Show, Kansas City. Box 1092, Minneapolis, Minn. 55440.

Int'l Motorama, Phoenix. Pacific Promotions Inc., P.O. Box 1518, Canoga Park, Calif. 91304.

Northeastern Retail Lumbermen's Assn. Expo, Boston. 339 East Ave., Rochester, N.Y. 14604.

Winter Consumer Electronics Show, Las Vegas. CES 1, IBM Plaza, Chicago, Ill. 60611.

TRADE SHOWS AND FAIRS

Men's Western Wear Market, Dallas. Dallas Market Ctr., 2100 Stemmons Freeway, Dallas, Tex. 75207.

Nat'l Handbag Market Weeks, New York City. 350 5th Ave., New York, N.Y. 10001.

Nat'l Audio-Visual Conv. & Exbn., New Orleans. Nat'l Audio-Visual Assn. Inc., 3150 Spring St., Fairfax, Va. 22030.

Nat'l Western Stock Show, Denver. 1325 E. 46th Ave., Denver, Colo. 80216.

Pulp & Paper World Conf./Expo, Atlanta. Nat'l Expositions, 14 W. 40th St., New York, N.Y. 10018.

Portland Gift Show, Atlanta. Western Exhibitors, Inc., 2181 Greenwich St., San Francisco, Cal. 94123.

Winter Home Furnishings Market, Dallas. Dallas Market Ctr., 2100 Stemmons Freeway, Dallas, Tex. 75207.

Nat'l Housewares Expos., Chicago. 1324 Merchandise Mart, Chicago, Ill. 60654.

Nat'l Assn. of Home Builders Conv. & Educ. Expo, Miami Beach. 15th & M St. NW., Washington, D.C. 20005.

Women's & Children's Apparel Market, Dallas. Dallas Market Ctr., 2100 Stemmons Freeway, Dallas, Tex. 75207.

Atlanta Home Furnishings Market, Atlanta. 240 Peachtree St. NW., Atlanta, Ga. 30303.

Int'l Expo for Food Processors, San Francisco. Food Processing Machinery & Supplies Assn., 7758 Wisconsin Ave., Washington, DC. 20014.

FEBRUARY

Southern Farm Show, Raleigh. Southern Shows, Inc., 1945 Randolph Rd., Charlotte, N.C. 28207.

Atlanta Int'l Sport & Travel Show, Atlanta. H & H Productions Inc., 1172 W. Galbraith Rd., Cincinnati, Ohio 45231.

San Francisco Gift Show, San Francisco. Western Exhibitors Inc., 2181 Greenwich St., San Francisco, Calif. 94123.

Southwestern Men's & Boys' Apparel Market, Dallas. Dallas Market Ctr., 2100 Stemmons Freeway, Dallas, Tex. 75207.

Int'l Turfgrass Conf. & Show, Atlanta. 1617 St. Andrews Dr., Lawrence, Kan. 66044.

World Fair for Technology Exchange, Atlanta. Dvorkovitz & Assoc., P.O. Box 1748, Ormond Beach, Fla. 32074.

Nat'l Sporting Goods Assn. Conv. & Show, Chicago. 717 N. Michigan Ave., Chicago, Ill. 60611.

Nat'l Automobile Dealers Assn. Equipment Expo, Las Vegas. 8400 Westpark Dr., McLean, Va. 22101.

Precast Concrete Industries Expo, Cincinnati. 20 N. Wacker Dr., Chicago, Ill. 60606.

Nat'l Antiques Show, New York City. 11 Warren St., New York, N.Y. 10007.

Decor Show, New York City. Int'l Trade Shows, 545 Fifth Ave., New York, N.Y. 10017.

Int'l Cycle Show, New York City. Int'l Trade Shows, 545 Fifth Ave., New York, N.Y. 10017.

TRADE SHOWS AND FAIRS

MARCH

Menswear Retailers of America Nat'l Conv. & Menswear Show, New Orleans. 390 Nat'l Press Bldg., Washington, D.C. 20045.

Dayton Sportsmen's Travel Trailer & Boat Show, 101 Shiloh Spr. Rd., Dayton, Ohio 45415.

Western New York Boat Show, Niagara Falls, N.Y. Creative Mall Promotions, Inc., 48 Landing Dr., Marlton, N.J. 08053.

Nat'l Home Ctr./Home Improvement Congress & Expo, Atlanta. 600 Talcott Rd., Park Ridge, Ill. 60068.

Pittsburgh Conf. on Analytical Chemistry & Applied Spectroscopy, Cleveland. Jane H. Judd, Pres., Westinghouse Bettis Plant, P.O. Box 70, W. Mifflin, Pa. 15122.

Birmingham Home & Garden Show, Birmingham. P.O. 20235, Birmingham, Ala. 35216.

Int'l Turbine Congress, San Diego, Stal-Laval Inc., 400 Executive Blvd., Elmsford, N.Y. 10523.

Electric Power & Farm Equipment Show, Madison. Wisconsin Power Equipment Retailers Assn., 3414 Monroe St., Madison, Wis. 53711.

Dallas Toy Show, Dallas. Dallas Market Ctr., 2100 Stemmons Freeway, Dallas, Tex. 75207.

WESTEC (Western Metal & Tool Conf. & Expo), Los Angeles. SME 20501 Ford Rd., Dearborn, Mich. 48128.

Mid-West Health Congress, Kansas City. 208 Nichols Rd., Kansas City, Mo. 64112.

Nat'l Mail Order Merchandise Show, New York City. Exhibition Mgmt. Inc., 40 W. Ridgewood Ave., Ridgewood, N.J. 07450.

Int'l Trucking Show, Anaheim. 1240 Bayshore Hgwy., Burlingame, Calif. 94010.

Nat'l Assn. of Broadcasters Conv., Dallas. Nat'l Assn. of Broadcasters, 1771 N St., NW., Washington, D.C. 20036.

Women's Apparel Show, Atlanta. Nam Sherry Hill, Atlanta Mart, 240 Peachtree St., NW., Atlanta, Ga. 30303.

Atlanta Toy Fair, Atlanta. 3384 Peachtree Rd., Suite 311, Atlanta, Ga. 30326.

Women's & Children's Apparel Market, Dallas. Dallas Market Ctr., 2100 Stemmons Freeway, Dallas, Tex. 75207.

APRIL

Photo Mktg. Assn. Int'l Conv., Chicago. 603 Lansing Ave., Chicago, Ill. 60606.

American Welding Soc., New Orleans. 2501 NW. 7th St., Miami, Fla. 33125.

Alabama Trade Fair & World Trade Expo, Birmingham. 90 Bagby Dr., Suite 222, Birmingham, Ala. 35209.

Chicagoland Business Services & Equipment Expo, Chicago. Industrial & Scientific Conference & Management Inc., 222 W. Adams, Chicago, Ill. 60606.

SAE Business Aircraft Marketing & Display, Wichita. Soc. of Automotive Engineers, 400 Commonwealth Dr., Warrendale, Pa. 15096.

Expo Pesca Pan Americana, San Juan, Puerto Rico. 21 Elm St., Camden, Maine 04843.

American Occupational Health Conf., New Orleans. 150 N. Wacker Dr., Chicago, Ill. 60606.

TRADE SHOWS AND FAIRS

AAPG Convention on Energy Resource, Oklahoma City. American Assn. of Petroleum Geologists, P.O. Box 979, Tulsa, Okla. 74101.

Nat'l Expo of Surgical Trade Industries, New York City. 139-1188 Rd., Jamaica, N.Y. 11435.

Louisville Retreaders' Conf. & Trade Show, Louisville. Box 17203, Louisville, Ky. 40217.

Puerto Rico Food & Equipment Expo, San Juan, Puerto Rico. Marketing Mgmt. Services Corp., P.O. Box 5171, Puerta de Tierra, P.R. 00906.

American College of Physicians Annual Session, Boston. 4200 Pine St., Philadelphia, Pa. 19104.

Design Engineering Show & ASME Design Engineering Conf., Chicago. Clapp & Poliak Inc., 245 Park Ave., New York, N.Y. 10017.

Nat'l Plant Engineering & Maintenance Show & Conf., Chicago. Clapp & Poliak Inc., 245 Park Ave., New York, N.Y. 10017.

Atlanta Home & Garden Show, Atlanta. Home Builders' Assoc. of Metro Atlanta, Atlanta, Ga. 30303.

Nat'l LP-Gas Assn. Intl Trade Show & Conv., Houston. 1301 W. 22nd St., Oak Brook, Ill. 60521.

MAY

Tri-State Hospital Assembly, Chicago. Alfred Van Horn III, Exec. V.P., 435 N. Michigan Ave., Chicago, Ill. 60611.

Accounting Show Conf., New York City. V.P., Charles Snitow Organization, 331 Madison Ave., New York, N.Y. 10017.

Premium Show, New York City. 98 Cutter Mill Rd., Great Neck, N.Y. 11021.

Nat'l SAMPE Symposium & Exbn., Anaheim. Soc. for the Advancement of Material Process Engineering, Box 613, Azusa, Calif. 91702.

Int'l Repro Graphic Blueprint Assn. Conv., Houston. 10116 Franklin Ave., Franklin Park, Ill. 60131.

Int'l Waste Equipment & Technology Expo, Miami Beach, Fla. National Solid Wastes Mgmt. Assn., Suite 930-1120 Connecticut Ave. N.W., Washington, D.C. 20036.

Int'l Save Conference, Indianapolis. Soc. of American Value Engineers, 2215 Allison Speedway Ave., Indianapolis, Ind. 46224.

American Ceramic Soc. Expo, Detroit. Exhibition Mgmt. Inc., 40 W. Ridgewood Ave., Ridgewood, N.J. 07450.

Aerospace Medical Assn. Scientific Meeting, New Orleans. 850 Third Ave., New York, N.Y. 10022.

Offshore Technology Conf., Houston. 6200 N. Central Expwy., Dallas, Tex. 75206.

NEPCON East & Semi Conductor/Hybrid Microelectronics, Symposium & Exbn., New York City. Industrial & Scientific Mgmt. Inc., 222 W. Adams, Chicago, Ill. 60606.

Puerto Rico Health Industries Expo, San Juan, Puerto Rico. Mktg. Mgmt. Services Corp., P. O. Box 5171, Puerta de Tierra, P.R. 00906.

Nat'l Micrographics Assn. Conf. & Expo, Boston. 8728 Colesville Rd., No. 1101, Silver Spring, Md. 20910.

Int'l Trucking Show, San Francisco. 1240 Bayshore Hgwy., Burlingame, Calif. 94010. FBP.

TRADE SHOWS AND FAIRS

Institute of Food Technologists Meeting & Food Expo, Dallas. 221 N. LaSalle St., Chicago, Ill. 60601.

Nat'l Fashion & Boutique Show, New York City. 393 7th Ave., New York, N.Y. 10001.

Portland Gift Show, Portland, Ore. Western Exhibitors Inc., 2181 Greenwich St., San Francisco, Calif. 94123.

Nat'l Computer Conf., Anaheim. AFIPS 210 Summit Ave., Montvale, N.J. 07645.

Nat'l Maintenance & Operations Meeting, Reading. P.O. Box 1201, Reading, Pa. 19603.

Miami Foreign & Custom Auto/Cycle Expo, Miami. 6915 Red Rd., Suite 228, Coral Gables, Fla. 33143.

Summer Consumer Electronics Show, Chicago. CES, 1 IBM Plaza, Chicago, Ill. 60611.

Housewares & Variety Merchandise Show, Los Angeles. 98 Cutter Mill Rd., Great Neck, N.Y. 11021.

Nat'l Material Handling Show, Detroit. W. P. Hakanson, Public Relations Exec., Material Handling Institute Inc., 1326 Freeport Rd., Pittsburgh, Pa. 15238.

Chicago Home Furnishings Market & America's Nat'l Lamp Show, Chicago. 666 Lake Shore Dr., Chicago, Ill. 60611.

Graphics '78, New York City. Conf. & Exbn., 3 Quintard Dr., Port Chester, N.Y. 10573.

Florida Furniture Mart, Orlando. 2373 Collins Ave., Miami Beach, Fla. 33139.

Nat'l Assn. of Plumbing/Heating/Cooling Contractors, Las Vegas. 1016 20th St. NW., Washington, D.C. 20036.

Las Vegas Gift Show, Las Vegas. Western Exhibitors Inc., 2181 Greenwich St., San Francisco, Calif. 94123.

Western Material Handling & Packaging Show, San Francisco. Suite 104, 3951 E. Huntington Dr., Pasadena, Calif. 91107.

Cosmesis Club of Texas Cosmetic Show, Dallas. Dallas Market Center, 2100 Stemmons Freeway, Dallas, Tex. 75207.

Christmas Gift Jewelry & Housewares Show, Dallas. Dallas Market Center, 2100 Stemmons Freeway, Dallas, Tex. 75207.

American Optometric Assn. Congress, New Orleans. 7000 Chippiwa St., St. Louis, Mo. 63119.

Transworld Housewares & Variety Exbn., Chicago. 466 Central Ave., Northfield, Ill. 60093.

Men's & Boys' Apparel Market, Atlanta. 4438 Lake Ivanhoe Dr., Tucker, Ga. 30084.

Int'l Housewares Marketplace, Chicago. Martin C. Dwyer, Inc., 400 N. Michigan Ave., Chicago, Ill. 60611.

Nat'l Fancy Food & Confection Show, New York City. Charles Snitow Organization, 331 Madison Ave., New York, N.Y. 10017.

Florida Furniture Mart, Tampa. 2373 Collins Ave., Miami Beach, Fla. 33139.

TRADE SHOWS AND FAIRS

Nat'l Handbag Market Weeks, New York City. 350 5th Ave., New York, N.Y. 10001.

American Conv. of Meat Processors, St. Louis. American Assoc. of Meat Processors, 224 East High St., Elizabethtown, Pa. 17022.

San Francisco Gift Show, San Francisco. Western Exhibitors, Inc., 2181 Greenwich St., San Francisco, Cal. 94123.

Midwest Mobile/Modular Home Recreation Vehicle Show, South Bend. 3210 Rand Rd., Indianapolis, Ind. 46241.

National Hardware Show, Chicago. Charles Snitow Organization, 331 Madison Ave., New York, N.Y. 10017. FBP.

Seattle Gift Show, Seattle. Western Exhibitors Inc., 2181 Greenwich St., San Francisco, Calif. 94123.

SEPTEMBER

Gift, Jewelry & Housewares Show, Dallas. P.R./Advertising, Dallas Market Ctr., 2100 Stemmons Freeway, Dallas, Tex. 75207.

Int'l Machine Tool Show, Chicago. Nat'l Machine Tool Builders, 7901 West Park Dr., McLean, Va. 22101. FBP.

Screen Print '79, St. Louis. 307-F Maple Ave. W., Vienna, Va. 22180.

Southeastern Shoe Show, Atlanta. Atlanta Mart, Suite 14-A-10, 240 Peachtree St., Atlanta, Ga. 30303.

Int'l Petroleum Expo, Tulsa. Martin C. Dwyer, Inc., 400 N. Michigan Ave., Chicago, Ill. 60611.

Int'l Assn. of Fire Chiefs Conf., Cincinnati. 1329 18th St., N.W., Washington, D.C. 20036.

American Hospital Assoc. Conv., Anaheim. 840 North Lake Shore Dr., Chicago, Ill. 60610. FBP.

SAE Off Highway Vehicle Meeting & Exbn., Milwaukee. Soc. of Automotive Engineers Inc., 400 Commonwealth Dr., Warrendale, Pa. 15096.

WESCON (Western Electronic Show), Los Angeles. Gen. Mgr. IEEE & ERA, 999 N. Sepulveda Blvd., El Segundo, Calif. 90245.

Eastern States Expos., W. Springfield, Mass. 1305 Memorial Ave., W. Springfield, Mass. 01089.

Int'l Woodworking Machinery & Furniture Supply Show, Louisville. 600 Talcott Rd., Park Ridge, Ill. 60068. FBP.

OCTOBER

Soc. of Petro Engineering Technical Conf. & Exbn., Houston. Meetings & Conv., 6200 N. Central Expressway, Dallas, Tex. 75206.

Water Pollution Control Federation Conf./Exbn. Anaheim. 2626 Pennsylvania Ave., NW., Washington, D.C. 20037.

Nat'l Safety Congress & Expo, Chicago. 425 N. Michigan Ave., Chicago, Ill. 60011.

Int'l Electric Vehicle Expo & Conf., Philadelphia. Charles Snitow Organization, 331 Madison Ave., New York, N.Y. 10017.

Nat'l Office Products Assn., Chicago. 301 N. Fairfax St., Alexandria, Va. 22314.

World Dairy Expo, Madison. 1707 S. Park St., Madison, Wis. 53713.

Nat'l Conv./Exbn. Vending & Food Service Mgmt., Atlanta. Nat'l Automatic Merchandise Assn., 7 S. Dearborn St., Chicago, Ill. 60603.

TRADE SHOWS AND FAIRS

Int'l Assn. of Chiefs of Police, New York City. Administrative Services, 11 First-field Rd., Gaithersburg, Md. 20760.

Nat'l Arts & Antiques Festival, New York City. 11 Warren St., New York, N.Y. 10007.

Incentive Travel & Meeting Expo Show, Chicago. 7237 Lake St., River Forest, Ill. 60305.

Int'l Mining Show, Las Vegas. Div., American Mining Congress, 1100 Ring Bldg., Washington, D.C. 20036. FBP.

Nat'l Premium Show, Chicago. 7237 Lake St., River Forest, Ill. 60305.

Nat'l Sporting Goods Assn. Fall Market, Anaheim. 717 N. Michigan Ave., Chicago, Ill. 60611.

NOVEMBER

AATCC Nat'l Technical Conf., Anaheim. American Assn. of Textile Chemists & Colorists, AATCC Technical Ctr., P.O. Box 12215. Research Triangle Park, N.C. 27709.

Int'l Film & TV Festival of New York. 251 W. 57th St., New York, N.Y. 10019.

Atlanta Int'l Marine Trades Expo, Atlanta. Southern Exposition Mgmt. Co., 3384 Peachtree Rd. N.E., Suite 311, Atlanta, Ga. 30326.

Keystone Int'l Livestock Expo, Harrisburg. Farm Show Bldg., P.O. Box 3362, Harrisburg, Pa. 17120.

Int'l Hotel/Motel & Restaurant Show, New York City. 141 W. 51st St., New York, N.Y. 10019.

DECEMBER

Nat'l Telecommunications Conf., Birmingham. S. Central Bell, P.O. Box 405, Birmingham, Ala. 35202.

Mini/Micro Computer Conf. & Expo., Anaheim. 5544 E. La Palma, Anaheim, Calif. 92807.

Dixie Farm Show, Atlanta. H & H Productions, Ltd., 1380 W. Paces Ferry Rd., Suite 100, Atlanta, Ga. 30327.

Chapter 25

SPECIALTIES FOR INCREASING SALES

"PROBABLY there is not an American living who, at one time or another, has not owned and used some piece of merchandise with advertising imprinted on it. The great majority of Americans at this very moment undoubtedly have on their persons or in their homes or offices one or more such items. The specialty advertising industry grosses approximately a billion dollars in sales, is comprised of 4100 suppliers and distributors, has a national trade association and a number of regional trade groups . . . yet is all but unknown to people who are not in the advertising business . . . and poorly understood and at times improperly used by (others) who are." So states Walter A. Gaw, Professor Emeritus of Marketing, Baruch College of the City University of New York, in the booklet "Specialty Advertising," published by the Specialty Advertising Association International, headquartered in Chicago.

Premiums and incentives have become an increasingly important part of a promotion executive's working tool. "From a simple in-pack to an expensive dealer incentive, there are few, if any, who would quarrel with the premium as a powerful sales promotion device," wrote editor Louis J. Haugh in an editorial in the defunct *Advertising & Sales Promotion.* "A premium and incentive offer can add dramatically to sales."

The use of premiums has spread astonishingly in the last few years and covers practically every field of business. Some major consumer goods manufacturers such as Van Heusen, Oneida, RCA, Brunswick (MacGregor Division), Owens-Illinois (Libbey Products) and numerous others now have special departments to develop and expand the use of their regular products as premiums by other advertisers. Considering all phases of the business, including coupons, trading stamps, contest prizes, sales incentives and other retail applications, it's a $4 billion dollar annual business, according to the premium manager of a large tobacco company. He suggests that it will probably be $8 billion in five years.

While there are successful companies which depend almost entirely upon specialties to advertise their business, this method of promotion has its greatest use as a supplement to other ways of increasing sales. One important use, for example, is as a door opener for salesmen. An industrial machinery company had a difficult time getting its story over to architects. Architects are busy people and are inclined to get rid of salesmen as quickly and as painlessly as possible. Yet the architect holds the fate of many an important installation in the palm of his hand. To break down this resistance and to help its salesmen get a higher ratio of interviews to calls, this machinery manufacturer decided to supply its salesmen with some small carborundum stones with their names and addresses on the back. These carborundum stones were just what the architect needed to put a point on his pencils as well as to sharpen knives and other tools he uses in his work. Armed with these sharpeners, the salesmen were able to get a far better reception and in a surprising number of cases the little friend-maker proved to be all that was necessary to give the salesman his big chance. They also helped him to make friends with the engineer who drew the specifications. That, of course, is most important where the first sales step depends upon getting your product specified.

In house-to-house selling operations the turnover in salesmen is a terrific load on sales costs. Not many salesmen can stand up day after day getting doors slammed in their faces. That is where the use of some little utility the salesman can give to the woman of the house proves indispensable. Thus a broom holder opened many doors, which might otherwise have been slammed closed, to salesmen selling cleaning compounds directly to the home. The Fuller Brush Company practically built its business on the skillful use of well-chosen "door openers." And in a similar way Swift & Company has capitalized the human desire to get something for nothing by giving farmers visiting its exhibit at state fairs a watch charm in the form of a miniature Swift's Premium Ham. The novelty of the thing intrigued the farm folks. Thousands were distributed. They proved to be excellent good-will builders. Later, packets of souvenir post cards were used for the same purpose. Friend-making gifts, with a sales purpose, have likewise been used by the big oil companies to introduce their products into foreign markets. Standard Oil scored a hit in China by giving away brilliantly colored pocket mirrors. They paved the way for converting the Chinese to the use of kerosene lamps. Actually the mirrors cost only a few cents, but to the average

Chinese they were a luxury which he probably would never own, if he had to buy it.

Basic Requirements of Specialty Advertising

It is a mistake, however, to look upon specialties as just something to give away, or a way to keep "our name before the public." They are an important part of any well-rounded plan for promoting sales, for any sales building program must be based upon customer good will. Specialties do that job.

Following are thirteen basic requirements to be considered in the selection and use of specialties:

1. FREQUENT USE

An advertising specialty should be an item that is used or referred to frequently. Since an advertising specialty is a tangible form of reminder advertising, the more often it is used, the more often it is seen, the more valuable is the advertising value. A clock meets this requirement ideally. In less expensive specialties the same purpose is served by calendars, desk pads, mechanical pencils.

2. PRIDE OF OWNERSHIP

An ideal advertising specialty is an item the average person has always wanted but may not buy because it would be considered a luxury. A leather desk set, a desk cigarette lighter, a pipe rack would fit into this category.

3. CIRCULATION

The more people who see an advertising specialty, the more its advertising value. Items which are kept *in* office desks or dresser drawers are not as valuable as items people carry on their persons and use in the presence of others, or items kept *on* the desk and seen by others. The advertiser wants his name to register frequently. Playing cards are an increasingly popular item for this reason.

4. LONG LIFE

Any item that is consumed immediately is less desirable than one with a normal, useful life of a year or more. Not only is it wasteful advertising to imprint consumable items, but the recipient will attach less value to such a gift. On the other hand, a specialty gift promising many years of service will be valued in direct proportion to its life expectancy. Edibles, except perhaps plum puddings or fruit cakes at Christmas, make poor advertising specialties for this reason, while merchandise like leather wallets, key cases, and pocket knives are perennial favorites.

5. NONBREAKABLE

If the specialty is one that can break or wear out quickly in use, it is liable to build bad-will instead of good-will. Experienced buyers look for foolproof mechanisms and sturdy construction. Cheaper brands of merchandise are usually ruled out on this score. The little extra cost for quality items more than pays back the difference in terms of recipient satisfaction and good-will.

6. Repair Service

If the item is one with moving parts, it is only natural that with use the gift will require servicing. If no provision has been made for repair service, the recipient may feel let down. And if the repair costs more than a very nominal sum, he is likely to feel imposed upon. This is one of the most difficult requirements to meet in a mechanical specialty item. One large manufacturer of pocket lighters used widely as an advertising specialty gives absolutely free repair or replacement service on a lifetime basis.

7. Easy to Mail

Bulky gifts that are difficult to wrap and mail or are open to possible breakage in shipping do not make ideal specialties. The smaller the item, the more acceptable it is to premium buyers for these packing and shipping reasons.

8. Good Display of Advertiser's Name

Almost all advertising specialties carry the name, insigne, or trade-mark of the advertiser. Gift specialties are just another form of advertising, and the purpose is to remind the user of the particular company. Items that allow for permanent engraving of the company name, insigne, or trade-mark, preferably in color, rate high with specialty purchasers. The calendar (wall or desk) allows the largest display of the advertiser's name.

9. Greatest Percent of Users

A big problem for the advertising specialty buyer is to pick up an item that will actually be used by the greatest percentage of recipients. Hardly any specialty will find 100% user acceptance; the trick is to get as near that as possible. Pens, pencils, memo pads, wallets appeal to almost everyone.

10. Personalized

Can the recipient's name or initials be put on the gift? People like personalized items, and if there is room for neatly engraved, or stamped, name or initials, the value is greatly enhanced.

11. It Must Not Offend

The company using advertising specialties to build good-will can't afford to take a chance of offending even one customer or prospect. That means the gift buyer had better avoid use of extreme color and design. Art work, if any is involved, should never be open to the criticism of being vulgar or in bad taste. The large calendar houses employ top artists at top prices to produce girl pictures that will attract the eye of any normal male but that cannot be accused of being sexy. Nor can a company afford to give something that may constitute an insult to sensitive souls—such as a gift of soap or a hairbrush (too many balding men) or anything to indicate a possible personal weakness.

12. Familiar Accepted Items

It is best not to try out as good-will specialties gadgets, or items, not yet accorded consumer acceptance. There must be no doubt in the mind of the recipient about the ability of the gift to do its job or about the general usefulness of the item. A new type of razor, one not yet accepted by the public, is not as good a specialty as some branded razor with consumer acceptance and national advertising behind it.

13. Tie-in Possibilities

Whenever possible, the specialty should have a possible tie-in with the product being advertised. A mechanical tool is not a good specialty for a cosmetic, any more than a manicure kit would be a suitable gift from an automobile tire company. A ball-point pen can be promoted to dealers by telling them they can "Write your own ticket with the X product," or "You'll write up more sales each month with the Z product." Similarly with a pocket lighter, the promotional tie-in allows the advertiser to say, "Light the way to more sales with X," or "X will spark up your sales volume." Likewise the advertiser using a wall clock as a gift can say, "It's time to see your XYZ salesman," or "It's time to reorder."

Successful Specialty Programs

To add glamor, excitement and impact to a new-business presentation, D'Arcy-McManus-Intermarco, Inc., a leading advertising agency, made good use of specialties with highly successful results.

Since the agency's proposed campaign featured an exclamation point, it was decided to use this symbol on advertising specialties during the presentation. When the prospective client audience entered the presentation room, writing portfolios were on the chairs, buttons were worn by agency personnel making the presentation, napkins were passed out with refreshments. Ties, cuff links and tie tacks were presented at the appropriate time, during which agency personnel also changed into new ties. All items bore the exclamation point symbol. Bracelets, key chains and jackets were displayed and given as take-home items.

Not only did the agency get the account but the client ordered additional quantities of the advertising specialties for use at regional sales meetings.

In another field, ITT General Controls, Glendale, California, manufacturer of heating controls, wished to stimulate sales efforts of factory salesmen and of distributors who also carried competing lines.

A racing theme design, incorporating racing stripes with the company name, was created for advertising specialties and trade journal advertising. The specialties used included imprinted coffee cups, ash trays (copy: "Win with General Controls"), lighters, vinyl correspondence folders, pens, playing cards, golf balls, and badges. Initially issued to salesmen at a sales meeting, the specialties were presented in person on sales calls.

The campaign produced a greater identity awareness on the part of distributor countermen, and the company reported a brisk increase in sales.

Southeast National Bank of Orlando, Florida, an established bank holding company wished to launch a bank in a new market area and to introduce a new range of financial services.

To achieve the greatest market impact, the bank employed an advertising agency, a public relations agency, and a specialty advertising distributor/counselor. Desk paperweights were presented at a pre-opening cocktail party for the financial community, and pencil caddies went to the working press of Central Florida at another pre-opening function. There were also drink stirrers and napkins, and for children of new accounts, kites and balloons. Golf tees and ball markers, imprinted with the bank logo only, were distributed to area golf courses. Other imprinted specialties included jar openers for women customers, piggy banks for new savings accounts, individual pillow items (first-aid kits, insect repellent, sun tan lotion) for distribution on the bank floor to all traffic. Officers calling on outside businesses distributed pillow items. Watches and charms were presented as thank-you gifts to personnel of motels where the parties were held.

The coordinated campaign was a prime factor in the new bank's immediate success. Deposits rose to nearly $10 million in less than a year of operation.

The Commonwealth of Pennsylvania embarked on a program to demonstrate to industry the production and distribution advantages of locating along a newly opened interstate highway and to encourage recreational investment.

As a follow-up to an invitation to attend a ribbon-cutting ceremony for new Interstate 80, a "Do-it-Yourself Time Saving Keystone Shortway Ribbon-Cutting Ceremony" kit was issued to enable the target audience, 1,000 presidents of the nation's largest corporations, to participate without leaving their offices. The kit included a ribbon-cutting scissors, a bottle of water (copy: "Water pure and plenty from Pennsylvania now available for industry, commerce and recreation"), an I-80 imprinted highball glass and drink stirrer, a flashlight battery (representing the power the state could generate for industry), and a red plastic bank with four pennies, the latter representing the state's plan for 100% financing for as low as 4% for new industries. These and other specialties in the kit were designed to tout the potential benefits that firms could avail themselves of.

The governor's office received 500 responses complimenting the promotion, and the kit received publicity on network radio and from a national news service.

If our orange juice turns you on, wait'll you turn on our orange.

Our orange is really plastic with a superb six-transistor radio inside. And great-sounding sound. To turn it on, pop in the battery (it's included) and twist the stem. To get it, send $4 and the white pull-tab from a can of TreeSweet frozen orange juice. TreeSweet is a natural. All pure orange juice. Nothing's added to water it down or flavor it up. Not even sugar. It's naturally sweeter, with the full, flavorsome, sunshiny goodness of Indian River oranges. And only TreeSweet has its own Indian River plant to make sure of that right-off-the-tree taste. Two great turn-ons. Wouldn't you know they're both from TreeSweet?

To: Orange Radio, P.O. Box 11625, Santa Ana, Calif. 92711
I'm enclosing $4.00* (check or money order) and 1 pull-tab from a can of TreeSweet frozen orange juice. Rush me—postage paid—the radio that looks like an orange. (Actual size: 3½" dia.)

Name

Address

City _____ State _____ Zip _____
*California residents add 5% sales tax. Zip code must be included. Offer good only in U.S.A. Void where prohibited. Allow six weeks for delivery. Offer expires 12/31/72.   FC-6

$4.00 Special Offer.

A novel promotional campaign, featuring a transistor radio that looks like an orange, was a highlight of TreeSweet Products Company's late marketing campaign. According to Vice President Robert E. Graves, the activity was unique to the citrus juice industry. The radios were available for $4 and two pull tabs from a can of TreeSweet orange juice.

743

How Specialties Are Used to Sell Insurance

Some idea as to the widespread use of advertising specialties to win friends and influence people is found in the insurance field. The Life Insurance Advertisers Association studied 125 leading companies, and found that 120 of them used specialties. Some used as many as 20 different kinds. The most popular were wall calendars, followed by celluloid pocket calendars, policy wallets, memo books, and blotters. Usually the agent pays part of the cost, and if he pays more than 50% of the cost the company imprints his name on the specialty.

The principal use for specialties in the insurance field is for building good will and paving the way for the agent. Sixty-three percent of the specialties are used as gifts to policyholders; 57% as door openers. Another widespread use is as gifts to people or institutions in a position to influence business, and then, of course, there is the dependable pocket wallet, offered by several companies in campaigns to get leads for their agents.

A majority of companies follow the practice of including advertising specialties in the regular advertising budget. A total of 56% do so, while 18% reported separate budgets, and 24% no special budgetary provision.

A total of 69 companies reported stocking all items themselves. Another 35 reported stocking most items while having manufacturers hold certain items subject to order. Only 8 companies said their regular practice is to have the manufacturer hold stocks subject to order.

The Plan Is the Thing

As in nearly every form of sales promotion, the way specialties are used is all-important. No matter how novel, useful, or engaging the thing you are going to give away may be, the return will depend upon the effectiveness of the plan for distributing it. The specialty must be given a job to do, and it should be a part of a well-rounded promotional program. Radio station WIBW, in Topeka, Kansas, for example, wanted to bring its facilities to the attention of a group of prospective time users in a dramatic way. The sales manager realized that with hundreds of stations in hundreds of other good cities competing for the advertisers' dollars, something more than the usual kind of radio ballyhoo was necessary. So he decided upon a promotional campaign, using useful specialties as a peg on which to hang his sales messages. One month, for example, the station sent prospects a silver-plated butter spreader attached to a special mailing card. With a maximum of 6 butter spreaders in filling each request, a total of 1,361 spreaders was required to fill requests from 273 prospects for time on the station. Another gadget was an aluminum holder for coat hangers, designed to fit on a car window and especially useful for travelers. The headline on this mailing piece was, "You'll Travel Far in the Kansas Market When You Hire WIBW." A mailing including a plastic coaster had this headline, "Are Your Sales Just Coasting in the Kansas Market? Hire WIBW."

An important part of the WIBW campaign was its consistency. Mailings were made approximately every 6 weeks to a selected list of advertising agencies, advertising managers, company executives, and other buyers and prospective buyers of WIBW radio time. The mailings were in the form of either four-page 8½- by 11-inch folders or of boxes containing the gadget affixed to a printed card that exactly fitted the size of the box. Some mailings were two colors, others three. Over a year "run" the campaign produced 1,135 replies.

Dealers attach considerable value to novelties which they can pass out to the small fry who come to shop with their parents. These do not have to be expensive. For example, rubber balloons printed with the advertiser's name and trade-mark, which the youngsters can blow up until they burst, go over big. The friends they make, both for the merchant and the advertiser, far outweigh the small expense involved. And in the same way wall calendars, corny as the idea may be, are still as popular as ever. Some companies appropriate thousands of dollars each year to furnish dealers with attractive calendars, imprinted with the dealer's name, which the housewife can hang up in the home. They are both ornamental and useful. Best of all, every time the lady of the house looks at it she is reminded of the friendly merchant who gave it to her. Because of the competition, such a calendar should be as attractive and useful as possible.

Premium Plans

The wide variety of premiums used to stimulate sales is indicated by a brief summary of some of the plans used by companies in different fields:

Company	Premium
American Oil Company	(Florida) One gas fill-up for staying at a participating hotel or motel.
Kitchen Bouquet	Modern airplane for two proofs of
Libby, McNeill & Libby	purchase of frozen lemonade and nominal cash.
Bic Pen Corporation	Four-piece Corning Ware free with each gross of Bic pens.

Company	Premium
Phillips 66	One Libbey glass with every ten-gallon purchase of Phillips gasoline.
Personna Blades	Free pair of panty hose plus 15c off.
General Foods	Oneida silver plated bowl for two labels from Cool Whip container plus $2.50.
Kimberly Clark Corporation	Coupon for one free package of Freedom Napkins for one premium seal.
Kitchen Bouquet	32-page recipe book free for one box top.
Scott Paper Company	$1 cash refund coupon for five proofs of purchase of Rediscover America Scotties.

The Oneida Incentive Planning Guide

The major uses and values of premiums are outlined by Oneida Ltd., Oneida, New York, in its Incentive Planning Guide, as follows:

A premium adds an "extra value" to your product or service. It attracts attention . . . creates interest . . . builds good will . . . and stimulates sales.

Case histories of many successful business organizations prove that premiums have played a vital role . . . in establishing a preference between equally good competitive brands . . . or to overcome a price differential.

A research study of manufacturers and wholesalers made by New York University produced the following list of *sales objectives most frequently achieved by premium users:*

- stimulating the sales force to achieve present objectives
- beating a sales slump
- building good will
- introducing a new product
- getting new customers for existing products
- offsetting competitors' activity
- improving shelf position
- increasing the size of orders
- making it easier to get orders, retailer displays, newspaper features, and other promotional support.

It is estimated that in a single year, $3-billion worth of premiums helped move up to $100-billion worth of goods and services. And 2200 programs took advantage of the persuasive power of premiums.

The Gruen Time-Teller

When dealers are supplied with inexpensive gadgets which they can give to customers, they will not only pay something for them but will advertise them as well. A few years ago Gruen Industries, Inc., developed a movable disc affair which told the corresponding time in the principal cities of the world. Somebody thought it was the sort of thing Gruen dealers might use to give to customers, since it was something nearly anyone would like to have. If a person had to go to a jewelry store selling Gruen watches to get it, there was a pretty good chance he might come away with a Gruen watch. At least the odds were in favor of his buying something while in the store. So the company offered to sell Gruen dealers as many "Time-Tellers" as they could profitably use at cost, provided the dealer would agree to advertise them either in his local newspaper or by mailing out to his customers a special letter which the company had prepared. Newspaper mats, display cards and other material for publicizing the Time-Teller, were supplied dealers without charge. As a result nearly 2 million of the gadgets were distributed and, according to a Gruen official, reorders are coming in regularly. It was a natural. A perfect tie-in for a watch dealer and the company which made them, or in this case, assembled them. Here is the letter, signed and mailed out by the local Gruen jeweler, which did the trick:

Dear Mr. Jones:

    You will be glad to know we have reserved for you a free copy of the fascinating new Gruen World Time-Teller disc which tells the time in all the important cities in the world!

    Increased interest in world events brought on by the recent war--news headlines from every corner of the earth--and the speed of trans-ocean air travel make the Gruen World Time-Teller a helpful device. By a simple turn of one dial in relation to the other, you can tell instantly the correct time in New York, Berlin, or any other major city.

    You and your whole family will be intrigued by this interesting gadget. Come in for your Time-Teller soon--we're holding it for you.

    And while you're here, we will be very happy to show you, without obligation, our suggestions for anything you may need in the way of gifts for Graduation, Weddings, or any of the other numerous gift occasions arising during this season of the year.

Sincerely yours,

General Electric Company made good use of a similar device in promoting the sale of electrical dishwashers. A disc was worked out which when dialed to the number of years the prospects had been married would show exactly how many dirty dishes they had washed and how many days they had spent in the kitchen. It also told what was in store for them unless they owned a dishwasher. General Electric sold the "Horrorscopes" to dealers for 2 cents, and the dealers had a lot of fun giving them away to likely buyers.

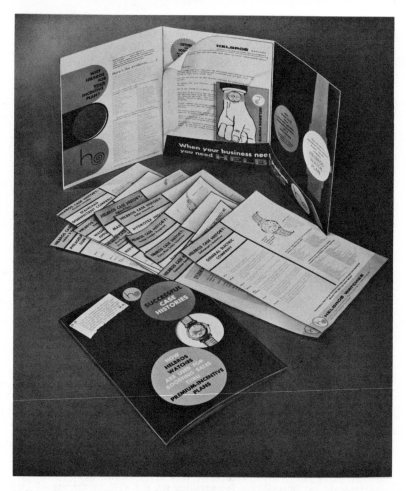

Helbros Watches tells incentive and premium buyers the complete story about its products in a colorful collection of catalogs, booklets, folders, letters and "spec" sheets. Here is one unit: the case history kit, in a six-page 3-color folder-with-pocket and die-cut front cover. Inside are an introductory letter, nine case history sheets and a reply card. The back cover features the company's lifetime guarantee and three different types of Helbros Watches.

Choosing the Premium

Owens-Illinois, Toledo, Ohio, has issued a Premium Merchandising Plan Book detailing how many companies have used its products for promotional purposes. One section contains some helpful tips on "Points to Consider when Choosing a Premium," such as:

1. It must have eye appeal. Eye appeal is most important, particularly when the premium is displayed at the point of sale.

2. It must readily lend itself to advertising and promotion. No premium deal is successful without strong advertising and promotional backing both at the time of introduction and for the duration of the offer. The premium must be such that it will create a demand in advertising copy and illustration.

3. It should be nationally advertised. A nationally advertised product with an established brand name has already gained consumer acceptance and thus makes the promotional task much easier.

4. It must be an outstanding value. The value of the premium should be easily recognized by the consumer.

5. The premium must have an easily recognized use. Gadgets which need detailed explanation as to their use are not good premiums. Articles of general use have greatest acceptance.

6. It should have household use. Almost all premium deals are directed to the housewife. Household articles of everyday use are by far the most popular.

7. It must have strongest appeal to the class of consumer buying your product. Your choice of premium should conform to income and territorial differences in consumer wants.

8. Can it be easily handled by the retailer? The premium distributed at point of sale must be properly packaged to ensure easy handling by the retailer.

9. It must serve as a constant favorable reminder of your product. The more often the premium is used, the more often the user is reminded of your product.

10. Will the manufacturer make deliveries to you promptly? Nothing will cause more ill will on the part of the consumer than non-delivery of the premium. Pick out a reliable supplier by all means.

Promotions which received First Place or Awards of Excellence in the Thirteenth Annual Specialty Advertising Awards Competition to recognize outstanding use of the medium.

Recipe Booklets

An old-time favorite with many food manufacturers is the recipe booklet. While it may seem that this method of promoting the use of a product is overdone, it seems as though women never tire of collecting recipes. Consequently recipe books with a sharp promotional angle make a worthwhile supplement to any campaign designed to increase the consumption of an ingredient used in the preparation of table foods. Some recipe books are written by famous cooking authorities and are quite elaborate. Others are very simple. Sometimes they are distributed by mail to lists furnished by dealers, other times they are offered for box tops or enclosed in packages. The favorite way for getting them into the hands of the housewife, however, is to make them available through local dealers. A "box" in magazine advertisements stating that a recipe book has been pre-

Industrial Marketing Promotion: First place. Awarded to D'Arcy-McManus-Intermarco, Inc., St. Louis, Missouri. Objective: To add impact to an advertising agency new-business presentation. Results: The agency won the account and the client ordered additional quantities of the specialties.

Industrial Marketing Promotion: Award to ITT General Controls, Glendale, California. Objective: To stimulate efforts of factory salesmen and distributors. Results: Greater identity awareness by distributor countermen with a brisk increase in sales.

Local-Regional Marketing Promotion: Award to Southeast National Bank of Orlando, Florida. Objective: To launch a bank in a new market area. Results: Immediate success; deposits rose to nearly $10 million in less than a year.

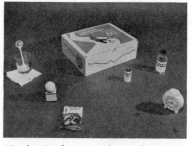

Not-for-Profit Promotion: First place, Awarded to Secretary of Commerce, Commonwealth of Pennsylvania. Objective: To attract industry interest in locations for new plants along a new highway. Results: The governor's office received 500 responses complimenting the promotion.

(Photos: Courtesy of the Advertising Specialties Association International)

pared and is available upon request from your favorite food store serves as an inexpensive way to get quick distribution and at the same time build dealer good will. If the food store does not have the recipe books, or does not carry the product in stock, these requests usually cause the dealer to order a supply from his wholesale supliers. Another good way to distribute recipe books is by spot radio or TV commercials, timed to catch the housewife while she is working in the kitchen, or at other appropriate times. A giveaway recipe book, for example, usually makes a perfect peg upon which to hang a short commercial.

Liquor companies also find it pays to provide dealers with booklets which they can pass out to customers. Some of these tell how to mix a variety of drinks, others are designed to give information of interest to those who may have occasion to serve liquor at parties. For example, Three Feathers whiskey dealers were supplied with booklets imprinted with their names containing all sorts of information helpful in putting on a party. It was called "The Life of the Party." The booklet included popular songs, games that could be played by the guests, and quizzes. One of the quizzes is the "Whisk-Quiz." It is intended to correct popular misconceptions about blended whiskies. Here are a few typical questions:

1. TRUE OR FALSE?

The "Proof" of a whiskey indicates only the alcoholic content—*not* the quality.

True: "Proof" in any whiskey means double the percentage of spirits by volume—nothing else. For instance: A 100 proof whiskey contains 50% spirits; an 86 proof whiskey contains 43% spirits, etc.

2. TRUE OR FALSE?

"Bottled in Bond under U.S. Gov't Supervision" on whiskey labels means that the Government guarantees the quality.

False: Not a chance! The Government does not guarantee the quality of *any* whiskey—*that's* the distiller's problem. "Bonding" indicates only that whiskey has been aged for at least 4 years and is bottled at 100 proof.

3. TRUE OR FALSE?

"Grain Neutral Spirits" is the lightest, most highly refined type of beverage distillate.

True: "Grain Neutral Spirits," made from the same ingredients as whiskey, is refined by distillation at higher proofs. The result: Lighter body—making neutral spirits ideal for blending with heavier whiskies for smoothness. Whiskies thus produced are known by law as "Blended Whiskies."

Paperback Books as Premiums

Paperbacks are increasingly popular with many advertisers because they are useful to the consumer, the advertisements they carry are more enduring than they would be in magazines or newspapers and they have a variety of applications as premiums.

Continental Oil Company used eight Purse Book titles, by Dell Publishing Company, in a "Book-a-Week" continuity promotion. A book was given free to each customer, regardless of the number of gallons of gas purchased. In addition, a tear-off coupon entitled the customer to 15 cents off on a can of Conoco Motor Oil. The premium campaign was promoted on TV, radio and billboards and in newspaper advertising.

Skinner Macaroni Company used a 208-page book with a four-color front cover illustrating the company's pasta products plus an eight-page, full-color center section, in a coupon promotion.

Banks have used Purse Books as free "give-aways" to build traffic and as inducements to open accounts.

Art Calendars

These are still the most widely used of all forms of specialty advertising, and thousands of business establishments, large and small, regard calendars as an important part of their sales promotional program. There are a number of calendar houses which annually prepare a wide selection of syndicated art calendars which they sell up and down Main Street, as well as to national advertisers for use by dealers. It is not unusual for a lithographer to pay as high as $5,000 for an especially good big name painting. It would, of course, be impractical for an individual advertiser to spend that kind of money for calendar art work although some of the air lines do.

It is not hard to understand the popularity of calendars. For one thing, every home, office, and shop needs calendars. They need a new supply every year. Moreover once a calendar is hung up, it usually stays up all year. It will be seen every day by those who live or work where it is hung, and by many others who may be visiting the home or office. It is therefore a form of bulletin advertising, doing much the same job inside that the outdoor bulletin does outside. Even if a percentage of the calendars sent out are never hung up, the advertising value of the space occupied by those which are hung makes it a good investment. They are especially popular with local merchants and dealers, who are usually quite willing to pay cost or better for them when offered as a dealer help by a manufacturer.

A near relative of the art calendar is the celluloid vest-pocket calendar with an appropriate advertising message on one side. Salesmen especially like to have these to pass out to customers and others whose good will they value. They are also used to enclose with the annual report to stockholders. As the number of owners of our business enterprises grows, management is becoming more conscious of the opportunity to get stockholders to boost the company's products to their friends. Placing these handy calendars in their hands, so that they can slip them into their pocket wallets, is about the least expensive way a company can keep its products before its friends and stockholders.

An objection to giving away calendars at the beginning of the year is that there are so many given away at that time. It is not unusual for a business office to receive a hundred or more during December and January, when actually the office only needs four or five. Some of those which fail to rate a spot on the office wall are given to employees who take them home. But this type of distribution is of questionable value. To get over this hurdle some companies send out midyear calendars, that is to say, calendars which start July 1 and cover the last 6 months of the year. This not only reduces the cost of the calendar, but many people tire of looking at the same calendar after 6 months and welcome a change. There is, of course, not nearly so much competition in June and July as there is in December and January. However, a really high-grade, well-done calendar, like the 3-months-at-a-glance art calendars sent out to customers by the American Colortype Company each year, is eager sought and usually occupies a preferred location the year around. In calendar advertising, as in so many other things, the best is the cheapest in the long run.

Books of Matches

A candy manufacturer in St. Louis, who wanted to promote the sale of Old Nick and Bit-o-Honey candy bars, hit upon the idea of advertising them on books of safety matches which he distributed to stores handling his product to give out at the cigar counter. One cover of each book featured the product, overprinted in bold type "Amazing Offer." The offer, described on the back cover of the book, was four stainless steel paring knives for 50 cents, with two "Old Nick" candy bar wrappers. The candy, of course, could be purchased right in the store. The inside of the cover was used (the long way) as a coupon for accepting the offer. The idea proved a winner, not because there was anything novel in giving away books of matches, but because of the plan by which the match books were distributed. Millions of match books are given away, or sold at cost to dealers, by advertisers who find their customers value them greatly.

Christmas Remembrances

It is estimated that American business concerns give away to customers more than $50 million worth of merchandise every Christmas. The average price paid for such gifts is about $7.50. Some companies send their customers a box of fruit, others a bottle of liquor, a box of cigars, or one of the attractive cheese samplers which are available from cheese makers and packers. It is felt that the sender's thoughtfulness will be appreciated, and since it is the Christmas season the gift will not be misunderstood.

But gifts of food or liquor, while appreciated, are soon consumed. So more and more companies are turning to gifts which the customer can keep and use the year through. A particularly popular and acceptable gift is an executive desk book, which the customer can use to keep track of his appointments, make daily entries of importance, and after the year is over file away as a permanent history of the year's activities. The Dartnell Corporation of Chicago, for

Philip Morris offered a set of three complexion brushes (one each for powder, eye brows and eye lashes) valued at $2.50, for ten bottom panels from packs of Virginia Slims. The company's agency reported that the response was overwhelming and that "we found ourselves constantly in the predicament of having to reorder to meet the demand. We plan to rerun a variation of the promotion."

example, issues a *Personal Record Book for Executives* each year, in November. Over the years it has won high acceptance from business and professional men. The books are offered in several leather bindings, at various prices, according to the type of binding. These books can be stamped with the customer's name in gold on the front cover and, if desired, with the trade-mark or firm name of the company on the back cover.

The user of advertising specialties should, wherever possible, test out the gift on a small group of people before extending the promotion to his entire list of prospects or customers. He should make a point of finding out what these test recipients think of the gift. If it meets with only mild favor it should be dropped and another item should be tested until one is found which evokes a majority of enthusiastic approval.

How Users Select Their Offerings

In connection with calendars, however, it should be noted that the most appropriate illustrative subjects are not always the most popular, for practically all surveys made on the question show pretty girl pictures to be far in the lead, regardless of the product promoted. Following one year's calendar mailing, for instance, the Pennsylvania Refining Company sent out a questionnaire to recipients soliciting information about what subjects would be preferred for the next calendar. Girls alone or girls with dogs got the great majority of the votes. The girl-and-dog theme appealed to 69% very much and to another 20% to lesser degree; with an 89% total preference the choice of a subject was easy to make.

As a long-time user of sales promotional specialties, the Panther Oil and Grease Manufacturing Company has experimented with many different kinds and, in the words of O. B. Swallow, sales manager, "It is always an item that normally can't be purchased from the local merchant." He enumerated as typical selections: "A magic mirror door detective; a combination pencil and cigarette lighter; a combination pencil and knife; a 12-in-1 tool that does practically everything except rock the baby to sleep; a hand-painted Western tie; a magic light that turns on automatically when it is lifted from the night stand."

Where several executives have a voice in deciding to whom the order will be given, a carefully selected and tactfully presented advertising specialty can be of great help. A manufacturer of air-conditioning machinery, for example, presents friendly persons in organizations likely to buy his equipment with a useful automobile trouble light.

PREMIUMS IN SALES PROMOTION

There are five basic types of premiums used in modern sales promotion, as classified by Frank H. Waggoner, in *Sales & Marketing Management* Magazine. They are:

1. Coupon plan.
2. Direct premium plan.
3. Self-liquidating plan.
4. Container premium plan.
5. Enclosure premium plan.

The coupon plan goes as far back as 1851, when Raleigh cigarettes were packed with a coupon "good for beautiful premiums" as an inducement to get purchasers to keep on using Raleigh long enough to get the habit. Direct premiums are given with a single purchase, as, for example, premiums that are given with magazine subscriptions. The self-liquidating premium is offered for a slight additional sum, usually enough to let the company which uses them out at about cost. Or the premium may be offered for a certain number of box tops, labels, or other evidence of purchases. In this case the number of purchases necessary to get the premium is usually sufficient to liquidate the cost of the premium. The premium which is packed with the product, as, for example, the free dishes once enclosed with Quaker Oats, is perhaps the most effective of all premiums and can be made nearly self-liquidating.

Self-Liquidating Premiums

Closely allied with the use of specialties in sales promotion are various premium plans in vogue. Most popular of these is the so-called "self-liquidating" premium, where the cost is covered by the added volume of sales. Speaking before the Sales Executives Club of New York, an official of the General Foods Corporation, extensive user of premiums, warned the sales executives present against using premiums to offset a poor product, a shabby package, or some other discrepancy in the sales program. "Essentially," he said, "a self-liquidating premium is a sampling device. Ordinarily, you are able to match your competitors' products from the standpoint of their physical qualities, as well as their consumer acceptance. Because of this, the differences in products are frequently so slight that you are limited severely by the Federal Trade Commission in the claims that you can make in your advertising. In circumstances such as this, a self-liquidating premium promotion can influence a given proportion of consumers to try your product who otherwise would not."

The actual returns from the use of self-liquidating premiums tell only part of the story of their success. There are people who buy the product in anticipation of sending for the premium but never get around to doing so. On the other hand, there are others who are already using the product but simply send for the premium. Among this group you are making better friends and enhancing good will.

Here is a short list of the more important objectives in using self-liquidating premiums:

1. Meeting competition.
2. Inducing use of a family of products.
3. Increasing size of purchase.
4. Inducing advance buying.
5. Holding established customers.
6. Reaching specific markets.
7. Widening distribution.
8. Boosting sales in dull or off-season periods.
9. Evaluating the effectiveness of certain media.

The manufacturer, after all, is in business to sell his *own* product at a profit. A premium to help him sell it is secondary. He is willing to pay the premium supplier a fair profit for the premium to help sell his own product. But he should *not* devote more than half of the advertising effort at most to plug the premium at the expense of his own product.

Promoting the Premium

In addition to the usual signs and posters at gasoline service stations, Marathon Oil ran a series of newspaper ads publicizing its premium of a B. C. glass with every purchase of eight or more gallons of gasoline. The ads were topped with a two-frame cartoon strip named B. C., by Johnny Hart, familiar to many newspaper comic strip readers as a copyrighted service of Field Enterprises, Incorporated. The text of the ad read:

Stop in now and pick up your B. C. glass. It's yours just for buying 8 or more gallons of gasoline at participating Marathon stations. Where you get it in writing: a guarantee of satisfaction or your money back on all petroleum products and automotive services. And while you're there, be sure to ask about our matching B. C. pitcher offer.

At the bottom of the ad was an illustration of the glass and the Marathon trademark.

Other companies have used newspaper ads and, posters or counter cards in addition, TV or radio spots to publicize their premium offerings. It should be noted that there are now some government restrictions on the use of the word "free" if the cost of the premium has been included in the price of the product it helps to sell.

Popularity of Premium Plans

A plan which is the foundation of some important sales programs is offering premiums of the customer's own selection for a certain number of purchases, evidenced by coupons or stamps. The basic appeal is to the collecting instinct. Saving soap wrappers, coupons, or trading stamps is a favorite indoor sport in many homes.

Colgate has used the premium coupon plan with certain of its soaps for over 50 years. Some 20 years ago the company combined premium operations with Borden and later with other companies. This combined operation now maintains 50 premium stores located in important cities and, in addition, over 2,000 redemption agencies where consumers may bring coupons and receive premiums. The coupons are interchangeable. Thus, it is possible for the consumer to accumulate coupons quickly.

It would be a mistake to judge the type of merchandise used as premiums in the coupon plan on the basis of those offered so successfully to the juvenile market. Effective as these juvenile premium offers are, they represent only a fraction of the wealth of merchandise offered to the housewife to influence her choice as she fills her daily or weekly market basket.

Tax Deduction Status

The U.S. tax laws do not limit the tax deduction status of advertising specialties that cost $4 or less and upon which the donor's name is imprinted. Business gifts that cost more than $4 or which are not imprinted are fully deductible for the first $25 per recipient. If a total of more than $25 is spent on any one recipient, the excess over $25 is not deductible. Employee awards, if in the form of merchandise, are deductible up to $100.

Limitations of the Medium

Every advertising medium has certain limitations as well as characteristic areas of strength and in this respect specialty advertising is not different. However, the two most commonly recognized limitations of specialty advertising need not be of major concern to advertisers who employ the medium properly. As the Specialty Advertising Association points out, specialty advertising is not a mass-circulation medium. Costs preclude the building of huge audiences which are obtainable through the use of some media. The most economical and effective use of specialty advertising is realized when the advertiser takes advantage of the selectivity and personal impact that may be achieved through this medium.

Specialty advertising often carries no more than an advertiser's name and address. This, however, is the fault of the advertiser more often than the result of space limitations imposed by the physical characteristics of the medium. In many cases the advertising copy on a specialty item can be made of considerably greater length than that which appears on the average outdoor poster. It is, of course, true that specialty advertising cannot deliver a long and detailed piece of copy. However, specialty advertising rarely is used as an advertiser's only medium, and when it is employed as a well-coordinated part of a complete campaign, its space limitations become unimportant. This is true because, when so used, large space is not vital to the job specialty advertising is designed to do.

Matchbook advertising is unlimited in its applications. One of the most exclusive shops in Atlantic City is that of Reese Palley who glories in the title of "merchant to the rich." The store features objets d'art, Boehme porcelain, oil paintings, glass statuary and $35 ash trays. One of his promotional items is the matchbook.

Chapter 26

TRAINING DEALERS AND SALESMEN

THE weak link in the distribution chain is at the point of sale. As a result of national advertising, or other sales promotional effort, Mrs. Consumer goes into an establishment where the product is for sale with the idea of "looking" at it. Mrs. Consumer is definitely interested and is receptive to reasons for making the purchase. But the dealer or the sales-person, not knowing the values which are built into the product or the advantages it offers, fails to turn Mrs. Consumer's interest into desire and she walks out of the store without buying—perhaps feeling definitely she does not want the product.

Here is a five-way loss. Mrs. Consumer lost the satisfaction which goes with the ownership of a quality product; the dealer lost his profit on a sale which was already half made; the salesperson lost the credit for having completed the sale; the distributor lost an opportunity to make a replacement sale to the dealer; and last, but perhaps most important of all, the manufacturer lost not only the profit on the sale, but his investment in getting Mrs. Consumer sufficiently interested in the product to go to the dealer and inquire about it.

Who is to blame for the loss? It could have been the salesperson, of course. The clerk might have been discourteous or indifferent. A great deal of business is lost because of that. A recent survey by the jewelry industry shows failure of clerks to be pleasant and to help the customer in buying wisely as the most common cause of lost sales. Perhaps the dealer is to blame for not training his clerks in the fundamentals of good retail salesmanship. Far too many dealers who distribute nationally advertised products are sound asleep when it comes to training store personnel to do a real selling job. In spite of all that has been said and printed on the importance of better selling at the retail level it is still a sad story. But actually the blame rests upon the manufacturer. The salesperson back of his dealer's counter is just as much a part of his sales organization as his own salesman. For after all, getting a product onto the shelf of a retail distributor means little, unless steps are taken to make sure it moves off the shelf quickly into the hands of the ultimate consumer. Only then is the sale complete. Only then has the factory or the wholesaler's salesman a chance to sell that dealer a repeat order. Without repeat orders a business dies.

The Manufacturer's Responsibility

Some large manufacturers, in long profit lines—building materials, for example—attach so much importance to educating the dealer's salespeople that they operate special training schools for them. A large camera company gives those who sell its products at retail an intensive 10-day training course at a company training center.

While the dealer pays the travel, salary, and living expenses of his salespeople the company makes all arrangements and supplies the necessary training facilities and materials. The whole emphasis of the course is upon selling. While there are some lectures and informal talks about the various markets and how to reach them most efficiently, the conference, upon discussion, or forum method is used to analyze the photographic selling story and to develop a well-rounded sales program that will actually increase a dealer's sales. Similar training centers are operated in the automotive, household appliance, and other "big ticket" merchandise fields. These companies find this type of sales training pays. With greater stability of personnel more and more of it will be done.

However, not all manufacturers are able, or willing, to spend lavishly for training dealer personnel. Since the responsibility rests as much upon the wholesale distributor as upon the manufacturer, there is a trend toward parceling out the job, so that part of the cost is absorbed by the distributor and the dealer themselves as well as by the manufacturer. The advantage of this is twofold. It puts the wholesaler and the dealer right up front in the picture, and since they are sharing the cost they take more interest in it. But regardless of how the cost is spread, it is the definite responsibility of the manufacturer to prepare an integrated plan for educating dealers and their salespeople, to package and present this plan to the distributors, and use every reasonable influence to enlist their active support and cooperation. No sales training plan was ever so good that it did not have to be "sold" to those who will benefit from it.

Early Experience with Dealer Training

There has always been dealer training. Even today, manufacturers who insist they don't spend money on that type of promotion require their salesmen to take time out to talk to dealers and their sales-people about resale problems. In fact, a smart salesman will do that without being told, for he knows that his best chance to increase territorial sales is to help his customers to sell more of the products he hopes to sell them. One of the first efforts to relieve salesmen of this educational job, and to provide a planned training program for the industry, so that the best experiences of all those distributing its product could be shared, was a "Course in Kid Glove Salesmanship" undertaken by a New York glove manufacturer in 1912. It was a series of multigraphed bulletins, punched for a loose-leaf binder, and issued periodically for the benefit of all dealers and clerks who wished to register. It was, of course, distributed free. At the time it was brought out it created a furor in marketing circles.

The next forward step was taken when a Kenosha hosiery manu-facturer brought all his dealers and salespeople into the factory for a short course in selling hosiery. This training was supplemented by texts and other educational literature which were sent to each person who attended the school. That proved quite successful. It was not long before there were correspondence courses for selling all sorts of products, but most of them were superficial and not too helpful.

Following through on that idea, a brass bed manufacturer decided to carry the idea a step further and trained his factory salesmen in the technique of organizing clubs for store salesmen. Those who con-ducted these clubs (merely an intriguing name for schools) were provided with texts and other educational material by the manu-facturer. Clerks from competitive establishments were invited, and the meetings were usually held at 7 o'clock in the morning—then a new idea.

Then the dealer school idea got another push forward when Johns-Manville employed Arthur A. Hood, then successful sales manager for one of its distributors and later editor of *American Lumberman,* to set up and conduct a training program for building material sales-men. It was called the National Housing Guild. These clinics were attended by as many as 500 building material salesmen at a time, where they were shown how to sell a "packaged" home. The Guild was later taken over and operated as an industry-wide project.

Tie-in with Over-All Training

The modern conception of training the dealer and those who sell for him is to treat it as a part of the over-all sales training program. Salesmen in all categories profit from it. There is nothing which will make a factory salesman more promotion-minded than attending a school for dealers. It really gives him a new point of view on his own and the company's problems. As to the value of over-all training, including both factory and distributor's salesmen, Fen Doscher gives the following nine ways it pays off for the company:

1. The more efficient your salesmen are, the more productive they will be in writing new business and expanding sales volume. This is vitally important when one considers that the average salesman actually spends from $2\frac{1}{2}$ to 3 hours a day face to face with prospects.

2. The salesman who is trained to organize his time more efficiently and to make shorter and more effective sales presentations will expose himself to more prospects and make more sales per interview. As a result, sales cost is reduced, salesmen on an incentive basis can make a larger income and this in turn will attract a higher type of salesman to your organization.

3. Top producing salesmen prefer to work for a company with a sound sales training program. They recognize the value to themselves in a well-integrated program of continuous sales training.

4. The influence of a well-developed sales training program can be extended to the whole company because all departments have a live interest in what the sales department is doing, and by exposing them to the sales training program you make everyone sales-minded even though their activities may be limited to operations.

5. A sales training program is an effective builder of morale. This is vitally important in not only the indoctrination period of new men but in keeping older men sold on the company and giving them a sense of confidence and security in their future. The higher the morale of a selling organization, the lower the turnover.

6. A broadly developed sales training program brings in sales, advertising, and all promotional activities with the result that you achieve a higher level of coordination among the direct and indirect selling activities which may be under various department heads.

7. A sales training program makes for more efficient direction on the part of sales managers and sales supervisors because the sales training program sets a pattern which everyone recognizes and understands.

8. A sales training program makes it easy to identify and correct the faults of new salesmen and, therefore, speeds up the training period and makes them effective sooner, and less costly than where there is no organized training plan.

9. It is wiser to invest in an effective sales training program than to pay the much higher cost of an inadequately selected, trained, and directed sales force which cannot meet the challenge of competitive selling.

Modernized Training

Tremendous strides are being made in training, not only dealer personnel, but *all* personnel, through the development of programmed electronic courses in which the individual trains himself. Throughout this HANDBOOK, references will be found to the latest advances in procedures and equipment, as a result of which training programs will be more widely applied in every field, in more convenient and more flexible ways.

The advent of self-teaching machines and programmed instruction is opening new vistas for the sales training manager in every area of marketing and sales promotion.

In the application of these modern methods to the retail field, the potentials are enormous and the surface has hardly been scratched at this point.

It is easily possible that entire training programs may be conducted at any time, any place, wherever needed, without any delay or preliminaries through the marvelous developments which have taken place in this field. Interestingly enough, the fullest use, up to this time, of the new facilities for self-instruction have taken place in the public-education field. It will not be much longer, then, for training machines to be more widely applied in business, particularly for training retail salespeople.

The Chevrolet Mini-Theater

A highly effective medium of sales training and sales promotion has been developed by the Chevrolet Division of General Motors through the use of its audio-visual Mini-Theater. In addition to its sales training functions it proved to be a creative sales tool as an effective point-of-sale product presentation.

The unit consists of a specially-mounted film projector that projects on a twelve-inch screen, about the size of a small television set. The viewing screen is ideally suited for small groups up to eight persons, but may be removed from its base and the picture projected on a larger screen.

With the help of the Mini-Theater, it was shown that inexperienced salesmen could out-sell the old pros; the rate of closing went up 25% and dealer grosses were up $50 per car, according to E. R. Torre, merchandising manager. When last reported, there were over 6,000 units in use.

The Chevrolet Manpower Development Catalog lists a broad selection of cartridge motion pictures for use with the Mini-Theater. The subjects covered include attitude development, sales training, management development. Other specialized services are included to make the manpower-development program easier and more effective.

The Mini-Theater proved so successful that it won an advertising campaign in its own right. The company provided dealers with posters, sample ads, radio spots and press releases.

See the new Chevrolets in action on the Chevrolet Mini-Theater.

Some things you have to see to believe. So we've made it easy for you.

We've installed a new Chevrolet Mini-Theater which is the *first* of its kind in the automotive industry. And have a set of 15 film cartridges that cover Chevrolet car and truck models. Plus such special subjects as trailering and recreation vehicles.

- See factual color, sound films that inform you about the cars you're interested in.
- See interesting, informative demonstrations of the value features of each car.
- See the many benefits built into every Chevrolet.

The Mini-Theater is simple to operate. One of our salesmen will be glad to help. Or, if you prefer, do it yourself. Just insert the film cartridge you want to see and press the start button.

Stop in and see all the new Chevrolets. In action. On the new Chevrolet Mini-Theater.

(Hometown Chevrolet)

In addition to its sales training function, the Chevrolet Mini-Theater served as an excellent point-of-sale product presentation. With the help of the Mini-Theater, inexperienced salesmen could outsell the old pros and the rate of closing went up 25%. It proved so effective that dealers advertised the Mini-Theater as a means of increasing show-room traffic and to create audiences for the Chevrolet sales story.

The unit has other applications in many sales promotion applications including showings to service clubs, driver education classes, shopping center demonstration and in automobile trade shows, passenger terminals at airports and on college campuses.

The film cartridges provided by the company include the following subjects: Chevrolet resources (engineering, styling, manufacturing, reliability); Chevelle wagons, Trailering, Factory options and accessories and such public relations films as a Tour of the U.S. National Park System and the Soap Box Derby.

Dealer reactions to the Mini-Theater have been highly enthusiastic. Some dealers use as many as ten of the units.

Indirect Approach Used by Parker Pen

Resistance to study on the part of retail sales personnel has caused some companies to experiment with an indirect approach to the problem. The Parker Pen Company developed a retail training program, consisting of moving pictures, sound-slidefilms, and a series of take-home booklets. Instead of labeling the program "A Course in Retail Salesmanship," which is the traditional approach to over-the-counter sales training, Parker built its whole program around the importance of good manners and speaking ability. The thinking back of this decision was that most training programs beamed at retail salespeople try to do too much at once. They confuse rather than educate. By concentrating the promotional effort on the clerk's relations with the customer, which are influenced very largely by the way the salesperson acts and talks, a real service was possible. The first and most important step in retail selling is for the salesperson to "sell" herself or himself to the customer. That constitutes "getting to first base" in making any kind of sale.

The backbone of the Parker program was the film and educational booklet, "Your Manners Are Showing." The title was calculated to appeal to all the people in a dealer's store who contacted the public. Everyone wants to be considered well mannered. But what is meant by good *sales* manners? "Manners, good or bad," the treatise points out, "are habits." If we work at them a while they will become easier and easier to practice. Finally they become as much a part of us as breathing. And then they really begin to pay off. You know, letting yourself get fat through overeating is really a kind of bad manners—but a fat pay check is always good form. Now there are five basic good manners of the good salesman—five qualities he must have to be something better than an "order taker":

"1. Cordiality.
2. Enthusiasm.
3. Attentiveness.
4. Good appearance.
5. Knowledge of merchandise."

That is the outline for the program, and the materials developed by Parker to carry it through, which takes up each of the five points, one by one, ending up with a checking chart which the salesperson can use to test his or her manners, and determine what kind of manners are showing. The "true or false" technique is used in making this test.

College of Practical Knowledge

A whimsical and effective training project was developed by Corning Glass Works in a program headed: "The Fluidics College of Practical Knowledge." The light touch was applied throughout, beginning with the invitation to participate, reading:

"To give long overdue recognition to those fellows of science who are friends of fluidics, The Fluidics College of Practical Knowledge extends this invitation to earn a slightly unaccredited degree in fluidics (Bachelor's, Master's, or Doctorate) . . . to participate in the Fluidics Honors Program . . . and to enjoy the unusual and beneficial privileges which are concomitant with enrollment in the alumni association of America's newest most exotic education institution."

The object of the training program was to have company representatives complete an examination form as a result of which three "degrees" would be awarded, with prizes. A cram kit was provided for review. Successful "graduates" would receive, according to the examination completed, a degree as Bachelor of Fluidics, Master of Fluidics or Doctor of Fluidics. In addition, the Honors Program provided three incentive prizes:

The Valedictorian Award

For the best paper on how fluidics can be applied in a new but practical application. The prize consisted of an engraved plaque plus two all-expense-paid weeks for two in a suburb of Corning, New York. Or, $1,000 in cash.

The Salutatorian Award

For the best paper on how fluidics is now being applied in an existing, practical, application. Prize: an engraved plaque plus a "College-Beer-Blast" for ten in a local rathskeller. Or, $500 in cash.

To give long overdue recognition to those fellows of science who are friends of fluidics, The Fluidics College of Practical Knowledge extends this invitation to earn a slightly unaccredited degree in fluidics (Bachelor's, Master's, or Doctorate)... to participate in the Fluidics Honors Program...and to enjoy the unusual and beneficial privileges which are concomitant with enrollment in the alumni association of America's newest and most exotic educational institution.

Corning Glass Works wrapped its sales training program for its electronic products representatives around the theme "The Fluidics College of Practical Knowledge." To attract and stimulate interest, the program, which was couched in humorous terms, included the award of "degrees" and three incentive prizes.

The Norbert P. No-No Fellowship Award

For the best thesis on an application where fluidics is not yet the best answer. Prize: engraved plaque plus selected memorabilia. Or, 500 Eisenhower silver dollars.

Experience of Sears Roebuck & Company

Most sales training programs fail to give consideration to the inability of the average retail salesperson to absorb information quickly, and undertake too much mass training.

The larger retail organizations, notably Sears Roebuck, have decentralized sales training as much as possible, placing the responsibility on older employees for training new employees, and thus training both. It realizes, of course, that training is a continuous operation and is never done. The training formula steps, after breaking down the knowledge, skills, habits, and attitudes to be learned into short teaching units, are these:

1. Determining what the trainee already knows.
2. Commenting on the facts to be learned. (Lecture, conference, film, manual study, etc.)
3. Discussion to fix the understanding of the content.
4. Telling back by the trainee.
5. Demonstration by the instructor, and then by the trainee.
6. Reteaching on points not understood.
7. Final demonstration of knowledge (skill, attitude) at end of organized instruction.
8. Performance under supervision.
9. Spot checking of performance for errors.
10. Reteaching or supplementary teaching to improve knowledge or skill.

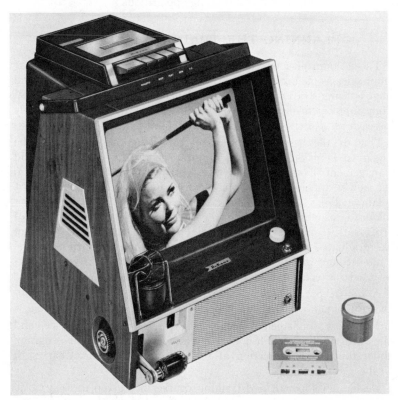

For individual or small group presentations, the Du Kane Cassette A-V Matic offers automatic tape sound-film-strip projection. The screen is 9 inches by seven inches in size.

A number of audiovisual, electronic salestraining and teaching systems are available. The Dukane Corporation, for example, has a response sound filmstrip projector which programs response and discussion into an audiovisual presentation and increases viewer participation and interaction. In the response system a two-second pulse advances the filmstrip, then stops both picture and sound. This pause provides time for the group to discuss the program, answer a problem or take a test on the material presented. The picture remains on the screen until the program is resumed by pressing the stop/start button. Audiscan® also has automated, portable, 16mm single cartridge sound filmstrip and projector systems that are highly appropriate. The Audiscan® 4000 is a portable front and rear projector combination which sells for under $400. The Audiscan® 4200 has a fast forward in sync. Their Audiscan® 3200 combines the above features and is excellent for educational and training applications.

PLANNING THE TRAINING PROGRAM

Those companies which are doing the most effective training of retail salespeople are making a liberal use of visual training aids and staged demonstrations, but do not depend entirely on these media. They supplement them with coaching literature. It is seldom possible to reach all dealers through sound-slidefilms.

One of the best-known training programs for dealers is The Chevrolet Division of General Motors' school of merchandising and management. This institution offers an intensive training program for newly appointed Chevrolet dealers and their sons. The curriculum includes business management, marketing, and the dealer's role as a responsible citizen in the community. The faculty includes professors from Wayne State University in Detroit. The program has graduated more than 7,000 retail and wholesale men from the United States and other countries. There is also a two-week Chevrolet sales executive academy for sales managers at Wayne State.

A similar program for dealers selling other GM products is conducted through the General Motors Institute at Flint, Michigan.

The most fundamental techniques of management service, and sales are taught through a dealer manpower development program, under the over-all direction of the Activity's Director, Charles B. Neely.

Dealer development and training courses are given in each of 30 training centers. Dealers and their staffs are invited to attend conference sessions, which generally are of one to five day's duration. Participation topped 104,000 in one year.

Local Schools for Specialized Training

Recently there has been a widespread movement within trade associations to assume responsibility for teaching the principles of salesmanship as applied to a particular industry. In that way the cost of this training may be shared by a number of concerns.

An example is the schools in printing salesmanship conducted by the Chicago printers. Each member of the local master printers' association is entitled to send as many salesmen as he wishes to the school for training. He pays the tuition for the salesmen, or a part of it.

The success of this plan depends a great deal upon the selection of the men. In some cities the instructor of the school has the right to reject any candidates for training whom he thinks might not be capable of doing a creative selling job.

When there is a shortage of salesmen in an industry, this plan is extended to young men without previous experience in selling the product. Trained men are thus made available to members of the organization. They are selected by the instructor from the candidates who present themselves for training.

"On the Job" Training

Not all companies, however, are in a position to operate training centers, or provide formal classroom training for dealers and their salespeople. So they bring the training to the dealers' salespeople instead of bringing the salespeople to the training center. There are several ways to do this:

1. Holding breakfast meetings to which dealers and clerks are invited, usually sponsored by the manufacturer, trade association, or by the manufacturer in cooperation with the local chamber of commerce.

2. Arranging "after hours" discussion groups, set up and conducted by some member of the promotion department for salespeople employed by local dealers who wish to participate. Attendance should be entirely voluntary to avoid conflict with Wages and Hours Act.

3. A specially fitted trailer, capable of seating from 10 to 20 salespeople, equipped for visual training. Trailers can be parked near a dealer's store so store personnel may attend in small groups at convenient hours.

4. Correspondence course, sometimes undertaken in connection with an extension university. Cost is partly paid by salesperson. Usually this is refunded when the course is completed and the student meets passing requirements.

5. Training film, either a movie or a talking strip film, which can be shown by territorial salesmen at informal store meetings. Suitable "take home" booklets tied into the film are used.

6. Manuals, with charts, suitable for store discussion groups, planned for use at store training programs conducted by store officials. This type of program favored over others by most dealers.

7. "Self-help" literature mailed direct by manufacturer to the salesperson's home periodically. These may be letters, bulletins, booklets, or a house organ.

The form which the training program should take depends upon: (1) What a company can afford to spend; (2) the type of training to be done; (3) the intellectual level of the dealer and his salespeople; (4) facilities available; and, (5) the competitive situation. If your competitor is conducting a training program, and sells through the same channels you do, you would want to use a different approach than you would if you were the only company in the field offering sales training to distributors.

The Dartnell sales-training film "Charge" is a 29-minute color film which features Arnold Palmer, the golf champion who has done so much for golf and in his way is a star salesman. With this film comes a sales campaign package which includes the meeting leader's "game plan," plus reminder cards, tee packet, trophy, incentive buttons and wall banner. This film is made available to sales executives on a purchase, rental or preview basis.

Films and Cassettes

The Sales Management Division of Bill Communications, New York, offers sales training managers a cassette-of-the-month program consisting of twelve 60-minute cassettes on the following subjects:

1. How to Set Up a Sales Training Program

2. How to Train Salesmen in Selling Skills

3. How to Train Salesman in Product Knowledge

4. How to Train Salesmen to Sell Benefits

5. Training Salesmen to Close More Sales

6. Training Salesmen in Persuasion Skills

7. Training Salesmen to Handle Resistance

8. Training Salesmen to Profitably Manage Time and Territory

9. Self-Training Program for Salesmen

10. Training Salesmen through On-the-job Coaching

11. Refresher Training for Experienced Salesmen

12. Training Salesmen through Sales Meetings

Color video-cassette systems have made great strides in promotional applications. Just as one example, Sony offers models for programs which can be recorded and played back instantly on con-

F. Leslie McEwen, Jr., CLU

**In recognition of his outstanding achievement, he will be honored
in the March 13 issue of TIME Magazine.**

THE **ROGER KENNEDY, JR.** AGENCY
648 Second Avenue South
St. Petersburg

*As a morale-building sales incentive, The Penn Mutual Life Insurance Company
features its Top Club salesmen in home-territory advertisements, headed by a
reproduction of a letter from the company's president.*

ventional color or black-and-white television sets. The cassette is a self-contained, sealed, unit, capable of playing tapes ranging in duration from 10 to 60 minutes in black-and-white or color with stereophonic sound.

Westinghouse Sales Audition Program

A novel idea for conducting a sales program was devised by Westinghouse. During a 4-month period the company had 6,000 retail salesmen make recordings of their sales talks. This gave each salesman or saleswoman a chance to hear his or her own voice in a sales presentation as it sounds to others. These records were then played at meetings of the salesmen conducted by the sales application supervisors. The voices heard were identified by number only, and after the records were played the men joined in group discussions regarding the good and bad points of each. After a few weeks' time in which they were supposed to study ways and means to improve their sales presentations, the salesmen were given another opportunity to make a recording. The second recordings showed a remarkable improvement in both organization of presentation and delivery. At a second meeting the men voted on the best records. Two $1,000 prizes were awarded to the two best talkers and smaller cash prizes were awarded according to district.

The purpose of the contest was to clarify sales principles involved in the retail sales of electrical appliances and to organize sales presentations in agreement with a formula set up by the company. The result was that all the salesmen taking part showed improvement in their sales talks after making these recordings.

What the Course Should Cover

Most sales training executives agree on two things: (1) More emphasis should be placed on the human relations side of retail salesmanship and less attention given to selling the product. (2) If all a sales training program accomplishes is to make retail salespeople realize their importance in distribution, and awakens them to their opportunities, the effort is worth while.

Even though the subject is a bit shopworn, every sales promotional activity aimed at increasing point-of-sale efficiency must directly and indirectly aim to make the retail salesperson courtesy-conscious. This is still a major weakness in retail selling, although it is a condition which has shown improvement since the end of the boom. The best test of the efficiency of a salesperson is what customers say about her when they go home. Nearly every woman, when she goes home from a shopping tour, tells the story of her adventures to her family.

She goes home with a story of success or frustration, of courtesy or the lack of it. She has a tale of pleasant or unpleasant people.

SALES DEMONSTRATION CHECK SHEET

OFFSET

MIMEOGRAPH

FOLDER

COPYING

FLUID

SALESMAN _____

CITY _____

DATE _____

RECOMMENDED GRADING STRUCTURE:

E   Excellent   O.K. Acceptable
V.G.   Very Good   N.I. Needs Improvement

SEQUENCE	DEMONSTRATION ELEMENTS	MANAGER'S RATING
GENERAL PREPARATION	Area neat and clean	....
	Equipment checked out and supplies in order	....
INTRODUCTION	Business-like and to the point	....
	Established points to prove during demonstration	....
OPERATING ABILITY	Was it smooth - operations performed with ease	....
	If mishap occurred, did he accept it calmly and	
	overcome it without embarrassment	....
	Careful to avoid talking while equipment operating	....
QUALITY	First copy consistently good	....
	Copy quality maintained thru entire demonstration	....
	Copies properly positioned on paper	....
	Folder (if applicable)	....
	First fold good and proper feeding maintained	....
FEATURES/BENEFITS	Were the important features covered adequately	....
	Were features converted into meaningful	
	benefits - or left as "Nuts & Bolts" explanations	....
	Were objections repeated and answered satisfactorily	....
	Was he able to obtain commitments from the prospect	
	and secure agreement as benefits were explained	....
VERBAL SKILLS/ ENTHUSIASM	Did he talk in a clear, easy to understand manner	....
	Was his sales pattern directed to prospect (eye contact)	....
	Did his voice convey a belief in what he's selling	....
	Was his enthusiasm strong enough to hold prospect's	
	interest	....
GENERAL BEARING	Did he appear to be confident and at ease	....
	Did he maintain eye contact with prospect or	
	did he look at equipment (Receiving Tray)	....
CLOSES	Did he summarize the demonstration	....
	Did he emphasize the important advantages (Benefits)	....
	Did he ask for the order enough times	....
	If you were a prospect would you have made the	
	purchase	....
	Manager's Signature _____	

At the end of their training period, A. B. Dick salesmen are required to make a product demonstration and are rated according to this check sheet.

She may say: "I'll never go to Blank's store again. One of the girls snapped my head off when I couldn't make up my mind."

Or she may say: "I did enjoy myself today when I was shopping at Smith's. Such a nice girl waited on me. I'll go to her again. She had a long search to get me just exactly what I wanted."

If the training helps more dealers and their salespeople to be "liked," much has been accomplished.

Then there is the job of making salespeople, who do not always have a natural aptitude for selling, appreciate and understand that customers are people, and people buy for certain reasons. They should be taught to recognize these buying motives and use them in making sales. There are two classes of buying motives: (1) Emotional, and (2) rational. These are listed by Professor Copeland as follows:

1. EMOTIONAL BUYING MOTIVES:
   Distinctiveness.
   Emulation.
   Economical emulation.
   Pride in personal appearance.
   Pride in appearance of property.
   Social achievement.
   Proficiency.
   Expression of artistic taste.
   Happy selection of gifts.
   Ambition.
   Romantic instinct.
   Maintaining and preserving
      health.
   Cleanliness.
   Proper care of children.
   Satisfaction of the appetite.
   Pleasing the sense of taste.
   Securing personal comfort.
   Alleviation of laborous tasks.

Security from danger.
Pleasure of recreation.
Entertainment
Obtaining opportunity for greater
   leisure.

2. RATIONAL BUYING MOTIVES:
   Handiness.
   Efficiency in operation or use.
   Dependability in use.
   Dependability in quality.
   Reliability of auxiliary service.
   Durability.
   Enhancement of earnings.
   Enhancing productivity of
      property.
   Economy in use.
   Economy in purchase.

The importance of helping the customer to buy, rather than trying to sell what you want him to buy, should be stressed. The use of suggestion and acquiring a professional attitude toward the work are likewise important to a salesperson's success. Other factors which should be covered in the course are:

1. Interest in work.
2. Alertness.
3. Speed.
4. Accuracy.
5. Knowledge.
6. Intelligence.
7. Tact.
8. Patience.
9. Adaptability.
10. Enthusiasm.

11. Memory.
12. Forcefulness.
13. Self-confidence.
14. Initiative.
15. Dependability.
16. Personal appearance.
17. Productivity.
18. Ambition.
19. Professional attitude.
20. Industry.

SALES PROMOTION

TO THE FIELD FORCE:

THE CENTURION COIN

'Mnemosyne' was the goddess of memory and the mother of the Muses
in mythology. Modern psychology has given an object which aids
memory the name "mnemonic device" in her honor.

We are practicing a bit of psychology, too, in coming up with
our own mnemonic device: THE CENTURION COIN, a tangible reminder to you that success begins by opening new sales every day.

Over the years coins have fascinated people for many reasons.
THE CENTURION COIN can be a good luck charm, a conversation
piece and a keepsake, but it should also help you to keep in
mind the value of your selling time.

Here is how it works. Put the Coin in your right pocket as you
leave home each working day. After you have had your first
opening interview for the day, then (and ONLY then) transfer it
to your left hand pocket. We hope it will "burn a hole in your
right pocket" until you can make an honest transfer to the left.

If you can honestly transfer the Coin from one pocket to the
other before 10 a.m. each day, you should not only become a
CENTURION, but a member of the MDRT as well!

THE CENTURION COIN will prompt you to open more new sales and
give added verve to your every interview. It will remind you
to insure at least 100 lives in 1972 and every year in the future.

Remember, NEW YORK LIFE wants YOU to be a CENTURION!

LIFE INSURANCE SALES PROMOTION

*The aggressive sales promotion department of the New York Life Insurance
Company sends out a constant stream of letters and bulletins to the company's
salesmen. To induce them to start making calls early in the day, two special
coins were attached to this letter. The plan was to put one of the coins in the
right pocket, to be transferred to the left pocket only after the first call was made.
The location of the coin was subject to question at any time by the local managers.*

It should be borne in mind that to appeal to a salesperson the training should be designed to make him or her a better all-round salesman—not alone of products you sell. Training programs which employ films to show the talking points of a specific product have their place, but should be incidental to the main coaching effort. In addition to teaching salesmen how to sell, the program should teach them how to be better cooperators; the importance of public relations; the principles of store management; and those functions which have to do with business success.

One of the mistakes made by those who have had little personal experience in working with retail salespeople is to think that these folks will read through page after page of type. They are human, and, being human, they like to look at pictures. Sales training manuals today recognize the fact, and *are picture books of selling.*

The A. B. Dick Salesman's Study Guide

A sales education program has been developed by the Sales Training Instructional Media Department of A. B. Dick Company, to teach company salesmen the features and user benefits of the company's equipment and to insure that the salesmen are able to make productive demonstrations to prospective customers.

The program includes a series of instructional meetings one of which covers a two-week session on the company's offset equipment. Following is a section of the study guide for the fifth day of the training program:

Materials Required

Equipment and Supplies	*Support Media*
Model 350/360 Offset Solution and Supplies Paper	• Study Guide
	• Offset Handbook
	• Offset Sales Manual
	• Technique of Offset
	• Fundamental of Offset

Audio Visual Aids

Du Kane Micromatic Projector
Filmstrips — Techniques of Offset Series
    Part IV — Offset Sales and Printing
       Papers
    Part V — Operating a Floor Model
       Offset

Study Section B of the *Offset Handbook* to further familiarize yourself with the *basic* specifications of A. B. Dick Offset Equipment. Learning sales specifications may appear to be boring, but this is basic knowledge which you absolutely must know in order to make successful sales contracts.

It is particularly important to know paper sizes and image areas (copy areas) as well as feed table and receiving tray capacities. This knowledge is the absolute minimum; to be conversant about your product you will need to have all the basic specifications on the tip of your tongue.

Review the 350/360 sales brochure carefully. It contains this basic information and points out the salient benefits of each piece of equipment.

Once you complete your review, plan to repeat the study pattern you did on the other filmstrips in the *Techniques of Offset* Series.

This time you will be viewing *Offset Inks and Printing Papers*, Part IV of the series.

Before you start this series, however, read pages 18-33 of *Techniques of Offset*. Also review Section H of the *Offset Handbook* — then take the pretest. As soon as you are ready to move on, view the filmstrip, taking brief notes as it is displayed on the screen. As you did earlier in the week, complete the Programmed Study Guide for Part IV.

Repeat the study pattern again, this time using Part V — Operating a Floor Model Offset Machine. Before actually getting involved in the pattern, review Project 1B of *Fundamentals of Offset*. Read pages 41-46 of *Techniques of Offset*, also. Now do Learning Inventory V as a pretest: view the filmstrip; then complete the Programmed Learning Guide for Part V.

At this point, you are ready to spend the remainder of the day actually operating the equipment. As you did with the tabletop unit, use the recommended masters from the demo set for practice. Doing this helps you become familiar with them immediately; you will be using them frequently later on.

Use your time judiciously as you practice with the equipment. The more familiar you are with all aspects of the equipment, the better chance you have of always making the hardware appear easy to operate. This, of course, helps sell the unit while it is being demonstrated. Be sure to make several paper size changes during the time you practice. Each change in masters, plates, paper and ink helps you become just that much better at the controls.

Good demonstrating, like good anything else, is simply a matter of well directed practice. When you complete running for the day, clean the equipment according to instructions on page 39, 40 and 41 of *Fundamentals of Offset*.

Review the section of the *Offset Sales Manual* covering survey and analysis.

Complete the 1st week exam included here.

At the completion of today's activities, you will have passed the embryo stage of your learning and you should be heading toward a solid base of Offset knowledge. Next week will concentrate on the application of knowledge in meeting sales objectives.

Over the week end, study the section on demonstration in the *Offset Sales Manual*. Monday will be spent largely in demonstrating the M-360.

Use of Standard Training Material

Smaller companies, unable to spend large sums for training dealers' salespeople, can do an effective job at a very low cost by coaching their own salesmen to form training groups, and equipping them with sound-slide-films, meeting guides, and instruction books. The aim is to get the salespeople of their customers to attend "sales clinics" at a local hotel or auditorium, usually after working hours.

A Chicago manufacturer of laundry supplies, for example, used the Dartnell sales training slidefilms and supplementary material that way. Each salesman was equipped with a portable projector and a series of six training films, with necessary guides and booklets. These were prepared by Richard C. Borden of Borden and Busse fame.

The salesman would suggest that the laundry owner hold a sales clinic at a central meeting place some evening. The route salesmen were invited to attend. After showing the film, which required about 30 minutes, another 30 minutes was used by the salesman to explain how the principles shown in the film could be applied to the laundry business.

The National Candy Wholesalers' Association conducts formal training courses for candy salesmen in cooperation with local schools in 86 cities. The association prepared 10 standard manuals for use by these student salesmen, and an outline of the training course for instructors. The association also issues a sales managers' guide outlining 45 meetings sales managers for candy wholesalers can conduct to teach "Balanced Selling." This is useful in planning meetings.

Sales promotional activities by trade associations are steadily expanding as the realization grows that pooling funds for this purpose is good business. While there are definite advantages accruing to the individual manufacturer who sponsors a training program for his dealers and their clerks, it is really a job which properly concerns the entire industry. What helps the industry helps all those who are engaged in it—manufacturers, wholesalers, retailers, and the sales personnel of each group.

"Making People Want to Trade with You"

The National Cash Register Company* allocates a considerable amount of its sales promotional appropriation to help merchants train their salespeople. Even back when John H. Patterson was at the helm, NCR operated on the principle that anything it did to help users of its registers to build up their businesses would help them need and buy more cash registers. Recognizing that in the eyes of the customer the clerk is the store, NCR merchants' service has

*Now NCR Corp.

consistently sought to keep dealers and their sales personnel customer-relations-conscious. A series of booklets on retail selling is one of the many NCR publications. Another booklet deals with what a store and its salespeople can do to give the store a good personality. It includes:

1. Friendliness.
2. Prompt attention to all customers.
3. Greeting customers by name.
4. Recognizing and greeting waiting customers.
5. Giving accurate directions to customers.
6. Suggesting related items.
7. Enthusiastic salesmanship.
8. Courtesy to "hard to please" customers.
9. Keeping every promise.
10. Telling the truth.
11. Knowledge about merchandise.
12. No betrayal of personal feelings or worries.
13. Prompt and cheerful adjustments.

NCR manuals of good retailing practices likewise cover some of the things which customers do not like about a store and its sales personnel. They include:

1. Limited assortments of merchandise.
2. Too much pressure to buy.
3. Indifferent attitude of salespeople.
4. Prices out of line with values.
5. Long waits for service, change, or parcels.
6. Carelessly wrapped parcels.
7. Being told they are hard to fit or please.
8. Unnecessary handling of food or candy.
9. Overheated, poorly ventilated stores.
10. Poorly lighted stores.
11. Idlers inside or outside of the store.

Automatic all-in-one portable audio-visual programming center is the way TMC describes its Model 2200 for cassette, slides and filmstrip operation. The audio section provides cassette recording and playback capacity up to two hours.

*Two scenes from the Dartnell sales-training film, "When You're Turned Down
... Turn On," featuring Joe Batten. This is one of four films in the series called
"Tough-minded Salesmanship."*

Sherwin-Williams Store Managers' Manual

Broadening the base of distribution by helping dealers to do a better selling job has two phases: (1) Training the sales personnel, and (2) training the dealer and his sales manager (if the operation is large enough) to train others. One company which has pioneered along these lines is the Sherwin-Williams Company, Cleveland paint manufacturer. For training the store personnel Sherwin-Williams program utilizes the pamphlets developed by the National Cash Register Company and the Ohio Bell Telephone Company, but these are geared into an over-all training program by the trainee manual for store operators. To encourage store discussion groups—one of the best methods of adult training—the Sherwin-Williams managers' manual includes questions, based on the supplementary material, which can be used to advantage. Here are a few typical questions:

QUESTION No. 1:

What obligation does a salesman owe to his customer?

Answer: Dependable service, helpful information, courtesy, and above all a genuine interest in the customer's problem, and sincere appreciation for his or her patronage.

QUESTION No. 2:

What obligation does every S-W salesman owe to his company?

Answer: Loyalty, integrity, dependability, capability, intelligent work, and results.

QUESTION No. 3:

Are you familiar with, and do you conscientiously follow, the S-W Code of Principles in your everyday selling contacts?

Answer: The Sherwin-Williams Code of Principles is a workable code of good business practices and as such should be followed in everyday selling contacts.

QUESTION No. 4:

What temptation must a salesman successfully deal with regarding customers' demands?

Answer: Temptation to cut price to meet a competitive price rather than talk quality; also unreasonable demands for "hot shot" deliveries. Also the practice of buying business by giving brushes, scrapers, etc., to painters. An inclination to agree with a customer to the disadvantages of the company instead of selling the merits of our policies and products.

QUESTION No. 5:

What is the salesman's duty to the customer when selling paint, varnish, enamel, or lacquer to the amateur?

Answer: To be helpful and suggestive, to show him the right products to use and why and how to use them. Never overestimate the qualities of the products and be patient and tactful in answering what are sometimes ridiculous questions. Be truthful always.

YOUR APPROACH

The purpose of the sales approach is to help put the customer in a buying mood.

You want him to have an open mind, receptive to your suggestions.

The three basic elements to a good approach in the selling of shoes are FRIENDLINESS, ATMOSPHERE, and RELAXATION.

FRIENDLINESS depends on the manager or floor man who first greets the prospect then the salesman's personality takes the responsibility A friendly sincere attitude toward the prospect is absolutely essential to successful selling.

2. ATMOSPHERE depends upon the store and the store's policies, as well as your ability to lead the prospect where his line of vision will stimulate him into a buying mood.

3. RELAXATION of your prospect is the final touch which opens his mind and makes him receptive to the demonstration. Place him in a comfortable chair —take one shoe off at once, and let him stretch his toes and relax the foot. Remember—COMFORT is his first subconscious consideration.

Having successfully handled the APPROACH, you are now ready to do a sales job on the DEMONSTRATION; your knowledge of the product and adapting it to the needs of the prospect should now be brought into play.

A careful study of the following pages will help you handle the demonstration.

THE JOHNSTON & MURPHY SHOE   THE STANDARD OF PERFECTION

Page from a training manual for retail shoe clerks developed by Johnston & Murphy. The aim is to teach store people how to deal with customers.

QUESTION No. 6:

What effect (good or bad) does "overloading" any customer have?

Answer: Destroys the good will and confidence placed in the store and salesman by the customer.

QUESTION No. 7:

Do you realize the importance of companion sales? What plans do you use in making them?

Answer: Yes. If you have gained the confidence of a customer, companion sales are easiest made through suggesting helpful ways to obtain the most satisfactory finish.

Distributing Training Materials

The easy, but not always effective, way of getting training literature into the hands of store personnel is to ship it in bulk to the store owner or, in the case of a large retail operation, to the executive responsible for personnel, and let him distribute it to clerks. An attractive portfolio, into which samples of the material are tipped, is prepared and sent to the dealer by mail, or handed to him by the company's salesman. From this portfolio the dealer requisitions what materials he needs to undertake the training, including the loan of the strip film, charts, and returnable material. But that plan has a weakness. The mere fact that the store operator asks for the training material does not mean he will use it *properly.* As a matter of fact, a good percentage of it may never be used at all.

So the trend is to relieve the store owner and his executives of as much detail connected with carrying out the program as possible. If the training lends itself to home study, an effort is made to secure the dealer's cooperation and get the names of his salespeople wishing to receive the literature *at home.* This adds to the expense of the promotion, but it pays. Some dealers object to giving out the names and home addresses of their employees, but most of them will cooperate if they are "sold" on the cash register benefits of the plan.

What to Leave Out of Training Literature

An examination of sales training material used by manufacturers shows over-emphasis on the theory of salesmanship, and not enough on business management. Some training courses create the impression that there are a lot of rules to salesmanship, and unless these rules are faithfully followed best results cannot be obtained. This is not true, because some of the most successful retail salesmen are just friendly, helpful, likable people who are first of all good businessmen.

An effective training program should strive to make every retail salesperson a good merchant and a good businessman, without confusing him with a lot of theories. The ideal employee in any well-managed and successful business is the one who most nearly duplicates the qualities of his employer—or, to quote a familiar expression, is "the lengthened shadow of his boss."

Group Training by the Retailer

One of the best jobs of training retail salespeople, by enlisting the

EVERHOT ● MODEL 900 ELECTRIC ROASTER OVEN

for all kinds of modern cooking

Precision manufacture and assembly, from the highest grade materials. Body of extra heavy gauge steel, insulated with Fiberglas glass wool.

Cover of 14-gauge aluminum alloy.

Knobs and handles of plastics.

Exterior finish is baked-on enamel. Interior finish acid-resisting porcelain enamel.

Equipped with drum type heating elements on all vertical sides and bottom. Electrical system conforms to highest standards.

Complete with lift rack, cord and cook book.

Utensil sets are optional equipment.

Listed by Underwriters Laboratories, Inc.

KEEP THIS CARD

This appliance was carefully inspected and should give trouble-free performance if used as directed. It is guaranteed (except cord) against defects in manufacture for a period of one year from date of purchase. If service is claimed during the guarantee period this card should accompany the appliance.

CAUTION: Do not dip body in water.

Purchased from

Date

EC—2134   Manufactured by

THE SWARTZBAUGH MFG. CO.

Toledo 6, Ohio   Established 1884

PRICE

Everhot ROASTER-OVEN

- Cooks a balanced meal for up to ten persons in one operation.
- Superb roasting—browns beautifully.
- Superior results in baking of all kinds.
- Ideal for simmering up to 18 qts. of soup, chili or stew.
- Saves shrinkage of meats, retains full flavors and food values.
- Saves hours of time, much work and uses current economically.

MANY EXCLUSIVE FEATURES

TURN-A-KNOB COVER LIFTER—opens, closes and locks cover. One hand control, both ways, all the way.

SELF-ADJUSTING VENTILATOR—preheats, browns and cooks without need for extra setting.

OBSERVATION WINDOW—of ovenproof glass, placed to minimize clouding.

ALUMINUM ALLOY COVER—self basting. Will not turn black in use. Extra heat reflecting properties. Note extra heavy gauge.

EXTRA DEEP COOKING WELL for better cooking results.

TIME AND TEMPERATURE CHART on roller of control panel.

AUTOMATIC THERMOSTAT controls heat—saves current.

A retail clerk who reads informative tags like these placed on products will be prepared to give a more complete demonstration.

cooperation of the dealer himself, is being done by the Armstrong Cork Company, maker of floor coverings. This national advertiser has prepared an effective series of sales training helps for the dealer, and Armstrong salesmen are carefully coached in selling dealers on the importance of continuous training of clerks.

Dealers are encouraged to put one capable clerk in charge of floor coverings, and then to make that salesperson a sales promotion manager for that section. He is held responsible for coaching the other clerks. This is done by personal discussion and group discussion at convenient times. Group training can be made doubly effective if the manufacturer will furnish his salesmen with suitable manuals or charts, which can be left with the dealer and which he in turn can turn over to the salesperson responsible for the promotion of the product within the store.

"Sales Point" tags attached to the product, notebooks which the salesmen can distribute to the clerks in which main sales points are printed, printing the selling points about a product on the back of counter displays, on the inside of boxes, etc., are recommended as methods for helping to educate retail salespeople on doing a better selling job.

Importance of Telephone Selling

Many training courses fall short of the mark because they overlook one tremendously important method for increasing sales: The proper use of the telephone.

Chevrolet dealers have long been encouraged to make better use of the telephone, and special bulletins on how to use the telephone have been prepared and furnished for distribution to salespeople.

The American Telephone and Telegraph Company makes available a number of motion pictures (16mm. sound) for showing salespeople, and others who contact the public by telephone, how to win friends by developing a more effective telephone personality. These films can be obtained without charge from local affiliates of the Bell System, and from some of the other telephone companies.

Chapter 27

SAMPLING AND COUPON PROMOTIONS

ACCORDING to the annual report to shareholders issued by Colgate-Palmolive, product samples delivered or mailed directly to the home are "the most conducive to securing consumer trials." Consumers gained this way according to the report, tend to be loyal and steady buyers. Widespread sampling supported the company's new products in the laundry and dental fields.

The company of course, is well established and well-known to consumers and this helps to assure the success of the sampling technique in introducing new models or improved products in already-established lines.

When it comes to the introduction of a brand-new product based on an original technical development, or innovative process, sampling offers its greatest value. It can help to develop a market by creating consumer demand, depending, of course, on other considerations such as price and distribution.

Sampling, in spite of its cost, is still an economical way to promote the sale of products which depend upon the sense of taste (or smell in the case of perfumes) for their sales appeal. The success of most advertised breakfast cereals, for example, was based upon systematic door-to-door sampling. The large tobacco companies still spend lavishly to sample cigarettes. They know that letting the smoker try a cigarette is the best way to convert him to its use. And they know, too, that once a smoker has formed the habit of smoking a particular brand of cigarettes it is likely to stay around a long time. When a product repeats as fast as cigarettes, a brand owner can well afford to put a good part of his sales promotional appropriation into sampling.

There is another side to sampling: It makes friends for the company as well as the product. People in all income brackets like to get something for nothing. Benson & Hedges offered to send a free sample of a new blend of cigarettes to 24,000 New Yorkers in the higher income brackets—people you might think would not be interested in free samples. However, 9,324 of those who received the invitation wrote in for the free samples—a 40% return. They were sent 3 packages of the new cigarettes. They may not have been wildly enthusiastic about the blend of tobacco used in them, but they certainly felt kindly toward Benson & Hedges for the gift, and according to the company's advertising department, the results from the sampling were very satisfactory. Most of those who received the gift cigarettes continued to use them after the 3 packs were gone.

Sampling Pays Off for Girard's

When backed by a sound merchandising plan, sampling can pay its way, and return a profit to boot. This is the experience of Girard's Incorporated, San Francisco salad dressing manufacturer. Girard mails post card certificates, good for a 15-cent credit on a bottle of French dressing, to selected lists in a locality where the product has distribution. A bottle of dressing retails at 55 cents. The post cards, when presented by the housewife to her grocer, are redeemed at their face value by the manufacturer. The president of the company states that he has found this to be the most effective sales promotion he has ever used. "It stirs up the trade," he said. "Brokers cooperate and we usually get a good display in the stores which come in on the plan," In Sacramento, where Girard mailed out 25,000 of these cards, enough new business was received from grocers who wanted to be in on the promotion to pay for the cards before they were released. As a result of the sampling plan, plus the repeat qualities of the product itself, Girard's grossed nearly double its previous year's income.

Another well-known advertiser who built up his business largely by sampling is William Wrigley, Jr. When Wrigley introduced "Spearmint" gum millions of sticks were mailed to telephone lists with the result that distribution was quickly completed. As a rule merchants are loath to put in a new chewing gum, since the unit of sale is small and they don't like to carry a number of different flavors on their counter. The Wrigley sampling campaign gave them little choice. People demanded Spearmint gum, and there was nothing for dealers to do but put it in stock. Another Wrigley sampling technique was to paste sample sticks of various flavored chewing gums on cards, mailing these cards in envelopes to people in a locality where sales were lagging. It seldom failed to stir up business.

Best Methods of Sampling a Product

Sampling presents three distinct problems. First, there is the mechanical problem of getting the product into the hands of potential future buyers. Second, there is the problem of creating acceptance so that the sample will accomplish its promotional mission. Third, there is the problem of following through to make sure any sales value the sample might have had will be fully capitalized. This last point is important and is too often overlooked. There is a tendency on the part of manufacturers to feel that their product is so good all they need to do is to get it into the hands of a potential user, and let nature take its course. Unfortunately, people have short memories. They are also procrastinators. They may think very highly of your sample, and fully intend to order a supply some time, but they forget. A thoroughgoing sampling campaign not only gets the sample into the hands of qualified purchasers effectively and economically, but there is usually a provision to follow up the sample for an order.

There are many ways to sample a product to consumers, but most of them fall into the following classifications, listed in the order of their promotional importance:

1. Cooking schools and educational demonstrations which feature specific products, such as those conducted by public service companies.

2. Church, parent-teachers, and other social gatherings where samples are provided by manufacturers for use or distribution at the affair.

3. State and county fairs where the company has space from which to distribute samples and discuss the product's merits with persons attending. Trade shows also fall into this category.

4. Displays in dealers' stores, with a clerk assigned to distribute samples to *interested* persons. If the service is made available to all stores on an equal basis the demonstrator's salary may be paid by the manufacturer. (See Chapter 21 — "Store and Home Demonstrations.")

5. Coupons, good for free samples or part payment for a full package, mailed to dealers' customers or widespread lists of people in a community.

6. Direct by mail sampling of either a full-size package or a miniature-size package, with specific instructions as to where additional supplies may be obtained, if the recipient likes the sample.

7. Display ads in magazines, newspapers, farm papers, spot radio broadcasts, etc. Samples offered free or for a nominal sum to help defray postage and mailing expense, or coupons which may be exchanged for product at dealer's store.

8. House-to-house sampling by salaried crews or by contract with distributing companies. Passing out samples to pedestrians in front of dealers' stores comes in this category, too.

9. Restaurants and other vendors in a position to sample the product, as, for example, miniature package of cigarettes, mixed drinks, honey, etc.

10. Service clubs and organizations which conduct sample nights or make up Christmas bags of samples for members.

Another effective method of sampling certain products is to require salesmen to "talk the product up" to their friends and acquaintances. Salesmen are furnished a supply of samples to distribute in that way. This scheme is used by cigarette manufacturers, especially in country territory. Some companies use stockholders, sending each stockholders two samples, one for his own use and one to hand to a friend whom he thinks might become a permanent user.

Hormel Girls' Caravan

Smartly uniformed salesgirls have been used to promote the sale of "Spam" and other canned meat products by George A. Hormel & Co. A typical campaign was described by a Hormel executive as follows:

"During a typical week the girls called on dealers for orders, held rehearsals for their weekly radio broadcast and stage revue, traveled another day on their cross-country journey, and were hostesses and performers at a two-hour 'Dealer Party' staged for food retailers.

"Starting in California, they staged parades, did house-to-house sampling, and created their original radio show. Their radio program, 'Music with the Hormel Girls,' was heard over 126 CBS network stations each week. The group included an orchestra, chorus, vocalists, dancers, and comediennes.

Millions of samples of "Hidden Magic" hair spray went through the mails to introduce this Procter & Gamble product. The gift was from "Wanda the Witch," at the time a new image for the product.

"The Hormel girls traveled continually, crossed the country three times, and appeared in most of the major towns in the nation. Operation of the show required a fleet of 39 spotless white cars, which the girls themselves drove; 7 trucks to carry costumes, instruments, music, and equipment; the cooperation of Hormel district men in each territory visited; and an advance crew for arrangements and publicity. This is now all past history, but it shows what can be done in the way of spectaculars to promote sales."

How Much for Sampling?

Companies selling a consumer product in fields where sampling is feasible should allocate a carefully determined portion of their total annual sales promotional appropriation for that purpose. Like any other form of advertising, sampling is most effective when done systematically, and according to a long-range plan. While it may be, and often is, used as a "shot in the arm" to pull up sales in a sluggish territory, that sort of sampling is expensive and usually not too satisfactory.

Sampling is most widely used by manufacturers of branded cigarettes and cleaning products. It is used to a varying extent in marketing food specialties, and to some extent in the toilet goods field. Some new companies spend as much as 50% of their total sales promotional appropriation for sampling, tapering off the percentage as distribution is secured. Generally, however, not over 5% of the total appropriation is spent for sampling, store demonstrations excluded.

The amount to be spent depends a great deal on the repeat qualities of the product, on the profit margin, and above all on what it is worth to the company to "create" a consumer of its product. This, of course, can only be determined by pretesting the plan in a typical sales territory. But even with careful tests, a certain amount of good will must be credited to any sampling effort, for it is seldom that a large-scale sampling operation pays off on its face. Sampling tends to "stir up business" in unexpected places. The value of word-of-mouth advertising is incalculable.

The amount of the appropriation depends also upon the nature of the sampling necessary to do the job. For example, it was the policy, following long experience, of the American Tobacco Company to mail important persons a carton of six full-size packages of Lucky Strike cigarettes. These were sent more as a gift than as a sample. No "sales talk" accompanied the cigarettes. The only clue as to who sent them was an engraved business card of Richard

Joseph Boylan, vice president. The recipient assumed the carton to be a gift from Mr. Boylan, whom he may or may not know personally. In any event he felt very kindly toward the American Tobacco Company for thinking of him and usually acknowledged the cigarettes. All of which served to impress the brand on his mind. There was a reasonably good chance, if he was a cigarette smoker, of his forming the habit of smoking Lucky Strikes after having smoked the six packages. If he was not a cigarette smoker he was reasonably sure to pass the carton along to a friend, with a comment to the effect that the vice president of the American Tobacco Company sent him the carton of Luckies to try. Obviously it takes a larger appropriation to do that kind of a sampling job than where sample packets of six cigarettes are placed at tables in swanky restaurants. More people can be sampled for the same expenditure by using the sample size packet, but there is a question as to the relative effectiveness saleswise of the two methods.

METHODS OF SAMPLING

Sampling Services

A number of companies are now offering special sampling services as a quick-and-easy means of distribution.

Gift-Pax, Incorporated, West Hempstead, New York, offers various sampling services with computer-controlled distribution. A partial listing includes:

Classification	Annual Distribution
Newlyweds	1,206,900
New Mothers	3,364,764
College Students	4,355,000
High School Students	2,012,500
Military	600,000

Gift-Pax kits are distributed every month on a local, regional or national basis, according to Nielsen Sales Areas and contain keyed receipt cards.

Segmented Sampling, Incorporated, New York, specializes in sample distribution to 1.4 million black middle class families in 25 major cities. Representatives of the company personally deliver an attractively-packaged box of non-competitive samples and coupons. Signed receipts guarantee delivery and 30 days later a follow-up sales letter is sent to each sampled family.

Value Package (Manufacturers Assortment Inc., New York) advertises its sample-package offers to the public at greatly reduced prices in full-page, four-color, ads in Parade Magazine, with its 17,000,000 circulation, at no expense for the manufacturers except for the cost of their sample products. According to Value Package, the number of samples distributed attains a total of 7,500 per advertisement.

Value Package advertisement in Parade Magazine offers a collection of sample units at greatly reduced cost. The only expense incurred by the manufacturers is the cost of the product.

Advertising agencies usually oppose sampling programs which tend to restrict or reduce the appropriation for display or commissionable advertising, on the grounds that it is too expensive as a medium for creating mass acceptance of a product. However, sampling has decided benefits, from a sales standpoint, which a sales manager is quick to appreciate.

Sampling Through Small Ads

When a product has restricted appeal, as in the case of an infant food or other specialty, it is not unusual for the manufacturer to offer free samples through magazine and newspaper advertisements, or spot radio broadcasts. To make sampling of this sort pay, the product should be quickly consumed. Some manufacturers who have had experience with curiosity seekers, such as school children, conducting sample gathering campaigns, make a small charge, usually 10 cents for samples. The 10 cents helps to pay the postage and mailing cost, but the principal advantage is that the charge, small though it might be, tends to get the samples into use channels. This is especially important if the inquiries are to be used as a means of getting distribution.

In the early days of sampling through magazine ads it was the practice to play up the word "Free," on the theory that people will be more inclined to send for samples if all that they risk is a post card. Publishers, advertising agents, and even advertising managers were eager to have the advertising "pull" as many inquiries as possible. No one cared too much about the quality of the inquiries. But advertisers soon awoke to the fact that indiscriminate sampling through easy offers was costing the company a lot of money. One beauty preparations manufacturer found that less than half of the samples he was mailing out went to potential users, the others went to teenagers who might eventually become customers, but who at the moment were not in a position to purchase beauty cream. So the practice shifted, and while some companies still play up "Free" in sampling "copy," the majority prefer to emphasize the product and what it will do in their ads, confining the sample offer to a small coupon at the bottom. The strategy is to *first* sell the product, and then when the reader's interest has been aroused, to offer the free sample. These coupons, of course, are keyed so that they can be traced to the publication in which they appeared, thus serving as an indication of the pulling power of an advertising medium, if and when large space advertising is used. Some companies consider this type of sampling worth its cost for that reason alone. It provides their advertising department with a yardstick for picking media. It not only indicates the relative pulling power of various magazines which might be under consideration, but it reveals the type of media best suited to advertising the product, that is to say, whether the bulk of the appropriation should be spent in magazines, newspapers, farm papers, business papers, radio, television, or what have you.

There are cases, reported in the advertising trade press, where these small 1-, 2-, and 3-inch single-column ads have not only produced enough direct business to pay the cost of space but have been the means of getting desirable distribution. For example, when Dennison Manufacturing Company introduced its diaper liners, a novelty product, the company ran 3-inch, single-column ads in a long list of women's publications. The sampling itself was profitable since the product was a fast repeater. But more important, mothers, noting from the ads the product was sold by department stores, infants shops, and drug stores, went to their local source of supply and were so insistent that the store ordered a supply rather than disappoint their customers. However, depending upon small ads to build distribution is not recommended. Larger, more impressive space, with a good "hook" in the coupon is preferred.

Coupons perform many valuable merchandising services and are applied in a variety of ways. They help to introduce new products, stimulate lagging sales, and test consumer acceptance.

Coupons in Newspaper Advertisements

This is one of the old and tried devices for forcing distribution or stepping up sales on an established product in a given locality. It has an advantage over national magazine advertising, since it enables a sales organization to move in behind the advertising and take full advantage of it, so far as getting distribution is concerned. When

Yuban Coffee was first introduced, this type of sampling enabled the company to obtain better than. 80% distribution in the metropolitan New York market. It has been used effectively in marketing such products as shortening, breakfast food, soaps and cleansers, toilet preparations, and cake mixes. While it calls for a considerable initial investment, if the product is a good repeater and the "deal" is attractive to the retailer, it is by far the quickest way to get intensive distribution in strategic markets. It permits concentrating sales promotional effort in cities which are known to the sales department as being receptive, and which offer the best prospects for sustained volume, *after* the sampling campaign has been terminated. (See Chapter 28—"Introducing the New Product.")

The usual procedure in conducting this type of sampling campaign is to first select a group of cities, or markets, to sample. Then, having determined the offer to be made to the consumer, prepare advertising to run in local newspapers. Usually, but not always, these advertisements carry a coupon which, when presented to a cooperating dealer, is good for a full-size sample of the product. Or the coupon and a certain amount of money entitle the holder to the product. The offer should be limited as to time, and is very often restricted in other ways, to prevent abuse. The "kick off" ads should be of good size, preferably full pages, and the amount of space can be tapered off during the last few days of the offer.

With the portfolios containing the proposed advertisements in hand, the territorial salesman or a member of the advertising department calls on the local newspaper and places a contract for the full schedule, subject to confirmation by the company's advertising agency. A letter from the publisher of the paper stating that such a contract has actually been signed is provided each salesman, so dealers will have no occasion to doubt that the advertising will be run. There have been cases when dealers were induced by fast-talking salesmen to stock up heavily on the strength of proposed advertising campaigns which failed to materialize, and some dealers have long memories. Newspapers, at least in most cities, will provide each salesman with a route list of dealers in the area, so that the trade can be covered quickly and with the least wasted effort.

The salesmen then call on each dealer, tell him about the product, and show him the proofs of the advertisements the company has contracted to run in the newspapers. On the strength of the advertising, the dealer agrees to place an initial order for delivery through the dealer's local wholesaler. When the dealer canvass is completed, the orders secured by all salesmen working the territory are pooled, and are sorted out by the wholesalers, who are asked to buy twice the total of the orders turned over by the salesmen, so that they will have a stock to take care of reorders. The coupons, at the conclusion of the campaign, are redeemed at their full face value by the manufacturer, so that both wholesaler and dealer make their full profit on each transaction.

If there is resistance to using coupons from customers, arrangements may be made with firms which make a business of calling on dealers weekly to redeem for cash all coupons of participating companies.

Sampling by Radio and Television

Spot commercials have proved profitable as a sampling device. Usually these offers are localized, so that full dealer effect may be secured. Radio and TV stations have been carrying a considerable number of accounts offering samples of this, that, and the other thing, sometimes free, sometimes for a nominal amount of money, sometimes with box tops of other products made by the same company. One successful promotion of this type intended to stimulate foreign interest, was put on by a soap manufacturer who offered to send a sample bar of soap to any relative or friend in a foreign country, free, upon receipt of two wrappers from the same brand of soap.

Best results of this type of promotion are obtained when the "spot" follows a popular program which has some relation to the product to be sampled. The minute spot following a popular show, for example, at approximately 6:55 in the morning, is ideal for "plugging" a food product, since it catches a large number of listeners at their breakfast.

Door-to-Door Sampling

Sampling can be made doubly effective, when the sample is personally delivered at the door to the housewife rather than laid on the doorstep, which is what happens too often when sampling is done by sample distributing companies. When delivering at the door the canvasser makes a brief "sales" talk, high-spotting the distinctive qualities of the product, and leaving a piece of literature, and possibly a card with the name and address of the neighborhood dealer.

To undertake that type of introductory work, a company needs to set up a full-scale sampling operation on a 3-year plan. A crew of canvassers should be hired and trained. A crew manager, whose job it is to supervise the canvassing and also contact the dealers in the territory so they will know about the work, is necessary. If the samples are bulky, it may be necessary to furnish each crew with a light truck as an operation headquarters. The sampling should tie in with the over-all sales plan, and the crew should be routed so as to get the full benefit of weather conditions. Operations are usually scheduled for the Southern part of the country in the winter months, and in the North during the summer, avoiding so far as possible rainy and other seasons which might slow down operations. Effective sampling requires favorable weather.

Daily reports are usually required from each crew manager, showing areas which were sampled, how many samples were distributed, and giving the result of calls upon dealers. Some companies go so far as to "spot check" sampled localities by mail to make sure samples were actually left at homes, and to get the housewives' reaction to the product. This tends to keep the canvassers on their toes.

In the case of a food product, for instance a new shortening, it is sometimes effective to explain to the person who comes to the door that the company is distributing samples of the product in order to give housewives in that particular community an opportunity to test it and give the company their opinion of it. The information sought is listed on the self-addressed post card which the canvasser leaves. People like to be asked for their opinions. The canvasser then expresses the hope that the lady of the house will like the shortening so much that she will use it regularly in her kitchen, and hands her a leaflet listing the names and addresses of local grocers who have it in stock.

Best results from door-to-door sampling are obtained when the campaign is backed up by strong newspaper and radio advertising. This serves to assure interest in the product when the sample is received. When Post's "Krinkles," a rice breakfast cereal, was introduced by sampling in four test markets, General Foods used newspaper space and spot radio broadcasts while the sampling was in progress to tell housewives about "Krinkles." The ads suggested that without waiting for their sample, they should get a package from their grocer and experience its delicious flavor.

Endorsed Sampling

Some years ago a man who had won fame on the stage hit upon the idea of making a soap scented with the fragrant pines of his native New England. Not being overendowed with funds, he used to make the soap backstage as he traveled about the country, and peddle it to drug stores. But to the druggist it was just one more brand of soap to stock. "I'll put it in," the druggists would say, "if you convince me someone will ask for it after I buy it."

This suggested to Billy B. Van that, since he had a trunk full of soap and no money, he might induce the local hotel to put a free sample cake of his Pine Tree Soap in every room. That would save the hotel from having to buy soap, and it would give him something to talk about to the drug store owners. Other hotels jumped at the proposition. They liked the idea of the small-sized bars of soap, and they liked the idea of having an exclusive brand of soap for their hotel. When Billy told the local druggists about the soap being in every bathroom of the leading hotel, and painted an action picture of the hotel's guests rushing out to lay in a supply of the soap to take home, they listened attentively and usually ended up by buying enough soap to cover Billy's outlay for hotel samples. At any rate, using that sampling technique, Billy built a unique business in a few years. He was one of the pioneers of the individual bars of soap in hotels. Today the hotels have to buy their soap, but the experience illustrates the possibilities of endorsed sampling. In this case the hotel, to get the samples, endorsed the soap.

In the same way when The Waldorf-Astoria Hotel prints on its menu that samples of Oscar's famous salad dressing will be served without extra charge on request, it gets the sample onto the table under most favorable circumstances. The same is true when a sample packet of Philip Morris cigarettes is put at your place, with the compliments of the hotel. The same is true with the coffee, or any number of things that people buy to consume. No one can estimate the cash register value of the favorable opinion, and the word-of-mouth advertising, this sort of sampling creates.

Sampling by Direct Mail

There are few easier ways of sampling a product than by compiling a list of likely consumers, and mailing each one a sample, with a card stating where the product may be purchased. But it is not the best way to sample. It lacks a build-up, and it lacks a follow-through. Too much is left to chance. When the product is to be sampled by direct mail, some way of dramatizing the distribution is needed. Recipients must be made sample-conscious.

For example, the Burry Biscuit Corporation of Elizabeth, New Jersey, wanted to intensify distribution for certain products in its line which were not making the most of their sales opportunity. These were all quality products for which a demand had to be created, but having been created could be easily sustained. It was decided to do a selective sampling job, backed by local newspaper advertising. The advertising agency handling the account prepared lists of important persons in various localities, people whose food preferences were likely to influence the buying habits of the community.

The agency sent each of these people a personally typed letter stating it had been commissioned to prepare a series of advertisements for these biscuits and it was planned to have the advertisements carry the endorsements of a few leaders in the community. The letter went on to say that the agency had asked the cracker manufacturer to send the recipient of the letter three packages of biscuits—one each of three different kinds—which the company wanted to advertise. In return the agency would appreciate a brief note, telling the agency frankly what she thought about the biscuits, keeping in mind an excerpt from the letter might be included in one of the advertisements later on—*but making no promises* to use the *endorsement*. This is important to avoid difficulty.

The sample packages of biscuits followed on the heels of the letter from the agency. The lady of the house, eager to express her opinion of such good products, sat down and wrote the agency what she thought about them, how they compared with other biscuits on the market, and why she planned to use them regularly hereafter instead of the brand she had been using. These letters made powerful sales ammunition for the salesman working that community. If the lady overlooked writing, the agency gave her a prod just to remind her that her opinion was important. A half-dozen or so of the best letters were held out, and excerpts used in the newspaper ads to indicate local acceptance.

This approach had the effect of registering the product firmly in the minds of those to whom the samples were sent. It provided the salesmen with written evidence the product had acceptance from people of importance in the community, and it supplied the advertising agency with names and comments it was able to use in the advertising copy. Results were thus multiplied many times over, and the modest sum invested in the sampling campaign laid the foundation for better distribution.

A commonplace method of using direct mail to distribute samples is to attach a money-like certificate to the letter (the coupon carries the recipient's name and address and serves as an address when a window envelope is used), which when presented to any listed dealer entitles the holder to a free sample. The coupons are redeemed from the dealer at full cash value, and while he may balk at having to mail them to the manufacturer in the stamped envelope provided, he likes the idea of having his store listed on a promotion to every housewife in the community. It ties his store directly into the sampling. It is obvious to him that a considerable number of women who will

Identa-Dials!

Wrist Alarms!

BUZZ-Z-Z

When it comes to <u>incentives</u>... you can cut corners with Helbros Watches.....by cutting this corner...

When you cut this corner, you cut down on your premium costs and still offer top-quality, top-performance watches every time. With Helbros' wide variety of styles in all price ranges, you can find watches to fit every premium need and every budget exactly: watches for men or women...for your salesmen...for retail salespeople...for executives, their wives and secretaries...and for customers. Whichever watch you choose, you can be sure the quality is the highest. With all this to offer, naturally Helbros has some truly astounding Premium success stories. They're available to you in a free kit just for the asking. Simply cut the coupon, cut your premium costs and add to your sales.

HELBROS WATCHES
2 Park Ave., New York, New York 10016 • (212) 685-6300

a Division of ELGIN NATIONAL INDUSTRIES, INC.

Creators of the World's first Moon-watch* — displayed
at the New York Hayden Planetarium. *(Patent Pending.)

Helbros Watches,
Dept._____
2 Park Avenue,
New York, N.Y. 10016

Please send me
complete information on:
_____WRIST-ALARM watch.
_____IDENTA-DIAL Service.
_____ELECTRIC watches.

Also rush to me:
_____Your Kit on Helbros Premium
      Success Stories.
_____Your Premium Information Kit.
_____Catalog and Confidential Price List.
_____Samples of promotional sheets available for our use.

Please contact me_____I'd like to discuss how
Helbros premium watches can be best used to increase sales for my firm.

Name_____
Title_____
Company_____
Address_____
City_____State_____Zip_____

Electrics!

As advertised in Incentive Marketing, Advertising & Sales Promotion, Premium/Incentive Business, Sales Management, Insurance News, Potentials and Premium & Incentive Product News.

Cutting the coupon is emphasized by Helbros Watches in the headline reading "... you can cut corners ... by cutting this corner."

want to get the free sample will come to his store for it, which means increased traffic and increased profits. And today, profits are profits.

This use of direct mail, where the name is typed or addressographed directly on the sample coupon, has one advantage over newspaper ad coupons—it automatically limits the number of coupons one woman can exchange for free merchandise. It is not unusual when coupons are used in newspaper ads for a smart housewife, with her eye on the dollar, to buy up several newspapers just for the coupons and have various members of the family present them to as many different stores. News vendors have been known to clip all the coupons from unsold papers, and exchange them for free samples. Some sampling plans require that each coupon be endorsed with the name and address of the person who presents it for redemption. While that precaution is not too effective, it provides a list for a follow-up letter.

Sampling Costs and Results Are Both High

The "in the mails" costs of sample mailings range anywhere from 30 or 45 cents to $10 or $15 per piece, depending on how much of the product is considered a fair sample and how elaborate a printed piece is designed as the vehicle for conveying it. One of the most expensive—and one of the most productive—sampling units is that prepared each fall and spring by the textile firm of A. D. Juilliard Company, Inc., for mailing to a list of 1,000 department store buyers, merchandise managers and promotion directors, the stylists of designing houses, and the fashion directors and editors of leading publications. One spring mailing consisted of a simulated phonograph record album called "Juilliard Folk Tones in Regional Colors." In addition to one actual record, the album contained three record-shaped boards with 20 swatches of woolen fabrics attached to each, plus additional pages of tipped-on samples. The fall mailing, equally elaborate, was 1,000 copies of "Juilliard's Theatre of Color in Woolens for Fall." Each piece cost between $10 and $15 but results proved that they were attracting fashion executives' attention to Juilliard lines and that leading stores were making use of the promotional suggestions offered in the albums and were displaying and advertising the fabrics sampled.

Sampling is especially good strategy in the introduction of new products or in the presentation of established products to new markets and new users. Specialties and novelties, being more in the nature of institutional and good-will pieces than actual sales instruments, are useful in keeping the products sold after the initial acceptance had been won.

Dealer Sampling

There are times when quick distribution for a new or novel product can be secured, at a relatively small cost, by mailing full-sized samples to a select list of dealers. A company manufacturing a detergent, for example, got initial distribution in New England that way. Two free bottles of the detergent, together with a letter explaining the product and quoting the price, were sent to a select list of drug stores, grocery stores, and department stores. At the same time, drug jobbers and grocery wholesalers were notified of the availability of the new product. Ten days after sending out the two bottles, promotion was started through newspaper advertisements, which included a coupon worth 10 cents, supplemented by radio advertising three times a week on three separate broadcasting systems. For 3 weeks, the radio advertising offered a 1-ounce bottle free to those who wrote in for it. In the door-to-door campaign bottles were sold and free 1-ounce samples and literature were distributed. Finally, direct mail was used. The company felt that the newspapers did the best job of all the types of promotion methods used.

Coupons That Help Sell

The power of coupons to trigger response at the cash register, to move merchandise, and build traffic was verified recently in a report from A. C. Nielsen, Jr., president of the Nielsen marketing research firm.

Writing in the *Journal of Marketing,* Nielsen noted that billions of coupons are distributed annually and that millions of dollars' worth of them are redeemed, often with dramatic impact on marketing programs.

"In recent years, alert manufacturers have come to appreciate that the coupon, when properly coded, can be a valuable supplement to marketing research programs," Nielsen observed. "Whether or not a coupon is redeemed or discarded, the manufacturer is learning something about his product, its price, and its appeal to the consumer."

Coupons may be classified into two major groups. In the first are the merchandising coupons, offering a free product or "cents off" when redeemed, either in the store, or by mail by the manufacturer

Money-savers, cents-off and free-offer coupons are widely used to stimulate package goods sales, especially in the food industries, because they are highly popular with cost-conscious shoppers.

Turn your ABCs into shorthand in as little as 6 weeks

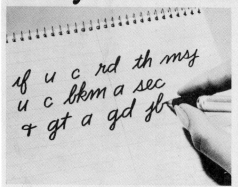

Can you read the message at left? If so, you are actually seeing for yourself just how simple it is to turn your ABCs into shorthand with Speedwriting.

There's no "mystery" to Speedwriting. No strange signs or symbols to learn. No expensive machines to buy.

With Speedwriting, you simply combine the individual letters of the alphabet in a systematic, common-sense way to make all the shorthand "notes" you need. You save time this way. And you develop your speed naturally.

Small wonder, then, that more than a million girls have been able to master shorthand the Speedwriting way. Many in as little as six weeks.

You can, too. And when you can take from 100 to 120 w.p.m., imagine the doors that will swing open to you in exciting fields like fashion, television, advertising, publishing—you name it.

You can learn Speedwriting at home, in your spare time, or attend classes in over 400 cities worldwide. But don't just take our word for it. See for yourself with a free sample Speedwriting lesson and information.

Mail the postage-paid coupon card at left. Or send your name and address to School of Speedwriting, 55 West 42nd Street, New York, N.Y. 10036. Mark it to the attention of Dept. 3110-1.

SCHOOL OF SPEEDWRITING
Dept. 9610-1
55 West 42nd Street, New York, New York 10036

Please send me, free, a sample Speedwriting lesson and full information. I am most interested in:

☐ Home study   ☐ Classroom instruction

☐ If under 17, check here for booklet "A"

Print
Name_____ Age_____

Street_____

City_____

State_____ Zip_____

----- FOLD IN HALF ALONG THIS LINE -----

BUSINESS REPLY MAIL
No postage stamp necessary
if mailed in the United States

FIRST CLASS
Permit No. 6341
New York, N.Y.

POSTAGE WILL BE PAID BY

Speedwriting
55 West 42nd Street
New York, New York 10036

----- CUT OUT ALONG THIS LINE -----

Speedwriting
Shorthand in 6 weeks
An Educational Service of ITT

MAIL POSTAGE-PAID COUPON CARD FOR FREE INFORMATION AND SAMPLE LESSON

1. Cut out coupon card along perforated line.
2. Complete top half (please print).
3. Fold in half along center line and seal with staple or tape. No stamp needed.

An unusual and innovative form of the traditional coupon was in its integration in a reply card in this magazine advertisement by the School of Speedwriting.

Courtesy: BBD&O

or the food processor. This type of coupon is useful in introducing a new product or in stimulating sales of an old product. The coupons may also be valuable in market-testing or consumer analysis.

A widely-distributed free-gift coupon was used by Planters Peanuts to attract visitors to its big store on the famed Atlantic City boardwalk.

Large retail services also frequently use coupons to attract new business. A good example of this was a coupon mailing sent by Holiday Cleaners to the residents of a new apartment-house complex in the outskirts of Philadelphia.

This was a well-printed, two-color circular containing 24 "money off" coupons totaling $23.52, plus a free offer of a liquor glass with every $1.50 dry cleaning order.

Extra attractions were one-hour service, custom-care, guaranteed satisfaction. How could it miss?

The second type of coupon simply makes it easy for the consumer to obtain product or service information in a very convenient way. For instance, Gift Stars coupon savers in Colorado had the choice of redeeming them for trading stamps, gifts, or cash. Housewives could redeem each 1,500 "Gift Stars" at any grocer's for $2. Grocers were paid a 50 cent handling fee for each set. The stars could also be redeemed on a one-for-one basis for stamps in multiples of 300 at authorized trading stamp gift centers.

According to H. W. Greenough, executive vice-president of the company, the stamp firms that participated in the offer were the Gold Bond Stamp Co., Affiliated Trading Co., Pioneer Savings Stamps, and Howdy Neighbor. Some of the supermarket chains that participated were Safeway Stores, Associated Grocers, Red Owl Stores, Miller's Super Markets, and King Soopers.

The Gift Star plan was introduced in Colorado and included Texas, the Southwest, California, the Pacific Northwest, and Hawaii.

For many years, the "cents-off" package has been a well-worn promotional device. However, with a growing revolt by the retail trade against the effort involved and with increased government regulations, there has been a major shift to another standby—the coupon. Rising costs of direct-mail have led to a resurgence of media coupons especially with free-standing inserts in Sunday newspapers.

A Nielsen study indicates that 58% of all United States households use coupons. Fifty-one percent of housewives claimed that they used their coupons within two weeks. The survey concluded with the statement that "availability of the couponed product in the retail store is of primary concern to marketers," because other reports said that 40% of the housewives stated that there were occasions when they could not find couponed products when they went shopping.

The Problem of Misredemption

The wrong use of coupons, whether at the retail or consumer levels, is one of the problems to be guarded against in coupon promotions. An old story is related about the store manager who became suspicious of a shopper with a handful of coupons. Inquiry disclosed that her son was a newsboy who brought them home in quantities every day.

In this connection, several associations issued a joint statement with recommendations that:

"The manufacturer, the advertising agency and the newspaper are encouraged to work with retailers and retail customers on procedures to avoid in-store misredemption of coupons.

"Tighten and maintain controls on the newsstand each day so that no unusually large number (of newspapers) can be ordered.

"Intensify and maintain in-plant security precautions to monitor printing and delivery practices and the disposition of returns and spoils.

"Increase and maintain controls on the use of voiding stamps, sales of sample back copies and public service desk sales."

Industrial Coupon Users

As a means of providing promotional assistance to their distributors, major producers of industrial products advertise to consumers. To stimulate inquiries and produce sales leads, coupons are often used. As stated by American Olean Tile Company:

"The intent of our coupon advertisements is to elicit more inquiries. This is especially important in our consumer program where the cost of consumer advertising is so high. We find that one of the most economical units is the $\frac{1}{4}$ page black-and-white advertisement promoting our 'Decorating Ideas' brochure. We analyze our advertising effectiveness on a cost/inquiry basis and this particular unit seems to do the job best. We place a charge of 10 cents for our brochure to eliminate coupon cutters."

American Olean aids its distributors and builders by promoting the use of its ceramic tile products in consumer magazines such as Better Homes and Gardens, the American Home, House and Garden. Ten cents is charged for the company's Home Decoration booklet to eliminate "coupon cutters."

Coupon-Campaign Costs

As a promotional medium, the popularity of coupons increases year after year, evidenced by their wide-spreading usage. One need only to go to a supermarket to see housewives clutching the newspaper and magazine coupon ads.

The test, of course, is the rate of coupon redemption versus costs. It offers the only definite measurement of cost-effectiveness. A summary in *Advertising Age,* based on an analysis according to publication in newspapers, magazines, direct mail and Sunday supplements, indicates that cost per coupon redeemed varies from 23 cents to as high as 44 cents per coupon. Naturally, these figures should be considered in relation to the cost of the product.

To give it greater attention value, Sheaffer Eaton throws the spotlight on the coupon by reversing the white-on-black pattern of the advertisement.

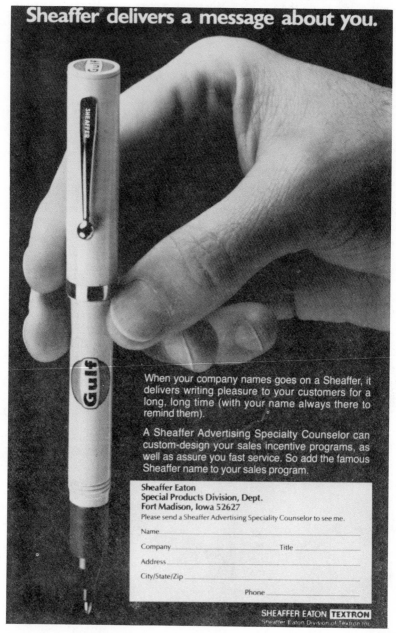

Sheaffer delivers a message about you.

When your company names goes on a Sheaffer, it delivers writing pleasure to your customers for a long, long time (with your name always there to remind them).

A Sheaffer Advertising Specialty Counselor can custom-design your sales incentive programs, as well as assure you fast service. So add the famous Sheaffer name to your sales program.

Sheaffer Eaton
Special Products Division, Dept.
Fort Madison, Iowa 52627
Please send a Sheaffer Advertising Speciality Counselor to see me.

Name

Company _____ Title

Address

City/State/Zip

Phone

SHEAFFER EATON **TEXTRON**
Sheaffer Eaton Division of Textron Inc.

PART 3

THE
CHANNELS
OF
DISTRIBUTION

Chapter 28

INTRODUCING THE NEW PRODUCT

THREE out of ten major new products marketed in a five-year period failed in some important respect to come up to expectations, according to a Conference Board survey among 87 companies. The major reasons given for new-product failure, in order of frequency of mention, were:

Inadequate market analysis	Competition
Product defects	Insufficient marketing effort
Higher costs than anticipated	Inadequate sales force
Poor timing	Weakness in distribution

More than half the companies mentioned the first three factors—inadequate knowledge of the market, product deficiencies and high costs—as contributing to failure.

All of these factors are subject to correction and control, but product defects involve the consumer and without consumer acceptance of course, any product is doomed. As a preliminary step, most companies expose their new products to juries or customer-panels.

Market tests are important because the launching of a new product is costly and entails high expenditures for promotion. Jacqueline Cochran, Incorporated, introduced Bigarade, a new fragrance line by Nina Ricci, with an estimated $500,000 campaign in women's magazines during an introductory six-month period. Purex Corporation spent "close to $1,000,000" in newspaper supplements to launch SweetHeart lime fabric softener. This did not include the cost of grocery trade presentations or trade advertising. Crazylegs, a new moisturized shaving gel for women, was introduced by S. C. Johnson & Sons with a campaign which included fifteen magazines, network television schedules and sponsorship of a six-mile marathon for women in New York.

The first step in the evaluation of a new or modified product should involve an exposure to unbiased consumers. Exposure can be made in a variety of ways: Through the use of juries or panels, or by house-to-house sampling.

The objective of such exposure is to obtain consumer reactions toward the proposed product after actual trial—particularly reactions after comparing the product with its strongest competition. This offers qualitative information on why the new product is acceptable —or even more important—why it is not.

If reasonable acceptance is indicated, or if any existing "bugs" can be ironed out on the basis of what was learned, sound procedure then calls for the marketing test. Otherwise, it is quite possible to learn— very expensively—that what consumers say they will do can differ quite remarkably from what they actually do later when purchasing in a free and competitive market!

In addition to measuring the performance of new products, test marketing is successfully used to determine the effectiveness of advertising-merchandising programs. Frequently such tests involve comparative appraisals of various amounts of promotion, types of media, and changes in combinations of advertising or merchandising efforts.

Test marketing is also used to measure the value of store displays, including effect of different locations within stores. It has reported accurately on promotions such as sampling and/or couponing, as well as on merchandising activities such as retail sales calls and detailing.

Changes in price, product, or type of packaging . . . all these are valid reasons for test marketing.

Steps to Successful Test Marketing

According to the A. C. Nielsen Co., these steps will serve as a guide to the basic requirements of test marketing—and to results which will serve to forecast "accurately" whether a product or idea merits broader investments on a sectional or national basis.

1. Decide on the primary purpose of the test. New product acceptance, promotional return, price revision, or some other basic question must be of predominant importance. The test should be designed to find an answer to a single major issue.

2. Plan ahead. Before entering the test market, develop a realistic, full-scale marketing strategy covering the entire area in which the product will eventually be advertised and sold. Set a price consistent with promotion and profitability needs.

3. Set test goals based on the over-all marketing plan. If national sales of a certain level are necessary to assure success, set goals for the test at the same level.

4. Seek the facts. Be completely objective and realistic in evaluating the performance of your product or your advertising-merchandising plan.

5. Benefit from comparative testing. Since the purpose of testing is to evolve a successful marketing program, a single test permits no comparative evaluation. Whenever possible, test several products or plans in different test markets ... so that a selection can be made of the most profitable plan.

6. Profit from professional advice. A call or letter to a firm dealing continuously with test marketing problems will not only provide much-to-be-desired objectivity, but will also help to avoid pitfalls.

7. Select representative test areas. Proper selection from the standpoint of size, geographical location, population characteristics, etc., permits results to be more closely duplicated on a regional or national scale. The test areas should also contain promotional facilities (i.e., television, radio, etc.) of the type contemplated for broader use later.

8. Employ proper research procedures. Budget adequately to permit accurate reporting of retail sales — at the point of sale where records are available and auditing techniques can be used. Allow the sample size and design to be determined by the test problem.

9. Establish a test base. Before the test is started, determine the individual and total sales of competitive brands. This provides a base against which subsequent changes may be compared and realistically appraised.

10. Follow competitors' shares of market. Some will hold established share, some will either gain or lose. Analyze those who are successful and locate their sources of strength. Ideas for improving your own strategy may evolve.

11. Welcome exposure to competitive retaliation during the test. This is the only way to tell how the product or plan will fare when normal competitive conditions prevail. Don't attempt to test in a vacuum.

12. Examine retailer cooperation and support. Are retailers carrying all package sizes ... providing adequate inventory ... conforming to prescribed pricing policies, etc.?

13. Wait for repeat sales after the initial purchase. Is your share continuing upward, leveling off, or declining?

14. Coordinate advertising and promotion. Poor timing can result in loss of full dealer support.

15. Avoid over-advertising or over-promotion during the test. Don't do more in a test than you plan to do on a broader basis. This suggestion may need modification when tests are determining ultimate potential and staying power of a new product.

16. Evaluate all possible sales-influencing factors (including those of competitors) such as sales force, season, weather conditions, distribution, inventories, out-of-stock, days' supply, age of stocks, location in store, and shelf space.

17. Avoid interference with the test once it is launched. If the test involves television advertising, for example, maintain that media. "Changing horses" will inevitably confuse the test results.

18. Adjust test findings to changes which occur during the test interval. Take into consideration changes in the economy, any major change in the total market for the product, the competitive situation, retailers' reactions to the product or merchandising plan, and consumers' reactions to the product or advertising appeal.

19. Allow the test to run its course. Many tests require only six months for preliminary appraisal; others, as long as three years. Unusually strong positive or strong negative results permit earlier decisions, as do high-volume products with a fast use-up in the home — provided that full distribution can be obtained early in the test period. Low-volume products with a long home life usually require a longer interval for test results to become conclusive. Also products with low distribution usually require a longer testing period.

Be sure to allow enough time for possible deterioration of product color or flavor, which might show up only after periods of two or three times normal shelf life. Allow also for merchandising and advertising to reach maximum effectiveness; many promotions need repeated impacts and the passage of time before they can be properly evaluated.

Above all, be patient — and don't be pressured into "getting into the market" before sales and market shares have stabilized ... the test is completed ... and its results analyzed.

"Today, most of our supposed modern marketers are using the methods of 1945, so we can predict the future: little change, for many.

"Many companies pay lip service to the marketing concept and continue the primitive practices of an outmoded era. It makes you wonder whether or not they really understand that a marketing evolution has changed the U.S. economy."

Thus began the outline of a new-product marketing plan by Remus Harris, then vice-president and director of marketing, McManus, John & Adams, New York, and published in a copyrighted article in *Advertising Age*.

According to Mr. Harris: "Marketing is the total procedure of creating new customers efficiently. Until it is understood that an entire business enterprise is a total marketing organization ... the concept cannot fully be implemented.

"To develop the marketing efficiency necessary even to survive today, the total marketing concept must be thoroughly understood by every employee of the company. Its meaning must be communicated to all levels by top management."

Craig S. Rice, author of *How to Plan and Execute the Marketing Campaign* (Dartnell Corp.), says: "Today, marketers of thousands of secondary brands are discovering that they too can increase sales substantially with marketing campaigns. Soon, brands not given this technique may suffer competitively."

In another study, by Booz, Allen and Hamilton, Inc., internationally-known management consultants, it was disclosed that two-thirds of the 366 new products surveyed were adequately successful, 10% were outright failures, and 23% were doubtful. A previous study had shown that only one out of two commercialized products was successful. One of the judgments verified by the survey was that most manufacturers cannot live without new products.

A.T. & T. Picturephone service is now available between major cities and is gradually being expanded. Shown is model Mod II which can easily transmit data as well as permit face-to-face contact. The control unit enables the user to adjust the volume, control the camera's field of view or prevent his picture from being transmitted.

The emphasis on new products is outstanding at Bristol-Myers'. In one year, over 30%, or approximately $80 million, of the company's total sales volume came from items that had been introduced nationally during the previous four years.

The existing older divisions—Products and Grove—had been increasing their new-product efforts but perhaps even more important sources of new-product diversification were the Clairol and Drackett acquisitions.

Qualifications for a New Product

It should not be assumed that appropriating money to finance a "packaged" promotion for a new product will insure its successful introduction. But if the product has the necessary basic qualifications, it has news value and interest which can profitably be capitalized. A good example of this is found in the automotive industry, where new models are made the basis for extensive, and sometimes expensive, sales promotional undertakings. But the mere fact it is new, in itself, is not the only requirement. Before spending any considerable sum on promoting a new product the following requirements should be kept in mind:

1. Stay close to your own field.
2. Be sure you have an intimate knowledge of your own market and the competitor in it.
3. Be sure that your product is preferably completely new or incorporates new features.
4. Be sure that your product can be made in commercial quantities and still preserve all its laboratory-tested qualities.
5. Consult legal and accounting counsel.
6. Never send an advertising boy out to do a man-sized job.
7. Thoroughly brief your salesmen with all scientific and advertising facts about your new product.
8. Organize a system of allocating orders based on planned production to assure the product of national distribution before advertising begins.
9. Remember point-of-sale displays and key your packaging and displays to impulse buying.

Another important factor in the success of the new product is the name it carries. A product which has a name that lends itself to sales promotion can be introduced with a smaller appropriation than one which is hard to remember and hard to pronounce. In the guide to developing and selling new products, issued by the U.S. Department of Commerce for small businessmen, the following characteristics of a good name are listed:

1. Short.
2. Simple.
3. Easy to spell.
4. Easy to read.
5. Easy to recognize.
6. Easy to remember.
7. Pleasing when read.
8. No disagreeable sound.
9. Easy to pronounce.
10. Pleasing when pronounced.
11. Cannot be pronounced in several ways.
12. Does not go out of date.
13. Adaptable to package or label.
14. Can be easily connected with trademark.
15. Available for use (not in use by another firm).
16. If to be exported, pronounceable in all languages.
17. Not offensive, obscene, or negative.
18. Not similar to some foreign word.
19. Descriptive or suggestive of product and use.

Crisco is an example of a good selection. The name is short, agreeable, easy to grasp, and sticks in the mind. Other examples of good names are: Caterpillar, Keen Kutter, Pestroy, Rinso, Duz, Sunkist, Band-Aid, Zerone, Yuban, and Lux. Names for use in Mexico should be identified by an illustration of a familiar thing like "Sun" or "Lion."

The name of the maker is perhaps the most common type of brand name for industrial goods, and it is also frequently used for consumer goods. Many manufacturers believe, too, that the names of industrial products should denote such qualities as strength, dependability, and durability. And for some industrial products it may be desirable that the name indicate what the product machine is or does; e.g., the "Premier Truck Tractor," or the "Acme Voltmeter."

To test customer acceptance of a new product, Monsanto Company's packaging division conducted a survey among foodmarket customers. The new product was a new "see through" plastic meat tray, designed for retail packaging of fresh meat and poultry. Of the housewives surveyed 97% liked the plastic tray better than a white-pulp meat tray. Of those who preferred the plastic tray, 73% cited its visibility and 24% thought the meat package had a cleaner, more sanitary appearance. The introduction of the plastic meat trays marked Monsanto's entry into a market estimated at eight billion units annually.

The Package as a Factor in Promotion

The advent of the self-service store, and the tendency in merchandising toward product display, has made the design of the product, the package, or the label, as the case might be, important.

When Monsanto introduced a new "see-through" plastic tray for retail packaging of meat and poultry, it conducted a survey among housewives to determine the product's acceptance. Results justified the company's entry in a market with a total potential of eight billion package-units.

Shopping goods are bought mainly on impulse, and product appearance has a lot to do with the kind of an impulse the shopper receives when she sees it on display. If it is drab and conventional, it is not likely to create a buying impulse, in fact that kind of a package does not even attract attention. A messy package is equally negative in advertising and sales promotion.

To have the most promotional influence the package, or whatever gives "appearance" to a product, should be simply designed. It should not have too many colors, since the colors may have to be reproduced in advertising and store display material. It should have billboard value, so far as the handling of the name is concerned, so that those looking for it by name on a dealer's shelf can quickly "spot" it. It should have a minimum of "bread and butter" (small type) copy. If recipes or directions for using it are necessary, the sides of the package, which do not show on the shelf, should be so used. If the product is one of a family of products made by the same company, there should be as much similarity as practical between the various packages in the line. This tends to pass on to the least known products in the family the good will and consumer acceptance which the others enjoy.

The People Finder Box

In launching its new FM radio pager, Pageboy II, Motorola introduced the product to its sales force in what National Market Promotion Manager G. R. Dawley described as "a highly unusual and very successful internal sales promotion campaign." The introduction was accomplished in a dramatic manner through the use of an attractively designed black cardboard box, 11½ by 11½ by 1½ inches in dimensions, housing a pullout-drawer with a separate compartment containing a non-working sample of the Pageboy II. The box was imprinted "People Finder II."

In addition to the Pageboy, the package contained a four-color catalog folder with specifications, national ad reprints, a complete series of direct mail pieces, a system-planner, a Product Feature/Customer Benefit Report, a User Booklet and Competitive Equipment Reports on three major competitive products.

An introductory sheet stated: "The purpose of this People Finder II box is twofold. First, it is an attractive announcement package. Secondly, and most important, it has been designed to use as a sales tool. The pager mounted on the inside of the box makes an attractive display case for use in a paging presentation."

Customer acceptance was overwhelming, reported Mr. Dawley,

Motorola's introduction of its FM radio pager, Pageboy II, was supported with national advertising in business publications.

largely because the Motorola sales force was greatly impressed and stimulated by the completeness and uniqueness of the announcement package.

LAUNCHING THE PRODUCT THROUGH SALESMEN

Since it is usually important to get distribution for a new product quickly, so that it can be profitably mass produced, most companies depend upon salesmen to do the spade work, backing them up with national advertising and intensive sales promotion. Sometimes the company's regular salesmen are used with the aid of special sales kits. Sometimes, if the regular salesmen are too busy or not very good at introducing a new product, special salesmen are used. A home appliance manufacturer brought out a new electric ironer. His established dealers put it on display in their stores but made no real effort to sell it. It did not carry a sufficient profit to interest them. They would rather sell washing machines, freezers, or refrigerators upon which they made far more money. But the small electrical shop, which sold electric fans, irons, and low-priced radios, jumped at the chance to sell apartment ironers. To them it was "big ticket" merchandise. So the manufacturer took the ironers away from the salesmen who called upon home appliance dealers, and organized a special sales force to introduce them to electrical stores. The plan worked fine until the appliance dealers ran into the competition and then they howled to high heaven. But the company was then in a position to tell the appliance dealers the facts of life, and get them to agree to really push the ironer if permitted to distribute it too.

Some companies hesitate to set up, what seems to them, a conflicting and overlapping sales organization. Yet that is being done more and more in marketing specialties. A good specialty salesman usually does a poor job selling a full line, and vice versa.

The Introductory Plan

The traditional method of introducing a new product which is sold through established trade channels is to use a "free deal"—that is to say, customers are given a small supply of the new product in consideration of the purchase of other products which the company sells. The Federal Trade Commission, however, objects to calling these "Free" deals, since actually the goods are not free but included in the price which the customer pays for the entire purchase. So the term "bonus goods" is commonly used. This sort of an introductory deal, however, actually amounts to cutting the price on the other products and sometimes leads a merchant to use the products as "loss leaders." Dealers, being human, are not likely to attach much value to something they get for nothing. However, it is one way to get quick distribution.

A better method than "bonus goods," is to offer an initial assortment of the new product at the regular price, but to include a "packaged" promotion, which might include store display material, newspaper mats, pass-out literature, etc. The offer, might also include an allowance for advertising in the local paper or for spot broadcasts. Usually, however, when the product is supported by extensive national advertising that is sufficient to get dealer cooperation.

Regardless of how the new product is to be merchandised it is important that salesmen be provided with presentation portfolios which they can use to explain the plan to the customer and secure his order cooperation. Before finally deciding upon the plan to be followed, these facts should be considered:

1. Do you know the sales promotion and advertising methods used by your competitors?

2. Do you know the sales promotion practices followed by distributors in reselling your type of product?

3. Do you intend to launch immediately into advertising and sales promotion activities or would it be better to begin later?

4. Are most of your prospects already accustomed to selling (or using) products of this type, or will they have to be taught?

5. If they have to be taught, do you have a plan for teaching them?

6. What design features of your product should you stress in your advertising and promotional work?

7. What, in general, will be the basis of your advertising appeal?

8. What will comprise the basis of your opening promotional effort?

9. Have you determined how much and what type sales promotion assistance you will need to give your own salesmen to help them sell to distributors or users, or both? (For example, what market data, catalogs, drawings, samples, brief-case portfolios, educational slides, or films, or scale models could they use?)

10. What general advertising and promotional support (for example, catalogs, hand-out circulars, dealer display materials) will you give your distributors? (Adapt such support carefully to the nature of your product. For example, some small specialty items handled by industrial distributors can be mounted on counter cards for most effective dealer sales promotion.)

11. Have you planned sales and service manuals, parts lists, tables of shipping weights and measures, and the like for the use of distributors and users of your product?

12. What advertising media will you use?
    a. Magazines?
    b. Business or farm papers?
    c. Daily newspapers?
    d. Direct mail?
    e. Telephone directories?
    f. Consolidated industrial catalogs?
    g. Manufacturer's registers?
    h. Other media? List.

If the new product lends itself to sampling, either to dealers or to consumers or both, the advantages and disadvantages of sampling plans should be carefully weighed. (See Chapter 27—"Sampling and Coupon Promotions").

Sell the Plan, Not the Product

Speaking before the New York Sales Executives Club, George P. Hall, star salesman and sales manager for James Jamison Company, sales agents for a group of hosiery mills, told of the method he used to open up enough new accounts to produce $5 million of business annually. When Hall went into a town where the company wanted distribution, he would contact the chamber of commerce, the newspaper publisher, or the banker and find out which merchant was doing the best merchandising job. He would get all the information he could about the merchant, and also information which gave him a line on the sales potential of the territory.

Hall then approached the merchant armed with the information he had gathered, and sought to convince the store owner he was only doing a fraction of the hosiery business he should be doing and could do with a plan he had prepared. The plan was simple. It gave the merchant exclusive retailing rights for the locality, provided he would lay in an adequate stock and agree to a continuous display of the products in his store. When the merchant objected he could not possibly sell that much hosiery in the community, Hall turned the objection into a reason for buying. He told him about merchandising plans other wide-awake merchants were using in towns of similar size, and about the sales they were making, and the money they were earning. He made him realize his sights needed lifting. In no time at all the merchant began to ask questions, and usually ended up by signing on the dotted line. "The worst thing a salesman introducing a new line to a merchant can do is to show his samples right off the bat," said Hall. "That buyer has hosiery all around him. He dreams of it at night; he gets worried that he may have overbought; and all day long a stream of salesmen are asking, 'Please look at my samples.'" Now it is a known fact that most hosiery is very much alike in appearance. One mill can turn out about the same grades as another. So why pester a buyer to look at something he is already tired of seeing.

The answer to this problem, says another hosiery salesman, is, "Talk about your mill, your company's personnel. Make the buyer feel that here is a mill he can trust. Then talk about a plan for getting a larger share of the local hosiery business, and what other stores are doing with the line. Finally, when the buyer has just about decided that other things being equal, he *wants* to do business with you, let him see the samples. Then, if they come anywhere near his needs, he will buy."

These principles hold good for selling almost anything. Unless an item has absolute novelty, unless there is something about it which can be interestingly demonstrated, do not pester the buyer to look at samples until you have sold the plan. Unless the samples are sensationally better than anything else he has seen his only answer is likely to be, "So what?"

"Detailing the Trade"

If the new product is to be distributed through wholesalers or mill supply houses, it is not always easy to get them to stock the product in advance of national advertising. They have heard so much about the "big" national campaigns manufacturers intend to run that it usually leaves them cold. "We will stock," they reply, "when the trade calls for it." To get over this hurdle some companies move a crew of salesmen into the territory and call on the principal merchants or dealers, soliciting orders to be shipped through a regional wholesaler. Or, depending upon the product, they may call upon garages, dentists, doctors, or even people who specify the product, such as architects. These detail men then sort out the orders they have written. The head salesman takes them to the different wholesalers. They try and usually succeed in getting the wholesaler to place a sufficiently large initial order to take care of the dealers' orders turned over to him, plus sufficient merchandise to fill repeat orders when the promotion gets under way.

These detail salesmen sometimes find it difficult to get orders in advance of introductory advertising, for the same reason salesmen calling on wholesalers get turned down. They, too, want to wait for demand, and then they will order from their wholesaler. The salesman cannot very well say the wholesaler won't be able to fill their orders. Here is how one salesman gets around that situation.

"When a merchant tells me he wants to wait for his customers to ask for my product before he places an order," this salesman said, "I dispose of the objection this way:

"Consider the dealer for a minute. When he decided to go into business, he selected his town and maybe the location of his store. Then he waited until the 'Citizens of our fair city' petitioned him to start his 'merchandise emporium.' In other words, he waited for 'a call' from the inhabitants before he opened up. He did all this, didn't he? Well, he did not. He opened up with the belief that he would have saleable goods for them when they did call, and if he is still awake to the game of today, he knows he must occasionally stock a new brand to keep pace with the consumer in his quest for something new. Don't you see that adding a new brand now and then without a call is the same thing in principle as opening up his store at the start without a call?

"Let's try to figure out how this dealer obtained his original stock. With his four bare walls and an empty showcase, did he wait until the folks came in and specified their choice, and then make purchases, and so at the end of 288 or 289 days have a fairly complete stock? Did he do this? I ask. Not on your life!

"All brands were new to him then and not one mite older than your brand is to him today. Your brand may be new to him, but can he say it is new and unwanted by his customers? Does he base its newness on the fact that he never had a call, and then change his views if John Smith comes in and asks for it? And with our advertising promotion work isn't he bound to 'have a call'? Does he strengthen his good will with his customers by waiting for a demand before he buys?

"Did you ever stop to think why you go to the post office for stamps? Funny question isn't it? But listen, you go to the post office for stamps because you know you can get them there! That's why, too, a lot of trade does not go to some stores for up-to-date merchandise, because they doubt if it can be purchased in the 'wait-for-a-call' store.

"Of course, this dealer will harp on being satisfied with the old brands—they suit his trade—why make a change? Is it really his love of these old brands, or his unreasonable dislike of a new one that inspires this prejudice? Don't you know that the oldest and best selling brand he now carries was at one time just as new as yours? Suppose he had always used this same argument on all the other one-time new brands! In a brief period his store would have run a race with a graveyard.

"When you get right down to it, what license has he to say that his trade is satisfied with his present brand? Might they not like a new brand better if they had a chance to compare its merits and wouldn't Mr. Consumer cuddle up a little closer to the dealer that put him next?

"Let me run in a little incident of my own experience. I wore a certain style of collar for years. Was apparently satisfied with it. Bought them here, there and everywhere. Had no choice of a haberdasher. One day I was purchasing my usual every-so-often half-dozen and the polite clerk showed me a collar with a new idea pertaining to the buttonhole and asked the privilege of putting in just two of the new ones with the four old style. Say, I would never go back to that old style, and now all my haberdasher wants go to the store that 'puts in new things without waiting for a call.'

"The simile may be a little farfetched, but it seems to me that waiting for a demand before making a purchase is just like waiting for Old Man Winter to 'make a call' before stocking up the coal bins."

Promotions to Get Inquiries

If the new product has qualities which lend themselves to publicity getting promotions, these may be developed in such a way that they result in inquiries which salesmen can follow up. Cronite Chemical Company, for example, made good use of this technique in marketing one of the pioneer products in the detergent field, which was put on the market in competition with soap. While traditional advertising methods were used to do a basic educational job, something was needed to convince the public that a detergent could take the place of soap. So the company embarked upon a program of demonstrations, such as washing a railroad train.

The train to be cleaned was backed at a speed of 3 or 4 miles an hour through a "wash shed," sprayed with the detergent and came out shiny new. Local newspapers gave the stunt publicity and the company's salesmen helped to spread the news. In another locality the new product was put through its paces washing streets. A busy downtown street in San Francisco, with the cooperation of the San Francisco Chamber of Commerce and the Department of Public Works, was roped off and given a bath. As a result hundreds of inquiries were received by the company from persons who had some sort of a water washing job to be done. These were followed up by salesmen and turned into orders. This type of promotion is

John H. Breck, Inc., Division of American Cyanamid Company, produced a merchandiser-display for its retailers as part of the introductory campaign for a new product.

claimed to have produced a 500% increase in sales for the company the second year.

When Trouble Develops

Most new products have bugs in them. When these begin to show up, there is an opportunity for the sales promotion department to communicate with customers so as to minimize the difficulty and, if possible, turn it to sales advantage. After all, it becomes a sales problem, and is no longer a production problem after the difficulty has been corrected, so long as the imperfect goods remain in the hands of customers. Such situations call for skillful and prompt action.

INTRODUCING THE PRODUCT BY MAIL

Since introducing a new product by personal contact is not always practical, or if practical too costly for a small operator, a number of companies are turning to direct mail, supported by business paper and local consumer advertising. This method, while somewhat less effective than when salesmen are used, does secure fairly good distribution at a reasonable expense, in fact if time permits, it can be obtained on a pay-as-you-go basis.

The Department of Commerce bulletin cites the case of a company which had developed a new intercommunication system which it desired to sell through radio parts jobbers. It had no sales force, so it had to depend upon the mail. The mailing piece consisted of a picture of the new product and a circular describing the important product features and the variations in models. Prices were also given.

For the introductory stage, the company took advantage of the practice of various trade publications to announce new products. A limited amount of paid advertising was also used.

About 6 months after the introductory work was completed, the company began to obtain sales representatives—manufacturers' agents handling other types of electronic equipment—to sell the product to distributors. The company now has sales representatives covering about 80% of the United States and, it believes, 90% of the United States market.

Teasers to Get Attention

Some sales promotion men contend that results from an introductory offer mailing can be stepped up by preceding the offer with one or two inexpensive teaser mailings. These may be penny post cards carrying an intriguing statement, usually in the nature of a question, designed to arouse curiosity. Like the advance card of a salesman it is slanted so as to induce the customer to withhold orders for that particular type of merchandise until he receives news about the new history-making product.

Checking the Results

It is important, after a reasonable period of time has elapsed, to check up and determine exactly how the new product is doing. If it is sold through dealers, is it moving off their shelves with sufficient speed to warrant extending the advertising and promotion? What do the consumers think of it? How do sales compare with those of competitive products in the same markets? Are there any "weak spots" either in the product itself or in the distribution plan which need correction? To get this information may not be as easy as it seems, especially if trade orders clear through regional distributors or wholesalers. So it is good practice at this point to do some intensive checking in the field, preferably using experienced research men rather than the company's own salesmen. For this purpose extensive (but not too involved) questionnaires may be needed—one for dealers and another for consumers.

The services of a market research organization may also be engaged for this work. These market-survey organizations usually inventory all competitive materials in the established group of retail outlets to determine the exact quantities sold both of the new item and competitive lines. These workers act without knowing which one of the commodities they are measuring.

If the test-run studies reflect a high degree of probable acceptance, the sales department then moves into national promotion as rapidly as production can be stepped up. If the test is unfavorable, the item is taken off the market, either as being undesirable or as needing further development.

As a rule, however, the introductory offer letter or announcement is sent "cold" without any build-up. Objection to the use of teasers is that the average buyer seldom pays much attention to them. As a result he fails to connect the teaser up with the offer, so little is accomplished. However, the answer probably lies in between these two extreme views. Teasers pay off, if the product lends itself to their use and if the spacing between the arrival of the teaser and the offer itself is not over 2 or 3 days. Teasers mailed out a week or more ahead of the offer are not recommended.

Lily-Tulip Introduces a New Container

"F. Norman Hartmann, president of the Lily-Tulip Cup Corporation, introduced publicly for the first time a new package in the field of round nesting containers.

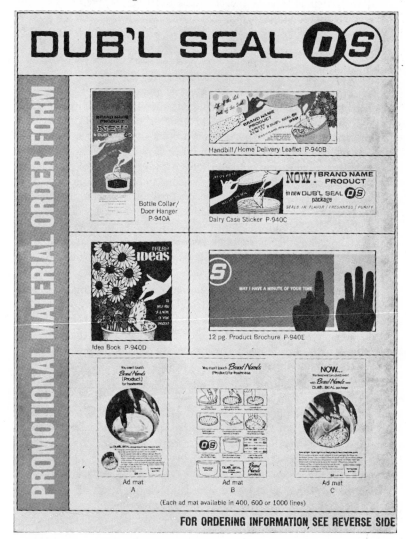

In introducing its food container, Lily-Tulip offered its food-processing customers such items as newspaper ad mats, counter cards, case-stickers, radio-commercial scripts, and other promotional aids.

"The new package, called Dub'l Seal, introduces improvements not heretofore available in this type of package; namely, air-tightness and liquid-tightness."

Thus started the announcement, in a publicity release, of a new Lily-Tulip container for food products.

Robert Ziselman, the company's sales promotion manager, said: "Along with a press introduction, there was a complete merchandising kit, supporting national ads, a complete point of sales program and an audio-visual presentation for our salesmen.

"The campaign for the new product included ads in the dairy trade papers, ad mats for food processors featuring the new container, promotional material illustrated on an order-form sheet, with free imprinting of the product and its brand name; 30- and 60-second radio commercials, handbills, counter stickers, door hangers, and other units.

"This packaging program was one of our most recent and successful efforts."

It should be borne in mind when planning a direct-mail effort to introduce a new product that a certain amount of showmanship is necessary to underscore the importance of the offer. This can be done by jazzing up the envelope, by sending the letter air mail, by using a large envelope that just can't be missed, and in other ways. Some promotion men take advantage of the low serial telegram rate offered by Western Union, and send a wire the same day the letter and offer are mailed to the customer. The telegram states the letter is in the mail, and asks the customer to be on the lookout for it since it is important to him. Or, and this may work even better, a telegram can be sent after the letter is mailed asking the buyer if he received the introductory announcement and offer mailed yesterday, and press him for an order. But make it easy for him to order, such as asking him to write his answer on the back of the telegram and hand it to the messenger.

The point is that unless you treat your new product as important, and show you do, you can hardly expect the recipient to take much interest in it. When you are introducing a new product is not, as a rule, a good time to pinch pennies.

Chapter 29

PROMOTING SALES THROUGH
WHOLESALERS

IT IS A FACT, not always recognized in sales management, that selling the wholesaler is one thing; getting him to sell your product is quite another.

Sales executives constantly exhort their wholesalers to go after bigger and better market coverage by selling retailers in every city and town in their territory and visiting them at frequent intervals. Manufacturers study industry statistics for every county or metropolitan area in the United States; market reports based on the latest census figures are available from the government; specialized trade publications offer periodic market figures; major newspapers and magazines provide market information for major trade classifications. All these provide a basis for evaluating any wholesaler's performance in his territory.

Other frustrating areas are sales training and advertising. The wholesaler leaves the training function to the manufacturer, who is in no position for daily or weekly implementation of programs. In advertising, wholesalers depend on the manufacturers' national campaigns and the retailers' local advertising; in between, they do little or nothing except, perhaps, to handle their share of their retailers' cooperative advertising and even this, in some cases, is refunded through various bonus and incentive plans.

Yet the role of the wholesaler, or distributor, is an important one: he has a definite function in the distribution and marketing process. Without the wholesaling channel, manufacturers would have to assume the function themselves, with extra costs and organization problems. This does not apply to all industries of course, as the direct-to-the-dealer approach has been found desirable with high price-ticket products, as in the case of automobiles. The wholesaler relieves the manufacturer of many headaches, such as retail credit, warehousing and local contact with dealers.

The reason wholesalers are indifferent to promoting any one product or line of products is not hard to understand. In the first place the average wholesale distributor is not promotion-minded. He may not admit it, but he operates on the theory that his function is to supply his customers with merchandise they can turn over quickly, and he is not interested in inducing them to buy anything for which a demand does not exist. Wholesalers are very much concerned with collecting the money for what they sell. And the tighter the credit situation becomes the more pronounced their caution. Then too, most wholesalers have private or pet brands which they want to push, if they are going to push anything. These are brands upon which they think they made the most money because they pay a longer profit. The high rate of turnover enjoyed by widely advertised brands does not affect their buying policy too much, although they will fill orders which come their way. In fact, it is not unusual for wholesalers to compensate salesmen on the basis of the margin of gross profit they make on the merchandise they sell, even going so far as to furnish salesmen with order blanks so arranged that the dollar sales of products in different profit groups can be entered in separate columns. This is done to keep the salesmen alert to the need of pushing the long profit items in the line, not dissipating effort on nationally advertised brands which some wholesalers still insist they handle at a loss.

So the first task of a manufacturer distributing through wholesalers is to make sure that they thoroughly understand the effect of turnover on operating profits. This is demonstrated in the success of many so-called "curb" jobbers who make good money by selling at cost, taking as their profit only the cash discounts they earn. But it is not always easy to convince a wholesaler that he can make more money by making more sales at a smaller profit. The average wholesaler runs a warehouse, and in spite of the inroads direct selling and syndicate buying have made into his business, he persists in averaging his selling costs as well as his selling prices. It costs him x cents out of every dollar in sales to operate, so he must have a margin of x plus 10% to stay in business. This, of course, is one of the fallacies which are driving some wholesalers to the wall, and give rise to talk about "eliminating" the jobber and thus reduce the high cost of distribution!

The Wholesaler's Function in Distribution

Our system of distribution, as many manufacturers who have attempted to bypass the wholesaler and sell direct can testify, requires a strong wholesale distributing set-up. The wholesaler who is on his toes and doing a constructive selling job is an economic necessity. The wholesaler who is dead on his feet and thinks of himself as a warehouseman is an economic liability. Hence the manufacturer has a long-range interest in strengthening the wholesaler by helping him to solve the many problems he faces, some of which stem from his lack of appreciation for modern sales promotion.

Promotion Objectives for Wholesalers

The promotional programs of wholesalers, unlike those of manufacturers which usually emphasize the company as well as what the company makes, have two parts. The first part consists of those operations which come under the head of "internal promotion." They consist of keeping salesmen inspired, stimulated, informed, and instructed. Since sales managers are usually engrossed in a variety of activities, they have little time to do all of their own writing. Their assistants must be properly instructed. An important task in promoting sales for a wholesale operation, therefore, is training and coaching the people in the organization who prepare letters and bulletins to the field.

An important element in training personnel to write effectively for wholesale salesmen is—how to present the merchandise so that it will give the fieldman the information he needs to help him sell it to his customers, and in turn help his customers to sell it to those who patronize their stores. To guide those in the home office in presenting sales points of merchandise to salesmen, a noted wholesaler prepared a checklist which was to be used in writing to salesmen, as follows:

I. Description of the Merchandise — The Name and So On —

1. Show sample and/or name it. Tell what it is, what it does, or how it's used.

2. Capacity to satisfy customers — why it's good.

3. Improvement over present or previous lines.

4. Is there any statement or guaranty as to quality and service?

5. The packing and assortment. Is there any advantage to this packing? Is it improved over previous packing?

6. Are there any exclusive qualities as to taste, wear, etc.?

7. Is there any trade-mark, trade name, or slogan worth playing up?

II. Advantages Due to Source

1. Where and how made?

2. What about the material used?

3. What about the reputation of goods due to source?

4. How about care in manufacture and packing?

5. Any patent rights?

6. Story of invention or discovery.

7. Inspection or tests.

8. Chain store supplier.

9. How to recognize goods of inferior quality.

III. TALKING POINTS BASED ON ADVANTAGES TO THE RETAILER

1. Easy to sell — quick turnover.

2. In demand by public.

3. The profit-markup for the merchant.

4. The value in repeat sales to the merchant.

5. Suitable for promotion or special selling?

6. Aid in building repeat business.

7. Transportation advantage—prepaid—freight allowance, pool cars or trucks.

8. Experience of other retailers.

9. Aid given by manufacturer in making sales.

10. Exclusive representation—if any.

11. Future plans regarding distribution.

12. When is the big wholesale selling season?

13. When is the big retail selling season?

14. Instances of purchase and result.

15. From the retailer's viewpoint would it pass this test:

    a. Is it the right type, style, or kind?

    b. Has it popular appeal — is it bought by a great number of people?

    c. How about the real value as compared with other products on the market?

    d. Is it a popular price?

    e. Is it packaged right?

IV. IMPORTANCE FROM D. S. STANDPOINT—

1. Checklist recommendations.

2. Current retail pricing.

3. Best selling price lines.

4. Recommended stock.

5. Type of fixture.

6. Location of display.

7. Amount of display space.

V. METHOD OF SELLING —

1. From samples, catalog, or factory listing.

2. Is it in stock or when will it be available for shipment?

3. Appeals generally used in selling.

4. Summary of main selling features.

5. Reason for price confidence—the immediate price—future price—outlook—reasons why the price is high or low.

6. Advantage of buying now!

The second important part of wholesale promotion comes under the head of "item promotions." Wholesalers have learned that in order to raise the sales effectiveness of their customers, it is desirable to conduct periodical promotions on certain fast selling items of merchandise. These promotions go further than merely getting orders for the merchandise, important though that may be. They must be "packaged" so that the customer who buys the merchandise can move it off the floor quickly and profitably, that is to say, there must be a planned promotional effort which the retailer can adapt to his needs and do a hard-hitting sales job. The long-range purpose of this type of promotion on the part of the wholesaler is to make good promoters out of as many of his customers as possible. Obviously, the retailer who is alert and eager for ideas which he can use to build his business is a far better outlet for a wholesaler than one who is content to let nature take its course, and sits around waiting for things to happen.

Wholesale Dry Goods Institute

The Wholesale Dry Goods Institute is a national organization of wholesalers of ready-to-wear, piece goods, domestics, floor coverings, notions, underwear, hosiery, furnishings, and other lines. This group has developed a plan for a store of the future, which includes standard shelving, standard flexible wall cases, self-service units, shelf units, island units, and backless windows. It is also developing a basic stock list for retail merchants, and attempting to help retailers with merchandising suggestions. The Institute's work in this respect is really in its infancy, but from now on it may be a real factor in helping to revive the independent merchant in the smaller towns and cities.

Apparently the Wholesale Dry Goods Institute looks upon its chief field as the towns with less than 25,000 population. At any rate, the Institute points out in all its promotion that:

> 43% of all department stores,
>
> 57% of all dry goods retailers,
>
> 60% of all variety stores,
>
> 98% of all general stores,

are in towns of 25,000 or less population. Of course, the Institute naturally contends that it is impossible to cover these markets economically without the use of wholesalers; in many cases this is true.

National Association of Wholesalers

This is a central group of wholesale associations. Some of its affiliates are (or have been): National Association of Tobacco Distributors; American Coal Sales Association; National Wholesale Druggists' Association; Wholesale Dry Goods Institute; National-American Wholesale Lumber Association; Wallcovering Wholesalers' Association; Motor Equipment Wholesalers' Association, etc.

The Association of Wholesalers issued a handbook of the wholesale industry, detailing the advantages of selling through wholesale channels, called, *The Miracle of Distribution.* While it is rather an elementary primer of the wholesalers' position, some manufacturers may find it helpful. Manufacturers seeking ideas for establishing better relations with wholesalers may find any or all of these groups helpful. There are, of course, many other wholesale associations; some make it a point to help manufacturers and others offer no service of this nature.

What Wholesalers Offer

In planning to promote sales through wholesalers it is important to study all means of reaching this market, and to decide on a sound distribution policy as the first step. This decision may be easier to reach if the facts about wholesalers are fully understood. The Wholesale Dry Goods Institute points out, in recent advertising, the wholesaler offers:

> National warehousing;
> Market surveys;
> Credit and accounting simplification;
> Services of many salesmen.

According to the Wholesale Dry Goods Institute the average wholesaler in this field has about 2,000 customers. The Institute claims that this means automatic coverage of 2,000 customers. Actually it means nothing of the kind, for the wholesaler may not sell more than 5 to 10% of his own customers any individual product or any manufacturer's line. But, of course, it is possible that the wholesaler may sell all his customers certain lines or products which have wide distribution possibilities. This would mean that 10 wholesalers would bring your goods to 20,000 stores—many more than some manufacturers have.

Importance of Adequate Stocks

There have been many instances where a manufacturer has been able to get a wholesaler to go along in undertaking a cooperative promotional effort, only to have it fail because of inadequate stocks. The very fact that wholesalers must stock so many different items makes them reluctant to buy heavily of any one item. They like to play it safe, and will argue that with air express shipments there is no need of carrying more than a week's supply of anything, promotion or no promotion.

To obtain maximum volume and profit, the distributor must not lose sales due to his unwillingness to carry complete stocks. One of the foremost automotive wholesalers in the business, Don Test of Indianapolis, told a Thompson Products executive that three cardinal principles, if faithfully followed, would practically guarantee success in the automotive parts business. These were: (1) Select and carry good lines; (2) stock those good lines completely and well; (3) use intelligent sales effort.

"In our 25 years in the automotive parts distributing business," he said, "we have seen these three cardinal principles followed almost inevitably to a successful conclusion. After all, customers will go where they get the best service and the best service can only be gotten when adequate stocks back up the efforts of your salesmen and your countermen."

Salesmen, especially, should be coached to discuss the high cost of letting stocks run down with their customers. Too many merchants are obsessed with the rapid turnover theory in store management. Credit men have pounded away on this theme for years, and it is good merchandising practice, but like all good things it can be overdone.

MARKET ANALYSIS FOR WHOLESALERS

Very few wholesalers, except possibly the large national houses, have any idea of their potential market. They take what business comes their way, and are happy if they can show a sales increase each year. This is especially true of the regional wholesaler. And even the big national establishments make little or no attempt to evaluate the potential possibilities of sales territories. They figure if a salesman produces a half-million dollars' worth of business from the territory assigned to him he is doing a grand job, and the aim of the sales department is to bring every man up to that level of production. If an accurate analysis was made of these territories in line with the practice of national manufacturers who sell direct, like The Borden Company, it would probably be found many of these "ace" territories should be producing a million dollars' worth of business. It would also be found there were "fringe" territories which could be made profitable by the use of better sales methods.

It is obviously to the advantage of manufacturers, as well as the wholesalers themselves, to know how much business is getting away because of inadequate coverage of highly potential territories. There are instances where regional wholesalers, following a change in management, have doubled sales and profits by rearranging territories and adding more young men to the sales staff. But before that can be safely and profitably done, it is important for the wholesaler to get the facts about the business he should have but is not getting.

Libbey-Owens-Ford "Customer Accounting" Service

The task of educating wholesalers to apply modern research techniques to their sales operations is too much for an individual manufacturer to assume, so they leave it to the wholesalers' trade associations. Sometimes that is sufficient, usually it is not. Trade associations are inclined to tackle projects which have more membership appeal than "selling" the idea of market analysis, which unfortunately requires an outlay of money before it begins to pay off. Regardless of what a trade association may or may not do to promote interest in market analysis, a few progressive manufacturers keep hammering at the need for better "customer accounting" on the theory that anything that can be done to raise the wholesaler's sights, and get him to increase his sales manpower, will help indirectly the sale of their products. This is especially true in the case of manufacturers who sell through limited line wholesalers.

Customer record, showing purchases by product, used by a glass manufacturer to analyze wholesale accounts. Purpose of this record is to spot wholesalers who are not purchasing the full line.

Libbey-Owens-Ford Company of Toledo has consistently promoted the sale of its products through wholesalers by doing a market analysis job for its wholesalers. Analysis sheets are arranged (see illustration on previous page so the wholesale distributor of Libbey-Owens-Ford products can list his accounts by territory. He then enters upon the recap sheet, under the proper column, (a) his annual sales to each account in dollars, (b) his approximate glass sales to that account, and (c) other sales. Another group of columns is provided for the wholesaler to break down the total glass sales to each account, as well as other products purchased by the customer over the year. These data are then analyzed by the manufacturer's Distribution Research Department. With that analysis, the wholesaler is better able to determine where sales emphasis should be placed. The value of the analysis to the wholesaler, together with instructions for making out the analysis blank, is explained as follows:

VALUE OF THE ANALYSIS

The value of our presentation, which will be based on the information supplied on the analysis sheets, will be to show: (1) The principal kinds of business which you do, i.e. "markets," and (2) the location of these "markets." Knowing this, it becomes possible to do things like the following:

1. Promote the most valuable kind of volume.
2. Determine the most profitable business.
3. Relate expenses to obtainable volume.

GENERAL INSTRUCTIONS

Omit *all* accounts (cash *and* charge) buying *less than $25* but keep a record of the *number* of such accounts omitted. Please show *total number* of such accounts without any sales figure.

After all 19.........*charge account* sales over $25 are listed, please show total *cash* sales for 19.......... The sum of the two will approximately total 19:....... gross sales. In addition, please supply the following estimates:

About ....% of 19......... cash sales were flat glass.

About ....% of 19......... cash sales were other than flat glass.

When tabulation is completed, be sure to tear off left side of the page (column 1) which shows names before sending the remainder of the sheets to:

Distribution Research Department

Libbey-Owens-Ford Glass Company

Nicholas Bldg.

Toledo, Ohio

together with any explanatory comments which will aid in understanding your method of classifying 19......... sales. Please number the pages submitted.

HOW TO FILL OUT THE FORMS

Column 1 — Put the name of the account in this column followed by

Columns 2 and 3 — the town and state.

Column 4—Someone familiar with the account should put down a trade classification abbreviation in accordance with the principal business done by the account. These abbreviations are shown on the attached sheet. For instance, if an account is a "Lumber Dealer," put down "L.D." in Column 4. This should be done with great accuracy.

Column 5—In Column 5, put down the total amount of sales you made to each account in the calendar or fiscal year 19......... Just enter the full dollar amount— not dollars and cents. In other words, $201.67 would be put down at the nearest dollar, i.e. $202. Dropping the pennies will save time for whoever fills out this column.

Columns 6 and 7—If you sell only "flat glass" products, skip these columns. If you sell other items besides flat glass products, someone familiar with the account should put down the approximate total dollar sales of flat glass products in Column 6, and the total dollar sales of other products in Column 7. The total of these two columns should always equal the total sales as shown in Column 5.

Column 8—If more than half of the total sales to an account were on contract work, mark "C" in this column. This means contract work which included glazing labor in the total figure.

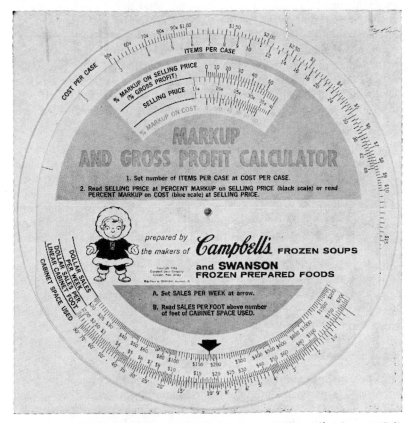

A very useful "Markup and Gross Profit Calculator" was supplied by Campbell Soup Company for distribution to retailers by brokers and distributors.

Column 9—Mark "D" whenever direct shipment was made.

Column 10—Indicate by marking with an "X" all products sold to the account. Then put a circle or parentheses around the principal product sold to them.

Column 11—Name the most important products, other than flat glass, purchased from you by the account.

How Diamond Match Dramatized Potentials

Another way to raise wholesalers' sights, by helping them to analyze their markets, was the match sales calculator developed by The Diamond Match Company. By turning the dial of the calculator to any size community, the calculator showed (a) the number of families in the community using matches; (b) the average food expenditure per family; (c) the average total lights used by family customers in that area per day and per month, broken down by kitchen matches, penny matches, book matches, and total matches. Another wheel in the indicator registered the total potential case match sales per month in an area of that population. The calculator was developed by the Statistical and Research Department of The Diamond Match Company using United States census figures. It was introduced to the sales organization, and then to jobbers' salesmen, by a 25-minute sound-slidefilm: "A Potential Idea."

In connection with the use of the calculator, wholesalers were furnished recap sheets which they filled out with the aid of The Diamond Match Company's representative. These sheets provided a space for the name and location of each store served by each jobber salesman, with a column for the actual sales by type of match, and a parallel column for the potential sales broken down the same way. This data provided the jobber with factual material he could use to raise the sights of each of his salesmen to convince them they were letting a lot of profitable match business go to competitors. To help the jobber's salesman locate weak spots in his operation, The Diamond Match Company provided each man with a similar indicator which used the number of families served by the store as a base of calculation. There were also forms which the storekeeper used to analyze his match sales by families served, thus establishing for each retailer a figure that represented his minimum monthly match sales.

When the information on the potential match sales of each jobber's territory were consolidated by the company's statistical department, a fairly accurate potential for each company sales territory was obtained. The data sheets used in setting these sales quotas, covering each jobbing territory, gave the following information:

1. Jobbers estimated percent of grocery volume (dry groceries) done by him in his area (per month). ....%

2. Population of jobbers trading area. ....

3. Number of families in trading area. ....

4. National average food expenditure (per month-per family) ....

5. Average monthly retail food volume in area (per month). ....

6. Less retailers .... percent markup in area. (Item 5.) $........................

7. Jobbing volume on food (all outlets per month) in area. $........................

8. Less half of item 7 for food items not sold by jobber (dry groceries only considered). $........................

9. Approximate average monthly volume (gross sales) done by jobber. $........................

10. Approximate percentage of food volume secured by jobber in area. ....%

11. Other distributors (dry groceries). ....%

While it is not easy to get the average wholesaler to gear his effort to his potential sales opportunity, it is a highly desirable objective for any sales promotional operation. As is true of nearly every business, one reason for the high cost of doing a wholesale business is inadequate volume. Attempting to cover overhead charges by increasing prices only makes a bad situation worse. It is infinitely better for the wholesaler and manufacturer to work together to increase the volume of sales in each wholesale territory even if such a policy might require the use of fewer wholesalers in a territory. The first step in carrying out such a plan is, of course, to determine how much business there is in the territory *if you go after it.*

COACHING DISTRIBUTORS TO TRAIN DEALERS

The increasing cost of training distributive personnel, essential to the successful marketing of many products today, can be reduced materially by getting wholesalers to assume their share of the responsibility. Wholesalers have good reason to cooperate because they profit, as well as the manufacturer, from the resulting sales increases. But before a wholesaler can effectively train his dealers to do a better selling job on the products he distributes, it is necessary for the manufacturer to train them to do the training job. It is the prevailing practice to bring in groups of wholesalers to the factory, where they are coached in the most effective training techniques and procedures. Such training usually requires from three days to a week, and involves the use of the various "props" and "visuals" such as are used in training factory salesmen.

American Central's Training Course

A typical program for training wholesalers was conducted by the American Central Manufacturing Company. Hundreds of distributors for that company's kitchen equipment were taught how to sell *complete* kitchens instead of only single appliances and cabinets. In connection with the 4-day course, 5 movies, 11 slidefilms, 16 chart presentations, and a skit were used. At the completion of the course, each wholesaler who had made the grade, was a qualified kitchen specialist, and was given a kit of materials which he in turn could use to train dealers. The "school" was known as the American Kitchens Institute. The 4-day curriculum was as follows:

TUESDAY MORNING

Registration—Train Reservations—etc.	9:05-9:35
Welcome—From Management	9:36-9:50
Opening Remarks and Introduction Chart	9:51-10:20
Trip Through Factory	10:21-11:05
Rest Period (It's at the end of the hall)	10 minutes

Company and Product
    "Designed for You"—Slidefilm
    Chart Presentation—Chart A
    Discussion using actual samples of product
	11:15-12:15

Lunch	12:40

TUESDAY AFTERNOON

Market—"In on the Ground Floor"—Slidefilm	1:35-1:50
Advertising—Chart Presentation and Discussion	1:51-2:20
Sales Promotion—Chart Presentation and Discussion	2:21-2:45
Publicity—Chart Presentation Motion Picture—"Tell It with Television"	2:46-3:05
Rest Period (Same Place)	10 minutes
Records and Reports—Chart Presentation	3:15-3:30

Display—"Give 'Em Ideas"—Slidefilm
    Chart Presentation—Chart B
    Motion Picture—"Opportunity Unlimited"
	3:31-4:30

Dinner	7:30

(Little man, you've had a busy day!)

PROMOTING SALES THROUGH WHOLESALERS

WEDNESDAY MORNING

(Don't you wish you had gone to bed?)

"Our Program for Kitchen Planning Service"— Lorine C. Mounce, Director of Kitchen Planning Service	9:05-9:15
Planning the American Kitchen Chart Presentation—Chart D Black Board Problems Student Planning—pencil and paper	9:16-10:16
Rest Period (It's still there)	10 minutes
Resume Planning	
The Plan-A-Kit Method of Planning American Kitchens	11:26-12:25
Lunch	12:40

WEDNESDAY AFTERNOON

Demonstration—"Step-Saving Kitchen—Believe It or Not"— Lorine C. Mounce, Director of Kitchen Planning Service	1:35-1:50
Continue Plan-A-Kit	1:51-2:51
Rest Period (Want a Coke?)	10 minutes
Locating Prospects "A Hunting We Will Go"—Slidefilm Chart Presentation—Chart C	3:01-3:45
Selling—"Simple as A B C"—Slidefilm Chart Presentation—Chart F Motion Picture—"Selling America" Hand out supplementary booklets	3:46-5:00
Bus leaves for Richmond	5:00

Free evening in Richmond—"Free" meaning you are free to choose your own entertainment, such as Blondes, Bourbon, or "B" pictures.

THURSDAY MORNING

(Are yuh listenin' huh................h?)

Installing the American Kitchen "According to Plan"—Slidefilm Chart Presentation—Chart E	9:05-10:00
Rest Period (You know where)	10 minutes
"Put on your coveralls—we're going to work"	
Problem Kitchens First Course—"Duck Soup Room"	10:20-12:10
Change clothes	
Lunch	12:40

Into your work clothes

Problem Kitchens
Introducing the Second Course—"Piece de Resistance"　　1:35-3:05

Change clothes

Rest Period (Yes—but is this trip necessary?)
How about a straight Coke?

Overcoming Objections
"Information Please"—Slidefilm
Chart Presentation—Chart G　　3:15-3:50

Closing the Sale
"Happy Ending"—Slidefilm
Chart Presentation—Chart H　　3:51-4:30

Dinner　　7:30

Shall we take our hair down this evening?

(Did you ever see a dream walking? Look around.)

Customer Follow-Up
"Every Customer a Salesman"—Slidefilm
Chart Presentation—Chart J　　9:05-9:30

How to Conduct a Sales Training Meeting
Chart Presentation with Student Participation　　9:31-10:10

Training Individuals　　10:11-10:25

Rest Period (Need we tell you?)　　10 minutes

Final Exam
Retire to the "Dagwood Special" Room and proceed according to
instructions　　10:26-12:15

Lunch　　12:40

Display—Your Distributor-Dealer Sales Training Equipment
You will use all this in *your* school　　1:35-1:55

Demonstration—How to use Charts, Script and all other material for
your Dealer Specialist School—Actual practice by students　　1:56-2:40

Rest Period (Again?)　　10 minutes

Motion Picture—"It Happened in the Kitchen"　　2:50-3:35

Graduation Exercises
Pass out "Kitchen Specialist Diplomas"
and "Kitchen Specialist Cards"

Pictures for posterity and expense account identification

Train Reservations O.K.? Didja like it?　　3:36-3:45
Bus leaves

You are now a full-fledged Kitchen Specialist!

While this type of training costs money, it is by far the best way to tackle the problem. It is too much to think, as so many do, that you can get the same results by sending out some printed material on how to train dealers. Wholesalers are no different than any other type of salesman, they can be taught best by *doing* rather than *telling*.

What the Training Should Cover

While the training procedure and program must differ with the business there are certain essentials necessary to any program for training distributors' salesmen, or dealers. On behalf of the National Society of Sales Training Executives, William Rados, a consulting sales manager, checked the distributors' training programs of 500 companies belonging to the National Sales Executives, Inc. He found that there were 10 basic sales subjects which were common to nearly every training operation studied. These were as follows:

1. Developing the customer's good will.
2. Determining the customer's needs for the product or service.
3. Overcoming objections.
4. Sales approach.
5. Guidance to the salesman on organization and use of his time.
6. The use of sales kits, manuals, visualizers, samples, models, and other things by the salesman can appeal to the eye as well as to the ear.
7. Methods of demonstrating or presenting the product.
8. Answering questions.
9. Getting repeat orders.
10. Salesmen's job duties.

You will notice that all of those subjects are aimed at two very practical objectives—how to make more calls and how to get more orders. Another major finding in the field of sales training was the repeated and very vigorous allegation of most sales executives that out of every $1,000 of sales training budget they would spend at least $500 on supervised application of sales training at the point of sale. In other words, out of every $1,000 of training budget they would spend half of that money on follow-up after formal schools and courses. In answer to the question: "Have you compared results of trained versus untrained groups of salesmen?" eighty-five concerns said: "Yes, we have definite proof that those men whom we have trained sell more than our untrained men," and they turned in figures showing that training was responsible for from 12 to 100% increase in sales, depending, of course, upon the company. Moreover, a majority of the companies that had made these comparisons between trained and untrained groups said that their sales went up from 50 to 100%.

Arranging for Speakers

The success of any meeting sponsored by a wholesaler, to which his customers are invited, depends upon an interesting and fast-moving program. Unfortunately, it is the practice of too many manufacturers, when asked by a wholesaler to supply a speaker for such a meeting, to send the territorial salesman. It is the easy and, obviously, the least expensive way to dispose of the matter. But it is seldom the best way. Salesmen are not usually good speakers. Yet these meetings present a real sales opportunity to the manufacturer, since it gives him the only chance he may have of personally contacting his customer's customers. The smart manufacturer, therefore, makes the most of the opportunity and assigns an executive experienced in platform work to the job. Sunshine Biscuits, for example, made thousands of friends among its dealers because of the peppery talks made by Gene Flack, formerly sales counsel and advertising manager. Flack was an accomplished public speaker. He knew the grocery trade and its problems, and always brought down the house. Wholesalers too, appreciate program building cooperation since it is no easy task for the average sales manager in that field to get good speakers for dealer meetings. The sort of cooperation a wholesaler asks from the manufacturers whose lines he handles is summarized in a folder, put out by the Automotive Advertisers' Council, to help wholesalers to conduct more profitable customer meetings. On the question of instructing manufacturers, the brochure suggests:

> Since the manufacturers are the wholesaler's "partners" in many of these trade activities, plan *with* them on all details and keep them advised of what they will be expected to do. First and foremost, call them in and be sure the proposed dates fit in with their plans and that they have reasonable opportunities to requisition their supplies, material, literature, and equipment well in advance. *Don't* keep plans secret until they are perfected to the point of issuing invitations before talking to the "factory" men. Bring them in right at the start. They may have a few ideas that will make the wholesaler's job simpler. Discuss with them the objectives of the program so that they may tie-in most effectively. Be sure that time allotments—for talks, demonstrations, etc.—are understood and agreed to. For clinics and shows, go

over the floor plans with them and agree on the amount of space and the grouping of various lines. Be sure they know what kind of a job is expected of them and be sure *you* know what they plan to do and what they expect of you. Give them complete written instructions, to be passed on to the factories, for the shipment of displays, literature and stock. State clearly how shipments are to be marked, how forwarded, the required arrival date, and who is to receive shipping notices. Make clear any restrictions as to size displays, current specifications, floor load, elevator size, local ordinances affecting operation of machines, projectors, or other equipment. *And be sure to talk over with the factory men the plans for registering, assigning, and following up the inquiries developed at the meetings.*

These suggestions indicate that no wholesaler should "spring" a meeting of any kind on his manufacturers—or expect them to be prepared to sell an unknown audience at a moment's notice. It's like jumping from a trapeze and then yelling for the net—but some wholesalers "plan" their meetings just that way.

Use of Syndicated Training Films

If the cost of specialized training at the factory is more than the margin of profit on the product will permit, it is possible to obtain syndicated film strips and motion pictures which can be shown to wholesalers in regional meetings. Wholesalers can purchase these films for their salesmen to use in training dealers and their sales personnel.

Among the most widely used films are those produced by The Dartnell Corporation's Film Division, which has specialized in sales training for over 55 years. A list of such films will be found on the next page.

Since it costs several thousand dollars to produce a 20-minute sound-slidefilm, and from $15,000 to $200,000 to bring out a good, well-planned sound motion picture, only the largest companies are inclined to produce their own films. Prints of syndicated films, on the other hand, may be purchased for a small fraction of this amount.

Naturally, a syndicated film cannot depict the exact products and selling situations of each individual company wishing to use it; such films, therefore, are made (1) with the greatest possible flexibility based on the most common denominators, and (2) are accompanied by meeting guides which suggest how best to adapt the film to the particular needs of each company using it.

Some companies prefer motion pictures; others prefer sound-slidefilms. Actually, each medium has its place. The slower pace of the slidefilm allows greater detail, as when discussing product construction, demonstration, or use; the faster-moving motion picture is better adapted to promotional use and for meetings where entertainment, as well as education, is a factor.

DARTNELL FILMS AND FILMSTRIPS

FOR TRAINING SALESMEN AND DEALERS

NOTE: *Several of these films are available in Spanish, French, German, Swedish, Norwegian, Dutch, Danish, and other languages. Details available from Dartnell.*

SECOND EFFORT. Vince Lombardi, famed coach of the Green Bay Packers, relates the tremendous drive of his team to salesmanship, and shows in this film how a "second effort" can often gain orders for business as well as yards on the football field.

SALESMAN. Entirely fresh in concept, "Salesman!" is a quiet but moving story about a salesman who likes his job . . . and tells you why. In 25-inspiring minutes, he reveals the challenges of selling, the satisfaction of doing the job right, and the rewards the dedicated salesman receives.

HOW TO CLOSE THE SALE. A fresh, new twist on a very basic technique of salesmanship—asking for the order. This British film zeroes in on 10 tried and true closing techniques demonstrated in a variety of sales situations. A must for every sales team.

MAKE IT HAPPEN. Professional golfer, Julius Boros, has made a compelling film with an inspiring, motivating message a sales team will never forget. A salesman in a slump finds himself teamed up on the course with the great Julius Boros and discovers that making a sale is very much like winning a championship tournament. 30 minutes, 16mm., full color film.

TAKE COMMAND. Astronaut Walter Schirra shows salesmen how to utilize the same success principles the astronauts use to overcome every obstacle and surmount every difficulty to reach their goals. 30 minutes, 16mm., full color film.

THINK WIN. George Blanda, the oldest active player in football, is also a great salesman. In this film he divulges his secrets of success both on the football field, and across the client's desk. 30 minutes, 16mm., full color film.

THE PROFESSIONAL. Two great actors, Van Johnson and Forrest Tucker have made an unforgettable film that will make all salesmen act and produce like true selling professionals. 30 minutes, 16mm., full color film.

CHARGE. The story line of this film centers on two salesmen—one young and pretty deep in a slump—the other a veteran. They find themselves teamed on the golf course one day with the great Arnold Palmer himself and discover that making sales is much like winning tournaments. 29 minutes — color.

PUT IT ALL TOGETHER. An entirely new kind of motivational film that reveals how three famous people, speaking independently about their own success, arrive at the same basic formula that your people can put to work for themselves. Starring Joe Paterno, Gene Cernan and Janet Guthrie.

TOUGH-MINDED SALESMANSHIP—ASK FOR THE ORDER AND GET IT. Joe Batten uses the same principles that made him famous as a tough-minded manager in this inspiring film. He shares his experience in showing salesmen how to overcome their fears in asking for the order. 28 minutes, 16mm., full color film.

POUR IT ON. Bobby Hull, the all-time hockey star, turns out to be as good an actor as he is a hockey player. The sterling principles that took him to the top in his chosen sport are immediately applicable to all phases of selling. 30 minutes, 16mm., full color film.

EXPLODE THOSE SALES MYTHS. Good sales people everywhere have been hampered and misled by old tales and beliefs that, when held up in the light of logic and fact, should have no bearing on their selling performance. And, if you sell through dealers or distributors, this film is an ideal entertainment/training vehicle for all dealer personnel.

RUN SMART. The star of "Run Smart" is one of the top life insurance salesmen in America. And while Frank Sullivan's field is insurance, the principles he believes in and the codes he practices are just as applicable to any sales field.

SELLING ON THE TELEPHONE. Effective use of the telephone can mean more sales and lower selling costs. Whenever any employee in your company talks to a customer on the telephone, there is an opportunity to sell. This superbly made, imaginative film shows how vital the telephone, as a selling tool, can be.

SELL PROUD. Earl Nightingale has surpassed himself in this 22-minute training film. It focuses on the need to develop pride, not only in yourself—but for the company you're working for. Earl outlines a three-point formula to help build self-confidence and improve sales know-how through increased product knowledge.

SELL LIKE AN ACE — LIVE LIKE A KING. Featuring John Wolfe, one of America's master salesmen and a successful sales trainer. In 30-powerful minutes, he reveals four principles of salesmanship that guided him as well as thousands of other successful salespeople he has trained.

YOUR PRICE IS RIGHT — SELL IT. In this 30-minute film, Joe Batten takes a mathematical approach to handling price objections because price itself is determined by arithmetic. The methods are simple—yet effective.

MANAGE YOUR TIME TO BUILD YOUR TERRITORY. Joe Batten's "tough-minded" approach can help your sales people organize their time for more profitable sales . . more productive sales. Five basic techniques comprise the system plus a personal "time log" which is used to tailor the system.

WHEN YOU'RE TURNED DOWN — TURN ON. Here are three power-packed techniques by which turndowns can be turned around into sales. This film shows you how to determine when a turndown is a true rejection.

THE CHALLENGE OF OBJECTIONS. This film tackles a vital part of sales training with rare insight into the salesman's hopes and frustrations—and presents the powerful techniques needed to turn objections into closed sales. It's presented in a fresh, imaginative manner.

REASON TO BUY. Business firms, like people, don't buy products. They buy benefits. Yet, how many of your salespeople—novice and veteran alike—tend to forget this all important principle of human nature?

LEARNING FROM EXPERIENCE. The difference between a good salesperson and a great one is the ability to analyze him/her-self and learn from experience. This 20-minute film shows your people how to achieve that big difference. And it does so in a way that is both entertaining and educating.

THE STRANGEST SECRET. Earl Nightingale possesses a rare talent: he has helped millions of people *do more, achieve more* and *enjoy more* in their lives and work than they ever thought possible. By showing this film to all your people, you can help them enrich their lives and make them more enthusiastic.

THE BOSS. There are rewards for those who observe Nightingale's four simple rules for the care and feeding of the BOSS. Recognition, personal growth and achievement, job satisfaction are some of the things we all want and can earn.

GETTING JOBBERS TO PUSH YOUR PRODUCT

A product, which may seem tremendously important to the company which makes it and whose profits depend upon selling it, is just another item in the line to the wholesale distributor. To be sure it is a good product, and he listens in a pained sort of way to your salesman who sings its virtues, but he seldom does much about it after your salesman leaves. It is not that the wholesaler does not want to make money, or that he is not awake to his opportunities. It is just that he sells so many thousands of different things that one more or less fails to excite him. If he pushes any product, it is likely to be one of his own private brands. But he will get behind a smart promotional *idea* if you make it easy for him to do so, and so will his salesmen.

Carborundum's "Missing Profits" Promotion

Carborundum "stones," like so many products sold through hardware stores, are good profit items but are relatively hard to sell. They are strictly "impulse" items. People don't usually go into a store looking for a carborundum stone. But when they are exposed to a display of abrasive products, they immediately think of all the knives at home which need sharpening, and are very apt to buy a stone before leaving the store. But competition for display space on the counters of good hardware stores was keen, and the company found it difficult to get the wholesalers who handled its products to get dealers to put in counter displays. Something more than persuasion was needed.

Carborundum's promotion department hit upon the idea of a packaged promotion built around missing profits, which wholesaler's salesmen would get behind and take out and present to their customers. The promotion involved six displays of related products, including Carborundum "stones." The purpose was to get abrasives out of the old-time all-purpose display cases where they are usually kept, into the modern, departmentalized group where they will sell themselves. There was a display designed to make extra sales to outdoor sportsmen; extra sales at cutlery and kitchenware counters; extra sales at paint and household supply counters—sales which were easily made simply by including an appropriate Carborundum display designed to point up the group with the related merchandise. There were other ideas too for increasing abrasive sales. But the glue that held the promotion together was a striking booklet, furnished to wholesalers for distribution to their customers, bearing the title: "The Case of the Missing Profits." It was done loosely with cartoons and was a take off on the mystery stories which are so popular now. There was in the plot, George Sellum, a hardware dealer now deceased; Sam Sharp, who wasn't born yesterday; The Inspector, as smart as they come; the Assistant to the Inspector, just another taxpayer; and Mrs. George Sellum, who steals the show, much to the disgust of the Inspector.

Motivating Jobber's Salesmen

Salesmen employed by wholesalers fall into two general classes: (1) Those who are satisfied to write up such business as a customer has "on the hook" or in his want book and let it go at that; and (2) those who make it a rule to plus the order by selling the customer something more than his current wants. The "something more" may be a special which his house is featuring that month, or it may be some item in the line which the salesman thinks would go well in the customer's store, or it may be a product which for one reason or another the salesman is enthusiastic about selling. Unfortunately most wholesale salesmen fall into the first classification and there isn't very much a manufacturer can do about them. But as competition grows keener, the mortality rate among the order-taker group may be expected to grow apace, so that gradually more and more wholesale salesmen will depend upon creative methods for building sales volume. To effectively employ such methods the salesman must build his sales talk around a specific product. It could be yours.

The Monthly Letter or Bulletin

As a rule wholesalers do not look with favor upon a manufacturer corresponding directly with their salesmen. The reason is obvious. If anyone is going to suggest products for their salesmen to push, they prefer to do it themselves. But they will pass along to their salesmen sales helps furnished in bulk by manufacturers of profitable products. Promotional literature of that sort should have an unselfish purpose. It should aim to help the salesman to be a better salesman, not merely a better salesman of the products which the manufacturer wishes to sell, but of all products sold by his house. A paper manufacturer selling through wholesalers was able to get a high degree of salesman cooperation by developing a series of talks on paper salesmanship, written by an outstanding authority in that field. These were issued in the form of a weekly letter from a "Self-Made Paper Salesman to His Son." Nowhere in the letters were the manufacturer's brands mentioned. The letters dealt exclusively with the problems of wholesale paper salesmen, and how they might be solved. To be sure the salesman knew who was sending him letters, because the letterhead carried the name of the mill. But so far as the salesman was concerned the manufacturer's only interest was to help him to make more money for himself and for his employer. Because of the unselfish nature of these letters, the wholesalers distributing the manufacturer's mill brands were glad to furnish the mill with the names and addresses of their salesmen so the letters could be mailed to them direct. Those who insisted on doing the mailing themselves changed their minds after a few letters had been released, and sent the mill the names of their men to save mailing expense.

An automobile manufacturer selling through independent distributors hit the jack pot by issuing a 3-month celluloid calendar every month, on the back of which was a timely suggestion for helping dealers to sell more cars. The little pocket calendars were supplied in quantities to the distributors who enclosed them in each salesman's mail, or handed them out at the monthly sales meeting. Over a period of months, these calendars added up to a short course on automotive salesmanship and proved very helpful. Salesmen who were flooded with promotional material from the factory, most of which they filed away without reading, carried the calendars in their vest pockets and read and reread the suggestion on the back. The utility feature did the trick.

Manufacturers who encourage their salesmen to hold meetings of jobber's salesmen whenever possible find it profitable to prepare sales educational materials for the salesmen to use as a basis of such meetings, and which they can leave with the jobber's men. Sometimes these are tied in with sound-slidefilms which the salesmen carry and show at such meetings. However, unless a salesman has a flair for this sort of work, and is a good platform man, it is better to depend entirely upon direct-mail promotions for motivating the jobber's salesmen.

Distributor's Salesman Advisory Board

Another device which has helped a number of manufacturers to "get over" sales stimulating ideas and viewpoints to distributor sales organizations is to establish a distributor's council or advisory board. This idea was used successfully some years ago by Nash-Kelvinator as a follow-up to its famous "Sales Mean Jobs" promotional activity. The plan is to have each wholesale distributor or, in the case of a smaller organization, each dealer appoint one member of his organization to represent the company on the council. These council members meet periodically, usually about twice a year, to discuss sales promotional projects which have been suggested for adoption by all distributing units.

At the first meeting the council elects officers and adopts a program of action. The purpose is to keep the meetings on the beam, confined to ideas which will help all distributors to do a better job. Transportation, out-of-pocket expenses, and housing of representatives attending the meetings is usually paid by the manufacturer, who profits from the exchange of ideas and the suggestions which come out of such meetings. Distributors are glad to pay their representative's salary while he attends the meetings, because it provides an incentive to salesmen to put forth extra effort.

Contests for Jobbers' Salesmen

No sales contest among distributors, wholesalers, or dealers ever achieves more than mediocre success without getting their cooperation in advance of the time the contest is scheduled to begin. Some companies go so far as to say that the degree of success of such a sales activity is wholly dependent on the thoroughness with which the advance work is done.

In those cases where there is a very close tie-up between distributors and the manufacturer, and where the sales volume of the manufacturer's products is a large percentage of the distributor's business, the advance work necessary can be completed with ease. But in those cases where less than 20% of the distributor's sales volume is in the manufacturer's line, there must be a thorough and comprehensive advance plan to get the necessary cooperation. The problem faced involves these factors:

1. The manufacturer must have the home addresses of distributor salesmen who are to receive not only an announcement of the sales contest but also frequent mailings to promote interest and activity.

2. He must have the consent of the distributor to offer prizes or some kind of an incentive to get extra effort on the part of individual salesmen.

3. The distributor must be shown that the sales contest will have a good effect on all of his business—not merely diverting the salesmen's efforts from other products to the manufacturer's line.

4. The distributor must be shown *how* the campaign will benefit his whole business—through the educational mailings that give salesmen selling ideas applicable to other products as well as the products of the manufacturer conducting the campaign. Or he has to be shown how stimulating sales activity on this line will increase sales activity on other related lines.

5. The manufacturer must get the distributor to cooperate in the promotion of the sales contest; by putting up scoreboards and keeping them posted daily; by turning in reports to the manufacturer to permit checking, or at least spot checking, the sales volume of individual salesmen for purposes of awarding prizes; by local mailings and meetings.

6. Sometimes the distributor must be sold on paying a part of the cost; or offering prizes locally to supplement the incentives set up by the manufacturer; or footing the bill and assisting in planning a local kick-off meeting.

Accomplishing this, therefore, becomes a campaign in itself. It is a job that becomes profitable by virtue of the fact that it greatly increases and often multiplies the sales results obtained in the sales contest.

How extra results are brought about is illustrated in the case of one large company which obtained a 33% increase in sales during a 60-day contest, when the best it ever did previously was to obtain a 10% increase which, in view of the size of the company, was considered satisfactory. The greater percentage came as the result of a well-planned advance activity lasting 30 days, in which the manufacturer's representatives turned in almost double the number of names registered in previous sales contests. From this the company knew in advance the activity would show increased sales volume even if the registrants averaged only a normal volume per individual, and they were certain to average better than normal.

In this case, during the campaign, many dealers interested new salesmen in going to work; they put inside help in the field, at least part time, to get some sales; and some even registered bookkeepers and delivery men who agreed to do some selling. As a result over 7,000 dealer salesmen were registered for the contest when the greatest number on other campaigns had never exceeded 4,000. This alone assured an increase. It would not have been possible without an effective advance activity to get a maximum number of registrants.

In plans of this nature, the advance work generally consists of the following steps:

STEP 1—The manufacturer has a meeting of representatives who contact distributors about 60 days in advance of the starting date of the sales contest, the purpose being to tell them of the coming sales contest and make plans to get registrations.

STEP 2—Manufacturer's representatives then schedule meetings with distributors' representatives for similar purposes in each local spot and these men are then equipped with:

  a. Portfolio outlining contest, including examples of mailings to be sent to dealer salesmen during contest to show sales educational job that will be done among these salesmen.

  b. Outline of local meeting for dealer salesmen to get campaign off to a good start.

  c. Registration blanks on which the home addresses of dealer salesmen are to be entered.

  d. Preview of any special advertising to be run during the contest—direct mail, newspaper, magazine—to place maximum sales power behind the sales contest.

  e. Order forms for bringing stock up to what it should be.

STEP 3—Distributor salesmen start making their calls on dealers 30 days in advance of the sales contest to get dealers ready for the contest and the home addresses of dealer salesmen on registration blanks.

STEP 4—Manufacturer conducts intensive follow-up by mail, telegram, and, finally, long distance telephone to get registrations from every dealer, and prepares list for campaign mailings that include, in addition to dealer salesmen, the dealer himself, all representatives, distributor executives, and others for a 100% coverage.

So important is the advance activity in obtaining the wholehearted cooperation of distributors and dealers that certain companies, having a record for exceptional attainment in sales contest results, design special campaigns.

Contests designed to motivate jobbers' salesmen are most effective when built around a sporting theme, and are developed so that every man has a chance to win. Baseball contests are unfailingly popular with jobbers' salesmen and permit offering prizes to those salesmen who have the highest batting average, as well as to the team (jobber organization) which gives championship performance. If cash or merchandise prizes are used, the method of awarding points must be simple so the salesman may report the prizes as income (as the law requires). All jobbers must be given an opportunity to participate on the same basis so that there can be no question of discriminating in favor of large buyers. If a manufacturer does not wish to stand the expense of the prizes, as well as providing the materials needed to successfully promote the contest, he can usually get the wholesaler to pay for the prize books and prizes in consideration of his assuming the cost of promoting and operating the contest. Actually the cost of the prizes is paid by the increased sales resulting from the contest.

Scoring the Salesmen

One of the secrets of putting a contest for jobbers' salesmen over in a big way is to furnish each wholesaler with an idea for a simple scoreboard, which he can erect in the office so that the entire organization will know who is who in the sales organization. It is not enough to just inform the salesmen.

One scoreboard which proved popular and which any wholesaler can easily and inexpensively make, if you provide him with a sketch, is based on the idea of keeping your light shining. Opposite each name on the scoreboard a small electric lamp (miniature size) is set loosely in a socket. When a salesman turns in an order, or makes his quota for the day or week, "his" lamp is screwed down until it lights up his name on the scoreboard. Office folks, as well as salesmen, get a big kick out of stopping by to see whose lamp is shining. It is just a small thing, but it is mighty important to the salesmen. It gives the sales manager an excellent peg on which to hang a whole series of bulletins, too.

WRITING TO WHOLESALER'S SALESMEN
By Milton G. Crume

A wholesaler's field publications are essentially the sales manager's own messages to his men. In addition to including centrally prepared pages, each deals with local selling assignments which would otherwise necessitate many individual letters. Their further purpose is to: (1) Inspire and stimulate, (2) inform and instruct, and (3) provide guidance and direction in selling.

The value of most articles can be improved by keeping the following general rules in mind:

1. Write each article as though you were talking to salesmen or superintendents. Tell them what you would want to know if you had to go into the field to do the job expected of them.

2. Don't assume that they will see and appreciate and make use of the main selling points in an item or line. Tell them what's important and *why* features of construction, or styling, or finish should be stressed ... tell a complete story.

3. Avoid like a plaque articles that say, "Let's rally 'round the banner and sell more turkey bells." What the man in the field wants to know is *how* to sell them. Unless you tell them *how,* the article isn't worth its ink. Don't just say *"sell it"*— say *how.*

4. Never scold publicly for failure to deliver. When it is necessary to check salesmen or superintendents on their shortcomings, do it in person or with a personal letter. Don't wash dirty linen in publications that others read. Besides, it doesn't help matters to tell them they fell down. What they want to know is how they can sell more successfully. You might review talking points or elaborate on selling facts previously given. Try to get salesmen and superintendents to invigorate their presentations with new material. These things help ... scolding doesn't.

5. Condense—don't bury thoughts and facts in too much verbiage. Go back and cut out useless words. Omit sentences that repeat.

6. The average weak article—the kind that lacks selling ideas or useful facts—

is half-baked because the man who wrote it did not dig deeply enough for his facts or he didn't have enough of them. You are writing to help the men do a better job and unless, when the article is written, you can look at it and say, "This will be helpful," don't use it. *Get more facts and write it again!*

7. Don't preach, give help. Make the man you are writing to realize you know what his problem is and that you are trying earnestly to help him. *Have a wholesome fear of swivel chair direction.* Try to make the man say, "The fellow who wrote this article is a merchant—he knows his stuff."

8. Assume that the man you are writing to is a capable Butler Brothers representative—most of our men are. Don't talk down to them. They appreciate helpful information, but resent ballyhoo and generalities which waste their reading time and mean nothing.

9. Avoid superlatives. Very few lines or items are the best, the most remarkable ever produced, or the greatest values on the market. The use of extravagant phrases weakens an article.

10. Whenever you say anything is particularly outstanding, *don't stop there, give the evidence*—say specifically why it is better, why it is cheaper, why it will sell, why customers want it. Be specific in giving facts and reasons. Old man "specific" is a great aid to good writing.

11. When writing an article get all of the facts together and then write it with some one man in mind, giving him information and advice he cannot help but feel will be for his own good. *Talk as though he were across the desk from you* ... and you won't use the ridiculous jargon that so many people employ in writing.

12. Avoid such overworked phrases as "Get the business," "This is the most wonderful line we ever had," "Cash in on the opportunity," etc. The fieldman wants to cash in on the opportunity. He wants to sell more goods. That's the only way he can improve his income. What he has a right to look for from you is *information* and *selling tools,* and *ideas* that will help him get the business.

13. Let's keep in mind that we are trying to get our men to sell things we want sold. Before we write, let's decide what we want them to do. Then, let's see what we can provide for them. And after that, set down the reasons that, for their own good, they should get going on the selling job we want accomplished. In short, sell them on what they have to work with.

14. When referring to merchandise that is listed, tell where it is—give page numbers, so anyone can find the particular line you are talking about. The men haven't time to page through their carrying case looking for material when it is a simple matter to give references.

15. Don't use the expression "dealers"—say "customers, store owners, merchants, retailers," etc.

16. Try to adjust the length of articles according to the importance of the material. It isn't consistent to write a short paragraph about an important volume line and give a full page to a 10-cent item of doubtful repeat value.

17. Try to express the substance of an article in the title. Follow the journalistic practice of newspapers. They state the story briefly in the heading. The body of the article should then agree with the title. Concentrate on a good headline and give particular thought to the opening paragraph—to do so strengthens any piece of writing. Put a punch in it. Make it attention arresting. Like the opening of a letter, it should gain attention and arouse interest.

18. All selling information is easier to understand when it is well organized. If talking points can be summarized in 1, 2, 3, 4 fashion, by all means do so. Usually you have to have material well organized to state it in this fashion.

19. Write *to* fieldmen—not about them. Sprinkle your sentences with "you" and "yours." No one is much influenced by the "I" and "we" type of article. Steer clear of "first person" constructions—use "you" and "your." It's good psychology and should be used in all written material. It's called the "you" approach.

20. Avoid breaks in the thought of an article.

21. Recommend a course of action. Don't leave your presentation up in the air. Tell the men what you want them to do. Tell them how to do it.

22. Decorative effects, fancy hand-lettering, and illustrations should be done well or not at all. Our publications are for businessmen so depend on solid informative facts and selling ideas rather than on fancy decorations to make pages interesting. For example, there is no need for an illustrated heading on a price change page. Where illustrations are needed in merchandise articles, by all means use them. Just be sure they are good enough to be businesslike.

23. Sales publications should not average more than 25 sheets or 30 reading pages. Consider the reader. The objective is "how good" not "how big."

24. Is the job you are asking the men to do practical and reasonable? Don't say, "Show this article in every store you visit." It may not fit some stores. Incomplete or impractical instructions destroy faith in management. Be practical.

When talking with merchandise department managers about articles, you will find that it is frequently difficult for them to give you specific talking points. They often assume that facts which would be helpful to salesmen are already known because they're so familiar to them. It is sometimes difficult to get talking points, and it is equally easy to overlook essential points. But remember this—all fieldmen depend upon your written material for their guidance. Their knowledge of lines and sublines is almost wholly dependent on what you tell them.

If our sales publications fail to do a good educational job, we reduce the effectiveness of your manpower in the field. Our aim then should be to so inform our men that they will be better posted and better able to write orders than the salesmen representing our competitors. Aim at providing a flow of selling ideas, of better ways and more workable plans to help our men in the field to get a greater volume of business.

Chapter 30

SELL AND DELIVER MERCHANDISING

THE sale of certain kinds of merchandise can often be economically and profitably promoted by selling the product and delivering it at the same time. Bakery goods, coffee, tea, candy, cigars, tobacco, cigarettes, magazines and periodicals, meat and packing house products were among the first to be delivered by the same man who sold the merchandise. But the field is constantly expanding. Automobile parts and accessories are sold in considerable volume by wholesalers whose salesmen are also truck drivers and delivery men.

Today there is a vast volume of merchandise sold and delivered at the same time. Potato chips, pies, cookies, peanut products, fish, confections, janitors' supplies, school supplies, and, in a few cases, clothing specialties, dresses, and similar merchandise are among the products sold in this fashion.

There is no limit theoretically to what can be sold and delivered at one stop, yet up to now the greatest volume has been in terms of small size, low weight, and quick turnover, which require servicing to eliminate the risk of selling stale merchandise to consumers.

Turnover is another factor. Current buying habits plus the desire for rapid turnover are both factors in the popularity of sell and deliver merchandising. Many small merchants cannot tie up money in more than a few days', or 2 weeks' supply of merchandise. It costs too much to employ one salesman to sell these customers and operate a separate delivery organization to deliver the merchandise.

The result is a combination driver salesman who calls frequently, delivers and collects for small quantities, and puts merchandise on display. Some observers call this automatic merchandising, because the salesman seldom asks the customer how much merchandise is needed. He simply puts in a previously agreed upon quantity, writes a sales ticket, collects the money upon delivery.

Economies of Sell and Deliver

Constantly increasing travel expense, higher salaries, smaller profit margins, rising transportation costs all combine to favor the seller who sells and delivers in one operation. One of the greatest savings is in time, formerly lost in selling small orders. The salesman often has to wait while the customer fries a hamburger, fills a prescription, weighs a pound of potatoes, or answers the telephone. The customer may even keep the salesman waiting just to show his own importance.

Once the sell and deliver salesman has made the rounds and completed arrangements with customers he loses little, if any, time waiting. In many cases the store cashier pays the salesman without consulting the owner. We have seen many truck or sell and deliver salesmen bring in an armload of coffee cartons, stack them under the restaurant counter, and collect the money from the cashier with no more delay than a customer encounters in paying his meal check.

Waiting time is the salesman's greatest bugaboo. Estimates of the time lost waiting for customers varies according to the territory, and the type of business, but many sales managers agree that some salesmen spend no more than 2 hours a day face to face with a customer or prospect. But the truck salesman eliminates much of this lost time.

There are other savings in selling from a truck. A considerable part of the packing cost is saved. Billing and invoicing charges, credit losses, collection expenses are additional savings. If the merchandise lends itself to the sell and deliver plan there is much to be said for it.

Wider Distribution Made Easier

When salesmen are employed, it is obviously unprofitable to call on many customers. Their orders are too small. For example: Many filling stations, or gasoline service stations, sell candy in small volume. The total candy sales of any given community add up to a considerable volume, but the cost of obtaining and maintaining distribution is often too high to leave any profit. Here the truck salesman seems to hold the answer to the problem. He can drive to a filling station, put in a dozen bars of candy, collect his money, and be on his way to the next customer in a few minutes.

Another factor which will probably increase truck salesmen's activities in the future is the increased cost of transportation. Express rates have increased appreciably. While parcel post shipments have replaced much express business, there is still a need for quick delivery of many products.

Many small merchants and service businesses, such as restaurants, cafes, hotels, service stations, cannot be expected to maintain stocks by sending in mail orders; nor can many companies afford to send salesmen to them for small orders, then ship the merchandise and expect to collect for it later. With the sell and deliver method the transaction is completed at each call.

Many Big Companies Use Sell and Deliver

Hormel and Company, Swift & Company, the Jewel Tea Company, many large bakeries, food products manufacturers, Tom Huston Peanut Company, The Lance Company—here are but a few large companies which have in the past built large volumes via the truck selling route. Duncan Coffee Company, aggressive coffee roasters of Houston, Texas, uses two methods. Small orders are delivered on the spot. Larger orders are booked for shipment later. Of course, the packing houses use both methods.

Service stations which carry a small line of automobile accessories and supplies depend mainly upon the arrival of a wholesaler's truck to replenish stocks. In some parts of the country, hotel and butcher supply companies have built passenger bus bodies into a sort of traveling wholesale house. From these converted busses deliveries are made at the time of the sale. Continental Coffee Company, which specializes in restaurant and institution trade, has built a large business through frequent deliveries of small quantities of coffee. Its drivers usually know what each customer requires without any preliminary call.

Compensation of Delivery Salesmen

In larger cities many salesmen who operate from trucks are members of unions and their wages are set by collective bargaining.

When this occurs, compensation arrangements are subject to union rule. Where driver salesmen are not members of a union, compensation arrangements are often set up to provide incentives to improve performance.

Straight salaries, salary and commission, salary and bonus, and straight commission plans are all used by different companies. Most favored arrangement is a basic salary, with extra compensation for definite performance results. Merit ratings for determining such bonuses are increasingly popular.

Some companies require salesmen to buy their own trucks. Other companies furnish trucks. One plan is to finance the truck for the salesman and permit him to pay for it out of earnings, with due compensation for use. Such a plan should be liberal enough to enable the salesman to accumulate funds toward paying for a replacement truck when it is no longer economical to operate the old one.

Bonding Salesmen

A number of companies require a cash deposit as a guarantee against loss where salesmen make collections. Others have bonding arrangements. The cash bond is, of course, simpler and less expensive from the company's standpoint, but some salesmen, who might be otherwise acceptable, do not have the required cash. Some companies do not require bonds, but investigate salesmen carefully. It is not always necessary to bond a salesman through a bonding company. A responsible friend or relative may be sufficient. Without a doubt the bonding company plan is better, for in case of a default it is usually extremely difficult to collect from a friend or relative.

Amount of bond should be at least equal to the average collections during one settlement period. If salesmen turn in collections daily, this sum can be small. If the turn-in and settlement period is weekly or monthly, the bond must be larger.

It is not prudent to employ a group of salesmen who collect money unless they are bonded. A certain number of men will default or get behind in payments and, without the protection of a bond, losses can quickly accrue to the point where the operation is without profit.

Training Driver Salesmen

Because many men recruited for jobs as driver salesmen have never had any previous selling experience, it is usually necessary to provide thorough training for sell and deliver salesmen. Without such training the chances of success are slim, and there will be a high turnover, in some cases so high that the operation cannot be maintained at a profit.

There are almost as many training plans as there are companies operating in the field. Some companies start potential salesmen in the warehouse to learn the line and become familiar with the types and quantities of merchandise being sold. Unless there is a definite timetable and a schedule of promotions, many potentially good salesmen, often the very best prospects, will become discouraged waiting for a territory and resign rather than remain indefinitely in a warehouse. This is perhaps the greatest objection to the inside training plan. Too often men are held in low-paying inside jobs too long; the best men leave before they have an opportunity for a try out as driver salesmen.

If a company has sufficient openings for salesmen occurring regularly and can promote men to sales jobs as fast as they actually familiarize themselves with the line, the warehouse plan seems to work reasonably well. But where men are put to work in warehouse, order-filling, or similar jobs, there to await a sales opening at some vague or distant date, the idea is almost hopeless. Men will not endure long training periods today, as they once did, unless the training job is a good job in itself.

It must be remembered that putting a man to work in a warehouse or similar job, with the promise that he will have a sales job as soon as a vacancy occurs, always seems, to the potential salesman, a means of getting a warehouse man cheaper than would otherwise be possible.

Delivery trucks make good mobile advertisements for many products. This truck carries three posters on each side for Arnold Bakeries, Inc.

Plan for Inside Training

Just putting a man to work filling orders, loading trucks, or putting away merchandise is not enough. There should be a regular training schedule. If the line is large, the salesman's first study should be the price book. He should learn every price, for every quantity, variety, and "deal," if deals are included in the company's selling plan. He should take an examination to prove his complete familiarity with all prices, terms, quantities, pack prizes, etc.

With the price book out of the way, move on to other subjects, such as company history, policy, selling methods, markets, types of customers sold. Once more an examination should be given to obtain a clue to the prospective salesman's ability to learn.

From this point the instruction should include the rudiments and principles of salesmanship. Give the young salesman one or two good books on selling for study. Set a time limit on completion of each book and give an examination at the end of the time set. Give a heavy penalty for failure to complete each section of the study course on schedule.

Training in Salesmanship

It must be admitted that some potentially excellent salesmen will not be studious. What they learn from books is limited. To overcome this tendency to dodge study of books on selling, many companies find it necessary to conduct classes in salesmanship with visual training aids.

Much time is often wasted on salesmanship classes. Too much time is taken up on the theories of salesmanship and many academic phases of the subject. What the new salesman needs to know, after he has learned the line is: How to introduce himself to the customer, what to say, what to show him, how to close.

In sell and deliver merchandising only the simplest forms of salesmanship need be used. It has been found time and again that the best way to teach salesmanship to green men is to tell them what others are doing. Case histories, therefore, are the quickest, perhaps the easiest, and certainly the most painless method of giving a new salesman some idea of what his job is all about.

If there is an executive who has been in actual sales work recently enough to understand current conditions, let him describe several sales at each meeting. Encourage him to tell just what he did, what he said, what he showed the customer, any suggestions he made, and how he closed the order.

Then call in salesmen who are on the job and have them discuss recent sales, telling in minute detail what occurred at each sale. If the salesman does not volunteer information, bring it out with questions. What sort of store was it? What was the buyer's attitude? What were his objections, if any?

There should be a session or two on company policy; another on reports, designed to sell the salesman on the importance and need for proper reports; a session on care, upkeep, driving, and safety measures for the truck or car used in the salesman's work.

It is a mistake to assume that because a man has been driving a truck or a car for a long time he knows the simple safety measures and the simplest facts about upkeep. Be sure that the salesman knows all the road rules, driving laws, parking and other regulations for the territory he covers. Make it clear that speeding, failure to stop, parking, and other fines will not be tolerated.

There should be one or two classes on outlets, planned to show the salesman how to find the out-of-the-way customers, how to work a town thoroughly, what unusual outlets may be worthwhile. Until a salesman has had long experience, or has been properly instructed, the tendency will be to visit only about 60% of the potential outlets for the line. In these classes on outlets the salesman should be given a checklist to use in his work. This checklist should show every conceivable type of outlet, so that the salesman can refer to it before he marks off a town or a community as completely worked.

Handbook or Sales Manual Preparation

Companies which have made the greatest success in this field furnish all salesmen with a complete manual containing all the instructions needed by salesmen. This handbook should be in a form that is easy to carry, and indexed for ready reference. Many companies find that a book which will fit the glove compartment of an automobile, or which can be carried easily, is best.

The most common form is a loose-leaf binder to which new sheets may be added and old sheets removed easily. Basic data in the handbook includes, in most cases, complete product information on every item in the line. Reproductions of all forms used in the salesman's work, with instructions for completing the forms, mailing dates, purpose of the information, etc., are also a basic part of the manual.

Every possible contingency which the salesman may meet should be covered. The manual should include a section on what to do in case of an automobile accident, reports to be made, witnesses' addresses obtained, and so forth.

Sales Bulletins and Letters

Sell and deliver salesmen need a constant flow of news, ideas, suggestions, and inspirational messages. Like all other salesmen they become discouraged, lose faith in themselves and the line they are selling. They want to know what other salesmen are doing, how their sales stack up with other men, and what progress is being made in the company generally.

Sell and deliver salesmen are not students. Messages to them must be simple, brief, and easy to understand. A minimum of reading matter, with plenty of charts, illustrations, pictures of the men at work, plus figures showing results of various men's work, constitute the best material for bulletins.

Stand-by of all bulletins to salesmen is the tabulation of weekly or monthly standings of the men. This tabular record can be presented in more than one way. For example: One tabulation showing the standing of the men can be supplemented by another showing men according to size of orders, number of sales, the standing of men according to size of orders, number of new accounts opened, or standing of salesmen in relation to cost of selling.

There is an endless variety of methods for getting across the message the company wants to impress upon the men. Sales in relation to miles traveled; sales in relation to population of territories; sales in relation to number of outlets.

If the operation is large enough there should be one man assigned to travel with salesmen, study their work, report on methods and results, and prepare bulletin material which will be a vital help to the men in the field. Do not expect sell and deliver salesmen to read long dissertations on salesmanship, on business conditions, or anything very general. Every item sent to them in a house magazine or in bulletin or letter form should be closely related to their daily work. Unless it is, the men simply will not read it.

Selling and delivering from a truck is hard work. It requires a man of excellent physical stamina; he must make every minute count. Of necessity, his paper work, his reading, and all other activities, except actual selling, must be kept to a bare minimum. Unless this is done he will lose valuable time on paper work and reading which ought to be devoted to selling.

Stale Merchandise Problem

One of the secrets of the fabulously successful Hershey chocolate operation was that Hershey learned, many, many years ago, never to overstock a merchant to the point where he had stale candy on hand. This is one of the prime advantages of the entire sell and deliver development. Merchandise can be kept fresh and salable. Nothing hurts a product more than staleness; once a consumer buys a product which has gone stale on the shelves, he is likely to stop buying that product.

Salesmen for many of the most successful sell and deliver companies are instructed to watch for and take up all stale, shopworn, soiled, frayed, or damaged merchandise. Simplest plan for this is to replace stale merchandise with new merchandise. This requires no bookkeeping for the merchant and means only a simple exchange at the warehouse or supply depot when the salesman turns in damaged merchandise.

Some record system must be set up to keep track of the amount of stale merchandise turned in by each salesman. Obviously, if too much stale merchandise comes back, the salesman is not doing the right sort of job in selling, displaying, or placing it.

Shall Salesmen Own Trucks?

Many of the larger companies find it best to buy trucks; smaller companies often require each salesman to buy his own truck, then compensate him for its use on a basis that will insure his being able to buy a new one when the time arrives.

Here are some of the advantages of company-owned trucks: (1) Better prices and larger discounts may be obtained. (2) Company has complete control of truck, and all complications incident to changes in personnel are eliminated. (3) Recruiting salesmen is simplified when the company owns the truck. (4) Standard operating, servicing, and storage methods can be used.

The disadvantages are obvious. There is a heavy investment necessary; the men do not care for company-owned property as well as if it is their own. Operating costs are frequently higher when company owns trucks.

The advantages of salesman-owned trucks are: (1) Capital is released for other purposes. (2) Salesmen who can buy own trucks are likely to be more stable and reliable than other salesmen. (3) Operating costs may be lower; repairs and replacements are less frequent.

It is important that a truck delivering merchandise be kept spic and span, in good condition, and that it have some advertising value. Where men own trucks this may be neglected unless there is a standard upkeep and maintenance requirement, rigid inspections, and minute supervision.

When a salesman has purchased his own truck, then fails to produce enough business to warrant keeping him on the payroll, it is sometimes difficult to release the man. Arrangements must usually be made to buy his truck, or to repaint it to remove all company lettering in case he intends to keep it and engage in other work. There are other complications in dealing with salesmen where they own the trucks which may more than balance the disadvantages of having a large investment in transportation equipment.

Recruiting Driver Salesmen

One sales manager reports excellent success in finding good driver salesmen in and around service stations. Many oil companies train young men carefully and teach them how to service customers. When such young men are ready for a bigger job, it may not always be available; hence this sales manager keeps a close watch every time he has his car serviced. He has trained all supervisors and all his assistants to watch for such men. Some of his best producers were formerly attendants in gasoline stations.

Advertising in classified sections of metropolitan newspapers is another method for obtaining men. When this is relied upon there should be some method of screening undesirable men quickly, because applicants may come in such quantities that an exorbitant amount of time is required to interview them. One company gives each applicant a tough application blank to fill out before any interview is granted. In this blank there is a question which eliminates the fly-by-nights quickly.

Retail stores are another good field for recruiting salesmen. Ever since there have been traveling salesmen it has been natural for store salesmen to step into road jobs. It is reported that a high percentage of all truck salesmen came from retail selling jobs.

It must be remembered that selling and delivering merchandise from a truck is basically a young man's job. He must be physically active, alert, energetic. It is no job for a drone. In recruiting men some sales managers find that the small towns, even villages, often offer good prospects. Here there are young men who have not quite found themselves. They may have tried several part-time jobs, or seasonal jobs. Often small-town merchants and businessmen can come up with the names of two or three possible candidates.

Variations of Sell and Deliver Merchandising

In considering a possible entry into this field many careful calculations must be made. The very nature of the transactions means that the unit of sale must be relatively small. It must be small enough so that the purchase becomes a routine matter, and not one which requires careful and lengthy consideration. If the sell and deliver salesman spends more than 5 to 10 minutes at a stop, his volume cannot be maintained. And it is obvious that a sale which can be completed in that many minutes must be a relatively minor transaction in the eyes of the buyer.

The fact that the transaction must be relatively minor means that the product must have good repeat value. Unless a high percentage of stops yield business at every visit, the method of selling and delivering at one stop will bog down under the weight of expense. Therefore the items sold in this manner must be well established and command steady, year-round sales.

While the field has grown and expanded and will probably continue to grow, there are many definite limitations to the type of merchandise which can be sold and delivered and collected for at one stop. Merchandise which sells steadily, supplies which are used steadily, or repair parts which are in constant demand seem to be about the limit of the field.

Chapter 31

EXCLUSIVE DISTRIBUTORS AND
THEIR PROBLEMS

ALTHOUGH the decision of the United States Supreme Court in the Standard Oil Company (California) case restricted the granting of exclusive dealerships, a growing number of manufacturers look with favor upon this method of distribution. Not the least of the advantages of selling through exclusive dealers (when the practice does not monopolize a market) is that such an arrangement assures the manufacturer of a larger degree of promotional cooperation. Since an exclusive distributor or dealer reaps full benefits from any creative sales effort in the territory covered by his franchise, he is more inclined to share the cost of introducing a product and in maintaining a satisfactory volume of sales for it. There are two very good reasons for this: First, the profit that accrues to the dealer; and second, the fear of losing his franchise.

Where there are several competing dealers in a territory all handling the same product or line of products, it is only natural they are hesitant to spend their own money to build up demand for a manufacturer's brand. They imagine, sometimes with good reason, that by so doing they are helping their competitors as much as, or even more than, they are helping themselves. Consequently they are indifferent to home office promotions. This tends to force a manufacturer operating through selected dealers, but not exclusive dealers, to assume most of the expense of promoting sales within these territories. In some instances, where the product has good national coverage, that job can be done without excessive cost through national advertising. If the advertising is adequate to give fairly good penetration within a dealer's trading area, he will usually cooperate to some extent. He feels it is to his advantage to identify himself with the manufacturer's quality reputation. Most dealers want to be regarded as headquarters for favorably known nationally advertised brands. But the cooperation they give the manufacturer is usually limited to merchandising displays, radio and newspaper advertising over their own name, or occasionally to direct mailings to customer lists. Under the circumstances it is difficult, if not impossible, to make "packaged" promotions pay unless some measure of control rests with the manufacturer.

Since the Standard Oil decision some manufacturers have backed away from any agreement with either distributors or dealers which might be construed as being in restraint of trade. However, the matter can be handled without any written agreement, if there is that danger, by establishing a firm company policy. Under such a policy the company might refuse to service any dealer or distributor who enjoys exclusive sale of its products, if the dealer withholds advertising cooperation, fails to conduct his business along constructive lines, or engages in any sales activity which might be harmful to the interests of the manufacturer. While the Standard Oil decision strengthens the position of dealers who insist upon their right to handle competitive products, and therefore makes the job of the manufacturer somewhat more difficult, selling through one dealer in a territory does offer many advantages in marketing products, the sale of which requires considerable promotional effort.

In the final analysis, however, the success of a distribution plan built around one dealer in a territory depends upon the value which the dealer or distributor attaches to his franchise. And the value of the franchise depends upon the sales promotional support the manufacturer puts back of it. Coca-Cola bottling franchises, for example, are valued highly and bring fancy prices, because of the extensive advertising constantly being done for that beverage by the syrup manufacturer. On the other hand, exclusive franchises are valued lightly by dealers, when the product is not identified to the consumer or where it is not supported by national or, at least, regional sales promotion.

Types of Exclusive Dealers

Exclusive dealerships are most common in the distribution of products which require creative selling. Included in that classification are automobiles, office appliances, household equipment, clothing, building materials, machinery, and mill supplies, etc. When there is considerable service required after the product has been sold, for example, in the case of an oil burner, it is not unusual for the manufacturer to localize his national advertising. Instead of spending most of the promotional appropriation in magazines and national radio broadcasts, it is customary to use newspapers in cities where there are well-established, aggressive dealers. These ads are run over the dealer's name. Sometimes the manufacturer pays the entire cost of this advertising, taking advantage, however, of the dealer's lower local rate, and sometimes the cost is divided—usually on a 50-50 basis. Rarely does the dealer pay the entire cost of such advertising. In most cases the lay-out, copy, and cuts are provided by the manufacturer.

RCA used a series of prize trips as incentives for increased distributor and dealer sales of home entertainment and industrial tubes. A post card illustration of the "wish you were here" theme whetted dealer appetites for the program.

When there is only one dealer or distributor in a trading area, the manufacturer can make special arrangements with his dealer or agent based upon sales and the extent of sales promotional cooperation the dealer agrees to give the manufacturer. Provided the arrangement with the dealer does not create a monopoly or restrain trade, such contracts are not contrary to the antitrust laws. Since the exclusive dealer has no competition within the area he serves, there can be no discrimination.

Patented products are usually distributed through sales agents who operate independently, yet work closely with the manufacturer. A typical set-up of this type is the National Cash Register Company. Its representatives operate their own businesses, employ their own salesmen, determine their own sales promotional policies, but their decisions are influenced by over-all company policy. It is important for agents to have the good will of the manufacturing company since they look to the manufacturer for financial assistance if the going gets tough. During a severe slump in business, for example, it is not uncommon for practically every sales agent to be in debt to the company. Naturally the home office insists upon the agent following any promotional plans it might develop.

In selling merchandise bought on impulse, exclusive agencies are less common. Some of the larger department stores, such as Marshall Field & Co., are more inclined to take on a line if they are assured of exclusive sales rights in the locality and will even go so far as to allocate advertising space to promote the sale of the product. As a rule, however, such advertising is paid for by the manufacturer. Hart Schaffner & Marx, Chicago clothing manufacturer, finds it desirable to distribute through exclusive dealers, and the prestige attached to that line of clothing gives the manufacturer considerable leverage in both opening and holding dealers. This same prestige, which is the result of long years of consistent national advertising, helps the manufacturer in securing a full measure of advertising cooperation from dealers. They usually maintain reliable mailing lists which they circularize with style announcements furnished by the manufacturer, spend considerable of their own money for local tie-in advertising and outdoor bulletins. Dealers are proud to identify their stores with Hart Schaffner & Marx clothes.

In the industrial field exclusive agents or distributors are the most widely used method of distributing the product. Usually they carry no stock of the product. In some cases manufacturer's representatives do maintain a small inventory. When large inventories are required, the agency is usually given to a mill supply house, which contacts the buyers and services them as well. Mill supply houses, because of the large number of items they sell, are not inclined to spend very much to promote a product, even though they may have exclusive sales rights in the territory for it. Some of the large houses get out catalogs, in which case they give more space to products they handle exclusively than they do to products they sell in competition with other local dealers. However, there is a growing tendency on the part of catalog dealers to charge the manufacturer for advertising space. Most manufacturers consider such advertising a good buy.

Still another type of exclusive dealer is the farm agent of which there are an increasing number. They carry no stock. Neither do they do much advertising. What they do is generally limited to "sniping"—highway signs tacked to barns and fences in the neighborhood. Some of the more progressive agents advertise regularly in local newspapers, but such advertising is not very effective even when a manufacturer's mat service is used.

Regardless of what type of exclusive dealer is used, the burden of creating demand for his products is largely upon the manufacturer. While the plan assures a larger degree of promotional cooperation than is the case where the product is sold by several dealers in a territory, it is seldom adequate to build the desired volume of territorial business. To suppose that because you go through dealers who have a vested interest in your product guarantees adequate promotional effort, without supporting national advertising and packaged sales promotions, is one of the greatest mistakes a manufacturer can make.

"Signing Up" Exclusive Dealers

It is the understandable aim of every company selling through one dealer in a territory to have the "best" dealer handle its products. For that reason prospective dealers are carefully checked, qualified, and rated. Unfortunately, however, the "best" dealer is very often committed to handling a competitive line on an exclusive basis, and is not in a position to take on another line. This is especially true where the dealer has a rather large inventory of a competitor's product on the shelf. It is no longer legal to buy up competing merchandise as used to be the practice. But if the sales promotional program is sufficiently powerful, it is possible to get a dealer to agree to making the switch at some future time, and replace the competitor's merchandise with yours, gradually. It takes something more than a good product and run-of-the-mill promotional help to get any dealer who has become identified with a well-advertised line to change over to another.

There are, in nearly every territory, up-and-coming dealers, who might not be rated quite as well as the one considered "best" but who are more aggressive and, in the long run, better distributors. The well-entrenched, highly rated dealer has usually reached an age where he is more interested in holding trade than in going out after new trade. But younger men are more promotion-minded, and more awake to the benefits which accrue to those who cooperate with their source of supply. Dealers of this type attach more importance to handling fast-turning lines, and will take on a line even if the margin of profit is not what they think it should be, for prestige

EXCLUSIVE DISTRIBUTORS AND THEIR PROBLEMS

reasons. It takes some effort to locate these dealers, but a company which is fortunate enough to have a number of such outlets is in an excellent position to carry nation-wide promotions through to success.

The Presentation Portfolio

Signing up dealers to distribute a product, or a line of products, on an exclusive basis requires a high order of salesmanship. Not only must the dealer be "sold" on taking on the line, but he must be enthusiastic about its possibilities. If that is not done, it is unlikely the dealer will put much promotional effort back of it. As a result the line will move slowly and the dealer may decide he made a mistake. Turnover in dealers is just as costly as turnover in salesmen, and should be held down by doing a thoroughgoing selling job in the beginning.

Salesmen responsible for opening new accounts require a special presentation which emphasizes opportunity—not just an opportunity to make money (important though that may be), but an opportunity to better serve the people in the community, and to build prestige for the store. The most effective presentations are those which tell what other dealers have done with the line, how they have done it, and what the line means in terms of customer satisfaction as well as store profits. If the line offers traffic building possibilities, that fact should be played up. The repeat qualities—representing satisfied customers—need heavy underscoring, especially if competitive products have not been giving as much customer satisfaction as the dealer has a right to expect. There is always a good chance that, for one reason or another, a dealer may be getting complaints about a competitor's product and has secretly resolved to switch to another line at the first opportunity.

Portfolios intended to help a salesman open up exclusive accounts, especially those which involve a considerable purchase of merchandise at the outset, should be impressive in size, and loaded down with FACTS. The facts should be dramatized but not overdramatized. The first page of the portfolio should be slotted to hold a typewritten survey of potential sales in the dealer's own territory, based upon data prepared by the home office sales research department. The letters can be quickly changed to fit different communities or markets the salesman may be working, and they have the highly desirable purpose of making it easy for the salesman to come to the profit part of his sales talk at the beginning rather than the end. The first job to be done is to make the dealer dissatisfied with the share of business he is currently getting; then tell him about your line, the advertising and promotional support given it, and how that support, plus a fast repeating product, adds up to leadership. The stage should be set in the presentation for promoting the product, for merchants today want to know how to sell the product, as well as being told what they *can* sell.

A Sales Manager for the Month

The results a dealer gets from a line he sells exclusively depend on many things, some of which have nothing to do with the product or the way the manufacturer promotes it. The *kind* of sales effort the dealer puts back of the line is equally important, and the place to awaken him to the need of unusual effort is at the time he is first sold. It is desirable that when the dealer takes on the line an aggressive effort will be made to introduce it to the store's customers. Yet not many stores today are doing an aggressive sales job. Dealers are inclined to think of themselves as "distributors" rather than "sales managers." To bring about a change in viewpoint, and at the same time pave the way for an influx of new energy and talent, one manufacturer embarked upon a program (following that pioneered by the Gamble-Skogmo stores) of getting dealers to appoint a lively clerk or assistant to act as store sales manager for the month. He is in charge of all promotions, as well as establishing his own sales and expense budget for the month. Measures of his success are the store's expenses and sales volume. Naturally he will want to take advantage of every opportunity to get a good sales increase. This particular manufacturer, who sold children's wear, suggested that one way these sales managers for the month could pick up extra volume was to push his line of children's wear. Too much emphasis in retailing today is on buying, when it should be on selling. In the case of a nationally advertised line, which a dealer is committed to carry and push, buying is relatively unimportant.

The old saying that "goods well bought are half sold" is only partly true today. It takes a lot of promotion know-how to succeed in business under present competitive conditions.

Westinghouse Contest for Dealers' Personnel

Educating the exclusive dealer in the sales points of new products as well as getting them to do a good merchandising job is another problem. When Westinghouse introduced a new heat and sun lamp, it was quite successful in getting acceptance for the product, both at the distributor and dealer levels, by putting on three simple prize contests. One contest was an essay competition for dealers' salespeople where prizes were awarded for the best answers to 14 pertinent questions. The contest was conducted by their distributor, in cooperation with the Lamp Division of the Westinghouse Electric Corporation. Informative booklets giving the salesmen all the details needed to enter the contest were supplied. The prize offer made sure that as many new dealers and their salespeople read it as possible. An effort was also made to get the salespeople to practice on the lamp in the store before attempting to answer the questions. The prize money awarded amounted to $1,000. There were also prizes for the best window and store displays for the new product.

An interesting angle to this Westinghouse contest was the inexpensive way it was promoted. Instead of flamboyant broadsides announcing the contest to the distributors and dealers, all the required information was produced in a sheaf of mimeographed sheets, each sheet different in color, and sized so that when assembled they looked like a ladder. The heading read, "What to Do and Who's to Do It in the Big $1,000,000 Sell Select-O-Ray Drive." The titles on seven sheets in the brief, each of which showed on the front, were:

1. What Headquarters Does.

2. What Wemco District Agency Sales Division Does.

3. What Wemco District Sales Promotion Division Does.

4. What Distributor Appliance Sales Manager Does.

5. What Distributor Promotion Manager Does.

6. What Distributor Salesman Does.

7. What You Should Consider.

The instructions to each factor in the drive were to the point and brief. Here, for example, is the work assignment to the Westinghouse District Sales Promotion Division, the key unit in the drive:

1. INSTRUCT DISTRIBUTOR SALESMAN

Hold meetings ... demonstrate sales features of SELECT-O-RAY ... how it's used ... who are prospects ... all pointing toward getting distributor salesmen to do the same with dealer salesmen. Make sure your entire sales staff knows the full details of the program—that during the weeks of January 27 and February 3 they get all dealers to tie-in with Malone radio promotion and Westinghouse newspaper advertising by displaying SELECT-O-RAYS and conducting local newspaper and radio advertising.

2. GET PROMPT DELIVERIES TO DEALERS

This is vitally important ... a 2-week drive to get dealers can't succeed unless deliveries are *fast*. You have the stocks. Can you get them delivered in 24 hours?

3. Report Progress in Getting Dealer Coverage

This is a *must* if you are to get for your dealers their full share of advertising support. Send reports to Wemco District Agency Sales Managers. *In addition*, Wemco Appliance Managers should send reports to J. T. Urban, New York.

Motivating Exclusive Dealers

Since the principal advantage of distributing through exclusive dealers is the greater interest they take in working closely with the manufacturer, so far as sales promotional programs are concerned, it is important that no stone be left unturned to make such promotions profitable to them. Exclusive dealers, like all dealers, need continuing motivation. They soon fall into the habit of waiting for things to happen, instead of making them happen. An editor of a trade magazine made a check of several small towns to determine which types of retailers were most aggressive and most prosperous as a result of using modern promotional techniques. The only businesses which seemed up to date were the several automobile dealers; the Frigidaire, Westinghouse, and GE dealers; the International Harvester dealer; and the better filling stations. In every case the prosperous dealers were the ones who followed the advice and instruction of big business. He took occasion to make a special check of the Frigidaire and Maytag dealer in one town, who seemed fabulously successful, considering his limited market. Here's what a banker told him: "This fellow is smart. Whenever the factory has a district meeting he is there. He comes home and does exactly what they recommend. The result is that he sells almost as many appliances as all the other dealers in town combined."

Bankers can do a lot to help retailers, especially those operating under an exclusive dealer franchise, to be better promoters. When a weak dealer comes to borrow money, the banker should insist that the dealer follow the merchandising policies laid down by the big companies whose sales franchise he holds. Business has not always done a good job of selling dealers on the true value of the franchises they hold.

Ralston Purina is a good example of a company which works closely with its dealers. In one small community there had been three successive failures in feed stores. Then Ralston Purina moved in and obtained a dealer willing to follow Ralston Purina's tested methods. In a couple of years that dealer was prospering despite dire predictions to the contrary. Today there are three prosperous feed stores in the community, and while Ralston leads them all, it was Ralston's merchandising help to the pioneer dealer which made the other two stores possible. Bankers know that such a franchise is good collateral for loans, because they have seen with their own eyes that a carload of Ralston Purina products loses no time in moving into consumption.

Sometimes it is necessary to give dealers a definite quota of sales they are expected to make in order to hold their franchise. This works very well when the franchise is considered of great value, or where the dealer knows his competitor would take on the franchise in a minute if he should lose it. However, more often than not, dealers are beseiged by manufacturers to take on their line, and they are not concerned over the possibility of losing one that is not too profitable. For that reason most companies selling through exclusive dealers are inclined to concentrate on making the franchise so valuable that no good dealer can afford to lose it. This calls for a fast-moving program of sales promotion, backed by local advertising, featuring the dealer as the territorial distributor.

The Dealer's Viewpoint

Finkbeiner's, a radio and TV retailer in Absecon, New Jersey, gave up his franchise and severed relations with his distributor because of serious dissatisfaction with the manufacturer's and distributor's sales and service policies. Deliveries were slow, parts were not always available, appeals for service information went unheeded, so Finkbeiner signed up with another company.

The dealer is on the firing line; he confronts the public. Unless he has the full support of his distributor, he cannot successfully build up his business and maintain it at profitable levels.

Some manufacturers appreciate this and try to guide and support their distributors accordingly; others give little consideration to distributor-dealer relationships and the fact that dealers are the backbone of their business. Dealers depend on their distributors.

Chapter 32

PROMOTING SALES THROUGH
SPECIALTY STORES

SPECIALTY STORES thrive, despite the rapid growth of chain and department stores, for several reasons. Specializing in one type of product, or one line, they offer their customers better product knowledge and a greater variety of sizes, colors, or other product variations, than is available from stores with departmental space limitations. To many shoppers they offer greater convenience by reducing department store weariness. Too, they usually find that sales personnel in specialty stores are friendlier and more agreeable than in chain or department stores. In fact, many are owner-operated and this also makes a difference in building customer satisfaction and good will.

In the same way there are thousands of independent druggists who have built up prosperous businesses in the very shadow of a big chain store, on personality and superior service. People like to do business with the man who owns the store. They feel their business is important to him, and his desire to please is usually reflected in the way he treats customers. The human equation is just as important in retailing as in any other type of selling.

The great handicap which the average specialty store has in competing with mass distributors is not price, as so many suppose, *but getting people into the store.* Americans like low prices as well as anyone, but a high percentage of shoppers are glad to pay a little more for better service than they might get from a mass distributor who operates on the principle that goods well displayed sell themselves. A man planning to decorate his home might conceivably go to a chain store and buy the paint and supplies he needs for less than he would have to pay at his neighborhood paint store. But stores specializing in paints are usually owned by a practical painter, and his advice and suggestions on painting are invaluable to an amateur home decorator. People who have a home painting job to do often buy the paint and brushes they need when they happen to be in a chain store for some other reason; whereas the only reason they would go to the paint store, and expose themselves to the owner's personality and desire to help, would be to buy paint, or a brush, or other supplies. So the problem of the painter who operates a paint store, like all retailers specializing in a particular type of merchandise, is building store traffic—getting people in town or in the neighborhood to think *first* of his store when they are in the market for the things he sells. That can best be done by promoting service and values, rather than price, in which area the mass distributor has the edge by virtue of larger buying power.

Importance of Store Services

Some independents fail to successfully compete with price-cutting competitors, because they themselves overrate the importance of price and underrate the importance of customer service—which includes being able to offer a larger selection of quality products, adequate stocks, better merchandising methods, ability to help the customer buy to better advantage, and so on.

The whole history of merchandising in this country proves that people are willing to pay for service. Europeans think it important to buy merchandise a few cents cheaper, as evidenced by the growth over there of consumer co-ops. But here in America one needs only to look at the dairy business to see the difference. In nearly every city milk depots, where milk may be bought at less than delivered prices, eke out a bare existence, while dairies which deliver the milk to your doorstep every morning (for a charge) thrive. And it is not unusual in the dairy business to see newcomers, who are able to offer a better grade of milk and dairy products at the same price, outdistance established competitors simply because, being new and eager to build up a business, they offer and give better service.

So in planning a promotional activity to help specialty stores increase their sales of a line of quality products, the manufacturer has a distinct advantage. Every merchant who has cut his eyeteeth in retailing knows that the least desirable of all trade (for a specialty store) is the shopper who is here today and across the street tomorrow, where he can buy for a few cents less. On the other hand, the most desirable of all customers are those who buy values rather than price, and who when they find a source of supply that offers good values and store service, become boosters and lifelong customers. It is therefore good sales strategy, in helping dealers who operate specialty stores, to aim the promotion at those people. True, there may be fewer of them, and getting them into the store is not always easy, but it pays off in the long run for both the manufacturer and the dealer.

It is for these reasons that the most successful promotions in the independent retailing field *first* aim to build store traffic among people who are willing to pay a little more for better service; and *second,* make it easier for the customer to buy wisely after he is in the store. This last point is especially important to manufacturers of quality products, since it has to do with helping the merchant or dealer do a more effective job *at the point of purchase.* This is recognized as the weak point in the distribution process.

PLANS FOR INCREASING STORE TRAFFIC

While the importance of display as a source of retail sales may be overrated, the claim has been made that one-third of the average store's sales are made by suggestion. That is to say, for every $2 spent in the store by people who come in to buy a specific thing, they spend an extra dollar while in the store for something they see advertised on the wall, displayed on the counter, or suggested to them by the salesperson. We know, for example, that druggists, stationers, and others consider the newsstand in their stores of great value, not because they make a lot of money selling a man a newspaper or a magazine, but because it brings people into the store. A man who comes in to buy the evening paper may, and often does, end up buying a box of cigars, a quart of ice cream, a box of candies, a tube of shaving cream, or a flock of coat hangers if they happen to be on display at the time. He may even buy some drugs.

In the same way big city stores spend considerable money to let the local garden club hold its floral arrangement contest in the store, even furnishing table linen and table silver for the contestants at no charge, not because the store expects to sell a lot of flowers, but because it brings a desirable class of potential buyers into the store, where they are exposed to displays of furniture, draperies, gifts, and clothing. Such exposure usually results in purchases.

More and more specialty, as well as department, stores are building meeting rooms over the store, or adjacent to the store, where civic and church groups can meet without cost or obligation. This device for increasing store traffic seems destined to grow in popularity. Some manufacturers, including at least one maker of

A somewhat difficult presentation problem was efficiently solved for Starr-Hollywood Ltd., by a display which shows off the clothing in a neat, orderly way and allows ample space for copy.

photographic goods, provide dealers with the promotional materials needed to organize and conduct local camera clubs whose meetings are held in the store's "Hobby Room." The "pay-off" comes in offering a ticket for the lectures in the club rooms with every $15 purchase of supplies in the store. Local camera enthusiasts give the lectures with the help of outline talks prepared by the manufacturer. Other promotional ideas used by Arel, Inc., to assist dealers, according to an officer of the company, are:

The tried and true demonstrator method has consistently proved effective. We have arranged, therefore, demonstrators of oil colors in various stores, coloring snapshots and photographs. Backed by a little advertising, in some instances stores have done, with this demonstrator, more business with these colors in 1 week than they previously did in a year. In smaller cities, it has proved effective to have the colorist use the customers' own pictures as samples. The personal touch is most effective.

In the sale of motor-driven toy movie projectors, retailing from $15 to $50, we have found it most effective to rig up the projector with a continuous belt so that movies are being shown constantly. Despite the fact that most of the customers are adults, cartoons nevertheless draw the largest crowd. Where possible, we like to include some color pictures in the continuous demonstration. The double use of color and motion almost always works, as is generally known.

Many camera stores use a spiff. In experimenting we discovered that it is foolish to offer one to the clerks on basic merchandise as that will be sold anyhow. It is the accessory items, like auxiliary lenses, which show tremendous increases when backed by a clerk's PM.

Several dealers have found it profitable to keep a book in the back of the store in which they list all new items received daily. Customers have learned to walk back and look at the last day's entries and also flip back the previous pages to see what new items might interest them. Some dealers have used a bulletin board merely listing the very current new items, but the book has proved more effective as the customers are able to go back for a considerable period. It is recommended that the book or bulletin board be placed in the back of the store to get the customers inside.

It has also proved effective to have a bulletin board featuring new items for the salespeople in the store.

It has proved effective to include folders on accessories in the original box of new items. When a camera is sold, for example, if the clerk forgets to mention extra lenses or filters, the consumer finds illustrated folders on both of these units with his camera instruction sheets. In the case of filters, it has proved very effective to have circulars enclosed with each package of finishing, calling the value of filters to the consumer's attention so that they will ask clerks about them.

Where possible, we recommend that each dealer keep an inventory list of every good customer's equipment. This list can be used for numerous personalized promotions and selling. It has proved extremely effective to send a letter early in the fall to the family and close friends of top customers suggesting a photographic item as a Christmas gift and listing various items in different price ranges that the dealer knows were things the individual did want. This is followed up by two other letters before Christmas, and the percentage of sales against same is astonishing.

Helping Dealers to Meet Competition

Parker Pen Company has spent as much as $25,000 to make a survey, the primary purpose of which was to help dealers to demonstrate the acceptance its pens had with folks in the store locality. On one occasion, for example, an independent research organization was retained to make a nationwide survey of pen preferences.

Advertising space was used in a national magazine for the purpose. A gift was offered to readers who filled out and mailed the question-coupon in the ad and 71,236 replies were received. To everyone who filled in the questionnaire a leatherette address book was mailed, although the recipients could not tell from the ad whether they were going to receive a washing machine or a bobby pin. The questionnaire was worded as follows:

1. What make (or brand) of fountain pen do you own? ....

2. Did you buy it, or was it a gift? ....

3. If you were to buy a fountain pen, which make would you choose? ....

4. What brand of writing ink do you now use? ....

5. What brand of ink will you buy next? ....

6. What make (or brand) of watch do you own? ....

7. Did you buy it or was it a gift? ....

8. What make (or brand) of watch would you choose:

   For yourself? ....

   Gift for man? ....

   Gift for a woman? ....

9. Check if you plan to buy in the next 6 months:

   For yourself? ☐   Gift, man? ☐   Gift, woman? ☐

NAME ....

(Please print)

STREET ....

CITY ....

COUNTY ....

STATE ....

Since there are, or were, 109 different brands of fountain pens on the market, the company took a chance on how the final tabulation would look. But it showed 32.7% of the pen owners who returned the questionnaire owned Parker pens; 80.2% were satisfied with their Parker pens; 57.7% of those owning Parker pens received them as gifts; 42.6% of those replying stated and this was important to dealers, that the next pen they bought would be a Parker. This information, when tabulated, was charted and furnished to all dealers for use in convincing hesitant customers that they would make no mistake if they bought a Parker, either for themselves or as a gift.

Included in the material sent to its retailers by U.S. Shoe Corporation was a very unique promotional piece. Housed in a paper-and-metal cannister labelled "The Selby Story" was a curled-up paper streamer, twelve feet long by seven inches wide, designed like a video tape, with printed film-perforation margins. The message on one side of the streamer was "Selby Makes Fashion News Across the Country on Radio, TV, Newspapers". The reverse side showed "stills" of TV and radio personalities or fashion experts with captions quoting their comments on the air about Selby shoes.

Other illustrations featured newspaper interviews by fashion editors with Selby Vice President, Charles Mincer.

The unusual format of the unit, so adequately and appropriately designed to accommodate 24 illustrations in sequence in one continuous piece, attracted considerable dealer comment, reflecting the impact of the distinctive streamer.

Getting Merchants to Poll Customers

A simple merchandising idea, which seldom fails to build business for a store owner who must watch his advertising dollars closely, is to invite the folks in the trading area to help decide what merchandise the store should carry. This stunt gives suppliers a chance to have their products listed in the letter, and it usually encourages the store owner to stock the full line, whereas he might have carried only a few items. A typical letter of this type, used by the Sunshine Feed Store of Washington Court House, Ohio, but with only about half the products which were used shown, follows:

Dear Friend:

We need your help.

It is our earnest desire to serve you and your neighbors to the fullest extent and in the best possible way. To accomplish this, we want to stock those items of merchandise which you may be able to use.

We will appreciate it if you will check the items of merchandise you are interested in now or in the near future, which we may be able to procure for you. This in no way, however, obligates you to purchase these items from our store.

When you have indicated your desires, just put this letter in the attached envelope, which requires no postage, and send it back to us, or if you can bring this letter to our store we have a souvenir for you.

Pay us a visit! We will be glad to see you! We can help you, by you helping us.

Sincerely,

SUNSHINE FEED STORE

Check items you would like to see your Sunshine Store carry. Some of these items are already in stock.

If parents knew as much about children's feet as you do, they wouldn't be crippling them.

Most parents choose their kid's shoes for sentimental reasons—when they should be buying them for health reasons.

But how many parents know that one-fourth of a child's bones are in his feet?

And that those 26 delicate bones can be easily and painlessly maimed by a succession of poorly designed shoes?

(Like the kind that dominate the market today.)

Yet, with a little knowledge, they would appreciate the necessity of a properly designed shoe.

Like Jumping Jacks.

The main idea behind all our shoes is to avoid any possible restriction to the normal growth pattern of the foot structure.

For example, we've engineered a shoe called the Cuddler.

It features a unique one-piece moccasin construction that covers the bottom and wraps around the sides of the shoe.

This cradles the entire foot securely, without inhibiting normal development in any way.

While a one-piece tongue replaces the ordinary seam, to prevent abrasion of the instep.

Jumping Jacks also innovated the sole-up-the-back design.

This provides greater stability while the child is learning to walk, without distorting the development of normal walking habits.

It also eliminates the back seam, so there's no irritation to the heel.

And a special ribbed plug in the sole helps prevent skidding and slipping.

Finally, we use only the softest leathers. Without linings. So the shoe is lighter and more flexible.

While letting the foot breathe freely.

Now we're not suggesting that all this is new to you.

But we are hoping you'll mention some of these points to the parents who depend on you for guidance.

We think you'll be surprised to find out how much *they* don't know.

Jumping Jacks

Most feet are born perfect. They should stay that way.

For free child foot care brochure, and additional information, write: Jumping Jacks, Division of U.S. Shoe Corp., Cincinnati, Ohio 45207

as advertised in: THE JOURNAL OF PEDIATRICS

United States Shoe Corporation, Cincinnati, helps bring business to its retailers by advertising to pediatricians, as in this advertisement in the Journal of Pediatrics.

FARM AND HOME ITEMS

1. ---Washing Machines	21. ---Pump Jacks
2. ---Electric Irons	22. ---Pruning Shears
3. ---Electric Toasters	23. ---Air Compressors
4. ---Electric Hot Plates	24. ---Cedar Kennel Bedding
5. ---Wearever Aluminum	25. ---Garden Sprayers
6. ---Pressure Cookers	26. ---Insecticides, Spray and
7. ---Bicycles, Boys and Girls	Dust Mat.
8. ---Flashlights	27. ---Tractor Wheel Cleaners
9. ---Low Temperature Food	28. ---Fertilizers
Freezers	29. ---Electric Water Heaters
10. ---Paint, Paint Supplies	30. ---Electric Light Bulbs
11. ---Radios	31. ---Cement Mixers
12. ---Automobile Seat Covers	32. ---Water Softener
13. ---Lawn Mowers	33. ---Tractor Air Pumps
14. ---Power Mowers	34. ---Roofing
15. ---Wheelbarrows	35. ---Fencing and Fence Posts
16. ---Garden Hose, Rakes, Shovels	36. ---Staples
17. ---Electric Fence Controller	37. ---Rope
18. ---Cultivators, Hand	38. ---Rat Poison
19. ---Seeders	39. ---Warehouse and Home Scales
20. ---Garden Hose	40. ---Sump Pumps

Proctor Electric "Lady Be Seated" Promotion

A standard technique used to get buyers into dealers' stores is the advertising "deal." A manufacturer who suspects sales could be increased if dealers and their salespeople did a better job at the point of purchase soon finds that is only half the battle. Along with better store salesmanship and display is the great need of getting more interested prospects to sell. So the manufacturer says to the dealer: "If you will agree to purchase and display a certain quantity of our product, and coach your salespeople to sell it more effectively, I will run these six two-column ads in your local newspaper over your signature at no cost to you. All I want is your promise that if the ads pull and you sell what you have on the shelf, you will run these six advertisements in the newspaper at your expense, at the same time placing a reorder for what you think you can sell in the next few months based on your experience with the first six ads." To keep within the law, of course, this offer must be made to all dealers and be so phrased that it cannot be construed as a special discount to a few favored customers. Such local promotions should be supported by national advertising, and carefully tested before being widely offered to dealers.

This matter of pretesting promotions designed to increase store traffic is most important. Illustrating how important it is, the Proctor Electric Company, making electric irons of a type which permitted a woman to do her ironing sitting down, found after two tests it was not necessary to use large ads to get the people into the dealer's store. A test "Lady Be Seated" campaign in Oklahoma, using a series of consumer demonstrations and very little advertising, brought more people into local stores than 8 full-page ads and 208 spot announcements on 4 radio stations in San Diego. As a result of these experiments Proctor reached the following conclusions:

> Any retailer who is going to be successful must meet advertising half way. We found that dealers can increase business by perfectly astonishing percentages if they adhere to simple sales fundamentals and associate their stores with the manufacturer's promotions.
>
> To do this, the dealer must:
>
> 1. Install window displays which say the same things as our ads.
>
> 2. Repeat the message inside the store.
>
> 3. Require the retail salesperson to demonstrate *all* features of the product.
>
> 4. Ask for the order, and overcome any objections if the order isn't forthcoming.
>
> It was quite apparent that many salesmen employed by both wholesalers and dealers are comparatively inexperienced in competitive selling and need additional training to equip them for full-scale operations. Dealers vary greatly, but the majority are not yet promotion-minded.
>
> Too many dealers believe the weight of the factory's advertising should carry the ball. This may be due in some measure to the overemphasis by distributor salesmen on the magnitude of our newspaper and radio advertising and other promotional activities.
>
> Little effort was made to encourage tie-in advertising. Mats were delivered to every retailer participating in the activity, but only 14 dealers ran a total of 32 such ads.

Despite these disadvantages, the San Diego campaign resulted in a substantial increase in the sales of all makes of irons, of which 52% were Proctor models. The campaign proved that it is possible for the manufacturer to pull his product through the dealership to the ultimate consumer by concentrated factory-sponsored sales promotion.

The Oklahoma campaign involved store demonstrations by pre-trained members of the dealer's own staff. In this case, the main push was not a matter of consumer advertising but of careful preliminary planning and training of personnel. The campaign was so successful that a number of dealers said afterward they were concerned about their inventories of competitive makes of irons because their clerks were so sold on Proctor. Figures like 9 to 1, 9.5 to 1, and 4 out of 5 were reported from the dealerships as to sales of Proctor versus other makes. Proctor's sales manager commented:

> "When a way was found to take a Never-Lift iron, an ironing board, and a sprinkler direct to the dealer and his salespeople, teach them the technique of sit-down ironing, and then show the dealer how to promote that technique to create store traffic and sell irons, we had a sure-fire promotion.

"A checklist was carefully prepared by Proctor and presented to the distributor for approval and support. This checklist proved to be very important to the success of the program. It gave each distributor, executive, and salesman a written copy of what had to be done. It gave Proctor personnel a clear-cut idea of Proctor's responsibility. Most important, it gave the Proctor district manager a tool with which to check distributor personnel and see that correct progress was being made in setting up the program."

Headquarters personnel and a wide-awake distributor opened the campaign by enlisting the support of top personnel in local utility companies. The distributor hired a home economist and a schedule of dealer meetings was prepared. Distributor executives and salesmen, in a meeting scheduled 3 days before the dealer meetings began, were taught to do "sit-down" ironing. This served the double function of training them and of showing them how easily others could be trained.

Only after this careful training was the program broken to the public. Results were highly satisfactory. Proctor has benefited in these ways.

1. Extensive dealer advertising.
2. Demonstrations before thousands of women.
3. Dealers can now effectively demonstrate the Never-Lift.
4. The utilities are cooperative.
5. The distributor realizes the profit in a small appliance promotion.

The dealer has profited from:

1. Floor traffic.
2. Iron sales.
3. Building good will by performing a service to customers.

Knowing the Dealer's Problems

The most effective promotions in the specialty field are usually those which are closely geared to the bread-and-butter problems of the small dealer. Too often the promotion has little else to recommend it to a merchant except the "cooperation" label placed on it by an advertising man at the home office.

To most independent merchants cooperation has a hollow sound. It suggests the desire of a manufacturer, whose products usually offer too small a profit, to get dealers to spend their money to advertise the manufacturer's products. This suspicion is a holdover from the days when "dealer helps" usually consisted of free electros for the dealer to run in his local newspaper, or selling a dealer "at cost" a display case to place in his store "alongside the cash register."

Here are some simple things most advertisers need to do to enlist the aid of dealers:

1. Determine reasonable sales expectancy in different types of stores by honestly conducted tests, or from carefully kept records.
2. Devise sales aids, store signs, price tickets, and other material in keeping with the importance of the product to total dealer sales. Thus, if your product sells to the extent of 1% of a dealer's total sales, do not attempt to make him spend 10% of his promotion and advertising money in behalf of your product. Gauge your newspaper electrotypes or mats, your booklets (if he is expected to pay mailing expense), and other helps, which either cost him money to buy or to use, to a reasonable relationship to the percentage of sales which can be made on your product.
3. Develop plans which enable the merchant to tie-in with your national advertising without spending too much money in the effort.

Failures have occurred so frequently in the past that some merchants will not attempt to cooperate with any manufacturer, at any time. If more sales managers would leave their comfortable offices and cover a few tank towns and whistle stops with the company's salesmen and really come to understand small stores and small-store problems, there would be fewer failures and more promotion material intelligently used.

What the Small Store Needs

The big city store usually has ample facilities to put on special promotions. But the smaller specialty store, or the general store in the smaller towns, is pretty much a "one man" enterprise. For better or for worse, he thinks of himself as being just about the busiest man in the county. He is, or thinks he is, too busy too read, let alone to plan. Yet he is keenly aware of the fact that to increase his profits and build his business, he needs merchandising ideas. Giving merchandising help to these small merchants—and those who are not so small—is like fertilizing a farm. It makes two dollars grow where only one grew before.

The problem of increasing store traffic is more than just a matter of buying space in the local newspaper, or contracting for a few highway signs to tie-in with a manufacturer's national advertising. These merchants need a constant flow of ideas and simple methods for improving the store's appearance, for perking up the window and interior displays, and all the many devices for building traffic. Obviously a manufacturer with a line which must be content with small volume, or on which the percentage of total store sales is very small, cannot spend a lot of money teaching dealers how to increase sales. But many manufacturers can well afford to plow back considerable sums in dealer helps. By "dealer helps" it is not meant the usual counter cards, signs, and similar gadgets which so often are wasted because they are not suitable, but similar helps which merchants have developed.

The great Garver store, which sells more than a half million dollars annually in a town of less than 2,000 (Strasburg, Ohio) offers as many services as possible to attract traffic. A shoe-repair department is one such service. Manufacturers and wholesalers can encourage merchant customers to lease space to shoe repair shops just to bring in more customers.

A shoe shining service is a real traffic puller, after a brief introductory period. In many small cities, women especially find it difficult to have their shoes shined without climbing up on a high chair in the barber shop. More small stores could profitably lease space to beauty parlors or beauty operators to attract more traffic and more frequent visits from customers.

It may be asked, "Where are these small stores going to find the space?" Gamble-Skogmo has found that nearly every small store has basement space which can be turned into customer service or selling space with little cost. This aggressive company urges all its customers to utilize basement space for selling. Even though basements are not always available, there is often a mezzanine floor, balcony, or some other space poorly utilized which can be turned to a profit producer after a little remodeling and decorating.

Other Traffic Builders

A small counter with an attendant to take orders for newspaper and magazine subscriptions, to take orders for photographic film developing, printing, picture framing, and enlarging, will increase traffic and pay its way in many stores. One merchant worked out a film and photo developing and printing service that brings a customer into the store three times for each set of films to be developed and printed: Once when the films are turned in, once to see if the prints are ready, and one more trip, when the films and prints are finally ready.

A money order service and a service for paying utility and telephone bills may also make a store more popular. Popular-priced books, especially the paperback pocket volumes, are both traffic builders and profit makers.

Food and Drink to Build Traffic

Americans, when they go to the races, to baseball, football, and basketball games, to a circus, carnival, fair, or almost anywhere else want to eat and drink. Small merchants paid little attention to this habit until the chain stores began to capitalize on it. Some of the

Neisner Brothers stores have as many as five places to eat or drink. A root beer barrel, a soda fountain and lunch counter, a popcorn machine, a hamburger or hot dog stand are the usual Neisner services. Many other chain stores have long soda fountain counters and luncheonette services. More independent merchants should be encouraged to operate such services.

A bottled soft-drink cooler will attract traffic. A small counter serving coffee has proved a traffic builder for the Herberger department store in Watertown, South Dakota. The famed $2,000-000-a-year independent Oneonta Department Store at Oneonta, New York (population 13,531), offers food service to its customers. Manufacturers can offer blueprints and plans with operating instructions for these small lunch counters or soft-drink departments to help merchants and encourage salesmen to "sell" the idea to their merchant customers as a traffic building service.

Fred Harvey, the well-known operator of railway diners, station stores, and services, found that an automatic, coin-operated photograph machine, which takes, develops, and prints small photographs is a great profit maker. Some stores may not have enough traffic to warrant installation of these machines, but the idea is worth investigating by many merchants.

International Harvester Company Methods

That knowing what is feasible in the small city market pays off is proved by the methods of International Harvester Company, which engaged in a campaign to improve small city outlets for the company's farm implements, motor trucks, and refrigerators.

International discovered that an excellent traffic builder is a modern building located at the edge of the city, usually on or near a highway leading to the neighboring communities served. One reason for this is the large amount of space required to display farm equipment properly.

The company's first step in deciding upon dealer locations was to determine the potential market in the area, and on a basis of this figure to determine the number of retail outlets needed to serve it. Finding the right dealer for each trade area was the next problem.

The company encouraged every dealer to take advantage of the planning which had gone into the Harvester prototype building and provided blueprints for its construction. From knowledge of the market potential for an area, and the specific dealer's probable share of it, plus the estimated income from equipment servicing, Harvester was able to tell the dealer almost to the penny how much he could profitably invest in a new building.

HAVE A NICE SPRING THIS WINTER!

With Healthful, Spring-like Comfort of Ideal Indoor Humidity Furnished by an

Aprilaire®
HUMIDIFIER

YOUR FAMILY BENEFITS

from Spring-like humidified air. *For Health*—to help repel upper respiratory ailments aggravated by too-dry air. *For Comfort*—to feel warmer at lower temperatures. *For Protection* — of furnishings from damaging dryness

THE ADVANTAGES

of an Aprilaire Humidifier are many. *Automatic, with High Capacity*—assures constant, proper humidity levels. *Rust-proof* — never rusts out. *Minimum Maintenance*—two-way elimination of trouble-causing minerals

JUST SET THE DIAL
. . . and the out-of-sight Aprilaire Humidifier takes over. Models for forced air furnaces — and for any other type heating.

Home appliance manufacturers run magazine and newspaper advertisements to attract customers to their dealers' stores.

Store Improvement Programs

Manufacturers who depend largely upon independent specialty stores for volume have just recently realized how important it is to them, saleswise, for their best dealers to modernize their stores. If they don't, they are certain to lose business to the more progressive and better arranged stores, such as Sears Roebuck is building in thousands of trading centers throughout the country. To keep the Main Street business, some national advertisers (especially those who sell through exclusive dealers) are putting store arrangement experts to work with dealers in strategic locations.

Store modernization activities of some alert manufacturers go so far as to give financial assistance to dealers who "go along" on a program of rearranging their stores. They not only help dealers to get a loan from the local bank, but extend credit terms to give them more time to benefit from the store improvements. There is some danger in such a policy, but how else can the small retailer compete? And in the last analysis, what is good for the dealer is good for the manufacturer.

POINT-OF-PURCHASE PROMOTIONS

After the prospective buyer has been brought to the store, there remains the need to make the sale. Back in the days when national advertising was supposed to "create demand" and "force distribution" of a product, manufacturers got into the habit of thinking when they spent their money for advertising, the public would make a beaten path to the doors of retailers stocking their products and in no time at all the dealers would have to order more. But it was not that simple.

National advertising does help to create consumer and trade acceptance for a product. When the product is favorably known, it is easier to sell. It turns over faster than the non-advertised product. There are fewer leftovers. If it is a quality product, and can live up to the reputation its advertising gives it, a dealer who ties in with the manufacturer's national advertising increases his local prestige. But none of the values found in a well-planned national advertising effort pay off if a poor selling job is done by the dealer or his sales staff, when people come in and ask to see the advertised product. It is an axiom of sales management that goods are not sold, "until they are moved off the dealer's shelf into the housewife's pantry." A home office salesman may do a wonderful job of getting the line into the store, but the number and size of the reorders he will get depend upon the ability of the dealer to get the goods out of the store.

The dealer and his salespeople are just as much a part of the manufacturer's sales organization as his own factory salesmen, which explains why sales managers seeking to expand their sales per dealer are giving more and more study to what happens at the point of purchase.

Types of Point-of-Purchase Promotions

Helping the dealer and his salespeople to do a more effective selling job is not only tremendous, but never ending. To do it thoroughly requires a larger appropriation than is usually available. The problem of training the salespeople in an important industry, if undertaken by a single manufacturer, requires an appropriation of $50 to $100 per salesman. Some companies spend that and more, but

Modern retail point-of-purchase display units capture attention by relying heavily on drama. This Sea & Ski Company diving tower display stands a full 11 feet high. It serves as a merchandiser as well as a display unit.

only a few can afford it. So a good deal of the basic training which salespersons require is now done by educational institutions under the George Dean Act, by trade associations, and by local chambers of commerce. Some manufacturers have developed home study courses for the sales personnel of dealers, the cost of which is divided between the manufacturer, the dealer, and the salesperson directly benefiting from the course. Considerable success is claimed for some of this training work, but, generally speaking, it is very difficult to get adults to study or even to read. The percentage of those who finish such courses is small.

As part of its "Eye Umbrella" campaign for prescription sun glasses, Bausch & Lomb supplied a free counter-card-holder with every order for patient folders.

Some very effective training is being done by well-financed associations, where the members pool the money they would spend for this sort of sales promotional work, employ competent counsel and training experts, and develop an industry-wide training program. It is then made available to the industry at a low cost. A typical program of this type is that of the American Gas Association. It is so designed that it can be built into the training program of individual members. For example, the dealer training plan used by George D. Roper Corporation (gas ranges) includes the following material:

> Series of 10 pamphlets providing topics for use at sales meetings.
>
> Booklets for the retail salesman (12 in all), each telling the story of one sales feature of the Roper range.

Salesman's visualizer.

Booklet on the advantages of gas over electricity.

Booklet on "The Power of Words" emphasizing the importance of what the salesman says.

A "How to Sell" booklet.

Refresher booklet on basic salesmanship.

The value of such materials, however, depends more upon the way they are used than upon the materials themselves. Best results are secured when the materials are used in connection with a series of dealer meetings, followed up by store meetings conducted by the dealer or his executive who previously attended the dealer meetings.

The dealer meetings are usually conducted by the territorial salesman, after being carefully coached, or if that is not practical, by a representative of the sales promotion department. In all cases, however, the meetings need a track upon which to run, and that track is provided by the manufacturer. The more visuals —that is to say, sound-slidefilms and moving pictures—which can be worked into the program the better. Visuals which provoke discussion are especially good.

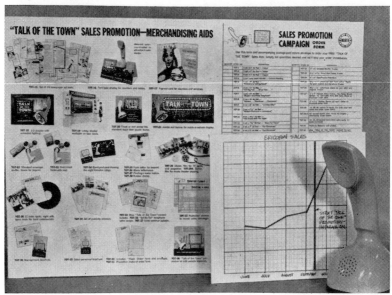

Photo courtesy Advertising & Sales Promotion magazine

A total concept in merchandising aids was the goal of North Electric Co. in a well-planned promotion of the unique Ericofon. In-store units, radio, TV and newspaper ads were available.

Product Education for Salespeople

In addition to whatever fundamental training it is feasible and profitable to give dealers, the rapid turnover among retail sales personnel makes it desirable to get the most important sales points about a product "across to the salesman" at the time he is making a sale. Sometimes a special sales tag is attached to the product listing the main sales points. In other cases the sales points are printed on the back of counter display cards large enough so that the salesman can read them easily. Or the information may be included on the carton or the label. This last-mentioned is favored in the case of products sold largely through self-service stores where the product must sell itself. In the food field, for example, the chains usually prefer to push private brands, and refuse permission to a manufacturer to display advertising for national brands. The only way to promote sales in such a case at the point of purchase is the package. It must not only attract favorable attention on the shelf, but should have enough information on the label to make the sale *quickly*.

Educational Product Contests

General Electric and other astute merchandisers go a step further than just passing out product literature to dealers and their clerks. Experience has taught that a distressingly small percentage of such material is ever read or, if read, remembered by the man behind the counter. So to get over that hurdle, these manufacturers, whenever practical, make a game out of studying the literature and award worth-while prizes to dealers or their salespeople who show the keenest understanding of the sales possibilities of the product.

Such contests, depending upon the unit of sale involved, are as a rule promoted through the local distributor or, if the company sells direct, through factory salesmen. One successful promotion of this type was based on the theme: "Cut Yourself a Big Slice of Cake." Dealers were encouraged to get their salespeople to send in suggestions for selling the product (a pressure cooker) over the counter. To help the contestants think of better ways to sell the cooker, the contest rules included considerable selling information about pressure cookers in general and this cooker in particular. Naturally, the dealer or the clerk interested in entering the competition had to study this part of the booklet carefully.

In this case, the pressure cooker was sold through stores operated by local gas utility companies, most of whom had a comparatively large number of inside salespeople. As a rule, they were quite intelligent and well able to do a selling job if coached on what the product would do. The unit of sale was fairly large so the manufacturer offered as a prize, for the best selling suggestion received from the sales force of each utility, a large fruit cake for the Thanksgiving feast. Actually what happened was that the winner received an order on the leading baker in town to bake and deliver such a cake to the person who presented the order. Or if that was not feasible, the company sent the winner a check for $10 and suggested he buy a cake at his bakery.

Contests of this type, to be successful, require that the competition be limited to small groups, in this case a single utility. This makes it look easy to win the prize, since every contestant knows personally those who are competing against him and does not feel his chance of winning is too remote. But the important thing is— he reads the literature.

Counter and floor displays, counter and wall cards, pass-out literature, novelties for the youngsters, and various other devices are also effectively used to help make the sale once the prospective buyer is in the store. While all of these have their place in modern sales promotion, as will be pointed out in subsequent chapters of this HANDBOOK, the real neck of the sales promotional bottle is the man or woman behind the counter. Depending upon how much, or how little, he knows about your product, the sale is made or lost.

It is for that reason that many companies, making products which do not sell themselves, go to such pains to keep their product continually before dealer's salespeople. Salesmen are required to submit lists of persons in each dealer's store who might be important to the company in a sales way. Periodical letters or news bulletins are then mailed to each name on these lists, or some sort of utility book (of value to them) is sent to them at Christmas.

BETTER MANAGEMENT PROMOTIONS

A criticism of sales promotion programs slanted at the smaller specialty store is—the cost to the merchant is too often out of proportion to the results. There is some justification for the criticism. Every credit manager has encountered, to his sorrow, merchants who spend so much money to get business that they find themselves short of working capital and unable to pay their bills. Ringing up sales is all very well, but if at the end of the month the merchant finds his outgo has exceeded his income, he is not only very unhappy about it, but blames the manufacturer who encouraged him to spend so much on cooperative sales effort.

Realizing that helping dealers to succeed involves more than just selling them to build store traffic, and to do a more effective selling job at the point of purchase, farsighted manufacturers supplement sales helps with management helps. These cover a wide variety of activities, such as plans for better inventory control, help in financing consumer credit, accounting systems, etc. Sylvania Electric Products, for example, furnishes dealers with a complete tax record system; U.S. Rubber supplies distributors with a guide to the compensation of personnel; Crane Company has worked out plans for extension of credit by its dealers; and a number of other companies have offered types of assistance which have no direct, immediate relationship to the sale of their products, but which, by helping the dealer to improve his profit position, ensure continued business relations between the buyer and seller.

The Inventory Headache

There is, for example, great need of educating small independent distributors and dealers on the importance of stock control. Obviously a merchant who builds up a heavy inventory of slow-moving goods soon finds himself with too much of his working capital frozen. When he is taken over by his creditors, his suppliers lose a retail outlet. Now it might be that this is not important, aside from the direct loss, since the consumer demand which exists for a product in any given locality will still exist. If one retailer does not get the business for you, another will. But that is not wholly true. The number of retail outlets for any product in any locality affects per capita consumption. The more retail outlets there are, where the product is exposed to purchase, where it is promoted and advertised, the greater the sales. To think otherwise would be to accept the philosophy that retailers are nothing more than warehousemen.

Even companies which sell through wholesalers assume responsibility for controlling the stocks of dealers handling their products, offering dealers standardized stock control plans. Such plans are designed to aid the retailer in maintaining adequate stocks of quick-moving goods, on one hand; and to avoid buying too heavily of slow-moving products, sizes, and styles, on the other. And, of course, there is always the problem of the dealer who buys too many unrelated lines, thus spreading his capital and energy too thinly for his own good, as well as his supplier's.

Ralston Purina's Credit Manual for Dealers

"Our company does not offer advisory service to dealers on any specific credit risks. We confine ourselves to discussing principles and let them make the applications," reported the manager of the dealer service department of Ralston Purina Company. The problem of working with independent dealers has certain aspects not present in the more closely controlled, company-owned or exclusively franchised setups. This Ralston Purina executive said:

"Our department simply has advisory functions with dealers and cannot control them in any way. We have, though, given rather wide circulation to our brochure, 'Credit Control for Purina Dealers.' In addition to making this credit control program available in this form, we write articles in our house organ for dealers periodically on this subject. In these we frequently quote credit control experiences in our company-owned stores, of which we have about 100, for their possible benefit to the 3,000 independent dealers who handle the bulk of our sales."

Purina's program was primarily for dealers selling on open account, but there is no reason why the same sort of discussion of basic credit principles could not be used in fields where time-payment contracts are employed.

The booklet offered a discussion of eight fundamentals of credit control:

1. Secure an application for credit from every credit customer.
2. Investigate the customer's ability to pay.
3. Have a definite understanding of terms.
4. Mail statements monthly to all unpaid accounts.
5. Follow all overdue accounts.
6. Put 60-day accounts on a cash basis.
7. Know when you are licked. Use past-due notices, letters, personal calls to collect, but when these fail—get a lawyer.
8. Make no exceptions. When you start making exceptions, your credit control is gone.

A somewhat similar but more elaborate program of assistance was offered to dealers by the Larro Division of General Mills, Inc. Dealers were given a merchandising bulletin on credits and collections which included samples of a form to obtain credit information, stickers for use with duplicate statements, and samples of effective collection letters.

In addition, the company made available two sizes of forms on which the dealer could keep a record of outstanding receivables, and emphasis on the importance of credits and collections was continued through featured articles in "The Larro Dealer," the bulletin for the dealer organization.

Complete Management Programs

In some large companies this area of dealer help has been pretty thoroughly explored. The United States Rubber Company supplied a complete package to distributors including:

A standard accounting system.

A sales and profit projection.

Credit and collection procedures.

Inventory control plan.

Cost-control system.

Compensation plans.

Personnel administration data.

Estimates of investment, space, and personnel requirements.

—and a running service based upon operating statistics from the dealerships which permitted any retailer to compare his figures with national averages on gross profits, expenses, and net profits.

The Goodyear Tire and Rubber Company, Incorporated, offered its dealers a similar package containing the following:

Store location service and assistance in lease negotiation.

Store identification materials and ideas.

Store lay-out and display planning service.

Recruiting, selection, and training aids.

Advice, assistance, and training aids for the service department.

Sales promotion and advertising materials.

Accounting, stock control, consumer credit, and other records.

Some of the automobile manufacturers have set up dealer-training programs in such fields as the following: marketing, advertising, public relations, business management controls, dealer accounting, selling techniques, financing and credit, and incentive compensation plans.

The Union Oil Company of California hired an expert to develop a model bookkeeping system for service station operators which would require a minimum of time or special training to maintain. The result, entitled the "Minute Man Profit Guide," sold for $10. It included a set of 12 spiral-bound volumes for keeping monthly accounts and a loose-leaf notebook for permanent records, and required the user to fill in only two pages a day.

Assistance to the dealer in extension of consumer credit is somewhat more common. A typical setup was that of Westinghouse, which financed both floor credit and retail sales through a tie-up with Universal C.I.T. Credit Corporation. All the forms needed in the program were supplied to the retailer, and his applications were handled by either the Westinghouse distributor or through C.I.T. directly.

Building Better Dealers Through Dealer Clubs

Another fairly new technique for improving dealers is through organizations sponsored by the manufacturer but in which the dealers have a substantial part. An example is the dealer clubs which are being used by one manufacturer. The company's merchandising manager said: "All of our promotional activity centers around our dealers. We use enough national advertising to keep our name before the public and create demand, and the dealers take it from there. As a result we don't have sales promotion in the usual sense; instead we push particular phases of a long-term program.

"We formed a dealers' club in each territory. Working through the clubs, we are planning for the hiring and training of 2,000 dealer salesmen. The clubs have been a great success, with an average 83% attendance at monthly meetings. Programs are laid out at headquarters. The territory salesman attends to help the dealer-president keep the meeting on the topic assigned. This setup gives us national coverage in 30 days."

Another interesting point about this company's activity is the emphasis placed on a long-range promotion plan. Closer cooperation between promotion men and the executives charged with long-range planning may offer a worth-while idea for incorporation in many programs.

METHODS FOR INCREASING STORE SALES

From "Handbook for Retailers" issued by Committee for Economic Development.

SALES RECORDS AS GUIDES TO THE FUTURE

A sales estimate for the volume which the store wants to do can be laid out now. This need not be an arbitrary figure to "shoot at," but a reasonable goal based on analysis of the store's own past operations.

Analyze past sales by line of goods, by departments, by brands, or by any type of records that the store now has or can secure.

Analyze charge accounts where these exist to show what kind of merchandise, by groups, has been sold to certain customers and to plan how to sell other goods to those customers.

If weakness in a line is disclosed, discover reasons, and strengthen it by better selection of goods and better selling methods.

On the basis of past records and all forecasts, set up a total estimate of sales for the store, by 6-month periods, and review as conditions require.

Increasing Stock Turn—Cleaning Out Dead Stock

The same amount of capital can buy more goods if turned more often. The most common cause of low stock turn is overbuying in lines that are not in active demand. Dead stock soon means a dead store. Capital tied up in old stock cannot be used for new, fresh goods that customers want most.

As new goods come into the market, watch inventories. No store can be "open to buy" new merchandise unless it cleans out its older inventories and "takes a licking" on its badly bought goods. Experienced merchandisers hear new stories every day of astonishing lack of attention to stock turn.

Train salespeople to rotate shelf stock so as to reduce spoilage and bring dying stock to light.

Clean out inventories by special sales, sales in special departments, bargain table or other means.

Rebuilding Good Will Now

Many studies show that stores have built heavy inventories of customer ill will through listless or impertinent service, and favoritism in allotting scarce merchandise. Not a day should be lost in correcting this condition.

Making "Related Sales" and "Suggestion Sales"

The success of the department store, the mail-order house, and the variety store is the principle of selling more goods to the same people.

Customers walk past many departments in making purchases from one department. Readers of a mail-order catalog thumb it over and are attracted by news about many kinds of goods. In a variety store customers see large assortments of goods at similar prices and buy on impulse.

The average sale can be increased most easily through selling related merchandise.

Consider each line of goods and each item in relation to other lines and items, and set up a program for training all salespeople in making related sales.

If a department store, consider circularizing customers who buy from one department with bulletins about goods in other departments.

Are Price Policies Right?

With a nation-wide price rise going on, a store needs to know costs and examine its price policy carefully to make sure it can meet new price competition.

As an over-all policy, analyze prices to see whether the store can meet present and future price competition.

..................Analyze all forms of overhead costs to see how they can be cut.

..................Consider making separate charges for services like delivery and alterations, and "selling" them to customers as economies that bring prices lower.

..................Analyze customer income to find out (a) whether incomes of former customers have decreased; (b) whether groups with recently increased incomes are becoming customers.

..................Decide whether customary markup makes the store's prices too high to appeal to the majority of the store's present or future customers.

..................Set markup according to lines and turnover, not store-wide.

INCREASING SALES PER SALESPERSON

As an over-all figure for average-sized stores, it is said that volume is likely to equal $12,000 per person employed, including sales and nonsales personnel. A department store authority, on the other hand, reports a lower amount. These figures are not to be taken as guides, but as suggestions.

..................Divide total sales by salespeople to give an over-all ratio.

..................If store records now provide for determining volume of sales made by each salesperson, analyze these records, and reasons for strength and weakness.

..................Discuss methods of increasing sales per salesperson, including incentive payment ideas.

DRAWING IN NEW CUSTOMERS

..................As a practical start toward increasing sales, list the families, stores, offices, etc., in the store's own block and immediate neighborhood, its natural trading area.

..................Set up a program, including all store personnel, for getting acquainted personally with more people, being a "good neighbor," knowing people by name, inducing friends to trade with the store.

..................Consider every method of incentive payment for sales traceable to such efforts, by individuals, or by share in increased store profits.

..................Discuss how the head of the business and other store people can take a more active part in community affairs, so as to make people feel better acquainted with the store and more friendly to it.

..................With the help of inside and outside counsel, consider how a store can be given a definite personality:

..................Through store policies, definitely established and well publicized.

..................Through redesigned lay-out, store front, and windows.

..................Through advertising copy, including institutional copy, and style of advertising lay-out.

..................Through featuring a line or lines of goods, store's brand or national brand.

..................Through impressing all policies and methods repeatedly on store personnel.

PROMOTING SALES THROUGH SPECIALTY STORES

Mailing Lists

In the face of high costs, direct mail efforts by stores are severely restricted, but they need not stop entirely. In the face of recent shifts in population, a store may not be giving its usual attention to keeping a mailing list up to date. But a store's best customers will expect to be informed instantly when merchandise is more plentiful.

Every store can have a mailing list. Names can be picked up in conversation and a list built up in a short time, or selected from a telephone directory of people in the store's natural trading area. Mimeographed post cards cost little. A short list is better than none. Make offerings specific, and aim them at bringing people into the store. Lists need constant revision, for they begin to "die" in a few months.

Lists of babies, births, birthdays, gathered from newspapers, provide opportunities for circulars that are particularly appreciated. Every day is a special day for somebody. Circularizing can be too expensive unless checked carefully, but if well used, it makes friends.

............With the help of all store personnel and store records, build up a mailing list and record it on 3- by 5-inch cards.

............From trade associations, trade papers, wholesalers and manufacturers, and books, gather information on how to build a mailing list.

............Investigate to find out what mailing material can be secured from manufacturers or wholesalers.

............Decide whether the store can prepare its own mailing matter, or should obtain help from local printers or advertising men.

Telephone Lists

Now that demands on telephone lines have declined, calls can be made to selected lists.

............Make up lists for calls announcing new merchandise or special prices.

............Encourage salespeople by incentive pay to develop a "following" of customers and to call them about seasonal or special offerings.

Giving an Overhaul to Advertising

Advertising should be looked on as the voice of the store, the representative of its personality, entering each home in its trading area. Alert, aggressive advertising will be the first notice served on the store's clientele that the management of the store is fully competent to meet the demands of its customers.

Analyze advertising to make certain that it meets these requirements:
............Presents news about merchandise that competes favorably for interest with the news columns.

............Appears in media that reach the store's actual or possible customers.

............Considers all available media, including handbills, outdoor, street car, motion picture slides, classified advertising in newspapers and telephone books.

............Makes full use of cards in one department calling attention to other departments.

............Bases its appropriation on a carefully determined percentage of net sales, and remains inside that figure but is set up so as to allow for special events.

................Makes an appeal that fits the store's actual class of trade, not too high or too low.

................Takes advantage of every event on the calendar, seasons, holidays, local events, etc.

................Makes use of other stores' advertising, mail-order catalogs, wholesalers' and manufacturers' catalogs, to get ideas on how to write copy and make lay-outs.

................Works in full cooperation with merchandising departments in planning events, and in making sure that merchandise is on hand when advertised.

INSTALLMENT SELLING AND HOUSE-TO-HOUSE SELLING

Installment selling is a valuable means of expanding volume. It gives the purchaser an incentive to work harder so as to pay for his purchase. Numberless young men have gotten their start in life by making a down payment on a house and lot, and then making greater efforts so as to own their own homes. The same principle applies to the purchase of furniture and other household equipment. But every installment salesman should be trained to ask a friendly question so as to protect the customer against over-extension. Not installment selling itself, but the reckless abuse of installment selling is a danger to individual and national credit.

House-to-house selling of goods adapted to this method can well be included as an element in a vigorous sales promotion program.

................Analyze what goods may be suitable for installment selling.

................Analyze what goods may be suitable for house-to-house selling.

BROAD REVIEW OF POLICIES

................Give a general review to policies, methods, personnel, and budget to enable the store's advertising to make a strong impression on its community for the changing days that lie ahead.

................Recognize that honesty and consistency in advertising have the same effect as honesty and consistency in the character of the head of the business.

Chapter 33

PROMOTING SALES THROUGH
DEPARTMENT STORES

THE department store or, as it is called in Great Britain, "the departmental store," exists by virtue of its ability to undersell the specialty store. Its advent into merchandising, which followed the success of the A. T. Stewart store in New York as far back as 1900, was an effort to apply organization to retailing. In the period from 1900 to 1940, department stores enjoyed a tremendous growth, so that by the beginning of World War II, this type of retailer was doing about 12% of the total retail business. The modern department store is a number of small stores under a central management and central control. In the early days of the era the most successful stores were usually dominated by an outstanding merchant, of whom John Wanamaker, Marshall Field, William Filene, and A. T. Stewart were typical examples. After the turn of the century, and especially after the death of A. T. Stewart and the subsequent closing of his New York store, a more enduring management was essential and decentralization of responsibilities began. One by one the big stores incorporated, and functionalized management was substituted for one-man management. This trend was accentuated with the growth of multiple-department stores, some of which, like the Field chain, operate a number of important stores.

Irreducible expense ratios have exerted a steady downward pressure upon the net profits of department stores, and the solution to the problem lies in increased sales volume on more profitable items. For example, in a recent survey of 237 department stores, 72% had higher expense ratios than in the previous year; 70% found their profit percentage lower; and on the average this net profit from merchandising operations had declined from 2.1% to 1.5%.

Five Principles of Retail Promotion

John A. Blum was senior vice-president and director of sales promotion for Macy's New York, the world's largest department store. Writing in one of advertising's publications, he posed the question: "What are the principles we have found most useful to observe in trying to do the sales promotion job for Macy's?"

To do the job effectively and at a profit, Macy's must offer the right goods at the right time and at the right price, Blum concluded.

"Too frequently in sales promotion, we succumb to the allure of a promotional approach that may be so attractive in itself that it takes our eye ... and the consumer's eye too ... away from the main thing, the merchandise we are above all else trying to pursuade our customers to buy.

"Its corollary stands by itself as principle number two. It is this: Promotion should never force merchandising. In other words, a promotional approach that is a good one per se is really not worth the powder to blow to the infernal regions if it involves merchandise that is not naturally right for the store, or if the timing is not naturally right for the contemplated push, or if promotional costs are out of line with probable results.

"Principle number three is an especially important one for those of us who work in metropolitan markets.

"The competition for attention, let alone for business, is fierce, so if you want to have a chance of being heard, principle number three becomes an essential one for you. Here it is: Whatever it is you have decided to do, do it importantly, do it in the biggest way possible, use every tool at your command and use them with the greatest drama, creatively, of which you are capable. If you are not willing to do things this way, then, I submit, it is better to skip the whole thing, for otherwise you risk wasting your most irreplaceable assets—time, money, people, and creative skill—and you will have achieved nothing worthwhile in the process.

"Principle number four, and certainly not in any order of priority, is that everything we say and do must in fact be true and that each one of our advertising and other promotional properties must. convey an entirely truthful impression in itself. Our business is repeat business, and certainly one of our greatest and most important assets is customer confidence.

"Principle number five is the determination to seek new and fresh approaches, to learn new ways of using old media and how best to use new media. In this connection, let me emphasize that our business in itself is one of risk-taking, of experimentation, of leadership in merchandise development. Therefore, if we in sales promotion do not also accept the responsibility for leadership, for innovation, the sales promotion job being done for Macy's will be less than Macy's requires."

The Division of Sales Promotion

At the head of the sales promotional function for most large department stores is a director of sales promotion. He reports directly to the general management and controller. A director of publicity and a director of personal selling form the two administrative arms of the sales promotional operation. The director of publicity is responsible for the store advertising, displays and exhibits, and special promotions. The director of personal selling is responsible for the recruiting, training, and over-all supervision of store sales personnel, customers' services, demonstrators, traveling sales units, telephone selling, etc. However, the importance of the department buyer is not overlooked in this reshuffling of responsibilities. The department or section buyer, who reports to the merchandising director, is still the backbone of a store's operations and the keystone to its success. But the emphasis has been shifted from buying to sales promotion. A store might have the best bargains in town and offer unusually good selections, but unless people in large numbers can be brought into the store and exposed to the values and the selections offered, the advantages which come with quick turnover will suffer. In other words, the principle upon which the modern department store operates is that goods well bought are more quickly sold with the aid of hard-hitting, customer-attracting store promotions.

This shift in organization recognizes that a good buyer is not always a good sales promoter. In fact the two qualities seldom go together. And while buying and selling are closely related, the trend today is toward developing better buyers by relieving them of the sales promotional responsibilities with which they were formerly burdened.

As a matter of fact, there are many instances where a department store has been an outstanding success in a location where competition is especially keen, simply because it did an exceptionally good sales promotional job.

One chain of department stores offers a case in point. This chain won a reputation for being good promoters by spectacular traffic-building promotions. For example, in a typical store in Watertown, Minnesota, a "Koffee Bar" with 28 seats at the rear of the main floor serves coffee and a doughnut for a dime; coffee alone is still only a nickel! At current costs this may result in a loss, but it draws men to the store, and men are notoriously diffident about visiting department stores.

The "Chain" Department Store

The desire to use great buying power to force price concessions from manufacturers, which was the underlying motive of the first department stores, now finds expression in the chain of department stores idea. The purchasing power of the Marshall Field group of department stores has reached a point where Field's operate a manufacturing division. At one time Field's operated a wholesale division, but it was discontinued to give store buyers greater freedom of action in the purchase of merchandise.

The stores comprising these chains of department stores are operated very much as individual stores, each store having its own buying and selling policies, but following an over-all policy laid down by a central management. In most store groups the central management has a sales division responsible for the merchandise in the stores, and the various district managers who, in turn, supervise and assist the individual store managers.

In this respect the department store chain (or group) differs from the variety store chain, like Penney, Woolworth, Kresge, and similar stores of this type, which, as explained in Chapter 34—"Promoting Sales Through Chain Stores," are more highly organized at national and regional levels. The merchandise they carry is usually standard to all stores in the chain, and is selected because of its mass selling possibilities. Thus what the variety store chain carries is determined by what the stores in a chain can sell rapidly, rather than with much thought to the needs of the community. A department store, as contrasted to a variety or general store, is generally accepted as handling women's ready-to-wear and accessories, and boy's wear, piece goods, small wears, home furnishings, and miscellaneous goods. There is some feeling, especially among independent retailers, that the chains of big department stores, with their tremendous purchasing power, are nearing the monopoly stage and there is a growing political pressure to "unscramble" them, or at least break them down into unit operations.

PROMOTING SALES THROUGH DEPARTMENT STORES

The population shift to suburban areas has been followed by department stores with keen interest. Freedom from parking problems, concentration of retail shops, and good purchasing power have encouraged the growth of suburban shopping centers, with their new buildings and modern stores, in uncrowded land areas.

The latest trend is the shopping mall, typified by the Cherry Hill Mall in New Jersey. Here the shopping areas are completely roofed over and self-contained, reducing the hazard of lower volume during inclement weather. To make the mall even more attractive to customers and to draw them away from the downtown stores, the Cherry Hill center has a large central area with fountains, tropical birds, and attractively landscaped spots where shoppers may rest. In addition, concerts, art exhibits, and special shows are staged, widely advertised in advance.

The growth of shopping centers and shopping malls provides new and challenging opportunities for productive promotional activities.

Department Store Specialists

To get maximum results from department store sales outlets some companies find it profitable to employ sales specialists, experienced in big store problems who devote their entire time to this operation. Sometimes these are sales managers, sometimes they are sales promotion men. There are other executives responsible for selling to wholesalers, chain stores, or independent merchants. This policy of servicing each major outlet classification has been successfully used by the Ekco Products Company in selling cutlery and kitchenware. Not only is there an Ekco executive responsible for sales to each major outlet, but he has his own sales organization of specialists. This means when an Ekco salesman calls on a department store he knows the language of that type of store and is in a position to do a constructive merchandising job.

The proper display of merchandise is an important matter with any retail store, and even the big stores are hungry for help. Ekco salesmen calling on big stores base their case on better display, and endeavor to get the management to use display cases which Ekco has developed to sell more cutlery. This cabinet is a complete sales unit, with space for the reserve stock as well as the stock on display. By combining units, the requirements of any size store can be met. A common mistake in designing display cases for big store promotions is that they take up too much space for the profit the store can expect to realize from its use. Even though a salesman may succeed in placing some of these oversized cases, they will soon be discarded because they just don't pay their freight.

STORE-WIDE PROMOTIONS

A department store, like a newspaper, should be a constructive factor in the life of the community as well as a profitable business undertaking. That is why the more progressive stores are spending more for activities of educational and cultural value to their customers and prospective customers. While these undertakings are primarily in the interest of better public relations, they also have definite sales promotional value since they bring people into the store.

These store-wide promotions differ from product promotions, such as a style show, in that they do not directly promote the sale of anything. They are usually of sufficient educational interest to get good press and word-of-mouth publicity. For example, during the war when the U.S. Navy took over the Navy Pier in Chicago, where the Illinois Garden Clubs had previously held their annual flower shows, Marshall Field & Company offered the clubs space to hold the show without charge. For the period of the war, the Chicago Garden Show was staged in this exhibition hall and was attended by many thousands of flower lovers in the Chicago area—many of whom no doubt took advantage of being in the store to make purchases. While Marshall Field & Company does not sell flowers, it does sell furniture and table accessories used in showing the flower arrangements. These were loaned for the occasion by the store. While it is hardly probable that the direct sales resulting from this promotion were sufficient to cover expenses, it did win thousands of friends for the store, especially among the members of the participating clubs.

Store-Wide Quality Exhibition

Another example of a type of educational promotion which brings traffic to a store, and offers an opportunity to manufacturers of products sold by the store, is the quality show successfully used by Marshall Field & Company and other large stores several years ago. The purpose of the exhibition was to show the people of the community the difference between products made to sell at a price, and comparable quality products. For example, one exhibit featured men's clothing. By means of charts and cross-sectional cuttings, with explanatory references, the store showed how a suit of ready-to-wear clothes was manufactured, beginning with the shearing of the sheep, and how the extra value put into a quality garment was well worth the small additional charge. The overall effect of this exhibition was to trade-up the store's customers, and get them to think about value first and consider price afterwards.

Store-wide promotions aimed principally at building store traffic likewise afford manufacturers opportunities to tie in their products. Barker Brothers of Los Angeles usually has one promotion of this type under way at all times. These promotions are slanted to arouse interest in merchandise which the store sells, such as home furnishing suggestions like the South Pacific bar on page 918.

The more modern stores, recognizing the value of these educational promotions, have allocated space on one of the upper floors for this purpose. Some stores equip their exhibition quarters with projection facilities where interesting educational movies, available from manufacturers, may be shown to passing customers.

Mass displays are effective as an attention-getting technique. Macy's, New York, presents an all-Libbey-products arrangement in its glassware department.

In the smaller communities store-wide promotions are less pretentious, but nonetheless effective as traffic builders. Cooking schools, sewing classes, and related promotions are never-failing attendance getters.

Community Events

Large department stores have developed major promotions which have practically become "institutions", such as Macy's Thanksgiving Day parade in New York and Gimbel's in Philadelphia. Hess, in Reading, Pennsylvania, is noted for its annual televised fashion shows, featuring two-thousand-dollar gowns. Marcus-Niemann, of course, is famous for its Texas-size promotions.

People are always looking for ideas to make their homes more attractive. A corner in the Barker Brothers store is set aside for displaying all sorts of equipment for the home bar. "Smart" merchandise is "punched" in these displays.

Intrastore Television Programs

What seems to have considerable possibilities for promoting the sale of suitable merchandise, such as style merchandise, is the development of television within the store. The program is projected from a central studio and may consist of a staged demonstration featuring merchandise on sale in the store, or it may be a showing of some educational sound movie borrowed from a manufacturer. To be suitable for this purpose, however, the movie should be relatively short. Television stations are located at strategic locations throughout the store where shoppers can sit down and rest while viewing the picture.

GETTING BIG STORES TO PUSH YOUR PRODUCT

It has been contended by sales promotion men that since a big department store is simply a group of specialty stores, with central control and management, any promotion which goes over well with specialty stores will prove equally successful with department stores. And to some extent that is true. But there is this difference. The big store, for example, Marshall Field & Company in Chicago, or Lord & Taylor in New York, or The Emporium in San Francisco, has more standing locally than most nationally advertised brands. Because of its local reputation the big store does not feel the need of handling a product just because it is nationally advertised. It thinks the name of the store, sponsoring a not too well known brand, has just as much sales appeal as some manufacturer's name.

While a store like Marshall Field's may sell, out of necessity, a certain number of nationally advertised products, it prefers to promote brands which it controls, or partly controls. This policy is a thorn in the side of manufacturers of nationally trade-marked and advertised goods, but it does give the merchant a better control of all repeat business. It also affords a longer profit. There are some manufacturers, especially when pressed for working capital, who will accept large orders for merchandise made to the same specifications as a national brand, but carry the department store's private brand, at a special "run on" price. The manufacturer figures his fixed charges are carried by sales to the regular trade, so he can lop them off and still come out with a tidy profit. This policy makes it difficult to "sell" the big department store like Field's or Macy's on tie-in promotions. But it can be done.

The Case of Mrs. Nellson's Chocolates

The argument of the big store that it cannot afford to promote a product unless it controls the repeat business can be overcome by limiting distribution to one big store in a town or locality. When that is done there is no other local store where a satisfied customer can go to place a repeat order. Whatever the store spends to promote your product is justified because of the exclusive rights you have granted the store. You may not do as much business as if you sold up and down Main Street, but you get a large volume at a relatively small selling cost, and that is important. It facilitates the task of getting national, or at least big city, distribution.

One manufacturer who elected to follow this plan of distribution, and concentrate sales in big store outlets, established a subsidiary company to tap the big store market. The candy sold for $1 a pound under the name of "Mrs. Nellson's Chocolates."

Distribution was confined to one major department store in a market and outlets chosen only on the basis of agreement that the store was willing to engage in aggressive promotion to ensure volume sales.

Mrs. Nellson's chocolates were introduced in March with an elaborate promotion in The Emporium, San Francisco. The promotion was preceded by a teaser campaign in newspapers. Two weeks before the premiere, tiny teaser advertisements began to

Cosmetics manufacturers long ago learned to offer promotional materials that impel retailers to make use of them. This L'Aimant window display created for Coty, Inc., is an example. Even the largest stores are eager to have good merchandising aids.

appear in San Francisco newspapers, asking "Who is Mrs. Nellson?" These increased in size and frequently until, on the final 2 days, half-page copy splashed the answer: "Mrs. Nellson's is the name of a box of candy."

During the week preceding the introduction, each store employee received a mimeographed announcement (on chocolate-colored paper) telling about the candy, its quality, and popular price, and the coming promotion. Each employee received a sample box containing three pieces of candy. Day before the premiere the store held an advance sale of the candy for employees at 75 cents a box.

Window displays consisted of a life-size cottage showing Mrs. Nellson's candy kitchen, and under the dome of the main floor a replica of the cottage was hung, with candy packages, pennant-wise, above. These were giant size, visible anywhere on the floor. Ten interior displays and sales counters were located at heavy-traffic spots on different floors. These were in addition to the mass display at the regular candy department.

Six of "Mrs. Nellson's Daughters," colorfully dressed, carrying sample trays, distributed samples to customers on each floor. On opening day chefs in the cottage window display packed the "kettle fresh" candy into boxes as crowds looked on. At a dramatic moment Mrs. Nellson arrived. On opening day 1,900 boxes were sold, and during the ensuing 3 weeks over 10,000 pounds. Emporium executives reported this record sale of chocolates represented more than they had previously sold of a single brand of candy in a full year.

Prior to the first promotion, Mrs. Nellson's had conducted a survey to find out what proportion and combination of the various kinds and pieces of candy most people preferred. With facts and photostat reproductions of the response and a mail presentation on the dramatic results of the Emporium test promotion, the company signed up selected outlets in a considerable number of other areas.

Establishing a New Department

Since a department store is organized on the stores-within-a-store principle, it is relatively easy to induce the store management to establish a new section, or sub-department, when the product lends itself to that type of promotion. When the Bernhard Ulmann Company undertook a campaign to extend its big store market, it "sold" the idea of putting in a needlework department, rather than a line of yarns. As a basis for the drive Ulmann engaged a research organization to determine the most satisfactory ways of selling needle-work. It was found that 65% of all customers knew the type of yarn they wanted, and more than 67% knew the amount required. So all that was necessary to expand the yarn business in a store was to provide space where the customers could make their own selections. This appealed to the store management since it meant a minimum of clerical help for the proposed new department.

The company then prepared a stock and display unit for selling yarns, so as to do the best job with the least space. These display cases were designed in various sizes to fit different situations and blueprints were offered to stores at a small charge. From these blueprints the store carpenter could easily build a display case. The display case was, as you may suspect, the backbone of the selling plan.

Along with the blueprints of the display case, the company prepared a list of 36 principles which should be incorporated in any needlework selling unit if maximum results were to be obtained. These were as follows:

Yarns

1. Are yarns well lighted and colors arranged to make an attractive display?

2. Is complete open selling used for all yarns?

3. Does display method give the impression of large assortment?

4. Is wall space used for "open" stock and display?

5. Is vertical space above counter height used?
   For stock?   For display?

6. Are bins adjustable?

7. Can fixtures be easily converted for use for other classifications?

8. Has the salesperson a fixed location?

9. Is it easy for customers to pick up, feel, and replace skein?

10. Do bins or shelves hold box of yarn or is stock easily available?

11. Are finished models displayed?
    Near yarn stock?

12. Are instruction books and needles near yarns?

13. Are informative signs used?
    Price, type, weight, uses?

14. Is section identified?

15. If open selling is used, do signs tell customer that it is for her convenience?

Stamped Goods

16. Are most of the designs displayed to give impression of assortment?

17. Are the items displayed in a minimum of space?

18. Is wall space or back fixture space used to display large pieces?

19. Is vertical space above counter height used?

> For stock?
> For display?

20. Is space in tables or counter used for stock?

21. Are featured items highlighted in display?

22. Is open selling method used for fast selling numbers?

23. Are items and designs given equal sales opportunity?

24. Is section identified?

25. Are small items segregated excepting where matched sets?

26. Is inside selling used with salesperson in fixed position?

27. Is floss displayed to remind customers?

28. Is floss near stamped pieces for fast service?

29. Are informative signs used?

COTTON YARNS

30. Does display give the impression of assortment?

31. Does section have complete open selling?

32. Do signs aid customer to make own selection?

33. Is section lighted?

34. Are bins adjustable?

35. Are instruction books near section?

36. Is the section identified?

The advantage of this method of selling a "packaged promotion" rather than mere merchandise is obvious. It combines a traffic building promotion with the opportunity for extra sales volume and profit. Every merchant knows that the "velvet" in storekeeping comes from sales over and above the store's budgeted business.

Big Store "Push" Plans

Department stores, as a rule, are not enthusiastic about sales contests sponsored by manufacturers. One reason is that the management has its own ideas as to what merchandise it wants to push. Then some stores regard a sales contest where prizes are awarded by the manufacturer as a sort of "spiff"—a practice which the Federal Trade Commission frowns upon. The Commission takes the attitude customers should be informed, when a clerk pushes one product at the expense of another, that he is doing so to earn a "spiff." However, "spiffs" and like inducements are widely used and actually are no more unethical than paying salespeople a bonus which varies with the profit they earn for the store.

Sales contests, both intra-store and inter-store, are best suited to promoting the sale of "big ticket" merchandise, such as home appliances, television or "hi-fi" sets, kitchen equipment, some furniture items, etc. One very successful inter-store contest was sponsored by a manufacturer of pressure cookers. The aim was to interest the salespeople in the advantages of pressure cooking, so that they could intelligently discuss it with' customers. A contest based around the "Hidden Treasure" theme was used. Points good for merchandise prizes of the contestant's own selection were offered to all wishing to use the promotion.

A feature of the plan which had much to do with its success was the way the department manager was tied in. In addition to prizes for the store personnel, points were also awarded the department manager on the basis of the store's purchases of pressure cookers during the contest period. While some overstocking resulted, due to some managers wishing to earn more points and placing orders for more cookers than could be moved quickly, it worked out all right. To justify the action, the department manager had to get busy and sell the stock before merchandise control began to ask questions.

Advertising and Promotion Allowances

This is one of the most popular methods of getting a big store to push a product. It gets the story across to the store's customers. It has the added advantage of buying advertising space or time, at the low local rates available to a store which contracts for advertising on an annual basis. However, in setting up this type of promotion, all stores, regardless of size, must be treated alike to conform to the Robinson-Patman Act. In the case of products like refrigerators, this may be done by gearing the allowance to the number of units sold. One, for example, has a fixed advertising budget of $6 for each refrigerator distributed. This is divided, $4 to be spent locally by the dealer, and $2 to be spent nationally by the manufacturer. All local advertising or promotion is handled by the store. Proof of the advertising, however, must be attached to the store's claim for the advertising allowance. The claim must be made within 60 days after the advertising appears. In the case of outdoor advertising, receipted bills from the local outdoor advertising company must be attached to claim. The dealer is reimbursed by a credit memorandum which he can apply toward the purchase of more refrigerators. Claims

Typical Buying Seasons at Department Stores

Department	Jan.	Feb.	Mar.	Apr.	May	June	July	Aug.	Sept.	Oct.	Nov.	Dec.	Year
PIECE GOODS													
Silks, Velvets, and Synthetics....	0.7	0.8	0.9	0.7	0.6	0.4	0.4	0.5	0.6	0.6	0.5	0.3	0.6
Woolen Yard Goods............	0.4	0.4	0.3	0.1	0.1	0.1	0.2	0.4	0.5	0.5	0.4	0.2	0.3
Cotton Yard Goods............	0.7	0.8	0.8	0.8	0.9	0.8	0.7	0.5	0.4	0.4	0.3	0.2	0.5
Linens and Towels.............	2.5	1.2	1.0	1.0	1.2	1.2	1.4	1.7	1.1	1.1	1.3	1.3	1.3
Blankets, Comforters, Spreads...	1.6	0.8	0.7	0.8	0.9	1.0	1.0	1.2	1.1	1.1	0.9	0.8	1.0
SMALL WARES													
Laces, Trimmings, etc..........	0.2	0.3	0.3	0.3	0.3	0.2	0.2	0.2	0.2	0.2	0.2	0.2	0.2
Notions......................	1.3	1.2	1.2	1.4	1.6	1.5	1.3	1.2	1.2	1.2	1.0	1.0	1.3
Toilet Articles, Drug Sundries....	2.8	2.9	2.4	2.5	2.6	2.8	2.9	2.5	2.5	2.3	2.4	3.6	2.7
Silverware and Jewelry..........	1.6	1.8	1.6	1.7	2.0	2.1	1.6	1.7	1.8	1.9	2.2	2.8	2.0
Art Needlework................	0.7	0.6	0.5	0.4	0.3	0.3	0.4	0.4	0.4	0.5	0.5	0.4	0.4
Books and Stationery...........	1.8	2.1	1.5	1.4	1.4	1.6	1.4	1.6	1.8	1.7	2.6	3.2	2.0
ACCESSORIES													
Neckwear and Scarves..........	0.8	1.0	1.0	1.1	1.1	1.1	1.0	0.8	1.1	1.2	1.2	1.4	1.1
Handkerchiefs.................	0.3	0.3	0.2	0.2	0.2	0.3	0.2	0.2	0.2	0.2	0.3	0.7	0.4
Millinery.....................	0.8	1.1	1.7	1.6	0.8	0.6	0.5	0.9	1.6	1.4	0.9	0.6	1.0
Women's and Children's Gloves..	0.5	0.6	0.6	0.8	0.6	0.4	0.3	0.3	0.5	0.7	1.0	1.1	0.6
Corsets and Brassieres..........	2.1	1.9	1.9	2.0	2.0	2.2	2.0	1.7	1.8	1.7	1.3	1.2	1.8
Women's and Children's Hosiery.	1.8	2.2	2.0	2.0	1.9	1.7	1.6	1.5	1.8	1.8	1.7	2.0	1.8
Negligees, Robes, Loung. Apparel.	0.4	0.5	0.5	0.5	0.6	0.5	0.6	0.5	0.4	0.5	0.8	1.1	0.6
Infants' Wear.................	2.4	2.6	2.9	2.7	2.2	2.2	2.3	2.9	3.2	2.9	3.0	2.8	2.7
Handbags, Small Leather Goods..	1.0	1.2	1.4	1.5	1.4	1.3	1.1	1.1	1.4	1.4	1.4	1.9	1.4
Women's and Children's Shoes...	3.1	3.4	4.1	4.2	3.6	3.3	3.1	3.3	4.1	3.5	2.6	2.3	3.3
APPAREL													
Women's & Misses' Coats, Suits..	4.3	3.7	4.5	3.4	1.8	1.2	1.5	2.8	3.5	4.1	3.2	1.9	2.9
Women's and Misses' Dresses....	4.4	4.4	5.0	5.5	6.1	5.0	4.2	3.8	4.6	4.1	3.2	2.6	4.2
Blouses, Skirts, Sportswear......	3.3	3.6	3.5	3.9	4.4	4.6	4.7	4.6	4.9	4.3	3.7	4.3	4.2
Girls' Wear...................	1.1	1.5	2.3	1.9	1.5	1.4	1.5	2.8	2.3	2.1	2.1	2.0	1.9
Furs.........................	1.4	0.9	0.7	0.6	0.3	0.2	0.5	1.1	0.8	1.1	1.1	1.0	0.9
MEN'S AND BOYS' WEAR													
Men's Clothing................	3.3	2.5	2.5	2.8	3.1	3.4	2.9	2.2	2.5	3.2	3.1	2.8	2.9
Men's Furnishings and Hats.....	3.4	3.8	3.1	3.6	3.9	5.9	4.3	3.2	3.4	4.0	5.5	8.1	4.6
Boys' Wear...................	1.1	1.3	1.9	2.0	1.4	1.4	1.3	2.1	2.0	1.8	2.0	2.1	1.8
Men's and Boys' Shoes, Slippers..	0.5	0.5	0.5	0.6	0.6	0.6	0.5	0.5	0.5	0.5	0.6	0.6	0.6
HOME FURNISHINGS													
Furniture and Bedding..........	7.1	7.0	5.5	4.9	5.6	5.6	6.7	7.1	5.6	5.6	4.6	2.6	5.4
Domestic Floor Coverings.......	2.6	2.6	2.1	1.9	2.1	1.8	2.0	2.1	2.3	2.6	2.3	1.1	2.0
Draperies, Curtains, Awnings, etc.	2.2	2.5	2.6	2.6	2.8	2.6	2.4	2.3	2.5	2.9	2.6	1.6	2.4
China and Glassware..........	1.3	1.5	1.2	1.1	1.2	1.2	1.2	1.2	1.2	1.2	1.4	1.5	1.3
Major Household Appliances.....	2.3	2.4	2.4	2.1	2.3	2.5	4.1	3.0	2.1	2.1	1.5	1.0	2.2
Housewares (incl. Sm. Appliances)	3.3	3.8	3.8	3.9	4.2	4.2	5.2	3.9	3.8	3.3	3.4	3.3	3.8
Radios, Phonos, TV, Records, etc.	1.8	1.8	1.5	1.1	1.1	1.3	1.4	1.5	1.7	1.8	1.6	1.8	1.6
MISCELLANEOUS													
Toys and Games...............	0.4	0.7	0.8	0.8	0.8	1.1	1.3	1.0	1.1	1.3	3.6	4.3	1.7
Sporting Goods and Cameras....	0.5	0.6	0.7	0.8	1.0	1.2	1.1	0.9	0.8	0.8	1.1	1.6	1.0
Luggage......................	0.4	0.4	0.3	0.4	0.6	0.8	0.7	0.6	0.4	0.3	0.5	0.7	0.5
Candy.......................	0.4	0.6	0.5	0.7	0.4	0.4	0.4	0.3	0.3	0.5	0.4	0.8	0.5
Store Totals.................	6.6	5.9	7.6	7.9	7.7	7.6	6.1	7.2	8.3	9.1	10.4	15.6	100

Figures show departments' percentages of stores' total monthly (or yearly) sales.

Courtesy National Retail Dry Goods Association

are not honored unless certain requirements are met. For newspaper ads these include:

1. Every advertisement must include the maker's logotype.
2. Every advertisement must include a picture of the maker's refrigerator, properly identified.
3. The refrigerator must be referred to in terms used by the manufacturer.
4. The dealer must submit a copy of the advertisement for approval by the manufacturer before it is published.

Outdoor copy must be approved by the company advertising department before posting, and radio and TV commercials must have prior approval.

Formulating a cost sharing promotional policy for general line products is more complicated and consequently less valued by the larger department stores, which are not inclined to devote advertising space, even if the manufacturer pays for it, to promote "thin" margin profits. If the product offers a good profit on each sale, and rapid turnover, it is usually possible to get the store to stand a share of the local advertising and promotion. Such a plan was used by Seidlitz Paint & Varnish Company in connection with a special line of mildew proof paints it was promoting. The plan provided:

We will pay one-half of the dealer's cost of local advertising expense in newspapers and telephone directory. The combined total of our share of the expenses for both the above media shall not exceed 5% of dealer's net purchases of Seidlitz manufactured products as shown in our dealer price list.

Other advertising features have been priced on a net basis to facilitate billing. In these prices we have absorbed an amount equal to or exceeding 50% of their total cost, and no further allowance will be made.

While we realize there are many good forms of advertising, some of which we have made no provision to use, we cannot include everything. We have provided a wide variety of features to make for a well-balanced program. *Our advertising plan is offered to all Seidlitz dealers on exactly the same basis.* Therefore, we cannot participate in any other advertising expense.

Samples, Donations, Etc. No credit will be allowed for contributions of paint for "advertising purposes" to any group or individual. The merchandise you buy is your property and we regret that we cannot credit any dealer for paint given in our name or otherwise without first securing our consent, any more than you would expect to allow us to give your merchandise away.

Samples will be furnished from our factory where necessary. As a general rule, we do not furnish samples with which to sell individual jobs. Such samples should constitute a part of the dealer's normal selling expense and may not be charged back to us.

Local Newspaper Advertising. All advertisements must be our regular mat service as shown on our current Proof Sheet. Where prices are shown in mats, permission is hereby granted to have your printer change them if you so desire. No other changes, alterations or additions will be permitted. Any mat may be used in a larger advertisement including other items such as roofing, hardware, etc., and we will share the expense for the space occupied by our mat only. *Only one mat may be used in any one issue of any paper.* All advertisements must be placed in regular daily or weekly newspapers and not in class publications such as school, church, and labor papers, programs, etc. You place the advertising and pay the newspaper at your *local* contract rate. Send us your paid statement together with the *full newspaper page* containing the advertisement and you will receive proper credit. Destroy all old mats. Order new mats now.

Telephone Directory Advertising. This type of advertising is of such little value in small towns that we will only cooperate in this expense in cities having a population of 25,000 or more. The copy used must be one of those shown on our own Proof Sheet and noted as being appropriate for telephone directory advertising. If other copy is used by the dealer it must be submitted to us in advance of use for our approval or we reserve the right to cooperate on only that part of the copy devoted to our products. Send *Paid Statement* showing such expense and copy of advertisement and proper credit will be issued.

Direct Mail. We have prepared a series of 8 beautifully printed, colorful direct mail folders for mailing with your name to your prospective customers. These will be most effective if you use at least four of the series, mailed about 2 weeks apart. You may select any one or all of them. Eight coupons with special offers are also available for your selection.

These folders will be imprinted, coupon inserted if you desire, addressed and mailed to the list of names you supply us. (Minimum of any one folder, 50.)

These coupons have no redemption value by Seidlitz Paint & Varnish Co.

Any one folder and any one special offer coupon, mailed, including postage, 2 cents each.

As a rule the advertising or sales promotional allowance is geared to a store's total purchases. Thus, American Lady Corset Company paid 50% of the cost of newspaper advertising at the lowest local rate. But a ceiling is placed on the total allowances by limiting the allowance to 5% of the store's purchases.

Use of Leaflets and Folders

Everyone is familiar with the literature which department stores mail with their statements to their charge account customers. These colorful, illustrated leaflets or folders are either provided by the manufacturers of the merchandise or their cost of production and mailing is shared on a cooperative basis.

One interesting example of a sales-producing piece was a four-page folder mailed out by Strawbridge & Clothier, Philadelphia, on Braggi Grooming Essentials for men (cologne, lotions, deodorant sprays, etc.,) distributed by Charles Revson, Inc. It featured "a bonus for you from Braggi: the executive trip kit" and was enclosed in a transparent glassine envelope because it was scented.

Utilizing Valuable Display Space

One of the problems faced by manufacturers is that major department stores jealously guard and control their available floor and shelf space because of the large number of displays offered to them and from which they may pick and choose. Store managers, naturally enough, also like to display merchandise in a neat and orderly fashion, with proper relation to other areas and traffic aisles.

To meet the situation, the Hamilton Beach Division of Scovill Manufacturing Company, in promoting its line of Gourmet small kitchen-appliances, developed a modular display of six movable Cubicon stacks, in varying sizes, which could be arranged vertically or horizontally to meet differing floor-space conditions. The cubes could be made to frame and house the individual appliance units or re-arranged as bases in a two-level horizontal layout.

Department managers more readily agreed to use the display because of its flexibility.

Bloomingdale's Cooperative Promotion

Fashions and beauty were combined to produce a highly effective promotion for Bloomingdale's, New York. Each day, for one week, a different fashion design, centered on the Coty American Fashion Critics' awards; and make-up created by Dina Merrill Inc., were featured in two-hour clinics.

The $5 entrance fee to the Coty Clinic could be applied toward purchase of Dina Merrill's products at Bloomingdale's cosmetics counter where tickets were available on a "first come" basis. Each clinic was limited to 30 participants.

Slides and live modeling of the award-winning designs highlighted the program. The members of the audience watched the make-up experts reproduce the fashion faces and were taught how to create the same effects. A sample kit of the cosmetics used in the presentation was given to each person in the audience.

TRAINING DEPARTMENT STORE PERSONNEL

Most large stores conduct systematic training programs for their salespeople. These are usually under the direction of a trained instructor, and clerks are coached in the fundamentals of good retail salesmanship, as well as in techniques for selling specific types of merchandise. It is often possible for a manufacturer to induce the store management to permit his representative to appear before groups of salespeople to discuss with them the best methods of selling his particular product. Such appearances are usually scheduled well in advance and, if possible, the sales techniques should be dramatized. The dramatization may take the form of a quick skit, a demonstration, or a sound-slidefilm. The Proctor Electric Company, for example, assigns a member of its sales department to conduct meetings for big store personnel. The executive is an experienced public speaker. He demonstrates the right and wrong way to sell an electric iron. With so many inferior quality irons on the market, selling at very low prices, it is important for store salespeople to appreciate that the cost of an electric iron depends on the current it will use during its normal life, rather than on its first cost. To show the loss of heat in a cheaply made iron, the demonstrator cooks a breakfast on the top of the iron utilizing the escaped heat. This type of presentation is always effective.

Arranging an Interesting Program

In the case of a store which is anxious to increase its sales of a certain line of products, the manufacturer can usually arrange to conduct a training meeting for clerks and executive personnel responsible for sales.

In that case the manufacturer should be prepared with an interesting and worth-while program. It should be dramatic but not too dramatic. A store in the Northwest opened a sales meeting with the lights turned down and just a few blue lights burning to enable the salesmen to find their places. A phonograph played doleful music. While the lights were dimmed and blue, the chairman called the meeting to order. He announced that the room had been darkened to resemble the mournful and gloomy point of view which most of the salesmen present held regarding conditions. Then he began to cite bright spots which the salespeople present had overlooked. As each point was mentioned, one white light was turned on. Gradually the room brightened, the mournful music stopped, and it was not long before the bright side of the picture completely dispelled the gloomy side. The "stunt" involved no large outlay of money, and proved tremendously effective to impress upon the store personnel the importance of being optimistic and cheerful. It got over the point that business is what we make it, and there are always people who will buy, if they are *sold*. The stunt paved the way for a demonstration of selling electrical appliances from the floor of a retail establishment.

Stunts That Keep Interest from Lagging

Aside from the use of demonstrations and skits, there are a

Sales meetings are most effective when the points to be emphasized are brought out in a short skit. The Minnesota Mining & Manufacturing Company makes good use of this technique in training Scotch Tape salesmen to help its dealers do a better sales promotional job.

number of ways to get action into a meeting, and drive home sales points about a product.

One method is to have two salesmen show how standard objections can be overcome most easily. Assign different problems to pairs of salesmen and give each pair 2 minutes to put on an act. One salesman takes the part of the customer, the other takes the part of the salesperson. In this way the principle of related sales can be effectively dramatized.

Mock trials also have possibilities. They can be staged with little preparation and do not call for much rehearsing. Care must be used not to let them drag, the snappier, the better. A simple idea should be hammered home. To attempt too much in a stunt of this kind is to kill the effect.

Interrupting the meeting with telegrams or telephone conversations is another popular method of getting over an idea. The chairman stops the meeting to read the message. To make this device effective, there should be a dash of humor to the telegram, but not so much that it will dull its constructive message. At one meeting the program was interrupted by a police officer who burst into the room looking for a thief. He searched all over the place, and finally dragged the culprit out of a closet in the corner. It turned out that he was a time thief—a fellow who stole his own time and thus robbed his family of comforts and luxuries they needed and should enjoy. The damning nature of his crime came out in the conversation between the chairman and the police officer who made the "arrest."

One store, which had the problem of keeping its salespeople sold on all of the many items in a popular selling line, created interest by erecting a great "Wheel of Fortune" and having each number on the wheel represent one product. Salesmen were called to the platform one at a time to spin the wheel, and were expected to tell the others how they sold the particular product represented by the number at which the spinning wheel stopped. The point was emphasized that there were no blanks in the line; that every number was a winner. The manufacturer's representative acted as judge and awarded prizes to the winners.

Handling the "Question" Problem

It is customary to have a period during the meeting for questions and answers after a film is shown. Salespeople come to the meeting loaded with questions, and need to get these questions off their chests. While quiz sessions have much in their favor, they also have a dangerous side. Some questions will be of such a nature that they will interest only a few of those present. Other questions will deal with matters which should not come before the meeting, but could better be discussed privately. There is a danger the meeting may get off on a side track.

To avoid undue loss of time (and it must be remembered that the combined time of the store's personnel represents a good deal of money), the practice is growing of asking salespeople to write out, prior to the meeting, any questions which they would like to ask. These questions are reviewed privately by the manufacturer's representative. Questions which should not come before the meeting are set aside or discussed personally with the salesman. A question box should be provided in the back of the room for this purpose. Put a spotlight on it.

Since many questions are of a technical nature, stores often have one session of a sales meeting devoted entirely to product questions. Tables for ten are set up in a room, and manufacturers' representatives act as hosts at each table. The men divide into groups of 10, and each group moves from one table to another at 15-minute intervals. A bell is rung for everybody to go to the next table. The groups are small enough that the table host can answer, informally and quietly, any questions which arise.

Summing Up at the End of the Meeting

A stunt used to close one meeting was to build a platform. Each plank symbolized one selling point that had been brought out during the conference. The various planks were all labeled, and as they were placed in position, the manufacturer's representative gave a short talk on each plank. This idea not only proved effective in holding interest, but also gave the salespeople something to remember.

Another meeting idea is to have a stenographic report made of the proceedings, and pass copies of the report out to the men, with a summary sheet on top. This report gives them something to study and think about after the meeting is over.

Still another idea is to have a sign painter letter up the principal sales points on 6-foot-high sheets of press board which are fastened together to make a giant book. The book is given an appropriate title, such as "How to Win Friends and Influence Orders." When the time comes to close the meeting, a pretty girl comes onto the stage and proceeds to turn the pages while the chairman of the meeting sums up.

Pass-Out Training Literature

It is the practice of those who attach importance to training big store personnel to do a better job of selling their products over the counter, to prepare some sort of an educational booklet or folder summarizing the principal sales points. These are handed to those attending a training meeting *as they leave*. If a film is shown the booklet should tie up with the film, and perhaps reproduce important frames from the film as memory joggers. If a mock trial is staged, the folder may take the form of the "verdict of the court." Or the piece may simply drive home the key points brought out during the meeting, arranged so that even the least experienced clerk can remember and use them when opportunity comes his way.

It is unwise, however, to attempt to do too much in training material for use of retail clerks. As a rule they are neither students nor readers. They must be taught as though they were taught not.

Charge Account Cards Open New Fields

Some of the major department stores are offering their charge-account customers special services in new fields, such as the health insurance policy offered to the charge-account customers of the eight Florida stores of Jordan Marsh. The announcement included a letter to the customers from the president of the retail organization.

Your bonus from Braggi
(an 11.00 value)

Cologne, Face Bronzer, Pre-Blade Beard Softener, After-Shave Balm

The Executive Trip Kit keeps a 'going man' going. It's packed with the Grooming Essentials a man needs for both kinds of travel... business and pleasure. This bonus is yours with a minimum 5.00 order from the Braggi Collection. Stop by to pick up your bonus. Or complete the attached order card.

Smell something warm and smoky? It's Braggi Cologne. The focal point of the entire Braggi Collection.

Braggi. Conceived and created for men by Charles Revson.

Please send me the following Braggi grooming essentials with my bonus of The Executive Trip Kit. (At least a 5.00 order is required.)

Cologne Spray	8.00 ☐
After Shave Lotion	5.50 ☐
Shave Lather	3.00 ☐
Face Bronzer	5.00 ☐
☐ Medium ☐ Ruddy Tan ☐ Extra-Deep	
Cologne Deodorant Spray	3.75 ☐
Icy After Shave	6.00 ☐
Private Deodorant Spray	5.00 ☐
Super Thick Shampoo	3.50 ☐
☐ Regular ☐ Oily	
Hair Management Spray	3.75 ☐
☐ Regular ☐ Hard to Hold	
Hair & Scalp Conditioner	5.00 ☐
Conditioning Hair Thickener	4.00 ☐
Anti-Dandruff Hair Dressing	4.00 ☐

Distr. by Charles Revson, Inc., N.Y. 10022   Made in U.S.A

Name_____

Address_____ Apt._____

City_____ State_____ Zip_____

Account No. _ _ _ / _ _ _ / _ _ _

Check ☐   Money Order ☐

Please add 75¢ service charge on orders under 5.01. Toll-Free Service from Suburbs within 15¢ toll area ... PENNSYLVANIA call UX 2-4500 ... CAMDEN (metropolitan area) call WO 6-4010 ... other NEW JERSEY points call WX 2500. Mail and phone orders will be delivered from within our motor delivery area. PENNSYLVANIA deliveries please add 6% for State sales tax. NEW JERSEY deliveries please add 5% for State sales tax.

Ardmore, Jenkintown, Wilmington, Cherry Hill, Springfield, Plymouth Meeting, Neshaminy

Strawbridge + Clothier

P.O. Box 358 · Philadelphia, Pa. 19105

A bonus valued at eleven dollars, consisting of four Braggi grooming products for men in a travel kit, was offered in a scented folder included with the statements mailed by Strawbridge & Clothier to its charge account customers.

Buying Power by Regions and States

REGION State	Population Estimate December 31, 1980		Effective Buying Income 1980 Estimate		Retail Sales 1980 Estimate	
	12/31/80 Total Population (Thousands)	% of U.S.	12/31/80 Households (Thousands)	% of U.S.	1980 Total Retail Sales ($000)	% of U.S.
NEW ENGLAND	12,386.1	5.4207	4,423.7	5.4011	51,929,598	5.3772
Connecticut	3,109.0	1.3606	1,106.2	1.3506	12,611,711	1.3059
Maine	1,134.3	.4964	403.4	.4925	4,578,088	.4740
Massachusetts	5,741.1	2.5126	2,056.0	2.5103	25,189,689	2.6084
New Hampshire	935.5	.4094	332.4	.4059	4,225,429	.4375
Rhode Island	949.6	.4156	343.2	.4190	3,326,007	.3444
Vermont	516.6	.2261	182.5	.2228	1,998,674	.2070
MIDDLE ATLANTIC	36,779.6	16.0963	13,227.2	16.1501	146,769,580	15.1976
New Jersey	7,380.2	3.2299	2,576.0	3.1452	31,761,939	3.2889
New York	17,526.3	7.6702	6,386.5	7.7978	68,385,105	7.0811
Pennsylvania	11,873.1	5.1962	4,264.7	5.2071	46,622,536	4.8276
EAST NORTH CENTRAL	41,800.9	18.2938	14,853.5	18.1359	173,847,576	18.0013
Illinois	11,452.7	5.0122	4,091.6	4.9958	48,060,409	4.9765
Indiana	5,512.9	2.4127	1,954.7	2.3866	21,541,075	2.2305
Michigan	9,287.9	4.0647	3,242.2	3.9587	40,545,384	4.1983
Ohio	10,813.3	4.7324	3,881.7	4.7395	44,742,092	4.6329
Wisconsin	4,734.1	2.0718	1,683.3	2.0553	18,958,616	1.9631
WEST NORTH CENTRAL	17,281.8	7.5633	6,308.3	7.7022	74,985,398	7.7645
Iowa	2,924.5	1.2798	1,067.9	1.3039	12,963,454	1.3423
Kansas	2,374.9	1.0394	885.7	1.0814	10,310,072	1.0676
Minnesota	4,103.6	1.7959	1,473.7	1.7993	18,053,915	1.8694
Missouri	4,947.9	2.1655	1,820.6	2.2229	20,751,534	2.1488
Nebraska	1,579.6	.6913	581.2	.7096	6,770,314	.7010
North Dakota	657.1	.2876	232.5	.2839	3,072,873	.3182
South Dakota	694.2	.3038	246.7	.3012	3,063,236	.3172
SOUTH ATLANTIC	37,481.6	16.4030	13,483.6	16.4631	158,370,462	16.3987
Delaware	599.4	.2623	211.5	.2583	2,709,052	.2805
District of Columbia	628.5	.2751	251.7	.3073	2,410,079	.2496
Florida	10,026.0	4.3878	3,877.6	4.7344	47,387,758	4.9068
Georgia	5,536.4	2.4230	1,917.7	2.3415	22,073,227	2.2856
Maryland	4,236.8	1.8542	1,484.6	1.8127	19,567,229	2.0261
North Carolina	5,930.6	2.5955	2,086.5	2.5475	21,567,399	2.2332
South Carolina	3,157.7	1.3819	1,055.0	1.2881	11,509,199	1.1918
Virginia	5,399.0	2.3628	1,900.5	2.3205	23,485,690	2.4318
West Virginia	1,967.2	.8610	698.5	.8528	7,660,829	.7933
EAST SOUTH CENTRAL	14,801.0	6.4776	5,152.4	6.2909	54,285,611	5.6211
Alabama	3,921.9	1.7164	1,367.3	1.6694	14,146,775	1.4649
Kentucky	3,698.4	1.6186	1,288.9	1.5737	14,527,730	1.5043
Mississippi	2,540.2	1.1117	842.6	1.0288	8,237,675	.8530
Tennessee	4,640.5	2.0309	1,653.6	2.0190	17,373,431	1.7989
WEST SOUTH CENTRAL	24,096.8	10.5458	8,479.6	10.3534	108,441,979	11.2289
Arkansas	2,311.3	1.0116	831.4	1.0151	8,851,973	.9166
Louisiana	4,251.2	1.8605	1,444.9	1.7642	16,071,506	1.6642
Oklahoma	3,059.5	1.3389	1,140.2	1.3921	13,488,260	1.3967
Texas	14,474.8	6.3348	5,063.1	6.1820	70,030,240	7.2514
MOUNTAIN	11,629.5	5.0895	4,121.9	5.0327	50,101,345	5.1879
Arizona	2,805.6	1.2278	999.6	1.2205	10,746,119	1.1127
Colorado	2,940.4	1.2869	1,093.1	1.3346	13,586,794	1.4069
Idaho	963.9	.4218	334.0	.4078	3,967,723	.4109
Montana	795.3	.3480	290.3	.3545	3,661,086	.3791
Nevada	822.0	.3598	316.5	.3864	4,515,475	.4676
New Mexico	1,323.1	.5790	454.8	.5553	5,576,939	.5774
Utah	1,497.1	.6552	462.1	.5642	5,453,214	.5647
Wyoming	482.1	.2110	171.5	.2094	2,593,995	.2686
PACIFIC	32,239.8	14.1094	11,851.6	14.4706	147,014,116	15.2228
Alaska	410.2	.1795	136.6	.1668	2,295,107	.2376
California	23,979.8	10.4945	8,814.2	10.7620	108,154,389	11.1990
Hawaii	979.1	.4285	301.6	.3682	4,518,261	.4679
Oregon	2,678.4	1.1722	1,019.4	1.2447	13,186,279	1.3654
Washington	4,192.3	1.8347	1,579.8	1.9289	18,860,080	1.9529
TOTAL UNITED STATES	228,497.1	100.0000	81,901.8	100.0000	965,745,665	100.0000

Source: Sales and Marketing Management's *Survey of Buying Power 1981*

Table of Dozen and Single Prices

Dozen	Each	Dozen	Each	Dozen	Each	Dozen	Each
$0.05		$3.80	$0.31 2/3	$7.55	$0.62 11/12	$11.30	$0.94 1/6
.10		3.85	.32 1/12	7.60	.63 1/3	11.35	.94 7/12
.15	$0.01 1/4	3.90	.32 1/2	7.65	.63 3/4	11.40	.95
.20	.01 2/3	3.95	.32 11/12	7.70	.64 1/6	11.45	.95 5/12
.25	.02 1/12	4.00	.33 1/3	7.75	.64 7/12	11.50	.95 5/6
.30	.02 1/2	4.05	.33 3/4	7.80	.65	11.55	.96 1/4
.35	.02 11/12	4.10	.34 1/6	7.85	.65 5/12	11.60	.96 2/3
.40	.03 1/3	4.15	.34 7/12	7.90	.65 5/6	11.65	.97 1/12
.45	.03 3/4	4.20	.35	7.95	.66 1/4	11.70	.97 1/2
.50	.04 1/6	4.25	.35 5/12	8.00	.66 2/3	11.75	.97 11/12
.55	.04 7/12	4.30	.35 5/6	8.05	.67 1/12	11.80	.98 1/3
.60	.05	4.35	.36 1/4	8.10	.67 1/2	11.85	.98 3/4
.65	.05 5/12	4.40	.36 2/3	8.15	.67 11/12	11.90	.99 1/6
.70	.05 5/6	4.45	.37 1/12	8.20	68 1/3	11.95	.99 7/12
.75	.06 1/4	4.50	.37 1/2	8.25	68 3/4	12.00	1.00
.80	.06 2/3	4.55	.37 11/12	8.30	.69 1/6	12.05	1.00 5/12
.85	.07 1/12	4.60	.38 1/3	8.35	69 7/12	12.10	1.00 5/6
.90	.07 1/2	4.65	.38 3/4	8.40	.70	12.15	1.01 1/4
.95	.07 11/12	4.70	.39 1/6	8.45	70 5/12	12.20	1.01 2/3
1.00	.08 1/3	4.75	.39 7/12	8.50	70 5/6	12.25	1.02 1/12
1.05	.08 3/4	4.80	.40	8.55	.71 1/4	12.30	1.02 1/2
1.10	.09 1/6	4.85	.40 5/12	8.60	.71 2/3	12.35	1.02 11/12
1.15	.09 7/12	4.90	.40 5/6	8 65	.72 1/12	12.40	1.03 1/3
1.20	.10	4.95	41 1/4	8.70	.72 1/2	12.45	1.03 3/4
1.25	.10 5/12	5.00	41 2/3	8.75	.72 11/12	12.50	1.04 1/6
1.30	.10 5/6	5.05	.42 1/12	8.80	.73 1/3	12.55	1.04 7/12
1.35	.11 1/4	5.10	.42 1/2	8.85	.73 3/4	12.60	1.05
1.40	.11 2/3	5.15	.42 11/12	8.90	.74 1/6	12.65	1.05 5/12
1.45	.12 1/12	5.20	.43 1/3	8.95	.74 7/12	12.70	1.05 5/6
1.50	.12 1/2	5.25	.43 3/4	9.00	.75	12.75	1.06 1/4
1.55	.12 11/12	5.30	.44 1/6	9.05	.75 5/12	12.80	1.06 2/3
1.60	.13 1/3	5.35	.44 7/12	9.10	.75 5/6	12.85	1.07 1/12
1.65	.13 3/4	5.40	.45	9.15	.76 1/4	12.90	1.07 1/2
1.70	.14 1/6	5.45	.45 5/12	9.20	.76 2/3	12.95	1.07 11/12
1.75	.14 7/12	5.50	.45 5/6	9.25	.77 1/12	13.00	1.08 1/3
1.80	.15	5.55	.46 1/4	9.30	.77 1/2	13.05	1.08 3/4
1.85	.15 5/12	5.60	.46 2/3	9.35	.77 11/12	13.10	1.09 1/6
1.90	.15 5/6	5.65	.47 1/12	9.40	.78 1/3	13.15	1.09 7/12
1.95	.16 1/4	5.70	.47 1/2	9.45	.78 3/4	13.20	1.10
2.00	.16 2/3	5.75	.47 11/12	9.50	.79 1/6	13.25	1.10 5/12
2.05	.17 1/12	5.80	.48 1/3	9.55	.79 7/12	13.30	1.10 5/6
2.10	.17 1/2	5.85	.48 3/4	9.60	.80	13.35	1.11 1/4
2.15	.17 11/12	5.90	.49 1/6	9.65	.80 5/12	13.40	1.11 2/3
2.20	.18 1/3	5.95	.49 7/12	9.70	.80 5/6	13.45	1.12 1/12
2.25	.18 3/4	6.00	.50	9.75	.81 1/4	13.50	1.12 1/2
2.30	.19 1/6	6.05	.50 5/12	9.80	.81 2/3	13.55	1.12 11/12
2.35	.19 7/12	6.10	.50 5/6	9.85	.82 1/12	13.60	1.13 1/3
2.40	.20	6.15	.51 1/4	9.90	.82 1/2	13.65	1.13 3/4
2.45	.20 5/12	6.20	.51 2/3	9.95	.82 11/12	13.70	1.14 1/6
2.50	.20 5/6	6.25	.52 1/12	10.00	.83 1/3	13.75	1.14 7/12
2.55	.21 1/4	6.30	.52 1/2	10.05	.83 3/4	13.80	1.15
2.60	.21 2/3	6.35	.52 11/12	10.10	.84 1/6	13.85	1.15 5/12
2.65	.22 1/12	6.40	.53 1/3	10.15	.84 7/12	13.90	1.15 5/6
2.70	.22 1/2	6.45	.53 3/4	10.20	.85	13.95	1.16 1/4
2.75	.22 11/12	6.50	.54 1/6	10.25	.85 5/12	14.00	1.16 2/3
2.80	.23 1/3	6.55	.54 7/12	10.30	.85 5/6	14.05	1.17 1/12
2.85	.23 3/4	6.60	.55	10.35	.86 1/4	14.10	1.17 1/2
2.90	.24 1/6	6.65	.55 5/12	10.40	.86 2/3	14.15	1.17 11/12
2.95	.24 7/12	6.70	.55 5/6	10.45	.87 1/12	14.20	1.18 1/3
3.00	.25	6.75	.56 1/4	10.50	.87 1/2	14.25	1.18 3/4
3.05	.25 5/12	6.80	.56 2/3	10.55	.87 11/12	14.30	1.19 1/6
3.10	.25 5/6	6.85	.57 1/12	10.60	.88 1/3	14.35	1.19 7/12
3.15	.26 1/4	6.90	.57 1/2	10.65	.88 3/4	14.40	1.20
3.20	.26 2/3	6.95	.57 11/12	10.70	.89 1/6	14.45	1.20 5/12
3.25	.27 1/12	7.00	.58 1/3	10.75	.89 7/12	14.50	1.20 5/6
3.30	.27 1/2	7.05	.58 3/4	10.80	.90	14.55	1.21 1/4
3.35	.27 11/12	7.10	.59 1/6	10.85	.90 5/12	14.60	1.21 2/3
3.40	.28 1/3	7.15	.59 7/12	10.90	.90 5/6	14.65	1.22 1/12
3.45	.28 3/4	7.20	.60	10.95	.91 1/4	14.70	1.22 1/2
3.50	.29 1/6	7.25	.60 5/12	11.00	.91 2/3	14.75	1.22 11/12
3.55	.29 7/12	7.30	.60 5/6	11.05	.92 1/12	14.80	1.23 1/3
3.60	.30	7.35	.61 1/4	11.10	.92 1/2	14.85	1.23 3/4
3.65	.30 5/12	7.40	.61 2/3	11.15	.92 11/12	14.90	1.24 1/6
3.70	.30 5/6	7.45	.62 1/12	11.20	.93 1/3	14.95	1.24 7/12
3.75	.31 1/4	7.50	.62 1/2	11.25	.93 3/4	15.00	1.25

Anniversaries of Various Events

Book Month
National Colorado Beef Month
National Blood Donor Month
Break-a-Cold Month

1—New Year's; Betsy Ross born, 1752
—Feast of the Circumcision of Christ
—Emancipation Proclamation, 1863
1-Mar. 31—Louisiana Yam Supper Season
2—Georgia 4th state to ratify, 1788
3—Alaska becomes 49th state, 1959
4—Sir Isaac Newton born, 1642
—Utah becomes 45th state, 1896
6—Epiphany
—New Mexico is 47th state, 1912
—Greek Cross Day
8—Battle of New Orleans, 1815
9—Connecticut 5th state to ratify, 1788
11-19—Stephen Foster Week
14—Dr. Albert Schweitzer born, 1875
16-22—International Printing Week
17—Benjamin Franklin born, 1706
17-23—Franklin Thrift Week
18—World Religion Day
19—Robert E. Lee born, 1807
21—Stonewall Jackson born, 1824
23-30—National YMCA Week
24—Gold discovered in California, 1848
—1st Boy Scout troop, England, 1908
25—Robert Burns born, 1759
26—Michigan becomes 26th state, 1837
—Septuagesima Sunday
27—Incandescent light patented, 1880
29—Tom Paine born, 1737
—Kansas becomes 34th state, 1861
30—Franklin D. Roosevelt born, 1882

FEBRUARY

Catholic Press Month
Heart and Hemophilia Month
Frozen Potato Month
Cherry Month

2—Candlemas Day
—Groundhog Day
3—Four Chaplains Memorial Day
6—Mass. 6th state to ratify, 1788
7-13—Boy Scout Week
8-15—Edison Pageant of Light
10-15—Gasparilla Pirate Invasion (Tampa)
11—Thomas A. Edison born, 1847
—Shrove Tuesday (Mardi Gras)
12—Lincoln and Darwin born, 1809
—Georgia Day: Oglethorpe lands, 1733
14—St. Valentine's Day
—Oregon becomes 33rd state, 1859
—Arizona becomes 48th state, 1912
15—Battleship *Maine* sunk, 1898
16-23—Brotherhood Week
17—Founders' Day (nat'l PTA)
18—*Pilgrim's Progress* published, 1678
—Italy united in one kingdom, 1861
19—Copernicus born, 1473
—Edison patents phonograph, 1878
—Marines land on Iwo Jima, 1945
20—Glenn orbits earth 3 times, 1962

22—Washington's birthday
—Spain cedes Florida to U.S., 1819
23—Rotary founded, Chicago, 1905
29—Bachelor's Day

MARCH

Pickle-Hamburger Month
Red Cross and Youth Art Month
Egg and Coffee Month

1—Ohio becomes 17th state, 1803
—Nebraska becomes 37th state, 1867
1-7—Return the Borrowed Books Week
—Weights and Measures Week
—Save Your Vision Week
1-Apr. 30—Spring Clean-Up Time
2—Texas Independence Day
3—Florida becomes 27th state, 1845
4—U. S. Constitution in force, 1789
—Vermont becomes 14th state, 1791
—Presidents' Day
6-12—Girl Scout Week
7—Feast of St. Thomas Aquinas
—Bell patents telephone, 1876
7-12—National Procrastination Week
12—Jane Delano Day (nursing)
—Girl Scouts founded, Savannah, 1912
13—Andrew Jackson born, 1767
—Ides of March
14—Whitney patents cotton gin, 1794
15—Maine becomes 33rd state, 1820
—Passion Sunday
17—St. Patrick's Day
—Camp Fire Girls' Founders Day
18—Grover Cleveland born, 1837
29—John Tyler born, 1790
30—Shut-Ins' Day
—Seward's Day

APRIL

Cancer Control Month
Freedom Shrine Month
National Automobile Month
America's Heartland Development Month
Easter Month

1—All Fools' Day
1-8—National Laugh Week
3—First pony express riders start, 1860
6—Peary at Pole, '09; U. S. at war, '17
6-7—Battle of Shiloh, 1862
8—Ponce de Leon lands in Fla. 1513
—Louisiana becomes 18th state, 1812
—Laetare Sunday
9—La Salle finds the Mississippi, 1681
—Lee surrenders at Appomattox, 1865
9-15—Let's All Play Ball Week
10—Congress creates Patent Office, 1790
10-16—Pan-American Week
11—Sertoma Founder's Day
—International Resistance Movement Day
12—Fort Sumter bombarded, 1861
—Salk polio vaccine successful, 1955
—Halifax Resolution Day (N.C.)
—National Christian College Day
12-17—National Cherry Blossom Festival

Some Dates Approximate

Anniversaries of Various Events

APRIL (cont.)

13—Thomas Jefferson born, 1743
17—National Library Week begins
18—Gen. Doolittle bombs Tokyo, 1942
19—Lexington and Concord, 1775
—John Howard Payne Memorial Day
22—Oklahoma Day
—Arbor Day
23—Shakespeare born, 1564
—First public movies (N.Y.), 1896
24—Arbor Day in 16 states
24-30—National YWCA Week
25-27—National Trout Festival
27—Ulysses S. Grant born, 1822
28—Maryland 7th state to ratify, 1788
—International Carillon Day (noon)
—Shenandoah Apple Blossom Festival
30—Washington our first President, 1789
—Louisiana Purchase, 1803
30-May 7—National Baby Week

MAY

Hearing and Speech Month
Car Care & Good Car-Keeping Month
Clean Up, Paint Up, Fix Up Month
Steel Mark Month
Senior Citizens Month
Touring Theater Month
It's Mattress Size-Up Time

1—May Fellowship Day
—May Day; Law Day, U.S.A.
—Admiral Dewey wins at Manila, 1898
5—U.S. space flight (Shepard), '61
5-8—Washington State Apple Blos'm Festival
7—Surrender of Germany, 1945
—Ascension Day
13—Mother's Day
—Harry S. Truman born, 1884
—World Red Cross Day
8-14—Hospital Week
8-June 19—Senior League Month
11—Minnesota becomes 32nd state, 1858
—Holland Tulip Time
—Israel's Independence Day
13—Jamestown settled, 1607
15—First regular airmail service, 1918
—Nat'l Defense Transportation Day
—Peace Officers Memorial Day
15,16—Cooper makes 22 earth orbits, 1963
15-21—Transportation Week
—Public Works Week
—Police Week
16—Armed Forces Day
19-24—Pickle Week
20-21—Lindbergh flies the Atlantic, 1927
22—National Maritime Day; first steam crossing of Atlantic begins, 1819
23—South Carolina is 8th state, 1788
24—Carpenter in 3 earth orbits, 1962
27—Golden Gate Bridge opened, 1937
29—Fall of Constantinople, 1453
—Rhode Island is 13th state, 1790
—Wisconsin becomes 30th state, 1848
—John F. Kennedy born, 1917
—Mt. Everest first climbed, 1953
30—Memorial or Decoration Day

JUNE

National Recreation Month
National Ragweed Control Month
Fight the Filthy Fly Month
National Rose Month
National Seat Belt Month

1—Kentucky becomes 15th state, 1792
—Tennessee becomes 16th state, 1796
—Fiesta of Five Flags (Pensacola)
3—Jefferson Davis born, 1801; Confed.
—Mem'l Day (also April 26, May 10)
—Pope John XXIII dies, 1963
3-12—Portland (Ore.) Rose Festival
4—Old Maid's Day
4-11—Let's Play Golf Week
5-11—National Humor Week
11—Kamehameha Day (Hawaii)
13-19—Little League Baseball Week
14—Flag Day; U.S. flag adopted, 1777
15—Franklin flies his kite, 1752
—Arkansas becomes 25th state, 1836
17—Bunker Hill Day
19—Father's Day
20—West Virginia is 35th state, 1863
21—New Hampshire is 9th state, 1788
24—Midsummer Day
25—Virginia 10th state to ratify, 1788

JULY

Souvenir Month
Hot Dog Month
National Barbecue Month

1—Dominion Day in Canada
1-3—Battle of Gettysburg, 1863
1-Aug. 31—Pickles for Picnic Time
2—Feast of the Visitation
2-9—Let's Play Tennis Week
3—Idaho becomes 43rd state, 1890
4—Independence Day
—U.S. Military Academy opened, 1802
—Stephen Foster born, 1826
—Adams and Jefferson die, 1826
—Fall of Vicksburg, 1863
—Statue of Liberty presented, 1883
—Calvin Coolidge born, 1872
7—U.S. annexes Hawaii, 1898
10—Wyoming becomes 44th state, 1890
—Transocean TV via Telstar, 1962
11—John Quincy Adams born, 1767
14—Bastille destroyed, 1789
15—St. Swithin's Day
16—First atomic bomb exploded, 1945
17-23—Rabbit Week
21—First Battle of Bull Run, 1861
—Grissom space flight, 1961
—Liberation Day
22-24—Maine Potato Blossom Festival
24-30—National Farm Safety Week
26—N. Y. 11th state to ratify, 1788
—Egypt seizes Suez Canal, 1956
27—Atlantic cable completed, 1866
—Korean armistice agreement, 1953
28—Austria declares war on Serbia, 1914
30—Henry Ford born, 1863
31—Maine Sea Foods Festival

Some Dates Approximate

Anniversaries of Various Events

AUGUST

National Sandwich Month

1—Colorado becomes 38th state, 1876
1—Stone House Day
1-6—Smile Week
2—Last G. A. R. veteran dies, 1956
—First successful Atlas ICBM, 1958
—Friendship Day
3—U. S. Nautilus at Pole, 1958
3—Colorado Day
4—Coast Guard Day
6—Tennyson born, 1809
—Trudy Ederle swims Channel, 1926
—Feast of the Transfiguration
6,9—Hiroshima, Nagasaki bombed, 1945
7—Tulagi, Guadalcanal landings, 1942
—Titov circles earth 17 times, 1961
8—Defeat of Spanish Armada, 1588
10—Missouri becomes 24th state, 1821
—Herbert Hoover born, 1874
13—E. Berlin escape routes closed, 1961
—AFL-CIO asks 35-hour week, 1962
14—Atlantic Charter Day: V-J Day, '45
—Mt. Blanc highway tunnels meet, '62
14-15—Allies invade southern France, 1944
15—Napoleon born, 1769
—Sir Walter Scott born, 1771
—Ft. Dearborn Massacre, Ch'go, 1812
—Panama Canal opened, 1914
—Will Rogers, Wiley Post crash, 1935
—Assumption of the Blessed Virgin
16—Battle of Bennington, 1777
—Alliance for Progress launched, 1961
17—David Crockett born, 1786
18—Virginia Dare born, 1587
19—National Aviation Day
21—Hawaii becomes 50th state, 1959
22—Red Cross Founded, Geneva, 1864
22,23—Sw't Corn Festival (Sun Pr., Wis.)
24—St. Bartholomew's Day
27—First oil well: Titusville, Pa., 1859
—Lyndon B. Johnson born, 1908

SEPTEMBER

National Better Breakfast Month
National Bowling Month
American Youth Month
Frozen Food Buy-Time Month
Home Sweet Home Month
National Pancake Month
Bourbon Month
Labor Day (first Monday after first Sunday)

1—Germany invades Poland, 1939
1-Oct. 31—Fall Clean-Up Time
1-Nov. 29—United Community Campaigns
6-10—Battle of the Marne, 1914
7—Labor Day (first celebrated, 1882)
8—Spanish settle St. Augustine, 1565
—Feast of the Nativity
9—California becomes 31st state, 1850
10—Perry wins on Lake Erie, 1813
12—Defenders' Day (Maryland)
13—British win Quebec battle, 1759
14-20—Lessons in Truth Week (Unity)
16—Cherokee Strip Day (Oklahoma)

17-23—Constitution Week
19-26—Tie Week
19-25—Sweater Week
20—World Peace Day
24-Oct. 1—4-H Club Week
25—American Indian Day
26—Kiwanis Kid's Day

OCTOBER

Country Ham Month
Indoor Games Month
National Wine Festival
Pizza Festival Time Month
Biscuit/Muffin Month
Yambilee; Cheese Festival
National Restaurant Month
Fish & Seafood Parade Month

1—First free rural mail delivery, 1896
1-7—Employ the Handicapped Week
2-8—Letter Writing Week
—Pharmacy Week
3—Schirra makes 8 earth orbits, 1962
—Missouri Day
4—Fire Prevention Week
4-10—National 4-H Week
9—Telephone bridges distance, 1876
9—Leif Ericson Day
10—Oklahoma Historical Day
11—Eleanor Roosevelt's Birthday
11—Pulaski Memorial Day (Nebraska)
11-17—National Y-Teen Week
12—Columbus Day
14—Dwight Eisenhower born, 1890
15—Ether first used publicly, 1846
15—International Credit Union Day
15-24—National Macaroni Week
17—Sweetest Day
19—Cornwallis surrenders, 1781
20—MacArthur lands on Leyte, 1944
20-Nov. 22—Chinese attacks on India, 1962
22—First parachute jump: Paris, 1797
23-29—Cleaner Air Week
—Pretzel Week
23-Nov. 20—Naval blockade of Cuba, '62
26-Nov. 1—National Honey Week
27—Theodore Roosevelt born, 1858
29—N. Y. Stock Market crash, 1929
30-Nov. 29—Jewish Book Month
31—Halloween; Nev. 36th state, 1864

NOVEMBER

International Marine Travel Month
National Retarded Children Month
Thanksgiving March (Muscular Dystrophy)
General Election Day (first Tuesday after the first Monday)
Thanksgiving (fourth Thursday)

1—All Saints' Day
2—All Souls' Day
—Daniel Boone born, 1734
—N.D. is 39th state, S.D. 40th, 1889
5—Guy Fawkes Day (England)
5-11—Cat Week
8—Montana becomes 41st state, 1889

Some Dates Approximate

Anniversaries of Various Events

NOVEMBER (cont.)
- 10—U.S. Marine Corps created, 1775
  - —Stanley finds Dr. Livingstone, 1871
- 11—Washington is 42nd state, 1889
  - —Feast of St. Martin
- 11-12—Germans at gates of Moscow, 1941
- 13-19—Asparagus Week
  - —Diabetes Week
- 13-Dec. 31—Christmas Seal Sale
- 14—Sadie Hawkins Day
- 14-20—Youth Appreciation Week
- 15-21—Children's Book Week
- 15—Articles of Confederation, 1777
  - —Lewis & Clark reach Pacific, 1805
- 16—Suez Canal opened, 1869
  - —Oklahoma becomes 46th state, 1907
- 17-23—Stamp Collecting Week
- 18—U.S. railroads use time zones, 1883
- 18-24—Farm City Week
- 19—Lincoln's Gettysburg Address, 1863
  - —James Garfield born, 1831
- 21—Mayflower Compact signed, 1620
  - —North Carolina is 12th state, 1789
  - —First balloon flight, Paris, 1783
- 21-Dec. 17—Aviation Month International
- 22-28—Latin American Week
- 24-25—Battle of Lookout Mountain, 1863
- 25—Andrew Carnegie born, 1835
- 30—Winston Churchill born, 1874

DECEMBER
- 2—Monroe Doctrine proclaimed, 1823
- 3—Illinois becomes 21st state, 1818
- 5—Prohibition repealed, 1933

- —AFL-CIO merger, 1955
- 6—Feast of St. Nicholas
- 7—Delaware 1st state to ratify, 1787
  - —Pearl Harbor attacked, 1941
- 8—Feast of the Immaculate Conception
- 9—Milton born, 1608
- 10—Mississippi becomes 20th state, 1817
- 10-17—Human Rights Week
- 11—Indiana becomes 19th state, 1816
  - —Edward VIII abdicates, 1936
- 12—Pennsylvania 2nd state to ratify, 1787
  - —Marconi's signals cross ocean, 1901
- 13—Festival of St. Lucia
- 14—Alabama becomes 22nd state, 1819
  - —Amundsen reaches South Pole, 1912
- 15—Bill of Rights adopted, 1791
- 15-31—Christmas Pageant of Peace
- 16—Boston Tea Party, 1773
  - —Beethoven's Birthday
- 16-Jan. 31—Belgian Bulge battle, 1944-45
- 17—Wrights fly, Kitty Hawk, N.C., '03
- 18—N.J. 3rd state to ratify, 1787
- 21—Pilgrims land at Plymouth, 1620
- 22—International Arbor Day
- 23,24—Apollo 8 orbits moon, 1968
- 25—Christmas; Delaware crossing, 1776
- 26—Boxing Day (England, Canada)
- 27—Pasteur born, 1822
- 28—Holy Innocents' Day
  - —Iowa becomes 29th state, 1846
- 29—Texas becomes 28th state, 1845
  - —First American YMCA, Boston, 1851
- 31—New Year's Eve.

Some Dates Approximate

Chapter 34

PROMOTING SALES THROUGH CHAIN STORES

LUCKY is the manufacturer who has established distribution through chain store networks. Whether they consist of department stores, supermarkets, variety stores, or discount stores, they offer volume sales and great promotional opportunities.

Special events are the keystone of chain store promotions. This is a never-to-be-forgotten principle of all successful effort in getting chain stores to push your merchandise or give it special attention.

Anyone who takes the trouble to walk along the streets of any downtown section, almost anywhere in America on Christmas Eve night, after the stores have closed, will see the window decorators and display men hard at work in the chain stores, putting up promotion material for the merchandising events of the day after Christmas.

Independent merchants may be slightly more leisurely in trimming windows and store interiors, but the chains work on a carefully planned schedule, permitting no delays or lulls between events. White sales and other special sales follow the Christmas holidays, without a day's delay. Soon after the January events displays, both window and interior displays are put up for Valentine's Day. On the morning of February 15, after St. Valentine's Day, something else is receiving chain store attention. Then other events may be hooked to Washington's birthday, and so on through the year.

Any promotion manager who wants chain store cooperation must key his own promotions to fit into established schedules, or make his promotional events so valuable that the chains will make room for them in their usually crowded schedules. It is easier to work in with some established event such as School Opening, Thanksgiving, Christmas, Vacation Sales, Fourth of

July events than to attempt some special promotion for which the chain must make special preparations.

Perhaps the next most important principle in chain store promotion is timing. Chain store promotion departments work a long way ahead of each seasonal event. Plans are made months in advance, and each promotion is "buttoned up," with all details arranged far in advance of the actual event.

This means that the manufacturers' or suppliers' promotion material and plans must be ready considerably in advance of the chains' early planning. Time and again some manufacturers have offered excellent promotional material and ideas to chains for certain dates, only to find the chains are already "set" on all plans for that date.

Timing Promotion for Chains

Close coordination with the sales department is necessary to win chain cooperation. The ideal way is to present the promotion at the time the salesman negotiates the sale or contract with each chain. This has a double advantage. Good promotional material may help the salesman land the sale. More than that, it may be the chief factor in the chains' decision to push certain merchandise. Another advantage is that when the promotional material is presented at the same time the sale is made there is little—certainly much less—chance of failure to use the promotion plan or material. Scheduling, therefore, is all-important in this area.

One advantage of working with chains for special promotions is that chains are nearly always more open-minded about what can be sold than the average independent. Chains are never content to rest on their oars. Independents are frequently indifferent to any promotion plan which requires work or expense. So many independent merchants are content to permit sales to rock along as they will, with little or no attempt to capitalize holidays, seasons, or other special days. With the chains there is usually a willingness to go along on an item that holds possibilities. When chain store promotion departments find an item responsive to sales stimulation they hit it hard and frequently.

What Chain Stores Need

While chains will frequently use the same material for store and window displays, some manufacturers find it profitable to prepare special material for the chains. It must be kept in mind that the majority of all chain store windows are made up of mass displays of a wide variety of merchandise. As a rule no one manufacturer's product is ever allowed to dominate a store, or a department, or a window. There may be slight exceptions to this rule when a promotion is on merchandise so important that the sales volume is large enough to warrant a promotion which dominates an entire department. But that is not very often true.

A number of additional sponsors aided the Red Owl stores in putting on the Mrs. Colorado, Mrs. Wisconsin, and Mrs. Minnesota contests. In Colorado, sponsors included Montgomery Ward, Howard Johnson's Motor Lodge, Sigman Meat Company, Inc., Fairmont Foods, and KBTV-TV and KBTR radio.

Firms participating in the Mrs. Minnesota competition included the Leamington Hotel, Fairmont Foods, Fleischmann Yeast, and Swift and Co. In Wisconsin, Fairmont Foods Co. shared the sponsorship.

As a rule a chain store promotion must fit into the regular sales promotion activity of the chain's own promotion department, and must be dovetailed with the department's own activities. Thus, if your product is one that belongs in a School Opening Sale it will be fairly easy to prepare some promotion which hooks into the store's own school opening event. But do not attempt to horn in on school opening week with some promotion which will interfere with it. Wait until there is no big store-wide promotion, or until your product fits naturally into some event which has been scheduled.

Chains Can Create a Market

When chains go to work on a product they can create a market for it if anybody can. During the war when so much merchandise was in short supply, one big national chain went to work on piggy banks and began to give them more promotion, and to stock them in larger quantities, give them better display and more attention. Before anybody realized it the country had a piggy bank boom and piggy banks were selling in tremendous volume. All because the chains saw possibilities in them.

The merchandise shortages of the war period opened up chain stores to many items of merchandise which they had never carried in the past. Low priced books are an example. Prior to the war few chains carried books in any volume, and what books were carried were almost entirely children's volumes. During the war one chain after another began stocking books until today many chains have regular popular priced book departments which are carrying their full share of the sales load. Chain stores do not devote space to slow selling items and if a department fails to produce the anticipated volume it is quickly abandoned.

Another important factor to be remembered in planning promotion for chain stores is the fact that the right sort of promotion will induce the chain to give more space to your merchandise. If the promotion plan actually moves merchandise and the chains see where it would be profitable to give it more space they will be quick to expand the space allowance for any "hot" lines.

Supermarket shoppers are losing their store loyalty. This was revealed in a study of supermarket shoppers released by one of the country's leading market research firms.

Several years ago, the study revealed nearly half of all shoppers did virtually all their grocery shopping in one favorite store. Today this figure has dropped to 12%.

The research firm attributes the change to greater competition plus increased customer desire for more specials, greater variety, and higher quality.

Changes in Store Needs

There are several trends in chain store development today which call for varied revisions in sales promotion programs. Chain stores today are vastly different from the chain stores of only a few years ago. No sales promotion program which is not built with modern trends in mind will produce maximum results. What are some of these changes?

Most important chain store changes are:

1. Higher prices, with constant upgrading.
2. Wider varieties of merchandise.
3. New lines and many new departments.
4. Larger, better lighted, better arranged stores.
5. More and more self-service departments.
6. Fewer clerks.
7. Suburban stores.

Every one of these developments has some influence on sales promotion methods and techniques.

In the food chain field the whole tendency is to eliminate smaller stores and concentrate all effort on larger stores, or super-

There are no salespeople in a true supermarket. The packaging of the product must sell the customer, and the quality must bring her back for repeat business.
(Courtesy CAMERIQUE, Philadelphia)

markets. The Great Atlantic & Pacific Tea Company's policy in this respect is perhaps typical. It has been closing smaller stores steadily for several years, as have National, Jewel, Safeway, and similar groups.

The trend toward supermarket layout and self-service in even smaller, privately owned stores has made new promotion methods mandatory.

As everybody knows, the modern chain drug store is a combined restaurant, soda fountain, drug, sundry, variety, and electrical goods store. Both of the two largest drug chains, Rexall and Walgreen, are building larger stores, more lavish stores, and adding new lines of merchandise. All this calls for sales promotion methods which are in keeping with present trends.

Department Store Chains

It is easy to think of our great department stores as individual units. But there are relatively few department stores which are not involved in some sort of chain operation, or some buying hook-up which is to all intents and purposes a chain store operation. Sales promotion men who think of Marshall Field & Company only as a store in Chicago should remember that this company has branches in all the principal Chicago suburbs and shopping centers.

Many other department stores have branches in shopping centers and even in distant cities. While each store is a separate and distinct unit, many policies are similar. The manufacturer's promotion manager must know, in all of these cases, intimate details of management in the various units of the big department store chains before he can work out sound promotions.

Other big units in the department store field tend more and more to embrace chain store methods. There is a movement in the department store field to curtail the heavy expense of buyers going to market so frequently. This has played into the hands of chain store promoters, and has increased the importance of the big buying organizations.

With the exception of the mail order department stores, nearly all the department store chains allow each store much more leeway than prevails in other chain store promotion programs.

In many drug and grocery and variety chain organizations the sales promotion material comes to the store manager with rigid instructions. It is to be put on display on a specific date, maintained for a given number of days and then "struck" to make way for the next promotion. The individual manager has no alternative but to do as he is told. This is not wholly true of the big department store chains, many of which maintain a complete advertising and sales promotion department at each store.

The Supermarket Distribution Channel

Supermarkets have become a highly effective distributing force for products other than food and household products. Their suc-

Brand names and attractive packaging are important factors in food store market-ing. The neat, orderly displays in supermarkets add to consumer appeal.

(Courtesy: Standard Brands)

cess in selling books and family-type magazines affords food for thought in other fields. For instance, Funk & Wagnalls is using supermarkets to sell its 25-book New Encyclopedia in 25,000 supermarkets, at the rate of one volume a week, with the first volume selling at 49 cents and $1.99 for each of the remaining books. To promote sales, the company features actress Donna Reed in TV spots filmed in individual markets and with other advertising and promotional helps. Supermarkets, of course, have also been engaged in sales of stationery products, toys, greeting cards and seasonal items.

Working with Associations

Many associations now take a strong hand in building sales for members. It is often possible to work in with an industry promotion which ensures better attention for a line of merchandise than would otherwise be possible. Every sales promotion manager whose company is a member of some group such as American Meat Institute, National Association of Bedding Manufacturers, Milk Foundation, or any of the other hundreds of associations should check all his sales promotion activities with these associations to determine whether or not some association activity will coincide or conflict with his own plans.

In nearly every field there is a trade association which does some type of industry-wide promotion. In addition there are varied phases of each industry which have special promotion activities, many of which can be used to advantage by the individual manufacturer.

For example, in the office furniture field there is the Wood Office Furniture Institute. This group, of about 20 leading manufacturers of desks and chairs, publishes a private magazine, advertises wood office furniture in business papers, publishes a merchandising manual, and makes and distributes other helps such as sales training films.

There is a national association of Ford motor car dealers, and many local groups of the same dealers. These groups engage in varied sales promotion activities which, at times, offer opportunities for tie-ups with other manufacturers. These are also local groups which can be useful in sales promotion to manufacturers.

Magazine and Newspaper Promotion Plans

Chain Store Age stages, once a year, a national promotion designed to promote the sale of larger sized packages. This promotion, which started in a relatively small way, has grown and grown until it is now almost a promotion classic in the chain store field. It is typical of others which seem to grow more and more important. *Esquire* magazine has all but taken over Father's Day and works out elaborate promotion plans, with considerable display material well in advance of the annual Father's Day event. One of the big advantages of these promotions being sponsored or guided by a magazine is that there is a tendency for an entire industry to work together and coordinate all sales promotional effort toward a common goal.

Many of the general magazines for women, as well as those of a more special nature, stage promotion events which have been embraced by chain stores. However, it should be pointed out that nearly all of these magazine promotions are available to independent as well as chain stores, and should not be considered special chain store events, although the chains are often quick to capitalize on them and make intelligent use of all the material offered.

No sales promotion plan should ever be entirely wrapped up without checking with all the magazines to determine what promotions the magazines may be planning for the period.

Newspapers in the larger cities stage a number of events which have chain store promotion possibilities. Food shows, cooking schools, sport and outdoor shows, garden shows, travel shows, and other similar events are common in our largest cities. These are often sponsored or managed by newspapers and, although they are not national, may swing considerable sales power in local areas.

Radio, Television, and Motion Picture Plans

Motion picture stars have been used in so many different promotion plans that it scarcely seems necessary to describe them. Unnumbered thousands of Western costumes, toy pistols, bandannas, hats, and other items were sold as a result of childish fascination with cowboy heroes.

Tie-ups with current motion pictures have at times produced terrific sales of various products and have been amazingly successful in tie-ups which have sold breakfast foods, given away bicycles in large quantities, and performed other almost miraculous sales events in which chain stores were a factor.

Building promotions around television programs is also so widely accepted that only passing mention is necessary.

It should be pointed out that it is often dangerous and difficult to confine one of these big, spectacular promotion campaigns to chain stores alone, unless the merchandise is sold only by chains. While it is true that the chains are often more willing and more capable of a tie-up with some big promotional event, the manufacturer of a product sold in all types of stores can scarcely favor one group of stores —i.e. a chain—above others.

This problem should not be difficult if the promotion plan is good enough to warrant both chains and independents using it. Certainly there are times when a special promotion designed only for a group of chains, or even for only one chain, is justified. Chief reason for this is that the chains take a plan and put it to work; whereas many independents will be almost wholly indifferent to an excellent promotion plan.

Training Chain Store Personnel

As a rule chain stores prefer to do their own sales training, rather than to work with suppliers. The reasons for this are readily understood. Chain stores feel that it is important for them to direct the sales efforts of store personnel so the sales emphasis will be placed on products and brands which show the most profit. Some of the larger chains operate well-organized training programs. These are usually decentralized, with the main responsibility placed upon older employees in the store. There is a trend, however, to use manufacturers' visual training aids, especially sound-slidefilms. These have a very definite advantage in *showing* clerks how to sell.

The training formula used by Sears, Roebuck & Company covers 10 points, as follows:

1. Determining what the learner already knows.
2. Telling the employee the facts to be learned. (Lecture, conference, film, manual study, etc.)
3. Discussion to fix the understanding of the content.
4. Telling back by the learner.
5. Demonstration by the instructor, and then by the learner.
6. Reteaching on points not understood.
7. Final demonstration of knowledge (skill, attitude) at end of organized instruction.
8. Performance under supervision.
9. Spot checking of performance for errors.
10. Reteaching or supplementary teaching to improve knowledge or skill.

The Unions and Sales Training

Retail chains which have contracts with labor unions have raised new problems in training store personnel. Unions view meetings held under company auspices with suspicion, and attempt to write into contracts that such meetings must be held on the company's time.

One oil company, as stated, which undertook to interest its filling station salesmen in a sales training course on their own time, ran into union difficulty in some cities. The management got over the hurdle by making it clear that the purpose of the training was self-improvement of the individual, and arranged for outside speakers who were not employees of the company.

The local business agent and union officials were invited to the initial meeting and asked to decide whether it was an activity which they should or should not support. The program for the first meeting was set up so as to appeal to the self-improvement desire of the filling station salesmen, and it was made crystal clear that enrollment in the course was entirely voluntary, that no one *had* to come, and that the purpose was to help the filling station salesman do a better job.

In most cases the union officials reacted favorably to the program after sitting in at the first meeting, and in some instances the union leaders actually volunteered to see that members of their union took the training. As a result this company regards its filling station salesmen training activities as one of the most important features of its public relations program.

Contest Plans for Chains

Many chain stores are great users of contest plans in which stores and store managers are pitted against each other in selling contests. The manufacturer's sales promotion department which can get a chain to include its merchandise in a contest is almost sure to enjoy stepped-up sales.

Arrangements for contests must be made with headquarters and, as in all other planning, arrangements must be made months in advance of the actual event. Contests can be planned among the personnel of a store, or between stores. Contests for one store are possible only in the larger stores where there are several employees in the department handling the merchandise on which the contest is staged.

Mrs. America state contests, which put a high value on home-making talents, have proved to be an excellent means of promoting food products and gaining community good will.

Such was the experience of Red Owl Food Stores, Minneapolis. This aggressive chain, with outlets in nine midwestern states, found the promotions so effective it handled the Mrs. America contest in three states in its trade area.

A leaflet offered in scores of Red Owl stores was one of the keys of the campaign. Slanted to the community-minded housewife, the brochure had an entry coupon to be filled out and mailed in.

Hundreds of housewives from communities in the three states sent in the brochure coupon. Each entrant was sent a four-page questionnaire based largely on homemaking problems and family life.

Special Week Plans

It is becoming a joke in this country that there are several times as many special week promotion events as there are weeks in the year. Nevertheless, the idea of a special week is difficult to beat in lining up chain store sales activity. For example, National Crochet Week was taken over by the chain stores and put to good use in selling crocheting materials. The Spool Cotton Company, perhaps better known by the famed old brand names of J. & P. Coats, and Clark's O.N.T. Crochet Cottons, made the most of this event. Prior to Crochet Week this company stocked the chains with two 10-cent books, "Crinoline Lady in Crochet," and "Floral Insertions," both in four colors. Chain stores used these books as the basis for window and interior displays during Crocket Week and not only sold many of the books, but a large volume of thread as well.

The company advertises in magazines reaching chain store executives and managers to line up cooperation with its national advertising. One year the company's big shot was a full page in four colors in the highest circulation magazine announcing a "Crochet Your Way Contest" with $10,000 in prizes. Chain stores hooked onto this contest and featured the books, even though the big advertising barrage followed Crochet Week by less than a month.

Crochet Week was a promotion of National Needlecraft Bureau, Inc. One of the features of its campaign was a $1,500 prize contest for window displays featuring crochet work during Crochet Week. There were prizes for department stores, independent variety stores, and for chain stores.

First prizes were $250 each in each group of stores. Only requirement for entry was an 8- by 10-inch photograph of the store. The Bureau paid $5 for each photograph submitted, whether it was a contest winner or not.

In addition to the various weeks in which chain stores often participate, chain stores are more than glad to have assistance on promotion of all other holiday events, such as Valentine's

Day, Mother's Day, Father's Day, Fourth of July, School Opening Week, etc.

Packages and Counter Cartons

Chain stores have always been partial to self-selling merchandise, and merchandise which lends itself to shelf display. This is more important today than ever before because chains are attempting to step up volume without employing additional help. Any piece of merchandise which can be mounted on a card, tucked into a display carton to sit on a counter, or hung on a wire frame or a plastic display rack has a better chance of winning chain store cooperation.

So important is this factor of self-selling that many manufacturers experiment constantly with display devices, and build entire sales campaigns around a counter display, or self-selling device of one kind or another. Here are some examples:

Sta-Rite Ginny Lou, Inc., has built a tremendous volume in chain stores on Sta-Rite Bobby Pins, mounted on die-cut cards, which carry an assortment of pins, state the price in large numbers, and show attractive illustrations in color of the pins in use. The company features two cards in business paper advertising because it has built a big business around properly displayed merchandise items.

Berkeley Industries, manufacturer of closet accessories, has been successful in getting many chains to use a large two-sided floor display which has 12 items mounted, ready for instant sale.

E. I. du Pont de Nemours & Company packs toothbrushes on a display card with 2 dozen brushes on each card. The same company furnishes a Lucite counter display which contains 3 dozen brushes. E. Z. Thread Company uses an attractive 4-color display carton to pack 6 or 12 dozen tapes with gripper fasteners. Griffon Cutlery Company promotes a counter display cabinet containing $140 (wholesale) worth of scissors and shears. The former Seiberling Latex Products Co. featured bathing caps in a counter display carton, with 2 dozen to a carton—12 white caps, 4 red, 4 green, 2 blue, and 2 yellow caps in each.

One visit to any chain store shows the importance of packaging merchandise so that it sells itself. In many stores today there is such a shortage of selling personnel that merchandise must literally sell itself or it just doesn't sell at all. This is almost 100% the case in many food stores, especially the large supermarkets, or other stores where the customers expect no help from store clerks. And it is rapidly becoming the custom in many other stores to permit the customer to select his or her own merchandise, bring it to a wrapping station to be wrapped, and "paid out." Packaging such products as meats has made it a lot easier for food stores to do away with the long waits customers had in getting service in that department.

The white space should be big enough to care for the varying sizes of stamps used for marking, and located with a view to ease both in price marking and in reading by the checker.

Fully as important as the design of the package itself is the matter of having the package *in stock* when the consumer is ready to buy it. While this is *always* important, it becomes a *crucial* matter when there is no clerk to assure the disappointed customer that the store is "expecting a shipment any day"—and persuade the consumer to wait. Today, in most chain stores, you are either *in stock* or *out of luck*.

Sales promotion men, with experience in conducting promotional programs aimed at stimulating sales of national brands in self-service stores, agree that the promotions which pay off the best in the long run are those built around the merit of the product, rather than those which appeal to the bargain instinct. These are in the nature of temporary price cuts. They include such promotions as 1-cent sales, combination offers, couponing, premiums, etc. They place all the sales emphasis on some product, other than your own, for example, a premium. The result is a "shot-in-the-arm" sales spurt and the inevitable morning after. Chain store promotions, like any promotion aimed to improve a competitive position, should recognize the fact that there is competition between commodities as well as brands, and the commodity which fails to promote itself is likely to be demoted.

Product Displays

The trend toward self-service in every type of store and the intense competition for display space on counters and islands means that it is all but suicidal to attempt to sell anything but staples without some type of window, counter, or ledge display. A prominent chain store promotion man lists the following requirements for a good display piece:

1. It must be easy to set up, and sturdy enough to stand up well. Should have its own easel or base and not require fastening, tacking, or attaching to any other fixture.

2. It should illustrate the product in use if there is the slightest chance the consumer cannot see at a glance exactly how to use it.

3. It should be colorful, well designed, and simple.
4. It should be informative, including the price.

This same executive added that the card or display device must not be so tall that it will obscure vision of adjoining departments. Today the majority of chain stores will not put up anything which interferes with a customer's line of vision. They want the customer to see all the way to the back, while standing at the entrance. For this reason some very tall cards sent to chain stores in the past have been discarded. Do not expect the chains to use counter display devices which "hog" a department or take up too much room. Counter and display space, as well as floor space, is carefully laid out in all chain stores, and space is allotted strictly on the basis of sales produced by each item. Many promotional devices planned for use in chain stores have been failures because the sales volume did not warrant the space required.

It is extremely important to check this matter of space. If the manufacturer's idea of space required does not coincide with a chain store management's experience and ideas, do not attempt to force chains to use larger displays than they desire to, for theirs is the final decision and must prevail. (See also Chapter 17, "Store Displays and Promotions.")

Selecting Sales and Dealer Helps

Many of the most astute and experienced promotion men make it a rule never to buy any display or counter device until dummies have been made up by hand and tested in an actual store. A device which looks excellent on their desk may have some glaring fault which will not be apparent until it goes on the store counters.

It is usually much cheaper to pay for a few hand-made dummy samples for checking and testing than it is to run the risk of producing a quantity of displays only to find they are too tall, clumsy, or otherwise unsuitable. Recently a manufacturer developed a display card on which were mounted one dozen items. In testing the card empty or dummy cartons were used. The card seemed attractive and just what was needed. When the cards were all printed and the merchandise mounted, it was found that the cards were unstable; the easel was not large enough and the cards had a tendency to topple over on the counters. The promotion was a flat failure.

This same principle must be applied to every step along the way in planning any promotion for chains. It is not enough to check with a store manager, or to make some sort of a test in a little corner store. Check everything with top men in the chain organization, then double check with the chain's own promotion and display men. It is necessary to become familiar with each chain's rules and regulations and policies, and to be currently familiar with chain promotional activities. Without this knowledge there is a big hazard that your carefully planned and expensive promotion will fail for some simple reason which could have been discovered by careful checking.

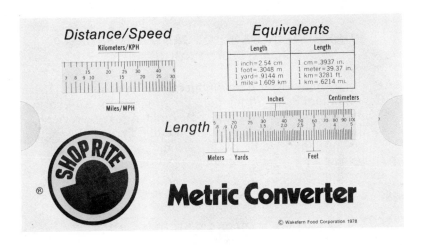

The chain of Shop Rite supermarkets offers its customers a free Metric Converter slide-chart. The front shows the equivalents for weights, liquids and temperatures; the reverse side converts lengths and distances.

Chapter 35

INDUSTRIAL SALES PROMOTIONS

THE American Management Association Conducted a "briefing" on the subject of "The Total Approach to Industrial Sales Promotion." Simply by listing the topics covered serves as an indication of the many aspects of industrial sales promotion. The subjects discussed included:

DEVELOPING AND ORGANIZING SALES PROMOTION PROGRAMS

A. Pre-Planning—Determining Objective, Theme and Approach
B. Coordinating Sales Promotion Programs with Advertising, Public Relations, Marketing, Sales and Agency Services
C. Evaluating and Selecting Most Suitable Type of Promotion
D. Organizing the Plan or Event—Promotional Checklist
E. Budgeting and Administration
F. Evaluating Results

SOLVING MAJOR PROBLEMS WITH SALES PROMOTION

A. Changing or Enforcing the Company Image
B. Attracting Distributors
C. Increasing the Effectiveness of Salesmen
D. Creating Sales Promotion to Meet Demands of Modern Purchasing Techniques
E. Launching New Products
F. Reaching New Markets
G. Creating the Sales Promotion Campaign for International Markets

Buying Motives of Industrial Prospects

It is not unusual in discussing sales problems with a manufacturer selling to industrial buyers for him to say: "We don't go for sales ballyhoo in our business. Our salesmen are trained engineers and they do business on an engineering plane. Sales promotion may be all right for the manufacturer of electric refrigerators, but our business is different." But is it? Actually they are faced with the problem which confronts every manufacturer sooner or later, that of making people want what they make.

A manufacturer of bearing metal built up a tight little business because he made a product of superior quality. But it was higher in price than competitive metals. When his salesmen called upon a machinery manufacturer, they usually contacted the purchasing agent who took the position that since the bearing metal now being used was satisfactory and lower in price, there would be no point to increasing the cost of the machine.

Then one of the salesmen learned, while talking with a user of this type of machinery, that it was not uncommon for bearings to burn out. When that happened the mill was down until the machine could be taken apart and a new bearing poured—all of which cost time and money, to say nothing of lost profits. This gave the salesman an idea.

The salesman went back to one of the large manufacturers of this type of machinery, but instead of calling on the purchasing agent he called on the sales manager. He reported his conversation with the mill owner, and asked the sales manager how much his company could afford to pay to have machinery which would cut down the customer's loss from such shut-downs. The sales manager didn't know the answer, but admitted he would have a big edge on his competitors if he could offer machinery which ran faster with less risk of burning out bearings. By converting the higher speed into terms of production, savings could be shown which would justify any reasonable price. The salesman asked if such an advantage would be worth $50,000 a year to the company. The sales manager felt sure it would. Then the salesman explained the company could add from 3 to 5 years to the life of its machines, run them at a much higher rate of speed, thereby increasing production per machine, and cut the breakdowns one-third to one-half, by spending not $50,000 a year, but $5,000 a year—the cost of his bearing metal over that which the engineering department was currently specifying and what the purchasing department was buying. The sales manager "sold" the engineering department on the idea of giving the salesman's metal a thorough test. The test proved out, and for more than 10 years thereafter this bearing metal was used in all machines made by that company.

The point, of course, is that this salesman went to town when he discovered that customers who were only mildly interested in quality, if it increased the cost of their products, were tremendously interested in increasing the operating efficiency of the machines they sold. He stopped talking about how much better his bearing metal was than that made and sold by his competitors, and concentrated instead upon convincing his customers they could place themselves in a stronger competitive position by increasing the life and wearing qualities of the bearings on their machines. He made them want that competitive advantage more than the money it cost, and his sales talk began to click. So did the company's sales promotion when it capitalized on this salesman's discovery and stopped bragging about how much better the product was, and emphasized what a better metal meant in terms of longevity. Thus a principle well established in the promotion of "unwanted" consumer products paid off for a manufacturer who had always believed that a product which was superior to those offered by competitors would sell itself, even if the price were higher. People will make a path to the door of the man who makes a better mousetrap, provided first of all they *want* a better mousetrap.

A common fault in much promotion for technical products is too much emphasis on technical points and too little attention to the basic fundamentals upon which every sale depends, regardless of what the product may be or the type of customer who is being sold. A proper balance should be maintained.

Breakdown of Promotional Effort

While there are certain groups in the industrial field which operate extensive sales promotional departments, as, for example, companies selling trucks, earth-moving machinery, and other heavy and relatively high-priced products, the majority of companies combine sales promotion with advertising. The tie-in with sales, rightly or wrongly, is less pronounced than in the consumer field.

A study of a typical year's breakdown of the industrial advertising budgets of 500 representative companies revealed the following percentages of expenditures:

Technical and trade magazine space	41.0%
Company catalogs	13.0
Direct mail	9.2
Production (space advertising)	8.0
Space in general magazines	5.2
Publicity	4.1
Salaries and administration (where charged)	4.0
Exhibits	3.5
Dealer and distributor helps	2.4
Motion pictures and slidefilms	1.3
Newspaper space	1.2
Market research	0.4
Other expenditures	6.7

Just what these figures cover in some cases is not certain. What comprises direct mail, for example, might be debated at length without general agreement.

Similarly, the word "publicity" is open to question. However, there can be no doubt but that the lion's share of industrial advertising money goes for publications of various kinds.

DEMONSTRATIONS AND EXHIBITIONS

Since most industrial products are sold on the basis of what they can do, manufacturers lean heavily on demonstrating the product to promote its sale. This is particularly true of machinery and heavy industrial products. There is a growing number of industrial shows, both national and regional, which offer an opportunity to display the equipment and even show it in action. Users of equipment are usually willing to cooperate and permit a manufacturer or his representatives to bring prospective buyers to their plants and see the equipment in operation. In the case of equipment or materials which can be easily transported, some manufacturers employ technically trained representatives to put on demonstrations in the plant or mine of the prospect.

Short of an actual demonstration of the product itself, the next best way to promote its sale is by "case studies" made by an independent research organization. These studies show how the product is used by a particular plant, the savings it has made possible, and other benefits obtained from its use. This type of sales promotion was popular prior to the depression of the 1930's.

The Open House

An excellent way of reaching industrial customers is by holding open houses.

Gulf Supply, Inc., Beaumont, Texas, an industrial supply company, staged its own trade show to help get product information to customers and prospects. According to Rudy Williams, Gulf Supply's president, the show produced at least 50 new customers and brought in an additional $1 million annually in sales.

The company displayed products of 57 different manufacturers. Two factors led to staging the show. First, the management felt that there was a need to quickly tell each product story to its increasingly sophisticated market. Second, with cooperation from the manufacturers, the distributor had staged smaller, but similar "open houses" and results indicated that a big show would bring even better response. A three-day show was planned at the company's Houston branch.

Five thousand prospects were formally invited to spend a day at the show. More than 3,600 accepted, and schedules were arranged so approximately 1,200 could attend each day. The distributor, impressed by results, scheduled shows in other cities.

Contests as a Promotional Aid

A type of promotion which is becoming popular in the industrial field is competitive demonstrations, such as an "Earth-Moving Contest" where manufacturers get together and put on a "show" for an interested audience. These competitions had their inception in the plowing contests which are the high spots in county fairs. They serve the double purpose of making onlookers dissatisfied with their present methods and equipment, and awakening interest in up-to-date methods.

The value of such promotions, however, depends on how the competition is publicized. The right people must be brought out to see the show, a means of registering them must be devised, and no opportunity missed to capitalize on the interest created. This can be done by developing special literature around the more interesting competitions, featuring results in paid advertising (rather than depending too much on free publicity) in industrial and other publications. Good photographs, offered gratis to the press, are a big help. Editors, who might not give a contest free publicity, find it hard to resist a good "action" photograph. Caterpillar Tractor secures thousands of dollars' worth of excellent publicity by furnishing high-grade photographs of its equipment *in action.*

Mailable Visual Aids

A manufacturer of spray nozzles for water treatment plants was recently faced with the problem of showing prospective customers what his products could do. He wanted to explain and demonstrate the variety of results that may be achieved. His solution was to use a miniature 8-frame film strip of 35mm. color slides mounted on stiff cardboard, mailed in an envelope together with a folding slide viewer. The slides showed aeration nozzles installed at such widely separated locations as Providence, Rhode Island; Newark, New Jersey; and Westfield, Massachusetts, and described the salient features of each nozzle.

Demonstrating nonportable products is only one of the many ways a mailable visual aid may be used. The depth, clarity and realism of 35mm. color transparencies mounted on a strip makes them ideal for:

> Generating interest in new products.
> Introducing new advertising campaigns.
> Previewing television commercials.
> Winning support of new ideas.

Psychologically, the attractive pocket kit commands attention. Few who receive it can resist looking through the eyepiece. Also, experience shows the kits have a long retention value. Recipients view the pictures again and again. Among other uses that have been made of the portable slide viewers:

> A roofing company depicted completed home improvement jobs, provided each of its door-to-door salesmen with kits.
>
> A leading electrical company introduced a new cable product to heads of engineering departments throughout the nation.
>
> An automobile company previewed new car models to 350,000 stockholders in advance of public showings.
>
> A soft drink company announced television commercials to salesmen, distributors, and regional bottlers.
>
> A manufacturing company portrayed a sequence of inplant facilities and community living advantages to aid in recruiting technical personnel.

Johns-Manville Campaign

To promote sales of its Rampart fiber glass shingles, Johns-Manville provided dealers with a promotion kit consisting of a counter display, a supply of "How To Buy A Roof" brochures which fit into a pocket on the display, proofs of consumer and trade ads and a sample copy of a new Rampart fiber glass shingle brochure. A card to order additional counter displays and brochures was also included. Dealer efforts were supported by general magazine and trade paper advertising.

To promote its fiber glass shingles, Johns-Manville provided dealers with a counter-card display containing a pocket for consumer brochures. Proofs of consumer and trade ads were also supplied in the dealer kit.

GETTING LEADS FOR SALESMEN

One of the most effective ways to promote the sales of industrial products, which may be purchased only occasionally or to fill a special need, is to keep "feeding" salesmen worth-while leads. This has a double value to the company, it conserves the salesman's time and increases his production and it also keeps the salesmen on their toes and reduces turnover and the cost of bringing new men into production.

However, there are leads and leads. Some sales managers make the mistake of thinking any kind of an inquiry is a good lead and get quite provoked at salesmen who won't follow them up. Not so long ago, one of the factory equipment manufacturers, after a favorable test, went all out on a program of obtaining leads for its salesmen. It issued a library of application booklets, featured them in advertisements in technical publications, and succeeded in getting hundreds of requests for them.

These requests were acknowledged, then sent to the salesmen to be followed up with a personal call. When the inquiry was sent to the salesman, he was sent a special form which he was required to fill out and mail back to the advertising department. The report indicated the date of his call, what transpired, whether he made a sale, and if not, why. If the salesman did not report in 10 days, he received a needling letter. If that didn't work, he got a letter over the sales manager's signature explaining that the inquiry had cost the company a lot of money, and the company expected him to call promptly and, if possible, turn the inquiry into an order.

On its face this looked like a good system, and the advertising manager was quite keen about it. It supplied him with some very useful figures to use on the board of directors when there was any doubt as to what the results were from all the money that was being spent for advertising. But the salesmen soon lost their enthusiasm for following up the inquiries after they had wasted a good deal of time following up curiosity seekers. They resented the needling from the advertising department, and before long the whole plan broke down. The advertising manager was replaced and advertising emphasis was placed on what the product would save, rather than on a free booklet. That type of advertising did not produce so many inquiries, but those it did produce were invariably closed by the salesman.

Republic Tells Its Story

Because of their nature, size or bulk, industrial products and raw materials lend themselves to the use of films and slides. To bring its story of degassed steels to its own sales force and, in turn, to their customers, Republic Steel Corporation used a packaged communications program for presentation to both of these important groups.

The tools employed included a flip chart, a meeting guide, a take-home piece for the salesman, and a 16mm. motion picture. The film was used to drive home the advantages of the Republic operation to the salesmen.

The program is, in fact, complete enough for the customer to conduct *his* own meeting if necessary.

To help salesmen to set up these meetings, an 8mm. sound film (shown on Fairchild repeater-type projectors) is available for management showings. The 11½-minute color film in this packaged program "Ladle Vacuum Degassing," is a straight-forward technical film report showing the actual process at work in the steel mill— from the melting furnace to the new induction-stirred vacuum degassing units. The exposition of these facts and the commentary are sufficiently nontechnical to be understood by men who have steel-related interests but who may not be technically-oriented. Produced in 16mm. Kodachrome, prints were reduced to 8mm. sound for field shows.

Inland's "Magic Show"

"Magic" was used by Inland Steel Co., Chicago, to dramatize the advantages of its new steel at a technical trade show. The company used a magician and his pretty assistant to capture the attention of show visitors. With the aid of a few props, a piece of carbon steel was magically brewed into a gleaming sheet of the new steel. Another piece of the new product took the shape of a square, a circle, and a diamond in rapid succession. The performances were presented 12 times daily during the four days of the show. The Inland Steel exhibit produced 850 requests for more information and 85 orders.

Reciprocal Sales Leads

A fertile source of leads for salesmen in the industrial field are companies who are buying what you sell, and to whom you are sending orders for what they make. Some sales executives frown upon "reciprocity" in sales relationships, contending that both sides usually get the worst of these deals. It is a form of "you scratch my back, and I'll scratch yours" selling which, they contend, undermines good business relations. On the other hand, when both buyer and seller publish prices, and there is not much chance of "loading the order" just because of the buyer-seller relationship, there is no reason why reciprocity should not be practiced. It is important, however, that the matter be approached in a constructive way, either in personal contact by the salesman or in correspondence. Nothing can destroy good will more quickly than a salesman who barges into the purchasing department of a company from which you buy to solicit business on these grounds alone.

A letter which worked out very well for the Quaker Rubber Corporation, in obtaining leads from sources of supply, yet which did not attempt to "strong arm" the supplier follows:

Gentlemen:

Did you ever split an axiom?

Well, let's try. Let's shatter the old axiom that states "Suggested Reciprocity Is Poor Business."

We feel that suggested reciprocity is NOT poor business and that it will NOT create a negative response if one does not try to hide the subject behind a fancy-worded letter.

To be very honest, Quaker Rubber Corporation, like every other company, is continually seeking new business. In this process, our suppliers came to our attention. We have purchased your goods for some time and we know you, for the most part, only by those products and materials we buy from you. May we suggest that you enlighten us further on other products we might be able to buy from you? In turn, may we have the opportunity to give you a more complete picture of the 9,001 industrial rubber goods we manufacture that you could possibly use in your operation?

The definition of reciprocity per Webster is, "Mutual dependence and cooperation." For the life of us, we can see nothing sinful or negative in that definition. The negative connotation was born, we feel, in the minds of those people who have deliberately applied it with unscrupulous intent.

In closing, let us put it this way--if we were not a customer of yours, we would not hesitate to try making you a customer of ours. Why should the situation be any different just because you happen to supply us with some of the products which you make?

There! Don't you think that old axiom is split wide open? Why not write us and let us know what you think?

Yours very truly,

Organizing Leads for Road Salesmen

If the business employs only a few salesmen who travel out of the home office, the cost of following up leads in far away places poses a problem. The cost can, however, be held to a minimum if as leads come in they are duly acknowledged and sent the proper sales literature at once. If the inquiry looks important and urgent a red tack, numbered to indicate the month of receipt, is stuck into a control map, in the city where the inquirer's plant is located. If it seems to be just a run of the mine type of inquiry, a dated blue tack is stuck in the map. If it is of doubtful value, possibly just a curiosity seeker, a white tack is used. Call slips for each inquiry, in duplicate, are made out and filed geographically, by state, city, and company.

Whenever a salesman is planning a trip, the sales manager can see at a glance where the "hot" prospects are located along the route he will follow. He pulls from the file the original call slips on all red, blue, or white prospects in those cities, hands them to the salesman, who uses them as a basis for making up his itinerary. At the same time the salesman's name is noted on the duplicate call slip remaining in the file, so that there is a record of the salesman to whom it was given and the date.

"Use the User" Contests

One of the most fruitful sources of leads is the satisfied user of a product or service. Some years ago a sales manager in the automobile field made the statement, and proved it, that any salesman could double his earnings if he so arranged his time that, in addition to his regular contacts, he called twice during the year on present users of the car sold by his company. His first call was to get better acquainted and show an interest in the car owner's problems, and then, having established a friendly basis, persuade the car owner to give him the names of friends who might be interested in buying a new car. It is common practice among life insurance underwriters, when having written a policy for a man, to get the names of his friends who might be in need of more insurance.

This same principle works in sales promotion as well as in personal selling. During the depression when utility companies were doing everything possible to build their lead, a number of them inaugurated "Bird Dog" contests for office employees. The purpose was to get these employees to check with their friends to learn whether they were planning to purchase any electrical appliances, and then turn in a prospect slip on them. The slips were sorted out by territories and given to outside salesmen who followed through. If a sale resulted, the employee who turned in the lead was awarded a certain number of points good for merchandise of his own selection. If no sale resulted, the employee still received a few points just for turning in the lead. To build up interest in the plan, prize books, featuring the merchandise with the number of points required to win it, were distributed. To qualify for the prizes an employee had to turn in five leads, and when he had done that, his light was lit on the office scoreboard. Each week the number of points to the credit of each contestant was posted on the board so the entire office force could see how the campaign was progressing and who was in the lead. To keep interest at high pitch weekly mailings of an educational nature were sent to the home of each employee, with a letter to interest the employee's homefolks in the opportunity the contest offered to get those long-wanted things for the home just by making a few calls of an evening.

The use of this type of contest received a setback in March 1949 as a result of an opinion by the Wage and Hour Administration that employees competing in such a contest are entitled to time and a half compensation for the hours they work outside of business. The opinion reads:

"Where the engagement in contest activities takes place outside of the normal working hours, it is necessary to keep accurate records of the time so spent and to compensate for such time according to the provisions of the Fair Labor Standards Act. The fact that such time is voluntarily spent by the employee and no compensation is promised, other than the prizes for employees accumulating the greatest number of points, does not affect this conclusion."

This ruling, of course, would not affect employees not covered by the Wages and Hours Act, and does not touch the contest status of professional and administrative personnel or outside salesmen.

Subscribing to press clipping services, new building reports, trade papers, and similar publications is another source of good leads which should not be overlooked.

COOPERATIVE CATALOGS AND BUYERS' GUIDES

A method of promoting the sale of "specified" products worthy of more thought and attention than it usually receives is "reference advertising." In the building, engineering, and other fields, it is an almost impossible task for those who design and specify products to keep on file up-to-date catalogs of even the leading manufacturers. Yet it is imperative that detailed information about materials and products to be specified should be available in the office when projects are under discussion or when the specifications for the job are being drawn.

This problem has been solved in some industries by the cooperative catalog, of which Sweet's is an outstanding example. These catalogs are simply the condensed catalogs of many different manufacturers supplying products in a certain field, standardized in size, and bound into one book or library of books. They are usually published by a house with contacts in the field, or as is the case with material handling equipment, by a group of manufacturers on their own. In such cases they employ an advertising agency to organize the book, handle mechanical and production details. Each cooperating manufacturer distributes his own reference books, or this may be done by a central office to avoid duplication.

Buyer's guides or trade directories are published for nearly every important industry. In addition to listing sources of supply, they carry the advertising of companies that wish to bring their product to the attention of the buyer at a time when he is wondering where to get it.

Type of Advertising Most Effective

Advertisements for cooperative catalogs or trade directories should give as much detailed information about a product as an architect or an engineer might require. Unlike "copy" for technical and trade publications, which must first catch the reader's eye to get attention, and therefore must be arresting and well displayed, copy for reference use can be relatively "dry" and still be read. It should give dimensions, list and describe the various grades and sizes in which the product is available, and give facts which will help the reader make an intelligent decision. Most reference advertising is too general and riddled with superlatives. While any advertisement must do a certain amount of selling, reference advertising should be planned to *serve* rather than sell.

Another weakness of reference advertising is that too much copy is usually crowded into too little space. It is better, if funds are inadequate to do a job in all reference books published in the industry, to buy more space in a few of the most widely used books and do a thorough job. If the coverage of a reference book is relatively small, and is used only by a fraction of the industry, it is better not to use it at all than to use billboard "copy." While such "copy" may result in a few people writing for catalogs, that objective can be attained at less cost, by the use of publications which are read for equipment news rather than used for reference. Advertising is not different from any other business undertaking—if it is worth doing at all, it is worth doing well. This is especially true of reference advertising, too much of which is poorly done.

FOLLOW-UP CAMPAIGNS

Making a sale has been likened to laying siege to a city. First of all you surround it and then you attack, and keep on attacking until you wear down its resistance and the city falls. So it is in selling. Some sales objectives are attained quickly and with relative ease by a single call. But more often it is a case of locating the prospect and then getting the order by "keeping everlastingly at it." It is not unusual in industrial selling to work on a prospective buyer for several months, or even years, before he signs on the dotted line. This is especially true in the case of heavy products the sale of which requires overcoming many prejudices and well-entrenched buying habits.

The Industrial Mailing List

Building a list of prospective buyers is relatively simple when the product is sold to stores. All that is necessary is to take a trade or city directory, check the names against credit rating books for buying ability, and from other sources get the name of the individual who owns or manages the store. In selling to industry, however, it is not enough to know the names of establishments which could profitably use what you are selling. You need to know (1) the name of the person or persons in the organization most likely to instigate the purchase of your product; (2) the name of the executive who will requisition the product; (3) the name of the officer who will approve the requisition; and finally (4) the name of the purchasing agent or executive who will actually place the order. They are all factors in the sale. In all probability the salesman sees only one or two of these persons. The others, when known, must be systematically followed up by mail. Failure to make sure that every factor in the sale was "sold" might mean the loss of not only the order, but the effort expended by the sales and sales promotion departments to get that establishment on the books.

This "penetration" of important prospective accounts presents a difficult problem in industrial marketing. It can be accomplished to some extent by well-planned advertising in publications known to cover all buying factors involved. Some technical publications are so well edited, and so newsworthy, that they are "must" reading for most of the executives and engineers in a plant. But that is assuming a great deal. Purchasing agents, for example, are usually so busy that they have little or no time for reading. They may read a publication edited expressly for purchasing executives, then again they may not.

The only safe way to be sure of getting deep penetration is to build up, with the help of the sales force, industrial directories, and other sources, as complete a mailing list as possible; painstakingly classify each name so it can be quickly selected for special mailings; and then work it systematically with "reason why" sales literature. The all too common practice of sending such pieces to the company with no individual names, while all very well under certain conditions, is inadequate if you want to penetrate a large industrial plant. Tests show that company-addressed mail is usually opened in a mailing department by the mail clerk, who uses his judgment (which may be good or bad) as to who should get the piece. Since mailing clerks rate promotional literature very lightly, if at all, the piece usually lands in the wastepaper basket of the third assistant in charge of purchasing. It should have been sent directly to the executive most likely to specify the purchase of your products.

On the theory that an industrial buyer who is once a prospect is always a prospect until he buys, and even after that, mailing lists used to promote sales to industry are usually embossed on metal address plates, of a style which permits selector tabbing. Thus the plates might be tabbed first to permit selection by line of business or according to the use of the product. Another arrangement of tabs might enable the promotion manager to select desired classification of executives. He might not want to send the same message to the engineer who is looking for ways to improve his product, as he would to the operations executive who is interested mostly in increasing production, or the purchasing agent who is interested above all in price. Or again, in the case of supplies or materials which are bought continuously, it may be desirable to select names according to when the company last purchased.

One company making and selling brass specialties to industry, for example, found that by classifying prospective customers according to the time of the year they were in the market for the products the company sold, and then timing mailings to each group of buyers to reach them at that time, paid big dividends. It almost doubled the returns from mailings. Another New England company, concerned because it was spending as much to promote sales to prospects of limited buying power as it was to prospects whose business was highly desirable and far more profitable, divided its mailing list into "blue" and "white" prospects. In addition to selections possible by the use of selector tabs, the blue cards were used on address plates of especially good prospects. The other cards were white.

With that distinction, it was possible for the addressing machine operator to address envelopes or mailing pieces only to "blue" prospects by simply skipping the white cards as the plates passed through the addressing machines. Blue names were worked once a month; white names three times a year. This permitted concentrating the bulk of the sales promotional budget on the most desirable names.

But no matter how painstakingly a mailing list may be compiled, it can soon become a liability unless constantly checked for dead names. This is especially true when the names of individuals are used. Trade papers should be watched and clipped for corporate and personnel changes. Mail returns should be handled as they come in, and not allowed to accumulate for weeks and months before the list is corrected. Once a year lists should be run on strips and forwarded to the salesman or distributed in the territory to make sure there are no dead names on the list. It is not always wise, however, to kill names which the salesman deems "duds" just because he hasn't been able to sell them. There is no such thing as a "dead" prospect.

Follow-Up Letters

There is no better device for following up names of prospective buyers than well-written, good-will building letters. They do not have to be filled in with the prospect's name, if his name is on the envelope to make certain the letter will go to his desk. Tests show that the extra cost of matched fill-ins is seldom justified. If a letter is that important, and sufficiently personal to call for a salutation, it is better to use an automatic electric typewriter for duplicating it. A paper "record" is cut, after the fashion of a player-piano roll, which when put in the machine operates the typewriter keys automatically. The machine can be stopped where desired and a special paragraph, line, or word can be typed in by the operator, who usually operates a battery of three or four machines at one time. To make doubly sure the prospect receives the letter, carbon copies can be made at the time the original is typed, and mailed a few weeks later with a penciled notation "Did you receive this letter?" These carbon copies often produce better results than the original.

Follow-up letters should be short and to the point if they are to be read by busy executives of industrial plants. They must come to the point quickly and talk about the prospect's problems rather than the writer's. They should be dignified in style, quickly get attention, create interest, prove your claim, and get action. They should not be loaded down with technical descriptions which can be presented better in a mimeographed or printed attachment accompanying the letter. A good rule is to let the enclosure describe, and the letter sell.

A stratagem which has worked well for many companies selling industrial equipment is to develop a series of letters, each on a different letterhead and each over the signature of a different executive. Thus the first letter may be from the manager of the service department, the second from the chief engineer, the third from the sales manager, and the fourth from the president. Each writer would, according to his position with the company, approach the sale from a different angle. The first two letters would be "warmer uppers" and the last two closers.

Service Bulletins

Periodical frequency of promotional mailings is desirable, not alone to keep the name of the company and its product before industry, but to obtain the cumulative values which accrue to any well-planned advertising effort. That is why so many companies selling to industrial markets favor the house organ as a sales promotional device. However, unless house organs are unusually well done and contain information of real value to technical-minded persons they are just one more piece of direct mail. Industrial house organs are too often started without consideration of the need of the industry. The manufacturer decides it would be a wonderful thing to have a company organ which would be read once a month, 12 times a year, by all his customers. The first few issues are lively and of real value, but all too soon the material runs thin and the editor is hard put to fill the pages. Before starting a house publication make sure a high degree of reader interest can be maintained, and that there is a need for the type of publication you intend to issue. It is, as a rule, foolish to spend money for a house publication in a field already served by a lively, newsy, trade or technical paper. You would only be doing in a less effective way what is already being well done. However, there are opportunities for well-edited house publications in specialized industrial fields. The *Value News*, published by Rockwell International, is an excellent example.

To get away from the stereotyped house organ format, and the obligation to get out a house publication every month, quarter or whatever period may be decided upon, some favor the bulletin service type of communication. This usually consists of one or more loose-leaf sheets, arranged for reference filing, with a brief covering letter. The letter personalizes the contact, and the loose-leaf sheets describe applications of interest to the reader, or other technical data which he is glad to receive and have on file. This type of promotion is flexible, and can be inexpensively produced by multilith or planograph process. Some of the sheets may be mimeographed, or if four colors are required for a special purpose, those sheets can be produced by letterpress. The number of sheets included in any given release may be changed according to the material to be released.

Standard Industrial Classification (SIC) Codes

Industrial marketers who wish to target specific industries may benefit from the Standard Industrial Classification codes issued by the U. S. Census Bureau. SIC starts with the broadest industrial groups and by a series of subdivisions, identifies and classifies industries down to the product level.

First is the manufacturing section. This is divided into 20 2-digit major groups, such as SIC 28, chemicals; or SIC 20, food. These are subdivided into 3-digit groups. The next classification lists specific industries, of which there are 457.

A complete list of industries and their definitions appears in the SIC Manual, available from the U. S. Government Printing Office, Washington D.C. 20402. Price $14.00.

SIC offers many uses for industrial marketers' sales and promotion departments, and research personnel; and for mailing list selection.

Chapter 36

THE MANUFACTURERS' AGENT

FOR thousands of manufacturers who are unable to stand the financial burden of maintaining a force of salesmen for exclusive representation the manufacturers' agent is, in a sense, a godsend.

While he may be, to some manufacturers, a heaven-sent blessing, he is at the same time a baffling problem. It seems that the chief ambition of every manufacturers' agent is to assemble as many lines, corral as much territory as possible. Then he can sit in his office and wait for orders to come in over the transom. This is, in some cases, literally what happens. Some manufacturers' agents are so well established, have so many lines, that a mere trickle of business on each line will earn them from $30,000 to $40,000 a year in commissions, with amazingly little effort.

Then there is another type of manufacturers' agent who has one or two good lines, gives them constant and aggressive sales work, and is altogether a great blessing and asset. Naturally, this latter variety is scarce. There is never enough of his brand to go around, and the good manufacturers' agent, who is doing a job for one or more manufacturers, usually is offered a new line about once a week. It is the insatiable demand for good agents that creates the problem. The agent has little incentive to take on some line on which there is little business in his territory, and put men to work on it on a missionary basis, so long as he has established lines which are showing a profit currently. Yet in the office of a good manufacturers' agent there is a constant stream of men from factories urging the agent to take on "just one more line."

The better the manufacturers' agent is, the less likely he is to take on another line. There are manufacturers' agents who have represented one or two, or possibly three, lines for 20 to 30 years. These agents have turned down hundreds of opportunities to represent other manufacturers.

There is also the manufacturers' agent who gets up a little office, hires a part-time secretary to answer telephone calls, and begins assembling a badly assorted group of lines, hoping to have enough windfall business to earn a living. He has little sales ability, is short of capital, and is a bad investment for any manufacturer. But it is often surprising to see how many good lines are tied up with agents who are unable or unwilling to put any creative salesmanship into the picture.

Types of Manufacturers' Agents

The manufacturers' agent differs from the sales agent in that he handles many different products and operates entirely free of control from the manufacturer. On the other hand, a sales agent such as those selling a line of cash registers, appliances, or machinery, operates under a franchise which defines the agent's area of operations, and while it may not be written into the agreement, it is thoroughly understood that if he takes on a competitive line, or fails to meet a required sales quota, the franchise will be cancelled. Unlike a distributor, the manufacturers' agent sells to whomever he pleases, and it is not unusual for such agents to sell wholesalers, dealers, and consumers alike.

Another advantage of the manufacturers' agent is that he offers manufacturers an economical, if not always a very satisfactory, way to cover sparsely settled or fringe territories where it would not pay to travel a salesman. Agents also serve, in the case of machinery and equipment manufacturers, to provide a way to show the product in strategically located centers. Inquiries are referred to the agent, who is in a position to demonstrate the product to interested prospects. There are certain things which cannot be sold from pictures; the product must be seen before it will be bought.

Then there are low-priced, nonrepeating products which require some selling effort, but are not sufficiently profitable to sell direct. These can be economically distributed by carefully chosen agents. And the same holds true of lines such as furniture, which repeat slowly, that can be sold by salesmen carrying a number of related lines about as well as if they sold only one line. Traveling salesmen today is rather expensive, and good salesmen are few and far between.

Another type of manufacturers' agent is the specialist who controls a number of large accounts, such as bottling plants, by virtue of his knowledge of the bottling business and his facilities to aid them in solving production and marketing problems. This type of agent can get business which the manufacturer's salesman might have some difficulty in obtaining. The creative nature of such customer service works to the advantage of the manufacturer too, since the more business the agent helps his customers develop, the more the agent will sell to them and the more the manufacturer, in turn, will sell. Specialist agents usually operate under agreements which restrict their sales to certain groups of customers, within a given territory or even nationally. For example, a bottle cap manufacturer desiring to build up his sales to Dr. Pepper bottlers might give a manufacturers' agent specializing in servicing Dr. Pepper bottlers the exclusive right to sell such bottlers a specific type of cap in a stated region, such as the Southwest or on the Pacific coast.

Selecting a Manufacturers' Agent

The sales manager of a well-known company manufacturing an established line of mechanical specialties had to find an agent to represent a new line the company was marketing. He came to Chicago and called on three large buyers of the product in question. All three recommended the same manufacturers' agent, who was handling related lines.

The sales manager felt that he had exactly the right man. He was able to sign up the man of many recommendations. Back to his offices he went, more or less elated that he had obtained such a promising man.

Weeks passed without orders. Then months passed. A stream of letters to the agent brought brief replies to the effect that they were "getting lined up." Other alibis followed in place of orders. When the sales manager finally returned to Chicago for investigation, he found that the agent he had signed was not interested in the line. He merely took it on with the hope that some windfall business would come his way.

This experience, which has been repeated thousands of times, clearly shows the problems of the sales promotion manager who works with manufacturer's agents. He must produce promotion aids, and sales aids: (1) which are easy to use; (2) which fit in with the agent's other sales aids; (3) which do not take up too much room, or weigh too much; and (4) which are complete, simple, and virtually self-explanatory.

While we understand that the sales promotion man usually has little to say in the selection of manufacturers' agents, it is true that the first step in building sales through agents is proper selection. Too often agents are selected without rhyme or reason. Agents should be selected for:

1. Knowledge of the product—or
2. Knowledge and following of buyers;
3. Reputation for honesty and good service;
4. Sales ability, and sound judgment;
5. Reputation for sticking to a few lines.

Do not anticipate best results from an agent who has a badly assorted group of lines. For example: One agent has a line of razor blades and cutlery, a line of fishing tackle, and a line of baking specialties sold to wholesale bakers. The trouble is that none of the lines are related or complementary. On the other hand, another highly successful manufacturers' agent has a line of office desks, and two lines of office chairs, all three of which are related and sold to substantially the same customers.

As a rule, the smart manufacturers' agent will stick to lines which have some relation to each other, and which do not require cultivation of a wholly different class of trade. It is the rare agent who can sell a jeweler on one call, then hit it off with a garage owner the next call; nor can the man who sells steam plant specialties make encouraging progress with a line of automobile accessories. A clothing man if he has a short specialty line may do all right with a notion line, but if he jumps the fence into a distant field, he may be worth little to the manufacturer.

Sample Equipment and Sales Kits

There are few manufacturers' agents who are equipped to do a creative selling job similar to what we expect from exclusive salesmen. They may have other lines; they cannot, or will not, carry too much material in the way of samples and sales kits. They want something which will fit into, or which can be combined with, their regular sales portfolio or sample case.

A sales manager whose line is sold in many territories by manufacturers' agents had this to say: "The average manufacturers' agent will not place new sheets in his catalog binder; he will not post price changes in his book; he will not carry a demonstrator, or samples. This is particularly true of the older, better established men. Day after day we get telegrams and telephone calls, as well as letters, asking for current prices, or other information, from agents who have neglected to read the mail and bulletins we send them.

This problem of getting agents to keep their catalog up to date, to post price and specification data, and to maintain samples is the biggest one we have. We have tried everything and are far from having the problem licked."

Pessimistic as this report is, it is typical enough to be studied carefully. It spotlights at least one of the most harrassing problems which occur in dealing with manufacturer's agents. But these are not all the problems. Manufacturers' agents often do not cooperate in sending in call reports or lists of prospects, or ask for mail assistance. They expect same day answers to all their inquiries,

Designed for personal selling or individual training, this portable audio-visual projector by La Belle Industries uses a synchronized cartridge with audio capacity up to 36 minutes (at 1⅞ I.P.S.) and 250 single-frame 16mm. visuals.

but will not answer letters, mail reports, or work with the promotion managers as they should.

Nor are they always active in going after leads sent to them, or in following up inquiries. In spite of all this, millions of dollars in sales are made through manufacturers' agents every year.

How much cooperation can be won from them depends almost entirely upon the sales promotion manager's understanding of their problems. To win and hold cooperation the sales promotion manager must produce a sample outfit or sales kit which will create profit for the agent. Otherwise it will not be used, no matter how beautiful or well done it may be.

How to Plan Sales Kits

Find out from each agent what sort of kit he is now using most frequently. If possible plan a kit which will fit into the cover he is already using. This is not to save the price of the cover, but to get it into the kit or portfolio he is already using. A number of promotion managers plan such kits, put them in a cover, but suggest to the agent that he remove the contents and incorporate it in his regular kit, or catalog cover.

Obviously it is better to have a complete presentation kit with cover, if we are sure the agents will use them. Hence it is customary to include good covers, but with rings, or posts, or other binding devices which will fit into the covers the agents are already using.

It may be that agents are using different sized kits. When this is true, select the size the largest number of agents are using and plan your material to fit those kits.

Several years ago a group of manufacturers in a small trade association were all using different sized catalogs—some considerably oversize. It was found that the larger catalogs were not popular with manufacturers' agents; they carried the standard 8½- by 11-inch catalogs and neglected the others. Today this group of manufacturers all use the same size catalogs, binders, and a standard punching arrangement.

After obtaining the agent's own ideas for a sales kit, produce a kit which carries a complete sales story, with a full-fledged sales presentation to enable the agent to present your proposition as it needs to be presented. The sales kit that does the double duty of educating the agent and selling the customer as well is the best investment. Such kits are costly and need expert preparation. They must be simple, forceful, and brief. Impressive illustrations are a big advantage. Include in the sales presentation all the necessary information such as specifications, prices, performance data, parts prices, so that in one package the agent has everything he needs. This may not be practical in some big lines, but it should be followed wherever possible.

Miniature Models and Lay-Out Devices

Much selling is done today with scale models. This is especially true of machinery, store and office equipment, furniture, refrigeration equipment, etc. Floor planning and lay-out sheets are also useful in closing sales and making presentations.

For example, one company furnishes manufacturers' agents with a special carrying case, containing a cork board divided into squares, each square representing one foot each way. With this it furnishes scale models of the equipment with tiny pins in the bottom. These pins are pushed into the cork board, in the exact position the equipment will occupy when installed.

In this particular case the manufacturer sold the case, scale models, and cork board mounting for about $75 to each manufacturers' agent. Some of them objected, others refused to buy, but enough did buy to make the venture profitable.

The manufacturers' agents in this case were selling to dealers and they were supposed to sell each dealer a kit for each salesman. The agents were reasonably successful in selling to dealers; but a fair percentage of the less active dealers declined to buy.

Preparation of sales kits for use of manufacturers' agents must be governed to a great extent by the kind and type of agent the manufacturer has. How many other lines does he carry? How much time does he devote to your line? Does he carry your samples or kit every day, or just on special occasions? Does he use it on the majority of calls, or only on calls where he is selling your line and nothing else?

In some offices of manufacturers' agents we find a vast array of samples, sample cases, brief cases, ring binders, and similar material piled in a corner, stacked in a closet, or buried in deep drawers of desks. These are, theoretically, hauled out for use when needed. But the trouble is that in too many cases the manufacturers' agent, or his salesman, goes out on a call forgetting all about the fine presentation portfolio he has back in the office.

It is obvious that all sales presentation kits, sample cases, lay-outs, or miniature model outfits must be so good the agent will decide he cannot do without them. Otherwise he is prone to attempt to sell without this help.

Educational Literature for Manufacturers' Agents

Many sales promotion managers believe that the best literature for manufacturers' agents is the type of material which they can pass on to customers. They feel that the agent, always hard pressed for time, will not be very studious in reading material addressed to him, for the purpose of keeping him informed. But he will pass along literature to prospects and customers on whom he calls, and in doing this will absorb part of the information.

When material addressed to the manufacturers' agent alone and not to be seen by customers is used, the best type is that which gives news, or experience. It should show:

1. What agents are doing with the line.
2. Who is buying, and what items are selling best.
3. What results the customers are obtaining.

A constant stream of experience data sent to manufacturers' agents will gradually build confidence, show sales opportunities, and induce the agents to give the line more attention.

Of course, each agent should be furnished with all the educational literature available for the lines or products he carries. When warranted it is a good investment to furnish racks or other equipment to store this literature. This is especially important where customers visit the agent's office or showroom.

Bulletins and Sales Letters

Almost without exception sales promotion managers are emphatic in asserting that the agents want and will read news about the product more than anything else. For example: One company got out a large

Manufacturers' agents are often aided in their selling efforts by industry promotions, as in this trade paper advertisement by the American Iron and Steel Institute.

folder showing a group of new and widely known buildings in which its equipment was used. Wherever it is possible tie product literature to some news event, such as the completion of a large hotel, a famous store, a skyscraper, or some other well-publicized building. One company produced a well-designed 8-page folder showing how its equipment was used in a new hotel under construction, and a data sheet on the use of its product in a new skyscraper being built in New York City.

News-type literature gives the agent something to pass on to his customers and prospects in selling. "This is the model selected for the new Mutual Life Building in New York," he tells the prospect. He has just picked up this bit of information from a company bulletin.

Another popular type of bulletin is a report sheet on performance. Give these sheets some special name such as "The Barometer," or "The Score Board," or even a less dignified name such as "The Dope Sheet." In it report, with as much detail as possible, activities of other agents. Tell who they are selling, what products they are selling, how many repeat orders they are getting.

In such bulletins it is an excellent idea to get in as much competitive news as possible. For example, "This week Cincinnati Office (name of representative) came in ahead of Cleveland, Pittsburgh, Detroit, St. Louis, Indianapolis, and Philadelphia, with the largest volume ever booked by Cincinnati."

After such a report give the figures, if your policy permits, and then chide the other cities, daring them to beat Cincinnati next week or next month.

Group cities according to size and publish their standings. Get one agent to challenge another agent. Offer prizes for specific performances. The big problem with agents is to snag your fair share of their selling time. This cannot be done unless each agent is kept constantly informed about the results achieved by other agents.

House Organs as Sales Promotional Devices

Any company which publishes its own house magazine should put all the agents on the mailing list. Even though it is strictly an internal house magazine, send it to the agents to help them become more familiar with the business.

While few companies publish house magazines wholly for manufacturers' agents it is usually profitable to send the agent regular editions of all house magazines published. If possible have a section for field agents. Better still publish a magazine just for them.

In publishing a house magazine for manufacturers' agents begin with obtaining each agent's photograph. Offer to pay for them if necessary. Then as fast as one agent produces business, find some excuse to use his picture. Here is a point to remember. In every news item written about a manufacturers' agent, write it so he can show it to customers.

The house organ or magazine should be written and edited very much like sales bulletins. It should feature news, news, news. Leave out the joke column, long and windy "inspirational" messages, material clipped from other house organs. Agents have precious little time for reading and they will not or cannot read a lot of general material. But they will devour news about your product, its performance, improvements, changes, new uses, and similar information.

Some companies publish house magazines, punched to fit binders used by the agents in sales work. A reasonable percentage of the agents will include these house magazines, if they are not too bulky, in their sales kits to show to customers and prospects. Pack the house magazine with case histories of other agents, case material of use and performance, and similar news material. Use as many pictures as possible, with informative (not boastful) captions under or above each picture.

If a manufacturers' agency is composed of a number of people, put each person on the list if possible. By all means put all names of active fieldmen or salesmen on the list. Do not think that the various members of the sales staff are going to be too careful in passing your magazine along to each other.

How a Typical Manufacturers' Agent Works

There may be no such thing as a thoroughly typical manufacturers' agent. But here is a story about one, perhaps better than average.

He has six others in his organization: His personal secretary; a bookkeeper, price clerk and general assistant, who also handles the switchboard; three salesmen; and one secretary for them.

The owner of the business spends all his time servicing two large and two smaller mail-order houses. One of the salesmen has two chain stores, several wholesale houses, one big retailer. The second salesman has a group of large retailers, three small wholesalers. The third salesman services all other retailers in the metropolitan area whose volume is large enough to warrant personal calls. The majority of retailers are serviced by wholesale salesmen.

These four active men spend the major part of each day away from the office. The clerical help handle correspondence and appointments, post price changes, and keep catalog pages and other literature available. Everybody is busy; no one has time for much reading or answering unnecessary correspondence.

Now suppose we look at the other side of the picture. Another manufacturers' agent uses his home as his office. He has eight lines, three of which are more or less competitive. He works practically the entire state of Texas. He is on the road perhaps an average of 4 days a week, 45 weeks a year. He has a real following of dealers whom he has been selling for years. In many towns he sells to dealers who are intensely competitive. For his three main lines he probably does a reasonably good job. From the others he merely obtains windfall business. He has been known, however, to force some of his secondary lines on certain dealers by threatening to take away his top lines. This man has no secretary, is slow in answering mail, neglects all paper work, and usually waits so late in all paper work that he uses long distance telephone instead of letters. Several of his manufacturers would be happy to make a change, but do not dare because they fear his influence with the dealers, and do not want to risk another man who might or might not turn in the volume he commands.

Such a man is a difficult problem from the sales promotion man's angle. He will not cooperate in many sales promotion activities. His long experience and his wide acquaintance with dealers insures a fair volume and he does no more than a routine promotional job on any dealer, or for any of his lines. He is independent, difficult to lead or manage, and claims he refuses many good lines each year.

Several younger men have attempted to establish themselves in his field, but only one has made much progress. They are unable to obtain lines which have the same merit or acceptance as his lines have. Manufacturers, although they profess much dissatisfaction with their present representative, are hesitant to risk their lines with younger men who have no "following."

Neither the one-man setup just described nor the seven-person agency in Chicago is aggressive in going after new business. Their established business keeps them busy. There seems to be little hope in getting agencies which are well established to put in much missionary work. They contend that it does not pay.

Miscellaneous Sales Aids

Manufacturers' agents will do a good job on one type of sales promotional material—useful gadgets to give away, otherwise known as advertising specialties. Book matches, pencils, blotters, calendars, and similar materials are enthusiastically welcomed by nearly all manufacturers' agents. One agent reports: "I have two men in addition to myself. We have tried, for many years, to have some useful device to present to customers on each call. One trip we will leave a handful of pens at every stop; next trip we will have book matches; again we will take a calendar, or a calendar card. We are constantly writing manufacturers for supplies of such material. We find it helps open up interviews, and is especially helpful where assistants, receptionists, telephone girls, and secretaries can pave the way toward an interview."

Manufacturers' agents are relatively inactive when it comes to using dealer helps, putting up displays, signs, or other advertising material. They do not have the time, and often feel it beneath their dignity. Chief exception to this is in the food field, where a manufacturers' agent employs several young men to detail retailers.

Winning Agent's Cooperation

It must be admitted that manufacturers' agents present a difficult sales promotion problem. Only in the rare case where the agent represents one or two noncompetitive manufacturers will he offer the full cooperation with the sales promotion manager that is needed to produce maximum results.

Misunderstandings and lack of confidence in the manufacturer are one cause of this failure to cooperate. One manufacturers' agent in Los Angeles told an editor of this HANDBOOK: "We have two lines on which we purposely hold sales to about $20,000 a year. It has been our experience that the minute volume jumps above this figure the manufacturer will hire his own man. On another line we stop work when sales seem likely to go over $100,000. We do not want to lose this account, yet we know that the manufacturer has hired his own representative in other cities as fast as sales reach $100,000. So we keep it at that figure. We might be able to produce considerably more if we were sure we could hold the line."

Another agent said: "I took on an extra line recently because volume on our three old lines had reached the point where we were fearful of losing the accounts if we increased sales any further."

There is just enough truth in what these manufacturers' representatives believe to make sense. They have seen other agents lose lines when the volume became big enough to warrant an exclusive salesman on a salary, or salary and commission basis. It is perhaps true that some manufacturers' agents have built up volume only to have the lines snatched away from them just when they became profitable. This is the chief reason why manufacturers' agents do not sell more. And it is the chief reason why sales promotion men find manufacturers' agents such a baffling problem.

Chapter 37

PROMOTIONS TO CONSUMERS
AND USERS

GASOLINE companies are selling other manufacturers' products by mail to their credit-card customers; department stores include manufacturers' leaflets with their statements and invoices; and prominent magazines are offering their subscribers encyclopedias, dictionaries and works of art. The South Jersey Gas Company offers accident and health insurance with premiums payable on the company's bills.

These are a few examples of companies capitalizing on their customer lists with promotions to produce more business through the sale of additional products. Other companies develop extra sales for their own products by offering them to other manufacturers for use as premiums, incentive awards or contest prizes.

It is rather astonishing, however, that more companies do not take advantage of ready-made opportunities to make additional sales to their own customers. For example, warranty cards are filled out by buyers of large and small electrical appliances and mailed to the manufacturers, never to be heard from again. Some companies produce full product lines, or several lines of products, but few include appropriate literature in the shipping cartons. When the suggestion was made to one sales promotion manager, he shrugged it off by saying: "We would need ten thousand full-line color folders; that costs money. Besides, somebody then has to drop them into the cartons!" Hardly credible, but true.

The value of well-planned and well-timed promotions to consumers is evidenced by the number of companies using them to outdistance strongly entrenched competition. Pepsodent toothpaste is a case in point. The continued success of this product can be attributed largely to the use of "plus incentives." In fact, Charles Luckman, former Lever Brothers president, won his spurs as sales manager for Pepsodent before the toothpaste was added to the Lever Brothers "stable," as the result of the ingenious plans he developed to sell Pepsodent. Luckman contends that if you can get the consumer to buy, sales to the dealer take care of themselves. All too often in sales work, manufacturers overdo themselves figuring out plans to force dealers to stock a product, on the theory that once he has his money invested in it, he will find a way to move the goods off his shelves. That does not always work. Usually what happens is that the dealer, awakening to the fact he overbought, cuts the price. In so doing he acquires a grudge against the maker of the product which lingers on long after the sale is forgotten.

A typical Lever Brothers promotion was the "Buy-Two Sale." It proved so successful that it has become a frequent promotional device among many other companies.

While this type of promotion is now so generally used that detailed description would be redundant, the details of the pioneer among such promotions are of historical interest.

The sale was ushered in with a four-color, full-page advertisement in *Life* and large color insertions in the country's leading Sunday comics from coast to coast. It was supported by all five of the top-ranking Lever radio shows of that time.

Discussing the success of this pioneer promotion, and the decision to repeat the offer, Lever's vice president in charge of sales said: "When our own records and reports from the trade showed that over 233,385 grocers took advantage of our big 'Buy-Two Sale' to empty their shelves, we knew that both dealers and consumers were enthusiastic about this promotion so we decided to repeat the offer.

"The sale was designed to bring customers back to the store for repeat orders of Lever products. Housewives received with every saucepan a reorder blank enabling them to order four additional pieces of Regal aluminumware at money-in-the-bank savings. With two more box tops or wrappers, customers obtained a 12-inch embossed serving tray worth $1.25 for 50 cents, a 10-inch oven broiler worth $1.50 for 75 cents, a 9-inch frying pan worth $1.75 for $1, and a 7-inch casserole worth $1.85 for $1.

"Grocers and supermarket operators were urged by Lever salesmen to expand the buy-two-and-save theme into store-wide sales that would bring in extra customers. To aid the retailers, 'Buy-Two Sale' newspaper and handbill mats in three sizes with space for store-wide listings were offered to dealers. Colorful theme banners, cut case cards with order blanks, double pennants, price posters, and take-one cards with order blanks also were supplied."

Special Events

In recent years, shopping centers have become focal points for many promotional events. Many of the larger shopping centers, in fact, employ promotion managers to develop activities beneficial to all the retailers within the location. Traffic is also stimulated through the use of malls, with gardens, water fountains, concerts, and exhibits.

Retailers have also organized for special promotional events at various times of the year.

The 69th Street Merchants Association, (Philadelphia) promoted the first annual Snow Bucks Festival, in which Miss Liz Cummings, an agency account executive, circled suburban areas in a helicopter, dropping hundreds of styrofoam snowballs containing one dollar discounts to participating merchants' stores. The Snow Bucks Festival was promoted by an extensive radio advertising campaign plus an advertising supplement in local area newspapers.

Backing Up House-to-House Salesmen

The tendency of many communities to enact anti-peddler laws has made it necessary for companies who sell door to door to devise plans which will give their salesmen a "guest" status. For example, Real Silk Hosiery salesmen make no effort to sell on the first call, but leave an introductory folder about their product, stating they will be back the next day with a gift—usually a hosiery mending kit. In this way the salesman, in a legal sense, calls the second time with the customer's permission—at least she made no objection. J. R. Watkins Company, operating about 1,000 salesmen selling food and home specialties door to door, backed them up with give-away calendars. The company spent the money its competitors (who sold through retailers) spent on national advertising for direct promotional helps, on the theory the national advertising would be helping competitors, whereas the calendars would help only the salesman who delivers them.

Lewyt's Market-Winning Promotions

Breaking into a hard-fought field, such as home appliances, requires hard selling backed by equally hard-hitting sales promotions. The Lewyt Corporation demonstrated how effective this combination can often be when it put a new vacuum cleaner on an already crowded market. In this case the advertising and promotion were released before the company had national distribution, or even before its sales organization was completed.

Outlining Lewyt merchandising plans, the company's president told the Sales Executives Club of New York that two programs were used to spark sales: The "Junior Demo" plan, a 10-second demonstration for use in stores; and the "Outside Selling Plan."

The demonstration is confined to a quick showing of cleaner performance in showrooms and is concluded with the question: "How old is your vacuum cleaner?"

The outside selling plan is not cold canvassing, but applies to selling in homes by prearranged appointments. Leads are obtained by the company from users, showroom sales personnel, newspaper advertising, and by direct mail, then turned over to specialists for follow-up.

Even after the sale is made, the interest of the dealer is maintained. Every sale is followed within 48 hours with a call from a qualified instructor.

Sampling Promotions

Many years ago, when prepared cereals were being introduced to the American housewife, large sums of money were spent for door-to-door sampling. Sampling crews, working a territory block by block, rang every doorbell, handed the occupant a sample package of the breakfast food with a few well-chosen remarks, usually to the effect that if she and the family liked the sample, they could get more from Jones Grocery. On the strength of the "plug" the company's salesman sold grocer Jones a good supply of the breakfast food, got him to put in a window display, and then at the end of the day took his orders over to the local jobber to be filled. That forced the jobber to stock the product, even though he insisted he was already overstocked on breakfast foods.

This method of promoting sales, except for a product like chewing gum, proved expensive and slow. It is occasionally used today, but only after the most careful testing. A more direct and usually more economical method of introducing a consumer product is to mail coupons good for a free sample to dealers' lists, or in the case of smaller communities to all the names in the telephone book. In that case the letter accompanying the coupon lists the stores at which the coupon will be honored. Introductory orders are obtained from these stores in advance of the mailing by either the local wholesaler's salesman or a company salesman. Sampling plans work best when backed up with newspaper or spot radio advertising.

A variation of the coupon sampling idea is to print coupons good for a free sample in connection with a display ad in the local newspaper. The advertiser, of course, must agree to redeem all coupons turned in at the full retail price. However, there are always a few merchants who see an opportunity to pick up some easy profit and buy up newspapers to clip the coupons. They fill them out with random names from the telephone book and mail them to the manufacturer for redemption. One way this problem has been solved is to offer the free sample to "The First Ten Women" who bring the coupon to any one of the stores listed in the advertisement. The effect is about the same, but the manufacturer is committed only to redeeming 10 coupons from a dealer. The company's salesman makes the original order sufficiently large, before listing the merchant's name in the local ad, to at least come out even on the deal. The cost of the advertisement itself is charged to the general advertising appropriation.

Sampling is still used extensively in promoting the sale of cigarettes. Small packages are distributed at conventions and banquets, or other meetings. Full-sized packages are handed out by the manufacturer's salesmen. The theory is that even if only 1 in 20, to whom samples are given, acquire the habit of buying the brand regularly, it is good advertising. A requisite for success in any sampling program is that the product must have a high degree of consumer acceptance, that it must be a fast repeater, and must carry a long profit, both to the distributor and the manufacturer. Sampling without adequate retail and wholesale distribution is a waste of money. The fond belief of so many manufacturers that their product is so good all they need to do is to let people sample it, and they will form in line to buy it, is wishful thinking. Changing the buying habits of the public is a tough job. It calls for much more than passing out samples. Selling begins when samples are placed in the consumer's hands.

Barbecue Cookbook Offered

Lark cigarettes offered consumers a popular, hard-cover barbecue cookbook free with the purchase of a carton of Lark, during a premium promotion.

The barbecue cookbook was the hard-cover Gourmet International Cookbook, a popular item that sold more than 1.3 million copies with a retail price of $3.95.

The cookbook promotion was supported in large outlets by floor displays, each containing 30 cookbooks and 60 cartons of Lark

The message, the product and the premium are all contained in this merchandiser-display offering a free cookbook with every purchase of the product. The display contained 60 cartons of cigarettes and 30 cookbooks.

cigarettes. In smaller stores, the free cookbook was offered, with proof of purchase, via tear-off pads at the point of sale.

During the same promotion period Lark participated in a Stratmar Intercept Co-op Coupon Program in which it offered a 40 cent coupon on the purchase of a carton of Lark 85 or 100 mm cigarettes. About 5.6 million coupons were distributed in 17 major markets.

Packages That Increase Unit Sales

The use of convenient cartons and packages to make the purchase of larger units easy is not new, but is finding increasing favor as a means of promoting sales to the consumer. Outstanding in this category was Coca-Cola's "Take Home a Carton" package of six bottles of "Coke" in a carton. This simple device added many thousands of dollars to the sales of this beverage. While the actual saving is not large, the convenience is enough to turn the scales in favor of taking home a carton, instead of a bottle or two.

The promotional package has also been used in the sale of light bulbs. In this case the package is designed to make lamps more convenient to buy. General Electric developed the idea when it became evident, some years ago, that there would soon be increasing competition for the household lamp business. GE wanted a package to step up the single lamp order, without making it necessary for the consumer to purchase a six-lamp carton of bulbs having a given wattage. The increasing importance of self-service retailing pointed to a smaller package. But how small? GE's marketing research manager said:

"The first step was to determine the number of lamps per package that would prove most satisfactory to our ultimate boss, the purchasing public. Half a million lamps (25-, 60-, and 100-watt) were first set aside for a large-scale sales test of package size. Special packages employing a nesting principle were designed for 3, 4, 5, and 6 lamps. These packages were of similar construction and art design. Every effort was made to have each of the sizes equally attractive.

"Five cities, each having a population of 25,000 to 30,000 as well as similar trade characteristics, were selected for the test. All the dealers handling our product in these cities were interviewed—electrical and hardware dealers, chain variety, chain and independent grocery, chain and independent drug stores. Because of their inherent interest in our product as well as the fact that they were assured of a free supply of the popular household sizes during a period of severe shortage, a high degree of cooperation was achieved. In no case were they told that this was a comparative test of different package sizes. It was described simply as a test of a new package to discover what sales appeal it would have compared with our standard method of packing. The cities were sufficiently separated so there was little possibility of knowledge of the other tests being communicated between them.

"All of the outlets in each of these cities were then given a free supply of our standard production for a period of 10 weeks. Each store was visited every 2 weeks to be sure that no out-of-stock condition had developed and to assure that display of lamps was on a normal and uniform basis throughout. No special promotional effort was made at any time during the test. As would be expected, the first several weeks of this conditioning period resulted in sales far above average. But, after 4 to 6 weeks of abnormal activity, sales dropped back to normal. However, the conditioning period continued for an additional month to insure quieting of the hoarding instinct.

"At the end of that time, 3-lamp packages were displayed in essentially all outlets in one city, 4-lamp packages in another, 5-lamp packages in the third city, and 6-lamp packages in still another city. The dealers in these cities were requested to provide equal display for the special and standard packages. Under no circumstances were they put on any promotional sales effort. Window displays were not permitted nor were any other special merchandising efforts with this package. Strict compliance was assured by having one of our men drop in at unexpected intervals (never to exceed 2 weeks) throughout the period of the test. The object was to permit the customer to select either single lamps, our standard packaged lamps, or the special package purely by his or her own preference. Through continuing normal counter display but simply putting half of it into the new packages, we felt we were rather successful in avoiding excessive attention to the new product on the part of the customer. Every effort was made to insure that sales conditions in all of the outlets in the four cities were comparable. This arrangement was maintained for a period of 4 months, and the data which we derived from it was based upon this period.

"In the fifth city, packages for the 60-watt lamp in all four package sizes were on display in all outlets. While we realized that this was not a normal sales condition, it was put in with the intention of checking the results in the other cities— particularly to see whether the proportionate sales of any given package would be greatly different when all of the packages were available from the ratios established in the main four-city test.

"Test results were expressed in terms of the number of lamps sold in special packages as a percent of the total sale of lamps in any given outlet. The data was also compiled for all stores of a given type as well as for the city as a whole. Likewise, estimates were made of the number of customers buying special packages compared to the number of customers who bought single lamps or the standard packaged lamps.

"There were some differences in the percent sale of the three different wattages, and, as might be expected, the most popular lamp sold better in the larger unit packages. However, it was conclusively determined that the unit of sale should not be greater than four. Concurrent tests in still different cities using our regular product only established that the over-all average of lamps of a single wattage sold per customer was two.

"It is much easier to define the desirable characteristics of a package than to achieve it. The new design must satisfy a number of criteria that had been established for a successful package. It must:

1. Have merchandising appeal:
    (a) Attractive.
    (b) Stack easily.
    (c) Adaptable to varying sales conditions.

2. Provide adequate protection to the product in shipment.

3. Obtainable:
   (a) Material must be readily available in quantities required.
   (b) The design must be practical to manufacture.

4. Adaptable to our manufacturing operations:
   (a) Not disturb existing factory operations unduly.
   (b) Be readily manipulated in the packing operation.

5. Economical:
   (a) Require minimum shelf and storage space.
   (b) Reasonable material cost.

"In all cases, comparison was made with our present standard package and the question always asked whether an improvement resulted.

"Over the following months several dozen packages were submitted and checked against the foregoing requirements. Most of them were rectangular packages, although we also investigated such peculiarities as a truncated four-sided pyramid and similar oddities. These packages were studied by merchandising experts, given forced shipping tests, sample packed in factories, and subjected to rigorous cost studies. The package which was finally selected more than fulfills our original objectives."

Building Sales with Re-Use Containers

It is probable that package design is in the field of sales promotion that will receive an increasing proportion of attention in the near future. A particularly adaptable idea in the shopping goods lines is that of packaging the product in a container which itself has further usefulness. Hickok belts, for example, were among a number of products sold in boxes which can be used later to hold cigarettes. A newcomer to this field has been the "Twintype" package developed by Schnefel Brothers Corporation. An executive of that company said:

"The origin of our Twintype package is quite interesting. We were anxious to bring out a popularly priced package featuring Naylon Nail Enamel and Lipstick, which would not be the usual paper type of presentation. We wanted to present these two dissimilarly shaped items to best advantage and our designer conceived the frame idea. He spent hours visiting antique shops and second-hand stores for the right idea.

"After conferring we had decided that in line with the new feminine look and the present nostalgic feeling in fashion it would be well to obtain a lovely old frame to serve as our model. When our designer had practically given up finding exactly what he had in mind he discovered a friend in an adjoining apartment had exactly what he wanted. It was loaned to us and resulted in our Twintype frame package. It was a natural outgrowth of the frame idea that it be so designed as to be used for snapshots after the Naylon Nail Enamel and Lipstick had been used.

"In promoting we tied in with major fashion stores throughout the country for our introduction. We introduced it directly ahead of Mother's Day, and many stores were using the 'I Remember Mama' theme in conjunction with the miniature frames, so our promotion on Twintype tied in beautifully with it. It has been successful from the first, so much so that we have retained it as a staple item in the Naylon line."

Visual Aids for the Salesman to Use

One of the most difficult problems in sales promotion is to get salesmen who sell to the consumer, whether they are direct or indirect salesmen, to properly present the product. Invariably they will leave out the most important points, or present them in disjointed sequence. It is an axiom of good salesmanship that to be most effective, each sales point should be presented in proper relation to the other points and no important point should be omitted.

To keep salespeople "on the track" most manufacturers depend upon some visual aid. These may be very simple and inexpensive, such as an easel chart which the salesman can set up on the prospect's desk or in his living room and use as a guide to his talk, or they may be more elaborate and do a complete selling job. When the United States Rubber Company introduced its "Air Ride" tire, dealers were provided with moving pictures demonstrating the ease with which the new tires took the bumps. The demonstration was so effective that little else in the way of sales talk was necessary.

Still another example was Dictaphone's talking picture: "Two Salesmen in Search of an Order." Ostensibly designed to train Dictaphone salesmen in the right and wrong way to sell, the picture packed a terrific sales wallop. The fact that primarily it was not intended to sell, seemed to add to its appeal, and hundreds of companies—most of whom were good prospects for dictating machine equipment—borrowed the picture to show to their salesmen and executives.

Vacuum cleaner salesmen have found it helpful to have available a moving picture showing how their cleaner operated under varying conditions, which they showed in the home of a prospective purchaser. It was far easier to get permission to bring in a projector to put on a parlor show in the evening, than to get permission to give a demonstration. People like to look at pictures, and it provides a way to get the man and woman of the house together so a joint sale can be made.

Imprinted Promotional Literature

One of the oldest forms of sales promotion to the consumer, using the dealer as a distributing agent, is imprinted booklets, folders, calendars, and other material. These are usually offered free to dealers in consideration of certain cooperation, or sold at a small charge. A pioneer in this type of promotion is Hart Schaffner & Marx, Chicago clothing manufacturer. This company offers dealers the following helps:

> Direct mail style booklets.
>
> Full-color outdoor posters.
>
> Complete newspaper advertising mat service.
>
> Full-color window display posters.
>
> Counter cards.
>
> Counter and window signs.
>
> Advertising match folders.

These dealer helps tie in with the extensive national advertising which this astute manufacturer depends upon to create consumer acceptance for its styles and fabrics. Some of the helps are offered free, others at a small charge. The letter announcing these helps stresses the national campaign and points out the reasons why a dealer should tie in with the effort. A typical letter follows:

Dear Sirs:

Here it is--the Hart Schaffner & Marx advertising service for spring and summer--twenty-two clean-cut ads designed to do a good selling and public relations job for your store.

Although the copy is brief, and planned essentially to point up your store as the home of quality merchandise, it has just the right amount of sales appeal. At the same time it avoids too specific mention of patterns, colors, models. In other words, these ads are designed to FIT THE NEEDS OF THE TIMES--to help you do an intelligent, effective advertising job with copy geared to today's conditions.

The spring Hart Schaffner & Marx national full-color advertising--more attractive this season than ever--breaks in national magazines early next month. Adaptations of these national ads for your use locally are attached.

After looking them over you'll certainly want to run each one as a simple tie-in which will enable you to reap the full benefit for your store. The beautiful Easter ad is included with this service to assist this year's Easter promotions.

Some ads on tropicals are included for our customers in the South who will want to advertise tropicals sooner than stores in the colder climates.

Look over all the ads. Choose what you need, and shoot in your order. Mats are ready for you now. To order, simply check the attached list and mail it in. Do it TODAY while it's on your mind.

Cordially yours,

REA Express "Quiz" Books

"Is Your Knowledge First Rate about the Way That Gets There First?" was the intriguing question which introduced 8 pertinent questions in a 20-page booklet which REA Express drivers gave out to shippers as they passed over their routes. It proved quite effective in getting shippers and potential shippers to *think* about their shipping problems. Similar quiz books for customers and prospects have been used to good effect by other companies, as well.

Timing Consumer Promotions

It is usually a waste of money to send dealers or distributors a supply of promotional material and let it go at that. All that happens is that it gets buried under a pile of incoming merchandise in a back room. Consumer mailings, whether they are by the dealer to his own mailing list or done by the manufacturer on behalf of the dealer, should be planned and timed to do a specific job. For example, record manufacturers plan some consumer promotions to hit the public just before or during Music Week, when music merchants all over the country are concentrating on getting people into music stores.

When more than one mailing a year is planned, it is important to provide dealers with a sales promotion schedule which not only suggests the best time to put on promotions but the kind of promotion to be used. It might be added that an organized presentation of this type also serves to clarify the planning in the manufacturer's sales promotion department as well.

These promotional calendars have been used in a variety of fields. For example, Culligan, Inc., produced a "quarterly plan book" whose suggestions were followed, according to a field check, by three-quarters of the firm's soft-water service dealers. The Fisk Tires Division of U.S. Rubber Company prepared a fine calendar for wall hanging in the dealership which suggested a weekly emphasis for promotions: "Tube Demonstration Week," "Recap Week," "Spare Fan-Belt Week," and so on.

One of the most comprehensive of these calendar promotions was the "Sales Planning Almanac" issued by Gruen Watch Company. The calendar offered a general promotional theme and suggested how it might be tied in with window display, free mats, radio spot announcements, direct mail, telephone selling talks, a suggested sales telegram, and a variety of selling tips which were as specific as these samples:

PROMOTIONS TO CONSUMERS AND USERS

Get on the telephone and contact either the presidents or program chairmen of local women's clubs and men's business and fraternal organizations. Offer a de luxe exhibit of Christmas gift suggestions for their next meeting. Arrange this on folding tables. Take along a good supply of order blanks and be sure to know the quantity of reserve stock in your store.

Most newspapers have a feature column in which they print brief interviews with men and women in the street. Speak to your local editor and suggest that he use the question, "What piece of jewelry would you like most to get as a Christmas present?" This will serve to plant the idea in the minds of many readers to give jewelry for Christmas.

In case of a good snowfall, arrange in advance for a horse-drawn, jingle-bell sleigh driven by a man dressed as Santa Claus. Hang a neatly lettered sign on the sleigh with this copy: "I'm going to (Jeweler's Name) for fine jewelry—the finest, most impressive gift of all!" Have this rig drive all over town, be sure it's seen by everyone.

It is unlikely that any one dealer will have the time or the personnel to carry out all the plans which Gruen suggested for a 2-month period. However, the range of ideas is so wide that any dealer can make up a program of his own, geared to his local situation, from these suggestions. The Almanac was accompanied by a folder of mats and offers of other materials—recorded singing commercials, imprinted post cards, and so on—either free or at cost. Flexibility in suggestions is important, since an idea which appeals to big stores may be impractical for small ones.

PROMOTION SCHEDULE DEVELOPED BY THE JEWELRY INDUSTRY COUNCIL

1. Helpful Publicity for Industry's Products

This campaign would provide national publicity, under the direction of a high-powered organization, which, through experts, would contact editors, write articles, supervise photos, place articles and photographs, arrange for newsreels, write radio scripts, arrange broadcasts, and keep in touch with film studios. A systematic and organized job for all products of the industry would be done—day-in and day-out. A recent survey shows that: 77% of a group of women's page editors say they want more material for their pages on jewelry products, and 92% of a group of women radio commentators have expressed a willingness to use more material than they now receive on the products of the jewelry industry. Everything possible will be done to keep jewelry before the American public in an exciting, tempting way.

2. Work with Women's Clubs

There are thousands of women's clubs in the country with a membership in excess of 6,000,000. These clubs want helpful information from industry. Sound films in color on all the products of the jewelry industry would get a warm welcome from them. Our planned program would give women's club audiences films that would tell a story for silver plate, sterling silver, clocks, men's and women's watches, jewelry for men, jewelry for women, precious stones, modern collections of gems, etc. At each showing there would be printed literature for viewers. Local retail store tie-ups would be arranged.

3. SCHOOL AND COLLEGE PROJECTS

About 4,000,000 girls pass through home economics and social study classes of the high schools of this country every year. The great majority get married within a few years after they leave high school. As prospective brides, and later as married women, they constitute a market for numerous products of the industry — sterling silver, silver plate, clocks, watches, rings, etc. About 200,000 a year move on to college, to marry some years later.

Here, in high schools and colleges, is an all-important market that should have the "jewelry story" year after year. It can be given that story, in a systematic way, by special study courses . . . by booklets and by films. It can be told what to own, what to wear, what to give . . . in sterling, plated ware, watches, costume jewelry, precious stones, pins, clocks, and all the products off the jewelry industry.

4. SET UP A CLEARING HOUSE

Create a central office, staffed with people experienced in the promotional, advertising, selling, and management problems of the jewelry retailer. Assign certain definite research duties to properly qualified experts. Make their knowledge and findings available to retail members in office consultations, and at industry conferences (local, state, regional, and national). Make findings and recommendations available also by mail. Make reports and recommendations available also to manufacturer, importer, and wholesaler membership.

5. CREATE A SYMBOL OF UNITY AND OF IDENTIFICATION

The name of the Jewelry Industry Publicity Board will be changed. Several names such as "Jewelers Council" and "Jewelers Institute" are under consideration. This new organization will adopt a symbol of unity and identification for its members. This insignia will be displayed in windows or in store interiors by retailers, and in offices by manufacturers and wholesalers. The insignia will be used in national advertising to direct the public to retail outlets displaying it. The public will come to know and recognize this symbol not only from advertising that will be put behind it by the Publicity Board, but also from publicity given it by member firms in their own advertising.

6. NATIONAL ADVERTISING FOR RETAILER JEWELERS

The purpose of such advertising would be to increase store traffic and to publicize the symbol created for members cooperating in this national campaign. Numerous themes and copy ideas for this national campaign have already been indicated by findings made in consumer studies. However, no final decision on copy themes or on advertising media to be used will be made until further studies are completed.

7. WINDOW DISPLAY RESEARCH AND RECOMMENDATIONS

This subject will get high priority because of the fact that the question "How can I make the most effective use of my windows" is a problem common to at least 95% of all retail jewelers. It is proposed to find a series of answers to this question by having window display experts make intensive studies of the problem. Such experts would carry on their research by living and working with this problem in different types of stores. Answers found to window display problems of different types of stores would be backed up with factual evidence, along with ways to "do something" about them.

8. STORE INTERIOR DISPLAY

Two-thirds of all the people who go into a jewelry store in a year have no definite purchase in mind. Only 1 in 11 makes a purchase. The majority of those who don't buy say they *saw* nothing they wanted for themselves or as a gift. Such a condition, obviously, warrants practical research on store interior display—research that would be carried on in the same manner, in different basic types of retail stores, as recommended with respect to window display.

9. RETAIL SALES TRAINING

Practical research on the selling techniques of retail salespeople and on methods of improving their sales efficiency would be carried on in retail stores by men experienced in such work. Minds trained to teach retail salesmen how to improve their selling methods would translate these research findings into information that could be put to everyday use.

10. IMPROVE RETAILER ADVERTISING COPY

Recent studies of some 1,700 retail jewelry newspaper advertisements indicate there is room for improvement in such advertising. Intensive study is therefore indicated. Such studies would take advantage of many thousands of dollars invested in readership studies of retail advertising of all kinds. Studies would also be made of direct-mail and radio advertising for retail jewelry outlets. It is estimated that the total advertising bill of retail jewelers last year in cities of 50,000 population and over was in excess of $26 million. Think of what a 10% improvement in the selling power of that $26 million might mean in increased sales volume for the jewelry industry!

11. KEEP A FINGER ON THE PUBLIC'S PULSE

You have read some of the findings obtained from a national cross section of the American public on its gift buying habits and its appraisal of the retail jeweler. A study of this nature for an industry should not be a one-time affair. It is a job to be repeated at proper intervals. Facts and trends thus obtained in the future will be analyzed and made available to members of this cooperative effort. This will be done so that the industry may intelligently adjust itself to overcome criticism quickly and capitalize on trends that are favorable.

PART 4

SPECIAL SUPPLEMENTS TO SALES PROMOTION

Chapter 38

CONTROLLING SALES PROMOTION EXPENDITURES

MORE money—both dollarwise and percentagewise—is being allocated for sales promotional activities and materials in many companies. A maker of fans has upped his share in cooperative advertising from 33 to 50%; an envelope company which has for years operated on a set sum is revising the figure upward to match the jump in company sales in the interval; a manufacturer of stoves who split his previous appropriation 60-40 between national advertising and sales promotion is now splitting it 50-50.

The sales promotional budget may be set up in a variety of ways (see Chapter 4, "The Budget for Sales Promotion"), but eventually the sales promotion man arrives at a point where he must decide what are the most effective ways of increasing sales through the expenditure of x number of dollars. In a typical "line" of sales promotional tools, which may have from 30 to 300 items, it is the sales promotion manager who determines how much emphasis should be given to each.

Controlling these expenditures is difficult, to say the least. In many cases there are intangible factors involved which can never be measured; for example, it would be difficult indeed to determine a dollars-and-cents value for billboard advertising, and it would be nearly impossible to prove that x dollars spent for billboards were more profitably employed than they would have been if used for direct mail promotion.

In spite of this, sales promotion funds can be used more effectively if a constant check is made on certain fundamental points. This type of control concentrates on the elimination of waste wherever possible.

Setting a Budget

An astonishing number of companies have no definite budget for their sales promotional activities. Even among those that do, executives generally admitted that if an item turns out to be particularly successful they will always exceed the budget to take advantage of the demand.

It is explaining the obvious to point out that sales promotional activities should be budgeted as definitely as are national advertising, accounting, production, or any other activities of a going business; the fact that so many intangible factors have discouraged the development of such budgets may make it advisable for many companies to review briefly the advantages of a definite allocation of funds.

"The most expensive thing about sales promotional materials is that the front office is in a rush to get them," an advertising executive recently said. The waste produced by haste can never be entirely eliminated, but it can be pared down by the kind of advance budgeting and planning used, for example, by Maurice Tiemann, director of advertising, Phelan-Faust Paint Mfg. Co.:

"Our sales promotion budget usually includes more than 35 different kinds of expenditures. We use a percentage of the previous year's sales as a base and then I go out and talk to dealers about their needs and wants. On the basis of their recommendations I develop a plan and spend 2 full days with our top management going over the total cost of each classification. This meeting is held around the beginning of the year; the budget is set in detail for spring, and some leeway is left in the fall plans.

"It's hard to analyze just how the breakdown is made. I get the dealers' ideas, add in my own experience, and then get the approval of seven members of top management. The budget is never exceeded without discussion and authorization by these seven men." Another company reported that the budget served as top management's signal of the way the sales promotion department was operating. Figures are set on a monthly basis; if the expenditures go either over or under the estimates, an explanation is required.

Allocating the Budget

Companies distributing through sales agents, such as the National Cash Register Company* and the Addressograph-Multigraph Corporation*, sometimes charge each agent with a pro-rata share of the total sales promotional expense. It becomes a part of his cost of doing business. Because it is something he pays to get, he is quite certain to make the best possible use of it. To properly allocate these expenses, so that each agent will pay his fair share

*Now NCR Corp and AM International.

according to his territorial potential, it is usual for the manufacturer to require a county-by-county break-down of the circulation of media used, the mailing list, and other factors. On the basis of this breakdown each agent is given a loading percentage, which represents his share of the total national effort.

To make this plan effective, however, each sales agent or distributor, as the case might be, should have a voice in determining how the sales promotional appropriation is to be spent. If this is not done, and if the sales agent is not "sold" on the loading given him, he will naturally feel the company is using the allocation plan to keep him from making "too much money."

A definite budget serves as a check on quick enthusiasms. Too often a red hot idea will occur to someone in the middle of the season and be jammed through ahead of regularly scheduled promotions. This is well and good if the idea happens to click; the subject is likely to be reviewed more critically and carefully if it is analyzed in terms of what must be dropped to make way for the brainstorm and still keep within the budget.

Still another advantage of a budget is in the analysis of the type of presentation to be used in terms of quantities required. A 4-color leaflet, for instance, will be extremely expensive if it is to be printed in small quantities, whereas the cost per copy will be a great deal smaller if it can be amortized over an edition of a million. However, budgets can be overdone. They sometimes prevent the sales executive from "hitting" a promotion, that shows promise, as hard as circumstances justify. In selling, when you find a sales plan that works, it pays to keep it working.

Record Keeping

Just as budgeting in advance is helpful, record keeping, as the basis of a post-mortem after the campaign, can be used to avoid errors in the future. The Cory Corporation, for instance, analyzed the results of a large expenditure for live demonstrators and found that the added volume was not enough in most outlets to justify the cost. As a result, the company is using a self-service merchandiser in low volume outlets; although the merchandiser has a substantial initial cost, it will not be as expensive in the long run as weekly salaries.

The type of records kept will of course depend on distribution channels used. One company whose salesmen sell direct to users has space on its territorial sales control sheet for records of number of calls, volume sold by product, and total cost of all sales promotional materials shipped into the territory. In this way variations, either in total cost or as a percentage of sales, can be spotted at a glance.

DISTRIBUTOR	DATA SHEET - SPECIAL PROMOTIONS
General Classification of Promotion Medium:	Amt. Allotted for Prev. Pro.: Date closed:
Description of Promotion:	Initiated By:
	Date.
	Effective Dates of Promotion: From: To:
	Ironrite Contribution:
Aim of This Promotion:	Distributor Contribution:
	Dealer Contribution:
	Total Cost of Promotion:
Results:	Approved by: Date:
	Approved by:. Date:
	Recommendations:

A leaking faucet in sales promotional costs is material sent to distributors which is never used, and money spent on special promotions. This form provides a record, by distributors, of what promotions they used and the results.

Companies which work through wholesalers very often keep such records by individual wholesale accounts, and those with direct-to-dealer setups by a similar control at the retail level.

A type of supplementary record which is handy is one which is kept by campaigns or by types of materials rather than by individual customers. Over a period of time such a record will give a fairly accurate picture of the amounts of different types of materials which are most important to a particular push; in addition, comparison of the record of a campaign with a similar campaign in the past is probably the best way to evaluate its effectiveness.

Like any other virtue, reference to records can be carried to such an extreme that it becomes a vice. The fact that a particular kind of promotional effort has been well received in a sellers' market is no proof that the same appeal will be successful in a price-conscious buyers' market. Further, long-term trends must be considered; as the tendency toward self-service grows in more and more kinds of outlets, it is probable that promotions with a self-service twist will do increasingly well.

SALES PROMOTION REPORT FROM_____ DATE_____ √ TYPE OF STORE

* FILL IN TYPE IF NOT LISTED

MFR'S ⎰ NAME _____   1.__ DEPARTMENT
☐ DEALER'S ⎱   2.__ FURNITURE
STREET_____   3.__ HARDWARE
     4.__ CURTAIN & DRAPERY
CITY _____ STATE _____   5.__ FLOOR COVERING
     6.__ PAINT
ATTENTION_____ DEPT. _____   7.__ VENETIAN BLIND
     8.__ BUILDING SUPPLY
MANUFACTURERS: _____   9.__ INTERIOR DECORATOR
     # 10.__

ADDRESSOGRAPH
DATE PROCESSED

HIGHLY PROMOTIONAL _____ MEDIUM_____ POOR_____

V B DISPLAYED: YES_____NO_____ FLEXALUM DISPLAYED YES_____NO_____

ADVERTISES FLEX: YES_____NO_____ADVERTISES V.B YES_____NO_____USES OUR ADV. MATTER. YES_____NO_____

PERCENTAGE OF SALES: CUSTOM_____% STOCK_____% FLEX_____% STEEL_____% WOOD_____%

WHOLESALE PRICE PER SQ. FT _____ RETAIL PRICE PER SQ. FT. FROM_____TO_____

TYPE OF V B OUTLET EXCELLENT_____GOOD_____FAIR_____POOR_____.

IF NOT CARRYING FLEXALUM IS THIS A DESIRABLE OUTLET? YES_____ NO_____

NEW	OLD	QUANTITY	MATERIAL TO BE SHIPPED	IMPRINT	CHARGE
___	___	___	8-PG FOLDERS	___	___
		___	4-PG FOLDERS (DEALERS ONLY)	___	___
		___	DECORATING BOOKS	___	___
		___	LABELS	___	NONE
___	___	___	BANNERS	NONE	NONE
___	___	___	IDENTIFICATION TAGS	___	NONE
___	___	___	SAMPLE FOLDERS: FILLED_____ BLANK_____	NONE	___
		___	DISPLAY CARDS SMALL	NONE	NONE
___	___		DISPLAY CARDS LARGE	NONE	NONE
		___	SLIDE RULE	___	___
___	___	___	DEALER BOOK (LIST DEALER IMPRINTS ON SEPARATE SHEET AND ATTACH TO THIS REPORT)	___	___
	___		DISPLAY STAND: FLOOR MODEL_____	NONE	___
			TABLE MODEL_____	NONE	___
___	___		MAT FOLDERS	NONE	NONE

     # _____ # _____ # _____

NEWSPAPER MATS
(SHOW QUANTITIES
OF EACH)   # _____ # _____ # _____

IMPRINT TO READ. _____

_____

_____I RECOMMEND SHIPMENT OF DESIRED QUANTITY FREE OF CHARGE. IRRESPECTIVE OF QUOTA (SEE COMMENTS)

_____SHIP ONLY FREE QUOTA _____CHARGE EXCESS. APPROVED BY_____

COMMENTS (USE REVERSE SIDE (THREE COPIES) — GIVE RESULTS OF CONTACT AND NOTE ANYTHING OUTSTANDING)

A useful form used to provide the sales promotion department with a check on dealers. It both rates the dealer on his promotional ability and serves as a blank for ordering out additional promotional material. Used by either territorial sales promotion men or salesmen. It gives the executive who must pass on the request a quick picture of the dealer to whom the material is being sent.

Sell the User

Whatever type of promotional aid is under consideration, an essential step in controlling the value of the expenditure is to make a definite part of the sum available for selling the user. This is equally true whether the sales tool is to be used by the company's own salesmen or by a retail clerk. More than one expensive and elaborate visualizer has been a flop because the company did not explain to its sales force why it had been prepared and how it could be used.

In the same way, a contest for distributor salesmen will probably fail unless its sponsor has taken the time and effort necessary to convince the distributor that the contest will be a good thing for his business. Just as a definite budget should be set up for this preselling, so should a definite time schedule be followed. In the case of a distributor's salesmen's contest, the presale should begin at least a month before the contest opens.

If the campaign is a consumer-level contest it may be wise to do this job in two steps as Lever Brothers Company did. Company salesmen were supplied with a visualizer to use in enlisting retail support, and a supplementary contest was run for the dealers to maintain their interest during the contest period.

The length of time and the amount of money involved in such a preparatory campaign are a function of the method of distribution. For example, an educational campaign for retail clerks, sponsored by a manufacturer who sells through wholesale channels, must be explained and enthusiastically sold to the wholesaler, to his salesmen, and to the dealers before it even reaches its audience.

Make Materials Flexible

A great deal of water could be squeezed out of many sales promotional packages by considering them in terms of their usefulness to a variety of users. The manager of sales promotion for the former American Stove Company, said on this point: "We can't make up a single package and sell the same thing to a utility with 50 outside salesmen and a hardware dealer who only has floor space for two models. Our salesmen are trained to do a merchandising job; they sit down with each dealer and go over a new campaign, cutting it down to fit his operation."

The need for flexibility of materials has probably been most widely recognized in connection with mat services for local advertising. It is common practice to produce such mats in a variety of sizes so that the retailer can pick the type best suited to his budget. Some work has been done in designing window display pieces which can be used in sections of different sizes, depending upon the amount of space the dealer has available, and a few companies have experimented with displays, both interior and window, which can be built up by repeating small standard units in as long a series as is necessary.

Actually this problem of making materials adaptable to varied outlets is part of the larger problem of making sure the dealer is getting what he wants. In a recent survey, nearly three-quarters of the 200 retailers participating reported that dealer helps from manufacturers were not "written in the required retail language and keyed to the local sales level."

Localize the Materials

It is an almost invariable rule that the more a sales campaign can be localized to a particular dealer, the more enthusiastically he will support it. Zenn Kaufman, when merchandising director of Philip Morris & Co., equipped the company's salesmen with cameras. The men took photographs of each of their retailer customers smoking; when the pictures were returned the dealer got a print for himself and another mounted in a special display card indicating that he personally smoked Philip Morris cigarettes. The display in thousands of instances drew that coveted counter space right next to the cash register.

In an entirely different field, James Klee, president of the Klee Waterproofing Corporation, offered to print a folder of local installations for any distributor who sent in photographs and data. Distributors simply paid the printing cost and mailed the folders to local prospects.

One of the larger paint companies will prepare a plated list of prospects for any dealer who will take the trouble to obtain names of property owners, present customers, or some other responsible group. These lists receive a broadside with the dealer's imprint, inviting them to go to his store for a free book of decorating ideas, and two mailings a year thereafter. In addition, dealers are given prospect cards for individuals who are known to be interested in some specific paint problem. These names receive a letter sent from the factory "at the request of Mr. Dealer," with folders on the types of paint he may use. A carbon of the letter goes to the company salesman; on his next call at the dealership he checks to see what follow-up has been made, and will go out with the dealer or his outside salesman to call on these prospects until the dealer is convinced that follow-up pays. The concern's vice president says this is "by far the best" of the company's sales promotional activities.

Just as a localized appeal is stronger, so is a personalized one. The insurance companies have a variety of premiums—small leather address books and so on—which are gold stamped with the individual prospect's name before they are mailed.

Perhaps one of the greatest wastes in sales promotion is producing more material than is really needed. One organization which sponsored four major retail promotions a year, found that it was getting only limited dealer backing. Investigation showed that the amount of work involved to participate was, in the dealers' opinions, excessive. The company now produces just three promotions, for spring, fall, and Christmas, and has found that its distributive organization can absorb these.

Many companies have issued such a tremendous line of sales promotional aids that it has been necessary to supplement them with a catalog so that dealers can keep track of just what is available. While this is not necessarily a bad idea, experience of a number of organizations indicates that such bulk makes it difficult for the dealers to see the forest for the trees. They become confused and then apathetic.

As a method of getting around this problem, some companies issue regular promotion calendars, usually for a month or 3 months. In such a calendar the dealer is shown the applicable items in the sales promotional line which he should stock and use.

The complicated line of promotional materials usually develops in companies which have a long product line. Chrysler Airtemp solved the problem by putting samples of all promotional pieces for each type of product in separate envelopes. The dealer could refer to the appropriate "Sales Kit" to see what was available for the type of promotion he was planning.

Another way to avoid overloading the dealer is to package goods and promotional materials in a single unit. The simplest version of this is the cigarette carton, which can be opened up into a counter display unit. David D. Doniger and Company, Incorporated, maker of men's sportswear, recently offered dealers a set of five ensembles which were then being advertised nationally; each ensemble was packaged as a unit so the display man would have everything he needed. By offering the five as separate units the program also achieved flexibility.

COOPERATIVE ADVERTISING

As in many other areas of merchandising, there has been a rise and fall in policies on cooperative advertising. Statistics have ranged, over the years, from 5 to 50% of advertising paid for by manufacturers. In some cases, this is 100%.

There is a wide range of payment arrangements in current use. A stove manufacturer splits the bill three ways among manufacturer, distributor, and dealer; a watchmaker absorbs half the cost and charges the retailer the other half; a maker of paper products charges the dealer one-third of the cost of catalogs and makes other materials available without charge; a soft drink manufacturer includes in the cost per case a definite sum for national advertising and another for local sales promotion.

Policies in this matter are far from standardized; however, the manufacturer usually absorbs all national advertising expense, makes some charge for the major portion of his sales promotional materials, and charges full cost—less of course the discount resulting from his quantity purchases—for such items as direct-mail programs, expensive premiums, uniform display cases, elaborate and permanent self-service merchandisers.

An indirect method of giving the dealer a feeling that he has an investment in his sales tools is to make them available only with a fairly substantial order for a model stock. Some manufacturers have offered to give an elaborate merchandiser to retailers who ordered enough goods, properly broken by lines, to stock it. Edwal Scientific Products Corp. offered with a model stock an identifying decal, a five-color window poster, an illuminated counter display, a training booklet for retail salesmen, a stock of nine consumer leaflets, newspaper mats, and a selection of electrotypes.

The Mechanics of Cooperative Advertising

Companies which do not charge the dealer a part of the cost of materials ordinarily follow this policy for two main reasons— a desire for administrative simplicity and fear of prosecution under the Robinson-Patman Act. The first of these is a real problem, although the activity can be so mechanized that the routine of checking is entirely clerical. The second can be solved by relating the individual dealer's allowance to a set percentage of his total pur-

---

VENDOR'S COPY

AUTHOR'S CHANGE COST SHEET

Please fill out and return the original copy of this form as soon as possible to —

Advertising Production Department
Remington Rand Inc.
315 Fourth Avenue
New York 10, New York

ALTERATIONS CHARGEABLE

Date _____ Job No. _____

Job Name _____

Description _____

_____

Page _____

_____

Galley _____ Ad _____

Kind of Work	Hrs. & Tenths of Hrs.	Kind of Work	Hrs. & Tenths of Hrs.
Hand Work	and	Mono K.B.	and
H.R. $	Total Cost $	H.R. $	Total Cost $
Linotype	and	Mono Caster	and
H.R. $	Total Cost $	H.R. $	Total Cost $

The immediate return of this form will expedite payment of your invoice for author's changes when it is rendered at the completion of this job.

Thousands of dollars are wasted making unnecessary changes in proofs of printed promotional literature. This waste can be cut by using a time slip for recording author's changes. It puts the finger on those who delight in moving commas around.

chases, embodying this arrangement in a written contract, and sticking to it under all circumstances.

An electric shaver manufacturer follows the policy of determining the individual dealer's fund by his purchases. The company matches his contribution up to $1 for each shaver purchased for advertising in any publication listed in *Standard Rate and Data;* the money to be spent in 30 days after authorization.

In the heavy consumer goods field, a heating equipment manufacturing company allows a $5 certificate with each unit sold.

The sum will be paid in cash when the dealer puts up an equivalent amount; ordinarily the only approved use of the fund is for local newspaper advertising.

Occasionally these arrangements are more elaborate, with credits varying according to the type of purchases. A leading refrigerator company pays 50% of the space cost in approved newspapers; the fund may also be used for billboard rental for which the company furnishes the paper, or in pre-OK'd spot radio announcements. A set amount, $1, $2, or $3, is credited to the wholesaler's advertising account for each refrigerator model purchased. The wholesaler passes the advertising credit on to the dealer in the same manner after the dealer provides tear sheets and receipted space bills.

The Robinson-Patman Act permits this type of activity provided it is available to all dealers on equal terms. Many companies take the precaution of explaining in their proposal that no dealer can get an increased appropriation by increasing his own contribution. At the same time, these plans permit a legal method of offering the same proposition to all dealers while allowing more help to the man who is doing a better selling job.

Contracts and Agreements

A standard agreement covering the terms of cooperative advertising plans has come into almost unanimous use. These agreements include the share to be contributed by each participant, the media in which the money may be expended, limitations on the time period in which the money must be spent, methods to be used in checking, a statement of the times at which the dealer is to be reimbursed, listing of things which the dealer must or must not do in his advertising to keep it in line with company policy, and provision for cancellation of the agreement by either party.

Such agreements are not necessarily in the form of legal contracts; many are simply outlines of company policy in which it is noted that the conditions specified apply to all members of the dealer organization.

Controlling Cooperative Expenditures

A few organizations have turned over the problem of controlling cooperative advertising to their advertising agencies; as one executive put it, "For 15% they do the scheduling and the arguing with the retailers." A majority of companies, however, control such programs through their own advertising departments.

The matter of selecting media to be used and determining times of insertion is generally left to the dealer, although many companies maintain some degree of control over media selection; for example, Holcomb & Hoke Manufacturing Company, Inc., specifies the type of publication in which ads may be run; distributors and dealers for Domestic Sewing Machine Company, Inc., work out their program jointly and submit it for factory approval; John Lucas & Company allows the fund to be used only for radio, newspapers, and billboards; Seidlitz Paint & Varnish Company restricts the program to daily and weekly newspapers.

Actual dates of insertion are generally left to the dealer and, in general, control is much less strict in this regard than in selection of media. A few companies, like the Tappan Company for example, require schedules to be submitted in advance for approval; a degree of control is maintained by furnishing seasonal ads which are only good for a limited period, as is done by Sewall Paint and Varnish Company; and other organizations, like Aeronca Manufacturing Corporation, require cooperative advertising to be placed within a particular period of time after approval.

Seasonal ads are not furnished to dealers to any great extent; as many as four sets of ads of this type are extremely unusual. It is probable that the growing demand from dealers for such aids, added to the fact that seasonal ads give the company a degree of control over insertion times, will lead to a growing emphasis on this type in the future.

A surprising number of companies impose no strict formal control at the home office over the cooperative program. Tear sheets which can be spot checked are almost always required, although a few companies permit their salesmen to approve the invoices in the field.

Restrictions on the Use of Cooperative Advertising Funds

The degree of choice given the dealer in spending cooperative funds varies greatly. Most companies which have this problem make it a matter of policy to refuse cooperative allowances for advertising in dance and theater programs and other media of the benefit or charity type. However, the advertising manager of a paint company was probably just being more frank than most when he said, "We do not encourage advertising of this type, as it has been proved to be uneconomical, but we do allow it to keep the good will of our dealers. Inasmuch as 50% of the money is theirs, we trust their judgment."

Another problem of recurring importance is that of the dealer who, as one executive put it, "Thinks he can design better advertising than our agency." Not many companies require that the dealer use the factory-prepared lay-outs and copy, although almost all make a service of this type available. In many cases the company will supply the dealer with mats of pictures, headlines, and so on, which he can use in preparing his own ads. Some companies require only that the company logotype appear in the ad. Others require only that the manufacturer's brand name be mentioned at least once in every ad.

A substantial majority of sponsoring companies permit their cooperative advertising material to run as part of larger ads.

A Typical Cooperative Program

While much of this discussion has been concentrated on cooperative newspaper advertising because of the special problems encountered in this field, the trend is for the extension of split payment systems to other types of sales promotional materials as well. As an example of such a setup, the text of the explanation to dealers of the program sponsored by the former American Stove Company, St. Louis, is reproduced here in its entirety:

American Stove Company introduces a completely new plan for cooperative advertising:

1. A plan designed to help you sell more American Stove Company products.
2. A plan designed to identify you as an American Stove Company dealer in your community.
3. A comprehensive plan designed to help you get the greatest results from your local promotion of American Stove Company products and to give you the necessary tie-up with national magazine advertising placed and paid for by American Stove Company.
4. A plan designed with flexibility to enable you to adjust it to fit your particular situation.

In short, it's a plan designed specifically for your use to build your sales of American Stove Company products, and thereby increase your profits.

Whatever advertising and promotion media you prefer:

Billboard	Car Card
Radio	Special Direct Mail Pieces
Newspapers	Indoor and Outdoor Store Displays
	Displays or Exhibitions

All are included in the current American Stove Company cooperative advertising plan.

American Stove Company will pay 50% and the dealer 50% of the cost of approved dealer advertising and approved dealer promotional material in accordance with the conditions outlined in this plan.

American Stove Company participation will be limited to 5% of an individual dealer's net purchases of all products specified below.

GENERAL PROVISIONS

1. Cooperative advertising credits must be used within the period between January 1 and December 31 and cannot be carried over. Unused balances are not available for use after December 31, except to apply on December advertising.

2. This cooperative advertising plan applies only to Domestic gas ranges, Dual Combination ranges, Kitchen Heater (Bungalow) ranges. No credit is allowed on the No. 500, 600, 5500, 5700, 9300, 9400 Series.

3. All local advertising is to be placed by the dealer and paid for by the dealer—at the dealer's local contract rates.

4. The dealer must send receipted bills for all advertising placed by him to his American Stove Company Sales Division Office. Invoices covering advertising placed during December must be in our hands not later than January 10.

5. The dealer will be invoiced for all charge material offered by American Stove Company and covered by this plan, at the full amount less 50% under the terms of this plan.

6. The dealer will be reimbursed by a credit memorandum issued by the American Stove Company Sales Division Office. When required, check will be issued in lieu of a credit memorandum.

7. If the entire advertisement is not devoted to the above-mentioned American Stove Company products, payment will be made only for that portion of the advertisement which is devoted to these American Stove Company products.

8. The specific provisions governing the use of each type of advertising or promotional activity appears on the following pages.

9. This plan may be amended or changed on 30 days' notice.

10. The American Stove Company Cooperative Advertising Plan does not provide cooperative funds if:

   a. The advertising or promotion, in the opinion of the American Stove Company, is misleading, contrary to company policy, or in violation of any Federal or State statute or municipal ordinance.

   b. Charges are made for local agency fees or advertisement preparation costs.

   c. The advertising or promotion violates any of the provisions of this plan.

11. All imprinting costs are considered to be included in this plan.

COOPERATIVE PLAN FOR NEWSPAPER ADVERTISING

1. See the General Provisions.

2. The dealer must send receipted bills from the newspapers supported by full-page tear sheets of ads to his American Stove Company Sales Division Office not later than 30 days after newspaper advertisement appears.

3. In order for the dealer to receive the greatest benefits from this plan, plus reimbursement, his newspaper advertisements must comply with the following provisions:

   a. Competitive ranges or their names must not appear in the same advertisement as American Stove Company products.

b. All ads must contain an illustration of any American Stove Company product together with the product trade name. It is suggested that the standard trade-mark logotype be used.

c. For greater product identification, use of the Magic Chef Man in all ads is always desirable. This man is available in different size mats.

d. Whenever possible, advantage should be taken of the American Stove Company newspaper mat service. This mat service provides a means for not only using tested ads, but also for getting greater results by tying-in more closely with the National Advertising Program.

e. When American Stove Company mat service is not used, the advertising copy should conform in general to features in the American Stove Company national advertising, or current retail literature and mats. Preferably, mention should be given to such American Stove Company features as the Swing Out Broiler, Red Wheel Regulator, Lifetime Burner Guarantee, One-Piece Top Burner Unit, etc.

f. The ad must appear in such newspapers as the dealer normally uses. This would include daily newspapers, weekly newspapers, class or foreign newspapers, or shopping news. These must be standard recognized publications. No premium will be paid for position.

4. No cooperative funds are provided if:

a. Charges are made for all or any portion of classified advertising.

b. Full-page tear sheets are not supplied properly identified as to date, locality, and name of newspaper.

COOPERATIVE PLAN FOR RADIO SPOT ANNOUNCEMENTS

1. See the General Provisions.

2. The dealer must send receipted bills and notarized affidavits from the radio stations, accompanied by exact copies of the script used in the announcement, giving the time of the broadcast(s), date, and name of station.

3. In order for the dealer to receive the greatest benefits from this plan, plus reimbursement, his radio spot announcements must comply with the following provisions:

a. The names or descriptions of competitive ranges must not appear in the same announcement as American Stove Company products.

b. Whenever possible, printed radio spot announcements should be used; these are available free of charge for use by the local announcer.

c. Or, whenever possible, prepared radio transcriptions should be used; these are available from American Stove Company for use by your local radio station. When transcriptions are used, the cost of the transcription is included in this plan and will be handled in accordance with Paragraph 5 of the General Provisions.

d. If radio spot announcements prepared by the American Stove Company or radio transcriptions are not used, your radio spot announcements should deal exclusively with (any or all of) the American Stove Company products specified in the General Provisions; the product should be mentioned by name at least every 30 minutes; preferably, American Stove Company exclusive features should be mentioned, and the announcement should be approved by your American Stove Company Sales Division Office prior to its being broadcast.

    e. Charges are to be made for station time cost only.

    4. The above requirements also apply to television broadcasts as sponsored by the dealer.

COOPERATIVE PLAN FOR BILLBOARD ADVERTISING

    1. See the General Provisions.

    2. The dealer must send receipted bills and location lists from the local outdoor advertising company. Charges must be made for space cost only.

    3. In order for the dealer to receive the greatest benefits from this plan, plus reimbursement, his billboard advertising must comply with the following provisions:

        a. Competitive ranges or their names must not appear in the same advertisement as American Stove Company products.

        b. It is highly recommended that the 24-sheet billboard posters furnished by the American Stove Company be used. When these posters are used, the cost of the poster is included in this plan and will be handled in accordance with Paragraph 5 of the General Provisions. When standard billboard posters as furnished by American Stove Company are not used:

            1. All ads must contain an illustration of an American Stove Company product as specified in this plan together with the product trade name. It is required that the standard trade-mark logotype be used.

            2. The advertising copy and design should conform in general to the features in the American Stove Company national advertising, or current retail literature.

            3. When standard billboard posters as furnished by American Stove Company are not used, copy and layout for dealer's poster must be approved by American Stove Company prior to its use.

COOPERATIVE PLAN FOR CAR CARD ADVERTISING

    1. See the General Provisions.

    2. The dealer must send receipted bills from the transit advertising firm. Charges must be made for space costs only.

    3. This fund applies to card advertising on street cars, buses, trains, and public conveyances.

    4. In order for the dealer to receive the greatest benefits from this plan, plus reimbursement, his car cards must comply with the following provisions:

        a. Competitive ranges or their names must not appear in the same advertisement as American Stove Company products.

        b. It is highly recommended that the car cards furnished by the American Stove Company be used. When these cards are used, the cost of the cards is included in this plan and will be handled in accordance with Paragraph 5 of the General Provisions.

        c. When standard car cards as furnished by American Stove Company are not used:

            1. All ads must contain an illustration of an American Stove Company product specified in this plan, together with the product trade name.

2. The advertising copy and design should conform in general to the features in the American Stove Company national advertising, or current retail literature.

3. Copy and layout for dealer's card must be approved by American Stove Company prior to its use.

COOPERATIVE PLAN FOR SPECIAL DIRECT MAIL PIECES

1. See the General Provisions.

2. All American Stove Company direct mail pieces and counter literature, as shown in the promotional material book and on the promotional material order blank, are included in this plan.

3. These pieces are prepared by American Stove Company for use by its dealers and are bought in large quantities to get a price discount. This savings in price is passed along to its dealers.

4. The dealer is credited with 50% of the price of the individual piece as shown on the order blank, in accordance with the provisions of crediting as explained in Paragraph 5 of the General Provisions.

5. When standard direct mail pieces and counter literature, as furnished by American Stove Company, are not used, prior approval of copy is required together with advance information regarding costs of material, distribution, and quantity involved on dealer initiated pieces. Provisions regarding copy, layout, etc., as stated under "Cooperative Plan for Newspaper Advertising" are applicable.

6. Distribution costs are not included in this plan.

COOPERATIVE PLAN FOR INDOOR AND OUTDOOR STORE DISPLAYS

1. See the General Provisions.

2. All American Stove Company store display pieces, as shown in the promotional material book and on the promotional material order blank, are included in this plan.

3. These pieces are prepared or purchased by American Stove Company for use by its dealers and are bought in large quantities to get a price discount. This saving in price is passed along to its dealers.

4. The dealer is credited with 50% of the price of the individual piece as shown on the order blank, in accordance with the provisions of crediting as explained in Paragraph 5 of the General Provisions.

5. When standard store display pieces, as furnished by American Stove Company, are not used, prior approval of each individual piece is required, together with information regarding costs of material, distribution, and quantity involved.

COOPERATIVE PLAN FOR LOCAL DISPLAYS OR EXHIBITIONS

1. See the General Provisions.

2. This plan covers only the costs for rental space used in exhibiting the American Stove Company products specified in this plan.

3. The dealer must send a receipted bill from the Exhibit Lessor and detailed explanation concerning the exhibit. If possible, a photograph of the booth should be furnished.

4. This plan does not cover the cost of display or preparation, except as included in the "Cooperative Plan for Window and Store Displays."

5. Should other products besides American Stove Company products be displayed, this plan covers only the costs for that part of the display devoted to American Stove Company products.

6. When a Magic Chef range is used as a prize, American Stove Company will pay 50% of the cost of the range. Prior approval for use of a range as a prize under this plan must be obtained from your American Stove Company Sales Division Office. American Stove Company participation will be limited to 5% of net purchases as described in this plan.

THIS IS A COOPERATIVE PLAN FOR YOU, MR. DEALER

Here is a plan whereby American Stove Company pays 50% of the cost for the local advertising you wish to do in promoting its products.

Here is a plan whereby you can tie-in locally ... cash in locally on the big American Stove Company national advertising program.

Here is a plan which allows you to select the advertising or promotional method you feel best suited to your community, and follow through on a cooperative basis.

Here is a plan designed to help you sell more American Stove Company products at a minimum of promotion expense to you.

Here is a plan that you can use ... use it, and you will realize greater sales of the highly profitable American Stove Company line of products.

If you have any inquiries, see your American Stove Company representative, or write your American Stove Company Sales Division Office.

ELIMINATING WASTE

All of the cooperative programs, whatever their details, have as one principal purpose the elimination of outright waste of sales aids by customers who order them and then don't use them. This is probably the most serious single headache in the field of sales promotion, and only an unending program of education seems to be a practical answer.

While training is necessary, there are several other very simple and obvious ways which can be profitably employed by a manufacturer to reduce this leakage. As a starter, many companies might profit by a cold-blooded analysis of the value of each item in the sales promotional line (see Chapter 39—"Measuring the Results of Sales Promotion"). Such a review will often indicate that certain items can be dropped entirely and others combined for both greater economy and greater efficiency.

Analysis of the size of order for promotional materials is another method of checking waste. If an over-optimistic dealer orders 5,000 copies of a catalog in a territory which has only 2,000 prospects, further investigation is obviously advisable before the order is filled. A company which is unable to develop market research data on the total potential can at least keep a running record of sales and orders for promotional materials and check on any discrepancies either over a period of time or from user to comparable user.

A clear distinction should also be made between spot promotions designed to pay off immediately and those intended to do a long-term job. When the Shell Oil Company inaugurated a direct-mail program for filling station operators, the participants were required to sign up for a full year. An arrangement of this sort is particularly important in a direct-mail campaign: otherwise the dealer will often send the first letter or two, become discouraged at the lack of response, and throw out the rest of the plan.

Eliminating Misuse of Materials

Almost as serious as the problem of the material that is never used is the situation in which the sales aids are used in the wrong way. A cheap offset folder, for instance, is much more appropriate for distribution at a county fair than an expensive four-color catalog.

In many cases this type of waste is the direct responsibility of the sponsor. A paint manufacturer, alarmed at the rate at which color-chip folders were being used, found on investigation that dealers were giving them away to all comers because they had no wall-hung display which showed the colors. The manufacturer issued a rather expensive wooden display board, and found that as soon as a dealer had used the board instead of the folder 20 times, the board was paid for.

Kold-Hold Manufacturing Company developed a simple single-sheet self-mailer which gave photographs and prices of six of its most popular lines. On the reverse side was an invitation to write for the complete catalog. By using the cheaper piece for their big mailings, distributors were able to cut catalog waste substantially.

Reproductions of four-color national advertising were being given less and less emphasis by Victor Comptometer Corporation. The same job could be done more effectively, in this organization's experience, by one-color offset sheets provided at a fraction of the cost of the reprints.

Although these three cases all involved a reduction in expense, it is sometimes paradoxically possible to save money by increas-

Number

NAME OF MAILING_____ Date released_____

Prepared by_____ Department_____

Total Inquiries Rec'd _____ % Inquiries _____ Quantity Mailed_____

Total Orders Rec'd_____ % Orders _____ "Returns" from P.O._____

List used_____ List was last used_____

Inquiry Results By Days (Record Orders Separately)

Month	1	2	3	4	5	6	7	8	9	10	11	12	13	14	15
Month	16	17	18	19	20	21	22	23	24	25	26	27	28	29	30
Month	1	2	3	4	5	6	7	8	9	10	11	12	13	14	15
Month	16	17	18	19	20	21	22	23	24	25	26	27	28	29	30

Daily record of orders, and amounts in dollars and cents.

Date Rec'd	No. of Orders	Amount	Date Rec'd	No. of Orders	Amount	Date Rec'd	No. of Orders	Amount

MAILING INSTRUCTIONS

Multigraph or Mimeograph

Letters_____

1. Fill-in _____
2. Dated _____
3. Date _____
4. Signature? _____
By hand_____ By machine _____

Enclosures (folders, etc.) x if to be imprinted

_____

_____

_____

Prepared Mailings

Show Packages_____

_____

_____

Return card enclosed? _____

Imprint _____

_____

Number_____

Date wanted _____

Where to be delivered_____

Instructions to Stenographic Department

_____

Deliver to_____ Dept._____

Marked as follows_____

Dept. O.K.	Detailed Figures of Cost		
	Printed matter		
	Letterheads		
	Envelopes		
	Addressing Envelopes		
	Fill-Ins		
	Fac-Simile Work		
	Stencil Addressing		
	Print Shop Labor		
	Mailing Room Labor		
	Postage @		
	Incidentals		
	Total Cost		
	Cost per piece		
	Cost per inquiry		
	Cost per order		

Approved_____ Acc't No._____

Supervisor of Sales

To provide a simplified method of keeping track of both costs and returns from direct-mail campaigns, some companies print the front of 9- by 12-inch envelopes. All papers, proofs, and three samples of the finished piece are placed in the envelope, which is filed away by number. Inquiries received from the mailing are tallied on the front of the envelope, which also carries cost and other data required by the promotion manager.

ing the original investment. A drug manufacturer checked on a window display unit to see how many retailers were planning to use it again, and found that nearly half had thrown it away because it had become soiled or faded. A more expensive unit which could be washed and reused was substituted the following year.

Misuse of materials often occurs simply because the manufacturer has not made clear to the user the purpose for which the tool was designed. The use of prospect mailings which offer an expensive premium, a stunt used by many of the insurance companies, would be very expensive unless it was made clear to the salesmen that these mailings were only for fully qualified prospects. The illustration of a page from Victor Comptometer Corporation's catalog of sales promotional aids shows how this organization spelled out the correct application of each item. When a new piece is introduced it is accompanied by a letter which does the same job.

Channeling Promotion to Best Prospects

"Getting thar fustest with the mostest" is not enough in planning sales promotional campaigns, they have to get to the right place. While a few companies believe that the area with the richest potential needs less cultivation than the underdeveloped area, a great majority make an effort to put the bulk of their materials where the greatest number of customers will see them.

Thanks to the activities of the space salesmen, this problem has been comparatively well solved as far as national advertising is concerned. Almost any publication can give a prospective advertiser a detailed break-down of its readership; by combining a group of these studies the advertiser can work out a schedule to get maximum coverage with a minimum of overlapping.

Direct mail, properly used, is of course the ideal medium for controlling the type of prospect who will get more expensive promotional materials. A close second is the use of inquiry coupons in advertising; these often require the prospect to send a dime or a quarter as a token of genuine interest. Names of these highly qualified prospects can then be forwarded to the salesman or dealer in whose territory the inquiry originated.

Pillsbury has a nation-wide promotion program supplemented by special extra promotional activities in those markets which its research department reported to have above the average potentials.

In a similar program, a leading electrical instrument manufacturing company checks sales for the preceding year and prorates the share of promotional money which is to be used in each territory.

A large life insurance company has developed a "Quality Rating Chart," which salesmen can work out for each prospect. The analysis involves 11 factors, each of which has point values. The total of the points indicates to the agent how much time, effort, and promotional material should be expended on the prospect.

A company selling to other industries has worked out annual purchase patterns for each industry. If a large account in the chemical field is buying only 8% of the company's product x, while the average percent of purchase in the chemical industry is 18% there is a plain indication not only of the amount of promotion which should be used, but also the type by product.

Competitive pressure is another factor involved in determining where to put sales promotional emphasis. A Texas oil products company has found that the promotional dollar is worth more in small towns because competition ignores these accounts, and the company urges salesmen to spend their time on county roads rather than on superhighways.

Eliminating Waste in Distribution

The method used to get sales promotional materials to the user is another leaking faucet. As a test, the Proctor Electric Company distributed mats to 250 retailers in the San Diego area during an all out promotion drive. Fourteen dealers ran a total of 32 ads during the period. The estimate by an advertising agency head of 75% waste in such distribution would be, in this case, overconservative.

As a result of this situation, the majority of manufacturers send only proofs of available mats to their dealer organizations and let them order from these proofs. One company has the mats delivered in person by a salesman, who then calls the local newspapers to tip them off that the dealer is considering the insertion of some advertising. The paper's space salesman can usually be counted on to follow up.

In cases where sales promotional materials are mailed from headquarters, there is a growing trend toward using this same sample system for other types of sales aids as well as mats. In the words of one executive, "If a dealer isn't interested enough to fill out a return card and mail it, he isn't going to use the material anyway."

The most effective way to deliver such materials, of course, is to have the company salesman take them to the dealership and explain them or install them himself. In many organizations, desirable as this might be, it 'cannot be done without cutting down too much on the man's selling time. Several systems have been developed to avoid this problem; Corning Glass Works employs in each territory an "assistant salesman," who does only merchandising. As vacancies occur in the senior sales force these men are moved up. Many organizations employ companies specializing in displays to do installations for them. In some fields the manufacturer's salesman rarely if ever takes an order; his entire job is to install displays and help the dealer plan promotions. Drug houses almost without exception employ detail men whose whole job is to acquaint doctors with new products and new uses for old products. The theory of course is that if the goods are moving the order is inevitable.

Waste in Duplicated Materials

For several years there has been a tendency for manufacturers to assume more and more responsibility toward their customers. A number of promotional programs have been set up which have no direct connection with the sales of the sponsors' goods, but are instead intended to strengthen the customers as businessmen. The idea is of course that strong customers, particularly retailers, will buy more goods and move them. Under present laws there is no reason why these generalized programs cannot be sponsored by an industry-wide group rather than developed and, in all probability, duplicated by individual manufacturers.

The Wood Office Furniture Institute, a group of 20 manufacturers, sponsored the publication of a 240-page manual which is actually a complete course in how to operate a retail wood office furniture store. The book was prepared by an outside consultant and sold to the dealers at cost.

Joint action by manufacturers and distributors has been undertaken by the American Supply and Machinery Manufacturers Association in collaboration with the National Supply and Machinery Distributors Association. This program is an extended research project into possible ways of cutting distribution costs.

The National Wholesale Druggists Association is still another group which has acted jointly on management problems. The usual method employed by this organization is to sponsor, through a scholarship or grant, independent research carried on by a graduate student or professor in a recognized college of business administration.

While most of such group activities have been of a general nature, there have also been promotional plans more directly under industry sponsorship. Twenty-three manufacturers sponsored a year-long selling contest for retail gas water heater salesmen. The promotion, run through the Gas Appliances Manufacturers Association, gave a heavier push than any one of the manufacturers acting alone would have found possible.

It isn't enough to sell a customer a particular brand of automobile; he must first be sold on the idea that he wants an automobile at all, rather than a refrigerator or a television set. As competition for the consumer dollar becomes keener, industry-wide activities within the limits imposed by the antitrust laws will in all probability be employed in many fields to avoid waste through duplication of sales promotional materials.

Chapter 39

MEASURING THE RESULTS OF
SALES PROMOTION

THERE are three periods of time at which an attempt can be made to evaluate a promotion: Before it is launched nationally; during the time that it is in operation in the field; and after the event has ended. Each period has advantages and disadvantages; in most cases all three can be profitably used in making a final evaluation.

For many businessmen, the word "pretest" calls up visions of bespectacled young women asking searching questions of housewives and punching the replies on statistical tabulating cards. Actually a pretest need not be that formal to be effective; merely obtaining the opinions of the company's salesmen will often suffice to get a lot of bugs out of a campaign in advance, and stopping 100 housewives in the nearest supermarket can be helpful in designing a consumer-level appeal. Since a pretest of a promotion or a promotion piece involves getting other people's ideas before a substantial investment is made, it is a safe generalization that any pretest is better than none.

One very valuable result of pretesting is that it supplies specific factual ammunition for selling the promotion to its users nationally. If a new sample kit can be sent to salesmen with a letter saying that Joe Doakes has been using it in the Oklahoma territory and has upped sales 30%, the kit will probably get better acceptance than if it is sent out cold. In the same way, a dealer is more likely to push a promotion if the manufacturer can give him case histories of the extra profits already made by retailers comparable to himself.

Whether pretesting is done on a scientific sampling basis or simply off the cuff, it is not a substitute for executive judgment. The very fact that pretesting must be done in advance is a handicap, since conditions may change rapidly from one season to the next or from the month of the test to the following month when the promotion is released generally. There are geographic differences in purchase pat-

RECORD OF COSTS and RESULTS OF ADVERTISING

DESCRIPTION OF MAILING _____ MAILING DATE _____

PURPOSE _____ QUANTITY _____ KEY _____

MAILING UNIT

☐ LETTERHEAD _____
☐ FOLDER _____
☐ CIRCULAR _____
☐ BOOKLET _____
☐ CATALOG _____
☐ ORDER BLANK _____
☐ REPLY CARD _____
☐ REPLY ENVELOPE _____
  ☐ STAMPED ☐ UNSTAMPED ☐ C.O.D.
☐ CARRIER ENVELOPE _____
  ☐ SEALED ☐ PENNYSAVER ☐ GUM SPOT
WEIGHT _____ POSTAGE _____

DUPLICATING LETTER

☐ HOOVEN FILL-IN
☐ MULTIGRAPH ☐ ONE LINE
☐ MIMEOGRAPH ☐ FOUR LINE
☐ TYPEWRITER TYPE SIGNED
☐ PRINTED TYPE ☐ HAND
☐ FACSIMILE ☐ MACHINE

DISTRIBUTION

☐ MAIL ☐ DOOR TO DOOR
☐ COUNTER ☐ PACKAGE INSERT

MAILING LIST

LIST _____
USED LAST _____
NUMBER UNDELIVERED _____

POSTAGE

☐ FIRST CLASS ☐ STAMP
☐ THIRD CLASS ☐ METER
☐ BULK THIRD ☐ PRECANCELLED
  ☐ PERMIT

ADDRESSING

☐ STENCIL ☐ TYPEWRITER ☐ HAND

PUBLICATION ADVERTISEMENT

PUBLICATION _____
CIRCULATION _____
ISSUE _____
SPACE _____
POSITION _____
COST _____

INQUIRY RESULTS BY DAYS				DAILY RECORD OF ORDERS				COSTS			
DAY	FOR MO. OF __	PER CENT	FOR MO. OF __	PER CENT	DATE REC'D	NO. OF ORDER	PER CENT	AMOUNT			
1								PREPARATION COPY			
2								ART WORK			
3								ENGRAVINGS			
4											
5											
6								TOTAL			
7								PRODUCTION LETTERHEADS			
8								ENVELOPES—OUTER			
9								ENVELOPES—REPLY			
10								POSTAL CARD			
11								PRINTING			
12											
13											
14											
15											
16								TOTAL			
17								DISTRIBUTION LIST			
18								MULTIGRAPHING			
19								FILL-IN			
20								ADDRESSING			
21								SIGNING			
22								FOLDING, INSERT, STAMP, ETC.			
23								POSTAGE			
24											
25											
26								OBJECTIVE COST TOTAL			
27											
28								TOTAL COST	$		
29								COST PER UNIT MAILED			
30								COST PER INQUIRY			
31								COST PER ORDER			
TOTAL			TOTAL								

SCHNEIDEREITH & SONS ● DIRECT MAIL ADVERTISING PRINTING OF CHARACTER ● 206-210 S. SHARP ST., BALTIMORE, MD.

A standard form widely used for scheduling, following through, and costing both direct-mail and publication advertising. Without some system of this sort it is difficult for the sales promotion manager to know which efforts are productive and which are not.

terns, too, which will not show up except in a very elaborate pretest. A campaign which sold a lot of beans in Boston, for example, might not necessarily do as well in the New Orleans market.

Too often pretests are made on the basis of intention to buy rather than on actual purchases. The result is an overoptimistic response. If a consumer is offered a choice of a very fancy fountain pen for $7.50 and a stripped-of-chromium version for $5.00, his preference will probably be for the more expensive model. However, when he must actually pay out the money, his decision may be reversed. The voting pollsters who ask the electorate which candidate they prefer, but not whether they intend to vote, are an extreme example of the fallacy found also in intention-to-buy testing.

Direct-Mail Testing

Pretesting of direct-mail campaigns is, of course, the simplest form of such activity. It is almost unanimously used as a result. The response to 2,000 or 5,000 of the mailing pieces can be obtained by simply mailing them, and total response of a comparable list of larger size can be projected with a fair degree of accuracy.

Very few companies, however, have gone one step further and used the mails to pretest other promotional materials. One of the big mail-order houses did test a variety of prices for selected items once by printing each million catalogs with different prices in them; the only result was that the curve of orders correlated directly with the amount of the price cut.

One company has made effective use of mail testing. A well-known cereal manufacturer has effectively used the following method of pretesting premium offers. Finished proofs of an advertisement offering a premium were sent to a group of consumers who had responded previously to a premium offer by the company. A letter explained that the company was making the premium available to old customers first. Since the ad was the same one that was scheduled to appear nationally later, the response indicated how well the promotion was likely to go.

Direct mail offers a method of testing the psychologically correct price for a consumer item. By sending to different sections of the same list promotion pieces which are identical except for the price, it is possible to get an evaluation of the difference in sales volume which can be anticipated between, for instance, $5.95 and $7.95.

Pretesting Advertising

Most of the big metropolitan newspapers offer a "split run" service to advertisers which can be used to pretest newspaper advertising before it is released nationally. The manufacturer submits two advertisements instead of one; half the papers carry one ad and the other half the other. By keying the ads differently, the sponsor can tell very quickly whether or not there is an appreciable variation in response.

A second method is to use different ads in papers in comparable communities; if the cities are really comparable in all essentials, this will also produce results which can be projected nationally.

Measuring the effectiveness of national magazine advertising is a wholly different problem. Many of these ads are not intended to encourage the reader to rush out and buy, but only to build brand acceptance to the point where, when the consumer is ready to redecorate, she will automatically think of a certain brand of rug, paint, or furniture.

Archibald Crossley, one of the pioneer experts in the survey field, told a Dartnell staff member, "We are particularly interested in the question of the effectiveness of national advertising, but we feel that this subject is only in its infancy. It is fairly easy to make pretty accurate counts of readers, but it is something else again to measure the real effectiveness of advertising. That work must necessarily be on an individual basis, tailor made to the specific need."

Panel Testing

For some types of promotions it is possible to assume that a small cross section of the audience can give the reaction of the whole. Actors know that if Monday night's audience laughs at a particular joke, in all probability the audiences will continue to laugh at that point for the rest of the week.

Sales promotional films, either at the dealer or the consumer level, are usually pretested in this way, just as Hollywood productions are. A group from the larger audience to whom the film is directed are given a "sneak preview" to obtain the typical reaction. In the case of training films the basic question is not so much whether the picture was esthetically enjoyable as whether it succeeded in imparting the desired information; for this type of picture a quiz on content is usually employed instead of a more general questionnaire.

Sales meetings are another type of promotion which can be evaluated by testing on a representative audience. If a skit bores an audience in Topeka, the chances are about 100 to 1 that it will bore other American audiences too.

Package and product design, which are at least partially the responsibility of the sales promotion department, can also be tested in this way. One manufacturer of refrigerators invites members of the Ladies' Aid societies in his headquarters city to a series of snack luncheons at which the line for the following year is on display. While the reactions of these housewives may not pay out on an exact scientific basis, the company found that they are typical enough to be used without further checking.

Field Testing

While valuable information about many types of promotions can be obtained in the manner just described, there are certain types of activities which must be tested under actual day-to-day conditions in real markets. A point-of-sale display, for instance, may get an enthusiastic OK from dealers when they see it at the factory and then be turned down by these same dealers because it's too big for their counters.

The simplest method of field testing is to release the new tool to a selected salesman or actually release the campaign in one distributorship. This type of testing is particularly advisable if it involves a new promotion or if the campaign is a rather complicated one; the sales promotion man who can foresee all his difficulties has not been born yet.

Tests of this type have also been used as the basis of decisions on sales promotional policies for the future. The Silex Company, toward the end of the war, needed information about how the market was likely to behave when normal supplies were again available. The company saturated the city of Peoria, Illinois, with merchandise and checked carefully to avoid "leakage" to other areas. The fact that the test was being made was not released to the public. On the basis of this actual field experience, the company was able to plan production schedules and promotional campaigns well in advance.

In the same way, the Proctor Electric Company has on occasion used two or more "guinea pig" communities to check on different types of promotions. Results are then evaluated in terms of dealer acceptance and promotional costs against sales, and the tests give

---

GENERAL ELECTRIC VISITORS' QUESTIONNAIRE
HOME BUILDERS' SHOW

DATE:

1. Did you find equipment in which you are interested displayed in the G-E exhibit?

_____ Yes _____ No

2. What impressed you most favorably about the exhibit?

_____

_____

3. Does the exhibit include any equipment of no interest to you?

_____

_____

4. Is there anything missing you would like to have seen displayed?

_____

_____

5. It is our purpose in this show to present General Electric appliances and heating equipment suitable for moderately-priced homes being built today.

(a) What class of home do you think the equipment displayed is practical for: $ _____

Comment _____

(b) Do you consider it practical for your home?

_____ Yes _____ No   Comment _____

_____

_____

POSITION OF RESPONDENT _____ TYPE OF CONCERN _____

Results from exhibits can be increased by passing out questionnaires to those who visit the exhibit asking how it impressed them. At the same time information can be obtained which will be useful in promoting the sale of the products shown in the exhibit. The above blank was used by General Electric Company to evaluate the interest in the company's exhibit of kitchen and house-heating appliances at the Home Builders' Show in Chicago. No signature was required, but the position and business connection of the person filling out the blank were asked for and usually given. Some excellent suggestions were secured in this way, which proved helpful in planning the next exhibit for this show.

a factual basis for the decision on which type of promotion to release nationally.

A guinea pig test is particularly helpful to the manufacturer whose sales peak moves north or south across the country with the changing seasons. A clothing manufacturer, for example, can iron the kinks out of his spring promotion plans on the Gulf Coast or in Southern California while the majority of his most profitable markets are still blanketed with snow.

Testing in Varied Markets

There are of course products, and promotional campaigns as well, whose appeal will be quite different in different sections of the country. In these cases it is usual for the manufacturer to pretest in several cities rather than one, and to select cities as completely different as possible, rather than trying to find nearly identical communities, as was done in the Proctor tests.

To be really effective, such tests should be based on known differentials in purchase rate. The failure of a promotion to move refrigerators among Eskimos is not a criticism of the promotion. In a less spectacular way these regional differences in purchase rate appear in the sales of consumer products from asparagus to automobiles.

These multi-town tests are of course more expensive to make, but they give more detailed information. Four key cities were used recently by a manufacturer to see what would happen to sales of a 35-cent item if the price went to 50 cents. In spite of intense promotion, the result was a big drop in sales in three communities. Had a decision been made without testing, or had a single city been used, the results might have been disastrous.

Testing by Random Sample

For premiums, consumer contests, package design, and other problems involving the verdict of the general consumer, a company can often obtain valuable information by interviewing a random sample of "man on the street." This type of interviewing is usually assigned to an independent research organization.

In the same way, the opinions of a company's salesmen, distributors, or dealers can be obtained. While the method makes no pretense of being exhaustive, it will often turn up enough new ideas or criticisms to be very worth while.

An important precaution in using random sampling is that the user must be sure that he has ruled out any factor in selecting the sample which will weigh their opinions in a particular way. The man on Broadway or the man on Wall Street is not the "man on the street" for most purposes. The classic example of a sample which turned out to be weighted was the *Literary Digest's* poll of subscribers on the Presidential election of 1936.

Testing by Scientific Sample

The most elaborate method of pretesting, and by far the most expensive to put into operation, employs accepted statistical techniques for building a "sample population" which has all the essential attributes of the larger group it represents.

Like any scientific application to human affairs, sampling technique is open to some criticism and involves problems that have not yet been solved. Whether a group of housewives will continue to be "representative" after they have been members of a panel for several years is typical of the comparatively hair-splitting points of debate.

For a company selling to other companies, which knows the names and has the essential information about every potential customer, or for an organization selling through dealers with whom close contacts are maintained, it is possible to build a rigidly accurate panel which will represent in correct proportions the 10 or 12 characteristics of most importance. The Frigidaire dealer panel is an example.

The company selling to a mass audience, however, cannot expect to achieve the same pin-point accuracy because there are too many human variables involved. Nonetheless, such a panel—2,000 members is the currently fashionable number—can give the answers to a tremendous number of questions with greater accuracy than is possible in any other form of pretesting.

Maintaining a panel of this size is obviously impossible for even the bigger individual manufacturers. Many advertising agencies have these panels and make them available to clients. It is also possible to obtain pretesting information from independent consumer panels.

EVALUATING A PROMOTION IN THE FIELD

Once a promotional campaign has been launched nationally, a different kind of evaluation begins. This study of the promotion in action is valuable both to make sure the program is clicking along on schedule and as the basis for planning more successful future activities.

The method used for this kind of evaluation naturally depends upon the type of promotion. In a display activity, the method of evaluating is to see how many dealers used the piece (and, if possible, whether its effect on sales can be directly determined). In a consumer-level promotion, the problem is whether or not goods are moving off retail shelves faster. In promoting a company film, the essential figure is the number of persons who have seen it.

If the estimate of the effectiveness of a selling promotion is to have any meaning, it must be checked against a base figure. This figure can be used as an indication of what sales would have been if the promotion had not been in effect during the period. One way of doing this is by keeping sales records in a test group of stores for a period of time preceding the promotion; another is to graph last year's sales and this year's on the same chart.

It is also advisable to keep a record of the period immediately following the promotion. If the jump in sales during the period recedes, but leaves total sales still considerably higher than they had been before, the promotion has obviously been of far more value in winning continued consumer acceptance than if at the end of the period sales promptly return to their pre-promotion level.

Using Salesmen to Check

Probably the most common method used for checking on a promotion while it is in use is by obtaining reports from the company's salesmen. The tremendous advantage of this method is its simplicity; no extra personnel are needed and, ordinarily, the salesman can gather the needed information in the course of his regular swing through a territory without waste by employing what would otherwise be waiting time.

In some cases the report need be only a "yes" or "no" as to whether a dealer is participating in a promotion or whether the salesman's new kit is satisfactory; in other instances the salesman is required to make periodic inventories either of the materials he himself is using or of the stocks on hand in distributorships and dealerships.

This system is most common in fields where the sales force is on salary and merchandising point-of-sale materials is an important part of the job. In such companies, if a merit-rating system is used, the amount of display obtained is an important factor for consideration before granting an increase. Very often in such a setup, common to the food, liquor, cigarette, and drug fields, it is part of the salesman's work to install the promotional materials himself.

Whether or not to use reports from the sales force depends upon the answers to two questions—how valuable the man's selling time is, and how much of that time will be required to make the report.

Using Direct Mail

A technique which has proved quite successful in running contests may offer an idea for checking on other types of promotions as well. The participant, whether he be a company salesman, an independent insurance agent, a jobber salesman, or a retail clerk, is required to register by mail his desire to take part in the contest and to submit reports either at definite time intervals or after he has made each sale.

Registering participants is an idea of particularly wide possibilities. As Zenn Kaufman, when merchandising director of Philip Morris & Co., Ltd., put it, "It's one thing for the manufacturer to tell people they are in a drive; it's something else when they tell him."

The Gas Appliance Manufacturers Association sponsored a year-long retail sales contest, sponsored by 23 manufacturers, with three different point awards for merchandise of differing values. In order to get reports without being flooded by detail work, the Association supplied each manufacturer with contest point credit tags which were attached to each appliance at the factory. When a retail salesman completed a sale he detached the tag, held part for his own records, and mailed the other section to contest headquarters. The utter simplicity of such a promotion appeals strongly to dealers and salesmen.

Periodic mail reports from retailers are easiest to obtain if the retailer gets something more than a word of thanks for his trouble. A monthly report of appliance sales for all the communities it serves is compiled by Southern California Edison Company. The form lists the number of dealers in the community, the number reporting sales for the month, and total sales of each of a dozen major appliances. Copies are released only to reporting dealers; each of these can quickly check his own sales against the area total to see if he is getting his share of actual business in each of the 12 lines. Although this is a continuous program, it does, as a by-product, give a monthly report on the effectiveness of current promotional activities, and a similar setup could be used only during a promotion period if the manufacturer wished.

If the letters are good, the mails can be used to obtain consumer-level reactions too. One advertising agency has developed a panel of 2,000 housewives which is used for mail surveys of product testing, copy testing, brand preferences, and other topics of interest to clients. Response runs 60% or over, and the members of the panel are not paid either in money or gifts. They reply because the letters are obviously from one human being to another; as an example of their style, here is the text of the first letter sent to a prospective panel member:

Dear Homemaker:

One of the nicest things about consumer research is getting to know people! You've shown such helpful enthusiasm and interest in answering my questionnaires that I'd like to have you as a member of my permanent consumer group. I'd like to know you better, personally, too. The more we know about you, the more helpful we can be to our clients and the more helpful they can be to you.

Since you women do the buying, if a manufacturer wants to sell to you, it's wise for him to know what you want...and our job is to find that out for him.

For example, I'd like to know your age, because if you're over 60, I wouldn't send you a panty girdle questionnaire, but I would send you one on cookies. I'd like to know your income, because if it's less than $50 a week I wouldn't ask about mink coats, but I would ask your opinion on cereals.

So, would you answer the questions on the reverse side of this letter and send it back to me in the enclosed envelope, please? No stamp is needed.

Since many of you have asked about me, I'll start the ball rolling by saying: My name is really Alice B. Day--I'm a widow--have six children (two boys and four girls) and my chief interests (besides the children, of course) are people and music.

Now won't you hurry and tell me about you?

For high ticket consumer items, it is easy to develop a user panel. Most manufacturers attach a tag to the product which must be returned to the factory before the guarantee becomes effective. In some cases an attempt is made on the registry tag to get sales information; in others the registrants are followed up by letter or questionnaire.

Almost anyone is flattered by being asked for his opinion. Mail questionnaires can give helpful information if it is kept in mind that the results are probably somewhat extreme; that is, the user of the promotion or the consumer whose experience has been either very unsatisfactory or extremely satisfactory is more likely to answer than someone who is indifferent.

Checking on Local Publicity and Advertising

It is standard practice for the manufacturer who participates in the cost of local advertising to require tear sheets of advertising insertions or receipted bills for radio time, accompanied by scripts, before the dealer's cooperative account receives credit. However, in cases where a mat service or electrotypes are furnished and the dealer pays the bill, it is impossible to get more than a minimum figure by this method. This is equally true of attempts to find out how much local publicity has been obtained through using the manufacturer's releases and how many dealers are using his radio spot announcements.

There are organizations which specialize in reporting in all three of these fields. Some will clip advertising, others news items, from the entire American press for a very reasonable fee per clipping. Another type of service monitors radio advertising by retailers.

Independent agencies will also check the complete promotional job being done by retail outlets. In cases where for some reason it is not practical to have this done by salesmen, the service, though expensive, is often well worth the investment.

Evaluating National Advertising

Just as services are available which will check the effectiveness of advertising, there are other groups which will measure how good a job is being done by national advertising in almost any medium. In most cases these services report how much attention the advertising is getting, rather than its cash register effectiveness—that is, for instance, the radio measurement services in general tell how many persons listened to a program rather than how many listeners went out and bought the product. Integrating this information with sales records is of course necessary to make final judgment on the worth of the activity. Current lists of organizations measuring the audience for newspaper and periodical advertising, radio and television shows, billboards, and car cards, can be found in the classified telephone directories of the major cities under the heading of MARKET RESEARCH & ANALYSIS.

MEASURING THE RESULTS OF SALES PROMOTION

The Worth of Inquiries

Too often a coupon advertisement will pull very well without appreciably affecting the sales curve of the sponsor. This may result from the presence, among those inquiring, of too many merely curious; it may also result from inadequate follow-up on the part of the company's salesmen, dealers, or advertising department. Or it might be, as has often happened, the total cost of processing the inquiries, including the time spent by salesmen making necessary call-backs, was more than the profit on the resulting business justified.

While there is a widely held impression among sales promotion men that one of the best things they can do to back up the salesmen is to figure out a way to provide them with a continuing stream of inquiries, there are sales managers who report that unless each inquiry can first be qualified for real buying interest, this stream-of-inquiries theory can do a sales organization more harm than good. This is especially true when a "needling system" is used to follow up salesmen to make certain they are calling on every inquirer.

When salesmen are given a crutch such as a continuing stream of *unqualified* inquiries, they lean on this instead of their own abilities. When they fail to produce sufficient business to cover their operating costs, they insist the inquiries are to blame. Were they permitted to develop their own leads, the story would be different. At any rate, many advertisers who formerly used free booklets as a device to get inquiries find it more profitable to put the salesmen on their own, and use the money formerly spent for free booklets, etc., for buyer-acceptance advertising.

One way of weeding out curiosity inquiries is to bury the offer in the advertising copy and omit any coupon. In this way the manufacturer is at least assured that the inquirer has read all of the advertisement and not simply clipped every coupon in the periodical. Most companies which have tried this plan report that it improves the quality of prospects.

There is little agreement as to the value of this procedure; a manufacturer of home building products tried both ways and found no appreciable difference in either quality or quantity of response.

A third method is by replying to an inquiry in such a way that a second inquiry is required, one which will involve a little work on the part of the prospect. A paint company, for example, sends the inquirer a form to be filled out and returned; on the basis of this information an individual recommendation covering the prospect's actual needs can be made.

Companies using this method agree that it tends to separate sheep from goats. To this arrangement, the Klee Waterproofing Corporation added one further refinement by asking on the second form for the name and address of the prospect's dealer. While this is not commonly done, it has several advantages: If the prospect is already on buying terms with one retailer, he will probably go there no matter what the manufacturer suggests; paper work in the home office can be substantially reduced if inquirers who know their dealers can be pulled before further checking; the charge of favoritism in assigning inquiries can be avoided; and, finally, the percentage of inquirers who already know their dealers offers an effective check on the company's distribution pattern and local tie-in advertising.

In many cases the value of inquiries is reduced by the failure to follow up on them. Two recent studies were made in which inquiries were addressed to all advertisers in a particular periodical. In both cases an astonishing number of advertisers made no acknowledgement whatever, and in only a minority of cases was the follow-up system so well worked out that eventually a retail salesman called. This, of course, is a sheer waste of promotional dollars.

To get full benefit from inquiries the routine should include acknowledgement by the manufacturer; a letter to the dealer giving the prospect's name and address; and carbons to the salesman and wholesaler in the territory. Another adaptable idea, which many companies might use with profit, is that employed by S. Augstein and Company, Incorporated: Inquirers are invited to return a post card if they wish to receive subsequent promotion pieces. In this way the manufacturer can build a substantial mailing list of his ultimate customers.

How to Use Inquiry Analysis

One of the most detailed studies of inquiries ever made was that undertaken some years ago by the Mullins Mfg. Co. (now part of American Radiator). The company analyzed 1 million coupon returns from mass periodicals and came to the following interesting conclusions:

> After you have included a certain number of mass magazines on your list, the new audience which you reach by adding another magazine is small indeed.

After you get as many as nine mass circulation magazines on your schedule, you could leave off any one of them and only lose about 5% of your audience.

Editorial content or lack of editorial content to "back up your advertising" does not materially affect our coupon returns.

The audience of one mass magazine (with circulation of 2 million or more) is remarkably similar to that of any other mass magazine.

In view of these conclusions, the company became interested in the sharp differences in magazine rates figured on the basis of cost per page per thousand circulation and of cost per inquiry. A second analysis was then made of 16,000 inquiries by obtaining reports from dealers as to the final outcome of each. The "good" inquiries—persons who bought or were rated by the dealers as good future prospects—formed an average of 72% of those inquiring from advertising in 17 different periodicals. The best periodical produced 82% and the least effective 69%.

Because of these facts, the company now rates periodicals on the basis of equal weighting of cost per good inquiry and of cost per page per thousand, and has made several shifts in its consumer publication advertising schedule.

Store Inventory Checks

Some industries market through channels where the double complication of wholesale inventories and nonexclusive wholesale distribution makes it impossible to quickly get figures back to the manufacturer through the distributive organization on what dealer is selling how much of what, where. In these cases about the only reliable measuring stick is a continuing retail inventory, which, of course, must be done on a sampling basis.

This can be done directly if the manufacturer makes a point of maintaining close relations with selected retailers. One company making heavy consumer appliances gets monthly inventory reports by agreeing in return to guarantee prices on the items reported on the inventories, but not on other stock.

Evaluating a Concluded Promotion

Until the last man is out in the ninth, the box score of a ball game is not complete. In the same way, there is much the sales promotion man can learn as a guide to future actions by making a careful post mortem of a campaign after it has been concluded.

At this point it is possible for the first time to make a qualitative analysis of results. If the primary purpose of the promotion was to introduce a product to new customers, sales for the period can be analyzed to find not only what total sales were, but how many new customers were brought in. If the activity was designed to beat competition, competitive sales can now be analyzed along with those of the sponsor to see whether or not he has improved his industry position.

A post-mortem analysis can also be done to evaluate the effectiveness of a promotion in comparison with previous efforts. One company in a seasonal industry tried putting a major promotional push in the slack months. Orders came in, but analysis afterward showed that the same amount of money and energy expended during the peak season brought more orders per dollar. As a result, the company now permits the slack season to remain slack.

If the promotion man determines in advance just what information he is going to need for his post mortem, records can be so set up as to make the job of tabulating much simpler. For instance, if a contest is run on a particular product, the salesmen can be given special contest report forms on which they can list sales of the product separately. When the time comes to add up the score it can be done very quickly.

Methods of Evaluation

The method used to figure out how successful a sales promotion has been will, of course, depend on what kind of promotion it was and its purpose. In some cases the results are necessarily a matter of opinion; the evaluation can be done by mail or personal interview. The merits of a catalog, for example, can be checked by asking users for suggestions on how to improve it. The value of a sales visualizer can be checked by taking a vote—an anonymous vote—among company salesmen as to whether they actually used it.

In other types of promotions the success of the activity can be gauged by direct measurement. Norge Division of Borg-Warner Corporation is among the companies which has prepared an extended program of training for dealership personnel. Each unit of the program includes a short written quiz, so that the man conducting the session can tell exactly how successful the activity has been. Similarly, an attempt to get dealers to put up "prototype buildings" of a type sponsored by the manufacturer can be evaluated by reports from the field.

A third group of activities requires comparison of the period under study with either a similar period or a "base line." In these cases the question is not so much how much was sold as how much better did the company do than it would have done without the promotion. In a sales contest in which participants receive credit for all business above quota, the base line has been determined before the promotion began. Other kinds of promotions which involve this problem include coupon deals on established products, extra goods deals for dealers, and direct-mail selling.

Factors to Consider in Evaluation

A west coast manufacturer, who supplies his men with company cars and asks them to install retail display material, found that installations were not approaching the desired level. Study of the problem was useless until an outside consultant, traveling with the men, found that an overwhelming majority of them objected to carrying the displays in the back seats of their 4-door cars, where they were plainly visible. After consultation with the men, the company agreed to supply business coupes, and the rate of installation rose sharply.

This case is included to illustrate an important point—evaluation of any sales promotional activity must include an awareness of all the factors involved. While it is true that "Nobody throws rocks at success," a good sales promotion man realizes that outside factors may distort his results favorably as well as unfavorably. It would take far less creative imagination, for example, to move expensive radio consoles which include television than to sell the same number of units without this equipment.

The experience of the Ralston Purina Company illustrates how effectively these factors can be isolated and controlled. A special sales research department was set up to study the results of sales effort and sales promotional effectiveness. The researchers found that costs had to be adjusted in different territories depending upon the state of their development; that advertising expense could be allocated to each territory on the basis of expected sales, and balanced by product groups within each territory; and that each product group required a distinctly different pattern of sales promotional expenditures. While all of this is obvious enough, very few companies have gathered the essential facts to make such decisions.

Value of Evaluation

A competent job of pretesting, checking in operation, and adding up the score afterward on a sales promotional activity requires time, effort, and money. At the present time, however, there are few companies which are doing so thorough a job in this field that they are in danger of spending more than the information obtained is worth.

When one company can, on the basis of tests, completely drop an annual expenditure of $100,000 a year for point-of-purchase displays, and another can find, by simply asking, that 96% of its dealers prefer window displays which provide space for articles other than those made by the sponsor; when one company finds that its competitive position is improved by omitting one of the four annual campaigns it has traditionally sponsored; and another finds a method of distributing materials results in 80% waste—and these are all actual cases—it seems obvious that careful evaluation is a good and necessary investment for part of the sales promotion man's time.

Market Research Services

There are many organizations specializing in market research, field testing, dealer surveys and studies of value in measuring advertising and sales results. Among them are Nielsen, Burke, Chilton, McGraw-Hill and other companies, some of which concentrate on specific areas according to product, industry, retailing and competition. Market studies are also available through the associations in the television, radio and print media fields, as well as through the major industry publications.

Whether they are obtained directly from dealers, or through the specialized research companies, the response of customers, industrial or consumer, especially if expressed in terms of sales, is the best measurement of promotional effectiveness provided the product is "right." Management must always remember that promotion, to be effective, depends on a good product and competitive pricing.

Chapter 40

MAIL ORDER SELLING

MAIL order selling is generally regarded as the most direct method of distribution and, therefore, the most economical. In fact, the growth of mail order merchandising in the United States is largely due to the widely held idea that because mail order houses employ no salesmen, they can sell their products for less. That, of course, does not always follow, but it is one of the psychological factors in selling by mail which must be considered. But mail order catalogs do establish a standard of prices for many classes of goods, especially in communities where there are no chain stores to compete with local merchants. Thus, mail order selling tends to keep down the cost of living, by holding down prices consumers pay for what they buy, and in so doing renders a useful public service.

Characteristics of Mail Order Selling

Today almost every business sells by mail. Some companies sell exclusively by mail or through mail order advertisements. Others operate mail sales departments to augment personal selling efforts, and to service customers in territories where potential sales volume is inadequate to profitably travel salesmen. Still others combine mail order selling with the operation of retail chains, finding therein a means of increasing their buying power and spreading executive overhead. It is safe to assume that the higher the cost of selling through personal salesmen climbs, the greater use businessmen will make of the mails to get business.

At first glance, there may seem no difference between mail order selling and direct mail advertising. However, there is a real and important distinction.

Mail selling attempts not merely to advertise a product, but to actually *sell* it. It is usually, but not always, considered a sales promotion function. Thus correspondence schools, publishers, and others refer to their mail sales department as the "Promotion Department." To successfully manage a mail sales department, or any mail order operation, highly specialized skills and more than the usual experience are required. In addition to being a good advertising man, the mail order executive must have the ability to obtain orders by mail (or through advertisements in mail order media) *at a profit*. The difference of a fraction of 1% in the returns from a large mailing, often spells the difference between a profit and a loss on the cost of the mailing.

For example, in selling a $10 book by mail, where the selling cost must not exceed $4, one order from every 100 circulars mailed to a list of book buyers might be satisfactory. Less than one order per 100 pieces mailed would put the list in the red. But if the mailing tested out 1¼ orders for every 100 pieces mailed, the publisher would consider he had "hit the jack pot." The difference between 1% and 1¼% returns on large mailings is usually, but not always, the difference in the experience, skill, and sales ability of the person who planned and prepared the mailing. While there are any number of promotion and advertising men who can write a good sales letter, or prepare a good-looking advertisement, only one in a hundred has the ability to plan and write profitable direct-selling copy.

Sales-Increasing Techniques

Some of the techniques which are being used to increase response from mail order catalogs, as presented by Bob Stone in *Advertising Age,* include:

Establishing a theme. Every catalog should have an underlying theme—a reason for being. Examples of themes: "Everything in Office Supplies," "Maintenance Supplies at Direct-To-You Prices," "Useful and Entertaining Hobbies," "Executive Gift Guide," "Wholesale Auto Parts for All Makes."

Overwraps. Dramatic increases in response are being attributed to catalog overwraps. Most overwraps consist of a letter overlaying the front of the catalog and an order form overlaying the back of the catalog. The letter serves to excite interest in the catalog. What's more, because the overwrap is printed separately, it's possible to use slanted letters directed at specific segments of the total market.

Order incentives. Substantially increased response is resulting from order incentives such as discount coupons, free gifts for minimum orders, or for ordering promptly.

Testimonials. Many firms which sell via the catalog method have developed the technique of spreading testimonials throughout their catalog. Testimonials are used to reinforce quality claims and speed of delivery.

Credit terms. Catalog firms which have sold for cash only for years are now offering bank charge privileges through Bank-Americard and Master Charge. Many report 10% to 15% of their orders are now being charged to one of the bank cards. And the average charge order is ranging anywhere from 10% to 40% more than the average cash order.

Leading with best sellers. Proper positioning of merchandise within a catalog is a key factor in increasing total sales from a catalog. Leading with your best sellers has proved to be the most profitable technique for most.

This makes sense in that theoretically, the more popular an item, the more likely that item is going to attract readership.

Conversely, less popular items up front in a catalog are likely to turn off readership.

Equating space to sales. Those who are expert at catalog selling long ago developed the technique of charging space to every item which appears in a catalog, just as they would if they were advertising in a magazine. Items which are profitable in small space earn larger space in a subsequent catalog. Items which don't make it are either relegated to smaller space, or eliminated.

Free trial periods. It's axiomatic that satisfaction is guaranteed for every item appearing in a catalog. But many catalog operations reinforce the guarantee by stating, "All items in this catalog may be ordered for 10 days free trial."

Envelope order forms. There's only one thing you want back from a catalog—a signed order form! Using a combination of order form and return envelope has proved to be a profitable technique. In small catalogs the envelope order form is usually bound into the center of the catalog. Another profitable technique is to offer additional items on the envelope flap and on the back of the order form.

Action verbs in headlines. Reader interest is being enhanced by making headlines interesting. For instance, instead of using labels like "Peach Trees," the headline goes something like this: "You Can Grow Peach Trees Like These In Only Three Years."

Book-of-the-Month Club

One of the early mail-order successes was the Book-of-the-Month Club, an outgrowth of the Little Leather Library, which was launched after World War I. Originally, the plan was to sell the little books through drug stores and for use as premiums. But it was not much of a success. Finally the owners, Max Sackheim and Harry Scherman, decided to experiment with selling the little books direct by mail. The first advertisement, written by Sackheim, appeared in the *Pathfinder,* and offered "30 of the world's great classics for $2.98. Send no money. Pay the postman when he delivers." During the period of 1920 to 1924 this technique, used in both publication ads and in direct mail, sold 40 million books. The almost finished Little Leather Library became a gold mine for the owners.

In the course of promoting the Little Leather Library, it occured to Sackheim and Scherman they should sell culture in small doses, rather than just a package of books. The idea of reading a classic a week was tried without success. Then the idea of a book club for the selection of popular current books was born and 4,000 members were enrolled the first month. It turned out to be one of the most profitable mail order ventures ever undertaken.

Max Sackheim's flair for writing result-getting copy was in large measure the secret of his success. He felt that much advertising is wasteful ... that too much emphasis was placed on the layout and art. He insisted that the layout should merely be the vehicle for the message and not the end in itself.

His credo: That mail order principles should be incorporated in every advertisement—that every device should be used to secure action immediately after reading the copy (rather than to permit human inertia to set in by restricting "clincher" statements to phrases like "go to your dealer"). He believed that if the product cannot be sold by mail, then offers of booklets, samples, premiums, box tops, etc., should be incorporated to produce immediate action. The purpose of an ad should be to make customers instead of only impressions.

In one split-run test it was found that dealers got only 10% of the business created by the ad, as against 90% of mail orders. In another test a department store sold nearly 10 times the units by mail as against counter sales. A coupon was used, and the item sold for a dollar. Many products are not *important* enough to an individual to induce him to rush to a store, but *are* important enough to produce an order by mail.

Sackheim was not sympathetic with big space ads for products that need *reminder* advertising instead of powerhouse sales arguments. He believed in the repetitive effect of small space advertising. It is advertising you can't escape. It's here, there, everywhere. It's done *not* with size, splash color, and argument, but with an interrupting idea that repeats and repeats itself in many insistent little ways. Even irritating advertising, if repeated often enough, gets in people's way—and despite their irritation, people buy. The basis of his copy was "think in terms of words that *sell,* for in the final analysis, advertising is selling."

1. Concentrate on the consumer. In the end you must sell him, no matter what method you use. In the beginning you must know him.

2. Know your product.

3. Find the "symptom" or "symptoms" that your product is qualified to cure. It may be a mental, physical, or financial "symptom" but your product must have an "excuse for existence."

4. Be exciting in your writing.

5. Advertising is essentially NEWS. It should inform, enlighten, instruct, or promise a reward. The news may take many forms. It may be price, it may be a new slant on quality, or both. It may be a new use for an old product. It may be a new twist to an old use of an old product. It may be startling language applied to a prosaic product. But always news.

A Great Catalog Promotion

Sunset House, Los Angeles, well-known specialty-novelty mail order house, has dramatically stimulated sales and increased the number of orders from its catalog by developing it into a complete promotional package. The 96-page catalog is its main sales vehicle and goes out as a self-mailer to a list of six million people approximately every six weeks, with the catalog overwrap computer-personalized to obtain utmost impact.

Each issue features a sweepstakes promotion. A recent edition offered a total of 1189 prizes and a fabulous first prize of a free vacation for at least ten years and possibly fifteen years, worth $1000 a year. The number of years was determined by a free-vacation number. The second prize was a Magnavox Stereo Theatre which included color television, record player and radio. There were ten third prizes of Sony TV sets. In addition there were 25 fourth prizes, 50 fifth prizes, 100 sixth prizes and 1000 seventh prizes!

But that was not all. As further inducements to buy, Sunset House offered two great "surprise bonuses." Bound into the center fold was a four-page section which included the order form, the contest rules and a return envelope. Folded over the order form were three covered flaps. When opened, the first disclosed the number of free-vacation years which might be won by the contestant; the second announced an early entry bonus prize of a Chevrolet Vega and the third panel proclaimed that whoever won the Chevrolet car would find a cash bonus of $1000 in the glove compartment of the car.

In addition, the front cover of the overwrap featured two certificates for second and third chances at the prizes.

The final touches were a free offer of four Tiffany "stained glass" appliques on any order over $4.95 and a money-back guarantee if not satisfied.

Hormel's Mail Order Activity

Some companies, while not making a practice of selling by mail direct to consumers, put out specialties for Christmas gift sale and go after corporations and other buyers of such products. Hormel & Company, for example, puts up carefully selected, uniform-weight hams in attractive wrappings and solicits quantity orders from companies which give gifts of that sort to customers and employees at Christmas. An apple grower in Michigan, who sells most of his crop through the usual channels of distribution, has built up a nice holiday mail order business. He features cartons of Jonathan apples. Cheese manufacturers also take advantage of the Christmas gift market to put on mail order campaigns. In selling products for Christmas gift distribution, it is usually the custom to quote delivered prices, with a sliding scale of prices so that the more a customer buys the larger his discount will be. Orders are secured from (1) lists of known buyers of Christmas gifts, (2) from small ads in Christmas shopping sections of mail order publications, (3) from ads in magazines reaching business executives, and (4) from spot radio and TV commercials.

Starting a Mail Order Department

A growing number of manufacturers, and to a lesser extent wholesalers and retailers, have established mail order departments to reduce selling costs in fringe territories, and to hold down selling costs in territories where high travel costs make it impractical to maintain frequent contact with all customers.

Many others would like to add a mail order department to their distribution pattern but have hesitated because of certain problems involved. Not the least of these is the problem of double selling costs, when the salesman must receive full credit on all orders arising in his territory. The problem exists, no matter how the salesman is compensated, but becomes especially acute when the salesman is working on a straight commission or a bonus on sales over quota.

One company solved the problem by rearranging territories. Instead of assigning territories on a county unit basis, territories were assigned by routes. Each route consisted of accounts located in communities on hard roads, or easily accessible by bus or train. Each town on the route was given a number, prefixed with the salesman's route number. It was his job to cover his route periodically, calling on all active accounts, with a quota of new business which the management expected him to secure each year. He was paid a bonus on the new business over quota. All accounts off the "beaten path" (i.e., the established routes) were assigned to the mail order department. Salesmen received no commission on orders received from customers by mail, unless the customers were located in communities on his route. In that case he received full credit. While the salesmen, as might be expected, opposed the idea at first, it was not long before they were making more money under the new arrangement as a result of the bonus on new business, which they did not receive under the straight salary plan previously in effect.

One well-known company financed its mail order department by increasing the compensation slightly on business sold directly by salesmen and reducing it on orders which came in by mail. It was explained to the salesmen they profited from the extra benefit they received from having their customers, who otherwise might give their business to a competitor, worked systematically by mail. Certainly mail order support makes it much easier for a salesman operating on the county unit plan to open up new accounts in out-of-the-way places. It is an axiom of sales management that a salesman can usually make more money, and do a better all-around territory-building job, if he can concentrate his effort on customers having the greatest potential.

But the national market is so large that even though a manufacturer credits his salesmen with all orders received by mail from his territory, the extra profit resulting from the increased volume thus obtained will usually more than carry the department and greatly broaden the base of a company's distribution. While initial operations of the department, in such cases, may not be very profitable, eventually, once a pattern is established and new salesmen join the organization, selling costs can be brought into line. Properly managed, the mail sales department can become increasingly important to the profits of the business. At any rate, the extra volume thus obtained permits spreading fixed expenses and enables a business to get considerable benefit from its ability to buy in larger quantities.

Duties of Manufacturer's Mail Order Department

An analysis of the failures in operating mail sales departments, to supplement personal sales efforts, shows the principal reasons are: (1) Inexperienced or incapable management; (2) failure of top management to give the mail order department its full support, especially during the initial year of operation. It is only natural that a management which has built the business by following some one method of distribution, will look with suspicion on any new method, especially a method which the sales organization may regard as competitive. This is especially true if the mail order department, as in the case of a wholesale house, seems to be in competition with established retail accounts. It is, therefore, important at the outset to set the operation up in such a way that it will actually help salesmen or dealers to do a better job. Since this value can be demonstrated, it need not be an impossible hurdle to get over.

Regardless of whether the mail selling operation is at the manufacturing or retailing level, it is generally best that the head of the department should report directly to top management, rather than to a sales officer who might not feel too kindly toward selling by mail.

The mail sales manager should be a trained mail order man, and not somebody picked at random from the office or sales staff to establish the department. Neither should he be an advertising man, nor should the job be given to the advertising manager along with his other duties. However, the advertising department can be used to good advantage in preparing the catalog, price lists, and promotional materials used in the operation. But the actual management should be the responsibility of a man who has demonstrated ability as a mail order merchandiser, and who is wholly "sold" on the opportunity the new department has to build a large volume of sales at a satisfactory cost. He should be skilled in mail order methods, not only of selling but of handling orders with the least clerical assistance. He will thus be in a position to install systems for expediting the business done by mail which might be very different from those presently in use.

Cost of Selling by Mail

In spite of the widespread opinion that it costs less to sell by mail than through established channels of trade, or direct through house-to-house salesmen, by and large it costs about the same when all factors, including the higher overhead, are considered. Because of the different methods used in computing costs by mail order houses and companies which sell through salesmen, comparisons are unreliable. A great deal depends upon the type of product, the price and, perhaps most important of all, upon the lists available. Obviously, the cost of selling any given product by mail to establish customers will be a great deal less than the cost of selling to "cold" lists or even to lists of persons who have purchased similar products by mail from other companies. It costs much more to sell a luxury by mail than it does a staple. In the case of products where the demand or want must be created, as compared with a product like shoes for which a demand exists, the cost is about double. Catalog houses, selling a variety of merchandise to consumers who have previously ordered from the company by mail, report selling costs ranging from 10 to 12% for fashions and jewelry, down to 3½% for automobile tires. The average selling cost of wearing apparel is about 8%. These figures include the actual cost of catalog preparation, printing, postage, and addressing. They do not include administration, shipping, or other expenses which accountants usually include when computing sales costs.

In selling magazine subscriptions by mail the cost of securing new subscriptions usually runs about 100%. About one-half the subscriptions usually renew at a cost of about 15%. Over a 3-year period then, the sales cost of maintaining a list of subscribers to a well-edited magazine is about 60%.

Mail Order Lists

It is possible to purchase, or rent, lists of persons who have bought products similar to those you wish to sell, by mail. One list broker in New York advertised lists of 2 million mail order buyers at an average cost of $25 a thousand names. Usually the lists are rented from the broker who divides the rental with the owner of the list, usually another mail order company. In some instances, the lists are furnished on strips of gummed paper, perforated so that they can be easily torn apart and pasted directly onto the envelope or mailing piece. Mail order merchandisers, who have built up sizable lists, can usually exchange mailings with other mail order companies. In this case the material to be mailed, already stuffed into penny-saver envelopes for mailing, is shipped to the list owner. He runs the envelopes through his addressing machine, mails them at his local post office, and reimburses the customer for returned mail.

The orders secured from lists of known mail order buyers usually produce enough additional orders over "cold" lists to more than justify the cost.

WRITING MAIL ORDER COPY

The purpose of an advertisement or a letter in mail order selling is *to get the order now*. Direct mailers are not especially concerned with making a good impression, creating consumer acceptance, or even building good will for the company. These are all valuable by-products of a successful mail order effort, but as one mail order man expressed it: "They are not negotiable down at the bank." When the unit of sale is large, as in the case of selling knock down boats by mail, the first need is to get an inquiry. But most of the things which are sold by mail are sold cash with order or cash on delivery. Firm orders are all that count. Consequently, copy used in mail selling, from the approach to the close, is slanted to get action. And, since the mail order field is highly competitive, not alone with other companies selling by mail but with local merchants as well, writing copy that gets an order is not easy.

How One Word Lost a Sale for Ward's

Richard Hodgson, whose book, *Direct Mail and Mail Order Handbook* (Dartnell) is based on many years of mail advertising and selling, tells of an Illinois farmer who made up his mind to buy a cream separator. Unable to make a decision from Ward's or Sears' catalogs, he got into his car and called on his neighbors. Those owning Sears' separators acknowledged they were good; those using Ward's were just as sure Ward's were the best. So he returned home more confused than ever. His wife pointed out that the copy in Sears' catalog read: "Guaranteed 225 pounds" and Ward's just read "190 pounds." Sears got the order. As a matter of fact, the lighter weight was an advantage but the Ward copy writer had failed to emphasize the fact. Because mail order copy sells "sight unseen" and depends upon words to fill out the picture and answer the many questions in a buyer's mind, it is most important that the copy cover *every* selling point. Dimensions, weights, speeds and details which seem unimportant to the copy writer, who thinks in general terms, may make or break the sale. The average mail order buyer spends hours considering a purchase before he puts his John Henry at the bottom of the order blank and mails his money order to you. Leaving a single doubt in his mind may cause him to lay the catalog or publication aside and postpone buying, perhaps for good.

Mail Order Buying Motives

People who buy by mail are the same people who buy from salesmen. They buy for the same reasons. They respond to the same appeals. They act only when they are made to want the product or service, more than they want the money it costs. Take, for example, the problem involved in writing an advertisement (or a letter) to sell a $35 dress. An advertising man, used to preparing ads to create consumer acceptance only, would probably come up with a short, snappy ad which would read about like this:

> "What woman would not be delighted to appear in this beautiful velvet gown—price $35?"

From a mail order standpoint the copy writer would have missed several points needed to close the sale. He said nothing about style, the use, the comparative value, the kind of velvet, its wearing qualities, the trimmings, whether suitable for misses or women, the colors, sizes, approximately length, and perhaps sweep. To really qualify as selling copy, of the bread and butter sort, the ad should run something like this:

> "What woman would not be delighted to appear in this last minute model of rich-looking silk chiffon velvet, smartly finished with new slashed sleeves of good quality silk satin? Just the thing for afternoon or informal party wear. The material will give you excellent wear and the price quoted represents unusual value. Length: 40 to 44 inches, according to size. Women's sizes 34 to 44. Colors: Navy blue, black, red, and dark brown. Special gown—price $35."

The secret of writing good mail order copy, like writing any other kind of advertising, is to put yourself in the shoes of the person you are selling. In all probability he is not especially interested in what you want him to buy or do. Like the farmer who wouldn't buy a book on farming because he wasn't farming as good as he knew how anyway, most people must be made to want a thing before they will even take the time to read your ad or letter. Their attitude is very much "Ho hum." They have so many places to put their money, why should they buy something else? So they ask: "Will it save enough to warrant spending the money?" "Will it make my work easier?" "Will it add to my prestige or standing among my friends and neighbors?" "Will it open new opportunities for my children?" "Will it help me to get ahead in my business or profession?" "Will it give me more old age security?"

These buying motives and the approach to them, while many in number, follow a defined pattern, which is as follows:

SECURITY—Appeal to buyer's desire for protection against adversity, loss of position, poverty, etc., by representing what you are selling as insurance against whatever it is he fears.

PROFIT OR GAIN—Show buyer that he is paying for what you offer in profit he is losing because he does not now have it. Since he is paying for it anyway why not get the benefit and satisfaction that goes with having it.

PRIDE—One of the strongest of human desires is the desire to be important. Tactfully impress upon the buyer that ownership of what you are selling carries with it the prestige of leadership.

COMFORT—People want to go places sitting down. Emphasize the leisure a buyer will have if the drudgery is taken out of his or her work. Stress the satisfaction that comes from doing things the easy and modern way.

VANITY—This involves the self-satisfaction one derives from possessing something very fine even though it may cost more. Appeal to every man's desire to be a "big shot" in the eyes of those whose opinions he values.

LOVE—Appeal to the finer instincts in men and women which cause them to make almost any sacrifice for those they love—especially their children. Play up the needs of those they love.

CURIOSITY—Most people have a large bump of curiosity. They will often buy a thing just to satisfy their curiosity, if in doing so they think they may find an answer to some problem of the moment.

Until you really know and understand the motives which cause people to buy your product you are not likely to write good selling copy. You have to know the "live nerve" to touch. And until you touch it you have not even reached first base. To find out why people will buy, find out why those you have already sold *bought*.

The "So What" Hurdle

Just as you cannot score in a ball game until you get to first base, you cannot profitably sell by mail until you first arouse favorable attention and interest. Most people, and especially farmers, are hard-boiled when it comes to parting with their money. They may be interested, but inwardly say to themselves: "So what?" To get to second base therefore, and to make sure you are not put out at first, your ad or letter, as the case may be, needs to create in the mind of the reader a strong desire to possess what you are selling. So your copy paints a word picture, with the prospect up in front enjoying or benefiting from having your product. If you are selling life insurance, you will picture the satisfaction which goes with knowing your loved ones are protected in case you should get hit by a truck tonight. If it is steaks, you make the reader drool over the pleasant prospect of eating such delicious steaks. As Elmer Wheeler put it: "Sell the sizzle and not the steak."

People seldom want things for what they are, they want them for what they will do. Picture them enjoying the fun, the pleasure, the comfort, or whatever it may be, that comes from ownership.

But a man may want your product very much, and still not buy because he has no confidence that the firm who is asking him to buy will give him a square deal. He does not know for sure that what he has read in the letter or advertisement is true. He may never have had any dealings with the firm, maybe they are just city slickers or racketeers. Is it safe to send money with his order? Suppose he is not satisfied, will he get his money back? Will he get it back without a lawyer or a lot of letters? Will the merchandise be as represented? These are just a few of the doubts in his mind. So to get to third base in our mail order ball game it is necessary to establish confidence.

The big mail order houses do this by guaranteeing complete satisfaction or money cheerfully and promptly refunded. Some mail order men even go further—they offer "double your money back" if not satisfied. If it is not practical to make unqualified guarantees (and "hedged" guarantees are worse than no guarantee at all, since they only arouse suspicion) then use the testimony of satisfied customers. Let them speak for you. But let them speak in an interesting way, so that what they say will register in the reader's mind and not be buried among a mass of testimonial statements. And be careful not to overdo proof. Too much back patting can slow down and, perhaps, kill the sale. It is the old story of boasting too loudly.

Getting Action

You have the reader's *favorable* interest, you have made him really want what you are selling, you have erased from his mind any doubt he may have about your treatment of him. You are on third base. To "come home" and score, one more thing is necessary, *getting him to act*. Some mail order men contend, with reason, that if a person really wants a thing hard enough, he will buy without using "closing strategy." They hold people resent being pressured into buying, and that corny last lines which urge them to take time by the forelock and send back the coupon *now*, are outdated. This is sometimes true. But that is like saying a salesman will get just as much business if he bows out before asking for the order as he will if he stays a minute longer and gives his prospect a valid reason for placing the order now. Thousands of dollars' worth of business is lost every year by companies whose salesmen don't think it is necessary to *ask for the order*. If you want maximum returns at a minimum cost, not only ask for the order but give your prospect a logical reason for acting while the matter is fresh in his mind.

Reply cards, with holes punched in them for each different list used, enable an advertiser to "tally" returns easily.

Providing a logical reason for immediate action sometimes requires special planning. Thus, in selling a set of books by mail, one publisher found it worth while to offer a special cross index to the books if the order was received by a certain date. Other publishers offer a slightly reduced price if the order with check attached is received before publication date. Old bromides—like the supply is limited, therefore the reader should send back the coupon today to make sure that he will not be disappointed—are discredited. They do more harm than good. They give the copy a flavor of insincerity which can undo everything that the copy has done before to make the sale.

The Agency to Handle Mail Order Sales

Preparing advertising copy for mail order publications is one of the most difficult jobs in advertising and calls for entirely different skills than are needed for preparing institutional and mass acceptance advertising. For that reason it is the usual practice to employ advertising counsel, experienced and skilled in planning and preparing direct selling copy, to handle any appropriation that is made to establish a mail sales operation.

Mail order copy writers and agency principals, by costly trial and error, are better able to tell in advance whether a certain appeal or a given piece of copy will pull, and which media should be most profitable to use. Because they understand the importance of 1/10 of 1% in the returns from an advertisement, mail order agencies are more inclined to make the necessary tests to evaluate the profitableness of an advertisement, and not "guess" that it will pull.

They understand the use of setting up a mail order "deal," of free trials, premium packages, keys, codes, and all the other devices which are so important in getting orders by mail. For example, one agency specializing in mail order advertising has developed 18 different methods of keying advertisements.

Scientific mail order advertising requires that the worth of an advertisement be measured by the cost per dollar of sale rather than the cost per inquiry. A further point, agencies specializing in mail order work are not as apt to spend unnecessary money on art work, "atmospheric" illustrations, and other advertising devices which make the ad look pretty, and help to "sell" it to the advertiser, but which actually do not produce enough extra sales volume to pay. Mail order men usually rate the layout as second in importance and hold the copy is most important. General advertising men, intent upon creating an impression rather than getting an order, place more importance on the layout.

Competition with Institutional Advertising

Companies which operate a mail sales department, in addition to selling through established dealers, hesitate to run direct selling copy for fear some dealers might object. The very fact that a supplier is actively soliciting orders by mail causes dealers to think they are losing business and they make an issue out of it the next time the salesman from the house calls. In some instances, it might be unwise to use mail order selling copy, even in mail order media which circulates outside of large cities where a company usually concentrates dealer sales efforts. But most companies, notably publishers, which sell through personal salesmen, dealers, and by mail, testify that while there are complaints, the net result to both the distributor and the company is favorable.

On this score, John Shrager, who has successfully handled a number of mail order accounts where the advertiser sold both ways, stated: "We answer such objections from distributors by explaining that without the mail order advertising to help pay for the cost of the ad, the product so advertised can seldom be fully exploited. Mail order advertising will not take away from the business of the distributors. The loss of a few "disgruntled" clients here and there will never compensate the advertiser as much as high-powered mail-order-type copy.

"Many of our advertisers contend that the distributors play only a passive part in the distribution of their products. We have sufficient proof by research organizations of decided benefits to distributors when mail order was used as the sole type of advertising for the promotion of the product. Where would the book industry and its distributors—the book stores—be if it were not for the millions of dollars invested in the last 20 years in mail order advertising by the book clubs? The mail order book club operations have in just 20 short years radically increased the reading habits of the nation, making many more customers for books than ever existed before."

But the objection some dealers have to a supplier selling by mail, in seeming competition to them, can be overcome by skillful copy writing. Somewhere in the ad it should be stated that the product or service may be purchased at most of the best stores, but if it is not so available, it will be sent directly at no additional cost, if the reader will fill out and return the coupon.

LETTERS THAT SELL BY MAIL

The fundamentals of writing any sales promotional letter (see Chapter 7—"Sales Promotion Letters") apply to writing letters intended to get orders. But the letters most effective in direct mail selling are those having a stronger appeal to the recipient's self-interest, and are long enough to do a complete selling job. They are usually produced more economically, with less attention to making a good impression. In fact some of the most profitable mail order letters have been duplicated on the cheapest sulphite bond, using both sides of the sheet, and enclosed in hand-addressed manila envelopes. In mail selling the message is all-important; the dress of the letter and the enclosures serve only as a vehicle for the message.

The Tone of the Letter

Mail order buyers are usually price-minded. They buy by mail because they think by so doing, they either save money or get products which they could not buy in local stores. Some buy because it is more convenient to buy by mail. But most small-town people buy on price. So it is important that your letters should be slanted in that direction, and sufficiently interesting to hold attention through the full length of the letter. And keeping in mind that mail order buyers are usually "folksy" people who just don't like "city slickers," the letter should not be imperative or in the least way "high brow." The best mail order letter are those like Bill Galloway used to write to his "folks"—kindly, friendly, chatty, with plenty of punch, but humble. To Bill Galloway the customer was king. It is not hard to give the customer the idea you think he is important, if you use tact.

A good example of a tactful person is Benjamin Franklin, who achieved a reputation at the French Court, and was able to accomplish many difficult feats of diplomatic salesmanship.

In his autobiography Franklin has this to say about humility in human relations: "I cannot boast of much success in acquiring the *reality* of this virtue, but I had a good deal in regard to the *appearance* of it. I made it a rule to forbear all direct contradiction to the sentiments of others, and all positive assertions of my own. I even forbade myself the use of every word or expression in the language that imported a fixed opinion, such as *certainly, undoubtedly,* etc. I adopted instead of them, I *conceive,* I *apprehend,* or I *imagine* a thing to be so and so, or it *so appears to me at the present.*

"When another asserted something that I thought an error, I denied myself the pleasure of contradicting him abruptly and of showing some absurdity in his proposition; and in answering I began by observing that in certain cases or circumstances his opinion would be right, but in the present case there *appeared* or *seemed* to be some difference.

"And to this habit I think it principally owing that I had early so much weight with my fellow-citizens when I proposed new institutions, and so much influence in public councils when I became a member; for I was but a bad speaker, never eloquent, subject to much hesitation in the choice of words, hardly correct in my language, and yet I generally carried my points."

To bring Franklin's philosophy home let us take a letter which came in just the other day. It was sent out to a list of dealers by a big Baltimore tailoring house. It started out: "Are you afraid that we will convince you against your will? At any rate don't answer our letters!"

How much more effective this opening would have been had it offered a suggestion which is nonchallenging, as for example: "May I offer a suggestion which could very easily add $5,000 to your profits this year?"

The more personal—the more "me and you"—a mail selling letter is, the better. People like to do business with people and not with those vague things we call "corporations." "I" is a stronger pronoun than "we," although for legal reasons it is sometimes necessary to use "we" when committing a corporation or a firm. Too many "we's" in a letter make it sound formal and stuffy. Write as you talk, and don't try to impress the person to whom you are writing with your command of English, your importance, or your education. None of these things add up to a reason for buying.

Use of Eye Catchers

More important than is generally realized by those who write letters to sell, is the need of something which will "stop" the casual reader when he first opens the letter. Here are a few suggestions from Howard Dana Shaw, a letter specialist who believes that any letter which does not catch the eye before the recipient gets to the opening paragraph, has two strikes against it:

> ... A sub-headline or two on the page. These can be centered, or even with the left edge of the text, or extending beyond the left edge into the margin.
>
> ... A paragraph in a different color, or typed in a narrower width *(indented both sides)*.
>
> ... Words or phrases can be underscored or typed in all capitals *(but don't overdo it)* ... An occasional sentence or short paragraph can be all capitals.
>
> ... And remember to use a regular paragraph indent *(don't use the "modern" block style)* because the rectangles of space are eye hooks.
>
> Another method that always proves to be effective when letters are tested is the use of imitation handwritten notations and marks. The letter will appear to have been doctored up by a pen in your hand, but it will still be processed in quantity.
>
> For example, you can underscore or ring a word or phrase, you can draw a bracket or arrow to emphasize a point, you can write a few words in the margin or add a postscript.
>
> To do this, you make the words or marks with black ink on tracing paper or glazed onion skin. The printer or offset shop will then photograph them so they will "register in" with the rest of the letter, and you should ask him to print in blue ink.

But just catching the eye is not enough to get the kind of favorable interest you must have to make a sale by mail. After you have the man's interest you must come to the point quickly, and the point is, so far as the customer is concerned: "What does this guy want now?" So, tell him the point of your letter—"what you are driving at"—and tell him as soon as you can. Particularly, tell him what you want him to do, or not to do.

How Long Should the Letter Be?

Somebody once asked Abraham Lincoln how long a man's legs should be. He answered: "Long enough to reach from his waist to the ground." This also applies to mail order letters. Make your letters long enough to do a complete selling job—no longer and no shorter. Most people will read long letters, as well as they read short letters, if the letters are made interesting. An exception to this rule might be letters undertaking to sell something to executives. People who are busy and who receive a lot of mail will not, as a rule, take time to read a letter more than two pages long. They may read at it. But usually they are in a hurry and want to get on with what they, at least, consider to be more important matters. This, of course, is not true in writing to farmers and others who do not receive much mail, and who regard even a form letter as a personal invitation to buy. Generally speaking, long letters pull better than short ones if an actual selling job is to be done, provided always that they *hold* interest.

MAIL ORDER TESTING

Mail order operators, while depending mainly upon direct mail for profits, usually supplement mail promotions with the use of mail order media. Even though the volume of business resulting from the use of mail order media may not be large, and sales may be somewhat more costly, the large circulation of such media gives the advertiser broad coverage at a very low rate per thousand circulation.

One mail order company spent $2,000 to test what appeared to be an excellent mailing list without getting a single order. The firm decided to make another try in a well-known magazine whose circulation was concentrated in small towns. With an investment of $70 for a small test ad, 140 orders were secured. After that experience the firm concentrated the bulk of its sales promotion in small-town media. Small ads in mail order media produce good names for the mailing list and build a certain amount of reader acceptance for any direct mail the reader subsequently receives from the advertiser. This is an important, but all too often overlooked, factor in the successful use of direct mail. The recipient of a direct mail piece, who knows the company through having seen its ads in publications is more likely to respond than one who never heard of the company before.

The usual practice in testing media is to prepare a series of three small ads, just large enough to include the essential information about the product or service, and run each ad in consecutive issues of a small list of media. Each ad, of course, is keyed so that all orders and inquiries received can be properly credited to the proper publication. By computing the cost per order, or inquiry, after a period of 90 days, each medium used in the test can be evaluated with some accuracy. Larger ads can then be scheduled in profitable publications, and unprofitable publications can be dropped or tested further with a different copy appeal.

Testing Mailing Lists

At a meeting of the Hundred Million Club, composed of companies doing large direct mailings to secure orders by mail, the various members described their experiences in conducting test mailings. It was interesting to note that tests, by conventional standards, are not at all conclusive and cannot be relied upon for long periods. Kiplinger's representative, for example, testified that poor mailing months one year turned into good months another year. Likewise his experience with copy, postage, lists, etc., convinced him of the need of constantly checking and rechecking every factor that might affect the results of a large mailing.

To be of value tests should be made quickly and acted upon quickly. A few months' lapse between the conclusion of a test and the beginning of the main mailing can be sufficient to change the results completely. Many tests are of questionable value because they are made on the first 1,000 to 10,000 names on a list. If the list is geographically filed, this means the names used will be from Alabama, Alaska, Arkansas, etc. Would those be typical? Tests should represent a 2% sampling to typical names. The best practice is to test every tenth or one hundredth name (depending upon the size of list) or to test all names in a typical state. Ohio and New Jersey are considered good test states. Another way is to use a certain number of "front" names in each state. If the list is arranged alphabetically, this matter of picking names is not so important. Any group of names within the list would be fairly typical provided the "sampling" is adequate.

Testing Letters or Advertisements

It is dangerous to go ahead with any program just because satisfactory returns are indicated by a single test. Not only should the mailing lists or media be carefully tested to determine which are the most profitable, but several letters or ads should be tested to sections of the same list (or the same media if time permits).

For example, if 6,000 names are being tested to evaluate a 100,000 mailing list, the recommended procedure is to prepare three letters using three different "schemes" and mail each letter to 2,000 of the test names. Do the same on several test lists. Carefully key and record all returns, so that an analysis can be made to determine (1) which letters or ads pull the best, (2) which media or lists produce the best. Then eliminate the least productive to ensure maximum results from the campaign.

Some mail order men test headings on ads or letters, too. They try out the same copy with different headings, on the theory that the headings are the most important factor in getting mail order letters or ads read. A correspondence school, for example, constantly tested ad captions in the hope of developing one which had more pulling power. This search went on for 10 years. But the school never was able to find a caption for its small display ads which pulled better than the one originally used which was "I Will Make You Prosperous." It carried a fingernail picture of the head of the outfit who was a venerable, though bald-headed, gentleman. People instinctively felt he was sincere.

The best months for mailings to farmers are after the crops are in and the farmer had received his money for his crops. In the Middle West and East this would be September and October. In the South it might be May after cotton is ginned. For most mail order solicitations June is usually the poorest month. For holiday items November is the best month to mail. Many people avoid mailing in July and August on the theory "everyone is away on his vacation." While this may be partly true, it is also true that during those months business firms and individuals receive less mail, and consequently there is less competition for the recipients' business. The only way to be sure when mailings are most profitable is to make annual tests. Here are some results of recent tests for your guidance:

Are letters better than circulars? Most tests indicate that the returns from a carefully written, Multigraphed letter are better than the returns from printed circulars. However, best results are usually obtained when both the letter and a circular are used together, with a return card. One test to one-third of a 3,000 mailing produced 3 orders using a circular and a card, 11 orders from the letter and a card, and 14 orders from a letter, circular, and card.

Testing experience likewise indicates relatively poor returns from flamboyant broadsides, even though they may be spectacular. The highest percentage of returns are from individually typewritten letters, with a change in the body of the letter to tie in with the prospective buyer's problems. The more personal a letter looks, the more orders it will pull.

Do filled-in letters pay? Not unless the fill-in is made to do double duty as an address or as the signature on a return card. Tests show that there is no great difference in the returns from a poorly matched filled-in letter, and the same letter with a caption which arrests attention and gets the letter into the hands of the right person.

In working business firms, where it is important to get the letter to the desk of a known executive, the one line filled-in letter, written on note size (7 by 10) stationery is just as effective and less costly to type. Some companies report good results from Addressograph fill-ins using a red ribbon and making no effort at all to try to "trick" the recipient. Similarly, a one line longhand fill-in pulls well, provided the person doing the fill-in writes a good Spencerian hand. Still another variation of the fill-in is a jumbo typed salutation. Such fill-ins are usually vivid green or red to arrest attention. They are natural stoppers.

First-class or third-class postage? Tests vary greatly according to the type of list, the need of getting the letter to the desk of the recipient and thus by-passing the clerk who opens and sorts incoming mail. If the unit of sale is large, and the prospect is used to receiving a lot of third-class mail, first-class with stamps affixed (especially commemorative issues) often pays in spite of the higher rate of postage.

On the other hand when runs are large, and the product is not high priced or is something everyone who receives the letter uses, and the list is composed of farmers or others who do not receive a lot of mail, dollar returns from third-class mailings will be better (postage savings considered) than first-class.

Careful tests indicate that best all-around results are obtained at the lowest cost, by using imprinted indicia (metered mail) and penny-saver envelopes. Some publishers, for example McGraw-Hill, have found they get almost as good returns from third-class mailing with penny-saver envelopes as they do from first-class mailings.

Hand-addressed versus typed envelopes. So far as third-class mailings are concerned, returns seem to be equally good regardless of whether the envelope is addressed in longhand or typewritten. Excepting in the case of facsimile longhand letters, letters to go out first class should be typewritten. The publishers of *Time* magazine state: "We prefer typing or stencil, if code numbers can be eliminated. Labels are objectionable. They usually represent cheap lists, are frequently blurred, and have a tendency to be affixed in a sloppy manner. Good handwriting seems to be a lost art. If stencils are used they must be good."

Does the second color on return cards pay? Usually not. Numerous tests made by mail order houses indicate that the extra cost of a second color is not justified by an offsetting increase in sales. There is a theory that an increasing number of persons who receive direct mail acquire the habit of reading the return cards first, since in that way they find out most quickly what the sender of the letter wants them to do. This hurts returns. It deprives the sender of the letter of an opportunity to create a want for what he is selling. Hence direct mailers reason, the less attention-attracting qualities given to return cards the better.

Second color on circulars and enclosures. On the other hand, tests to determine whether it pays to use a second color on promotional literature to accompany sales letters show in favor of the use of red or orange in addition to black. However, color must be used to "punch" important sales points, and not just to ornament a piece of printed matter. Inexperienced mail order men often make the mistake of using too much color, thus losing emphasis.

Second color in form letters. Judicious use of the second color in Multi-graphed or processed letters is usually profitable and according to numerous tests, especially in selling books by mail, increased returns from 10 to 20%. Use of the second color in sales letters should be restricted to paragraphs containing the offer, or sentences to get favorable attention for the letter. Such paragraphs are usually indented, or set off, in some way. The psychological effect of a red paragraph is to give it added weight and make sure it will be read.

Air-mail reply cards and envelopes. Tests indicate that the use of the red, white and blue air-mail markings on return envelopes and cards pays only when there is a real need for prompt action, as in the case of a special offer which expires on a certain date.

If there is no need for a prompt response, the use of air-mail return cards might suggest high-pressure selling and, of course, there is the extra cost of postage on the returned mail. Air mail return cards look pretty, and add a measure of importance to the offer, but numerous tests do not show the increased returns justify the increased cost.

Adhesive stamps against metered postage. Hundreds of tests show that there is practically no difference in the results when metered indicia or ad-hesive stamps are used on first- or third-class mail. Most advertising men insist that this is not the case, but tests have proved otherwise. So many large companies now use metering machines for dividend checks, personal communications, and other purposes that even farmers, who scan mail closely, are so used to metered indicia on letters that they give it the same consideration. An exception might be newly issued commemorative stamps which have an appeal to stamp-minded persons.

What kind of order forms are best? That depends upon how important it is to have a formal order. In the solicitation of commitments from responsible businessmen, where the mailing is highly personalized and it may not be desirable to give it a "circular" appearance by enclosing supplementary printed matter (other than a Multigraphed second sheet) best returns are secured when the recipient is asked merely to initial and return the letter. Make it easy for him to say "okay."

On the other hand, when mailing is third class and includes a circular as well as a letter, tests show it pays to enclose a return card which does not tell too much of the story, and use a coupon on the last page of the circular. Placing the return coupon on the circular helps should it be laid aside by the recipient.

In the case of long letters—that is to say form letters that run two or three pages—the best strategy is to use a printed return coupon on the bottom of the last page of the letter and a Multigraphed (rather than a printed) re-turn envelope. You not only save the cost of the return cards, but you intro-duce the order form at the logical time.

Where orders for merchandise are being solicited, as in the case of dealer mailings, an envelope blank is recommended. Dealers are used to filling out order blanks.

Who should pay the postage on return cards? It is almost standard practice in mail order selling to use C.O.D. return cards and envelopes, on the theory that it saves the buyer from having to hunt up a postage stamp. In that case the seller pays the return postage, plus the extra fee charged by the post office for making the collection. Tests show that the increased returns when the "seller pays the freight" more than justify the added expense.

On the other side of the argument, some large mailers, who make examination or approval orders, find that while the percentage of returns are lower when the recipient must pay the return postage, they are of a higher quality with a minimum of curiosity seekers. Then, too, in the case of business executives, it involves no extra effort on their part to toss the envelope or card into the outgoing mail basket, and the stamp is affixed automatically by the mail clerk. Prepaid cards usually arrive in the first mail, whereas C.O.D. mail arrives in the second mail, or if there is no second mail, the following day.

Front and back form letters. Where it is not important to create an atmosphere of quality and prestige, tests show that returns from a form letter, where it is *printed* from typewriter type using both the front and the back of the letterhead, are just as good as when each page of the letter is Multigraphed on one side only. It is not practical to Multigraph both front and back of the letterhead, unless low commas and periods are used. Otherwise they will punch the paper. Letterheads to be printed front and back should be of not less than 20-pound weight to get opacity. Sixteen-pound paper shows through.

Filled-in versus blank reply cards. In theory, the easier you make it for a person to say "yes," the more return cards you will receive. Hence it should pay to type in the recipient's name and address on the return card so that all he needs to do is to initial and return it. This is sometimes, but not always, true.

Direct mailers report that when an order is involved, returns are about the same regardless of whether the card is filled-in or blank. But in getting inquiries, returns are higher if the card is filled-in. Whether the quality of the returns is equally good, however, is a debatable question. Careful tests should be made before incurring the expense of filling in return cards.

Is it better to offer merchandise on a free trial basis or try to get cash in advance? It is far superior, according to all our past experiences, to the records of and experience of other mail order advertising agencies, to offer merchandise on a free trial basis, whenever possible. The majority of people are honest. The proportion of results from a free trial type of ad are usually so much more superior to an ad which insists on cash, that even with the small percentage of bad debts which result, the advertiser is usually ahead in the end.

Is "send no money—pay postman nothing" superior to "send no money—pay postman on delivery"? Put yourself in the other man's shoes—suppose you wanted to buy a horse—two farmers came to you, each with the same kind of horse, the same age, weight, and price—$200. The first farmer said to you "Buy my horse. Pay me $200 when I deliver him to you in good condition. Use him for 2 weeks at my risk. If you don't like him, send him back and I will refund your $200." The second farmer said, "Buy my horse. Pay me nothing on delivery. Use him for 2 weeks. Then at the end of that time, if you like him, keep him and pay me $200. If you don't like him, send him back and owe me nothing." Which horse would you buy?

Chapter 41

SALES PROMOTION EQUIPMENT

JUST as the manufacturing divisions need the latest and best tools, the sales promotion department needs good equipment, room in which to work, and the proper tools with which to do its important work.

Good tools are not an expense. In most cases a company is paying for them in lost time, delayed mailings, poor quality of work, mistakes, and other ways. An important responsibility of the sales promotion manager is to undertake a periodical survey of equipment, and determine what it cost the company to operate obsolete and out-of-date equipment, or to do by hand operations which can be done better by specialized appliances now available. The results of such a survey should be presented annually to top management so that in setting up the budget for the year, consideration can be given to the purchase of all, or at least most, of the required equipment.

The growing emphasis on sales promotion in marketing gives new importance to the company's facilities to effectively and efficiently carry through an expanding program of sales promotion. This can best be dramatized to top management, or to the board of directors as the case may be, by getting all the recommendations and proposals together, and presenting them at the proper time, in one package. At least, it brings home to those who hold the purse strings, the losses the company is taking as a result of using outmoded equipment and horse and buggy methods. Since the company is paying for the equipment in either case, is it not better business to buy it and get the benefit from it, as well as whatever tax savings may be involved?

Audio-visual Programs

Sound slide strips and motion picture films provide forceful attention and retention values for sales presentations, sales training and sales promotion purposes. Cassettes, or cartridges, have given new impetus to the development of all types of projectors. Bell & Howell projection systems, for instance, use Autoload cartridges for 35mm. film-strip projector with synchronized film strips and standard tape cassettes.

The Kalavox Sound Slide System is a recording and playback unit with a tray of 40 audio-slide cassettes sitting atop an Eastman Kodak Carousel or Ektagraphic slide projector, with facilities for direct voice recording, background music, signal cueing and automatic playback.

The Singer Graflex Division produces a 35mm. sound film strip projector with synchronized film strip and tape cassette. Techni-

Viewlex Model 1600, for 16mm. sound projection, features automatic film threading; 15 watt amplifier and operates at two light levels. The entire system, including the speaker, is housed inside the projector.

color Instant Theatre Systems comprise a large rear-screen, cartridge-loading movie projector and continuous-loop sound motion picture cartridges. Norelco advertises its PIP models as combining all the major audio-visual techniques in one self-contained unit. The Norelco Synchroplayer is a cassette playback unit for music, speech, and synchronized slide/filmstrip presentations. Another unit which combines the Norelco system with the Kodak Ektagraphic projector is offered in a Syncromedia model manufactured by Setco. Other manufacturers in the field include, among others, Du Kane Corporation, Sony, Taylor Merchant Corporation, LaBelle Industries, Viewlex, A. B. Dick Company.

EQUIPMENT NEEDED FOR BETTER CONTROL

As pointed out elsewhere in this HANDBOOK the effectiveness of any sales promotional activity depends upon the plan back of it. And the first essential of good planning is to get the *facts*. In all too many cases sales promotions are somebody's "hot" idea and, without stopping to analyze the chances of success or even make an estimate of the situation, the activity is undertaken. Millions of sales promotional dollars have been wasted in just that way. "Analyze—deputize—supervise" is just as good a rule for successfully promoting sales as it is in conducting any business operation. The sales promotion graveyard is full of the tombstones of campaigns that failed because somebody guessed.

Sales Analysis Equipment

A profitable source of facts for planning sales promotional operations are the orders which come into a business every day. "Who is buying what, and why?" is a question which has spelled added sales for many businessmen. It has been well said that to succeed in business you must first find out what people want, and then make it easy for them to get it. By the use of punched cards, it is a simple matter now for a sales manager to keep a running analysis of where his business is coming from, what items are in greatest demand at different times, and which territories offer the most promising sales opportunities.

One cereal food company, for example, handles all accounting records in connection with its premium program such as control of cash, shipping labels, and inventory control by the IBM punched card method. In addition, the same cards are used to analyze premium redemption by location, type of package, and type of premium. Radio, television, and magazine advertising are pin pointed to the needed areas, "tailor-made" to suit changing customer preferences and competition.

Another corporation uses this method to control and formulates policies with regard to its display advertising. As the salesmen call on its accounts, they mark cards to indicate the condition of their merchandise on retailers' shelves, its location, types of displays, retailer preference, etc. These cards, automatically processed, aid in "eliminating guesswork about the most effective point-of-purchase display pieces and about how much to send out and where to send it."

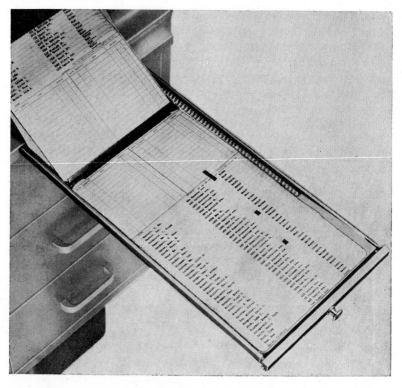

Visible Kardex records, filed in slides, permit a sales promotion manager to keep track of the results of sales promotional mailings, advertising media, and other data useful for planning future programs.

The punched card system of sales analysis requires first, listing all the kinds of information about an order or a market that the sales promotion department needs; then designing, with the help of the machine manufacturer, a card on which the information, as it is taken from an order, can be punched. The punched cards are then run through a sorting and tabulating machine, and totaled for executive use. There is also another system, which operates without the more costly installations required to tabulate punched cards, which tells: (1) What is selling and what is not selling; (2) what is on hand and how long it has been there; (3) what must be bought or made. This card carries the information on the margin. When notched, the coded holes along the edge make it possible to take off the information desired quickly and accurately.

Keeping Sales Promotion Records

Any sales promotion department will have some lists to be maintained. There may be lists of customers, dealers, salesmen, wholesalers, users, or branch offices. We strongly urge use of the latest equipment for lists. If at all possible, maintain all lists on modern visible record equipment, properly indexed.

Before you begin work on any list, look at all the equipment available. There are visible indexes in trays, housed in cabinets, with almost any kind of "tab" equipment for call-up or follow-up purposes. Then there are wheel and rotary filing devices, files in sliding trays, visible rotary equipment, and others.

Take pains to select filing equipment which has these advantages: Cards must be quickly and easily removable; it must be easy to write on cards without removing; there must be some way of indexing or tabbing; major data must be visible at a glance; and there should be facilities for signaling. Thus, a red signal at a given point may call for a follow-up letter, a reorder or some other action.

In many lines of business, and particularly in a wholesale or retail operation, there is an unlimited opportunity to promote sales by systematically "working" customers who are buying only from certain departments, or certain lines, when they could and should be buying from all departments. By automatic selector devices on the addressing equipment, operating from tabs or notches on the address plate or stencil, it is possible to direct special sales appeals at selected groups of customers periodically. Usually the customer information required to evaluate an account is posted right on the addressing plate, eliminating one

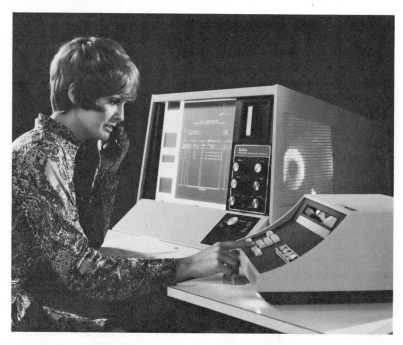

Kodak's Miracode II system compacts millions of documents into a few square feet of instantly accessible information. It scans 16mm. roll microfilm at a speed of 350 documents per second, selects the one document, or group of documents, sought, then makes paper copies as desired. To microfilm an invoice 337941, for example, the operator would merely key in those numbers, verify the work via a lighted display, then push a button to microfilm the document. To retrieve the invoice, the operator enters the numbers 337941, the film is scanned in seconds and the document displayed. At the press of a button, the terminal produces a paper copy of any document on the screen.

set of records. It is a mistake to maintain duplicate sets of records, which involve double posting, twice the opportunity for errors, and require space which can often be used to better advantage for other purposes.

Saving Space with Microfilm

Permanent records maintained by the sales promotion department which occupy a great deal of floor space should be photographed on microfilm. Film can be run through a reading screen at the rate of 150 feet a minute, making it possible for the operator to select needed records quickly. A typical microfilm application in sales promotion is keeping survey records of dealers' stores. Burroughs Corporation uses a prepared microfilm to acquaint salesmen with salient selling points of its equipment and as a means of point of sale demonstration. The microfilm equipment in most general use photographs documents up to 11 inches wide by any length and projects the image in one of three standard ratios on a reader screen which is approximately 14 by 16 inches in size. While it would hardly pay to install microfilm equipment for that purpose alone, there are so many ways microfilm can be profitably used in the over-all operations of a business that an increasing number of companies are using the equipment to save record storage space. In such cases, the sales promotion records might very well be included.

DUPLICATING EQUIPMENT

Copiers and Duplicators

Copying equipment has proved to be a great boon to business and industry and many companies are vying with each other to produce better and more sophisticated models each year. One of the best known, of course is Xerox, which now produces copiers, duplicators, copier-duplicators and microfilm printers and enlargers. The models range from desk-top copiers to the Model 2400 which produces 40 copies per minute. The Microfilm Enlarger Printer 600 feeds up to 200 aperture cards, prints up to 99 copies of each at 10 a minute and offers a choice of four magnification ratios.

Pitney Bowes offers a series of desk-top models with models 252 and 253, for low-volume users, to the Model 262 book copier with "strobostatic lighting" and built-in reduction lens.

The Bell & Howell Combomatic 9000 produces 150 copies a minute, makes copies with up to five colors on each page, makes masters, stencils, and projection transparencies.

Stencil Duplicating

Duplication of typewritten, handwritten, or drawn images by means of a paperlike stencil is perhaps the most common form of office duplicating or printing. Principle of this type of duplicating is the cutting of a stencil on a typewriter (without the ribbon) or with a stylus. The stencil is placed upon a revolving cylinder, with an ink fountain attachment which inks the stencil. Machines come in various sizes, and handle from post-card to legal-size paper. Hand-operated machines are available for small runs; and automatic feed, electrically operated machines are made for longer runs and heavier duty. Office forms, bulletins, letters, sales bulletins, price lists, instruction sheets, and a wide variety of other duplicating is done on these machines.

One or more colors may be used. There are many advantages to this type of production, chief of which is the brief time required to produce a job.

The Bell & Howell Statesman: Produces 1800 copies per hour. The handsome cabinet includes a 12-bin collating rack and occupies six square feet of floor space. Each roll of paper provides 1125 letter-size copies.

Copies can be produced in the time required to type a stencil; a few minutes later, after the stencil is placed in the duplicator, copies are coming off the machine at the rate of several thousand an hour. Costs are low, and for many different types of work the stencil duplicator is advantageous. There is almost no limit to the number of copies which can be made from one stencil. If the run is long enough another stencil may be cut. Stencils may be put away and saved for future use. Preprinted stencils are available for special purposes, such as business forms, on which in-

Savin Model 880 produces 30 copies a minute while its document feed allows originals as large as 10" x 14" to be fed continuously. It is intended for 5,000 to 30,000 copies per month.

tricate patterns are necessary. Changeable information can be typed on these preprinted stencils, or added to them as the occasion requires. Line drawings, cartoons, line-drawn illustrations, shaded illustrations, diagrams, trade-marks, copies of blueprints, and many other designs may be reproduced on stencil duplicators.

Offset Duplicators

In recent years many improvements on offset printing equipment have given the sales promotion manager a valuable tool. The office offset presses are available from several companies, in sizes up to

The A. B. Dick Copier holds an oversize roll of copier paper and a fluid reservoir that handles up to ten thousand copies from one filling. It turns out copies at the rate of 25 a minute.

11 by 17 inches, and the high speed of these machines makes it possible to produce a large volume of work. Larger, professional sizes are also available.

The offset process is exactly what its name implies. The image is drawn or photographed on a master. From this master the image is transferred or offset to a roller, instead of directly to the paper. The printing is accomplished by transferring the image from the roller to the paper stock.

Photographs, printing, drawings—anything typed, written, printed, or drawn may be reproduced at high speed on these machines. Good color work is possible on offset duplicators. Several types of plates (masters) are available. The most common and most satisfactory plate is a metal sheet, sensitized to "take" photographic images. These plates are made very much in the same way that a photograph is developed. Platemaking equipment is available for office use, although many office users have plates made outside by professional platemakers who specialize in such work.

Masters on which printing is done directly from a typed master are also used in the offset process. These masters are available in both metal and paper—the paper masters are for shorter runs and for use when highest type reproduction is not necessary.

PRINTING EQUIPMENT

More and more companies are producing some of their printed matter in their own printing shops. There are many reasons for this. First, and probably most important, is the saving in costs. For a given number of dollars more printed material can usually be produced in the promotion man's own department than can be purchased outside.

Another reason is the delays incident to buying printing. For many years now the commercial printers have been handicapped by help shortages and inability to obtain modern, fast equipment. It is not uncommon to produce a job in a sales promotion department in 24 or 48 hours which would require 1 to 2 weeks if the same job were turned over to an outside printer.

There is a limit, however, to the amount of work which the average sales promotion manager should attempt to produce in his own department. Good printing requires costly machinery, and the office type printing equipment was never intended to produce large broadsides containing many halftone illustrations, fine catalogs, brochures, or the higher type booklets. Such work requires an investment in large presses, typesetting machinery, such as Linotypes, Intertypes, or Monotype keyboard and casters, bindery equipment, folding machines, and other equipment which requires skilled operators.

For all kinds of forms, letters, many different promotion pieces, price lists, campaign literature, envelope inserts, instruction sheets, sales and dealer bulletins, and the less elaborate house magazines, there is available, at reasonable costs, equipment which will speed production, save time, and reduce costs. The first step in planning a production section for a sales promotion department is to analyze the various types of work to be done. Then buy the equipment needed to produce this work.

One common error in many organizations is an attempt to produce work on office machines which these machines were never intended to do. Perhaps a sound rule is to buy only such equipment for office printing or reproduction as can be kept reasonably busy. Care should be taken to ascertain that enough work is available as needed to keep the operators busy. Nothing raises costs of office-produced printing more than idle operators.

Caterpillar Tractor Company at Peoria is one of the country's largest buyers of high-quality printing. This company patronizes one of the largest and best-known printing and engraving companies in the country. Yet in its own office millions of pieces of printed matter are produced. But Caterpillar does not make the mistake of attempting to produce major printing jobs on its office equipment.

How to Survey Needs

Before purchasing and installing any office reproduction or printing equipment a careful survey of annual needs should be conducted. One method is to assemble all printing bills for a year. Divide these bills into two categories: (1) Work which could be produced on office equipment; and (2) work which requires a major investment in large presses, composing room machinery, folders, stitchers, trimmers, and similar equipment. It is better to err on the side of conservatism where there is any doubt. Give the outside printer the benefit of every doubt. Do not say, "We can produce this job, and fold it by hand." Office wage rates are too high today, and are likely to remain too high to warrant much hand folding. Where there are complicated gathering or assembly jobs, as in the case of multiple copy office forms, allot this work to outside printers. Stuffing one-time carbons, printing order books, or invoices, where many copies are needed, is a job for specialists, not for office production.

After all jobs for a year have been analyzed call in the salesmen for office printing equipment and buy the proper tools to produce the work.

Another way to analyze the need for office reproduction devices is to assemble every form and put down the quantities ordered of each form.

In analyzing the need for equipment get the following facts on each form or printed piece:

1. Quantity.
2. Frequency of purchase.
3. Stock used.
4. Colors (registration problems).
5. Cost of composition.
6. Type of printing (offset or letterpress).
7. Folding, gathering, stitching required.
8. Cost when purchased outside.
9. Cost if produced in office.
10. Probable saving on year's requirements.

Where an office is situated in a large city it may be possible to do the actual printing or duplicating in the office shop, and send out the finishing, such as folding, binding, inserting, and carbon interleaving to trade shops. But, as a rule, this is unsatisfactory.

It is for these reasons that most experts advise a careful limitation on the type of work which the office shop attempts to produce, unless there is a large volume of work—enough to justify investment in all the necessary incidental equipment.

When it is determined how many different jobs can be economically produced, and how large the runs are, as well as how frequently the jobs will be required, it is then comparatively easy to select the equipment needed.

Letterpress Printing

There was a time when many companies, using large quantities of printing thought it necessary to own their own full-scale printing plants. Many of the private plants were later sold to professional printers because the investment, the space required, and the high payrolls necessary, cost so much that the product of these private plants was more expensive than printing bought from specialists.

It would be difficult to set a definite figure, but as a rough estimate it appears that any company having less than $100,000 a year in printing bills would scarcely be justified in attempting to operate a private letterpress printing plant.

For such a plant there is a large investment in type; one or more typesetting machines ($10,000 and up) are necessary. Since a one-press shop is seldom practical, because there is always a feast or a famine of work, several presses are required. Prices of modern automatic presses begin at around $5,000 for smaller sizes and range up to $30,000 for even the simpler types of machines.

Add to this the folders, stitchers, cutters, staplers, make-up tables, and a thousand and one other incidental items of equipment and there is an investment of $25,000 to $50,000 before even simple printing is feasible.

Another factor enters into the decision of whether to install a letterpress printing plant for private use. This is the problem of specialization. Nearly all types of printing today call for special equipment, and much of today's large-scale printing is done by specialists. Labels are printed by label-printing specialists; sales-books, order books, report forms are printed by other specialists, with costly, high-speed automatic equipment. Catalogs are often handled by printers who have special equipment and highly skilled organizations of catalog specialists.

Overlooking this factor may cause an enthusiastic sales promotion man to lump all his printing bills in one sum and decide to install his own private plant. Then, when the plant is set up he will find that one job after another requires special equipment which, in a private plant, would be idle nearly all year. For this reason it is often better to take advantage of the many printing specialists and send work out.

General Foods Corporation is probably one of the country's largest users of printed matter. At the company's headquarters it has a battery of offset printing equipment, but it does not attempt many special jobs. Labels, package inserts, and much similar printing are purchased from specialists.

Several General Motors units produce their own parts books, but much of this company's promotional printing goes to large printers who are set up to handle large-scale work. If these companies find it profitable to buy printing outside, rather than invest the large sums necessary to equip private plants, it scarcely seems likely that smaller companies can afford to attempt to enter the printing business on a private scale. One of the largest plants in the country was once operated by a large insurance company, which decided, a few years back, to stop producing its own printing and turn to big printers with the specialized equipment required.

Setting Up an Offset Plant

In large cities it is scarcely necessary to own all the equipment necessary for offset printing. The plates or masters can be made outside in trade shops. But in a smaller city or town, where no trade shops are nearby, it is almost imperative to have a complete shop, equipped for platemaking as well as printing.

Sending the plates to an outside shop eliminates some of the savings incident to doing all the work in your own plant; on the other hand, the platemaking equipment requires a considerable investment.

For platemaking, a camera, vacuum frame, whirler, drier, and complete darkroom equipment are usually needed. An operator to photograph the copy, mount it, and make the plates is also necessary. The key to good offset printing lies in the quality of the work done in the darkroom and if your platemaker is a bungler you cannot avoid bad reproduction.

To prepare masters it is a distinct advantage to own a typewriter with a variable spacing attachment so that the right-hand margins of all typed matter will be flush, just as in your newspaper, or in a book. The typewriters used for preparing offset copy should not be used for any other purpose, and it is better to purchase machines designed for using carbon paper ribbons which produce a sharp, black character.

There has been constant improvement in the quality of offset printing. Today a good platemaker can turn out halftone work that is the equal of letterpress in good quality. The old muddy tones, the "off-white" appearance of highlights in halftones, are gone from the better class of offset printing today. Many companies produce house magazines on small offset presses; others produce letters, mailing pieces, price lists, parts lists, small display pieces, envelope inserts, sales bulletins, and a wide variety of printing at a considerable saving when compared with prices charged by printing companies.

The IBM Word-Processing System

There are more people creating paper work and relatively fewer office workers to do it. Categories of people most likely to originate letters, memos, reports and other paperwork have jumped by 87% in a decade. And the cost of the average business letter can range from $4.00 to $15.00. Furthermore, clerical productivity has not risen to any great degree—it's not much greater than it was 20 years ago.

A new approach has been developed—one that incorporates two principles of modern technology; automation and systemization. The new term to describe the method of dealing with paperwork is "word processing."

Word processing is defined by IBM as a combination of people, procedures and equipment that transforms ideas into printed communications and facilitates the flow of related office work . . . at a savings over prior methods, when properly organized and managed.

Using a magnetic media typewriter rather than an ordinary electric typewriter, transcription speed rises to over 30 words per minute. Magnetic typewriters record copy either on magnetic tapes or cards, therefore, the typist can work at rough-draft speed, correcting errors by merely backspacing and retyping over the error. This creates perfect, error-free documents in recorded form ready to play back immediately at a speed of 150 words per minute.

Magnetic typewriters also eliminate the necessity for complete retyping of author-revised documents. Only the changes need to be re-keyboarded, unchanged portions are played out automatically.

Storage capability is another advantage of such machines. Individually typed form letters and other standard documents may be produced automatically at any time.

Utilizing the same tapes on composing equipment, fully justified copy in a variety of type sizes and styles can be produced. Such equipment can also be used for in-house direct impression typesetting when mass reproduction of documents is required.

Another outstanding characteristic of composing equipment is proportional spacing. Proportional spacing requires less space than ordinary spacing so more type can be fitted on a page resulting in faster reading. This can result in savings in paper costs that sometimes amount to 25% or more, and is thus a vital factor in large-scale reproduction.

Transmission of material over long distances can be handled easily by using the IBM Communicating Mag Card "Selectric" Typewriter. Separated by thousands of miles, Mag Card "Selectric" Typewriters are able to send information to each other over voice-grade telephone lines. Material may be pre-recorded in error-free form on magnetic cards and sent at a speed of 150 words per minute. An original typewritten document is received on another Communicating Mag Card "Selectric" Typewriter at the other end of the line. Input and output to computers is also possible with this machine.

As well as equipment and procedures, word processing also

The IBM Magnetic Tape Selectric Typewriter (MT/ST) produces error-free typing at speeds up to 150 words a minute. The typist is retyping work on which changes have been made. By pressing a button on the console, she can instruct the machine to search a magnetic tape on which the original typed material is stored for the point where the change is to be made. She then "erases" the tape by retyping over the unwanted material, thus storing the new data at the same time for mass typing and future reference.

requires a systemization. A possible systems change is the establish-ment of a central word-processing center. There, highly qualified and trained personnel using magnetic media typewriters perform the correspondence duties of the secretary. They can produce more work of higher quality and uniformity than secretaries at scattered typing stations.

The administrative duties and telephones which often inter-fered with the production capabilities of the secretary may now be handled by administrative secretaries. Released from typing cor-respondence, they are free to assume additional responsibilities.

Systemization is also applied to the equipment used by the authors of paperwork. Individual dictating machines can be re-placed by PBX telephone or remote microphone systems. That way, many ordinary telephones or specially installed microphones feed into one or more central recorders located in a word processing center. More authors may thus make use of the same equipment.

With equipment taking verbal ideas and information from the point of inception to the point of distribution, the task of processing words has become faster, easier and more economical.

PHOTOGRAPHIC EQUIPMENT

In any sales promotion department where there is a large pro-duction of sketches, layouts, "roughs" of advertisements, and similar work, a photographic reproduction unit of one kind or another is a time- and money-saver.

There are two basic kinds of photocopy machines. One, the simpler variety, copies anything written, drawn, or printed by contact. There is no enlargement or reduction possible on these machines. The reproduction is the same size as the original to be copied.

The other type of machine is actually a large camera, combined with a developing unit and a drier. Most common name for this equipment is Photostat, but this is a private trade-mark, owned by one company. Several other companies make and sell similar machines. With this type of equipment, enlargement and repro-duction of any type of original is easy and rapid. Any man or woman can be quickly trained to operate such a machine, and a very small floor space is required—say about 12 by 18 feet for a minimum.

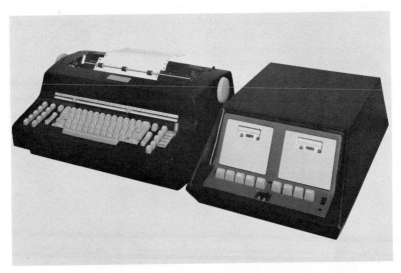

A cassette automatic revision typewriter, Model QuinType 80, developed by QuinData Incorporated, permits high-speed original typing, stores all typewritten material on tape, corrects errors electronically and reads back the tape to produce finished copy at speeds in excess of 175 words per minute. It makes duplicates, modified or personalized copies.

Photocopy equipment may save an endless amount of retyping, redrawing, and hand lettering. Where a sales organization is small this equipment is especially valuable for reproducing statistical material which must be sent to salesmen. In cases where there are many salesmen or others to receive the same material it is better to reproduce it by one of the printing or duplicating processes, but for small quantities the photocopy equipment is economical.

When a Camera Department Is Needed

A well-equipped photographic or camera department is a useful adjunct to many sales promotion departments. Chief advantage of a private photographic unit is the ability to make pictures with far less formality and in less time than is usually required when an outside photographer must be summoned.

Where a house magazine, either for employees or for customers or dealers, is part of the sales promotion manager's task, a photographic department is almost a "must." By assigning one man to the business of illustrating the house magazine he can roam the plant and take pictures of individuals whose names will appear in the magazine; he can "cover" all plant meetings and conferences; he can photograph the installation of new equipment; and provide a running record of all plant and office improvements. The same man can photograph prominent visitors to the plant, new employees, and all manner of personnel activities.

The same photographic department, if manned by skilled men, can produce photographs of the product, record stages in product development, go into the field to photograph dealer displays, win-

There are many occasions when sales promotion, art department or agency personnel need quick, on-the-spot, photo prints. Polaroid's Square Shooter 2 is an all-purpose color camera with built-in flash producing 60-second color prints measuring 3¼ by 3⅜ inches. Transistorized electronic shutter teamed with an electronic eye provides automatic exposure control.

dows, field sales meetings, and make records of the product in actual use.

Relatively few companies expect private photographers to turn out the high quality work required for the best catalog illustrations, for magazine advertising, and important sales promotion material. This is a job for the professional.

Another job for the company photographer is production of publicity photographs to be sent to newspapers, magazines, and business papers. Where photographs are used in sales portfolios the company photographer can often be kept busy a considerable part of his time.

As in all other attempts to set up private or company equipment to produce different types of work, it is necessary to draw the line between "run of the mill" jobs and jobs which require highly skilled specialists.

Your company photographer may be excellent for making quick shots of plant meetings, of new employees, and baseball games for the plant magazine, but unless he is far better than the average do not expect him to turn out a beautifully posed, skillfully lighted illustration for your season's most important sales promotion piece. Call in a professional for such work.

National Cash Register Company was one of the earliest large-scale operations of a private photographic unit. At Dayton headquarters a staff of men are busy turning out all sorts of photographs for use in the company's tremendous production of printed material. The same shop photographs prominent visitors to the plant, many different meetings, athletic and recreational activities, sales meetings, and other gatherings. The company has a tremendous file of photographs which is actually a visual record of N.C.R. activities over the years.

Photographs in Sales Promotion

There is a very definite trend to making more use of photographs in all forms of sales promotion. This trend has become especially pronounced since the advent of TV. People are lazier so far as reading habits go. They like to get a sales story by looking at interesting pictures, rather than having to read hundreds of words. So we find more and more pictures being used to flag attention, to underscore key points, to describe complex processes, to show products in action, and in many other ways.

Illustrating some of the ways photographs are being used to

promote sales, directly and indirectly, Eastman Kodak comes up with the following list, which readers may find suggestive:

Plans and Presentations—Slidefilms—Movies—Easel presentations—Portfolios.

Advertisements—Illustrations for magazines—Newspaper—Direct Mail—Sales and service literature—Calendars—Car cards—Billboards.

Market Research—Product application photos—Customers' buying habits—Displays—Merchandising ideas—Photocopying charts and reports.

Packaging—Product pictures—Labels—"How to" explanations—Photo lettering—Photo composition.

Merchandising—Displays—Background photos—Jumbo cutouts—Installation or application photos—Demonstrations.

Trade Shows—Background murals—Motion pictures—Slidefilms—Descriptive booklets and pamphlets—Plant and product photos.

Sales Training and Service—Salesmen's portfolios and bulletins—Stills—Slides—Movies—Installation and service manuals—Customers' instruction books.

Television Production—Set backgrounds—Spot commercials—Animation.

Printed Production — Illustrations — Transparencies — Photoengraving — Photocopying.

Public Relations—Stockholder notices—Employee papers—Institutional movies—House organs—News releases—Slidefilms.

Administration—Office layout plans—Progress reports—Office copying—Microfilming of records for storing—Miniature prints of ads for schedule boards.

Actually, good photography is the result of experience and training and it is not a job to be taken lightly, even though several men in the sales promotion department may be confident that they can handle any photographic assignment that comes along.

Consider a photographic unit as a part of the sales promotion department only when (1) there is enough work to keep one man busy half his time, or (2) where good professional photographers are not readily available, as is the case in some small towns. Do not rely on the belief that anybody can make a picture good enough for reproduction. Be sure the man selected to head your photographic unit is either a professional, or at least an advanced amateur, who has long since graduated from the "drug store" type of development and processing. Be sure he has had experience in a darkroom and knows something about lighting, posing, processing, and, above all, has some knowledge of reproduction processes and requirements.

The Photograph File

Ordinary 8½- by 11-inch metal filing cabinets are usually favored for the photograph file. Here are several rules for preventing trouble in maintaining a useful file of photographs.

1. A photograph is no photograph unless it is identified. Never permit a photograph to go to file without a number, without proper identification of ALL people appearing, the date, subject, and any other necessary data. It is better to destroy a photograph than to file it without number and caption or identification data.

2. Cross index all photographs in the file. If you use the subject index and have a tab labeled "Meetings," list the names of people appearing in meeting pictures, and put a duplicate print under each name, or make a slip for each name and file in proper alphabetical sequence with a notation, "See meeting file."

3. Set up a negative and print numbering system so that prints can be matched with negatives for duplicates when needed.

4. Never allow the last print to be removed from the file. Take its number and have a duplicate printed.

5. Do not file under too broad classifications—such as "Exteriors," "Interiors," etc. Do not file under such broad classifications as "New Products." Give them a date, a model number, an experimental department number, or some other data to pin them down to more definite identity.

The same rules for filing and finding photographs should apply to all other exhibit material, drawings, blueprints, cuts, masters for duplicating machines, etc.

Investment in blueprint cabinets, cut and electrotype cabinets, proper storage space for printed material will save the cost of such equipment in a year or so. A vast quantity of costly printed material is ruined each year in many departments because of lack of adequate storage space.

MAILING ROOM EQUIPMENT

Steadily rising costs of labor in the mailing room have made it imperative that facilities for getting out promotional matter quickly and efficiently should be modernized. Hand-addressing, sealing, stamping, and sorting are no longer economical and are now done by machinery. Even gathering, a tedious operation, is now done mechanically in mailing rooms where large quantities of the same type of mail matter are handled. Such equipment should be the best.

Many addressing or mailing departments prerun envelopes or

COLLATORS	NO. OF BINS	CAPACITY PER BIN	OPERATING SPEED OF EQUIPMENT*	
			SETS PER HOUR	SHEETS PER HOUR
(Semi-Automatic)				
7308	8	250 Sheets	1320	10,560
7312	12	450 Sheets	1320	15,840
7218	18	450 Sheets	1320	23,760
7224	24	300 Sheets	1320	31,680
(Automatic)				
7012/7112**	12	450 Sheets	1200	14,400
7020/7120	20	450 Sheets	1200	24,000
7024/7124	24	450 Sheets	1200	28,800
7040/7140	40	250 Sheets	1200	48,000

Collator Attachments	
7001	Single Stitcher
7002	Double Stitcher
7005	Folder
S	Receding Stacker
7010	Programmer for 20, 24, 40 bin models
7011	Programmer for 24, 40 bin models

Manufacturers produce a variety of automatic and semi-automatic collators, in different sizes, to meet specific requirements. This A. B. Dick chart shows the range of available speeds and capacities.

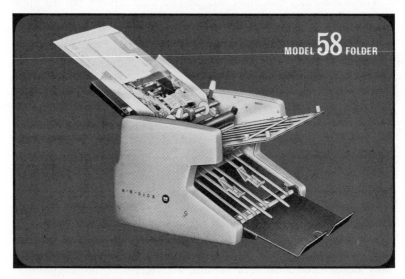

MODEL 58 FOLDER

The A. B. Dick Model 58 folds a variety of paper sizes and weights at speeds of 12,000 letter folds per hour.

labels for all branch offices, salesmen, dealers, or other groups which receive mail regularly. These labels or envelopes are kept in special racks, and as the mail reaches the mailing room the contents are sorted into racks which already contain a supply of preaddressed envelopes or labels. This plan speeds the work and tends to level out peaks and valleys on schedules, because the addressing can be done at times when the staff is not busy.

Selection of mailing and addressing equipment can be done intelligently only after a careful analysis of every piece of mail handled in the organization. Salesmen for the office appliance companies are usually well informed and no one should hesitate to call them in for consultation and help.

Addressing Equipment

We have considered various types of reproductive equipment. There is no point in producing a quantity of material unless there are facilities for mailing or distributing it. The finest set of photographs of your product are of little value packed away in a filing cabinet. Nor is the company magazine worth very much if it is mailed too late, or haphazardly. Much excellent sales promotion material fails to produce expected results because mailing facilities are not available. Therefore we need to consider, very carefully, the ways and means for addressing and mailing everything the various printing, duplicating, and photographic units produce.

At present wage rates for white-collar help, hand addressing is usually too costly for any consideration. It is both too slow and too inaccurate. Hence machine addressing is a "must."

Basically, there are two types of addressing jobs. The first, and most important, is the addressing job which must be done over and over again. In this category we find the list of employees for mailing house magazines, announcements, etc.; then there is the list of dealers, wholesalers, or customers. Add to this the list of salesmen, manufacturers' representatives, fieldmen, branch offices, agents, or others who receive regular mailings.

The second type of addressing job involves the special mailing, in which a list, large or small, is addressed perhaps only once or twice, or perhaps once or twice a year.

For the regular mailing which is mailed weekly, monthly, or at some other frequent interval, the addressing machine, working from pre-cut or pre-embossed metal plates is fully justified. It is usually the cheapest in the long run.

Whether you use metal plates or the paperlike stencil variety depends upon the frequency of use, the value of each name, and the investment which seems justified.

Address stencils are made on a regular typewriter with a special attachment. These stencils are mounted in a card frame and may be used over and over again.

Metal address plates are embossed on a special machine for the purpose. These plates have a very long life, and may be used over and over again without appreciable signs of wear.

Addressing machines are available for either kind of name plate in a wide choice of models, ranging from the simplest hand-operated models on up to fully automatic, high-speed models which handle a tremendous variety of work.

For really big operations there are addressing machines which print from a roll of paper and print an entire label, insurance premium notice, or bill, inserting items, such as premium amounts, automatically.

Equipment required in an addressing department is the stencil cutting or embossing units, the addressing machines, and cabinets for the address plates.

For regular mailings it is customary to address labels or envelopes in advance, have them ready when the contents of the mailing—letters, magazines, catalogs, or folders—arrive.

Folding Machines for Sales Promotion Use

When you buy an office folding machine buy the best. It will pay in the long run. There is nothing in the way of office appliances that will waste so much time, cause so many work interruptions and headaches, as a folding machine that only folds when the spirit moves it. The trouble with most office folders is that they depend on rubber rolls to pick up the sheet and feed it into the machine. They work all right so long as the rolls are kept roughed up. But they soon become slick and slippery, failing to pick up the sheet or, if there is too much static electricity in the air, the sheets are apt to cling together and jam the folder.

The roll-fed office folder is useful in small offices where most of the work to be folded is of the same size, as, for example, standard-sized two-fold letterheads. But if the range of work varies, and it is necessary to "set up" the folding machine frequently for different folds and different kinds of paper stock, it is well to buy a folding machine of the type used in commercial binderies.

They usually feed by suction, and are far more dependable. This type of folder is now available in small sizes to take the direct mail which goes out from the sales promotion department.

Gathering and Mailing Equipment

There are still offices which lay out work to be gathered on a long table, and the gatherer assembles the brief or whatever it might be, while walking back and forth. In most commercial shops the

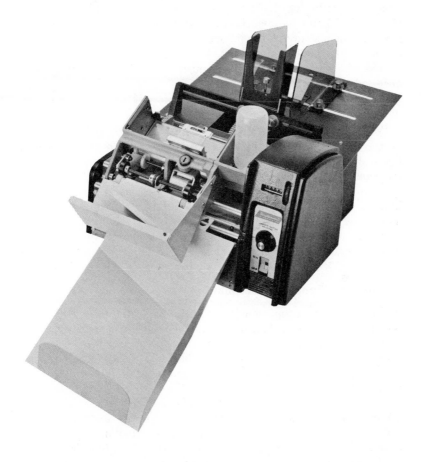

Operating from card masters, this desk top Scriptomatic Model 72 will address practically any type or size of mailing piece at the rate of 4,000 per hour. Other models can handle up to 7,500 pieces per hour.

gathering operation is speeded by placing the "pick ups" on a rotating table, which is slowly turned by a motor. Several girls sit around the table and pick up the sheets as it turns. The most up-to-date method of gathering stapled materials for sales promotional use is an electrically operated collator, of which the manufacturers offer many models with various capacities.

When a company's direct mail is well standardized, with long runs of the same piece, there are automatic gathering and sealing machines for the work. These machines, operating on the principle of a gathering machine used in a commercial bindery, automatically pick up most enclosures; stuff them into the envelopes; and seal them ready to stamp, sack, and mail. These machines cost about $3,000. Unless a company has long runs they should not be purchased. They take too much time to set up and adjust. But once adjusted and kept going on the same mailing, they will gather, insert, and seal up to 2,000 pieces of mail an hour, day in and day out.

While there are several good sealing and stamping machines on the market, most mail users today meter their mail and depend upon that equipment for these operations. The latest metering machines are very fast, reliable, and pay for themselves several times over in stamp savings, advertising benefits from special indicia, and labor. Not many modern sales promotion departments use adhesive stamps for the run of their outgoing mail. However, when adhesive stamps are called for, affixing machines which operate like a numbering machine save postage and time.

Sorting and Typing Direct Mail

There are many opportunities for savings in the way the mail is handled after being sealed and stamped. In the case of large metered mailings, where it is not necessary to cancel adhesive postage stamps, delivery will be greatly expedited if it is tied into packages by cities, and then sacked by train routes. Mail thus treated will usually go right out as soon as it lands in the post office. Otherwise, under the prevailing practice of handling "slow" mail, it may lie around the post office several days until someone feels inclined to sort it. For this operation the well-equipped mailing room should have a good tying machine, and enough racks to hold four to eight mail sacks during the sorting. If the sizes of the mailings are not sufficient to use sacks (supplied upon request by the local post office) a wall sorting rack can be constructed with pigeon-holes for each of the 50 states and the principal cities.

EQUIPPING THE MEETING ROOM

In most sales operations the sales promotion manager is responsible for dealer and other meetings at which a "program" or "campaign" is presented to a group of people. If the presentation takes the form of a series of regional or district meetings, some sort of a portable stage with the required "props" is used. Such stages may be purchased outright, or they may be rented from companies which specialize in dramatizing sales conventions. These portable stages can be taken down in a few hours, and quickly reassembled. They are complete with lighting equipment, drops, side boxes, and other facilities. Some companies have special trailers, in which these portable stages are packed, then hitched to a car or truck, and transported from town to town.

Projectors

Depending upon the kind of material to be used at a sales meeting, the projection room (or traveling equipment) should include a 16mm. talking motion picture projector, a long-range slide projector for throwing stills and charts over the heads of an audience from the rear of the room, and sound film-strip equipment. New developments in the sound/strip field call for a complete investigation at the time of purchase. Units are available that automatically

Overhead projectors have been efficiently used by the Minnesota Mining and Manufacturing Company in training representatives. A special advantage of this type of projector is that it permits the speaker visually to pinpoint his comments.

project 35mm. strip film and 2- by 2-inch slides. Prices vary according to the sophistication of the equipment, and both portable and permanent machines are available.

Another useful piece of equipment for conducting meetings is an overhead projector which throws a letter, chart, or drawing directly upon a screen from a transparency. The speaker can write on the transparency with a crayon as he talks. Using overlays, a chart can be built up or changed to fit the talk. One advantage of this type of projector is that it does not require an operator. The conference leader places the films in position as he talks. He faces the audience while using the projector.

In late years the use of talking movies has greatly increased. Some companies have produced educational pictures which are shown at sales meetings of various sorts. They may also be used at luncheon meetings of service clubs and trade conventions. To make the best use of such films, and to get the benefit of the extensive rental libraries of sales films, in 16mm. size, many companies equip their sales promotion department with an up-to-date talking picture projector. Where a company invests $35,000 and up in a promotional picture it is usually wise to purchase several projectors and keep them at division points, so that they can be used in the division area for dealer and other meetings at which the pictures will be shown. The White Motor Company, for example, equips each branch with a 16mm. movie projector (with sound) for showing pictures of interest to its dealer organization, including its own pictures which show the wide-spread use of motor trucks in solving transportation problems.

A less expensive, but very effective, projector is available for use with Kodachrome slides (stills). The slides are particularly good for demonstrating mechanical products, or equipment sold to industry. They are used both in group selling and in personal selling instead of the usual type of portfolio. While most projectors operate fairly well on a white wall, for best results a silver screen, large enough to permit a good-sized projection is required. This folds compactly into a carrying unit, and comes with a stand so it can be quickly set up in a meeting room without having to hunt up the hotel carpenter (see Dartnell *Sales Manager's Handbook* for information on portable projectors and other equipment for salesmen's use).

Blackboards

Two variations of the traditional blackboard of our school days is the "white board" and the "slap board" for use in making presentations. The "white board" has an advantage in that it can be used as a projection screen as well as a writing board. While the image is not as sharp as it is when a silver screen is used, it is quite all right for working with small groups. The slap board is a plush-covered board upon which cut-outs, signs, segments of charts, and other matter can be "slapped" as a speaker delivers his talk. These boards are popular for presenting standardized talks to dealers and groups.

In using any of these devices two things are important—they should be placed high enough on the platform so that they can be seen easily by everyone in the group, and they should be lighted with *double* spots, one from each side of the platform.

Traveling Exhibits

For "trading up" dealers and bringing demonstrations to the front door of customers, instead of requiring them to take time out to go to a showing at some local hotel, a number of companies employ specially equipped trailers for that purpose. These trailers have proved quite effective and are used for promoting the sale of a wide variety of products, ranging from carborundum wheels to high-speed printing machinery. They are sometimes operated by the sales department, in which case the trailer is usually in charge of a salesman who takes orders on the spot. Others are intended for educational purposes only, and are in charge of a member of the sales promotion department.

Audio Tape Cassettes

Tapes used in producing audio-visual programs cover the four main time periods of 30, 60, 90 or 120 minutes; record or play back at $1\frac{7}{8}$ or $3\frac{3}{4}$ inches per second (I P S) and are housed in polystyrene cassettes which load and unload in projectors in a second.

The tapes are tensilized, splice-free and usually coated to provide uniform winding and to eliminate jamming. Some manufacturers also use coatings to prevent static build-up.

Many tapes have one recording track with a separate track for registering pulses (inaudible signals at 50 Hz) which automatically advance the pictures in complete synchronization with the sound. In the Du Kane Cassette Recorder/Pulser, audio and signals are recorded on the same track.

Norelco Compact Cassette tapes, for the company's Synchroplayer model, have four tracks. Tracks 1 and 2 are for narration, track 4 is used for the inaudible picture cues and track 3 is a safety zone to prevent cross talk or inadvertent cueing.

The convenience of tape cassettes is also available for film-strips. As with cassettes, in the Du Kane and La Belle projector models, one simply plugs in a film-strip cartridge and starts the program.

A magnetic audio tape and a continuous-loop 16mm. film-strip have been combined in a permanently synchronized single cartridge for La Belle Series 16 projectors. The cartridge has an audio capacity of 36 minutes at 1⅞ IPS and can show up to 250 single-frame 16mm. visuals.

The Sony Video Cassette System records and reproduces two-track sound on erasable magnetic tape and reproduces color or black-and-white pictures. Inserting a color Video Cassette into the player reproduces the program on the screen of a standard television set.

With blank magnetic tape cassettes and standard slides or film-strips any company may produce its own training or sales presenta-

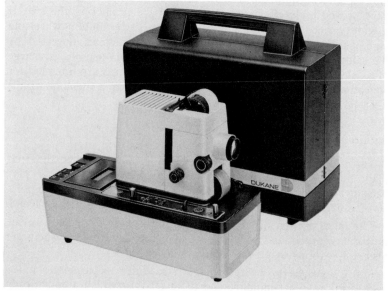

This Dukane Automatic Sound Filmstrip Projector, Micromatic II, is designed to meet audiovisual requirements for product presentations or for sales training. Pictures are changed automatically in synchronization with the sound by means of an inaudible 50 Hz cue signal recorded on the tape. It projects 35 mm film-strips or 2 x 2 slides.

tion programs with or without the aid of independent professional services.

Equipment for the Salesmen

While the sales promotion department is often charged with the responsibility for *producing* the equipment carried by a salesman, it is usually instigated and developed by the operating division of the sales department. This is especially true in the case of demonstration kits, miniature models of the product, sample cases and, to a lesser extent, presentation portfolios and visualizers. The effective equipment of salesmen to increase sales call efficiency is fully covered in the Dartnell *Sales Manager's Handbook*. The development and production of portfolios and visualizers for use by salesmen in promoting the sale of a product also is covered in that handbook.

The sales promotion department is, however, frequently in a position to offer suggestions to the sales operating department for increasing sales call efficiency. For example, salesmen of gas refrigerators have the problem of underscoring, in the prospective buyer's mind, the silent operation of this type of refrigerator. Merely stating this fact was not enough. So the sales promotion department of Servel came up with the idea of providing salesmen with books of giant matches, one of which they handed to a prospect and asked him to strike one match. As the big match burned, the salesman pointed out that Servel refrigerators operated just as quietly as the match burned, since there were no moving parts and gas burned noiselessly. While this device was essentially a sales tool, it also served a sales promotional purpose, since the books of matches carried the Servel advertising, and were used as advertising specialties as well.

If we take the salesman's advice we would furnish a small binder of about 12 pages which he can carry in his coat or shirt pocket. Such a presentation might not be very useful in increasing sales, but it would please salesmen. The problem is to produce a presentation kit—not one to look impressive on the sales promotion manager's desk, but one which the salesmen will use constantly. To achieve this, the kit must be:

Small enough to be carried easily.

Compact enough to fit into the salesman's ordinary luggage.

Foolproof—requiring no complicated folding or unfolding.

Easy to open and close in a moment's time.

Brief—to the point where the average prospect will pay attention to the end.

Simple—so that the language and arguments are within the salesman's mental range.

The best presentation kits leave out nearly all introductory pages, such as pictures of the plant, company history, pictures of company officers. Such kits are designed to open with the very heart of the sales story and present it fully in the fewest number of pages. They are planned so as to appeal to the prospect and win his interest quickly—and hold it.

Reduce the basic sales story to the fewest possible words and illustrations. Plan to include only the sharpest cutting facts, the most telling illustrations. One great objection to many sales presentations is the time required to go through them with the prospect. Do not include language which does not come naturally to the salesman; there may be times when he has to repeat the material from memory, or cannot use the kit, hence the facts and material must be written and presented in a way the salesman himself would use to do the same job if he did not possess a kit—or in case he leaves it at home on half his trips.

MISCELLANEOUS EQUIPMENT

One of the sales promotion manager's jobs is to "sell" his department to top management. The sales manager, the director of sales, the general manager, the treasurer, and the president—all these men should be familiar with the work of the sales promotion manager and his department.

Many of our best sales promotion managers find it profitable to provide large display fixtures on which all current samples of the department's work can be displayed. Fixtures mounted on casters for easy mobility are best, because they can be rolled into a conference room or to some officer's office for exhibit. If mobile display racks are unavailable, cork boards, for easy "pinups," or simple wall racks are useful. An excellent idea is to have glass panels mounted on walls, so that pieces can be slipped under the glass. Molding tacked in horizontal lines on the wall and notched to admit the glass is a simple way to provide adequate display facilities.

The same displays of all current production are useful when there are visiting salesmen. Good sales promotion managers make it a point to nab visiting salesmen and show them all current sales promotion pieces. Without a good exhibit space, planned for the purpose, this is difficult.

Drafting tables, special drawing instruments, a quiet conference room, and good lighting are not luxuries in the average sales promotion department. Do not expect an artist or a lay-out man to do good work at an ordinary desk. Give him the equipment he needs if you demand good work. Do not expect good stencils for the duplicating machine from a typewriter with the type faces worn flat or nicked from long use.

When the planning of printed material comes within the province of the sales promotion department, considerable time can be saved by maintaining a convenient file of paper samples. These are available without charge from the paper merchants from whom you purchase your paper. The samples should be carefully filed and arranged in a suitable cabinet, and classified according to the uses for paper, rather than by the paper house which supplies them. For example, cover papers from all suppliers with whom you do business should be arranged in a separate drawer and filed by grades and finish, so that when you are looking for a cover for a new booklet you can go to the cover paper drawer and find a suitable sample. The brand name, weight, color, and source of supply can then be written into the specifications for the job. This is especially desirable when competitive bids are to be secured, as it assures each printer bidding on uniform paper specifications. Too often the sales promotion department specifies only the kind of paper stock, as, for example, "80-pound cover, antique finish, medium price." This gives bidders an opportunity to use some stock they may have on the floor.

Some sales promotion men even go so far as to have an assortment of booklet dummies of various sizes and folios on hand, so that when they are called upon to prepare a booklet they can pull from their file a suitable dummy without waiting for the printer or paper house to make one for them. In the same way it is smart to have on file ink sample books, showing the various grades and colors of ink stocked by reputable manufacturers. In that way *exact* ink specifications can be given to printers. When fuzzy color instructions are issued as, for example, "bright red," the printer's idea of "bright red" may run all the way from a crimson to an orange red.

Installation of reproductive and addressing equipment in the sales promotion department nearly always brings up the question, "Can't we use this equipment for other departments?"

The practice of using the equipment full time to reduce sales promotion costs, and to help reduce other printing or mailing costs, can become a perpetual headache if the major purpose for which the equipment was purchased is not fully understood.

When the sales promotion department purchases and installs duplicating equipment, for example, it should be made clear to everybody and to every department manager especially, that the prime purpose of the equipment is to produce sales promotion material. When the equipment is not in use it may be used to turn out other items such as factory forms on the same machine. But if the sales promotion manager is not firm and careful he may find his presses busy running a factory shipping ticket, or time ticket, when he wants to get out a sales promotion piece, a sales letter, or a bulletin to the salesmen.

The same problem comes up constantly in the mailing room. While the addressing machine may have been purchased primarily to address dealer bulletins, the treasurer may commandeer the equipment for a dividend check mailing, or for sending a letter to the stockholders. Before any equipment is installed, careful consideration should be given to the question of who is to have prior rights in using the equipment. Chief problem is to make it clear that certain work must be considered as "fill-in" jobs, produced only when the equipment and personnel are not busy on the major job assigned to the equipment.

At today's high wages, which prevail everywhere, good tools are quickly amortized in the time saved, better work, and in improved morale. It is part of the sales promotion manager's job to sell management on providing all the necessary and proper tools.

Finally, the sales promotion manager should consider how to make the best use of his own precious time. So many executives, throughout any corporation, will schedule projects and processes on a weekly, daily, even hourly basis, but give little if any thought to the question of meeting the daily demands on their working hours. With some exceptions, such as when they are involved in a specific project, or when the boss dictates the need for action, time is subject to chance, circumstance, visitors and telephone calls. Time, for the busy sales promotion manager, is a valuable working tool.

This Fairchild Super-8 has made my job a lot lighter...

...I'm a businessman. Nowadays, I need all the help I can get to tell my story to my customers. So I use Fairchild's new Galaxy 900. It's the most effective, dependable, easiest-handling sales assistant I've ever had!

I carry it with me right to my customer's office. In seconds it's set up on his desk, telling my product story with all the drama and impact of sound, color and action.

This Galaxy is a beauty. It's compact, light as a feather and really low cost. And full of all the features you need.

The case, for example. Tough and rugged and styled just like a handsome attache case. It opens with a touch to show a big, bright rear projection screen.

My presentations are problem free. They're on fully self-contained, continuous loop film cartridges that pop right in for immediate playing. For big groups, I just flip a mirror for any-size front projection.

So, take it from me. If you have a selling job to do — or a teaching or training job — think Galaxy 900! It will make your job a lot lighter. And that's a promise.

FAIRCHILD
INDUSTRIAL PRODUCTS

Fairchild Industrial Products
75 Mall Drive, Commack, N.Y. 11725/516-864-8500
☐ Yes, show me how to make my job a lighter.

Name
Company
Address
Phone
Title

Fairchild made a strong appeal to salesmen with this ad featuring its Super-8 Galaxy Model 900. With most of the space devoted to an illustration of the model and the headline, it included an inquiry-coupon in a lower corner.

Chapter 42

PUBLIC RELATIONS*

PUBLIC RELATIONS can be defined as the sum total of an organization's philosophies, policies, and practices (its "three P's") through effective communication with each of its target publics, in the public interest, in order to achieve and maintain the goodwill and understanding it wants. This means that while the prime thrust of public relations work is to persuade—to shape or mold public opinion or to reinforce opinions which are already favorable—public relations entails adherence to a code of professional ethics which supercedes any organization's profit and loss statement.

(For a complimentary copy of the professional standards for the practice of public relations in the U.S., write to the Public Relations Society of America, 845 Third Ave., New York, New York 10022.)

Public relations, despite the diverse activities of its so-called practitioners, is not synonymous with publicity as many nonprofessionals are prone to believe. Too often publicity is fallaciously considered to be the ultimate PR function; it is not. Positive publicity, as vitally important as it is in sales promotion work, may score when it points to wants, needs, or achievements, or when it is used as a tool to extol the virtues, wonders and glories of people, places, or things.

Public relations, on the other hand, when geared to realistic, measurable objectives, can help attain wants, satisfy needs, and earn virtues and glories for those in sales promotion and related work areas.

Publicity focuses upon what has been done or on what needs to be done; public relations focuses on how to get things done and, as a supporting staff function, assists those "on the line" to get things done.

Publicity is a major legitimate tool for those in the profit and nonprofit sectors but it is only one of many communications functions and tools used in the practice of effective public relations which can do the following:

• Develop new markets for products and services, improve an organization's internal and external communications, and thus its public relationships, help prevent labor controversies, educate con-

---

*Especially written by Leonard J. Snyder, Ph.D., School of Business, San Francisco State University.

(Dr. Snyder teaches public relations, marketing, and sales promotion management courses. He is also a management consultant in communications for profit and nonprofit organizations.)

sumers, and provide many other publics, including suppliers and distributors, with indirect sales aids.

- Help determine public attitudes and opinions; plan and implement programs to change or mold them.
- Work to overcome misconceptions and prejudices and build goodwill of various publics, including consumers, distributors, shareholders, suppliers, employees, customers, labor union officials, government representatives, students, specific professional groups, and myriad others with common, identifiable interests.
- Build confidence in an organization and point the way toward making an affiliation with it an honor and privilege.

Astute PR professionals are inclined to assist and counsel because, by temperament, training, and education, they know the value of keeping abreast of their organization's affairs. They are usually knowledgeable in interpreting public opinion so as to correctly give other members of top management the feedback and other information needed for judicious, efficient organizational performance.

Publicity Is News

Publicity is news and news is *a report* of an event, happening, product, person, place, or thing which is of significant interest to someone else. A reporter or editor for a news medium may or may not agree on what is newsworthy and, consequently, may or may not use a given news release written by a publicist or public relations practitioner.

Because sales promotion involves nonpersonal selling efforts, those who use publicity techniques such as news releases to extol the virtues of a good or service would do well to "cool" their enthusiasm by using specific facts, not adjectives, to "sell" their story to a skeptical editor. Accuracy, unvarnished truth, and detailed exactness will likely succeed in getting a story told to a potentially interested audience, especially if what is written is described in an objective, credible way. Above all, it must be understood that any newsworthy story must be viewed from the perspective of the reader or viewer and not from that of the sponsor. Generally, there's a thin but clearly-delineated line which identifies a publishable news release from one which is not; it's whether the report has a sufficiently strong impact upon the reader/viewer to warrant and justify interest and time spent pursuing it. And this creates numerous opportunities in sales promotion work.

This Handbook itself indicates countless areas of sales promotion publicity opportunities. New ideas, concepts, products, and activities all merit publicity consideration. Yet one must be wary about believing that self-interest insofar as news is concerned is tantamount to public interest. It is not, of course. Criteria-type questions to ask to determine whether a given news release is newsworthy, and therefore in the publishable category, are:

Is what is written significant or at least more than of momentary interest to the target audience? Is it timely? Does it affect people emotionally or touch upon their lives in some other important way? Is it likely to stimulate action or counteraction by someone? Will those who read a specific release be affected by its contents in some positive or negative way? Will it be of interest to many people or a relatively few?

Proximity, the "distance" between what is read and the effect this has upon the reader, contributes much, of course, to the impact of any story and therefore its publishability.

While it's usually beneficial to know, in advance, which specific medium you will want to place a hard news story or feature article, a glance at such media directories as *Bacon's Publicity Checker, Gebbie Press All-in-One Directory, Ayer Directory of Publications, Editor & Publisher Yearbook, Broadcasting Yearbook, TV Publicity Outlets Nationwide, Ulrich's International Periodical Directory, Working Press of the Nation,* and other media information guides will readily suggest thousands of outlets which exist for publicity placement. The best source for access to these and many other excellent directories are university or major city libraries, although established public relations agencies and major advertising agencies may be willing to lend an assist with placement tips, or the names and addresses of directories suitable for your activity. Of course, if your organization needs professional counsel and assistance with publicity or more involved public relations activity, it would be prudent to pursue it.

Publicity Is Often Difficult To Measure

The 1980s have brought an increasing awareness by all segments of business and industry as well as those organizations in the nonprofit sector for the need to do more than to seek to publicize an event, product, idea, or other activity. One principal reason is that, even if successful, it's becoming relatively difficult to assess the bottom line effects of publicity. A comparison of editorial and advertising time or space cannot be measured by using such criteria as cost because of different perceptions people have of these two different forms of exposure. While the former is uncontrolled by a publicity sponsor and the latter is controlled by the buyer of the paid time or space, the messages conveyed will be viewed differently simply because of the mediums used. It is therefore ill-advised to compare the value of publicity space or broadcast time with what it costs an advertiser to purchase equal space or time in a given medium. Too many practitioners do this today in an attempt to justify their professional efforts to their employers; they contrast the dollar value of their skills in producing publicity against the cost of buying an equal amount of space or time in the same hard news or news feature medium.

Unfortunately, most often overlooked is that while comparative editorial versus advertising space and time can be measured in column inches or minutes respectively, the knowledge of how many in a target audience have seen or heard the controlled or uncontrolled messages is not known. More importantly, perhaps, is whether, as a result of a publicity placement, a predetermined minimum number of persons among the target public are known to have been motivated, i.e., persuaded, to do what the sponsor wants or plans. And this introduces the concept of PR planning or programming.

Public Relations Programming

Public relations programming has become more sophisticated and precise during the decade which began in the mid-1970s because there has been top management pressure in many organizations for their internal and/or external PR personnel to justify their existence and their missions. This, in turn, coupled with the desire of professionals to upgrade their expertise, has generated increased emphasis upon research measurement and evaluation techniques in public relations.

The decade of the 1980s will predictably see further advances in PR programming, to be brought about in large measure through more knowledge and training in research methods and techniques.

Research marks the beginning and end of any worthwhile public relations program. The program itself generally entails four major steps:

1) Defining the problem or opportunity which, in PR terms, refers to a situation capable of being resolved or addressed *through communicative means.*

2) Determining what strategies should be taken to tackle the problem or opportunity.

3) Devising appropriate communicative tools or vehicles—the tactics—for resolving or addressing the problem and/or opportunity.

4) Evaluating the effectiveness of the program and its component parts to assure that the specific problem(s) or opportunities—the

objectives—were adequately addressed and whether anything further needs to be done to achieve the desired results.

The first step is a research effort because problems from the PR perspective must be validated in public relations terms. Public relations is an applied science as well as a creative art. As an applied science its principal thrust is to identify accurately attitudes and other psychographic characteristics or behavioral profiles of a target audience. It is neither prudent nor practical to beam messages to a target public which have little or no prospects for effectiveness. Thus, *effective communication* can be defined as *more* than a two-way exchange of ideas or meaning; it is viewed here as a behavioral act which results in a voluntary, persuasive effect brought about by deliberate, intentional design by a persuader. Therefore, like a solid hard-sell advertising or other type of promotional campaign activity, research is the bedrock upon which any public relations program must rest.

Often the cost of such research is negligible compared to the results obtained. When practiced by experienced specialists, public relations can be successful in motivating or persuading a target group as well as in providing that group with the tools or techniques needed to persuade other groups to climb on the bandwagon. For example, a manufacturer who provides salient data to wholesalers or distributors that they can use to increase sales also benefits from the use of the information.

Let's look at four specific cases to see the practical benefits of survey research used by public relations counselors to assess the force of public opinion for a bank, a food processing company, an airline, and a metal products manufacturer.

• A large California bank which felt it had nothing to fear wondered whether its size and power constituted some sort of hidden threat to its continued growth. Its directors, understanding that PR is a top-management function, suggested a survey. The finding was that while the bank was solidly respected, it had a reputation for being aloof and for tending to give poor service. Customers attributed this to the bank's size.

Moreover, the bank was becoming vulnerable to competition from smaller banks which played up their personalized services. Fortunately, the survey caught this trend and, using a remedial public relations program, the bank was able to return to the good graces of its widespread community customers.

• A food processing company could not understand why it was failing to attract greater stockholder interest despite its excellent earnings record and prospects. It retained a PR consultant who tapped the attitudes of the community toward the firm. As a result, a shareholder relations program was launched which ultimately succeeded in winning stockholder support.

• An airline, looking toward the introduction of new jets, polled many of its passengers to find out their likes and dislikes about jet flying. Not only did the results of the airline's poll make nationwide news—and excellent product publicity for the company—but fear and apprehension provoked by the new jets was detected in time to mount an impressive educational campaign to offset the gossip and misleading information which the public had conjured up about the new model.

• A metal products manufacturer, mindful that it was losing some good employees to competitors who paid prevailing wage scales, decided to poll its employees about their opinions on work conditions. What the manufacturer found out was a shock since top management's ideas about employee attitudes and opinions clashed sharply with the findings of the public relations survey. The survey validated the real public relations problem and a new successful employee relations program was promptly launched.

Surveys—primary research—were directional finders for the public relations specialists involved in these actual cases. These were typical of countless others that proved to be much less costly than the consequences of the problematic situations which prompted managements to undertake them. The surveys revealed that prevailing opinions of many of those polled were based not on facts, but on ignorance. Knowledge about sources of information as well as of the information itself is essential; therefore, applied PR techniques must be successful in resolving a troublesome situation or addressing a promotional or public relations opportunity.

Post-campaign surveys, part of the evaluation process in a PR program, are generally enlightening, too, because they provide a means of determining how successful are the communication strategies and tactics—stages two and three above—in reaching the goals and objectives sought. If a public relations program is sound initially it will have built into it specific yardsticks or other measurement devices so that, during the evaluation stage, it will be fairly easy to determine the relative strengths and/or weaknesses of the program. Periodic mini-surveys, taken while a campaign is underway, are also useful for keeping a campaign on target, inasmuch as unforeseen environmental factors, such as legal restraints or competitive inroads, may affect its ultimate outcome.

Qualifications of PR Personnel

The diverse knowledge and skills needed in the performance of successful sales promotion work have been alluded to throughout this Handbook. While experience may also be a good teacher, it should be emphasized that the future can never be planned entirely by the past. It's for this reason, perhaps, that imagination and creativity along with the ability to exercise sound judgment seem to be necessary prerequisites in all promotional work.

Public relations specialists who do sales promotion work well should not be confused or mistaken for other public relations experts in other areas of the profession. Therefore, the selection of public relations personnel should depend upon the nature, scope, and range of work activities to be performed. For example, an experienced product publicity writer or speech writer will need more than excellent writing skills to produce a company's annual report; in addition to conceptual planning, the qualifications of a publication editor involves knowledge about design and layout, typography, photography, and other facets of art illustrations and graphics as well.

Surprisingly, perhaps, even chief executive officers of some of the most prestigious and best-known organizations in the U.S. and Canada—with corporate budgets of many millions of dollars—have been found to have difficulty in trying to determine the kind of background, skills and experience they would look for if they had to fill their top communication staff position. This apparently stems from their own uncertainty or lack of what constitutes substantive knowledge about communication and public relations which many CEOs seem to take for granted.

This was borne out in a study by the International Association of Business Communicators, headquartered in San Francisco, which the author of this chapter was commissioned to analyze. However, it can be surmised from the study that among the CEOs surveyed, many are looking in the 1980s for personnel with some knowledge of the field they'll be working in, media experience, preferably in journalism, with a master's degree in some area of communication. In addition to excellent writing and verbal skills, CEOs feel that knowledge of graphics and good design is helpful and that strong managerial ability, problem solving, and research skills are decided pluses. A number of these chief executive officers stressed that they would want their principal communication aides to be imaginative, cost-conscious planners and organizers with good judgment.

The following matrix can be helpful in determining either the type of public relations personnel your organization may need for a particular position or, if used as a career chart, may help a beginner or mid-career individual to define and identify desired job qualities for a specified public relations position.

PR Qualifications Chart

How to use this chart: Attempt to reach a consensus among top management policy-making executives on desired job qualities perceived to be needed for a designated position by asking each to check off all qualities listed here. Using this chart as a guide, feel free to add, change, or substitute other job characteristics as you wish. Then, when all executives involved in the decision-making process have made known their preferences, you will have identified the qualities wanted to fill a needed position.

If you are already employed in a company in which you seek promotion, you could write a brief covering letter or memo and submit it with the chart among those select executives who you believe may be instrumental in shaping your career aspirations. Your letter or memo would request your respondent to check off the personal qualities such as background, skills, and experience he or she would like to see in the person who will fill the job you have in mind. While your returned charts might provide an opportunity to personally discuss your future with a superior, they may be helpful in identifying areas of professional development worthy of further consideration.

The preceding public relations qualifications chart—depending upon how it is used—indicates the scope and depth of contemporary public relations practice. The chart is not wholly exhaustive because approaches used for reaching specific goals and objectives within different organizations can be as varied as the unique qualities, characteristics, personalities, and backgrounds of their managements. For instance, press agentry, a form of media hucksterism which borders more on entertainment than on an attempt to reach out for organizational goodwill based upon solid informational understanding of an idea or issue, is considered by many PR professionals to be passé nowadays. Yet, it's still being practiced, just as advertising hyperbole has become part of the U.S. lifestyle and will remain so long as it is considered to be successful by its adopters. Sound, long-term growth public relationships depend upon goodwill in good times and bad, however, and these attributes must be honestly and candidly conveyed if public relations and sales promotion activities are to be lastingly credible and respectable.

Therefore, if knowledge about the use of public relations techniques and skills is to be of tangible benefit in the field of sales promo-

Defining Job Needs/Qualities for the Position of: _____

(Check off the background, skills and experience you deem vital, very important, important, helpful, or unimportant for this position.)

	Vital	Very Important	Important	Helpful	Unimportant
Management/administrative experience					
More knowledge/experience in this field, business					
MBA degree					
Master's degree in Journalism, Communication or related field					
Promotional skills. e.g., special events, exhibits, and special showings; contests and award programs; visual aids					
Writing/editing, e.g., reports, news releases, pamphlets, radio/TV copy, speeches, trade features, product releases					
Speaking, e.g., before select groups and finding suitable opportunities for appearances; speakers' bureau					
Production, e.g., knowledge of layout & design & graphics for brochures, special reports and publications					
Counseling, e.g., public contact recommendations for senior executives and mid-management officials					
Research skills, e.g., surveys, audits, methodology & design techniques, analysis of quantitative/qualitative data especially with primary data					
Decision making, particularly in areas of public relations and/or public affairs					
Photography, art, illustrations, and graphics					
Marketing and/or public relations research especially in gathering data from secondary sources					
Financial knowledge and preparation of financial documents and reports					
Lobbying and/or representing company at special events, hearings, with public or industry groups					
Training non-professionals in public relations and public affairs					
Formulation and implementation of policy programs in areas of employee and community relationships					
Planning and executing corporate PR programs, including institutional advertising					
Media contact, including placement of news and features in newspapers, radio, TV, magazines, & trade journals					

tion, it must be grounded on practical and workable principles, terms, and concepts.

Useful PR Principles, Terms, and Concepts

Here are key terms, concepts, and principles in public relations practice which, when properly understood and used, will have a positive affect on an organization's entire public relations program:

News or press conferences—should probably not be arranged unless there's a sufficiently compelling reason to do so. This means providing a format for questions and answers which are exchanged in an open, give-and-take news media forum. Publicity ploys, especially those which lend themselves to news releases, disseminated by mail or messenger, should not be used to call news conferences. To do so will negatively affect one's credibility, as will attempting to dodge or skirt answers to legitimate questions newspeople feel the public has a right to know. Hold or stage a news conference only at a place likely to enhance its news impact; a hotel room is no substitute for a place where needed visuals can be shown by television or still camera crews.

Effective communication—is a two-way plus process which involves listening, seeing, and interpreting or monitoring of public attitudes as well as transmitting information or instructions. To a knowledgeable PR practitioner, effective communication is influenced behavior —the transmission and reception of ideas, feelings, and attitudes which, by intent, produce a favorable response. Therefore, effective communication is not to be confused with tools of communication such as house organs, bulletin boards, films, news releases, phone conversations, speeches, interviews, letters and the like . . . it's also the less obvious, the *action* of people talking, listening, seeing, feeling and *reacting* to one another as *intended* by the communicator. This requires planning. "More" communication is not effective communication in anybody's language.

Persuasion—not to be confused with coercion—is a *voluntary* behavioral act and a practical way to remember the three essential characteristics of the process is "ICE"—intent, communication, and effects. That is, for persuasion to occur there must be a willingness to accept an argument, a point of view, etc., which a persuader *intends* to *communicate* with a message that has a demonstrable *effect* in the person or persons who are the targets of the communication. Thus, one needs to first capture attention before trying to communicate, which is an art unto itself. But the end or culmination of persuasion is action—the effect which the message(s) produce(s) within a human being.

Propaganda—contrary to popular belief this is not necessarily a negative concept inasmuch as it refers to the dissemination of truth or fiction. Like public relations itself, which is a process which can be either good or bad, propaganda is an amoral concept whose users *intentionally* aim to direct a course of action; usually the users are a *hidden* source. The difference between propaganda and advertising, for instance, is that while advertising is public persuasion—to get someone to take a course of action—the public *knows* the advertiser because the advertising source is identified. In propaganda, the would-be public persuader is usually not identified. Thus, it can be deceptive.

Channels of communication—are the media through which messages pass to reach a target audience. Advertising and sales promotion, which involve "hard" selling in contrast to public relations which involves "soft" selling, rely more on the acquisition of time and space in the mass media to provide maximum exposure for a product or service. Public relations, on the other hand, uses noncommercial newsspace and time to "sell" the organization, not its products, by dissemination of truthful, accurate information. Ways of verifying or disproving that a news report, an editorial, or a speech are propaganda, for example, involve identifying not only the source of messages but the channels of communication—and who controls them—through which the messages pass to reach a target public. The reliability of the sources as well as of the channels used must be above reproach. Therefore, one should look to past performances to determine reliability. Ask whether the channels of information have been dependable or whether these channels are likely to be biased or prejudiced.

Institutional advertising—is also known as public relations, advocacy, corporate, or organizational advertising. It should be distinguished from product advertising which uses the hard sell. Institutional (PR) advertising uses a somewhat softer sell through paid-for space or time to convey a message. Reason, understanding, and the credibility of logic to convince and persuade are the pervading forces behind the institutional advertising concept. Thus, a company's display ad in an urban newspaper wishing readers "the best of the Holiday Season" is institutional because the focus is to generate goodwill and understanding and not direct sales. Likewise, a message which attempts to explain a corporate position during a strike by employees is defined as institutional because the message's theme is not to sell the company's product(s) but the company itself.

*Rumors—and how to control them—*are of paramount importance, particularly during a crises situation. PR people, as other communicators, have a responsibility and obligation to disclose facts as promptly and accurately as possible. Groundless rumors should not be allowed to persist because they can detrimentally affect employee morale and productivity and adversely affect an organization's other publics, i.e., customers, suppliers, distributors, etc. Therefore, move fast to correct misconceptions because if rumors are repeated often they may get out of hand. When dealing with the news media, keep in mind they may have gathered "facts" from varied sources and may already know more about a situation than your organization may want to disclose. While it may not be wise to say more than is necessary, be cautious with what is said. The organization's reputation (not image) and your credibility may be at stake. When a fact cannot be readily confirmed, say so, but verify facts promptly and get back to your news media caller. Ultimately, the truth will be told. Meanwhile, do not give credence to a rumor by referring to it in attempting to quell or refute it. The less said about it the better.

*Social responsibility—*a particularly important concept in PR—refers to the public posture or behavior of those who make up the organization, in accord with social norms or expectations. It holds that those in the organization, because they are an integral part of it, are responsible for the organization's public negligence or misconduct and should, accordingly, be held accountable. Thus, while a company may not be legally responsible for social ills or other discomforting conditions which exists in its environment, it's considered to be socially responsible when it makes an overt effort to correct those conditions. The firm, by being a good corporate citizen, extends its hand of welcome and goodwill to others and, by so doing, generates positive public attitudes towards itself; it demonstrates, among other things, its genuine desire to side with societal concerns and to be a part of their solution instead of the communal problem. This concept may be viewed as an extension of the corporate conscience theory which has long existed in public relations. The theory holds that, because an organization's public relations staff is primarily involved in cultivating sound and better public relationships which affect the institution, the PR function becomes the corporate conscience.

Corporate responsibility today, more perhaps than in past decades, means coming to grips with the reality of what it means to build better business climates in which companies can operate. Major corporations are continually judged, praised or condemned by their various publics—whether they realize it or not—and there is growing recognition among many of them for the need to devote more time, energy, and money to improving their own measurements of public opinion.

Employees, consumers, shareholders, government, labor, suppliers and other groups are all identifiable publics affected by the affairs of a business or other organization, large or small. And, attitudes of individuals in each of these key groups often ferment to a point where group thought (public opinion) affects an organization's operation for better or worse. Social responsibility does not start with recognition of public consumer or activist groups, however. It signifies a commingling with them for the common good. Therein lies the measure of understanding and goodwill, the result of intelligent public relations philosophies, policies, and practices for the organization as a whole and not solely for its marketing function, as vital as this is for its economic survival.

Chapter 43

INTERNATIONAL SALES PROMOTION

INTERNATIONAL marketing, to those who are not familiar with it, is cloaked in mystery and framed in a complex of strange and unusual procedures. It does not take long, however, to become acquainted with the procedures of making overseas shipment or of handling the financial requirements of international selling. There are many agencies, governmental and private, to help. Once these become routine, the problem resolves itself into the fundamentals of sales promotion.

International marketing usually falls into three classifications. To begin with, sales are made to independent local distributors who maintain their own facilities for local distribution. They place orders for merchandise; payment is made through the banks with overseas correspondents or branches through letters of credit or sight drafts; and shipments are handled by freight forwarders who handle all the necessary details.

In fact, it is possible to sell overseas through independent export sales agencies, which pay for the merchandise in the U.S., obtain local distribution, and take care of all the shipping details. The U.S. Department of Commerce, the export trade papers and some of the larger international advertising agencies are very helpful in developing the necessary arrangements to bring the manufacturer and the importer together. Of course, the larger companies maintain their own export departments and do the entire job themselves.

In major overseas markets, import restrictions by local governments often lead to the establishment of manufacturing subsidiaries which import raw materials or technical components and do a local assembly job. These subsidiary companies become fairly autonomous, since they cannot depend on bringing in U.S. products in either finished or semiassembled form. In recent years, larger corporations with overseas manufacturing plants have been obliged to permit their subsidiaries to buy their requirements from company plants in a variety of countries. This multinational policy is justified on the ground that sales would otherwise be lost. In any event, it produces dividends which eventually return to the home country.

The third application of international marketing is through licensees. In this situation, where it is impossible to export from the U.S., and the formation of a subsidiary manufacturing company is not warranted because of costs, U.S. companies license local organizations to produce their products and use their trademark for a predetermined annual fee. Formerly known as a "royalty," this is now called a "technical assistance fee." In return, the American company provides management, technical, and marketing assistance to the local licensee.

Which of these three aproaches employed depends on the market. As a rule, manufacturing subsidiaries are organized in such countries as Canada, Mexico, Argentina, Brazil, and some of the large European markets.

Licensees are justified where imports are restricted and the market is too small to warrant the cost of organizing a subsidiary with its own manufacturing plant. This would apply to some of the smaller markets in Latin America, Europe, and the Far East. The major advantages of licensing are that it is less costly than building a plant and the U.S. manufacturer acquires a ready-built distributing organization.

The Common Markets

Licensing agreements are necessary for American companies wishing to introduce their products or expand their sales in Europe and other countries with great sales potentials but which, for economic reasons, have restricted import policies.

The European Common Market, which when joined by the countries in the European Free Trade Association, will include sixteen countries from the Baltic to the Mediterranean, with a population of over 300 million, is a tremendous market for American products if they could be imported. The main avenue available to United States manufacturers, however, is through licensing, whereby local producers manufacture and distribute American products under licensing arrangements. There are favorable conditions, for certain products, in which a licensee in Italy, for example, could be licensed to sell, not only in the home market but in other Common Market countries as well.

The concept of the common market has spread to Central and South America, where many countries have been compelled, for economic reasons, to impose import restrictions as a result of which American companies have had to resort either to licensing agreements with local producers or to the establishment of subsidiary manufacturing companies.

The United States government is attempting to alleviate the potential risks involved through the development of insurance programs and by tax-preference policies for special export corporations.

In other countries, where there are few or no import restrictions, shipments are made directly from the U.S.

This diversification leads us to a consideration of the sales promotion policies which must be developed for each type of international marketing. The subsidiaries develop their own, they are on the scene and they frequently have products which differ from the parent organization's merchandise. The licensees, in many cases, have their own complete selling and advertising organizations; the products they introduce to the local market are not the same as the U.S. models, and, if they are, lag from one to two years behind schedule. That leaves the distributors who depend on direct shipments from the U.S.

The selection of the proper distributor will "make or break" the position of the manufacturer in any market. A brief checklist which may help to serve as a guide includes the following points:

1. Character and reputation of owners.
2. Capital available.
3. Quality of organization.
4. Location and nature of quarters.
5. Territory to be covered.
6. Volume and quotas by products.
7. Market coverage (dealers or agents).
8. Dealer quotas.
9. Personnel.
10. Service facilities.
11. Display space.
12. Advertising and sales promotion.

One chief difference between export and domestic merchandising is the lack of dependable information in foreign areas on

B4700...B3700...B2700...MCP V

Burroughs presenta tres series de computadores de gran capacidad y un quinto adelanto importante en Software de Sistemas.

He aquí noticias importantes para quienes usan computadores de tamaño medio. La "familia" Burroughs 700 está aumentando con . . .

...Computadores Más Productivos y Poderosos

Serie B4700: Cinco modelos adicionales con un potencial de entrada y salida hasta un 100% mayor que el de los modelos actuales.

Serie B3700: Cuatro nuevos modelos basados en el comprobado diseño de la Serie B4700 . . . su productividad es hasta un 70% mayor que la de los bien conocidos B3500.

Serie B2700: Tres modelos que extienden la avanzada tecnología de las Series B2500 y B3500 ofreciendo una gama aún mayor en productividad y precio.

Estos avanzados sistemas le ofrecen a Ud.—

• "Madurez instantánea"—aceptan los programas de aplicaciones de las Series B2500 y B3500 procesándolos de manera óptima.

• Económica expansión modular dentro de una Serie y de una Serie a otra, sin necesidad de reprogramar o aún de recompilar.

• Extensa biblioteca de "generadores de programas" que ahorran substancialmente el tiempo y costo de programación.

• Poderosos compiladores FORTRAN, COBOL, y BASIC así como Software avanzado para RJE y manejo de "bancos de información".

• Multiprogramación automática bajo el control de MCP . . . auto-regulación . . . memoria virtual . . . asignación dinámica de recursos . . .

• Multiprogramación paralela y procesamiento en multisistemas compartiendo el mismo archivo en discos.

• Pre-procesadores de comunicación de datos para una mayor capacidad y eficiencia en el manejo de terminales remotos.

Un Programa Maestro de Control más Productivo y Poderoso

Pruebas efectuadas indican que el MCP V aumenta la productividad del 10% al 20% tanto en los nuevos sistemas como en los ya instalados. El MCP V está ahora disponible para *todos* los sistemas Burroughs de tamaño medio. El MCP V confirma la posición de prominencia conquistada por Burroughs en la tecnología de sistemas operativos.

Sin duda, Burroughs le pone a Ud. "a la vanguardia" mediante computadores más productivos, económicos, así como más fáciles de instalar y de operar . . . manteniendo siempre excelente flexibilidad y modularidad de crecimiento para satisfacer a cabalidad el aumento en sus actividades de procesamiento de datos.

Burroughs

Burroughs advertises its three computer series models in the Spanish edition of Vision magazine, New York-based publication for business men overseas.

which to base sales objectives. Some countries have never taken a census! Population figures mean little anyway; it's purchasing power that counts. Most companies, of course, are guided by past performance, but this does not take into account the real market potentialities. Some organizations use the Department of Commerce figures, showing the total U.S. exports each month by individual product and country as a readily available and practical guide to sales performance. If a company obtains 5% of the total domestic volume, it should have at least 5% of the total exports of its industry to any country.

Export Management Companies

Small, medium-size, and even some large manufacturers have found they can expand into profitable world trade without the financial risks or complications involved in setting up their own export departments. They are doing this through the services of the Export Management Company—the EMC—which acts as their "export department," selling their products overseas along with other allied but noncompetitive products. The EMC's service is extensive and includes:

Research of foreign markets for its principal's product.

Travel overseas to determine the best methods of distributing the product.

Appointing distributors or commission representatives as needed in individual foreign countries, frequently within an already existing overseas network created for similar goods.

Exhibiting the principal's product at international fairs.

Granting the customary finance terms to the trade abroad and assuring payment to the manufacturer for his product.

Preparation of advertising and sales literature in cooperation with the manufacturer, and adapting it to overseas requirements for use in personal contacts with buyers abroad.

Corresponding in the necessary foreign languages.

Making sure that goods being shipped are suitable for local conditions, and meet overseas legal and trade norms, including labeling, packaging, purity, electrical characteristics, etc.

Advising overseas patent and trademark protection requirements.

Some EMC's do not use their own names when selling abroad for their principals. Instead, they use special letterheads showing their address as the manufacturer's "export department" or "international division." Correspondence and export documents are then signed by the EMC in the manufacturer's name.

In short, the EMC takes full responsibility for the export end of the business, relieving the manufacturer of all details except filling orders.

Valuable Government Assistance

The Bureau of International Commerce of the United States Department of Commerce can be of tremendous assistance to manufacturers marketing their products abroad. Many companies began to sell internationally through the commercial exhibitions program developed by the Bureau of International Commerce.

The marketing program uses exhibitions as vehicles to bring the United States manufacturer into the overseas marketplace. The exhibition may bet set up in permanent United States Trade Centers strategically located in eight major markets around the world. Or it may be part of a well-known international trade fair, such as the Paris Air Show, the Frankfurt Chemical Show, and the Japan Electronics Show.

In each case the exhibition is organized to help an American businessman quickly and easily to locate customers and build a prospect list tailored to his marketing needs.

It puts him into contact with potential agents, distributors, and licensees who want to handle his product overseas. For example, a United States exhibitor in one year signed up 975 agents as a direct result of their participation in commercial exhibitions overseas.

Most importantly, the exhibition places the manufacturers' product line before an audience that represents up to 80% of the purchasing power in that market.

It is relatively easy for a United States company to participate in a Bureau-sponsored exhibition in a trade center, trade fair, or solo fair. Here's what the company must do:

Provide products for display;
Supply adequate quantities of technical and promotional literature;
Ship the products to the exhibit site;
Assign a representative qualified to man the booth and transact business;
Make the specified contribution.

In return, here's what the Bureau of International Commerce will do:

Promote the attendance of qualified buyers and agents;
Provide exhibit space and facilities;

Design and construct the exhibit;

Advise regarding the shipment of products to the site;

Unpack and position the display;

Supply all utilities and housekeeping services;

Provide a translator/demonstrator, if appropriate;

Provide an attractive lounge or meeting rooms for exhibitor-customer conferences;

Pay the cost of returning any unsold exhibit items to the United States.

To aid exporters locate and develop overseas markets, the Department of Commerce publishes a wide variety of publications including:

Foreign Markets for United States Products and Services

Economic Facts on Foreign Countries

Foreign Buyers and Suppliers

Firms with Marketing Facilities in Foreign Countries

Trade and Investment Opportunities Abroad

Foreign Government Procurement in the United States

Government Financing Aid to Exporters

Quotas and Tariffs

FCIA Insurance Against Commercial and Political Risks Abroad

Export and Import Licenses

Foreign Exchange Regulations and Procedures

Export and Import Statistics

Operations of the Export-Import Bank of the United States

Assistance available from the Regional Export Expansion Council.

Trade Fairs and Trade Centers

Fairs and exhibits have a special degree of importance in overseas markets. Some of the better-known fairs date back to the sixteenth century and still have considerable promotional impact, as attested to by the interest of the United States government in stimulating participation by American companies in order to increase exports from this country.

European companies sell as much as 50% of their total production at trade fairs, leading quite naturally to a marked difference of emphasis in the place allocated in their budgets to exhibiting. American corporations apportion from one-half of one percent to five percent of their advertising budgets to exhibiting while European companies set aside between 10% and 25% of their advertising budgets for the same function!

In addition, the United States Department of Commerce has established a number of Trade Centers in major cities abroad, in which American manufacturers may exhibit their products at little or no cost except for inland delivery to a United States port of embarkation. One of the best sources of assistance is the United States Department of Commerce with its vast knowledge of overseas markets. In order to encourage American firms to market abroad, the Department's Bureau of International Commerce provides marketing counseling, promotion, professional exhibition services, arrangements for moving of exhibitors' materials to United States trade centers in many parts of the world. All is done at a very nominal fee. Many American corporations have used BIC's services with success to make their first penetration of a foreign market. Complete information along these lines is available through the:

U.S. Exhibition Manager
Trade Center Director
Bureau of International Commerce
U.S. Department of Commerce
Washington, D.C. 20230

There are two types of advertising available to the American exporter interested in developing his foreign sales. The first is through the magazines and trade publications produced in various languages in the United States for circulation abroad.

U.S. Trade Centers are overseas "merchandise marts" or commercial showrooms, permanently established in central marketing areas where the potential for American products is high and continuous. Providing U.S. manufacturers with a unique method of testing and selling key foreign markets, Centers are located in London, Frankfurt, Milan, Stockholm, Tokyo, Paris, Sydney and Mexico City. Trade Centers provide year-round facilities for display and demonstration of U.S. products and have proved highly successful.

Every year each Center holds seven to nine major product showings, featuring displays by 25 to 35 U.S. firms, built around a product theme selected on the basis of continuing market research that indicates need for, and acceptance of, the product, and also identifies the audience for the exhibit. Technical seminars, often held in conjunction with specially selected exhibits, enhance interest in the products and help boost sales. Participation fees are only $450 for Trade Center shows.

Das kleine bißchen „Mehr" entscheidet.

Für Sie oder gegen Sie!

Lesen Sie deshalb Deutschlands
große Wirtschaftszeitung.

HANDELSBLATT-INDUSTRIEKURIER **Deutschlands
große Wirtschaftszeitung**

*West German industrial advertisers
aim straight at lead-producing inquiries
by emphasizing the coupon. One company placed it at the very top of the ad.*

The second, and perhaps the more important, is the local advertising through the publications and radio and TV stations in each country. The best method for doing this, and one which has been adopted by most experienced exporters, is the cooperative advertising plan.

Many versions of local cooperative advertising have been developed, but the best plan is one which includes the dealer as well as the distributor and the manufacturer. Under this plan, the dealer contributes half the cost of his local advertising, with the distributor and the manufacturer contributing 25%. The manufacturer's contribution is limited by a percentage of his sales to the distributor. This may range anywhere from 2 to 5% of sales, depending on the product and other conditions. This contribution takes the form of a credit issued when the distributor submits a properly substantiated statement at the end of each month.

The production and distribution of promotional materials for use abroad presents some complex problems. First, the local distributor is not inclined to pay for displays and literature, so he

A Few U.S. Department of Commerce District Offices

Albuquerque, N.M., 87102, 505 Marquette, N.W., Suite 1015.

Anchorage, 99501, 632 Sixth Ave., Hill Bldg., Suite 412.

Atlanta, 30309, Suite 600, 1365 Peachtree St., NE.

Baltimore, 21202, 415 U.S. Customhouse, Gay and Lombard Sts.

Birmingham, Ala., 35205, Suite 200-201, 908 S. 20th St.

Boston, 02116, 10th Floor, 441 Stuart St.

Buffalo, N.Y., 14202, Room 1312, Federal Bldg., 111 W. Huron St.

Charleston, W.Va., 25301, 3000 New Federal Office Bldg., 500 Quarrier St.

Cheyenne, Wyo., 82001, 6022 O'Mahoney Federal Center, 2120 Capitol Ave.

Chicago, 60603, Room 1406, Mid-Continental Plaza Bldg., 55 E. Monroe St.

Cincinnati, 45202, 10504 Federal Office Bldg., 550 Main St.

Cleveland, 44114, Room 600, 666 Euclid Ave.

Columbia, S.C., 29204, Forest Center, 2611 Forest Dr.

Dallas, 75202, Room 7A5, 1100 Commerce St.

Denver, 80202, Room 165, New Custom House, 19th and Stout Sts.

Des Moines, Iowa, 50309, 609 Federal Bldg., 210 Walnut St.

Detroit, 48226, 445 Federal Bldg., 231 W. Lafayette.

Greensboro, N.C., 27402, 203 Federal Bldg., W. Market St., P.O. Box 1950.

Hartford, Conn., 06103, Room 610-B, Federal Office Bldg., 450 Main St.

Honolulu, 96813, 286 Alexander Young Bldg., 1015 Bishop St.

Houston, 77002, 2625 Federal Bldg./ Courthouse, 515 Rusk St.

Indianapolis, 46204, 357 Federal Office Bldg., 46 E. Ohio St.

Los Angeles, 90049, Room 800, 11777 San Vicente Blvd.

Memphis, 38103, Room 710, 147 Jefferson Ave.

Miami, 33130, Rm. 821, City National Bank Bldg., 25 W. Flagler St.

Milwaukee, 53203, Federal Bldg., 517 E. Wisconsin Ave.

Minneapolis, 55401, 218 Federal Bldg., 110 S. Fourth St.

New Orleans, 70130, Room 432, International Trade Mart, 2 Canal St.

Piet Zeutemelk finds worldwide understanding – at the ICC Berlin.

Although hardly any of the 2,000 delegates in Hall 1 can understand him in his mother tongue. The speech is simultaneously translated into 8 different languages. Frank Dwight of Texas, for example, can hear it in American, and Pedro Gonzales in Spanish... The simultaneous translation system is just one of many distinctive features at the biggest, most versatile convention center there'll be in Europe as of April 1979: the ICC Berlin.

We thank Herr Zeutemelk for his remarks...

International
Congress Center Berlin

☑AMK Berlin
Company for Exhibitions, Fairs and Congresses, Ltd.
Box 191740, Messedamm 22, D-1000 Berlin 19

Win the Winner's Chair

Here's your chance to win an advance souvenir of the ICC Berlin. We're raffling off 11 genuine Congress Chair combinations. Just send in the coupon and we'll forward your entry card, plus additional ICC Berlin information.

Name _____

Company _____

Position _____

Address _____

Contact address: German American Chamber of Commerce,
One Farragut Square South, Washington, D. C. 20006, (202) 347–0247

International Congress Center Berlin
Congress Hall Berlin
Exhibition Grounds Berlin
Deutschlandhalle/Ice Palace Berlin

AMK Berlin
Company
for Exhibitions, Fairs and Congresses, Ltd.

Box 191740, Messedamm 22
D-1000 Berlin 19
Telephone: (030) 30 38-1
Telex: 0182908 amkb d

Companies holding international sales meetings, with attendance by distributors from many countries around the world, ensure the effectiveness of their presentations through simultaneous translations, as featured in this advertisement by the International Congress Center in Berlin.

limits his orders to samples, or to very small quantities. This small-quantity factor increases the cost of printing material in foreign languages with the result that it is generally limited to Spanish editions.

Further, dependably accurate or perfect translations of copy into languages other than Spanish are rather difficult to obtain. This is due to several reasons. For example, French copy, written in France, is not fully acceptable in French-speaking Canada, because of many variations. Even Spanish, as spoken in one Latin American country, may vary in some respects from that in another. The Spanish word for radio-tube is different in each of five countries. The best way to ensure a good translation is to have it made in the country in which the material is to be used.

One solution to the problem is to authorize the local distributors to print their own material and include its cost in the manufacturer's cooperative advertising plan.

Overseas distributors are particularly fond of exhibits. Perhaps this may be due, in part at least, to lower literacy levels among consumers in many countries.

Foreign distributors are eager for promotional plans and selling ideas from the U.S., and many subscribe to American business publications and trade journals. When they visit their principals' offices in this country, one of their questions is: "What do you have in advertising and sales promotion?"

Regardless of the language differences, however, all the larger American corporations apply the full range of promotional techniques to their international merchandising and promotion. This includes not only literature, catalogs, and displays, but world-wide contests, special promotional campaigns, export house organs in English and Spanish editions, dealer meetings, sales training programs, and prize-trip incentives. International marketing and sales promotion, with its many distinct markets scattered throughout the world, and with its prospects for future growth, is a challenging area of business expansion and sales-stimulating activity.

Tax Advantages

Marketing and sales promotion executives with international responsibilities will note that sales and use taxes do not always apply to materials and supplies which go into the design and production of advertising and sales promotion materials destined for use in other countries. This is a cost-saving precept which applies particularly to advertising agencies which do not distinguish applicable costs between domestic and international advertisements and sales promotional material. There is a difference which in some cases, could amount to sizable amounts of money.

Of special interest to top management, too, is that Congress has provided that special export corporations—Domestic International Sales Corporations (or DISCs)—are entitled to special tax treatment for taxable years beginning on or after January 1, 1972.

For example, if a DISC has $100,000 of export earnings $50,000 is taxed currently to its shareholders as a dividend and $50,000 is eligible for deferral while retained by the DISC.

The DISC may, as principal or agent, engage in the business of exporting products manufactured, produced, grown or extracted in the United States. It can export articles produced by related and unrelated producers and can export to related and unrelated purchasers. In addition, it may lease or sublease such products for use outside of the United States or perform engineering or architectural services for foreign construction projects.

INTERNATIONAL ADVERTISING AGENCIES IN THE U.S.

Adler, William Hart, Inc.
64 Old Orchard, Skokie 60076

Advertising Associates, Inc.
300 W. Main St., Richmond, Va. 23220

Ally, Carl, Inc.
437 Madison Ave., New York 10022

Ayer & Son, N. W., Inc.
W. Washington St., Philadelphia 19106

Basford, Inc.
(now Coordinated Communications, Inc.)
1301 Ave. of Americas, New York 10019

Bates, Ted & Co., Inc.
666 5th Ave., New York 10019

Batten, Barton, Durstine & Osborn, Inc.
383 Madison Ave., New York 10017

Benton & Bowles, Inc.
909 3rd Ave., New York 10022

Black-Russell-Morris
231 Johnson Ave., Newark, N. J. 07108

Botsford, Ketchum, Inc.
114 Sansome St., San Francisco 94111

Bowes Company, The
1010 S. Flower St., Los Angeles 90015

Bozell & Jacobs, Inc.
655 Madison Ave., New York 10021

Burnett, Leo, Company, Inc.
Prudential Plaza, Chicago 60601

Carson/Roberts, Inc.
8322 Beverly Blvd., Los Angeles 90048

INTERNATIONAL ADVERTISING AGENCIES
IN THE U.S.

Communications Affiliates
1345 Ave. of Americas, New York 10019

Compton Advertising, Inc.
625 Madison Ave., New York 10022

Coordinated Communications, Inc.
1301 Ave. of Americas, New York 10019

Culver Advertising, Inc.
535 Boylston, Boston 02116

Cutler & Edmonds International, Inc.
222 W. Adams St., Chicago 60606

Dancer-Fitzgerald-Sample, Inc.
347 Madison Ave., New York 10017

D'Arcy-MacManus-Intermarco, Inc.
Bloomfield Hills, Michigan

DeGarmo, McCaffery, Inc.
605 3rd Ave., New York 10016

Denhard & Stewart, Inc.
20 W. 43 St., New York 10036

Doremus & Company, Inc.
120 Broadway, New York 10005

Doyle Dane Bernbach, Inc.
20 W. 43 St., New York 10036

Dreher Advertising, Inc.
45 Rockefeller Plaza, New York 10020

Drew, A., & Co., Advertising, Inc.
66 Glen Ave., Glen Rock, N.J. 07452

Erwin Wasey, Inc.
5455 Wilshire Blvd., Los Angeles 90036

Esty, William, Company, Inc.
100 East 42nd St., New York 10017

Foote, Cone & Belding, Inc.
200 Park Ave., New York 10017

Frohlich, L. W. & Co./Intercon
34 East St., New York 10022

Fuller & Smith & Ross, Inc.
665 5th Ave., New York 10019

Gardner Advertising Company
915 Olive St., St. Louis 63101

Geer, DuBois & Company, Inc.
220 E. 42nd St., New York 10017

Glenn Advertising, Inc.
4700 Republic National Tower,
Dallas 75201

Graff, Harry W., Inc.
380 Madison Ave., New York 10017

Grant Advertising, Inc.
10 S. Riverside Plaza, Chicago 60606

Gray & Kilgore, Inc.
18845 W. McNichols Rd., Detroit 48219

Grey & Davis, Inc.
777 3rd Ave., New York 10017

Griswold-Eshleman Company
55 Public Square, Cleveland 44113

Hodes-Daniel Company, Inc.
500 Saw Mill River Rd.,
Elmsford, N.Y. 10523

Holley-Thomas, Inc.
800 Second Ave., New York 10017

Howard, Edward & Co.
1 Riverview Plaza, Cleveland 44114

**ICITA—Int'l Chain of Industrial and
Technical Advertising-Agencies**
231 Johnson Ave., Newark, N.J. 07108

Infoplan International, Inc.
1345 Ave. of Americas, New York 10019

JBS International Associates
655 Madison Ave., New York 10021

Kenyon & Eckhardt, Inc.
200 Park Ave., New York 10017

Ketchum, MacLeod & Grove, Inc.
4 Gateway Center, Pittsburgh 15222

Knoth & Meads Advertising
426 Pennsylvania Ave., San Diego 92103

Lennen & Newell, Inc.
380 Madison Ave., New York 10017

Leon, S. R., Company, Inc.
515 Madison Ave.,, New York 10022

INTERNATIONAL ADVERTISING AGENCIES
IN THE U.S.

Lief, B. W., Advertising, Inc.
304 W. 58th St., New York 10019

Magna, Ltd.
9570 Pico Blvd., Los Angeles 90035

Marplan
1414 Ave. of Americas, New York 10019

Marsteller, Inc.
866 3rd Ave., New York 10022

Mathes, J. M., Inc.
260 Madison Ave., New York 10016

McCann-Erickson, Inc.
485 Lexington Ave., New York 10017

Meltzer, Aron & Lemen, Inc.
165 Post, San Francisco 94108

Meyerhoff, Arthur Associates
410 N. Michigan Ave., Chicago 60611

Modern Merchandising Bureau, Inc.
183 Madison Ave., New York 10016

National Bakers Service, Inc.
1747 Van Buren St.,
Hollywood, Fla. 33020

National Export Advertising Service, Inc.
271 Madison Ave., New York 10016

Needham, Harper & Steers, Inc.
909 3rd Ave., New York 10022

Norman, Craig & Kummel, Inc.
488 Madison Ave., New York 10022

Ogilvy & Mather, Inc.
2 East 48th St., New York 10017

Oliver-Beckman, Inc.
748 Lexington Ave., New York 10022

Papert, Koenig, Lois, Inc.
488 Madison Ave., New York 10022

Passante, D. L. Associates, Inc.
1619 Broadway, New York 10019

Post-Keyes-Gardner, Inc.
827 N. Michigan Ave., Chicago 60611

Pritchard, Wood, Inc.
1345 Ave. of Americas, New York 10019

Publicis Corp.
610 5th Ave., New York 10020

Quadrant International, Inc.
1271 Ave. of Americas, New York 10020

Reuter & Bragdon, Inc.
4 Gateway Center, Pittsburgh 15222

Roy, Ross, Inc.
2751 E. Jefferson Ave.,
Detroit, Mich. 48207

Ruder & Finn, Inc.
110 E. 59 St., New York 10022

SSC&B, Inc., Advertising
575 Lexington Ave., New York 10022

Scott, M. B., Inc.
8721 Sunset Blvd., Los Angeles 90069

Swink, Howard, Advertising, Inc.
372 E. Center, Marion, Ohio 43302

Taylor & Associates Advertising, Ltd.
222 S. W. Harrison, Portland 97201

Thompson, J. Walter, Company
420 Lexington Ave., New York 10017

Tyson, O. S. and Company, Inc.
475 Park Ave. S., New York 10016

Universal Public Relations, Inc.
420 Lexington Ave., New York 10017

Van Brunt & Company, Inc.
711 3rd Ave., New York 10017

Warwick & Legler, Inc.
375 Park Ave., New York 10022

Waters, Norman D., & Associates, Inc.
360 Lexington Ave., New York

Wells, Rich & Greene, Inc.
767 5th Ave., New York

Woods, Donegan & Company, Inc.
400 Madison Ave., New York 10017

Wunderman, Ricotta & Kline, Inc.
575 Madison Avenue, New York

Young & Rubicam, Inc.
285 Madison Ave., New York 10017

Reprinted by permission of Dun-Donnelley Publishing Corporation

Overseas Advertising Directory

A Geographical Listing of American Agencies Having
Overseas Branches and Affiliates

ARGENTINA

Benton & Bowles, Inc.
Burnett, Leo Co.
Coordinated Communications, Inc.
Grant Advertising
Kenyon & Eckhardt
Marplan
McCann-Erickson
Ogilvy & Mather
Thompson, J. Walter
Van Brunt & Co., Inc.

AUSTRALIA

Bates, Ted & Co.
Burnett, Leo Co.
Compton Advertising
Coordinated Communications, Inc.
Foote, Cone & Belding
Graff, Harry W., Inc.
Grant Advertising
Gray & Kilgore, Inc.
Grey & Davis, Inc.
Howard, Edward & Co.
ICITA
Infoplan
Marplan
McCann-Erickson
Needham, Harper & Steers
Ogilvy & Mather
Pritchard, Wood
Quadrant International
Thompson, J. Walter
Van Brunt & Co., Inc.
Young & Rubicam

AUSTRIA

Batten, Barton, Durstine & Osborn
Cutler & Edmonds International
Dancer-Fitzgerald-Sample, Inc.
Graff, Harry W., Inc.
Grey & Davis, Inc.
McCann-Erickson
Needham, Harper & Steers
Ogilvy & Mather
Thompson, J. Walter
Van Brunt & Co., Inc.
Young & Rubicam

BARBADOS

Compton Advertising
McCann-Erickson

BELGUIM

Bates, Ted & Co.
Batten, Barton, Durstine & Osborn
Benton & Bowles
Compton Advertising
Coordinated Communications, Inc.
D'Arcy-MacManus-Intermarco, Inc.
Foote, Cone & Belding
Gardner Advertising
Gray & Kilgore, Inc.
Grey & Davis, Inc.
Griswold-Eshleman Co.
ICITA
Kenyon & Eckhardt
Marplan
Marsteller, Inc.
McCann-Erickson
Needham, Harper & Steers
Norman, Craig & Kummel
Ogilvy & Mather, Inc.
Pritchard, Wood
Publicis Corp.
Thompson, J. Walter
Van Brunt & Co., Inc.
Young & Rubican

BERMUDA

Compton Advertising

BRAZIL

Burnett, Leo Co.
Grant Advertising
ICITA
Infoplan
Kenyon & Eckhardt
Marplan
McCann-Erickson
Ogilvy & Mather
Pritchard, Wood
Quadrant International
Thompson, J. Walter
Van Brunt & Co., Inc.

CANADA

Advertising Associates
Bates, Ted & Co.
Batten, Barton, Durstine & Osborn
Benton & Bowles, Inc.
Burnett, Leo Co.
Communications Affiliates

Overseas Advertising Directory

A Geographical Listing of American Agencies Having
Overseas Branches and Affiliates

CANADA (Cont'd.)

Coordinated Communications, Inc.
D'Arcy-MacManus-Intermarco, Inc.
Doyle Dane Bernbach, Inc.
Dreher Advertising
Foote, Cone & Belding
Fuller & Smith & Ross
Grant Advertising
Gray & Kilgore, Inc.
Grey & Davis, Inc.
Hodes-Daniel Co.
ICITA
Kenyon & Eckhardt
Lennen & Newell
Leon, S. R. Co.
Marplan
Marsteller, Inc.
Mathens, J. M. (Freeman, Mathes
& Milne Ltd.)
McCann-Erickson
Meyerhoff, Arthur Associates
National Bakers Service
Needham, Harper & Steers
Norman, Craig & Kummel
Ogilvy & Mather
Roy, Ross
Ruder & Finn
Swink, Howard Advertising
Thompson, J. Walter
Van Brunt & Co., Inc.
Young & Rubicam

CEYLON

Grant Advertising
Gray & Kilgore, Inc.
Thompson, J. Walter

CHILE

Grant Advertising
Kenyon & Eckhardt
Marplan
McCann-Erickson
Thompson, J. Walter

COLOMBIA

Burnett, Leo Co.
Kenyon & Eckhardt
McCann-Erickson
Ogilvy & Mather
Van Brunt & Co., Inc.

COSTA RICA

McCann-Erickson
Van Brunt & Co., Inc.

DENMARK

Bates, Ted & Co.
Compton Advertising
Dancer-Fitzgerald-Sample, Inc.
D'Arcy-Manus-Intermarco
Foote, Cone & Belding
Grant Advertising
Gray & Kilgore, Inc.
ICITA
Needham, Harper & Steers
Norman, Craig & Kummel
Thompson, J. Walter
Van Brunt & Co., Inc.
Young & Rubicam

EAST PAKISTAN

Grant Advertising

ECUADOR

McCann-Erickson
Van Brunt & Co., Inc.

EL SALVADOR

McCann-Erickson
Oliver-Beckman

ENGLAND

(see United Kingdom)

FIJI

Gray & Kilgore, Inc.

FINLAND

Compton Advertising
D'Arcy-MacManus-Intermarco
Gray & Kilgore, Inc.
ICITA
Marplan
McCann-Erickson
Quadrant International
Van Brunt & Co., Inc.

FRANCE

Bates, Ted & Co.
Batten, Barton, Durstine & Osborn
Benton & Bowles, Inc.
Black-Russell-Morris

FRANCE (Cont'd.)

Burnett, Leo Co.
Compton Advertising
Coordinated Communications, Inc.
Dancer-Fitzgerald-Sample, Inc.
D'Arcy-MacManus-Intermarco, Inc.
DeGarmo, McCaffery
Doyle Dane Bernbach, Inc.
Foote, Cone & Belding
Gray & Kilgore, Inc.
Grey & Davis, Inc.
ICITA
Infoplan
Kenyon & Eckhardt
Ketchum, MacLeod & Grove, Inc.
Lennen & Newell
Leon, S. R. Co.
Lief, B. W. Advertising
Marplan
Marsteller, Inc.
McCann-Erickson
Needham, Harper & Steers
Norman, Craig & Kummel
Ogilvy & Mather
Pritchard, Wood
Publicis Corp.
Quadrant International
Reuter & Bragdon
Ruder & Finn
Scott, M. B., Inc.
Thompson, J. Walter
Van Brunt & Co., Inc.
Waters, Norman D., & Associates
Wells, Rich & Greene
Woods, Donegan & Co.
Wunderman, Ricotta & Kline, Inc.
Young & Rubicam

GERMANY

Bates, Ted & Co.
Batten, Barton, Durstine & Osborn
Benton & Bowles
Black-Russell-Morris
Burnett, Leo Co.
Compton Advertising
Coordinated Communications, Inc.
Dancer-Fitzgerald-Sample, Inc.
D'Arcy-MacManus-Intermarco, Inc.
Doyle Dane Bernbach, Inc.
Foote, Cone & Belding
Frohlich, L. W. & Co.

Graff, Harry W.
Gray & Kilgore, Inc.
Grey & Davis, Inc.
Infoplan
Kenyon & Eckhardt
Ketchum, MacLeod & Grove, Inc.
Marplan
Marstellar, Inc.
McCann-Erickson
Needham, Harper & Steers
Norman, Craig & Kummel
Ogilvy & Mather
Oliver-Beckman
Pritchard, Wood
Publicis Corp.
Reuter & Bragdon
Thompson, J. Walter
Van Brunt & Co., Inc.
Young & Rubicam

GREECE

Gray & Kilgore, Inc.

GUATEMALA

Marplan
McCann-Erickson

HONDURAS

McCann-Erickson

HONG KONG

Bates, Ted & Co.
Burnett, Leo Co.
Compton Advertising
Grant Advertising
Gray & Kilgore, Inc.
Marplan
McCann-Erickson
Needham, Harper & Steers
Taylor & Associates Advertising
Van Brunt & Co., Inc.
Wells, Rich & Greene

INDIA

Grant Advertising
ICITA
McCann-Erickson
Needham, Harper & Steers
Thompson, J. Walter
Van Brunt & Co., Inc.

IRAN

ICITA
Van Brunt & Co., Inc.

Overseas Advertising Directory

A Geographical Listing of American Agencies Having
Overseas Branches and Affiliates

IRELAND

Van Brunt & Co., Inc.

ISRAEL

Ruder & Finn

ITALY

Ayer & Son, N.W., Inc.
Bates, Ted & Co.
Batten, Barton, Durstine & Osborn
Benton & Bowles
Burnett, Leo Co.
Compton Advertising
Dancer-Fitzgerald-Sample, Inc.
D'Arcy-MacManus-Intermarco, Inc.
Foote, Cone & Belding
Gray & Kilgore, Inc.
Grey & Davis, Inc.
ICITA
Kenyon & Eckhardt
Marplan
McCann-Erickson
Needham, Harper & Steers
Norman, Craig & Kummel
Ogilvy & Mather
Oliver-Beckman
Pritchard, Wood
Rudder & Finn
Thompson, J. Walter
Van Brunt & Co., Inc.
Young & Rubicam

JAMAICA

Compton Advertising
Kenyon & Eckhardt
McCann-Erickson
Norman, Craig & Kummel

JAPAN

Adler, William Hart, Inc.
Bates, Ted & Co.
Botsford, Ketchum, Inc.
Burnett, Leo Co.
Communications Affiliates
Compton Advertising
Coordinated Communications, Inc.
Culver Advertising, Inc.
Frohlich, L. W. & Co./Intercon
Grant Advertising
Gray & Kilgore, Inc.
Grey & Davis, Inc.

Infoplan
Marplan
McCann-Erickson
Ruder & Finn
Thompson, J. Walter
Van Brunt & Co., Inc

KENYA

Grant Advertising
Needham, Harper & Steers

LEBANON

Grant Advertising
Gray & Kilgore, Inc.
Young & Rubicam

MALAWI

Burnett, Leo Co.

MALAYSIA

Bates, Ted & Co.
Burnett, Leo Co.
Grant Advertising
McCann-Erickson
Needham, Harper & Steers

MALTA

Van Brunt & Co., Inc.

MEXICO

Burnett, Leo Co.
Compton Advertising
D'Arcy-MacManus-Intermarco, Inc.
Doyle Dane Bernbach, Inc.
Foote, Cone & Belding
Glenn Advertising
Grant Advertising
Infoplan
Kenyon & Eckhardt
Knoth & Meads Advertising
Lennen & Newell
Leon, S. R. Co.
Marplan
McCann-Erickson
Norman, Craig & Kummel, Inc.
Ogilvy & Mather
Oliver-Beckman
Pritchard, Wood, Inc.
Thompson, J. Walter
Van Brunt & Co., Inc.
Young & Rubicam

Overseas Advertising Directory

A Geographical Listing of American Agencies Having
Overseas Branches and Affiliates

NETHERLANDS

Bates, Ted & Co.
Batten, Barton, Durstine & Osborn
Benton & Bowles
Burnett, Leo Co.
Compton Advertising
Coordinated Communications, Inc.
Dancer-Fitzgerald-Sample, Inc.
D'Arcy-MacManus-Intermarco, Inc.
Foote, Cone & Belding
Gardner Advertising
Gray & Kilgore, Inc.
Grey & Davis, Inc.
ICITA
Kenyon & Eckhardt
Marplan
McCann-Erickson
Needham, Harper & Steers
Norman, Craig & Kummel
Ogilvy & Mather
Thompson, J. Walter
Van Brunt & Co., Inc.
Young & Rubicam

NEW ZEALAND

Burnett, Leo Co.
Gray & Kilgore, Inc.
McCann-Erickson
Ogilvy & Mather
Van Brunt & Co., Inc.

NIGERIA

Grant Advertising

NICARAGUA

McCann-Erickson

NORWAY

Bates, Ted & Co.
Compton Advertising
D'Arcy-MacManus-Intermarco, Inc.
Gray & Kilgore, Inc.
ICITA
Norman, Craig & Kummel
Van Brunt & Co., Inc.
Young & Rubicam

OKINAWA

McCann-Erickson

PAKISTAN

Grant Advertising

ICITA
Thompson, J. Walter
Van Brunt & Co., Inc.

PANAMA

Grant Advertising
McCann-Erickson

PERU

McCann-Erickson
Thompson, J. Walter
Van Brunt & Co.
Wells, Rich, Greene

PHILIPPINES

Compton Advertising
Grant Advertising
Marplan
McCann-Erickson
Thompson, J. Walter
Van Brunt & Co., Inc.

PORTUGAL

Burnett, Leo Co.
Gray & Kilgore, Inc.
ICITA
Marplan
McCann-Erickson
Needham, Harper & Steers
Norman, Craig & Kummel
Van Brunt & Co., Inc.

PUERTO RICO

Burnett, Leo Co.
Compton Advertising
Esty, William, Company, Inc.
ICITA
Kenyon & Eckhardt
Lennen & Newell
McCann-Erickson
National Export Adv. Service, Inc.
Norman, Craig & Kummel
Passante, D. L. Associates
Quadrant International
Roy, Ross
SSC&B
Thompson, J. Walter
Young & Rubicam

RHODESIA*

Burnett, Leo Co.
Grant Advertising
Thompson, J. Walter

*ZIMBABWE

Overseas Advertising Directory

A Geographical Listing of American Agencies Having
Overseas Branches and Affiliates

SANTO DOMINGO

Compton Advertising
Kenyon & Eckhardt
Young & Rubicam

SAUDI ARABIA

Gray & Kilgore, Inc.

SCOTLAND

Graff, Harry W., Inc.

SINGAPORE

Bates, Ted & Co.
Burnett, Leo Co.
Grant Advertising
McCann-Erickson

SOUTH AFRICA

Burnett, Leo Co.
Grant Advertising
Gray & Kilgore, Inc.
Ogilvy & Mather
Quadrant International
Thompson, J. Walter
Van Brunt & Co., Inc.

SPAIN

Bates, Ted & Co.
Burnett, Leo Co.
Cutler & Edmonds International
D'Arcy-MacManus-Intermarco, Inc.
Foote, Cone & Belding
Graff, Harry W., Inc.
ICITA
Kenyon & Eckhardt
Lennen & Newell
Marplan
McCann-Erickson
Needham, Harper & Steers
Norman, Craig & Kummel
Posner & Mitchell
Pritchard, Wood
Publicis Corp.
Thompson, J. Walter
Van Brunt & Co., Inc.
Young & Rubicam

SWEDEN

Bates, Ted & Co.
Compton Advertising
D'Arcy-MacManus-Intermarco, Inc.

Drew, A., & Co. Advertising, Inc.
Foote, Cone & Belding
Gray & Kilgore, Inc.
ICITA
Marplan
McCann-Erickson
Needham, Harper & Steers
Norman, Craig & Kummel
Oliver-Beckman
Pritchard, Wood
Quadrant International
Van Brunt & Co., Inc.
Young & Rubicam

SWITZERLAND

Ally, Carl, Inc.
Coordinated Communications, Inc.
Dancer Fitzgerald Sample, Inc.
D'Arcy-MacManus-Intermarco, Inc.
Graff, Harry W., Inc.
Gray & Kilgore, ,Inc.
ICITA
Marsteller, Inc.
McCann-Erickson
Norman, Craig & Gummel
Oliver-Beckman
Publicis Corp.
Taylor & Associates Advertising
Thompson, J. Walter
Van Brunt & Co.
Young & Rubicam

TAIWAN

Grant Advertising
Van Brunt & Co., Inc.

THAILAND

Bates, Ted & Co.
Burnett, Leo Co.
Coordinated Communications, Inc.
Grant Advertising
Marplan
McCann-Erickson
Van Brunt & Co., Inc.

TRINIDAD, W.I.

Compton Advertising
Kenyon & Eckhardt
McCann-Erickson
Norman, Craig & Kummel

Overseas Advertising Directory

A Geographical Listing of American Agencies Having
Overseas Branches and Affiliates

UNITED KINGDOM

Bates, Ted & Co.
Batten, Barton, Durstine & Osborn
Benton & Bowles
Black-Russell-Morris
Bows Company, The
Botsford, Ketchum, Inc.
Compton Advertising
Culver Advertising
Dancer-Fitzgerald-Sample, Inc.
D'Arcy-MacManus-Intermarco, Inc.
DeGarmo, McCaffery
Denhard & Stewart
Doremus & Co.
Doyle Dane Bernbach, Inc.
Free, F. William & Co., Inc.
Foote, Cone & Belding
Fuller & Smith & Ross
Gardner Advertising
Geer, DuBois
Graff, Harry W.
Gray & Kilgore, Inc.
Grant Advertising
Grey & Davis, Inc.
Holley-Thomas
ICITA
Infoplan
Kenyon & Eckhardt
Ketchum, MacLeod & Grove, Inc.
Lief, B. W. Advertising
Lennen & Newell
Les Strang Advertising
Marplan
Marsteller, Inc.
Mathes, J. M. (Freeman, Mathes & Milne)
McCann-Erickson
Meltzer, Aron & Lemen
Modern Merchandising Bureau

Needham, Harper & Steers
Norman, Craig & Kummel
Ogilvy & Mather
Oliver-Beckman
Papert, Moenig, Lois
Post-Keyes-Gardner
Pritchard, Wood
Publicis Corp.
Quadrant International
Ruder & Finn
Taylor & Associates
Thompson, J. Walter
Universal Public Relations
Van Brunt & Co., Inc.
Warwick & Legler, Inc.
Wells, Rich & Greene, Inc.
Wunderman, Ricotta & Kline, Inc.
Young & Rubicam

URUGUAY

McCann-Erickson
Thompson, J. Walter
Van Brunt & Co., Inc.

VENEZUELA

Compton Advertising
Grant Advertising
Grey & Davis, Inc.
Kenyon & Eckhardt
McCann-Erickson
Ogilvy & Mather
Thompson, J. Walter
Van Brunt & Co., Inc.
Young & Rubicam

ZAMBIA

Grant Advertising
Thompson, J. Walter

Thiokol international newsletter

Case Histories of Polysulfide Polymer Base Products
Number 15

Shortly before this photograph was taken, there was a parking lot on the corner. A conventional foundation and basement were first constructed and then, the seven story building was assembled in just five days.

Built by Co. Montagebau Hamburg, G.m.b.H., this demonstration project proved that it is possible to build a defect-free building in a very short time using prefabricated components. More important, it proved that with proper planning and timing, such a building can be precisely assembled with no sacrifice of quality or workmanship.

The saving of time demonstrated through this experiment can be attributed to the long experience of the people involved, combined with considerable planning, preparation and coordination. It is an excellent example of how time-proven materials can be effectively combined with modern building technology.

The facade of the building is quite plain though pleasing; without non-functional frills. The structural form essentially arises from the construction methods employed.

The sandwich panels were fabricated by the contractor, using heavy concrete, styrofoam slabs, some concrete facings with others of glass and ceramic. The panels were produced by the Camus process, with hot-air hardening, according to a definite time-proven schedule. The efficiency of this process was demonstrated during the assembly period when one of the panels had to be newly fabricated. Even with the little time available, the panel went through the normal production cycle.

The assembly of the panels went as well as their fabrication. The joints between the panels were not tapered at all. What little variation that could be measured was negligible and certainly not noticeable to the naked eye. A primer was first used on all of the joints. These were then sealed with "Formflex VM-350," a building sealant based on Thiokol's LP® polysulfide polymers supplied by Formflex, G.m.b.H.

SEVEN STORIES IN FIVE DAYS

...a product of successful timing.

Thiokol Chemical Corporation publishes a four-page, two-color newsletter for builders, architects and contractors abroad. Each issue features a case history of some project in which its product was used.

Chapter 44

COMPUTERS IN SALES PROMOTION

"IN EFFECT, the computer is a very-high-speed clerk with a perfect memory and zero intelligence," writes Charles G. McGee in *Graphic Arts Monthly.* "Once you have explained to the computer (programming) exactly what you want it to do, it will do it without fail. ... All *you* have to do is learn the language."

Computers are the greatest advance in marketing and advertising since the creation of the human mind, said Vincent M. Petrilli, vice-president of Young & Rubicam, Chicago, at the annual meeting of the eighth district, Advertising Federation of America.

Mr. Petrilli said computers ought to be described as relation machines, or "What will happen if I do?" machines.

"Very simply, what these machines have to offer is multiple-dimensional experimentation with the object of providing us with better questions to ask," he said.

"Dependent and interdependent marketing relationships are something we have never had a chance to investigate before. With computers we have begun to get the tools to think about marketing problems in a number of dimensions at the same time."

Washington researcher Stanley Foster Reed, in his remarks titled, "The Outlook for Computers in Direct Mail Promotion," at the Direct Mail Advertising Association annual conference in Washington, said: "I've never seen an industry which could use computers better."

Here are some of the other comments which were made at the conference:

"I personally believe that the punched card is on the way out as an input device to computers—especially for direct mail.

"It seems to me entirely possible, with an elaborate shorthand, or abbreviations of commonly used words and phrases, that the input effort could be reduced to 25% of that for the typing of the entire name and address.

"With our names in the computer, duplicates can easily be eliminated and names can be rearranged in any order, totaled by area of any of the other classifications that might be desired, depending on the depth of the coding.

"With our names in the computer, it is also possible to do some market analysis. You can set up yield criteria for your sales promotion targets so that when returns do come in, you can discover the low yield areas and search for the reasons.

"It might be possible to write individual letters to individual people, millions of them, and all the letters would be different.

"With the high-speed printer, it should be possible to put together a constant succession of new and different letters, to correlate the response with the characteristics of the person, and to optimize the mailings to people of a similar nature. I believe that if this were done in an actual mailing—say for a subscription campaign, it could have the effect of doubling the return from half the list, provided that the list is big enough.

"In a few years you will have line-printers in elite type that will be able to duplicate a typewritten letter exactly."

Quoting *The Philadelphia Inquirer,* computers will permeate and invade almost every field of human endeavor and they will particularly affect communications.

Communications is nothing more than the movement and transmission of information. Computers, like the human brain, can handle, process, manipulate, and correlate information.

The world now finds computers aiding in the diagnosis and care of patients in clinics and hospitals, the teaching of students in schools, the operation of manufacturing in factories, the presentation of legal arguments in court, the looking-up of information in libraries, the apprehension of criminals by police departments and the direction and control of traffic on land, on sea, and in the air.

Computers operate so swiftly they can handle many different tasks "at the same time." They perform their operations in microseconds (millionths of a second), an interval too short to be comprehended by man. One microsecond is to an hour as an hour is to a century.

IBM System/370 Models: Computers range, in functions, size and capacity, from desk-top models to great complex systems. IBM has now marketed two very complex System/370 models 158 and 168. They use new programming systems and are equipped with memory faculties that enable them to run many kinds of programs

IBM System 370, Model 135, extends advanced technology to thousands of users of medium-size and smaller computers. It offers large-capacity memory, direct access storage and optional features that provide economical data communications.

automatically. The new models cost from $2.3 million to $7.3 million each. Some existing medium-size System/370's will be able to use the new programs without change; larger systems can be converted for $200,000 to $400,000. Other IBM computers are available, of course, for less complex functions.

A computer anyone can use: Low-cost IBM System 3, Model 6, is designed for use in any office. Here, a manager looks over a sales report printed from data entered through the keyboard. An optional television-like display unit (left) can be used to answer quickly a customer inquiry or to display other needed material.

Electronic Newspapers of the Future

The "newspaper" of the future may be electronic. Readers may get their news on a television screen or on a wall panel or on a private teleprinter, or on some combination of these.

One thing is certain: Computers will play a major role in the collection, editing, and distribution of news in 1985. Not only will they affect the nature of the final "news product" that the public sees, but computers will radically change the "internal workings" of newspapers and of radio and TV stations.

The Oklahoma Publishing Company's two newspapers, the *Daily Oklahoman* and the *Oklahoma City Times,* have a capacity for producing 24,000 lines of type per hour through the use of two powerful computers.

Each of the computers can produce justified and hyphenated paper tape for automatic typesetting machines at up to 12,000 30-character lines an hour.

Robert B. Spahn, production manager of the newspapers, said the system is also being used for the photocomposition of display advertising. Similar to the linecasting operation, the teletype operator includes a series of short codes in the paper tape. These instructions are recognized by the computer which determines font, size, measure, and position of copy on film or paper. The computer-produced tape is then fed directly to the photocomp machine.

Another feature of the computer is a disk-storage device giving the computer direct access to any number of type fonts and to an "exception word" dictionary. This provides the computer with 99% hyphenation accuracy.

The computer uses the new microelectronic circuits which operate at billionths-of-a-second speeds. It can perform as many as 120,000 additions in one second.

Among good examples of computer application to the preparation of editorial and sales promotion copy is the IBM Administrative Terminal System.

This system eliminates the tedious, repetitious steps of text preparation. Graphic reproduction specialists, writers, secretaries, and technicians can enter data or edit information by operating their own typewriters, which are on-line to a computer.

A writer can transmit his information directly from a keyboard to computer files. Data is held in accessible storage while he proofreads and edits what was typed on the printer as he transmitted his information. He can make editorial changes and they will be accommodated automatically in the stored data.

The system consists of a combination of operating programs, data-processing and related equipment, especially prepared to handle text. It will handle any combination of spaces, characters, words, sentences, or paragraphs in any sequence and entered at any period of time.

The system stores information in the computer and, upon demand, returns the information automatically as typewritten data.

Some of its capabilities are: (a) to enter information through a typewriter keyboard; (b) to replace a word, phrase, or sentence in text which has been entered or recalled from storage; (c) add or delete lines or sentences; (d) copy information; (e) transmit information to any other terminal or to a card punch or magnetic tape; (f) store or retrieve any definite set of information, and (g) produce precisely formated output from rough input, including such features as automatic page heading, footing, pagination, and right-margin justification.

The IBM Type Composition Program allows the computer to accept unjustified paper-tape input. This input not only contains the copy to be set, but also instructions telling how it is to appear on the printed page. The program then justifies and hyphenates the copy, and produces new tape for controlling the operation of line-casting equipment. The program is flexible enough to handle a wide variety of type fonts, formats, and column measures.

Since both copy and format definition instructions are combined on the input tape, the system must be able to distinguish between them. This is accomplished by a single character, the format instruction signifier, represented by the familiar dollar sign ($). If this dollar sign is followed by an appropriate alphabetical character, the information that follows is interpreted as an instruction. The instruction indicates how the basic program is to be modified to perform the function designated. Upon sensing the $ signifier, the program is placed in a special operating mode, which interprets the instruction and performs the required modification.

Of course, computers are valuable in marketing, research, and in controlling sales promotion expense.

Instant Advertising Analysis

Sales executives of Schenley Industries have instant access to a complete breakdown of advertising, merchandising, and promotion expenditures on their brands in any of the country's trade areas.

The advertising data will be added to a two-way, computerized, data-reporting system, which links Schenley's offices with a computer memory drum in Bunker-Ramo Corporation's Telecenter.

With the system, Schenley personnel may punch a keyed code into a transmitter-receiver desk console and receive an answer from the Telecenter in less than a second. In addition to expenditures by brand, region and medium, the system also will provide comparable data for the previous year or an increment of the previous year.

Computerized Mailing Lists

A good example of computerized mailing list selection and maintenance is afforded by R. L. Polk & Co. One hundred and twelve years old, employer of more than 5,000 persons, and international in scope, R. L. Polk & Co. furnishes business and industry with a wide range of services.

Sperry Univac System 90/25 is designed to satisfy a wide range of information processing requirements with speed and power. The company states that it offers users "simplicity of operation, stability of performance. It may be augmented by an array of peripherals which can be integrally attached to the central processor."

These include the publishing of more than 1,200 city directories, the compilation of statistics on new vehicle registrations and truck ownership for the automotive and allied industries, the semi-annual publication of *Polk's Bank Directory,* and complete direct mail marketing services. The company also offers banks and savings associations syndicated promotion packages.

A pioneer in electronic data processing, Polk constantly has upgraded its electronic equipment to keep up with the ever-growing volume of information it must process.

Today, the computer centers include two IBM 370/155 computer systems and an IBM 370/145.

A chief function of the computers is to select from Polk's huge file of more than 85 million car owners those prospects identified by name, address, and make, year model, series, and body style of car owned. Selection also is available on America's truck owners on the basis of make, age, weight, and number of trucks owned.

The L 7500 magnetic record computer is the newest and most powerful of Burroughs Series L commercial mini-computers. Series L systems extend the power of electronic data processing to thousands of small businesses.

Prospects also can be picked on the basis of where they live—even down to certain postal zones, census tracts, or dealer areas. Once the prospects are selected, their names and addresses are printed out for addressing mail advertisements.

Clients using this list may select their prospects by such factors as occupation, size of family, age range of children, whether wife works, whether home is owned or rented and, finally, but economic quality of the neighborhood. Since most of Polk's city directories are recompiled annually, about 80% of this list will be updated every year.

What of the Future

We have seen how the computer has made its presence felt in printing, in market research, and in mailing-list selection and maintenance. That is only the beginning. As with the desk-type photo copier, some day there will be a desk-type computer in every office. As more uses are found, more units produced, and new engineering developments facilitate manufacturing, prices will lower and markets widen.

Obviously, any device which can perform intricate tasks with such amazing speed will be increasingly applied throughout industry. Its economic effects are already visible in its use in automatic manufacturing. As a marketing tool, its future is practically unlimited. As a social instrument, it will surely create a different world through its applications in education, communications, travel, and the creation of leisure time.

APPENDIX

Media for Advertising and Publicity

A list of newspapers and radio and television stations for advertising, publicity and public relations purposes. For rates, write direct to media or consult the current *Standard Rate and Data Service* catalogs.

State and City	Newspapers	Radio		TV
ALABAMA Birmingham	News (e) Post-Herald (m)	WAPI WAPI(FM) WATV WBUL WCRT WDJC(FM) WENN WENN(FM) WERC WJLD	WKXX(FM) WLPH WQEZ(FM) WSGN WVOK WVOK(FM) WYAM WYDE WZZK(FM)	WAPI-TV (NBC) WBMG-TV (CBS) WBRC-TV (ABC)
Huntsville	News (m) Times (e)	WAAY WAHR(FM) WEUP	WFIX WNDA(FM) WVOV	WAAY-TV (ABC) WHNT-TV (CBS) WYUR-TV (NBC)
Mobile	Press (e) Register (m) Press-Register (S)	WABB WABB(FM) WBLX WGOK WKRG WKRG(FM) WKSJ	WKSJ(FM) WLIQ WLPR(FM) WMOB WMOO WUNI	WALA-TV (NBC) WKRG-TV (CBS)
ALASKA Anchorage	News (m) Times (e)	KANC KBYR KENI KFQD KGOT	KHAR KKLV KNIK(FM) KYAK	KENI-TV (NBC) KIMO (ABC) KTVA (CBS)
ARIZONA Phoenix	Gazette (e) Republic (m)	KASA KBBC(FM) KDKB KDKB(FM) KDOT(FM) KHCS KHEP KHEP(FM) KIFN KIOG(FM) KJJJ KMEO KMEO(FM) KNIX KNIX(FM) KOOL	KOOL(FM) KOY KPHX KQXE KRDS KRFM KRIZ KRUX KSGR KTAR KUPD KUPD(FM) KWAO KXIV KXTC(FM)	KOOL-TV (CBS) KPHO-TV KTAR-TV (N°C) KTVK-TV (ABC)
Tucson	Citizen (e) Star (m)	KAIR KCEE KCEE(FM) KCUB KEVT KFMM(FM) KHYT KIKX	KJYK(FM) KMGX KOPO KRQQ(FM) KTKT KTUC KWFM(FM) KXEW	KGUN-TV (ABC) KOLD-TV (CBS) KVOA-TV (NBC) KZAZ-TV
ARKANSAS Little Rock	Arkansas Democrat (e) Arkansas Gazette (m)	KAAY KARN KDXE KEZQ(FM) KKYK(FM) KLAZ	KLAZ(FM) KLRA KOKY KSOH KXLR KXXA(FM)	KARK-TV (NBC) KATV (ABC) KTHV (CBS)

Source: Standard Rate & Data Service, Inc.

Media for Advertising and Publicity

State and City	Newspapers	Radio		TV
CALIFORNIA Bakersfield	California (e)	KAFY KERN KGEE KGFM(FM) KKXX	KLYD KLYD(FM) KPMC KUZZ KWAC	KBAK-TV (ABC) KERO-TV (NBC) KJTV (CBS)
Fresno	Bee (m)	KARM KBIF KEAP KFIG(FM) KFRE KFRY KFYE(FM) KGST	KIRV KKNU(FM) KMAK KMJ KMJ(FM) KXEX KYNO KYNO(FM)	KAIL-TV KFSN-TV (CBS) KFTV KJEO (ABC) KMJ-TV (NBC) KMPH-TV
Los Angeles- Long Beach	Herald-Examiner(e) Indep. (m) (Long Beach) Press-Telegram (e) (Long Beach) Times (m) (L.A.) Indep.-Press-Telegram (S) (Long Beach)	KABC KBCA(FM) KBIG KFAC KFAC(FM) KFI KFOX KFWB KGBS(FM) KGER KHJ KHOF(FM) KIIS KIIS(FM) KIQQ(FM) KJOI	KLAC KLOS(FM) KLVE(FM) KMET(FM) KMPC KNAC KNOB KNX KNX(FM) KOST(FM) KPOL KPOL(FM) KRTH(FM) KTNQ KWST(FM)	KABC-TV (ABC) KCOP KHJ-TV KMEX-TV KNBC (NBC) KNXT (CBS) KTLA KTTV KWHY
Oxnard-Ventura	News Chronicle (e) (Thousand Oaks) Press-Courier (e) (Oxnard)	KAAP KAAP(FM) KACY KACY(FM) KBBQ KBBY(FM)	KDAR KGAB KHAY(FM) KOXR KVEN	
Riverside-San Bernardino-Ontario	Enterprise (m)(Riverside) Press (e) (Riverside) Press-Enterprise (Sat., S) (Riverside) Sun-Telegram (m) (San Bernardino)	KBBL(FM) KBON KCAL KCAL(FM) KCKC KDUO(FM) KFXM	KHNY KHNY(FM) KMEN KOLA(FM) KPRO KQLH(FM)	KHOF-TV
Sacramento- Stockton	Bee (e) (Sacramento) Union (m) (Sacramento) Record (e) (Stockton)	KCRA KCTC(FM) KEWT(FM) KFBK KFBK(FM) KGMS KJAY KNDE	KPIP(FM) KPOP KRAK KROI(FM) KROY KXOA(FM) KZAP(FM)	KCRA-TV (NBC) KLOC-TV KMUV-TV KOVR-TV (ABC) KXTV (CBS)
Salinas-Seaside- Monterey	Californian (e) (Salinas) Peninsula Herald (e) (Monterey)	KBEZ(FM) KCTY KDON KDON(FM) KIDD	KMBY KTOM KWAV(FM) KZEN(FM)	KMST (CBS) KSBW-TV (NBC)
San Diego	Tribune (e) Union (m)	KCBQ KEZL(FM) KFMB KFMB(FM) KFSD(FM) KGB KGB(FM) KIFM KITT(FM)	KLRO(FM) KMJC KOGO KOZN(FM) KPRI(FM) KSDO KSON KSON(FM) KYXY(FM)	KCST-TV (NBC) KFMB-TV (CBS) KGTV (ABC)

State and City	Newspapers	Radio		TV
CALIFORNIA—*Cont.*				
San Francisco-Oakland	Chronicle (m) (S.F.) Examiner (e) (S.F.) Tribune (Oakland) (e) Examiner & Chronicle (S) (S.F.)	KABL KABL(FM) KBRG(FM) KCBS KCBS(FM) KDFC(FM) KDIA KEST KFAX KFOG(FM) KFRC KGO KIOI(FM) KIQI KJAZ(FM) KKHI KKHI(FM)	KMEL KMPX(FM) KNBR KNEW KOFY KOIT KRE KRE(FM) KSAN(FM) KSFO KSFX(FM) KSOL(FM) KTIM KTIM(FM) KYA KYA(FM)	KBHK-TV KDTV KEMO-TV KGO-TV (ABC) KPIX (CBS) KRON-TV (NBC) KTVU KVOF
San Jose	Mercury (m) News (e) Mercury News (Sat.) Mercury-News (S)	KARA(FM) KBAY(FM) KEEN KEZR(FM) KLIV KLOK	KNTA KOME(FM) KPEN(FM) KSJO(FM) KXRX	KGSC-TV KNTV (ABC)
Santa Barbara	News-Press (e)	KDB KDB(FM) KIST KKIO KRUZ(FM)	KTMS KTMS(FM) KTYD KTYD(FM)	KCOY-TV (CBS) KEYT (ABC) KSBY (NBC)
COLORADO				
Colorado Springs	Gazette Telegraph (m,e,S) Sun (m)	KIIQ KIIQ(FM) KINX KKFM(FM) KPIK KPIK(FM) KRDO	KRDO(FM) KSPZ(FM) KSSS KVOR KWYD(FM) KXXV KYSN	KKTV (CBS) KOAA-TV (NBC) KRDO-TV (ABC)
Denver	Post (e) Rocky Mt. News (m)	KAAT KADX(FM) KAZY KBNO KBPI(FM) KDEN KDKO KERE KFML KHOW KIMN KIMN(FM) KLAK	KLAK(FM) KLIR(FM) KLZ KOA KOAQ(FM) KOSI KOSI(FM) KPPL(FM) KQXI KRKS KTLK KVOD(FM) KXKX(FM)	KBTV (ABC) KMGH-TV (CBS) KOA-TV (NBC) KWGN
CONNECTICUT				
Bridgeport	Post (e) Telegram (m)	WEZN(FM) WICC	WNAB	
Hartford-New Britain	Courant (m) (Hartford) Herald (e) (New Britain)	WCCC WCCC(FM) WDRC WDRC(FM) WHCN(FM) WINF WKND WKSS(FM)	WLVH(FM) WPOP WRCH(FM) KRCQ WRYM WTIC WTIC(FM)	WFSB (CBS) WHCT WHNB-TV (NBC)
New Haven	Journal-Courier (m) Register (e)	WAVZ WCDQ WELI WKCI(FM)	WNHC WPLR(FM) WYBC(FM)	WTNH-TV (ABC)

Media for Advertising and Publicity

State and City	Newspapers	Radio		TV
CONNECTICUT—*Cont.* Norwich-Groton- New London	Bulletin (m) (Norwich) Day (e) (New London)	WCTY WICH WNLC	WSUB WSUB(FM) WTYD(FM)	
Stamford	Advocate (e)	WSTC	WYRS	
Waterbury	American (e) Republican (m)	WATR WIOF(FM) WOWW	WQQW WWCO WWYZ(FM)	WATR-TV (NBC)
DELAWARE Wilmington	Journal (e) News (m) News-Journal (Sat.,S)	WAMS WDEL WILM	WJBR(FM) WSTW(FM) WTUX	
DISTRICT OF COLUMBIA	Post (m) Star (e)	WASH(FM) WAVA WAVA(FM) WCTN WDON WEAM WEEL WFAN(FM) WFAX WGAY WGAY(FM) WGMS WGMS(FM) WHFS(FM) WHUR(FM) WINX	WJMD(FM) WKYS WMAL WMZQ(FM) WOL WOOK WPGC WPGC(FM) WPIK WRC WRQX WTOP WUST WWDC WWDC(FM)	WDCA-TV WHAG-TV (NBC) WJLA-TV (ABC) WRC-TV (NBC) WTOP-TV (CBS) WTTG
FLORIDA Ft. Lauderdale- Hollywood	News (e) (Ft. Lauderdale) News & Sun-Sentinel (Sat., S) Sun-Sentinel (m) (Ft. Lauderdale) Sun-Tattler (e) (Hollywood)	WAVS WAXY(FM) WCKO(FM) WEXY WFTL WGLO(FM)	WGMA WHYI(FM) WLOD WRBD WSHE(FM) WSRF	WKID
Jacksonville	Fla. Times-Union (m) Journal (e)	WAIV(FM) WAPE WBIX WCGL WCMG WERD WEXI WIVY(FM) WJAX WJAX(FM)	WJNJ WJNJ(FM) WKTZ WKTZ(FM) WOZN WPDQ WQIK(FM) WSNY WVOJ	WJKS-TV (ABC) WJXT (CBS) WTLV (NBC)
Lakeland- Winter Haven	Ledger (e) (Lakeland) News-Chief (e) (Winter Haven)	WGTO WONN WPCV(FM) WQPD	WSIR WVFM(FM) WWAB	
Miami- Miami Beach	Herald (m) News (e) Sun-Reporter (m) (Miami Beach)	WAIA(FM) WAXY(FM) WCMQ WCMQ(FM) WEDR(FM) WFUN WGBS WIGL(FM) WINZ WINZ(FM) WIOD WKAT	WLYF(FM) WMBM WMJX WOCN WQAM WQBA WRHC WTMI(FM) WVCG WWOK WWWL(FM) WYOR(FM)	WCIX-TV WCKT (NBC) WHFT-TV WLTV WPLG-TV (ABC) WTVJ (CBS)

Media for Advertising and Publicity

State and City	Newspapers	Radio		TV
FLORIDA—*Cont.* Orlando	Sentinel-Star (all day)	WBJW WDBO WDBO(FM) WDIZ(FM) WHOO WHOO(FM)	WKIS WLOF WLOQ(FM) WNBE WORL	WDBO-TV (CBS) WESH (NBC) WFTV (ABC)
Pensacola	Journal (m) News (e) News-Journal (S)	WBOP WBOP(FM) WBSR WCOA WHWM	WJLQ(FM) WMEZ WNVY WPFA	WEAR-TV (ABC)
Tampa- St Petersburg- Clearwater	Independent (e) (St. Petersburg) Sun (e) (Clearwater) Times (m) (St. Petersburg) Times (e) (Tampa) Tribune (m) (Tampa)	WAVV WAZE WDAE WDCL WFLA WFLA(FM) WFSO WHBO WINQ WJYW WLCY WOKF(FM) WQXM(FM)	WQYK(FM) WRBQ(FM) WRXB WSOL WSST WSUN WTAN WTIS WTMP WWBA WWBA(FM) WYNF(FM) WYOU	WFLA-TV (NBC) WLCY-TV (ABC) WTOG-TV WTVT (CBS) WXLT-TV (ABC)
West Palm Beach	Palm Beach Post (m) Palm Beach Times (e) Palm Beach Post- Times (Sat., S)	WEAT WEAT(FM) WGMW(FM) WIRK WIRK(FM) WJNO	WJNO(FM) WKAO WLIZ WPBR WPOM	WPEC (ABC) WPTV (NBC)
GEORGIA Atlanta	Constitution (m) Journal (e) Journal- Constitution (Sat.,S)	WAOK WBIE(FM) WCOB WFOM WGKA WGST WGUN WIGO WIIN WKLS(FM) WLTA(FM) WPCH(FM) WPLO	WQXI WQXI(FM) WRNG WSB WSB(FM) WSSA WTJH WVEE(FM) WXAP WXLL WYNX WYZE WZGC(FM)	WAGA-TV (CBS) WANX-TV WATL-TV WSB-TV (NBC) WTCG (NBC) WXIA-TV (ABC)
Augusta	Chronicle (m) Herald (e) Chronicle-Herald (S)	WAUG WAUG(FM) WBBQ WBBQ(FM) WBIA WFNL	WGAC WGUS WGUS(FM) WRDW WTHB WZZW(FM)	WATU-TV (NBC) WJBF (ABC) WRDW-TV (CBS)
Columbus	Enquirer (m) Enquirer-Ledger (Sat.) Ledger (e) Ledger-Enquirer (S)	WCGQ(FM) WCLS WDAK WEIZ(FM) WHYD	WOKS WPNX WRBL(FM) WRCG WWRH(FM)	WRBL-TV (CBS) WTVM (ABC) WYEA-TV (NBC)
Macon	News (e) Telegraph (m) Telegraph—News (Sat.,S)	WBML WCRY(FM) WDDO WDEN WDEN(FM)	WIBB WMAZ WMAZ(FM) WNEX	WCWB-TV (NBC) WMAZ-TV (ABC,CBS)

Media for Advertising and Publicity

State and City	Newspapers	Radio		TV
HAWAII Honolulu	Advertiser (m) Star-Bulletin (e) Star-Bulletin & Advertiser (S)	KAHU KAIM KAIM(FM) KCCN KGMB KGU KHSS(FM) KHVH KIKI KIOE KISA	KKUA KNDI KOHO KORL KPOI KQMQ(FM) KULA(FM) KUMU KUMU(FM) KZOO	KGMB-TV (CBS) KHON-TV (NBC) KIKU-TV KITV (ABC)
ILLINOIS Chicago	Sun-Times (m) Tribune (all day)	WAIT WBBM WBBM(FM) WCFL WCRW WDAI(FM) WEDC WEFM(FM) WFMT(FM) WFYR(FM) WGCI WGN WIND	WJJD WJPC WLAK(FM) WLOO WLS WLUP WMAQ WMET(FM) WNIB(FM) WNIS WSBC WVON WXRT(FM)	WBBM-TV (CBS) WCIU-TV WFLD-TV WGN-TV WLS-TV (ABC) WMAQ-TV (NBC) WSNS
Peoria	Journal Star (all day)	WIRL WKZW(FM) WMBD WPEO WSIV	WSIV(FM) WSWT(FM) WWCT(FM) WXCL WZRO(FM)	WEEK-TV (NBC) WMBD-TV (CBS) WRAU-TV (ABC)
Rockford	Register-Republic (e) Star (m) Register-Star (Sat.,S)	WKKN WLUV WLUV(FM) WROK	WRRR WYFE(FM) WZOK(FM)	WIFR-TV (CBS) WREX-TV (ABC) WTVO (NBC)
INDIANA Evansville	Courier (m) Press (e) Courier & Press (S)	WGBF WIKY WIKY(FM)	WJPS WROZ WVHI(FM)	WEHT-TV (CBS) WFIE-TV (NBC) WTVW (ABC)
Fort Wayne	Journal-Gazette (m) News-Sentinel (e)	WCMX(FM) WFWR WGL WLYV	WMEE WMEF(FM) WOWO WPTH(FM)	WANE-TV (CBS) WFFT-TV WKJG-TV (NBC) WPTA (ABC)
Gary	Post-Tribune (e)	WLTH	WWCA	
Indianapolis	News (e) Star (m)	WATI WBRI WFBQ(FM) WFMS(FM) WIBC WIFE WIRE	WNAP(FM) WNDE WNTS WTLC(FM) WXLW WXTZ(FM)	WHMB-TV WISH-TV (CBS) WRTV (NBC) WTHR (ABC) WTTV
South Bend	Tribune (e)	WHME(FM) WJVA WNDU WNDU(FM)	WRBR(FM) WSBT WWJY(FM)	WHME-TV WNDU-TV (NBC) WSBT-TV (CBS) WSJV-TV (ABC)
IOWA Davenport- Moline (Ill.)- Rock Island (Ill.)	Argus (e) (Rock Island) Dispatch (e) (Moline) Quad Cities Times (all day)	KIIK(FM) KRVR KSTT KWNT WEMO(FM)	WHBF WHBF(FM) WHTT(FM) WOC WQUA	WHBF-TV (CBS) WOC-TV (NBC) WQAD-TV (ABC)

Media for Advertising and Publicity

State and City	Newspapers	Radio		TV
IOWA—*Cont.*				
Des Moines	Register (m)	KCBC	KRNQ(FM)	KCCI-TV (CBS)
	Tribune (e)	KDMI(FM)	KRNT	KVFD-TV (NBC)
		KGGO(FM)	KSO	WHO-TV (NBC)
		KIOA	KWKY	WOI-TV (ABC)
		KLYF(FM)	WHO	
		KMGK		
KANSAS				
Wichita	Beacon (e)	KAKE	KFDI(FM)	KAKE-TV (ABC)
	Eagle (m)	KARD(FM)	KFH	KARD-TV (NBC)
	Eagle-Beacon (Sat.,S)	KBRA(FM)	KICT(FM)	KAYS-TV (ABC,CBS)
		KBUL	KLEO	KCKT (NBC)
		KEYN(FM)	KWBB	KGLD
		KFDI		KTVC (CBS)
				KTVH (CBS)
				KUPK (ABC)
KENTUCKY				
Louisville	Courier-Journal (m)	WAKY	WLOU	WAVE-TV (NBC)
	Times (e)	WAMZ(FM)	WLRS(FM)	WDRB-TV
		WAVE	WQHI(FM)	WHAS-TV (CBS)
		WCSN(FM)	WREY	WLKY-TV (ABC)
		WFIA	WSTM(FM)	
		WFIA(FM)	WTMT	
		WHAS	WVEZ	
		WINN	WXVW	
		WKLO		
LOUISIANA				
Baton Rouge	Advocate (m)	WAFB(FM)	WLUX	WAFB-TV (CBS)
	State-Times (e)	WAIL	WQXY(FM)	WBRZ (ABC)
		WFMF	WXOK	WRBT (NBC)
		WIBR	WYNK	
		WJBO	WYNK(FM)	
		WLCS		
New Orleans	States-Item (e)	WBOK	WRNO(FM)	WDSU-TV (NBC)
	Times-Picayune (m)	WBYU(FM)	WSHO	WGNO-TV (ABC,
		WEZB(FM)	WSMB	CBS, NBC)
		WGSO	WTIX	WVUE-TV (ABC)
		WNNR	WVOG	WWL-TV (CBS)
		WNOE	WWL	
		WNOE(FM)	WWL(FM)	
		WNPS	WYLD	
		WQUE(FM)		
Shreveport	Journal (e)	KBCL	KOKA	KSLA-TV (CBS)
	Times (m)	KCIJ	KRMD	KTAL-TV (NBC)
		KEEL	KRMD(FM)	KTBS-TV (ABC)
		KEPT(FM)	KROK(FM)	
		KFLO	KTAL(FM)	
		KJOE	KWKH	
		KMBQ(FM)		
MARYLAND				
Baltimore	News American (e)	WAYE	WJRO	WBAL-TV (NBC)
	Sun (m & e)	WBAL	WKTK(FM)	WBFF-TV
		WBKZ(FM)	WLIF(FM)	WJZ-TV (ABC)
		WBMD	WLPL(FM)	WMAR-TV (CBS)
		WCAO	WMAR(FM)	
		WCBM	WPOC(FM)	
		WDJQ	WRBS(FM)	
		WEBB	WSID	
		WFBR	WTOW	
		WITH	WWIN	
		WIYY(FM)		
MASSACHUSETTS				
Boston	Globe (m & e)	WACQ	WCAS	WBZ-TV (NBC)
	Herald American (m)	WBCN(FM)	WCOZ(FM)	WCVB-TV (ABC)
		WBOS(FM)	WCRB	WLVI-TV
		WBZ	WEEI	WNAC-TV (CBS)

Media for Advertising and Publicity

State and City	Newspapers	Radio		TV
MASSACHUSETTS—*Cont.*				
Boston—*Cont.*		WEEI(FM)	WNTN	WSBK-TV
		WEZE	WRKO	
		WHDH	WROR(FM)	
		WHET	WRYT	
		WHRB(FM)	WSSH(FM)	
		WILD	WTTK(FM)	
		WJIB(FM)	WUNR	
		WKOX	WVBF(FM)	
		WLYN	WWEL	
		WMEX	WWEL(FM)	
		WNSR		
Lawrence-Haverhill	Eagle-Tribune (e) (Lawrence) Gazette (e) (Haverhill)	WCCM WCGY(FM)	WHAV WHAV(FM)	
Lowell	Sun (e)	WCAP WLLH	WSSH(FM)	
Springfield	News (e) Union (m) Republican (S)	WACE WAQY(FM) WDEW WHMP WHMP(FM) WHYN WHYN(FM)	WIXY WMAS WMAS(FM) WNUS WREB WSPR	WHYN-TV (ABC) WWLP (NBC)
Worcester	Gazette (e) Telegram (m)	WAAF(FM) WFTQ WNEB	WORC WSRS(FM) WTAG	WSMW-TV
MICHIGAN				
Ann Arbor	News (e)	WAAM WIQB WPAG	WPAG(FM) WSDS WYFC	
Detroit	Free Press (m) News (e)	WABX(FM) WBFG(FM) WCAR WCAR(FM) WDEE WDRQ(FM) WGPR(FM) WJLB WJR WJR(FM) WJZZ	WLDM(FM) WMUZ(FM) WMZK(FM) WOMC(FM) WQRS(FM) WRIF(FM) WWJ WWJ(FM) WWWW(FM) WXYZ	WGPR-TV WJBK-TV (CBS) WKBD-TV WWJ-TV (NBC) WXON-TV WXYZ-TV (ABC)
Flint	Journal (e)	WAMM WFDF WGMZ(FM) WKMF	WLQB WTAC WTRX WWCK(FM)	WJRT-TV (ABC)
Grand Rapids	Press (e)	WCUZ WFUR WFUR(FM) WGRD WGRD(FM) WJFM(FM) WLAV	WLAV(FM) WMAX WMLW(FM) WOOD WOOD(FM) WYGR WZZM(FM)	WKZO-TV (CBS) WOTV (NBC) WUHQ-TV (ABC) WZZM-TV (ABC)
Lansing	State-Journal (e)	WFMK(FM) WILS WILS(FM) WITL WITL(FM)	WJIM WJIM(FM) WVIC WVIC(FM)	WILX-TV (NBC) WJIM-TV (CBS)
Saginaw	News (e)	WIOG(FM) WKCQ(FM) WKNX	WSAM WSGW WWWS(FM)	WEYI-TV (CBS) WNEM-TV (NBC)
MINNESOTA				
Duluth-Superior (Wisc.)	Herald (e) News-Tribune (m)	KAOH KAOH(FM) KDAL WAKX WAKX(FM)	WDSM WEBC WGGR(FM) WWJC	KBJR-TV (NBC) KDAL-TV (CBS) WDIO-TV (ABC)

Media for Advertising and Publicity

State and City	Newspapers	Radio		TV
MINNESOTA—*Cont.*				
Minneapolis- St. Paul	Dispatch (e) (St. Paul) Pioneer Press (m) (St. Paul) Star (e) (Minneapolis) Tribune (m) (Minneapolis)	KANO KDAN KDWB KDWB(FM) KEEY KEEY(FM) KFMX(FM) KQRS KQRS(FM) KRSI KSTP KSTP(FM) KTCR	KTCR(FM) KTWN(FM) KUXL WAYL WAYL(FM) WCCO WCCO(FM) WDGY WLOL WLOL(FM) WMIN WWTC	KMSP-TV (ABC) KSTP-TV (NBC) WCCO-TV (CBS) WTCN-TV
MISSISSIPPI				
Jackson	Clarion-Ledger (m) News (e) Clarion-Ledger & News (S)	WJDX WJFR WJMI(FM) WJQS WJXN WKXI(FM)	WLIN(FM) WOKJ WRBC WSLI WYIG WZZQ(FM)	WAPT-TV (ABC) WJTV (CBS) WLBT (NBC)
MISSOURI				
Kansas City	Star (e) Times (m)	KAYQ KBEA KBEQ(FM) KBIL KCCV KCEZ(FM) KCKN KCKN(FM) KCMO KCNW	KMBR(FM) KMBZ KPRS KPRT KUDL(FM) KWKI(FM) KXTR(FM) KYYS WDAF WHB	KBMA-TV KCMO-TV (CBS) KMBC-TV (ABC) WDAF-TV (NBC)
St. Louis	Globe-Democrat (m) Post-Dispatch (e)	KADI KADI(FM) KATZ KCFM(FM) KEZK(FM) KIRL KKSS(FM) KMOX KMOX(FM) KSD KSHE(FM) KSLQ(FM)	KSTL KXEN KXOK WCBW(FM) WESL WEW WGNU WGNU(FM) WIL WIL(FM) WMRY(FM)	KDNL-TV KMOX-TV (CBS) KPLR-TV KSD-TV (NBC) KTVI (ABC)
NEBRASKA				
Omaha	World-Herald (m&e)	KEFM(FM) KEZO(FM) KFAB KGOR(FM) KOIL KOOO	KOOO(FM) KOWH KOWH(FM) KQKQ(FM) KRCB WOW	KETV (ABC) KMTV (NBC) WOWT-TV (CBS)
NEVADA				
Las Vegas	Review-Journal (e) Sun (m)	KDWN KENO KENO(FM) KFMS(FM) KLAV KLUC	KLUC(FM) KNUU KORK KORK(FM) KRAM	KLAS-TV (CBS) KORK-TV (NBC) KSHO-TV (ABC) KVVU
NEW JERSEY				
Jersey City	Jersey Journal (e)			
New Brunswick- Perth Amboy	Home News (e) News Tribune (e)	WCTC	KMGQ(FM)	
Newark	Star-Ledger (m)	WHBI(FM) WNJR	WVNJ WVNJ(FM)	WNJU-TV WTVG-TV
Paterson-Passaic- Clifton	Herald-News (e) (Passaic-Clifton) News (all day) (Paterson)	WPAT	WPAT(FM)	WXTV
Trenton	Times (e) Trentonian (m) Times-Advertiser (S)	WBJH(FM) WBUD WCHR(FM)	WPST(FM) WTNJ WTTM	

Media for Advertising and Publicity

State and City	Newspapers	Radio		TV
NEW MEXICO Albuquerque	Journal (m) Tribune (e)	KABQ KAMX KDAZ KHFM(FM) KKIM KOB KOB(FM) KPAR	KQEO KRKE KRKE(FM) KRST(FM) KRZY KUFF KZIA KZZX	KGGM-TV (CBS) KMXN-TV KOAT-TV (ABC) KOB-TV (NBC)
NEW YORK Albany- Schenectady- Troy	Gazette (m) (Schenectady) Times-Union (m) (Albany) Knickerbocker News (e) (Albany) Times Record (e) (Troy) Record (S) (Troy)	WABY WFLY(FM) WGFM(FM) WGNA WGY WHAZ WHRL(FM) WHSH(FM)	WOKO WPTR WQBK WQBK(FM) WROW WROW(FM) WTRY WWOM(FM)	WAST (ABC) WRGB (NBC) WTEN-TV (ABC)
Binghamton	Press (e) Sun-Bulletin (m)	WAAL(FM) WENE WINR WKOP	WMRV(FM) WNBF WQYT(FM)	WBJA-TV (ABC) WBNG-TV (CBS) WICZ-TV (NBC)
Buffalo	Courier-Express (m) News (e)	WADV(FM) WBEN WBEN(FM) WBLK(FM) WBNY(FM) WBUF(FM) WDCX(FM) WGR WGRQ(FM)	WKBW WNIA WPHD WUFO WWOL WWOL(FM) WXRL WYSL	WGR-TV (NBC) WIVB-TV (CBS) WKBW-TV (ABC) WUTV
New York City	Daily News (m) Post (e) Times (m) Newsday (Long Island) (e) Trib	WABC WADO WBLS(FM) WBNX WCBS WCBS(FM) WEVD WEVD(FM) WHN WINS WJIT WKTU(FM) WLIB WMCA WNBC	WNCN(FM) WNEW WNEW(FM) WOR WPIX(FM) WPLJ(FM) WPOW WQXR WQXR(FM) WRFM(FM) WRVR(FM) WWRL WXLO(FM) WYNY(FM)	WABC-TV (ABC) WCBS-TV (CBS) WNBC-TV (NBC) WNEW-TV WOR-TV WPIX
Poughkeepsie	Journal (e)	WEOK WHPN WHVS	WKIP WPDH(FM) WSPK(FM)	
Rochester	Democrat & Chr'cl (m) Times-Union (e)	WAXC WBBF WCMF(FM) WDKX(FM) WEZO(FM) WHAM WHFM(FM)	WMJQ(FM) WNYR WPXY(FM) WROC WSAY WVOR(FM)	WHEC-TV (CBS) WORK (ABC) WROC-TV (NBC)
Syracuse	Herald-Journal (e) Post-Standard (m) Herald-American (S)	WEZG(FM) WFBL WHEN WMHR(FM) WNDR WNTQ(FM)	WOLF WONO(FM) WSOQ WSYR WSYR(FM)	WENY-TV (ABC) WNYS-TV (ABC) WSYR-TV (NBC) WTVH (CBS)
Utica	Observer-Dispatch (e) Press (m)	WBVM WIBQ(FM) WIBX WKAL WKAL(FM) WKGW(FM)	WOUR(FM) WRNY WRUN WTLB WTLB(FM)	WKTV (NBC) WUTR-TV (ABC)

Media for Advertising and Publicity

State and City	Newspapers	Radio		TV
NORTH CAROLINA Charlotte	News (e) Observer (m)	WAME WAYS WBT WBT(FM) WEZC(FM) WGIV	WHVN WIST WROQ(FM) WRPL WSOC WSOC(FM)	WBTV (CBS) WCCB-TV (ABC) WHKY-TV WRET-TV WSOC-TV (NBC)
Fayetteville	Observer (e) Times (m) Observer & Times (S)	WFAI WFLB WFNC	WIDU WQSM(FM)	
Greensboro	News (m) Record (e)	WBIG WCOG WEAL WGBG	WPET WQMG(FM) WRQK(FM)	WFMY-TV (CBS) WGHP-TV (ABC) WXII-TV (NBC)
Raleigh-Durham	Herald (m) (Durham) Sun (e) (Durham) News & Observer (m) (Raleigh) Times (e) (Raleigh)	WDBS(FM) WDCG(FM) WDNC WDUR WKBQ WKIX WLLE WPTF	WQDR(FM) WRAL(FM) WRNC WSRC WTIK WYNA WYYD(FM)	WRAL-TV (ABC) WRDU-TV (NBC) WTVD (CBS)
OHIO Akron	Beacon Journal (e)	WAEZ(FM) WAKR WCUE WHLO	WKDD WKNT WKNT(FM) WSLR	WAKR-TV (ABC)
Canton	Repository (e)	WHBC WHBC(FM) WHLQ(FM) WINW	WNYN WQIO WTIG WTOF(FM)	WJAN-TV
Cincinnati	Enquirer (m) Post (e)	WCIN WCKY WCLU WEBN(FM) WHKK(FM) WKRC WKRQ(FM) WLQA(FM) WLVV	WLW WLYK(FM) WNOP WSAI WSAI(FM) WUBE WUBE(FM) WWEZ(FM) WZIP	WCPO-TV (CBS) WKRC-TV (ABC) WLWT (NBC) WXIX-TV
Cleveland	Plain Dealer (m) Press (e)	WABQ WCLV(FM) WDBN(FM) WDMT WDOK(FM) WELW WERE WGAR WGCL(FM) WHK WJMO	WJW WKSW WLYT(FM) WMGC WMMS(FM) WQAL(FM) WSUM WWWE WWWM(FM) WZAK(FM)	WEWS (ABC) WJKW-TV (CBS) WKYC-TV (NBC) WUAB-TV
Columbus	Citizen-Journal (m) Dispatch (e)	WBBY(FM) WBNS WBNS(FM) WCOL WCOL(FM) WLVQ(FM) WMNI	WNCI(FM) WRFD WRMZ(FM) WTVN WVKO WVKO(FM)	WBNS-TV (CBS) WCMH (NBC) WTVN-TV (ABC)
Dayton	Journal Herald (m) News (e)	WAVI WDAO(FM) WHIO WHIO(FM)	WING WONE WTUE(FM) WVUD(FM)	WDTN (NBC) WHIO-TV (CBS) WKEF (ABC)

Hamilton-
  Middletown
	Journal (e) (Middletown)
	Journal-News (e)
	  (Hamilton)
		WCNW
		WLVV
		WLWS(FM)
		WMOH
			WPBF(FM)
			WPFB
			WYCH(FM)	

Media for Advertising and Publicity

State and City	Newspapers	Radio		TV
OHIO—*Cont.* Lorain-Elyria	Chronicle-Telegram (e) (Elyria) Journal (e) (Lorain)	WBEA(FM) WEOL	WLRO WZLE	
Toledo	Blade (e)	WCWA WGOR WIOT(FM) WKLR(FM) WLQR(FM)	WMHE(FM) WOHO WSPD WTOD WXEZ(FM)	WDHO-TV (ABC) WSPD-TV (NBC) WTOL-TV (CBS)
Youngstown	Vindicator (e)	WBBW WFMJ WGFT WHOT	WKBN WKBN(FM) WNIO WQOD(FM)	WFMJ-TV (NBC) WKBN-TV (CBS) WYTV (ABC)
OKLAHOMA Oklahoma City	Journal (m) Oklahoman (m) Oklahoman & Times (Sat.) Times (e)	KATT KATT(FM) KBYE KEBC(FM) KLTE KGOU(FM) KGOY(FM) KKNG(FM) KNOR KOCY KAKC	KOFM(FM) KOMA KQCV KRMC KTOK KKLR KXXY(FM) KZUE(FM) WKY WNAD	KOCO-TV (ABC) KTVY (NBC) KWTV (CBS)
Tulsa	Tribune (e) World (m)	KAKC(FM) KCFO KELI KFMJ KGOW(FM) KKUL(FM) KTFX	KMOD KRAV(FM) KRMG KTOW KVOO KWEN(FM) KXXO	KOTV (CBS) KTUL-TV (ABC)
OREGON Eugene- Springfield	Register-Guard (e)	KASH KATR KBDF KBMC(FM) KEED KFMY(FM)	KORE KPNW KPNW(FM) KSND KUGN KZEL(FM)	KEZI-TV (ABC) KVAL-TV (NBC)
Portland	Oregon Journal (e) Oregonian (m)	KEX KGAR KGON(FM) KGW KINK(FM) KJIB(FM) KKEY KLIQ KMJK KPAM KPAM(FM) KPDQ KPDQ(FM)	KQFM(FM) KQIV(FM) KRDR KUIK KUPL KUPL(FM) KVAN KWJJ KXL KXL(FM) KYTE KYTE(FM) KYXI	KATU (ABC) KGW-TV (NBC) KOIN-TV (CBS) KPTV
PENNSYLVANIA Allentown- Bethlehem	Call (m) (Allentown) Chronicle (e) (Allentown) Call-Chronicle (S) (Allentown) Call Weekender (Sat.) Globe-Times (e) (Bethlehem)	WAEB WEEX WEST WEZV(FM) WFMZ(FM) WGPA	WHOL WKAP WLEV(FM) WQQQ(FM) WSAN WXFW(FM)	
Erie	News (m) Times (e) Times-News (S)	WCCK(FM) WJET WLKK	WLVU WRIE WWGO	WICU-TV (NBC) WJET-TV (ABC) WSEE (CBS)
Harrisburg	News (e) Patriot (m) Patriot-News (S)	WCMB WFEC WHP	WHP(FM) WKBO WSFM(FM)	WHP-TV (CBS) WTPA (ABC)
Johnstown	Tribune- Democrat (all day)	WCRO WFMM WJAC	WJAC(FM) WJNL WJNL(FM)	WJAC-TV (NBC) WJNL-TV (CBS)

Media for Advertising and Publicity

State and City	Newspapers	Radio		TV
PENNSYLVANIA—*Cont.*				
Lancaster	Intelligencer J'l (m) New Era (e) News (S)	WDAC(FM) WDDL WLAN	WLAN(FM) WNCE	WGAL-TV (NBC) WLYH-TV (CBS)
Philadelphia	Bulletin (e) Inquirer (m) News (e) WKBS-TV	KYW WCAU WCAU(FM) WDAS WDAS(FM) WDVR(FM) WFIL WFLN WFLN(FM) WHAT WIFI(FM) WIOQ(FM)	WIP WMMR(FM) WPEN WRCP WSNI WTEL WVSL(FM) WWDB(FM) WWSH(FM) WYSP(FM) WZZD	KYW-TV (NBC) WCAU-TV (CBS) WCMC-TV WKBS-TV WPHL-TV (NBC) WPVI-TV (ABC) WTAF-TV
Pittsburgh	Post-Gazette (m) Press (e)	KDKA KQV WAMO WBCW WBVP WDVE(FM) WEDO WEEP WEEP(FM) WFFM(FM) WHJB WIXZ WJOI(FM) WKPA WKTQ	WLOA WMBA WNUF(FM) WOKU(FM) WPEZ(FM) WPIT WPIT(FM) WPLW WQTW WSHH(FM) WTAE WWKS WWSW WXKX WYDD(FM)	KDKA-TV (CBS) WIIC (NBC) WPGH-TV WTAE (ABC)
Reading	Eagle (e) Times (m)	WEEU WHUM	WRAW WRFY(FM)	
Scranton	Times (e) Tribune (m) Scrantonian (S)	WARD WARM WEJL WEZX(FM) WGBI WGBI(FM)	WICK WMJW WNAK WSCR WWDL(FM)	WDAU-TV (CBS) WNEP-TV (ABC)
Wilkes-Barre	Times-Lead'r, News Record (all day)	WBAX WBRE WBRE(FM)	WILK WYZZ(FM)	WBRE-TV (NBC)
York	Dispatch (e) Record (m)	WNOW WQXA(FM) WSBA	WSBA(FM) WYCR WZIX	WSBA-TV (CBS)
RHODE ISLAND				
Providence	Bulletin (e) Journal (m) Journal-Bulletin (Sat.)	WARV WBRU(FM) WEAN WGNG WHIM WHJY(FM) WICE WJAR	WKRI WLKW WLKW(FM) WPJB(FM) WPRO WPRO(FM) WRIB	WJAR-TV (NBC) WPRI-TV (CBS) WTEV (ABC)
SOUTH CAROLINA				
Charleston	News & Courier (m) Post (e) Standard (e)	WCSC WEZL(FM) WKTM(FM) WNCG WOKE	WPAL WPXI(FM) WQSN WTMA WXTC(FM)	WCBD-TV (ABC) WCIV (NBC) WCSC (CBS)
Columbia	Record (e) State (m) Sun News (m)	WCAY WCOS WCOS(FM) WIS WNOK WNOK(FM)	WOIC WQXL WSCQ(FM) WXRY(FM) WZLD(FM)	WIS-TV (NBC) WNOK-TV (CBS) WOLO-TV (ABC)

Media for Advertising and Publicity

State and City	Newspapers	Radio		TV
SOUTH CAROLINA—*Cont.*				
Greenville	News (m) Piedmont (e) News -Piedmont (Sat.,S)	WASC WESC WESC(FM) WFBC WFBC(FM) WHYZ WKDY	WMRB WMUU WMUU(FM) WORD WQOK WSPA WSPA(FM)	WAIM-TV WFBC-TV (NBC) WLOS-TV (ABC) WSPA-TV (CBS)
TENNESSEE				
Chattanooga	News-Free Press (e) Times (m)	WDEF WDEF(FM) WDOD WDOD(FM) WDXB WFLI WGOW	WMOC WNOO WOWE(FM) WRIP(FM) WSIM WYNQ(FM)	WDEF-TV (CBS) WRCB-TV (NBC) WRIP-TV WTVC (ABC)
Knoxville	Journal (m) News-Sentinel (e)	WBIR WBIR(FM) WEZK(FM) WIVK WIVK(FM) WJBE	WKGN WKVQ WKXV WNOX WRJZ WSKT	WATE-TV (NBC) WBIR-TV (CBS) WTVK (ABC)
Memphis	Commercial Appeal (m) Press-Scimitar (e)	KSUD KWAM KWAM(FM) WDIA WEEF(FM) WEZI(FM) WHBQ WHRK(FM) WLOK	WMC WMC(FM) WMPS WMQM WQUD WREC WWEE WZXR(FM)	WHBQ-TV (ABC) WMC-TV (NBC) WREG-TV (CBS)
Nashville	Banner (e) Tennessean (m)	WAMB WBYQ(FM) WJRB WKDA WKDF(FM) WLAC WLAC(FM) WMAK	WNAH WSIX WSIX(FM) WSM WSM(FM) WVOL WWGM WZEZ(FM)	WBKO (ABC) WNGE (ABC) WSM-TV (NBC) WTVF (CBS)
TEXAS				
Austin	American-Statesman (m & e)	KASE(FM) KHFI(FM) KIXL KLBJ KLBJ(FM)	KMXX(FM) KNOW KOKE KOKE(FM) KVET	KTBC-TV (CBS) KTVV-TV (NBC) KVUE-TV (ABC)
Beaumont	Enterprise (m) Journal (e)	KAYC KAYD(FM) KIEL(FM) KJET	KLVI KQXY KTRM KWIC(FM)	KBMT-TV (ABC) KFDM-TV (CBS) KJAC-TV (NBC)
Corpus Christi	Caller (m) Times (e) Caller-Times (S)	KCCT KCTA KEYS KIOU(FM)	KRYS KSIX KUNO KZFM(FM)	KIII (ABC) KORO-TV KRIS-TV (NBC) KZTV (CBS)
Dallas	News (m) Times Herald (e)	KAFM(FM) KBOX KKDA KKDA(FM) KLIF KMEZ(FM) KMGC KNUS(FM) KOAX(FM)	KPBC KRLD KSKY KVIL KVIL(FM) KZEW(FM) WFAA WRR WRR(FM)	KDFW-TV (CBS) KXTX-TV WFAA-TV (ABC)

Media for Advertising and Publicity

State and City	Newspapers	Radio		TV
TEXAS—*Cont.* El Paso	Herald-Post (e) Times (m)	KAMA KAMA(FM) KELP KEZB(FM) KHEY KINT KINT(FM) KISO	KLOZ(FM) KPAS KROD KSET KSET(FM) KTSM KTSM(FM)	KDBC-TV (CBS) KTSM-TV (NBC) KVIA (ABC)
Fort Worth	Star-Telegram (m & e)	KAMC KESS(FM) KFJZ KFJZ(FM) KFWD(FM) KJIM KNOK	KNOK(FM) KPLX(FM) KRXV KSCS(FM) KXOL WBAP	KTVT KXAS-TV (NBC)
Houston	Chronicle (e) Post (m)	KAUM(FM) KBUK KCOH KENR KEYH KFMK(FM) KIKK KIKK(FM) KILT KILT(FM) KLEF(FM) KLOL(FM) KLVL	KLVL(FM) KNUZ KODA KODA(FM) KPRC KQUE(FM) KRBE(FM) KRLY(FM) KTRH KULF KXYZ KYND(FM) KYOK	KDOG-TV KHOU-TV (CBS) KHTV KPRC-TV (NBC) KTRK-TV (ABC)
San Antonio	Express (m) Express-News (Sat., S) Light (e) News (e)	KAPE KBUC KBUC(FM) KCOR KDRY KEDA KISS(FM) KITE KITE(FM) KITY(FM) KKYX	KMAC KMFM(FM) KONO KQAM KQXT(FM) KTFM(FM) KTSA KUKA KZZY WOAI	KENS-TV (CBS) KMOL-TV (NBC) KSAT-TV (ABC) KWEX-TV
UTAH Salt Lake City	Deseret News (e) Tribune (m)	KALL KALL(FM) KCPX KCPX(FM) KLUB KLUB(FM) KPRQ KRGO KRSP	KRSP(FM) KSFI KSL KSOP KSOP(FM) KSXX KWHO KWHO(FM) KWMS	KSL-TV (CBS) KTVX (ABC) KUTV (NBC)
VIRGINIA Bristol-Johnson City-Kingsport	Herald-Courier (m) Virginia-Tennessean (e)	WFHG WKYE	WOPI WZAP	
Newport News- Norfolk	Ledger-Star (e) (Norfolk) Press (m) (Newport News) Times-Herald (e) (Newport News) Virginian-Pilot (m) (Norfolk)	WCMS WCMS(FM) WCPK WFOG WFOG(FM) WGH WGH(FM) WKEZ WNOR WNOR(FM) WOKT	WOWI(FM) WPCE WPMH WQRK(FM) WRAP WTAR WVAB WVEC WVHR(FM) WXRI(FM) WZAM	WAVY-TV (NBC) WTAR-TV (CBS) WVEC-TV (ABC) WYAH-TV

Media for Advertising and Publicity

State and City	Newspapers	Radio		TV
VIRGINIA—*Cont.* Richmond	News-Leader (e) Times-Dispatch (m)	WANT WDYL(FM) WEET WENZ WEZS(FM) WGOE WIKI WLEE	WRGM WRNL WRVA WRVQ(FM) WRXL(FM) WTVR WTVR(FM) WXGI	WTVR-TV (CBS) WWBT (NBC) WXEX-TV (ABC)
WASHINGTON Seattle	Post-Intelligencer (m) Times (e)	KAAR KAYO KBIQ(FM) KBLE KBLE(FM) KEUT KEZX(FM) KGDN KING KING (FM) KIRO KISW(FM) KIXI KIXI(FM) KJR KMPS	KOMO KQIN KRKO KSEA KTAC KVI KVI(FM) KWYZ KXA KYAC KYYX KZAM KZAM(FM) KZOK KZOK(FM)	KING-TV (NBC) KIRO-TV (CBS) KOMO-TV (ABC) KSTW-TV
Spokane	Chronicle (e) Spokesman-Review (m)	KEZE KEZE(FM) KGA KHQ KHQ(FM) KJRB KREM KREM(FM)	KSPO KUDY KXLY KXLY(FM) KXXR KXXR(FM) KZUN KZUN(FM)	KHQ-TV (NBC) KREM-V (CBS) KXLY-TV (ABC)
Tacoma	News Tribune (e)	KBRD(FM) KLAY(FM) KMO	KNBQ(FM) KTAC KTNT	
WEST VIRGINIA Charleston	Gazette (m) Mail (e) Gazette Mail (S)	WBES(FM) WCAW WCHS WKAZ WKLC	WKLC(FM) WTIO(FM) WTIP WVAF(FM) WXIT	WCHS-TV (CBS)
Huntington	Advertiser (e) Herald-Dispatch (m)	WAMX(FM) WCMI WEMM(FM) WGNT WHEZ(FM) WIRO	WITO(FM) WKEE WKEE(FM) WTCR WWHY	WOWK-TV (ABC) WSAZ-TV (NBC)
WISCONSIN Appleton- Oshkosh	Northwestern (e) (Oshkosh) Post-Crescent (e) (Appleton)	WAGO WAPL WAPL(FM) WHBY WKAU WKAU(FM)	WMKC WNAM WOSH WROE(FM) WYNE WYTL	
Madison	Capital Times (e) Wisconsin State	WIBA WIBA(FM) WISM WISM(FM	WTSO WWQM WWQM(FM) WZEE(FM)	WISC-TV (CBS) WKOW-TV (ABC) WMTV (NBC)
Milwaukee	Journal (e) Sentinel (m)	WAUK WAWA WAWA(FM) WBCS WBCS(FM) WEMP WEZW(FM) WFMR(FM) WISN WKTI(FM) WLPX(FM)	WKTI(FM) WMIL(FM) WNOV WNUW(FM) WOKY WQFM(FM) WTMJ WZMF(FM) WZUU WZUU(FM)	WISN-TV(ABC) WITI-TV (CBS) WTMJ-TV (NBC) WVTV

Business and Professional Publications

Publication	Address
Administrative Management	51 Madison Ave., New York, N.Y. 10010
Advertising Age*	740 Rush St., Chicago, Ill. 60611
Advertising & Sales Promotion	740 Rush St., Chicago, Ill. 60611
American Banker	525 W. 42nd St., New York, N. Y. 10036
American Bar Association Journal	1155 E. 60th St., Chicago, Ill. 60637
American Builder*	30 Church St., New York, N. Y. 10007
American City	757 Third Ave., New York, N. Y. 10017
American Druggist*	1790 Broadway, New York, N. Y. 10019
American Journal of Nursing (ANA)	10 Columbus Circle, New York, N. Y. 10019
Architectural Forum	111 W. 57th St., New York, N. Y. 10019
Army Times	200 Park Ave., New York, N, Y. 10017
Automotive News	965 E. Jefferson Ave., Detroit, Mich. 48207
Aviation Week & Space Technology	330 W. 42nd St., New York, N. Y. 10036
Banking (ABA)	90 Park Ave., New York, N. Y. 10016
Billboard*	165 W. 46th St., New York, N. Y. 10036
Bowling Magazine (ABC)	1572 E. Capitol Dr., Milwaukee, Wis. 53211
Building Maintenance & Modernization	407 E. Michigan St., Milwaukee, Wis. 53201
Building Materials Merchandiser	300 W. Adams St., Chicago, Ill. 60606
Burroughs Clearing House	P.O. Box 418, Detroit, Mich. 48232
Business Automation	288 Park Ave., Elmhurst, Ill. 60126
Business Management	22 W. Putnam Ave., Greenwich, Conn. 06830
Business Publication Rates & Data*	5201 Old Orchard Rd., Skokie, Ill. 60078
Business Week	330 W. 42nd St., New York, N. Y. 10036
Buyers' Purchasing Digest	918 N.E. 20th Ave., Fort Lauderdale, Fla. 33304
The Carpenter (UBCJA)	101 Constitution, N.W., Washington, D. C. 20001
Case and Comment	Aqueduct Bldg., Rochester, N. Y. 14603
Chain Store Age (5 editions)	2 Park Ave., New York, N. Y. 10016
Chemical & Engineering News	1155 16th St., N. W., Washington, D. C. 20036
Chemical Week; Chemical Engineering	1301 Avenue of the Americas, New York, N. Y. 10019
Civil Engineering (ASCE)	345 E. 47th St., New York, N. Y. 10017
Coal Age	330 W. 42nd St., New York, N. Y. 10036
Commercial Car Journal*	Chestnut & 56th Sts., Philadelphia, Pa. 19139
Commercial & Financial Chronicle	25 Park Place, New York, N. Y. 10007
Computer Decisions	850 Third Ave., New York, N. Y. 10022
Construction Equipment & Materials	205 E. 42nd St., New York, N. Y. 10017
Construction Methods & Equipment*	330 W. 42nd St., New York, N. Y. 10036
Contractors & Engineers	757 Third Ave., New York, N. Y. 10017
Cooking for Profit	1202 S. Park St., Madison, Wis. 53715
Credit World (ICCA)	375 Jackson Ave., St. Louis, Mo. 63130
Current Medical Digest	428 E. Preston St., Baltimore, Md. 21202
Daily News Record; Women's Wear*	7 E. 12th St., New York, N. Y. 10003
Dental Survey* (PFA)	4015 W. 65th St., Minneapolis, Minn. 55424
Department Store Economist*	60 East 42nd St., New York, N. Y. 10017
Dun's Review	P.O. Box 3088, Grand Central Stn., N. Y., N. Y. 10017
Editor & Publisher, The 4th Estate	850 Third Ave., New York, N. Y. 10022
Electrical World; Electrical Mdsg. Wk.	1301 Avenue of the Americas, New York, N. Y. 10019
Electrified Industry	20 N. Wacker Dr., Chicago, Ill. 60606
Electronic Industries	Chestnut & 56th Sts., Philadelphia, Pa. 19139
Electronics World	1 Park Ave., New York, N. Y. 10016
Engineering News-Record*	330 W. 42nd St., New York, N. Y. 10036
Financial World	17 Battery Place, New York, N. Y. 10004
Firemen (NFPA)	60 Batterymarch St., Boston, Mass. 02110
Fleet Management News*	300 W. Lake St., Chicago, Ill. 60606
Flying	1 Park Ave., New York, N. Y. 10016
Food Processing	111 E. Delaware Place, Chicago, Ill. 60611
Food Service Magazine	2132 Fordem Ave., Madison, Wis. 53701
Food Topics	205 E. 42nd St., New York, N. Y. 10017
Forbes	60 Fifth Ave., New York, N. Y. 10011
Fortune	541 N. Fairbanks Court, Chicago, Ill. 60611
Gasoline Retailer	19 Union Square West, New York, N. Y. 10003
Grade Teacher	866 Third Ave., New York, N. Y. 10022
Harvard Business Review	Soldiers Field Station, Boston, Mass. 02163
Heating & Plumbing Merchandiser	260 Fifth Ave., New York, N. Y. 10001
Home Furnishings Daily	7 E. 12th St., New York, N. Y. 10003
Hospitality Restaurant Combination	5 S. Wabash Ave., Chicago, Ill. 60603
Hospitals (AHA)	840 N. Lake Shore Dr., Chicago, Ill. 60611
House and Home	330 W. 42nd St., New York, N. Y. 10036
Industrial Bulletin	450 E. Ohio St., Chicago, Ill. 60611
Industrial Equipment News*	461 Eighth Ave., New York, N. Y. 10001
Industrial Machinery News	16171 Meyers Rd., Detroit, Mich. 48235
Industrial Maintenance & Plant Operation	1 West Olney Ave., Philadelphia, Pa. 19120
Industrial Marketing*	740 Rush St., Chicago, Ill. 60611

*Also one or more related publications

Business and Professional Publications

Publication	Address
Inland Printer/American Lithographer........	300 W. Adams St., Chicago, Ill. 60606
Institutions Magazine*......................	1801 Prairie Ave., Chicago, Ill. 60616
The Instructor.............................	Dansville, N. Y. 14437
Instrument & Apparatus News*..............	56th & Chestnut Sts., Philadelphia, Pa. 19139
Insurance Salesman* (life insurance)..........	1142 N. Meridian St., Indianapolis, Ind. 46204
International Musician (AFM)................	220 Mt. Pleasant Ave., Newark, N. J. 07104
Investment Dealers' Digest..................	150 Broadway, New York, N. Y. 10038
Iron Age; Hardware Age....................	Chestnut & 56th Sts., Philadelphia, Pa. 19139
Journal of Accountancy (AICPA)............	666 Fifth Ave., New York, N. Y. 10019
Journal of American Medical Association*......	535 N. Dearborn St., Chicago, Ill. 60610
Law and Order............................	72 W. 45th St., New York, N. Y. 10036
Leatherneck...............................	Box 1918, Washington, D. C. 20013
Life Association News (insurance) (NALU)....	1922 F St., N. W., Washington, D. C. 20006
Machine and Tool Blue Book*...............	Hitchcock Bldg., Wheaton, Ill. 60187
Magazine of Wall Street & Business Analyst....	120 Wall St., New York, N. Y. 10005
Maintenance Engineering....................	1 River Road, Cos Cob, Conn. 06807
M D Medical Newsmagazine.................	30 E. 60th St., New York, N. Y. 10022
Mechanical Engineering* (ASME)............	345 E. 47th St., New York, N. Y. 10017
Medical Economics.........................	550 Kinderkamack Rd., Oradell, N. J. 07649
Metlfax Magazine..........................	Box 2454, Cleveland, Ohio 44112
Mill and Factory..........................	205 E. 42nd St., New York, N. Y. 10017
Modern Beauty Shop.......................	300 W. Adams St., Chicago, Ill. 60606
Modern Drugs*............................	466 Lexington Ave., New York, N. Y. 10017
Modern Medicine*.........................	4015 W. 6th St., Minneapolis, Minn. 55435
Modern Office Procedures...................	614 Superior, W. Cleveland, Ohio 44113
Modern Photography.......................	165 W. 46th St., New York, N. Y. 10036
Modern Plastics...........................	1301 Avenue of the Americas, New York, N. Y. 10019
Modern Sanitation & Building Maintenance....	855 Avenue of the Americas, New York, N. Y. 10001
Modern Stores & Offices....................	20 N. Wacker Dr., Chicago, Ill. 60606
Motor....................................	250 W. 55th St., New York, N. Y. 10019
Motor Service.............................	205 W. Monroe St., Chicago, Ill. 60606
NAHB Journal of Homebuilding.............	1625 L St., N. W., Washington, D. C. 20006
NARGUS Bulletin (retail grocers)...........	360 N. Michigan Ave., Chicago, Ill. 60601
National Business Woman (NFBPWC).......	2012 Massachusetts Ave., N. W., Wash., D. C. 20036
National Petroleum News....................	330 W. 42nd St., New York, N. Y. 10036
National Provisioner (meat packing)..........	15 W. Huron St., Chicago, Ill. 60610
National Safety News* (NSC)................	425 N. Michigan Ave., Chicago, Ill. 60611
National Underwriter (insurance; 2 editions)....	175 W. Jackson Blvd., Chicago, Ill. 60604
Nation's Business (CCUS)...................	1615 H St., N. W., Washington, D. C. 20006
New Equipment Digest......................	1213 W. Third St., Cleveland, Ohio, 44113
Occupational Hazards.......................	614 Superior Ave., W., Cleveland, Ohio 44113
Official Airline Guide.......................	2000 Clearwater Dr., Oak Brook, Ill. 60521
Oil and Gas Journal*......................	211 S. Cheyenne Ave., Tulsa, Okla. 74101
Ordnance.................................	815 17th St., Washington, D. C. 20006
Plant Engineering*.........................	1301 S. Grove Ave., Barrington, Ill. 60010
Power....................................	1301 Avenue of the Americas, New York, N. Y. 10019
Practical Builder Product Data File..........	5 S. Wabash Ave., Chicago, Ill. 60603
Proceedings of the IEEE (radio engineers)......	345 East 47th St., New York, N. Y. 10017
Product Engineering*......................	330 W. 42nd St., New York, N. Y. 10036
Progressive Grocer.........................	420 Lexington Ave., New York, N. Y. 10017
Public Works Magazine.....................	200 S. Broad St., Ridgewood, N. J. 07451
QST (American Radio Relay League).........	225 Main St., Newington, Conn. 06111
Radio Electronics..........................	200 Park Ave. S. New York, N. Y. 10003
Railway Age..............................	30 Church St., New York, N. Y. 10007
Roads and Streets.........................	209 W. Jackson Blvd., Chicago, Ill. 60606
Sales Management*.........................	630 Third Ave., New York, N. Y. 10017
Salesman's Opportunity.....................	875 N. Michigan Ave., Chicago, Ill. 60611
Scholastic Teacher*........................	50 W. 44th St., New York, N. Y. 10036
School Management.........................	22 W. Putnam Ave., Greenwich, Conn. 06830
Super Service Station.......................	7300 N. Cicero Ave., Chicago, Ill. 60646
Supermarket News..........................	7 E. 12th St., New York, N. Y. 10003
Textile World.............................	330 W. 42nd St., New York, N. Y. 10036
Today's Secretary..........................	245 Park Ave., New York, N. Y. 10017
Traffic World.............................	815 Washington Bldg., Washington, D. C. 20005
Transport Topics (ATA)...................	1616 P St., N. W., Washington, D. C. 20036
U. S. News & World Report	2300 N St., N. W., Washington, D. C. 20037
Wall Street Journal........................	New York Chicago Dallas San Francisco
What's New in Home Economics..............	466 Lexington Ave., New York, N. Y. 10017
Your Church (Protestant pastors)............	Box 397, Valley Forge, Pa. 19481

COMMUNICATIONS DATA*

(How to save money on wired messages)

Because charges for telegrams go by word count, telegrams customarily are brief and staccato, with such words as *I, we, the, is, are,* etc., trimmed out.

There is a danger, however, that the drafter may go too far in condensing his message, with the result that ambiguity may occur. It is therefore a useful practice to have every telegram read by someone other than the drafter before it is sent, to be sure that the meaning will be clear to the recipient.

The practice of typing telegrams in CAPITAL LETTERS arose because telegraph machines were equipped only with capitals.

Capitals are harder to type and harder to read; *therefore a telegram should be typed like any other communication, with caps and small letters.*

The original of a telegram should be sent out for transmission; a carbon should be retained for the drafter. In preparing the telegram, the following points should be observed:

1. SENDING INSTRUCTIONS. Indicate in the spaces provided on the form whether the wire is CHARGE or COLLECT; also whether TELEGRAM, or NIGHT LETTER. (As the number of words allowed in various classes changes from time to time, the latest telegraph-company data should be kept at hand.)

2. DATE. Type in upper right corner.

3. INSIDE ADDRESS. Be sure address of consignee is complete and accurate.

4. SALUTATION. Not used in telegrams.

5. COMPLIMENTARY CLOSE. Rarely used. If *Regards* or *Best wishes,* etc., are included, they are typed as part of the message, at the end.

6. BODY OF MESSAGE. As noted above, this should be typed in the normal way, and NOT in ALL CAPS. Double spacing should be used.

7. SIGNATURE. Type sender's name a double space below text of message, a half inch to right of center of form. If title and/or company name are to be included, type them directly below sender's name. (See SIGNATURES, following.)

NOTE WELL: The practice of writing STOP instead of using periods has gone out of style. (See PUNCTUATION, following.)

From Dartnell's Professional Secretary's Handbook.

Tips for Typing Telegrams

ABBREVIATIONS: In general, single words should be spelled out, but common abbreviations like *f.o.b., c.o.d, a.m., p.m.* are used.

ADDRESSES: Any number of words may be used in address of domestic wires, so long as the purpose is to help delivery. In international use, each word in the address is charged for. Thus the use of code names saves money in foreign telegrams.

"CARE OF": No extra charge when used in address of domestic wires.

CODE: No limitations on use in domestic wires; counted at five letters to a word. In international use, some countries have restrictions; check with telegraph company.

COINED WORDS: Like *Retel,* will be counted as a single word if they contain no more than five letters. Thus *Reurtel* would count as two words.

DELIVERY INSTRUCTIONS: Special instructions, such as *deliver before noon,* or *deliver after 2 p.m.,* may be included after address in domestic wires without extra charge.

FIGURES: Word count for figures is based on the rule that each five characters or fraction thereof equals a word. Decimal points do not count as characters; symbols like $ are counted as one character.

FOREIGN LANGUAGES: Dictionary words in Dutch, French, German, Italian, Latin, Portuguese, or Spanish are counted as one word each, regardless of length. Words in all other languages are counted on the basis of five characters equaling one word.

GREETINGS: Holiday, birthday, and other special-occasion greetings are delivered on decorated blanks at no extra cost.

"HOLD FOR ARRIVAL": May be written after address at no extra cost in domestic wires.

MONEY: Any amount may be sent by wire (subject to international regulations).

MULTIPLE COPIES: If the same message is to be sent to several addresses, only one copy need be sent to the telegraph office, with a list of addresses.

"PERSONAL DELIVERY": A message so marked will be delivered only to the person addressed. NOTE that the word *PERSONAL* alone is not enough; such messages will be left with a clerk or other employee who may or may not observe the "personal" marking.

PUNCTUATION: No charge is made for punctuation marks in domestic telegrams. If spelled out, however, a charge is made. Therefore *STOP* should not be used. In international wires, each punctuation mark is charged for.

"REPORT DELIVERY": If wires are so marked, the sender will be notified (by collect wire) as to time of delivery and person to whom delivered.

SIGNATURES: A personal name (*J. C. Smith*), a company name (*Mohawk Mills*), or a combined personal and company name (*J. C. Smith, Mohawk Mills*) are not charged for in domestic wires. (Every word IS charged for in international wires.) A title may be used with a personal name (*J. C. Smith, President*) without charge; but in a compound signature (*J. C. Smith, President, Mohawk Mills*) an extra word is charged for.

Examples of Domestic Word Count

(Applicable between points within the United States and to points in Alaska, Canada, Mexico, and Saint Pierre-Miquelon Islands. For complete statement of word count regulations see Rule 4 in Western Union Tariff Book.)

Basic principles in counting chargeable matter in message texts:

(1) Dictionary words count as one word each.
(2) Place names and proper names count as normally written.
(3) All other groups count at five characters per word.

Free punctuation marks are: period or decimal point (.), comma (,), colon (:), semicolon (;), dash or hyphen (-), question mark (?), apostrophe ('), quotation marks (" "), and parentheses ().

Chargeable "other characters" are: dollar sign ($), fraction bar or diagonal stroke (/), ampersand (&), number or pound sign (#), sign for feet or minutes ('), and sign for inches or seconds (").

	Number Chargeable Words
DICTIONARY WORDS *(Single count regardless of length)*	
EXCURSION CANCELED (English)	2
HERZLICHEN GLUECKWUNSCH (German)	2
NOUS ARRIVERONS DIMANCHE (French)	3
DOLCE FAR NIENTE (Italian)	3
MIJNE GROETE AAN ME VROUW (Dutch)	5
TUDO ESTA PERDIDO (Portuguese)	3
UN CABELLO HACE SOMBRA (Spanish)	4
ERRARE EST HUMANUM (Latin)	3

NOTE—Words in other languages are subject to 5-character count.

COMBINATIONS OF DICTIONARY WORDS *(Counted and transmitted per dictionary)*	
AIRBILL (for AIR BILL)	2
AIREXPRESS (for AIR EXPRESS)	2
ALLRIGHT (for ALL RIGHT)	2
AND/OR (Stroke counts as separate word in this case)	3
BACKORDER (for BACK ORDER)	2
CARLOAD (dictionary word)	1
CARRYALL (dictionary word)	1
DON'T (dictionary contraction—apostrophe is punctuation)	1
DOTHE (for DO THE)	2
ENROUTE (for EN ROUTE)	2
EXTRAFANCY (dictionary word)	1
FIBERGLAS (dictionary word)	1
FORTYFOURONEHALF (for FORTY FOUR ONE HALF)	4
FULL-RATE (hyphen is punctuation)	2
GLUTENFEED (for GLUTEN FEED)	2
HAVEN'T (dictionary contraction—apostrophe is punctuation)	1
HIGHSCHOOL (for HIGH SCHOOL)	2
HOOKUP (dictionary word)	1
ITIS (for IT IS)	2
NEWYEARS (for NEW YEARS)	2
NIGHTLETTER (for NIGHT LETTER)	2
NON-EXCLUSIVE (dictionary word)	1
PEASIZE (for PEA SIZE)	2
PERCENT (dictionary word)	1
PER CENT (if so written)	2
POLICYHOLDER (dictionary word)	1
RECORRESPONDENCE** (for RE CORRESPONDENCE)	2
RELETTER* (dictionary word)	1

Examples of Domestic Word Count (Cont.)

	Number Chargeable Words
REMYPHONE** (for RE MY PHONE)	3
REORDER* (dictionary word)	1
REPHONE* (dictionary word)	1
RETELEGRAM** (for RE TELEGRAM)	2
RETELEGRAPH* (dictionary word)	1
RETELEPHONE* (dictionary word)	1
REWIRE* (dictionary word)	1
REYOUR** (for RE YOUR)	2
SHARKSKIN (dictionary word)	1
SHORTSHIPPED (for SHORT SHIPPED)	2
SHOULDN'T (dictionary contraction—apostrophe is punctuation)	1
SOYBEANMEAL (for SOYBEAN MEAL)	2
STOREDOOR (for STORE DOOR)	2
TANKCAR (for TANK CAR)	2
THEY'LL (dictionary contraction—apostrophe is punctuation)	1
TRUCKLOAD (dictionary word)	1
T-SHIRTS (hyphen is punctuation)	2
WESTERNUNION (for WESTERN UNION)	2

Combinations of "re" with verb form are acceptable as dictionary words at single count, regardless of meaning conveyed in particular context.

**These are combinations of "re" with noun or pronoun which cannot properly be used as verb forms and are not dictionary words.*

MUTILATED AND NONDICTIONARY WORDS (*5-character count*)

AIREX (5 characters)	1
ALRIGHT (7 characters)	2
BESCANDO (8 characters)	2
FOURBA (6 characters)	2
HABYU (5 characters)	1
MAZELTOV (7 characters)	2
OURLETS (7 characters)	2
PERTEL (6 characters)	2
RAILEX (6 characters)	2
REOURLET (8 characters)	2
RETEL (5 characters)	1
REURTEL (7 characters)	2
REURTELETYPE (12 characters)	3
SATEVEPOST (10 characters)	2
URORDER (7 characters)	2
USONES (6 characters)	2
USTWOS (6 characters)	2

TRADE NAMES (*5-character count*)

DURA-GLO (7 characters, hyphen is punctuation)	2
EATMORE (7 characters)	2
EUCODOL (7 characters)	2
FLAKEWHITE (10 characters)	2
FLEXISOLES (10 characters)	2
LINMEAL (7 characters)	2
REDIFORM (8 characters)	2
REZISTAL (8 characters)	2
STAZYME (7 characters)	2
SUNSOY (6 characters)	2
SWEETOSE (8 characters)	2
SWIFTNING (9 characters)	2
UNAFLO (6 characters)	2

Examples of Domestic Word Count (Cont.)

ABBREVIATIONS AND LETTER GROUPS (*5-character count*)

ABCDE (5 characters)	1
ABCDEF (6 characters)	2
A.M. (if written without spaces)	1
A. M. (if written with spaces)	2
BANDO (5 characters)	1
CNR (if written without spaces)	1
C.N.R. (if written without spaces)	1
C. N. R. (if written with spaces)	3
LB (for POUND)	1
LOSA (for LOS ANGELES)	1
N.Y. (if written without spaces)	1
PM (if written without spaces)	1
S. C. (if written with spaces)	2
TP-CRIP (hyphen is punctuation)	2
U.S.A. (if written without spaces)	1
U.S.S.R. (if written without spaces)	1
WASHDC (6 characters)	2
W. N. E. W. (if written with spaces)	4
W.N.E.W. (if written without spaces)	1

Courtesy of THE WESTERN UNION TELEGRAPH CO.

CODE FOR AVOIDING CONFUSION IN SPELLING

To avoid confusion between letters sounding alike—like *b* and *d* or *f* and *s*—when spelling out names over the phone, in dictating, and so on, there are several codes in use. Choice is optional.

	General	*Military-Naval*	*International*
A for:	Adam	Able	Alfa
B for:	Boston	Baker	Bravo
C for:	Chicago	Charlie	Coca
D for:	Denver	Dog	Delta
E for:	Edward	Easy	Echo
F for:	Frank	Fox	Foxtrot
G for:	George	George	Golf
H for:	Henry	How	Hotel
I for:	Ida	Item	India
J for:	John	Jig	Juliet
K for:	King	King	Kilo
L for:	Lincoln	Love	Lima
M for:	Mary	Mike	Metro
N for:	New York	Nan	Nectar
O for:	Ocean	Oboe	Oscar
P for:	Paul	Peter	Papa
Q for:	Queen	Queen	Quebec
R for:	Robert	Roger	Romeo
S for:	Samuel	Sugar	Sierra
T for:	Thomas	Tare	Tango
U for:	Union	Uncle	Union
V for:	Victory	Victor	Victor
W for:	William	William	Whiskey
X for:	X-ray	X-ray	Extra
Y for:	Yellow	Yoke	Yankee
Z for:	Zero	Zebra	Zulu

ADVERTISING LINEAGE CONVERSION TABLE

ADVERTISING LINEAGE CONVERSION TABLE

AGATE LINES TO INCHES
(14 Agate Lines to One Inch)

14 = 1	504 = 36	994 = 71	1484 = 106	1974 – 141
28 = 2	518 = 37	1008 = 72	1498 – 107	1988 = 142
42 = 3	532 = 38	1022 = 73	1512 = 108	2002 = 143
56 = 4	546 = 39	1036 = 74	1526 = 109	2016 – 144
70 = 5	560 = 40	1050 = 75	1540 = 110	2030 = 145
84 = 6	574 = 41	1064 = 76	1554 = 111	2044 = 146
98 = 7	588 = 42	1078 = 77	1568 = 112	2058 – 147
112 = 8	602 = 43	1092 = 78	1582 = 113	2072 = 148
126 = 9	616 = 44	1106 = 79	1596 = 114	2086 – 149
140 = 10	630 = 45	1120 = 80	1610 = 115	2100 = 150
154 = 11	644 = 46	1134 = 81	1624 = 116	2114 – 151
168 = 12	658 = 47	1148 = 82	1638 = 117	2128 = 152
182 – 13	672 = 48	1162 = 83	1652 = 118	2142 = 153
196 = 14	686 = 49	1176 = 84	1666 = 119	2156 = 154
210 = 15	700 = 50	1190 = 85	1680 = 120	2170 – 155
224 = 16	714 = 51	1204 = 86	1694 = 121	2184 – 156
238 = 17	728 = 52	1218 = 87	1708 – 122	2198 = 157
252 = 18	742 = 53	1232 = 88	1722 = 123	2212 – 158
266 = 19	756 = 54	1246 = 89	1736 = 124	2226 = 159
280 = 20	770 = 55	1260 = 90	1750 – 125	2240 – 160
294 = 21	784 = 56	1274 = 91	1764 = 126	2254 = 161
308 – 22	798 = 57	1288 = 92	1778 – 127	2268 = 162
322 = 23	812 = 58	1302 = 93	1792 = 128	2282 = 163
336 = 24	826 = 59	1316 = 94	1806 – 129	2296 = 164
350 = 25	840 = 60	1330 = 95	1820 = 130	2310 – 165
364 = 26	854 = 61	1344 = 96	1834 = 131	2324 – 166
378 = 27	868 = 62	1358 = 97	1848 = 132	2338 = 167
392 = 28	882 = 63	1372 = 98	1862 = 133	2352 = 168
406 = 29	896 = 64	1386 = 99	1876 – 134	2366 = 169
420 = 30	910 = 65	1400 = 100	1890 = 135	2380 – 170
434 – 31	924 = 66	1414 – 101	1904 – 136	2394 = 171
448 = 32	938 = 67	1428 = 102	1918 = 137	2408 – 172
462 = 33	952 = 68	1442 – 103	1932 = 138	2422 = 173
476 = 34	966 = 69	1456 = 104	1946 = 139	2436 – 174
490 – 35	980 = 70	1470 – 105	1960 – 140	2450 = 175

An agate line is a traditional standard of measurement for depth of columns in newspaper advertising space. Fourteen lines equal one column-inch.

Courtesy: The Sacramento Union

Time Differences of Foreign Cities

(Standard Time Around the World at Noon, Eastern Standard Time)†

City and Country	Time	City and Country	Time
Aberdeen, Scotland	5:00 p.m.	Leningrad, U.S.S.R.	8:00 p.m.
Adelaide, Australia	2:30 a.m.*	Leopoldville, The Congo	6:00 p.m.
Addis Ababa, Ethiopia	8:00 p.m.	Lima, Peru	12:00 noon
Algiers, Algeria	6:00 p.m.	Lisbon, Portugal	5:00 p.m.
Alexandria, Egypt	7:00 p.m.	Liverpool, England	5:00 p.m.
Amsterdam, Netherlands	6:00 p.m.	London, England	5:00 p.m.
Anchorage, Fairbanks, Alaska	7:00 a.m.	Lyons, France	6:00 p.m.
Ankara, Turkey	7:00 p.m.	Madras, India	10:30 p.m.
Antwerp, Belgium	6:00 p.m.	Madrid, Spain	6:00 p.m.
Asuncion, Paraguay	1:00 p.m.	Manchester, England	5:00 p.m.
Athens, Greece	7:00 p.m.	Manila, Philippines	1:00 a.m.*
Auckland, New Zealand	5:00 a.m.*	Marseille, France	6:00 p.m.
Baghdad, Iraq	8:00 p.m.	Melbourne, Australia	3:00 a.m.*
Bangkok, Thailand	12:00 mid.	Mexico City, Mexico	11:00 a.m.
Barcelona, Spain	6:00 p.m.	Milan, Italy	6:00 p.m.
Belfast, Northern Ireland	5:00 p.m.	Montevideo, Uruguay	2:00 p.m.
Belgrade, Yugoslavia	6:00 p.m.	Montreal, Canada	12:00 noon
Berlin, Germany	6:00 p.m.	Moscow, U.S.S.R.	8:00 p.m.
Birmingham, England	5:00 p.m.	Munich, Germany	6:00 p.m.
Bogota, Colombia	12:00 noon	Nagoya and Nagasaki, Japan	2:00 a.m.*
Bombay, India	10:30 p.m.	Naha, Okinawa	2:00 a.m.*
Bonn, Germany	6:00 p.m.	Nairobi, Kenya	8:00 p.m.
Bordeaux, France	6:00 p.m.	Nanking, China	1:00 a.m.*
Brasilia, Brazil	2:00 p.m.	Naples, Italy	6:00 p.m.
Bremen, Germany	6:00 p.m.	New Delhi, India	10:30 p.m.
Brisbane, Australia	3:00 a.m.*	Nome, Alaska	6:00 a.m.
Bristol, England	5:00 p.m.	Odessa, U.S.S.R.	8:00 p.m.
Brussels, Belgium	6:00 p.m.	Osaka, Japan	2:00 a.m.*
Bucharest, Rumania	7:00 p.m.	Oslo, Norway	6:00 p.m.
Budapest, Hungary	6:00 p.m.	Ottawa, Canada	12:00 noon
Buenos Aires, Argentina	2:00 p.m.	Panama City, Panama	12 00 noon
Cairo, Egypt	7:00 p.m.	Paris, France	6:00 p.m.
Calcutta, India	10:30 p.m.	Peiping, China	1:00 a.m.*
Calgary, Canada	10:00 a.m.	Perth, Australia	1:00 a.m.*
Canberra, Australia	3:00 a.m.*	Prague, Czechoslovakia	6:00 p.m.
Canton, China	1:00 a.m.*	Quebec, Canada	12:00 noon
Cape Town, South Africa	7:00 p.m.	Rangoon, Burma	11:30 p.m.
Caracas, Venezuela	12:30 p.m.	Reykjavik, Iceland	4:00 p.m.
Casablanca, Morocco	5:00 p.m.	Rio de Janeiro, Brazil	2:00 p.m.
Chungking, China	1:00 a.m.*	Rome, Italy	6:00 p.m.
Cologne, Germany	6:00 p.m.	Rotterdam, Netherlands	6:00 p.m.
Copenhagen, Denmark	6:00 p.m.	Saigon, South Vietnam	1:00 a.m.*
Dakar, Senegal	5:00 p.m.	San Juan, Puerto Rico	1:00 p.m.
Darwin, Australia	2:30 a.m.*	Santiago, Chile	1:00 p.m.
Dublin, Eire (Ireland)	5:00 p.m.	Sao Paulo, Brazil	2:00 p.m.
Durban, Union of South Africa	7:00 p.m.	Seoul, Korea	1:30 a.m.*
Edinburgh, Scotland	5:00 p.m.	Shanghai, China	1:00 a.m.*
Edmonton, Canada	10:00 a.m.	Sheffield, England	5:00 p.m.
Frankfurt, Germany	6:00 p.m.	Shenyang (Mukden), Manchuria	2:00 a.m.*
Geneva, Switzerland	6:00 p.m.	Singapore	12:30 a.m.*
Genoa, Italy	6:00 p.m.	Sofia, Bulgaria	7:00 p.m.
Glasgow, Scotland	5:00 p.m.	Stockholm, Sweden	6:00 p.m.
Guayaquil, Ecuador	12:00 noon	Sydney, Australia	3:00 a.m.*
Halifax, Canada	1:00 p.m.	Taipei, Formosa	1:00 a.m.*
Hamburg, Germany	6:00 p.m.	Teheran, Iran	8:30 p.m.
Hamilton, Bermuda	1:00 p.m.	Tel Aviv, Israel	7:00 p.m.
Helsinki, Finland	7:00 p.m.	Tientsin, China	1:00 a.m.*
Hobart, Tasmania	3:00 a.m.*	Tokyo, Japan	2:00 a.m.*
Hong Kong, off China	1:00 a.m.*	Toronto, Canada	12:00 noon
Honolulu, Hawaii	7:00 a.m.	Tripoli, Libya	6:00 p.m.
Irkutsk, U.S.S.R.	1:00 a.m.*	Turin, Italy	6:00 p.m.
Istanbul, Turkey	7:00 p.m.	Valparaiso, Chile	1:00 p.m.
Jakarta (Batavia), Indonesia	12:30 a.m.*	Vancouver, Canada	9:00 a.m.
Jerusalem, Israel and Jordan	7:00 p.m.	Venice, Italy	6:00 p.m.
Johannesburg, South Africa	7:00 p.m.	Veracruz, Mexico	11:00 a.m.
Juneau and Sitka, Alaska	9:00 a.m.	Victoria (Hong Kong)	1:00 a.m.*
Karachi, Pakistan	10:00 p.m.	Vienna, Austria	6:00 p.m.
Kiev, U.S.S.R.	8:00 p.m.	Vladivostok, U.S.S.R.	3:00 a.m.*
Kingston, Jamaica	12:00 noon	Warsaw, Poland	6:00 p.m.
Kobe and Kyoto, Japan	2:00 a.m.*	Wellington, New Zealand	5:00 a.m.*
La Paz, Bolivia	1:00 p.m.	Winnipeg, Canada	11:00 a.m.
Leeds, England	5:00 p.m.	Yokohama, Japan	2:00 a.m.*
Leipzig, Germany	6:00 p.m.	Zurich, Switzerland	6:00 p.m.

†Add an hour to the times given here for British cities since England is now on year-round daylight-saving time. *On the following day.

INDEX

INDEX

1178

INDEX

INDEX

INDEX

INDEX

INDEX

INDEX

INDEX

INDEX

INDEX

INDEX

INDEX

INDEX

INDEX

INDEX

INDEX

INDEX

INDEX

INDEX

INDEX

INDEX

INDEX

INDEX

INDEX

INDEX

Westinghouse Electric Corp., 774
what course for wholesalers' salesmen should cover, 847
what retail salespeople need to know, 774
Your Manners Are Showing, 766
Trans World Airlines, 660

TRANSIT ADVERTISING
bus posters, 614
car cards, 613-615
exposure, 614
users of, 614
Transit Advertising Assn., 613
Tree Sweet Products Co., 743
Trucks for delivery salesmen, 864
Truth About Business Mailing Lists, 456

TYPE
classification, 369
faces, chart showing, 373-377
Linotype, 364
Ludlow, 364
measurement tables, 33, 337, 338, 339
Monotype, 364
tables (Hooper's) for fitting copy, 335

TYPOGRAPHY
American Type Founders, Inc., 365
Bauer Type Foundry, Inc., 365
Berté, Jean, 359
Bodoni Book, 364
chart of type faces, 373-377
Clason's Rapid Copy Fitter, 336
classification and selection of type faces, 369
copy-fitting systems, 336-337
copy preparation, 371
CRT typesetters, 366
Dartnell style chart, 340
factors influencing selection, 369
Gordon press, 354
Hopper's Type Tables, 335
Intertype, 363
Linotype, 364
Ludlow, 364
Manual of Style, A., 329
methods of typesetting, 363
Monotype, 364
Old Style vs. Modern, 369
PDQ Copymeter, 335
PDQ Printometer, 335
Phototypesetting, 365
printers' calculat, 336
Roto-Typometer, 335
table of type measurements, 333, 338, 339

USM Corporation, 148, 153
Ulmann, Bernhard, Co., 921

Union Oil Company of Calif., 905
Unions and sales training, 949
United Air Lines, 272
U.S. Department of Commerce, 817, 828, 1117
U.S. Employment Service, 71
United States Envelope, 402-403
U.S. Government Printing Office Style Manual, 329
U.S. Post Office Department operations, 461, 467, 585
U.S. Postal Service, 693
U.S. Rubber Co., 676, 678, 680, 905, 996, 998
U.S. Shoe Corp., 887, 889
U.S. Steel Corp., 299
U.S. Supreme Court, 872
U.S. Tire Co., 98-99, 574
U.S. Tire Dealers Mutual Corporation, 98, 574
Universal C.I.T. Credit Corp., 906
"Use the User" contest, industrial, 966
User's Service Bureau, 522

Value News, 972
Venetian and Vertical Blind Assn., 686
Victor Adding Machine Co., 430
Victor Computometer Corp., 1021
Video-cassette systems, 772
Visual aids for consumer selling, 996
Visual aids, mailable, 961
Vogue, 174, 546, 631

Wage and Hour Act, 165
Wage and Hour Administration, 967
Wages and Hours Act, 967
Walgreen Co., 945
Wall hangers for getting contest entries, 702
Wall posters and hangers, 549
Wanamaker, John, 911
Warren, S. D., Co., 358, 389
Water color process, 359
Watkins, J. R., Co., 989
Webster's *New International Dictionary,* 329
Western Electric Corp., 546
Western Union Telegraph Co., 171, 718
Westinghouse Electric Corp., 572-574, 706, 774, 878, 906
Westinghouse incentive program for salesmen, 706
Wholesale Dry Goods Institute, 836-837

WHOLESALERS
American Central Manufacturing Co., 844
American Coal Sales Assn., 837
American Kitchen Institute, 844

INDEX